T0214877

Lecture Notes in Artificial Intelligence   9183

Subseries of Lecture Notes in Computer Science

More information about this series at http://www.springer.com/series/1244

Dylan D. Schmorrow · Cali M. Fidopiastis (Eds.)

Foundations of Augmented Cognition

9th International Conference, AC 2015
Held as Part of HCI International 2015
Los Angeles, CA, USA, August 2–7, 2015
Proceedings

 Springer

Editors
Dylan D. Schmorrow
Soar Technology Inc.
Vienna, VA
USA

Cali M. Fidopiastis
United Technologies Research Center
East Hartford, CT
USA

ISSN 0302-9743   ISSN 1611-3349 (electronic)
Lecture Notes in Artificial Intelligence
ISBN 978-3-319-20815-2   ISBN 978-3-319-20816-9 (eBook)
DOI 10.1007/978-3-319-20816-9

Library of Congress Control Number: 2015943035

LNCS Sublibrary: SL7 – Artificial Intelligence

Springer Cham Heidelberg New York Dordrecht London

Printed on acid-free paper

Springer International Publishing AG Switzerland is part of Springer Science+Business Media
(www.springer.com)

Foreword

The 17th International Conference on Human-Computer Interaction, HCI International 2015, was held in Los Angeles, CA, USA, during 2–7 August 2015. The event incorporated the 15 conferences/thematic areas listed on the following page.

A total of 4843 individuals from academia, research institutes, industry, and governmental agencies from 73 countries submitted contributions, and 1462 papers and 246 posters have been included in the proceedings. These papers address the latest research and development efforts and highlight the human aspects of design and use of computing systems. The papers thoroughly cover the entire field of Human Computer Interaction, addressing major advances in knowledge and effective use of computers in a variety of application areas. The volumes constituting the full 28-volume set of the conference proceedings are listed on pages VII and VIII.

I would like to thank the Program Board Chairs and the members of the Program Boards of all thematic areas and affiliated conferences for their contribution to the highest scientific quality and the overall success of the HCI International 2015 conference.

This conference could not have been possible without the continuous and unwavering support and advice of the founder, Conference General Chair Emeritus and Conference Scientific Advisor, Prof. Gavriel Salvendy. For their outstanding efforts, I would like to express my appreciation to the Communications Chair and Editor of HCI International News, Dr. Abbas Moallem, and the Student Volunteer Chair, Prof. Kim-Phuong L. Vu. Finally, for their dedicated contribution towards the smooth organization of HCI International 2015, I would like to express my gratitude to Maria Pitsoulaki and George Paparoulis, General Chair Assistants.

May 2015

Constantine Stephanidis
General Chair, HCI International 2015

HCI International 2015 Thematic Areas and Affiliated Conferences

Thematic areas:

- Human-Computer Interaction (HCI 2015)
- Human Interface and the Management of Information (HIMI 2015)

Affiliated conferences:

- 12th International Conference on Engineering Psychology and Cognitive Ergonomics (EPCE 2015)
- 9th International Conference on Universal Access in Human-Computer Interaction (UAHCI 2015)
- 7th International Conference on Virtual, Augmented and Mixed Reality (VAMR 2015)
- 7th International Conference on Cross-Cultural Design (CCD 2015)
- 7th International Conference on Social Computing and Social Media (SCSM 2015)
- 9th International Conference on Augmented Cognition (AC 2015)
- 6th International Conference on Digital Human Modeling and Applications in Health, Safety, Ergonomics and Risk Management (DHM 2015)
- 4th International Conference on Design, User Experience and Usability (DUXU 2015)
- 3rd International Conference on Distributed, Ambient and Pervasive Interactions (DAPI 2015)
- 3rd International Conference on Human Aspects of Information Security, Privacy and Trust (HAS 2015)
- 2nd International Conference on HCI in Business (HCIB 2015)
- 2nd International Conference on Learning and Collaboration Technologies (LCT 2015)
- 1st International Conference on Human Aspects of IT for the Aged Population (ITAP 2015)

Conference Proceedings Volumes Full List

1. LNCS 9169, Human-Computer Interaction: Design and Evaluation (Part I), edited by Masaaki Kurosu
2. LNCS 9170, Human-Computer Interaction: Interaction Technologies (Part II), edited by Masaaki Kurosu
3. LNCS 9171, Human-Computer Interaction: Users and Contexts (Part III), edited by Masaaki Kurosu
4. LNCS 9172, Human Interface and the Management of Information: Information and Knowledge Design (Part I), edited by Sakae Yamamoto
5. LNCS 9173, Human Interface and the Management of Information: Information and Knowledge in Context (Part II), edited by Sakae Yamamoto
6. LNAI 9174, Engineering Psychology and Cognitive Ergonomics, edited by Don Harris
7. LNCS 9175, Universal Access in Human-Computer Interaction: Access to Today's Technologies (Part I), edited by Margherita Antona and Constantine Stephanidis
8. LNCS 9176, Universal Access in Human-Computer Interaction: Access to Interaction (Part II), edited by Margherita Antona and Constantine Stephanidis
9. LNCS 9177, Universal Access in Human-Computer Interaction: Access to Learning, Health and Well-Being (Part III), edited by Margherita Antona and Constantine Stephanidis
10. LNCS 9178, Universal Access in Human-Computer Interaction: Access to the Human Environment and Culture (Part IV), edited by Margherita Antona and Constantine Stephanidis
11. LNCS 9179, Virtual, Augmented and Mixed Reality, edited by Randall Shumaker and Stephanie Lackey
12. LNCS 9180, Cross-Cultural Design: Methods, Practice and Impact (Part I), edited by P.L. Patrick Rau
13. LNCS 9181, Cross-Cultural Design: Applications in Mobile Interaction, Education, Health, Transport and Cultural Heritage (Part II), edited by P.L. Patrick Rau
14. LNCS 9182, Social Computing and Social Media, edited by Gabriele Meiselwitz
15. LNAI 9183, Foundations of Augmented Cognition, edited by Dylan D. Schmorrow and Cali M. Fidopiastis
16. LNCS 9184, Digital Human Modeling and Applications in Health, Safety, Ergonomics and Risk Management: Human Modeling (Part I), edited by Vincent G. Duffy
17. LNCS 9185, Digital Human Modeling and Applications in Health, Safety, Ergonomics and Risk Management: Ergonomics and Health (Part II), edited by Vincent G. Duffy
18. LNCS 9186, Design, User Experience, and Usability: Design Discourse (Part I), edited by Aaron Marcus
19. LNCS 9187, Design, User Experience, and Usability: Users and Interactions (Part II), edited by Aaron Marcus
20. LNCS 9188, Design, User Experience, and Usability: Interactive Experience Design (Part III), edited by Aaron Marcus

Augmented Cognition

Program Board Chairs: Dylan D. Schmorrow, USA
and Cali M. Fidopiastis, USA

- Rosario Bruno Cannavò,Italy
- David Combs, USA
- Andrew J. Cowell, USA
- Martha Crosby, USA
- Wai-Tat Fu, USA
- Rodolphe Gentili, USA
- Michael W. Hail, USA
- Monte Hancock, USA
- Ion Juvina, USA
- Joe Keebler, USA
- Philip Mangos, USA
- David Martinez, USA
- Yvonne R. Masakowski, USA
- Santosh Mathan, USA
- Denise Nicholson, USA
- Banu Onaral, USA
- Robinson Pino, USA
- Tiffany Poeppelman, USA
- Lauren Reinerman-Jones, USA
- Victoria Romero, USA
- Amela Sadagic, USA
- Anna Skinner, USA
- Robert Sottilare, USA
- Ann Speed, USA
- Roy Stripling, USA
- Polly Tremoulet, USA
- Eric Vorm, USA
- Peter Walker, USA

The full list with the Program Board Chairs and the members of the Program Boards of all thematic areas and affiliated conferences is available online at:

http://www.hci.international/2015/

HCI International 2016

The 18th International Conference on Human-Computer Interaction, HCI International 2016, will be held jointly with the affiliated conferences in Toronto, Canada, at the Westin Harbour Castle Hotel, 17–22 July 2016. It will cover a broad spectrum of themes related to Human-Computer Interaction, including theoretical issues, methods, tools, processes, and case studies in HCI design, as well as novel interaction techniques, interfaces, and applications. The proceedings will be published by Springer. More information will be available on the conference website: http://2016.hci.international/.

General Chair
Prof. Constantine Stephanidis
University of Crete and ICS-FORTH
Heraklion, Crete, Greece
Email: general_chair@hcii2016.org

http://2016.hci.international/

Contents

Cognitive Performance and Workload

Adaptive Tutoring and Training

Applications of Augmented Cognition

Cognitive Performance and Workload

Error Visualization and Information-Seeking Behavior for Air-Vehicle Control

Lewis L. Chuang[✉]

Department of Perception, Cognition and Action,
Max Planck Institute for Biological Cybernetics,
Tübingen, Germany
lewis.chuang@tuebingen.mpg.de

Abstract. A control schema for a human-machine system allows the human operator to be integrated as a mathematical description in a closed-loop control system, i.e., a pilot in an aircraft. Such an approach typically assumes that error feedback is perfectly communicated to the pilot who is responsible for tracking a single flight variable. However, this is unlikely to be true in a flight simulator or a real flight environment. This paper discusses different aspects that pertain to error visualization and the pilot's ability in seeking out relevant information across a range of flight variables.

1 Introduction

Man-machine systems, such as a human pilot and an aircraft, can be considered as a closed-loop control system. In accordance with the approach popularized by McRuer and colleagues [1], such a system can be generalized as a control schema, as illustrated in Fig. 1.

In this schema, the aircraft controller is approximated by a function, Y_c, that describes how the control dynamics of the aircraft ought to interpret the command inputs, $u(t)$, from the human pilot to generate a joint system state, $y(t)$. External disturbances, such as modeled wind turbulences, can be input into the controller to perturb the overall output. The changing objective of the system (e.g., the flight trajectory) is represented by a target function, $f_t(t)$. Deviations between this target function and the current system state represent the error, $e(t)$, that the human pilot has to resolve by submitting new command inputs to the aircraft controller. This control behavior of the human pilot can be approximated by a linear function, Y_p, which is typically derived by fitting data that is obtained from human participants. During behavioral experimentation, parametric properties of the target function, $f_t(t)$, and characteristics of the machine controller, Y_c, can be systematically manipulated to determine this model of a generic pilot's response characteristics.

The appeal of this approach in describing the relationship of a pilot and an aircraft is apparent. It allows the control behavior of a pilot to be modeled as a simple linear mathematical function, which consists, for example, of

© Springer International Publishing Switzerland 2015
D.D. Schmorrow and C.M. Fidopiastis (Eds.): AC 2015, LNAI 9183, pp. 3–11, 2015.
DOI: 10.1007/978-3-319-20816-9_1

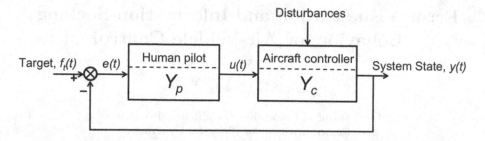

Fig. 1. Basic control schema of a human-machine system.

the operator's input gain and the time delay of the same input. An overview of such pilot models are provided in [2]. More importantly, such an approach allows for the human operator to be simulated in closed-loop control systems, which can include engineered machine controllers and modeled disturbances. In other words, possible interactions between the pilot and the vehicle can be simulated and evaluated for different aviation scenarios. Situations that merit further investigation can be thus identified for actual behavioral experimentation. Moreover, this framework unifies the, otherwise, separate efforts of human behavioral research and control engineering in an integrated framework. It also presents the opportunity to systematically evaluate how a human operator might respond to a novel aircraft controller, such as a personal aerial vehicle for daily commuting [3].

In its most basic form, this schema makes several implicit assumptions. First, it assumes that error feedback, $e(t)$, is perfectly communicated to the human operator. However, the mode of communication — that is, how this error feedback is presented to the pilot — can result in a non-veridical perception of error feedback. This will be discussed in Sect. 2. Second, the schema only accounts for the tracking of a single flight variable. However, controlling an aircraft is a complex task that involves tracking multiple flight variables simultaneously, which are themselves coupled to each other. Thus, pilots have to shift their gaze across different instruments periodically so as to update themselves on the overall state of the aircraft. This will be addressed in Sect. 3. Third, the human pilot is typically modeled as a consistent stationary unit. However, the operational state of the human pilot can be expected to be influenced by situational factors such as anxiety, perceived workload, attentional fatigue and overload. Some of these factors might themselves be influenced by the presentation mode of error feedback or the need to manage the tracking of multiple flight objectives. This is considered in several studies that are presented across Sects. 2 and 3.

2   Influences of Error Visualization

Accurate visual communication of error feedback to the human operator is necessary to support stable closed-loop control performance. This section discusses three aspects of error visualization, namely the issue of instrumentation versus outside-world feedback, the influence of feedback latencies, and how the available field-of-view could have a long-term impact on flight control behavior.

A basic control schema does not specify the communication channel through which error is displayed to the pilot. Given ideal meteorological conditions, a pilot is permitted by visual flight rules to navigate and maintain aircraft stability by monitoring terrain features and the horizon. When outside world visibility is compromised, a pilot is compelled by instrument flight rules to refer to instruments, such as a heading indicator and an attitude indicator that serve as proxies for supporting navigation and orientation control.

On the one hand, outside-world feedback contains rich visual cues, such as optic flow that serves as a visceral cue for both self-heading and -orientation. Increasing terrain realism by including buildings and hills in a fixed-wing approach display has been shown to improve the accuracy of horizontal, vertical and altitude perception [4]. More specifically, increasing the density of objects (i.e., number of trees) in the outside-world visualization of a flight simulator has been shown to support better estimates of altitude, which resulted in less control variability in a low-altitude flight task [5]. On the other hand, instruments that track specific flight variables (e.g., heading indicator) can be better than outside-world cues (i.e., optic flow) in supporting control behavior, especially under unpredictable, fast-varying conditions [6]. In a recent study, we directly compared participants who relied on either outside-world cues (i.e., terrain features and a visible horizon) or its instrument equivalent (i.e., attitude indicator) to correct for instabilities in the roll orientation of their aircraft [7]. Although self-reports of workload did not vary significantly between the two types of error visualizations, stability control was less variable when it was supported by the instrument visualization. To understand this difference in control performance between the two visualization conditions, control output was separated into two components — one that reflected the perceptual bias of the target function (i.e., a constant signed error off the zero-point) and another that reflected the variance around this perceived (and possibly biased) target function. This separation revealed that participants exhibited substantial perceptual bias when they relied on the realistic outside-world visualization. In other words, relying on visual cues from an outside world environment can cause pilots to systematically mis-estimate the desired target function. In agreement with these findings, highly experienced rotorcraft pilots have been observed to rely less on looking at the "outside-world" and more on their instruments, as compared to their less experienced counterparts [8].

Another important aspect of error visualization is the latency in its presentation. Latencies can be introduced into a control system due to a lag in the vehicle dynamics or as a result of a transport delay between the system state, $y(t)$, and visualization of the error feedback, $e(t)$. The latter could be especially perceptible in remote visualization systems, such as Helmet Integrated Display Sight Systems (HIDSS), that are intended to compensate for reduced visual flight conditions by presenting error visualizations that are computed from on-board sensors (e.g., forward looking infrared radar) [9]. Pronounced delays can impair control performance and reduce the perceived handling qualities of the aircraft [10,11]. Furthermore, we found that pilots often increase their stick input activity, $u(t)$, in the presence of such delays in order to compensate for unintended over-shooting. This can result in pilot-induced oscillations that are generated by stick inputs at higher frequencies than is required to resolve the target function of the task objective itself [12,13]. With time, these pilot-induced oscillations can grow and destabilize the entire control system. In addition, visualization delays have a impact on perceived as well as physiological workload. Increased visualization delays have been associated with larger self-reported workload [14] and electrodermal activity [13], suggesting that the human operator suffers considerable stress under delay conditions.

A final aspect of error visualization that merits discussion is the size of the field-of-view. Restricting the field-of-view of the outside-world can curtail the availability of visual cues. However, its detrimental influence on control performance is surprisingly limited. Although improvements in roll stabilization can be achieved by supplementing a central display with the use of peripheral displays [15], any improvements that can be gained from increasing the field-of-view of the central display to cover peripheral vision tend to be exhausted after 40° [16]. From this, it might appear that an arguably small field-of-view contains sufficient information for the purposes of a roll disturbance task. Nonetheless, it remains worthwhile to question how a small field-of-view could restrict other aspects of flight control besides limiting the availability of visual information. For example, a restrictive field-of-view could impair flight control by inducing non-optimal looking behavior. A basic control schema assumes that error feedback is submitted to the pilot just in time for its immediate resolution. However, a pilot can move his eyes to look ahead 'in time' and to predict the consequence of the current system state (e.g., course deviation) on achieving the final objective (e.g., landing target). Therefore, a restrictive field-of-view of the outside world environment in a flight training simulator could inhibit a trainee pilot in acquiring look-ahead behavior that is presumably advantageous in the real world. Preliminary findings in my lab support this conjecture. We have found that restricting the horizontal (but not the vertical) field-of-view during flight training can have a long-term influence on acquired eye-movement behavior. When tested in a large 230° field-of-view environment, participants who learned to perform a side-step maneuver in a 60° horizontal field-of-view condition exhibited a greater tendency to restrict their eye-movements to near objects than those who were trained in a 180° field-of-view environment.

3 Information-Seeking Behavior

Gazetracking technology allows us to monitor how a pilot seeks out task-relevant information during flight control. This section deals with how this unobtrusive method of pilot observation can inform us on the relevance of instrument scanning to control performance, the pilot's operational state, and how attention might shift between different flight variables during a more complex flight maneuver.

A cockpit environment presents a diverse array of instruments that has to be attended to. Each instrument tends to be looked at as frequently as it delivers relevant information [17]. Thus, tracking the gaze of the human operator during task performance enables us to make inferences concerning the perceived relevance of the information that is communicated by each instrument.

Controlling a real aircraft requires a pilot to track more than one flight variable. Fixation on a single flight variable will cause the pilot to lose control over other variables, since flight variables tend to be dynamically coupled to each other. For example, increasing the airspeed of a rotorcraft (e.g., Bo-105) by pitching it downwards brings about the unintended consequence of losing altitude. Therefore, a pilot should adopt a regular and efficient instrument scanning strategy, also referred to as "cross-checking", in order to be proficient. Only by looking periodically between instruments can a pilot ensure that all flight variables continue to be maintained at their desired values, regardless of adjustments to any single variable. In fact, instrument scanning techniques form an integral part of a pilot's training. Different flight maneuvers tend to be associated with recommended instrument scanning techniques, so as to ensure that flight variables that are relevant to the maneuver are not neglected (for examples, see [18] pp. 6-10–6-12). In some cases, flight instructors rely on playbacks of eye-movements to identify inappropriate scanning strategy in trainee pilots [19]. Some studies have further validated that scanning behavior differs across different levels of flight experience in tasks ranging from approach and landing [20] to combat engagement [21].

The regularity of scanning instruments for task relevant error feedback has an impact on control performance. We have shown that scanning regularity distinguishes between good and bad performance, even across naïve participants with no formal training in instrument scanning techniques [22]. In this study, participants were first introduced to the control dynamics of a rotorcraft, namely a Bo-105, without explicit instructions on how they were expected to look at the instruments. They were trained to perform a flight mission that consisted of several consecutive maneuvers, such as straight-and-level flight, altitude adjustments, and airspeed adjustments. We recorded flight control performance and instrument scanning behavior. Flight control performance was measured in terms of the overall stability of airspeed and altitude maintenance, and instrument scanning was described by a probability matrix that described the statistical dependencies of gaze transitions between instruments. Control performance and instrument scanning behavior were found to be closely related. More specifically, participants who were able to maintain stable airspeed and altitude also demonstrated more regular and self-consistent patterns of gaze transitions between instruments. In contrast, unstable flight control behavior tended to be accompanied by unpredictable gaze transitions.

The statistical dependencies of gaze transitions between specific regions-of-interest (i.e., instruments) can be computed as a visual scanning entropy score, whereby a low score indicates regular (i.e., predictable) scanning behavior [23]. A recent study demonstrated that pilot anxiety can influence visual scanning entropy [24]. Here, participants were first trained to perform an approach-and-landing fixed-wing aircraft maneuver without receiving any specific instrument scanning instructions. The training objective was to ensure that participants could perform this maneuver using only cockpit instruments, under low visibility conditions. Upon attaining satisfactory performance, participants were subjected to a battery of manipulations that were designed to induce anxiety — this included monetary incentives for the best performer as well as informing participants that video-recordings of subpar attempts could be used as public teaching material. Induced anxiety, as validated by increased heart-rate and self-reported anxiety scores, had the effect of increasing visual scanning entropy across the trained flight maneuver. In other words, artificially induced anxiety had an effect of increasing the randomness of instrument scanning behavior.

A complex flight mission, such as an Instrument Landing System (ILS) approach of a fixed-wing aircraft, would require the pilot to juggle between attending to multiple task objectives, namely vertical, horizontal, and airspeed tracking. Given that instrument scanning patterns are most likely generated by the pilot's task objectives, an analysis of instrument scanning behavior could allow us to infer how pilots allocate attention between basic task objectives during a complex mission. In a notable example [25], a Hidden Markov Model was proposed that initially assumed that pilots switch between tracking three of the above-listed flight variables during an ILS approach. The model further assumed that each of these task objectives would give rise to scanning behavior across their relevant set of instruments, as specified by the Federal Aviation Administration, USA (see Chapter 6, [18]). Fitting instrument scanning behavior to this model resulted in a description of how pilots switched their attention between the three task objectives across the comprising phases of an ILS approach, namely straight-and-level, intercept, and final descent phases. The fitted model also indicated that the least experienced pilot devoted most of his efforts towards tracking the vertical and horizontal variables at the cost of monitoring airspeed. Unexpectedly, the three pre-specified task objectives were not sufficient in accounting for all of the instrument scanning behavior that was observed in the most experienced pilot, especially during the final descent phase. Instead, the most experienced pilot was found to be tracking an additional flight variable, namely the attitude of the aircraft. This resulted in an additional and unexpected instrument scanning behavior that had to be included in the model. Interestingly, post-experimental interviews revealed that this instrument scanning behavior is well-known among experienced pilots. However, it is not typically endorsed during training for an approach-and-landing maneuver and was, thus, not included in the initial model. This example highlights how gazetracking can facilitate our understanding how pilots switch their attention between multiple single-variable control schemata in order to execute a complex flight maneuver. In addition, it allows task objectives, which were not originally modeled for a particular flight maneuver, to be raised for consideration.

4   Discussion and Outlook

To summarize, this paper began by introducing a basic control schema, which can serve as a starting point for integrating a human operator in a closed-loop control system. Given good approximations of human and machine behavior, it can be used to simulate their joint performance. Nevertheless, a realistic aviation scenario raises certain challenges to some of the assumptions that are implicitly held by such a control schema.

In this paper, I have addressed several aspects of real flight behavior that run counter to the implicit assumption, held by a basic control schema, that error feedback is perfectly transmitted to a human pilot that is merely reactive. More specifically, I have discussed the various influences of error visualization on the human pilot as well as how the human pilot acquires relevant information by shifting his attention across multiple sources of error feedback. Less than ideal transmission of error feedback can not only result in systematically biased and unstable performance; it can also have non-negligible consequences on the experienced workload and looking habits of the pilot. In addition, I have explained how regular instrument scanning behavior is a critical component of proficient flight control. Gazetracking provides us with the means to observe how the human pilot shifts his attention between tracking multiple and inter-dependent flight variables. With this in hand, we might be able to extend a basic control schema that allows for the tracking of only a single flight variable to one that is able to accommodate the full complexity of a flight maneuver.

Most of the research that is presented in this paper was conducted under controlled experiment settings, including certified flight simulators. For safety reasons, it might not be feasible to manipulate visual conditions in real flight scenarios. Nevertheless, gazetracking in real flight conditions could provide us with the opportunity of monitoring the specific error feedback that is attended to by the pilot. Recent advances in technology are starting to allow for unencumbered gazetracking. Improved calibration algorithms [26] as well as lightweight hardware (e.g., mobile eyetracking glasses by SensoMotoric Instruments GmbH) contributes toward this possibility.

While it is tempting to treat gaze fixation as a proxy for visual attention, this need not necessarily be true. A gazetracker cannot discriminate between a purposeful fixation and a blank stare. In order to determine the extent to which fixated information is actually processed, it might be necessary to evaluate cortical responses that proceed from a visual fixation. The lightweight nature and high temporal resolution of electroencephalography (EEG) presents itself as a likely candidate for this purpose. However, several technical issues have to be resolved before simultaneous gazetracking and EEG can be achieved in field conditions [27]. Predominant among these is the fact that eye-movements generate large electrical signals that can be confounded with the recording of cortically-generated activity. In spite of this, signal processing algorithms (e.g., independent component analysis) could be employed that are generally effective in separating these two sources of recorded activity. Still, reliable methods continue to be computationally expensive and only allow for off-line analysis.

To conclude, the transmission and acquisition of information is a vital aspect of how a human pilot interacts with an aircraft. The advantages of relying on a control schema to describe this interaction can be further expanded upon by a careful consideration of the issues that can impinge on how error feedback is communicated to the human pilot.

References

1. McRuer, D.: Human dynamics in man-machine systems. Automatica. **16**, 237–253 (1980)
2. McRuer, D.T., Jex, H.R.: A review of quasi-linear pilot models. IEEE Trans. Hum. Factors Electron. **3**, 231–249 (1967)
3. Nieuwenhuizen, F., Jump, M., Perfect, P., White, M., Padfield, G., Floreano, D., Schill, F., Zufferey, J., Fua, P., Bouabdallah, S., et al.: myCopter – enabling technologies for personal aerial transportation systems. In: Proceeding of the 3rd International HELI World Conference, pp. 1–8 (2011)
4. Barfield, W., Rosenberg, C., Kraft, C.: The effects of visual cues to realism and perceived impact point during final approach. Proc. Hum. Factors Ergon. Soc. Annu. Meet. **33**(2), 115–119 (1983)
5. De Maio, J., Rinalducci, E.J., Brooks, R., Brunderman, J.: Visual cueing effectiveness: comparison of perception and flying performance. Proc. Hum. Factors Ergon. Soc. Annu. Meet. **27**(11), 928–932 (1983)
6. Zaal, P.M.T., Nieuwenhuizen, F.M., van Paassen, M.M., Mulder, M.: Modeling human control of self-motion direction with optic flow and vestibular motion. IEEE Trans. Syst. Man Cybern. B Cybern. **43**(2), 544–556 (2012)
7. Scheer, M., Nieuwenhuizen, F.M., Bülthoff, H.H., Chuang, L.L.: The influence of visualization on control performance in a flight simulator. In: Harris, D. (ed.) EPCE 2014. LNCS, vol. 8532, pp. 202–211. Springer, Heidelberg (2014)
8. Yang, J.H., Kennedy, Q., Sullivan, J., Fricker, R.D.: Pilot performance: assessing how scan patterns navigational assessments vary by flight expertise. Aviat. Space Environ. Med. **84**(2), 116–124 (2013)
9. Rash, C.E. (ed.): Helmet Mounted Displays: Design Issues for Rotary-wing Aircraft. SPIE Press, Washington (1999)
10. Wildzunas, R.M., Barron, T.L., Wiley, R.W.: Visual display delay effects on pilot performance. Aviat. Space Environ. Med. **67**, 214–221 (1996)
11. Jennings, S., Reid, L.D., Craig, G., Kruk, R.V.: Time delays in visually coupled systems during flight test and simulation. J. Aircraft. **41**, 1327–1335 (2004)
12. Middendorf, M., Lusk, S., Whitley, J.: Power spectral analysis to investigate the effects of simulator time delay on flight control activity. In: IAA Flight Simulation Technologies Conference, pp. 46–52 (1990)
13. Flad, N., Nieuwenhuizen, F.M., Bülthoff, H.H., Chuang, L.L.: System delay in flight simulators impairs performance and increases physiological workload. In: Harris, D. (ed.) EPCE 2014. LNCS, vol. 8532, pp. 3–11. Springer, Heidelberg (2014)
14. Middendorf, M., Fiorita, A., McMillan, G.: The effects of simulator transport delay on performance, workload, and control activity during low-level flight. In: AIAA Flight Simulation Technologies Conference, pp. 412–426 (1991)
15. Hosman, R.J.A.W., Van der Vaart, J.C.: Effects of vestibular and visual motion perception on task performance. Acta Psychol. **48**(1), 271–287 (1981)

16. Kenyon, R.V., Kneller, E.W.: The effects of field of view size on the control of roll motion. IEEE Trans. Syst. Man Cybern. **23**(1), 183–193 (1993)
17. Senders, J.W.: The human operator as a monitor and controller of multidegree of freedom systems. IEEE Trans. Hum. Factors Electron. **5**, 2–5 (1964)
18. Federal Aviation Administration, U.S. Department of Transportation Instrument Flying Handbook FAA-H-8083-15B (2012)
19. Wetzel, P.A., Anderson, G.M., Barelka, B.A.: Instructor use of eye position based feedback for pilot training. Proc. Hum. Factors Ergon. Soc. Annu. Meet. **42**, 1388–1392 (1998)
20. Anders, G.: Pilot's attention allocation during approach and landing: Eye-and head-tracking research in an A330 full flight simulator. Focusing Attention on Aviation Safety (2001)
21. Yu, C.S., Wang, E.M.Y., Li, W.C., Braithwaite, G.: Pilots visual scan patterns and situation awareness in flight operations. Aviat. Space Environ. Med. **85**(7), 708–714 (2014)
22. Chuang, L.L., Nieuwenhuizen, F.M., Bülthoff, H.H.: A fixed-based flight simulator study: the interdependence of flight control performance and gaze efficiency. In: Harris, D. (ed.) EPCE 2013, Part II. LNCS, vol. 8020, pp. 95–104. Springer, Heidelberg (2013)
23. Ellis, S.R., Stark, L.: Statistical dependency in visual scanning. Hum. Factors J. Hum. Factors Ergon. Soc. **28**(4), 421–438 (1986)
24. Allsop, J., Gray, R.: Flying under pressure: effects of anxiety on attention and gaze behavior in aviation. J. Appl. Res. Mem. Cogn. **3**(2), 63–71 (2014)
25. Hayashi, M.: Hidden markov models to identify pilot instrument scanning and attention patterns. In: IEEE International Conference on Systems, Man and Cybernetics, **3** (2003)
26. Browatzki, B., Bülthoff, H.H., Chuang, L.L.: A comparison of geometric-and regression-based mobile gaze-tracking. Front. Hum. Neurosci. **8**, 200 (2014)
27. Plöchl, M., Ossandón, J.P., König, P.: Combining EEG and eye tracking: identification, characterization, and correction of eye movement artifacts in electroencephalographic data. Front. Hum. Neurosci. **6**, 278 (2012)

DataShopping for Performance Predictions

Michael Collins[1]([⊠]), Kevin A. Gluck[2], and Tiffany S. Jastrzembski[2]

[1] ORISE at Air Force Research Laboratory, 2620 Q Street, Building, 852,
Wright-Patterson Air Force Base, OH 45433, USA
`michael.collins.74.ctr@us.af.mil`
[2] Air Force Research Laboratory's Cognitive Models and Agents Branch, 2620
Q Street, Building, 852, Wright-Patterson Air Force Base, OH 45433, USA
`{kevin.gluck, tiffany.jastrzemski}@us.af.mil`

Abstract. Mathematical models of learning have been created to capitalize on the regularities that are seen when individuals acquire new skills, which could be useful if implemented in learning management systems. One such mathematical model is the Predictive Performance Equation (PPE). It is the intent that PPE will be used to predict the performance of individuals to inform real-world education and training decisions. However, in order to improve mathematical models of learning, data from multiple samples are needed. Online data repositories, such as Carnegie Mellon University's DataShop, provide data from multiple studies at fine levels of granularity. In this paper, we describe results from a set of analyses ranging across levels of granularity in order to assess the predictive validity of PPE in educational contexts available in the repository.

Keywords: Performance prediction · Datashop · Repository · Learning optimization · Mathematical models

1 Introduction

In many real world domains, there is a recurring need to educate both workers and students in order to equip them with new skills or to ensure that a baseline standard of knowledge and performance is met. Time and cost are relevant factors when deciding whether continuing education or refresher training should be required, as are the potential risks associated with ignorance or decreased proficiency. This complex and consequential trade space is motivating the development of learning management systems that attempt to improve either the quality or rate at which individuals learn or can allow training to be tailored to specific individuals. One way that these goals can be accomplished is for these systems to employ different mathematical models of learning that can be used to generate predictions of future performance of either an aggregate sample or specific individuals in order to inform education and training decisions. This presents an opportunity for basic cognitive science research to find real-world application.

Psychological research has long noted that humans exhibit certain mathematical regularities when learning new knowledge and skills [2, 8]. The Predictive

© Springer International Publishing Switzerland 2015
D.D. Schmorrow and C.M. Fidopiastis (Eds.): AC 2015, LNAI 9183, pp. 12–23, 2015.
DOI: 10.1007/978-3-319-20816-9_2

Performance Equation (PPE) (described in the following section) is a mathematical model of learning, forgetting, and the spacing effect that uses the historical performance of individuals to generate a prediction of their future performance [4]. The PPE was developed from Anderson and Schunn's [1] General Performance Equation (GPE), which captured the important influences of the power laws of learning and forgetting as determinants of performance. To improve upon the GPE, Jastrzembski et al. [4] introduced the PPE, taking into account the effects on performance of temporal spacing between instances of practice [2]. The PPE has been validated across many samples of data from laboratory studies on learning and retention [5].

A typical limitation of archival publications in the literature regarding learning and retention is that data are only reported at the sample level of analysis. In other words, data regarding measures of central tendency and variability are only reported at the level of the entire sample, or at best the level of the experimentally manipulated sub-samples of interest. This is understandable and generally serves the proximal scientific objective of each particular study quite well. However, most of the real world applications of technologies like learning management systems involve assessment at a finer level of granularity, down at the level of the individual learners. For that level of analysis we generally need source data, rather than archival, summative publications. This is the sort of niche intended to be filled by online data repositories. Repositories can be used to test model predictions and explore new uses of different models of learning. One such data repository is DataShop located on Learnlab.org, created by the National Science Foundation-funded Pittsburgh Science of Learning Center [7]. It holds a large set of publicly available data that can be used to further learning research objectives, and this paper describes a case study using DataShop for exactly that purpose. In this case, we used data available on DataShop to advance our performance prediction research using fine-grained third-party data available on its public database.

A primary intended application of the PPE is in adaptive scheduling of continuing education and refresher training. To accomplish this we will use a real-time calibration update method, which has PPE make multiple sequential predictions about the performance of a sample or individual over time, re-calibrating and updating it prediction of future performance each time a new data point becomes available. Implementing the PPE in this way may be beneficial in two ways. The first possible benefit is, that the PPE can take into account the entire historical performance of a group or individual in order to generate a prediction of what their future performance might be. Using the entire available historical performance of a sample or individual to generate a prediction is useful especially within applied domains where more variability is seen in human performance compared to the performance seen in controlled short-term laboratory studies. The second possible benefit is, by allowing the model to calibrate to all of the available instances of learning, the PPE can make a more informed prediction of what the sample or individual's performance will be during the next event, a prediction that would be useful to inform training decisions. However, it is currently unknown whether the calibration update method gives rise to better predictions over time, or if it allows for informative predictions to be made at different levels of aggregation (e.g., the aggregate performance of an individual across multiple tasks or the aggregate performance of a sample over multiple or single tasks).

In this paper, data collected from thirteen different classroom tutoring studies[1] exported from DataShop were used to perform a validation analysis of PPE using the calibration update method. The PPE was used to predict the performance of multiple samples across several levels of aggregation over different numbers of events, mimicking how PPE would be used in an applied domain. We examined how both the level of aggregation and the number of calibration and prediction events affected PPE's general ability to both fit the initial performance and predict future performance when implemented using the calibration update method.

2 The Predictive Performance Equation

The PPE is a hybrid model of learning and forgetting that predicts future performance by exploiting the mathematical regularities seen when individuals acquire a skill or learn new information, based on the amount of experience they have had on a given task and the amount of time in between instances of practice. The PPE works by calibrating to historical performance data using three free parameters (Eq. 1).

$$Performance = S * ST * N^c * T^{-d} \tag{1}$$

The three free model parameters are S (scalar), used to accommodate the performance measure of interest (e.g., Error Rate, Percent Correct, Response Time, etc.), c (learning rate), and d (decay rate). There are also fixed parameters determined by the timing and frequency of events in the protocol, such as T, the amount of true time passed since the onset of training, and N, the discrete number of training events that occurred in the training period. ST (Eq. 2) is the stability term that "captures the effects of spacing, by calibrating experience amassed as a function of temporal training distribution and true time passed" [6, p. 110].

$$St = \frac{\sum lag}{P} \cdot \frac{P_i}{T_i} \cdot \frac{\sum_i^j (lag_{max_{i,j}} - lag_{min_{i,j}})}{N_i} \tag{2}$$

Lag denotes the amount of wall time that has passed since the last training event and P is the amount of true time amassed during practice. Once the PPE has calibrated to the set of historical data points, it uses the learning and decay rates, the amount of experience on a task(s), and the time since its previous instance of practice to generate a quantitative point prediction of future performance for the sample or individual [5].

---

[1] The thirteen studies used in this paper are listed in the acknowledgement section, per instructions of DataShop.

3   Studies Collected from DataShop

DataShop is a repository of data collected from different learning and tutoring studies. A single sample on DataShop is referred to as a dataset, which is composed of a record of performance of individuals who attempted to solve a set of problems in a specific domain within a certain period of time [3]. For example, one dataset in the repository contains a record of students' performance when solving physics problems in a tutoring system used at the United States Naval Academy over the Fall 2007 semester. Each dataset contains a record of the performance of each individual across that curriculum's content. Each curriculum is made up of *problems*, defined as "a task [attempted by] a student usually involving several steps" [3]. An example of a problem in the physics tutor is comparing the difference in velocity between train *A* and *B*. Successfully solving a problem involves completing a series of *steps*, which are "an observable part of a solution to a problem" [3], such as finding the velocity of train *A*, which subjects attempted to solve over the course of the study. In the analysis presented here, we examined performance on the individual steps within a dataset, because they represented the distinct pieces of knowledge and skills learners were acquiring, over the course of the study.

3.1   Data Organization

All of the data from each dataset was organized into three different levels of aggregation. The first and highest level of aggregation was a sample's performance across multiple steps, defined as a sample of data from a single dataset composed of individuals who all had the same number of opportunities to complete the same steps. The second level of aggregation was a sample's performance on a specific step, defined as a sample of individuals from the same dataset who all had the same number of opportunities to attempt the same step. The third level of aggregation was an individual's performance across multiple steps, defined as a sample of steps done by the same participant.

Due to the fact that a majority of the datasets used for these analyses were recorded on tutoring systems that students used to complete their homework throughout the semester or year, each individual within a dataset did not have the same number of opportunities to complete each step (e.g., One individual could have had four opportunities to attempt a single step, while another individual had eight opportunities to attempt the same step). Each student did not have the same number of opportunities to attempt all steps because either an individual dropped out of the class or showed a high enough competence on a particular problem and was not presented with any more opportunities to solve that step. In order to create equivalent samples (subsets), that included the same individuals, attempting the same steps, for the same number of times for each of the three levels of aggregation, multiple subsets from each dataset were created. Subsets were constructed based on the number of opportunities that individual participants had with specific steps within a dataset.

For example, one participant could have had six opportunities to attempt steps A and B and eight opportunities with steps C and D, while only having four opportunities to attempt step E. In order to formulate a subset whose performance is aggregated over this individual's data where each step was done for the same number of times, one subset can be composed from this individual's first four opportunities with steps A, B, C, D, and E, creating four unique events where each step was done once. A second subset can also be composed from the individual's first six opportunities with steps A, B, C, and D, creating a subset of data with six unique events. This process of separating the data in order to create multiple subsets comprised of four to nine events was repeated across all thirteen datasets for each level of aggregation.

Error rate was used as a dependent measure, determined by the individual's first attempt at each step (i.e., correct or incorrect). The error rate was calculated by the percentage of incorrect first attempts across all of the steps done at each event within a subset. It is expected that the error rate will be highest at the subset's first event, because it is the first time participant(s) will have attempted to solve these steps. Additionally, error rate should decrease in subsequent events as individual(s) gain more experience solving these steps over time.

After each dataset was sorted into multiple subsets for each of the three different levels of aggregation, two different criteria were used to decide whether a subset was included or excluded from the exploratory analysis. The first criterion was that the subset's performance had to improve over the period of time that it was observed, and was assessed by comparing the error rate of the first and last event. Subsets of data where the error rate was higher on their final event than on their first event were excluded from our analysis, due to the fact that the PPE would not be able to account for their performance. Of all the subsets that were compiled from the thirteen datasets, 18 (26 %) of subsets aggregated over a multiple steps, 1745 (56 %) of subsets aggregated over a single step, and 2006 (47 %) subsets aggregated over an individual were excluded from our analysis for not meeting the first criterion. The second criterion was that the number of steps present at each trial had to be greater than or equal to the number of events within a subset. Thus, if a subset whose performance was aggregated over an individual participant was observed over nine events, their performance had to be aggregated over a minimum of nine individual steps. The same criterion was used for subsets aggregated over a single step, though to be included in our analysis a minimum number of participants were required. A minimum number of steps or participants were required for each subset because it was found that the error rates of subsets aggregated over a few steps or participants (e.g., one or two steps) were highly variable. Minimal changes in performance of subsets aggregated over a few steps or individuals caused large fluctuations in their error rates (e.g., a subsets error rate could go from 100 % on event one to 0 % on event two and 50 % on event three), which PPE could not account for. From the subsets that met the first criterion, 551 (58 %) of subsets aggregated over multiple subsets and 652 (33 %) of subsets aggregated over an individual were excluded for not also meeting the second criterion. All remaining subsets, which met both criteria, were used in the exploratory analysis (Table 1).

Table 1. Shows the total number of subsets comprised of different numbers of events across all three levels of aggregation that were included in the exploratory analysis.

Level of aggregation	Number of events in a subset						Total
	4	5	6	7	8	9	
Subsets aggregated over multiple steps	14	12	12	10	8	10	66
Subsets aggregated over a single steps	331	136	105	81	61	57	771
Subsets aggregated over an individual	410	314	234	203	104	90	1355

3.2   Calibration Updating with the Predictive Performance Equation

The PPE was run the same way on each subset across all three levels of aggregation, following the calibration update method. The PPE began by calibrating to the performance of the first three events of each subset (the minimum number of events needed for the PPE to make an initial prediction), then made a prediction about the subset's performance on their remaining events. After its initial prediction, PPE then updated its prediction by calibrating to all of the previous events plus one additional event and again generated a prediction for the subset's performance on the remaining events. The PPE continued to predict the performance of a subset's remaining events until it had calibrated up to the second to last event.

4   Results

The goal of this study was to examine PPE's ability to both account for and predict performance of subsets across multiple datasets at different levels of aggregation. In order to address these goals, we assessed PPE's ability, (a) to calibrate to the initial performance of a subset (calibration period) and (b) to predict the performance of future events (prediction period). To examine the overall ability of PPE to calibrate to the subsets' initial performance, the R^2 and RMSD of the calibration period for each prediction was computed and averaged over subsets where PPE had calibrated to the same number of events from the same level of aggregation (e.g., subsets whose performance was aggregated over a single individual and where PPE had only calibrated to the performance of the first three events). In order to examine PPE's ability to predict the performance of subsets' future events, the R^2 and RMSD of the prediction portion for each prediction made by PPE was computed and averaged over subsets from the same level of aggregation where PPE had both calibrated to and predicted the performance of the same number of events (e.g., subsets whose performance was aggregated over multiple steps, where PPE had calibrated to its first three events and predicted the performance of on its last three events). The overall R^2 for each of PPE's predictions were not recorded when predicting the performance of a subsets' last two events, because the R^2 of the prediction portion was always one between the PPE's prediction and the subset's performance of their last two events – it is simply a best fitting straight line. The overall R^2 of the prediction period could not be computed when only predicting the performance of the last event because a R^2 could not be calculated with only one event. To examine the change in PPE's predictions of performance of a single event while calibrating to additional instances of performance, the residual between PPE's prediction and a subset's performance on the last event was recorded after each prediction. The absolute value of the last residual of each prediction was then averaged across subsets from the same level of aggregation where PPE had predicted over the same number of events.

4.1   Calibration Period

Calibration period R^2 and RMSD varied only slightly as a function of aggregation. Looking across the three levels of aggregation, the average R^2 for subsets whose performance was aggregated over multiple steps ($M = .83$, $SD = .20$) did not differ greatly from subsets aggregated over a single step ($M = .78$, $SD = .29$) (Fig. 1). The average R^2 of subsets whose performance was aggregated over a single individual ($M = .73$, $SD = .28$) was slightly lower still (Fig. 1). The level of aggregation was found to have a similar effect on the overall RMSD values, with fit quality (in this case meaning a *lower* RMSD) positively correlated with the level of aggregation (Fig. 2). The average RMSD when PPE calibrated to the first three events of a subset's performance was lowest in subsets' aggregated over multiple steps ($M = .01$, $SD = .03$), with little difference being seen in subsets' aggregated over a single step ($M = .04$, $SD = .06$) or individual ($M = .05$, $SD = .03$) (Fig. 2). The results from the average R^2 and RMSD of the calibration period across each of the three levels of aggregation show that the ability of PPE to fit the initial performance of a subset's performance in part depends on the granularity of the data.

The pattern holds across levels of aggregation, as we increase the number of calibration points, but fits deteriorate as the number of calibration data points increases. The highest average R^2 and the lowest RMSD at each level of aggregation, occurred when PPE calibrated only to the performance of a subset's first three events (Figs. 1 and 2). The average R^2 of the calibration period decreased and the average RMSD increased, meaning that the calibration fits get worse, as PPE calibrated to each additional event. The impact of adding calibration events is stronger on the R^2 than on the RMSD, which increased but only slightly as PPE calibrated to additional events. Although, the overall ability of PPE to calibrate to additional events decreased as the number of events calibrated to increased, it is how these results affect PPE's ability to predict future performance that is the more important question when assessing the effectiveness of the calibration update method.

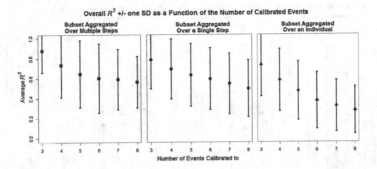

Fig. 1. Shows the average R^2, ± one standard deviation (SD) of the calibration period as a function of the number of events calibrated to, across the three levels of aggregation.

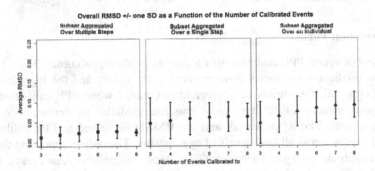

Fig. 2. Shows the Average RMSD, ± one standard deviation (SD) of the calibration period as a function of the number of events calibrated to, across the three levels of aggregation.

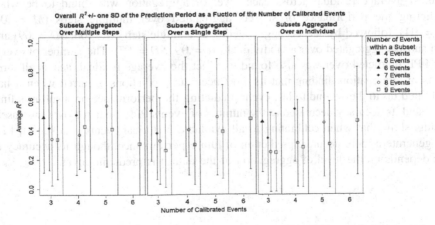

Fig. 3. Shows the average R^2, ± one standard deviation (SD) of the prediction period as a function of the number of events calibrated to, across the three levels of aggregation.

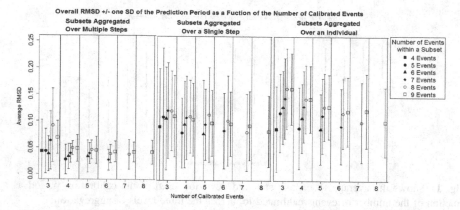

Fig. 4. Shows the average RMSD, ± one standard deviation (SD) of the prediction period as a function of the number of events calibrated to, across the three levels of aggregation.

4.2 Prediction Period

The number of events PPE calibrated to affected its prediction accuracy (Figs. 3 and 4). The worst prediction accuracies (lowest average R^2 values and the highest average RMSD) across all three levels of aggregation occurred when PPE calibrated to the subsets' performance on their first three events and predicted the performance of their remaining events. The R^2 increased, and the RMSD decreased as PPE calibrated to additional events across all three levels of aggregation. The only exception to this trend occurred in subsets aggregated across multiple steps comprised of nine events. In these subsets, the overall R^2 of the prediction period decreased after PPE calibrated to the first five and six events and predicted the performance on the remaining four and three events.

The average last residual between the PPE's prediction of a subset's performance on their final event varied as a function of the level of aggregation (Fig. 5). The smallest average residual across each level of aggregation was found to be when predicting the performance of subsets aggregated over multiple steps ($M = .04$, $SD = .04$), followed by subsets aggregated over a single step ($M = .08$, $SD = .09$) and then subsets aggregated over an individual ($M = .09$, $SD = .07$). The number of events that PPE predicted over was also found to affect the average residual, across all three levels of aggregation, finding that its most accurate predictions occurred when it had calibrated up to the second to last event predicting the performance on a subset's final event and its accuracy decreased as the number of events PPE predicted over increased. Results show that when calibrating to all available historical events in a subset, PPE can generate a more accurate prediction of future performance, though its accuracy in part depends on the level of aggregation of the data it is predicting over.

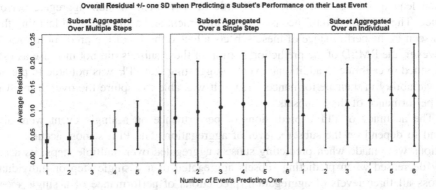

Fig. 5. The average absolute value of the residual between the PPE's predictions and a subset's performance on their last event as a function of the number of events predicting over, across all three levels of aggregation.

5 Discussion

The goal of this study was to perform an exploratory analysis on datasets available on DataShop to implement PPE using the calibration update method across different levels of aggregation, examining its ability to both fit and predict the performance of different subsets. During the calibration period, the level of aggregation and the number of calibration events both affected PPE's overall fit to a subset's initial performance. The PPE calibrated to subsets aggregated over multiple or single steps better than subsets which were aggregated over of an individual, as measured by the average R^2 and RMSD values of the calibration period. The effect the level of aggregation had on the calibration period is understandable due to the noise within a sample being decreased when a subset's performance is averaged over multiple individuals and steps; it is the statistical smoothing benefit of the law of large numbers.

The number of events to which PPE calibrated also affected its ability to fit the initial performance of a subset, decreasing the R^2 and increasing the RMSD with each additional event calibrated to. When PPE calibrates to the initial performance of a subset, it attempts to minimize the RMSD between the subset's initial performance and PPE's calibration, by manipulating its three free parameters. As PPE repeatedly calibrates to additional events within a subset, it must attempt to minimize the RMSD between more events, which may not all clearly fall along a best fit line. This pattern of results was seen across each level of aggregation showing that as PPE calibrates to additional events, it loses some of its ability to fit the initial performance of a subset.

Although as PPE calibrated to additional events its ability to fit a subset's performance decreased, the opposite results were seen during the prediction portion. As the number of events PPE calibrated to increased, so did its overall ability to predict the performance of future events across all three levels of aggregation. The only exception to this trend was observed in subsets aggregated over multiple steps comprised of nine events. This group of subsets was comprised of a higher proportion of steps which learners showed no improvement on, over the period of time they were observed, which lead to inconsistent and overall little improvement in their aggregate performance. The combination of inconsistent improvement and a small overall learning that was seen in the performance of these subsets affected the R^2 of the prediction portion. However, the RMSD of the prediction portion of these subsets did not increase as PPE continued to calibrate to additional events, suggesting that PPE was not able to predict the variability in their performance, though it was able to capture the overall trend in the performance of these subsets.

The accuracy of PPE's predictions of performance on a single event were also found to depend on the subset's level of aggregation. The PPE's most accurate predictions were made when predicting subsets aggregated over multiple steps; its accuracy decreased when predicting subsets aggregated over a single step or individual. Across all three levels of aggregation, predictions of performance of a single event were most accurate when PPE calibrated to all but one of the events within a subset and predicted the performance on its final event and its accuracy decreased as the number of events it predicted over increased. The results from both the accuracy of PPE predictions of a single event, the R^2, and RMSD of the prediction period suggest that by calibrating to additional events, PPE can better predict the future performance of a subset, despite the decrease in its ability to calibrate to the additional instances of a subset's initial performance.

The results obtained from using PPE on the datasets collected from DataShop shed light on two points for our prediction performance research. The first was, across each level of aggregation, PPE's predictions were overall improved by continually calibrating to additional events, in order to update its predictions. The second was, that the accuracy of PPE's predictions were able to be examined across three different levels of aggregation, which were seen to affect the accuracy of its predictions. If mathematical models of learning are to be implemented in learning management systems developed to help improve the rate or quality of training and education that specific individuals receive, it is not enough for them to be able account for a sample's aggregate performance, but the performance at lower levels of aggregation, such as the performance of an individual on a single task or the individuals within a sample, need to be able to be accounted for as well. One way to account for the inherent variability in the performance seen in data at low levels of granularity is to include prediction intervals in addition to making quantitative point predictions of future performance. Prediction intervals would allow PPE to predict a range that future performance might fall within, depending on both the granularity of the data and time period predicting over, two factors which were seen to affect PPE's predictions. Jastrzembski et al. [6] have previously addressed the need for incorporating prediction intervals into PPE. The results reported here show the additional benefit that prediction intervals could add, by being able to address the uncertainty seen in the performance at low levels of aggregation.

In conclusion, the data collected from DataShop allowed for a large scale exploratory analysis to examine the utility of implementing PPE using the calibration update method. Datasets with a record of each individuals' performance at the individual-step level allowed for a far more in depth analysis of PPE's predictions, which archival aggregate sample data from the published literature would not have allowed for. We hope that others will use this case study as an example of how DataShop's public database can be used as a source of data from applied domains and will take advantage of the data being available at a such a fine level of granularity to improve other mathematical models of learning, so that they may find real world application.

Acknowledgements. We would like to thank Carnegie Learning, Inc., for providing the Cognitive Tutoring data supporting this analysis. We used the "Handwriting/Examples Dec 2006", "Geometry Area (1996–1997)", "USNA Physics Fall 2006", "USNA Physics Fall 2007", "USNA Introductory Physics Fall 2009", "USNA Physics Spring 2007", "USNA Physics Spring 2008", "USNA Introductory Physics Spring 2010", "Watchung Hills Regional High School AP Physics 2007–2008", "Watchung Hills Regional High School AP Physics 2008–2009", "Watchung Hills Regional High School Honors Physics 2007–2008", "Watchung Hills Regional High School Honors Physics 2008–2009" and "Watchung Hills Regional High School Honors Physics 2009–2010" accessed via DataShop. We would also like to thank Michael Krusmark for the work he was done implementing the PPE into R. This research was supported by the Air Force Research Laboratory through AFOSR grant 13RH15COR and through Early Career Award Winner funds provided to the third author.

References

1. Anderson, J.R., Schunn, C.: Implications of the ACT-R learning theory: no magic bullets. In: Glaser, R. (ed.) Advances in Instructional Psychology: Educational Design and Cognitive Science, vol. 5, pp. 1–33. Erlbaum, Mahwah (2000)
2. Bahrick, H.P., Bahrick, L.E., Bahrick, A.S., Bahrick, P.E.: Maintenance of foreign language vocabulary and the spacing effect. Psychol. Sci. **4**, 316–321 (1993)
3. Glossary. https://pslcdatashop.web.cmu.edu/help?page=terms
4. Jastrzembski, T.S., Gluck, K.A., Gunzelmann, G.: Knowledge tracing and prediction of future trainee performance. In: 40th I/ITSEC Annual Meeting, pp. 1498–1508. National Training Systems Association, Orlando, FL (2006)
5. Jastrzembski, T.S., Gluck, K.A.: A formal comparison of model variants for performance prediction. In: Proceedings of the International Conference on Cognitive Modeling (ICCM), Manchester, England (2009)
6. Jastrzembski, T.S., Addis, K., Krusmark, M., Gluck, K.A., Rodgers, S.: Prediction intervals for performance prediction. In: International Conference on Cognitive Modeling (ICCM), pp. 109–114, Philadelphia, PA (2010)
7. Koedinger, K.R., Baker, R.S.J.D., Cunningham, K., Skogsholm, A., Leber, B., Stamper, J.: A data repository for the EDM community: the PSLC DATASHOP. In: Romero, C., Ventura, S., Pechenizkiy, M., Baker, R.S.J.D. (eds.) Handbook of Educational Data Mining, pp. 43–56. CRC Press, Boca Raton (2010)
8. Newell, A., Rosenbloom, P.S.: Mechanisms of skill acquisition and the law of practice. In: Anderson, J.R. (ed.) Cognitive Skills and Their Acquisition, vol. 1, pp. 1–55. Lawrence Erlbaum Associates, Inc., Hillsdale (1981)

Using Context to Optimize a Functional State Estimation Engine in Unmanned Aircraft System Operations

Kevin Durkee[1(✉)], Scott Pappada[1], Andres Ortiz[1], John Feeney[1], and Scott Galster[2]

[1] Aptima, Inc, Fairborn, USA
{kdurkee, spappada, aortiz, jfeeney}@aptima.com
[2] Air Force Research Laboratory, Dayton, USA
scott.galster@us.af.mil

Abstract. As UAS operations continue to expand, the ability to monitor real-time cognitive states of human operators would be a valuable asset. Although great strides have been made toward this capability using physiological signals, the inherent noisiness of these data hinders its readiness for operational deployment. We theorize the addition of contextual data alongside physiological signals could improve the accuracy of cognitive state classifiers. In this paper, we review a cognitive workload model development effort conducted in a simulated UAS task environment at the Air Force Research Laboratory (AFRL). Real-time workload model classifiers were trained using three levels of physiological data inputs both with and without context added. Following the evaluation of each classifier using four model evaluation metrics, we conclude that by adding contextual data to physiological-based models, we improved the ability to reliably measure real-time cognitive workload in our UAS operations test case.

Keywords: Context · Human performance · Modeling and simulation · Physiological measurement · Workload · UAS

1 Introduction

Unmanned Aircraft Systems (UAS) have grown to become a central capability of the modern United States Air Force by providing essential mission support while preserving the safety of its pilots. Although UAS operations physically remove the human from the aircraft, the human operators of these systems remain an essential component for achieving mission success. As the volume and complexity of UAS operations continues to expand, warfighters will become increasingly vulnerable to undesired cognitive states, such as high workload, stress, fatigue, and vigilance decrements. The ability to monitor these states throughout a mission would be a valuable asset to modern Air Force systems. Measuring cognitive states in relation to task and mission performance would provide the requisite data to detect if, and when, a warfighter has met his/her limits while diagnosing what intervention is best suited to sustaining good performance and obtaining the desired outcomes. By introducing this capability,

© Springer International Publishing Switzerland 2015
D.D. Schmorrow and C.M. Fidopiastis (Eds.): AC 2015, LNAI 9183, pp. 24–35, 2015.
DOI: 10.1007/978-3-319-20816-9_3

assessments of UAS operators would become integral system parameters about the mission to be proactively monitored and addressed before potential problems occur [1].

There has been a great deal of research on model-based classification techniques to provide real-time operator state monitoring capabilities. Physiological signals have been relied upon as a prominent source of data under the assumption that changes in cognitive activity produce a predictable associated response in physiology. Physiological data are also compelling given their potential to be available at all times and in any work domain, particularly with the emergence and growing affordability of wearable sensors. The majority of research has employed some combination of electroencephalography (EEG) [2], electrocardiogram (ECG) [3], pupillometry [4], or galvanic skin response (GSR) [5]. DARPA's Augmented Cognition (AugCog) was one of the first large-scale efforts to bring this research into warfighter applications [6]. In the Air Force Multi Attribute Task Battery (AF_MATB) environment, Wilson and Russell [7] introduced a novel application of artificial neural networks (ANNs) trained to each individual human performer for real-time mental workload classification using six channels of brain electrical activity, as well as eye, heart, and respiratory signals [7]. Wang et al. (2012) also employed the AF_MATB to introduce a novel hierarchical Bayesian technique that showed promise for cross-subject workload classification [8].

In spite of the many advancements in this line of research, the potential benefits remain inhibited by the inherent noisiness of physiological data. The term "noisy data" refers not only to the robustness of the raw signal itself, but also to the inconsistent and often ambiguous patterns in the processed signals and derived data features. This inconsistency can occur not only across humans, but also within the same individual person over time. Many previous operator state classification efforts have been forced to cater to these caveats and limitations in a variety of ways. For instance, in order to achieve 88 % classification accuracy, Wilson and Russell (2003) focused on highly discrete classifications of "low" versus "high" mental workload, and trained unique ANN models to each individual person [7]. For Wang et al. (2012) although a cross-subject workload classification method was introduced with approximately 80 % classification accuracy across low, medium, and high workload conditions, all eight of their participants' data appeared in both the model training and model testing data sets [8]. Furthermore, the model evaluation metrics reported across much of the published literature tend to focus on how well a *single* output matches that of the intended condition as a whole, rather than evaluating classifier outputs at specific points in time.

While prior research has provided the necessary stepping stones toward a deployable solution, there remains significant room for further innovation. Our recent work has sought to fill several key gaps in physiological-based cognitive state assessment through the development of the Functional State Estimation Engine (FuSE^2), a system designed to derive real-time cognitive state measurements that update frequently (e.g., second-by-second) and provide high-granularity measurement (e.g., 0–100 scale). The FuSE^2 system was initially developed and tested in the AF_MATB [9], and more recently has been applied within a realistic UAS simulation, the Vigilant Spirit Control Station (VSCS) [10]. Although FuSE^2 is capable of on-line supervised learning to adapt to an individual for improving model accuracy, we restrict the scope of this paper solely to cross-subject workload classification since a universal "plug and play" model that does not require per-subject training would be an ideal technological milestone.

The prospect of a cross-subject, physiological-only cognitive state classifier is very challenging, particularly one that can obtain high-resolution measurement. To some extent, there is no guarantee that subtle changes in a person's cognitive state will consistently be reflected in their physiological signals, and any patterns that exist are likely to vary across individuals. This begs the question of what other data sources could be available to help a model classifier "sift through the noise" of physiological signals and ultimately produce more precise measurements. One approach that has not been extensively studied in the operator state modeling literature is the addition of "contextual data" as model inputs alongside a human's real-time physiological signals. Context can generally be defined as any information that can be used to better characterize the situation of an entity [11]. In computer science literature, there is ample evidence that the utilization of contextual data can be used to greatly improve how system applications behave for a variety of purposes [12]. A similar approach could be explored to further optimize physiological-based operator state classification systems. A drawback of this approach is that a particular model classifier could become closely tied to the specific task environment on which it was trained. However, this may be an acceptable tradeoff for system developers since it could reduce a system's dependency on training separate model classifiers for each individual human performer. In addition, by selecting con-textual data that are available in a variety of domains – such as system interactions and task performance measures – this maintains the possibility that a cross-person classifier would transfer across some (though assuredly not all) work domains.

The objective of this work was to explore to what extent contextual data inputs can increase the accuracy of physiological-based cognitive state classifiers in a UAS task environment. In the following sections we review a UAS study that was used to produce data for building real-time workload classifiers within the FuSE^2 system, followed by an analysis with four model evaluation metrics of both second-by-second and aggregated model outputs. We specifically opted to examine the effects of adding two contextual data inputs – human computer interaction (HCI) rate and primary task performance – since these measures were hypothesized to have a predictive relationship with cognitive workload in the UAS study environment, and would be obtainable data inputs in a variety of other task environments.

2 Methods

2.1 Data Collection

Data were collected within a simulated UAS task environment at the Human Universal Measurement and Assessment Network (HUMAN) Laboratory located at Wright-Patterson Air Force Base. We focused exclusively on cognitive workload for this study and the ensuing model development effort so as to constrain the problem space to a single human functional state that has wide applicability, particularly to UAS operations, and a large body of literature to draw from as needed. The UAS task simulation employed the VSCS operator interface (Fig. 1) paired with a Multi-Modal

Communication (MMC) tool for issuing communication requests [13] and a custom-built lights and gauges monitoring display. The primary task objective was to track a high value target (HVT) while keeping the HVT continuously positioned on the center of the UAS sensor crosshairs. Simultaneously, participants conducted two secondary tasks: (1) monitor the lights/gauges display and acknowledge each system event via button presses; and (2) verbally respond to each communication request via the MMC tool. Task difficulty was manipulated by modifying the HVT speed and motion complexity, the number of communication requests, and the number of light/gauge events in each 5 min trial. This task paradigm allowed for a gradual titration of task difficulty across 15 five-minute conditions ranging from easy to hard, which was intended to induce variations in workload and performance for each participant.

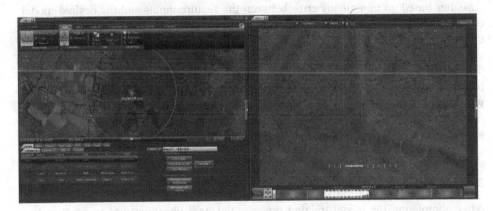

Fig. 1. The VSCS operator interface

There were 25 participants with each person completing one training session and one data collection session each. Dependent measures were threefold: (1) a suite of physiological metrics collected during each task condition consisting of six-channel EEG, ECG, off-body eye tracking, respiratory activity, electrodermal activity, and voice analysis features; (2) self-reported NASA Task Load Index (TLX) responses collected at the end of each trial [14]; and (3) system-based performance measures derived from Aptima, Inc.'s Performance Measurement Engine (PM Engine™) that utilized behavioral and situational data to estimate continuous performance for all three task requirements. NASA TLX responses and condition difficulties yielded a correlation of $r = 0.75$ across all subjects and $r = 0.89$ mean correlation within subjects, suggesting the manipulations were successful at inducing the intended variance in workload.

2.2 Model Development

Using the data collected from this study, a set of model-based classifiers was developed within the FuSE^2 system using machine learning techniques that train each classifier to output second-by-second workload estimates on a 0–100 scale. Adhering to the approach in Durkee et al. [9], we first applied a noise injection algorithm to all NASA TLX responses under the assumption that workload does not remain perfectly static over time. This algorithm derives an estimate of "ground truth" on a second-by-second basis to which the model classifiers are subsequently trained. Because it is impractical to obtain operator responses at very frequent intervals, this algorithm relies on a theoretically-grounded correlate of workload as the basis for injecting this noise. We refer to each series of ground truth estimates as the "desired model output" given each model classifier's attempt to find the best fit based on its feature inputs. A comprehensive training set was then prepared containing all selected feature inputs and the desired model outputs. The training set included data from 19 of the 25 study participants, while the other six participants were randomly selected for model evaluation. A training process was initiated to derive model weights for each classifier based on minimizing error between the feature inputs and the desired model outputs. Three levels of physiological inputs were selected: (1) a "reduced" model consisting of three EEG channels (Fz, Pz, O2) and ECG; (2) a "standard" model consisting of six EEG channels (Fz, Pz, O2, F7, F8, T3) and ECG; and (3) an "expanded" model consisting of the same physiological inputs as the standard model, but with pupillometry included. For each level of physiological input, one classifier was trained with contextual data included and another classifier was trained without contextual data included. A seventh model was also trained consisting solely of contextual data inputs (i.e., no physiological inputs).

2.3   Model Evaluation

After completing the model training process, the next objective was to produce test results in order to evaluate the accuracy of each workload classifier, particularly to assess how the addition of contextual data impacted model accuracy. Workload classifier results were produced through a batch playback of data collected from the six participants excluded from the training set. All six test participants completed the same 15 five-minute trials used to train the model classifiers, thus totaling 90 trials used for evaluation. The batch playback process simulated the production of real-time classifier results by outputting one workload estimate per second on a 0–100 scale for each of the seven models, totaling 300 values per model within each trial. Model accuracy was analyzed via summary statistics in two general ways: (1) second-by-second classifier results (see Sect. 3.1); and (2) aggregated classifier results averaged over entire 5 min trials (see Sect. 3.2). Two model evaluation metrics (similarity score and relative classification accuracy) were used to assess the degree to which each classifier accurately replicated the desired model outputs on a second-by-second basis. In contrast, two other metrics (correlation and absolute difference between average model output and NASA TLX) were used to assess how closely mean classifier output for each trial resembled its respective NASA TLX rating. These four metrics – described further in Sect. 3 – were chosen to balance analyses across the micro- and macro-levels, and to evaluate both patterns and absolute differences compared to ground truth estimates. A secondary objective was to assess the degree to which model accuracy changed as the volume of physiological data inputs is manipulated. A graphical plot is provided for each of the four model evaluation metrics along with discussion of observable trends. Each figure includes results for the three physiological-based model configurations (reduced, standard, and expanded inputs) both with and without contextual data inputs. Results for the context-only model using the specified evaluation metric are also provided as a basis for comparison. Error bars in each graphical plot are shown to illustrate the standard error derived from averaging each metric across the 90 trials.

3 Results and Discussion

3.1 Second-by-Second Workload Classifier Results

The first model evaluation metric is a nonlinear similarity measure known as the correntropy coefficient [15]. For this analysis, we refer to this metric as a "similarity score" in which a higher score indicates a higher degree of pattern similarity between a particular model's actual outputs and the desired model outputs. For the 90 test trials, a correntropy coefficient was derived and each coefficient was adapted to a 0–100 scale to represent the similarity score. A zero value indicates there is no degree of similarity between actual and desired model output, while 100 indicates the actual and desired outputs are identical. We consider the similarity score to be a particularly important metric because it directly gauges how closely each model's second-by-second classifier outputs and trending information matches that of our desired model outputs. This metric's strength is that it focuses squarely on the *shape* of the trend line for each trial's second-by-second model output, while not taking into account whether each individual state classification is at the desired level in an absolute sense. This supplements our other second-by-second model evaluation metric, relative classification accuracy.

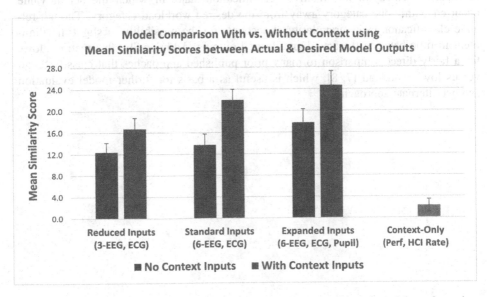

Fig. 2. Comparison of with-context and without-context results for each model configuration using mean similarity scores between 6 test participants' actual & desired model outputs.

Figure 2 illustrates the mean similarity scores for each model as averaged across the 90 test trials. The six physiological-based models yielded two primary trends. First, the additional of contextual data inputs increased the mean similarity score for all three levels of physiological model inputs; the reduced input model increased by 35 %, the standard input increased by 61 %, and the expanded input model increased by 39 %. By comparison, immediately it can be seen this metric highlights a key limitation with the context-only model configuration. With a mean similarity score of only 2.2, the contextual data features by themselves were not able to closely produce the desired model output trend. This is a particularly notable finding given that a context-only model achieved a very low similarity score, yet the addition of contextual data to physiological data produced similarity scores considerably higher than either model could achieve alone. Secondly, as a more general finding, the mean similarity scores increased as the number of physiological inputs increased, resulting in the expanded input model with context producing the highest mean similarity score (24.6). To some extent this pattern is not surprising since this metric most directly reflects the machine learning processes employed during model training. Thus, by increasing the number of feature inputs, the chances of finding reliable model weights will typically increase.

The next metric is classification accuracy of each model's second-by-second outputs relative to desired model output. This metric is intended to supplement the similarity score by examining how frequently the desired *amount* of workload is successfully being measured at any point in time. For this metric we first identified four discrete categories of workload – low, medium-low, medium-high, and high – the boundaries of which were derived from the distribution of all NASA TLX responses. Each individual classifier result was then compared to desired model output at each corresponding point in time for all seven models. Values were flagged as either correct or incorrect based on its "relative" classification state, in which the actual value occurred within one category away from the desired workload category. Though relative classification lacks granularity, it accounts for the possibility of slight misalignment in time between the actual and desired outputs. Additionally, this metric allows for a fairly direct comparison to many prior published approaches that classify "high versus low" workload [7, 8], which is useful as a basis for further model evaluation against alternate approaches.

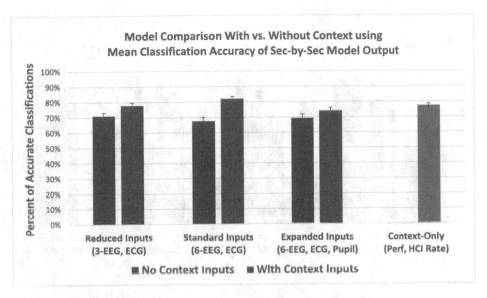

Fig. 3. Comparison of with-context and without-context results for each model configuration using mean classification accuracy of 6 test participants' second-by-second model output.

Figure 3 illustrates the mean classification accuracy of each model's second-by-second outputs across all 90 test trials. Overall, there is low variability across the seven models with a range from 67 % to 82 %. However, there is a consistent trend that by adding context to each of the three physiological-based model configurations, classification accuracy improved in all three cases. The most notable improvement occurred for the standard input model, which produced the lowest classification accuracy without context, yet produced the highest classification accuracy with context added. Furthermore, by adding context to the reduced input and standard input models, this provided another example (much like similarity score) of combining physiological and contextual inputs to provide more accurate classifications than either set of inputs could alone.

3.2 Aggregated Workload Classifier Results

The remaining two model evaluation metrics are: (1) correlation between average model output and NASA TLX; and (2) absolute difference between average model output and NASA TLX. For the correlation analysis, we believed it would be most suitable to derive a Pearson's correlation coefficient (r) on a per-person basis to better reflect how a given model tends to track any given person's cognitive workload across the entire length of each trial. As such, the correlation coefficients for each of the six individual test participants and for all seven model classifiers are illustrated in Fig. 4.

Perhaps the most noticeable finding in Fig. 4 is the high correlations achieved by

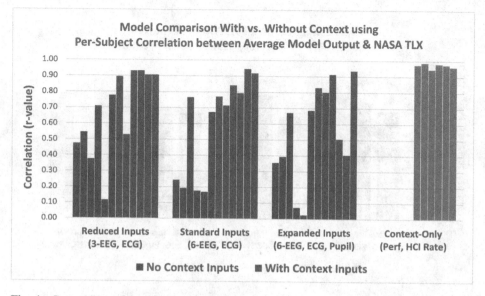

Fig. 4. Comparison of with-context and without-context results for each model configuration using per-subject correlation of NASA TLX and 6 test participants' average model output.

the context-only model ($r = 0.95$–0.99). Although a strong relationship was anticipated between performance, HCI rate, and NASA TLX responses given the nature of the task environment, this result was more pronounced than expected. Another key finding is the degree to which adding context to the three physiological-based models consistently improves each correlation. While these correlations are not quite as high as the context-only model, half of the correlation coefficients are boosted to approximately $r = 0.90$ or higher with the addition of context, and only three of the 18 coefficients remain below $r = 0.70$. Considering the physiological-based models also achieved considerably higher mean similarity scores than the context-only model (see Sect. 3.1), as well as comparable relative classification accuracy, this suggests the blend of physiological and contextual data features may provide the ideal real-time workload assessment capability within this UAS test case. Lastly, one final observation from Fig. 4 is that the correlation coefficients tend to decrease overall as the number of physiological inputs increases. At face value, this finding appears to contrast the observation from mean similarity scores in which a larger number of physiological features resulted in a higher similarity score. This may simply be random chance due to the small number of test participants, or could imply an undesired effect caused by the additional physiological inputs that is not observable in the other metrics. Further evaluation work is needed to gain deeper insight into this observation.

The final model evaluation metric is the absolute difference between average model output and NASA TLX for each trial. This metric provides insight into each model's ability to produce workload classifications that accurately reflect the overall workload induced over the course of an entire trial.

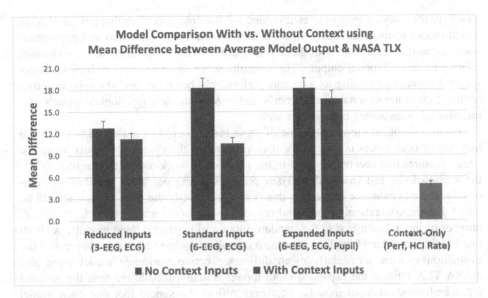

Fig. 5. Comparison of with-context and without-context results for each model configuration using mean difference between NASA TLX and 6 test participants' average model output.

As shown in Fig. 5, the overall trend of these data largely mirrors the correlation results. The context-only model produced the smallest mean difference (5.0) between average model output and NASA TLX rating. Likewise, the addition of contextual data inputs reduced the mean difference for all three levels of physiological-based models (reduced, standard, and expanded inputs). Out of the physiological-based models, the standard input model with context produced the smallest mean difference (10.6) between average model output and NASA TLX ratings, followed closely by the reduced input model (11.3). The standard input model was boosted the most through the additional of contextual data inputs by reducing the mean difference by nearly half (from 18.3 to 10.6). The reduced input model (from 12.8 to 11.3) and expanded input model (from 18.2 to 16.7) were only marginally boosted through the additional of contextual data, though the reduced input model already had a notably smaller difference than the other two models before adding context. Similar to the correlation results in Fig. 4, the model with the largest number of inputs produced the largest mean difference.

4 Conclusions

In summary, we conclude that contextual data collected from our UAS task environment generally enhanced the FuSE^2 system's ability to accurately classify workload for 90 new trials across six test participants. This trend is observed across all four model evaluation metrics and remains consistent, albeit with differing levels of impact, across all three levels of physiological data inputs: 3-channel EEG and ECG ("reduced input model"), 6-channel EEG and ECG ("standard input model"), and 6-channel EEG, ECG, and pupillometry ("expanded input model"). Thorough consideration was given based on the varying perspectives provided by the four model evaluation metrics, in which model results were analyzed on both a second-by-second basis and aggregated basis, as well as analyzing both the absolute differences and patterns of state changes relative to desired model outputs. These results serve as an example of how carefully selected context pertaining to a human performer's behaviors and the mission environment can support a model classifier's ability to translate physiological signals into meaningful assessments of cognitive state.

From a skeptical viewpoint, some of these results could be attributed to either the increase of data inputs in general, or perhaps even to the contextual inputs being the "best" features that account for most of the variance in workload by themselves. While the scope of our test case and analyses prevents ruling out these possibilities completely, there is evidence suggesting this is not necessarily the case. First, it should be noted that the context-only model and reduced input model with context have a small number of inputs compared to the standard input and expanded input models, yet both rated highly on three of the four metrics. It can also be observed that for several of the evaluation metrics, particularly mean difference between average model input and NASA TLX ratings, the expanded input model actually rated lower than the reduced input and standard input models. This may reflect the simple fact that each model depends less on the volume of inputs, and more on having data inputs that provide a discoverable and generalizable indicator of state changes.

It is also necessary to cover an important and perhaps obvious question stemming from these results: is it better to rely simply on a context-only model consisting solely of performance and HCI inputs, while omitting physiological data altogether? This question bears consideration since the context-only model outperformed the six physiological-based models when comparing aggregated model output and NASA TLX ratings (i.e., correlation and absolute difference). At face value, this may challenge the value of physiological data acquisition and convince system developers to rely exclusively on task-specific behavioral data, particularly due to the added cost of introducing physiological sensors. However, there are several counterarguments to this assertion. First, while the aggregated context-only model output was highly predictive of NASA TLX ratings, these model assessments are limited to entire 5 min trials and thus not available on a second-to-second basis. This could be problematic since it may imply the context-only model would not be capable of detecting a sudden and drastic shift in workload with sufficient time to intervene. The similarity scores suggest the physiological-based models with context would be more likely to detect such an occurrence. Second, it bears mentioning that in most cases, contextual data such as HCI rates and primary task performance are likely to be very "task-specific", whereas physiological signals are always present and have some degree of similarity regardless of a person's task requirements. Hence, the accuracy of a context-only model could be more likely to degrade if it were used to assess human operators in new task environments that a trained model has not been exposed to before. Third, it is important to note that as cognitive state monitoring capabilities are developed and tested in different work domains, the utility of different types of contextual data as model inputs is likely to vary substantially. An extensive feature selection process must be accomplished to identify which task-specific indicators exist within a work domain, and the degree of utility they provide to optimize physiological-based models for assessment.

Acknowledgement. Distribution A: Approved for public release; distribution unlimited. This material is based on work supported by AFRL under Contract FA8650-11-C-6236. Any opinions, findings, conclusions, or recommendations expressed in this material are those of the authors and do not necessarily reflect the views of AFRL.

References

1. Blackhurst, J., Gresham, J., Stone, M.: The quantified warrior: how DoD should lead human performance augmentation. Armed Forces Journal (2012)
2. Gevins, A., Smith, M.E., Leong, H., McEvoy, L., Whitfield, S., Du, R., Rush, G.: Monitoring working memory load during computer-based tasks with EEG pattern recognition methods. Hum. Factors **40**, 79–91 (1998)
3. Hoover, A., Singh, A., Fishel-Brown, S., Muth, E.: Real-time detection of workload changes using heart rate variability. Biomed. Signal Process. Control **7**, 333–341 (2012)
4. Just, M.A., Carpenter, P.A.: The intensity dimension of thought: pupillometric indices of sentence processing. Can. J. Exp. Psychol. **47**(2), 310–339 (1993)
5. Setz, C., Arnrich, B., Schumm, J., La Marca, R., Troster, G.: Discriminating stress from cognitive load using a wearable EDA device. Technology **14**(2), 410–417 (2010)
6. John, M., Kobus, D.A., Morrison, J.G., Schmorrow, D.: Overview of the DARPA augmented cognition technical integration experiment. Int. J. Hum. Comput. Interact. **17**(2), 131–149 (2004)
7. Wilson, G.F., Russell, C.A.: Real-time assessment of mental workload using psychophysiological measures and artificial neural networks. Hum. Factors **45**(4), 635–644 (2003)
8. Wang, Z., Hope, R.M., Wang, Z., Ji, Q., Gray, W.: Cross-subject workload classification with a hierarchical bayes model. NeuroImage **59**(1), 64–69 (2012)
9. Durkee, K., Geyer, A., Pappada, S., Ortiz, A., Galster, S.: Real-time workload assessment as a foundation for human performance augmentation. In: Schmorrow, D.D., Fidopiastis, C.M. (eds.) AC 2013. LNCS, vol. 8027, pp. 279–288. Springer, Heidelberg (2013)
10. Rowe, A.J., Liggett, K.K., Davis, J.E.: Vigilant spirit control station: a research testbed for multi-UAS supervisory control interfaces. In: Proceedings of the 15th International Symposium on Aviation Psychology, Dayton, OH (2009)
11. Dey, A.: Understanding and using context. Pers. Ubiquitous Comput. **5**(1), 4–7 (2001)
12. Dey, A., Abowd, G., Salber, D.: A conceptual framework and a toolkit for supporting the rapid prototyping of context-aware applications. Hum. Comput. Interact. **16**(2), 97–166 (2001)
13. Finomore, V., Popik, D., Dallman, R., Stewart, J., Satterfield, K., Castle, C.: Demonstration of a network-centric communication management suite: multi-modal communication. In: Proceedings of the 55th Human Factors and Ergonomics Society Annual Meeting. HFES, Las Vegas (2011)
14. Hart, S.G., Staveland, L.E.: Development of NASA-TLX (Task Load Index): results of empirical and theoretical research. In: Peter, A.H., Najmedin, M. (eds.) Advances in Psychology, vol. 52, pp. 139–183. Elseiver, North-Holland (2006)
15. Xu, J., Bakardjian, H., Cichocki, A., Principe, J.: A new nonlinear similarity measure for multichannel signals. Neural Netw. **21**, 222–231 (2008)

Methods for Determining the Role of Fatigue and Cognitive Load on Behavior Detection Officers (BDOs) Performance in the Field

Robert Kittinger[1](✉) and James Bender[2]

[1] Sandia National Laboratories, Albuquerque, NM, USA
rskitti@sandia.gov
[2] Deloitte, Washington, DC, USA
jambender@deloitte.com

Abstract. Job analysis and cognitive task analysis (CTA) are two methods for identifying all job tasks, both observable and unobservable respectively, which correlate to successful job performance. These methods will be applied to the Transportation Security Administration's (TSA's) Behavior Detection Officers (BDOs) to identify the elements which compose their job and to identify what elements are most difficult, important and frequently accomplished in the support of our national security. This paper will describe one method for conducting a job analysis on the BDO job and then a method for following that work with a cognitive task analysis. The described JA and CTA will provide a scientific foundation for future research and analysis of the BDO job position and successful performance of that job.

Keywords: National security · Homeland security · Transportation security administration · TSA · Behavior detection officers · BDO · Job analysis · Work analysis · Cognitive task analysis · Cognitive load · Cognitive fatigue · Fatigue · Job performance · Methodology

1 Introduction

In 2006, the Transportation Security Administration (TSA), under the Department of Homeland Security (DHS), shifted from primarily screening passengers and their baggage and started training officers to identify suspicious behaviors and/or activities at airports. The officers chosen to receive this training and execute this mission are selected from the existing pool of Transportation Security Officers (TSOs) to join the Behavior Detection and Analysis (BDA) Program. Once training is completed, these officers become certified Behavior Detection Officers (BDOs). As recently as 2013, there were over 3,000 BDOs deployed to 176 airports though today both numbers are reduced (Pistole 2013). In 2012 alone, their work resulted in 30 plane boarding denials, 79 law enforcement investigations, and 183 arrests (Pistole 2013).

BDOs observe individuals' behavior for indications that they are experiencing stress, fear, and/or deception which could indicate a passenger is participating in illicit activity. These officers are trained to assess the environment, create a baseline of normal behavior, and then identify potential high-risk passengers based on deviations

© Springer International Publishing Switzerland 2015
D.D. Schmorrow and C.M. Fidopiastis (Eds.): AC 2015, LNAI 9183, pp. 36–43, 2015.
DOI: 10.1007/978-3-319-20816-9_4

from the normal behavior baseline. BDOs, from 2006 to December 2014, were trained using a method called SPOT (Screening Passengers by Observational Techniques) – now labeled as Behavior Detection (BD), under TSA Behavior Detection & Analysis Program (BDA). SPOT was originally created for Boston's BOS airport and later rolled out nationally (Hallowell 2011; Seidman 2011). SPOT was created using subject matter experts (SMEs) who based much of the system on similar behavior detection systems deployed in international sectors and federal entities. SPOT was tailored to American airports and has continued to evolve since it was launched. Two notable SMEs utilized in the creation and modifications of SPOT include Rafi Ron, former Israeli airports security chief, and Paul Ekman – famous for his 40 year career in interpreting the emotions coded in facial expressions (Burns 2010). Since October 2014, TSA has been piloting an updated version of the BDO protocol, referred to as the optimized BD indicator protocol, or Optimization.

The BD system provided BDOs with a large list of nearly 100 behaviors (behavioral indicators) to watch for while passengers are in the TSA checkpoint queue and other locations. BDOs observe for these indicators and when a specific threshold has been met, that individual would undergo additional screening before crossing into the sterile area of the airport (i.e., the area beyond the TSA checkpoint with access to the plane terminals). If the passenger in question passed the additional screening they would proceed, without further intervention, into the sterile area of the airport. If, however, the passenger in question failed to pass the additional screening, or excessive BDO points were assigned to that passenger, a Law Enforcement Officer (LEO) would be summoned to take over.

The piloted Optimized indicator protocol training was deployed in the field in October of 2014 (Bugler 2013). It was created to address several of the criticisms and concerns of the program (Government Accountability Office [GAO] 2013). Previously, there had been criticisms that there was no scientific evidence that SPOT worked and through the optimization effort, TSA has provided scientific support from various fields associated with deception detection, verbal and non-verbal communication, and physiological areas of academic research.

The purpose of the current paper is to discuss the methodology of conducting a job analysis on the occupation of BDOs, how the job analysis will navigate the recent BD-to-Optimized indicator protocol changes in the standard operating procedures (SOP), and how to conduct a cognitive task analysis (CTA).

2 Literature

Job analysis is the foundation of industrial-organizational (I-O) psychology, and it paves the way for many other types of work to be done (e.g., CTA, assessment centers, recruitment, selection systems). A job analysis is a structured process of identifying and measuring the elements (i.e., tasks and sub-tasks; equipment, machines, tools, technology; knowledge, skills, abilities, etc.) that compose a single job (Van De Voort and Whelan 2012). Based on how the resulting job analysis will be used the more detailed aspects can be tailored to the expected need [e.g., collecting SME job task difficulty, importance, and frequency ratings (DIF analysis) to support an HR/training department].

Several methods for conducting a job analysis exist including Threshold Traits Analysis, Ability Requirements Scales, Position Analysis Questionnaire, Critical Incidents Technique, Task Inventory/CODAP, Functional Job Analysis, and Job Elements Method, to name a few (Levine et al. 1983). Each of these has different strengths and weaknesses but job analysis experts consistently rate the Task Inventory/CODAP and the Functional Job Analysis as two of the best for the purposes of defining and describing the job and also meeting legal requirements (Levine et al. 1983). To paraphrase Levine et al., ultimately, job analysis experts overwhelmingly endorse a strategy of using a combination of multiple job analysis methods (1983, p. 346). With this in mind, for legal purposes, the Uniform Guidelines on Employee Selection Procedures (Equal Opportunity Employment Commission 1978), clearly states their preference for a job analysis method which identifies job tasks that are "observable behaviors" (p. 228).

Identifying the job tasks, sub-tasks, and other elements that compose a job with a job analysis is helpful in informing high-level organizational leadership decisions to more effectively guide their personnel's employee lifecycles (i.e., recruitment, selection, training, promotions, teams, job duties, etc.). It can also be used to perform an even deeper analysis of the work being done, as is the case with a CTA.

A CTA is used to systematically identify the critical human worker's cognitive activities (e.g., decision making, goal forming) related to the successful completion of job tasks. Where a quality job analysis produces a list of observable tasks and work behaviors, a CTA captures many of the internal processes and steps that are not immediately observable - without specialized cognitive measures. In many ways, "Cognitive task analysis is the extension of traditional task analysis techniques to yield information about the knowledge, thought process, and goal structures that underlie observable task performance" (Schraagen et al. 2000, p. 3). A CTA is also used to understand the cognitive demands various job tasks require (Hoffman and Militello 2012). The CTA utilizes a combination of worker observations, surveys, and in-depth SME interviews to identify and map worker's cognitive processes (Wei and Salvendy 2004).

The recent rise in popularity of CTAs has been attributed to the growing prevalence of job specialization, the growing use of smart machines, and workplace modernization in our society (Hoffman and Militello 2012). For these reasons, CTA has been used extensively in the aerospace industry (Seamster et al. 2000), as well as with air traffic controllers (Seamster et al. 1993). Indeed CTA is a great fit for assessing the BDOs at airports as well because CTA's strength is in supporting jobs that require cognition in the form of inference, diagnosis, judgment, and/or decision making.

In 2011, a Science and Technology (S&T) validation study of the BDO program was conducted in partnership with the American Institutes for Research (AIR). This research showed just how effective and important the job tasks of BDOs were. Their study found that across approximately 70,000 random samples of passengers submitted to secondary screening, BDOs using the BD method were nine times more likely to catch a high-threat passenger than random screenings (Pistole 2013). This type of validation study demonstrates that while cognitive load may have an effect on BDO performance, the BDO's work is still effective in contributing as one layer of TSA security keeping passengers safe. A cognitive task analysis will demonstrate where various forms of cognition support BDO work and ultimately how to improve that work process so that BDO screening is even more effective.

3 Method

The current research is ongoing and will conduct both a job analysis and a CTA. The job analysis will assess the full scope of the BDO occupation. To do this, the researchers first acquired all possible existing sources of BDO job information including job descriptions, training materials, standard operating procedures (SOPs), other relevant HR documents and policies, and any related previous job analysis research or data.

During the document review phase, a previous job analysis covering all TSA screening positions (TSO, LTSO, STSO, STI, CCO, and BDOs) was discovered called the "OJAS" (Job Analysis of Transportation Security Officer Jobs), which was conducted by HumRRO. In this job analysis, 97 of the 416 job tasks were linked to BDOs.

A second job analysis was also found, the Human Performance Requirements Analysis (HPRA) which was conducted by Applied Research Associates (ARA). This job analysis identified a total of 3,164 TSA officer screening tasks (including Behavioral, Cognitive and Communication job tasks). Unfortunately, the BDO job fell out of the scope of that research so none of the identified screening tasks were linked to BDOs – though many likely apply based on overlap between TSO and BDO job tasks identified in the OJAS. A small group of BDO SMEs will be consulted to analyze the 3,164 tasks and to identify which tasks are relevant to the BDO job and which are not.

A third job analysis, specific to the BDO job, was conducted by American Institutes for Research (AIR) and was completed in March 2010. This job analysis identified 107 BDO job tasks, of which 95 were organized under 10 duties (Hendrickson et al. 2010). This research also identified and linked 56 knowledge, skills, abilities and other factors (KSAOs) to the related job tasks they supported. Additionally, 64 competencies from the TSA Competency Catalog were linked to the relevant job tasks they supported (Hendrickson et al. 2010).

Once the document review phase is concluded, a job analysis will be conducted to validate the currency of the job tasks being performed and to analyze differences between the former protocol and the Optimized protocol. Twelve incumbent BDO subject matter experts will be sampled from airports around the country, with the minimum qualifications of at least 1 year on the job, presently holding the BDO position, and being trained in both BD and Optimized indicator screening methods. A minimum of 6 months of job experience has been suggested as a rule of thumb (Gatewood and Field 1994; Harvey et al. 2007) though the experience necessary is expected to vary from job to job and BDO work is highly cognitive.

The national sample would be selected to increase the representativeness of the SME sample for the national population. The national sample will also help transcend regional and airport specific training differences. The SMEs would convene as a group in a conference room for 2 weeks. Each SME would be given a laptop with custom job analysis software loaded on it – created to leverage the existing BDO job tasks identified in the OJAS and HPRA.

The researcher would lead the team of SMEs through the existing job tasks and add additional job tasks as needed (i.e., tasks specific to the optimized indicator protocol). During this time the researcher would also add any subtasks below tasks that were not fully described; identify a list of KSAOs that supported all of the tasks and subtasks;

and identify the equipment, machines, tools and technology (EMTTs) that supported BDO job task performance.

Once all additions and modifications to the list of job tasks had been made, the list would be uploaded to their laptops. The SMEs would then, working independently, screen each job task and related subtasks in a series of steps to (a) Verify it is accurate and current; (b) Check boxes to indicate if it applies "only to Optimized" or "only to BD" (the default would be that it applies to both); (c) Identify all of the relevant KSAOs that supported each task; (d) Identify all of the relevant EMTTs that supported each task; and finally the SMEs would rate each task based on its difficulty, importance and frequency (DIF analysis), and complexity. The difficulty and complexity ratings will serve to ensure the following cognitive task analysis sufficiently explores the highly difficult and/or complex tasks (Fig. 1).

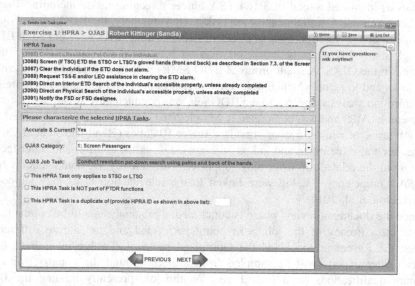

Fig. 1. Sandia's existing job analysis software, formerly used with S/L/TSOs, would be tailored to the BDO job

Once all of the SMEs complete the task of linking and rating the job tasks, the researcher will lead the group in conducting a CTA. Prior to conducting this CTA, the researcher will coordinate with TSA to understand its specific downstream use of the CTA outputs. This will ensure that all relevant and necessary data is collected during the CTA.

The CTA will be used to map out the chronology for various sequences of job tasks and sub-tasks, identify where decisions are made, what criteria on which those decisions should be based, and in general where the cognitive work is being done (Crandall et al. 2006; Jonassen et al. 1999). To complete the CTA, the researcher would begin to create a chronological flow diagram of job tasks and subtasks in a software package (i.e., Euterpe, Hierarchical Task Analysis, Cognitive Analysis Tool, Microsaint, or MS

Visio). The SMEs would guide the creation of the task chronologies adding to and modifying the design until it was complete. Disagreements in the design would be discussed until there was a group consensus (Fig. 2).

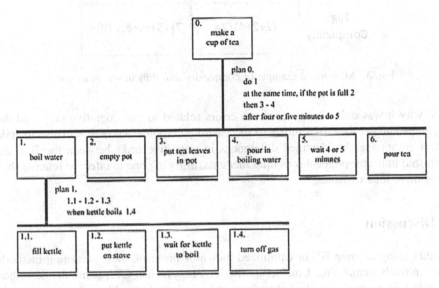

Fig. 2. Generic example from a Hierarchical Task Analysis

Once the observable tasks were accurately diagrammed, the researcher would walk through each sequence with the SMEs and add all of the unseen tasks (e.g., mental processes, planning, calculations, judgments, strategies, decisions, knowledge accessed, etc.) into the sequence while noting any critical cues, potential errors, strategies used, and branching in various directions as when decisions lead to different actions (Militello and Hutton 1998).

To help the same twelve incumbent BDO subject matter experts think through specific job task processes, related critical incidents will be collected from their group during interviews and then the group will be lead through a discussion to identify the specific steps in decision making and all the variables that were considered. Once the cognitive task map is completed, the SMEs will independently rate the cognitive tasks for difficulty, importance, frequency and complexity. Complex tasks are defined as those that have many steps or considerations, while task difficulty pertains to the likelihood of doing it incorrectly or producing the wrong outcome (Fig. 3).

Once the CTA is completed, the researcher will validate the data by observing SMEs on the job for a few days and asking questions about why they did various things or made various decisions. The observed cases and answers to the questions will then be mapped to the CTA diagram to demonstrate alignment between the map and what was observed.

The final products of the CTA will be the task process map and a Cognitive Demands Table. The Cognitive Demands Table will identify all difficult cognitive

	Low Difficulty	High Difficulty
Low Complexity	1+2 =	$\sqrt{5}+7 =$
High Complexity	(2+2+4)/2=	$7(\sqrt{5}+6)+8(\sqrt{79})=$

Fig. 3. Math-based example of complexity and difficulty interactions

tasks, why it was difficult, any common errors related to that cognitive task, and the cues and strategies the BDOs utilize to successfully complete a task. It will also include a chart comparing the identified differences in cognitive tasks between the BD and Optimized indicator protocol screening methods, allowing one to infer the relative shift in cognitive load demands.

4 Discussion

Whether using existing BD or Optimized indicator protocol, these screening methods are cognitively demanding. Conducting the job analysis and CTA using the described methods will ensure that all of the observable and unobservable tasks are not only identified but also related to one another and qualified with important information. The outputs of this important work will ensure that the TSA leadership has all of the information they need to assess and compare the SPOT and Optimized screening methods. This research could also provide valuable information to help the newly created Optimized training evolve over time to most effectively train BDOs to make the best decisions at the decisions points, and increase training time for the most difficult job tasks. Future empirical research could build on this BDO CTA by measuring BDO cognitive load in the field, in real time, while officers perform the most cognitively demanding tasks. The job analysis and CTA could also be used to create better tests and measures for selecting future BDO candidates in order to maximize the human capital and minimize BDO attrition – lowering program-wide BDO training costs.

References

Pistole, J.S.: Statement of Administrator John S. Pistole Transportation Security Administration U.S. Department of Homeland Security Before the United States House of Representatives Committee on Homeland Security Subcommittee on Transportation Security, pp. 1–5 (testimony of John S. Pistole). http://www.tsa.gov/sites/default/files/assets/pdf/11-14-13_testimony_jsp.pdf. Accessed 2013

Burns, B.: The TSA Blog: TSA SPOT Program: Still Going Strong, 21 May 2010. http://blog.tsa.gov/2010/05/tsa-spot-program-still-going-strong.html. Accessed 9 Feb 2015

Hallowell, B: TSA Launches Israeli-Style Behavior Detection at Boston's Logan Airport, 2 Aug 2011. http://www.theblaze.com/stories/2011/08/02/tsa-launches-israeli-style-behavior-detection-at-bostons-logan-airport/Katherine. Accessed 9 Feb 2015. Walsh interview of Ron Rafi. 1 Feb 2006, http://www.csoonline.com/article/2120522/investigations-forensics/behavior-pattern-recognition-and-why-racial-profiling-doesn-t-work.html

Seidman, A.: TSA launching behavior-detection program at Boston airport, 17 Aug 2011. http://articles.latimes.com/2011/aug/17/nation/la-na-tsa-logan-20110818. Accessed 12 Feb 2015

Bugler, E.: Written testimony of TSA administrator for a house subcommittee on transportation security hearing titled "TSA's SPOT Program and Initial Lessons From the LAX Shooting", 12 February 2015. http://www.dhs.gov/news/2013/11/14/written-testimony-tsa-administrator-house-homeland-security-subcommittee. Accessed 14 Nov 2013

Government Accountability Office. TSA should limit future funding for behavior detection activities (GAO Publication No. 14-159). U.S. Government Printing Office, Washington, D.C. (2013)

Van De Voort, D.M., Whelan, T.J.: Work analysis questionnaires and app interviews. The Handbook of Work Analysis, pp. 41–80. Routledge, New York (2012)

Levine, E.L., Ash, R.A., Hall, H., Sistrunk, F.: Evaluation of job analysis methods by experienced job analysts. Acad. Manag. J. 26(2), 339–348 (1983)

Equal Employment Opportunity Commission, C. S. C. U. S. D. L. U., Equal Employment Opportunity Commission. Uniform guidelines on employee selection procedures. Fed. Reg. 43(166), 38295–38309 (1978)

Schraagen, J.M., Chipman, S.F., Shalin, V.L. (eds.): Cognitive Task Analysis. Psychology Press, New York (2000)

Hoffman, R.R., Militello, L.G.: Perspectives on Cognitive Task Analysis: Historical Origins and Modern Communities of Practice. Psychology Press, New York (2012)

Wei, J., Salvendy, G.: The cognitive task analysis methods for job and task design: review and reappraisal. Behav. Inf. Technol. 23(4), 273–299 (2004)

Seamster, T.L., Redding, R.E., Kaempf, G.L.: A skill-based cognitive task analysis framework. Cogn. Task Anal. 135–146 (2000)

Seamster, T.L., Redding, R.E., Cannon, J.R., Ryder, J.M., Purcell, J.A.: Cognitive task analysis of expertise in air traffic control. Int. J. Aviat. Psychol. 3(4), 257–283 (1993)

Hendrickson, C., Myers, T.L., Loignon, A.C., Gilbert, S.N., Kurtessis, J., Clayton, T.P., Norris, D.G., Davies, S.A.: Updating the personnel selection system for behavior detection officers: job/task analysis report, vols. 1, 2. American Institutes for Research, Washington, D.C. (2010)

Gatewood, R.D., Field, H.S.: Human Resource Selection, 3rd edn. Dryden Press, Fort Worth (1994)

Harvey, J.L., Anderson, L.E., Baranowski, L.E., Morath, R.A.: Job analysis: gathering job-specific information. In: Whetzel, D.L., Wheaton, G.R. (eds.) Applied Measurement: Industrial Psychology in Human Resource Management, pp. 57–95. Lawrence Erlbaum Associates, Mahwah (2007)

Crandall, B., Klein, G.A., Hoffman, R.R.: Working Minds: A Practitioner's Guide to Cognitive Task Analysis. MIT Press, Cambridge (2006)

Jonassen, D.H., Tessmer, M., Hannum, W.H.: Task Analysis Methods for Instructional Design. Lawrence Erlbaum Associates, Mahwah (1999)

Militello, L.G., Hutton, R.J.B.: Applied cognitive task analysis (ACTA): a practitioner's toolkit for understanding cognitive task demands. Ergonomics 41(11), 1618–1641 (1998)

Workload Is Multidimensional, Not Unitary: What Now?

Gerald Matthews[✉], Lauren Reinerman-Jones, Ryan Wohleber,
Jinchao Lin, Joe Mercado, and Julian Abich IV

Institute for Simulation and Training (IST), University of Central Florida (UCF),
Orlando, FL, USA
{gmatthews,lreinerm,rwohlebe,jlin,
jmercado,jabich}@ist.ucf.edu

Abstract. It is commonly assumed that workload is a unitary construct, but recent data suggest that there are multiple subjective and objective facets of workload that are only weakly intercorrelated. This article reviews the implications of treating workload as multivariate. Examples from several simulated task environments show that high subjective workload is compatible with a variety of patterns of multivariate psychophysiological response. Better understanding of the cognitive neuroscience of the different components of workload, including stress components, is required. At a practical level, neither subjective workload measures nor single physiological responses are adequate for evaluating task demands, building predictive models of human performance, and driving augmented cognition applications. Multivariate algorithms that accommodate the variability of cognitive and affective responses to demanding tasks are needed.

Keywords: Workload · Task demands · Psychophysiology · Electroencephalogram (EEG) · Electrocardiogram (ECG) · Stress · Performance · Individual differences

1 Introduction

Mental workload is most simply defined in terms of the allocation of processing resources to meet task demands [1]. It is acknowledged that both sources of demand and resources are multifaceted, but, as a recent review states, explaining workload "in terms of demand/resource balance offers an attractive and parsimonious approach to this otherwise multidimensional construct" (p. 2) [2]. Thinking of workload in relation to a single ratio, i.e., demands: resources, is also attractive to systems designers, as it allows the definition of a "redline" as the ratio approaches 1.0 [3]. Subjective workload assessments, such as the NASA-TLX [4], typically provide an overall workload score that may be used to inform systems evaluation and design.

But what if the unitary workload model is incorrect? Suppose that there is no scalar value that adequately captures workload - how can we then understand workload conceptually and apply workload assessments in practical ergonomics? In this chapter, we review some of the evidence that calls into question the utility of the unitary model,

© Springer International Publishing Switzerland 2015
D.D. Schmorrow and C.M. Fidopiastis (Eds.): AC 2015, LNAI 9183, pp. 44–55, 2015.
DOI: 10.1007/978-3-319-20816-9_5

taken primarily from recent studies conducted in our lab. We also consider the prospects for developing workload models in the absence of a unitary construct.

1.1 General Workload: An Elusive Construct

General unitary workload is an intuitively appealing concept, given that cognitive overload is a universal human experience. However, it may be questioned from a variety of perspectives. First, in experimental studies that vary task demands, different workload metrics may dissociate, calling into question the validity of one or more of the metrics concerned [5]. Usually, dissociations are interpreted as indicating measurement problems; for example, subjective measures may not be sensitive to task differences associated with data limitations. However, they may point towards more fundamental uncertainties over construct definition. Second, multiple resource theories have become increasingly popular as a means for explaining dual-task interference data [1, 6]. Such theories may be compatible with some general integration of the loads imposed on different pools of capacity [2], but questions remain about how to weight multiple load factors to derive overall workload [7]. Third, the conventional stress/strain metaphor for workload [2] assumes some passive deformation of cognitive functioning (strain) as the external load (stress) increases. However, there are various dynamic factors that the metaphor does not capture, such as people's attempts to actively manage workload [8] and regulate task goals [9], and the malleability of resources over various timespans [2, 10].

The most basic objection to the assumption of unity is lack of psychometric support. Human factors has a history of embracing broad-based constructs such as workload, stress and arousal because of their potential for synthesizing findings and design recommendations across a variety of task contexts. These approaches have often failed to fulfill their potential because of the lack of a psychometrically sound metric for the construct concerned. For example, research on general arousal effects on performance devolved into futile attempts to work backwards from stressor interactions to fit data to the Yerkes-Dodson Law inverted-U curve post hoc [11]. Workload measurement is on a stronger footing because there appears to be a general factor underpinning the subjective experience of workload. The six rating scales of the NASA-TLX typically intercorrelate, suggesting they measure a common construct. However, modern psychometric techniques for identifying latent factors such as confirmatory factor analysis and item response theory have been largely neglected in the workload domain.

Given the limitations of self-report, especially in high-stakes test settings, objective workload assessments are essential. A range of psychophysiological techniques have shown considerable promise (see [12] for a review). However, the literatures on leading techniques, such as those using the electrocardiogram (ECG), electroencephalogram (EEG), or recent brain hemodynamic methods, have tended to develop in isolation from one another. The few comparative tests that have been performed typically do not include sufficient participants for standard psychometric analyses, such as factor analysis, to be performed.

Psychometric studies of psychophysiological response are challenging for a range of reasons, including the expense of running substantial numbers of participants, and the sensitivity of responses to extraneous physiological factors, such as general metabolic activity. Nevertheless, if workload is unitary, the assumption is that different metrics reflect some common latent factor. A basic difficulty is that standard workload criteria, such as sensitivity, diagnosticity, selectivity, and others [13] are designed (quite effectively) for evaluating outcomes of experimental studies in which task load manipulations produce changes in mean response across groups of participants. However, building a strong psychometric case requires analysis of inter-subject correlations of the various metrics to demonstrate a unitary latent factor, a standard neglected in conventional workload criteria [14].

1.2   Psychometrics of Physiological Workload Indices

Recently, we investigated the psychometric properties of multiple psychophysiological metrics secured from a fairly substantial sample of individuals ($N = 150$) performing a simulation of unmanned ground vehicle (UGV) operation, under various task demands [14, 15]. We employed a suite of sensors selected to assess a range of previously validated workload responses [16]. Sensors included ECG and EEG, from which conventional workload metrics were extracted, such as heart-rate variability (HRV) and frontal theta. Hemodynamic indices of workload were obtained bilaterally from two sensors: functional near infrared spectroscopy (fNIR) which indexes prefrontal oxygen saturation, and transcranial Doppler sonography (TCD) which yields measures of cerebral blood flow velocity (CBFV) in the middle cerebral arteries. Eye tracking metrics including frequencies and durations of fixations were also obtained.

Twelve independent measures of each response were obtained from the different conditions, defined by task load factors such as task difficulty, multi-tasking needs, and event rate. These proved to be highly internally consistent. That is, we can measure a given response at the individual level reliably. As further discussed below, several responses were sensitive to task manipulations, such as single- vs. dual-task performance. However, while data generally met conventional workload criteria [13], responses from different sensor systems were mostly independent from one another, and there was no prospect for modeling a unitary latent factor. The lack of covariance of alternate measures represents a major failure in convergent validity. Furthermore, while the NASA-TLX was also sensitive to task demand manipulations, correlations between this subjective measure and psychophysiological response hardly exceeded chance levels resulting in strongly divergent subjective and objective metrics.

Standard psychometric models, such as those derived from confirmatory factor analysis and structural equation modeling, are made up of two parts [17]. First, there is a measurement model that attaches measured variables to latent factors. Second, there is a structural model that specifies the relationships between latent factors. The failure of convergence of alternate workload metrics might be attributed to failures in the measurement model. Response measures may be poor indicators of activity in the brain systems that control workload. There may also be variability in the measurement model across individuals, in line with the response specificity principle [18], e.g., HRV but not frontal theta might be sensitive to task demands in one person, and vice versa in another. Studies identifying individualized workload classifier algorithms [19] support this possibility.

It is plausible that measurement model issues contribute to the lack of convergence, and improvements in psychophysiological recording and analysis may alleviate the problem in the future. However, there are also reasons to question whether workload response is controlled by a unitary neurocognitive system, and we may thus need to elaborate the structural model of workload components. Imposing external task loads on operators impose multiple, concurrent neurocognitive responses, including cortico-reticular arousal, changes in brain metabolic activity, specific processing routines, high-level executive processing, task- and state-directed effort and regulation of stress and coping [20]. While these various responses may commonly occur together, they may not be strongly correlated within the individual. That is, there is not a single 'strain' response. Instead, there are various layers of regulation of the response to task stimuli, including anticipation of task demands based on prior expectancies. Correspondingly, even relatively simple but demanding tasks such as vigilance are supported by a complex network of brain areas [21], which may operate somewhat independently in supporting different neurocognitive functions.

At this point, we emphasize that the ultimate value of treating workload as unitary remains open. Improved measurement technology and models, as well as accommodation of individual variability in response, may yet salvage the construct. The practical utility of general subjective workload assessments is also well-established [22]. However, we will proceed to explore the consequences of abandoning a unitary workload construct in favor of a multidimensional conceptualization, should this step prove to be necessary.

2 Multivariate Workload Evaluation

Extant criteria for evaluating workload metrics [13, 22] already contain an inbuilt tension between sensitivity and diagnosticity. The idea behind diagnosticity is that the workload measure should identify the source of workload, as the NASA-TLX does in distinguishing mental demands, physical demands and other sources. However, maximizing diagnosticity requires that the measure is insensitive with regard to task-irrelevant sources of workload, a requirement that may limit the overall sensitivity of the instrument. Existing measures may not adequately discriminate sources of workload directly tied to task demands (e.g., rate of stimulus input) from those that reflect workload management strategy (e.g., effort). For example, the Multiple Resources Questionnaire (MRQ) [6] is geared primarily towards demand factors that can be specified objectively, such as auditory and visual task load, whereas the NASA-TLX includes more elusive, psychologically-defined qualities such as effort and frustration.

A multivariate conceptualization of workload avoids such difficulties by treating each index as a distinct diagnostic metric. The NASA-TLX and other subjective metrics provide an estimate of the participant's awareness of task demands. However, given that the NASA-TLX does a rather poor job of capturing physiological response [14], it does not provide a comprehensive 'gold-standard' workload assessment.

Contrasting findings from two recent studies [14, 23] illustrate the multivariate approach. One study ($N = 81$) applied the sensor set previously described [16] (without eye tracking) to investigate workload response in simulated Generalized Pressurized Water Reactor Nuclear Power Plant (NPP) Main Control Room (MCR) operation. The participant, in the role of a Reactor Operator (RO), works with a Senior Reactor Operator (SRO) to perform tasks requiring (1) checking that controls are appropriately set, (2) detecting changes in gauges, and (3) implementing responses that changed the state of controls. Designing plants to provide manageable workloads requires attention to different task elements of these kinds.

NASA-TLX data suggested that workload was highest for detection, and lower for checking and response implementation. However, psychophysiological data suggested a more complex pattern. Response magnitudes were calculated as the percentage change from a no-task baseline. Figure 1 shows these data by task for selected measures. Several responses were insensitive to the task manipulation and are omitted from the figure. Generally, responses to workload were bilateral, and so most of the indices graphed are averaged across hemisphere: the exception was CBFV which showed a lateralized (left-hemisphere) response. EEG responses (spectral power densities: SPDs) were averaged across three frontal sites (F3, F4, Fz).

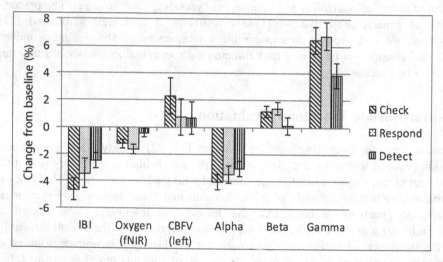

Fig. 1. Selected workload responses in three task conditions

Consistent with NASA-TLX data, bilateral prefrontal cortex blood oxygenation (fNIR) was higher for the detection task than the other two. By contrast, EEG data suggested that workload was lowest for detection. This task was associated with the highest level of alpha, but also with the lowest levels of high-frequency EEG (beta, gamma). Yet another pattern was implied by TCD and ECG data suggesting that workload was actually highest in the checking task. Left-hemisphere CBFV, measured by TCD, is elicited by demanding verbal tasks, including working memory [24, 25]. The checking task produced elevation of left-hemisphere CBFV, relative to the other two tasks. Cardiac IBI was also lowest for this task, although HRV was insensitive to task differences. Thus, concordance between subjective and objective metrics was poor, and any conclusion about workload differences between the tasks depended entirely on the choice of metric. However, we can identify patterns of response that correspond to the unique demands of each task.

A second study [14, 15], introduced above, profiled workload response during simulated UGV operation. Two key manipulations were task type and multi-tasking. (A third manipulation, event rate, is beyond our current scope). In single-task conditions, the operator was required either to detect threatening human figures (enemy insurgents) in a video feed, or to detect changes in icons representing friendly and unfriendly forces on a map display. The subjective workload imposed by threat detection was substantially lower than that of change detection, perhaps because of the evolution of the visual system to process realistic human character stimuli. In multi-tasking conditions, participants performed both tasks simultaneously.

NASA-TLX data confirmed that both change detection and multi-tasking elicited substantially higher workload. Performance data tended to follow the TLX; for example, multi-tasking produced interference. However, the psychophysiological data again provided a more nuanced picture of workload response which contrasted with findings from the NPP study [23]. Several indices were diagnostic of task type but not multi-tasking. Specifically, change detection induced higher EEG theta (including frontal theta), lower HRV, higher prefrontal oxygenation (fNIR), and higher values for the pupillometric Index of Cognitive Activity (ICA). By contrast, multi-tasking did not affect any of these indices but it reduced eye fixation duration. As noted, TLX scores were not significantly correlated with any of the metrics that were sensitive to the manipulations, again calling into question the meaningfulness of any overall workload score. Speculatively, we might suggest that processing arbitrary symbols or icons (change detection) is more effortful than processing realistic human character stimuli. By contrast, with the UGV simulation, the need to exert cognitive control over scan patterns in order to monitor two task windows renders eye fixations the most sensitive metric for multi-tasking.

3   Extension to Task Stress

In a recent, unpublished study [26], we used the sensor suite [16] (less eye tracking) to examine responses to a simulated UAV task, in which task manipulations were expected to be stressful. UAV operation typically requires coordination of multiple subtasks, making the operator vulnerable to both overload and concerns about maintaining adequate performance [27]. One manipulation was intended to cause cognitive overload, by increasing the number of UAVs controlled from two to six, and reducing the time available to perform elements of the mission. A second manipulation involved the presentation of negative feedback messages suggesting that the person was failing to perform adequately (irrespective of actual performance).

The study also used the short Dundee Stress State Questionnaire (DSSQ) [28] to monitor subjective stress response. This multidimensional instrument assesses distress, task engagement, and worry. Typically, in performance studies, distress elicited by task stressors follows subjective workload. For example, unpublished analyses for the simulated UGV study [14] showed that DSSQ distress was substantially higher both for change detection and for multi-tasking. In the UAV study, however, we considered that the qualitative difference between overload and negative evaluation as sources of stress might provoke differing multidimensional patterns of DSSQ response. The workload issue is then the extent to which both subjective stress response and psychophysiological response correspond to overall subjective workload as indexed by the NASA-TLX.

Subjective data from the study are shown in Fig. 2, confirming that the two tasks differ qualitatively in response pattern. These represent mean levels for each variable in paired low demand and high demand conditions. "Stress" associated with high workload took the form of highly elevated NASA-TLX scores and increased distress, with little change in task engagement. However, negative evaluation produced only modestly increased distress and workload, together with a decline in task engagement, implying that noncontingent negative feedback is demotivating.

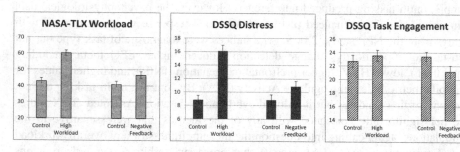

Fig. 2. Effects of high workload and negative feedback on three subjective measures

Turning to the psychophysiological metrics, we found yet another pattern of response, differing from that found in both the NPP [23] and UGV [14] studies. The metrics that were sensitive to the task manipulations were high-frequency EEG power (beta and gamma), which increased, and HRV, which also increased. The two manipulations did not differ significantly in their impacts on these responses. The effects on high-frequency EEG suggest that simulated UAV operation may produce a rather subtle, "cognitive" stress response that is not expressed either in increased mental effort (e.g., frontal theta) or in classic arousal response (e.g., reduced alpha and IBI).

The increase in HRV was particularly unexpected, given that increased cognitive demand is traditionally considered to *lower* HRV [29]. A resolution to the paradox is suggested by a meta-analysis [30], which coordinated HRV response with activation of discrete brain areas in functional Magnetic Resonance Imaging (fMRI) studies. Higher HRV may signal increased top-down regulation of emotional processing in structures such as the amygdala. High frequency EEG might also reflect the processing associated with emotion-regulation. The impact of cognitive load on HRV may then depend on the extent to which task demands are perceived as threats requiring initiation of emotion-regulation. However, at least in the present paradigm, the subjective data are necessary to differentiate the threat of cognitive overload from the threat of negative evaluation; in this respect, the DSSQ was more diagnostic than the psychophysiology. The notion of general workload appears inadequate to capture the nature of the similarities and differences of the response patterns elicited by the two task manipulations.

4   Modeling Individual Differences in Performance

The standard demand/resource model [2] suggests that workload should be diagnostic of performance at the individual level, to the extent that the demand: resource ratio is indicative of poor performance. (Note that secondary task performance may be more sensitive than primary task performance to resource insufficiency [1]). However, existing research already shows that it is difficult to find any single index of resource utilization that is uniquely associated with performance. In relation to psychological measures, a previous study found that cognitive ability, task-focused coping, and task engagement all predicted vigilance task performance, but each had unique effects [20]. "Resources" appeared to be a construct that emerged from several personal characteristics, rather than being identified with any single measures. Similarly, a study showed that task engagement and phasic CBFV response were correlated but uniquely predictive of vigilance [24].

Unpublished data from the UGV simulation study [14, 15] suggest a similar conclusion. Performance levels varied across task conditions that differed in task demands. However, there were consistent individual differences in performance on the change detection and threat detection tasks. Thus, we can calculate average accuracy scores on these performance tasks, across the different conditions. Table 1 shows correlations between averaged workload and stress indices and these performance criteria. Omitted psychophysiological measures did not correlate with either performance index. Only change detection was related to psychophysiological as well as subjective metrics. Several indices of low workload (low TLX scores, three psychophysiological metrics) were linked to more accurate performance.

Table 1. Correlations between averaged performance accuracy and selected measures

Task	Subjective scales				Psychophysiology		
	NASA-TLX	Distress	Engagement	Worry	HRV	Beta	Fixation duration
Change detection	−.39**	−.39**	.45**	−.32**	.26**	−.30**	.26**
Threat detection	−.12	−.21**	.28**	−.33**	−.07	−.14	.16

Note. **p < .01

A multiple regression showed that the seven predictor variables together explained 40.4 % of the variance in change detection (adjusted R^2 = .37). With the four subjective measures entered into the equation first, the three psychophysiological measures added significantly to the variance explained ($\Delta R^2 = .08$, $p < .01$). Conversely, the subjective measures contributed significantly to prediction with the psychophysiological variables controlled ($\Delta R^2 = .20$, $p < .01$). In the final equation, five predictors remained significant at $p < .05$ or better (i.e., TLX, task engagement, HRV, fixation duration, beta). That is, we can identify individuals who are sufficiently vulnerable to overload that their change detection is impaired quite effectively, but we need multiple subjective and objective indicators to do so. No single index represents a "gold standard" for behavioral impairment resulting from overload. Indeed, the different measures may correspond to different psychological processes which work together to preserve or threaten performance competency [20].

5 Augmented Cognition

Greater validity in predicting individual performance may support augmented cognition applications, especially adaptive automation or intelligent tutors. The accurate assessment of workload is critical for creating closed-loop systems to augment performance [31]. Such systems require a valid workload metric to drive adaptive allocation of task functions between human and machine. In the absence of such a metric, adaptation of automation to match the cognitive demands being experienced is likely impossible. Similarly, in training applications, developing a system that effectively provides feedback relies on valid, near real-time workload assessment. Data such as those in Table 1 suggest that determining a valid metric for practical applications is not such a simple task as suggested by unitary resource theory, but instead might require individuation that is also task dependent and domain dependent. That is, implementing augmented cognition is not task and domain agnostic.

Acceptance of multiple workload components allows progress to be made. It remains true that psychophysiological metrics are more powerful than subjective ones for application. Within a given task domain, it is possible to develop multivariate algorithms for predicting performance vulnerability. For example, in the UGV operation scenario [14, 15], a person showing low HRV, high beta and short fixation durations may be especially vulnerable. This pattern of response might be used to drive an automated aid for the task concerned. Individuals may vary in relation to which indices are most diagnostic of compromised performance. One operator may be especially taxed by overload of executive processing, another by misdirection of effort, and yet another by stress. Multivariate modeling may allow adaptive automation to be directed towards the specific vulnerabilities of individual operators. Efforts at developing idiographic workload classifiers based on techniques such as neural net analysis show the promise of this approach, although defining cross-task classifiers remains problematic [19]. The limitation of such approaches is loss of diagnosticity; it may be difficult to determine *why* different workload processes are more or less predictive of performance across different individual operators.

6 Future Directions and Challenges

Table 2 summarizes the central dilemma for unitary workload assessment. Each row of the table corresponds to a task paradigm in which we have identified demand manipulations which influence NASA-TLX workload predictably. In addition, each manipulation is associated with poorer performance and higher workload (although it is difficult to compare performance levels across the NPP tasks [23]). However, at the physiological level, each workload response appears quite different, with each inducing a unique pattern of response. Indeed, in some cases, changes in metrics were unexpected, such as increased HRV in the high cognitive load condition of the UAV study [26], and reduced high frequency EEG during the NPP detection task. Increases in subjective workload are rather poorly diagnostic of changes in neural function.

Another challenge is that subjective and objective indices are not mutually reducible to one another. Both are necessary to optimize performance prediction [24]. In a research context, both may be validly assessed, but subjective assessments lose validity in high-stakes real-life settings where the person may be motivated to distort subjective response. It remains to be seen whether future developments in sensor technology will allow objective metrics to be effectively substituted for subjective ones.

Our principal argument is that, from a psychometric perspective, the structural model of workload cannot be identified with a single latent factor. Instead, there appear to be multiple latent dimensions, which should be identified with more narrowly defined characteristics than global workload. A challenge to better definition of multiple factors is uncertainty over the measurement model, i.e., the best response measures to identify each factor. It remains plausible that there is individual variation in the mappings of responses onto latent factors.

An applied approach that might address the limitations imposed by individual differences is to examine clustering patterns across individuals to determine if a subset of classificatory patterns emerge. Ideally, then, a person newly entering a system or task environment would complete a short baseline multivariate assessment of workload

Table 2. Task-sensitive workload metrics in four task paradigms

Study	Task or manipulation	Metric(s) for elevated workload (expected)	Metric(s) for reduced workload (unexpected)
NPP simulation [23]	Detection (vs. other tasks)	Frontal oxygenation (fNIR)	Lower beta Lower gamma Higher alpha
UGV simulation [14]	Change detection (vs. threat detection)	Higher frontal theta, lower HRV, prefrontal oxygenation (fNIR), higher ICA	
UGV simulation [14]	Dual-task (vs. single task)	Shorter fixation duration	
UAV simulation [26]	Cognitive demands (vs. low demands)	Higher beta Higher gamma	Higher HRV

response that enabled the correct pattern to be identified. Furthermore, it is not enough to assume that tasks that are similar theoretically or in processing structure produce an equivocal workload response, but rather the tasking environment (domain) must be considered when developing a closed-loop system. Accommodating the complexities of individual workload response may be critical for realizing the real-world potential of augmented cognition.

Acknowledgements. This work was in part supported by the Air Force Office of Scientific Research (AFOSR) (FA 9550-13-1-0016) and the US Army Research Laboratory (ARL) (W91CRB-08-D-0015). The views and conclusions contained in this document are those of the authors and should not be interpreted as representing the official policies, either expressed or implied, of AFOSR, ARL or the US Government.

References

1. Wickens, C.D.: Multiple resources and mental workload. Hum. Factors **50**, 449–455 (2008)
2. Young, M.S., Brookhuis, K.A., Wickens, C.D., Hancock, P.A.: State of science: mental workload in ergonomics. Ergonomics **58**, 1–17 (2014). (advance online publication)
3. Colle, H.A., Reid, G.B.: Context effects in subjective mental workload ratings. Hum. Factors **40**, 591–600 (1998)
4. Hart, S.G., Staveland, L.E.: Development of NASA-TLX (task load index): results of empirical and theoretical research. In: Hancock, P.A., Meshkati, N. (eds.) Human Mental Workload, pp. 139–184. North-Holland, Amsterdam (1988)
5. Yeh, Y.Y., Wickens, C.D.: Dissociation of performance and subjective measures of workload. Hum. Factors **30**, 111–120 (1988)
6. Boles, D.B., Bursk, J.H., Phillips, J.B., Perdelwitz, J.R.: Predicting dual-task performance with the multiple resources questionnaire (MRQ). Hum. Factors **49**, 32–45 (2007)
7. Finomore, V.S., Shaw, T.H., Warm, J.S., Matthews, G., Boles, D.B.: Viewing the workload of vigilance through the lenses of the NASA-TLX and the MRQ. Hum. Factors **55**, 1044–1063 (2013)
8. Saxby, D.J., Matthews, G., Warm, J.S., Hitchcock, E.M., Neubauer, C.: Active and passive fatigue in simulated driving: discriminating styles of workload regulation and their safety impacts. J. Exp. Psychol. Appl. **19**, 287–300 (2013)
9. Hockey, G.R.J.: Compensatory control in the regulation of human performance under stress and high workload: a cognitive-energetical framework. Biol. Psychol. **45**, 73–93 (1997)
10. Young, M.S., Stanton, N.A.: Malleable attentional resources theory: a new explanation for the effects of mental underload on performance. Hum. Factors **44**, 365–375 (2002)
11. Matthews, G., Davies, D.R., Westerman, S.J., Stammers, R.B.: Human Performance: Cognition, Stress and Individual Differences. Psychology Press, London (2000)
12. Brookhuis, K.A., de Waard, D.: Monitoring drivers' mental workload in driving simulators using physiological measures. Accid. Anal. Prev. **42**, 898–903 (2010)
13. O'Donnell, R.D., Eggemeier, F.T.: Workload assessment methodology. In: Boff, K.R., Thomas, J.P. (eds.) Handbook of Perception and Human Performance. Cognitive Processes and Performance, vol. 2, 2nd edn, pp. 1–49. Wiley, Oxford (1986)
14. Matthews, G., Reinerman-Jones, L.E., Barber, D.J., Abich, J.: The psychometrics of mental workload multiple measures are sensitive but divergent. Hum. Factors **57**, 125–143 (2014)

15. Reinerman-Jones, L.E., Matthews, G., Barber, D.J., Abich, J.: Psychophysiological metrics for workload are demand-sensitive but multifactorial. Proceed. Hum. Factors Ergon. Soc. Annu. Meet. **58**, 974–978 (2014)

16. Reinerman-Jones, L., Guznov, S., Mercado, J., D'Agostino, A.: Developing methodology for experimentation using a nuclear power plant simulator. In: Schmorrow, D.D., Fidopiastis, C.M. (eds.) Foundations of Augmented Cognition, pp. 181–188. Springer, New York (2013)

17. Loehlin, J.C.: Latent Variable Models: An Introduction to Factor, Path, and Structural Equation Analysis. Lawrence Erlbaum, Mahwah (2004)

18. Stephens, C.L., Christie, I.C., Friedman, B.H.: Autonomic specificity of basic emotions: evidence from pattern classification and cluster analysis. Biol. Psychol. **84**, 463–473 (2010)

19. Baldwin, C.L., Penaranda, B.N.: Adaptive training using an artificial neural network and EEG metrics for within-and cross-task workload classification. NeuroImage **59**, 48–56 (2012)

20. Matthews, G., Warm, J.S., Shaw, T.H., Finomore, V.S.: Predicting battlefield vigilance: a multivariate approach to assessment of attentional resources. Ergonomics **57**, 856–875 (2014)

21. Langner, R., Eickhoff, S.B.: Sustaining attention to simple tasks: a meta-analytic review of the neural mechanisms of vigilant attention. Psychol. Bull. **139**, 870–900 (2013)

22. Vidulich, M.A., Tsang, P.S.: Mental workload and situation awareness. In: Salvendy, G. (ed.) Handbook of Human Factors and Ergonomics, 4th edn, pp. 243–273. Wiley, Hoboken (2012)

23. Mercado, J.E.: Assessing the effectiveness of workload measures in the nuclear domain. Doctoral dissertation, University of Central Florida (2014)

24. Matthews, G., Warm, J.S., Reinerman, L.E., Langheim, L., Washburn, D.A., Tripp, L.: Task engagement, cerebral blood flow velocity, and diagnostic monitoring for sustained attention. J. Exp. Psychol. Appl. **16**, 187–203 (2010)

25. Stroobant, N., Vingerhoets, G.: Transcranial doppler ultrasonography monitoring of cerebral hemodynamics during performance of cognitive tasks: a review. Neuropsychol. Rev. **10**, 213–231 (2000)

26. Wohleber, R.W., Matthews, G., Reinerman-Jones, L.E., Sollins, B., Panganiban, A.R., Scribner, D.R.: Manuscript in preparation (2015)

27. Lin, J., Matthews, G., Wohleber, R., Calhoun, G., Funke, G.: Manuscript in preparation (2015)

28. Matthews, G., Szalma, J., Panganiban, A.R., Neubauer, C., Warm, J.S.: Profiling task stress with the Dundee stress state questionnaire. In: Cavalcanti, L., Azevedo, S. (eds.) Psychology of Stress: New Research, pp. 49–91. Nova Science, Hauppage (2013)

29. Mulder, L.J.M., De Waard, D., Brookhuis, K.A.: Estimating mental effort using heart rate and heart rate variability. In: Stanton, N.A., Hedge, A., Brookhuis, K., Salas, E., Hendrick, H.W. (eds.) Handbook of Human Factors and Ergonomics Methods, pp. 201–210. CRC Press, Boca Raton (2004)

30. Thayer, J.F., Åhs, F., Fredrikson, M., Sollers, J.J., Wager, T.D.: A meta-analysis of heart rate variability and neuroimaging studies: implications for heart rate variability as a marker of stress and health. Neurosci. Biobehav. Rev. **36**, 747–756 (2012)

31. Parasuraman, R., Wickens, C.D.: Humans: still vital after all these years of automation. Hum. Factors **50**, 511–520 (2008)

Time Dependent Effects of Transcranial Direct Current Stimulation and Caffeine on Vigilance Performance During Extended Wakefulness

R. Andy McKinley[1]([⊠]), Lindsey K. McIntire[2], Ryan Schilling[3], Chuck Goodyear[2], and Justin Nelson[2]

[1] Applied Neuroscience Branch, 711th HPW, 2510 Fifth Street, BLDG 840, Dayton, OH, USA
Andy.McKinley@wpafb.af.mil
[2] Infoscitex Inc., Dayton, OH, USA
[3] ORISE, Dayton, OH, USA

Abstract. Background: Previously, we found that transcranial direct current stimulation (tDCS) preserved vigilance performance approximately twice as well and three times as long as caffeine during a period of extended wakefulness. Vigilance performance often declines linearly over the period of watch, but in our previous study the performance trends over the period of watch were not analyzed. Hence, it was not known whether the intervention applied reduced the vigilance decrement, or simply shifted the performance to a higher mean value while maintaining a similar slope.

Objective: Our objective was to evaluate the time-dependent effects (within each period of watch) of anodal transcranial direct current stimulation (tDCS) applied to the pre-frontal cortex at 2 mA for 30 min. We then compared these results to those of caffeine as well as the effects of both interventions on arousal.

Methods: The period of watch was segregated into equal time segments and target identification accuracy was averaged across subjects in each group. These values were used in an analysis of covariance (separately for each session) as the dependent variable. Factors were group and subject nested in group.

Results: The results indicated there is not a significant difference in slope (i.e. vigilance decrement) between the treatment conditions (tDCS, caffeine, and sham) within each period of watch. However, as reported previously, there was a significant difference in mean change from baseline between the treatment conditions.

Conclusion: Our data suggests that tDCS does not prevent the vigilance decrement within the period of watch. Rather, it shifts performance to higher mean values by a scalar multiple while maintaining a similar slope.

Keywords: Transcranial direct current stimulation · Sleep deprivation · Caffeine · Cognition · Vigilance

© Springer International Publishing Switzerland 2015
D.D. Schmorrow and C.M. Fidopiastis (Eds.): AC 2015, LNAI 9183, pp. 56–62, 2015.
DOI: 10.1007/978-3-319-20816-9_6

1 Introduction

As work demands and pressures continue to increase, sleep deprivation induced fatigue has continued to plague many occupations. Notably, sleep deprived individuals suffer from cognitive performance declines analogous to being legally intoxicated [1] as well as undesired mood states such as increased hostility and anger [2]. In particular, vigilance and psychomotor reaction times are highly susceptible to performance losses during periods of sleep-deprivation or extended wakefulness [3, 4]. Caffeine is perhaps the most readily available and commonly used stimulates to assuage the effects of sleep deprivation. However, caffeine has many limitations. As the period of sleep deprivation increases, individuals often require greater doses to have the desired effects in subjective feeling of drowsiness and fatigue. However, in high doses (above 400 mg) caffeine can cause caffeine intoxication, an undesirable condition with symptoms such as declines in mood, insomnia, nervousness, hallucinations, and intestinal complaints [5–7]. Likewise, the effect is reduced as the level of sleep deprivation increases [8] while the effects are short-lived (i.e. less than 2 h) [3]. Chronic use further reduces its beneficial effects [9]. As a result, we have begun to investigate other means of preserving performance when sleep deprived, such as non-invasive brain stimulation.

Recently, we have discovered that observed linear declines in vigilance performance over time, known as the vigilance decrement [10], can be reduced or eliminated with a form of non-invasive brain stimulation known as transcranial direct current stimulation (tDCS) [11]. This technique applies weak currents between two electrodes placed on the scalp, although the reference electrode is sometimes placed in an extracephalic location [12–14]. The stimulation is believed to modulate activity in a polarity dependent manner, which can have beneficial effects on performance [12, 13]. In a previous study, we found just 30 min of tDCS applied to the dorsal-lateral prefrontal cortex (DLPFC) prevented vigilance performance declines for up to 6 h in participants who were kept awake for 30 h [3]. However, the exact mechanism causing this effect remains somewhat ambiguous. To examine this further, it is necessary to first understand existing theories regarding the vigilance decrement.

Currently, arousal theory and resource theory are the two primary competing theories that attempt to explain the vigilance decrement [15]. Arousal theory attributes the increased rate of missed critical signals to a reduction in overall arousal (i.e. the participant becomes uninterested) while resource theory contends the performance drop is driven by depletion of some critical cognitive resource [15, 16]. Previously, we concluded that tDCS supported the resource theory due in part to the fact that we did not observe a significant change in response bias. Modulating arousal generates a significant increase in response bias (i.e. increases in target detections and false alarms). However, we only found significant increases in signal (i.e. target) detection that was not accompanied by increases in false alarms [3]. Of note, vigilance performance was assessed by taking the cumulative signal detection percentage over the entire session essentially making each session a signal data point. Hence, we did not examine the trends within a session which is more commonly the case in the vigilance literature. To further assess how tDCS is creating the previously observed performance improvements, we decided to decompose the data within each session and examine possible trends.

The first possibility was that tDCS produces its beneficial effect by reducing or eliminating the negative slope of the vigilance decrement curve. In fact, Nelson found this to be the case in fully rested participants [11]. The other possibility is that tDCS simply shifts the vigilance curve to higher values by a scalar factor without impacting the overall slope. Hence, by starting at a higher level of performance at beginning of the vigil, the participant could achieve a higher level of number of signal detections while also having a performance decrement within the individual session. To answer this question, we reanalyzed the data to examine the effects within each session.

2   Methods and Materials

2.1   Procedures

The original data set from our previous publication was further analyzed and reported herein. For details on the original methods and procedures used to collect the data set, please see McIntire et al. [3].

2.2   Analysis

The Mackworth clock test data collected in McIntire et al. [3] were further decomposed into temporal segments within each session and analyzed. Only sessions occurring during or after the intervention was applied were included (i.e. sessions occurring at 4 am, 6 am, and 8 am). The 10 am session was not included due to the fact circadian rhythms had shifted in a positive direction creating improvements in performance not influenced by the intervention applied. Each 30 min session contained a total of twelve targets. The signal (i.e. critical target) detection accuracies were segregated into three time segments with 4 targets in each segment. These accuracies were then averaged within each segment for each subject. Slopes were calculated with a simply linear fit. To quantify the effect of the intervention (i.e. tDCS or caffeine) on the slope of the vigilance decrement, these accuracy values were used in an analysis of covariance (separately for each session) as the dependent variable. Factors were group and subject nested in group. Time segment (coded as 1, 2, 3) was used as a covariate. The p-values reported are from an F-test for the group*segment interaction.

A second analysis was used to examine effects on accuracy levels (i.e. shifts in performance). Each subject had an accuracy mean (n = 12) for each session (2 am, 4 am, 6 am, 8 am). For each subject, the change in mean accuracy from 2 am to each subsequent session was used as the dependent variable in a one-way analysis of variance (separately for each session) with group as the factor. The p-value is from an F-test for the main effect of group.

3   Results

3.1   Mackworth Clock Test

There were no significant differences in slope between the three treatment groups for any of the sessions tested as denoted by the F-test. Figure 1 displays the linear fit slopes for each session along with the p-values for the group*segment interaction. However, similar to the results presented the original study, we did find significant main effect of group in the mean percentage change from baseline (i.e. 2 am session) in both the 4 am (p = .001) and 8 am (p = .003) sessions. The post hoc t-tests showed that the tDCS group performed significantly better than both the sham and caffeine groups in both 4 am and 8 am sessions. The sham and caffeine groups were not statistically different from one another in either session (Fig. 2).

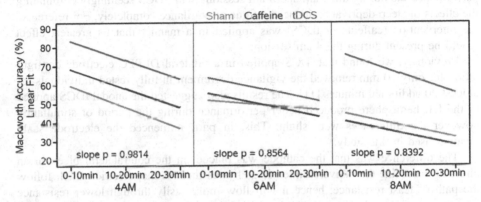

Fig. 1. Mackworth clock test accuracy slopes for the 4 am, 6 am, and 8 am sessions. The 4 am session denotes the time point at which the intervention was applied. Slopes were the result of a linear fit to the accuracy percentages in each of the three time segments.

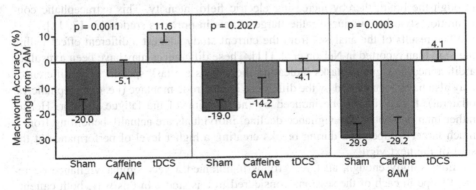

Fig. 2. Mackworth clock test accuracy mean change from 2 am (Baseline). Caffeine was given at 3:15 am (requires 1 h to be fully effective); tDCS was applied at 4 am. Changes in performance were measured for each subject and averaged across groups (n = 10).

4   Discussion

We previously discovered large effects of anodal tDCS applied to the DLPFC on vigilance performance that remained over a period of hours. However, we did not examine the effects within sessions as such analyses are not common in the fatigue/sleep deprivation literature. Still, the vigilance decrement is typically found within the vigil itself begging the question of whether the effects of tDCS manifested in a reduction of the vigilance decrement (i.e. performance slope), or whether it improved performance overall (i.e. shifting the performance values to higher levels at each time point) without influencing the slope.

The results reported herein seem to suggest the latter as there were no significant differences in the slope of the vigilance decrement between groups. As reported in our original publication [3], there was a significant difference between groups in mean performance the during the 4 am and 8 am sessions with tDCS seemingly eliminating the effects of sleep-deprivation induced fatigue on vigilance completely. For reference, the intervention (caffeine or tDCS) was applied in a manner that its greatest effect would be present during the 4 am session.

Previously, we found that tDCS applied in a bilateral DLPFC electrode configuration for only 10 min removed the vigilance decrement in fully rested individuals for at least 20 additional minutes [11]. The results also suggested the anodal tDCS applied to the left hemisphere produced better performance during the period of stimulation however the differences were slight. This, in part, influenced the electrode scalp location used in this study.

The difference was that the cathode was placed on the contralateral bicep in an effort to maximize the delivered intensity. Physics dictates that electricity will follow the path of least resistance; hence it will flow more easily through lower resistance tissues such as the skin and cerebral spinal fluid before entering brain tissue. Theoretically, by placing the electrodes close together, the current will remain superficial, reducing the intensity of the electric field delivered to the cortical tissue. Conversely, by placing the electrodes far apart, the current is forced to take a longer pathway through the brain, thereby increasing electric field intensity. This extracephalic configuration style has produced rather large effects in previous studies [3, 17, 18].

The results of the analyses from the current study suggest a different effect within the vigil than reported in Nelson et al. [11]. These differences may have been a result of a difference in vigilance tasks indicating the effects are task specific. The differences may also have been caused by the difference in electrode montage (i.e. extracephalic vs. bilateral). It may instead be induced by the addition of the fatigue stressor. Hence, rather than preventing the vigilance decline, individuals are actually benefiting from a much larger recuperation during breaks creating a higher level of performance at the start of the next vigil.

Interestingly enough, all three groups maintained a very similar vigilance decrement slope in each of the sessions considered in this study. In this way, both caffeine and tDCS produced the same type of benefit where performance was increased at the start of the vigil, but suffered from a linear decline over time. This consistency between the treatments may suggest similar mechanisms of action, as reported in our previous manuscript [3]. It does appear that when sleep deprived, neither intervention is capable of preventing the vigilance decrement. Even with these similarities, the results still show a differential effect on mean performance over longer timelines (i.e. multiple sessions). This difference is better explained by resource theory given that there was no change in response bias and a separate test of arousal showed no difference in performance between the caffeine and tDCS groups [3]. If the effect were due to arousal alone, the effects on vigilance should have been the same in the tDCS and caffeine groups.

This study has potentially raised more questions than it has answered. The robustness of the effects of tDCS on vigilance should be examined across tasks to test for sensitivity to the task itself. Likewise, the extracephalic electrode configuration should be replicated in a study of rested individuals to look for consistency in the findings reported in Nelson et al. [11]. However, the current results may have significant implications for scheduling and duty cycle for many occupations, if the effects of tDCS are actually derived from improved recuperative value of the breaks. Regardless, these results warrant further investigation of tDCS as an intervention for fatigue.

Acknowledgments. We'd like to acknowledge the Air Force Office of Scientific Research for funding this project. A special thanks to our entire research team for working so quickly and tirelessly through this process.

Financial Disclosures. None of the authors have any financial disclosures or conflicts of interest.

References

1. Williamson, A.M., Feyer, A.M.: Moderate sleep deprivation produces impairments in cognitive and motor performance equivalent to legally prescribed levels of alcohol intoxication. Occup. Environ. Med. **57**, 649–655 (2000)
2. Hart, R.P., Buchsbaum, D.G., Wade, J.B., Hamer, R.M., Kwentus, J.A.: Effect of sleep deprivation on first-year residents' response times, memory, and mood. J. Med. Educ. **62**, 940–949 (1987)
3. McIntire, L.K., McKinley, R.A., Goodyear, C., Nelson, J.: A comparison of the effects of transcranial direct current stimulation and caffeine on vigilance and cognitive performance during extended wakefulness. Brain Stimulation **7**, 499–507 (2014)
4. Lim, J., Dinges, D.F.: Sleep deprivation and vigilant attention. Ann. N.Y. Acad. Sci. **1129**, 305–322 (2008)
5. Griffiths, R.R., Bigelow, G.E., Liebson, I.A.: Reinforcing effects of caffeine in coffee and capsules. J. Exp. Anal. Behav. **52**(2), 127–140 (1989)
6. Stern, K.N., Chait, L.D., Johanson, C.E.: Reinforcing and subjective effects of caffeine in normal human volunteers. Psychopharmacology **98**, 81–88 (1989)
7. Loke, W.H., Hinrichs, J.V., Ghoneim, M.M.: Caffeine and diazepam: separate and combined effects on mood, memory, and psychomotor performance. Psychopharmacology **87**, 344–350 (1985)
8. McLeelan, T.M., Kamimori, G.H., Voss, D.M., Bell, D.G., Cole, K.G., Johnson, D.: Caffeine maintains vigilance and improves run times during night operations for special forces. Aviat. Space Environ. Med. **76**, 647–654 (2005)
9. Miller, N.L., Matsangas, P., Shattuck, L.G.: Fatigue and its Effect on Performance in Military Environments. Naval Postgraduate School Operation Research Department (Report No. 0704-0188) Monterey, CA (2007)
10. Davies, D.R., Parasuraman, R.: The Psychology of Vigilance. Academic Press, London (1982)

11. Nelson, J.T., McKinley, R.A., Golob, E.J., Warm, J.S., Parasuraman, R.: Enhancing vigilance in operators with prefrontal cortex transcranial direct current stimulation (tDCS). NeuroImage 15(85), 909–917 (2014)
12. Paulus, W.: Outlasting excitability shifts induced by direct current stimulation of the human brain. Adv. Clin. Neurophysiol. 57, 708–714 (2004)
13. Priori, A.: Brain polarization in humans: a reappraisal of an old tool for prolonged non-invasive modulation of brain excitability. Clin. Neurophysiol. 11(14), 589–595 (2003)
14. McKinley, R.A., Weisend, M.P., McIntire, L.K., Bridges, N., Walters, C.M.: Acceleration of image analysts training with transcranial direct current stimulation. Behav. Neurosci. 127(6), 936–946 (2013)
15. Nelson, J.T.: Modulating the dorsolateral prefrontal cortex during sustained attention. Unpublished doctoral dissertation, Tulane University (2012)
16. Smit, A.S., Eling, P.A., Coenen, A.M.: Mental effort causes vigilance decrease due to resource depletion. Acta Psychol. 115(1), 35–42 (2004)
17. McKinley, R.A., Weisend, M.P., McIntire, L.K., Bridges, N., Walters, C.M.: Acceleration of image analysts training with transcranial direct current stimulation. Behav. Neurosci. 127(6), 936–946 (2013)
18. McKinley, R.A., Nelson, J.T., McIntire, L.K., Nelson, J., Weisend, W.: Improved skill learning: enhancing formation and retention of non-declarative memories with transcranial direct current stimulation. Presented at the Society for Neuroscience, New Orleans, LA, Oct 2012

Towards a Translational Method for Studying the Influence of Motivational and Affective Variables on Performance During Human-Computer Interactions

Jason S. Metcalfe[1,2(✉)], Stephen M. Gordon[1], Antony D. Passaro[1,2], Bret Kellihan[1], and Kelvin S. Oie[2]

[1] Scientific Research Department, DCS Corporation, Alexandria, VA, USA
{jmetcalfe, sgordon, apassaro, bkellihan}@dcscorp.com
[2] Human Research and Engineering Directorate, US Army Research Laboratory, Aberdeen Proving Ground, Aberdeen, MD, USA
kelvin.s.oie.civ@mail.mil

Abstract. A primary goal in operational neuroscience is to create translational pathways linking laboratory observations with real-world applications. Achieving this requires a method that enables study of variability in operator performance that does not typically emerge under controlled laboratory circumstances; the present paper describes the development of such a paradigm. An essential aspect of the design process involved eliciting subject engagement without using extrinsic incentive (e.g. money) as a motivating stressor and, instead, tapping an appropriate intrinsic incentive (i.e. competitive stress). Two sources of competition were initially considered including one based on self-competition and another based on competition with another individual; ultimately, the latter approach was selected. A virtual competitor was designed to affect individual valuation of momentary successes and failures in specific ways and preliminary results revealed early indicators of success in meeting this goal. Discussion focuses on implications and challenges for future research using similar translational paradigms.

Keywords: Competitive stress · Affect · Motivation · Translational science

1 Introduction

Research on operational performance in defense contexts increasingly leverages the knowledge, methods, and technologies of modern cognitive neuroscience to improve decision making within complex, high-risk, time-limited circumstances [1, 2]. The future success of such efforts relies partly on the ability to outfit warfighters with lightweight, wearable sensor suites that, in concert with the application of advanced computational techniques, facilitate the inference of a variety of cognitive and/or emotional processes (i.e. attention control, decision-making, event appraisal) and states (i.e. stressed, frustrated, fatigued; [3]). Ultimately, to make full use of such technologies, these types of efforts must establish clear translational pathways linking laboratory

© Springer International Publishing Switzerland 2015
D.D. Schmorrow and C.M. Fidopiastis (Eds.): AC 2015, LNAI 9183, pp. 63–72, 2015.
DOI: 10.1007/978-3-319-20816-9_7

observations of operator state changes with real-world implications for the development of systems and methods that will improve operational effectiveness.

Traditional research in cognitive neuroscience has tended to focus on delineating changes in psychological constructs, such as mental fatigue or attention, using narrow sets of variables derived from physiological and behavioral data recorded during simplified tasks that were performed in tightly controlled laboratory environments. For instance, some studies assess brain activity that has been averaged across hundreds of isolated stimulus presentations using neuroimaging techniques that are limited in spatial and/or temporal resolution (e.g. functional near-infrared spectroscopy, fNIRS, or electroencephalography, EEG). While these paradigms have provided important understandings of average brain dynamics and behavioral response patterns across populations of individuals, they do not provide much power for understanding precisely how these patterns may vary within any given operator or from moment to moment during individual performance instances within more complex task and stimulus environments. A precise and individualized understanding, however, is necessary to enhance real-time, real-world operational effectiveness of systems and technologies intended to work for individuals in varied operational circumstances. New paradigms are thus needed to enable detailed understandings of brain-behavior relationships in individuals as they perform real-world operational tasks and make real-time appraisals thereof [4].

The overarching goal of the project described in this paper was to develop and validate methods for enabling and drawing inferences about event appraisal processes (i.e. determining the value of actions and outcomes) as reflected in motivational and emotional state variables. Specifically, we aimed to develop an understanding of factors that influence the event appraisal processes expected to be revealed by subjective changes in affect, task-specific motivation, and their associations with performance.

2 Method

2.1 Assumptions

The research described herein was designed based on certain assumptions about the information available for inference and classification of affective and motivational states within realistic operational environments. Even in highly constrained operational settings, such as tactical vehicle environments, there are sources of information that have considerable potential to improve the estimation of operator states, particularly when applied in combination with those already commonly used in neuroscience laboratories (e.g. [5]). Further, we believe that such information may be mined to help identify states with unique, yet consistent, neural, cognitive, and behavioral dynamics. For example, the use of computer-vision technologies that register graph topologies with individual facial features may be applied simultaneous with facial electromyography (EMG) and electrodermal activity (EDA) recordings to assess and reliably characterize operator affective variables during a variety of task conditions. The present research was based on a method that we developed to leverage these approaches through the capture of continuous streams of data related to individual facial expressions, head orientation, and manual behavior, EEG, EDA, ECG (electrocardiography) and eye motion tracking, while subjects performed operationally relevant tasks. In addition to the behavioral and physiological modalities, state data from common task interface devices (keyboards, response pads, vocal inputs, etc.) as well as environmental event data were also expected to enhance the performance of traditional machine learning-based state prediction and classification systems.

2.2 Primary Task

Subjects were asked to perform an object detection and classification task in a semi-realistic virtual environment that emulated a modern military-relevant urban setting. There were four object types and each required a button-press response. The objects appeared within moving imagery that represented the out-the-window view of a tactical vehicle driving through an urban environment. As the vehicle proceeded, the objects appeared in a randomized order at a variety of radial distances and eccentricities. The subjects did not have any control over the simulated vehicle's path.

For each 15-min condition, there were 300 object presentations divided among four types. The object types included a male figure holding a large gun (human threat), a male figure with no gun (human non-threat), a table that the subject could not see under (table threat), and a table that the subject could see was clear underneath (table non-threat). Objects each appeared for 1 s and the inter-stimulus interval was chosen from a uniform random distribution between 1 and 3 s. Subjects were responsible for reporting the threat status (threat/non-threat) of each object by pressing one of two buttons on a response pad. For each subject, threats (regardless of human or table) were to be indicated using one hand and non-threats with the other; the assignment of hand to stimulus category was balanced across the subjects.

3 Design Considerations

The main goal of this research was to examine motivational and affective influences over variability in operational task performance. Among the avenues towards achieving this goal in a way that provided translational value (i.e., having a clear pathway through which it may be applied in operational settings) it was essential to have a means of facilitating a sense of investment in the task outcome that was analogous to motivational sources in the operational environment. Typically, research aiming to provoke a sense of personal investment in the task has accomplished this by linking performance outcomes to extrinsic rewards; most commonly these rewards have been in the form of financial incentives. Here, our concern was within the domain of defense application. Though financial incentives are indeed "real-world" (i.e. most adults are familiar and have daily experience with valuing things in financial terms and, further, have some motivational orientation towards financial gain), their function as a motivator on the battlefield, where most decisions have a potential cost of human life or overall mission failure, is not as clear. Indeed, it seems clear that not all types of incentives are equally rewarding; the behavioral context is an important indicator of how a given decision or behavior is best valuated [6]. For the current research, it thus was considered appropriate to implement a different reward mechanism. In particular, we were interested in a reward mechanism that was more internally driven and, at least in terms of face validity, was more relatable to a defense context than would be financial gain. As such, we developed the translational paradigm around competitive challenge. There were a few crucial design considerations driven by the goals just described. These considerations included the definition of the basis for competitive reward, the design of a scoring function for the reward feedback, and the appropriate selection of the subject population given the reward paradigm used.

3.1 Competitive Reward Basis

In considering what it might mean to motivate participants with a so-called competitive stressor, the first question encountered was who, or what, should serve as the basis for competitive evaluation. That is, against whose performance would the subjects evaluate their own performance? Immediately, it was decided that actual human confederates, though most preferred [7], were not feasible for several reasons including cost, time, and experimental control. Thus, the remaining options necessarily involved the use of a computerized competitor. Nevertheless, even within the domain of computerized competition, the reward structure has several options. Most generally, rewards can essentially be with the self or with another. That is, the rewards can be chosen to focus the individual on evaluations of their current performance with respect to their own recent performance history (self-competition). Alternatively, the reward structure can be chosen to focus the individual on their current performance in comparison with that of another. Therefore, during initial development of the software that served as the basis for this study, two variants of the competitive reward were developed and overlaid on the exact same game.

One of the two game variants that was considered was based on the concept of an "Infinite Runner". In this competitive format, game evaluators played to achieve the highest score possible. There was no direct competitor. Instead, the competitive feedback was structured such that the cost of an incorrect response increased with each correct response. That is, each correct response would earn the player a flag and an uninterrupted sequence of flags was required to score points, which were the main objective. Importantly, an incorrect response would cost the loss of all current flags, thus requiring the subject to start over in accumulating to the next point value. Further rewards and protections were possible; for example, enough points could earn "shields" that would offer protection against loss of flags. Thus, there were different levels of achievement combined with different degrees of consequence for performance errors. Ultimately, game evaluators indicated that the complex scoring structure of this game, while more interesting, was less intuitive and thus less preferred for a single session of game play (i.e. it would take longer to learn).

The second game variant, which was ultimately selected for the formal experiment, was based on a model of more direct competition. That is, players were told that they were in direct competition with a virtual competitor (VC) that they could out-perform if they played well enough. Their score was displayed in direct opposition to that of the

VC. In reality, the score of this VC was driven by a scoring function that accumulated or lost points as a transformation on the recent performance history of the human player (algorithm described in Sect. 3.2 below). Research advantages of this paradigm became immediately apparent. Though the game evaluators reported that this variant was less interesting, it was more intuitive and therefore, they had a more immediate understanding of what was needed to "win" the game. Moreover, a degree of simplicity in experimental control was afforded by the use of the VC scoring function. That is, the function was tunable to achieve a specific level of competition in terms of the percentage of time that the VC was ahead of or behind the performance of the player.

3.2   Structuring the Scoring Function

In order for the competitive stimulus to function properly (elicit subject investment and engagement to the point of provoking affective state changes), it was not only important that the subjects perceived the presence of the competition but also that the competition was of a nature that it made sense to fully engage with the game. That is, the players of this game needed to judge that there was a legitimate chance they could win even if the apparent difficulty was high. Indeed, if and when subjects perceived that the game was not "winnable" or was otherwise "rigged", their personal sense of agency and investment in the task would diminish. This risk was apparent in the formal data sample when one subject noted "I lost competitive interest when I figured out it was a slingshot AI" (implying fixed outcome). Now, despite the fact that the subject was incorrect about the precise nature of the VC (it was not, in fact, a "slingshot AI"), the important thing was that this resulted in complete disengagement in the task in terms of personal investment in the outcome. Further, without a sense of personal investment, the competitive reward would fail in provoking the kinds of motivational and affective state changes that were actually of interest in this study.

Therefore, a primary task in the development of this translational paradigm was to define the VC such that it tracked with the performance of the subjects in particular ways, was tunable to particular levels of competitive challenge (see below), and that its functional connection to the subject's own performance was not immediately apparent. The subjects must also have had a fair chance to win, even when winning was more or less difficult. Several mechanisms were attempted through early development and evaluation phases, including tracking of a weighted running average of the subject's performance as well as a number of different variations on proportional-integral-derivative (PID) based feedback control schemes. Ultimately, a manually-tuned proportional-gain feedback control model was the basis of the scoring function, with specific VC scores determined by the control system plus a stochastic value added as a mask against detection by the subjects.

3.3   Subject Selection

Logically, when choosing any particular reward mechanism to affect motivational and emotional states, it is essential to ensure that the subjects actually value the rewards in the manner expected. For instance, during the initial design phase for the stimuli to be used in the current paradigm, subjects who were self-identified "gamers" were thought to be important to include as the game and competitive reward were evaluated. The rationale for focusing on gamers as system evaluators was that they would already maintain an intrinsic reward system based on the gain and loss of points and, therefore, they would be motivated by this assumed value system. In the initial informal system tests, a number of the evaluators who self-identified as both gamers and non-gamers played the game under the two variants of the competitive reward system. Ultimately, the responses to the game versions appeared independent of whether an individual was a self-identified gamer. However, all evaluators were also asked additional questions about their game-playing experiences and, as it turned out, the key variable that appeared to elicit differing perceptions was whether the evaluators self-identified as feeling competitive when playing the games. Moreover, not all evaluators who self-identified as competitive were also gamers. While no formal analyses were conducted on these early evaluations, the lesson was that the match of reward to personality traits was likely to be critical as expected. Moreover, because the manipulation targeted competitive challenge, it was clear that self-identified competitiveness was more important than gaming experience.

4 Translational Paradigm

Sixteen adult male participants[1] who self-identified as being competitive were recruited to participate in this experiment. Each subject played the game in two conditions, with each condition representing a different level of competitive challenge. Subjects were instructed to play the object detection and classification game with the primary goal of outscoring the VC. The subject's score was clearly displayed along with the score of the VC and both were updated in real time. Immediate score feedback was shown per target, with the numeric value for each response displayed as a brief pop-up overlaid on the screen. Correct and incorrect responses were associated with specific sounds connoting success or failure. The sound cues were intended to help the subjects more readily evaluate their responses. To provide a persistent reminder of the competitive aspect of the game, the difference between the subject's score and that of the VC was graphically represented with a color-coded bar at the bottom of the screen. The size, direction, and color of the bar changed as a function of the score difference to indicate whether the subject was winning (blue bar growing to the right of screen center) or losing (red bar growing to the left of screen center).

Although subjects were told that the other score that appeared on the screen was based on a computerized competitor (the VC), they were also told that the outcome of the game was not fixed. Though the outcome was not fixed, the score of the VC was controlled in a systematic manner relative to the subject's real-time performance. To give the impression of two levels of competition, the VC either closely matched the subject (high challenge) or was clearly losing a majority of the time (low challenge). The actual

---

[1] All participants in this research provided their voluntary, fully informed consent [8, 9], and investigators adhered to U.S. Army policies for protecting human subjects [9].

difficulty of the task was comparable across conditions. Figure 1 shows distributions of the score differences between the subjects and the VC for each condition.

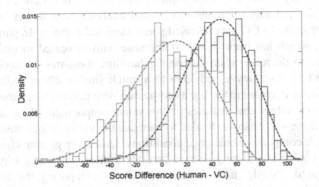

Fig. 1. Empirical distributions of the score differences between the subjects and the VC. The distribution centered on 0 points (red) was from the high challenge condition and the one centered on 50 points (blue) was from the low challenge condition. (Color figure online)

In addition to the level of persistent competitive challenge, the stimulus environment was varied to change the task difficulty within each condition. The intention of this manipulation was to shift the task context, within each competitive circumstance, in order to enable assessment of corresponding changes in affective state variables as a function of the ambient context. Here, the task difficulty was periodically increased with a fog that was overlaid onto the video stream. Shown in Fig. 2, these periods of fog (shaded regions) were nearly identical across the two challenge conditions.

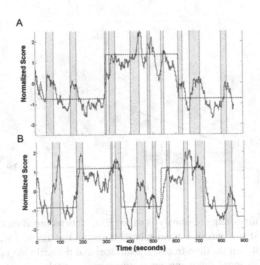

Fig. 2. Actual vs targeted score differences in the (A) low and (B) high challenge conditions. The square trace is the target scoring function and the irregular trace is a representation of the actual score differences observed. Shaded regions are times when the fog was enabled.

5 Initial Results

Though formal analyses are as yet incomplete, initial assessments are encouraging for the success of this paradigm. For instance, initial analyses on a subset ($n = 7$) of the subjects with processed ECG data revealed some expected patterns. In particular, heart rate variability, which has been shown to decrease with increased mental effort [10], was also shown to decrease when comparing baseline measures to recordings when performing the task; meanwhile, although to a much smaller effect, indications were present for a similar decrease in the fog as compared with periods when the fog was not present. Moreover, subsequent analyses on this same sample using K-means clustering suggested that those subjects who tended to increase the visual search area when going from low to high competitive challenge conditions, indicating greater visual searching for targets, also tended to show greater reductions in heart rate variability as the task difficulty increased. Finally, time frequency analyses comparing the low and high competitive challenge conditions on a separate subset of subjects ($n = 9$) with processed EEG are shown in Fig. 3. Here, a negative cluster (right-most scalp map; blue) was statistically significant ($p < 0.05$) while a positive cluster (left-most scalp map; red) was also observed although this did not reach significance for this small group size. In both clusters, the low-challenge condition appeared to be associated with greater event-related changes than in the high-challenge condition. Beta event-related synchronizations following an incorrect button-press response, as seen in these preliminary analyses, has been shown to increase in medial regions [11] and is likely reflected in the present data. One interpretation of such preliminary results is that the subjects were evaluating the meaning of their errors differently as a function of the perceived competitive challenge induced with this translational paradigm.

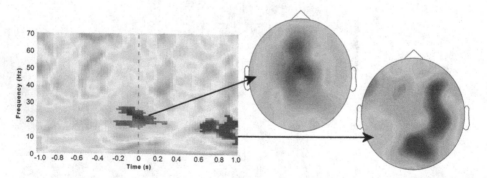

Fig. 3. Results from a time-frequency analysis of the EEG data recorded on the initial 9 subjects. Scalp map on the left shows positive event-related activation associated with the button press (vertical dashed line at 0 s on the time-frequency surface) and the scalp map on the right shows a negative event-related response following erroneous response trials.

6 Discussion

While the currently observed patterns in subject physiology and behavior have yet to be clearly and unequivocally associated with known affective state changes, these results reinforce the premise that performance differences can be modulated through an appropriately constructed competitive challenge. The results also suggest that subjects respond in different ways to the increased competition, as well as to actual changes in task difficulty (i.e., fog vs no fog). However, it is unlikely that any individual variable will embody the entire influences of competitive challenge. Rather a comprehensive view across multiple variables, simultaneously recorded and synchronized, should be employed. The paradigm described in this work was effective in reaching its initial objectives and well-suited for such operational analyses as suggested by the preliminary results.

Acknowledgements. The authors would like to our colleagues in the Translational Neuroscience Branch of the Army Research Laboratory for their help in designing and vetting this research project. This research was sponsored by the Army Research Laboratory and was accomplished under Cognition and Neuroergonomics Collaborative Technology Alliances (CaN CTA; Cooperative Agreement #W911NF-10-2-0022). The views and conclusions contained in this document are those of the authors and should not be interpreted as representing official policies, either expressed or implied, of the Army Research Laboratory or the U.S. Government. The U.S. Government is authorized to reproduce and distribute reprints for Government purposes notwithstanding any copyright notation herein.

References

1. Committee on Military and Intelligence Methodology for Emergent Neurophysiological and Cognitive/Neural Research in the Next Two Decades, N. R. C.: Emerging Cognitive Neuroscience and Related Technologies. The National Academies Press, Washington, DC (2008)
2. Committee on Opportunities in Neuroscience for Future Army Applications, N. R. C.: Opportunities in Neuroscience for Future Army Applications. The National Academies Press, Washington, DC (2009)
3. McDowell, K., Lin, C.-T., Oie, K.S., Jung, T.-P., Gordon, S., Whitaker, K.W., Li, S.-Y., Lu, S.-W., Hairston, W.D.: Real-world neuroimaging technologies. IEEE Access 1, 131–149 (2013)
4. Kerick, S.E., McDowell, K.: Understanding brain, cognition, and behavior in complex dynamic environments. In: Schmorrow, D.D., Estabrooke, I.V., Grootjen, M. (eds.) FAC 2009. LNCS, vol. 5638, pp. 35–41. Springer, Heidelberg (2009)
5. Kerick, S., Metcalfe, J., Feng, T., Ries, A., McDowell, K.: Review of fatigue management technologies for enhanced military vehicle safety and performance. Technical report #ARL-TR-6571. US Army Research Laboratory, Aberdeen Proving Ground, MD (2013)
6. Rangel, A., Camerer, C., Montague, P.R.: A framework for studying the neurobiology of value-based decision-making. Nat. Rev. Neurosci. 9, 545–556 (2008)

7. Ravaja, N., Saari, T., Turpeinen, M., Laarni, J., Salminen, M., Kivikangas, M.: Spatial presence and emotions during video game playing: does it matter with whom you play? Presence 15(4), 381–392 (2006)
8. U.S Department of Defense Office of the Secretary of Defense. Code of federal regulations, protection of human subjects. 32 CFR 219. Government Printing Office, Washington, DC (1999)
9. U.S. Department of the Army. Use of volunteers as subjects of research. AR 70-25. Government Printing Office, Washington, DC (1990)
10. Allanson, J., Fairclough, S.H.: A research agenda for physiological computing. Interact. Compt. 16(5), 857–878 (2004)
11. Koelewijn, T., van Schie, H.T., Bekkering, H., Oostenveld, R., Jensen, O.: Motor-cortical beta oscillations are modulated by correctness of observed action. Neuroimage 40(2), 767–775 (2008)

Impact of Acute Stress on Attentional Orienting to Social Cues in Special Operations Personnel

Charles A. Morgan[1], Harlan M. Fichtenholtz[2,3(✉)],
and Bartlett Russell[4]

[1] Henry C. Lee College of Criminal Justice and Forensic Sciences, University of
New Haven, West Haven, CT, USA
camorgan3rd@gmail.com

[2] Department of Veterans Affairs, National Center for PTSD,
West Haven, CT, USA

[3] Child Study Center, Yale University, New Haven, CT, USA
harlan.fichtenholtz@gmail.com

[4] Department of Kinesiology, University of Maryland, College Park, MD, USA
bartlett.a.russell@lmco.com

Abstract. The goal of the present study was to characterize the effects of an
acutely stressful situation on attentional orienting to social cues. Participants
were tested before and during a highly stressful military training course. During
the task, participants shown faces at fixation that concurrently displayed
dynamic gaze shifts and expression changes from neutral to fearful or happy
emotions. Military-relevant targets subsequently appeared in the periphery and
were spatially congruent or incongruent with the gaze direction. Participants
showed faster responses during fearful face trials during the high stress condition compared to baseline, while the response on happy face trials did not
change. Additionally, enhanced performance was related to self-report reappraisal use during emotion regulation at baseline. Reaction times to threatening
targets were faster on validly cued trials during both tests. Trials with safe
targets showed no differences at baseline. These results suggest that acute stress
plays a role in how individuals respond in the presence of a fearful cue, and
during the evaluation of potentially threatening targets.

Keywords: Facial affect · Shared attention · Stress

1 Introduction

Gaze direction and emotional expression are used in social contexts to direct visuo-
spatial attention to salient features of the environment. The attentional focus and
motivational state of another individual can be discerned in part by interpreting his or
her communicative facial cues. Attentional focus is most readily inferred by noticing
the direction of a partner's gaze, although other cues such as body and vocal gestures
are also used in social communication. Emotional facial expressions provide information about the motivational state of the actor (Ekman and Oster 1979) as well as

© Springer International Publishing Switzerland 2015
D.D. Schmorrow and C.M. Fidopiastis (Eds.): AC 2015, LNAI 9183, pp. 73–81, 2015.
DOI: 10.1007/978-3-319-20816-9_8

changes in one's level of safety and threat. People rely on their understanding of changes in facial behaviors and gaze direction in social situations to respond appropriately to both a partner as well as to the stimulus that elicited his or her change in affect and attentional deployment.

Effects of gaze and emotion on attention have been experimentally investigated in studies that vary the standard Posner attentional cuing paradigm by using faces as attention-directing cues (Friesen and Kingstone 1998). In this task, the peripherally or centrally presented symbolic cues are replaced with a socially relevant cue, a face. At the start of each trial a face with direct gaze is presented at fixation, after a short interval the pupils shift to represent leftward gaze or rightward gaze, or hold position for a direct gaze. Targets are randomly presented at a location in the periphery of the left or right visual field. Participants are faster at responding to targets (detection, localization, or identification) when presented at the gazed-at location (valid) compared to the opposite visual field (invalid) or when there was a direct gaze.

Using this approach, behavioral studies have directly investigated the relationship between emotional expression and gaze during attentional target detection or identification tasks. Previous studies (Fichtenholtz et al. 2009; Graham et al. 2010) have shown that targets are responded to more quickly when observing faces that express a change in emotional expression (fearful, happy, or disgust) regardless of the match between gaze direction and target location. However, some studies have shown that facial expression can interact with gaze validity, with larger validity effects in the presence of a fearful face (Putman et al. 2006; Tipples 2006) or a happy face (Hori et al. 2005; Putman et al. 2006) relative to a neutral face. Another group of studies have found no effect of facial expression (fearful, angry, disgust or happy) and no interactions between gaze direction and facial expression on attention (Bayliss et al. 2007; Hietanen and Leppanen 2003). A few studies have interrogated the influence of anxiety on orienting to social cues (Holmes et al. 2003; Mathews et al. 2003; Putman et al. 2006). Those that have demonstrated a greater influence of facial expression on the orienting to gaze shifts compared to non-anxious controls. The limitation of these studies is the focus on trait anxiety, not state anxiety or current stress.

In the current study, a modified gaze-cuing paradigm was used in which dynamic gaze shifts and dynamic expression changes were incorporated in face cues (neutral to fearful, or neutral to happy) and attentional targets were objects that varied in emotional meaning (adapted from Fichtenholtz et al. 2007). Changes in gaze shifts, cue emotion and target emotion were fully crossed. Thus, participants were presented with a complex attention-directing face cue that had the appearance of emotionally reacting (happy or fearful expressions) just prior to the appearance of either a threatening or safe target.

2   Methods

2.1   Participants

Thirty-one male, active duty personnel (mean age, 25.42 years; SD 3.42) enrolled in U. S. military Survival School training at the Marine Corps Special Operations Command in Camp Lejeune, North Carolina, participated in this study. Before enrollment in Survival School, MARSOC medical and psychiatric teams cleared all students medically and psychiatrically. No students with clinically significant medical or psychiatric conditions are permitted to participate in Survival School training. Results of psychiatric screenings are not available to the public and, as in our prior studies of Special Operations personnel, are not part of our research assessments. The MARSOC medical and psychiatric teams were able to provide assurances that no students with known medical or psychiatric conditions were enrolled in this study.

Recruitment of participants was conducted by the principal investigator (C.A.M.). It was explicitly stated to the prospective participants by the Command that the investigator was a civilian and that participation in the study was voluntary; furthermore, prospective participants were informed that their decision to participate in the research project would not influence their status in the Survival School course. After explaining the study, the PI conducted a question and answer period with prospective participants. Individuals who chose to participate in the study (100 %) then provided written informed consent. The study was approved by Institutional Review Boards of VA Connecticut Healthcare System and the University of Maryland.cc

2.2 Venue

Numerous studies from have established that military Survival School training represents a valid, reliable venue for assessing the impact of acute stress in humans (Morgan et al. 2000, 2006). The stress is intense and produces alterations of both psychological and biological processes similar to those elicited by life threatening events. This venue offers a unique opportunity to evaluate how stress affects affective-cognitive functioning.

Survival school training is comprised of two phases. The first (didactic) phase consists of classroom instruction, and "hands on" practice to learn specific survival skills. The second (experiential) phase consists of the students demonstrating the skills they learned in a semi-controlled environment. During the first day of the non-stressful, didactic phase of the course, participants completed valid, reliable, self report measures of individual's emotional expressivity (BEQ; Gross and John 1997), and emotion regulation strategies (ERQ; Gross and John 2003).

On the third classroom day, participants completed a baseline administration of social orienting task. The social orienting task was also administered during the Captivity/Isolation phase of Survival School training. This test took place approximately 17 days after the baseline test (see Fig. 1). Each participant was tested separately in a private area without external distractions. Evaluators who administered the social orienting task during this phase were the same individuals who performed data collection during the didactic phase.

2.3 Task Parameters

The task consisted of one run. Each run contained 120 trials, 5 each of 24 stimulus categories, and lasted approximately 7 min. Trials were pseudorandomized in an

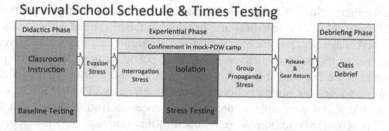

Fig. 1. Order of events at MARSOC survival school.

event-related design across participants. Each trial consisted of a dynamic facial cue stimulus that changed gaze direction (left, right) and facial expression (happy, neutral, fearful), followed by presentation of a target individual (fellow Marine – SAFE, known terrorist – THREAT). All of these variables were fully crossed in the experimental design. The nomenclature for the direction of gaze is based upon the participants' frame of reference so on a leftward gaze shift trial the pupils move to the left of center. Trial with affective cues consisted of three phases. The first phase was the presentation of a neutral face for 300 ms. The second phase consisted of the presentation of a 50 % fearful or 50 % happy expression and a left or right eye gaze presented for 75 ms. The third phase consisted of the presentation of a 100 % fearful or 100 % happy expression and a left or right eye gaze presented for 75 ms. Following this third phase, the cue stimulus maintained its facial configuration and remained on the screen for the remainder of the trial (1000 ms). Spatial location of the target was validly cued by gaze shifts 50 % of the time, and congruency of emotion in cues and targets (e.g., Marine following happy faces) occurred 50 % of the time. This task is a modified version of the task used by Fichtenholtz and colleagues (2007, see Fig. 2).

The dynamic expression change created a situation where the participant saw the cue stimulus become either afraid or pleased in response to the upcoming stimulus. Additionally, previous research has shown that emotional expressions are more accurately identified when presented dynamically (Ambadar et al. 2005) which should enhance the perceived emotional experience of the participant. 150 msec after the onset of the gaze shift, the attentional target was presented for 100 ms. The attentional target consisted of a rectangular image of either a fellow Marine or a known terrorist presented in the periphery (2.1° above fixation, 7.4° left or right of fixation) of the upper left or right visual field (see Fig. 1 for a visual depiction of the task). There was a random inter-trial interval between 1500–2000 ms.

Throughout the entire run, participants were asked to fixate on a centrally-presented cross. The participants' task was to identify the content (Marine or terrorist) of the target image using two buttons on the keyboard. Responses were made with the index finger of each hand. Response mapping was balanced across subjects.

2.4   Stimuli

One male actor (P.E.) was selected from the Ekman and Friesen (1978) pictures of facial affect to act as the centrally-presented cuing stimulus. One actor was used and

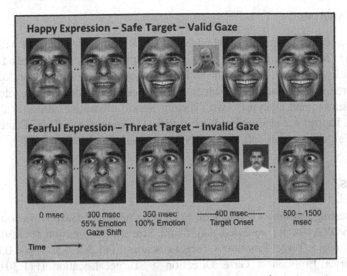

Fig. 2. This novel variation on the gaze direction cueing task uses both dynamic expression and gaze shifts, as well as an emotionally salient target.

compared across emotion categories because previous studies have established that facial identity modulates the perception of facial expression (e.g., Schweinberger and Soukup 1998). The original photos posed fearful, happy, and neutral facial expressions with direct gaze. Adobe Photoshop (Adobe Systems Incorporated, San Jose, CA) was used to manipulate gaze direction so that irises were averted between 0.37° and 0.4° from the centrally-positioned irises in the faces with direct gaze. Thus, five digitized greyscale photographs were used – a neutral face with direct gaze as the initial anchor for the morph and the factorial combination of two facial expressions (fear, happy) and two gaze directions (left, right) from the same actor. In order to create realistic dynamic emotional expressions, fearful and happy facial expressions of intermediate intensity were created using the morphing methods outlined in LaBar and colleagues (2003) using MorphMan 2000 software (STOIK, Moscow, Russia). Three morphs depicting 55 % fearful or happy/45 % neutral expression were created with left- and right-looking gaze and were used to create a more natural-looking appearance of apparent motion. The greyscale facial cuing stimuli were presented at fixation and subtended approximately 6.3° of horizontal and 8.9° of vertical visual angle.

Target stimuli consisted of two photos that were found online to represent the appropriate categories. One stimulus was positively-valent and depicted the face of a fellow Marine; the other was negatively-valent and depicted the face of a known terrorist and was taken from the FBI terrorist watch list (http://www.fbi.gov/wanted/wanted_terrorists). The stimuli were chosen, for their opposing valence, military relevance, and shared similar features (i.e., both were pictures of faces with some facial hair and closed mouths). The original photos were cropped to include only the face area and were converted into grey scale photos. The contrast and luminance of the target photos was equated to that of the facial cues. Targets measured approximately 2.5° of visual angle.

2.5 Data Analysis

Accuracy was approaching ceiling (M 95.98, SD 2.19) so the data analysis will focus on reaction time. Mean reaction time (RT) was computed for correct trials from each condition and participant. Any trials with RTs shorter than 100 ms or longer than 1000 ms (duration of the face on the screen after target presentation) were excluded from this and all subsequent analyses. Two (Testing Session: baseline, stress) × 2 (Expression: fearful, happy) × 2 (Target Emotion: positive, negative) × 2 (Gaze Direction: left, right) × 2 (Target Location: left, right) ANOVAs were conducted for RT.

3 Results

The Stress (testing session) × Expression × Target Emotion × Gaze Direction × Target Location ANOVA for RT revealed significant Stress × Expression ($F(1,30) = 5.58$, $p < 0.025$), Stress × Target Emotion × Target Location ($F(1,30) = 5.79$, $p < 0.022$), and Stress × Target Emotion × Gaze Direction × Target Location ($F(1.30) = 5.28$, $p < 0.029$) interactions.

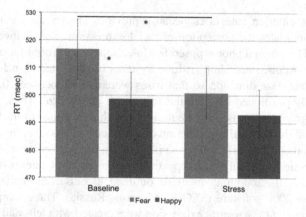

Fig. 3. Stress improves reaction time during fearful face trials but not happy face trials

Reaction time decreased from baseline (M 516.65, SD 60.78) to stress (M 500.79, SD 51.45); $t(30) = 2.24$, $p < 0.032$. On trials with happy faces RT remains constant (Baseline: M 498.58, SD 54.95; Stress: M 492.91, SD 51.51), $t(30) = 0.86$, $p > 0.05$ (see Fig. 3). Additionally, the change in RT from the baseline to the stress test sessions was significantly correlated with self-reported use of cognitive reappraisal as an emotion regulation strategy ($r(30) = 0.42$, $p < 0.02$) but not use of suppression to regulate emotions ($r(30) = -0.12$, $p > 0.05$) (see Fig. 4).

Follow-up analyses on the Stress × Target Emotion × Gaze Direction × Target Location interaction by Target Emotion revealed a significant Gaze Direction × Target Location interaction ($F(1,30) = 12.66$, $p < 0.001$) for Threat target trials. RT was faster

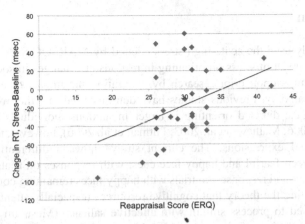

Fig. 4. The performance benefit on fearful face trials is predicted by lower self-report of cognitive reappraisal.

for trials where the gaze direction and target location matched (M 495.93, SEM 9.99) compared to trials where the gaze direction and target location did not match (M 508.29, SEM 9.19). On trials with the Safe target there was a significant main effect of Stress (F (1,30) = 6.13, p < 0.019) and a significant Stress × Gaze Direction × Target Location interaction (F(1.30) = 5.14, p < 0.031). Post Hoc comparisons showed that during the baseline test there was no difference in RT was on trials where the gaze direction and target location matched (M 508.85, SEM 10.24) compared to trials where the gaze direction and target location did not match (M 513.15, SEM 11.40), t(30) = −0.82, p > 0.05. During the stress testing session RT was faster for trials where the gaze direction and target location did not match (M 489.29, SEM 8.16) compared to trials where the gaze direction and target location matched (M 489.96, SEM 8.89) (see Fig. 5).

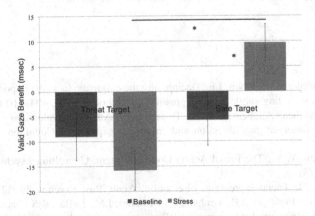

Fig. 5. Reaction times to threatening targets were faster on validly cued trials during both tests. Trials with safe targets showed a benefit for invalidly cued trials during stress.

4   Discussion

The current study used the acute high stress elicited by MARSOC Survival School to investigate the impact of stress on orienting in response to changes in social cues. The current study builds upon prior research by examining the impact of acute stress in contrast to trait anxiety. Previous studies have demonstrated that the impact of facial expression on gaze directed orienting is larger in anxious individuals than controls (Holmes et al. 2006; Mathews et al. 2003; Putman et al. 2006), however, this effect was seen across facial expressions. The current study shows a differential pattern of responding between fearful and happy face cues, with responses on trials with fearful faces getting faster and responses on trials with happy faces remaining constant. This is evidence supporting the theory that cognitive resources (especially attention) are preferentially allocated to process stimuli with affective salience (Mesulam 1999). Additionally, this increase in performance on fearful face trials is inversely related to the use of cognitive reappraisal as an emotion regulation strategy. The relationship between less efficient processing of fearful facial cues and increased cognitive reappraisal may be indicative of the increased resources necessary to regulate emotions in this manner, potentially decreasing the cognitive flexibility necessary to perform the task.

In addition to these findings relating to the facial cue, we also show an interaction between stress, target status and gaze validity. During the baseline assessment, participants were faster responding to looked-at compared to looked-away targets for both threatening and safe conditions. While under stress, responses to threatening targets remained faster when looked-at compared to the responses to safe targets which were faster to looked-away targets. This interaction suggests that when experiencing an acutely stressful situation, the emotional salience of external stimuli is a significant factor in engaging attentional mechanisms (Mesualm 1999).

Acknowledgements. Preparation of this manuscript was supported by the Clinical Neurosciences Division of VA National Center for PTSD. The opinions reflected in this study are not to be considered policy or guidance of the U.S. Government, U.S. Marine Corps, U.S. Navy, or the Department of Defense, but reflect solely the opinions of the authors.

References

Ambadar, Z., Schooler, J.W., Cohn, J.F.: Deciphering the enigmatic face: the importance of facial dynamics in interpreting subtle facial expressions. Psychol. Sci. **16**, 403–410 (2005)

Bayliss, A.P., Frischen, A., Fenske, M.J., Tipper, S.P.: Affective evaluations of objects are influenced by observed gaze direction and emotional expression. Cognition **104**, 644–653 (2007)

Ekman, P., Friesen, W.V.: The Facial Action Coding System. Consulting Psychologists Press, Palo Alto (1978)

Ekman, P., Oster, H.: Facial expressions of emotion. Annu. Rev. Psychol. **30**, 527–554 (1979)

Fichtenholtz, H.M., Hopfinger, J.B., Graham, R., Detwiler, J.M., LaBar, K.S.: Facial expressions and emotional targets produce separable ERP effects in a gaze directed attention study. Soc. Cogn. Affect. Neurosci. **2**, 323–333 (2007)

Fichtenholtz, H.M., Hopfinger, J.B., Graham, R., Detwiler, J.M., LaBar, K.S.: Event-related potentials reveal temporal staging of dynamic emotional expression and gaze shift effects on attentional orienting. Soc. Neurosci. **4**, 317–331 (2009)

Friesen, C.K., Kingstone, A.: The eyes have it! Reflexive orienting is triggered by nonpredictive gaze. Psychon. Bull. Rev. **5**, 490–495 (1998)

Graham, R., Friesen, C.K., Fichtenholtz, H., LaBar, K.: Facial expression facilitates target detection but does not modulate rapid reflexive orienting to gaze. Vis. Cogn. **18**, 331–368 (2010)

Gross, J.J., John, O.P.: Revealing feelings: facets of emotional expressivity in self-reports, peer ratings, and behavior. J. Pers. Soc. Psychol. **72**, 435–448 (1997)

Gross, J.J., John, O.P.: Individual differences in two emotion regulation processes: implications for affect, relationships, and well-being. J. Pers. Soc. Psychol. **85**, 348–362 (2003)

Hietanen, J.K., Leppanen, J.M.: Does facial expression affect attention orienting by gaze direction cues? J. Exp. Psychol. Hum. Percept. Perform. **29**, 1228–1243 (2003)

Holmes, A., Vuilleumier, P., Eimer, M.: The processing of emotional facial expression is gated by spatial attention: evidence from event-related brain potentials. Cogn. Brain Res. **16**, 174–184 (2003)

Hori, E., Tazumi, T., Umeno, K., Kamachi, M., Kobayashi, T., Ono, T., Nishijo, H.: Effects of facial expression on shared attention mechanisms. Physiol. Behav. **84**, 397–405 (2005)

LaBar, K.S., Crupain, M.J., Voyvodic, J.B., McCarthy, G.: Dynamic perception of facial affect and identity in the human brain. Cereb. Cortex **13**, 1023–1033 (2003)

Mathews, A., Fox, E., Yeind, J., Calder, A.: The face of fear: effects of eye gaze and emotion on visual attention. Vis. Cogn. **10**, 823–835 (2003)

Mesulam, M.-M.: Spatial attention and neglect: parietal, frontal and cingulate contributions to the mental representation and attentional targeting of salient extrapersonal events. Philos. Trans. R. Soc. B Biol. Sci. **354**, 1325–1346 (1999)

Morgan III, C.A., Doran, A., Steffian, G., Hazlett, G., Southwick, S.M.: Stress-induced deficits in working memory and visuo-constructive abilities in special operations soldiers. Biol. Psychiatry **60**, 722–729 (2006)

Morgan III, C.A., Wang, S., Mason, J., Southwick, S.M., Fox, P., Hazlett, G., Charney, D.S., Greenfield, G.: Hormone profiles in humans experiencing military survival training. Biol. Psychiatry **47**, 891–901 (2000)

Putman, P., Hermans, E., van Honk, J.: Anxiety meets fear in perception of dynamic expressive gaze. Emotion **6**, 94–102 (2006)

Schweinberger, S.R., Soukup, G.R.: Asymmetric relationships among perceptions of facial identity, emotion, and facial speech. J. Exp. Psychol. Hum. Percept. Perform. **24**, 1748–1765 (1998)

Tipples, J.: Fear and fearfulness potentiate automatic orienting to eye gaze. Cogn. Emot. **20**, 309–320 (2006)

Live-Virtual-Constructive (LVC) Training in Air Combat: Emergent Training Opportunities and Fidelity Ripple Effects

Kelly J. Neville[1]([⊠]), Angus L.M. Thom McLean III[2],
Sarah Sherwood[3], Katherine Kaste[1], Melissa Walwanis[1],
and Amy Bolton[4]

[1] Naval Air Warfare Center Training Systems Division, Orlando, FL, USA
{Kelly.Neville,Katherine.Kaste,
Melissa.Walwanis}@navy.mil
[2] Georgia Institute of Technology, Atlanta, GA, USA
Thom.Mclean@gmail.com
[3] Embry-Ridde Aeronautical University, Daytona Beach, FL, USA
Sherwoo9@my.erau.edu
[4] Office of Naval Research, Arlington, VA, USA
Amy.Bolton@navy.mil

Abstract. Live training is where air combat personnel gain practice and experience with situations as close to real combat as possible. Computer-generated entities could expand the range and complexity of scenarios used in live training and could offer instructors a new means of manipulating the training environment. These new capabilities might help aircrew boost their proficiency beyond what is currently achieved in live training. On the other hand, computer-generated entities add artificiality to the live training environment, reducing its similarity to real combat. As part of a research program conducted to examine how the introduction of Live, Virtual, Constructive (LVC) training technology may change air combat training, we identified strategies to support learning and the acceleration of proficiency development. In this paper, we present these new possibilities for live training and discuss their implications for the fidelity of the training experience, related research, and research needs.

1 Introduction

When a change is introduced into a system, especially a complex system, it can trigger ripple effects and interact with existing system dynamics in ways that produce emergent behaviors and capabilities [1, 2]. This holds true for the introduction of new technology into a training program, as a training program can be considered a system. In this paper, we discuss the introduction of the Live, Virtual, Constructive (LVC) training paradigm and associated technology into live air combat training. The LVC training paradigm involves augmenting a live training environment using *virtual* and *constructive* (VC) entities. Virtual entities are controlled from simulators operated by trained domain professionals—i.e., an aircraft simulator operated by

D.D. Schmorrow and C.M. Fidopiastis (Eds.): AC 2015, LNAI 9183, pp. 82–90, 2015.
DOI: 10.1007/978-3-319-20816-9_9

a trained pilot or an intelligence platform simulator operated by intelligence professionals. Constructive entities are computer-generated, controlled by a software program and often with oversight from a person who adjusts their behavior as a scenario unfolds.

The primary appeal of including VC entities in live air combat training events is that they will allow aircrew to interact with greater numbers of adversaries and within an artificially enlarged training space. LVC technology also may offer additional benefits, many of which may emerge only as the training technology begins to be used. Likewise, the technology could have negative training impacts that only emerge over time and use. This paper describes the partial results of research conducted to predict potential interactions of LVC technology with existing Navy air combat training practices, capabilities, and culture. Specifically, this paper focuses on a portion of the research that addresses ways LVC technology might be used to benefit aircrew proficiency beyond the basic goals of virtually expanding the training range and increasing the numbers and capabilities of adversaries in training exercises. Research results are expected to guide the design and implementation of an LVC training system for air combat.

2 Method

2.1 Participants

Thirty-six participants were interviewed over the course of the study. Twenty-two were active-duty F/A-18 pilots reporting an average of 1310.5 flight hrs ($SD = 460.9$). All but one was qualified to instruct. Five participants were active-duty Naval Flight Officers who either worked as Weapons Systems Officers (WSOs; $n = 4$) or performed command-and-control on the E-2C Hawkeye ($n = 1$), with an average of 1074 h ($SD = 270.1$) in their position. Six participants were former military aviators; five of these were fighter pilots, one was a former WSO, and one had been both a fighter pilot and a WSO. These interviewees had an average of 1938.0 flight hrs ($SD = 1417.0$). Other interviewees were an air intercept controller with 9 years of experience and two military modeling and simulation experts.

2.2 Data Collection

Informed consents were obtained from all participants except the two M&S experts, who considered the interview to be a discussion among colleagues. Permission to audio record was obtained for 19 individual participants and one group interview of five participants. (Nine individuals and the group were interviewed in facilities where recording devices were not allowed). When audio recording was not permitted, researchers took detailed notes. Audio recordings were transcribed and interviewees were given the opportunity to review the notes and transcripts and offer corrections.

Semi-structured Interviews. One-hour semi-structured interviews based on the Critical Decision Method (CDM) [3] were conducted with two groups of five active

duty instructors (one instructor participated in both groups) and 10 individual partic
ipants. Participants were briefed on the LVC training concept and the Navy's goal of
using it to improve training efficiency and virtually extend training ranges. They were
then told that the purpose of the interview was to identify potential *training concerns*
(ways LVC technology might interact negatively with current training practices),
training benefits (ways LVC could enhance or supplement current training), and
training hazards (ways that LVC might negatively impact training safety if the LVC
system was to be implemented into naval air combat training without mitigation).

Some interviews followed the CDM protocol closely. In these, researchers asked
the participant or one participant of a group to recall a memorable and challenging
event that they experienced during a past air-to-air training exercise. The participant
was then asked to give a verbal "walkthrough" of the event and, once he or she
finished, researchers posed (to the individual or group if a group interview) "what-if"
questions about the potential impacts of LVC technology on the training event that had
just been described (e.g., "what if the adversary pilot(s) had been constructive?").

Other interviews were only loosely based on the CDM. In these, interviewees
volunteered their concerns about training impacts and hazards related to flying with VC
entities in the live environment. The researchers prompted them to describe how each
concern could manifest within the context of a training exercise and, if possible, a past
event in which a similar problem had occurred.

Discussion-Based Data Collection. Following assessment of the interview data,
additional data were collected using a discussion-based approach. Discussion sessions
of approximately one hour (30 to 90 min) were held with one group of five participants
(one WSO and four pilots) and nine individual participants. At the beginning of each
session, a respected, high ranking Navy reservist and former expert F/A-18 pilot gave
an approximately 20-min, in-depth description of the LVC paradigm and ways it could
be used to support Navy air combat training. He concluded the description by iden
tifying a challenge identified in the semi-structured interview data assessment and
asked the participant(s) what his/their thoughts on the challenge and resolving it were.
The participant or group's response was followed by a discussion of various solutions
and their pros and cons for the initially posed challenge and then for a number of other
challenges that were brought up by the expert pilot. During individual interviews,
research team members also suggested challenges for discussion.

2.3   Data Analysis

Identification of Potential Hazards and Training Concerns. Thematic analysis [4]
of the interview data was performed to identify and categorize excerpts about potential
LVC hazards, training concerns, strategies for avoiding hazards and training concerns,
and training opportunities. Excerpts addressing these topics were assigned a code
corresponding to the specific hazard or training issue being described. As excerpts were
identified, the set of topics and corresponding codes expanded and previously coded
data were reassessed in light of the new codes.

Coded data extracts, labeled by participant number, were reorganized by code so that all data related to a given hazard or training issue could be considered together and synthesized. Each set of grouped excerpts was organized into contrasting positions, as applicable. (Participants did not always agree on how features of LVC training might affect safety and training).

Two naval air combat experts separately reviewed the identified hazards and training issues, along with the associated interview data, during meetings with members of the research team. (The experts had 2,200 and 2,800 Navy fighter jet flight hours, including experience as adversary pilots; had been on three deployments; were qualified range training officers; and still flew F/A-18 s in the Navy Reserves). They elaborated on conditions that might cause each hazard and training concern to become a reality and described strategies that Navy air combat personnel use or could use to avoid them. Expert reviews were recorded in researchers' notes and added to the categorized interview data.

For the present paper, the discussion-based transcripts were reviewed to identify potential design and implementation solutions. Because the solutions were provided by instructor-level personnel at the Naval Strike and Air Warfare Center (NSAWC) and were viewed as reasonable by the naval air combat expert who led the discussions, they are being treated as equally valid and worthy of further evaluation.

Potential hazards, training concerns, and recommendations for training opportunities were additionally proposed for evaluation by members of the research team.

3 Results

The current paper focuses on live air combat training opportunities made possible by the LVC paradigm. Four categories of potential LVC training opportunities were identified: increased scenario options, scaffolding, attentional support, and repetition. For all but one of the training opportunities in the latter three categories, potential negative impacts on realism were identified for some aspect of the live training experience. These emergent training opportunities and their potential effects on fidelity are presented below.

3.1 Emergent Training Opportunities

New scenario options that LVC technology makes possible include the two basic goals noted in the introduction:

- Supporting the training of long-range combat operations and tactics by allowing VC aircraft to fly outside the physical boundaries of the training range (i.e., by virtually extending a given training range). (Source: U.S. Navy)
- Presenting large numbers of adversaries. (Source: U.S. Navy)

In addition, LVC technology could potentially be used to:

- Present advanced adversary aircraft profiles, including advanced aircraft electronic signatures, speeds, and aerodynamics. (Sources: Interviews, Discussions)

– Expose aircrew to better perceptual cues for post-engagement and re-attack decision making by displaying realistic simulated radar data of an aircraft hit by a missile. (Currently, when aircraft are "killed", they execute a series of exit maneuvers that initially can be mistaken for tactical maneuvering.) (Source: Discussion)

Potential **scaffolding opportunities** found in the LVC training paradigm involve using LVC technology to prepare aircrew to understand and learn more complex or difficult aspects of air combat. Three scaffolding strategies that air combat instructors might find useful are:

– Exposing aircrew to scenarios of the next complexity level in the live environment and populating them with VC adversaries and some VC "friendlies" to reduce the risk of a mishap while aircrew acclimate to the new complexity level. (Source: Research Team)
– Helping aircrew learn the perceptual patterns of different adversary set ups and configurations on their radar display by presenting them as if the radar system operated perfectly and then systematically degrading its detection range and track maintenance capabilities. (Source: Expert)
– Giving instructors controls to vary the complexity of the training environment; for example, controls that allow them to vary the amount of noise and ambiguity in radar data, the sophistication of electronic attack effects, and the shape of the adversary's weapons engagement zone. (Source: Discussions)

Four strategies were identified that involve using LVC technology to help aircrew focus on specific training objectives or on learning specific elements of the work and the environment. These **attentional support opportunities** consist of:

– Teaching aircrew about weaknesses of different radar systems by laying the data from that system over simulated radar data of a perfectly performing advanced radar system. (Source: Research Team)
– Allowing instructors to fly as a virtual (simulator-based) section (i.e., two-ship) leads with a less experienced pilot to draw pilot's attention to aspects of the exercise that relate to the training objectives. The virtual presence of the instructor means the less experienced pilot would be able to focus on training objectives without worrying about running into the section lead. (Source: Expert)
– Allowing instructors to upload performance-support graphics onto radar displays of less experienced pilots as sources of real time guidance and feedback about, e.g., optimal merge geometry, coverage by electronic protection sources, expected flow, the mission timeline, and adversary tactics and flow possibilities to anticipate. (Source: Research Team)
– Practicing the air-to-air phase of an exercise (i.e., the merge) with VC adversaries to reduce the mishap risk while focusing on aspects of the merge that can be practiced in the absence of a live adversary. Flying with reduced consequences of error allows pilots to safely learn from mistakes (assuming mistakes are detected) and may reduce stress levels associated with the merge, which can also facilitate learning. (Source: Research Team)

Repetition opportunities are made possible by the LVC paradigm because VC adversaries can be recycled immediately and repeatedly to practice an engagement or mission phase and without drawing on costly fuel resources. Valuable uses of this repetition capability could be to support:

- Refresher training while an air combat unit is between deployments. During that time, unit aircraft undergo maintenance and only a small number tend to be available to support training at any given time. Funding allocated for fuel during this time is another major limiting factor. (Sources: Expert, Discussion)
- Practicing the merge. The low cost of using VC adversaries and the ability to quickly re-position them means VC adversaries can be used to support a quick succession of practice runs. The merge is complex, high stress, and difficult to master; thus, repetition in the live LVC training environment could contribute to the proceduralization and automatization of the basic skills involved. (Source: Research Team)

3.2 Ripple Effects: Fidelity Trade-Offs

Table 1. Emergent training opportunities and associated impacts on training experience realism

Emergent training opportunity	How fidelity could be impacted
Using friendly VC aircraft to reduce exercise complexity	Relative to live pilots, friendly VC pilots may produce fewer or artificial-sounding communications
Using simulated radar data to develop perceptual skill	The perceptual portion of perceptual-motor radar work (e.g., radar tuning) is artificially separated from the motor portion
Flying with a virtual instructor	The cognitive work of *maintaining separation* is not practiced as interwoven with the rest of the mission execution work
Using VC adversaries to increase repetition and decrease the complexity of going to the merge	The stress of the merge and merge skills that depend on seeing an aircraft out the window are excluded from the fabric of merge practice
	Feedback that live aircraft can provide in the merge phase of an exercise is absent
Uploading graphics that provide real-time guidance and feedback.	Graphics would introduce perceptual artificialities and change the information pilots process

The above scaffolding, attentional support, and repetition strategies represent a variety of ways instructors could leverage the LVC paradigm and technology to train more strategically and efficiently. However, many were associated with trade-offs in the realism of certain aspects of the live training environment (see Table 1). Of the realism tradeoffs, those in Rows 3–6 of Table 1 were explicitly identified as concerns during interviews, with multiple pilots raising each. Artificialities described in the other rows are consistent with and derived from the explicitly identified concerns, as well as with safety concerns raised about introducing other artificialities (e.g., an LVC on-off switch in the cockpit) into the live environment.

4 Discussion

The LVC training paradigm has the potential to increase the fidelity of certain aspects of training scenarios and even the training environment (e.g., by showing a realistic representation of a shot-down aircraft); however, a number of training opportunities made possible by the paradigm could negatively impact some aspect of the realism of operating in a live training environment (e.g., the ability to see adversary aircraft by looking out the cockpit window). Since live air combat training is considered the last stop before real combat, fidelity in that environment is viewed as highly desirable: most interviewed aircrew asserted that interacting with VC entities should involve the same flow and interplay of cognitive activities as interacting with real aircraft. This means, that, for example, there should be no LVC-off option to consider activating nor VC entities in the merge phase when pilots are supposed to be looking out their window and not at their displays. This is consistent with the importance researchers place on *cognitive fidelity*: To support the acquisition of expert, combat-ready levels of perception, decision making, and response fluency, changes to live air combat training should not change the cognitive work such that what is practiced is no longer the work to be performed in the operational setting [5].

Also critical to proficiency is the availability of corrective feedback [5]. Aircrew must be able to detect when their performance would be unacceptable or unsafe in the operational environment—they need to develop a sensitivity to the *selective pressures* of that environment. They need to be able to test the boundaries of effective and safe performance and recognize when they have been reached.

It can be difficult to know what aspects of the rapidly shifting, information intense air combat environment can be reduced in fidelity without changing cognitive work or critical feedback in some way. However, aircrew would not need to do all their live training as LVC training; nor would all LVC training have to be the same. This raises the question of whether cognitive-work-changing artificialities are important to avoid if they (a) are recognized by the aircrew as artificialities and (b) will not exist in all live training and practice. In other words, how much is proficiency affected by intermittent exposure to an acknowledged artifact in the midst of extended practice without the artifact?

Yet another research question is whether expertise contributes to a resistance to negative training that might be produced by artifacts. Research suggests that artificialities, (the use of simplifications and metaphors to explain complex system dynamics and relationships) can produce misconceptions that persist and may never be recognized as misconceptions and corrected [6]. Based on these findings, new learning might be more susceptible to artificialities in the training environment, compared with fluency development at the upper reaches of proficiency. Possibly even new learning can be rendered immune to artificialities, however, if the artificialities are varied across learning experiences. Thus, if a metaphor used to explain a system relationship is alternated with other metaphors or with a range of learning materials and experiences that address that relationship, misconceptions should be detectable and correctable.

In the absence of varied learning experiences and opportunities, fluency at the upper reaches of proficiency is likely to be just as prone to negative training effects as new learning. In other words, at all levels of proficiency, it is likely worthwhile to take advantage of training opportunities that benefit some aspect of expertise acquisition, even if their artificialities detract from another aspect, so long as they are used in combination with training opportunities not featuring the same artificialities.

Faced with practicalities such as resource limitations, instructors will not always be able to provide a variety of training opportunities. It would be useful in these instances to know which would be more valuable—practice and training in as high-fidelity an environment as possible or practice and training that includes learning aids such as scaffolding, attentional support, and other instructional interventions at the expense of certain aspects of realism and cognitive fidelity. The above arguments for the importance of cognitive fidelity and corrective feedback could suggest that realism is most valuable; however, it is nonetheless possible that certain artificialities could integrate into a high fidelity environment to support the cognitive work of learning.

In summary, the keys to augmenting learning in a live complex performance environment may be realism and variety. In addition, we hypothesize that instructional interventions that compromise realism can be more valuable than pure realism if there is variety in instructional methods, materials, and scenarios. To the extent that the realism of the cognitive work and feedback is preserved and a given training experience featuring a given artificiality is alternated with other training experiences featuring other artificialities, learning and proficiency development should benefit from training interventions made possible by the LVC paradigm and technology. Additional research is needed to assess this hypothesis and to better understand the ways realism distortions in the live training environment interact with variables such as level of expertise, variety of training experiences, and the intensity (time and effort) of the training experience.

Acknowledgements. This research was sponsored by the Office of Naval Research (ONR). We wish to thank our interviewees for taking time out of their busy schedules to talk to us in-depth about the domain. The views expressed in this paper are those of the authors and do not represent the official views of the organizations with which they are affiliated.

References

1. Bar-Yam, Y.: Making Things Work. NECSI Knowledge Press, Boston (2004)
2. Kauffman, D.L.: Systems One: An Introduction to Systems Thinking. Future Systems Inc., Minneapolis (1980)
3. Klein, G.A., Calderwood, R., MacGregor, D.: Critical decision method for eliciting knowledge. IEEE Syst. Man Cybern. **19**, 462–472 (1989)
4. Braun, V., Clarke, V.: Using thematic analysis in psychology. Qual. Res. Psychol. **3**, 77–101 (2006)

5. Hoffman, R.R., Feltovich, P.J.: Accelerated proficiency and facilitated retention: recommendations based on an integration of research and findings from a working meeting. Technical report, Air Force Research Laboratory, Mesa, AZ (2010)
6. Feltovich, P.J., Coulson, R.L., Spiro, R.J.: Learners' (mis) understanding of important and difficult concepts: a challenge to smart machines in education. In: Forbus, K.D., Feltovich, P.J. (eds.) Smart Machines in Education, pp. 349–375. MIT Press, Cambridge (2001)

A Composite Cognitive Workload Assessment System in Pilots Under Various Task Demands Using Ensemble Learning

Hyuk Oh[1(✉)], Bradley D. Hatfield[1,2], Kyle J. Jaquess[2], Li-Chuan Lo[2],
Ying Ying Tan[1], Michael C. Prevost[5], Jessica M. Mohler[6],
Hartley Postlethwaite[7], Jeremy C. Rietschel[8], Matthew W. Miller[9],
Justin A. Blanco[7], Shuo Chen[4], and Rodolphe J. Gentili[1,2,3]

[1] Neuroscience and Cognitive Science Program, University of Maryland,
College Park, MD 20742, USA
hyukoh@umd.edu
[2] Department of Kinesiology, University of Maryland,
College Park, MD 20742, USA
[3] Maryland Robotics Center, University of Maryland,
College Park, MD 20742, USA
[4] Department of Epidemiology and Biostatistics, University of Maryland,
College Park, MD 20742, USA
[5] Naval Survival Training Institute, Pensacola, FL 32508, USA
[6] Midshipmen Development Center, United States Naval Academy, Annapolis,
MD 21402, USA
[7] Electrical and Computer Engineering Department, United States Naval
Academy, Annapolis, MD 21402, USA
[8] Maryland Exercise and Robotics Center of Excellence, VA Maryland Health
Care System, Baltimore, MD 21201, USA
[9] School of Kinesiology, Auburn University, Auburn, AL 36849, USA

Abstract. The preservation of attentional resources under mental stress holds particular importance for the execution of effective performance. Specifically, the failure to conserve attentional resources could result in an overload of attentional capacity, the failure to execute critical brain processes, and suboptimal decision-making for effective motor performance. Therefore, assessment of attentional resources is particularly important for individuals such as pilots who must retain adequate attentional reserve to respond to unexpected events when executing their primary task. This study aims to devise an expert model to assess an operator's dynamic cognitive workload in a flight simulator under various levels of challenge. The results indicate that the operator's cognitive workload can be effectively predicted with combined classifiers of neurophysiological biomarkers, subjective assessments of perceived cognitive workload, and task performance. This work provides conceptual feasibility to develop a real-time cognitive state monitoring tool that facilitates adaptive human-computer interaction in operational environments.

Keywords: Attentional reserve · Mental workload · Simulated visuomotor task · Ensemble of classifiers

© Springer International Publishing Switzerland 2015
D.D. Schmorrow and C.M. Fidopiastis (Eds.): AC 2015, LNAI 9183, pp. 91–100, 2015.
DOI: 10.1007/978-3-319-20816-9_10

1 Introduction

In a variety of everyday situations, we observe that different people process identical stimuli in different ways. Specifically, we can focus our attentional resources on particular parts of a stimulus (e.g., spatial locations or shapes of a target object in visual scene) for detailed analysis and optimal decision-making, and overlook irrelevant aspects. Particularly in cognitive-motor performance studies, attention refers to the allocation of limited cognitive resources to execute a task [1], and our previous works have confirmed that it is consumed in proportion to task demand [2–4]. From these findings, three critical facets of attention and task demand can be inferred; (a) attention is a limited resource that can be focused on a single task or divided among several tasks, (b) individuals can shift their attentional focus between tasks having different requirements in terms of the size of the focus, and (c) cognitive-motor performance is sensitive to these differences including task demands.

It was suggested that attentional reserve (i.e., the unused portion of attentional capacity) is a main factor to measure mental workload (i.e., the used portion of attentional capacity) along with task demand [5]. Moreover, many studies have assessed mental workload by means of various metrics such as subjective ratings, the secondary-task paradigm, and psychophysiological measures (e.g., heart rate, galvanic skin response, evoked potentials, and pupil diameter) [2–4, 6, 7]. Overall, these results imply that the excessive mental workload from a failure to conserve adequate attentional reserve would result in an overload of attentional capacity, the failure to execute critical brain processes, and suboptimal decision-making for effective motor performance. As such, assessment of mental workload and attentional reserve is particularly important for individuals such as pilots who must retain adequate reserve to respond to unexpected events when executing their primary task. In this context, our previous work examined subjective report (Visual Analog Scale (VAS) and NASA Task Load Index (NASA-TLX)) as well as electroencephalographic (EEG) and electrocardiographic (ECG) biomarkers in conjunction with detailed monitoring of task-specific behavioral performance during a flight simulation task characterized by various task demands [4]. This result revealed that multiple metrics could index mental workload in ecologically valid situations.

Although this finding identified selective biomarkers to construct a composite metric sensitive to mental workload, there is still a need to further investigate a set of quantifiable features to assess the operator's cognitive workload in a wide variety of operational situations. However, this is very challenging as the data originates from various sources and possess different characteristics. Surprisingly, only a handful of studies have classified multimodal metrics derived from EEG, ECG, or pupillometry, according to the task demands in a pilot task (e.g., [8, 9]). Although interesting, their approaches ended up in studying individual classifiers to achieve higher accuracy rather than examining the relationship between features as well as classifiers.

Therefore, we propose to employ an advanced machine learning algorithm called *ensemble learning* to better understand how multiple metrics from various modalities correlate in feature space, and how the selected heterogeneous features relate to the operator's cognitive state. Ensemble learning is a process that creates and combines a set of independent expert classifiers to improve the prediction performance of a model

[10]. In other words, if data obtained from multiple sources contain complementary information (e.g., amplitudes and latencies of event-related potentials (ERP), standard deviation of the N-N interval (SDNN), the root mean square of the successive differences (RMSSD) of N-N intervals for heart rate variability (HRV), etc.), a proper fusion of such information can lead to improved accuracy of the prediction, even if the predictions from each individual data is less accurate. Thus, this study aims to devise an ensemble model that is able to select optimal features from multiple metrics for a more accurate classification according to three levels of task demand to determine an operator's current cognitive workload in ecologically valid tasks.

2   Methods

2.1   Data Acquisition

Subjects. Thirty-nine healthy volunteers (35 men and 4 women) between the ages of 19 and 24 years (mean and standard deviation age of 20.79 and 1.18), who were midshipmen in the United States Naval Academy (USNA), participated in this study. All subjects had received basic flight training covered in Aviation Preflight Indoctrination before participating in the study.

Apparatuses. Three systems were employed: (1) electrocortical and physiological data acquisition system, (2) a flight simulator cockpit and the Flight Data Recorder (FDR) known as one part of the black box, and (3) auditory stimuli with synchronous trigger delivery system. First, EEG and ECG recordings were accomplished using a single amplifier (g.USBamp®, g.tec medical engineering). Specifically, four active gel-free EEG electrodes (g.SAHARA electrodes®) were placed on the scalp along the frontal, frontocentral, central, and parietal midline sites (Fz, FCz, Cz, and Pz respectively) according to the 10–20 System. In addition, one-lead ECG electrode was placed below the 8th rib for basic heart monitoring. The system was grounded to the right mastoid and referenced to the left ear (A1); recording from the right ear (A2) was used for later EEG re-referencing purpose. Second, the simulator cockpit was equipped with a 22-inch widescreen LCD monitor, a computer with external stereo speakers, a Hands On Throttle-And-Stick set, and rudder pedals. Prepar3D® (v1.4, Lockheed Martin) was installed in the simulator computer, and a custom FDR was used to log operating conditions of the flight such as time, airspeed, and heading that will reflect the pilot's motor response and quality of flight operational performance. Finally, Presentation® (v18.1, Neurobehavioral Systems) delivered auditory probes to the subjects through earphones [2], and sent digital TTL pulses to the g.USBamp through a parallel port to mark stimulus-dependent synchronous triggers on the EEG and ECG data. The volume on the earphones was adjusted to a comfortable and yet audible level for each subject to ensure that the subjects could hear the engine and other mechanical noises played through the external speakers.

Scenarios and Task. Three scenarios were selected from the flight training program and adjusted with advice from naval aviators. Specifically, S1 was to keep straight and level flight, S2 was to repeat straight descending and climbing flight, and S3 was to

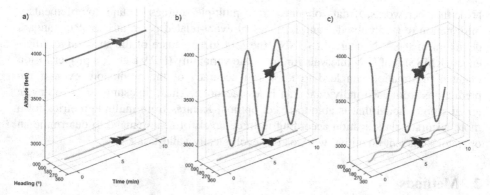

Fig. 1. A brief outline of three challenging scenarios; the red aircraft and blue line respectively depict the manned aircraft and its trajectory for 10 min, and they are represented by gray shadows. (a) S1 is to maintain straight and level flight. (b) S2 is to repeat straight descending and climbing flight. (c) S3 is to repeat diving in left turns and climbing in right turns.

Fig. 2. A flight simulation task; (a) EEG, ECG, and flight data were monitored while the subjects were engaged in the task. (b) the main instrument console in virtual cockpit contains all instrumentation and systems displays for the aircraft. The cockpit layout is based on the US air force and navy joint primary aircraft training system training documentation.

repeat diving in left turns and climbing in right turns (Fig. 1; [4, 11]). Thus, they represented relatively low, moderate, and high demand scenarios, respectively. Scenario sequence was counter-balanced. Participants controlled a single-engine turboprop aircraft (Beechcraft T-6A Texan II). They were instructed to use the primary flight controls (i.e., the control stick, the rudder pedals, and the throttle), without the use of secondary flight controls and other controls (e.g., rudder/elevator/aileron trim systems, etc.; Fig. 2). The flight was programmed to begin at 0900 virtual time, and at an initial altitude of 4000 feet.

Data Acquisition. Each participant sat in the simulator cockpit and was allowed 5 min of free practice along with exposure to the novel sounds. After the practice session, they were prepared for placement of the EEG and ECG sensors. The amplifier was calibrated, and all electrode impedances were maintained below 5 kΩ during data acquisition. The signals were sampled at a rate of 512 Hz with an online Butterworth filter from 0.01 to 60 Hz. Participants were then assigned an initial scenario with relevant instructions. Each scenario was composed of a 1 min preparation period followed by a 10 min scenario. During each scenario, up to 30 stimuli were randomly presented with an inter-stimulus interval randomly ranging from 6 to 30 s, and all relevant flight data were sampled at a rate of 2 Hz. After the completion of each scenario, participants were provided the five VAS questions and the NASA-TLX survey to report their subjective experience. The same order of procedures was followed until all scenarios were completed.

2.2 Preprocessing

EEG. The re referenced EEG were processed using an IIR filter with a 20-Hz low-pass cut-off frequency and 48-dB/octave roll-off. Next, each baseline of 1-s epochs that were time-locked to the auditory stimuli was corrected using the pre-stimulus interval (-100 to 0 ms). Those epochs retaining significant artifacts (e.g., eye-blink, etc.) were excluded. The remaining epochs were averaged per sensor for each scenario. The average ERP amplitudes were derived for the novelty P3 (P3a; 270 to 370 ms).

ECG. HRV was measured through the following methods along with average heart rate, which are appropriate for short 5 min samples from the middle section of the whole 10 min experiment: (1) SDNN, (2) RMSSD, (3) the low (LF; 0.04 to 0.15 Hz) and high frequency (HF; 0.15 to 0.4 Hz) ratio (LF/HF) of R-R intervals using a Welch's method.

FDR. Acceptable operational performance was defined as deviations from the tolerance limits of the target goals: at most ± 200 feet of altitude, ± 10 knots of airspeed, $\pm 5°$ of heading, $\pm 5°$ of bank angle, and ± 500 fpm of ascent/descent rate. Each deviation was bounded above and below the acceptable decision boundary. The performance was calculated once a minute using the area under bounded curves, and normalized in the early (0 to 2 min), middle (4 to 6 min), and late (8 to 10 min) segments of the tests.

Subjective Response. All VAS and NASA-TLX variables were measured to range from 0 to 100, where greater value indicates the respondent felt relatively more efforts in the corresponding scenario.

2.3 Classification

First, attribute sets were constructed by joining preprocessed metrics. This allows each data to be expressed uniquely as a combination of basis vectors (i.e., selective attributes), which means that the attributes for the optimal classifier can better represent the relationship between the data and the task demands. Five individual classifiers were examined: classification trees (CTREE), k-nearest neighbors (kNN), quadratic discriminant analysis (QDA), naïve Bayes (NB), and error-correcting output codes using support vector machine (ECOC-SVM). For an ensemble of classifiers, bagging, boosting, stacking, and voting algorithms were scrutinized. Specifically, bagging derived the final prediction through a simple majority rule from multiple CTREEs.

Boosting combined weak CTREEs using a weighted majority rule, where each classifier was sequentially built as a better model than previous classifiers by considering misclassified observations. Unlike bagging and boosting, stacking employed a higher level model (CTREE) to combine five base learners (i.e., individual classifiers) rather than using one algebraic rule, and voting averaged the predictions of the five base learners. For each classifier, various tests were simulated to find the optimal parameters, and to determine the optimal classifier. Specifically, the optimal model was selected by taking the minimum balance (BAL) error (ε_{BAL}) to balance large biases due to a small sample size [12], which is a convex combination of resubstitution (RESB) and cross-validation (CV) errors. Lastly, the classifiers were assessed using the confusion matrix and the Receiver-Operating Characteristic (ROC) curve, and the rank of attributes was assessed through the ReliefF algorithm.

3 Results

Up to 117 samples (39 subjects in 3 scenarios) with 35 attributes (EEG, SDNN, Airspeed, etc.) from 4 metrics (P3a Amplitude, HRV, FDR, and Subjective Response) including missing data were used to train and test the classifiers.

3.1 Individual Classification

Each optimal classifier was constructed by exhaustively searching various possible parameters and CV settings (Table 1). According to our empirical tests, ECOC-SVM outperformed other classifiers in terms of RESB error (ε_{RESB}), but leave-one-out

Table 1. Optimal individual classifiers for each metric

Metric	Assessment	CTREE	kNN	QDA	NB	ECOC-SVM
P3a Amplitude	ε_{RESB}	0.2105	0.2807	0.5088	0.4912	0.0351
	ε_{CV}	0.6316	0.4211	0.7018	0.5789	0.5439
	ε_{BAL}	0.4211	0.3509	0.6053	0.5351	0.2895
	Accuracy	0.5000	0.7143	0.3750	0.5714	**0.8571**
HRV	ε_{RESB}	0.2464	0.4348	0.6667	0.4928	0.0290
	ε_{CV}	0.7826	0.5797	0.6812	0.8986	0.7681
	ε_{BAL}	0.5145	0.5072	0.6740	0.6957	0.3986
	Accuracy	0.6667	0.5000	0.3333	0.3333	**0.7500**
FDR	ε_{RESB}	0.0601	0.1021	0.2583	0.2763	0.0601
	ε_{CV}	0.1862	0.1411	0.2583	0.2973	0.2823
	ε_{BAL}	0.1232	0.1216	0.2583	0.2868	0.1712
	Accuracy	0.8000	**0.9333**	0.8333	0.8333	0.8667
Subjective Response	ε_{RESB}	0.1282	0.2478	0.2112	0.2821	0.0769
	ε_{CV}	0.3590	0.2743	0.4431	0.3419	0.3846
	ε_{BAL}	0.2436	0.2611	0.3272	0.3120	0.2308
	Accuracy	0.7333	0.7333	0.6000	0.8000	**0.8667**

cross-validated kNN surpassed all the other classifiers regarding CV error (ε_{CV}). Thus, no single classifier can unvaryingly outperform the others over all datasets. Each algorithm has its unique strengths, so it is difficult to decide which method is most appropriate on each dataset. However, the results revealed that εBAL could be a reliable indicator to select the optimal model, although the predictive accuracy is not proportional.

The predictive accuracy rates were 85.71 % for P3a Amplitude; 75.00 % for HRV; 93.33 % for FDR; 86.67 % for Subjective Response. However, to exaggerate, the three weaker classifiers have no contribution to assessing overall mental workload, because the assessment will be still robust with accuracy of 93.33 % even if three less accurate classifiers and corresponding data are excluded from the system. On the other hand, it will be impractical to mix all mutually unrelated metrics into one container to construct a single individual classifier that generates precise and accurate results for all datasets, because it will increase the overall complexity concerning system architecture as well as data representation, classification, and interpretation.

3.2 Ensemble Classification

There is no clear and comprehensive picture of which ensemble methods are optimal. In Table 2, bagging, boosting, and stacking respectively reached an accuracy of 88.0, 95.7, and 94.0 %, while voting had the highest 97.44 %.

The bagging showed that the ensemble learning did not guarantee good performance all the time, although it was still reasonable. Possible reasons may include several missing values on some variables (e.g., certain subjects skipped some VASs), small data sizes, unexpectedly correlated classifiers, noise in samples, and suboptimal parameters. Another critical reason may be due to ill-conditioned data, because some subjects were overwhelmed during high demanding scenarios and had given up halfway through the task. However, the boosting, stacking, and voting showed very reliable performance as expected. In particular, stacking and voting could be easily extensible through a hierarchical structure particularly when any new feature set is included in the future to produce more reliable results.

Table 2. Optimal ensemble classifiers and assessment measurements

a) Bagging

Accuracy	0.880	True Class			Precision	ROC
Kappa	0.821	S1	S2	S3		
Predictive Class	S1	33	4	2	0.846	0.927
	S2	6	31	2	0.886	0.897
	S3	0	0	39	0.907	0.958
Recall		0.846	0.795	1.000		

b) Boosting (AdaBoost)

Accuracy	0.957	True Class			Precision	ROC
Kappa	0.936	S1	S2	S3		
Predictive Class	S1	37	0	2	0.974	0.992
	S2	1	36	2	1.000	0.984
	S3	0	0	39	0.907	0.989
Recall		0.949	0.923	1.000		

c) Stacking

Accuracy	0.940	True Class			Precision	ROC
Kappa	0.910	S1	S2	S3		
Predictive Class	S1	37	2	0	0.974	0.996
	S2	1	36	2	0.900	0.984
	S3	0	2	37	0.949	0.974
Recall		0.949	0.923	0.949		

d) Voting

Accuracy	0.974	True Class			Precision	ROC
Kappa	0.962	S1	S2	S3		
Predictive Class	S1	38	0	1	0.974	0.995
	S2	1	37	1	1.000	0.999
	S3	0	0	39	0.951	1.000
Recall		0.974	0.949	1.000		

Table 3. Importance of selective attributes by means of ReliefF algorithm using 8-fold CV

Average Merit	Average Rank	Attribute	Average Merit	Average Rank	Attribute
0.1813	2.37	Heading	0.0190	23.40	P3a Amplitude on Pz
0.1073	7.67	Altitude	0.0140	27.10	P3 Amplitude on Cz
0.0430	17.66	VAS	0.0110	27.40	RMSSD
0.0290	18.90	P3a Amplitude on Fz	0.0130	27.40	P3a Amplitude on FCz
0.0303	20.23	Vertical Speed	0.0100	28.10	SDNN
0.0247	21.23	Airspeed	0.0080	28.30	LF/HF
0.0248	22.87	NASA-TLX	0.0070	29.40	HR

ReliefF evaluator showed that most of the attributes related to FDR and self-reports better represent task demands in the optimal ensemble classifier (Table 3). It is no wonder that both features are strongly related with task demands, because FDR directly reflects how the operators are performing to achieve a given task, and subjective responses quantify their internal status about the task demands. Interestingly, this result revealed that the P3a Amplitudes (7.5 %) and RMSSD (1.1 %) had a fair amount of contribution to the assessment of the operator's mental workload even considering strong attributes such as FDR (34.36 %) and self-reports (6.78 %). In addition, this revealed that there is a proportional relationship between the importance of attributes and their statistical significance according to our previous work [4].

4 Discussion

This study proposed a novel approach to assess the operator's mental workload under various task demands in ecologically valid situations. Although other research groups have reported the feasibility of mental workload assessment with specific classifiers for each metric, they have mainly focused on individual-level analysis instead of providing results for combined classification [9, 13]. Moreover, only a few studies have examined even individual-level classifiers using multimodal data from operational environments (e.g., [9, 14]). Thus, this study complements previous efforts in that both individual and ensemble learning of multiple classifiers were employed to examine the relationship between mental workload and various feature vectors in an ecologically valid task. Particularly, compared to other methods, while providing accurate and reliable classification accuracy, our approach is able to handle diverse new datasets (e.g., functional near-infrared spectroscopy) and other task specific performance measurements by combining them with existing classification models considering the characteristics of ensemble learning.

We showed that mental workload is a predictable variable with high accuracy if ensemble classifiers are optimally configured. Specifically, high classification accuracy can be achieved when each expert detects distinct but common directional patterns from each feature set, and the final arbiter of classification makes a decision considering a majority vote from each expert. Moreover, the ReliefF indicates that even statistically non-significant metrics (e.g., HRV in our previous study [4]) could contribute to constructing the correct classification if they are discriminable.

Our current research efforts were limited to classification, where the model could predict categorical dependent variables. This method could not predict graded cognitive states, because the task demand and mental workload are intrinsically continuous. Thus, ensemble regression is worth considering in the future. However, constructing such approximation models require highly complex computation, but such a burden can be alleviated by constructing surrogate models. Other possible future work is to pursue more practical approaches. For example, current ERP analysis was highly dependent on the novel sounds, which will be inappropriate when cognitive tasks include auditory stimulus or a silent environment such that the introduction of extraneous sounds could be destructive. One solution is to employ the eye-tracking technology to extract the fixation-related potential (FRP) on the areas of interest, while another solution is to use other signal processing methods that do not rely on ERPs as suggested by our colleagues at the USNA [11].

In summary, the results revealed that both individual and combined classifiers could effectively assess properly constructed feature sets that were extracted from multimodal data. Particularly, ensemble classifiers are expected to outperform individual classifiers, because a single strong referee of classification could merge information collected from multiple weaker experts. As a long-term goal, this work provides conceptual feasibility to develop a real-time cognitive state monitoring tool that facilitates adaptive human-computer interaction in operational environments.

Acknowledgement. The authors would like to express their appreciation for the guidance and supports provided by Kenneth T. Ham (Captain, USN) who was a naval astronaut and the chair of the Aerospace Engineering Department at the USNA, and all student aviators who were midshipmen at the USNA and volunteered to participate in the study. In addition, this research was supported by the Lockheed Martin Corporation (Bethesda, MD, USA) under grant 4-321830.

References

1. Kahneman, D.: Attention and Effort. Prentice-Hall, Englewood Cliffs (1973)
2. Miller, M.W., Rietschel, J.C., McDonald, C.G., Hatfield, B.D.: A novel approach to the physiological measurement of mental workload. Int. J. Psychophysiol. **80**, 75–78 (2011)
3. Rietschel, J.C., Miller, M.W., Gentili, R.J., Goodman, R.N., McDonald, C.G., Hatfield, B. D.: Cerebral-cortical networking and activation increase as a function of cognitive-motor task difficulty. Biol. Psychol. **90**, 127–133 (2012)
4. Gentili, R.J., Rietschel, J.C., Jaquess, K.J., Lo, L.-C., Prevost, M.C., Miller, M.W., Mohler, J. M., Oh, H., Tan, Y.Y., Hatfield, B.D.: Brain biomarkers based assessment of cognitive workload in pilots under various task demands. In: 36th Annual International Conference of the IEEE Engineering in Medicine and Biology Society, pp. 5860–5863. IEEE, Chicago (2014)
5. Kantowitz, B.H.: Mental workload. In: Hancock, P.A. (ed.) Human Factors Psychology, pp. 81–121. Elsevier, Amsterdam (1987)
6. Hankins, T.C., Wilson, G.F.: A comparison of heart rate, eye activity, EEG and subjective measures of pilot mental workload during flight. Aviat. Space Env. Med. **69**, 360–367 (1998)

7. Kok, A.: Event-related-potential (ERP) reflections of mental resources: a review and synthesis. Biol. Psychol. **45**, 19–56 (1997)
8. Wilson, G.F., Russell, C.A.: Real-time assessment of mental workload using psychophysiological measures and artificial neural networks. Hum. Factors **45**, 635–643 (2003)
9. Noel, J.B., Bauer, K.W.J., Lanning, J.W.: Improving pilot mental workload classification through feature exploitation and combination: a feasibility study. Comput. Oper. Res. **32**, 2713–2730 (2005)
10. Dietterich, T.G.: Ensemble methods in machine learning. In: Kittler, J., Roli, F. (eds.) MCS 2000. LNCS, vol. 1857, pp. 1–15. Springer, Heidelberg (2000)
11. Johnson, M.K., Blanco, J.A., Gentili, R.J., Jaquess, K.J., Oh, H., Hatfield, B.D.: Probe-independent EEG assessment of mental workload in pilots. In: 7th International IEEE EMBS Conference on Neural Engineering. IEEE, Montpellier (2015)
12. Raudys, S.J., Jain, A.K.: Small sample size effects in statistical pattern recognition: recommendations for practitioners. IEEE Trans. Pattern Anal. Mach. Intell. **13**, 252–264 (1991)
13. Henelius, A., Hirvonen, K., Holm, A., Korpela, J., Müller, K.: Mental workload classification using heart rate metrics. In: Proceedings of 31st Annual International Conference of the IEEE Engineering in Medicine and Biology Society, EMBC 2009, pp. 1836–1839 (2009)
14. Kohlmorgen, J., Dornhege, G., Braun, M.L., Blankertz, B., Müller, K.-R., Curio, G., Hagemann, K., Bruns, A., Schrauf, M., Kincses, W.E.: Improving human performance in a real operating environment through real-time mental workload detection. In: Dornhege, G., del Millán, J.R., Hinterberger, T., McFarland, D., Müller, K.-R. (eds.) Toward Brain-Computer Interfacing, pp. 409–422. MIT Press, Cambridge (2007)

Sensitive, Diagnostic and Multifaceted Mental Workload Classifier (PHYSIOPRINT)

Djordje Popovic[1]([✉]), Maja Stikic[1], Theodore Rosenthal[2],
David Klyde[2], and Thomas Schnell[3]

[1] Advanced Brain Monitoring Inc., Carlsbad, CA, USA
{dpopovic,maja}@b-alert.com
[2] Systems Technology Inc., Hawthorne, CA, USA
{trosenthal,dklyde}@systemstech.com
[3] Operator Performance Laboratory, University of Iowa, Iowa City, IA, USA
thomas-schnell@uiowa.edu

Abstract. Mental workload is difficult to quantify because it results from an interplay of the objective task load, ambient and internal distractions, capacity of mental resources, and strategy of their utilization. Furthermore, different types of mental resources are mobilized to a different degree in different tasks even if their perceived difficulty is the same. Thus, an ideal mental workload measure needs to quantify the degree of utilization of different mental resources in addition to providing a single global workload measure. Here we present a novel assessment tool (called PHYSIOPRINT) that derives workload measures in real time from multiple physiological signals (EEG, ECG, EOG, EMG). PHYSIO-PRINT is modeled after the theoretical IMPRINT workload model developed by the US Army that recognizes seven different workload types: auditory, visual, cognitive, speech, tactile, fine motor and gross motor workload. Preliminary investigation on 25 healthy volunteers proved feasibility of the concept and defined the high level system architecture. The classifier was trained on the EEG and ECG data acquired during tasks chosen to represent the key anchors on the respective seven workload scales. The trained model was then validated on realistic driving simulator. The classification accuracy was 88.7 % for speech, 86.6 % for fine motor, 89.3 % for gross motor, 75.8 % for auditory, 76.7 % for visual, and 72.5 % for cognitive workload. By August of 2015, an extended validation of the model will be completed on over 100 volunteers in realistically simulated environments (driving and flight simulator), as well as in a real military-relevant environment (fully instrumented HMMWV).

Keywords: Mental workload · Assessment · EEG · IMPRINT · Wearable

1 Introduction

The construct of mental workload – defined as the degree to which mental resources are consumed by the task at hand - is difficult to quantify. This is due largely to the nature of the construct, a latent or hidden variable that results from an interplay of several other variables such as the objective task load, external distractions (task-irrelevant stimuli that draw one's attention and temporarily occupy mental resources), internal

© Springer International Publishing Switzerland 2015
D.D. Schmorrow and C.M. Fidopiastis (Eds.): AC 2015, LNAI 9183, pp. 101–111, 2015.
DOI: 10.1007/978-3-319-20816-9_11

distractions (e.g. task-related stress, task-irrelevant mentation), capacity of one's mental resources and strategy of their utilization (Fig. 1). The overall capacity of mental resources and strategy of allocating them to the tasks are, in turn, strongly dependent on individual traits (e.g. personality profile, stress resiliency), previous training and factors such as motivation, fatigue and stress. Furthermore, for any given individual, different types of mental resources such as attention, audio-visual perception, cognition or motor control will be mobilized to a different degree in different tasks even though the subjective perception of their 'difficulty' may be the same [1, 2]. An ideal measure of mental workload therefore needs to be multifaceted and diagnostic, such that is had the ability to quantify the engagement levels of each of mental resources before eventually combining them into a single global measure. Moreover, it should be able to model the impact of individual traits and psychophysiological states onto the capacity and utilization of mental resources to a degree that does not hamper its ease of use.

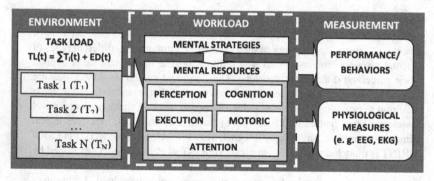

Fig. 1. Schematic presentation of the concept of mental workload and its relationship with pertinent variables: task load (TL), capacity and management of mental resources (MR, MS), individual traits and states (e.g. fatigue), and external and internal distractions (ED and ID).

The standard techniques for workload assessment include self-report scales, performance-based metrics, and physiological measures. Self-report scales are popular due to their low cost and consistency (assuming that the individual is cooperative and capable of introspection). Some of these scales are one-dimensional such as the Rating Scale of Mental Effort (RMSE) and the Modified Cooper-Harper scale (MHC) [3], whereas some scales comprise subscales that measure specific mental resources, e.g., NASA Task Load Index (TLX) [6], Subjective Workload Assessment Technique (SWAT) [5], and Visual Auditory Cognitive Psychomotor method (VACP) [4]. The major drawback of these measures is that they cannot be unobtrusively administered during the task, but are assessed retrospectively at its conclusion. Furthermore, the inherent subjectivity of self-ratings makes across-subjects comparisons difficult. Self-report scales are, therefore, often complemented with performance measures, such as reaction time to different events or accuracy of responses. The performance assessment is relatively unobtrusive and can be accomplished in real time at low cost, but it is not sensitive enough because of the complex relationship between the two variables [7, 8]. Moreover, performance measures cannot tap into all cognitive resources with comparable accuracy. Lately, there has been renewed interest in physiological measures as workload assessment metrics, and signals [9–16] such as electro-oculography (EOG), electromyography (EMG), pupil diameter, electrocardiography, respiration, electroencephalography and skin conductance. Until recently, their utility was limited by the obtrusive nature of earlier instrumentation, but this has changed with the advent of miniaturized sensors and embedded platforms capable of supporting complex signal processing techniques. Still, physiological workload measures have multiple drawbacks. First, the physiological workload scales are often derived empirically on a set of tasks assumed to represent different workload levels and selected ad hoc, without detailed consideration of their ecological validity and ability to tap into different mental resources (e.g., cognitive, visual, auditory, or motor workload). As a result, the models trained on such atomic tasks may not perform well when applied to the physiological signals acquired during other non atomic tasks even though they seemingly require the same mental resources. Second, in spite of the well known fact of considerable between- and within-subject variability of nearly all physiological signals and metrics, the majority of physiological workload models have been developed and validated on a relatively small sample of subjects. Third, the classifiers used in the models introduced hitherto have typically lacked mechanisms for an adjustment of the model's parameters in relation to individual traits, which leads to models that do not generalize well. Finally, the models have mostly ignored the considerable amount of noise inherent in the acquired physiological signals. Thus, poor performance of some models could be attributed to their reliance on rather simple mathematical apparatus.

This paper introduces PHYSIOPRINT - a workload assessment tool based on physiological measures that is built around an established theoretical model called Improved Performance Research Integration Tool (IMPRINT) [17]. The proposed model distinguishes among seven different workload types, and is trained on tasks chosen to represent the key anchors on the respective workload scales. Its mathematical apparatus is not computationally expensive, so it is applicable in real time on a fine timescale.

The rest of the paper is organized as follows. In Sect. 2 we outline the experimental setting while Sect. 3 reports on the experimental results. Finally, in Sect. 4, we summarize our results and give an outlook on future work.

2 Methods

2.1 IMPRINT Workload Model

The IMPRINT Workload Model, developed by the Army Research Laboratory (ARL) [17], discriminates between seven types of workload: visual, auditory, cognitive, fine motor, gross motor, speech, and tactile. Each workload type is quantified on an ordinal/interval scale, similar to the VACP scales [4]. Each of the seven scales is defined by a set of behaviors of increasing complexity that are associated with a numeric value between 0 and 7. Furthermore, for each point in time, IMPRINT produces a composite measure of the overall workload, which is defined as a weighted sum of the type-specific workload values calculated across all tasks that are being simultaneously performed. The model has been successfully applied to estimate mental workload in a number of settings of military relevance, including a strike fighter jet, a mounted combat system [18], and the Abrams tank [19].

2.2 Study Design

Twenty-two healthy subjects (11 females, 25 ± 3 years) who had reported no significant previous or existing health problems participated in the study. They were required to maintain a sleep diary for 5 days prior, and refrain from alcoholic and caffeinated beverages 24 h prior to the experiment. The experiment would typically start at 9AM, when the attending technician would set up the subject with the sensors and recording equipment (Figs. 2 and 3). The wireless X24 sensor headset (Advanced Brain Monitoring Inc., Carlsbad, CA, USA) was used to acquire 20 channels of electroencephalography (EEG) along with electrocardiography (ECG), respiration and head movement data, while a smaller X4 device from the same manufacturer recorded the forearm electromyography (EMG). Following the setup, the subject would engage in a series of computer-based auditory, visual, cognitive and memory tasks that corresponded to the key anchors of the respective workload scales from the IMPRINT model (*atom tasks*, Table 1). The subject would next perform a set of physical exercises on a treadmill (3 min of walking at 2 mph at 0° inclination, 3 min of running at 6 mph at 0° inclination, 3 min of walking at 2 mph at 15° inclination, 3 min of walking at 6 mph at 15° inclination) and with weights (lift-ups with 5–10 lb in each hand). The subject would then participate in a 30 min session in a driving simulator, and, finally, repeat the computer-based atom tasks. The entire session was recorded with a microphone and video camera that were mounted on the PC or treadmill displays in front of the participant. The protocol was approved by a local Institutional Review Board; all subjects signed an informed consent before the experiment began, and were financially compensated for their participation in the study.

Setup (30 min)	Atom tasks (90 min)	Exercises (15 min)	Driving tasks (30 min)	Atom tasks (90 min)

Fig. 2. Sequence of experimental activities and their estimated duration

2.3 Data Processing and Analyses

All computerized tasks, physical exercises and driving scenarios were scored on a second-by-second basis with respect to the workload they impose in accord with the IMPRINT workload model [17, 18]. Each EEG channel was processed with proprietary algorithms to eliminate artifacts and derive spectral features for each subsequent 2-s data segment with 1 s (50 %) overlap. ECG signals was filtered, QRS complexes were detected, and beat-to-beat heart rate (HR) were converted into second-by-second values. Time- and frequency-domain measures of heart-rate variability (HRV) were derived from the HR data in accord with the literature [20]. EOG signals were

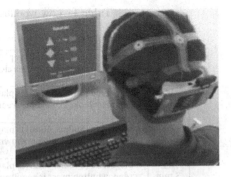

Fig. 3. A subject during a driving simulator task (left) and computer-based atom tasks (right)

processed with our proprietary algorithms for detection for eye blinks and eye fixations. EMG levels and body and limb motion were quantified in each second of the data using the bin integration. In addition to these 'absolute' or primary variables, a number of secondary or 'relative' variables were derived by computing ratios and/or differences between different time instances of the same primary variable or between different but functionally or spatially related primary variables (e.g. anterior-posterior gradient of the alpha EEG power). Finally, brain-state variables quantifying fatigue, alertness and distraction were derived using our validated classifiers [15, 16]. Step-wise regression analysis was used to identify variables derived from the physiological signals that are most predictive of the IMPRINT workload profiles and performance. The analyses took into account the existing relationship between specific workload types and certain physiological signals (e.g. speech workload scale and respiration, gross motor workload and heart rate or body/limb motion).

3 Results

3.1 Speech Workload Scale

The impedance-based respiration signal and sound envelope from our X12 device sufficed for a very precise identification of speech episodes across the pertinent tasks (A2, A4, C3, C4, S1 and S2). Between-subject variability was not significant, and overall classification accuracy amounted to 88.7 % (Table 2).

3.2 Fine Motor Workload Scale

The EMG acquired from the forearm was a good source for identification of fine motor activities in the pertinent tasks (B4, B5, C1, C2, A1, F1). Between-subject variability was relatively large, and normalization with respect to the baseline EMG activity (defined as the EMG activity during tasks B1 and B2) was required for obtaining the classification accuracy of 86.6 % (Table 3). As one can observe, the sensitivity was high for no activity and short discrete activities (on/off EMG pattern), but there was

Table 1. Low workload PHYSIOPRINT tasks

Task	Description
B1 3min	A brief tone (500ms, 40dB) is played through the earphones every 5 seconds; the participant keeps the eyes closed; no response to the stimulation is required.
B2 3 min	A brief tone (500ms, 40dB) is played through the earphones every 5 seconds; the subject looks at a blank screen; no response to the stimulation is required.
B3 3 min	A brief tone (500ms, 40dB) is played through the earphones every 5s; concurrently, 2 images are shown on a screen as a distraction; no response required.
B4 3 min	A brief tone (500ms, 40dB) is played every 5s; the subject looks at a blank screen; a button press is required in response to each stimulus.
B5 3 min	A brief tone (500ms, 40dB) is played every 5 seconds; concurrently, two images are shown on a screen; a button press is required in response to each stimulus.
V1 3 min	Every 5s a pair of images is shown on the screen, and the subject is asked to communicate if the images are associated.
V2 3 min	Every 5s a pair of images with virtual knobs is displayed: one in a neutral, the other in a target position. The subject uses a real knob to align the two.
V3 5 min	Every 10s 9 objects appear in the left half of the screen, then drift to the right half via pseudo-random paths. The subject is expected to track 1-3 of them
V4 3 min	Every 5s two completely or nearly identical images are shown on the screen; the participant is expected to find the difference, if it exists.
V5 3 min	Every 5s a complex image and a simple image (object) are displayed; the subject is expected to find/locate the displayed objects within the complex image.
A1 3 min	Every 5s a brief tone is played to one (20%) or both ears (80% of the cases); a key press is required in response to the unilateral tone.
A2 5 min	Every 5s a verbal command is issued; a response requested by the command is expected (eye blink, button press, verbal response, body position change)
A3 3 min	The participant uses a joystick (held in the dominant hand) to balance (i.e. cancel out) the sound levels in the left and right ears
A4 5 min	A combination of A1 and A2: tones OR commands delivered every 5s, a differential response is required (key press for unilateral tone, or as instructed)
C1 3 min	Every 20 seconds a sequence of 3-9 digits is displayed (1 digit/s). The subject is expected to type them into a text box after a variable pause period (1-10s)
C2 3 min	Every 20 seconds a sequence of 3-9 digits is read aloud (1 digit/s). The subject is expected to type them into a text box after a variable pause period (1-10s)
C3 3 min	Every 20 seconds a sequence of 3-9 digits is displayed (1 digit/s). The subject is expected to reproduce them verbally after a variable pause period (1-10s)
C4 3 min	Every 20 seconds a sequence of 3-9 digits is read aloud (1 digit/s). The subject is expected to reproduce them verbally after a variable pause period (1-10s).
C5 3 min	Every 20s the participant is shown an arithmetic problem on the screen (addition, subtraction, multiplication or division). The response is typed in.
S1 3 min	Every 5s a command is shown on the screen: to hold his breath, keep breathing normally, or read aloud a brief (<3 words) or a long (up to 8 words) sentence.
Task	Description
S2 3 min	Same as S1, except that the subject may also be instructed to repeat (say aloud) the last sentence that has been displayed on the screen
F1 3 min	Every 5s various a contour of an object is shown on the screen of a tablet; the participant uses a stylus to track the contour.

Table 2. Classification of speech events

CLASSIFIED AS	BEHAVIORS			
	Breath hold	Normal breathing	Short speech (<5s)	Long speech (>5s)
Breath hold	1946	33	43	23
Normal breathing	59	1928	77	79
Short speech (<5s)	105	127	2591	272
Long speech (>5s)	0	24	215	1911
TOTAL	2110	2112	2926	2285
Sensitivity (SE)	92.2%	91.3%	88.6%	83.6%
PPV	95.1%	89.9%	83.7%	87.4%

Table 3. Classification of fine motor events

CLASSIFIED AS	BEHAVIORS				
	None	Discrete actuation (key press)	Keyboard typing	Contour tracking	Continuous adjustment
No activity	6902	73	2	0	15
Key press	337	4896	176	0	112
Keyboard typing	374	507	863	12	120
Contour tracking	402	67	6	1193	995
Driving	76	59	4	379	3056
TOTAL	8091	5602	1051	1584	4298
Sensitivity (SE)	85.3%	87.4%	82.1%	75.3%	71.1%
PPV	98.7%	88.6%	63.1%	44.8%	85.5%

more confusion between the continuous activities (steering wheel adjustments vs. contour tracking).

3.3 Gross Motor Workload Scale

The X-, Y-, and Z-axis signals from the accelerometer within our head-worn EEG recorder and arm-worn peripheral recorder proved to be an excellent source for differentiation of gross motor activities (push-ups and treadmill exercises). Between-subject variability was not significant, and the classification accuracy reached 89.3 % (Table 4).

3.4 Auditory Workload Scale

The classifier attempted to distinguish among 5 conditions: 'no activity' (silent breaks during tasks B1–B3), register a sound (beeps delivered throughout tasks B1–B5), 'discriminate sounds' (uni- vs. bilateral beeps in tasks A1 and A4), 'interpret speech'

Table 4. Classification of gross motor events

CLASSIFIED AS	BEHAVIORS			
	Sitting	Walking	Running	Push-ups
Sitting	2992	13	9	2
Walking	68	5554	379	198
Running	0	272	5628	228
Push-ups	93	473	293	2720
TOTAL	3153	6312	6309	3148
Sensitivity (SE)	94.9%	88.0%	89.2%	86.4%
PPV	99.2%	89.6%	91.8%	76.0%

Table 5. Classification of auditory events

CLASSIFIED AS	CONDITIONS				
	No activity	Register a sound	Discriminate sounds	Interpret speech	Interpret pattern
No activity	7097	2334	28	56	59
Register a sound	1874	8938	72	63	67
Discriminate sound	275	147	2194	119	103
Interpret speech	113	49	383	6465	322
Interpret patterns	79	125	385	1738	1576
TOTAL	9438	11593	3062	8441	2107
Sensitivity (SE)	75.2%	77.1%	71.6%	76.6%	74.8%
PPV	74.1%	81.1%	77.3%	88.2%	40.4%

(digits read during tasks C2 and C4), and interpret sound patterns (different honking patterns during the driving task). The overall classification accuracy (shown for a classifier developed on combination of subsets of feature vectors from both times of the day) amounted to 75.8 % (Table 5).

3.5   Visual Workload Scale

The classifier attempted to distinguish among 5 conditions: 'no activity' (silent breaks during tasks B1–B3), register an image (tasks B4, B5), 'detect a difference' (task V4), 'read a symbol' (digits read during tasks C1 and C3), and scan/search (task V5). The overall classification accuracy (shown again for a classifier developed on combination of subsets of feature vectors from both times of the day) amounted to 76.7 % (Table 6).

3.6   Cognitive Workload Scale

The classifier attempted to distinguish among four (4) conditions: 'no activity' (silent breaks during tasks B1–B3), alternative selection (task A2, A4), 'encoding/recall' (tasks C1–C4), and calculation (task C5 and sign task during the driving). The overall

Table 6. Classification of visual events

CLASSIFIED AS	CONDITIONS				
	No activity	Register an image	Detect difference	Read a symbol	Scan / search
No activity	7182	1153	23	31	29
Register an image	1783	5019	30	693	43
Detect difference	203	69	1821	827	410
Read a symbol	152	35	56	6420	53
Scan / search	118	22	429	589	1843
TOTAL	9438	6298	2359	8560	2378
Sensitivity (SE)	76.1%	79.7%	77.2%	75.0%	77.5%
PPV	83.3%	66.3%	63.1%	44.8%	85.5%

Table 7. Classification of gross motor events

CLASSIFIED AS	BEHAVIORS			
	No activity	Alternative selection	Encoding/recall	Calculation
No activity	7069	1003	241	193
Selection	1847	4587	493	472
Encoding/recall	382	426	2948	481
Calculation	140	285	511	2458
TOTAL	9438	6301	4193	3604
Sensitivity (SE)	74.9%	72.8%	70.3%	68.2%
PPV	83.1%	62..0%	69.6%	72.4%

classification accuracy (shown again for a classifier developed on combination of subsets of feature vectors from both times of the day) amounted to 72.5 % (Table 7).

4 Discussion

The current study sought to develop a physiologically-based method for workload assessment applicable in the challenging automotive setting. We addressed this need by designing a comprehensive, sensitive, and multifaceted workload assessment tool that incorporates the already established theoretical workload framework that both: (1) covers the different types of workload employed in complex tasks such as driving, and (2) helps define the necessary atomic tasks for building the model. The experimental results suggested that the classifier benefits from combination of complementary input signals (EEG and ECG), better coverage of the scalp regions by an increased number of EEG channels, inclusion of concurrent physiological measurement of fatigue and alertness levels, and short-term signal history. We aimed to overcome the individual variability inherent in the physiological data by including the relative PSD variables in the feature vector. The generalization capability of the trained model was tested by using leave-one-subject-out cross-validation. The proposed method demonstrated that physiological monitoring holds great promise for real time assessment of mental workload.

In the future, we plan to extend the model validation to other simulated environments (flying simulator at Systems Technology Inc.) and real pertinent environments (fully instrumented HMMWV at the Operator Performance Laboratory at the University of Iowa). We also plan to refine the existing atom tasks, especially in the cognitive and visual areas. Alternative classification algorithms such as multi-label learning [21] will be evaluated to facilitate the process of resolving the conflicts between different workload types. The classifier will, finally, be validated on a much larger sample of subjects (target N = 150 subjects).

The ultimate PHYSIOPRINT workload assessment tool is envisioned as a flexible software platform that consists of three main components: (1) an executable that runs on a dedicated local (client) machine to acquire multiple physiological signals from one or more subjects, processes them in real time, and determines global and resource-specific workload on a fine time scale; (2) a large server-based database of physiological signals acquired during relevant atomic tasks from a large number of subjects with different socio-demographic and other characteristics (e.g., degree of driving experience); and (3) a palette of real-time signal processing, feature extraction, and workload classification algorithms. The platform will support a number of recording devices from a wide range of vendors (via the appropriate device drivers), and enable visualization of the workload measures. The users will essentially be able to build their own workload assessment methods from the available building blocks of feature extraction methods and implemented classifiers. Initially, the database will include 100–150 subjects, but we envision that the database will continue to evolve as the community grows in the following years.

Acknowledgments. This work was supported by the Army Research Laboratory grant W91CRB-13-C-0007. The views, opinions, and/or findings contained in this article are those of the authors and should not be interpreted as representing the official views or policies, either expressed or implied, of The Army Research Laboratory or the Department of Defense.

References

1. Huey, F.M., Wickens, C.D.: Workload Transition: Implications for Individual and Team Performance. National Academy Press, Washington (1993)
2. Gopher, D., Donchin, E.: Workload – an examination of the concept. In: Boff, K.R., Kaufman, L., Thomas, J.P. (eds.) Handbook of Perception and Human Performance: Cognitive Processes and Performance, vol. 2, pp. 41-1–41-49. Wiley, Oxford (1986)
3. Jex, H.R.: Measuring mental workload: problems, progress, and promises. In: Hancock, P.A., Meshkati, N. (eds.) Human Mental Workload, pp. 5–39. Elsevier Science Publishers B.V., Amsterdam (1988)
4. Wickens, C.D., Hollands, J.G.: Engineering Psychology and Human Performance. Prentice Hall, Upper Saddle River (1999)
5. Eggemeier, F.T., Wilson, G.F., et al.: Workload assessment in multi-task environments. In: Damos, D.L. (ed.) Multiple Task Performance, pp. 207–216. Taylor & Francis, Ltd., London (1991)

6. Wickens, C.D.: Engineering Psychology and Human Performance. HarperCollins Publishers, New York (1992)
7. De Waard, R.: The Measurement of Driver's Mental Workload, p. 198. Traffic Research Centre (now Centre for Environmental and Traffic Psychology), University of Groningen, Heran (1996)
8. Farmer, E., Brownson, A.: Review of workload measurement, analysis and interpretation methods. Eur. Organ. Saf. Air Navig. 33 (2003)
9. Castor, M.C.: GARTEUR Handbook of Mental Workload Measurement, p. 164. GARTEUR, Group for Aeronautical Research and Technology in Europe, Flight Mechanics Action Group FM AG13 (2003)
10. Wilson, G.C., et al.: Operator Functional State Assessment, p. 220. North Atlantic Treaty Organization (NATO), Research and Technology Organization (RTO) BP 25, F-92201, Neuilly-sur-Seine Cedex, France, Paris (2004)
11. Fahrenberg, J., Wientjes, C.J.E.: Recording methods in applied environments. In: Backs, R. W., Boucsein, W. (eds.) Engineering Psychophysiology: Issues and Applications, pp. 111–135. Lawrence Erlbaum Associates Inc., Mahwah (1999)
12. Kramer, A.F.: Physiological metrics of mental workload: a review of recent progress. In: Damos, D.L. (ed.) Multiple Task Performance, pp. 279–328. Taylor & Francis Ltd., London (1991)
13. Sirevaag, E.J., Stern, J.A.: Ocular measures of fatigue and cognitive factors. In: Backs, R.W., Boucsein, W. (eds.) Engineering Psychophysiology: Issues and Applications, pp. 269–287. Lawrence Erlbaum Associates Inc., Mahwah (1999)
14. Wilson, G.F.: An analysis of mental workload in pilots during flight using multiple psychophysiological measures. Int. J. Aviat. Psychol. 12(1), 3–18 (2001)
15. Berka, C., Levendowski, D., Ramsey, C.K., et al.: Evaluation of an EEG-workload model in an aegis simulation environment. In: Caldwell, J.A., Wesensten, N.J. (eds) Proceedings of SPIE Defense and Security Symposium, Biomonitoring for Physiological and Cognitive Performance during Military Operations, pp. 90–99. SPIE: The International Society for Optical Engineering, Orlando (2005)
16. Berka, C., Levendowski, D., Davis, G., et al.: EEG indices distinguish spatial and verbal working memory processing: implications for real-time monitoring in a closed-loop tactical tomahawk weapons simulation. In: 1st International Conference on Augmented Cognition, Las Vegas, NV (2005)
17. Mitchell, D.K.: Mental workload and ARL workload modeling tools. Final report. Army Research Laboratory, Aberdeen Proving Ground MD. ADA377300 (2000). http://handle. dtic.mil/100.2/ADA377300
18. Mitchell, D.K., Samms, C., Henthorn, T., Wojciechowski, J.: Trade Study: A Two- Versus Three-Soldier Crew for the Mounted Combat System (MCS) and Other Future Combat System Platforms, ARL-TR-3026. U.S. Army Research Laboratory, Aberdeen Proving Ground, MD (2003)
19. Mitchell, D.K.: Workload analysis of the crew of the Abrams V2 SEP: phase I baseline IMPRINT model. Final Report. Army Research Laboratory, Aberdeen Proving Ground, MD. Human Research and Engineering Directorate. ADA508882 (2009). http://handle.dtic. mil/100.2/ADA508882
20. Task Force of the European Society of Cardiology and North American Society of Pacing Electrophysiology. Heart rate variability: standards of measurement, physiological interpretation, and clinical use. Circulation 93, 1043–1065 (1996)
21. Tsoumakas, G., Katakis, I.: Multi-label classification: an overview. Int. J. Data Warehouse. Min. 3, 1–13 (2007)

The Neurobiology of Executive Function Under Stress and Optimization of Performance

Ann M. Rasmusson[1(✉)] and John M. Irvine[2]

[1] VA Boston Healthcare System and Boston University, Boston, USA
ann.rasmusson@gmail.com
[2] Draper Laboratory, Cambridge, USA
jirvine@draper.com

Abstract. Much basic and clinical research to date has investigated predictors of stress resilience and vulnerability, indicating, for example, that broad impact neurobiological factors, such as neuropeptide Y (NPY) and neuroactive steroids, are mechanistically related to short term stress resilience, as well as longterm patterns of stress-related medical and neuropsychiatric comorbidities. The problem is that we lack good methods for identifying predictors of stress resilience or vulnerability at an individual level, so that human performance and therapeutic interventions can be targeted precisely to underlying points of malfunction for maximum effectiveness. We thus propose modified experimental designs that capitalize on our growing capacities to query and analyze multimodal data across the translational levels of human biology and behavior. We propose that use of these methods in studies of individuals participating in intense military training or returning from deployment could enable better prediction of performance, and development of more effective personalized interventions aimed at optimizing and maintaining stress resilience over time.

Keywords: Resilience · PTSD · Translational neuroscience · Neuropeptide Y · Allopregnanolone · Neuroactive steroids · Predictive algorithms · Functional data analysis · Non-linear modeling · Machine learning

1 Introduction

Hallmarks of resilience in the face of threat to survival, which is typically accompanied by intense psychological and physiological demand, include the capacity to: (1) respond physiologically and behaviorally as needed in the moment, (2) moderate arousal, so as to think rapidly and flexibly, (3) recover rapidly, and (4) adaptively upregulate systems under demand so that the challenge can be met more easily the next time. Then, should environmental threat recede over time, the downregulation of formerly adaptive stress reactions promotes readjustment. The failure of these capacities may present immediate risk, as well as the potential for longterm psychological, interpersonal, vocational and medical disabilities. As a result, there is great interest in enhancing the stress resilience of military personnel who confront life threat as a routine part of their duties.

From a research perspective, four major developments from studies of stress resilience and posttraumatic stress disorder (PTSD) conducted over the past 15 years

© Springer International Publishing Switzerland 2015
D.D. Schmorrow and C.M. Fidopiastis (Eds.): AC 2015, LNAI 9183, pp. 112–123, 2015.
DOI: 10.1007/978-3-319-20816-9_12

promise to advance this goal. First, a plethora of relatively small scale studies, appropriately constrained in breadth and depth by data analytic attention to risk for Type I error, have demonstrated that *multiple individually variable* biological components of the complex stress response *interact* to influence both: (a) *short-term* physiological, psychological, cognitive and behavioral reactions *during acute stress*, as well as (b) *longterm adaptive and maladaptive responses to stress*. The latter include posttraumatic stress disorder (PTSD) and a number of PTSD-comorbid conditions, such as depression, chronic pain, substance abuse disorders, traumatic brain injury, autoimmune disorders, cardiovascular disorders and metabolic syndrome [1–3]. Secondly, there is now much evidence to suggest that many biopredictors of acute stress resilience *reciprocally* predict PTSD risk [1, 4]. Third, advances in epigenetics have both dispelled the notion that genotype is "determinant" and revealed means by which dysregulated stress systems may be modified or even restored to normal function— using techniques likely to evolve quickly over the coming years. Fourth, new and rapidly evolving bioinformatics tools now allow multimodal, multi-level data analysis to help: (a) elucidate the multiple interacting *translational mechanisms* that contribute to higher order *behavioral phenotypes*, and (b) develop algorithms for prediction of stress resilience or PTSD risk on an individual basis. Combined, these capacities promise to facilitate development of individualized interventions to enhance human performance or therapeutically restore normal function.

These new opportunities in the field of stress research also have generated new prospective study designs aimed at identifying individual level predictors of stress resilience or vulnerability amenable to modification. Such studies *collect a dense translational array of known as well as prospective resilience relevant biomarkers from individual participants* exposed to field relevant stress conditions or more convenient proxy conditions validated against field relevant conditions. While more costly and labor intensive in the short term, this approach seems most likely to accelerate our understanding of "how stress resilience works"—a prerequisite to effective individual targeting of performance enhancers and therapeutics.

In contrast, previous neurobiological predictors of military performance and selection, or of PTSD risk and severity, have been studied alone or, at most, a few at a time in different populations. For example, in the seminal series of studies by Morgan et al. [5–8], each hormone predictor [e.g., peak stress plasma levels of neuropeptide Y (NPY) or ratios of salivary dehydroepiandrosterone sulfate (DHEAS) to plasma cortisol, or resting plasma DHEA(S) levels measured across intense training] accounted for about ~ 16–30 % of the variance in military performance and ~ 16–40 % of the variance in dissociation at peak stress. Thus, it is clear that other factors must be considered in addition to these in order to achieve adequate predictive power. In addition, these hormone predictors were not correlated within individuals when more than one predictor was measured. This suggests that diverse physiological systems mediate stress resilience in different individuals. This observation is consistent with a study [9] showing that PTSD symptoms were uniquely exacerbated by noradrenergic (NA) system activation in about one-third of Viet Nam veterans tested, by serotonergic system activation in another third, and by activation of either system in yet another third.

These earlier military stress resilience studies demonstrate another principle to consider in the design of future studies. Dissociation, as measured by the Clinician Administered Dissociative States Scale [10], was a stronger predictor of military performance than hormone levels or ratios that predicted dissociation. This is to be expected. As indicated in Fig. 1, the contribution of a particular predictive factor to the variance in a behavioral phenotype (e.g., selection for Special Forces, PTSD risk) increases as the translational level of organization increases (i.e., from genes to gene products to physiological processes to higher order neuropsychological function to observable behavior). This is generally due to the fact that higher order phenomena emerge from combinations of lower order components that vary and interact.

2   Broad Impact Biological Contributors to Stress Resilience

Some stress-sensitive neurobiological factors, however, have particularly large effects on stress-related outcomes due to their *broad impact* in the brain and peripheral physiological systems. Pathological variations in such broad-impact factors, in turn, have *manifold* pathological effects—which may account for the high rates of comorbidity among what might otherwise appear to be discrete clinical phenomena resulting from stress. High rates of association among apparently discrete stress-related disorders thus may signal the presence of shared underlying pathophysiologic processes amenable to common therapeutic approaches. The precise point of dysfunction within such broad impact systems may, however, vary from one individual to another. The following subsections therefore discuss the subcomponents of two broad-impact stress-sensitive systems previously found to influence stress resilience and/or stress vulnerability. Knowledge of the translational subcomponents of each system, as well as of extra-system factors that may impact each system, will be critical to developing maximally effective, individually targeted interventions to enhance stress resilience.

2.1   Neuropeptide Y

As previously reviewed [2, 4], NPY is co-localized with a variety of neurotransmitters in the brain and periphery. During the resting state, extra-neuronal NPY reduces the release of neurotransmitters with which NPY is co-localized intra-neuronally by activating pre-synaptic NPY-Y_2 autoreceptors. Once released in response to intense neuronal stimulation, NPY facilitates the post-synaptic effects of its co-localized neurotransmitter. NPY thus functions generally as a neurobiological capacitor or high-pressure valve, effectively conserving bioenergy for use under high demand situations. NPY also promotes adaptive anabolic processes when environmental demands exceed physiological capacities. For example, NPY stimulates growth of cardiac collateral vessels in response to ischemia [11] by inducing platelet-derived growth factor (PDGF) and exerting mitogenic effects on vascular smooth muscle and endothelial cells [12]. As previously reviewed [1], NPY promotes post-stress feeding and lipogenesis, which is advantageous in the aftermath of stress that drains energy reserves. However, NPY acting at NPY-Y_2 receptors, promotes metabolic syndrome when stress is coupled

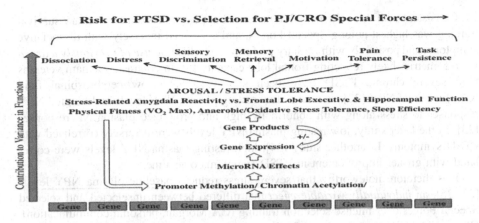

Fig. 1. Interactive translational processes that determine and define stress resilience

with excess sugar and fat calories [13]. NPY also has anti-inflammatory and anti-nociceptive properties [3], preventing opiate tolerance and withdrawal, and the progression of acute pain to chronic pain. It also promotes sleep [14] and likely enhances function of the recently discovered "glymphatic system", which clears damaging byproducts of oxidative stress from brain during sleep [15]. In addition, NPY stimulates neurogenesis [16] and enhances nucleus accumbens mediated reward [17]. Thus it is not surprising that dysregulation of the NPY system has been related to risk for PTSD, chronic pain, neurodegeneration, cardiovascular disease, metabolic syndrome, and immune system dysfunction—clinical phenomena that frequently co-occur among persons exposed to chronic severe or traumatic stress.

The importance of investigating sub-components of the NPY system that contribute to resilience or PTSD risk is particularly well exemplified by the sympathetic NPY-NA subsystem. As reviewed and illustrated in Pitman et al. [4], mild to moderate stress increases arousal by activating the release of norepinephrine (NE), which at moderate levels acts at high-affinity NA α_2 receptors in the frontal lobe to enhance frontal lobe executive capacities and frontal lobe inhibition of the amygdala. Intense stress, however, may induce hyperarousal by releasing NE in greater amounts, resulting in activation of low-affinity NA α_1 receptors in the frontal lobe and degradation of frontal lobe function [18]. This results in a lifting of the frontal lobe brake on amygdala-mediated reactions, including defensive behaviors, cardiovascular system responses, hypothalamic-pituitary-adrenal (HPA) axis activation, and brain monoamine release [19].

During resting and low stress conditions, NPY restrains NE release from sympathetic neurons by activating pre-synaptic NPY-Y_2 receptors that interact with NA-α_2 autoreceptors [20] —thus moderating arousal and facilitating calm. However, during intense stress, NPY is released from sympathetic neurons along with NE to facilitate post-synaptic NA effects. In the meantime, dipeptidyl peptidase 4 (DPP-4) cleaves the first two N-terminal amino acids from NPY to produce NPY$_{3-36}$, a selective NPY-Y_2 receptor agonist with low NPY-Y_1 receptor affinity [21]. Activated NPY-Y_2 receptors likely then interact with NA-α_2 receptors to reduce the firing rate of sympathetic neurons and release of NE—restoring calm and frontal lobe function.

Consistent with this schema, NPY measured at peak stress during military survival training was highest among Special Forces, and correlated inversely with dissociative symptoms and positively with military performance reliant on *use of previously learned tactics*, metrics likely reflecting frontal lobe capacity [5]. In contrast, Vietnam veterans with severe chronic PTSD have been shown to have low cerebrospinal fluid (CSF) levels of NPY [22], as well as low resting plasma NPY levels and blunted NPY responses to stress along with abnormally high and prolonged plasma NE responses [23]. In the latter study, low resting plasma NPY levels were inversely correlated with PTSD symptoms. In another study [24], high resting plasma NPY levels were correlated with greater improvement in PTSD symptoms over time.

It is therefore noteworthy that severe stress reduces baseline plasma NPY levels [25, 26], an *individually variable effect* that differed between unselected and selected Special Forces over intense selection training (CA Morgan, personal communication). Of possible relevance to these findings, NPY gene expression and synthesis are upregulated by glucocorticoids [13] and testosterone, but downregulated by estrogen [21], a basis for possible general gender differences in the mediation of military relevant stress resilience and PTSD risk. Both NE and NPY release during stress are also influenced by genotype [27–29], including possible alterations in the Kozak sequences of two NPY gene start codons that determine whether NPY is made available for release or targeted to mitochondria [30]. In mitochondria, NPY diminishes oxidative metabolism, which may be immediately protective during stress, but promote longterm stress intolerance, "burn-out", depression, fatigue, or weight gain. The NPY gene also has a large CpG island in its promoter, suggesting the potential for methylation dependent epigenetic downregulation, a potentially reversible process that may contribute to stress-induced downregulation of NPY synthesis.

We therefore believe that full characterization of NPY-NA system subcomponent function could enable more effective prediction of military performance. For example, possession of a gain-in-function NPY gene polymorphism might predict short-term stress resilience [5], but in the longer term, metabolic syndrome [13] —although perhaps not if compensated by possession of a loss-of-function NPY-Y_2 receptor polymorphism. A gain-in-function NPY gene polymorphism might not be predictive of resilience in a model relying just on genotype data, however. Combining genotype and gene methylation data may be more effective, as a normal NPY gene with a methylated promoter conferring loss-of-function can be equated with loss-of-function NPY gene polymorphisms to predict risk.

Knowledge of precise points of NPY-NA system malfunction may also enable more precise treatment targeting. For example, selective NA α_1 receptor antagonists (e.g., prazosin) have been shown to enhance sleep and moderate daytime reactivity to stressors in PTSD [31]. These medications might be prescribed as a temporary measure to individuals in whom the NPY-NA system has been temporarily re-programmed by exposure to extreme stress, but they may need to be prescribed chronically to those with gene polymorphisms associated with excessive NE release even at baseline (e.g., the NA α_{2C}Del322-325 gene polymorphism [27] or loss-of-function NPY gene polymorphisms [29]). Intranasal NPY could potentially be used to facilitate engagement of the frontal lobe during cognitive reprocessing therapies to promote fear extinction or extinction recall. Deacetylase inhibitors perhaps could be prescribed briefly to reduce

NPY promoter methylation and thereby enhance NPY gene expression. Exercise or use of ketogenic diets may have similar benefits. Moderate progressive exercise has been used in already trained male rowers to further increase the capacity for NPY release during intense exercise challenge [32]. We hypothesize that global stimulation of free fatty acid oxidation to acetyl CoA by exercise or use of a ketogenic diet may enhance chromatin acetylation, and thus facilitate access of regulatory elements (e.g., testosterone or cortisol) to DNA response elements in the NPY gene promoter during stress exposure—with consequent upregulation of NPY synthesis.

2.2   GABAergic Neuroactive Steroids

As reviewed [2, 4], the neuroactive progesterone metabolites, allopregnanolone and its equipotent stereoisomer, pregnanolone (collectively termed ALLO), potently and positively modulate GABA action at brain $GABA_A$ receptors by increasing Cl- influx 7–10 fold [33]. ALLO thus function generally as a resistor in stress sensitive brain circuits connecting somatosensory cortex, thalamus, prefrontal cortex and the amygdala [34]. However, ALLO is also critical for production of myelin, which speeds neurotransmission in select circuits, suggesting a broader role for ALLO in coordinating neuronal networks. Of note, ALLO has highest affinity for extrasynaptic benzodiazepine-resistant $GABA_A$ receptors that *reduce gain* in neuronal firing rates during periods of increased activation, as occurs during stress [35]. This is an important characteristic, because synaptic benzodiazepine-sensitive $GABA_A$ receptors and GABA synthesis are downregulated in the amygdala in response to fear conditioning [36], which in the extreme, models exposure to traumatic stress. Thus restraint of amygdala reactivity after trauma exposure may rely on extrasynaptic $GABA_A$ receptor activation by ALLO synthesized locally or released from the adrenal gland.

Like NPY, ALLO has broad impact in the brain and periphery, exerting potent anxiolytic, anti-conflict, anticonvulsant, anti-nociceptive, anesthetic, sedative, anti-inflammatory, pro-myelination, neurogenerative and neuroprotective effects. ALLO levels peak about an hour after stress exposure [37], to provide delayed negative feedback and return stress responses back to baseline [38]. Thus it is noteworthy that CSF levels of ALLO were found to be low (39 % of normal) in women with PTSD and to correlate inversely with PTSD reexperiencing and negative mood symptoms [39]. Similarly, male OEF/OIF veterans showed a reduction in the plasma ratio of allopregnanolone to progesterone, in association with increased depression and PTSD symptoms [40]. Pilot work showing a correlation between maximum load exercise-induced plasma ALLO levels and pain tolerance is also consistent with the anti-nociceptive properties of ALLO (E. Scioli-Salter and A. Rasmusson, personal communication). In addition, ALLO synthesis deficits have been induced by binge alcohol consumption in a rodent model [41]. Together, these studies support the idea that PTSD and comorbid conditions such as depression, chronic pain, and alcohol abuse may share underlying pathophysiological processes—that may respond to common therapeutics.

Two enzymes are involved in the synthesis of ALLO from progesterone, 5α-reductase and 3α-hydroxysteroid dehydrogenase (3α-HSD). A rodent model of PTSD

[42] and a recent genotype study in humans [43] suggest that diminished function of 5α-reductase contributes to PTSD symptomatology in males. In contrast, Rasmusson et al. [39] suggest that a block in ALLO synthesis at 3α-HSD promotes PTSD in women. Cortisol and testosterone upregulate expression of the 3α-HSD gene, suggesting that low levels of these steroids might also contribute to deficient ALLO production and PTSD risk. Alcohol-induced reductions in nicotinamide adenine dinucleotide phosphate (NADPH), a protective antioxidant and 3α-HSD enzyme cofactor may also contribute. Such causes for ALLO synthesis deficits may apply to both males and females. The enzymes 5α-reductase and 3α-HSD also synthesize GABAergic neuroactive steroids from testosterone, androstenedione and cortisol. Thus, measurement of the full complement of GABAergic neuroactive steroids may be needed to accurately assess stress resilience across gender and at the individual level in order to improve predictive models and best target potential therapeutics.

Based on these studies, it seems reasonable to consider ALLO "replacement" by synthetic derivatives (e.g., ganaxolone) in the prevention or treatment of PTSD and its comorbidities. Recent work suggests that ganaxolone blocks fear memory reconsolidation during extinction training and promotes extinction retention [44]. Of note, the beneficial effects of ganaxolone were not observed in animals without ALLO deficiency. Alternatively, administration of selective brain steroidogenic precursors such as pregnenolone [45] or other stimulants of GABAergic neuroactive steroid production [46] may be helpful. The presence of a CpG island in the 5α-reductase gene promoter also suggests the potential for epigenetic regulation of ALLO synthesis [47].

3 Modeling and Analysis of Contributors to Stress Resilience

Development of prediction models is a multi-step process that begins with investigation of individual measurements and builds to a multimodal characterization of the data. Traditional analytic methods employ standard statistical techniques, such as linear modeling, to examine specific factors in isolation or in limited combinations. While these approaches have yielded valuable insights about groups of people as described above, they have yet to reveal a richer understanding of the mechanisms operating at the level of the individual. Recent advances in functional data analysis, non-linear methods, and machine learning offer the potential to develop new models that consider a broader set of factors to predict stress resilience or stress vulnerability for the individual. A brief discussion of these methods is presented here.

3.1 Functional Data Analysis

An individual's performance can vary over time with repeated exposures to stress or life threat followed by periods of recovery. While traditional statistical methods can analyze a point in time, understanding trajectories is necessary to characterize short-term responses, recovery, and long-term adaptations. Functional data analysis is a new approach to handling these challenges by representing values across time as mathematical functions [48]. Measurements collected at various times, representing various stages of stress exposure and recovery, can be expressed as a simple function of time, such as a polynomial. The parameters that define the function relationship then become the variables employed in the statistical analysis. The terms of the functional representation provide a powerful method for characterizing resilience over time. The constant and linear terms, for example, represent the level and general trend in performance over time. Quadratic and higher-order terms indicate the temporal dynamics of the process within such overall trends and thus can capture changes in performance more finely. Functional data analysis methods have proven useful in other biomedical applications, such as modeling acute limb ischemia and reperfusion injury [49]. For modeling resilience, functional data analysis provides a natural framework for analyzing temporal changes in individual performance.

3.2   Non-linear Modeling

Multi-modal data acquired through studies of stress resilience and vulnerability yield rich data sets, providing new opportunities for discovery and analysis. However, the size and complexity of the data pose challenges. Variables of interest can include psychophysiological indices, levels of various neurotransmitters, and performance scores for various cognitive and physical tests. Taken at face value the number of variables can appear daunting, but the underlying physiology will constrain the relationships among the measurements, causing the data to be in some lower dimensional arrangement within the high dimensional space implied by the full set of measurements. Standard methods for data reduction, such as principal component analysis (PCA) or factor analysis, seek to identify the implicit dimensions, which capture the major variance in the data. These methods work well when a simple affine procedure will transform the data into an appropriate low-dimensional space. However, because of complex and possible mechanistic mediational relationships among the various measurements, in many cases the very high-dimensional data actually exist on a much lower dimensional manifold. A new class of methods, known as manifold learning [50], has emerged to handle these problems. These methods for non-linear dimensionality reduction seek to discover the underlying structure of the data. A number of techniques have been proposed for this type of analysis – principal curves, Gaussian process latent variable models, and kernel PCA, to name a few. The goal of these techniques is to learn the low-dimensional manifold and thereby develop a compact representation of the data that is more tractable. Once this new representation is known, data analysis and prediction modeling can operate off of the lower-dimensional representation to achieve robust prediction modeling.

3.3   Machine Learning

Machine learning encompasses a class of methods for discovering relationships by letting the data speak, producing a mapping from a set of measurements to a set of class labels. For analyzing resilience, the class labels might represent different trajectories that were identified during the functional data analysis. The common approach is to use a set of "labeled data" (i.e., a set where the class labels and the various measurements are known) as the training data for learning the mapping between the measurements and the classes. This learning stage produces a classifier that is then evaluated on new data to assess its accuracy. For predicting trajectories of human performance capacity, a major challenge is the multi-model nature of resilience relevant data. To develop a robust classifier requires finding a common framework for merging the diverse set of measurements. For similar research problems, where data arise from a diverse set of measurements and observations, multiple kernel learning (MKL) has proven successful. This novel machine learning technique mathematically "homogenizes" different types of data through an optimized estimation of the contributions from each data type. MKL has proven effective in modeling heterogeneous data for a number of applications [51, 52]. Use of this approach will allow for comparisons of different variable combinations to identify the most predictive set of variables, while ensuring the model is stable and does not over fit to the data.

4 Summary

Much research to date has investigated predictors of stress resilience and vulnerability, and indicates that broad impact neurobiological factors such as NPY and neuroactive steroids may be mechanistically related to short-term military performance and long-term stress-related medical and neuropsychiatric outcomes. The problem is that we lack good methods for identifying predictors of stress resilience and vulnerability at the individual level. We thus propose modified experimental designs that capitalize on our growing capacities to query and analyze multimodal data across the translational levels of human biology and behavior. This approach allows consideration of critical interactions among multiple stress reactive systems that vary across individuals along the translational spectrum. It also allows discovery of novel factors that may contribute to resilience. In addition, use of new data analytic methods may help define underlying mechanisms shared among stress-related outcomes. We propose that use of these methods will enhance our ability to both predict human performance under high stress conditions, as well as diagnose dysfunction of resilience-related systems, at the individual level—thus, enabling personalization of performance interventions and therapeutics to increase, maintain and restore stress resilience over time.

References

1. Rasmusson, A.M., Schnurr, P., Zukowska, Z., Scioli, E., Forman, D.E.: Adaptation to extreme stress: PTSD, NPY, and metabolic syndrome. Exp. Biol. Med. 235, 1150–1156 (2010)
2. Rasmusson, A.M., Shalev, A.: Integrating the neuroendocrinology, neurochemistry, and neuroimmunology of PTSD to date and the challenges ahead. In: Friedman, M., Keane, T., Resick, P. (eds.) Handbook of PTSD, 2nd edn. Guilford Publications Inc, New York (2014)
3. Scioli-Salter, E.R., Otis, J.D., Forman, D.E., Gregor, K., Valovski, I., Rasmusson, A.M.: The Shared Neuroanatomy and Neurophysiology of Comorbid Chronic Pain & PTSD: Therapeutic Implications (PAP 12 August 2014, in press)

4. Pitman, R.K., Rasmusson, A.M., Koenen, K.C., Shin, L.M., Orr, S.P., Gilbertson, M.W., Milad, M., Liberzon, I.: Biology of posttraumatic stress disorder. Nat. Rev. Neurosci. **13**, 769–787 (2012)

5. Morgan III, C.A., Rasmusson, A.M., Wang, S., Hoyt, G., Hauger, R.L., Hazlett, G.: Neuropeptide-Y, cortisol and subjective distress in humans exposed to acute stress: replication and extension of previous report. Biol. Psychiatry **52**, 136–142 (2002)

6. Morgan III, C.A., Southwick, S., Hazlett, G., Rasmusson, A., Hoyt, G., Zimolo, Z., Charney, D.: Relationships among plamsa dehydroepiandrosterone sulfate and cortisol levels, symptoms of dissociation, and objective performance in humans exposed to acute stress. Arch. Gen. Psychiatry **61**, 819–825 (2004)

7. Morgan III, C.A., Rasmusson, A., Pietrzak, R.H., Coric, V., Southwick, S.M.: Relationships among plasma dehydroepiandrosterone and dehydroepiandrosterone sulfate, cortisol, symptoms of dissociation, and objective performance in humans exposed to underwater navigation stress. Biol. Psychiatry **66**(4), 334–340 (2009)

8. Morgan 3rd, C.A., Hazlett, G., Dial-Ward, M., Southwick, S.M.: Baseline dissociation and prospective success in special forces assessment and selection. J. Spec. Oper. Med. **9**, 87–92 (2009). (Reprint of Psychiatry, pp. 53–58, 5 July 2008)

9. Southwick, S.M., Krystal, J.H., Bremner, J.D., Morgan 3rd, C.A., Nicolaou, A.I., Nagy, L.M., Charney, D.S.: Noradrenergic and serotonergic function in posttraumatic stress disorder. Arch. Gen. Psychiatry **54**, 749–758 (1997)

10. Bremner, J.D., Krystal, J.H., Putnam, F.W., Southwick, S.M., Marmar, C., Charney, D.S., Mazure, C.M.: Measurement of dissociative states with the clinician-administered dissociative states scale (CADSS). J. Traumatic Stress **11**, 125–136 (1998)

11. Robich, M.P., Matyal, R., Chu, L.M., Feng, J., Xu, S.-H., Laham, R.J., Hess, P.E., Bianchi, C., Sellke, F.W.: Effects of neuropeptide Y on collateral development in a swine model of chronic myocardial ischemia. J. Mol. Cell. Cardiol. **49**, 1022–1030 (2010)

12. Pons, J., Kitlinska, J., Hong, J., Lee, E.W., Zukowska, Z.: Mitogenic actions of neuropeptide Y in vascular smooth muscle cells: synergetic interactions with the beta-adrenergic system. Can. J. Physiol. Pharmacol. **81**, 177–185 (2003)

13. Kuo, L.E., Kitlinska, J., Tilan, J., Lijun, L., Baker, S., Johnson, M., Lee, E., Burnett, M.S., Fricke, S., Kvetnansky, R., Herzog, H., Zukowska, Z.: Neuropeptide Y acts directly in the periphery on fat tissue and mediates stress-induced obesity and metabolic syndrome. Nat. Med. **13**, 803–811 (2007)

14. Held, K., Antonijevic, I., Murck, H., Kuenzel, H., Steiger, A.: Neuropeptide Y (NPY) shortens sleep latency but does not suppress ACTH and cortisol in depressed patients and normal controls. Psychoneuroendocrinology **31**, 100–1007 (2006)

15. Xie, L., Kang, H., Xu, Q., Chen, M.J., Liao, Y., Thiyagarajan, M., O'Donnell, J., Christensen, D.J., Nicholson, C., Iliff, J.J., Takano, T., Deane, R., Nedergaard, M.: Sleep drives metabolite clearance from the adult brain. Science **342**, 373–377 (2013)

16. Howell, O.W., Silva, S., Scharfman, H.E., Sosunov, A.A., Zaben, M., Shatya, A., Gray, W.P.: Neuropeptide Y is important for basal and seizure-induced precursor cell proliferation in the hippocampus. Neurobiol. Dis. **26**, 174–188 (2007)

17. Brown, C.M., Coscina, D.V., Fletcher, P.J.: The rewarding properties of neuropeptide Y in perifornical hypothalamus vs nucleus accumbens. Peptides **21**, 1279–1287 (2000)

18. Arnsten, A.F.: Stress signaling pathways that impair prefrontal cortex structure and function. Nat. Rev. Neurosci. **10**, 410–422 (2009)

19. Goldstein, L.E., Rasmusson, A.M., Bunney, B.S., Roth, R.H.: Role of the amygdala in the coordination of behavioral, neuroendocrine and prefrontal cortical monoamine responses to psychological stress in the rat. J. Neurosci. **16**, 4787–4798 (1996)

20. Colmers, W., Bleakman, D.: Effects of neuropeptide Y on the electrical properties of neurons. Trends Neurosci. **17**, 373–379 (1994)
21. Zukowska-Grojec, Z.: Neuropeptide Y: a novel sympathetic stress hormone and more. Ann. N.Y. Acad. Sci. **771**, 219–233 (1995)
22. Sah, R., Ekhator, N.N., Strawn, J.R., Sallee, F.R., Baker, D.G., Horn, P.S., Geracioti Jr., T. D.: Low cerebrospinal fluid neuropeptide Y concentrations in posttraumatic stress disorder. Biol. Psychiatry **66**, 705–707 (2009)
23. Rasmusson, A.M., Hauger, R.L., Morgan III, C.A., Bremner, J.D., Charney, D.S., Southwick, S.M.: Low baseline and yohimbine-stimulated plasma neuropeptide Y (NPY) levels in combat-related PTSD. Biol. Psychiatry **47**, 526–539 (2000)
24. Yehuda, R., Brand, S., Yank, R.K.: Plasma neuropeptide Y concentrations in combat exposed veterans: relationship to trauma exposure, recovery from PTSD and coping. Biol. Psychiatry **59**, 660–663 (2005)
25. Corder, R., Castagne, V., Rivet, J.M., Mormede, P., Gaillard, R.C.: Central and peripheral effects of repeated stress and high NaCl diet on neuropeptide Y. Physiol. Behav. **52**, 205–210 (1992)
26. Morgan III, C.A., Rasmusson, A.M., Winters, B., Hauger, R.L., Morgan, J., Hazlett, G., Southwick, S.: Trauma exposure rather than posttraumatic stress disorder is associated with reduced baseline plasma neuropeptide-Y levels. Biol. Psychiatry **54**, 1087–1091 (2003)
27. Neumeister, A., Charney, D.S., Belfer, I., Geraci, M., Holmes, C., Sharabi, Y., Alim, T., Bonne, O., Luckenbaugh, D.A., Manji, H., Goldman, D., Goldstein, D.S.: Sympathoneural and adrenomedullary functional effects of alpha2C-adrenoreceptor gene polymorphism in healthy humans. Pharmacogenet. Genomics **15**, 143–149 (2005)
28. Kallio, J., Pesonen, U., Kaipio, K., Karvonen, M.K., Jaakkola, U., Heinonen, O.J., Uusitupa, M.I., Koulu, M.: Altered intracellular processing and release of neuropeptide Y due to leucine7 to proline7 polymorphism in the signal peptide of pre-proneuropeptide Y in humans. FASEB J. **15**, 1242–1244 (2001)
29. Zhou, Z., Zhu, G., Hariri, A.R., Enoch, M.-A., Scott, D., Sinha, R., Virkkunen, M., Mash, D. C., Goldman, D.: Genetic variation in human NPY expression affects stress response and emotion. Nature **452**, 997–1001 (2008)
30. Kapio, K., Kallio, J., Pesonen, U.: Mitochondrial targeting signal in human neuropeptide Y gene. Biochem. Biophys. Res. Commun. **337**, 633–640 (2005)
31. Raskind, M.A., Peskind, E.R., Hoff, D.J., Hart, K.L., Holmes, H.A., Warren, D., McFall, M. E.: A parallel group placebo controlled study of prazosin for trauma nightmares and sleep disturbance in combat veterans with post-traumatic stress disorder. Biol. Psychiatry **61**, 928–934 (2007)
32. Ramson, R., Jurimae, J., Jurimae, T., Maestu, J.: The effect of 4-week training period on plasma neuropeptide Y, leptin and ghrelin responses in male rowers. Eur. J. Appl. Physiol. **112**, 1873–1880 (2012)
33. Puia, G., Mienville, J.M., Matsumoto, K., Takahata, H., Watanabe, H., Costa, E., Guidotti, A.: On the putative physiological role of allopregnanolone on GABA A receptor function. Neuropharmacology **44**, 49–55 (2003)
34. Agis-Balboa, R.C., Pinna, G., Zhubi, A., Maloku, E., Veldic, M., Costa, E., Guidotti, A.: Characterization of brain neurons that express enzymes mediating neurosteroid biosynthesis. Proc. Natl. Acad. Sci. U.S.A. **103**, 14602–14607 (2006)
35. Semyanov, A., Walker, M.C., Kullmann, D.M., Silver, R.A.: Tonically active GABA A receptors: modulating gain and maintaining the tone. Trends Neurosci. **27**, 262–269 (2004)
36. Chhatwal, J.P., Myers, K.M., Ressler, K.J., Davis, M.: Regulation of gephyrin and GABAA receptor binding within the amygdala after fear acquisition and extinction. J. Neurosci. **25**, 502–506 (2005)

37. Purdy, R.H., Morrow, A.L., Moore Jr., P.H., Paul, S.M.: Stress-induced elevations of gamma-aminobutyric acid type a receptor-active steroids in the rat brain. Proc. Natl. Acad. Sci. **88**, 4553–4557 (1991)
38. Barbaccia, M.L., Roscetti, G., Trabucchi, M., Mostallino, M.C., Concas, A., Purdy, R.H., Biggio, G.: Time-dependent changes in rat brain neuroactive steroid concentrations and GABAA receptor function after acute stress. Neuroendocrinology **63**, 66–172 (1996)
39. Rasmusson, A.M., Pinna, G., Paliwal, P., Weisman, D., Gottschalk, C., Charney, D., Krystal, J., Guidotti, A.: Decreased cerebrospinal fluid allopregnanolone levels in women with posttraumatic stress disorder. Biol. Psychiatry **60**, 704–713 (2006)
40. Payne, V.M., Morey, R.A., Hamer, R.M., Tupler, L.A., Calhoun, P.S., Beckham, J.C., Marx, C.M.: Neuroactive steroids are related to psychiatric symptoms in veterans who served in operation enduring freedom/operation Iraqi freedom. In: Annual Meeting of the International Society for Traumatic Stress Studies (2007)
41. Cagetti, E., Pinna, G., Guidotti, A., Baicy, K., Olsen, R.W.: Chronic intermittent ethanol (CIE) administration in rats decreases levels of neurosteroids in hippocampus, accompanied by altered behavioral responses to neurosteroids and memory function. Neuropharmacology **46**, 570–579 (2004)
42. Pibiri, F., Nelson, M., Guidotti, A., Costa, E., Pinna, G.: Decreased allopregnanolone content during social isolation enhances contextual fear: a model relevant for posttraumatic stress disorder. Proc. Natl. Acad. Sci. **105**, 5567–5572 (2008)
43. Gillespie, C.F., Almli, L.M., Smith, A.K., Bradley, B., Kerley, K., Crain, D.F., Mercer, K.B., Weiss, T., Phifer, J., Tang, Y., Cubells, J.F., Binder, E.B., Conneely, K.N., Ressler, K.J.: Sex dependent influence of a functional polymorphism in steroid 5-alpha-reductase type 3 (SRD5A2) on post-traumatic stress symptoms. Am. J. Med. Genet. B Neuropsychiatr. Genet. **162B**, 283–292 (2013)
44. Pinna, G., Rasmusson, A.M.: Ganaxolone improves behavioral deficits in a mouse model of post-taumatic stress disorder. Front. cell. Neurosci. **8**, 1–11 (2014)
45. Sripada, R.K., Marx, C.E., King, A.P., Rampton, J.C., Ho, S., Liberzon, I.: Allopregnanolone elevations following pregnenolone administration are associated with enhanced activation of emotion regulation neurocircuits. Biol. Psychiatry **73**, 1045–1053 (2013)
46. Pinna, G., Rasmusson, A.M.: Upregulation of neurosteroid biosynthesis as a pharmacological strategy to improve behavioral deficits in a putative mouse model of PTSD. J. Neuroendocrinol. **24**, 102–116 (2012)
47. Pinna, G., Agis-Balboa, R., Pibiri, F., Nelson, M., Guidotti, A., Costa, E.: Neurosteroid biosynthesis regulates sexually dimorphic fear and aggressive behavior in mice. Neurochem. Res. **33**, 1990–2007 (2008)
48. Ramsay, J.O., Silverman, B.W.: Functional Data Analysis, 2nd edn. Springer, New York (2005)
49. Irvine, J.M., Regan, J. Spain, T., Caruso, J.D., Rodriguez, M., Luthra, R., Forsberg, J., Crane, N.J., Elster, E.: Analysis of temporal dynamics in imagery during acute limb ischemia and reperfusion. In: SPIE Medical Imaging, Image Processing Section (2014)
50. Izenman, A.J.: Modern Multivariate Statistical Techniques: Regression, Classification, and Manifold Learning. Springer, New York (2008)
51. Cocuzzo, D., Lin, A., Ramadan, S., Mountford, C. Keshava, N.: Algorithms for characterizing brain metabolites in two-dimensional in vivo MR correlation spectroscopy. In: Conference Proceedings: Annual International Conference of the IEEE Engineering in Medicine and Biology Society, pp. 4929–4934 (2011)
52. Stanwell, P., Siddall, P., Keshava, N., Cocuzzo, D., Ramadan, S., Lin, A., Herbert, D., Craig, A., Tran, Y., Middleton, J., Gautam, S., Cousins, M., Mountford, C.: Neuro MRS using wavelet decomposition and statistical testing identified biochemical changes in people with SCI and pain. NeuroImage **53**, 544–552 (2010)

Objective-Analytical Measures of Workload – the Third Pillar of Workload Triangulation?

Christina Rusnock[✉], Brett Borghetti, and Ian McQuaid

Air Force Institute of Technology, Wright-Patterson AFB, Fairborn, OH, USA
{christina.rusnock,brett.borghetti,
Ian.mcquaid.ctr}@afit.edu

Abstract. The ability to assess operator workload is important for dynamically allocating tasks in a way that allows efficient and effective goal completion. For over fifty years, human factors professionals have relied upon self-reported measures of workload. However, these subjective-empirical measures have limited use for real-time applications because they are often collected only at the completion of the activity. In contrast, objective-empirical measurements of workload, such as physiological data, can be recorded continuously, and provide frequently-updated information over the course of a trial. Linking the low-sample-rate subjective-empirical measurement to the high-sample-rate objective-empirical measurements poses a significant challenge. While the series of objective-empirical measurements could be down–sampled or averaged over a longer time period to match the subjective-empirical sample rate, this process discards potentially relevant information, and may produce meaningless values for certain types of physiological data. This paper demonstrates the technique of using an objective-analytical measurement produced by mathematical models of workload to bridge the gap between subjective-empirical and objective-empirical measures. As a proof of concept, we predicted operator workload from physiological data using VACP, an objective-analytical measure, which was validated against NASA-TLX scores. Strong predictive results pave the way to use the objective-empirical measures in real-time augmentation (such as dynamic task allocation) to improve operator performance.

Keywords: Workload measurement · Machine learning · VACP · IMPRINT

1 Introduction and Background

With the rising use of automation and recent interest in adaptive automation (e.g. Kaber and Kim 2011; Sheridan 2011; Parasuraman et al. 2007; Scerbo 2007), the human factors community has become highly motivated to find an effective and accurate means for measuring operator workload. The ability to measure operator workload is critical for the dynamic task allocation envisioned in adaptive systems, because workload is typically the impetus that determines whether an operator should be allocated a more or fewer tasks (e.g., Bailey et al. 2006; Parasuraman et al. 2009; De Visser and Parasuraman 2011). In this context, operator workload refers to the amount of attentional resources required of a specific person to perform a specific task (Hart and Staveland 1988). Due to the personal nature of workload, workload measurements

© Springer International Publishing Switzerland 2015
D.D. Schmorrow and C.M. Fidopiastis (Eds.): AC 2015, LNAI 9183, pp. 124–135, 2015.
DOI: 10.1007/978-3-319-20816-9_13

are difficult to accomplish and verify, and human factors professionals must choose from numerous workload measurement tools that often provide incompatible measurements.

1.1 Workload Measurement Taxonomy

These workload measurement tools can be categorized across two dimensions: objective–subjective and empirical–analytical (Fig. 1). Objective workload measurements are gathered from facts; subjective workload measurements are gathered from individual opinions. Thus, objective workload measurements use information and data about the real world, and are independent of the person gathering the measurement. Subjective workload measurements, on the other hand, are highly dependent on the person gathering the measurement.

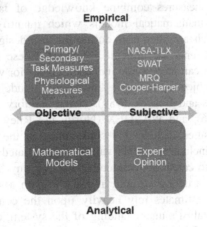

Fig. 1. Dimensions of workload measurement

Orthogonal to the objective-subjective dimension is an empirical–analytical dimension. Empirical workload measurements are derived from experience; analytical workload measurements are derived from analysis. Thus, empirical workload measurements are a posteriori; they entail an actual data collection process, and are often used in conjunction with laboratory experiments or field observations. Analytical workload measurements can be thought of as a priori measurements, since they rely heavily upon the analytical reasoning of the human factors specialist. While they do not necessarily rely upon empirical data, in practice analytical workload measurements are often derived from extensive task analyses. The distinction is that empirical measures aim to measure workload directly, whereas analytical measures infer workload based on knowledge of the task, operator, and environment. These two orthogonal dimensions form natural axes which facilitate categorizing various workload measurement tools.

Subjective-empirical measures assess workload directly by gathering individual opinions–frequently in the form of self-report questionnaires. Due to the nature of these tools, the measurements do not provide real-time feedback on the subject's mental workload, do not capture changes in workload over the course of the task, and may be subject to memory biases. Widely used subjective measurement tools include the NASA-TLX (Hart and Staveland 1988), SWAT (Reid and Nygren 1988), Cooper-Harper (1969), MRQ (Boles and Adair 2001), Overall workload (Jung 2001), and workload profile (Tsang and Velazquez 1996).

Subjective-analytical measures rely upon subject matter experts or experienced users to provide estimates for anticipated workload. These estimates are essentially expert opinions which can vary widely between raters. As can be expected, this method of estimating workload is not utilized in academia; however, it is commonly used in the public and private sector for product and system development, especially when making early design decisions early on in a program's life cycle. Before initial prototypes are developed, empirical methods are not feasible, thus workload evaluation must rely upon analytical methods.

Objective-analytical measures combine knowledge of task, environment, and individual as inputs to mathematical models which quantify estimated workload. Objective-analytical models are often used during the task design or re-design process, when empirical measurements are difficult to obtain. These models are built from detailed task analyses and can incorporate individual behavior when the information is available. Examples of objective-analytical measures include time-line analysis and prediction (TLAP) (Parks and Boucek 1989), visual auditory cognitive psychomotor (Aldrich and Szabo 1986), and W/INDEX (North and Riley 1989). Advantages of objective-analytical measures include: (1) consistency in the workload values produced, (2) the ability to include workload values differentiated for resources or channels, and (3) the ability to calculate workload values on any time scale. However, it should be noted that constructing accurate models is both a science and an art; the quality of the workload estimates rely heavily upon the completeness of the task analysis as well as the analyst's understanding of the system, operator, task, context, and the modeling methodology.

Objective-empirical measures feature direct measurement of either task performance or physiological states. Task performance measures focus on error frequency, number of errors, response time, and response accuracy to determine the level of cognitive workload. Direct measurement of task performance can be conducted in a way that is transparent to the user, and it can be conducted continuously throughout the performance of the task. However, the relationship between performance and workload is non–linear, with both high and low workload associated with poor performance, with higher task performance between these workload extremes (Teigen 1994). Furthermore, despite task performance measures ability to monitor real-time changes in performance, performance changes likely lag causal changes in workload. That is, an operator may experience excessively high workload for a period of time before the change becomes apparent in their performance. Lag is especially detrimental to adaptive systems: if the system only alters workload after a performance change is detected, it is too late to *prevent* that performance degradation. These problems with using performance as an indicator of workload: non-specificity, non-linearity and lag, have encouraged the expedited search for other objective-empirical measures of workload.

Technological advances in sensor development and computer processing have enabled the use of physiological measures for assessing operator workload. Objective-empirical physiological measures use biological feedback to estimate cognitive workload. Common physiological measures include heart rate, heart rate variability, respiration, skin response, pupil dilation, eye movement/fixation, blink rate, and brain activity. Physiological measures are particularly well suited for adaptive automation purposes because they provide immediate feedback, are highly sensitive to change, and can be designed for minimal–to–no intrusiveness in task performance. In order for objective-empirical physiological measures to be effective, researchers need to be able to distinguish useful, workload-relevant information from physiological fluctuations caused by environment and irrelevant biological processes. Just as workload does not have a linear correlation with performance, it is likely that the relationship between physiological data and workload will be highly complex.

1.2 Workload Measurement Application

While subjective-empirical, or self-report measures, are relatively easy to use and widely accepted, the measurements are typically taken after task completion and often consist of a single, cumulative rating. These features make self-reported workload unrealistic for incorporation into adaptive systems. Thus, while workload measurement has historically defaulted to subjective-empirical measures, more recently interest has grown in using physiological measures to estimate workload (Parasuraman and Wilson 2008; Warm and Parasuraman 2007). Physiological measures have the advantage of being specific to the individual, relatively un-intrusive to the task, continuously measurable, and available in real-time. However, using physiological measures for workload estimation has challenges, one being that physiological state is affected by numerous factors besides workload. Separating the workload "signal" from the biological and environmental "noise" is a daunting task, especially when the relationship between the physiological measure and workload is not well-established.

In order to define this relationship between workload and physiological measures, researchers have begun to use a dual collection approach, collecting both self-reported measures and physiological measures (e.g. Wilson and Russell 2004; Taylor et al. 2013). This dual collection provides an opportunity to interpret and validate objective-empirical physiological data using the subjective-empirical self-reports. However, this validation is difficult because–in order to reduce task interruptions– subjective-empirical measures are sampled infrequently, sometimes only at the completion of the task. In contrast, objective-empirical measurements are recorded continuously, and provide frequently-updated information over the course of a trial. Thus, linking the low-sample-rate subjective-empirical measurement to the high-sample-rate objective-empirical measurements poses a significant challenge. While the series of objective-empirical measurements could be down–sampled or averaged over a longer time period to match the subjective-empirical sample rate, this process discards potentially relevant information, and may produce meaningless values for certain types of physiological data which could vary rapidly in the time between the less-frequently measured samples.

Objective-analytical measures posses the unique potential of being able to bridge the gap between subjective-empirical and objective-empirical measurements. Objective-analytical measures are produced from detailed task analyses of the individual's behavior when performing the task. The task analysis assigns workload estimates to each low-level activity the subject performs during the task. Regardless of task duration, workload can be estimated by aggregating workload values from all the activities the subject was performing in an arbitrarily-sized time interval. As a result, workload values are generated bottom-up from the lowest level of activity. While objective-analytic values are scale–compatible with the subjective workload estimates subjects normally provide at the end of a trial, objective-analytical measures avoid being influenced by estimation biases occurring when subjects have to recall their experiences and declare their cumulative workload over long time intervals.

Objective-analytical measures can be calculated continuously over the course of a task, allowing for comparison on the natural (continuous) time-scale of the objective-empirical measurements. Moreover, objective-analytical measurements can be consolidated in meaningful ways (time-weighted average, peak value, and sustained peak-value) to validate against well-established subjective-empirical measures. This bridge between self-reported subjective-empirical measures and objective-empirical measures will enable a time-series characterization of workload based on physiological measures in real time, a necessary feature of workload-based dynamic task allocation, such as adaptive automation.

2 Purpose

This paper argues that objective-analytical measures of workload possess numerous benefits that can significantly enhance current empirical workload measurement and analysis techniques. Specifically, objective-analytical methods have the unique ability to be able to connect subjective-empirical workload measures, such as NASA-TLX to objective-empirical measures, such as physiological readings. This connection enables the creation of predictive machine learning algorithms, which paves the way to use physiological measures in real-time augmentation (such as dynamic task allocation) to improve operator performance.

3 Method

Our study begins by collecting subjective- and objective- empirical data from a human-in-the-loop experiment. Next, objective-analytical workload measurements are generated using the improved performance research integration tool (IMPRINT). IMPRINT simulation models are created for each subject for each trial in order to calculate continuous workload values that correspond directly to the physiological data collected for each trial. These workload values are established using the visual, auditory, cognitive, psychomotor (VACP) method (Bierbaum et al. 1989). Next, the objective-analytical models are validated using the subjective-empirical data. The continuous workload profiles generated through IMPRINT allow for the training of a model tree to discover the relationship between physiological data and VACP workload values. To demonstrate efficacy of our method, the model tree algorithms are evaluated on their ability to infer objective-analytic VACP workload from objective-empirical physiological measurements. Algorithm performance is reported using root mean squared error (RMSE).

3.1 Human-in-the-Loop Study

The human-in-the-loop study was conducted by the HUMAN Lab, Air Force Research Laboratory, at Wright-Patterson AFB. The study included 12 participants (8 male, 4 female; ranging from 18–46 years of age, with a mean of 25.66), performing remotely piloted aircraft tasks using a synthetic task environment. The participants performed two tasks, a surveillance task and a tracking task. In the surveillance task, the participant operated a simulated drone-mounted video camera to search through a desert marketplace for a high-value target designated as the figure holding a rifle. Upon finding the target, the participant used the camera to track the target (who was on foot) until the target left the observation area. The task difficulty was affected by manipulating the number of distracter figures (12 or 48) and the video image quality (high or low noise), creating a 2 × 2 factorial design. Each of the 4 surveillance conditions was completed 4 times by each participant.

The second task was the tracking task, which consisted of operating the video camera to follow a high–value target whose position is already known. In the tracking task, the target is on a motorcycle, and moves at considerably faster speed than the surveillance targets, making it more difficult to keep the target in the camera image and requiring faster reaction time from the participants. The task difficulty was altered by manipulating the number of targets to follow (either one or two) and the terrain type (urban or rural), creating a 2 × 2 factorial design. Each of the 4 tracking conditions was completed 4 times by each participant.

NASA-TLX scores were collected at the end of each trial: each participant provided 16 surveillance scores and 16 tracking scores. Physiological data collected included 49 electroencephalography (EEG) measurements (7 cranial node sites, 7 brainwave frequency bands), 4 pupilometry measurements ([diameter, quality] × [filtered, raw]), 2 electrooculography (EOG) measurements (blink rate, fixation), 2 electrocardiography (ECG) measurements (heart rate and heart rate variability) and 2 respiration measurements (amplitude, frequency).

3.2 IMPRINT Models and Model Validation

A task analysis was conducted on the surveillance and tracking tasks in order to develop task networks that captured the task flows, decision logic, and user interactions. Participant performance and response times were used to calculate timing for each of the lowest level tasks. Workload demand values were assigned to each of the lowest level tasks using the VACP method. VACP builds upon multiple resource theory (Wickens 2002) to capture workload demand across 7 resource channels: visual, auditory, cognitive, fine psychomotor, gross psychomotor, speech, and tactile. Each channel has a 0–7 demand scale, with specific values tied to descriptive anchors (e.g. a visual reading task has a value of 5.9). Each of the lowest level tasks in the network is assigned a demand value for each channel. Demand values are then summed across channels and tasks at each point in time to generate an overall workload score. This workload score for each point in time enables the generation of a workload profile (Fig. 2).

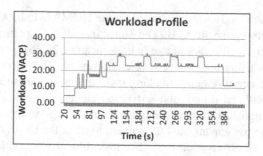

Fig. 2. Example VACP workload profile

Workload is validated using a correlation analysis that pairs model VACP predicted workload per trial with self-reported NASA-TLX values for each participant for each task (tracking and surveillance). The subjective interpretation of the NASA-TLX scale, makes this dimension unique to each individual, thus it is necessary to perform separate correlations for each participant. This validation produces a set of 24 correlations (12 subjects × 2 tasks). The tracking task correlations ranged from 0.31–0.87 with a mean of 0.61. Correlations values above 0.60 are considered as having a "marked degree of correlation" (Franzblau 1958), and thus the correlations from the tracking task meet the criteria for satisfactory validation. The surveillance task correlations ranged from 0.1–0.63 with a mean of 0.37. Lower correlations for the surveillance task are largely due to the lack of differentiation in the NASA-TLX self-reported scores; an ANOVA for the NASA TLX by condition does not find any statistical difference between the four surveillance conditions. Thus, the inability to validate these models is attributed to the design of the human-in-the-loop experiment rather than an issue with the models.

3.3 Inferring Workload with Machine Learning Algorithms

Validated IMPRINT models generate profiles which characterize operator workload throughout the course of a task. As workload varies, operator physiological response is affected. By determining the relationship between workload and physiological response, physiological state can be used to infer the workload the operator is experiencing. This section describes machine learning methods for inferring operator workload.

Our proposed method estimates operator workload in real time from physiological measurements using supervised machine learning algorithms to train predictive models.

We evaluated this method using algorithms trained on a subset of the objective-empirical physiological measurements and their corresponding objective-analytic workload values computed using IMPRINT. Once trained, the ability of the models to infer workload from physiological data was assessed on hold-out data that was not used for training.

IMPRINT produces a log of discrete workload changes. The log contains a series of timestamps and new workload values which were captured as each workload-change event in the simulation of the task occurred. Between any two events in the log, workload is constant. These discrete-event workload values were sampled at 1 Hz to create a time-series interpretation of operator workload which could be associated with corresponding physiological data. Time series data for all seven VACP channels of cognitive workload were captured and summed to produce an overall workload value at 1 Hz for each of the 32 scenarios the twelve subjects accomplished during the experiment.

During the execution of the sixteen surveillance and sixteen tracking tasks, operator physiological data was recorded for each of the twelve subjects. The researchers who conducted the study performed additional processing on the sensor data to generate physiological data in commonly-used formats, then re-sampled at 1 Hz. Sixty brain, heart, respiratory and eye physiological data features were collected.

Inferring real-valued workload from real-valued physiological data is a specific example of a more general activity known as regression. Three supervised-learning regression algorithms were evaluated for their ability to infer workload from physiological data: linear regression, model trees, and the multi-layer perceptron (also known as an artificial neural network). Due to space limitations, and because it had the best performance of the algorithms evaluated, only the model tree algorithm (Quinlan 1992, Wang and Witten 1997, Fong 2010) are discussed further in this section, although the performance of all three algorithms is presented in Sect. 4. Before a model can be used for prediction, it must be trained. We discuss the training and testing process for model trees next.

During training, a model tree uses an iterative hierarchal process to split a dataset according to a particular feature value. Each branch in the tree captures the value of a single feature which best splits the remainder of the data into evenly-sized subgroups. Once the training is complete, the tree can be used to infer workload from the feature values observed in the physiological data. To infer workload value from an observation, the algorithm evaluates the observation in the context of the first node in the tree, and decides which branch to follow based on the value of the feature being evaluated in that branch. This process is repeated until the observation is evaluated at a leaf node. At a leaf node of the tree, an inference is made on the value of workload.

4 Results

To be useful, our method must demonstrate that objective-empirical physiological measurements can be used to infer objective-analytic workload. This section examines the efficacy of the supervised machine learning algorithms to infer workload from physiological data. Figure 3 depicts an example of overall actual and inferred

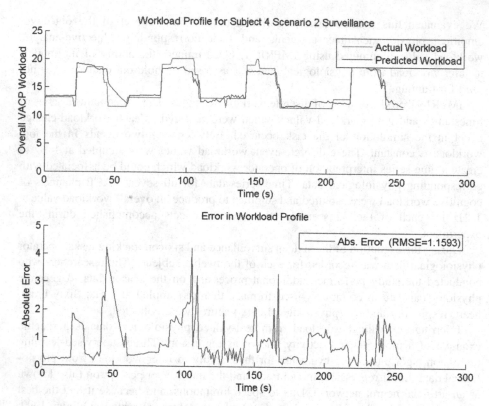

Fig. 3. Inferring operator workload. (*Top*) Workload profile and model tree prediction for surveillance task. (*Bottom*) Absolute prediction error of tracking task.

(predicted by model tree) VACP workload for one subject's surveillance task. The distance between the inferred workload and the actual workload is the absolute prediction error.

Efficacy was evaluated for three supervised learning algorithms: model tree, multilayer perceptron (60-30-1), and linear regression. For training, each model used 75 % of the data and tested on the remaining unseen 25 % of the data. The workload prediction results are presented in Fig. 4. Accuracy of three prediction algorithms with error bars representing the standard deviation of root mean squared errors (RMSE) and 95 % confidence intervals. Root mean squared error (RMSE) is used as the figure of merit for model performance. Low, medium, and high accuracy thresholds are depicted for reference. These accuracy thresholds have meaning in the workload prediction task:

Low (RMSE < 3.2): At low accuracy in a two-target scenario the model could differentiate between the situation where the operator is tracking both targets or tracking no targets.

Med (RMSE < 2.6): At medium accuracy the algorithm could determine if the secondary task (question and answer) was being performed or not.

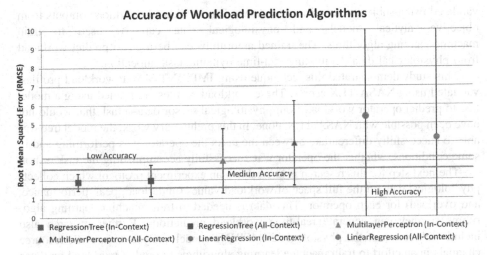

Fig. 4. Accuracy of three prediction algorithms with error bars representing the standard deviation of root mean squared errors (RMSE) and 95 % confidence intervals. "In-context" workload prediction performance is measured using a model trained on the same person in the same conditions as the testing scenario. "All-context" workload prediction performance is measured using a model trained using more general data from all scenarios.

High (RMSE < 1.6): At high accuracy in the one-target scenario, the algorithm could differentiate between an operator who was successfully tracking the target and one who was attempting to reacquire a lost target.

Our evaluation suggests model trees are the most accurate supervised learning algorithm for inferring workload from physiological data. In most cases, this predictor can differentiate between tasks the operator is performing, and in some cases the algorithm is able to indicate whether or not the operator is successfully at performing the task. This finding suggests the algorithm's ability to infer workload from physiological sensor data may be accurate enough to facilitate dynamic task allocation in real-time.

5 Discussion and Future Directions

Subjective-empirical workload measures such as NASA-TLX provide quick, well-accepted measurements of workload, but are not practical for use in adaptive systems, which require continuous, real-time measurements of operator workload. Objective-empirical workload measures, especially physiological measures, possess the ability to fill this gap, by enabling an adaptive system to directly monitor operators and predict their cognitive states. However, predicting cognitive workload requires a means of interpreting or connecting physiological readings to levels of workload.

Objective-analytical measures, such as IMPRINT's VACP, can fill this gap, by providing workload values that correspond to the change in demand on an individual's cognitive resource during task performance. These objective-analytical outputs can be validated using subjective-empirical measures. Once validated, workload outputs from objective-analytical models and physiological data can be used to train machine-learning algorithms. The trained algorithms can be used to predict workload from physiological data, facilitating real-time dynamic task allocation.

This study demonstrated this technique using IMPRINT VACP workload profiles, validated using NASA-TLX scores. These workload profiles are trained using a model tree to predict operator workload from physiological sensor data–a task that would not have been possible with NASA-TLX alone. In this preliminary work, the model tree was able to successfully differentiate between the tasks the operator was performing and in some conditions, whether the operator was successfully accomplishing the task or not.

The next step for this research is to establish an experiment protocol which collects physiological data on the full space of workload values (underload, peak performance, and overload) for each operator. This data is needed to train machine learning algorithms so they can generate real-time workload predictions. Further research also includes extension of the physiological-IMPRINT model analysis to specific resource channels in an effort to train machine learning algorithms to predict workload on those specific resource channels. This channel-specific analysis will enable identification of tasks that are appropriate for dynamic task allocation or for adaptive presentation of information via alternate modalities (e.g. moving information from visual to audio modality).

References

Aldrich, T.B., Szabo, S.M.: A methodology for predicting crew workload in new weapon systems. In: Proceedings of the Human Factors Society 30th Annual Meeting (1986)

Bailey, N.R., Scerbo, M.W., Freeman, F.G., Mikulka, P.J., Scott, L.A.: Comparison of a brain-based adaptive system and a manual adaptable system for invoking automation. Hum. Factors 48(4), 693–709 (2006)

Bierbaum, C.R., Szabo, S.M., Aldrich, T.B.: Task analysis of the UH-60 mission and decision rules for developing a UH-60 workload prediction model No. AD-A210763. U.S. Army Research Institute for the Behavioral and Social Sciences, Alexandria (1989)

Boles, D.B., Adair, L.P.: The multiple resources questionnaire (MRQ). In: Proceedings of the Human Factors & Ergonomics Society Annual Meeting, pp. 1790–1794 (2001)

Cooper, G.E., Harper, R.P.: The use of pilot ratings in the evaluation of aircraft handling qualities No. NASA Ames Technical Report NASA TN-D-5153). NASA Ames Research Center, Moffett Field (1969)

De Visser, E.J., Parasuraman, R.: Adaptive aiding of human-robot teaming: effects of imperfect automation on performance, trust, and workload. J. Cogn. Eng. Decis. Making 5(2), 209–231 (2011)

Fong, A., Sibley, C., Cole, A., Baldwin, C., Coyne, J.: A comparison of artificial neural networks, logistic regressions, and classification trees for modeling mental workload in real-time. In: Proceedings of the Human Factors and Ergonomics Society Annual Meeting, vol. 54, pp. 1709–1712 (2010)

Franzblau, Abraham N.: A Primer of Statistics for Non-Statisticians. Harcourt, Brace & World, New York (1958)

Hart, S.G., Staveland, L.E.: Development of NASA-TLX (task load index): results of empirical and theoretical research. In: Hancock, P.A., Meshkati, N. (eds.) Human Mental Workload, pp. 139–183. Elsevier, Amsterdam (1988)

Jung, H.S.: Establishment of overall workload assessment technique for various tasks and workplaces. Int. J. Ind. Ergon. **28**(6), 341–353 (2001)

Kaber, D.B., Kim, S.H.: Understanding cognitive strategy with adaptive automation in dual-task performance using computational cognitive models. J. Cogn. Eng. Decis. Making **5**(3), 309–331 (2011)

Parasuraman, R., Barnes, M., Cosenzo, K.: Adaptive automation for human-robot teaming in future command and control systems. Int. C2 J. **1**(2), 43–68 (2007)

Parasuraman, R., Cosenzo, K.A., De Visser, E.J.: Adaptive automation for human supervision of multiple uninhabited vehicles: effects on change detection, situation awareness, and mental workload. Mil. Psychol. **21**(2), 270–297 (2009)

Parasuraman, R., Wilson, G.F.: Putting the brain to work: neuroergonomics past, present, and future. Hum. Factors **50**(3), 468–474 (2008)

Parks, D.L., Boucek Jr., G.P.: Workload prediction, diagnosis, and continuing challenges. In: McMillan, G.R., Beevis, D., Salas, E., Strub, M.H., Sutton, R., Van Breda, L. (eds.) Applications of Human Performance Models to System Design, pp. 47–64. Plenum, New York (1989)

North, R.A., Riley, V.A.: W/Index: a predictive model of operator workload. In: Mc-Millan, G., Beevis, D., Salas, E., Strub, M., Sutton, R., Van Breda's, L. (eds.) Applications of Human Performance Models to System Design, pp. 81–90. Springer, USA (1989)

Quinlan, R.J.: Learning with continuous classes. In: 5th Australian Joint Conference on Artificial Intelligence, pp. 343–348 (1992)

Reid, G.B., Nygren, T.E.: The subjective workload assessment technique: a scaling procedure for measuring mental workload. In: Hancock, P.A., Meshkati, N. (eds.) Human Mental Workload, pp. 185–218. Elsevier, Amsterdam (1988)

Scerbo, M.W.: Adaptive automation. In: Parasuraman, R., Rizzo, M. (eds.) Neuroergonomics: The Brain at Work, pp. 238–252. Oxford University Press, New York (2007)

Sheridan, T.B.: Adaptive automation, level of automation, allocation authority, supervisory control, and adaptive control: distinctions and modes of adaptation. IEEE Trans. Syst. Man Cybern. Part A Syst. Hum. **41**(4), 662–667 (2011)

Taylor, G., Reinerman-Jones, L., Szalma, J., Mouloua, M., Hancock, P.: What to automate: addressing the multidimensionality of cognitive resources through system design. J. Cogn. Eng. Decis. Making **7**(4), 311–329 (2013)

Teigen, K.H.: Yerkes-Dodson: a Law for all seasons. Theory Psychol. **4**(4), 525–547 (1994)

Tsang, P.S., Velazquez, V.L.: Diagnosticity and multidimensional subjective workload ratings. Ergonomics **39**(3), 358–381 (1996)

Wang, Y., Witten, I.H.: Induction of model trees for predicting continuous classes. In: Poster Papers of the 9th European Conference on Machine Learning (1997)

Warm, J.S., Parasuraman, R.: Cerebral hemodynamics and vigilance. In: Parasuraman, R., Rizzo, M. (eds.) Neuroergonomics: The Brain at Work, pp. 146–158. Oxford University Press, New York (2007)

Wickens, C.D.: Multiple resources and performance prediction. Theor. Issues Ergon. Sci. **3**(2), 159–177 (2002)

Wilson, G.F., Russell, C.A.: Psychophysiologically determined adaptive aiding in a simulated UCAV task. Human Performance, Situation Awareness, and Automation: Current Research and Trends, pp. 200–204. Erlbaum Associates, Mahwah (2004)

Eye-Tracking Technology for Estimation of Cognitive Load After Traumatic Brain Injury

Ashley Safford[1,2(✉)], Jessica Kegel[1,2], Jamie Hershaw[2],
Doug Girard[1,3], and Mark Ettenhofer[2]

[1] Henry M. Jackson Foundation for the Advancement of Military Medicine,
Bethesda, MD, USA
[2] Department of Medical and Clinical Psychology, Uniformed Services
University of the Health Sciences, Bethesda, MD, USA
{ashley.safford.ctr,jessica.kegel.ctr,jamie.hershaw,
mark.ettenhofer}@usuhs.edu
[3] Loyola University Maryland, Baltimore, MD, USA
doug.girard@gmail.com

Abstract. The goal of this study was to develop an eye-tracking based tool to measure cognitive effort as an approach to assess injury-related changes in brain function. A set of novel tasks were developed to examine changes in manual and saccadic reaction time under varying levels of cognitive load and cuing conditions. Twenty-six healthy individuals completed these working memory and continuous monitoring tasks while eye movements were recorded. Results indicate that these tasks, in combination with eye-tracking measures, are sensitive to cognitive difficulty as manual and saccadic response times increased under the higher load and invalid cuing conditions. These procedures show promise for utility in measuring cognitive effort and track the subtle changes associated with mild TBI.

Keywords: Eye-tracking · Cognitive load · Mild TBI

1 Introduction

Traumatic brain injury (TBI) is a significant and prevalent health concern for military and civilian populations alike. TBI is often considered to be the "signature injury" of the ongoing military campaigns as an estimated 1 in 6 deployed U.S. military personnel have sustained a mild TBI [1, 2]. Similarly, events including motor vehicle accidents and sport related concussion result in a large number of head injuries among the civilian population. Although most who suffer a mild TBI recover successfully, many others experience chronic post-concussive symptoms that lead to poorer outcomes. Accurate characterization of injury is important for directing treatment and making informed decisions regarding return to duty, work, or play.

Currently, the clinical tools commonly used to assess mild TBI have failed to show differences in performance, indicating that these measures are insensitive to persistent injury-related changes in cognitive function, behavior, or symptoms [3, 4]. However,

© Springer International Publishing Switzerland 2015
D.D. Schmorrow and C.M. Fidopiastis (Eds.): AC 2015, LNAI 9183, pp. 136–143, 2015.
DOI: 10.1007/978-3-319-20816-9_14

anecdotal reports indicate that greater levels of effort are required by individuals with TBI in order to achieve these similar levels of performance. Additionally, previous research using fMRI has demonstrated that after mild TBI, larger groups of neurons are required to maintain the same level of task performance [5]. This pattern of activation could reflect greater degree of effort extended by the mild TBI group, and suggests that measures of cognitive effort may provide a basis for estimating injury-related changes in brain function.

The aim of this study was to develop a novel tool for assessment of mild TBI by incorporating physiological correlates of cognitive load, as measured by eye movements. Eye movements are often considered to be a reflection of cognitive processes, especially attention, and provide a rich source of data to objectively assess neural functioning. In addition to sharing cortical regions with attention, eye movements have also been shown to be impaired in several neuropsychiatric disorders including Alzheimer's disease [6], Parkinson's disease [7], schizophrenia [8] and even mild TBI [9–11].

The eye movement related measure utilized in this project is saccadic reaction time (RT), or the amount of time it takes for an individual to respond to a stimulus by moving their gaze from one point to another. Saccadic RT was used because RT is a well-established framework for computer assessment of cognitive performance. Also, saccadic RT has been shown to be influenced by both top-down and bottom-up cognitive processes [12] but is minimally influenced by verbal, visual spatial and other motor processes, allowing these measures to be embedded in a variety of other task contexts [13, 14].

2 Methods

2.1 Cognitive Efficacy Tasks

To measure cognitive capacity, a set of novel tasks were developed to systematically manipulate load. The complex dual tasks consisted of a saccadic target detection task combined with either a working memory or continuous monitoring task. The saccadic target detection task (Fig. 1) involved cuing participants to the location of subsequently appearing targets. Participants were asked to fixate on the target as soon as it appeared, then return their gaze to central fixation. Cues, left- or rightward facing arrows, were presented centrally for 200 ms and provided either valid or invalid information about the location of the target. Targets, white, blue or green circles, were presented immediately following the cue for 1500 ms on either the right or left side of the screen. Additionally, some trials were uncued. This combination of cues was designed to elicit various attention processes with varying degrees of difficulty, corresponding with a range of saccadic reaction times.

Simultaneous to the target detection task, participants performed one of two cognitive tasks: (1) a modified n-back task to activate working memory processes (fusion N-back), or (2) a continuous perceptual monitoring task (fusion color matching) to activate sustained attention processes. Each task included three levels of difficulty.

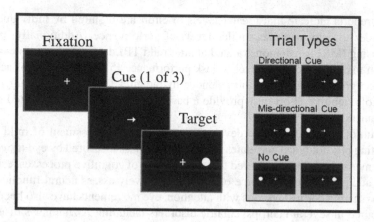

Fig. 1. Saccadic target detection task

In the fusion N-back task, participants were asked to respond with a button press to indicate the presence of the target (simple RT), the color of the target (choice RT), or whether the current target matched the color of the previous target (1-back). In the fusion color matching (CM) task, participants pressed a button to make the grey-scale shade of a continually changing box match the shade of another simultaneously present box that remained a constant shade; in this task, difficulty was manipulated by the rate at which the dynamic box changed color (low, moderate, and high).

2.2   Data Acquisition

Stimuli were presented during eye-tracking data acquisition using presentation software (neurobehavioral systems) on a Thermaltake PC with 4.01 GHz processing speed and a 19" LCD monitor with 1440 × 900 pixel resolution. Manual responses were recorded using a Cedrus RB-530 response pad.

Consistent with previous research conducted in our laboratory [15], participants were seated approximately 24" from the stimulus display and instructed to limit head and body movements as much as possible. Gaze data were acquired at 120 Hz using an Applied Science Laboratories (ASL) D6 high-speed (HS) desktop eye tracker. Gaze vectors were calibrated using a 9-point rectangular calibration screen. Gaze data and manual responses were synchronized with task event markers during data acquisition.

2.3   Data Processing and Analysis

Data were processed using ASL results standard (Version 2.4.3; ASL, 2011) to filter blinks and identify fixations and saccades. Custom scoring software was then used to perform a series of validity checks, remove invalid trials, and aggregate RTs across trials as median scores. A minimum of 10 valid trials were required to obtain a summary median RT for each task condition.

Statistical analyses were conducted using the SPSS 22.0 statistical package. Analyses included 3(load) × 3(cue type) repeated measures ANOVAs for manual and saccadic RT. Participants without the required number (10) of valid trials to calculate median RTs were excluded from the relevant analyses. Additionally, a one-way repeated measures ANOVA was used to evaluate the influence of load (3 levels) on performance of the color matching task.

3 Results

Manual and saccadic RTs were collected from 26 healthy control participants while they completed a series of novel cognitive efficacy tasks. One individual was excluded due to a failure to properly follow task instructions and another individual was missing data for the CM task due to limited testing time. Additionally, due to technical difficulties with recording eye movement data, some individuals did not have a sufficient

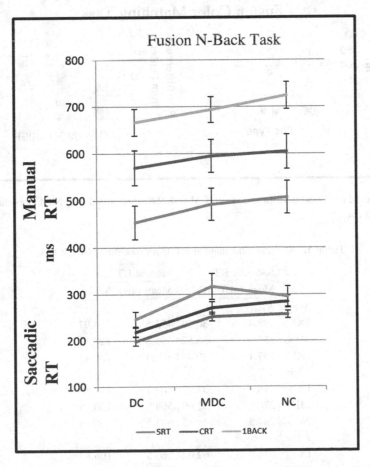

Fig. 2. Saccadic and manual RT from fusion N-back Task. SRT-simple reaction time; CRT-choice reaction time; DC-directional cue; MDC-mis-directional cue; NC-no cue.

number of valid trials (10) and were excluded from the analysis for which they had insufficient data. Accordingly, the final sample was as follows: N-back saccadic RT n = 16, N-back manual RT n = 15, color match saccadic RT n = 17, color match manual performance n = 24.

Results demonstrate that both the fusion tasks were sensitive to increased cognitive difficulty. Results from the fusion N-back task are shown in Fig. 2 and Table 1. These results showed significant main effects of both load and cue type for saccadic RT (load: $F(2,30) = 8.506$, $p < 0.01$, $\eta p^2 = .362$; cue type: $F(2,30) = 19.979$, $p < .01$, $\eta p^2 = .571$) and manual RT (load: $F(2,28) = 21.980$, $p < .01$, $\eta p^2 = .611$; cue type: $F(2,28) = 17.412$, $p < .01$, $\eta p^2 = .554$). However, there were no interactions between load and cue type for either saccadic RT ($F(4,60) = 1.169$, $p > 0.01$, $\eta p^2 = .072$) or manual RT ($F(4,56) = 0.844$, $p > 0.01$, $\eta p^2 = .057$).

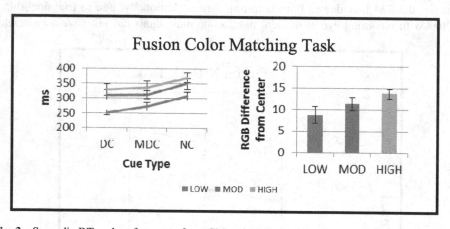

Fig. 3. Saccadic RT and performance from CM task. DC-directional cue; MDC-mis-directional cue; NC-no cue.

Table 1. Saccadic and manual RT from modified N-back task

	Saccadic RT		Manual RT	
	Mean (ms)	SD	Mean (ms)	SD
Simple RT				
DC	198.4	36.19	453.5	134.97
MDC	251.6	36.52	491.8	128.12
NC	257.1	30.40	507.3	130.45
Choice RT				
DC	218.4	37.77	569.7	137.85
MDC	270.8	51.69	594.9	130.85
NC	284.5	49.85	604.5	136.75
1-Back				
DC	246.2	62.02	666.5	106.82
MDC	316.5	108.56	693.5	102.36
NC	295.5	85.09	723.9	108.46

DC-directional cue; MDC-mis-directional cue; NC-no cue.

These results demonstrate that both saccadic and manual responses were influenced by cognitive load as well as cueing conditions. As would be expected, for both modalities, RT slows as cognitive load increases. The effect of cue type indicates that presenting spatially invalid information also slows response times relative to valid information, but is still more helpful than not having a cue at all.

Results from the fusion CM task are shown in Fig. 3, Table 2. These results showed significant main effects of load and cue type for saccadic RT (load: $F(2,32) = 19.236$, $p < .01$, $\eta p^2 = .546$; cue type: $F(2,32) = 22.807$, $p < .01$, $\eta p^2 = .588$). Again, there was no significant interaction between load and cue type ($F(4,64) = 0.593$, $p > 0.01$, $\eta p^2 = .036$). There was also a main effect of load for CM manual performance, $F(2,46) = 17.269$, $p < .01$, $\eta p^2 = .429$.

Table 2. Saccadic RT from CM task

	Mean (ms)	SD
Low		
DC	251.6	33.49
MDC	272.8	49.10
NC	307.9	49.90
Moderate		
DC	311.0	59.04
MDC	312.4	52.16
NC	350.5	69.91
High		
DC	329.0	73.44
MDC	335.9	79.51
NC	370.1	63.10

DC-directional cue; MDC-mis-directional cue; NC-no cue.

These results demonstrate that, similar to the fusion N-back task, in this task saccadic responses are influenced by cognitive load as well as cueing conditions. Again, increasing cognitive load leads to slower RTs and presenting cues reduces RTs, especially when the cues provide spatially valid information.

4 Discussion

This study examined methods and tasks for manipulating and measuring cognitive load using eye-tracking technology. Results demonstrated that analysis of eye-movements, specifically saccadic reaction times, is a useful technique for measuring cognitive processing. Additionally, the novel fusion tasks developed in this study were shown to successfully manipulate cognitive load.

In the fusion N-back task, in addition to being influenced by cognitive load, both manual and saccadic RT varied based on cue type such that compared to validly cued target locations, responses were slower when invalid cueing information was presented.

However, the presence of some type of cueing information yielded an advantage over the trials where there was no cue, suggesting that the cues (both valid and invalid) provide valuable information about the timing of the impending target onset. Importantly, under the highest working memory load (1-back), saccadic RT is impacted more by invalid directional information than a lack of timing information (MDC is slower than NC). This pattern suggests that, for this task, when cognitive resources were limited, there was a greater cost associated with processing invalid information. Similarly, in the fusion color match task, results demonstrate that saccadic responses were influenced by cognitive load as well as cueing conditions. For this task, the influence of cue validity seems to be reduced in the moderate and high load conditions, suggesting that under the higher workloads, only the timing information provided by these cues is used and perhaps the spatial information is not fully processed. Interestingly, the two fusion tasks, which activate different cognitive processes (N-back, working memory; CM, perceptual monitoring and sustained attention), seem to have different effects on participants' use of directional cues; possibly reflecting how they access different networks and processing streams.

These preliminary data from healthy controls demonstrate that these fusion tasks, when used in conjunction with eye-tracking methodology, are sensitive to cognitive load. These procedures will be useful for measuring the cognitive effort extended to perform a task and establish a unique profile of the subtle deficits associated with mild TBI. Follow-up research, currently underway, will evaluate the hypothesis that TBI is associated with reduced efficiency of performance at increasing levels of cognitive load. Ultimately, this technology could be generalized to detect and characterize other changes in cognitive capacity such as those associated with training, stress, aging, or other cognitive conditions.

Acknowledgements. Support for this research was provided by Congressionally Directed Medical Research Program (CDMRP) Award #W81XWH-13-1-0095. The technology described in this manuscript is included in U.S. Patent Application #61/779,801, with rights assigned to USUHS. The views and opinions presented in this manuscript are those of the authors, and do not necessarily represent the position of USUHS, the Department of Defense, or the United States government.

References

1. Hoge, C., McGurk, D., Thomas, J., Cox, A., Engel, C., Castro, C.: Mild traumatic brain injury in U.S. Soldiers returning from Iraq. New Engl. J. Med. **358**, 453–463 (2008)
2. Okie, S.: Traumatic brain injury in the war zone. New Engl. J. Med. **352**, 2043–2047 (2005)
3. Coldren, R., Kelly, M., Parish, R., Dretsch, M., Russell, M.: Evaluation of the military acute concussion evaluation for use in combat operations more than 12 h after injury. Mil. Med. **175**, 477–481 (2010)
4. Coldren, R., Russell, M., Kelly, M., Parish, R., Dretsch, M.: Re: automated neuropsychological assessment metrics (ANAM). Mil. Med. **176**, IV (2011)
5. McAllister, T., Sparling, M., Flashman, L., Guerin, S., Mamourian, A., Saykin, A.: Differential working memory load effects after mild traumatic brain injury. Neuroimage **14**, 1004–1012 (2001)

6. Crawford, T., Higham, S., Renvoize, T., Patel, J., Dale, M., Suriya, A., et al.: Inhibitory control of saccadic eye movements and cognitive impairment in Alzheimer's disease. Biol. Psychiatry **57**, 1052–1060 (2005)
7. van Stockum, S., MacAskill, M., Anderson, T., Dalrymple-Alford, J.: Don't look now or look away: two sources of saccadic disinhibition in Parkinson's disease? Neuropsychologia **46**, 3108–3115 (2008)
8. Schwartz, B., O'Brien, B., Evans, W., Sautter, F.J., Winstead, D.: Smooth pursuit eye movement differences between familial and non-familial schizophrenia. Schizophr. Res. **17**, 211–219 (1995)
9. Heitger, M., Jones, R., Macleod, A., Snell, D., Frampton, C., Anderson, T.: Impaired eye movements in post-concussion syndrome indicate suboptimal brain function beyond the influence of depression, malingering or intellectual ability. Brain **132**, 2850–2870 (2009)
10. Heitger, M., Anderson, T., Jones, R., Dalrymple-Alford, J., Frampton, C., Ardagh, M.: Eye movement and visuomotor arm movement deficits following mild closed head injury. Brain **127**, 575–590 (2004)
11. Heitger, M., Jones, R., Anderson, T.: A new approach to predicting postconcussion syndrome after mild traumatic brain injury based upon eye movement function. In: Proceedings of Conference in IEEE Engineering in Medicine and Biological Society, vol. 2008, pp. 3570–3573 (2008)
12. Pierrot-Deseilligny, C., Milea, D., Muri, R.: Eye movement control by the cerebral cortex. Curr. Opin. Neurol. **17**, 17–25 (2004)
13. Hutton, S.: Cognitive control of saccadic eye movements. Brain Cogn. **68**, 327–340 (2008)
14. Stuyven, E., Van der Goten, K., Vandierendonck, A., Claeys, K., Crevits, L.: The effect of cognitive load on saccadic eye movements. Acta Psychol. **104**, 69–85 (2000)
15. Ettenhofer, M.L., Hershaw, J.N., Barry, D.M.: Multi-modal assessment of visual attention: preliminary evaluation of the bethesda eye & attention measure (BEAM) (under review)

Measuring Expert and Novice Performance Within Computer Security Incident Response Teams

Austin Silva[✉], Glory Emmanuel, Jonathan T. McClain,
Laura Matzen, and Chris Forsythe

Sandia National Laboratories, Albuquerque, NM, USA
{aussilv,jtmccl}@sandia.gov

Abstract. There is a great need for creating cohesive, expert cybersecurity incident response teams and training them effectively. This paper discusses new methodologies for measuring and understanding expert and novice differences within a cybersecurity environment to bolster training, selection, and teaming. This methodology for baselining and characterizing individuals and teams relies on relating eye tracking gaze patterns to psychological assessments, human-machine transaction monitoring, and electroencephalography data that are collected during participation in the game-based training platform Tracer FIRE. We discuss preliminary findings from two pilot studies using novice and professional teams.

Keywords: Cybersecurity · Training · Teams · Visual search · Eye tracking · EEG · In situ testing · Measuring individual differences · Psychological measures

1 Introduction

As the trend towards highly sophisticated cyber-attacks continues to rise in the U.S., the need for more highly skilled professionals to counter these attacks has become critical. There is an increased demand for qualified individuals across the nation in both private and government domains. Currently, cyber incident responders (IRs) are generally selected through an interview-based hiring process and trained through tool-centric workshops. There is little understanding of the progression from novice to competent to expert to elite, within cyber security, nor is there a clear understanding of the ideal structure and allocation of duties within cyber IR teams. This lack of basic understanding is compounded by the fact that the number of individuals training for positions in cyber security is insufficient to meet the demands projected over the next decade. In order to defend against dynamic and intelligent cyber-attacks, there is a need for a rigorous, quantitative approach to selecting and training IRs that will produce more world-class experts, at the individual and team level.

An interdisciplinary team of researchers at Sandia National Laboratories ("Sandia") has developed an empirical methodology to quantify novice and expert differences. Performance data was collected through the instrumentation of a training environment known as Tracer FIRE. Cognitive and behavioral processes were quantified through the

D.D. Schmorrow and C.M. Fidopiastis (Eds.): AC 2015, LNAI 9183, pp. 144–152, 2015.
DOI: 10.1007/978-3-319-20816-9_15

use of eye tracking, electroencephalography (EEG), self-report measures, and computer instrumentation. The purpose of the current project is to test the hypothesis that we can differentiate between effective and ineffective individuals and teams by utilizing cognitive measures such as EEG, eye tracking, self-report measures, and human-machine transactions during domain-specific and domain-general tasks. The integration of technical capabilities to develop a human performance measurement system for IR teams will offer a cornerstone for cyber security training programs.

This work is challenging for two reasons. At the psychological level, identifying causal relationships in an unstructured environment is very challenging. At the instrumentation level, capturing and synchronizing the data from a network of machines and other sensors (e.g., EEG and eye tracking) at the millisecond level in a way that supports causal analysis at the psychological level is a significant data fusion problem. In this way, this work is unique in its close approximation to an operational environment while allowing controlled quantitative measurement.

In our paper, we separately discuss the relationship of Tracer FIRE, eye tracking, human-machine transaction tracking capabilities, EEG, and self-report measures to cyber security. We specifically present how each of these technologies can be used to collect data and quantify attributes related to cyber expertise. From there we highlight the methodology we used to collect data from expert and novice IRs. This methodology is unique and innovative due to the combination of these various technologies in a single cyber training environment. We are aware of both the strengths and weaknesses of our methodology and present how this experimental design can be used on a larger scale to understand the human dimension in cyber security environments.

While cybersecurity relies heavily on software tools that are used to protect and analyze a network and its traffic, the human in the system is sometimes understated. The human-centric approach to understanding cybersecurity personnel and their aptitude was developed and piloted. This approach leveraged metrics that range from psychological, behavioral, and neuronal measurements. There is a heavy emphasis on visual search since the tools used by IRs tend to include an abundance of text information that requires downselection through search. Overall, our methodology provides a mechanism to acquire a deeper understanding of the characteristics of high performing individuals in cyber security, as well as their impact on incident outcomes. Such understanding could lead to a broad range of capabilities such as:

1. The ability to identify individuals with a high aptitude to excel in the cyber security domain in order to inform recruiting and enhance training.
2. The ability to build a better cyber security workforce that will directly contribute to the crucial task of protecting organizations' information and infrastructure.

2 Design and Instrumentation

2.1 Tracer FIRE

Tracer FIRE is a multi-day training method that uses lectures regarding cybersecurity techniques and tools that culminates in a two-day competitive team event. During the lectures, the participants learn in a classroom setting with hands-on examples of the tools and topics of study. The final days allow students to team up together in groups of up to six students and compete in a challenge-based puzzle game in which the teams must analyze and solve a forensic narrative. During the main event, teams are allowed to allocate challenges to one another or team up to collectively solve aspects of the narrative. Teams are then given points for each of the challenges they solve, in addition to unlocking new content (i.e., challenges).

The Tracer FIRE environment has been used before to study the dynamics of teams including communication and task delegation [1]. But there were problems in comparing performance based on point awards, with questions arising concerning the degree to which points were meaningful and comparable across teams and challenges [2]. The new scenario presented a linear story line, which allowed for teams to be compared against each other. Using this test bed, a number of data collection methods were used: psychological measures for understanding individual decision-making styles as well as team composition; human-machine transaction monitoring of the activity of each team member; eye tracking on a domain-specific task to compare metrics to experts in the field; and EEG assessment of the relationship between memory processes and performance in the cyber exercise.

2.2 Participants

The data collected in the pilot consisted of participants from two separate events. The first Tracer FIRE was for experienced cyber IR professionals and had 9 participants out of 20 that were willing to complete out the psychological measures. It should be noted that the EEG and eye tracking tasks were not available at this time. The second population consisted of student interns in a separate Tracer FIRE exercise. The novice teams were self-selected and ranged from students with limited exposure to cyber security to students that were graduate students specializing in cybersecurity. Some participants volunteered for data collection that occurred within an instrumented training exercise environment, as well as a test battery outside of the exercise setting. For the student exercise, 31 of 40 participants consented to data collection. Of this group, twelve participants agreed to undergo the EEG and eye tracking tasks. Participation in the any of the measures was completely voluntary.

2.3 Eye Tracking

Eye tracking was used to examine if there would be differences between visual search patterns of novice IR personnel compared to experts. The tools used by IRs are mostly text-centric and require the users to scan through vast data in the form of logs files and other visual output. The process of how experts downselect this information tends to be user specific and changes through experience. More experienced users are able to ignore extraneous data, but novice tool users may spend more time inspecting every visual element. Metrics to examine differences included response accuracy, reaction time, and time until first fixation within the region of interest (the area on the screen in which the answer was contained). While the data collected during the Tracer FIRE exercise were only novice information, a subject matter expert provided an "optimal search path" for a notional expert data reference.

Materials. The equipment used in the eye tracking experiments was the Smart Eye Pro 6.0 eye tracking system. This system consisted of a three-camera configuration, which is key to ensuring a large head box since often the text on the screen in many of the cyber tools was small and required the user to lean in towards the screen. This is often a problem with a two-camera system where users can freely move in and out of the head box and camera frame. The SmartEye system recorded raw gaze patterns and sampled at 60 Hz. The raw gaze data was also time synced with the on-screen video recording through the use of EyesDX's Record Manager and Video Streamer software packages. The combined data was then processed in the MAPPS data analysis software for determination of fixations and gaze length.

Procedure. The first task was domain-specific and consisted of ten questions regarding screenshots from common cyber tools used in the field. These screenshots used static images instead of letting the user dynamically operate the software to provide comparable measures of reaction times and eye tracking, making it unnecessary to adjust for on-screen differences. The software tools that were used in this experiment include Network Miner, Wireshark, ENCASE Enterprise, AccessData Registry Viewer, PDF Dissector, and Hex Workshop. Subjects were displayed a question regarding a static screenshot prior to being shown the screenshot. This allowed the subject to read the question and get a preview of what tool was about to be shown. After the subject determined they understood the question, they pressed the space bar, and a one-second fixation cross appeared in the center of the screen. Then, they were presented with a full-screen static image. The image would stay on the screen until the participant pressed a key that corresponding to their answer. All answers were single character answers such as the last number of an IP address or the first letter of a password. This allowed the subject to respond using a single button.

After completing the cyber tools task, subjects were asked to complete a domain-general visual cognitive battery. This battery was developed by Sandia National Laboratories and has been used for research in domains involving visual search such as studies of radar analysts and TSA baggage screeners [11]. The battery includes a mental rotation task, an attentional beam task, a rotation span task, an O/Q visual search task, a T/L discrimination task, and the Sandia Progressive Matrices task.

Preliminary Findings. The preliminary findings suggest that the there are differences between the expert and novice population. The expert reference was based on a subject matter expert that was able to provide an expected gaze path for each of the trials. The novice users often took longer to find the region of interest and were often distracted by extraneous text that drew their attention. Thus, reaction time and time to the first fixation were longer (approximately 3 times on average) in our sample.

2.4 Psychological Measures

Self-report measures allowed quantification of attributes associated with individuals' personality, cognition, and social processes. Using these measures, the gaze search patterns identified by the eye tracking system were compared to the attributes identified by the measures. Three specific attributes were measured, with the general hypothesis that these attributes would differentiate across individual skill level. The following was expected:

- High performing individuals that responded quickly or entered the regions of interest fast would have a higher level of need for cognition, indicating a strong desire to pursue and solve hard problems.
- High performing individuals that answered soon after entering the region of interest would be rational, intuitive decision makers while low performing with individuals eye tracking demonstrating participants entered the region of interest, but failed to answer without first investigating the screen in its entirety, would be avoidant or spontaneous. High performing teams would have higher levels of dependent decision-making style.
- High performing individuals would demonstrate higher levels of conscientious and openness to experience. Roughly half of high performers would be extroverted, indicating that extroversion is not a predictor of performance.

The three assertions were assessed using the following scales. For personality, the Big Five was used. The Big Five Personality Inventory consists of items used to measure neuroticism, agreeableness, conscientiousness, and openness to experience as well as characteristics of extraversion and introversion [3]. Respondents are asked on a Likert scale of 1 to 5 to state how strongly they disagree (1) or agree (5) with a statement about themselves. Example statements are: "Is outgoing, sociable," "Is talkative," and "Is sometimes shy, inhibited." The desire to pursue and solve problems was measured using the Need for Cognition Scale. This is a self-report assessment instrument that quantitatively measures "the tendency for an individual to engage in and enjoy thinking" [4]. Cacioppo and Petty created the Need for Cognition Scale in 1982. The original scale included 34 questions. Two years later, Cacioppo and Petty collaborated with Chuan Feng Kao to shorten the scale to the 18-item format, which is used in the Wabash National Study of Liberal Arts Education. Based on previous research, the Need for Cognition Scale appears to be a valid and reliable measure of individuals' tendencies to pursue and enjoy the process of thinking—that is, of their "need for cognition" [4, 5]. Need for Cognition scores are not influenced by whether an individual is male or female, or by differences in the individual's level of test-taking anxiety or cognitive style (the particular way that an individual accumulates and merges information during the thinking process). In general, scores on the Need for Cognition Scale are not impacted by whether or not the individuals are trying to paint a favorable picture of themselves [4]. Finally, decision-making style was quantified using the General Decision-Making Style inventory (GDMS) [6]. The GDMS measures five different decision-making styles: rational, intuitive, dependent, avoidant and sponta- neous. The instrument has 25 questions (5 items for each dimension) rated on a 5-point Likert-type scale ranging from "strongly disagree" to "strongly agree". The GDMS has been shown to be a reliable and valid scale for assessing decision-making. Reliability (Cronbach's alphas) for the different dimensions vary between 0.62 and 0.87 and patterns of correlations with values, measure of social relations, work conditions and other variables provide convergent validity for the GDMS [7–9].

2.5   Cyber Environment Instrumentation

Instrumenting a highly distributed competitive cyber training exercise, such as Tracer FIRE is fraught with difficulties. First, the distributed nature of the exercise, meaning the fact that much of the target behavior is occurring across networks of multiple machines, means any data collection solution must also be distributed. Second, because it is a competitive environment, data collection solutions must not interfere with the task at hand, nor be presented as a target for attack within the training environment.

Within the Tracer FIRE environment, we chose three distinct targets for behavioral data collection; the individual participant's workstations, the game server from which challenges are obtained, and the news server from which task-relevant contextual information is presented. We outline each instrumentation approach below.

Hyperion. One of the key sources of behavioral data within the cyber environment is the individual actions taken by participants at the machine level. This includes information such as when the user is active, what tools they are using, and how they are using them. To capture this information, we developed a low-level tool called Hyperion. The Hyperion agent is installed on each of the workstations within the Tracer FIRE environment. Hyperion is capable of logging individual keystrokes, mouse clicks, and window switches. In addition, Hyperion has a window-pathing collection method, which generally allows us to understand exactly which part of an application received an event.

Game Server Instrumentation. We couple the low-level behavioral data collected by Hyperion with high-level Tracer FIRE-specific game information by instrumenting the Tracer FIRE game server. This instrumentation provides information such as a team's progress within the training scenario, challenge receipt, and correct and incorrect solutions. This can be linked with Hyperion data to understand what tools and methodologies were being used during specific aspects of the game scenario.

News Server Instrumentation. Another source of data is the news server. The news server provides non-technical information contextual injects throughout the Tracer FIRE scenario in the form of a CNN-like news site (e.g., media claims by a hacktivist organization). This information can be used within the exercise to facilitate the solution of challenges. The news site also contains "red-herring" type information, which can lead teams astray. Our instrumentation collects when a news article becomes available within the scenario and when a participant actually accesses the information. This information can be correlated with game server and Hyperion data to better understand the impact of outside information on team performance.

Preliminary Findings. Analysis of the cyberspace specific behavioral data is still ongoing. However, initial analysis of the first Tracer FIRE data indicates that there may be a relationship between an increased use of general-purpose tools, such as command-line and scripting tools, and performance in the Tracer FIRE exercise [10]. We hypothesize that one aspect of expertise within cyber security may be knowing the limitations of existing cyber security-specific tools, and knowing when to use general purpose tools to "do it yourself." These findings will then be compared to see if a relationship between tool use, eye tracking gaze patterns, and personality style exists.

2.6   Electroencephalography (EEG)

The EEG task used in this experiment was a recognition memory task that incorporated repeated and quizzed items. Prior research has shown that the amplitude of event-related potential (ERP) repetition effects elicited by repeated words can indicate whether or not an individual is using an effective learning strategy and can be predictive of future memory performance [12]. Participants with larger repetition effects, indicative of self-quizzing, outperform participants with smaller repetition effects, indicative of more passive study strategies. We hypothesized that participants who used effective learning strategies on a simple memory test would also be high performers on the cyber security training tasks.

Materials. The materials for the memory task consisted of 255 common English nouns. They were divided into 16 counterbalanced study/test lists such that every word appeared in every condition. During the study block, each participant studied 30 words that were presented once, 15 words that were presented and then repeated after a short lag (one intervening item), 30 words that were repeated after a long lag (nine intervening items), 15 words that were studied once and then quizzed after a short lag, 30 words that were quizzed after a long lag, and 45 words that were quizzed but had not been studied previously in the list. After the study block, participants took a short break before beginning the test block. On the test block, participants were tested on all of the studied words (120 total), plus 90 new, unstudied words.

Procedure. A fixation cross appeared in the center of the screen throughout the experiment. Participants were asked to fixate on the cross and to avoid blinking or moving their eyes during the presentation of a word. Prior to the presentation of a study word, a yellow dot appeared above the fixation cross for one second. This was a cue to the participant, indicating that he or she should prepare to memorize a word. Prior to the presentation of a quiz word (during the study block) or a test word (during the test block), a red dot appeared. This meant that participants would be asked to respond to the next word, indicating whether or not they believed they had studied that word previously. After the dot disappeared, the word appeared above the fixation cross. The interval between the disappearance of the dot and the appearance of the word varied randomly between 600 and 800 ms. The word remained on the screen for one second. On quiz and test trials, the word was followed by a question mark. The question mark remained on the screen until the participants pressed a button on the keyboard to indicate their response (yes or no). The next trial began after 250 ms. EEG was recorded using a 16-channel Emotiv headset, a widely-available consumer-grade EEG headset with electrodes soaked in saline solution.

Preliminary Findings. The behavioral results of the memory test were consistent with prior studies. Participants had the lowest memory for words that were only studied once. They had improved memory for the words that were repeated during study, and the best memory performance for words that were quizzed during study. However, the EEG signal from the Emotiv headset proved to be too noisy to extract useable ERPs. The repetition effect is relatively small and it typically centered over the top of the scalp. The position of the Emotiv electrodes and the signal-to-noise ratio were insufficient for calculating the magnitude of the repetition effects. In future research, a lab-grade EEG system with electrodes on the top of the scalp would be needed to test our ERP hypotheses.

3   Discussion

The preliminary findings and data collection proved that it is feasible to perform in situ testing on cybersecurity individuals while performing domain-specific tasks. These strategies can be leveraged to then compare and contrast difference between high- and low-performers to understand if there are different attributes associated with each group. While some testing, such as EEG, may be suited better for isolated testing outside of the main operations location, others metrics can be collected in real-time to assess behavior, strategy, and teaming dynamics.

While the data collection was mostly focused on the individual, team dynamics can be understood using the answer submissions of each team and its members. However, it was noted that attribution of action is essential to understand if the behavior that is collected under user screen name is what had actually occurred in the scenario or if the other users were operating the keyboard under someone else's name. If the correct data is collected, the team composition and cohesion could be assessed such that personnel with similar decision-making styles are paired together to ensure positive social outcomes. However, with a larger sample of experts, there may be a need to disperse and intermingle the different psychological styles assessed in the self-report measures for optimal success.

For future data collection, the team seeks to acquire more physiological and behavioral data from experts to further compare the differences in the novice data set. For instance, using the SME-generated gaze patterns was enough to provide interesting anecdotal evidence of differences, with a large population of experienced cyber defenders and incident responders, the appropriate statistical measures could be calculated. The combination of all the measurements during the same domain-specific task would also enable more robust comparison of how visual search styles may be related to various neural and behavioral activity in the task.

Acknowledgments. Sandia National Laboratories is a multi-program laboratory managed and operated by Sandia Corporation, a wholly owned subsidiary of Lockheed Martin Corporation, for the U.S. Department of Energy's National Nuclear Security Administration under Contract DE-AC04-94AL85000, Sandia Report SAND2015-1796 C.

References

1. Stevens-Adams, S., Carbajal, A., Silva, A., Nauer, K., Anderson, B., Reed, T., Forsythe, C.: Enhanced training for cyber situational awareness. In: Schmorrow, D.D., Fidopiastis, C.M. (eds.) AC 2013. LNCS, vol. 8027, pp. 90–99. Springer, Heidelberg (2013)
2. Reed, T., Nauer, K., Silva, A.: Instrumenting competition-based exercises to evaluate cyber defender situation awareness. In: Schmorrow, D.D., Fidopiastis, C.M. (eds.) AC 2013. LNCS, vol. 8027, pp. 80–89. Springer, Heidelberg (2013)

3. Benet-Martínez, V., John, O.P.: Los Cinco Grandes across cultures and ethnic groups: multitrait-multimethod analyses of the big five in Spanish and English. J. Pers. Soc. Psychol. **75**(3), 729–750 (2013)

4. Cacioppo, J.T., Petty, R.E., Feng Kao, C.: The efficient assessment of need for cognition. J. Pers. Assess. **48**(3), 306–307 (1984)

5. Cacioppo, J.T., Petty, R.E., Feinstein, J.A., Jarvis, W.B.G.: Dispositional differences in cognitive motivation: the life and times of individuals varying in need for cognition. Psychol. Bull. **119**(2), 197–253 (1996)

6. Scott, S.G., Bruce, R.A.: Decision-making style: the development and assessment of a new measure. Educ. Psychol. Measur. **55**(5), 818–831 (1995)

7. Loo, R.: A psychometric evaluation of the general decision-making style inventory. Personality Individ. Differ. **29**(5), 895–905 (2000)

8. Spicer, D.P., Sadler-Smith, E.: An examination of the general decision making style questionnaire in two UK samples. J. Manage. Psychol. **20**(2), 137–149 (2005)

9. Thunholm, P.: Decision-making styles and physiological correlates of negative stress: is there a relation? Scand. J. Psychol. **49**(3), 213–219 (2008)

10. Silva, A., McClain, J., Reed, T., Anderson, B., Nauer, K., Abbott, R., Forsythe, C.: Factors impacting performance in competitive cyber exercises. In: Proceedings of the Interservice/Industry Training, Simulation and Education Conference (I/ITSEC2014) (2014)

11. Matzen, L.E.: Effects of professional visual search experience on domain-general and domain-specific visual. Paper presented at the HCI International, Los Angeles, CA (2015)

12. Haass, M.J., Matzen, L.E.: Using computational modeling to assess use of cognitive strategies. In: Schmorrow, D.D., Fidopiastis, C.M. (eds.) FAC 2011. LNCS, vol. 6780, pp. 77–86. Springer, Heidelberg (2011)

Bracketing Human Performance to Support Automation for Workload Reduction: A Case Study

Robert E. Wray[✉], Benjamin Bachelor, Randolph M. Jones,
and Charles Newton

Soar Technology, Inc., 3600 Green Court Suite 600, Ann Arbor, MI 48105, USA
{wray,ben.bachelor,rjones,
charles.newton}@soartech.com

Abstract. Semi-automated Forces (SAFs) are commonly used in training simulation. SAFs often require human intervention to ensure that appropriate, individual training opportunities are presented to trainees. We cast this situation as a supervisory control challenge and are developing automation designed to support human operators, reduce workload, and improve training outcomes. This paper summarizes a combined analytic and empirical verification study that identified specific situations in the overall space of possible scenarios where automation may be particularly helpful. By bracketing "high performance" and "low performance" conditions, this method illuminates salient points in the space of operational performance for future human-in-the-loop studies.

Keywords: Simulation-based training · Semi-automated forces · Cognitive workload

1 Introduction

Semi-automated Forces (SAFs) are commonly used in training simulation to represent the behavior of enemy, friendly, and neutral entities within the training exercise. Most SAFs in current simulations are adaptive to the doctrinal context of the mission, such as the application of appropriate tactics in the situation. However, they are typically unaware of the learning context, such as the current training objectives, the estimated level of skills of the trainee, and assessment of trainee actions, relative to the training objectives, as the scenario progresses.

When there is a mismatch in the appropriate tactical decision and the learning context, human intervention is required. For example, a pilot trainee might be expected to achieve or demonstrate specific competencies within a defined training event. As a consequence, human intervention during the simulation to enable achievement of training objectives is often a requirement for effective training.

When variation from pre-programmed SAF behavior is appropriate, whether to reflect real-world situations or to reinforce instruction (e.g., consequences of an error), the instructor must recognize this need, choose a course of action, and then issue direction to operators. The instructor desires to control or "steer" the training scenario

D.D. Schmorrow and C.M. Fidopiastis (Eds.): AC 2015, LNAI 9183, pp. 153–163, 2015.
DOI: 10.1007/978-3-319-20816-9_16

toward particular milestones and outcomes. The instructor has, by design, limited control over the trainee, so a dynamic control process is needed to adjust scenario evolution in response to trainee actions.

For tactical aircraft pilot training, we have developed an instructional support tool, the Training Executive Agent (TXA), designed to facilitate and simplify this control problem [1]. This paper describes the results of a software verification experiment to evaluate the functionality of the TXA. The primary goal of the study was to compare the relative quality of training experiences without and with the TXA as scenario complexity increased. In conjunction with this empirical evaluation, analytic methods were used to estimate anticipated operator workload over routine and non-routine control profiles. Together, the results provide high-end and low-end expectations (brackets) for human-in-the-loop experimentation. The importance of this bracketing it helps to identify salient points in a large space of possible training scenarios and differing complexities to sample for actual human-in-the-loop experimentation. We describe goals, methodology and results and consider the potential value of this combination of analytic and empirical methods in the design of supervisory control systems more generally.

2 Context and Motivation

As suggested above, today's training typically requires some direct human control of SAFs to achieve desired training outcomes. SAFs are reactive to the doctrinal context of the mission. However, they unaware of the learning context, such as the current training objectives, the estimated level of skills of the trainee, and an assessment of actions, relative to the training objectives, as the scenario progresses. When there is a mismatch in the tactical context and learning context, human intervention is required. For example, a pilot trainee is expected to achieve or demonstrate specific competencies within a defined training event. As a consequence, human manipulation of the simulation to enable the presentation of situations appropriate for the training objectives is a critical part of the training: a missed bogey (enemy aircraft) may be manually relocated to support a trainee's inefficient or misdirected radar search to ensure that the trainee also has an opportunity to engage ("intercept") the bogey; an extra bogey may be inserted to challenge a trainee that is excelling in demonstrating basic intercept tactics.

When deviation from the pre-programmed SAF behavior is appropriate, the instructor must recognize this need, choose a course of action, and then issue tell operators to modify the simulation. From a control perspective, the instructor desires to drive the training scenario toward particular milestones and outcomes. The instructor has, by design, limited control over the trainee, so a dynamic control process is needed to adjust scenario evolution in response to trainee actions. Further, the simulation presents only a tactical summary of the situation to the instructor, which requires the instructor to maintain a separate mental representation of the learning context and possible implications of the current situation on the learning context.

From this assessment, the instructor determines which adjustments are necessary and acts to execute them. In the operational training context, the recommended adjustments are verbally communicated to a human operator who then issues command to individual

SAFs, monitors their execution, and makes low-level adjustments to behavior. A consequence of this distribution of control, however, is that the operators may not necessarily understand the intent of the instructor's directives because the learning context that motivates the adjustments may remain implicit (e.g., not verbalized).

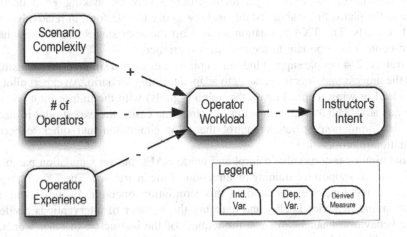

Fig. 1. Summary of relationships between independent and dependent variables for constructive simulation.

From this perspective, the targeted functions of the TXA are two-fold. First, it provides a more explicit representation of the scenario and learning context to the instructor and operator. Second, it shifts the manual control process for individual SAFs to a supervisory control process [2] in which an operator (or instructor/operator) uses the summary information from the TXA to make comparatively infrequent or periodic adjustments to the system via a higher-level action representation. In this role, the TXA acts as a mediator or controller of individual SAFs, similar to the role of a real-time strategy game player [3]. However, unlike previous SAF control approaches, the TXA makes decisions and recommendations based on both the tactical situation (as do most controllers do) and the learning context (uncommon).

The hypothesized relationships between human-control variables in the context of constructive simulation are illustrated abstractly in Fig. 1. We assume that quality of training is consonant with meeting instructor intent; that is, if the training scenario delivers the experiences that the instructor intends to deliver, the training experience is high quality. Meeting instructor intent is negatively correlated with operator workload: as workload increases, the ability of the overall system to match instructor intent decreases. Operator workload is itself a dependent variable. It positively correlates (goes up) with scenario complexity, and it negatively correlates with number of operators and operator experience.

3 Experimental Goals and Methodology

The primary use case for TXA testing and evaluation is a current U.S. Navy program of instruction. The training focuses on teaching new pilots (i.e., pilots recently graduated flight school) how to fly a specific platform. The initial stages of training focus on cockpit familiarization; later stages focus progressively on making good decisions relative to the platform capabilities; that is, how to use the platform in relatively simple tactical contexts. The TXA evaluation focuses on the later stages of training where a mission context is important to the training experience.

Currently, 2–4 people support individual pilot training in a simulation. An instructor guides the process and directs operators to adapt a training scenario. An expert pilot may fly as a lead or wing (depending on the training goals) with the trainee pilot when the trainee has advanced to section-level tactics. In some cases, the expert pilot is also the instructor. Simulation operators control the pilot simulation and other technology coordination/interoperation.

Simulation operator(s) also control and guide SAFs and set simulation parameters and variables to support the training (at direction of the instructor). The TXA is targeted primarily at reducing the workload of this simulation operator, by improving mis-sionization and behavior fidelity and reducing the number of interventions needed to achieve behavioral changes made at the request of the instructor. In other words, the TXA should enable a high span of control while maintaining high scenario quality/satisfy instructor's intent. The TXA is not designed to improve the fidelity that can be provided by human operators but rather provide force multiplication for the operator, making it possible for a human operator to maintain high levels of scenario quality in more complex scenarios than is currently feasible with manual control.

We conducted a software test evaluation to begin to assess the specific relationships illustrated in Fig. 1. We assumed in this initial test design that the number of available

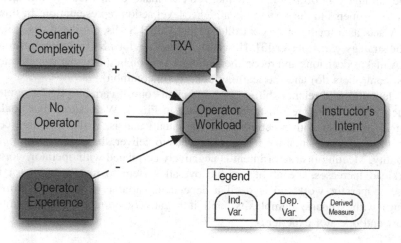

Fig. 2. The TXA is hypothesized to reduce workload and improve the ability of the training system to meet instructor's intent.

operators and the level of operator experience/capability are scarce resources that cannot be significantly improved without increasing training costs. The implication then is that increased scenario complexity will increase operator workload, which in turn will decrease presentation quality (match with instructor intent), thus decreasing overall training quality.

The further hypothesis is that the TXA's functions will positively influence the quality of presentation or match to instructor intent (Fig. 2). By providing operators and instructors with high-level control actions, operator workload will decrease which will improve (or maintain) presentation quality.

We manipulated scenario complexity as the primary independent variable. To conduct actual tests, we developed 20 aviation-training scenarios, reflecting differences in subjective complexity as determined by subject matter experts. Each test case scenario was composed from individual setups, representing tactical situations one might encounter in a training program and the training goals associated with each scenario. For example, in the example in Fig. 3, the training goal is to give the trainee (blue pilot) the experience of combating two distinct groups of aggressor (red) aircraft. The instructor's goal is to present these groups as two successive but independent engagements for the trainee.

For each setup, we had subject matter experts define criteria for assessing the overall quality of the training experience as presented to a trainee. For example, in the situation illustrated in Fig. 3, maintaining some distance between the groups is

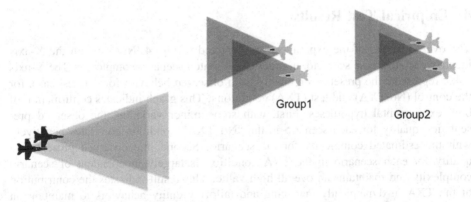

Fig. 3. Experimental testcases are composed from relatively simple tactical situations

important, but the trailing group needs to remain close enough to the blue aircraft that when the first engagement is completed the trainee has the experience of a "successive" engagement. Subject matter experts provided specific criteria and parameters. We used a scenario monitoring tool, the Goal Constraint System [4] to encode these criteria and automatically "score" individual setups.

We then developed (simple) computational models of trainees, representing "normal" or expected trainee actions and "novice" trainee actions that could diverge from the pre-programmed scenario assumptions. For example, in the situation illustrated in

Fig. 3, a "normal" trainee would directly engage the first group. A "novice" trainee might take doctrinally unnecessary evasive action to attempt to separate the two groups. The role of these models is to provide some sampling of the variation one might expect to encounter in the training program.

Finally, based on the setups and testcases, we developed analytic models of the workload demands for each setup. We used the Goals, Operators, Methods, and Selection Rules (GOMS) modeling paradigm [5, 6]. We developed a methodology and estimates of workload for each setup and testcase [7]. For the purposes of this paper, the results of this analysis provided estimates of the time it would take an operator to monitor a setup and to intervene under certain anomalous conditions. Table 1 summarizes the prediction for the setup illustrated in Fig. 3. It says the minimum amount of time the operator can attend to the setup and it remain close to 100 % of its performance quality is about 22 s over the course of 1 min of execution time. Based on this lower bound, the analysis tells us that the operator could successfully manage up to two of these setups simultaneously (i.e., managing three setups perfectly would require 66 s of operator monitoring and action/minute).

Table 1. Example operator performance bounds predicted by GOMS for Fig. 3 setup

	Lower bound	Max. number of manageable setups
Successive intercepts	22.2 s	2

4 Empirical Test Results

The overall results of the experiment are depicted in Fig. 4. Numbers on the X-axis identify each test case scenario, in order of estimated scenario complexity. The Y-axis value represents the presentation quality from observed behavior for that test case, for the control (No TXA) and test (TXA) conditions. This graph indicates confirmation of both experimental hypotheses. First, with some minor variation, the observed presentation quality for each scenario in the "No TXA" condition correlates negatively with the estimated complexity for the scenario. Second, the observed presentation quality for each scenario in the TXA condition is largely independent of scenario complexity and maintains an overall high value. This result indicates the contribution of the TXA in dynamically managing and tailoring entity behaviors to maintain an instructor's goal for the exercise in response to variations (e.g., mistakes) in trainee actions.

Figure 5 presents the experimental results organized by estimated complexity. These figures also contain the quantitative presentation quality scores omitted in Fig. 4. For these summaries, we divided the test-case results into three categories. Low complexity test cases are those test cases that we predict a human operator would find manageable to perform the same types of tailoring as the TXA performed to maintain high presentation qualities. That is, in a future experiment with humans in the loop, we predict human performance to be comparable to automated TXA performance.

We predict medium complexity scenarios to be near the edge of manageability for human operators. We predict that human operators would, for the most part, not be able

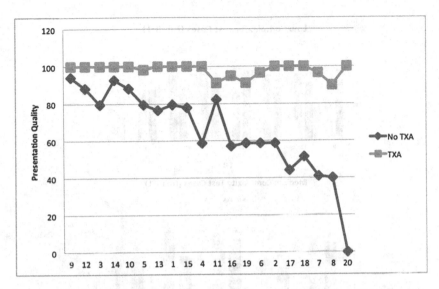

Fig. 4. Overall summary of the verification results with and without TXA automation

to produce the same quality of presentation as TXA is able to produce, for these test cases, although human performance results in this band may differ widely based on expertise and innate capacities. However, high complexity test cases are predicted to be of such significant complexity that they are completely beyond the abilities of human operators to manage them. We predict low presentation quality scores by human operators for these scenarios.

We see that relatively high quality scores are observed even without the assistance of the TXA for the low-complexity scenarios (Fig. 5a). For the medium-complexity scenarios, we see larger differences in presentation quality for most of the scenarios (Fig. 5b). For the high-complexity scenarios, there is a significantly large difference in quality between the No TXA and TXA conditions (Fig. 5c). The most complex scenario (Scenario 20) produces the worst possible quality score in the No TXA condition, and the best possible quality score in the TXA condition.

5   Bracketing for Human-in-the-Loop Experimentation

The results of these experiments suggest some potential value of automation. However, comparing a system that requires intervention to achieve its goals without the means to deploy interventions, as in the "No TXA" case, offers little insight for estimating the operational impact of the automation. Further, replicating this experiment with human operators, across all the scenarios, would be prohibitively costly. Instead, we can combine the empirical results and some additional analysis using the GOMS approach to attempt to "bracket" expected human performance. This bracketing heuristic is adopted from Kieras and Meyer [8]. The intention is that the GOMS analysis provides a priori predictions of expected performance across the range of scenarios. We can then

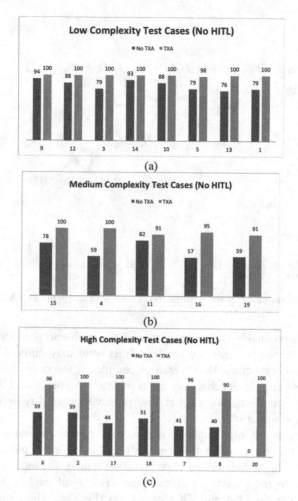

Fig. 5. Quantitative experimental results for low-complexity test cases (a), medium-complexity (b) and high complexity (c).

choose specific scenarios to test the predictions. But we choose scenarios that would also help most fully contrast the impact of automation without exploring the full set of scenarios.

Figure 1 illustrated the prediction that a training scenario's presentation quality will decrease as the estimate of the operator's workload increases for a particular scenario. However, there is a "workload threshold" below which the operator will be able to maintain a close to perfect presentation quality. We would like to determine where this threshold occurs because testing scenarios "below the threshold" is unlikely to show much value for automation. According to the GOMS analysis, this threshold can be determined primarily by "the number of times an operator switches attention between setups." This specific value for any individual is dependent on the switching strategy they choose for that individual testcase as well as operator expertise and tendencies. For

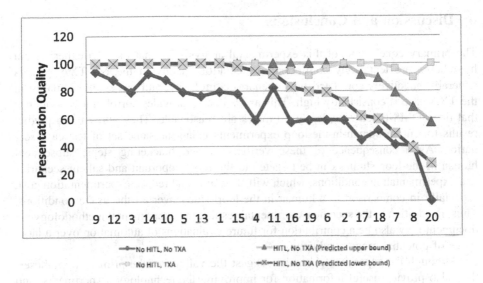

Fig. 6. Bracketing predictions of expected human performance

example, some operators might cycle deliberately thru each testcase while others might attempt to anticipate time-critical events in individual setups. These factors are targets for a future more refined GOMS analysis.

Rather than attempt to explicitly model the impact of these different strategies (as is done by Kieras and Meyer), we instead generated thresholds based on pilot-study observations of operator performance (both on the test cases and more generally). Figure 6 illustrates the predicted operator performance bracket from the GOMS analysis for the "No TXA" condition. The brackets were generated from the workload analysis illustrated in Table 1. The upper bound assumes that an operator can perfectly use all available time (60 s). Thus, if a testcase with three setups had limits of 20 s, 30 s, and 10 s, the upper bound assumes that the operator would manage all of these cases without error. We expect that most operators will use some time within each minute to perform switching. Thus, this upper bound is likely to be liberal in its estimate of operator performance. The lower bound assumes that the operator is half as efficient as the high bound (30 s of work per 60 s of simulation time).

The brackets suggest that even for the "medium" complexity cases, some operators may be able to maintain very high presentation quality. Pilot studies focused on test cases between 11 and 6 (11, 16, 19, 6) should help to determine how optimistic the upper performance bound is and localize the actual "bend in the curve" in human performance data. Our expectation is that the operator's sense of subjective workload would be quite high under these conditions in comparison to the low workload conditions, even if presentation quality differences were not evident. As they stand prior to any pilot testing, the brackets suggest that human in the loop studies should focus primarily on the high complexity cases. Further, we should work with subject matter experts to evaluate points in the curriculum that require or would benefit from presentation of scenarios with comparable levels of complexity.

6 Discussion and Conclusions

The primary conclusions of this experimental analysis are that the two experimental hypotheses are tentatively confirmed: presentation quality in the No TXA case is generally negatively correlated with scenario complexity, and presentation quality in the TXA case is consistently high. This analysis also provides corroborative evidence that the GOMS-based complexity estimates are reasonable. They allow us to predict results for future human-in-the-loop experiments using the same set of test-case scenarios. As a consequence of these verification and bracketing steps, subsequent human-in-the-loop studies can be targeted to the most important and salient scenarios and experimentation conditions, which will save time and reduce experimentation cost, especially in comparison to a human-in-the-loop study over all the usage conditions. Thus, in addition to the specific experimental results, the experimental methodology we document may also be a contribution for future evaluations of automation over a large space of potential usage conditions.

Although the experimental results suggest the validity of the primary hypotheses, they also provide useful information for improving the technology, experiments, and analyses in future work. For example, the quality measures in the experimental results do not completely correlate with the test-case complexity scores. It is not necessarily the case that these two measures must correlate, but the fact that there are inconsistencies between the mappings and the subsequent results point to potential opportunities to examine assumptions. These assumptions include the criteria for scoring presentation quality, as well as assumptions about estimating scenario complexity. Although we worked with SMEs to generate the presentation quality criteria, the rationale for some of the scoring formulas was not always straightforward. For example, we conceived of presentation quality as a continuous function, but some types of setups are more "binary" in nature ("perfect" or "unacceptable" was the way the SME framed the scoring in this case). Because there are both "binary" and "continuous" forms of presentation quality in the setups, some additional effort to analyze the qualitative differences between these two classes of setups may be justified, which would potentially result in refinements to the scoring criteria. Additionally, we should further analyze the question of whether presentation quality ought to correlate negatively with scenario complexity in all cases. It may be that complexity and cognitive workload manifest themselves in different ways for different types of setups.

Acknowledgments. This work is supported by the Office of Naval Research project N00014-1-C-0170 Tactical Semi-Automated Forces for Live, Virtual, and Constructive Training (TACSAF). The views and conclusions contained in this document are those of the authors and should not be interpreted as representing the official policies, either expressed or implied, of the Department of Defense or Office of Naval Research. The U.S. Government is authorized to reproduce and distribute reprints for Government purposes notwithstanding any copyright notation hereon. We would like to thank collaborators and sponsors at NAWC TSD and ONR who have provided insights and operational perspectives in the development of TXA: LCDR Brent Olde, Ami Bolton, Melissa Walwanis, and Heather Priest.

References

1. Wray, R.E., Woods, A.: A cognitive systems approach to tailoring learner practice. In: Laird, J., Klenk, M. (eds.) Proceedings of the Second Advances in Cognitive Systems Conference, Baltimore, MD (2013)
2. Sheridan, T.B.: Humans and Automation: System Design and Research Issues. Wiley, New York (2002)
3. Wray, R.E., van Lent, M., Beard, J.T., Brobst, P.: The design space of control options for AIs in computer games. In: IJCAI 2005 Workshop on Reasoning, Representation, and Learning in Computer Games, pp. 113–118. US Naval Research Laboratory (2005)
4. Jones, R.M., Bachelor, B., Stacy, W., Colonna-Romano, J.: Automated monitoring and evaluation of expected behavior. In: International Conference on Artificial Intelligence, Las Vegas (in preparation)
5. John, B.E.: Why GOMS? Interactions 2, 80–89 (1995)
6. John, B.E., Kieras, D.E.: The GOMS family of user interface analysis techniques: comparison and contrast. ACM Trans. Comput. Hum. Interact. 3, 320–351 (1996)
7. Jones, R.M., Wray, R.E., Bachelor, B., Zaientz, J.: Using cognitive workload analysis to predict and mitigate workload for training simulation. In: Proceedings of the Applied Human Factors and Ergonomics Conference 2015, Las Vegas (2015)
8. Kieras, D.E., Meyer, D.E.: The role of cognitive task analysis in the application of predictive models of human performance. In: Schraagen, J.M.C., Chipman, S.E., Shalin, V.L. (eds.) Cognitive Task Analysis. Lawrence Erlbaum, Mahwah, NJ (2000)

References

1. Wray, R.E., Woolley, B.: [illegible] cognitive [illegible] approach to [illegible] performance. In: [illegible] Proceedings of the Second Annual Conference on Advances in Cognitive Systems, Baltimore, MD (2013)
2. Sheridan, T.B.: Humans and Automation: System Design and Research Issues. Wiley, New York (2002)
3. Wray, R.E., [illegible] [illegible] in computer games. In: IJCAI 2009 Workshop on Representation and Learning in Computer Games, [illegible] U.S. Naval Research Laboratory (2009)
4. Jones, R.M., [illegible]: Automated [illegible] and [illegible] of [illegible]. In: [illegible] Conference on Artificial Intelligence, Las Vegas, [illegible]
5. [illegible] (1995)
6. John, B.E., Kieras, D.E.: The GOMS family of user interface analysis techniques: comparison and contrast. ACM Trans. Comput. Hum. Interact. 3, [illegible] (1996)
7. [illegible], R.E., Bach, L., [illegible]: [illegible] in [illegible] and [illegible] Simulation. In: Proceedings of the Applied Human Factors and Ergonomics Conference 2015, Las Vegas (2015)
8. [illegible]: The [illegible] of cognitive task analysis [illegible] of the application of cognitive models of human performance. In: [illegible], J.M., Chipman, S.F., Shalin, V.L. (eds.) Cognitive Task Analysis. Lawrence Erlbaum, Mahwah, NJ (2000)

BCI and Operational Neuroscience

Phylter: A System for Modulating Notifications in Wearables Using Physiological Sensing

Daniel Afergan[✉], Samuel W. Hincks, Tomoki Shibata, and Robert J.K. Jacob

Tufts University, Medford, MA 02155, USA
{afergan,shincks,tshibata,jacob}@cs.tufts.edu

Abstract. As wearable computing becomes more mainstream, it holds the promise of delivering timely, relevant notifications to the user. However, these devices can potentially inundate the user, distracting them at the wrong times and providing the wrong amount of information. As physiological sensing also becomes consumer-grade, it holds the promise of helping to control these notifications. To solve this, we build a system Phylter that uses physiological sensing to modulate notifications to the user. Phylter receives streaming data about a user's cognitive state, and uses this to modulate whether the user should receive the information. We discuss the components of the system and how they interact.

Keywords: fNIRS · Adaptive interfaces · Brain-computer interfaces · Google glass

1 Introduction

Wearable technology such as Google Glass has the capability to capture and deliver information to its user with an immediacy that surpasses the current generation of input/output devices. Combined with Google Now, Search, and a rich store of personalized, situation-sensitive data, the capability to swiftly display information enables a new genre of consumer grade human-computer interaction, where the computer ceases to be the focus, and instead becomes an inconspicuous assistant to ordinary activities. But this immediacy and amalgamation with the user carries a steep price when the bond is broken with an untimely interruption.

Delivering information at the wrong moment or delivering the wrong information for the user's current situation can disrupt work or social interactions, and exacerbate the very problems that wearables such as Glass might solve. Muting all notifications is an option, but frequent manual muting and unmuting would itself be disruptive. Instead imagine a "magic" knob that is driven by the moment-to-moment measured interruptibility of a user. As such, Glass may attain the sweet spot of being actively informative without being overly obtrusive. It would deliver notifications to users precisely when they have the time and capacity to perceive them. For example, it would be capable of prioritizing

D.D. Schmorrow and C.M. Fidopiastis (Eds.): AC 2015, LNAI 9183, pp. 167–177, 2015.
DOI: 10.1007/978-3-319-20816-9_17

incoming emails or social network messages to present the most important items first and defer others to a more opportune time; it could also summarize or suppress lower level detail display such as those on a map when it detects that the user is busy. However, high-priority notifications that might be important regardless of state can bypass this filter and be shown to the user immediately. In a dual-task scenario, this system can let the user focus on a primary task and only interrupt the user to work on another task when it detects the user can handle the additional effort.

This paper introduces a physiological-based notification filtering system, Phylter, that sends pertinent notifications to a user only when the user is in the proper cognitive state to handle additional information. The system uses physiological sensing as a means to time, suppress, and modulate information streams in real time. We posit that *functional near-infrared spectroscopy (fNIRS)*, a lightweight brain-monitoring technology, has promise to control this framework because of its access to measures of blood flow in the brain, an overarching barometer of the user's level of cognitive workload – the degree to which present engagements have posed computational demands on short term working memory. Using machine learning algorithms trained to distinguish known instances of high cognitive workload and low cognitive workload exclusively from fNIRS data, our brain-augmented Glass prototype distinguishes the neural signature of its user's state of short-term memory cognitive workload and applies this knowledge to capitalize on the most opportune moments to deliver information.

2   Related Work

2.1   Short-Term Memory Workload and Interruptions

In the age of mobile computing and social media, interruptions from e-mail [17], instant messages [7], and other services which are granted unsupervised access to the browser, cell phone, or wearable computer's output threaten to destabilize a user's ability to focus on a singular task. In one study by Bailey and Constan, multitasking participants reported twice the anxiety, committed twice the number of errors, and required up to 25 % longer time on a primary task when interruptions arrived during rather than in-between tasks [5]. To mitigate the costs of interruption, research has explored a breakpoint-based method for mediating notifications in which statistical models infer likely points of transition between tasks and schedule notifications for these moments [15]. But this method requires complete knowledge about all of the user's concurrent tasks, and assume that the sum of the user's cognition can be understood within the digital environment. The second assumption, in particular, loses validity in a wearable computing context – where the interface is no longer the main object of the user's attention. Horvitz and and Apacible devised a mathematical model of the cost and utility of interruptions, but their model assumes knowledge of the attentional state of the user and the the utility of interruption [13].

In cognitive science, working memory refers to the mental resources dedicated to storage, retrieval, and manipulation of information on a short timescale – measured in seconds, not minutes. It is involved in higher cognitive processes such as language, planning, learning and reasoning [3]. Some of the most popular models of working memory [29,39] posit that the system operates under severe constraints with competition for the limited pool of resources for the numerous tasks that might at any moment engage it. A task pushing the upper-bound of working memory's phonological loop (the working memory component engaged by subvocal mental rehearsal) may not directly undermine the processing done by the visuospatial sketchpad (another component for visual simulation and recall), but, drawing from a common pool of computational resources, two simultaneous working memory tasks nonetheless limits overall performance. Cognitive workload is dependent on the characteristics of the task, of the operator, and of the environment [40]. Working memory and executive function engage areas in the prefrontal cortex, and the amount of activation increases as a function of the number of items held in WM [23].

Research has explored the interruptibility of a user through physiological input such as heart rate variability and EEG [6] and pupil dilation [4,16]. In these studies, the physiological sensor is calibrated to detect cognitive workload, as it has long been acknowledged that moments of low cognitive workload present the most opportune time for interruptions [21], in part since workload diminishes at task-boundaries [4]. Tremoulet et al. found that by queuing questions and alerts until the user is in a state of low workload (measured by EEG, heart rate, and galvanic skin response), they could increase the number of tasks that the user could complete, reduce error rate, and also decrease decision making time for the interrupting alert tasks [37].

2.2 Passive Brain-Computer Interfaces

Passive physiological interfaces portray the user's present state of mind without continuously involved human effort. As such, they can supplement direct input with implicit input (derived from a physiological sensor attached to the user) and apply gleanable information to trigger adaptations that aid the user's short-term or long-term goals. When the underlying physiological interface measures brain activity, these systems, known as passive or implicit brain-computer interfaces (BCIs), benefit the user by deducing state without additional effort on their part. In contrast to the much wider usage of brain sensors in active BCIs (where the user consciously manipulates mental activity in order to trigger an intended command) [41], passive BCIs support a practical defense mechanism towards inevitable physiological misclassifications and the small-but-not-negligible lag-time between the physical manifestation of a thought and the deliverable command [8].

In controlled experiments, real-time passive BCIs have proven to yield measurable improvements to users' performance compared to static counterparts. Prinzel et al. used EEG signals to modulate levels of automation in simultaneous auditory and hand-eye coordination tasks [28] and Wilson and Russell used an EEG engagement index to decelerate UAVs or present alerts depending on what would most effectively sustain the user's focus. Stripling et al. built a system where an operator could create rules for the user's physiological state that triggered pre-recorded macros in order to manipulate a virtual environment when physiological conditions were met [36]. Recently, real-time adaptive systems have used passive fNIRS input to modify robot autonomy [33], control a movie recommendation engine [24], and modify the number of UAVs for an operator [1].

2.3 FNIRS

Propelled primarily by scientific and medical motives, brain monitors have improved dramatically in price-performance and resolution, and two devices, distinguished by their relative non-invasiveness and ease-of-use, have trickled into the field of Human-Computer Interaction, initially serving a small but significant community of disabled users. The more common tool for brain-computer interfacing, electroencephalography (EEG) provides a measurement of neuroelectrical firing in large populations of neurons situated by the scalp. EEG has high temporal resolution and is reliable for measuring responses to quick stimuli, but has low spatial resolution and suffers from motion artifacts as its reliability in depicting actual cognitive activity is undermined when the user is moving (Fig. 1).

Fig. 1. An fNIRS sensor with light sources and a detector.

As an alternative, functional near-infrared spectroscopy (fNIRS) measures blood-oxygenation levels in neural tissue as deep as 3 cm. The technique relies on the fact that infrared light penetrates bone and other tissues but is absorbed and scattered by oxygenated and deoxygenated hemoglobin. Conveniently, the optical properties of oxygenated and deoxygenated hemoglobin differ, and so, the relative proportion of the two can be deduced by the infrared light returned to the detector [38]. It measures the same blood-oxygenation level-dependent signal as fMRI [35], but only measures the part of the brain where the sensor is applied. FNIRS has high spatial resolution, but because the changes in blood flow take several seconds to reach the brain, fNIRS is not suitable for direct input. Instead, fNIRS can portray more stable trends in the users mental state, and can be used to distinguish workload levels [9,12] or multitasking [2,33].

In many cases, fNIRS continues to provide moderate descriptions of its wearer's brain even when the user is in motion. Head movements, heartbeats, and respiration can be corrected with filters, and standard computer-interactions like typing and clicking do not interfere with the signal [10,19,32]. FNIRS sensors consist primarily of multiple infrared light sources (at two wavelengths to detect oxygenated and deoxygenated hemoglobin) and detectors, usually attached to a processing unit by fiber-optic cables. With advancements in signal processing, microelectronics, and wireless communications in recent years, fNIRS has become portable, supporting light sources and detectors in a self-contained unit. These wireless devices can accurately measure activity while users are performing real-world tasks such as running [18] or bicycle riding [27], with only slightly higher error rates than a traditional clinical device [34]. Feature selection can be used to improve the efficiency and accuracy of machine learning algorithms translate fNIRS signals to classifications in real time [25].

3   System Design

Phylter is a software tool that uses physiological input to schedule the delivery of notifications. It attempts to solve one of the main challenges of a wearable device (the ease with which it can bother its wearer at any moment) by using one of its key affordances (the proximity to skin and state-indicative biological markers). In technical terms, Phylter is a server with the capability to communicate with clients that deliver packets of messages and physiologically-based classifications about the user's present state. It bases its decision to deliver the message on its specified importance (contained in the message) and prediction about the user's interruptibility. Although Phylter generalizes to a variety of physiological sensors and any wearable devices that accept TCP/IP or Bluetooth input, the current software is calibrated to receive messages from a Unity virtual environment and physiological input for an fNIRS-based classification scheme written in Matlab; it redirects messages that meet the changing threshold to a Google Glass (a protocol shown in Fig. 2). The source code can easily be modified for other devices. Phylter builds off of the framework described by Shibata et al. but incorporates the three major components *(1) subscribing or receiving passive sensor information, (2) accumulating or holding implicit input, and (3) interpreting the wearer's state* [30].

3.1   Physiological Input

Because individuals have different values of raw physiological signals, a back-end engine creates a machine learning classifier for each individual using our system, and then feeds real-time data into this model. We used the online fNIRS analysis and classification (OFAC) tool, shown to produce real-time classifications of fNIRS data with high accuracy [11]. Participants first complete trials of a task that stimulates known cognitive states – reference points that can later be used to determine the user's state when the ground truth is otherwise impossible to

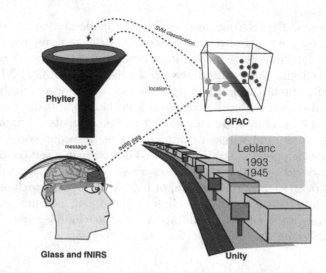

Fig. 2. Framework of the Phylter system. Phylter processes a continuous stream of physiological data, and when it receives a notification, it decides based on user state if it should send the notification to the user.

gauge. For example, participants might complete trials of the n-back task [22], generating multiple labeled time-series which, after being described in terms of appropriate statistical features, serve as instances to the open source machine learning library LIBSVM. Trained on both high workload and low workload instances, LIBSVM ultimately allows for rapid binary classification on a moving window of time-segments in real-time. This system has been used to adapt a scenario where an interactive human-robot system changed its state of autonomy based on whether it detected a particular state of multitasking [33], measure preference signals to control a movie recommendation engine [24], and expand the motor space of high-priority targets in a visual search task [2].

The client receives a continuous stream of machine learning classifications in a string format. Each classification comes in the form of a colon-delimited string, containing the first letter of the most probable prediction as well as the associated confidence value of it and the other (potentially numerous)possibilities. Based on Afergan et al.'s [1] method of triggering adaptations from a moving window of the most recent confidence values, we store a running confidence of each classification over a user-defined period of time (typically 5–20 s). Less sensitive to erratic swings in classification, the sliding window provides a more conservative estimate of the user's state, as a small number of misclassifications will not necessarily provoke incorrect adaptations, an important design principle to mitigate negative effects of BCIs [31].

Phylter accepts data from any number of physiological sensors without confusing the origin of any given stream, enabling sensor fusion, a popular method for merging data (or already processed predictions) from multiple devices in the hope of arriving at more accurate estimates of a particular state [14,20].

The system is configurable to create complex rules using Boolean logic to combine the different sensor input (Fig. 3).

Fig. 3. Phylter screenshot. The left panel displays a stream of physiological classifications ('l' for low workload, 'h' for high workload). The center panel shows a log of notifications, if the notifications were sent, and the running average of the user's physiological state at the time. The right panel displays a log of the notifications sent to the wearable device.

3.2 Notification Input and Output

Phylter can process notifications from an email server, a messaging service, or a custom application as long as it adheres to a basic string or XML format and includes a marker at the beginning of the packet specifying the level of notification. It handles three levels of notifications: *never send* (only useful for archival or experimental purposes), *always send* for high-priority notifications, and *adaptively send* for physiological-based filtering. It displays and logs when it receives notifications so that whatever system utilizes the service knows whether or not the user has received a message.

As a prototype of the wearable device that ultimately receives the message, we built a custom message handler for Google Glass that receives notifications and displays them for a set period of time before clearing the screen. If running as a background service, the application can turn on the screen to display the message, and then deactivate the screen once the notification ceases to be relevant. The message handler is built on a simple shell script that can be customized for the protocol of other wearable devices.

3.3 Server Architecture

The core functionality of Phylter relies on client-server architectures. Phylter runs two concurrent threads to receive information over TCP/IP, opening separate ports for physiological input and notifications. It acts as the server in these connections so that it can handle multiple sources for each type of input. Every time Phylter receives a new physiological classification, it updates its running average of the physiological state by discarding the oldest classification and adding this new data point. When it receives a notification marked as adaptive, it checks the user's physiological state, and sends the notification to the wearable device via an Android device bridge communication channel triggered by a shell script.

3.4 Data Logs

Phylter records a detailed, timestamped log of its activity in plain text. It saves (in separate files) a record of all of the physiological input, as well as a list of notifications and what messages were ultimately sent to the user. This allows an operator to see the efficacy of a system and what information a user did and did not receive.

4 Discussion

As computing devices continue to battle for users' attention, Phylter limits less significant notifications that distract the users from focusing on a single task. It serves as a framework to prevent information overload by modulating the display of notifications to the user. While our initial setup is designed for fNIRS brain data and Google Glass, it uses generic network protocols and a framework that can be extended to other input or output devices.

Phylter is composed of several self-contained systems which communicate with each other wirelessly. As these components and their requirements reduce in size and computational and power requirements, we envision that this system could become completely portable and run with commercial electronics in the near future. With future improvements to the system, Phylter could control not only the timing of notifications, but the delivery mechanism, distributing notifications across multiple wearable devices or even between devices [26] to balance user-awareness with the cost of interruption.

This software suggests an important step in physiological-based notifications, and that turning notifications on and off can make a discernible difference. In order to assess the validity of this system, we plan on running a controlled laboratory experiment to see if user performance does indeed improve by the user only receiving pertinent notifications at opportune times.

Acknowledgments. We thank Shiwan Zuo, Beste Yuksel, Alvitta Ottley, Eli Brown, Fumeng Yang, Lane Harrison, Sergio Fantini, and Angelo Sassaroli from Tufts University, Erin Solovey from Drexel University, and Michael Rennaker, Timothy Jordan, and Alex Olwal from Google. We also thank Google Inc. and the NSF for support of this research (NSF Grants Nos. IIS-1065154 and IIS-1218170). Any opinions, findings, conclusions, or recommendations expressed in this paper are those of the authors and do not necessarily reflect the views of Google Inc. or the National Science Foundation.

References

1. Afergan, D., Peck, E.M., Solovey, E.T., Jenkins, A., Hincks, S.W., Brown, E.T., Chang, R., Jacob, R.J.K.: Dynamic difficulty using brain metrics of workload. In: Proceedings of the SIGCHI Conference on Human Factors in Computing Systems, pp. 3797–3806. ACM (2014)
2. Afergan, D., Shibata, T., Hincks, S.W., Peck, E.M., Yuksel, B.F., Chang, R., Jacob, R.J.K.: Brain-based target expansion. In: Proceedings of the ACM Symposium on User Interface Software and Technology, pp. 583–593. ACM (2014)
3. Baddeley, A.: Working memory. Science 255(5044), 556–559 (1992)
4. Bailey, B.P., Iqbal, S.T.: Understanding changes in mental workload during execution of goal-directed tasks and its application for interruption management. ACM Trans. Comput.-Hum. Interact. (TOCHI) 14(4), 21 (2008)
5. Bailey, B.P., Konstan, J.A.: On the need for attention-aware systems: measuring effects of interruption on task performance, error rate, and affective state. Comput. Hum. Behav. 22(4), 685–708 (2006)
6. Chen, D., Vertegaal, R.: Using mental load for managing interruptions in physiologically attentive user interfaces. In: CHI 2004 extended abstracts on Human Factors in Computing Systems, pp. 1513–1516. ACM (2004)
7. Cutrell, E.B., Czerwinski, M., Horvitz, E.: Effects of instant messaging interruptions on computing tasks. In: CHI 2000 extended abstracts on Human Factors in Computing Systems, pp. 99–100. ACM (2000)
8. Cutrell, E., Tan, D.: BCI for passive input in HCI. In: Proceedings of the SIGCHI Conference on Human Factors in Computing Systems. ACM (2008)
9. Girouard, A., Solovey, E.T., Hirshfield, L.M., Chauncey, K., Sassaroli, A., Fantini, S., Jacob, R.J.K.: Distinguishing difficulty levels with non-invasive brain activity measurements. In: Gross, T., Gulliksen, J., Kotzé, P., Oestreicher, L., Palanque, P., Prates, R.O., Winckler, M. (eds.) INTERACT 2009. LNCS, vol. 5726, pp. 440–452. Springer, Heidelberg (2009)
10. Girouard, A., Solovey, E.T., Hirshfield, L.M., Peck, E.M., Chauncey, K., Sassaroli, A., Fantini, S., Jacob, R.J.K.: From brain signals to adaptive interfaces: using fNIRS in HCI. In: Tan, D.S., Nijholt, A. (eds.) Brain-Computer Interfaces, pp. 221–237. Springer, London (2010)
11. Girouard, A., Solovey, E.T., Jacob, R.J.K.: Designing a passive brain computer interface using real time classification of functional near-infrared spectroscopy. Int. J. Auton. Adapt. Commun. Syst. 6(1), 26–44 (2013)
12. Hirshfield, L.M., Solovey, E.T., Girouard, A., Kebinger, J., Jacob, R.J.K., Sassaroli, A., Fantini, S.: Brain measurement for usability testing and adaptive interfaces: an example of uncovering syntactic workload with functional near infrared spectroscopy. In: Proceedings of the SIGCHI Conference on Human Factors in Computing Systems, pp. 2185–2194. ACM (2009)
13. Horvitz, E., Apacible, J.: Learning and reasoning about interruption. In: Proceedings of the International Conference on Multimodal Interfaces, pp. 20–27. ACM (2003)

14. Hussain, M.S., Calvo, R.A., Aghaei Pour, P.: Hybrid fusion approach for detecting affects from multichannel physiology. In: D'Mello, S., Graesser, A., Schuller, B., Martin, J.-C. (eds.) ACII 2011, Part I. LNCS, vol. 6974, pp. 568–577. Springer, Heidelberg (2011)
15. Iqbal, S.T., Bailey, B.P.: Effects of intelligent notification management on users and their tasks. In: Proceedings of the SIGCHI Conference on Human Factors in Computing Systems, pp. 93–102. ACM (2008)
16. Iqbal, S.T., Zheng, X.S., Bailey, B.P.: Task-evoked pupillary response to mental workload in human-computer interaction. In: CHI 2004 extended abstracts on Human Factors in Computing Systems, pp. 1477–1480. ACM (2004)
17. Jackson, T., Dawson, R., Wilson, D.: The cost of email interruption. J. Syst. Inf. Technol. 5(1), 81–92 (2001)
18. Jones, B., Hesford, C.M., Cooper, C.E.: The use of portable NIRS to measure muscle oxygenation and haemodynamics during a repeated sprint running test. In: Huffel, S.V., Naulaers, G., Caicedo, A., Bruley, D.F., Harrison, D.K. (eds.) Oxygen Transport to Tissue XXXV, pp. 185–191. Springer, New York (2013)
19. Maior, H.A., Pike, M., Sharples, S., Wilson, M.L.: Examining the reliability of using fNIRS in realistic HCI settings for spatial and verbal tasks. In: Proceedings of the SIGCHI Conference on Human Factors in Computing Systems (In Press). ACM (2015)
20. Mandic, D.P., Obradovic, D., Kuh, A., Adali, T., Trutschell, U., Golz, M., De Wilde, P., Barria, J.A., Constantinides, A.G., Chambers, J.A.: Data fusion for modern engineering applications: an overview. In: Duch, W., Kacprzyk, J., Oja, E., Zadrożny, S. (eds.) ICANN 2005. LNCS, vol. 3697, pp. 715–721. Springer, Heidelberg (2005)
21. Miyata, Y., Norman, D.A.: Psychological issues in support of multiple activities. In: Norman, D.A., Draper, S.W. (eds.) User Centered System Design: New Perspectives on Human-Computer Interaction, pp. 265–284. Lawrence Elbaum Associates, Hillsdale (1986)
22. Owen, A.M., McMillan, K.M., Laird, A.R., Bullmore, E.: Nback working memory paradigm: a meta analysis of normative functional neuroimaging studies. Hum. Brain Mapp. 25(1), 46–59 (2005)
23. Parasuraman, R., Caggiano, D.: Neural and genetic assays of human mental workload. In: McBride, D.K., Schmorrow, D. (eds.) Quantifying Human Information Processing, pp. 123–149. Rowman & Littlefield Publishers Inc., Lanham (2005)
24. Peck, E.M., Afergan, D., Jacob, R.J.K.: Investigation of fNIRS brain sensing as input to information filtering systems. In: Proceedings of Augmented Human International Conference, pp. 142–149. ACM (2013)
25. Peck, E.M., Afergan, D., Yuksel, B.F., Lalooses, F., Jacob, R.J.K.: Using fNIRS to measure mental workload in the real world. In: Fairclough, S.H., Gilleade, K. (eds.) Advances in Physiological Computing, pp. 117–139. Springer, London (2014)
26. Pierce, J.S., Nichols, J.: An infrastructure for extending applications' user experiences across multiple personal devices. In: ACM Symposium on User Interface Software and Technology, pp. 101–110. ACM (2008)
27. Piper, S.K., Krueger, A., Koch, S.P., Mehnert, J., Habermehl, C., Steinbrink, J., Obrig, H., Schmitz, C.H.: A wearable multi-channel fNIRS system for brain imaging in freely moving subjects. Neuroimage 85, 64–71 (2014)
28. Prinzel, L.J., Freeman, F.G., Scerbo, M.W., Mikulka, P.J., Pope, A.T.: Effects of a psychophysiological system for adaptive automation on performance, workload, and the event-related potential P300 component. Hum. Factors J. Hum. Factors Ergon. Soc. 45(4), 601–614 (2003)

29. Repovš, G., Baddeley, A.: The multi-component model of working memory: explorations in experimental cognitive psychology. Neuroscience **139**(1), 5–21 (2006)
30. Shibata, T., Peck, E.M., Afergan, D., Hincks, S.W., Yuksel, B.F., Jacob, R.J.K.: Building implicit interfaces for wearable computers with physiological inputs: zero shutter camera and phylter. In: Proceedings of the adjunct publication of the ACM Symposium on User Interface Software and Technology, pp. 89–90. ACM (2014)
31. Solovey, E.T., Afergan, D., Peck, E.M., Hincks, S.W., Jacob, R.J.K.: Designing implicit interfaces for physiological computing: guidelines and lessons learned using fNIRS. ACM Trans. Comput.-Hum. Interact. (TOCHI) **21**(6), 35 (2015)
32. Solovey, E.T., Girouard, A., Chauncey, K., Hirshfield, L.M., Sassaroli, A., Zheng, F., Fantini, S., Jacob, R.J.K.: Using fNIRS brain sensing in realistic HCI settings: experiments and guidelines. In: Proceedings of the ACM Symposium on User Interface Software and Technology, pp. 157–166. ACM (2009)
33. Solovey, E., Schermerhorn, P., Scheutz, M., Sassaroli, A., Fantini, S., Jacob, R..J.K.: Brainput: enhancing interactive systems with streaming fNIRS brain input. In: Proceedings of the SIGCHI Conference on Human Factors in Computing Systems, pp. 2193–2202. ACM (2012)
34. Sthalekar, C.C., Koomson, V.J.: A CMOS sensor for measurement of cerebral optical coefficients using non-invasive frequency domain near infrared spectroscopy. IEEE Sens. J. **13**(9), 3166–3174 (2013)
35. Strangman, G., Culver, J.P., Thompson, J.H., Boas, D.A.: A quantitative comparison of simultaneous BOLD fMRI and NIRS recordings during functional brain activation. Neuroimage **17**(2), 719–731 (2002)
36. Stripling, R., Coyne, J.T., Cole, A., Afergan, D., Barnes, R.L., Rossi, K.A., Reeves, L.M., Schmorrow, D.D.: Automated SAF adaptation tool (ASAT). In: Schmorrow, D.D., Reeves, L.M. (eds.) HCII 2007 and FAC 2007. LNCS (LNAI), vol. 4565, pp. 346–353. Springer, Heidelberg (2007)
37. Tremoulet, P., Barton, J., Craven, P., Gifford, A., Morizio, N., Belov, N., Stibler, K., Regli, S.H., Thomas, M.: Augmented cognition for tactical Tomahawk weapons control system operators. In: Schmorrow, D., Stanney, K., Reeves, L. (eds.) Foundations of Augmented Cognition, pp. 313–318. Strategic Analysis Inc., Arlington (2006)
38. Villringer, A., Chance, B.: Non-invasive optical spectroscopy and imaging of human brain function. Trends Neurosci. **20**(10), 435–442 (1997)
39. Wickens, C.D.: Multiple resources and mental workload. Hum. Factors J. Hum. Factors Ergon. Soc. **50**(3), 449–455 (2008)
40. Young, M.S., Brookhuis, K.A., Wickens, C.D., Hancock, P.A.: State of science: mental workload in ergonomics. Ergonomics **58**(1), 1–17 (2015)
41. Zander, T.O., Kothe, C., Welke, S., Roetting, M.: Utilizing secondary input from passive brain-computer interfaces for enhancing human-machine interaction. In: Schmorrow, D.D., Estabrooke, I.V., Grootjen, M. (eds.) FAC 2009. LNCS, vol. 5638, pp. 759–771. Springer, Heidelberg (2009)

Monitoring Mental States of the Human Brain in Action: From Cognitive Test to Real-World Simulations

Deepika Dasari[1], Guofa Shou[1], and Lei Ding[1,2(✉)]

[1] School of Electrical and Computer Engineering,
University of Oklahoma, Norman, OK 73019, USA
{deepika,gshou,leiding}@ou.edu
[2] Center of Biomedical Engineering, University of Oklahoma,
Norman, OK 73019, USA
leiding@ou.edu

Abstract. Functional mental state of operators in real-world workspaces is a crucial factor in many cognitively demanding tasks. In this paper, we present our recent efforts in studying electroencephalograph (EEG) biomarkers to be used to assess cognitive states of operators. We studied these biomarkers from a simple cognitive task to low- and high-fidelity simulated air traffic control (ATC) tasks, with both novices and professional ATC operators. EEG data were recorded from 25 subjects (in three studies) who performed one of three different cognitively demanding tasks up to 120 min. Our results identified two EEG components with similar spatial and spectral patterns at the group level across all three studies, which both indicated the time-on-task effects in their temporal dynamics. With further developments in the future, the technology and identified biomarkers can be used for real-time monitoring of operators' cognitive functions in critical task environments and may even provide aids when necessary.

Keywords: Functional brain imaging · EEG · Independent component analysis · Mental state · Human factors

1 Introduction

The functional mental state of operators is a determinant factor in task performance. It depends on various cognitive factors including mental fatigue, mental workload, and mental engagement, etc. In operational environments where high cognitive attention is required, these factors can contribute to lapse in attention directly or indirectly, which consequently lead to performance degradation [1]. Task-related behavioral measures like errors or response time, or subjective evaluations like NASA task load index are simple means in assessing performance variations [1, 2]. In recent years, many researchers have attempted to identify and evaluate reliable metrics in electroencephalography (EEG) to assess various cognitive states of operators [1, 3, 4].

Challenges remain in building portable, ease-to-use, and reliable EEG recording systems to be used in real-world situations and in developing novel computational algorithms in extracting useful information from recordings of such EEG systems.

© Springer International Publishing Switzerland 2015
D.D. Schmorrow and C.M. Fidopiastis (Eds.): AC 2015, LNAI 9183, pp. 178–186, 2015.
DOI: 10.1007/978-3-319-20816-9_18

In comparison to classic EEG systems with electrodes using gel, wireless EEG systems designed to collect high-density EEG data (64, 128 or 256 channels) at high sampling frequencies using dry electrodes have been recently pursued [5]. These systems enable data collection in naturalistic environments with minimal interference to users.

In most EEG studies on assessing mental states and/or cognitive functions in real-world situations, frequency-specific oscillatory activities at channels of interest are major targets to be investigated in identifying patterns. Besides limiting the assessment to pre-defined channels, these methods usually emphasize only on temporal patterns and cannot reveal complete spatial patterns of activities of interests. Furthermore, channel-level EEG signals suffer from superimposition of multiple neural sources due to the volume conduction effect [6].

In this paper, we summarized three of our recent studies in monitoring mental/cognitive functions from lab bench experimental protocol, i.e. a speeded color-word matching task, to low-fidelity simulation protocol, i.e. training oriented air traffic control (ATC) task, and then to high-fidelity ATC simulation protocol. We implemented a spatial filtering method called independent component analysis (ICA) [7], based on the principle of statistical independence of source components in EEG data, which are potentially associated with distinct neural substrates. The method has been further advanced into the time-frequency ICA in one of our recent studies [6]. Our current results indicate that oscillatory activities in EEG components of interest in each study showed consistent spatial patterns across studies and indicated increasing dynamic patterns with the time-on-task effect.

2 Methods

2.1 Experimental Design

Figure 1 illustrates the three studies in the order of varied fidelity and realistic configurations. The details of each study are described as follows. Written informed consents were obtained from all subjects prior to their participation in the study.

Study I. Ten healthy college students (20−29 years, all males) were recruited at the University of Oklahoma. Subjects performed a speeded color-word matching Stroop task [7] implemented using E-prime (for further details see [8]). They were required to judge the congruency between word meaning and ink color, and respond by pressing a button within 1400 ms. Each subject took part in two sessions of about 20 min each with a pseudo-randomized sequence of 390 trials, divided into 3 blocks.

Study II. Ten subjects (21−33 years, all males) were recruited at the University of Oklahoma. Subjects participated in two 2-h sessions of ATC tasks in low-fidelity simulation generated by CTEAM V2.0 [9, 10]. They were required to perform control actions (i.e., change direction of heading, speed and altitude level) on aircraft to regulate and maintain smooth air traffic flow using mouse.

Study III. Five certified professional controllers (54−60 years, all males) were recruited at FAA CAMI, Oklahoma City. Subjects performed 2-h ATC tasks in an high-fidelity en route environment on En route automation modernization (ERAM)

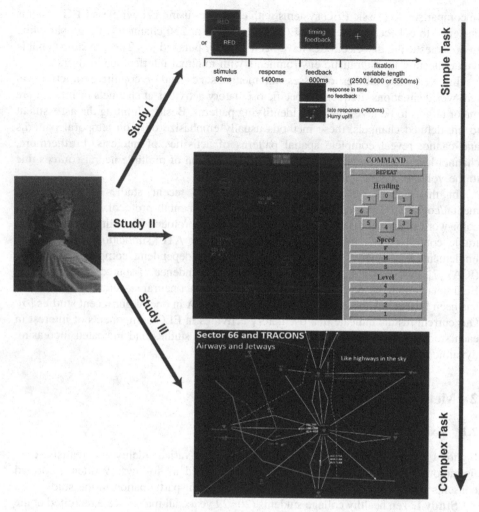

Fig. 1. Illustration of tasks in three studies

interface [11]. They were asked to safely navigate aircrafts across designated airspace using slew-ball, keyboard and voice commands.

2.2 Data Analysis

In Study I and II, 128-channel EEG data were recorded at sample frequency of 250 Hz using an Amps 300 amplifier (Electrical Geodesics, Inc., OR, USA). In Study III, 64- channel EEG data were recorded at sample frequency of 1000 Hz using a Brain-Amp amplifier (Brain Products GmbH, Munich, Germany).

All EEG data were offline filtered with a band-pass filter of 0.5−30 Hz. Preprocessing steps of bad channel removal, bad epoch removal and artifactual independent components (ICs) subtraction, were sequentially performed at each session data. In Study I, data in epochs from 1500 ms before to 2300 ms after stimulus onset were selected. In Study II and III, data points at peaks of global field power (GFP) data were selected for each session. The selected data from each study were combined and a group-wise ICA method was applied to identify ICs of interest [12]. Similar brain related IC patterns of interest among three studies were selected from individual studies based on spatial patterns. Then oscillatory power dynamics from each IC were calculated and transformed to dB to probe the time-on-task effect as follows. In Study I, an epoch of 700 ms pre-stimulus to stimulus onset for each trial was selected. The spectral powers of all epochs in each block were averaged and repeated measures analysis of variance (ANOVA) was performed using blocks as an independent variable. In Study II, each IC's spectral-temporal dynamic was fitted with a linear regression line for each session and the detection of significant positive slopes of the fitted lines was tested via a binomial test. In Study III, the period of first (T1) and last (T2) 10 min of the task were selected and their spectral powers in each IC were compared using t test for individuals.

3 Results

3.1 ICs of Interest

Two distinct brain activities related ICs (named as the frontal IC and the parietal IC; Fig. 2) were similarly identified in terms of spatial and spectral patterns in each study. The frontal IC indicated a spectral peak in the theta band (5- < 8 Hz), while the parietal

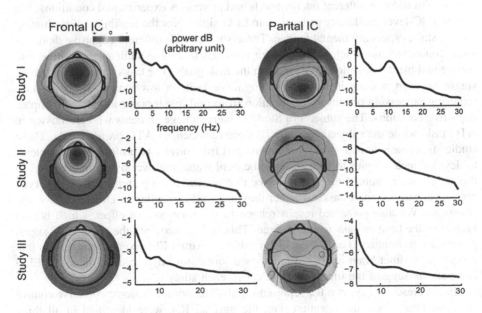

Fig. 2. The spatial and spectral patterns of two selected ICs

IC indicated a spectral peak in the alpha band (8 - < 13 Hz). Consequently, subsequent analysis was only performed on these frequency bands for each IC.

3.2 Dynamics of EEG Components

In Study I, the oscillatory dynamics from all ICs augmented within each session, which revealed the tendency of significance in ANOVA tests (Table 1). For the frontal IC, t tests indicated a significant increase of the theta power from Block 1 to Block 3 ($p = 0.01$) and Block 2 to Block 3 ($p = 0.02$) in session 1 and from Block 1 to Block 3 ($p = 0.04$) in session 2. Similarly, for the parietal IC a significant increase of the alpha power was observed in both sessions from Block 1 to Block 3 ($p < 0.001$) and Block 2 to Block 3 ($p < 0.005$).

In Study II, the linear regression analysis indicated a significant ($p < 0.05$) regression model of positive slope (PRS) in most subjects for the frontal IC (8 out of 10 subjects in both sessions) and for the parietal IC (all subjects in session 1, and 8 out of 10 subjects in session 2), which were significant from a binomial test (Table 1).

In Study III, for the frontal IC, t tests indicated a significant increase of the theta power from T1 to T2 in subject 3 and 4, while a significant decrease in subject 2. For the parietal IC, a significant increase of the alpha power from T1 to T2 was detected in subjects 1, 4 and 5 (Table 2).

4   Discussion and Conclusion

In this paper, we presented our recent studies in monitoring mental/cognitive performance with tasks of different fidelity levels and at various experimental conditions. We explored IC-level oscillatory patterns from EEG signals for the feasibility of evaluating mental state, especially mental fatigue. Three studies with different cognitive demands were conducted, in which subjects were required to utilize sufficient cognitive reasoning and mental attention to accomplish the task goals. The tasks varied from simple single decision making in a repetitive cognitive task, to low- and high-fidelity task requiring processing of sensory information from multiple inputs and making complex cognitive decisions. The subjects in Study II were college students who are novice in ATC task, while the subjects in Study III were experienced ATC professionals. These studies from basic to real-world simulations and from novice to professionals enable us to develop technologies to inch closer to be deployable real-world task monitoring. In this paper, we presented the first evidence that similar brain patterns can be observed across various cognitive tasks, whether they are well-controlled or close to real-world situations. We also presented results related to the time-on-task effect, which is also known as the time-on-task mental fatigue. This is achieved with the novel EEG signal processing techniques (i.e. ICA), which is able to extract EEG component signals that arise from distinct brain regions. Variations in oscillatory dynamics of identified EEG components suggest the time-on-task effect in each study.

In the present study, two ICs representing distinct brain functions: cognitive control (i.e., the frontal IC) and attention (i.e., the parietal IC), were identified in all three

Table 1. Average and std of spectral powers (dB) of identified ICs in all blocks of two sessions for Study I and the detections of PRS in Study II.

	Study I														Study II			
	Session 1							Session 2							Session 1		Session 2	
	Block 1		Block 2		Block 3		F/p	Block 1		Block 2		Block 3		F/p	PRS	p	PRS	p
	mean	std	mean	std	mean	std		mean	std	mean	std	mean	std					
Frontal IC - Theta	25.15	3.12	25.53	3.46	26.08	3.78	7.87 / <0.005	25.21	3.04	25.48	3.46	25.94	3.69	4.33 / 0.03	8/10	<0.05	8/10	<0.05
Parietal IC - Alpha	25.73	6.25	25.99	6.04	26.87	6.13	10.92 / <0.001	25.78	6.25	25.86	6.14	26.84	6.02	14.49 / <0.001	10/10	<0.001	8/10	<0.05

Table 2. Averaged spectral powers (dB) of identified ICs in two time periods (T1 and T2: first and last 10 min respectively).

		Subject 1		Subject 2		Subject 3		Subject 4		Subject 5	
		mean (std)	p / t	mean (std)	p / t	mean (std)	p / t	mean (std)	p / t	mean (std)	p / t
Frontal IC -Theta	T1	-3.46 (1.74)	0.08	-3.85 (1.78)	0.04	-4.36 (1.77)	<0.001	-2.35 (1.78)	<0.001	-6.99 (2.26)	0.68
	T2	-3.63 (1.69)	1.73	-4.06 (1.87)	1.99	-0.42 (2.60)	-30.7	-0.90 (2.45)	-12.2	-6.94 (2.56)	-0.41
Parietal IC - Alpha	T1	-7.23 (1.66)	<0.001	-7.28 (1.67)	0.50	-7.75 (1.65)	0.32	-4.56 (1.78)	0.04	-10.02 (1.65)	<0.01
	T2	-6.56 (1.87)	-6.45	-7.22 (1.90)	-0.66	-7.76 (1.69)	-0.98	-4.34 (2.30)	-2.09	-9.71 (1.78)	-3.13

studies. The frontal theta activity has been observed in many cognitive tasks that require concentration, attention, and short-term working memory [13], while the parietal alpha is thought to be critical in attention control mechanism during a complex human-computer interaction [14]. Two IC-based oscillatory dynamics suggest gradual increasing patterns in dominant spectral band with time on task in all studies. The increasing parietal alpha power suggests deteriorated attention levels in subjects while the increasing theta power indicates that more cognitive resources needed to fulfill cognitive demands from the tasks. Both phenomena have been reported as indicators of mental fatigue [15]. More complex dynamic patterns of the frontal theta power in professionals in Study III might suggest the effect of their training and working experience in battling the time-on-task mental fatigue in tasks that have zero tolerance to errors and failures. Furthermore, our recent data using engagement indices based on the ratio of the beta to the sum of alpha and theta band power showed consistent dynamic patterns across subjects [16], which suggests better biomarkers might be developed with information from multiple frequency bands.

Compared to Study I, both Studies II and III, which mimicked realistic ATC tasks and duration, allowed us to evaluate these phenomena in real-world condition. Our findings from these three studies indicate the consistent pattern of the time-on-task effect on different tasks, similar to some previous studies [15]. It is noted that, although we only reported data related to the time-on-task effect here, other behavioral metrics like response time, mouse clicks or key presses have been used to evaluate our EEG component data [6, 8, 10, 17, 18], in which significant correlations have been identified and indicated that these phenomena can be used to study other factors in monitoring mental/cognitive functions, e.g., mental workload and effort. In the future, more studies, including real ATC tasks, should be conducted to further explore the capability of the proposed technique and associated discoveries from its implementation.

EEG is a direct measure of neuronal electrical activities, and has been largely used to evaluate mental states of human being in neuroergonomics [4]. Compared to behavioral data, EEG data has the advantage that it can be obtained and analyzed continuously. Our recent efforts on computational data analysis method development have advanced the capability of using EEG in real-world situations. Together with recent non-prep sensor and portable and wireless hardware developments, this technology can be translated to in-field uses in many areas. In terms of monitoring mental/cognitive functions, our recent data suggest that brain processes including working memory, performance monitoring and decision-making from a brain network are required to accomplish cognitive tasks. Our technique reveals oscillatory dynamics of EEG components indicative of these brain processes. The present results indicate that the proposed technique can assess mental state of, such as, ATC operators in real-world conditions that need to be error free for public safety.

Acknowledgments. This work was supported in part by NSF CAREER ECCS-0955260 and DOT-FAA 10-G-008.

References

1. Boksem, M.A., Meijman, T.F., Lorist, M.M.: Effects of mental fatigue on attention: an ERP study. Cogn. Brain. Res. **25**(1), 107–116 (2005)
2. Cao, A., et al.: NASA TLX: Software for assessing subjective mental workload. Behav. Res. Methods **41**(1), 113–117 (2009)
3. Wilson, G.F., Russell, C.A.: Operator functional state classification using multiple psychophysiological features in an air traffic control task. Hum. Factors: J. Hum. Factors Ergon. Soc. **45**(3), 381–389 (2003)
4. Lorist, M.M., et al.: The influence of mental fatigue and motivation on neural network dynamics; an EEG coherence study. Brain Res. **1270**, 95–106 (2009)
5. Gargiulo, G., et al.: A mobile EEG system with dry electrodes. In: IEEE Biomedical Circuits and Systems Conference BioCAS 2008, IEEE (2008)
6. Shou, G., Ding, L., Dasari, D.: Probing neural activations from continuous EEG in a real-world task: time-frequency independent component analysis. J. Neurosci. Methods **209** (1), 22–34 (2012)
7. Mager, R., et al.: Mismatch and conflict: neurophysiological and behavioral evidence for conflict priming. J. Cogn. Neurosci. **21**(11), 2185–2194 (2009)
8. Shou, G., Ding, L.: Ongoing EEG oscillatory dynamics suggesting evolution of mental fatigue in a color-word matching stroop task. In: 2013 6th International Conference on Neural Engineering (NER), IEEE (2013)
9. Bailey, L.L., et al.: Controller teamwork evaluation and assessment methodology: A scenario calibration study, DTIC Document (1999)
10. Dasari, D., Shou, G., Ding, L.: Investigation of independent components based EEG metrics for mental fatigue in simulated ATC task. In: 2013 6th International IEEE/EMBS Conference on Neural Engineering (NER), IEEE (2013)
11. Willems, B., Hah, S., Schulz, K.: En route data communications: Experimental human factors evaluation (2010)
12. Kovacevic, N., McIntosh, A.R.: Groupwise independent component decomposition of EEG data and partial least square analysis. Neuroimage **35**(3), 1103–1112 (2007)
13. Klimesch, W.: EEG alpha and theta oscillations reflect cognitive and memory performance: a review and analysis. Brain Res. Rev. **29**(2), 169–195 (1999)
14. Smith, M.E., et al.: Monitoring task loading with multivariate EEG measures during complex forms of human-computer interaction. Hum. Factors: J. Hum. Factors Ergon. Soc. **43**(3), 366–380 (2001)
15. Lal, S.K., Craig, A.: A critical review of the psychophysiology of driver fatigue. Biol. Psychol. **55**(3), 173–194 (2001)
16. Dasari, D., Shou, G., Ding, L.: EEG index for time-on-task mental fatigue in real air traffic controllers obtained via independent component analysis. In: 2013 6th International IEEE/EMBS Conference on Neural Engineering (NER) (2013)
17. Shou, G., Ding, L.: Detection of EEG spatial–spectral–temporal signatures of errors: a comparative study of ICA-based and channel-based methods. Brain topography, pp. 1–15 (2014)
18. Shou, G., Ding, L.: Frontal theta EEG dynamics in a real-world air traffic control task. in Engineering In: 2013 35th Annual International Conference of the IEEE Medicine and Biology Society (EMBC), IEEE (2013)

Discrimination in Good-Trained Brain States for Brain Computer Interface

Mariko Funada[1(✉)], Tadashi Funada[2], and Yoshihide Igarashi[3]

[1] Department of Business Administration, Hakuoh University,
Oyama, Tochigi, Japan
mfunada@fc.hakuoh.ac.jp
[2] College of Science, Rikkyo University, Toshima-ku, Tokyo, Japan
[3] Professor Emeritus, Gunma University, Kiryu, Gunma, Japan

Abstract. BCI (brain computer interface) is particularly important for HCI. Some of recent results concerning BCI made a great contribution to the development of the HCI research area. In this paper we define "good-trained brain states", and then propose a method for discriminating good-trained brain states from other states. We believe that repetitious training might be effective to human brains. Human brain reactions can be quantified by ERPs (event related potentials). We analyze the data of ERPs reflecting the brain reactions, and then discuss the effect of repetitious training to the brain states.

Keywords: Good-trained brain states · BCI · ERP · EEG · Individual difference

1 Introduction

In order to achieve a satisfactory stage of the effective BCI, we consider a method of how to discriminate good brain states from other states. Some skills can be improved by repetitious training. Using a BCI system we can observe some changes in brain states by the repetitious training. In our experiments, we use such training for simple calculation tasks by subjects. We recognize some noticeable changes [5, 6] in their ERPs [8, 12–14] during the repetitious tasks [4]. At a certain stage of each experiment, we notice that their ERPs reach a stable state within minor fluctuation [1, 5]. We call such a stable state a good-trained brain state. In our experiments, the good-trained brain state shows that the skill for the simple calculation reaches the proficient level as the result of the repetitious training. That is, the good-trained brain state reflects the effect of the repetitious training. By analyzing the ERPs obtained from our experiments, we propose a method for discriminating good-trained brain states from other states [6].

According to the review of BCI [9], BCI can be considered to be an artificial intelligence system recognizing a certain set of patterns in brain signals through the following five consecutive stages: signal acquisition, preprocessing or signal enhancement, feature extraction, classification, and the control interface. In this paper we focus our attention on the first four stages of the BCI.

© Springer International Publishing Switzerland 2015
D.D. Schmorrow and C.M. Fidopiastis (Eds.): AC 2015, LNAI 9183, pp. 187–198, 2015.
DOI: 10.1007/978-3-319-20816-9_19

2 Methods

2.1 An Experimental Method

Each of the following experiments is repeatedly carried out (eight times per each task on the average).

The subjects are 10 men and 2 women from 20 to 23 years old. All of them are right-handed. Each of the subjects is identified by a letter from a to l. The experiments were carried out in the laboratory of the first author at Hakuoh University. We use two kinds of stimuli. One is a division question and the other is a circle, as shown in Fig. 1. Each stimulus is displayed in a CRT (cathode ray tube) of 19 inches with 80×240 pixels.

$$144 \div \square = 18 \qquad\qquad \circ$$

a stimulus of a division   a stimulus for an answer

Fig. 1. A set of stimuli, a division question and a circle.

A subject starts his/her calculation work when a division question is displayed. He/she inputs his/her answer to the question when a circle is displayed.

We call the calculation work, from when a division question is displayed until when its answer is given by a subject, a *task*. A sequence of sets of stimuli is displayed in the CRT placed in front of the subject. Each sequence consists of 100 tasks. A circle displayed after each division question is to inform the subject the timing for answering (as shown in Fig. 1). The circle is displayed for 1 s. The time interval between two consecutive stimuli is randomly chosen within the range from 800 [ms] to 1200 [ms]. EEGs as a response to the stimuli, a set of a division question and a circle followed by the question, are recorded in real time (strictly speaking, it requires 1 s to record the EEGs). Consequently about 10 min are required to record the data for one experiment (i.e., 100 division questions together with answers). The single polar and four channels of the "international 10–20 method" are used to measure the EEGs. The positions of the measurement are at C3, C4, Cz, and Pz. The base is A1 that is connected to A2. The sampling frequency for the A/D converter is 1 kHz.

2.2 An Analytical Method

The recorded EEGs shown in Fig. 4 are filtered by an adaptive filter [10, 11], and the EEGs are normalized by taking the average of their waveforms and using the standard deviation of the data (see Fig. 5). Then we obtain the ERPs of 100 repetitious tasks by using the normalized EEGs, the AM (averaging method), the DSAM (data selecting and averaging method) [3], and the m-DSAM (multi-DSAM) [6].

2.2.1 Data Selecting and Averaging Method (DSAM)

The data of EEGs are sieved and normalized by using a threshold value, and then the selected and normalized data are averaged. In this way ERPs are derived from EEGs.

This method is called the DSAM (data selecting and averaging method). The outline of the data process by the DSAM is as follows:

Let $x_i(t)$ be a filtered and normalized data, where i is a data index and t is the latency (the time delay from the time when a division question is displayed). Let D be a data set of $x_i(t)$.

- Step 1: For each i, $x_i(t)$ is translated into the binary sequence $b_i(t)$ by threshold L (in this paper $L = 0.5$, which is determined by signal-noise ratios), i.e.

$$b_i(t) = \begin{cases} 1 & if \quad x_i(t) > L \\ 0 & if \quad x_i(t) \le L \end{cases}.$$

- Step 2: The sum $B(t)$ of all $b_i(t)$ is calculated.
- Step 3: The maximum value MB of $B(t)$ around the latency of a positive peak P is found. Let T_P be the latency such that $B(T_P) = MB$. In our analysis of the data obtained by DSAM, P = P3 is chosen.
- Step 4: We find the subset D_{P3} of D such that

$$D_{P3} = \{x_i(t) | x_i(T_{P3}) > L, \quad x_i(t) \in D\}.$$

- Step 5: We calculate
$ERP_{DSAM}(t) = \frac{1}{n_{P3}} \sum_{x_i(t) \in D_{P3}} x_i(t)$, where n_{P3} is the number of elements in D_{P3}.

2.2.2 Multi-data Selecting and Averaging Method (M-DSAM)

The m-DSAM is a method to find the potential of an ERP for each target (peak) by using the DSAM. For each potential obtained in this way, we estimates the ERP by a normal distribution. The outline of the data process by the m-DSAM is as follows:

We modify the process in Step 1 of Sect. 2.2.1 in order to detect negative peaks.

- Step 1: For each i, $x_i(t)$ is translated into the binary sequence $b_i'(t)$ by threshold L' $(= -0.5)$, i.e.

$$b_i'(t) = \begin{cases} 0 & if \quad x_i(t) \ge L' \\ 1 & if \quad x_i(t) < L' \end{cases}.$$

- Step 2: We calculate the sum $B(t)$ of all $b_i(t)$ and the sum $B'(t)$ of all $b_i'(t)$.
- Step 3: For each positive peak P, we find the maximum value MB_P of $B(t)$. For each negative peak N, we find the maximum value MB_N of $B'(t)$, too. The interval between two peaks can be predicted from the past data.
- Step 4: We find the subsets D_P and D_N of D such that

$$D_P = \{x_i(t)|x_i(T_P) > L, \ x_i(t) \in D\}, \quad D_N = \{x_i(t)|x_i(T_N) < L', \ x_i(t) \in D\}.$$

- Step 5: We calculate

$$ERP_P(t) = \frac{1}{n_P} \sum_{x_i(t) \in D_P} x_i(t), \quad ERP_N(t) = \frac{1}{n_N} \sum_{x_i(t) \in D_N} x_i(t),$$

where n_p and n_N are the numbers of elements in D_p and D_N, respectively.
- Step 6: For each peak P or N, we estimate $ERP_P(t)$ or $ERP_N(t)$, respectively. These values are calculated as the values of ERPs at peaks P or N, by the following formulae (a normal distribution determined by a certain algorithm [2]):

$$ERP_Q(t) \approx f_Q(t) = (-1)^h w_Q \frac{1}{\sqrt{2\pi}s_Q} \exp\left(-\frac{(t - T_Q)^2}{2s_Q^2}\right), \tag{1}$$

where Q is a P or an N, $h(Q)$ is the function such that if $Q = P$ then $h = 0$, otherwise $h = 1$, w_Q is the amplitude of peak Q, s_Q is the standard deviation, and T_Q is the latency of Q.
- Step 7: We calculate
$ERP_{m-DSAM}(t) = \frac{1}{\bar{n}} \sum_Q n_Q f_Q(t)$, where $\bar{n}$ is the average of all n_Q's.

2.2.3   The Definition of the Distance Between Potentials

In our experiment, positive peaks P1, P2 and P3, and negative peaks N1, N2 and N3 are closely related to the task. Let Q denote one of these peaks. Let j and k be experimental days. We let $\mathbf{v}_{jQ} = (w_{jQ}, s_{jQ}, T_{jQ}, n_{jQ})$.

Then we can construct formulae (1) from this vector, too. We consider that vector $\mathbf{v}_{jQ}$ represents the potential at the peak Q on the j-th experimental day. Let $\mathbf{v}_{jQ}$ and $\mathbf{v}_{kQ}$ be the vectors for experimental days j and k, respectively. We let

$$\mathbf{u}_{j/kQ} = \left(\frac{w_{jQ}}{w_{kQ}}, \frac{s_{jQ}}{s_{kQ}}, \frac{T_{jQ}}{T_{kQ}}, \frac{n_{jQ}}{n_{kQ}}\right) \text{for each } j.$$

Then we can write $\mathbf{v}_{jQ} = \mathbf{u}_{j/kQ} * \mathbf{v}_{kQ}$, where the operation "*" is the Hadamard product. Next we define a distance between $\mathbf{u}_{j/kQ}$ and $\mathbf{u}_{k/kQ}$ of ERPs at peak Q on j-th experimental day and k-th experimental day as the Euclidean distance, denoted by $d(\mathbf{u}_{j/kQ}, \mathbf{u}_{k/kQ})$.

An ERP can be reconstructed by the m-DSAM and the linear combination of the normal distributions. Four parameters for each potential are determined by the m-DSAM: three of these parameters are shown in Fig. 2. Then we define a distance between vectors of these parameters with the coordinates determined by the m-DSAM. Using this distance, we discriminate the *good-trained brain states* from other brain states.

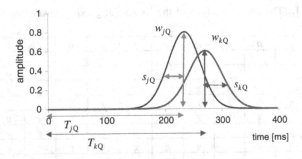

Fig. 2. The parameters defined by the formulae (1)

3 Results

3.1 The Ratios of Correct Answers

We calculate the ratios of correct answers (RCA) for all subjects and experimental days. Then we calculate the average of them and the standard deviations for each experimental day. These values are shown in Fig. 3, where the maximum value of the averaged RCA is 76.1 %. In Fig. 3, the horizontal line marked by tiny triangles on the line shows 95 % of 76.1 %. The area of the graph above the horizontal line can be considered to be the area showing that the subject reaches the proficient level of the calculation task.

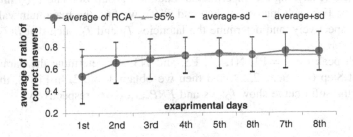

Fig. 3. Averages, standard deviations, and 95 % of the average of the maximum values

3.2 The Definition of a *Good-Trained Brain State*

We analyze the RCAs by the cluster analysis regarding to the experimental days for each subject. As shown in Table 1, the RCAs can be classified into two groups. The RCAs used for the classification are different among the subjects. Comparing Fig. 3 and Table 1, we consider that this classification is reasonable. In Table 1, the brain states indicated by "*g*" are *good-trained brain states*. The entries with oblique lines in Table 1 indicate that we could not carry out the calculation for the cluster analysis due to the loss of the experimental data.

Table 1. The cluster analysis of the RCAs (g: *good-trained brain state*)

experiments	a	b	c	d	e	f	g	h	i	j	k	l
1st												
2nd			g							g		g
3rd			g	g					g	g		g
4th	g		g	g	g		g	g	g	g	g	
5th	g	g	g	g	g	g		g	g	g	g	g
6th	g	g	g	g		g		g	g	g	g	g
7th	g	g		g	g	g	g	g	╱	g	g	g
8th	g	g		g	g		g	g	╱	g	g	g

3.3 ERPs Calculated by the m-DSAM

In this section, we give a number of examples calculated by the m-DSAM. The graph in Fig. 4 shows the recorded data (EEGs), which were obtained from the 3rd data measurement of subject g at the 2nd experimental day. The data contains 50 Hz alternative current noise and other types of noise as well. The graph of $x_i(t)$ ($i = 3, t = 1, ..., 1000$) in Fig. 5 shows the data after filtering and normalizing the data given in Fig. 4. Then we translate $x_3(t)$ into the binary sequences $b_3(t)$ and $b_3'(t)$. These translated data are shown in Fig. 6. Then we calculate $b_i(t)$, $b_i'(t)$, the summation $B(t)$ of $b_i(t)$, and the summation $B'(t)$ of $b_i'(t)$ for $i = 1, ..., 100$. The summations $B(t)$ and $B'(t)$ are shown in Fig. 7. It was previously reported that the potentials P1, N1, ..., P3, and N3 were noticed on the graph of the ERPs, and that the latencies of the ERPs were also estimated. Analyzing the experimental data, we group $B(t)$ and $B'(t)$ into several time intervals. For each interval of $B(t)$ and $B'(t)$, we find the maximum values MB_P and MB_N, respectively, and determine the latencies T_P and T_N such that $B(T_P) = MB_P$ and $B'(T_N) = MB_N$.

For each peak of Q = P1, N1, ..., P3, and N3, we determine the parameters as described at Step 6 in Sect. 2.2.2, and then we obtain Table 2. In Fig. 8, the dashed curves and the solid curve show $f_Q(t)$'s and $ERP_{m\text{-}DSAM}(t)$, respectively.

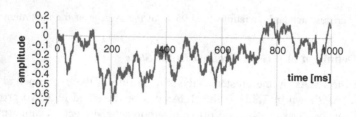

Fig. 4. Recorded data (EEGs) after a stimulus is displayed (subject: g, position: Cz)

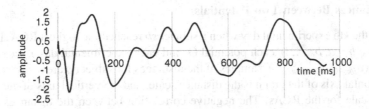

Fig. 5. The data shown in Fig. 4 are filtered and normalized

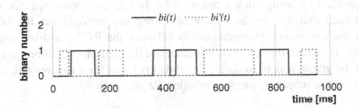

Fig. 6. The binary sequences translated from the data shown in Fig. 5

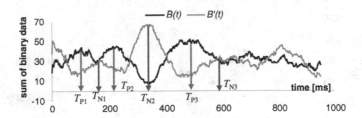

Fig. 7. The time distribution of binary sequences $B(t)$ and $B'(t)$

Table 2. Parameters obtained by the m-DSAM.

Q	h	w_Q	s_Q	T_Q	n_Q
P1	0	61.0	20	105	44
N1	1	74.8	28	165	32
P2	0	99.8	32	215	45
N2	1	112.5	31	335	67
P3	0	131.0	45	482	52
N3	1	107.0	38	593	35

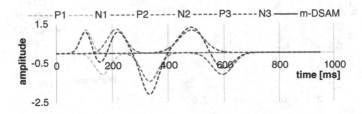

Fig. 8. ERPs calculated by the m-DSAM and $f_Q(t)$'s (Q = P1, N1, ..., P3, N3).

3.4   Distances Between Two Potentials

Let k_{sb} be the kth experimental day when a subject sb reached the highest RCA. For each subject sb ($sb = a, b, \ldots, l$), each potential Q, and each experimental day j, we calculate distance $d(\mathbf{u}_{j/ksbQ}, \mathbf{u}_{ksb/ksbQ})$. Examples of the distances for subject b are shown in Fig. 9. The horizontal axis of the graph is the distance scale, and the vertical axis of the graph is the ratio scale for the RCAs. The negative correlation between the distances and the RCAs shows high when Q is N1, P2, or P3. For each subject there exists a potential Q such that the correlation is less than -0.5. It is suggested that *good-trained brain states* could be specified by using such a potential Q. In the same way, we can specify a potential Q such that the absolute value of correlation between the RCAs and the distances is the maximum. The relationship between the RCAs and the distances is shown in Fig. 10, where the symbolic sequences at the rightmost column, just after the right end of the graph, denote subjects, electrode positions for measurement, and peaks (e.g., aPzP1 means subject a, measure position Pz and peak P1).

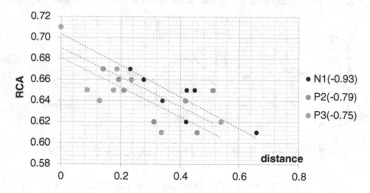

Fig. 9. Distances between peaks of ERPs (subject: b)

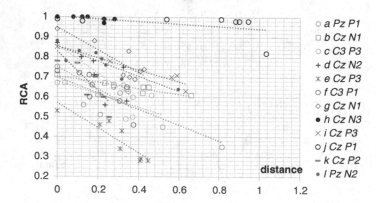

Fig. 10. Relationship between the distances and RCAs

3.5   Discrimination of the *Good-Trained Brain States*

We apply the discriminant analysis to the experimental data for 6 peaks and 4 electrodes. We obtain the discriminant function [7] for each subject such that the discrimination ratios are 100 % for all the subjects except for subject i (subject i repeated each task only 6 times). The discrimination ratio of subject i is 83 %.

Each ij-component in Table 3 shows the frequency (the number of times) of being selected by the discriminant analysis. Position Cz is the most frequently selected among all the electrode positions, and peaks N1 and P2 are the most frequently selected ones among all the peaks. However, for all the subjects we cannot remark any particular pair (electrode position and a peak) that are frequently selected together compared with other pairs.

Table 3. Selected distances to discriminate the *good–trained brain states*

Peaks	Cz	Pz	C3	C4	Total
P1	3	1	4	1	9
N1	4	2	4	5	15
P2	6	1	4	4	15
N2	2	2	1	3	8
P3	3	2	2	2	9
N3	2	2	1	1	6
Total	20	10	16	16	62

4   Discussions

4.1   Discussions on the Effectiveness of the m-DSAM

The sufficient amount of data for the m-DSAM, is relatively small. For an experiment, an ERP is usually the collection of 1000 data. However, the ERP can be represented by a normal distribution of 6 potentials × 4 parameters (i.e., about 24 data by the m-DSAM). Some of the potentials detected by the m-DSAM cannot be detected by the AM. Although the potentials of the data by the DSAM appear clearly, they are not sharp enough compared with the data by the m-DSAM. Furthermore, the latencies of the data by the DSAM are biased (see N1 and P2 in Fig. 11).

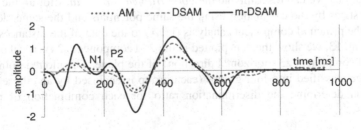

Fig. 11. Waveforms of the ERPs obtained by the AM, the DSAM, and the m-DSAM

4.2 Discussions on the Discrimination by Eliminating Individual Differences

Adopting the results of the cluster analysis for the RCAs of all the subjects, we can define the *good-trained brain states* for all the subjects, too. That is, when the RCA of a subject reaches 94.0 % or more, he/she is considered to be at a *good-trained brain state*. The discrimination defined in this way reflects our educational view point or the traditional learning method.

For each potential Q, let $\bar{v}_{0Q} = (v_{5_hQ} + v_{7_hQ})/2$. This value is the average of the 5th and the 7th parameters of subject h. Subject h has the highest RCA among all the subject. Using the vector introduced above, we calculate all $\mathbf{u}_{j/0Q}$ and the distances $d(\mathbf{u}_{j/0Q}, \mathbf{u}_{0/0Q})$ for all the subjects and the electrode positions. Next we find potential Q_{max} and electrode position E such that the correlation between the distances $d(\mathbf{u}_{j/0Qmax}, \mathbf{u}_{0/0Qmax})$ at E and RCAs is the maximum. The relationship between the distances $d(\mathbf{u}_{j/0Qmax}, \mathbf{u}_{0/0Qmax})$ at E and the RCA's for all the subjects is shown in Fig. 12. The meaning of symbolic sequences given in the rightmost part of the graph in Fig. 12 is the same as in Fig. 10.

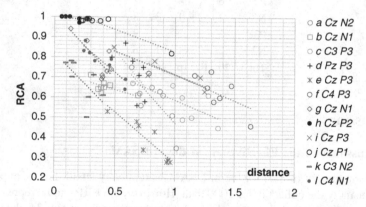

Fig. 12. Relationship between distances and RCAs

Using all the distances $d(\mathbf{u}_{j/0Q}, \mathbf{u}_{0/0Q})$ in Fig. 12, the discriminant analysis for the *good-trained brain states* (for all the subjects) is applied to the data. Then we obtain the discrimination ratio 78.7 %.

It is nice that we can discriminate the *good-trained brain states* for all the subjects from other states by the calculation using the same potentials and the same electrodes. We apply the principal components analysis (PCA) to the data of the distances and the RCAs. In Fig. 13, we show the data plotted in the 2nd component $z2$ (vertical direction) and the 3rd component $z3$ (horizontal direction) of the plane. The plotted points in the graph can be classified into four groups (each group is enclosed by an ellipse). In this way we can determine the discrimination ratio for each combination of principal components.

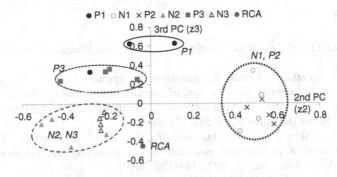

Fig. 13. Data plots for the combination of the 2nd and the 3rd principal components

We apply the discriminant analysis to the data for various combinations from the 25 principal components. The following are discrimination ratios for them:

$\{z2, z3, z8\}$:	97.8%,	$\{z1, z2, z3, z8\}$:	96.7%,
$\{z2, z3\}$:	79.3%,	$\{z1, z2, z3\}$:	80.4%,
$\{z2, z3, z18, z20\}$: 83.7%,		$\{z1, z2, z3, z18, z20\}$: 87.0%.	

For the combinations including $z8$ (the 8th principle component), which is the principal component highly related to the RCAs, the discrimination ratios are about 97 %. On the other hand, for the combinations of components related only to the distances, the discrimination ratios are at most 87.0 %. These results show that the combinations of various principal components without considering individual differences are useful to determine the *good-trained brain states*.

5 Conclusions

The problems and the results discussed in this paper are summarized as follows:

(1) We proposed a method called the m-DSAM for translating the original data of ERPs into clear waveforms of the ERPs.
(2) We defined the distances of ERPs between potentials.
(3) By using the cluster analysis, we defined the *good-trained brain states* for each subject.
(4) By using the distances, we could determine whether a subject is in a *good-trained brain state* or not.
(5) We defined the *good-trained brain states* for all the subjects as the states when the RCAs of subjects reach 94.0 % or more.
(6) By the principal component analysis, we extract the combinations of components, which give discrimination ratios more than 80 %.

In Sect. 2.2.3, we introduced a vector $\mathbf{v}_{jQ}$ to define the distances between potentials in the waveforms of the ERPs. It would be nice if we could find a suitable vector better than the vector $\mathbf{v}_{jQ}$ for our purpose. Such a problem would be worthy for further investigation.

References

1. Carlson, N.R.: Physiology of Behavior, pp. 27–100. Pearson Education Limited, Edinburgh (2014)
2. Funada, M., Igarashi, Y., Funada, T., Shibukawa, M., Igarashi, Y., Ninomija, S.P.: Models of event related potentials using the sum of normal distributions and their evaluation by simulations. In: The 16th IASTED International Conference on Applied Simulation and Modelling, Palma De Mallorca, pp. 581–159 (2007)
3. Funada, M., Shibukawa, M., Igarashi, Y., Funada, T., Ninomija, S.P.: Some characterizations of event-related potentials by reconstructing the distribution of the potentials. Jpn. J. Hum. Factors 46(2), 144–156 (2010)
4. Funada, M., Igarashi, Y., Funada, T., Shibukawa, M.: A model reflecting the changes of ERPs during iterative learning of calculations. In: The Second IASTED Asian Conference on Modelling, Identification and Control, Phuket, pp. 769–086 (2012)
5. Funada, M., Funada, T., Shibukawa, M., Akahor, K.: Quantification and analysis of efficiency of iterative learning by using event related potentials. Educ. Technol. Res. 35, 103–113 (2012)
6. Funada, M., Funada, T., Shibukawa, M.: ERPs composited by multi-data selecting method. In: Proceedings of the 42nd Annual Meeting of the Behaviormetric Society of Japan, pp. 300–301 (2014)
7. Härdle, W., Simar, L.: Applied Multivariate Statistical Analysis, 2nd edn, pp. 215–247. Springer, Heidelberg (2007)
8. Luck, S.J.: An Introduction to the Event-Related Potential Technique. The MIT Press, Cambridge (2005)
9. Luis, F.N.A., Jaime, G.G.: Brain computer interface, a review. Sensors (Basel) 12(2), 1211–1279 (2012)
10. Minami, S.: Data Processing for Scientific Instrumentation, pp. 84–99. CQ Shuppansha, Tokyo (1992)
11. Motiya, E.: Operations Research, pp. 55–66. Nihon Rikou Syuppankai, Tokyo (1988)
12. Nittono, H.: Guidebook Event-Related Potential for Psychology. Ojishobou, Kyoto (2005)
13. Picton, T.W., Bentin, S., Berg, P., Conchin, E., Hillyard, S.A., Johnson Jr., R., Miller, G.A., Ritter, W., Ruchkin, D.S., Rugg, M.D., Taylor, M.J.: Guideline for using human event-related potentials to study cognition: recording standards and publication criteria. Psychophysiology 37, 128–152 (2000)
14. Tsuru, N.: Clinical Electroencephalography and Analysis of Electroencephalography. Shinko Igaku Shuppansha, Tokyo (2000)

BCI and Eye Gaze: Collaboration at the Interface

Leo Galway[✉], Chris Brennan, Paul McCullagh,
and Gaye Lightbody

Computer Science Research Institute, University of Ulster,
Coleraine BT37 0QB, UK
{l.galway, pj.mccullagh, g.lightbody}@ulster.ac.uk,
brennan-c15@email.ulster.ac.uk

Abstract. Due to an extensive list of restraints, brain-computer interface (BCI) technology has seen limited success outside of laboratory conditions. In order to address these limitations, which have prevented widespread deployment, an existing modular architecture has been adapted to support hybrid collaboration of commercially available BCI and eye tracking technologies. However, combining multiple input modalities, which have different temporal properties, presents a challenge in terms of data fusion and collaboration at the user interface. The use of cost-effective and readily available equipment will further promote hybrid BCI as a viable but alternative interface for human computer interaction. In this paper, we focus on navigation through a virtual smart home and control of devices within the rooms; the navigation being controlled by multimodal interaction. As such, it promises a better information transfer rate than BCI alone. Consequently, an extended architecture for a personalised hybrid BCI system has been proposed.

Keywords: Hybrid brain-computer interface · Eye tracking · Domotic control modalities

1 Introduction

Brain-computer interface (BCI) is a paradigm in assistive technology that aims to empower users' capabilities by providing a consistent and reliable input modality that does not require the involvement of peripheral nerves and muscles [1]. In recent years, our increased understanding of the human brain, coupled with advances in modern technology, has led to this type of system becoming a reality, albeit in a more logical and believable form. Whilst the dream of thought controlled devices and applications lives on, the reality, however, focuses on signal processing algorithms that utilise specific patterns in acquired brain signals across both spatial and temporal domains. Increasingly as the algorithms become more complex, the resulting systems may be endowed with more intelligent, contextual processing, thereby leading to increased augmentation for the user.

© Springer International Publishing Switzerland 2015
D.D. Schmorrow and C.M. Fidopiastis (Eds.): AC 2015, LNAI 9183, pp. 199–210, 2015.
DOI: 10.1007/978-3-319-20816-9_20

While it is possible to monitor this type of brain activity via electrocorticogram (ECoG), functional magnetic resonance imaging (fMRI), magnetoencephalogram (MEG), or near-infrared spectroscopy (NIRS), the most commonly employed approach in BCI is via EEG [2]. In this case, the mental state of the user is stimulated in order to generate brain activity patterns that facilitate control, which will vary in accordance with the underlying BCI operating protocol (also referred to as the BCI *paradigm*) [3]. Commonly employed paradigms include event-related desynchronisation/synchronisation (ERD/ERS), slow cortical potentials (SCP), steady state visually evoked potentials (SSVEP), or the P300 and error-related potential (ErrP) components of event-related potential (ERP) waveforms [4]. Nevertheless, each of these paradigms is hindered by a corresponding set of limitations, including slow information transfer rates, inter/intra-subject variability, inconvenient set up procedures, and the need for carefully controlled environments. This is particularly disappointing as such restrictions adversely affect those that could potentially benefit from this technology the most, individuals who suffer from disease and traumatic injury, which, in severe cases, can lead to Amyotrophic Lateral Sclerosis (ALS) [5]. To reduce the impact of such limitations and utilise the advantages of different BCI methods recent emphasis has been placed upon hybrid architectures. A possible architecture may combine the use of BCI paradigms with separate technologies, such as eye tracking, in order to permit the use of a sequential or collaborative set of input modalities [5]. Systems that follow such a structure are typically known as hybrid BCIs (hBCI) and have the potential to improve classification accuracy for specific tasks, by facilitating individual modalities for distinct aspects of user input processing or cooperative command classification.

In this work, a custom BCI system, originally developed within the EU FP7 BRAIN project to provide BCI control within a virtual domestic environment [6], has been extended to facilitate an approach that makes use of hBCI. Comprising a set of tools for interface development, along with SSVEP and ERD/ERS recording, the system known as the intuitive graphical user interface (IGUI) has been augmented in order to support the combination of eye tracking and BCI control through the use of inexpensive, portable and commercially available devices. Consequently, it is anticipated that the use of such commercially available technology in the hybrid system will facilitate improvements in human-computer interaction over more traditional BCI-based approaches.

2 Related Work

BCI is a potential solution for individuals that suffer from a variation of neuronal dysfunction and similar afflictions, but it endures various technical limitations, which have hindered its exploitation. There is a gap between what is considered to be an acceptable accuracy for a usable system and what is achievable outside the laboratory, in addition to differences in the performance of such systems between users suffering from brain injury and control subjects [6]. Thus, solutions based on hBCI architectures could prove to be the next logical step by harnessing the best features from complementary technologies [5, 7].

Previous research studies have focused largely on singular paradigms in order to facilitate control using BCI systems. Yet these studies have noted accuracy, performance and reliability limitations [8, 9]. The combination of a number of different input modalities may improve upon these results, thus providing a greater level of communication and control [10]. For instance, an active BCI paradigm, such as SSVEP, can deliver a method of direct control, whereas a passive BCI paradigm, such as ErrP, can potentially provide implicit control [11]. Such a system could benefit from reinforced decisions while autonomously correcting false positive *no-control* states, thereby improving upon the performance that the use of a single paradigm can offer [12]. Furthermore, eye tracking technology, which can aid severely disabled individuals by providing them with a level of control, also experiences its own set of limitations. In general, eye tracking, which is often used by patients with peripheral muscular dysfunction, uses both infrared signals and reflected light to determine the trajectory of a user's gaze. This technology is known to provide efficient cursor control but suffers from intended selection restrictions, an area of significant attention in BCI. Earlier research studies have focused on the frequency of blinks and dwell times as the selection criteria, however, the results are far from promising [1], thus increasing the demand for further technological innovation within this area. Subsequently, the collaboration of both BCI and eye tracking as input modalities may mitigate the limitations associated with the individual modalities, thereby providing a more powerful hybrid system. For example, Lee et al. [13] proposed a method to combine BCI and eye tracking for 3D interaction using a bespoke head-mounted eye tracker with attached EEG sensors. According to the experimental results, the feasibility of the proposed 3D interaction method using eye tracking and BCI was confirmed [13]. However, there remains a gap in the efficacy of such systems outside of laboratory conditions, particularly in terms of usability and user interaction [6]. Subsequently, the primary motivation for this research is that solutions based on hBCI architectures could harness features from complementary technologies [5], thereby closing this gap.

3   Navigation and Control of a Virtual Domestic Environment

As previously discussed, the IGUI is a system designed to interact with a virtual representation of a domestic environment, which has the overarching purpose of providing alternative channels for communication and domotic control. The system was originally developed to provide all users with a method to interact with their external environment using a traditional BCI in conjunction with the SSVEP paradigm [6]. Implemented using the Java programming language, thus permitting operating system-independent deployment, the IGUI provides an interactive menu system that has been specifically structured to facilitate four-way directional control and item selection, whereby each selected item controls an event that can be triggered within a corresponding smart environment. As illustrated in Fig. 1, the IGUI presents users with four directional arrows (*Up, Down, Left, Right*), which are utilised to navigate through a hierarchy of environment-related events. The current event, or level of the hierarchy, appears in the middle of the interface, which then permits users to trigger the event,

Fig. 1. The IGUI interactive menu system facilitates domotic control within a smart environment. Navigation through levels of an event hierarchy is conducted though 4-way directional control. A distinct event or current level is positioned in the centre of the interface.

or move to a sub-level of the hierarchy, by selecting the *Down* arrow. Likewise, to navigate to upper levels of the hierarchy, or to exit the system, the user must select the *Up* arrow.

While the IGUI provides the user interface, the overall system has been realised as a customisable and practical application architecture that can be easily extended to support various input modalities. Subsequently, the two primary components of the system are the IGUI and the universal application interface (UAI), which is an application programming interface that provides a generic platform for bridging the IGUI, BCI platform, and both applications and devices within a smart environment.

3.1 Intuitive Graphical User Interface System Architecture

To facilitate BCI-based domotic device control, the UAI interacts with the BCI device through the IGUI. Accordingly, the UAI aims to interconnect heterogeneous networked devices and provide a common controlling interface for the rest of the system. In order to achieve this, UPnP has been chosen as the communication protocol, thus providing an interoperable specification with common protocols to other technologies. As UPnP is a distributed, open networking architecture that uses TCP/IP and HTTP, proximity networking may be enabled in a seamless manner, along with control and data transfer among networked devices. As a result, device interaction with the IGUI system may be implemented through an UPnP interface. Where this is the case, implementation of the UPnP standard will be conducted using a dedicated module in the UAI, which is accessible to all applications. Consequently, the IGUI and UAI interact based upon command structure; in conjunction with both the IGUI and UAI components, the IGUI system architecture utilises a set of user datagram protocol (UDP) packets to facilitate both input and output to/from the overall system. In terms of system inputs, the IGUI has been designed in order to act as a UDP listener. Employing external components to perform processing and analysis of the raw EEG signal, processed signals are translated into directional commands, which are further encapsulated within a set of UDP packets before transmission to the IGUI system. Each packet is assigned an arbitrary code, which is determined in correspondence with the appropriate classification result obtained during signal processing. For example, in the original IGUI system, the SSVEP paradigm was employed to provide four-way directional control in which the *Up*, *Down*, *Left* and *Right* commands were determined from classification of the raw EEG signal. Upon receipt of a UDP packet, the IGUI is updated to reflect the resulting command. In the case where a directional command is used to trigger an environment-related event (i.e. the icon for an event, such as switching on a light, is shown in the centre of the IGUI and the user selects the *Down* command), the command corresponding to the event is processed by the UAI, which, in turn, transmits the command encapsulated in another UDP packet to a UAI receiver for the external device associated with the event. Thus, the IGUI and UAI synthesize in order to facilitate BCI-based navigation and control of devices within a smart environment. However, during initial trials, some users found the use of the directional control system a cognitive challenge as the navigation arrows and manipulation of a central event icon caused confusion and difficulties when attempting to locate specific environment-related events. Additionally, when using the IGUI with a BCI paradigm, several unintended exits would occur due to miss-classification of the raw EEG signal into an *Up* command when the user was at the topmost level of the event hierarchy. Consequently, using alternative input modalities, or hybrid combinations of input modalities, can potentially mitigate the effects of this. In addition, each BCI paradigm utilised with the original IGUI system followed the same command structure and was allocated an individual set of command codes. Although there was no in-built mechanism to automate a switch between paradigms, the modular nature of the IGUI architecture and use of arbitrary codes further promotes development of an hBCI system that can utilise a number of input modalities in either a sequential or collaborative manner.

3.2 Hybrid Intuitive Graphical User Interface System Architecture

In order to provide more intuitive navigation, an eye tracking system was initially implemented whereby a user could select a directional command within the IGUI by navigating to it with their gaze. In keeping with the original design of the IGUI system, the user could then perform selection of an environment-related event using the *Down* command. Essentially, this approach attempts to simulate a more natural input method where the user's gaze acts as both cursor control and mouse click. The eye tribe tracker [14] was chosen as the alternative input modality because it is available at a much lower cost than other eye tracking systems, and yet it retains sufficient accuracy for this type of application. At first glance, the eye tracking-only variation of the IGUI system appeared to significantly outperform the original BCI-only variation in terms of accuracy of user control. However, after extensive testing, a substantial rate of false positives was detected, especially when a user paused to think, as this often resulted in excessive dwell times occurring on targeted directional commands, which substantially reduced the reliability and usability of the system.

To overcome this issue, a further iteration of the IGUI system was developed to integrate a brain-neuronal computer interaction approach, thereby permitting inclusion of devices that monitor additional physiological signals, not only from signals acquired directly from the brain. Utilising the Emotiv EPOC [15] as a BCI device for the acquisition of EEG activity, it was possible to mitigate the dwell time with a teeth clench component as a proxy for an EEG feature, which was subsequently employed to trigger usage of the eye tracker component. The EPOC was employed to extract the representative features from scalp locations AF3, AF4, F3, F4, F8, F7, FC5, FC6, T7, T8, P7, P8, O1, and O2. In order to extend the base IGUI architecture, a *Data Fusion* component was implemented within the IGUI, which was responsible for determining an authoritative control signal from the receipt of UDP packets from both the BCI device and eye tracker. An overview of the data flow through the various components of the IGUI system is illustrated in Fig. 1.

In terms of multimodal interaction, the current system supports two modalities for selection and control. The eye tracker can facilitate navigation and selection by generating a set of co-ordinates that are representative of the users gaze, divided among the four quadrants of the IGUI. In the centre of the IGUI is a *No State Zone*, which is a predefined location where the user can verify selection of an environment-related event. Additionally, the BCI device can facilitate explicit operation of the eye tracker by permitting the user to initiate and suspend use of the eye tracker when required. In essence, the BCI device acts as a *switch*, therefore simple EEG-based features, such as an increase in overall EEG power initiated by the user, can be potentially utilised. Correspondingly, more sophisticated features can be initiated by relaxation (e.g. an increase in the alpha activity ratio of the EEG signal) or in response to screen-based visual stimulation, such as the use of a pattern reversal stimulus at a pre-determined frequency, thereby invoking an SSVEP response. As the IGUI system must also handle quickly repeated correct commands, due to variations in the frequency of responses from the individual input modalities, in conjunction with the variable nature of user interaction, the frequency of the response from the eye tracker has been reduced in order to moderate responsiveness. The following sections of the paper cover details of the experimental protocol used and analysis of the corresponding results from testing of both the eye tracker-only and hybrid variations of the system (Fig. 2).

4   Methodology

Within the BCI literature it is common to measure performance by calculating the information transfer rate (ITR) in bits/min, which takes into account values for both accuracy and time. Accordingly, the literature suggests that BCI systems generally

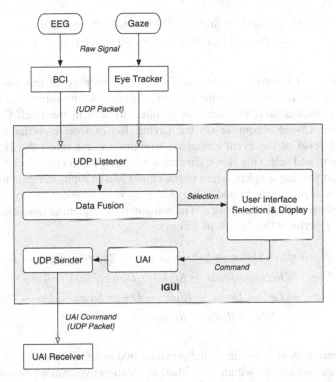

Fig. 2. The internal dataflow of the hybrid system featuring a BCI-based input modality and an eye tracking input modality.

achieve an ITR between 10–25 bits/min whereas conventional input devices, such as a mouse and keyboard, have been known to achieve an ITR in excess of 300 bits/min. ITR as defined in [16] is shown below:

$$ITR = (log_2M + Plog_2P + (1 - P)log_2[(1 - P)/(M - 1)]) * (60/T). \quad (1)$$

where M is the number of choices, P is the accuracy of target detection, and T is the average time for a selection. Subsequently, this metric has been used in order to conduct an evaluation of the performance of the two variations of the IGUI system. A cohort of 12 users were asked to carry out 3 tasks within the associated virtual domestic environment, as follows:

Task 1 (Domotic Control): The purpose of this task is to simulate navigation and control within the virtual domestic environment. Starting in the Back Garden, the user is asked to navigate to the Dining Room, turn on a lamp, and then return to the Back Garden. The sequence of sequential operations required to successfully perform this task is as follows:

$$Right \rightarrow Right \rightarrow Right \rightarrow Right \rightarrow Down \rightarrow Right \rightarrow Right$$
$$\rightarrow Down(LampON) \rightarrow Up \rightarrow Left \rightarrow Left \rightarrow Left \rightarrow Left$$

Task 2 (Multimedia Control): Similar to Task 1, the purpose of this task is also to simulate navigation and control within the virtual domestic environment. For successful completion of this task, the user was required to start in the Back Garden, then navigate to the Living Room, select the Living Room icon in order to enter the corresponding level of the event hierarchy, navigate to and select the Home Media icon, navigate to and select the Home Cinema icon, navigate to and select a Video icon in order to start playing a video, return to the Home Media icon, navigate to and select the Controls icon, navigate to and select the Stop icon in order to stop playing the video, then return to the Back Garden. The sequence of sequential operations required to successfully perform this task is as follows:

$$Left \rightarrow Left \rightarrow Left \rightarrow Down \rightarrow Left \rightarrow Down \rightarrow Right \rightarrow Right \rightarrow Down$$
$$\rightarrow Right \rightarrow Right \rightarrow Right \rightarrow Down(Play) \rightarrow Up \rightarrow Left$$
$$\rightarrow Left \rightarrow Down \rightarrow Right \rightarrow Down(Stop) \rightarrow Up \rightarrow Up \rightarrow Up$$
$$\rightarrow Right \rightarrow Right \rightarrow Right$$

Task 3 (Communication): Similar to the previous two tasks, the purpose of this task is also to simulate navigation within the virtual domestic environment, however, rather than direct selection of an environment-related event, the user is asked to indicate their desire to eat using the iconography provided within the environment. For successful completion of this task, each user was required to start in the Back Garden, then navigate to and select the Talk icon, navigate and select the Eat icon, then return to the Back Garden. The shortest series of sequential operations required to successfully complete this task is follows:

$$Left \rightarrow Down \rightarrow Left \rightarrow Left \rightarrow Down(Eat) \rightarrow Up \rightarrow Right$$

For both variations of the IGUI system, the ITR was determined according to Eq. (1) for individual users on each task.

5 Evaluation Results

A comparison of the mean ITR values from each task using both variations of the IGUI system is given in Fig. 3. In order to determine the mean ITR for each task, the ITR from each task for each user was first determined and the overall set of ITR values for a task averaged. Subsequently, when Task 1 was carried out using the eye tracker-only variation of the IGUI system, a mean ITR of 122.79 (SD: 28.53) bits/min was obtained, whereas a mean ITR of 168.70 (SD: 21.17) bits/min was obtained for Task 1 when the hBCI variation of the IGUI system was used. Likewise, Task 2 also showed an increase

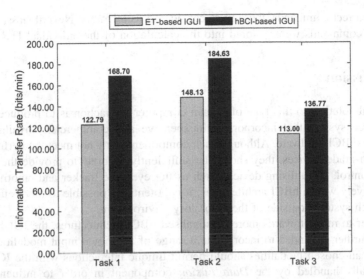

Fig. 3. Comparison of mean information transfer rate values for each task performed by all users when utilizing the eye tracker-only version of IGUI system (denoted *ET-based IGUI*) and hybrid version of IGUI system combining eye tracker for directional control and EEG-based signal for switch (denoted *hBCI-based IGUI*).

in the mean ITR obtained, from 148.13 (SD: 14.98) bits/min, when using the eye tracker as the only input modality, to 184.63 (SD: 25.05) bits/min when using a combination of eye tracking and an EEG-detected teeth clench as input modalities. The improvement in the ITR is also observed for the results obtained from Task 3, with the single input modality achieving a mean ITR of 113.00 (SD: 22.27) bits/min in comparison to the combination of input modalities, which achieved a mean ITR of 136.77 (SD: 18.02) bits/min. Consequently, the results indicate that regardless of the complexity of the task, a higher ITR is achieved when utilising a combination of an eye tracker for directional navigation and selection, and a BCI-based switch to trigger the use of the eye tracker, as input modalities.

During the evaluation of the eye tracker-only variation of the IGUI system, a number of false positives were detected, which triggered an incorrect command that needed to be rectified by the user, or in the case of an unintended exit, by the experimenter. In the cases where an unintended exit occurred, the interaction time was paused and the IGUI manually returned to the state prior to the unintended exit. All unintended commands were considered as false positive commands and any commands used to rectify a mistake were considered as true positive commands, which were factored into the calculation of the individual ITR values.

By contrast, during evaluation of the hybrid variation of the IGUI system, a significant reduction in the number of false positive commands was observed. As a result, no unintended exits were triggered by any of the users during the evaluation. However, unintended commands still needed to be rectified by the user. In addition, the hybrid system also experienced a rate of false negatives, which were not present during the evaluation of the eye tracking-only version of the system. As false negatives do not trigger incorrect commands, these were considered as tolerable. Nevertheless, all such erroneous commands were factored into the calculation of the individual ITR values.

6 Discussion

A potential solution to this type of human computer interaction is to produce a fully open source system that incorporates inexpensive and commercially available eye tracking and BCI hardware. Although such components may not meet the performance of research-grade devices, they should be sufficiently accurate to provide the desired level of control. By utilising devices such as the eye tribe tracker and emotiv EPOC collaboratively within hBCI architectures, it is potentially possible to more effectively deploy such systems outside of the laboratory environment.

In order to move towards more personalised hBCI architectures, the IGUI system could be further expanded to incorporate a range of additional input modalities. Subsequently, all chosen modalities should permit unique interactions with the IGUI and be eventually handled by the *Data Fusion* component in order to influence user commands. Furthermore, modalities should be weighted by the *Data Fusion* component and operate either collaboratively or competitively, whereby weightings are automatically adjusted as the system is utilised in order to provide a degree of personalisation. Moreover, in order to further expand and exploit the IGUI system architecture, two key application domains should be taken into consideration: affective computing and ambient intelligence. Subsequently, Fig. 4 illustrates a proposed personalised hBCI architecture that utilises the IGUI as a core component.

As depicted in Fig. 4, integration of an affective computing sensor platform would facilitate input to the IGUI from a range of pre-processed features acquired by physiological and affective sensors, in conjunction with the use of passive BCI. By passively monitoring physiological and emotion-related signals, including the EEG signal, the

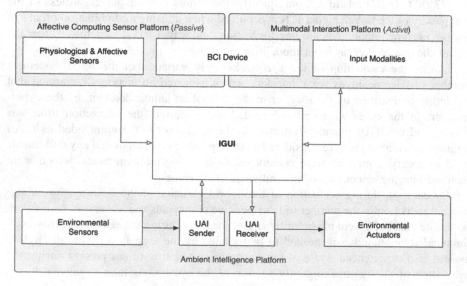

Fig. 4. A proposed architecture for personalised hybrid BCI that expands on the IGUI system

resulting affective state of a user may be determined and subsequently utilised by the IGUI in order to permit a degree of personalisation and system adaptation [17, 18], through the weightings and control signals associated with the data fusion component of the IGUI. In essence, the affective computing sensor platform, in conjunction with usage statistics from the IGUI, could be used to generate an affective model of the user, which acts as an enabler for personalisation of the overarching user interface and set of input modalities. Additionally, the ambient intelligence platform may be used to facilitate feedback of external environmental information to the IGUI. Such feedback, in conjunction with the IGUI usage statistics, could potentially provide a further degree of contextual information that could subsequently be utilised to provide enhanced context awareness that contributes to the adaptation of the IGUI and choice of input modalities. For example, menus within the IGUI could be arranged according to frequent usage depending on current tasks, historical patterns, time of day, etc. Again, this leads to a greater degree of personalisation, as the iconography employed within the IGUI could be adapted to support the current context of the user. Furthermore, a hBCI system that utilises the collaboration of active BCI, eye tracking and other technologies as input modalities may be employed to provide a multimodal interaction platform that mitigates the limitations associated with these individual modalities, thereby providing a more natural set of active inputs for the personalised hBCI architecture.

7 Conclusion and Future Work

In this work we have shown the feasibility of using collaborative input modalities based on a hybrid BCI approach. Both of the devices utilised are cost-effective, highly usable and sufficiently accurate, which makes them particularly suited for deployment outside of laboratory conditions. A benefit of such a hybrid approach is in the system's ability to facilitate interaction only when desired by the user, rather than unintentionally when the user is distracted or idle. In the evaluation presented, we have also shown that the fusion of BNCI and eye tracking technologies improves upon the performance of singular approaches. Consequently, a key objective for future work is to investigate how the current BNCI component can be replaced with the use of more traditional BCI paradigms. Furthermore, an extended hybrid architecture has been proposed, which substantially expands upon the range of input modalities to incorporate environmental, physiological and affective features, thus facilitating the creation of a truly personalised hybrid BCI system. It is anticipated that collaboration at a central interface will enfranchise such personalisation.

References

1. Zander, T.O., Kothe, C., Jatzev, S., Gaertner, M.: Enhancing human-computer interaction with input from active and passive brain-computer interfaces. In: Tan, D.S., Nijholt, A. (eds.) Brain-Computer Interfaces: Human-Computer Interaction Series, pp. 181–199. Springer, London (2010)

2. Volosyak, I., Valbuena, D., Malechka, T., Peuscher, J., Gräser, A.: Brain-computer interface using water-based electrodes. J. Neural Eng. **7**(6), 066007 (2010)
3. Wolpaw, J.R., Birbaumer, N., McFarland, D.J., Pfurtscheller, G., Vaughan, T.M.: Brain-computer interfaces for communication and control. Clin. Neurophysiol. **113**(6), 767–791 (2002)
4. Allison, B.Z., Brunner, C., Kaiser, V., Müller-Putz, G.R., Neuper, C., Pfurtscheller, G.: Toward a hybrid brain-computer interface based on imagined movement and visual attention. J. Neural Eng. **7**(2), 026007 (2010)
5. McCullagh, P., Galway, L., Lightbody, G.: Investigation into a Mixed Hybrid Using SSVEP and Eye Gaze for Optimising User Interaction within a Virtual Environment. In: Stephanidis, C., Antona, M. (eds.) UAHCI 2013, Part I. LNCS, vol. 8009, pp. 530–539. Springer, Heidelberg (2013)
6. Ware, M.P., McCullagh, P.J., McRoberts, A., Lightbody, G., Nugent, C., McAllister, G., Mulvenna, M.D., Thomson, E., Martin, S.: Contrasting levels of accuracy in command interaction sequences for a domestic brain-computer interface using SSVEP. In: 5th Cairo International Biomedical Engineering Conference. IEEE Press, New York, pp. 150–153 (2010)
7. Pfurtscheller, G., Allison, B.Z., Brunner, C., Bauemfeind, G., Solis-Escalante, T., Scherer, R., Zander, T.O., Mueller-Putz, G., Neuper, C., Birbaumer, N.: The hybrid BCI. Front. Neurosci. **4**(42), 1–11 (2010)
8. Allison, B., Luth, T., Valbuena, D., Teymourian, A., Volosyak, I., Gräser, A.: BCI demographics: how many (and what kinds of) people can use an SSVEP BCI? IEEE Trans. Neural Syst. Rehabil. Eng. **18**(2), 107–116 (2010)
9. McFarland, D.J., Miner, L.A., Vaughan, T.M., Wolpaw, J.R.: Mu and beta rhythm topographies during motor imagery and actual movements. Brain Topogr. **12**(3), 177–186 (2000)
10. Durka, P.J., Kuś, R., Żygierewicz, J., Michalska, M., Milanowski, P., Łabęcki, M., Spustek, T., Laszuk, D., Duszyk, A., Kruszyński, M.: User-centered design of brain-computer interfaces: OpenBCI.pl and BCI appliance. Bull. Polish Acad. Sci. Tech. Sci. **60**, 427–431 (2012)
11. George, L., Lécuyer, A.: An overview of research on "passive" brain-computer interfaces for implicit human-computer interaction. In: International Conference on Applied Bionics and Biomechanics ICABB 2010 – Workshop W1 "Brain-Computer Interfacing and Virtual Reality", Venise (2010)
12. The Future BNCI Project: Future BNCI: a roadmap for future directions in brain/neuronal computer interaction research (2012)
13. Lee, E.C., Woo, J.C., Kim, J.H., Whang, M., Park, K.R.: A brain-computer interface method combined with eye tracking for 3D interaction. J. Neurosci. Methods **190**(2), 289–298 (2010)
14. The Eye Tribe Tracker: https://theeyetribe.com/products/
15. Emotiv EPOC / EPOC+: http://www.emotiv.com/epoc.php
16. Gao, S., Wang, Y., Gao, X., Hong, B.: Visual and auditory brain-computer interfaces. IEEE Trans. Biomed. Eng. **61**(5), 1436–1447 (2014)
17. Molina, G.G., Tsoneva, T., Nijholt, A.: Emotional brain-computer interfaces. In: 3rd International Conference on Affective Computing and Intelligent Interaction and Workshops ACII 2009. IEEE Press, New York (2009)
18. Zander, T.O., Jatzev, S.: Detecting affective covert user states with passive brain-computer interfaces. In: 3rd International Conference on Affective Computing and Intelligent Interaction and Workshops ACII 2009. IEEE Press, New York (2009)

Using Behavioral Information to Contextualize BCI Performance

Stephen M. Gordon[✉], Jonathan R. McDaniel,
Jason S. Metcalfe, and Antony D. Passaro

DCS Corporation, Alexandria, VA 22310, USA
{sgordon, jmcdaniel, jmetcalfe, apassaro}@dcscorp.com

Abstract. Brain-computer interface (BCI) systems often require millisecond-level timing precision in order to function reliably. However, as BCI research expands to an ever-widening array of applications, including operation in real-world environments, such timing requirements will need to be relaxed. In addition, overall BCI system design must be improved in order to better disambiguate the numerous, seemingly similar, neural responses that may arise in such environments. We argue that this new area of operational BCI will require the integration of neural data with non-neural contextual variables in order to function reliably. We propose a framework in which non-neural contextual information can be used to better scope the operational BCI problem by indicating windows of time for specific analyses as well as defining probability distributions over these windows. We demonstrate the utility of our framework on a sample data set and provide discussion on many of the factors influencing performance.

Keywords: Brain-computer interface (BCI) · Electroencephalography (EEG) · Asynchronous event detection

1 Introduction

Previous work to monitor individuals in operational environments using electroencephalography (EEG) has focused on continuous state monitoring. Systems have been developed to estimate states such as a user's alertness or fatigue [1, 2]. In order to perform reliably in operational settings many of these systems focus on, relatively, slowly varying signals that often exhibit broad scalp topologies. These systems do not attempt to monitor the moment-to-moment dynamics associated with event-related, phase-locked, processing unless precise event timing information is available. Within the field of brain-computer interfaces (BCI) there has been little work in developing tools capable of detecting such events in real-time without precise timing.

Most BCI classifiers are built using some form of time-locked signal representation, which in turn is based on the onset of some known event. However, in real-world applications the onset of events is often not known. Without knowing the time periods to which the classifier should be applied it is very difficult to control the number of false positives produced. This problem is exacerbated when one considers that in real-world environments there are numerous tasks and side-tasks that an individual may perform.

© Springer International Publishing Switzerland 2015
D.D. Schmorrow and C.M. Fidopiastis (Eds.): AC 2015, LNAI 9183, pp. 211–220, 2015.
DOI: 10.1007/978-3-319-20816-9_21

Therefore one of the major problems associated with asynchronous, online, EEG-based event detection is one of scope. Furthermore, we argue that it is unlikely that advances in EEG technology or signal processing methods for EEG analysis alone will be able to clearly disassociate the myriad brain states and phase-locked events that a system could encounter in operational settings.

In this regard, researchers and system developers must find alternative methods to analyze and interpret real-time EEG data. In order to facilitate application of current BCI tools to operational settings we feel that well-designed systems need the following three critical components:

1. *Trigger mechanism*: This mechanism indicates a period of high likelihood for an event's occurrence and, thus, scopes the classification problem.
2. *Likelihood function*: Even with an appropriate trigger mechanism, the temporal ambiguity of the neural event must be quantified or estimated in order to optimize classifiability.
3. *Decision criterion*: This enables a go/no-go decision to be made using the current data. In the case of a no-go response, the classifier may wait for more data, or output that there is insufficient information to make a decision.

Our approach is based on the notion that in operational settings there is an inextricable link between behavior and brain dynamics [3, 4] that must be taken advantage of in order to build functioning BCI systems.

2 Operational BCI Model

2.1 Trigger Mechanism

Most of the prior work in the field of asynchronous BCI [5, 6] has focused on strategies to reason over the output of multiple classifiers without utilizing additional information, such as that provided by other physiological and behavioral sources, to contextualize or scope the problem. Scoping the problem, however, is a critical need that must be met in order to perform BCI analysis in operational environments. In its most basic form, scoping the problem defines an analysis window over which the BCI system must reason and may be used to select the appropriate set of classifiers to apply to that analysis window. We propose the use of a trigger mechanism to initially scope the problem.

In operational environments there may be a number of potential trigger mechanisms. Triggers may occur before, during, or after an event and, in some cases, may only occur with a particular probability. However, when present, the trigger mechanism determines an analysis window for the underlying BCI components. In addition, the trigger itself may form one layer of event detection with the presence or absence of a neural signature forming a subsequent layer for event detection. Trigger mechanisms may be unique to each data set and to each cognitive event.

Specific trigger mechanisms could come from behavior, such as saccadic eye movements or changes in pupil dilation in response to the onset of visual stimuli or gross movement patterns in response to actual or perceived errors. Alternatively, triggers could come from more general state changes such as changes in attentional focus or current task. In the prior case, the analysis window may be a relatively short, well defined period of time, whereas in the latter case the trigger may indicate a shift from one set of asynchronous BCI tools to another.

2.2 Likelihood Function

The second need for operational BCI is that, even given an approximate analysis window, there will still be a significant amount of temporal variability associated with the precise timing of the cognitive event. This is due, in large part, to the ambiguity of the natural world and the difficulty associated with determining the precise timing, both at the physiological level and at the hardware level, of events. It is important to establish, to the extent possible, a likelihood function describing the probability of the event within the analysis window. There has been recent work to account for temporal ambiguity in the event response, e.g. Marathe et al. [7], but such approaches have not incorporated probability distributions derived from known behavior and event dynamics.

There are many ways in which likelihood functions may be obtained, but the key is that these functions link measurable properties of the situation, e.g. the trigger mechanism, to the probability of the cognitive event. These functions allow the system to interpret the output of the BCI classifier, or an ensemble set of classifiers, at each time point in the analysis window. In addition, if the likelihood function can be linked to other measurable signals, either physiological or behavioral in origin, then this allows the integration of the BCI output into a more structured belief network describing the current state of the operator. Integration strategies that could be used include approaches such as generalized linear models, multivariate regression, Bayesian belief networks, Markov chains, or fuzzy methods. In addition, the likelihood function could be used to integrate the output of multiple classifiers in a manner similar to the approach of [7].

2.3 Decision Criteria

Given the ambiguity associated with defining both the analysis window and the likelihood function, operational BCI systems will also need some form of confidence metric or decision criteria to determine whether the current output should be accepted or rejected. If the output is rejected, the system may continue to analyze additional data as it arrives or assert that insufficient information was available to make the decision. Incorporating a likelihood function allows a natural extension to develop confidence values in the BCI output. An appropriate decision criterion must be tuned for each scenario to balance (1) the speed with which a decision is reached, (2) the number of misclassifications produced by the system, and (3) the number of missed cognitive events. There has been much prior work in machine learning to develop confidence metrics for both the input data and the output of the classifier [8]. We simply suggest using metrics that take advantage of the known dynamics of the situation, e.g. the likelihood function, the analysis window, and the signal to be classified.

3 Methods

We illustrate our proposed framework using an experiment in which participants were required to detect and report targets that appeared in the environment. Target reports were made by pushing a button with either the left or right index finger. We focus on classifying the target reports (i.e. distinguishing which hand the participants used). We use saccadic eye movements as the trigger mechanism and use empirically derived estimates of the distribution of response times given a saccadic eye movement as the likelihood function. We compare our approach with an asynchronous method in which no such information is available.

3.1 Participants

Participants were 13 right-handed males age 20–40 (mean, 31.3 std. 2.6). All subjects reported normal, or corrected to normal, vision and reported no known neurological issues. All participants provided written, informed consent in accordance with procedures approved by the Institutional Review Board of the US Army Research Laboratory, and all testing conformed to the guidelines set forth by the 1964 Declaration of Helsinki.

3.2 Stimuli and Procedure

Participants completed a simulation task in which they were driven, as passengers in a vehicle, through a simulated environment and were responsible for detecting and classifying targets and reporting the type of target, by pressing a button with either the left or right index finger. The simulated environment was an urban landscape and targets appeared at random, but in logically congruent, locations in that environment. There were two basic types of targets: threats and nonthreats. Participants were trained to recognize each type of target during an initial training phase. Training continued until each participant reached a minimum performance level of 80 % classification accuracy. Targets were presented roughly every three seconds and participants were asked to respond as quickly and accurately as possible. Participants completed two 15 min blocks, each comprising approximately 180 targets.

3.3 Physiological Recording

Electrophysiological recordings were sampled at 1024 Hz from 64 scalp electrodes arranged in a 10–10 montage using a BioSemi Active Two system (Amsterdam, Netherlands). External leads were placed on the outer canthus and below the orbital fossa of the right eye to record monopolar electrooculography (EOG). External leads were also placed on both mastoids to provide electrical reference as well as on the forehead and along the ridge of the masseter to record electromyographic (EMG) signals. The continuous data were referenced offline before being digitally filtered 0.3–50 Hz. To reduce muscle and ocular artifacts in the EEG signal we removed EOG and EMG components using independent components analysis (ICA) by finding the ICA components that maximally correlated with the horizontal and vertical EOG channels [9].

Eye tracking was recorded at 60 Hz using the Facelab (www.seeingmachines.com) two-camera, video-based eye tracking system. Participants were calibrated for the eye tracker prior to the start of the experiment. In addition, participants performed a baseline eye tracking task involving a quick saccade task in which the participant had to saccade to different points on the screen and click on colored targets using the mouse pointer. This task was completed before and after the experiment.

3.4 Contextualized BCI System Construction

Baseline Classifier. We built a classifier for each participant to detect the finger movements associated with target responses. We used ICA to derive a set of components that captured the phase-locked, event-related potentials (i.e. ERPs) and non-phase-locked (i.e. spectral changes in the alpha and beta frequency bands) but event-related features associated with motor control for each subject. We used these components as features and a forward feature selection algorithm to select the best components for each subject. Classification was performed using a support vector machine with a radial basis function kernel implemented with the LibSVM toolbox for Matlab [10]. For each subject we trained on the first 15 min block of data and tested on the second.

Integrating Context. To improve detection and disassociation of cognitive events associated with target onset, target discrimination, and reporting, we developed the model shown in Fig. 1. For the results described in the following section, we focused on the model components highlighted by the dashed line.

We analyzed the relationships between target onset and the saccadic eye movement and between the saccadic eye movement and the motor response. We first smoothed the

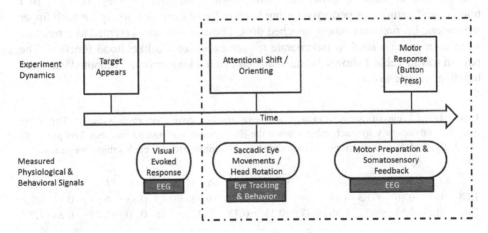

Fig. 1. Time course of experiment dynamics and measurable physiological and behavioral changes associated with target onset, detection, and reporting.

eye tracking data and then performed threshold-based saccade detection. For our current analysis we used the saccade as the trigger mechanism. We then used the probability of response given a saccade as the likelihood function, which was empirically estimated from the available training data.

We analyzed subsets of this data by stepping the BCI system over the analysis window. The analysis window extended from the onset of the saccade for 1.5 s. We limited our analysis to this window because no motor responses occurred outside of this time range for any subject. For each participant a set of classifiers were trained using different subsets of the available training data to predict the motor response. The classifiers were each trained using one second of data. We then stepped these classifiers over the analysis window in 100 ms increments and for each of these analysis points we summed the output from this ensemble of classifiers to obtain a single value. We used the distribution of reaction times given a saccadic eye movement to combine the outputs within a single analysis window.

Eye Tracking Quality. Eye tracking quality was determined using the baseline saccade task. As previously stated, the task required participants to saccade to different points on the screen. For each trial, the minimum distance between the gaze coordinates measured by the eye tracker and the known screen coordinates for the current point was used to create an error for that trial. These errors were z-scored and then averaged over all trials for each participant and used to compute a total quality for each subject. We standardized these values before averaging because we found that the errors produced at the end of the experiment were significantly larger than those produced before the experiment.

4 Results

4.1 Epoch BCI

The top row in Table 1 shows the classification results for all subjects when BCI training and testing was performed using knowledge of the exact timing for each finger movement, i.e. precisely timed, epoched data. These results are presented as a baseline since there was no need to incorporate trigger events or the likelihood function. The bottom row in Table 1 shows the standardized eye tracking error as computed using the baseline saccade tasks.

Table 1. BCI classification accuracy and eye tracker error for each subject. Top row: classification accuracy for each subject when the BCI system was trained and tested on precisely timed, epoched data. Bottom row: standardized mean-square error for each subject's eye tracking data.

	S1	S2	S3	S4	S5	S6	S7	S8	S9	S10	S11	S12	S13
BCI	0.75	0.80	0.83	0.64	0.84	0.77	0.74	0.76	0.85	0.83	0.84	0.71	0.73
Eye	−0.39	0.56	−0.17	1.35	0.47	−0.39	−0.73	−0.77	−0.25	0.30	−0.41	−0.58	1.22

4.2   Contextualized BCI

Next, we performed asynchronous BCI detection using the same data that was used to generate the results in Table 1. As described previously, we focused on analysis windows starting with the onset of the saccade, but we removed all experimental information describing the timing of those events within the analysis window. We performed two types of asynchronous detection. First we used the continuous fire approach where we obtained final BCI output by integrating the individual outputs computed over the entire analysis window. Second, we used the likelihood function that related the probability of a motor response to the onset of the saccade. We applied these likelihood values to the individual outputs produced at each analysis point in the analysis window. This likelihood function was determined using the same training data that was used to develop the BCI classifiers. Finally, we compared the performance of both approaches by analyzing how the accuracy varied as a function of confidence level.

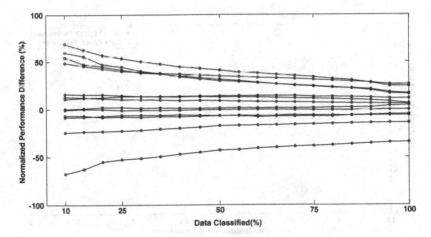

Fig. 2. Percent improvement in classification for the contextualized BCI over the non-contextualized approach. For each subject the differences have been normalized by the baseline classification level achieved with the epoch-based classifiers from Sect. 4.1.

Figure 2 shows the performance differences between the contextualized approach and the non-contextualized approach for each subject as we iteratively relaxed the decision criteria to capture more of the motor events. The x-axis shows the percent of data classified based on selecting the data with the strongest confidence values. The y-axis shows performance differences between the two approaches, normalized for each subject by the baseline classification levels achieved in Table 1. Positive values indicate that the contextualized approach performed better.

As can be seen from Fig. 2, the results are mixed. Four subjects showed substantial improvement and had, generally, monotonically decreasing curves indicating that the confidence metrics were functioning properly. One subject performed substantially worse and the remaining eight subjects were distributed within the approximately ±15 % range, indicating a net zero effect on performance across these subjects.

To better understand the performance differences we next analyzed the extent to which these differences were a function of eye tracker quality as well as baseline performance on the epoch-based BCI. These results are presented in Fig. 3. The x-axis shows the standardized eye tracker error (from Table 1), while the y-axis shows the standardized averaged performance gains (from Fig. 2). Blue o's indicate the top six performers on the baseline epoch-based BCI (from Table 1). Black x's indicate the bottom seven performers on the baseline epoch-based BCI. While the conclusions that can be drawn from such a small data set are limited, there appears to be general trend among the best performers (blue o's) that the performance gains are a negative function of eye tracker error. In other words, as the quality of the eye tracking data decreases the utility of our approach also decreases. For the worst performers (black x's) the trend is less clear. It is unclear the extent to which the performance differences are a function of eye tracking quality, poor BCI classifiability (as measured using the epoch-based BCI), other factors not discussed here, such as EEG quality, or some combination of multiple factors.

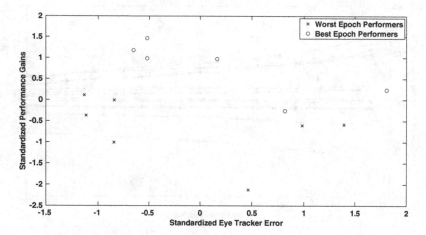

Fig. 3. Performance differences between the contextualized BCI and the non-contextualized BCI as a function of eye tracker error. Both axes have been standardized. Higher values indicate the contextualized BCI performed better. Data points marked by (o) indicate the six best performers on the epoch-based BCI. Data points marked by (x) indicate the seven worst performers on the epoch-based BCI (Color figure online).

5   Discussion

The results presented here suggest that, under the right circumstances, physiological and behavioral signals can be used to improve online BCI performance. While the results comparing the performance of the contextualized approach to the non-contextualized approach for all subjects were mixed, a more detailed analysis showed a possible trend between the quality of the contextualizing information and the performance gains for those subjects with better baseline BCI performance. We believe that this can be explained, in part, by the fact that these subjects had more robust BCI classifiers allowing us to see the trend in eye tracking quality. However, further data is needed to substantiate this claim.

In addition, we did not focus on comparing different types of BCI classifiers. We attempted to optimize an SVM-based classifier for each subject, but future work should compare performance gains with our approach across a range of different classifier methods. In addition, future work should also attempt to model, to the extent possible, the moment-to-moment variations in signal quality for both the EEG and contextualize resources. As these sources of variability become better understood, this can pave the way for more comprehensive systems that incorporate multiple forms of trigger events as well as multivariate probability distributions.

As BCI research and development extends into more complex domains, we believe that approaches, such as the one presented here in which contextual information is incorporated into the BCI problem, will provide the best opportunities to build functioning, reliable systems. This represents a new challenge for traditional BCI but it is also an opportunity to expand towards a more comprehensive view of brain-body-behavior modeling.

Acknowledgements. The authors would like to thank Dr. Kelvin Oie of the Army Research Laboratory for his help in designing the research study. This research was sponsored by the Army Research Laboratory and was accomplished under Cooperative Agreement Number W911NF-10-2-0022. The views and conclusions contained in this document are those of the authors and should not be interpreted as representing official policies, either expressed or implied, of the Army Research Laboratory or the U.S. Government. The U.S. Government is authorized to reproduce and distribute reprints for Government purposes notwithstanding any copyright notation herein.

References

1. Lin, C.-T., Wu, R.-C., Liang, S.-F., Chao, W.-H., Chen, Y.-J., Jung, T.-P.: EEG-based drowsiness estimation for safety driving using independent component analysis. IEEE Trans. Circuits Syst. I Regul. Pap. **52**(12), 2726–2738 (2005)
2. Berka, C., Levendowski, D.J., Lumicao, M.N., Yau, A., Davis, G., Zivkovic, V.T., Olmstead, R.E., Tremoulet, P.D., Craven, P.L.: EEG correlates of task engagement and mental workload in vigilance, learning, and memory tasks. Aviat. Space Environ. Med. **78** (Supplement 1), B231–B244 (2007)
3. McDowell, K., Lin, C.-T., Oie, K.S., Jung, T.-P., Gordon, S., Whitaker, K.W., Li, S.-Y., Lu, S.-W., Hairston, W.D.: Real-world neuroimaging technologies. IEEE Access **1**, 131–149 (2013)
4. Makeig, S., Gramann, K., Jung, T.-P., Sejnowski, T.J., Poizner, H.: Linking brain, mind and behavior. Int. J. Psychophysiol. **73**(2), 95–100 (2009)
5. Leeb, R., Friedman, D., Müller-Putz, G.R., Scherer, R., Slater, M., Pfurtscheller, G.: Self-paced (asynchronous) BCI control of a wheelchair in virtual environments: a case study with a tetraplegic. Comput. Intell. Neurosci. **2007**, 79642 (2007)

6. Townsend, G., Graimann, B., Pfurtscheller, G.: Continuous EEG classification during motor imagery-simulation of an asynchronous BCI. IEEE Trans. Neural Syst. Rehabil. Eng. **12**(2), 258–265 (2004)

7. Marathe, A.R., Anthony, J.R., McDowell, K.: Sliding HDCA: single-trial EEG classification to overcome and quantify temporal variability. IEEE Trans. Neural Syst. Rehabil. Eng. **22**, 201–211 (2014)

8. Schapire, R.E.: The boosting approach to machine learning: an overview. In: Denison, D.E., Hansen, M.H., Holmes, C.C., Mallick, B., Yu, B. (eds.) Nonlinear Estimation and Classification. Lecture Notes in Statistics, pp. 149–171. Springer, New York (2003)

9. Makeig, S., Bell, A.J., Jung, T.-P., Sejnowski, T.J.: Independent component analysis of electroencephalographic data. In: Advances in Neural Information Processing Systems, pp. 145–151 (1996)

10. Chang, C.-C., Lin, C.-J.: LIBSVM: a library for support vector machines. ACM Trans. Intell. Syst. Technol. (TIST) **2**(3), 27 (2011)

How Low Can You Go? Empirically Assessing Minimum Usable DAQ Performance for Highly Fieldable EEG Systems

W. David Hairston[✉] and Vernon Lawhern

Human Research and Engineering Directorate, US Army Research Laboratory,
Aberdeen Proving Ground, MD, USA
william.d.hairston4.civ@mail.mil,
Vernon.Lawhern@utsa.edu

Abstract. Electroencephalography (EEG) as a physiological assessment technique holds high promise for on-line monitoring of cognitive states. Examples include detecting when a user is overly fatigued, if they are paying attention to a target item, or even detecting sub-conscious object recognition, all of which can be used for greatly enhanced human-system interaction. However, because EEG involves measuring extremely small voltage fluctuations (microvolts) against a potential background that is very large (milivolts), conventional EEG data acquisition (DAQ) systems utilize very high-resolution components, such as low-noise amplifiers and 24-bit sigma-delta analog-to-digital converters (ADCs) on the ideal premise of acquiring a maximal resolution signal to guarantee information content from the data. Unfortunately this comes at the cost of high power consumption and requires expensive system components. We hypothesize that, for many targeted research applications, this level of resolution may not be necessary, and that by intelligently allowing a reduction in the signal fidelity, substantial savings in cost and power consumption can be obtained. To date though a pragmatic minimum resolution remains unexplored. Here, we discuss the utility of using a parametric approach of simulating signal degradation analogous to decreasing ADC bit (vertical) resolution and amplifier fidelity. Results derived from classification of both drowsiness (alpha oscillation) and oddity (P300) detection show strong overall robustness to poor-quality signals, such that classifier performance remains unaffected until resolution is well outside of typical recording specifications. These observations suggest that researchers and system designers should carefully consider that resolution trade-offs for power and cost are entirely reasonable for targeted applications, enabling feasibility of ultra-low power or highly fieldable data collection systems in the near future.

1 Introduction

Electroencephalography (EEG) is a technique of measuring voltage fluctuations on the scalp, arising from large pools of electrical currents generated by regional neural activity. Although EEG is largely viewed as a medical technique used for diagnosis of brain dysfunction and injury [1], it has also been used as a research tool for several decades,

© Springer International Publishing Switzerland 2015
D.D. Schmorrow and C.M. Fidopiastis (Eds.): AC 2015, LNAI 9183, pp. 221–231, 2015.
DOI: 10.1007/978-3-319-20816-9_22

especially in conjunction with cognitive and perceptual neuroscience studies aimed at identifying the neural basis of behavior. In more recent years, a wide range of studies have shown the utility of using EEG to identify or classify different cognitive states (such as drowsiness and fatigue [2], or anxiety [3]) as well as a the detection and identification of novel events [4, 5]. Based on these successes, there is increasing promise that EEG can be a useful tool as a component of human-computer interactive systems [6], many of which could be embedded within every day, typical-life scenarios.

However, currently most implementations of such algorithms remain constrained to laboratory or fairly limited short usage cases, leaving a lack of transition into real-world environments. While there is increasing interest in performing so-called real-world neuroimaging [7] – that is, monitoring brain activity within its full, natural context of the real world – current designs for EEG systems are not amendable to usage in a truly fieldable format, and a number of technical hurdles must be addressed. For example, because the brain-source voltage fluctuations represented by EEG are extremely small (microvolts) against a potential background that is heavily contaminated by larger fluctuations (milivolts to volts) created by movement artifacts [8, 9], environmental electrical noise, and long-term capacitive drift effects [10], the overall signal-to-noise (SNR) is very poor. As a result, EEG data acquisition (DAQ) systems must be extremely sensitive.

The conventional approach for addressing this problem is to use very high-resolution components, such as low-noise amplifiers and 24-bit sigma-delta analog-to-digital converters (ADCs), on the ideal premise of acquiring a maximal resolution signal in order to guarantee information content from the data. Targeting ideal, high-resolution signals is particularly pertinent in research settings where the user may not know exactly what features of the data will be the most critical for a successful outcome, or in medical cases where very small differences may have critical health relevance. Unfortunately this demand for high resolution comes at the cost of systems tending to be being very expensive and power-draining. This is generally a trivial concern for typical laboratory or patient-care environments where the benefits of having a high-quality DAQ system outweigh the disadvantages of size, cost, and power consumption of the system. However, it creates substantial limitations on the ability to build and use truly fieldable, long-application-time systems designed for use in every-day settings [7, 11] or use in large scale "crowdsourced" implementations where cost would play a major factor [12].

In many targeted research and translational neuroscience settings, as well as brain-computer interaction technologies, the user typically already has a specific use identified for the acquired data stream, and knows what the relevant signal properties are ahead of time. In these cases, having perfectly "ideal", high-resolution DAQ systems may not be necessary as long as the most critical features for the application can be extracted, and considerable savings in both power and expense can be garnered. For example, the power consumption of an ADC increases exponentially with bit resolution, with each additional bit requiring nearly $10\times$ the power draw [13, 14]. Since the analog front end is a major portion of the total power consumption of a typical EEG DAQ system, this equates to a substantial difference between, for example, 24, 16, or even 10-bit resolution. Meanwhile, ultra low-noise amplifiers are costly and challenging to design in a low-power format, and in many cases the added sensitivity results in more susceptibility to artifacts.

This suggests that, at least for targeted applications, there may be room for considerable power and cost savings by sacrificing the resolution of certain components of the DAQ system. To date, however, this issue has been largely ignored, with no systematic analyses of the pragmatic minimum technical specifications necessary to detect or assess particular brain mental states. While a practical minima will vary between applications, at the very least there is a need to establish paradigms or test methods for answering this question.

Here, we highlight results from two target mental-state detection applications, with the goal of providing initial insight into the necessity for such analyses and the relationship between DAQ signal fidelity and performance for specific applications. Applications include: (1) detection of alpha spindle oscillations representative of "drowsiness" during a driving task, and (2) the detection of P300 visual evoked responses a rapid serial visual presentation (RSVP) paradigm. In each case, we examine the effect of simulating degraded DAQ performance (decreased vertical resolution and increased RMS noise) on the performance of classifiers already shown to have reasonable success at differentiating the target states [15–18].

2 Methods

We empirically assessed the practical impact of EEG signal record fidelity by evaluating the performance of several classifiers at various stages of signal degradation. Here we chose to classify two different neural events of interest: alpha spindle oscillations [15, 16] which have been associated with fatigue and drowsiness in prolonged experiments, and P300 visual evoked responses elicited during a rapid serial visual presentation (RSVP) experiment [19, 20], a neural feature associated with the detection and recognition of novel visual stimuli. For each neural event class (alpha oscillations and P300 responses) two separate classifiers were used. Details about the data and classifiers used in each paradigm are described below.

2.1 Datasets

Driving Task – Drowsiness Detection. The datasets used here have been analyzed previously [15]; a brief description is presented here. Two healthy males, both right handed, were instructed to drive in a simulated driving environment in a sound-attenuated room. The subjects were presented with a straight four-lane highway with minimal scenery (highway, roadside, and horizon) except for an occasional speed limit sign. Subjects were requested to maintain the posted speed limit (25 mph or 45 mph) while keeping their vehicle in the center of the lane. A perturbation force would occasionally cause the vehicle to veer left or right in a manner similar to the effects experienced when a gust of wind crosses a real vehicle [21]. Subjects drove for approximately 70 min after a 10–15 min practice period. The EEG was recorded using a 64-channel Biosemi ActiveTwo system, and offline referenced to the average of the two mastoids.

RSVP Task – Target Object Recognition. The data used here has been analyzed previously [17, 22]. Short video clips were used in an rapid serial visual presentation (RSVP) paradigm. Video clips included two classes of scenes, either those containing people or vehicles on background scenes, or containing background scenes alone. Observers were instructed to make a manual button press with their dominant hand when they detected a person or vehicle (targets), and to abstain from responding when a background scene (distractor) was presented. Video clips consisted of five consecutive images of 100 ms in duration each; each video clip was presented for 500 ms without pause between, such that the first frame was presented immediately after the last frame of the prior video. If a target appeared in the video clip, it was present on each 100 ms image. The distracter to target ratio was 90/10. RSVP sequences were presented in two minute blocks after which time participants were given a break, and participants completed a total of 25 blocks.

2.2   Classifiers

Drowsiness Detection. Two classifiers were used for detecting alpha spindle oscillations in EEG. The first method, proposed by Simon and colleagues [16] defines the Full-Width at Half-Max (FWHM), which is a measure of peak amplitude and frequency distribution in the alpha band in sliding EEG windows. The method starts by determining if the largest peak of the power spectrum from 4–50 Hz in the EEG window lies in the alpha band (8–13 Hz). If the peak lies in the alpha band, the width of the peak at half maximum is calculated. If this width is less than two times the bandwidth of a Hamming window, it is identified as an alpha oscillation. The second method is based on sequentially discounted autoregressive modeling (SDAR) of a narrowband filtered EEG signal [15]. The goal of the SDAR approach is to detect statistically irregular time segments in a time-adaptive nature. The statistics of specificity, precision and recall are used to evaluate the performance of both algorithms under varied levels of signal fidelity (see below).

P300 Object Recognition. Two classifiers were used for detecting target object recognition (e.g., P300 visual evoked potentials) during the RSVP task. The first method, Hierarchical Discriminant Component Analysis (HDCA) [19, 23], is a two stage binary classification method which is based on an ensemble of logistic regression classifiers. In the first stage, the EEG data window, relative to image onset, is divided into K non-overlapping segments. In each segment, a logistic regression classifier is trained to segregate between two different sets of stimuli. This logistic regression is trained for each segment independently. The outputs of these regressions are then used as parameters in another logistic regression to make the final overall classification. The first stage classification collapses information across channels in a small time window, while the second classification collapses information across time. We used K = 10 windows for discrimination as this value has been used previously in similar studies [20].

The second classification method employed here used a combination of the xDAWN spatial filtering technique coupled with a Bayesian linear discriminant analysis (BLDA) classifier. Collectively this technique will be referred to as XDBLDA; a full description can be found in [24–26]. xDAWN spatial filtering results in a set of spatial filters that are rank ordered such that the highest rank filters maximize the signal to signal plus noise ratio in the EEG signals. Our implementation uses the top eight spatial filters for classifier input, and the input vector is obtained by concatenation of the eight spatially filtered EEG signals. The BLDA classifier is then used to discriminate targets from non-targets. For both classifiers, the area under the receiver operating characteristic (AUC) curve was used to evaluate overall classifier performance under each level of signal fidelity. In order to assess baseline control (chance) AUC values for each classifier, performance was re-assessed with data event tags randomly intermixed between target and non-target classes for each dataset and trained using cross-validation.

2.3   Simulated Degradation of Signal Fidelity

In order to simulate the effects of data acquisition using different bit-rate ADCs, the previously-acquired data from each subject were iteratively re-quantized using a rounding quantization scheme for a series of 6 to 24 bit depths covering a range of ± 4 mV (8 mV total). Values outside this range were clipped. This yields a net effect of decreasing the effective vertical resolution (increased step size) between possible data points and likewise increasing "blockiness" of continuous waveforms and loss of discrimination of small-amplitude fluctuations (See the top row of Fig. 1 for examples). This step was performed at the earliest stage prior to any further processing and application of each classification algorithm. We created a total of 13 datasets per subject ranging from a minimum resolution of 62.5 nV to 256 µV in log2 scale.

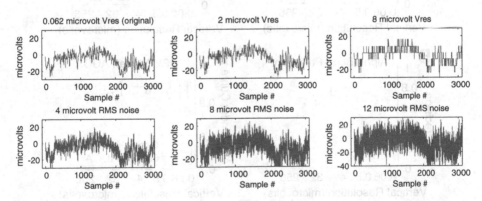

Fig. 1. Examples of how the recorded signal is affected by decreasing vertical resolution (top row) and increased RMS random noise (bottom row). As the vertical resolution decreases (top row, left to right), signal features of low amplitude are effectively removed, while the overall signal becomes similar to that of a step function. Also, as the RMS noise increases (bottom row, left to right), small changes in the overall signal become masked and more difficult to observe.

To simulate effects of amplifier random noise on data acquisition, a series of noise files with uniform random distribution were iteratively created and added to the original data. Noise data were zero-centered with uniform distribution, each with root-mean-square power (across the entire waveform). Amplitude values tested ranged from 2 to 62 μV RMS. The bottom row of Fig. 1 shows an example of how this affects the data. Note that these steps were applied to the raw data prior to any signal processing required for each classification method.

3 Results

3.1 Decreased Vertical Resolution

First, we examined the importance of the vertical resolution of the acquired signal, simulated by re-quantizing pre-recorded data to represent a range of different ADC bit rates. Figure 2 shows results for two types of experimental paradigms, alpha-oscillation detection during a driving task (Panels 2A–2C) and P300/target object detection during an RSVP task (Panel 2D). For alpha oscillation detection, we tested the performance of two existing classifiers, the SDAR method of Lawhern and colleagues [15] (blue lines

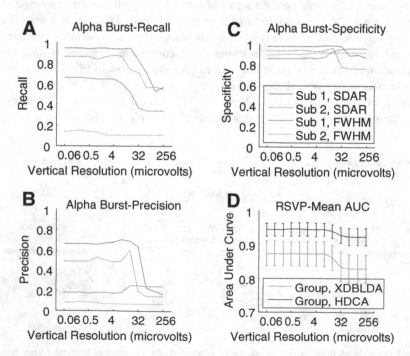

Fig. 2. Classifier performance per vertical resolution for alpha oscillation detection evaluated as (a) Recall, (b) Precision, and (c) Specificity; and group mean AUC for P300 detection (d). Blue lines: SDAR performance (2 subjects); Red FWHM (2 subjects); Black: XDBLDA (mean ± SD); Green: HDCA (mean ± SD) (Color figure online).

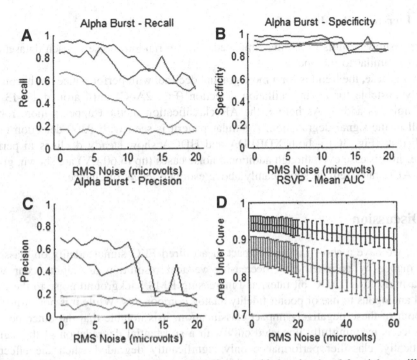

Fig. 3. Classifier performance per increased RMS noise added to the signal for alpha oscillation detection evaluated as (a) Recall, (b) Precision, and (c) Specificity; and group mean AUC for P300 detection (d). Blue lines: SDAR performance (2 subjects); Red FWHM (2 subjects); Black: XDBLDA (mean ± SD); Green: HDCA (mean ± SD) (Color figure online).

in Fig. 2) and the FWHM-based method of Simon and colleagues [16] (red lines) for each of two subjects (separate similar colored lines in Fig. 2). Each panel depicts scores based on recall (Panel 2A), precision (2B) and specificity (2C) per ADC rate.

Similar to previous reports, overall performance for the AR-based method (blue lines) is stronger than for the spectral method [15], especially for subject 2 (lowest line). More notably however, this overall trend is fairly consistent through vertical resolutions as large as 16 µV. Beyond this point, all three statistics become less stable, especially recall and sensitivity for the spectral classifier, suggesting substantially higher false positive rates.

Meanwhile a similar trend is seen when examining P300 detection performance (Fig. 2D) with XDBLDA (black lines) and HDCA (green lines). Here, group mean values for area under the curve (AUC) are shown for a set of 15 subjects. As has been reported, overall performance with XDLBDA is very accurate, superseding HDCA; however both classifiers follow similar patterns with consistent performance through 8 µV of vertical resolution. Notably, even above this point, performance plateaus above chance, confirmed in our randomized control simulation averaged to 0.70 ± 0.025 AUC for XDLBDA and 0.51 ± 0.026 AUC for HDCA.

3.2   Increased Random Noise

Figure 3 shows results of adding simulated uniform random noise to each dataset and classifier similar to the above.

In this case, the trend is for a more gradual decline, with performance not becoming notably unstable for alpha-oscillation detection (Fig. 2A–C) until around 11–13 μV RMS noise is added. As before, the AR classification method appears more robust overall to the signal degradation. A similar pattern is seen with P300 detection in an RSVP task (Fig. 3C) – both XDBLDA and HDCA show steady declines in performance. In this case even though additional noise cases (up to 60 μV) are shown, group mean AUC rates remain significantly above estimate levels of chance.

4   Discussion

Above, we have a shown a clear impact of acquired EEG signal fidelity on classifier performance by parametrically decreasing vertical resolution as might occur with decreasingly lower ADC bit rates, and increasing RMS background noise to the EEG signal analogous to use of poorer fidelity analog components. While it is not surprising that both of these negatively impact classification, it is notable that the outcome performance is meaningfully impacted only with a substantial degradation of the signal. Specifically, classifier performance only significantly degraded when the effective vertical resolution was at least 8 μV or background RMS added noise exceeded about 10 μV. Although initial baseline performance differed, this trend appears to be independent of the type of classifier used. These results suggest that tailored systems can functionally operate with substantially lower signal fidelity than is considered a typical requirement, and that it is important to carefully consider what are the truly necessary minimum performance specifications for the application at hand. While the traditional approach to system design for experimental settings (where the emphasis is on maximizing signal quality) has served those purposes well, the approaches in use for those applications currently suffer a number of challenges regarding overall usability [27] and are not tenable for truly mobile applications where power, size, and cost are considerable factors. In contrast, technological design for targeted real-world application must be prepared to address these challenges in light of potential tradeoff regarding idealistic signals.

Our vision of "real-world neuroimaging" (RWN) involves conducting neuroimaging within realistic, non-contrived situations, where neural responses reflect what is expected in real-life situations [6, 7, 11]. While some RWN scientific endeavors can be managed using currently available DAQ approaches without the need for high mobility or long-term recording, in order to fully realize our goals of measuring and monitoring brain activity in truly unconstrained circumstances, we must re-think the way DAQ occurs with EEG. In particular, our vision is to develop and utilize systems which are completely "user transparent" – that is, require no direct interaction or intervention from the user. One facet of this is operation solely on locally-harvested power, so as to have no requirement for recharging or battery replacement [28]. In order to meet such stringent constraints, we advocate a careful re-examination of the logic by which we collect neurophysiogical data, and focus on the specific needs of the system given it's intended use. Some initial prototype integrated circuit designs suggest such ultra-low power operation is feasible [29–31]; however an empirical evaluation of performance trade-off, such as carried out here, is necessary in order to validate the utility of these approaches.

While promising, much follow-up work remains. Regarding the examples highlighted here, the performance of HCDA and XDBLDA for P300 discrimination are surprisingly robust to the manipulations of vertical resolution and RMS noise. Even above 8 μV resolution, the performance plateau for both classifiers remains above statistical chance. It is likely that the reason for the plateau is that once resolution exceeds about 25 μV the data becomes functionally binary in nature – no meaningful brain-related change in amplitude will be observed. Thus a functional floor effect would be expected. We hypothesize that the remaining accuracy that occurs despite the overall lack of information in the amplitude domain stems from the power of pooling across multiple channels (in this case, 64). Future efforts will focus on exploring this additional feature domain, and pooling multiple signal features into a single multivariate analysis, so that we can ascertain the relative pragmatic impact of each feature, as well as the interactions between them from combined analyses. With that approach, we can develop models which focus on and refine only the most critical system design components which affect overall utility of the system. Such a refined approach is critical due to the complexity of fieldable system design, where numerous factor affect overall utility for research applications [27, 32, 33]. The cases highlighted here are only some examples from a wide variety of potential uses for EEG in fieldable application. Undoubtedly the performance of any classifier is very tightly coupled to the circumstances under which it is used and the data to which it is applied. Therefore the data presented here alone cannot be used to set overall standards for EEG data acquisition even for targeted applications. Rather, this report is intended to highlight the importance of this issue by using some specific example cases. The degree to which other applications are dependent on signal fidelity, and the specific signal features which may be lost due to decreasing fidelity, is likely to vary widely across domains. For example, successful discrimination of extremely small amplitude but highly localized signals, such as an auditory brainstem response, would likely be substantially more dependent on both vertical resolution and higher-fidelity noise, but with minimal dependence on spatial pooling. Our suggestion is for future work to focus on large-scale parametric analyses involving several datasets and classifiers covering a wide range of domains, with the goal of establishing the most critical DAQ features tied to a particular class of applications.

In summary, we have shown that successful discrimination of multiple classes of neural state is entirely feasible using signals acquired with relatively low fidelity without a direct consequence to accuracy. These results suggest that, for targeted research applications, acquiring data at the typical high-fidelity resolution is not necessary. This has direct implications for programs utilizing EEG in real-world domains where data acquisition methods are critical to success. For example the ability to use lower-resolution components, such as lower bit-rate ADCs and amplifiers, dramatically increases opportunities for design and use of ultra-low power systems, or low-cost systems that can be easily distributed and managed on a large scale.

References

1. Rapp, P.E., Keyser, D.O., Albano, A., Hernandez, R., Gibson, D.B., Zambon, R.A., Hairston, W.D., Hughes, J.D., Krystal, A., Nichols, A.S.: Traumatic brain injury detection using electrophysiological methods. Front. Hum. Neurosci. **9**, 11 (2015)
2. Borghini, G., Astolfi, L., Vecchiato, G., Mattia, D., Babiloni, F.: Measuring neurophysiological signals in aircraft pilots and car drivers for the assessment of mental workload, fatigue and drowsiness. Neurosci. Biobehav. Rev. **44**, 58–75 (2014)
3. Moore, N.C.: A review of EEG biofeedback treatment of anxiety disorders. Clin. EEG Neurosci. **31**, 1–6 (2000)
4. Dien, J., Spencer, K.M., Donchin, E.: Localization of the event-related potential novelty response as defined by principal components analysis. Cogn. Brain. Res. **17**, 637–650 (2003)
5. Ranganath, C., Rainer, G.: Cognitive neuroscience: Neural mechanisms for detecting and remembering novel events. Nat. Rev. Neurosci. **4**, 193–202 (2003)
6. Lance, B.J., Kerick, S.E., Ries, A.J., Oie, K.S., McDowell, K.: Brain Computer Interface Technologies in the Coming Decades. Proc. IEEE **100**, 1585–1599 (2012)
7. Mcdowell, K., Lin, C.-T., Oie, K.S., Jung, T.-P., Gordon, S., Whitaker, K.W., Li, S.-Y., Lu, S.-W., Hairston, W.D.: Real-world neuroimaging technologies. IEEE Access **1**, 131–149 (2013)
8. Gramann, K., Jung, T.-P., Ferris, D.P., Lin, C.-T., Makeig, S.: Toward a new cognitive neuroscience: modeling natural brain dynamics. Front. Hum. Neurosci **8**, 444 (2014)
9. Gwin, J.T., Gramann, K., Makeig, S., Ferris, D.P.: Removal of movement artifact from high-density EEG recorded during walking and running. J. Neurophysiol. **103**, 3526–3534 (2010)
10. Usakli, A.B.: Improvement of EEG signal acquisition: an electrical aspect for state of the art of front end. Comput. Intell. Neurosci. **2010**, 1–7 (2010)
11. Kellihan, B., Doty, T.J., Hairston, W.D., Canady, J., Whitaker, K.W., Lin, C.-T., Jung, T.-P., McDowell, K.: A real-world neuroimaging system to evaluate stress. In: Schmorrow, D.D., Fidopiastis, C.M. (eds.) AC 2013. LNCS, vol. 8027, pp. 316–325. Springer, Heidelberg (2013)
12. McDowell, K., Whitaker, K., Hairston, W.D., Oie, K.S.: Concepts for Developing and Utilizing Crowdsourcing for Neurotechnology Advancement. US Army Research Laboratory Technical Report SR-266 (2013)
13. Zhang, D., Svensson, C., Alvandpour, A.: Power consumption bounds for SAR ADCs. ECCTD, pp. 556–559 (2011)
14. Murmann, B.: A/D converter trends: Power dissipation, scaling and digitally assisted architectures. CICC, pp. 105–112 (2008)
15. Lawhern, V., Kerick, S., Robbins, K.A.: Detecting alpha spindle events in EEG time series using adaptive autoregressive models. BMC Neurosci. **14**, 101 (2013)
16. Simon, M., Schmidt, E.A., Kincses, W.E., Fritzsche, M., Bruns, A., Aufmuth, C., Bogdan, M., Rosenstiel, W., Schrauf, M.: EEG alpha spindle measures as indicators of driver fatigue under real traffic conditions. Clin. Neurophysiol. Off. J. Int. Fed. Clin. Neurophysiol. **122**, 1168–1178 (2011)
17. Marathe, A.R., Ries, A.J., McDowell, K.: A novel method for single-trial classification in the face of temporal variability. In: Schmorrow, D.D., Fidopiastis, C.M. (eds.) AC 2013. LNCS, vol. 8027, pp. 345–352. Springer, Heidelberg (2013)

18. Marathe, A.R., Ries, A.J., McDowell, K.: Sliding HDCA: single-trial eeg classification to overcome and quantify temporal variability. IEEE Trans. Neural Syst. Rehabil. Eng. **22**, 201–211 (2014)
19. Gerson, A.D., Parra, L.C., Sajda, P.: Cortically coupled computer vision for rapid image search. IEEE Trans. Neural Syst. Rehabil. Eng. **14**, 174–179 (2006)
20. Sajda, P., Pohlmeyer, E., Wang, J., Parra, L.C., Christoforou, C., Dmochowski, J., Hanna, B., Bahlmann, C., Singh, M.K., Chang, S.-F.: In a blink of an eye and a switch of a transistor: cortically coupled computer vision. Proc. IEEE **98**, 462–478 (2010)
21. Brooks, J.R., Kerick, S.E., McDowell, K.: Novel Measure of Driver and Vehicle Interaction Demonstrates Transient Changes Related to Alerting. J. Mot. Behav. **47**, 1–11 (2014)
22. Ries, A.J., Larkin, G.B.: Stimulus and Response-Locked P3 Activity in a Dynamic Rapid Serial Visual Presentation (RSVP) Task. US Army Research Laboratory, TR-6314 (2013)
23. Parra, L., Christoforou, C., Gerson, A., Dyrholm, M., Luo, A., Wagner, M., Philiastides, M., Sajda, P.: Spatiotemporal linear decoding of brain state. IEEE Signal Process. Mag. **25**, 107–115 (2008)
24. Cecotti, H., Rivet, B., Congedo, M., Jutten, C., Bertrand, O., Maby, E., Mattout, J.: A robust sensor-selection method for P300 brain–computer interfaces. J. Neural Eng. **8**, 016001 (2011)
25. Cecotti, H., Eckstein, M.P., Giesbrecht, B.: Effects of performing two visual tasks on single trial detection of event-related potentials. Presented at the August (2012)
26. Rivet, B., Souloumiac, A., Attina, V., Gibert, G.: xDAWN algorithm to enhance evoked potentials: application to brain–computer interface. IEEE Trans. Biomed. Eng. **56**, 2035–2043 (2009)
27. Hairston, W.D., Whitaker, K.W., Reis, A.J., Vettel, J.M., Bradford, J.C., Kerick, S.E., McDowell, K.: Usability of four commercially-oriented EEG systems. J. Neural Eng. **11**(4), 046018 (2013)
28. Hairston, W.D., Proie, R.M., Conroy, J., Nothwang, W.: Batteryless Electroencephalography (EEG): Subthreshold Voltage System-on-a-Chip (SoC) Design for Neurophysiological Measurement. U.S. Army Research Laboratory, TR-7234 (2015)
29. Bhargava, P., Hairston, W.D., Proie, R.M.: A 262nW analog front end with a digitally-assisted low noise amplifier for batteryless EEG acquisition. IEEE S3S, pp. 1–2 (2014)
30. Zhang, Y., Zhang, F., Shakhsheer, Y., Silver, J.D., Klinefelter, A., Nagaraju, M., Boley, J., Pandey, J., Shrivastava, A., Carlson, E.J., Wood, A., Calhoun, B.H., Otis, B.P.: A batteryless 19 microW MICS/ISM-band energy harvesting body sensor node SoC for ExG applications. IEEE J. Solid-State Circuits **48**, 199–213 (2013)
31. Zhang, F., Mishra, A., Richardson, A.G., Otis, B.: A low-power ECoG/EEG processing IC with integrated multiband energy extractor. IEEE Trans. Circuits Syst. Regul. Pap. **58**, 2069–2082 (2011)
32. Ries, A.J., Touryan, J., Vettel, J., McDowell, K., Hairston, W.D.: A comparison of electroencephalography signals acquired from conventional and mobile systems. J. Neurosci. Neuroeng. **3**, 10–20 (2014)
33. Guger, C., Krausz, G., Allison, B.Z., Edlinger, G.: Comparison of dry and gel based electrodes for p 300 brain-computer interfaces. Front. Neurosci. **6**, 60 (2012)

Investigation of Functional Near Infrared Spectroscopy in Evaluation of Pilot Expertise Acquisition

Gabriela Hernandez-Meza[1]([⊠]), Lauren Slason[2], Hasan Ayaz[1],
Patrick Craven[2], Kevin Oden[3], and Kurtulus Izzetoglu[1]

[1] School of Biomedical Engineering, Science & Health Systems,
Drexel University, Philadelphia, PA, USA
{gh88, hasan.ayaz, ki25}@drexel.edu
[2] Applied Informatics Group, CCI, Drexel University, Philadelphia, PA, USA
{lrs75, plc35}@drexel.edu
[3] Lockheed Martin Corporation, Orlando, FL, USA
kevin.oden@lmco.com

Abstract. Functional Near-Infrared (fNIR) spectroscopy is an optical brain imaging technology that enables assessment of brain activity through the intact skull in human subjects. fNIR systems developed during the last decade allow for a rapid, non-invasive method of measuring the brain activity of a subject while conducting tasks in realistic environments. This paper examines the hemodynamic changes associated with expertise development during C-130j simulated flying missions.

Keywords: Near-infrared spectroscopy · Optical brain imaging · fNIR · Human performance assessment · Pilot training

1 Introduction

Improving the operational safety and efficacy of human-computer interactions is of interest for aerospace applications. Understanding the underlying neural processes that are associated with mental workload and expertise development is the first step in the development of a method for their accurate assessment. The current study is based on earlier work [24–30] that investigated the relationship of the hemodynamic response in the anterior prefrontal cortex to changes in mental workload, level of expertise, and task performance during learning of simulated piloting tasks utilizing functional near-infrared spectroscopy (fNIR).

fNIR is a safe, non-invasive and portable optical method that can be used to monitor activity within the prefrontal cortex of the human brain [15–22]. Making use of specific wavelengths of light fNIR provides measurements of oxygenated (oxy-Hb) and deoxygenated (deoxy-Hb) hemoglobin that are in direct relation with hemodynamic changes in the brain [2]. Research on brain-energy metabolism has elucidated the close link between hemodynamic and neural activity [3]. Traditional neuroimaging techniques, such as fMRI cannot be used to measure hemodynamic changes for a variety of

© Springer International Publishing Switzerland 2015
D.D. Schmorrow and C.M. Fidopiastis (Eds.): AC 2015, LNAI 9183, pp. 232–243, 2015.
DOI: 10.1007/978-3-319-20816-9_23

real-life applications that could yield important discoveries and lead to novel uses. On the other hand, fNIR is well-suited for the flight simulator environment as it is capable of obtaining continuous measurements of the cerebral hemodynamics without restricting the testing location or the participant's movements.

In this paper we present an examination of the relationship between hemodynamic and performance measures as a C-130j pilot develops expertise during a flight simulator task. The main goals of this study is to understand the hemodynamic changes occurring in the pre-frontal cortex as an individual's expertise increases during flight simulator missions. Based on earlier work we hypothesize that a decrease in brain activity, measurable by fNIR, will occur as a result of skill acquisition in a flight simulator task.

To examine our hypothesis, 10 healthy adult individuals volunteered for a one day session consisting of eight trials in the flight simulator. Throughout the session the participants faced scenarios that reflected typical flying tasks while their behavioral and anterior prefrontal cortex (PFC) brain activation were recorded by Prepar3D and fNIR respectively.

1.1 Physiological Principles of FNIR in Brain Activity Assessment

Understanding the brain energy metabolism and associated neural activity is important for realizing principles of fNIR spectroscopy in assessing brain activity. The brain has small energy reserves and the great majority of the energy used by brain cells is for processes that sustain physiological functioning [4]. Furthermore, glucose utilization by various brain regions increased several fold in response to physiological stimulation or in response to pharmacological agents that affect physiological activity [4]. Oxygen is necessary for the metabolism of glucose and therefore for energy production. Oxygen is transported to the neural tissue via oxy-Hb which gives up the oxygen to the surrounding tissues in the capillary bed and is transformed to deoxy-Hb. The need for oxygen in active brain regions is satisfied by a rise in local cerebral blood flow (CBF) [23]. Based on the brain energy metabolism fNIR is capable of providing correlates of brain activity through the oxygen consumption of neurons via measurements of deoxy and/or oxy-Hb [27–34]. Because oxy-Hb and deoxy-Hb have characteristic optical properties in the visible and near-infrared light range, the change in concentration of these molecules during increased brain activation can be measured using optical methods.

1.2 Physical Principles of FNIR in Brain Activity Assessment

Most biological tissues are relatively transparent to light in the near infrared range between 700-900 nm, largely because water, a major component of most tissues, absorbs very little energy at these wavelengths (Fig. 1). Within this window the spectra of oxy- and deoxy-hemoglobin are distinct enough to allow spectroscopy and measures of separate concentrations of both oxy-Hb and deoxy-Hb molecules [5]. This spectral

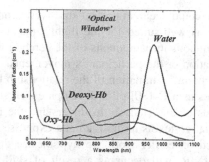

Fig. 1. Absorption spectrum in NIR window: spectra of oxy-Hb and deoxy-Hb in the range of 700 to 900 nm allows spectroscopy methods to assess oxy-Hb and deoxy-Hb concentrations, whereas water absorption becomes substantial above 900 nm, and thus majority of photons are mainly absorbed by water [5].

band is often referred to as the 'optical window' for the non-invasive assessment of brain activation [6].

If wavelengths are chosen to maximize the amount of absorption by oxy-Hb and deoxy-Hb, changes in these chromophore concentrations cause alterations in the number of absorbed photons as well as in the number of scattered photons that leave the scalp. These changes in light intensity measured at the surface of the scalp are quantified using a modified Beer–Lambert law, which is an empirical description of optical attenuation in a highly scattering medium [1]. By measuring absorbance/scattering changes at two wavelengths (730 nm and 850 nm), one of which is more sensitive to deoxy-Hb and the other to oxy-Hb, changes in the relative concentration of these chromophores can be calculated. Using these principles, researchers have demonstrated that it is possible to assess hemodynamic changes in response to brain activity through the intact skull in adult human subjects [7–11].

Typically, an optical apparatus consists of a light source by which the tissue is radiated and a light detector that receives light after it has interacted with the tissue. Photons that enter tissue undergo two different types of interaction, namely absorption and scattering. According to the modified Beer-Lambert Law [5], the light intensity after absorption and scattering of the biological tissue is expressed by the equation:

$$I = GI_o e^{-(\alpha_{HB}C_{HB} + \alpha_{HBO2}C_{HBO2})*L} \tag{1}$$

where G is a factor that accounts for the measurement geometry and is assumed constant when concentration changes. I_o is input light intensity, α_{HB} and α_{HBO2} are the molar extinction coefficients of deoxy-Hb and oxy-Hb, C_{HB} and C_{HBO2} are the concentrations of chromophores, deoxy-Hb and oxy-Hb respectively, and L is the photon path which is a function of absorption and scattering coefficients μ_a and μ_b.

By measuring optical density (OD) changes at two wavelengths, the relative change of oxy- and deoxy-hemoglobin versus time can be obtained. If the intensity measurement at an initial time is I_b (baseline), and at another time is I, the OD change due to variation in C_{HB} and C_{HBO_2} during that period is:

$$\Delta OD = \log_{10} \frac{I_b}{I} = (\alpha_{HB} \Delta C_{HB} + \alpha_{HBO_2} \Delta C_{HBO_2})L \qquad (2)$$

Measurements performed at two different wavelengths allow the calculation of ΔC_{HB} and ΔC_{HBO_2}. Change in oxygenation (Oxy) and blood volume or total hemoglobin (Hbt) can then be deduced:

$$Oxygenation = \Delta C_{HBO_2} - \Delta C_{HB} \qquad (3)$$

$$BloodVolume = \Delta C_{HBO_2} - \Delta C_{HB} \qquad (4)$$

1.3 Near-Infrared Spectroscopy Based Brain Imaging Systems

The continuous wave (CW) fNIR system used in this study was originally described by Chance et al. [7]. The current generation consists of a flexible headband sensor with 4 LED light sources and 10 detectors (Fig. 2) and was developed in the Drexel's Optical Brain Imaging laboratory. In CW systems, light is continuously applied to tissue at constant amplitude. The CW systems are limited to measuring the amplitude attenuation of the incident light [33].

CW systems have a number of advantageous properties that have resulted in wide use by researchers interested in brain imaging. Compared to other near-infrared systems it is minimally intrusive and portable, affordable, and easy to engineer relative to frequency and time domain systems [12].

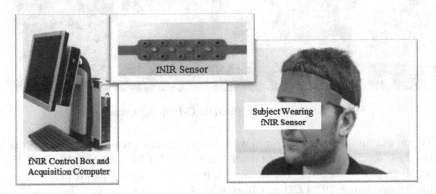

Fig. 2. Overview of the continuous wave 16-channel fNIR system

The fNIR sensor, illustrated in Fig. 2, reveals information in localizing brain activity, particularly in dorsolateral prefrontal cortex. Figure 3 shows the spatial map of the 16-channel fNIR sensor on the curved brain surface, frontal lobe [13].

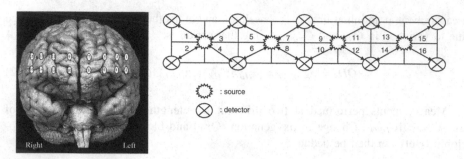

Fig. 3. Spatial map of the 16-channel fNIR sensor on the curved brain surface, frontal lobe

2 Method: Brain Activity Monitor During C-130j Flight Simulations

During each session the prefrontal cortex of the subjects was monitored using a 16 channel CW-fNIR system from the start until the end of the session. The simulation environment was constructed using Prepar3D (©2014, Lockheed Martin Corporation) with a model of a C-130 J airplane. The flight scenarios were developed to allow for the evaluation of skill development during a series of eight scenarios within the mission. The simulated scenarios reflect typical flying tasks such as adhering to a heading and altitude provided by an air traffic controller, navigation to way points, controlling vertical speed, completion of smooth turns, and following safety guidelines for the C130-J.

Fig. 4. Screenshot of prepared3D C-130j flight simulation

To run the simulation reliably and with a high degree of realism, high performance hardware is specified, including an Intel Core i7 925 CPU and an nVidia GeForce GT × 280 graphics processor. The simulation is presented on a triple-display system by Digital Tigers, using 19" LCD monitors with 4:3 aspect ratios in a horizontal configuration (Fig. 4).

The C-130 J simulator is controlled using the Saitek Pro Flight Yoke System. The research team developed customized logging software that tracked specific performance-related values within the simulator environment, and real-time algorithms calculated feedback to the participants during the course of the trials as well as logged

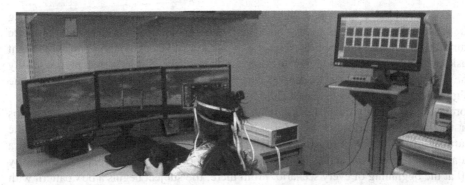

Fig. 5. Subject operating the C-130j simulator with fNIR sensor attached and data acquisition apparatus on far right.

performance values for later analysis. This custom software then communicated specific events for fNIR recording via serial port which allows time synchronization and the delivery of markers to the fNIR data acquisition computer (Fig. 5).

2.1 Experimental Procedure

Prior to the study, all participants are given an overview of the experiment and signed approved informed consent statements. After being given an overview of the experiment and providing informed consent, each subject completes (a) the Edinburgh Handedness Inventory, (b) a background questionnaire, and (c) a brief questionnaire regarding previous flight and video game experience. The flight scenarios were developed in conjunction with both an experienced C-130 pilot and an air traffic controller, and was designed to simulate a circuit (e.g., see Fig. 6). The scenarios require the subject to adhere to a heading and altitude provided by an air traffic controller, navigate to way points, control vertical speed, complete smooth turns, and follow safety guidelines for the C-130 J in the vicinity of New Castle Airport, home of the 166th Airlift Wing of the Delaware Air National Guard.

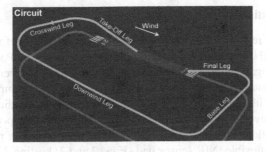

Fig. 6. Example of flight circuit around an airport

Each subject performs one flight session lasting approximately one hour. During the session the participants are first presented with a theoretical introduction to promote familiarization with the controls, a brief explanation of select aviation concepts, flight tasks within the scenario and how to complete these tasks. Subjects then proceed to fly the C-130 J plane in a mock scenario where they can familiarize themselves with the flight controls and expected task. The fNIR sensor is then placed on the participant's forehead and they fly the plane during a one hour session that contains eight scenarios or trials. The scenarios consist of a series of gates placed on a flight path that the participants will attempt to reach by flying the C-130 J plane. The subject begins at a heading of five degrees and an altitude of 950 feet shortly beyond the end of the runway 10 at the beginning of every scenario. From there, the subject begins a box pattern with waypoints marked to assist in following the pattern. In order to guide the inexperienced participants, the waypoints are displayed as large gates floating in space. The participant will complete more sections of the box pattern with each successive scenario by adding additional gates along the flight path. By the sixth and seventh scenario, the participant is expected to complete a full box pattern and pass through 10 gates. The subject is then presented with a modified flight path and gates for the 8th scenario. A schematic of the gates completed in each trial is presented in Fig. 7.

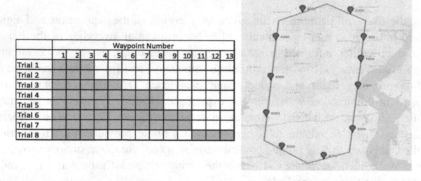

	Waypoint Number												
	1	2	3	4	5	6	7	8	9	10	11	12	13
Trial 1													
Trial 2													
Trial 3													
Trial 4													
Trial 5													
Trial 6													
Trial 7													
Trial 8													

Fig. 7. Schematic of gates/waypoints per trial and map of flight circuit with labeled waypoints

2.2   Data Acquisition

Throughout the entire session, the following physiological and performance measures were collected: i. fNIR sensor recordings acquired at every half second; ii. events including the heading, bearing, relative bearing, distance from gate center and scores for heading, altitude, and smoothness of the approach upon gate completion within the Prepar3D scenario, iii. events including the C130-J's altitude, heading (true and magnetic), bearing, relative bearing, bank, pitch, latitude, longitude, airspeed, vertical speed, roll and yaw in addition to the gear, flaps, throttle and yoke controller positions recorded at 1/8 s intervals. A flexible fNIR sensor pad (Figs. 2 and 3) hosting 4 light sources with built in peak wavelengths at 730 nm and 850 nm is placed over subject's forehead to scan cortical areas. With a fixed source-detector separation of 2.5 cm, this configuration generates a total of 16 measurement locations per wavelength. For data acquisition and visualization, COBI Studio software (©2010, Drexel University) was used.

2.3 Participants

Ten participants between ages of 18 and 28 with varying levels of 3D videogame experience volunteered for this study. The volunteers consisted of five male and five female participants. Prior to the study all participants signed informed consent forms approved by the Drexel University Institutional Review Board.

2.4 Data Analysis

For each participant, raw light intensity measures (16 optodes x 2 wavelengths) were low-pass filtered with a finite impulse response, linear phase filter with order of 20 and cut-off frequency of 0.1 Hz to attenuate the high frequency noise, respiration and cardiac cycle effects. Saturated and undervalued channels were excluded from analysis. fNIR data epochs for each task period were extracted using event markers recorded during task execution. Oxygenation (Oxy) within each of the 16 optodes was calculated from the difference between the calculated oxy-Hb and deoxy-Hb values using the modified Beer Lambert Law for each waypoint task period with respect to a 10 s baseline.

The main effect of expertise acquisition during the tasks was tested using two-way repeated measured analysis of variance (ANOVA), with subject, waypoint and trial as fixed effects. Greenhouse-Geisser (G-G) correction was used when violations of sphericity occurred in the omnibus test. The False Detection Rate (FDR) was applied to control for type I error [31, 32]. For this analysis, only the first 3 waypoints were evaluated as they are ones purposely repeated across all trials. Intergroup differences for significant optodes were examined using Tukey's post hoc test with a significance criterion of $\alpha = 0.05$. Additionally, to determine differences in oxygenation related to skill acquisition or expertise level in the flight simulator task, the trials were divided into *Initial* trials (mean of the first 3 waypoints during the first 3 scenarios) and *Final* trials (mean of the first 3 waypoints during the last 3 scenarios). Differences in oxygenation between the Initial trials and Final trials groups were tested in significant optodes using repeated measures ANOVA with subject and expertise level as fixed effects.

A variety of behavioral measures were generated from the logged simulator data in order to determine the participant's skill in navigating the scenario trials. These measures included *average heading difference*, *average altitude difference*, *average deviation from x and y* in coordinate space, and *average distance* from the gate. Average scores were calculated for each of these measures as high level view of an individual's overall performance, and these scores were compared (correlated using Pearson's product-moment correlation coefficient) with the survey results to see how demographic information relates to performance.

3 Results

3.1 fNIR Measures

The average oxygenation (Oxy) concentration change throughout the first 3 waypoints in each trial was analyzed using two-way repeated measures ANOVA for each optode. The response was significant after applying FDR for Trial in optodes 4 and 6 (F(7,49) = 4.609, p = 0.001 and F(7,49) = 5.268, p < 0.001 respectively) and reveals a decrease in oxygenation across trials as expected from previous result and in support of the hypothesis of this study (see Fig. 8A). The effect of the waypoints was not found to be significant (p > 0.05). Tukey Post hoc test for optode 6 revealed significant differences between trial 1 (M = 0.50, SD = 0.96) and trials 5 (M = −0.17, SD = 0.42), 6 (M = −0.013, SD = 0.46) and 8 (M = −0.01, SD = 0.49). A decrease in brain oxygenation as a function of expertise development was observed, see Fig. 8B where oxygenation is calculated as a function of *Initial* trials and *Final* trials. The difference in oxygenation between *Initial* and *Final* trials was found to be significant in optode 4 (F (1,1) = 8.879, p = 0.021) and optode 6 (F(1,1) = 10.782, p = 0.013).

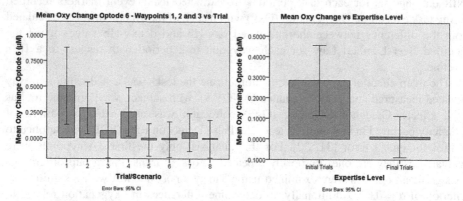

Fig. 8. A and B. (A). Mean Oxygenation Change in Optode 6 for Waypoints 1, 2 and 3 during 8 Trials. (B) Mean Oxy Change for Waypoints 1, 2 and 3 during Initial and Final Trials. Error bars represent the 95 % Confidence interval.

3.2 Behavioral Measures

The questionnaire responses were related to the prime behavioral measures, and the following results were observed. Participants' reported hours playing video games was correlated with both altitude difference (r = −.246, p < .05) and heading difference (r = −.252, p < .05), with smaller differences (i.e., better performance) were associated with more hours playing video games. These results were echoed in the more specific question asking participant's hours playing first-person video games in which the response was related to deviation from the airplane's optimal x (r = −.295, p < .05) and y (r = −.303, p < .05) position in coordinate space. Finally, performance results suggest that age matters and that a participant's age correlated with heading difference

($r = -.312$, $p < .01$), x deviation ($r = -.305$, $p < .05$), and y deviation ($r = -.272$, $p < .05$). It must be noted that all of the participants were between 18 and 28 years of age.

4 Discussion

The goal of this study was to examine the influence of pilot expertise development on the hemodynamic response in the prefrontal cortex during the complex cognitive task of flying a plane using a flight simulator.

The neurophysiological measures captured by fNIR show a decrease in oxygenation as the subjects become more proficient in the task. The oxygenation pattern that occurs in the process of skill acquisition during flight simulator task is consistent with neurophysiological results from previous work that examined expertise development using fNIR [24, 26, 27]. The significant differences observed between *Initial* and *Final* trials are hypothesized to be the result of expertise development, which is associated with lower brain activation in the prefrontal areas of the brain [14].

The results obtained in this study support the hypothesis that brain activity decreases (measured as Oxygenation by fNIR) as the level of expertise of a subject increases during flight simulator tasks.

The initial investigation of behavioral measures and how they relate to demographic survey responses reveal correlations in the expected direction. For example, a participants' reported hours playing video games was related to better performance, and reported hours playing first-person video games was related to one's ability to better maintain an ideal plane position in coordinate space. These results are in-line with similar studies revealing improved ability to manipulate objects in 3D space [34]. In addition, within the 18–28 age range of the participant population, age was positively related to performance. These results would be expected as the older participants within this range may benefit from increased experiences across a variety of domains without any associated decline of neural processing speed.

Acknowledgments. This investigation was in part funded by Lockheed Martin (University Research Agreement S14-009). The views, opinions, and/or findings contained in this article are those of the authors and should not be interpreted as representing the official views or policies, either expressed or implied, of the funding agency.

References

1. Cope, M., Delpy, D.T.: System for long-term measurement of cerebral blood and tissue oxygenation on newborn infants by near infra-red transillumination. Med. Biol. Eng. Comput. **26**, 289–294 (1988)
2. Kruggel, F., von Cramon, D.Y.: Temporal properties of the hemodynamic response in functional MRI. Hum. Brain Mapp. **8**, 259–271 (1999)
3. Magistretti, P.J.: Cellular bases of functional brain imaging: insights from neuron-glia metabolic coupling. Brain Res. **886**, 108–112 (2000)

4. Ames, A.: CNS energy metabolism as related to function. Brain Res. Rev. **34**, 42–68 (2000)
5. Cope, M.: The application of near infrared spectroscopy to non-invasive monitoring of cerebral oxygenation in the newborn infant. vol. Ph.D. University of London (1991)
6. Jobsis, F.F.: Noninvasive, infrared monitoring of cerebral and myocardial oxygen sufficiency and circulatory parameters. Science **198**, 1264–1267 (1977)
7. Chance, B., Zhuang, Z., Unah, C., Alter, C., Lipton, L.: Cognition-Activated Low-Frequency Modulation of Light-Absorption in Human Brain. Proc. Natl. Acad. Sci. USA **90**, 3770–3774 (1993)
8. Gratton, G., Corballis, P.M., Cho, E., Fabiani, M., Hood, D.C.: Shades of gray matter: noninvasive optical images of human brain responses during visual stimulation. Psychophysiology **32**, 505–509 (1995)
9. Hoshi, Y., Tamura, M.: Dynamic multichannel near-infrared optical imaging of human brain activity. J. Appl. Physiol. **75**, 1842–1846 (1993)
10. Kato, T., Kamei, A., Takashima, S., Ozaki, T.: Human visual cortical function during photic stimulation monitoring by means of near-infrared spectroscopy. J. Cereb. Blood Flow Metab. **13**, 516–520 (1993)
11. Villringer, A., Planck, J., Hock, C., Schleinkofer, L., Dirnagl, U.: Near infrared spectroscopy (NIRS): a new tool to study hemodynamic changes during activation of brain function in human adults. Neurosci. Lett. **154**, 101–104 (1993)
12. Chance, B., Anday, E., Nioka, S., Zhou, S., Hong, L., Worden, K., Li, C., Murray, T., Ovetsky, Y., Pidikiti, D., Thomas, R.: A novel method for fast imaging of brain function, non-invasively, with light. Opt. Express **2**, 411–423 (1998)
13. Ayaz, H., Izzetoglu, M., Platek, S.M., Bunce, S., Izzetoglu, K., Pourrezaei, K., Onaral, B.: Registering fNIR data to brain surface image using MRI templates. Conf. Proc. IEEE Eng. Med. Biol. Soc. **1**, 2671–2674 (2006)
14. Milton, J.G., Small, S.S., Solodkin, A.: On the road to automatic: dynamic aspects in the development of expertise. J. Clin. Neurophysiol. **21**, 134–143 (2004)
15. Chance, B., Zhuang, Z., UnAh, Z., Alter, C., Lipton, L.: Cognition-activated low-frequency modulation of light absorption in human brain. PNAS **90**, 3770–3774 (1993)
16. Villringer, A., Chance, B.: Non-invasive optical spectroscopy and imaging of human brain function. Trends Neurosci. **20**, 435–442 (1997)
17. Hoshi, Y., Onoe, H., Watanabe, Y., Andersson, J., Bergstrom, M., Lilja, A., Langstom, B., Tamura, M.: Non-synchronous behavior of neuronal activity, oxidative metabolism and blood supply during mental tasks in man. Neurosci. Lett. **172**, 129–133 (1994)
18. Villringer, A., Planck, J., Hock, C., Schleinkofer, L., Dirnagl, U.: Near infrared spectroscopy (NIRS): a new tool to study hemodynamic changes during activation of brain function in human adults. Neurosci. Lett. **154**, 101–104 (1993)
19. Strangman, G., Boas, D.A., Sutton, J.P.: Non-invasive neuroimaging using near-infrared light. Biol. Psychiatry **52**(7), 679–693 (2002)
20. Gratton, E., Toronov, V., Wolf, U., Wolf, M., Webb, A.: Measurement of brain activity by near-infrared light. J. Biomed. Opt. **10**(1), 011008 (2005)
21. Hoshi, Y.: Functional near-infrared optical imaging: utility and limitations in human brain mapping. Psychophysiology **40**, 511–520 (2003)
22. Izzetoglu, M., Izzetoglu, K., Bunce, S., Ayaz, H., Deveraj, A., Onaral, B., Pourrezaei, K.: Functional Near-Infrared Neuroimaging. IEEE Trans. Neural Syst. Rehabil. Eng. **13**(2), 153–159 (2005)
23. Buxton, R.B., Uludag, K., Dubowitz, D.J., Liu, T.T.: Modeling the hemodynamic response to brain activation. NeuroImage **23**(Suppl. 1), S220–S233 (2004)

24. Ayaz, H., Onaral, B., Izzetoglu, K., Shewokis, P.A., McKendrick, R., Parasuraman, R.: Continuous monitoring of brain dynamics with functional near infrared spectroscopy as a tool for neuroergonomic research: Empirical examples and a technological development. Front. Hum. Neurosci. **7**, 1–13 (2013). doi:10.3389/fnhum.2013.00871

25. Ayaz, H., Bunce, S., Shewokis, P., Izzetoglu, K., Willems, B., Onaral, B.: Using brain activity to predict task performance and operator efficiency. In: Hussain, A., Liu, D., Zhang, H., Wang, Z. (eds.) BICS 2012. LNCS, vol. 7366, pp. 147–155. Springer, Heidelberg (2012)

26. Ayaz, H., Cakir, M. P., Izzetoglu, K., Curtin, A., Shewokis, P. A., Bunce, S., Onaral, B.: Monitoring expertise development during simulated UAV piloting tasks using optical brain imaging. Paper presented at the IEEE Aerospace Conference, BigSky, MN, USA (2012)

27. Ayaz, H., Shewokis, P.A., Bunce, S., Izzetoglu, K., Willems, B., Onaral, B.: Optical brain monitoring for operator training and mental workload assessment. NeuroImage **59**(1), 36–47 (2012)

28. Harrison, J., Izzetoglu, K., Ayaz, H., Willems, B., Hah, S., Ahlstrom, U., Onaral, B.: Cognitive workload and learning assessment during the implementation of a next-generation air traffic control technology using functional near-infrared spectroscopy. IEEE Trans. Hum.-Mach. Syst. **44**(4), 429–440 (2014). doi:10 1109/THMS.2014.2319822

29. Izzetoglu, K., Ayaz, H., Hing, J., Shewokis, P., Bunce, S., Oh, P., Onaral, B.: UAV Operators Workload Assessment by Optical Brain Imaging Technology (fNIR). In: Valavanis, K.P., Vachtsevanos, G.J. (eds.) Handbook of Unmanned Aerial Vehicles, pp. 2475–2500. Springer, Netherlands (2014)

30. Izzetoglu, K., Ayaz, H., Menda, J., Izzetoglu, M., Merzagora, A., Shewokis, P.A., Pourrezaei, K., Onaral, B.: Applications of functional near infrared imaging: case study on UAV ground controller. In: Schmorrow, D.D., Fidopiastis, C.M. (eds.) FAC 2011. LNCS, vol. 6780, pp. 608–617. Springer, Heidelberg (2011)

31. Benjamini, Y., Hochberg, Y.: Controlling the false discovery rate: a practical and powerful approach to multiple testing. J. Roy. Stat. Soc. Ser. B (Methodol.) **57**, 289–300 (1995)

32. Singh, A.K., Dan, I.: Exploring the false discovery rate in multichannel NIRS. NeuroImage **33**, 542–549 (2006)

33. Strangman, G., Boas, D.A., Sutton, J.P.: Non-invasive neuroimaging using near-infrared light. Biol. Psychiatry **52**, 679–693 (2002)

34. Lynch, J., Aughwane, P., Hammond, T.: Video games and surgical ability: a literature review. J. Surg. Educ. **67**, 184–189 (2010)

Measuring Situational Awareness Aptitude Using Functional Near-Infrared Spectroscopy

Leanne Hirshfield[1(✉)], Mark Costa[1,2], Danushka Bandara[1,3], and Sarah Bratt[1,2]

[1] M.I.N.D. Lab, Newhouse School of Communications, Syracuse, NY, USA
{lmhirshf,mrcosta,dsbandar,sebratt}@syr.edu
[2] School of Information Studies, Syracuse University, Syracuse, NY, USA
[3] Electrical Engineering and Computer Science, Syracuse University, Syracuse, NY, USA

Abstract. Attempts have been made to evaluate people's situational awareness (SA) in military and civilian contexts through subjective surveys, speed, and accuracy data acquired during SA target tasks. However, it is recognized in the SA domain that more systematic measurement is necessary to assess SA theories and applications. Recent advances in biomedical engineering have enabled relatively new ways to measure cognitive and physiological state changes, such as with functional near-infrared spectroscopy (fNIRS). In this paper, we provide a literature review relating to SA and fNIRS and present an experiment conducted with an fNIRS device comparing differences in the brains between people with high and low SA aptitude. Our results suggest statistically significant differences in brain activity between the high SA group and low SA group.

Keywords: Situational awareness · fNIRS · HCI · Brain measurement

1 Introduction

Recent advances in biomedical engineering have enabled the measurement of cognitive and physiological state changes non-invasively, allowing for the quantification of user states that were not measurable even a few years ago. Researchers have used non-invasive brain measurement to successfully measure mental states with great relevance to the human-computer interaction (HCI) domain, such as cognitive workload, deception, trust, engagement, and emotion [1–4]. Others have used brain measurement to compare the brain activation between groups of people with different traits while they complete the same task. For example, experiments have found that novices and experts show different patterns of brain activation during difficult tasks [5], and it has also been shown that people with high IQ have different patterns of brain activation than lower IQ counterparts [6]. One construct that remains difficult to define and quantify involves situational awareness (SA). SA remains an ill-defined buzzword, but Mica Endsley's three stage model of SA remains the most widely accepted description used in SA research [7]. The model, which is discussed in further detail in the next

© Springer International Publishing Switzerland 2015
D.D. Schmorrow and C.M. Fidopiastis (Eds.): AC 2015, LNAI 9183, pp. 244–255, 2015.
DOI: 10.1007/978-3-319-20816-9_24

section, breaks SA into three high-level cognitive stages. High SA aptitude is a necessary quality for many jobs, both in the military and civilian domains.

Measurement of SA is done primarily through surveys and/or viewing task performance. However, surveys are not reliable because they are subjective and must be administered post-task completion. Similarly, task performance only gives a small piece of overall information related to SA. No successful measurement of SA in the brain has been reported yet; this research provides a first step in that direction. The accurate quantitative, real-time assessment of SA aptitude could be used to screen individuals' for employment in both the military and civilian domains. We leveraged our expertise using functional near-infrared spectroscopy (fNIRS) to measure brain activity of users while they completed tasks that require high SA aptitude. The fNIRS tool is safe, portable, non-invasive, and can be implemented wirelessly, allowing for use in real world environments.

The paper proceeds as follows: First, we describe background literature relating to our research goals. Then, we describe the challenges faced, guidelines established, and the hypotheses formulated while conducting this research. We then provide step-wise details of an experiment administered in our lab comparing high-SA and low-SA participants. The paper concludes with a thorough discussion of the next steps that follow naturally from our work to measure SA in the brain.

2 Background and Literature Review

There are several brain measurement devices available in medical and research domains. These devices monitor brain activation by measuring several biological metrics. When a stimulus is presented, neurons fire in the activated region(s) of the brain fire causing an electric potential, an increase in cerebral blood flow in that region, an increase in the metabolic rate of oxygen, and an increase in the volume of blood flow. All of these factors contribute to the blood oxygen level dependent (BOLD) signal, which can be detected (in various forms) by a number of brain measurement techniques such as fMRI, fNIRS, and PET. Ideally, a brain measurement device suitable for measuring brain activity in typical HCI activities would be non-invasive and portable. It would have extremely fast temporal resolution (for use in adaptive systems) and it would have high spatial resolution, enabling the localization of brain activation in specific functional brain regions. Electroencephalograph (EEG) and fNIRS are the two most popular devices for non-invasive imaging of the brain. However, when compared to EEG, fNIRS has higher spatial resolution, lower set-up time, and a higher signal-to-noise ratio [2, 8]. We focus on fNIRS, as this is one of the best suited technologies for non-invasive brain measurement during naturalistic HCI.

2.1 Functional Near-Infrared Spectroscopy

FNIRS is a relatively new non-invasive technique that was introduced in the late 1980s [9] to overcome many of the drawbacks of other brain monitoring techniques. The tool, still primarily a research modality, uses light sources in the near infrared wavelength range (650–850 nm) and optical detectors to probe brain activity.

Light source and detection points are defined by means of optical fibers held on the scalp with an optical probe. Deoxygenated (Hb) and oxygenated hemoglobin (HbO) are the main absorbers of near infrared light in tissues during hemodynamic and metabolic changes associated with neural activity in the brain [10]. These changes can be detected measuring the diffusively reflected light that has probed the brain cortex [10]. FNIRS has been used in recent years to measure a myriad of mental states such as workload, deception, trust, suspicion, frustration, types of multi-tasking, and stress [2]. With its high spatial resolution, fNIRS can also localize brain regions of interest in order to measure more granular cognitive states such as verbal working memory load, spatial working memory load, response inhibition load, visual search load, executive processing, or emotion regulation load [2, 3, 11]. We posit that fNIRS can also be used to measure the cognitive correlates of situation awareness.

2.2 Situation Awareness

As described previously, the first stage of Endsley's model focuses on one's **perception** of the elements in the current situation. Many SA-demanding tasks involve extremely complex environments where the human operator must be able to perceive relatively small environmental changes while working on the complex task at hand. For example, an air traffic controller who is keeping track of a particular region of airspace must easily be able to perceive the entry of a new plane into that space. Stage 1 of SA is very important in a practical sense, as it can be responsible for many SA-related accidents. A review of SA-related aircraft accidents revealed that SA errors related to **perception and attention** (Stage 1), constituted the majority of such accidents [18]. If users successfully meet the multitasking related demands of SA Stage 1 while working with their complex system, they will immediately perceive when their environment has changed. At this point, SA Stages 2 and 3 become important. SA stage 2 is involved with one's **comprehension** of the elements in the current situation. Simultaneous to comprehending the nature of a given scenario, someone with high SA must be able to make **projections** about how the newly-evolved situation will affect the future. This projection involves SA Stage 3, the ability to plan and project into the future.

Several techniques have been developed to assess SA. For example, SA has been measured subjectively, using the Situation Awareness Rating Techniques (SART) and the Participant Situation Awareness Questionnaire (PSAQ). The questions in Table 1 are representative of the questions presented in the SART and PSAQ surveys [12, 13].

One of the most widely used measures of SA is provided by Endsley's Situation Awareness Global Assessment Technique (SAGAT) [14]. With SAGAT, task

Table 1. Example questions from the SART and PSAQ surveys

PSAQ	Please circle the number that best describes how aware of the evolving situation you were during the scenario
SART	Please circle the number indicating the degree to which the situation at the low level, is confusing and contradictory, or, at the high level, is straightforward and understandable.

simulations are frozen at randomly-selected times, and the operators quickly answer questions about their current perceptions of the situation. The questions correspond to their situation awareness requirements as determined from the results of an SA requirements analysis. Operator perceptions are then compared to the real situation, based on simulation computer databases, to provide a qualitative measure of the operator's SA.

Although Endsley's model and the popular SA measurement techniques of SA-GAT, SART, and PSAQ, are widely accepted in the SA research domain, they all view SA on a very abstract level, and they involve distracting the subject from the task at hand in order to complete the questionnaire(s). From a human factors research point of view, it is acceptable to speak about user states such as SA or mental workload in high level terms, and survey techniques such as SART, SAGAT, and PSAQ may suffice to measure these states abstractly. However, if we are to measure these states objectively and in real-time, there is a need to understand the cognitive and physiological correlates that are related to SA. We use Endsley's SA model throughout this next section as a general reference while we describe the low level cognitive resources that we posit are involved in maintaining high SA.

2.3 Cognitive Correlates of Situation Awareness

Visual perception and search involves searching for items within a set of distracter items, and being able to notice subtle changes in a dynamic environment, which is directly related to Stage 1 in Endsley's SA model. Visual search has been explored extensively in the neuroscience and psychology literature [15]. It is well known that people differ in their aptitude at conducting visual search tasks. We hypothesize that: *H1: A person with superior SA will have a higher aptitude at visual perception and scanning than their lower SA counterparts.*

A fundamental adaptive challenge for humans is that of regulating our emotions in order to successfully complete a given task. To meet this challenge, we have the ability to exert control over the emotions we experience. Emotion regulation entails controlling or changing one's emotions through both extrinsic means (managing overt behaviors and social situations) and intrinsic means (recruiting cognitive and neuro-physiological systems) [16]. It is well known that stress can cause catastrophic breakdowns in the ability to concentrate, pay attention to a task, or make complex decisions. Emotion regulation is a component for maintaining high SA during all three stages of Endsley's SA model. Emotion regulation has been successfully measured with fNIRS [3]. Thus, we hypothesize that: *H2: A person with superior SA will have a higher aptitude at emotion regulation than their lower SA counterparts, as measured by fNIRS.*

SA Stage 3 considers one's ability to take new information and to project how that information or event will affect the future. *Prospection* is the act of thinking about the future. The term prospection is very similar to the term projection, which Endsley uses in her third stage of SA. When we think about the future, we use a common functional brain region that includes frontal and medial temporal systems that are associated with planning and episodic memory [17]. As with all of the other brain functions mentioned in this paper, some people are better at prospection than others. Thus, we hypothesize that: *H3: A person with superior SA will have a higher activation in brain regions responsible for prospection than their lower SA counterparts, as measured by fNIRS.*

There is an interesting body of literature focusing on the neural efficiency debate that is of direct relevance to SA. The basic premise behind the neural efficiency approach is that individuals with higher IQ's use less brain activation in order to complete the same tasks as their less apt counterparts. However, recent research has shown that the neural efficiency hypothesis is heavily dependent on task difficulty:

1. When the underlying task is easy or of a moderate level of difficulty, the neural efficiency approach is correct; high IQ people have less, and more focused, brain activation, while completing the same task as their lower IQ counterparts.
2. When the underlying task is very difficult and/or complex, the opposite of the neural efficiency hypothesis occurs: high IQ individuals show brain activation than their lower IQ counterparts while doing the same task.

In both scenarios above, the high IQ groups outperform their lower IQ counterparts, but it is interesting to note that the amount of brain activity is directly related to the difficulty of the task. People with high SA aptitude would likely show brain activation that clearly fits with the neural efficiency hypothesis. Since many tasks that require high SA are complex, we hypothesize that: *H4: When completing a complex multi-tasking scenario, a person with superior SA will have more brain activation than their lower SA counterparts measured with fNIRS.*

3 Experiment

Before conducting our experiment, we conducted a set of exploratory pilot studies that were designed to help us determine the best testbed that would be complex enough to enable us to differentiate between participants with high and average SA aptitude. We worked with the Research Environment for Supervisory Control of Heterogeneous Unmanned Vehicles (RESCHU) [18], the Warship Commander Task [19], and the Air Force's updated version of the Multi-Attribute Task Battery (MATB) [20]. In the end, we decided that the MATB testbed provided the ideal environment that would require aptitude at each of Endsley's three SA stages in order to achieve high accuracy.

We also tested the PSAQ and SART surveys (described in the prior section) out during pilot testing of our testbeds. During exit interviews with our pilot participants, they reported these subjective surveys to be difficult to understand. The sampling of PSAQ an SART questions from Table 1 supports this finding; the questions shown in Table 1 could be difficult for subjects' to accurately respond to. One pilot participant noted that a participant can think that he or she understands the situation well, but this misconception may lead to high amounts of user error. These subjective surveys do not account for users who are not fully aware of the situation. The popular saying: "You don't know what you don't know', rings very true in this situation. We purchased the SAGAT assessment tool and found that, within the context of our task, the SAGAT results were directly related to participants' performance data. Performance data has been shown to directly relate to SA. One advantage of using performance data is that you don't have to interrupt users during the task, as must be done with SAGAT. Although performance is usually directly related to SA, Endsley found that high SA does not always lead to good performance, and low SA does not always result in poor performance [21]. However, in the context of the AF_MATB, our pilot data suggested that performance data did directly relate to SA (as assessed by SAGAT) as long as all participants had an equal amount of training time with the system.

With the information gained from our pilot testing, we designed an experiment to help us explore the four hypotheses listed above. The primary goal of the experiment was to use fNIRS to measure differences in the brains between people with high and average SA aptitude.

3.1 Experiment Testbed

Our task involved a complex multi-tasking scenario using a variation of the Multi-Attribute Task Battery (MATB) [20, 22]. This difficult task made it imperative that high achieving users not become overloaded or overly stressed, forcing them to prioritize their actions based on the most time sensitive or important needs of the task at the time. We used the Air Force's updated version of the Multi-Attribute Task Battery (AF_MATB) [20], and we chose a difficulty level (based on pilot testing) that required a good deal of mental effort and multi-tasking.

With the difficulty of the task and the high level of multi-tasking required, the task was nearly impossible to complete perfectly, and our pilot tests showed that all subjects had to remain extremely engaged during the entire task to receive an adequate performance score. Like the original version, AF_MATB consists of six windows which provide information about four different subtasks (see Fig. 1); these subtasks include: System Monitoring, Communications, Resource Management, and Tracking. The last two windows, which contain Scheduling and Pump Status information, are resources that the user can use to improve performance during the task. The AF_MATB keeps track of, and outputs, a thorough report of each subject's performance data on the

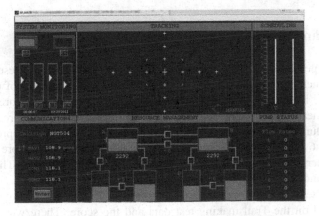

Fig. 1. A screen shot of the MATB testbed

various subtasks. In our pilot studies, we selected a MATB difficulty level that would result in the majority, if not all, of the subjects having difficulty executing every task perfectly. They would have to multi-task, prioritize, and accept that while their performance would likely be imperfect, they must keep from becoming frustrated in order to complete the demanding MATB scenario.

3.2 Experimental Protocol

Eight subjects completed this experiment (3 female). After providing informed consent, subjects completed a Trail Making Test [23], as well as a visual perception and scanning aptitude test called the finding A's task from the Educational Testing Service [24]. The Trail Making Test is a neuropsychological test of visual attention and task switching. It consists of two parts in which the subject is instructed to connect a set of 25 *dots* as fast as possible while still maintaining accuracy. Subjects then spent 45 min learning about AF_MATB. We wanted to ensure that they would fully comprehend the many rules and goals included in the experiment task before beginning the experiment. Subjects then completed two experimental conditions, and repeated these conditions 5 times, resulting in 5 trials of data. In each trial, the subject completed 2 min of working with the AF_MATB (MATB condition), and then they rested for 2 min while making similar mouse movements as those caused by the AF_MATB (control condition). They repeated this process 5 times.

We collected fNIRS data using the Hitachi ETG-4000 device. Subjects wore a cap with 52 channels that take measurements twice per second. As fNIRS equipment is sensitive to movement, subjects were placed at a comfortable distance from the keyboard and mouse and were asked to minimize movement throughout the experiment. Prior research has shown that this minimal movement does not significantly corrupt the fNIRS signal with motion artifacts [24]. We also gathered performance data throughout the experiments. Based on our pilot studies with the SAGAT, SART, and PSAQ surveys, we chose to use performance data as our primary metric to assess SA. This objective metric, which has been shown to directly relate to SA, could be measured in real-time while users worked with the MATB.

4 Results and Analysis

We gathered performance data for each of the 6 multi-tasks represented in the AF_MATB. Each of the performance outputs represented an amount of error on that task: therefore, lower numbers indicate better performance. We z-score normalized each of these measures, and then summed them up for each individual, resulting in the **total score** column in Table 2. A lower score is better in this case (representing less error across all 6 sub-tasks). We sorted our data by the subjects' total score and selected the top three performers (subjects 7, 6, and 4) as the high SA group. The rest of the subjects were included in our average SA group.

We conducted a Pearson product correlation on the visual scanning data and the total score, and on the Trail making test data and the score. There was not a strong

Table 2. Performance results on MATB

	Visual Scan (s)	TMT A (s)	System Monitoring	Track	Resources	Communicate	Total score
s7	17.0	12.0	0.8	-0.5	-0.2	-1.9	-1.7
s6	10.0	15.8	-0.8	0.3	-0.7	-0.5	-1.7
s4	15.0	15.0	0.2	-0.9	-1.0	0.2	-1.5
s2	10.0	27.0	0.2	-1.0	-0.1	0.6	-0.4
s5	14.0	21.6	-1.8	1.9	1.0	0.0	0.3
s3	10.0	22.0	0.5	-0.7	-0.3	0.8	1.2
s1	14.0	21.0	-0.5	0.2	0.2	1.4	1.3
s8	15.0	12.0	1.4	0.7	-1.4	-0.5	0.2

correlation between visual scanning test scores (the finding A's task) and the final score, but there was a strong relationship (r = −0.69, p = .058) between subjects' scores on the Trail Making Test (neuropsychological test of visual attention and task switching) and their overall score. Thus, it seems that the same high level resources that caused one to be superior at the Trail Making test were recruited to help them during the AF_MATB task. With the contradictory results from the Trail Making Test and Visual Scanning Tests, we only had partial support for *H1: A person with superior SA will have a higher aptitude at visual perception and scanning than their lower SA counterparts.*

We used the NIRS_SPM Matlab suite of tools to analyze the fNIRS data [25]. We first converted our raw light intensity data into relative changes of oxygenated (HbO) concentrations. We then preprocessed all data using a band-pass filter (between .1 and .01 Hz) to remove noise and motion artifacts. We used a general linear model (GLM) to fit our fNIRS data. Because the GLM analysis relies on the temporal variational pattern of signals, it is robust to differential path length factor variation, optical scattering, or poor contact on the head. By incorporating the GLM with the *p*-value calculation, NIRS-SPM not only enables calculation of activation maps of HbO but also allows for spatial localization. We used Tsuzuki's 3D-digitizer-free method for the virtual registration of NIRS channels onto the stereotactic brain coordinate system. Essentially, this method allows us to place a virtual optode holder on the scalp by registering optodes and channels onto reference brains. Assuming that the fNIRS probe is reproducibly set across subjects, the virtual registration can yield as accurate spatial estimation as the probabilistic registration method. Please refer to [26] for further information. Based on performance data, participants were placed into two groups: high SA and average SA groups. Statistical tests were run on the data from each group to determine significant regions of activation (p < .05) for each group when participants were completing MATB, as compared to the control condition. NIRS_SPM results are shown in Fig. 2.

It appears that the high SA group had more brain activation than the average SA group during the MATB tasks. All participants were undergoing a very challenging

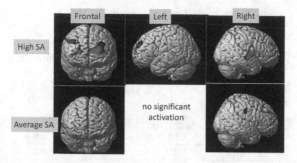

Fig. 2. Results from the NIRS_SPM toolkit showing significant areas of activation at p < .05

multi-tasking scenario that involved their constant vigilance and information process-ing, and projection of future events. Our results are in line with the recent neural efficiency research that suggests that high aptitude (in this case, high SA) subjects elicit more brain activity than their peers when undergoing highly complex tasks. The brain activation shown in the frontal view shows that the high SA group had more brain activation in areas directly responsible for cognitive load processing (i.e., concentrating and thinking hard during the task) than the average SA group. These regions corre-spond with executive functioning, memory, and planning and coordinating activities. This supports H4: *When completing a complex multi-tasking scenario, a person with superior SA will have more brain activation than their lower SA counterparts, which is in in the neural efficiency research, as measured with fNIRS.*

The left side of the high SA group's brain shows activation in Brodman's area 9, or the dorsolateral prefrontal cortex (DLPFC) for the high SA group. The DLPFC is recruited during workload inducing tasks, and in particular, it is responsible for emotion regulation. It is possible that the high SA group may have been expending cognitive effort to regulate their emotions, keeping them from becoming stressed by the demands of the MATB task. In stark contrast to the high SA group, there was no significant activation on the left side of the brain of the average SA group. This sup-ports H2: *A person with superior SA will have a higher aptitude at emotion regulation than their lower SA counterparts, as measured by fNIRS.*

On the right side of the brain, the high SA group and the average SA group had activation in the Superior Frontal Sulcus, which is heavily involved in working memory, but the high SA group had a good deal more activation than the average SA group in that region. The high SA group also had activation in the Inferior Frontal Sulcus and Supramarginal Gyrus. The Supramarginal Gyrus is involved in language processing and perception. The activation on the right side of the brain of the high SA group also has some overlap with regions responsible for prospection. As described previously, prospection involves thinking into the future about upcoming events and situations. It is interesting to note that high SA users may have been predicting future events in the task, which is a key element of Endsley's SA stage 3. This is in line with prior research, discussed in the literature review, that people with higher IQ's spend more cognitive resources 'planning ahead' than their average IQ counterparts when doing the same task [17]. This supports H3: *A person with superior SA will have a higher activation in brain regions responsible for prospection than their lower SA counterparts, as measured by fNIRS.* When completing a complex multi-tasking scenario, a person with superior SA will have more brain activation than their lower SA counterparts, which is in in the neural efficiency research, as measured with fNIRS.

5 Study Limitations

One limitation of this study is that we used performance metrics to get our 'ground truth' values of SA. Although performance and SA often have a positive correlation, they do not always have a direct mapping. However, we did not choose performance as our 'ground truth' lightly; we evaluated SAGAT, PSAQ, and the SART SA assessment techniques before deciding to use objective performance measures as our 'ground truth'. Future work should further explore the relationship between SA assessments like SAGAT, PSAQ, and SART with performance data.

6 Conclusion

Attempts have been made to evaluate people's SA through subjective surveys and assessment of speed and accuracy data acquired during target tasks that require SA. However, it is well known in the SA domain that more systematic measurement is necessary to test theories of SA, to screen personnel for SA, and to find ways for individuals to maximize their SA in a variety of real world contexts [7]. While preliminary attempts have been made to measure the psychophysiological correlates of SA, no research has looked deeply into this issue, even though the benefits of such research have been recognized [27]. Recent advances in biomedical engineering have enabled us to measure people's cognitive and physiological state changes non-invasively, allowing us to quantify user states that were not measurable even a few years ago. While there are many non-invasive sensors available to take measurements of users during naturalistic HCI, fNIRS is a relatively new brain measurement device that holds great potential in the HCI domain [2, 3, 10, 28]. The fNIRS tool is safe, portable, and non-invasive, enabling use in real world environments. As with many high-level user states (such as workload, trust, and flow), SA remains an oft misunderstood buzz term. Although Mica Endsley's well respected model of SA [7] provides us with a useful guide for our work, we found that viewing SA in the brain requires a more precise view of SA than that described in past research. This research provides a first step in that direction.

In this paper, we described an experiment conducted with a 52-channel fNIRS device to measure differences in the brains between people with high and average SA aptitude. Our task involved a complex multi-tasking scenario using a variation of the Multi-Attribute Task Battery (MATB). This difficult task made it imperative that high achieving users not become overloaded or overly stressed, forcing them to prioritize their actions based on the most important needs of the task at the time. Our results suggest that: When completing the MATB, people with superior SA have more brain activation than their lower SA counterparts, which is in line with neural efficiency research. Also, people with superior SA have a higher aptitude at emotion regulation than their lower SA counterparts, as measured by fNIRS. We also found that people with superior SA have a higher activation in brain regions responsible for prospection than their lower SA counterparts, as measured by fNIRS. Lastly, we had partial support that people with superior SA have a higher aptitude at visual perception and scanning than their lower SA counterparts. Many military and civilian jobs require high SA aptitude. Screening for SA is already a part of many of these jobs, but these screenings are based largely on survey and performance data. An objective measure of SA, based on cognitive data during completion of complex tasks, would provide an unbiased way to get these measurements in real-time. Our research makes measurable steps toward this goal.

References

1. Grimes, D., et al.: Feasibility and pragmatics of classifying working memory load with an electroencephalograph. In: CHI 2008 Conference on Human Factors in Computing Systems, Florence (2008)
2. Hirshfield, L., et al.: This is your brain on interfaces: enhancing usability testing with functional near infrared spectroscopy. In: SIGCHI. ACM (2011)
3. Hirshfield, L.M., et al.: Using non-invasive brain measurement to explore the psychological effects of computer malfunctions on users during human-computer interactions. Adv. Hum.-Comput. Interact. **2014**, 1–13 (2014)
4. Berka, C., et al.: Real-time analysis of EEG indexes of alertness cognition, and memory acquired with a wireless EEG headset. Int. J. Hum. Comput. Interact. **17**(2), 151–170 (2004)
5. Gevins, A., Smith, M.: Neurophysiological measures of working memory and individual differences in cognitive ability and cogntive style. Cereb. Cortex **10**(9), 829–839 (2000)
6. Grabnera, R., Neubauera, A., Stern, E.: Superior performance and neural efficiency: The impact of intelligence and expertise. Brain Res. Bull. Sci. Direct **69**(4), 422–439 (2006)
7. Endsley, M.: Situation awareness. In: Salvendy, G. (ed.) Handbook of Human Factors and Ergonomics. Wiley, New York (2006)
8. Parasuraman, R., Rizzo, M.: Neuroergonomics: The Brain at Work. Oxford University Press, Oxford (2008)
9. Chance, B., et al.: A novel method for fast imaging of brain function, non-invasively, with light. Opt. Express **10**(2), 411–423 (1988)
10. Izzetoglu, K., et al.: Functional near-infrared neuroimaging. In: Proceedings of IEEE EMBS (2004)
11. Hirshfield, L.M., et al.: Brain measurement for usability testing and adaptive interfaces: an example of uncovering syntactic workload in the brain using functional near infrared spectroscopy. In: Conference on Human Factors in Computing Systems: Proceeding of the Twenty-Seventh Annual SIGCHI Conference on Human Factors in Computing Systems (2009)
12. Matthews, M.D., et al.: Measures of infantry situation awareness in a virtual MOUT environment. In: Human Performance, Situation Awareness and Automation Conference, Savannah (2000)
13. Taylor, R.M.: Situational awareness rating technique (SART): the development of a tool for aircrew systems design. In: Situational Awareness in Aerospace Operations (AGARD-CP-478), Neuilly Sur Seine (1990)

14. Endsley, M.R., Garland, D.G.: Situation Awareness Analysis and Measurement. CRC Press, Atlanta (2000)
15. Anderson, E.J., et al.: Involvement of prefrontal cortex in visual search. Exp. Brain Res. **180** (2), 289–302 (2007)
16. Gross, J., Thompson, R.: Emotion regulation: conceptual foundations. In: Gross, J. (ed.) Handbook of Emotion Regulation. Guilford Press, New York (2007)
17. Buckner, R., Carrol, D.: Self-projection and the brain. Trends Cogn. Sci. **11**(2), 49–57 (2006)
18. Donmez, B.D., Nehme, C., Cummings, M.L.: Modeling workload impact in multiple unmanned vehicle supervisory control. IEEE J. Syst. Man Cybern. **40**(6), 1180–1190 (2010)
19. John, M.S., et al.: Overview of the DARPA augmented cognition technical integration experiment. Int. J. Hum.-Comput. Interact. **17**(2), 131–149 (2004)
20. Miller, W.: The US Air Force-Developed Adaptaion of the Multi-Attribute Task Battery. AFRL-RH-WP-TR-2010–0133 (2010)
21. Endsley, M.: Predictive utility of an objective measure of situation awareness. In: Proceedings of the Human Factors Society 34th Annual Meeting. Human Factors Society, Santa Monica (1990)
22. Arnegard, R., Comstock, R.: The multi-attribute task battery for human operator workload and strategic behavior research. NASA Technical Report (1992)
23. Arnett, J., Labovitz, S.: Effect of physical layout in performance of the Trail Making Test. Psychol. Assess. **7**(2), 220–221 (1995)
24. Eckstrom, R., et al.: Kit of Factor-Referenced Cognitive Tests. Educational testing service, Princeton (1976)
25. Ye, J.C., et al.: NIRS-SPM: statistical parametric mapping for near-infrared spectroscopy. Neuroimage **44**(2), 428–447 (2009)
26. Tsuzuki, D., et al.: Virtual spatial registration of stand-alone functional NIRS data to MNI space. NeuroImage **34**, 1506–1518 (2007)
27. Wilson, G.: Strategies for psychophysiological assessment of situation awareness. In: Endsley, M., Garland, D. (eds.) Situation Awareness: Analysis and Measurement. Lawrence Earlbaum Associates, NJ (2000)
28. Chance, B., et al.: Cognition activated low frequency modulation of light absorption in human brain. Proc. Nat. Acad. Sci. **90**(8), 3770–3774 (1993)

Neurocognitive Correlates of Learning in a Visual Object Recognition Task

Ion Juvina[1]([⊠]), Priya Ganapathy[2], Matt Sherwood[3],
Mohd Saif Usmani[4], Gautam Kunapuli[2], Tejaswi Tamminedi[2],
and Nasser Kashou[4]

[1] Department of Psychology, Wright State University, Dayton, OH, USA
ion.juvina@wright.edu
[2] UtopiaCompression Corporation, Los Angeles, CA, USA
[3] Wright State Research Institute, Wright State University, Dayton, OH, USA
[4] Department of Biomedical Industrial, and Human Factors Engineering,
Wright State University, Dayton, OH, USA

Abstract. Preliminary results of a longitudinal study aimed at understanding the neurocognitive correlates of learning in a visual object recognition task are reported. The experimental task used real-world novel stimuli, whereas the control task used real-world familiar stimuli. Participants practiced the tasks over 10 weeks and reached a high level of accuracy. Brain imaging data was acquired in weeks 2, 6, and 10 and eye-tracking data was acquired in the other seven weeks. Quantitative and qualitative changes in brain activity were observed over the course of learning and skill acquisition. Generally, in the experimental task, brain activity increased at week 6 and decreased at week 10, whereas in the control task, brain activity decreased at week 6 and further decreased at week 10 compared to week 2. New clusters of brain activity emerged at week 6 in the experimental task. Eye-fixation and pupil-dilation data showed that fast learners tend to inspect the stimuli more thoroughly even after a response was given. These results are used to inform the development of computational cognitive models of visual object recognition tasks.

Keywords: Longitudinal study · Learning · Brain imaging · Eye tracking

1 Introduction and Background

Practice related changes in brain activity have been reported in a variety of laboratory tasks and paradigms. Here we report preliminary results form a study aimed at investigating patterns of brain activity associated with practice and learning in a visual object recognition task. What distinguishes this study from similar ones is the use of real-world, complex stimuli (i.e., military aircraft) and a variety of measurements, such as accuracy, response time, eye fixations, pupil size, and fMRI BOLD signal. The purpose of this investigation is to inform the development of computational cognitive models (Anderson et al. 2007) that can be used to suggest instructional interventions that maximize learning and engagement and can be embedded in intelligent, adaptive tutoring systems. Anderson et al. (2010) have put forward a compelling argument for

© Springer International Publishing Switzerland 2015
D.D. Schmorrow and C.M. Fidopiastis (Eds.): AC 2015, LNAI 9183, pp. 256–267, 2015.
DOI: 10.1007/978-3-319 20816-9_25

the value of combining behavioral and brain imaging data with computational cognitive modeling for the purpose of informing the development of intelligent tutoring systems.

The most robust result in the literature is that repeated practice is associated with reductions in activity in task-specific and task-general brain regions (Chein and Schneider 2005). However, this result applies only when there is a consistent mapping between stimuli and responses and no change in strategy is expected to occur with practice and learning. Increases in activity with practice are reported in paradigms that aim to develop skills (e.g. mirror reading, Poldrack and Gabrieli 2001) or capacities (e.g., working memory, Olesen et al. 2004). In these paradigms, strategy shifts are expected and even seen as a desirable effect of training. We expect our task to be more prone to strategizing than simpler laboratory tasks and conceive of strategy learning as an intrinsic component of skill acquisition. We expect participants to develop strategies to inspect stimuli and their features, search for relevant information, encode, keep, and retrieve information in/from long-term memory. These activities will likely be associated with changes in neural activity that can be detected with fMRI. Given the purpose of our study, we are not just interested in quantitative changes such as increases or decreases in activity with learning. Qualitative changes are more interesting because we can learn something about the structure of thought, for example, whether a participant changes strategies or allocates different resources to the task at hand. In addition, since our main purpose is to inform the development of cognitive models, the temporal dimension of task performance is very important. We assume that the brain reacts differently at different stages of skill acquisition. Thus, the question is not whether activation increases or decreases but rather when it increases and when it decreases.

A number of theoretically informed regions of interest (ROI) were defined based on the literature on neural correlates of practice and learning (e.g., Anderson et al. 2011; Borst and Anderson 2014; Supekar et al. 2013). These were brain regions associated with visual recognition (fusiform gyrus, middle occipital gyrus), manipulations of spatial representations (posterior parietal), storage and retrieval of declarative memories (hippocampus, prefrontal cortex), cognitive control (anterior cingulate), motor control (areas around the central sulcus), automaticity (basal ganglia), and workload (insula). We also used a control ROI that was known a priori to be insensitive to the experimental manipulation – the auditory cortex.

1.1 Tasks

In the experimental task (Fig. 1A), participants saw an aircraft image and had to select its name out of four options. There were 75 different aircraft images in total. The control task (Fig. 1B) was similar except it used familiar stimuli. There were 52 different control images in total.

2 Method

2.1 Participants

Fifteen participants were recruited for this study from Wright State University's undergraduate and graduate student population. Throughout the 10-week duration of

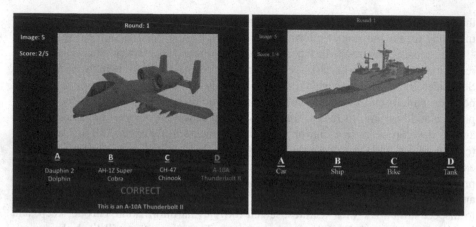

Fig. 1. A (left side): The experimental task and B (right side): The control task

the study, over 50 % of the participants dropped out of the study or were excluded for various reasons. This attrition rate is not uncommon for longitudinal studies.

2.2 Design

A pilot study was run with five participants to determine the length of the study necessary to achieve asymptotic performance in terms of both accuracy and response time for an average participant. Based on what we learned from the pilot study, we decided to include 10 sessions in the main study, one session per week, and insert the brain imaging sessions at weeks 2, 6, and 10. Table 1 shows a schematic of the design.

Table 1. Layout of the experimental design

Week	Session type	Number and type of rounds	Number and type of trials
1	Behavioral	1 Training + 1 Testing	2 x (75 Air + 52 Ctrl)
2	Imaging	1 Testing	1 x (75 Air + 52 Ctrl)
3	Behavioral	3 Training + 1 Testing	4 x (75 Air + 52 Ctrl)
4	Behavioral	3 Training + 1 Testing	4 x (75 Air + 52 Ctrl)
5	Behavioral	3 Training + 1 Testing	4 x (75 Air + 52 Ctrl)
6	Imaging	1 Testing	1 x (75 Air + 52 Ctrl)
7	Behavioral	3 Training + 1 Testing	4 x (75 Air + 52 Ctrl)
8	Behavioral	3 Training + 1 Testing	4 x (75 Air + 52 Ctrl)
9	Behavioral	3 Training + 1 Testing	4 x (75 Air + 52 Ctrl)
10	Imaging	1 Testing	1 x (75 Air + 52 Ctrl)

2.3 Apparatus

Eye fixations and pupil size were recorded using a video-based eye tracker (EyeLink). Neuroimaging was performed using a 1.5 Tesla MR scanner (General Electric Excite HDX; General Electric, Milwaukee, Wisconsin) with an eight-channel head coil. Visual stimuli were projected onto a screen positioned at the foot end of the bore. A mirror affixed to the head coil enabled the participants to view the screen. A fiber-optic button response unit was used to record participants' behavioral performance.

3 Results and Discussion

Here we present exploratory analyses and preliminary results, mainly descriptive statistics and visualizations. More detailed quantitative analyses, including inferential statistics, will be presented at the conference and in a subsequent journal paper.

3.1 Pilot Study Results

The purpose of the pilot study was to get a sense of how many sessions were needed in order to achieve asymptotic performance. In addition, we were interested to learn about the participants' strategies and how they organized their learning in the aircraft task. Figure 2 shows how (A) accuracy and (B) response time changes as a function of session. It is not clear whether the average performance has reached an asymptote, particularly with regard to response time. Based on this observation we decided to increase the number of sessions to 10 to ensure solid learning and skill acquisition.

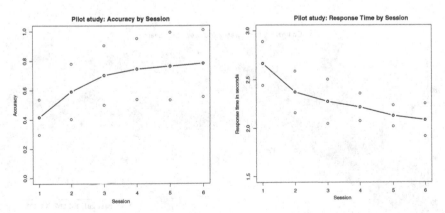

Fig. 2. (A) Accuracy (left plot) as a function of session. (B) Response time (right plot) as a function of session. Error bars are 95 % confidence intervals.

After task completion, we debriefed the participants with regard to their learning strategies. A variety of strategies were reported such as: directly associating aircraft shapes and names, finding distinctive features of aircraft to aid with distinguishing among similar aircraft, selecting most memorable part of a name (e.g., the word "sea", animal names) and discarding apparently irrelevant parts (e.g., numbers), using features and labels to group aircraft in categories, look for logical associations (e.g., helicopters without wheels have "sea" in their name), give ad hoc names to particular shapes, etc. We concluded that the task is conducive to strategizing and performance in this task may be a function of how participants organize their learning (strategic learning and executive control) in addition to visual processing and memory per sec.

3.2 Behavioral Results

Extending the study to 10 sessions proved to be a good decision because performance continued to improve after session 6, although it did not reach the maximum possible level (100 % accuracy). Since the accuracy variable was somewhat bimodal in distribution, we chose to show descriptive statistics for two ad hoc groups that we call "fast learners" and "slow learners", respectively. We show the two groups separately to illustrate an interesting difference in learning strategy (see also the section on eye tracking results); we do not claim that the two groups are statistically distinct.

Figure 3 shows how accuracy increases over the 10 sessions, starting from slightly above chance level (25 %) in session 1 and ending at almost ceiling level (100 %) in session 9 for fast learners. Figure 4 shows reductions in response time associated with practice in the two groups. Performance in the fMRI scanner (sessions 2, 6, and 10) tends to be lower than expected based on the learning trajectory (i.e., accuracy is lower and response time is higher in the scanner than out of scanner). This effect has been attributed to specific attentional and motor deficits caused by the scanner environment and the scanning procedure (Van Maanen et al. 2015).

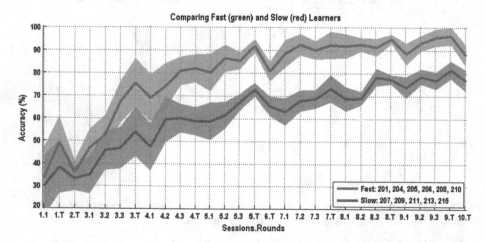

Fig. 3. Accuracy by session and round for fast and slow learners: for each session, the training rounds are indexed numerically (1 to 3) and the testing round is indexed with the letter "T". The shaded areas represent 95 % confidence intervals (Color figure online).

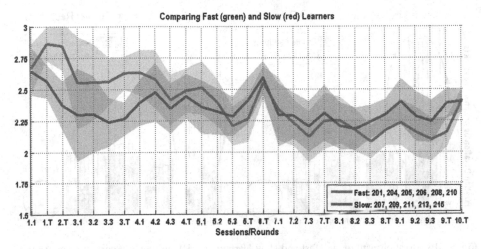

Fig. 4. Response time (in seconds) by session and round for fast and slow learners. Eye tracking results (Color figure online)

The tipping point of the separation between the two groups is around sessions 3 and 4, where accuracy of the fast learners increases significantly faster than that of the slow learners. The confidence intervals are also wider around this point, suggesting that the cause of separation between groups is also an important determinant of individual differences among learners. The response time pattern (Fig. 4) suggests an interesting strategic difference between the two groups: fast learners tend to be more deliberative; they spend more time inspecting the stimuli in the first 3 sessions than slow learners (see the section of eye tracking results for a corroboration of this interpretation).

Eye-tracking data provided additional insights into the learning strategies of slow and fast learners. We analyzed the amount of time each participant looked at each of the following five components of the interface: object image, correct name option, incorrect name options, feedback, and progress (i.e., image index and score). We grouped the eye tracking data in two classes based on when it occurred in a given trial: (1) before a response was made and (2) after feedback was provided. Figure 5 shows the eye fixation patterns for (A) fast and (B) slow learners in trials in which they gave correct responses. The interface components of interest are shown on the X-axis. Each vertical bar represents a behavioral session (note: eye tracking data was not collected in the fMRI sessions). We notice that fast learners look longer at the aircraft image than slow learners, particularly after a response was made. In contrast, slow learners look longer at feedback and progress regions. Another interesting observation is that fast learners tend to increase the time they spend looking at the object as they learn. This increase occurs around sessions 3 and 4, which coincides with the moment in which fast learners clearly differentiate themselves from slow learners. Arguably, the extra time in which fast learners inspect the object after a correct response was given is spent rehearsing and attempting to consolidate their memories by use of mnemonic strategies.

We also analyzed changes in pupil diameter as a function of task and practice. Pupil dilation has been interpreted as an index of cognitive resources allocated to the task at

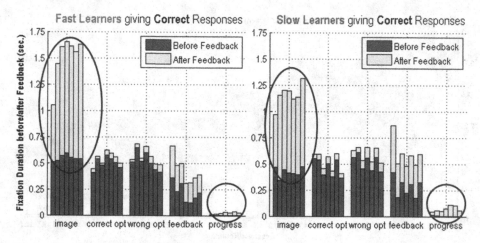

Fig. 5. Eye fixation patterns for fast and slow learners in trials in which a correct response was given.

hand (Granholm and Steinhauer 2004; Siegle et al. 2003). We assumed that pupil size of a given individual should be higher in the aircraft task than in the control task and took the difference between the two measures (here referred to as pupil dilation for brevity) to represent a normalized index of an individual's resource allocation strategy. Figure 6A shows that pupil dilation is higher in fast learners and peaks around sessions 3 and 4. Paradoxically, in some sessions, slow learners show "negative" pupil dilation, that is, higher pupil size for control vehicles than for aircraft. This is obviously an inappropriate resource allocation strategy that may be responsible for the poorer performance observed in slow learners. Figure 6B shows that pupil dilation in session 1 strongly predicts aircraft accuracy over the entire experiment ($r = 0.63$, $p = 0.04$). Recall from Fig. 3 that aircraft accuracy in session 1 was similar in the two groups and close to chance level. This result suggests that the overall performance in this study was determined to a large extent by the participants' willingness to allocate cognitive resources to the aircraft task at the outset of the study.

3.3   Region of Interest Analysis

Overall, across all brain regions of interest, in the control task, we see the usual pattern of activation reported in the literature: activation decreases with practice (Chein and Schneider 2005). In the aircraft task, we see a different pattern: activation increases in the learning phase from week 2 to week 6 and decreases in the consolidation phase from week 6 to week 10 (Fig. 7A). This distinction is even clearer in the activation extent data (Fig. 7B). These data represent to what extent (percentage) a region is activated above threshold.

We investigate further the distinction between the aircraft task and the control task in each region of interest (see Fig. 8). We see that the distinction is more pronounced in particular regions of interest and almost inexistent in others. The largest differences are

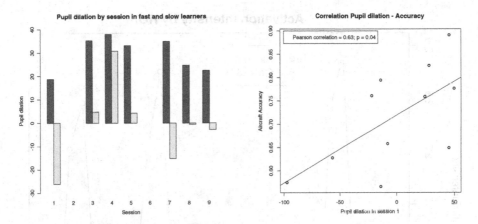

Fig. 6. A (left side): Pupil dilation by session (except fMRI sessions 2, 6, and 10) in fast learners (dark bars) as compared to slow learners (light bars). B (right side): Correlation between pupil dilation in session 1 and overall aircraft accuracy.

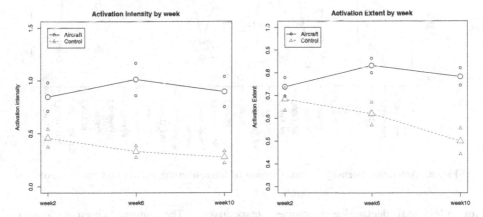

Fig. 7. A (left side): Activation intensity by fMRI session (week). B (right side): Activation extent by fMRI session (week). Error bars represent 95 % confidence intervals.

seen in fusiform gyrus, middle occipital gyrus, and superior parietal lobule. These are areas involved in developing visual object representations and operating on them. Part of this effect can be a "set size effect" considering that there are much more aircrafts than control vehicles. More interesting are the differences seen in the inferior, middle, and medial frontal gyri thought to reflect retrieval and cognitive control operations.

Thus, there seem to be more than just quantitative differences between the two tasks. The participants seem to employ different strategies in the aircraft task as compared to the control task. The control task seems to be executed in a more automatic way, while the aircraft task is performed in a more controlled and deliberate manner.

Next we analyzed the dynamics of activation in the two tasks as the participants advanced in their learning. In the aircraft task, we notice increases in activation from week 2 to week 6 in caudate and hippocampus reflecting development of procedures

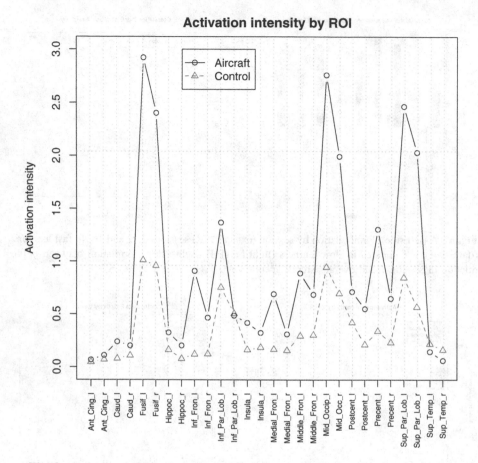

Fig. 8. Activation intensity by brain region of interest in the aircraft and control tasks

(or rules) and declarative memories, respectively. The anterior cingulate cortex (ACC) also shows an increase in activation at week 6. This probably reflects the increased conflict and interference that occur with learning to distinguish between somewhat similar objects and features. The control task shows different dynamics. Activation is much lower in magnitude to start with and decreases with practice. There is not much change of activation in areas related to memory and strategy development or deployment (ACC, caudate, hippocampus, and frontal gyri), reflecting the high level of automaticity reached by this task.

3.4 Whole-Brain Exploratory Analysis

A theoretically agnostic exploratory analysis was performed to uncover potential activation patters that were not found in previous research or may be specific to our task and experimental setup. We identified all clusters of activity (i.e., adjacent voxels activated above threshold) as a function of task (aircraft vs. control) and session (weeks

2, 6, and 10). For each cluster, we determined its size (i.e., number of voxels), identified all the local maxima, and listed the brain regions that these maxima belonged to. The overall pattern of changes in brain activity is consistent with the one observed in the ROI analysis (see Sect. 3.4).

With regard to the content of the clusters, the general trend that emerges across individuals is as follows. The first cluster tends to capture visual and representational areas in the occipital, temporal and parietal lobes, and cerebellum. The second cluster and the subsequent ones capture frontal areas (inferior frontal gyrus, middle frontal gyrus, superior frontal gyrus, and cingulate gyrus), motor areas (precentral and postcentral gyri), and subcortical areas (e.g., thalamus, basal ganglia). In the aircraft task, we see a qualitative shift from week 2 dominated by occipital areas to week 6 and week 10 showing the emergence of the fusiform gyrus and other areas in the temporal lobe (inferior and middle temporal gyri) reflecting complex object representation and memory. Frontal and parietal areas involved in cognitive control, interference resolution, attention, and memory retrieval tend to be activated throughout the entire study in the aircraft task. In the control task, at week 2 the pattern looks much like the aircraft task, but by week 6 we see the emergence of medial frontal gyrus, possibly indicating a strategy shift. By week 10, we see the emergence of posterior parietal areas and the decline of frontal and temporal involvement, which suggests that by week 10 the strategy might be based on direct representations bypassing memory and control.

3.5 Correlations of Brain Activation and Behavioral Performance

We examined correlations between brain activity in our predefined regions of interest and behavioral performance (i.e., accuracy in identification of aircraft images). Most of these correlations were not statistically significant due to the very low number of participants (7). However, an interesting pattern emerged from the analysis of the correlations from all regions of interest (Fig. 9). The correlations tend to be negative at week 2, turn to positive at week 6, and decrease significantly approaching zero at week 10. This pattern is similar for both activation intensity (Fig. 9A) and activation extent (Fig. 9B).

The negative correlations at week 2 can be interpreted as indicating higher and perhaps inefficient metabolic expenditure for low performers and relatively lower metabolic expenditure for high performers. This can also be associated with higher anxiety or stress for low performers. By week 6, all participants have significantly increased their accuracy. Their brain activity at this level could reflect how much of relevant brain resources participants recruit for the task. The participants who are able to recruit more of these resources perform better, which explains the positive correlation. By week 10, most participants reach a high level of performance (around 80 %), the task has become less challenging for everybody, which explains the decrease in the magnitudes of the correlations. Thus, the participants who gradually recruit more brain resources as they learn the task tend to perform better. When their performance reaches a high level, they may decrease the level of metabolic expenditure. The participants who show relatively higher levels of brain activity and relatively lower performance in the early stages of learning tend to learn at a slower rate.

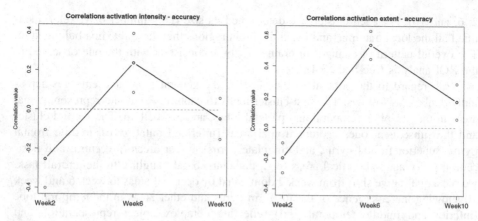

Fig. 9. Pattern of correlations between brain activation (A, left side) intensity and (B, right side) extent and task performance (aircraft accuracy) at start, midpoint, and end of study. Error bars represent 95 % confidence intervals.

4 Conclusion

The preliminary analyses reported here suggest that learning progresses differently in the two tasks. The control task reaches high levels of automation, which is associated with decreases in most brain regions. The aircraft task recruits more brain resources as the participants learn to master it, particularly from brain regions involved in memory, representation, and control. Learners would benefit from a tutoring process aimed at aiding memory encoding and retrieval, making correct associations, and resolving ambiguity and interference among representations and associations.

Acknowledgements. The work presented here was funded by the Office of Naval Research Contract # N00014-13-C-0138. The authors would like to thank Scott Watamaniuk, Assaf Harel, and Cody Otten for help with eye tracking, fMRI data analysis, and literature search.

References

Anderson, J.R.: How Can the Human Mind Occur in the Physical Universe? Oxford University Press, New York (2007)

Anderson, J.R., Betts, S., Ferris, J., Fincham, J.M.: Neural imaging to track mental states while using an intelligent tutoring system. Proc. Natl. Acad. Sci. **107**(15), 7018–7023 (2010)

Anderson, J.R., Bothell, D., Fincham, J.M., Anderson, A.R., Poole, B., Qin, Y.: Brain regions engaged by part- and whole-task performance in a video game: a model-based test of the decomposition hypothesis. J. Cogn. Neurosci. **23**(12), 3983–3997 (2011)

Borst, J.P., Anderson, J.R.: Using the ACT-R cognitive architecture in combination with fMRI data. In: Forstmann, B.U., Wagenmakers, E.-J. (eds.) An Introduction to Model-Based Cognitive Neuroscience. Springer, New York (2014)

Chein, J.M., Schneider, W.: Neuroimaging studies of practice-related change: fMRI and meta-analytic evidence of a domain-general control network for learning. Cogn. Brain. Res. 25(3), 607–623 (2005)

Granholm, E., Steinhauer, S.R.: Pupillometric measures of cognitive and emotional processes. Int. J. Psychophysiol. 52(1), 1–6 (2004)

Olesen, P.J., Westerberg, H., Klingberg, T.: Increased prefrontal and parietal activity after training of working memory. Nat. Neurosci. 7(1), 75–79 (2004)

Poldrack, R.A., Gabrieli, J.D.: Characterizing the neural mechanisms of skill learning and repetition priming: evidence from mirror reading. Brain 124, 67–82 (2001)

Siegle, G.J., Steinhauer, S.R., Stenger, V.A., Konecky, R., Carter, C.S.: Use of concurrent pupil dilation assessment to inform interpretation and analysis of fMRI data. NeuroImage 20(1), 114–124 (2003)

Supekar, K., Swigart, A.G., Tenison, C., Jolles, D.D., Rosemberg-Lee, M., Fuchs, L., Menon, V.: Neural predictors of individual differences in response to math tutoring in primary-grade school children. PNAS Early Ed. 110(20), 8230–8235 (2013)

Van Maanen, L., Forstmann, B.U., Keuken, M.C., Wagenmakers, E-J., Heathcote, A.: The impact of MRI scanner environment on perceptual decision-making. Behav. Res. Methods, 1–17 (2015)

Neural Adaptation to a Working Memory Task: A Concurrent EEG-fNIRS Study

Yichuan Liu[1,2(✉)], Hasan Ayaz[1,2], Banu Onaral[1,2],
and Patricia A. Shewokis[1,2,3,4]

[1] School of Biomedical Engineering, Science & Health Systems,
Drexel University, Philadelphia, PA, USA
yl565@drexel.edu
[2] Cognitive Neuroengineering and Quantitative Experimental Research
(CONQUER) Collaborative, Drexel University, Philadelphia, PA, USA
[3] Nutrition Sciences Department, College of Nursing and Health Professions,
Drexel University, Philadelphia, PA, USA
[4] Department of Surgery, College of Medicine, Drexel University,
Philadelphia, PA, USA

Abstract. Simultaneously recorded electroencephalography (EEG) and functional near infrared spectroscopy (fNIRS) measures from sixteen subjects were used to assess neural correlates of a letter based n-back working memory task. We found that EEG alpha power increased and prefrontal cortical oxygenation decreased with increased practice time for the high memory load condition (2-back), suggesting lower brain activation and a tendency toward the 'idle' state. The cortical oxygenation changes for the low memory load conditions (0-back and 1-back) changed very little throughout the training session which the behavioral scores showed high accuracy and a ceiling effect. No significant effect of practice time were found for theta power or the behavioral performance measures.

Keywords: Multimodality · EEG · fNIRS · Working memory · Mental workload · Practice time · Adaptation

1 Introduction

Assessment of mental workload directly from the brain with functional neuroimaging techniques has been an active field of research for many years [1]. Monitoring the human operator's workload levels are desirable for preventing under- and overloading that can increase human errors, and hence potentially improve working efficiency by maintaining a balanced workload level. An early demonstration of using brain measures to assess working memory has been reported by Gevin et al. [2] in which EEG data from subjects across three days were collected during which time they performed n-back tasks that induced two memory load levels. Artificial neural networks were adopted to recognize patterns in the EEG signal for mental workload level classification [2]. Since then, mental workload classification has been investigated by numerous researchers using various neuroimaging techniques [3, 4], for different types application

© Springer International Publishing Switzerland 2015
D.D. Schmorrow and C.M. Fidopiastis (Eds.): AC 2015, LNAI 9183, pp. 268–280, 2015.
DOI: 10.1007/978-3-319-20816-9_26

areas [5, 6], with many signal processing approaches [7] and across affective contexts [8].

Although promising, previous mental workload classification results did not take in to account the effect of practice time on the neurophysiological signals and how it would affect the classification results. Indeed, the dynamics of the acquired signals with time were either not considered, or were controlled by allowing sufficient training time before data acquisition so that the behavioral performance reached an asymptotic level [2]. However, several studies have reported a significant effect of practice time on the neurophysiological signals of subjects performing mental tasks [4, 9–11]. These studies suggested that the brain adapts with each practice session and the effect of practice time should not simply be ignored. In the interim, if the task is complex, it may not be feasible to allow enough practice time so the subjects are 'trained'. Additionally, the mental workload level of novices who are learning a new task is also of interest in some studies [4] and practicing before the recording session should not be allowed in this case.

In this study, we investigated the brain's adaptation to a working memory task using a multimodality approach. This work is part of a larger project in which the ultimate goal is to investigate mental workload classification with concurrent EEG and fNIRS for building a passive brain-computer interface (BCI). The multimodality approach offers two fundamental benefits over traditional single modality methods. First, EEG and fNIRS are highly complementary techniques. EEG records scalp electrical activities and has a time precision of micro-second level but is spatially blurred due to the volume conductive effect. EEG also has EOG artifacts especially in the prefrontal areas. fNIRS, on the other hand is an optical brain imaging technique that measures the hemodynamic response in the cortical areas. It provides measures that are closely related to functional Magnetic Resonance Imaging (fMRI) [12] with enhanced ecological validity. fNIRS has been adopted to study working memory [13] and the effect of practice time on working memory inducing tasks [4]. As well, fNIRS has the advantage of spatial specificity and it is immune to EOG artifacts however fNIRS has low time resolution and is sensitive to head orientation. Second, in addition to the complimentary information that they can provide, estimating the correlations between EEG and fNIRS can potentially reveal new biomarkers which cannot be accessed using only a single modality. This is evidenced by the concurrent fMRI-EEG studies in the literature [14]. Previously, we adopted concurrent EEG-fNIRS to study performance monitoring for improving a P300 BCI [15]. Recently, EEG-fNIRS has been adopted to improve the classification of motor imagery [16], mental workload [17], and the behavioral performance of a working memory task [18].

The objective of this preliminary work is twofold. First, to test the efficacy of multimodal assessment of working memory practice using concurrent EEG-fNIRS setup and verify the results of previous work [4, 9, 10]. Specifically, we would expect an increase in alpha/theta activity and a decrease in blood oxygenation with increased practice time. Second, is to provide some initial insights into the relation between EEG and fNIRS signals. The focus of assessing the relation between EEG and fNIRS is to identify how these modalities interact with the two experimental factors of memory load and practice time as we develop the next stage objective of mental workload classification under the influence of practice time.

2   Materials and Methods

2.1   Participants

Sixteen healthy individuals (six female) volunteered for the study. All participants were right handed (LQ = 80 ± 18, Decile = 6.3 ± 3.1, mean ± SD) and aged between 18 and 30 years (mean ± SD = 22 ± 3). One participant was rejected from the study because the fNIRS data was not recorded. Two more participants were excluded from the study due to excessive motion artifacts. All participants gave written informed consent approved by the institutional review board of Drexel University prior to their involvement in the study.

2.2   Recording

We simultaneously recorded EEG and fNIRS from subjects while they were performing the n-back tasks. Figure 1 shows a schematic of the recording setup.

EEG was recorded using a Neuroscan Nuamp amplifier from 28 locations according to the International 10–20 system. The two prefrontal sites Fp1 and Fp2 were not recorded due to the placement of fNIRS sensor over the forehead. Two additional electrodes, one placed below the left eye and the other placed at the right outer canthus were used to record electrooculography (EOG) activities. All 30 channels (28 EEG + 2 EOG) were referenced to the right mastoid, digitally sampled at 500 Hz and low-pass filtered at 100 Hz for analysis.

Prefrontal fNIRS were recorded using COBI Studio [19] from a 16-optode continuous wave fNIRS system developed at Drexel University [4] and manufactured by fNIR Devices, LLC. The sampling rate was 2 Hz. To ensure repeatable sensor placement, the center of the sensor was aligned to the midline and the bottom of the sensor was touching the participant's eye brow.

The EEG and fNIRS signals were synchronized offline using stimulus triggers that have been sent from the stimulus presentation software BCI2000 [20] to the EEG and fNIRS data acquisition devices during recording.

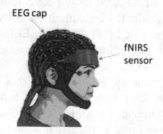

EEG cap

fNIRS sensor

Fig. 1.   Schematic of recording setup

2.3   Experimental Paradigm

Participants sat comfortably facing a LED screen which was placed at about 70 cm in front of them. Letter targets (1.7° visual angle) were presented on the center of the screen. The stimulus duration was 500 ms and the inter-stimulus interval was 2000 ms. The sequence of the stimuli was pseudo randomized so that no letters appeared more than twice in succession.

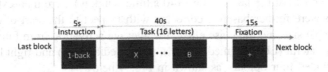

Fig. 2. Time line of an n-back block

There were three experimental conditions: 0-back, 1-back and 2-back. One n-back block timeline is depicted in Fig. 2. The instruction period informed the subject which task (0-, 1-, or 2-back) to perform. During the task period, 16 letters (5 targets) would be shown to the participant on a screen in pseudo random order. For 0-back condition, letter 'X' was the target, while other letters were non-targets. For 1-back and 2-back conditions, a letter was the target if it was shown in the previous screen and two screens back, respectively. Subjects were instructed to press a key as soon as they identified a target letter. During the fixation period, subjects were instructed to fix their eye gaze on a white cross and do nothing which allowed the fNIRS signals to return to baseline levels.

The entire experiment included four sessions while each session encompassed four repetitions. One repetition included three n-back blocks, one from each of the conditions. Hence, there were 48 n-back blocks for the entire experiment, 16 from each condition. The order of the blocks was randomly shuffled so that no condition was repeated twice in succession within a session. One session would typically take approximately 12 min to complete. Subjects took a 5 min break between sessions. The entire recording time was about 60 min. Figure 3 displayed the protocol outline.

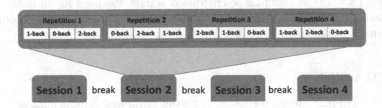

Fig. 3. Protocol outline

2.4   fNIRS Analysis

The raw light intensities were first visually inspected to reject problematic optodes over the hairline or in areas that had non-usable contacts. In this manner, optode 1 was rejected from seven subjects, optode 15 was rejected from six subjects and optode 14 was rejected from one subject (See Fig. 4 for optode configuration). We then converted the raw light intensities to oxygenation (ΔOxy) and total hemoglobin (ΔHbt) concentration changes by applying the modified Beer-Lambert law [21]. The ΔOxy and ΔHbt signals were low-pass filtered at 0.1 Hz using a 20-order finite impulse response (FIR) filter. The fNIRS epoch of each n-back block from the onset of the first stimulus to 2 s after the onset of the last stimulus (40 s time window) were then extracted. The fNIRS epochs were further baseline corrected with respect to the start of each epoch. To reduce sample size and the noise effect, the average activation from four areas were calculated: left lateral (LL), left medial (LM), right medial (RM) and right lateral (RL). Each area included four optodes as shown in Fig. 4 below.

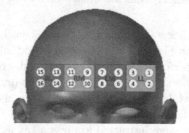

Fig. 4. The four prefrontal areas: left lateral (LL), left medial (LM), right medial (RM) and right lateral (RL).

A 4 × 4 × 3 [*Area* (LL; LM; RM; RL) × *Session* (1–4) × *Load* (0-back; 1-back; 2-back)] ANOVA with repeated measures on all factors was applied for analysis. A similar approach was adopted in previous cognitive-motor executive function adaptation studies [22]. The η_p^2 effect sizes were calculated to assist in data interpretation. To assess the effect of practice time, we fitted linear models with session as the independent variable and ΔOxy/ΔHbt as the dependent variable. A separate model was fitted for each load condition, brain area and subjects. The group effect of the slopes of fitted models were tested employing a Wilcoxon signed rank test using one subject as one sample (N = 13). A significance criterion α = 0.05 was used for all tests. For the linear effect of practice time, false discovery rates (FDR) [23] was applied to control for Type I error.

2.5   EEG Analysis

EEGs were band-pass filtered 0.1–50 Hz applying zero-phase infinite impulse response (IIR) filter, epoched from −500 ms to 1500 ms and baseline corrected with respect to the 500 ms prior to the stimulus onset at 0 ms. We adopted a threshold based approach to reject artifact contaminated epochs. Wrongly responded epochs, i.e. key-press responded to a non-target and non- responses to a target were also rejected from analysis. Taken together, about 19 % epochs were rejected.

The periodogram of each EEG epoch was estimated with application of a Hann window. The average power spectral of all correctly responded blocks of a session for each memory load condition was calculated for analysis. For this preliminary study, we only considered EEG channels along the midline.

A 6 × 4 × 3 [*Channel* (Fz; FCz; Cz; CPz; Pz; Oz) × *Session* (1–4) × *Load* (0-back; 1-back; 2-back)] ANOVA with repeated measures on all factors was applied for analysis. The η_p^2 effect sizes were calculated to facilitate result interpretation. As with fNIRS, we fitted linear models with session as the independent variable and alpha/theta power as the dependent variable. A separate model was fitted for each load condition, channel and subjects. The group effect of the slopes of fitted models were tested employing a Wilcoxon signed rank test using one subject as one sample (N = 13). For the linear effect of practice time, false discovery rates (FDR) [23] was applied to control for Type I error.

3   Results

3.1   Behavioral Measures

We considered two behavior measures: (1) *Target accuracy*, which is the percentage of correctly responded targets; and (2) *Key-press delay*, which is the time delay from stimulus onset to key-press response for a correctly responded target. The measures were standardized across load and session within each subject before analysis. Figure 5 showed the average behavior performance. A 4 × 3 [*Session* (1–4) × *Load* (0-back; 1-back; 2-back)] repeated measures ANOVA revealed a significant main effects of *Load* for target accuracy ($F_{(1.14,13.69)}$ = 6.22, p < 0.05, η_p^2 = 0.34) and key-press delay ($F_{(1.38,16.55)}$ = 13.59, p < 0.001, η_p^2 = 0.53). Target accuracy was 98.0 % (SD = 2.5) for 0-back, 97.2 % (SD = 2.9) for 1-back and 94.0 % (SD = 5.8) for 2-back condition. And the key-press delay was 450 ms (SD = 54) for 0-back, 450 ms (SD = 88) for 1-back and 549 ms (SD = 145) for 2-back condition. No significant effect has been found for *Session*.

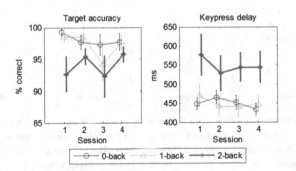

Fig. 5. Average behavior performance of task load across Sessions (error bars are standard error of the mean).

3.2   fNIR Measures

The average fNIRS measures for each task load condition across sessions are shown in Fig. 6.

ΔOxy. The 4 × 4 × 3 ANOVA revealed a significant interactions of *Area* × *Load* ($F_{(6, 72)} = 4.42$, $p < 0.001$, $\eta_p^2 = 0.27$), and *Session* × *Load* ($F_{(6, 72)} = 3.28$, $p < 0.01$, $\eta_p^2 = 0.21$) and a significant main effect of *Load* ($F_{(2, 24)} = 6.34$, $p < 0.01$, $\eta_p^2 = 0.35$). Pairwise comparison revealed a significant lower medial prefrontal activation in 2-back compared to 1-back and 0-back conditions (See Table 1 for detail). For 2-back condition, a significant lower activation in Session 4 was detected when compared to Session 1 ($t_{(12)} = 4.68$, adjusted $p < 0.05$). No significant session-wise differences have been found for 1-back and 0-back conditions. Wilcoxon signed rank test showed a significant linear fit for 2-back only (See Fig. 7). The topography of prefrontal activations were shown in Fig. 8.

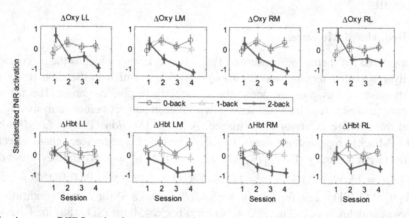

Fig. 6. Average fNIRS activations (and standard error) after subject-wise standardization. LL – left lateral; LM – left medial; RM – right medial; RL – right lateral.

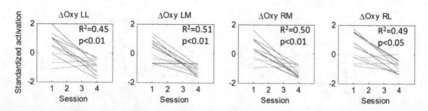

Fig. 7. Linear fit results for ΔOxy as a function of practice time in the 2-back condition. Each line represented the linear fit of a subject (N = 13). The p-values shown here were FDR adjusted across the four brain areas and the three workload levels. The median coefficient of determination (R^2) across all subjects was shown in addition. No significant results have been found for 0-back, 1-back and ΔHbt.

Alpha. The 6 × 4 × 3 ANOVA revealed a significant interaction *Session* × *Load* ($F_{(6, 72)} = 3.87$, $p < 0.05$, $\eta_p^2 = 0.21$) and main effect of Session ($F(3, 36) = 4.27$, $p < 0.05$, $\eta_p^2 = 0.30$), Load ($F(2, 24) = 47.67$, $p < 0.001$, $\eta_p^2 = 0.83$). Post hoc contrasts revealed a significant linear trend for both Session ($F(1,10) = 19.64$, $p < 0.001$) and

Table 1. Significant pair-wise comparison results (*Area × Load*)

fNIRS signal		0-back vs 2-back	1-back vs 2-back
ΔOxy	Left medial	$t_{(12)} = 3.63$, $p < 0.05$	$t_{(12)} = 5.65$, $p < 0.005$
	Right medial	$t_{(12)} = 4.01$, $p < 0.01$	$t_{(12)} = 4.53$, $p < 0.005$
ΔHbt	Left lateral	Not significant	$t_{(12)} = 2.65$, $p < 0.05$
	Left medial	$t_{(12)} = 3.92$, $p < 0.005$	$t_{(12)} = 4.00$, $p < 0.005$
	Right medial	$t_{(12)} = 4.14$, $p < 0.005$	$t_{(12)} = 5.35$, $p < 0.005$
	Right lateral	Not significant	$t_{(12)} = 4.30$, $p < 0.005$

Note: p-values are FDR-adjusted

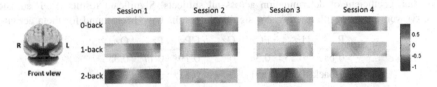

Fig. 8. ΔOxy topography plots. Data were standardized subject-wise across all conditions and sessions before averaging.

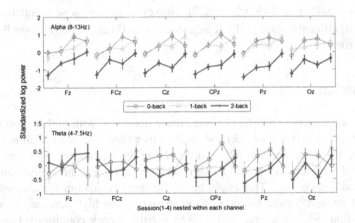

Fig. 9. Average alpha and theta band power (and standard error) after subject-wise standardization.

Load ($F(1,10) = 56.08$, $p < 0.001$). Alpha amplitudes increased with increasing session number and decreased with increasing memory load as shown in Fig. 9. Pair-wise comparison revealed a significantly lower alpha activation in session 1 compared to session 4 ($t(12) = 5.04$, adjusted $p < 0.01$). Wilcoxon signed rank test showed a significant linear fit for all memory load conditions (See Table 2). We further compared the coefficient determination (R^2) values of the fitted linear model across the load conditions with Wilcoxon signed rank test. Results showed in Pz a significantly higher R^2 in 2-back compared to 0-back conditions (adjusted $p < 0.005$).

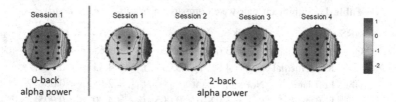

Fig. 10. Topography of alpha power (created with EEGLAB [24]). Alpha powers were standardized subject-wise across all conditions and sessions before averaging.

Table 2. Linear fit results for alpha activity as a function of practice time. Results showed are the median coefficient of determination across all subjects. Significant results (FDR-adjusted p < 0.05) were marked with asterisk. No significant results have been found for theta activity.

R^2	Fz	FCz	Cz	CPz	Pz	Oz
0-back	0.35*	0.34*	0.22	0.19*	0.17*	0.35
1-back	0.41*	0.51	0.53	0.51*	0.41*	0.32
2-back	0.66*	0.41*	0.31*	0.54*	0.72*	0.41

Theta. The $6 \times 4 \times 3$ ANOVA revealed a significant interaction Channel × Load (F(10, 120) = 3.05, p < 0.05, η_p^2 = 0.23). However, no pair-wise comparison results passed the significant threshold (FDR-adjusted p < 0.05) and no significant linear trend have been found.

4   Discussion

Our main results showed that EEG alpha power decreased with higher workload level (2-back compared to 0 and 1-back) and on the other hand, increased with practice time (throughout the task period). These results are in agreement with the previous work [10]. Theta activity, however, showed only a significant interaction between memory load and channel. This might be due to the fact that our n-back task was not challenging enough for the subjects as evidenced by the high accuracy achieved for target detection (96.4 % overall and 94.0 % for the 2-back condition). For the same reason, the behavioral performance was affected by workload level but not affected by practice time. The fNIRS oxygenation and total hemoglobin levels were also compared and results for the first session of the protocol is aligned with previous reports in which increased activation is observed with increased task load [3, 4].

Interestingly, a significant decrease in the 2-back related activation was observed across the sessions from the beginning to the end of the recording period although there was no change in behavioral performance. These findings suggest that an adaptation to the current task took place with the recording session as the EEG alpha power also increased. There was no change in cortical oxygenation measures for 0- and 1-back as they are extremely low task load conditions. The decrease in the cortical activation of 2-back task with practice time leads to a reversal of the load related activation pattern when compared to the beginning session. These reversals of load activation patterns might be due to a combination of effects from adaptation and task difficulty. We also need to take into consideration that the current protocol is longer than many previous experiments. Since the task was not challenging enough for the subjects, one explanation is that the effect of practice time is dominated by the cortical oxygenation. Another possibility is that after practicing the task for some time, more effort might be required by the subjects to focus on the easier 0-back and 1-back task compared to 2-back due to boredom.

The practice time effect we observed in the current study was also presented in a previous fNIRS-based n-back classification study [3]. A similar decrease in cortical oxygenation and also in total hemoglobin levels can be seen for the most highest load condition (3-back) in the dataset published by authors (See Fig. 11).

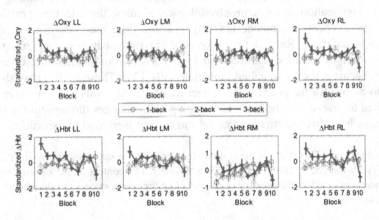

Fig. 11. Average fNIRS of data collected in [3]. The change of 3-back activation pattern over time showed similar decreasing trend as reported in the current study. Data were baseline corrected respect to the start of each block and standardized across block and conditions (1-, 2-, 3-back) for each optode. The four region of interests were defined as: LL – Channel 7 and 8; LM – Channel 5 and 6; RM – Channel 1 and 2; RL – Channel 3 and 4.

From the effect size estimation, we can see that mental workload level has the largest effect on alpha power ($\eta_p^2 = 0.83$) followed by key-press delay ($\eta_p^2 = 0.53$), ΔHbt ($\eta_p^2 = 0.42$), ΔOxy ($\eta_p^2 = 0.35$) and target detection accuracy ($\eta_p^2 = 0.34$). This suggested that alpha power is better than behavioral performance metrics for characterizing mental workload, especially when there is a ceiling effect in the performance. The fNIRS measures provided an effect larger than target detection accuracy and may provide valuable information for mental workload classification. Furthermore, we observed a large practice time effect on alpha power ($\eta_p^2 = 0.30$) and a large interaction effect between load and practice time on alpha power ($\eta_p^2 = 0.21$) and ΔOxy ($\eta_p^2 = 0.21$) which suggested that these effects cannot be simply ignored.

Our study is aligned with previous EEG and fNIRS works and demonstrated that the effect of brain adaptation with practice time can be observed in both types of brain signals [4, 10]. The increased alpha activity and decreased cortical oxygenation in the 2-back condition suggested lower brain activation and the brain's tendency toward the idle state with increased practice time. It should be noted there are many other studies that showed different brain activation patterns before and after practicing. In [25], the authors categorized these patterns into four classes: (1) increased brain activation after practicing; (2) decreased brain activation after practicing; (3) a combination of increased and decreased activation, suggesting a *functional reorganization* [9] of brain activity; and (4) changed brain activation areas. In the same paper, the authors concluded that the exact reason for these inconsistent patterns is still unknown but could be caused by certain factors such as task complexity, task load demand and the length of practice time which can range from 20 min to two months. Other factors such as fatigue and boredom need to be considered.

In summary, these preliminary results suggest that when performing mental workload classification using neurophysiological signals, the effect of practice time needs to be carefully examined. Ignoring practice time may result in a degraded classification accuracy. Related to the practice time effect is work regarding a substantial number of machine learning and EEG classification studies that investigated how to compensate for the so called 'covariate shift' [26]. These studies may shed light on how to control for the practice time effect we observed in this study. Further studies are required to investigate the brain activation pattern changes throughout the task and to determine how this information can inform mental workload classification.

Acknowledgement. This study is made possible in part by a research award from the National Science Foundation (NSF) IIS: 1065471 (Shewokis, PI). The content of the information herein does not necessarily reflect the position or the policy of the sponsors and no official endorsement should be inferred.

References

1. Parasuraman, R., Christensen, J., Grafton, S.: Neuroergonomics: the brain in action and at work. NeuroImage **59**, 1–3 (2012)
2. Gevins, A., Smith, M.E., Leong, H., McEvoy, L., Whitfield, S., Du, R., Rush, G.: Monitoring working memory load during computer-based tasks with EEG pattern recognition methods. Hum. Factors: J. Hum. Factors Ergon. Soc. **40**, 79–91 (1998)
3. Herff, C., Heger, D., Fortmann, O., Hennrich, J., Putze, F., Schultz, T.: Mental workload during n-back task-quantified in the prefrontal cortex using fNIRS. Front. Hum. Neurosci. **7**, 935 (2014)
4. Ayaz, H., Shewokis, P.A., Bunce, S., Izzetoglu, K., Willems, B., Onaral, B.: Optical brain monitoring for operator training and mental workload assessment. Neuroimage **59**, 36–47 (2012)
5. Mehta, R.K., Parasuraman, R.: Neuroergonomics: a review of applications to physical and cognitive work. Front. Hum. Neurosci. **7**, 889 (2013)
6. Ayaz, H., Onaral, B., Izzetoglu, K., Shewokis, P.A., McKendrick, R., Parasuraman, R.: Continuous monitoring of brain dynamics with functional near infrared spectroscopy as a tool for neuroergonomic research: Empirical examples and a technological development. Front. Hum. Neurosci. **7**, 1–13 (2013)

7. Grimes, D., Tan, D.S., Hudson, S.E., Shenoy, P., Rao, R.P.N.: Feasibility and pragmatics of classifying working memory load with an electroencephalograph. In: Proceedings of the SIGCHI Conference on Human Factors in Computing Systems, pp. 835–844. ACM, Florence, Italy (2008)
8. Muhl, C., Jeunet, C., Lotte, F.: EEG-based workload estimation across affective contexts. Front. Neurosci. **8**, 114 (2014)
9. Kelly, A.M.C., Garavan, H.: Human functional neuroimaging of brain changes associated with practice. Cereb. Cortex **15**, 1089–1102 (2005)
10. Gevins, A., Smith, M.E., McEvoy, L., Yu, D.: High-resolution EEG mapping of cortical activation related to working memory: effects of task difficulty, type of processing, and practice. Cereb. Cortex **7**, 374–385 (1997)
11. Ayaz, H., Cakir, M.P., Izzetoglu, K., Curtin, A., Shewokis, P.A., Bunce, S.C., Onaral, B.: Monitoring expertise development during simulated UAV piloting tasks using optical brain imaging. In: 2012 IEEE Aerospace Conference, pp. 1–11 (2012)
12. Cui, X., Bray, S., Bryant, D.M., Glover, G.H., Reiss, A.L.: A quantitative comparison of NIRS and fMRI across multiple cognitive tasks. Neuroimage **54**, 2808–2821 (2011)
13. Ayaz, H., Izzetoglu, M., Bunce, S., Heiman-Patterson, T., Onaral, B.: Detecting cognitive activity related hemodynamic signal for brain computer interface using functional near infrared spectroscopy, pp. 342–345. IEEE (2007)
14. Huster, R.J., Debener, S., Eichele, T., Herrmann, C.S.: Methods for simultaneous EEG-fMRI: an introductory review. J. Neurosci. **32**, 6053–6060 (2012)
15. Liu, Y., Ayaz, H., Curtin, A., Onaral, B., Shewokis, P.A.: Towards a hybrid P300-based BCI using simultaneous fNIR and EEG. In: Schmorrow, D.D., Fidopiastis, C.M. (eds.) AC 2013. LNCS, vol. 8027, pp. 335–344. Springer, Heidelberg (2013)
16. Fazli, S., Mehnert, J., Steinbrink, J., Curio, G., Villringer, A., Müller, K.-R., Blankertz, B.: Enhanced performance by a hybrid NIRS–EEG brain computer interface. Neuroimage **59**, 519–529 (2012)
17. Coffey, E.B.J., Brouwer, A.-M., van Erp, J.B.F.: Measuring workload using a combination of electroencephalography and near infrared spectroscopy. In: Proceedings of the Human Factors and Ergonomics Society Annual Meeting, vol. 56, pp. 1822–1826 (2012)
18. Merzagora, A.C., Izzetoglu, M., Polikar, R., Weisser, V., Onaral, B., Schultheis, M.T.: Functional near-infrared spectroscopy and electroencephalography: a multimodal imaging approach. In: Schmorrow, D.D., Estabrooke, I.V., Grootjen, M. (eds.) FAC 2009. LNCS, vol. 5638, pp. 417–426. Springer, Heidelberg (2009)
19. Ayaz, H., Shewokis, P.A., Curtin, A., Izzetoglu, M., Izzetoglu, K., Onaral, B.: Using mazesuite and functional near infrared spectroscopy to study learning in spatial navigation. J. Visualized Exp.: JoVE, 3443 (2011). doi:10.3791/3443
20. Schalk, G., McFarland, D.J., Hinterberger, T., Birbaumer, N., Wolpaw, J.R.: BCI2000: a general-purpose brain-computer interface (BCI) system. IEEE Trans. Biomed. Eng. **51**, 1034–1043 (2004)
21. Cope, M., Delpy, D.T.: System for long-term measurement of cerebral blood and tissue oxygenation on newborn infants by near infra-red transillumination. Med. Biol. Eng. Compu. **26**, 289–294 (1988)
22. Gentili, R.J., Shewokis, P.A., Ayaz, H., Contreras-Vidal, J.L.: Functional near-infrared spectroscopy-based correlates of prefrontal cortical dynamics during a cognitive-motor executive adaptation task. Front. Hum. Neurosci. **7**, 277 (2013)
23. Benjamini, Y., Hochberg, Y.: Controlling the false discovery rate: a practical and powerful approach to multiple testing. J. Roy. Stat. Soc.: Ser. B (Methodol.) **57**, 289–300 (1995)

24. Delorme, A., Makeig, S.: EEGLAB: an open source toolbox for analysis of single-trial EEG dynamics including independent component analysis. J. Neurosci. Methods **134**, 9–21 (2004)
25. Buschkuehl, M., Jaeggi, S.M., Jonides, J.: Neuronal effects following working memory training. Dev. Cogn. Neurosci. **2** (Supplement 1), S167–S179 (2012)
26. Shimodaira, H.: Improving predictive inference under covariate shift by weighting the log-likelihood function. J. Stat. Plan. Plann. **90**, 227–244 (2000)

The Effect of Limiting Trial Count in Context Aware BCIs: A Case Study with Language Model Assisted Spelling

Mohammad Moghadamfalahi[1]([✉]), Paula Gonzalez-Navarro[1],
Murat Akcakaya[2], Umut Orhan[3], and Deniz Erdogmus[1]

[1] Northeastern University, Boston, USA
moghadam@ece.neu.edu
[2] University of Pittsburgh, Pittsburgh, USA
[3] Honeywell International, Morristown, USA

Abstract. Deflections in recorded electroencephalography (EEG) in response to visual, auditory or tactile stimuli have been popularly employed in non-invasive EEG based brain computer interfaces (BCIs) for intent detection. For example, in an externally stimulated typing BCI, an accurate estimate of the user intent might require long EEG data collection before the system can make a decision with a desired confidence. Long decision period can lead to slow typing and hence the user frustration. Therefore, there is a trade-off between the accuracy of inference and the typing speed. In this manuscript, using Monte-Carlo simulations, we assess the speed and accuracy of a Language Model (LM) assisted non-invasive EEG based typing BCI, RSVPKeyboard™, as a function of the maximum number of repetitions of visual stimuli sequences and the inter-trial interval (ITI) within the sequences. We show that the best typing performance with RSVPKeyboard™ can be obtained when ITI=150 ms and maximum number of allowed sequences is 8. Even though the probabilistic fusion of the language model with the EEG evidence for joint inference allows the RSVPKeyboard™ to perform auto-typing when the system is confident enough t o make decisions before collecting EEG evidence, our experimental results show that RSVPKeyboard™ does not benefit from auto-typing.

1 Introduction

Non-invasive electroencephalography (EEG)-based brain computer interfaces (BCIs) provide means for people with severe motor and speech impairments to communicate their needs and desires to their family members, friends and care takers. A typing interface is a very common application domain for these EEG-based BCIs [1]. A well established signal paradigm used for intent detection in typing BCIs is based on event related potentials (ERPs) which are responses to presented visual, auditory or tactile stimuli [1–4].

Rapid serial visual presentation (RSVP) is a presentation scheme that distributes the symbols chosen for intent communication in time to induce ERPs.

© Springer International Publishing Switzerland 2015
D.D. Schmorrow and C.M. Fidopiastis (Eds.): AC 2015, LNAI 9183, pp. 281–292, 2015.
DOI: 10.1007/978-3-319-20816-9_27

This paradigm is popularly used in visual stimuli based typing BCIs, in which the presented sequence of symbols on the screen usually consists of the 26 letters of the English Alphabet, 10 numerical digits, and space and backspace symbols [5–9]. A sequence is usually repeated multiple times to improve the accuracy in intent detection, due to the low signal-to-noise ratio in the recorded EEG data in response to the presented visual stimuli. This repetition in turn decreases the speed of the typing interface. A faster typing on the other hand usually decreases the typing accuracy [10]. However, any typing interface can benefit from a proper language model to enhance both speed and inference accuracy. In this manuscript, we analyze the effect of the repetition counts of the presented symbols and the time delay between consecutive symbols on the typing performance in the presence of a language model.

We have designed a language model assisted non-invasive EEG based letter by letter typing interface, RSVPKeyboard™. This system presents a subset of 28 symbols (26 letters and space and backspace symbols) as a sequence after which the BCI attempts to make a decision. If a preset confidence level is reached, a decision is made. Otherwise the sequences are repeated multiple times until the confidence level or a bound on the maximum number of repetitions of the sequences is reached. Such a decision period is denoted as an epoch. To analyze the effect of (1) bound on the maximum number of repetitions in an epoch and (2) the minimum number of sequences before a system can make a decision in an epoch on the typing performance of RSVP Keyboard™, we use Monte Carlo simulations. Note here that setting the minimum number of sequences to "0" allows the system to auto-type if the maximum of the symbol probabilities provided by the language model exceeds the desired confidence threshold. Therefore, our analysis in this manuscript will also investigate the effects of auto-typing on typing performance.

2   RSVPKeyboard™

As illustrated in Fig. 1, RSVPKeyboad™ consists of three major components (A) presentation component, (B) feature extraction component, (C) decision making component; in the following we will describe each component in detail.

2.1   Presentation Component

Presentation component is utilized to present the stimuli for ERP induction and also for providing feedback to the user. RSVP paradigm in which the trials are rapidly presented one at a time at a predefined fixed location on the screen in a pseudo-random order is utilized as the presentation scheme [1,5–9]. As also described in Sect. 1, a presented sequence consists of a subset from the dictionary $\mathcal{A} = \{26$ alphabetical symbols, "<" as the backspace, and "_" for the space character$\}$. After a sequence, the typing interface makes a decision on the user intended symbol if a desired confidence level is reached; otherwise, sequences are repeated until the desired confidence or a preset maximum bound on the number

presentation component

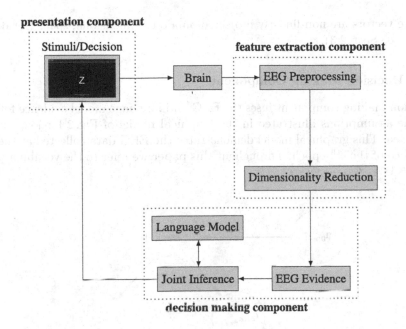

Fig. 1. The RSVPKeyboard^{TM} flowchart.

of sequence repetitions is reached and a decision is made accordingly. This time period in which a decision is made is denoted as an epoch.

2.2 Feature Extraction Component

EEG Preprocessing: EEG signals are acquired using a g.USBamp bio-signal amplifier with active g.Butterfly electrodes at a sampling rate of 256 Hz, from 16 EEG locations (according to the International 10/20 configuration): Fp1, Fp2, F3, F4, Fz, Fc1, Fc2, Cz, P1, P2, C1, C2, Cp3, Cp4, P5 and P6 . Recorderd signals are filtered by a finite impulse response (FIR) linear-phase bandpass filter cut-off frequencies 1.5 and 42 Hz with zero DC gain, and a notch filter at 60 Hz to improve the signal to noise ratio (SNR), and to eliminate DC drifts.

EEG data from a time window of $[0, 500)$ ms time locked to each trial is processed as the raw data for that trial in order to capture the P300 signal and avoid motor related potentials [11].

Dimensionality Reduction: EEG dimensionality reduction is performed in two steps. First, considering the upper limit of the FIR filter, EEG data is downsampled by the factor of 2. Then, to remove directions with negligible variance at each channel, Principle Component Analysis (PCA) is utilized and the EEG data are projected onto a lower dimensional feature space. Finally, this component concatenates the data from all channels corresponding to the same trial to form a feature vector for each trial. In decision making component, the concatenated feature vectors are non-linearly projected on a one dimensional space (for detail please see Sect. 2.3).

2.3   Decision Making Component

Decision making component fuses the EEG and language model evidence following the assumptions illustrated in the graphical model of Fig. 2 for joint intent inference. This graphical model demonstrates the EEG data collected at the sth sequence of the eth epoch. Throughout this paper we refer to the vocabulary set as $\mathcal{A} = \{a_1, a_2, ..., a_{|\mathcal{A}|}\}$.

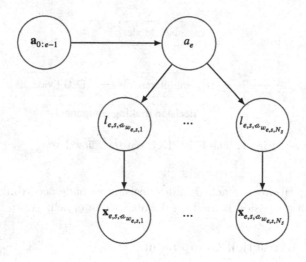

Fig. 2.

Here "a_e" is the desired character for epoch "e" and "$\mathbf{a}_{0:e-1} = \{a_0, a_1, a_2, ..., a_{e-1}\}$" is the set of all previous characters which define the context and accordingly a prior probability over the epoch's possible outcomes. In RSVP paradigm, each trial contains only one symbol and $\mathbf{w}_{e,s} = \{w_{e,s,1}, w_{e,s,2}, ..., w_{e,s,N_s}\}$ is the index set of symbols, presented in epoch "e" and at sequence "s". Also N_s is the number of trials in each sequence. The label set for epoch "e" and sequence "s" is defined as $\mathbf{l}_{e,s} = \{l_{e,s,a_{w_{e,s,1}}}, l_{e,s,a_{w_{e,s,2}}}, ..., l_{e,s,a_{w_{e,s,N_s}}}\}$

where:

$$l_{e,s,a_{w_{e,s,i}}} = \begin{cases} 1, & a_e = a_{w_{e,s,i}} \\ 0, & a_e \neq a_{w_{e,s,i}} \end{cases}$$

Finally, $\mathbf{X}_{e,s} = \{\mathbf{x}_{e,s,a_{w_{e,s,1}}}, \mathbf{x}_{e,s,a_{w_{e,s,2}}}, ..., \mathbf{x}_{e,s,a_{w_{e,s,N_s}}}\}$ is the set of EEG evidence for trials in epoch "e" and sequence "s".

EEG Evidence: Regularized discriminant analysis (RDA) is applied to the features extracted as explained in Sect. 2.2. RDA is a generalization of the quadratic discriminant analysis and it allows full-rank estimation of high dimensional covariance matrices from proportionally few number of supervised realizations by applying shrinkage and regularization on the maximum likelihood covariance estimates [12]. Assume $\mathbf{x}_i \in \mathbb{R}^p$ is p dimensional feature vector and $l_i \in \{0, 1\}$ is the class label for $\mathbf{x}_i$ which can represent the target class ($"l_i = 1"$) or the non-target class ($"l_i = 0"$). Then the maximum likelihood estimator of the mean and covariance for each class are as in (1).

$$\boldsymbol{\mu}_k = \frac{1}{N_k} \sum_{i=1}^{N} \mathbf{x}_i \delta_{l_i,k}$$
$$\boldsymbol{\Sigma}_k = \frac{1}{N_k} \sum_{i=1}^{N} (\mathbf{x}_i - \boldsymbol{\mu}_k)(\mathbf{x}_i - \boldsymbol{\mu}_k)^T \delta_{l_i,k}$$

(1)

where $\delta_{i,j}$ is the Kronecker-δ such that it is equal to 1 when $i = j$ and zero otherwise, $k \in \{0,1\}$ is the class indicator, and N_k is the number of training data in class k. Define $N = N_0 + N_1$, as the total number of feature vectors from both classes, then through the shrinkage the class conditional covariance estimators are defined as in (2).

$$\hat{\boldsymbol{\Sigma}}_k(\lambda) = \frac{(1 - \lambda)N_k\boldsymbol{\Sigma}_k + (\lambda)\sum_{k=0}^{1} N_k\boldsymbol{\Sigma}_k}{(1 - \lambda)N_k + (\lambda)\sum_{k=0}^{1} N_k}$$

(2)

The shrinkage parameter $\lambda \in [0, 1]$, defines the similarity between the class conditional covariances such that when $\lambda = 1$ both covariances become equal and the RDA reduces to linear discriminant analysis (LDA). Regardless of the shrinkage step, if the dimensionality of the feature space is higher than the total number realizations in every class, (2) cannot produce invertible covariance matrices. Then, the next step in RDA, known as regularization, is applied and it changes the estimator as in (3).

$$\hat{\boldsymbol{\Sigma}}_k(\lambda, \gamma) = (1 - \gamma)\hat{\boldsymbol{\Sigma}}_k(\lambda) + (\gamma)\frac{1}{p}tr[\hat{\boldsymbol{\Sigma}}_k(\lambda)]\mathbf{I}_p$$

(3)

$tr[.]$ is the trace operator, $\mathbf{I}_p$ is a $p \times p$ identity matrix and $\gamma \in [0, 1]$ is the regularization parameter which determines the circularity of the covariance matrix. Finally, the discriminant score in RDA is defined as in (4).

$$d_{RDA}(\mathbf{x}) = log\frac{f_\mathcal{N}(\mathbf{x}; \boldsymbol{\mu}_1, \hat{\boldsymbol{\Sigma}}_1(\lambda, \gamma))\hat{\pi}_1}{f_\mathcal{N}(\mathbf{x}; \boldsymbol{\mu}_0, \hat{\boldsymbol{\Sigma}}_0(\lambda, \gamma))\hat{\pi}_0}$$

(4)

In (4), $f_\mathcal{N}(\mathbf{x}; \boldsymbol{\mu}, \boldsymbol{\Sigma})$ is the Gaussian probability density function when $\mathbf{x} \sim \mathcal{N}(\boldsymbol{\mu}, \boldsymbol{\Sigma})$ and $\hat{\pi}_k$ is the prior probability of class k. After this projection, we utilize kernel density estimation (KDE) to compute the class conditional distributions over the RDA scores using (4).

$$f(\mathbf{x} = \mathbf{y}|l = k) =$$
$$f_{KDE}(d_{RDA}(\mathbf{x}) = d_{RDA}(\mathbf{y})|l = k) =$$
$$\frac{1}{N_k} \sum_{i=1}^{N} \mathcal{K}_{h_k}(d_{RDA}(\mathbf{x}_i), d_{RDA}(\mathbf{y}))\delta_{l_i,k} \tag{5}$$

In (5), $\mathcal{K}_{h_k}(\cdot, \cdot)$ is a suitable kernel function with bandwidth h_k. In our work, we employ Gaussian kernels and compute h_k using the Silverman rule of thumb [13].

Language Model: The language model in our system is utilized both for prioritizing the symbols for presentation in an iterative Bayesian framework, and for making inference after each sequence by imposing a prior distribution on symbols. We use an n-gram language model that provides a probability distribution over the vocabulary based on $n - 1$ previously type characters as shown in (6) [14].

$$p(a_e = a|\mathbf{a}_{(0:e-1)} = \mathbf{a}) = \frac{p(a_e = a, \mathbf{a}_{(0:e-1)} = \mathbf{a})}{p(\mathbf{a}_{(0:e-1)} = \mathbf{a})} \tag{6}$$

Here a_e is the symbol to be typed at the eth epoch and $\mathbf{a}_{(0:e-1)}$ are the typed symbols prior to epoch e. RSVPKeyboard^{TM}, utilizes a 6-gram letter model, which is trained on the NY Times portion of the English Gigaword corpus [14].

Joint Inference: Maximum a posterior (MAP) inference mechanism is used in our system for joint inference after each sequence. According to the graphical model presented in Fig. 2, the posterior probability distribution over the vocabulary is calculated using

$$Q = p(a_e = a|\mathcal{X}_e = \mathbf{X}_e, \mathbf{a}_{(0:e-1)} = \mathbf{a}) \propto$$
$$p(\mathcal{X}_e = \mathbf{X}_e, \mathbf{a}_{(0:e-1)} = \mathbf{a}|a_e = a)P(a_e = a) \tag{7}$$

Then, using the conditional independence assumption on the trials within a sequence, the fusion rule is simplified to

$$Q \propto \left(\prod_{s=1}^{N_e}\prod_{t=1}^{N_s} \frac{f(\mathbf{x} = \mathbf{x}_{e,s,w_{e,s,t}}|l = 1)}{f(\mathbf{x} = \mathbf{x}_{e,s,w_{e,s,t}}|l = 0)}\right) P(a_e = a|\mathbf{a}_{(0,e-1)} = \mathbf{a}) \tag{8}$$

In (8), N_e represents the number of sequences presented in the eth epoch in N_s number of sequences. The inference mechanism in our system requires that the posterior probability of the estimated target reaches a predefined threshold. Otherwise, more sequences will be presented until either the mentioned confidence level is reached, or the number of sequences in the epoch e, N_e, attains its upper limit.

2.4   System Operation Modes

RSVPKeyboard^{TM} can be used in five different operation modes.

(i). *Calibration mode:* The inference mechanism of the system requires supervised EEG data, which are collected during a calibration task. Typically, each calibration session consists of 100 sequences of symbols. Before each sequence the user is asked to attend to a particular symbol. Then a sequence consisting of the target symbol and 9 other non-target symbols is presented to the user in a random order.

(ii). *Copy phrase task mode:* In this mode, a user is asked to type missing words in a set of phrases. Utilizing the language model, 5 difficulty levels for phrases based on the predictability of the missing phrases have been defined: 1 as the most and 5 being the least predictable. The sentences used in a standard copy phrase task are selected such that their difficulty level span a uniform distribution.

(iii). *Mastery task mode:* A complete mastery task consists of 5 levels. To complete each level, the user should successfully copy the missing words in two different phrases with the same difficulty level. The level index is assigned by the difficulty level of the phrases. This mode is specifically designed for user training.

(iv). *Free spelling mode:* In this mode, the system can be employed by the user to type the desired text.

(v). *Simulation mode:* In a simulation session, with Monte Carlo simulations, many copy phrase tasks are completed using the samples drawn from class conditional KDEs (see (5)). These samples are specifically used to construct the EEG scores and are fused with the language model for joint inference as in (8) [7]. Simulation mode reports the system performance in terms of the probability of phrase completion (PPC) and total task duration (TTD).

3   Experiment and Results

In this manuscript, to analyze the typing performance of the RSVPKeyboard^{TM}, we employ the simulation mode. We set the sequence size as 15 symbols/trials (always including a backspace symbol in a sequence); choose the time difference between two consecutive trials, known as inter trial interval (ITI), from the set $\{0.085, 0.1, 0.15, 0.2\}ms$; and assign the minimum ($SN_{min} \in \{0, 1\}$) and maximum ($SN_{max} \in \{2, 4, 8, 16\}$) number of sequences in an epoch. Note here that setting $SN_{min} = 0$ represents the auto-typing scenario.

3.1   Participants

In the simulation mode, we employ the calibration data obtained from eleven healthy volunteers (two females, nine males), aged between 24 and 38 years old. The data is collected according to the IRB-approved protocol (IRB130107). Specifically, calibration data with different ITI values were collected in one

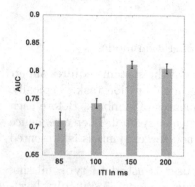

Fig. 3. The bar chart with error bars for average AUC values of classifier when trained one the data collected at each ITI.eps

Table 1. Hypothesis testing results between AUC values for different ITIs. The null hypothesis is that the expected AUC difference of the two considered ITIs is zero. Here we used $\alpha = 0.05$.

Paired t-test results between different ITI values	
ITI_1 v.s. ITI_2	P-values
85 v.s. 100 ms	0.157
85 v.s. 150 ms	0.001
85 v.s. 200 ms	0.009
100 v.s. 150 ms	0.0008
100 v.s. 200 ms	0.027
150 v.s. 200 ms	0.693

session from each user. To reduce the effect of fatigue and tiredness in group based analysis, we quasi-randomized the ITI values over the four calibration tasks among all users such that, the number of tasks with a specific ITI value for a particular order index are kept equal.

3.2 Data Analysis and Results

Area under the receiver operating characteristics curve (AUC) values, an indication of the classification accuracy, are calculated for every calibration data set using 10-fold cross validation. A paired t-test is run over the AUC values for different ITI conditions. The test results are illustrated in Table 1. This table shows that the classification accuracy significantly depends on the ITI. Moreover, as shown in Fig. 3, the average AUC is higher when the ITI=150ms suggesting that in average we expect to observe a better typing performance from the system when ITI=150ms.

The total typing durations (TTDs), performance metric computed by the simulation mode, for different users are summarized in Fig. 4. More specifically, sub-figure 4a,b,c and d represent the scatter plot of TTDs with (y-axis) and without (x-axis) auto-typing capability of the system at different ITI=85, 100, 150 and 200 ms. Different colors correspond to different SN_{max}. Every data point represents the mean and the variance of TTD, as a dot and a rectangle around that dot, respectively. The TTD variance for $SN_{min} = 0$ (auto-typing enabled) defines the vertical length of the rectangle while the horizontal length represents the variance when $SN_{min} = 1$ (auto-typing disabled). According to these plots, regardless of SN_{max}, auto-typing is not helping the users to type faster especially when the AUC is low (see the most top right data points of every color at each sub-figure). Moreover, in general among all SN_{max}, the TTD values are lower for ITI= 100 ms and ITI= 150 ms while most of the data points demonstrate values less than 2000 s at ITI= 150 ms.

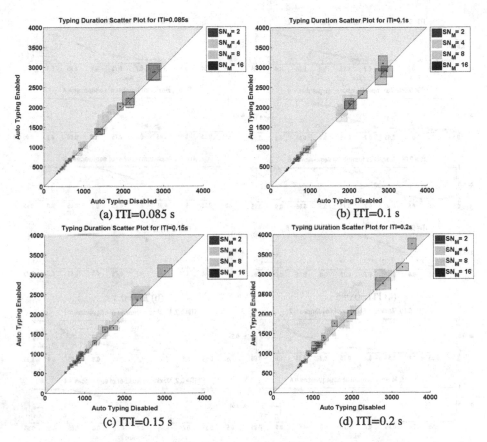

Fig. 4. Total typing duration (TTD) scatter plot. X-axis represents the total typing duration when the auto-typing is allowed and Y-axis corresponds to the TTD when auto-typing is disabled. Each point in these plots shows the mean value, and the horizontal and vertical skewness of the box around each point visualizes the variance of the results from 20 Monte-Carlo simulations.

Moreover, the simulation mode of the RSVPKeyboard^{TM} measures the probability of phrase completion (PPC) as an accuracy measure of the simulated typing tasks. The effects of SN_{max} and ITI on PPC are demonstrated in Fig. 5. Different sub-figure 5a,b,c and d, illustrate the PPC as a function of AUC for different ITI values. In every figure, blue and red curves are used when auto-typing is enabled ($SN_{min} = 0$) or disabled ($SN_{min} = 1$), respectively. From these figures, we observe that increasing the SN_{max} improves the PPC at every ITI especially for lower AUC values. However, the comparison of the blue and red curves does not show any significant gain in PPC when the auto-typing is enabled. Also, as expected from Table 1, in average $ITI = 150$ms has in average higher PPC as shown in sub-figure 5c.

In conclusion, as all results suggest, for RSVPKeyboard^{TM}under the current design assumptions, not only auto-typing does not offer any improvement in typing

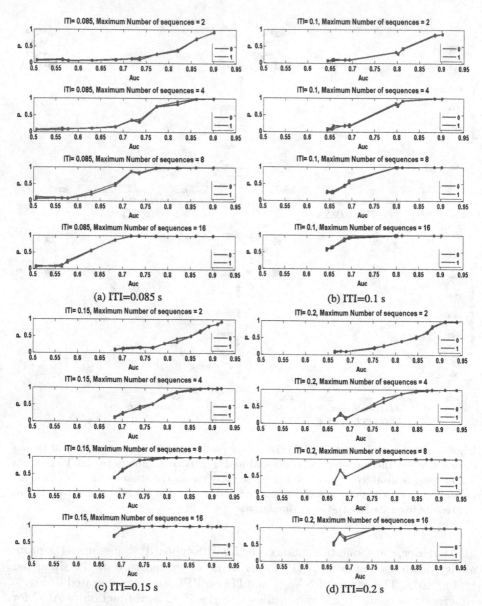

Fig. 5. Probability of phrase completion v.s. AUC. The blue curves correspond to the simulation results when auto-typing is enabled and the red curves represent the performance when auto-typing is disabled.

performance, but it also may decrease the typing speed. Furthermore, the combination of ITI= 150 ms, $SN_{max} = 8$ and $SN_{min} = 1$ provides the best performance of the system in terms of AUC, PPC and TTD for most of the users who participated in these experiments.

4   Discussion and Future Work

In this manuscript, we analyzed the effect of variations in inter-trial interval, maximum number of sequences and minimum number of sequences in an epoch on the typing performance of the RSVPKeyboard™, a language model assisted non-invasive EEG based letter by letter typing interface. Probability of phrase completion and total typing durations were obtained from 20-Monte-Carlo copy phrase tasks using the simulation mode of the typing interface over the calibration date collected from 11 healthy users. We observed that under the current design assumptions, the system does not benefit from auto-typing. In our future work, we will consider different graphical models to design joint inference engines that can enable the typing interface to benefit not only from auto-typing, but also from error related negativity for auto-correction.

References

1. Akcakaya, M., Peters, B., Moghadamfalahi, M., Mooney, A., Orhan, U., Oken, B., Erdogmus, D., Fried-Oken, M.: Noninvasive brain computer interfaces for augmentative and alternative communication. IEEE Rev. Biomed. Eng. **7**(1), 31–49 (2014)
2. Halder, S., Furdea, A., Varkuti, B., Sitaram, R., Rosenstiel, W., Birbaumer, N., Kübler, A.: Auditory standard oddball and visual p300 brain-computer interface performance. Int. J. Bioelectromag. **13**(1), 5–6 (2011)
3. van der Waal, M., Severens, M., Geuze, J., Desain, P.: Introducing the tactile speller: an erp-based brain-computer interface for communication. J. Neural Eng. **9**(4), 045002 (2012)
4. Farwell, L.A., Donchin, E.: Talking off the top of your head: toward a mental prosthesis utilizing event-related brain potentials. Electroencephalogr. Clin. Neurophysiol. **70**(6), 510–523 (1988)
5. Acqualagna, L., Blankertz, B.: Gaze-independent BCI-spelling using rapid serial visual presentation (RSVP). Clin. Neurophysiol. **124**(5), 901–908 (2013)
6. Acqualagna, L., Treder, M.S., Schreuder, M., Blankertz, B.: A novel brain-computer interface based on the rapid serial visual presentation paradigm. In: Proceedings of Conference on IEEE Engineering in Medicine and Biological Society, vol. 1, pp. 2686–2689 (2010)
7. Orhan, U., Erdogmus, D., Roark, B., Oken, B., Purwar, S., Hild, K., Fowler, A., Fried-Oken, M.: Improved accuracy using recursive bayesian estimation based language model fusion in erp-based bci typing systems. In: Annual International Conference of the IEEE on Engineering in Medicine and Biology Society (EMBC), vol. 2012, pp. 2497–2500. IEEE (2012)
8. Orhan, U., Erdogmus, D., Roark, B., Oken, B., Fried-Oken, M.: Offline analysis of context contribution to ERP-based typing BCI performance. J. Neural Eng. **10**(6), 066003 (2013)
9. Orhan, U., Hild, K. E., Erdogmus, D., Roark, B., Oken, B., Fried-Oken, M.: Rsvp keyboard: An eeg based typing interface. In: 2012 IEEE International Conference on Acoustics, Speech and Signal Processing (ICASSP), pp. 645–648. IEEE (2012)
10. Orhan, U., Akcakaya, M., Erdogmus, D., Roark, B., Moghadamfalahi, M., Fried-Oken, M.: Comparison of adaptive symbol presentation methods for rsvp keyboard

11. Sutton, S., Braren, M., Zubin, J., John, E.: Evoked-potential correlates of stimulus uncertainty. Science **150**(3700), 1187–1188 (1965)
12. Friedman, J.H.: Regularized discriminant analysis. J. Am. Stat. Assoc. **84**(405), 165–175 (1989)
13. Silverman, B.W.: Density Estimation for Statistics and Data Analysis, vol. 26. CRC Press, Boca Raton (1986)
14. Roark, B., Villiers, J. D., Gibbons, C., Fried-Oken, M.: Scanning methods and language modeling for binary switch typing. In: Proceedings of the NAACL HLT 2010 Workshop on Speech and Language Processing for Assistive Technologies. Association for Computational Linguistics, pp. 28–36 (2010)

Improving BCI Usability as HCI in Ambient Assisted Living System Control

Niccolò Mora(✉), Ilaria De Munari, and Paolo Ciampolini

Information Engineering Department, University of Parma,
Parco Area delle Scienze 181/A, 43124 Parma, Italy
{niccolo.mora, ilaria.demunari,
paolo.ciampolini}@unipr.it

Abstract. Brain Computer Interface (BCI) technology is an alternative/
augmentative communication channel, based on the interpretation of the
user's brain activity, who can then interact with the environment without relying
on neuromuscular pathways. Such technologies can act as alternative HCI
devices towards AAL (Ambient Assisted Living) systems, thus opening their
services to people for whom interacting with conventional interfaces could be
troublesome, or even not viable. We present here a complete solution for
BCI-enabled home automation. The implemented solution is, nonetheless,
more general in the approach, since both the realized hardware module and the
software infrastructure can handle general bio-potentials. We demonstrate the
effectiveness of the solution by restricting the focus to a SSVEP-based,
self-paced BCI, featuring calibration-less operation and a subject-independent,
"plug&play" approach. The hardware module will be validated and compared
against a commercial EEG device; at the same time, the signal processing chain
will be presented, introducing a novel method for improving accuracy and
immunity to false positives. The results achieved, especially in terms of false
positive rate containment (0.26 min^{-1}) significantly improve over the literature.

Keywords: Brain computer interface (BCI) · Steady state visual evoked
potential (SSVEP) · Self-paced BCI · Subject-independent BCI

1 Introduction

A Brain Computer Interface (BCI) is an alternative, augmentative communication
channel [1] which aims at providing the user with an interaction path based on the sole
interpretation of her/his brain activity. It is thus natural considering such technology in
the realm of HCI devices; as a consequence, comparison with "conventional" user
interfaces suggests several desirable features for BCI interaction. For the ease of discussion, but without loss of generality, let us focus on a possible use of BCI as a HCI,
namely in Ambient Assisted Living (AAL) system control [2].

In such a scenario, user interactions are quite limited and sparse in time, so the need
for user-friendly approaches becomes capital: in order to foster BCI acceptance and
effectiveness, the user needs to perceive BCI-enabled control as easy and natural as
possible.

© Springer International Publishing Switzerland 2015
D.D. Schmorrow and C.M. Fidopiastis (Eds.): AC 2015, LNAI 9183, pp. 293–303, 2015.
DOI: 10.1007/978-3-319-20816-9_28

Within such perspective, the user should be allowed to interact with the system without needing neither complex, time-consuming, "ad personam" calibration procedures, nor demanding training sessions. This means that a "plug & play" approach is highly desirable, and such behavior should be uniform across different users; i.e. they should be able to consistently use the device with the same settings (realizing a so-called subject-independent BCI), and limiting fine performance tuning to just a few high-level parameters. This implies a shift of paradigm in BCI design: instead of looking for the optimal set of user-specific features, compatibility across users needs to be sought for.

Moreover, other relevant features for a practical BCI include the ability to operate in real-time, in a so-called self-paced (asynchronous) way [3], i.e., having the ability to run continuously and recognize actual "commands" without having any information whether the user is actively trying to control the device or not. This calls for a reliable method for discerning between intentional control and no-control periods, having false positive minimization as primary concern.

Finally, another major aspect worth considering in promoting accessibility to this kind of technology is its cost. Lowering costs does not merely means saving money, but rather broadening the spectrum of users and uses for BCI-enabled devices, generating new concepts and ideas, just as in the commercial electronic realm happens. Closely related to this aspect is the adoption of scalable, compact technological solutions; future BCI-embedded implementations could potentially allow to discover new methods and applications, just as wearable devices are re-inventing the way we intend sensors. In [4, 5], a cost-effective EEG hardware solution was presented; in this paper we present an upgraded version, which will significantly improve performance and flexibility.

These considerations led us to develop, from scratch, a solution which will be presented, in this context, tailored to a practical BCI-enabled AAL system control. In this sense, the application layer of our solution is highly focused; nonetheless, the underlying hardware and infrastructure layers are designed to be as general purpose as possible, thus allowing further experiments to be designed.

2   BCI as HCI in Ambient Assisted Living: Practical Context

CARDEA [6] is the AAL-system which will be used to control the home environment. It is a versatile, highly-scalable system which can deal with multiple input devices, including switches, touch-panels and web-based interfaces. Our goal is to devise a complete BCI solution which could act, with respect to the automation system, just as a conventional input device.

Using a BCI as an input channel to an automation system implies, as previously stated, a (usually) limited amount of user interactions, and such events are, moreover, sparse with respect to time. This led us to consider adopting calibration-less approaches, since long training phases could be perceived as an excessive burden by the user. Moreover, we also stressed the importance of adopting methods which are maximally re-usable across different users, without having to re-train the whole system.

All these considerations led us to choose SSVEP (Steady State Visual Evoked Potentials) as our operating protocol. A SSVEP is a periodic brain response elicited by a visual stimulus, flickering at a constant frequency: a peak in the brain power spectrum, synchronous with such frequency, can be produced just by looking at the visual stimulus. SSVEP are regarded as robust features for BCI [7], given their inherently higher SNR (Signal to Noise Ratio) with respect to other paradigms (e.g., motor imagery [8]). Moreover, since it exploits an involuntary response, SSVEP do not require, in principle, any specific user skill and thus involve no user training. SSVEP is, hence, a suitable paradigm for implementing BCI aimed at control applications or, more generally speaking, at building interface systems involving choices among a discrete and finite set of values.

The user interaction will then be as follows: he/she will be presented with 4 simultaneously flickering LED (Light Emitting Diodes), placed, for example, at the vertices of an LCD screen about 1 m from the user. The choice of LED is necessary for achieving arbitrary flickering frequencies, allowing to flash in a medium-high frequency band (e.g. 15–25 Hz), for improved user comfort. By selectively focusing on one visual stimulus, the user is able to provide a command which, for example, will allow him to navigate through a menu. In the simple, demonstrative setup shown in Sect. 4.2, the users are presented with 4 simultaneous flickering visual stimuli, arranged in a rectangular pattern over a box; each LED is associated with a specific action (light on/off, shutter open/close), and the user must focus on one of them (at his own pace) to perform the desired action. Although demonstrative, this approach is general, and more sophisticated UI can be designed. Once a SSVEP response is detected and classified, the BCI issues commands to the home automation system, which takes care of executing the decoded action.

3 EEG Hardware Realization

A dedicated hardware module was designed and realized for acquiring bio-potentials. The module features 16 input channels in a small, 100×130 mm form factor; moreover, the module is battery operated (4xAA alkaline batteries), given its power consumption (as low as 160 mW, which represents a 45 % improvement, in power per channel, over the previous release [2]). Production costs are also contained, with respect to current, commercial EEG devices: in medium scale, device manufacturing amounts to, approximately, 300 €. The module connects to a computer via a full-speed USB 2.0 link (12 Mbps), and its main parameters (such as data rate and gain) can be adjusted on-the-go directly via software.

At the core of the module are two high-resolution (24-bit) δ-Σ Analog to Digital Converters (ADCs), featuring DC-handling capability. Data rate can be adjusted in the range of 250-16 kSPS (Samples Per Second), although, for EEG acquisition, we usually set 250 SPS (for better noise performance), with an input applied gain of 24 (input dynamic range is, thus, ± 188 mV).

Experimental Validation and Results. In order to validate and compare our device against a commercial one, several tests were performed. At first, the Referred To Input

(RTI) noise was measured, acquiring a total of 150 s waveforms, with shorted input terminals (at the connector level, to account for the noise coupled across the whole board). Our device, from here on referred to as DUT, was set for 250 SPS, whereas the REF device, a g.tec USBamp, was set for 512 SPS instead. Table 1 summarizes the results, which are also referred to a common [0–40] Hz band, in order to perform a homogeneous comparison. These results highlight the good performance of the proposed solution.

Another test was performed with real EEG data, to assess the performance of the device in dynamic conditions. In order to do so, a p300 experiment was set up; two subjects participated to this test, totaling 12 runs, during which 10 series of 23 flashes were presented. The probability of a target stimuli (green square, vs. distracters, i.e. red squares) appearing is set to, approximately, 0.13. The EEG was acquired, holding the cap and electrode set fixed, and simply switching the input connectors for recording waveforms in an interleaved scheme (i.e. run1 REF, run2 DUT, run3 REF etc.). The collected waveforms were compared, assessing the differences between target vs. non-target epochs, at each time instant: REF and DUT show consistent behavior, as exemplified in Fig. 1, where waveforms from the POz electrode are displayed, along with the significance test. Also, standard tests with ocular artifacts, EMG artifacts and alpha burst were performed, proving good detectability.

Table 1. Noise performance comparison between the proposed device (DUT) and a reference one (REF, *g.tec USBamp*).

	Peak-to-Peak	[0–40] Hz integrated
REF	7.16 µVpp	0.405 µVrms
DUT	1.39 µVpp	0.126 µVrms

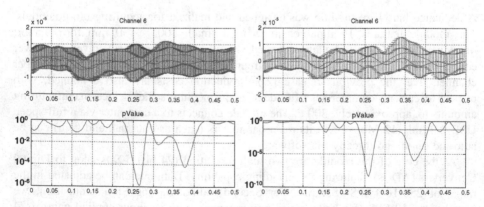

Fig. 1. Example of P300 waveform comparison between two runs (left: REF, right: DUT). The top figures report the temporal domain waveforms acquired from POz electrode (mean and std. dev., targets in red, non-targets in blue). The bottom ones are the related *p-value* plots (Colour figure online).

All these hints allow us to conclude that the realized module does not introduce significant noise or bias, when compared with a high-end, reference device, and can, therefore, be equivalently used in BCI experiments.

4 SSVEP and Related Signal Processing

Many algorithms exist in literature for SSVEP classification; among the most popular ones are: MEC [9] (Minimum Energy Combination), AMCC [10] (Average Maximum Contrast Combination) and CCA [11] (Canonical Correlation Analysis). Also, in [12], a SSVEP classification algorithm is introduced, particularly optimized for low computational demand. Mentioned algorithms are considered state of the art and allow, in general, to achieve better performance with respect to methods based on pure PSDA (Power Spectrum Density Analysis) methods. A review of such methods goes beyond the scope of this article; the interested reader could refer, for example, to [12, 13]. In the following, we refer to CCA algorithm, and build up on top of it in order to achieve optimal performance in terms of accuracy and immunity to false positives.

CCA is a statistical method, generally used for finding the correlations between two sets of multi-dimensional variables. It seeks a pair of linear combinations (canonical variables, characterized by weight vectors $\mathbf{w_x}$, $\mathbf{w_y}$) for the two sets, such that the correlation between the two linear combinations $\mathbf{x_L} = \mathbf{w_x^T} X$ and $\mathbf{y_L} = \mathbf{w_y^T} Y$ is maximized:

$$\max_{w_x, w_y} \rho = \frac{E[x_L y_L^T]}{\sqrt{E[x_L x_L^T]E[y_L y_L^T]}} = \frac{w_x^T XY^T w_y}{\sqrt{w_x^T XX^T w_x w_y^T YY^T w_y}}. \tag{1}$$

Here X, Y are the input and the SSVEP reference matrix, respectively. Y is composed by N_h (sin, cos) couples representing a steady state sinusoidal response, with N_h representing the number of considered harmonics:

$$X = \begin{bmatrix} \sin(2\pi f t_1) & \cos(2_1) & \cdots & \sin(2\pi N_h f t_1) & \cos(2\pi N_h f t_1) \\ \vdots & \vdots & \cdots & \vdots & \vdots \\ \sin(2\pi f t_{Nt}) & \cos(2_{Nt}) & \cdots & \sin(2\pi N_h f t_{Nt}) & \cos(2\pi N_h f t_{Nt}) \end{bmatrix}. \tag{2}$$

CCA is performed for every target stimulus frequency, and a classifier picks the largest correlation coefficient in this set.

4.1 Offline Performance

With reference to the 4-class SSVEP dataset introduced in [12], the performance of this signal processing method can be assessed; Table 1 reports the average accuracy (and standard deviation) as a function of the observed EEG window length. It is worth remarking that, consistently with the "plug & play" goal, no user-specific calibration

Table 2. Mean accuracy (std. dev.) vs. EEG window length (without neutralization)

$t_{window} = 1.5$ s	$t_{window} = 2$ s	$t_{window} = 3$ s	$t_{window} = 4$ s
88.71 %	90.30 %	90.69 %	90.20 %
(2.56 %)	(1.86 %)	(1.49 %)	(2.11 %)

procedure is required and that all of the EEG waveforms coming from different users were considered as a whole, seeking for a method suitable for general use (Table 2).

A Strategy for Enhancing Accuracy. Accuracy is the main performance indicators for the aimed control application. Thus, we developed a methodology for optimizing it, introducing an estimate of the confidence level in the classification [14]. Should such indicator result in a low confidence, classification is not validated: we call this new "no-reliable-decision" state a neutral state. The neutralization mechanism can positively impact on the overall prediction accuracy, at the expense of discarding information embedded anyhow in the ruled out epochs.

Of course, the choice of such a confidence indicator depends on the actual algorithm: with reference to the CCA method, we assume the absolute difference between the largest correlation coefficient and the second largest one as such indicator, from here on referred to as parameter d.

In Fig. 2, distribution of correctly and wrongly classified epochs with respect to d parameter is shown by a histogram approximation (each epoch contains a SSVEP, as per dataset in [12]). Ideal behavior should associate all errors (red bars) to low values of d, with correct classification (blue bars) associated to largest values instead. Then, one could choose a suitable threshold value $d*$ to separate the two cases: whenever $d \leq d*$ we rule the epoch as neutral, otherwise a decision is made. However, since actual data show overlaps between the correct and wrong classification distributions, a tradeoff between prediction accuracy and data yield (i.e. the fraction of non-neutral epochs) is needed. In order to address such tradeoff, the following procedure was adopted: for a given value of $d*$, a subset of epochs is selected, fulfilling the condition $d \geq d*$; then, wrong and correct classification are counted within the subset, keeping track of the fraction of rejected epochs, and errors and accuracies computed accordingly. Such procedure is repeated, sweeping the parameter $d*$, in order to assess its effect on error count (or accuracy) and neutralization rate. We characterized the method on the whole population of the test, instead of relying on a per-user basis analysis: this is in line with our view of subject-independent approach.

Figures 3 and 4 graphically report such results for errors and accuracy, respectively. In order to appreciate the improvement carried by neutralization strategy, the performance achieved with no neutralization is also reported (red dashed line). Consistent improvement in both the accuracy and the error count are attained over the reference case, even at lower neutralization rates, i.e., without implying too relevant data loss.

The quality metric introduced above can also be exploited to introduce some adaptive features in the SSVEP classification stage. In particular, we can check the quality of the current prediction at runtime by looking at the indicator d: we may start with a short time window length, to be increased whenever d does not exceed a given

Fig. 2. Distribution of wrong (red) and correct (blue) epochs classification (normalized to the sample size) as a function of the parameter d. The distributions are also plotted for different EEG window lengths (Colour figure online).

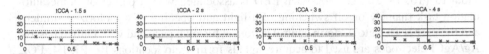

Fig. 3. Classification errors as a function of neutralization rate, at different values of threshold d*. The red dashed line represents the reference error count, i.e. without neutralization (i.e. d* = 0). The graphs are also plotted for different EEG window lengths (Colour figure online).

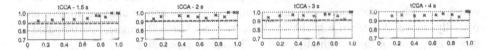

Fig. 4. Accuracy as a function of neutralization rate, at different values of threshold d*. The red dashed line represents the reference accuracy level, without i.e. neutralization (i.e. d* = 0). The graphs are also plotted for different EEG window lengths (Colour figure online).

threshold. This could potentially improve the user's experience and comfort: each time, the required SSVEP persistence time for classification is dynamically chosen, so as to be as short as possible (i.e. the user needs to focus for less time on the stimulus, provided sufficient quality of the SSVEP response is reflected in the d value); at the same time, avoiding to choose a fixed, short window, may help in improving immunity to false positives.

A simple proof-of-concept test has been carried out: just a couple of window lengths were exploited here, switching from 2 s to 3 s whenever the d threshold test fails. Statistical analysis performed shows that the method does not degrade accuracy, with respect to fixed window implementation; on the other hand it is effective in reducing the fraction of rejected epochs (p ≈ 0.05 for the 2 s window, p ≈ 0.02 for the 3 s one, with mean neutralization rates of 18 %, 21 %, 13 % for the 2 s, 3 s and adaptive windows, respectively), this meaning that information in the epoch is maximally exploited, thus achieving, potentially, a more responsive system.

4.2 Online, Self-Paced Operation

Based on the algorithms described so far, a self-paced, online BCI, exploiting a 4-class SSVEP paradigm was implemented and tested.

Experimental setup is very close to that in [12]: 4 visual stimuli (LED, organized in a rectangular pattern over a box) are shown simultaneously, with blinking frequencies

Table 3. Online performance on the self-paced, 4-class experiment: mean (std. dev.)

	True Positive Rate	False Negative Rate	False Positive Rate [min⁻¹]
No smoother	96.44% (0.77)	3.56% (0.77)	0.74 (0.08)
Smoother	94.62% (0.83)	5.38% (0.83)	0.26 (0.03)

equal to {16, 18, 20, 22} Hz. Each LED is associated with a particular home automation task (namely on/off switching of a light and opening of a motorized shutter), and the user is asked to perform control action, at his own pace and will. Only 6 passive Ag/AgCl electrodes are used to acquire signals form scalp locations Pz, P3, P4, POz, O1, O2.

With respect to [12], the main difference in the protocol is that the subject here is not given any cue on when to start looking at an LED; instead, he is free to decide when to focus on the visual stimulus and when to rest. Also, in order to assess the immunity to false positive events, long idle periods are introduced on purpose, during which the subject does not make any intentional choice and is allowed to talk and, partially, move. A total of 6 healthy volunteers (age 24-61, 2 females) participated in this study, none of them with any prior BCI-control experience.

As far as the online signal processing is concerned, a classification is attempted every 200 ms, using the neutralization technique we introduced before, to ensure classification reliability. The adaptive window-length choice mechanism is also used: at first, classification is attempted using the shortest available window (2 s). In case no prediction can be made reliably (at least according to the confidence indicator d), the window is allowed to grow in pre-determined steps, attempting classification at each time step until either a reliable choice is obtained or an upper time limit is reached (4 s).

In addition, in order to further improve immunity to false positives, a post-smoother is optionally added, which averages the last 5 classification outputs for each class (the 4 targets plus the neutral state): if the average for a class exceeds a given threshold, the choice is validated, otherwise a null output is assumed

4.3   Results of the Online, Self-Paced Operation

As previously stated, in order to provide smoother operation in BCI-enabled control applications, we are primarily concerned with maximizing the accuracy (i.e. correctly classifying the command when the user is trying to issue one) and, at the same time, minimizing the false positives. That also requires being able to discern when the user is actively controlling the device, or is just resting or performing other tasks.

Table 3 reports the online experiment results (mean and standard deviation), in terms of true positive, false negative and false positive rates.

A very good performance is achieved, both in terms of true positive and false positive rates. In Table 3, influence of the optional post-smoothing step is also accounted for: when no smoothing is applied, the "raw" performance of the neutralization mechanism can be assessed. In this case, false positives are kept to a very small amount (0.74 min^{-1} on average), improving over literature data [15, 16]. Such performance is further boosted by switching on the smoother stage: a 0.26 min^{-1} false positive frequency is attained, at the expense of an increase in latency time (due to the summing stages of the smoother, which introduce an additional 1 s delay, in our implementation) and of an almost negligible decrease in the true positive rate (– 1.82 %), which nevertheless does not jeopardize the user ability to effectively control the BCI.

In evaluating such results, it is worth remarking that the parameters for the neutralization mechanism and the post-smoother are kept constant across all users and that no user-specific setup adjustment was made. Results therefore show that the signal processing chain is quite stable with respect to user variations, supporting the aimed "plug & play" vision.

Finally, the entire setup was put to test in a relatively harsher environment, in the context of the *Handimatica 2014* exhibition. Here, high background luminosity, noise, electromagnetic interference, are not controlled as lab environments, and may potentially hinder the effectiveness of the solution. Furthermore, the subject was relatively free to move and speech, in order to interact with people. Overall, 6 live demos were performed, for the approximate duration of 30 min each. Although non-conclusive from a statistical point of view, promising results were achieved: the subject was able to successfully operate the BCI (controlling the on/off switching of a light and the opening of a mechanical shutter thanks to the CARDEA system, as mentioned in Sect. 2), and the false positive rate was as low as 0.14 min^{-1}. This encourages the transition of such technology also outside of lab environments.

5   Conclusions

In this paper, we discussed a complete implementation of a SSVEP-based BCI and demonstrated its effectiveness in a concrete BCI-enabled AAL system control.

A dedicated EEG hardware module was realized and its performance assessed and compared against a reference, commercial device, highlighting good performance.

The whole signal processing chain for a self-paced, SSVEP-based BCI was presented. Given the application scope of home automation control, in which user interactions are quite rare and sparse in time, the accuracy and robustness constraints prevail over high data throughput requirements. From this perspective, undergoing long or periodical system calibration phases could be perceived as an excessive burden by the user (this spoiling acceptance and usability chances), so that a calibration and training-free approach was pursued. Subject-independent operation was demonstrated, at the same time achieving remarkably good performance.

To this purpose, a CCA-based algorithm was exploited: after assessing its reference performance, improvement in accuracy and robustness were obtained by accounting for neutralization of unreliable choices, based on the estimation of a classification confidence index. Such an index was also exploited to implement adaptive, dynamic selection of optimal duration of EEG epoch, thus increasing efficiency of the classification process and consequently allowing to improve the BCI responsiveness towards the user.

Finally, devised methods were implemented and tested in an online, self-paced BCI experiment. Obtained results are very promising: high true positive rates (> 94 %) and low false positive rates (0.26 min^{-1}) were achieved, outperforming literature data.

Moreover, the entire setup was also replicated outside lab-controlled conditions, in the scope of the *Handimatica 2014* exhibition, with very promising results. This may encourage the adoption of such technology in more realistic contexts.

As a future development, the adoption of hybrid BCI technology [17], exploiting EMG (ElectroMyoGraphy) as informative channel, will allow to improve and enhance user experience, for example by providing a viable on/off switch for the visual stimuli (thereby improving immunity to false positives), or by constituting a parallel/alternative input channel.

References

1. Wolpaw, J.R., Birbaumer, N., McFarland, D.J., Pfurtscheller, G., Vaughan, T.M.: Brain-computer interfaces for communication and control. Clin. Neurophysiol. **113**(6), 767–791 (2002)
2. Mora, N., Bianchi, V., De Munari, I., Ciampolini, P.: A BCI platform supporting AAL applications. In: Stephanidis, C., Antona, M. (eds.) UAHCI 2014, Part I. LNCS, vol. 8513, pp. 515–526. Springer, Heidelberg (2014)
3. Millan, R.J., Mourino, J.: Asynchronous BCI and local neural classifiers: an overview of the adaptive brain interface project. Trans. Neural Syst. Rehabil. Eng. **11**(2), 159–161 (2003)
4. Mora, N., Bianchi, V., De Munari, I., Ciampolini, P.: Controlling AAL environments through BCI. In: IEEE/ASME 10th International Conference on Mechatronic and Embedded Systems and Applications (MESA), 2014, pp. 1–6, 10-12 September 2014
5. Mora, N., Bianchi, V., De Munari, I. Ciampolini, P.: A low cost brain computer interface platform for AAL applications. In: AAATE 2013 Conference Proceedings. Vilamoura, Portugal, 19–22 September 2013
6. Grossi, F., Bianchi, V., Matrella, G., De Munari, I., Ciampolini, P.: An assistive home automation and monitoring system. In: ICCE 2008. Digest of Technical Papers, pp. 1–2 (2008)
7. Cecotti, H.: A self-paced and calibration-less SSVEP-based brain-computer interface speller. IEEE Trans. Neural Syst. Rehabil. Eng. **18**(2), 127–133 (2010)
8. Pfurtscheller, G., Brunner, C., Schlögl, A., Lopes da Silva, F.H.: Mu rhythm (de) synchronization and EEG single-trial classification of different motor imagery tasks. NeuroImage **31**(1), 153–159 (2006)
9. Volosyak, I.: SSVEP-based Bremen-BCI interface - boosting information transfer rates. J. Neural Eng. **8**(3), 1–11 (2011)
10. Garcia-Molina, G., Zhu, D.: Optimal spatial filtering for the steady state visual evoked potential: BCI application. In: 5th International IEEE/EMBS Conference on Neural Engineering, pp. 156–160 (2011)
11. Lin, Z., Zhang, C., Wu, W., Gao, X.: Frequency recognition based on canonical correlation analysis for SSVEP-based BCIs. IEEE Trans. Biomed. Eng. **54**, 1172–1176 (2007)
12. Mora, N., Bianchi, V., De Munari, I., Ciampolini, P.: Simple and efficient methods for steady state visual evoked potential detection in BCI embedded system. In: IEEE International Conference on Acoustics, Speech and Signal Processing (ICASSP), pp. 2044–2048 (2014)

13. Mora, N., De Munari, I., Ciampolini, P.: Subject-independent, SSVEP-based BCI: trading off among accuracy, responsiveness and complexity. In: 7th International IEEE/EMBS Conference on Neural Engineering (NER) (2015)

14. Millan, R.J., Mourino, J.: Asynchronous BCI and local neural classifiers: an overview of the adaptive brain interface project. Trans. Neural Syst. Rehabil. Eng. **11**(2), 159–161 (2003)

15. Pfurtscheller, G., Solis-Escalante, T., Ortner, R., Linortner, P., Muller-Putz, G.R.: Self-paced operation of an SSVEP-based orthosis with and without an imagery-based "brain switch:" A feasibility study towards a hybrid BCI. IEEE Trans. Neural Syst. Rehabil. Eng. **18**(4), 409–414 (2010)

16. Pan, J., Li, Y., Zhang, R., Zhenghui, G., Li, F.: Discrimination between control and idle states in asynchronous SSVEP-based brain switches: a pseudo-key-based approach. IEEE Trans. Neural Syst. Rehabil. Eng. **21**(3), 435–443 (2013)

17. Mueller-Putz, G.R., Breitwieser, C., Cincotti, F., Leeb, R., Schreuder, M., Leotta, F., Tavella, M., Bianchi, L., Kreilinger, A., Ramsay, A. Rohm, M. Sagebaum, M., Tonin, L., Neuper, C., Millán, R.J.: Tools for brain-computer interaction: a general concept for a hybrid BCI (hBCI). Front. Neuroinform. **5**(30) (2011)

Human Computer Confluence in BCI
for Stroke Rehabilitation

Rupert Ortner[1], Danut-Constantin Irimia[1,2], Christoph Guger[1,3],
and Günter Edlinger[1,3(✉)]

[1] Guger Technologies OG, Herbersteinstrasse 60, 8020 Graz, Austria
{ortner,irimia,guger,edlinger}@gtec.at
[2] Faculty of Electrical Engineering "Gheorghe Asachi",
Technical University Iasi, Iasi, Romania
[3] g.tec medical engineering GmbH, Sierningstrasse 14,
4521 Schiedlberg, Austria

Abstract. This publication presents a novel device for BCI based stroke
rehabilitation, using two feedback modalities: visually, via an avatar showing
the desired movements in the user's first perspective; and via electrical stimulation of the relevant muscles. Three different kinds of movements can be
trained: wrist dorsiflexion, elbow flexion and knee extension. The patient has to
imagine the selected motor movements. Feedback is presented online by the
device if the BCI detects the correct imagination. Results of two patients are
presented showing improvements in motor control for both of them.

1 Introduction

Stroke is the second leading cause of death in the world. According to the WHO,
around 6.7 million people suffered a stroke in the year 2012 [1]. In 2010, the absolute
number of stroke survivors was 33 million worldwide [2]. Brain-Computer Interface
(BCI) based motor rehabilitation has the potential to improve the rehabilitation outcomes of stroke survivors compared to standard treatment [3, 4]. In this approach, well
known rehabilitation strategies are complemented by real-time feedback about the
patients' cortical activations.

Evidence suggests that motor imagery (MI) provides additional benefits over
conventional therapy [5–7]. In chronic stroke training, patients may be able to overcome "learned nonuse", resulting in cortical hand expansion and functional gains [8].
The disadvantage of standard motor imagery is that neither the patient, nor the therapist, receives any feedback about the performed task and the patient's compliance.
This lack can also reduce the motivation to perform or continue the training.

Robotic rehabilitation has become popular with recent technological progress.
Several robots and orthoses have been developed and tested. A systematic review
found that robot-aided therapy appears to improve motor control more than conventional therapy [9]. Meanwhile, several rehabilitation robots for upper and lower limbs
are commercially available and are used widely in rehabilitation clinics. The approach

© Springer International Publishing Switzerland 2015
D.D. Schmorrow and C.M. Fidopiastis (Eds.): AC 2015, LNAI 9183, pp. 304–312, 2015.
DOI: 10.1007/978-3-319-20816-9_29

is to assist the patient with movements he or she cannot perform without help. It is known that by performing these movements highly repetitive, functional recovery is applied [10]. Robotic rehabilitation with BCI was proven to result in significantly larger motor gains than standard arm treatment [4, 11].

Functional electrical stimulation (FES) for post stroke patients showed a statistically significant recovery of muscle strength after stroke [12]. FES has been used to restore hand grasp and release in people with tetraplegia, and standing and stepping in people with paraplegia [13]. With FES, one can define distinct movement patterns that are performed by the patient even if he is not able to perform these movements without external help. A big advantage of FES, compared to robots, is its flexibility to stimulate any desired muscle, and hence the possibility to implement a number of different movement patterns for upper and lower limbs within one device.

In BCI based motor rehabilitation, the patient is supported by feedback if the BCI detects correct imagination of motor movements in the cortex and then performs or supports the patients in performing a predefined motor task. With this approach, the sensory feedback loop is closed during rehabilitation, and thus Hebbian brain plasticity is enforced due to coincident activation of motor and sensory neurons [14].

In 2013, we introduced a prototype providing robotic and visual feedback [15]. In the present manuscript, we present a system integrating FES for feedback and wireless EEG acquisition for reduced movement artifacts and enhanced user comfort.

2 System Architecture

An overview of the system is shown in Fig. 1 on the left side. The laptop controls the paradigms, performs the signal processing and displays the results to the therapist. The patient views a second screen where the visual feedback is presented. Electrodes for functional stimulation are placed on the muscles to perform the selected movement

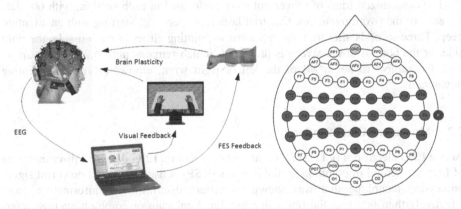

Fig. 1. Left: System overview: The wireless EEG cap records EEG data from 29 positions. The computer classifies the MI and drives the two feedback devices. Right: Electrode setup. The red positions show the 29 EEG electrodes used. The ground is placed on FPz (yellow), with the reference on the right earlobe (blue) (Colour figure online).

pattern. The stimulation of muscles is done by a Motionstim 8 (KRAUTH + TIMMERMANN GmbH, Germany) electrical stimulator, which is controlled by the laptop. EEG is acquired from 29 positions over the sensorimotor cortex. The electrode setup can be seen in Fig. 1, right. The physiotherapist can select one of three different movement paradigms (see below) including moving the wrist, elbow or knee.

2.1 Movement Paradigms

In each movement paradigm, the user's task is to perform one of two possible movements. The visual feedback adapts according to the paradigm, while the electrodes for electrical stimulation have to be placed on the muscles that are doing the selected movements. The three movements can be seen in Fig. 2.

In the wrist dorsiflexion paradigm (i), the two movements are the dorsiflexion of the left and right wrist. In the elbow flexion paradigm (ii), the patient is asked to perform a flexion of the left or right elbow. For the knee extension paradigm (iii), the patient is asked to perform an extension of the left knee or a flexion of the left elbow. The side of the body could be selected to be the extension of the right knee versus the flexion or the right elbow.

Fig. 2. Movement paradigms: wrist dorsiflexion, elbow flexion and knee extension.

120 randomized trials of movement were performed in each session, with 60 trials for each of the two movements. One trial lasts eight seconds, starting with an attention beep. Three seconds after trial onset, the arrow pointing either to the left side, the right side, or the bottom of the screen is presented, which remains until 4.25 s. This arrow cues the subject to begin MI of the left or right wrist, elbow, or knee, if pointing downwards.

2.2 Movement Classification

Active EEG electrodes (g.LADYbird) are used to acquire EEG data. For discrimination of MI, the method of common spatial patterns (CSP) is used. CSP is a powerful signal processing technique that was shown to extract discriminative information more effectively than other spatial filters like bipolar, Laplacian or common average reference [16, 17].

Before applying the spatial patterns, the EEG data are bandpass filtered between 8 Hz and 30 Hz. Then, the variance is calculated within a time-window of 1.5 s.

These features are normalized, log transformed and classified with a linear discriminant analysis (LDA). Finally, the LDA classification result drives the feedback devices. After each session, a set of spatial patterns and a LDA classifier is generated that can be loaded in the next session. If no subject specific set of spatial patterns and classifier exist, a generic one can be used, which was generated out of a pool of twenty subjects.

2.3 Paradigm Feedback

Feedback is presented visually via the avatar showing the hands and feet in the first perspective (see Fig. 2), and via FES. The two devices operate in parallel to give the patient the illusion that what he sees on the computer screen is what he feels in his hands. Necessary instructions are presented on a computer screen and via voice commands on headphones. Feedback is only activated if the detected MI fits the given instruction, e.g. if the task is to perform a dorsiflexion of the left wrist, then feedback starts only if MI of the left wrist is detected. Otherwise, the feedback devices will not move.

3 System Validation

Tests were performed on two patients. The paradigm used for both patients was the wrist dorsiflexion paradigm. 21 feedback sessions were done with the first patient (P1, female, 61 years) within a time frame of 12 weeks. The patient suffered from a stroke event of the right hand, which occurred 75 days before the first BCI feedback session was performed. The second patient (P2, female, 40 years) suffered from a chronic stroke, four years before the BCI feedback training started. The stroke resulted in a complete paralysis of her left hand. 10 feedback sessions where performed with this patient. All tests were done at the rehabilitation hospital of Iasi, Romania, and both participants gave written informed consent to participate to the study.

For patient selection, the following inclusion criteria were applied: survivor of a cerebrovascular accident in the territory of the middle cerebral artery, with residual spastic hemiparesis; significant upper limb deficit, defined by the patient as disability in performing daily activities and objectively quantified through submaximal values of the Fugl-Meyer score, ARAT test and Brunstromm scale; stable neurologic status during the last 60 days; and willingness to participate in the study expressed by signing the informed consent.

Exclusion criteria were: significant speaking/understanding and/or cognitive disorders, which do not allow the patient to understand the informed consent and the activities to perform within the study; inability to independently maintain the seat position (without assistance) for about 90 min; presence of pacemakers or other cardiac/cerebral/medullar implants which do not allow the use of FES; presence of a history of epilepsy or seizures uncontrolled by proper treatment.

3.1 Control Accuracy

An evaluation of control accuracy, based on the presented cue and the classified movement, was done after each session. The classifier was applied in steps of 0.5 s of all 120 trials across the session. If the detected MI fitted the given cue, this sample was counted as correct; otherwise, it was counted as incorrect. The average accuracy over all trials was then calculated. Examples can be seen in Figs. 3 and 4. The blue line shows the performance of right wrist dorsiflexion, the green line the performance of the left wrist dorsiflexion, and the black line shows the performance of both hands. The red line marks the time where the cue was presented to the patient. The maximum accuracy level of both sides is marked with a red spot.

3.2 9 Hole Peg Test

For assessment of rehabilitation process, a 9-hole PEG test [18], which measures the time to perform certain tasks, was done before the first session. After every three sessions, the test was repeated. This test could not be performed with Patient P2, because the complete paralysis of her affected hand prevented her from successfully performing the task.

4 Results

Table 1 shows, for every third session, the results of the control accuracy of both patients and the 9-hole PEG test from P1.

The control accuracy stayed relatively constant and even slightly decreased for P1, who performed well from the beginning. Her accuracy in the first and the last sessions can be seen in detail in Fig. 3. In the latter session, she was able to reach the maximum peak faster. P2 showed a clear increase in control accuracy from session one to session ten. The results of the first and the last sessions can be seen in Fig. 4. It shows that she

Table 1. Performance of the two patients. The table lists the control accuracy of P1 and P2 and the results of the 9-hole PEG test from P1.

P1				P2	
Session	Control accuracy (%)	9-hole PEG test		Session	Control accuracy (%)
		Left hand (s)	Right hand (s)		
0	–	31	65	1	63,7
3	95,0	32	54	4	86,2
6	91,2	32	45	7	96,2
9	92,5	31	42	10	96,2
12	95,0	31	42		
15	91,2	29	38		
18	91,2	29	34		
21	88,7	29	30		

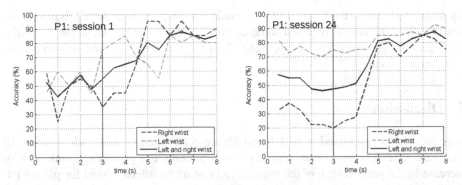

Fig. 3. Control accuracy of patient P1 after the first session (left) and the last session (right). The red line marks the time where the arrow appeared on the screen (Colour figure online).

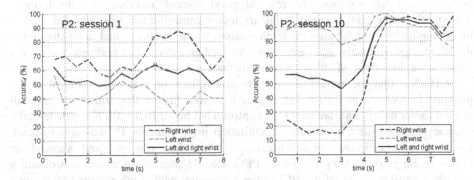

Fig. 4. Control accuracy of patient P2 after the first session (left) and the last session (right). The red line marks the time where the arrow appeared on the screen (Colour figure online).

Fig. 5. Movement of P2 with her affected hand after ten sessions. This movement is done without any external support or functional electrical stimulation.

was not able to control the BCI during the first session, but had good control in the last session.

For P1, the time to complete the 9-hole PEG test with the affected hand decreased from 65 s before the treatment to 30 s after the last session. With the unaffected hand, the time to completion remained nearly constant during the whole treatment.

As mentioned above, the 9-hole PEG test could not be performed for P2, but after the tenth session, the patient regained some control of her affected hand, in the form of a wrist dorsiflexion and a hand grasp. Figure 5 shows the movement she was able to do with her left hand.

5   Discussion

This publication presented a BCI based stroke rehabilitation tool with multimodal feedback. The first evaluation results on two patients are promising, with a clear increase in the performance of the 9-hole PEG test of the affected hand for patient P1.

The random control accuracy of P2 in the first session could be due to the long time of chronic stroke wherein she had no motor control of her affected hand, resulting in learned nonuse [19]. The BCI training seemed to help her overcome this learned nonuse. After ten sessions, she reached good control accuracy, but much more importantly, she started to regain voluntary motor control of her affected hand. P2 left the rehabilitation hospital after the tenth session, so the treatment had to be stopped at this time. It would have been interesting to further explore her performance over a longer time, including additional improvements.

It is clear that the control accuracy cannot reflect the real motor control of the patients. In addition to the present results, it is well known that some persons with normal motor movements are unable to control a MI based BCI [20]. Nevertheless, the accuracy can provide a hint about rehabilitation improvements. P1 was able to reach faster to her maximum control accuracy in the last sessions, and showed an improvement in performing the 9-hole PEG test. P2 showed no motor control and a random control accuracy of the BCI in the beginning, while both changed after some sessions.

This system's use of FES, instead of a rehabilitation robot, allows high flexibility in selection of movement paradigms. Therefore, three different paradigms are implemented; further ones could easily be introduced. Only wrist dorsiflexion has been tested so far. Decisions about which movements should be trained are within the responsibility of the medical doctors and physiotherapists, and depend on each patient's condition. By developing and validating new paradigms with additional movements, we could extend this approach to help a broader variety of patients. For example, a system that can work with knee dorsiflexion could help persons seeking gait rehabilitation.

6   Conclusion

Our overall aim is to combine several feedback modalities for BCI based motor rehabilitation into one device. With this approach, we aim to further foster the stimulation of sensory neurons and thus strengthen the effect of brain plasticity. The chosen modalities, the virtual reality and FES feedback allow us to easily integrate a number of different movement paradigms for upper and lower limbs and hence adjust the rehabilitation to the conditions and needs of the patients.

While the results of the first patients are promising, further patients need to be assessed. We also intend to explore additional movement paradigms and extend this approach to persons with movement disabilities from other causes.

Acknowledgements. This research has been partially supported by the European projects ComaWare (GA no. 650381), DeNeCor (ENIAC JU 2012 GA on. 324257) and CREAM (GA no. 265648).

References

1. World Health Organization: The top 10 causes of death. Available from: http://who.int/mediacentre/factsheets/fs310/en/
2. Feigin, V.L., Forouzanfar, M.H., Krishnamurthi, R., Mensah, G.A., Connor, M., Bennett, D. A., et al.: Global and regional burden of stroke during 1990–2010: findings from the global burden of disease study 2010. The Lancet **383**, 245–255 (2014)
3. Daly, J.J., Wolpaw, J.R.: Brain-computer interfaces in neurological rehabilitation. Lancet Neurol. **7**, 1032–1043 (2008)
4. Ang, K.K., Guan, C., Phua, K. S., Wang, C., Zhou, L., Tang, et al.: Brain-Computer Interface-based robotic end effector system for wrist and hand rehabilitation: results of a three-armed randomized controlled trial for chronic stroke. Front. Neuroengineering, vol. 7 (2014)
5. Zimmermann-Schlatter, A., Schuster, C., Puhan, M.A., Siekierka, E., Steurer, J.: Efficacy of motor imagery in post-stroke rehabilitation: a systematic review. J Neuroeng Rehabil. **5**, 8 (2008)
6. Sharma, N., Simmons, L.H., Jones, S., Day, D.J., Carpenter, A., Pomeroy, V.M., et al.: Motor imagery after subcortical stroke: a functional magnetic resonance imaging study. Stroke **40**, 1315–1324 (2009)
7. Liu, K.P., Lee, T.M., Chan, C.C., Hui-Chan, C.W.: Mental imagery for promoting relearning for people after stroke: a randomized controlled trial. Arch. Phys. Med. Rehabil. **85**(9), 1403–1408 (2004)
8. Liepert, J., Bauder, H., Miltner, W.H.R., Taub, E., Weiller, C.: Treatment induced cortical reorganization after stroke in humans. Stroke **31**, 1210–1216 (2000)
9. Prange, G.B., Jannink, M.J., Groothuis-Oudshoorn, C.G., Hermens, H.J., IJzerman, M.J., et al.: Systematic review of the effect of robot-aided therapy on recovery of the hemiparetic arm after stroke. J. Rehabil. Res. Dev. **43**, 171 (2006)
10. Barreca, S., Wolf, S.L., Fasoli, S., Bohannon, R.: Treatment interventions for the paretic upper limb of stroke survivors: a critical review. Neurorehabilitation Neural Repair **17**, 220–226 (2003)
11. Ramos-Murguialday, A., Broetz, D., Rea, M., Läer, L., Yilmaz, O., Brasil, F.L., et al.: Brain-machine-interface in chronic stroke rehabilitation: a controlled study. Ann Neurol. **74**, 100–108 (2013). doi:10.1002/ana.23879
12. Glanz, M., Klawansky, S., Stason, W., Berkey, C., Chalmers, T.C.: Functional electrostimulation in poststroke rehabilitation: a meta-analysis of the randomized controlled trials. Arch. Phys. Med. Rehabil. **77**, 549–553 (1996)
13. Triolo, R.J., Bogie, K.: Lower extremity applications of functional neuromuscular stimulation after spinal cord injury. Top. Spinal Cord Injury Rehabil. **5**, 44–65 (1999)

14. Grosse-Wentrup, M., Mattia, D., Oweiss, K.: Using brain–computer interfaces to induce neural plasticity and restore function. J. Neural Eng. **8**, 025004 (2011)
15. Ortner, R., Ram, D., Kollreider, A., Pitsch, H., Wojtowicz, J., Edlinger, G.: Human-Computer Confluence for Rehabilitation Purposes after Stroke. In: Shumaker, R. (ed.) VAMR 2013, Part II. LNCS, vol. 8022, pp. 74–82. Springer, Heidelberg (2013)
16. Guger, C., Ramoser, H., Pfurtscheller, G.: Real-time EEG analysis with subject-specific spatial patterns for a Brain-Computer Interface (BCI). IEEE Trans. Rehab. Eng. **8**, 447–456 (2000)
17. Blankertz, B., Tomioka, R., Lemm, S., Kawanabe, M., Müller, K.-R.: Optimizing spatial filters for robust EEG single-trial analysis. IEEE Signal Process. Mag. **25**(1), 41–56 (2008)
18. Beebe, J.A., Lang, C.E.: Relationships and responsiveness of six upper extremity function tests during the first 6 months of recovery after stroke. J. Neurol. Phys. Ther. JNPT **33**, 96 (2009)
19. Taub, E., Uswatte, G., Mark, V., Morris, D.: The learned nonuse phenomenon: implications for rehabilitation. Europa medicophysica **42**, 241–256 (2006)
20. Allison, B., Neuper, C.: In: Tan, D.S., Nijholt, A. (eds.) Brain-Computer Interfaces, pp. 35–54. Springer, London (2010). at http://dx.doi.org/10.1007/978-1-84996-272-8_3

Relevant HCI for Hybrid BCI and Severely Impaired Patients

José Rouillard(✉), Alban Duprès, François Cabestaing,
Marie-Hélène Bekaert, Charlotte Piau, Christopher Coat,
and Jean-Marc Vannobel, and Claudine Lecocq

CRIStAL Laboratory, University of Lille,
59655 Villeneuve D'Ascq Cedex, France
{jose.rouillard,alban.dupres,francois.cabestaing,
marie-helene.bekaert,charlotte.piau,christopher.coat,
jean-marc.vannobel,claudine.lecocq}@univ-lille1.fr

Abstract. In this paper, we are studying the possibility to enhance the relevance of hybrid Brain-Computer Interfaces for severely impaired patients by improving the relevance of Human-Computer Interfaces. Across virtual reality tools and serious games approaches, we believe that users will be more able to understand how to interact with such kind of interactive systems.

Keywords: Human-computer interaction · BCI · Hybrid BCI · Handicap · Virtual reality

1 Introduction

Although the concept of Brain-Computer Interface (BCI) had been introduced by Vidal [1] in 1973, it really emerged as a new field of research in the early nineties when systems allowing real-time processing of brain signals became available. Since then, BCI research has seen an impressive growth in the domains of neuroscience, computer science, and clinical research. However, there are still a significant number of theoretical and technological issues that have to be dealt with, probably with a maximum efficiency if following an interdisciplinary approach.

BCI is considered as an effective tool for rehabilitation and/or assistance of severely impaired patients. In our team, we are particularly working on BCI for Duchenne Muscular Dystrophy (DMD). DMD is a severe pathology of the skeletal musculature. This genetic disorder causes an absence of dystrophin, a protein that supports muscle strength and muscle fibers cohesion, which leads to progressive muscle degeneration and weakness. This dystrophy is described by Moser as the most common sex linked lethal disease in man (one case in about 4000 male live births). The patients are wheelchair bound around the age of 8-10 years and usually die before the age of 20 years [2]. It affects mostly males and is due to a progressive degeneration of the skeletal muscles but also of digestive, respiratory and heart muscles. Other disorders appear such as bone fragility, microcirculation disorders, nutritional disorders and anxiety syndromes. Recent advances in medicine may help delay the symptoms of DMD, and

© Springer International Publishing Switzerland 2015
D.D. Schmorrow and C.M. Fidopiastis (Eds.): AC 2015, LNAI 9183, pp. 313–323, 2015.
DOI: 10.1007/978-3-319-20816-9_30

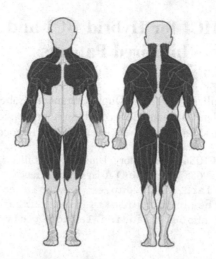

Fig. 1. In the early stages, DMD affects the shoulder and upper arm muscles and the muscles of the hips and thighs (in red). These weaknesses lead to difficulty in rising from the floor, climbing stairs, maintaining balance and raising the arms (Colour figure online). (Source: http://mda.org/disease/duchenne-muscular-dystrophy/overview)

increase life expectancy of patients, but unfortunately fail to stop the natural evolution that leads to progressive loss of motor skills to extremely severe quadriplegia (see Fig. 1).

The residual motor ability of the most advanced patients is characterized by very low amplitude movements associated with loss of degrees of freedom and severe muscle weakness in the fingers. The residual distal movements are maximized to control an electric wheelchair or a computer, thanks to palliative existing solutions on the market such as mini-joystick, mini-trackball or touchpad. Using these devices requires an extremely precise installation. However, at a very advanced stage, these assistive technologies no longer meet the needs: there are some losses of efficiency despite the custom configurations and some equipment usability fluctuations. These fluctuations are related to the duration of use, combined with excessive physical load, or may be due to the environment: humidity, coldness (causing microcirculation disorders) or minor modifications of the system (when moving a wheelchair, for example).

In the context of progressive, degenerative and very disabling disease such as DMD, the recommendation of assistive technology must adapt to the constant changes in the functional state of the user. Anticipating needs is not trivial because we need flexible human-computer interfaces at different stages of the evolution of the user's functional profile without requiring a change in strategy (material, equipment, behavior) each time the disease evolves.

The recent development of BCI allows one to consider new control options for these patients, eager for autonomy, particularly in the use of computers, electric wheelchairs and home automation [3, 4].

The purpose of our study is to observe various muscle and brain signals, when users push joysticks, typically to move a character in a 2D or 3D maze, or a car on a road, for instance.

We want to check the level of correlation between movements performed by the patients (finger and foot) and changes in electrophysiological potentials (EEG and EMG). This correlation is well known for healthy people.

For example, in the preparation of a motor action, a desynchronization of cortical rhythms in the beta and mu frequency band can be detected on the EEG signals recorded over motor areas. This desynchronization precedes the appearance of bursts of action potentials in EMG signals and the realization of movement. Our goal is to check whether similar correlations are present in DMD subjects, and if so at what level of repeatability and robustness they can be identified, at different stages of disease progression.

In this context, the challenge is therefore to propose to the patient a series of manipulations he/she is able to do now (time t), and to look how it will be possible in the future (time t + n months) to reproduce them, without necessarily using the same data source as that used initially to control the system (EEG instead of EMG, or a mix of them, for example).

In this study, we focus our attention particularly on asynchronous non-invasive BCI [4]. Our work is oriented towards two main questions: (a) how to help people with better human-computer interfaces for BCI? and (b) how to propose hybrid BCI able to adapt themselves to the context of use (user profile, progression of his/her disease in time, type of wheelchair, adaptation intra and inter session, etc.)?

The paper is organized as the following: part 2 presents our motivation in helping people suffering from muscular dystrophy or schizophrenia with better HCI for BCI; part 3 describes our approach around Hybrid BCI and Virtual Reality; part 4 and 5 describe the conducted experimentation and the obtained results; the last part gives a short conclusion and some perspectives for this work.

2 Helping People with Better HCI for BCI

We have noticed that most of the BCI proposed to people are not very pleasant and ergonomic to use. Most of the time users can only see some graphics on the screen, but it's not easy for them to understand how to interact with such interactive systems. For instance, how to perform mentally the task "push" with an Emotiv EPOC system, while nothing in the documentation explains how to do this, concretely? We believe that giving more feedback and feedforward to the users, before, during and after performing a task will lead to better user experiences and better results.

In the early stages of progressive disease such as DMD, the patient is still able to use his/her muscles. Thus, he/she can be trained to use a hybrid BCI with channels measuring his/her motion, his/her muscle activities through electromyography, as well as the activity of his/her motor and pre-motor cortical areas [5]. Later, with the disease evolution, motion-related channels will become less informative and the challenge will be to allow the control channels related to brain activity to take over. Clinicians of the physical medicine and rehabilitation service of Lille University Regional Hospital will define user needs, recruit and manage DMD patients for long term experiments. Colleagues of the clinical neurophysiology service at Lille University Hospital help us define the most appropriate markers of cortical activity for each interaction task.

2.1   For People Suffering from Muscular Dystrophy

As we said before, our first target population will be people suffering from Duchenne Muscular Dystrophy (DMD), but for the moment, we are improving our interactive system by testing it on non-disabled people, as presented on other work on DMD [6].

Concerning HCI aspects, we are focusing on virtual reality in order to provide a better feedback to users. The goal of virtual reality is to enable a person to obtain a sensorimotor and cognitive activity in an artificial world, created digitally, which can be imaginary, symbolic or a simulation of certain aspects of the real world. For instance, Fig. 2 presents hybrid BCIs developed in our laboratory, where the user can see in a virtual world (NeoAxis or Unity3D), realistic effects of his/her interaction in the world, when he/she pushes Arduino scanned buttons (left hand, right hand or both simultaneously) and/or when he/she thinks of pushing the buttons.

Fig. 2. (Left): Hybrid BCI developed in our team (EEG, EMG and Arduino). (Right): Hybrid BCI and virtual reality showing on the screen the hand(s) to move

We are also planning to use this approach (hybrid HCI and virtual reality) with other kinds of patients, such as schizophrenic people, where serious games will hopefully help to detect and manage their psychiatric disorders.

2.2   For People Suffering from Schizophrenia

As explained previously, DMD patient sometimes suffer from anxiety syndromes. Thus, we are also interested in the observation of brain signals detected on people suffering from schizophrenia. And so, our maze designed with Unity3D to study DMD pathologies could also be used with psychiatric disorders such as schizophrenia.

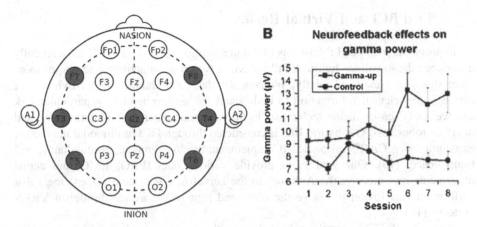

Fig. 3. Left: International 10-20 system and chosen electrodes. Right: Neurofeedback effect on gamma power (30-60 Hz) [8].

The maze would allow working on 2 items: occurrence of Auditive Verbal Hallucination (AVHs) and spatial memory. Many studies have characterized profiles of abnormal neuronal oscillations of schizophrenic (SCZ) patient. For example, reduction of the amplitude of theta waves and delayed phase are significant clues to detect such profiles [7]. We propose the use of a virtual maze because theta waves are involved in the spatial orientation. The complexity of the maze would depend on the amplitude of SCZ's theta waves that will be measured in temporal area (see Fig. 3, left).

A recent study [8] demonstrated that the repeated use of a playful serious game allows increasing the amplitude of gamma waves. The working assumption is that the same phenomenon could be observed with theta waves.

In first time, increase of the theta wave would allow to resolve the problems of spatial orientation. In second time, as suppose McCarhy [9], this increase could reduce the severity of the AVHs or their occurring.

The use of this serious game would also allow interacting with objects triggering the AVHs. Recent study [10] demonstrates that SCZ patients can identify these objects. We propose to place/hide/animate such objects in the maze. The aim would be to observe the effect these objects cause on profiles of neuronal oscillations of schizophrenic patient.

In parallel we propose to work with the SCZ patient to develop strategies to be adopted during AVHs. McCarthy [8] proposes to use the humming, based on studies showing less AVHs occurred in periods when SCZ patients are humming [11].

The aim would be to develop these strategies based on the song then to ask the SCZ patient to apply these strategies in front of the elements met in the maze. Among them the object activing would be hidden. The objective would be to re-educate the patient in its fear and to validate the use of the humming.

3   Hybrid BCI and Virtual Reality

To improve the speed and robustness of communication, Leeb et al. [12] have recently introduced the so-called "hybrid BCI" notion, in which brain activity and one or more other signals are analyzed jointly. We consider that each channel of our hybrid BCI carries some relevant information to understand the achievement of a particular task and we apply sensor fusion techniques to improve man-machine communication and interface robustness. Our hydrid BCI is considered through HCI multimodal interaction paradigm using CARE properties (Complementarity, Assignment, Redundancy, and Equivalence) [13]. Our goal is to provide various data (EEG, EMG and actual movements measured by the Arduino) to the kernel of our system (OpenVibe[1]) that performs a data fusion to derive the command sent to the avatar through a VRPN protocol [14].

Analysis of EEG signals collected over the scalp provides guidance on the amplitude and phase of cortical rhythms, allowing to identify synchronizations or desynchronizations related to a real or an imagined event (movement of a limb, for example) [15, 16].

The electromyography (EMG) detection allows the analysis of electrical phenomena that occur in the muscle during voluntary contraction. This examination detects an electrical signal transmitted by peripheral motor neuron to the muscle fibers it innervates, called motor unit action potential (MUAP) [17]. Standard techniques use invasive electrodes, usually with concentric needles. The explored area is reduced and the exploration is very precise.

But there are also non-invasive "global" EMGs, using a surface electrode, exploring a larger territory, applicable to many muscles. A compound muscle (or motor) action potential (CMAP) is then collected [18]. There are mainly used in the study of muscle strength and fatigue in patients with neuromuscular diseases [19].

Patients with Duchenne muscular dystrophy have a myogenic EMG pattern during physical effort. Abnormally high compared to the effort, it is composed of potential polyphasic motor units, with low amplitude and short duration. Abnormal spontaneous activity can also be detected in the form of potential fibrillation waves of positive sharp waves and complex repetitive discharges. In very advanced forms, some areas may become electrically silent [20].

The analysis of the EMG signal can be made on motor unit potential (MUP) [21, 22] or compound muscle action potential (CMAP) parameters [19], to check various elements such as duration, peak to peak amplitude, total area under the curve, number of phases, etc.

---

[1] http://openvibe.inria.fr, retrieved on 13/02/2015.

4 Experimentation

The experiment was realized by nine healthy subjects (6 men and 3 women) aged between 20 and 53 years. Subjects' approval was verbally required. Two of them had previously used the system. Participants were asked to seat comfortably in an armchair and to keep their indexes on each joystick. They were asked to avoid blinking their eyes or contracting their jaws during the experiment in order to prevent recording ocular and muscular artifacts.

Subjects were wearing an electrode cap (GAMMAcap, g.tec), with Ag/AgCl electrodes located according to the international 10/20 system. Ten mono-polar channels were recorded from the central, parietal and frontal lobe: C1, C2, C3, C4, C5, C6, FC3, CP3, FC4 and CP4 with an electrode clipped on the right ear as a reference and another one on the forehead as mass. A gel was applied between skin and electrodes to increase conduction of electrical signal. Signals were amplified and sampled at the frequency Fe = 512 Hz.

Two bipolar channels were placed on the forearms in order to record muscular activities when users manipulate the joysticks.

Figure 4 shows our system which is composed of a physiological signals amplifier with 16 channels (g.USBamp, g.tec), two DELL computers using XP and windows 7 operating systems. Two joysticks are connected to the USB port of one computer via an Arduino UNO. On one computer runs OpenVibe software which collects data from EEG, EMG and Arduino sources. OpenVibe allows controlling online signal acquisition, signal processing and commands sending for application control. On the other computer runs the application developed under Unity 3D. The two computers are linked with an ethernet cable which enables commands sending from OpenVibe to Unity 3D application thanks to VRPN protocol.

The experiment was composed of a calibration phase followed by two online phases. During those second and third parts of the experiment, participants were asked

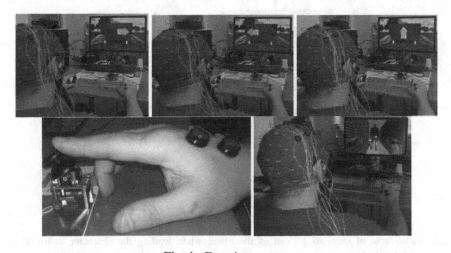

Fig. 4. Experiment setup

to control a character in a maze thanks to the joysticks. The experiment lasted about one hour. The calibration phase enables to record EMG and EEG data at specific moment. During this phase, the user has to push on the left, right or on both joysticks according to orange arrows displayed on the screen (see Fig. 4). Virtual hands are displayed and move according to the activated joystick.

During online phase users have to get the character out of the maze, following a yellow path. The character rotates to the right or left or goes straight by activating respectively right, left or both joysticks. In the first online phase the user controls the character using an immersive view whereas an aerial view is used during the second online phase. No time indication is displayed to avoid competition effects and stressing people. Experiment ends with a questionnaire in order to get qualitative data.

5 Results

Figure 5 shows the average time needed by users to get the character out of the maze in immersive (A) and aerial (B) views. The average time in immersive view (152 s) is slightly higher than in aerial view (130 s). Nevertheless, a Wilconxon non-parametric test doesn't show a significant difference (p-value = 0.141) of time between immersive and aerial view, with an alpha risk of 5 %.

Moreover, qualitative data indicate that users' concentration is slightly better in aerial view than in immersive view. This can explain why the average time to get out

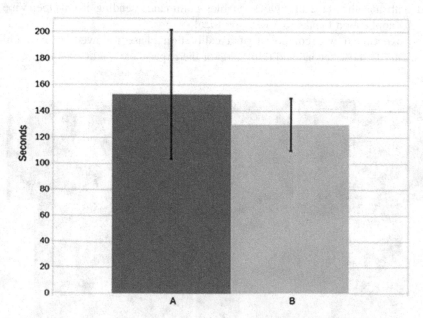

Fig. 5 Mean time of users to get out of the maze when leading the character in immersive (A) and aerial (B) view. Vertical bars show standard deviation.

the maze is lower in aerial view. This result seems to show that we can easily switch from one view to the other.

According to Fig. 5, time to get out of the maze, in immersive and aerial view, is correct. Our control mode with two degrees of freedom for rotating and moving the character forward in the maze seems efficient.

This is supported by qualitative data which indicate that all users feel comfortable with the proposed HCI. More over a majority of people (55 %) estimated that the character control is intuitive, unlike to other one who felt it moderately intuitive.

6 Conclusion and Perspectives

In this paper we have shown the relevance of our approach to controlling a character with two degrees of freedom. Indeed time to get out of the maze for all participants is satisfying. It is supported by qualitative data, indicating that participants feel comfortable with the proposed HCI.

Moreover time comparison, thanks to a Wilcoxon test, between character control in immersive and aerial view doesn't indicate a significant difference.

According to users, their concentration in aerial view was slightly better than in immersive view. These results seem to show that users can easily switch from one view to the other. It is interesting if we want to switch from a 3D to a 2D application. User can firstly learn to control the proposed HCI thanks to a 3D gaming. Then he/she can switch to a 2D application such as controlling cursor movements on a computer screen. This proposed HCI is promising for handicaped people like DMD (Duchenne Muscular Dystrophy) patients who have a weak motor activity and can control a system with only very few degrees of freedom.

During calibration and online phases, virtual hands were displayed on the screen. Right and left virtual hands move when users handle respectively right and left joysticks. According to qualitative data, half the people consider that virtual hands allow a good feedback of their interaction on the system during calibration phase. So it will be beneficial to display virtual hands animations as feedback for users during the calibration phase. It allows them to know if they perform the correct movement. However a large majority (89 %) of participants don't find these animations useful during online phase. Maybe it will be removed from the application in next experiments.

Furthermore this first study indicates that sending commands via VRPN protocol allows an efficient application control in real time. Nevertheless, when Arduino data, recording during online phase, are replaying several times, character's trajectories are never the same. It is a drawback if character moving analysis is needed after the experiment.

Further experiments will be performed soon in order to assess our system with DMD patients. Given that muscular strength of a DMD patient is lower than healthy people, joysticks need to be adapted. Movement sensors requiring a lower effort and yielding a better sensitivity to fingers movements will also be integrated.

References

1. Vidal, J.J.: Toward direct brain-computer communication. Ann. Rev. Biophys. Bioeng. **2**(1), 157–180 (1973)
2. Moser, H.: Duchenne muscular dystrophy: pathogenetic aspects and genetic prevention. Hum. Genet. **66**(1), 17–40 (1984)
3. Wolpaw, J.R., Birbaumer, N., McFarland, D.J., Pfurtscheller, G., Vaughan, T.M.: Brain–computer interfaces for communication and control. Clin. Neurophysiol. **113**(6), 767–791 (2002)
4. Wolpaw, J.R., McFarland, D.J., Neat, G.W., Forneris, C.A.: An EEG-based brain-computer interface for cursor control. Electroencephalogr. Clin. Neurophysiol. **78**(3), 252–259 (1991)
5. Bermudez i Badia, S., Garcia Morgade, A., Samaha, H., Verschure, P.F.M.J.: Using a hybrid brain computer interface and virtual reality system to monitor and promote cortical reorganization through motor activity and motor imagery training. IEEE Transactions on Neural Systems and Rehabilitation Engineering, 21(2), 174–181 (2013)
6. Power, S.D.: Toward an optical brain-computer interface based on consciously-modulated prefrontal hemodynamic activity. Doctoral dissertation, University of Toronto (2012)
7. Uhlhaas, P.J., Singer, W.: Abnormal neural oscillations and synchrony in schizophrenia. Nat. Rev. Neurosci. **11**(2), 100–113 (2010)
8. Keizer, A.W., Verschoor, M., Verment, R.S., Hommel, B.: The effect of gamma enhancing neurofeedback on the control of feature bindings and intelligence measures. Int. J. Psychophysiol. **75**(1), 25–32 (2010)
9. McCarthy-Jones, S.: Taking back the brain: could neurofeedback training be effective for relieving distressing auditory verbal hallucinations in patients with schizophrenia?. Schizophrenia bulletin, sbs006 (2012)
10. Escher, S., Romme, M., Buiks, A., Delespaul, P., Van Os, J.I.M.: Independent course of childhood auditory hallucinations: a sequential 3-year follow-up study. Br. J. Psychiatry **181**(43), s10–s18 (2002)
11. Green, M.F., Kinsbourne, M.: Subvocal activity and auditory hallucinations: Clues for behavioral treatments? Schizophr. Bull. **16**(4), 617 (1990)
12. Leeb, R., Sagha, H., Chavarriaga, R., del R Millan, J.: Multimodal fusion of muscle and brain signals for a hybrid-BCI. In: Engineering in Medicine and Biology Society (EMBC), 2010 Annual International Conference of the IEEE, pp. 4343–4346 (2010)
13. Coutaz, J., Nigay, L., Salber, D., Blandford, A., May, J., Young, R.M.: Four easy pieces for assessing the usability of multimodal interaction: the CARE properties. InterAct **95**, 115–120 (1995)
14. Taylor II, R.M., Hudson, T.C., Seeger, A., Weber, H., Juliano, J., Helser, A.T.: VRPN: a device-independent, network-transparent VR peripheral system. In: Proceedings of the ACM symposium on Virtual reality software and technology, pp. 55–61, ACM (2001)
15. Pfurtscheller, G., Aranibar, A.: Event-related cortical desynchronization detected by power measurements of scalp EEG. Electroencephalogr. Clin. Neurophysiol. **42**(6), 817–826 (1977)
16. Derambure, Ph, Defebvre, L., Bourriez, J.L., Cassim, F., Guieu, J.D.: Désynchronisation et synchronisation liées à l'évènement. Etude de la réactivité des rythmes électrocorticaux en relation avec la planification et l'évolution du mouvement volontaire. Neurophysiol. Clin. **29**, 53–70 (1999)
17. Bouche, P.: Electromyographie clinique. EMC – Neurol. **5**(3), 1–32 (2008)

18. Labarre-Vila, A.: Électromyographie de surface et fonction musculaire en pathologie. Revue Neurologique **162**(4), 459–465 (2006)
19. Lindeman, E., Spaans, F., Reulen, J.P., Leffers, P., Drukker, J.: Surface EMG of proximal leg muscles in neuromuscular patients and in healthy controls. Relations to force and fatigue. J. Electromyogr. Kinesiol. **9**(5), 299–307 (1999)
20. Yiu, E.M., Kornberg, A.J.: Duchenne muscular dystrophy. Neurology India. **56**(3), 236–247 (2008)
21. Zalewska, E., Hausmanowa-Petrusewicz, I.: Global and detailed features of motor unit potential in myogenic and neurogenic disorders. Med. Eng. Phys. **21**(6), 421–429 (1999)
22. Sonoo, M., Stålberg, E.: The ability of MUP parameters to discriminate between normal and neurogenic MUPs in concentric EMG: analysis of the MUP "thickness" and the proposal of "size index". Electroencephalography and Clinical Neurophysiology/Evoked Potentials Section **89**(5), 291–303 (1993)

Brain-in-the-Loop Learning Using fNIR and Simulated Virtual Reality Surgical Tasks: Hemodynamic and Behavioral Effects

Patricia A. Shewokis[1,2,3,4(✉)], Hasan Ayaz[1,2], Lucian Panait[3],
Yichuan Liu[1,2], Mashaal Syed[1,2], Lawrence Greenawald[3],
Faiz U. Shariff[3], Andres Castellanos[3], and D. Scott Lind[3]

[1] School of Biomedical Engineering, Science and Health Systems,
Drexel University, Philadelphia, PA 19104, USA
Shewokis@drexel.edu
[2] Cognitive Neuroengineering and Quantitative Experimental Research
(CONQUER) Collaborative, Drexel University, Philadelphia, PA 19104, USA
[3] Department of Surgery, College of Medicine, Drexel University, Philadelphia,
PA 19102, USA
[4] Nutrition Sciences Department, College of Nursing and Health Professions,
Drexel University, Philadelphia, PA 19102, USA

Abstract. Functional near infrared spectroscopy (fNIR) is a noninvasive, portable optical imaging tool to monitor changes in hemodynamic responses (i.e., oxygenated hemoglobin (HbO)) within the prefrontal cortex (PFC) in response to sensory, motor or cognitive activation. We used fNIR for monitoring PFC activation during learning of simulated laparoscopic surgical tasks throughout 4 days of training and testing. Blocked (BLK) and random (RND) practice orders were used to test the practice schedule effect on behavioral, hemodynamic responses and relative neural efficiency ($EFF_{rel-neural}$) measures during transfer. Left and right PFC for both tasks showed significant differences with RND using less HbO than BLK. Cognitive workload showed RND exhibiting high $EFF_{rel-neural}$ across the PFC for the *coordination* task while the more difficult *cholecystectomy* task showed $EFF_{rel-neural}$ differences only in the left PFC. Use of brain activation, behavioral and $EFF_{rel-neural}$ measures can provide a more accurate depiction of the generalization or transfer of learning.

Keywords: Cognitive effort and learning · fNIR · Simulation · Virtual reality · Transfer · Brain sensors and measures · Contextual interference

1 Introduction

Functional near infrared spectroscopy (fNIR) is a noninvasive, emergent optical imaging tool to monitor changes in hemodynamic responses (i.e., oxygenated hemoglobin (HbO)) within the prefrontal cortex (PFC) in response to sensory, motor or cognitive activation [1–6]. The PFC serves as the highest cortical area responsible for motor planning, organization and regulation and it plays an important role in the

© Springer International Publishing Switzerland 2015
D.D. Schmorrow and C.M. Fidopiastis (Eds.): AC 2015, LNAI 9183, pp. 324–335, 2015.
DOI: 10.1007/978-3-319-20816-9_31

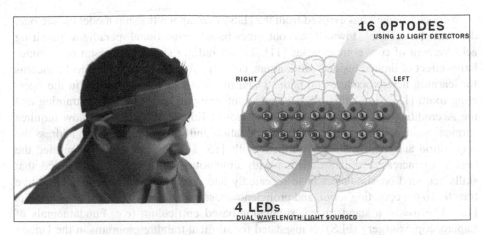

Fig. 1. Functional near infrared spectroscopy sensor (head band) covers forehead of participants (left) and sensor overlaid on brain image with sensor configuration of light sources, detectors and optodes (right).

integration of sensory and mnemonic information, the regulation of cognitive function and action, and works with other cortical circuits with executive functions including working memory [7]. fNIR (Fig. 1) is a portable brain imaging tool for the identification of neurophysiological markers of human learning and performance [4–6]. It can monitor brain activity in both ecologically valid environments (i.e., surgical suites, classrooms, offices) or in the laboratory. The use of portable, safe and accessible neuroimaging technologies, i.e., fNIR, allows for data collection to occur in real time settings thereby permitting the simultaneous testing of cognitive and motor task related brain activations along with behavioral performance metrics [4–6]. These hemodynamic brain activation biomarkers could lead to the development of training and assessment protocols that incorporate cognitive workload (i.e., mental effort via cortical processing) and behavioral performance measures for assessments of task and goal attainment [4].

Cognitive Load Theory (CLT) focuses on designing instructional methods and exemplars that enhance cognitive processing and facilitate the application of acquired skills and knowledge to novel situations or skills [8–10]. Paas and colleagues [8] differentiated between cognitive load, mental load and mental effort regarding CLT with *cognitive load* representing multiple dimensions associated with the burden a performed task imposes on a learner's cognitive system. *Mental load* is the section of cognitive load that reflects task demands interacting with learner characteristics (i.e., expertise level, abilities) while *mental effort* concerns the demands placed on the cognitive capacity to perform the task [8]. Paas [8] discussed the applications of relative instructional efficiency to different contexts along with the use of self-report measures of effort [9, 10] and some physiological measures (i.e., heart rate variability and eye movement tracking). However, no one has explicitly applied and assessed objective neural measures of cognitive effort with exception of Ayaz et al.'s work with Unmanned Aerial Vehicles [e.g., 22].

Surgical training has evolved from the Halstedian apprenticeship model of 'see one, do one, teach one' towards an outcomes-based educational paradigm requiring achievement of core competencies [11]. This paradigm shift is the result of a cumulative effect of limited resident work hours, concerns for patient safety, ethical concerns for learning new procedures on patients and the cost of resident training in the operating room [12]. Simulation has become an integral part of surgical skills training and the Accrediting Committee for Graduate Medical Education (ACGME) now requires surgical residency programs to include simulation and skills laboratories to address the acquisition and maintenance of surgical skills [13, 14]. Several studies identified the benefit of increased skill acquisition with simulation training. Stefanidis noted that skills acquired on simulators have repeatedly and consistently demonstrated positive transfer to the operating room, and proficiency-based training maximizes these benefits [15]. The use of a standardized, simulation-based curriculum (e.g. Fundamentals of Laparoscopic Surgery (FLS)) is mandated for surgical training programs in the United States. While there are a myriad of studies establishing the efficacy of simulation in teaching operative skill, there is no consensus on the ideal practice model for the most efficient method of acquiring these skills. The use of educational and movement science theories in the development of curricula for teaching surgical skills is a relatively new concept in the surgical literature; as well the use of neurophysiological markers in the evaluation of skill acquisition is equally novel.

Practice organization when acquiring multiple tasks is a learning phenomenon called the contextual interference effect, which incorporates, blocked (BLK) and random (RND) practice schedules into the specific order the learner will perform the tasks during the acquisition phase [16–18]. Low contextual interference (BLK practice) is created when the tasks to be learned are presented in a predictable order while high contextual interference (RND practice) occurs when the tasks to be learned are presented in a non-sequential, unpredictable order. Laparoscopic training curricula utilize BLK orders where trainees perform the same task for a fixed number of times, or until a predefined proficiency level is achieved, before being allowed to move to the next task in the curriculum [19]. Given the natural training environment of surgical skill curricula combined with the importance of patient safety and high performance accuracy under stress (i.e., cognitive workload), we conducted an experiment to test brain measures of cortical activation, selected behavioral performance metrics and cognitive workload when five different surgical laparoscopy simulation tasks were acquired with different practice schedules. The specific aim of this pilot study is to identify brain based biomarkers of neural activity and cognitive workload of transfer of learning using simulated laparoscopic surgical tasks performed in a virtual environment.

2 Methods

2.1 Participants and Experimental Protocol

Fifteen medical students between the ages 24 to 28 years volunteered for the study. Three were rejected due to technical issues during recording and missing sessions and another was rejected during transfer for poor data quality on the majority of the optodes. Eleven medical students with no previous exposure to laparoscopic surgery were randomly assigned to either a BLK ($n = 2_F$; $n = 3_M$) or RND ($n = 2_F$; $n = 4_M$) practice order using a virtual reality (VR) laparoscopic simulator (LAPSIM®). The medical students provided written informed consent for participation in the study via a Drexel University Institutional Review Board approved protocol. All participants were medication-free, with normal or corrected-to-normal vision.

Each student performed 36 acquisition trials each of three VR laparoscopic tasks (i.e., *camera navigation, grasping* and *fine dissection*) across three days and approximately 72 h following acquisition, 6 retention (2 each of the acquisition tasks) and 6 transfer trials ("*coordination*" – involved *camera navigation* and *grasping* tasks; "*cholecystectomy*" - dissection, application of clips and cutting vessels using scissors). PFC activity was monitored during all phases for 16 optode sites using fNIR.

2.2   Simulation Tasks

A total of five tasks from the LapSim 2013 Simulator (www.surgical-science.com) were used in this study (See Table 1 for an image and description of each task). These tasks represented the basic laparoscopy skills a surgeon would perform during an operation (*Camera Navigation, Lifting and Grasping* and *Fine Dissection*), and also serve as a comprehensive basis for the participant to complete the two transfer tasks, *Coordination* and *Cholecystectomy* (removal of the gallbladder), on day 4 of the experiment.

2.3   Data Collection

The optical brain imaging data was recorded using a continuous wave fNIR system (fNIR Devices LLC; www.fnirdevices.com) that has a flexible wearable sensor pad,

Table 1. Descriptions and images of the laparoscopic tasks from LAPSIM®

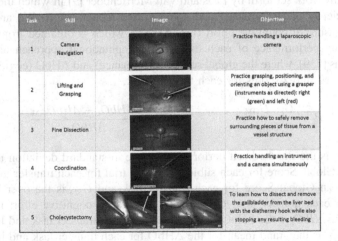

Task	Skill	Image	Objective
1	Camera Navigation		Practice handling a laparoscopic camera
2	Lifting and Grasping		Practice grasping, positioning, and orienting an object using a grasper (instruments as directed): right (green) and left (red)
3	Fine Dissection		Practice how to safely remove surrounding pieces of tissue from a vessel structure
4	Coordination		Practice handling an instrument and a camera simultaneously
5	Cholecystectomy		To learn how to dissect and remove the gallbladder from the liver bed with the diathermy hook while also stopping any resulting bleeding

hardware control box and data collection computer. The sensor houses 4 light sources with built in peak wavelengths at 730 nm and 850 nm and 10 detectors designed to sample cortical areas underlying the forehead. With a fixed source detector separation of 2.5 cm and a rectangular grid layout, sensor samples from 16 measurement locations (optodes) were collected and assessed (see Fig. 1) [4, 18]. For data acquisition and visualization, COBI Studio software [18] (Drexel University) was used on the data collection laptop with the sampling rate of the system was 2 Hz. During the task, the start and end of each session and simulation task were marked on the fNIR computer for time synchronization during post-processing [20].

2.4 Signal Processing

Raw light intensity signals were first visually inspected to reject problematic optodes such as over hairlines or bad optical coupling. To reject portions of the data with motion artifact contamination, an automated sliding window motion artifact (SMAR) algorithm [21] that uses a coefficient of variation-based approach was adopted. To eliminate the high frequency noise and physiological artifacts, such as heart rate and respiration rate, a low-pass finite impulse response filter of cut-off frequency 0.1 Hz and a 20th order was applied to raw light intensity data.

Hemodynamic changes (ΔHbO) within the anterior PFC for all optodes were calculated using the Modified Beer Lambert Law [4]. The data epochs for each surgery simulation trial were then extracted using time synchronization markers and they were baseline corrected with respect to the start of the trial.

2.5 Relative Neural Efficiency Analyses

A multidimensional computational approach was used to simultaneously evaluate behavioral performance and a neural measure of cognitive effort during performance using the framework set forth by Paas and van Merriënboer [9] in which they assessed relative efficiency of performance and self-reported mental effort. We are using an objective measure of cognitive effort (i.e., ΔHbO), which is obtained from each participant during performance of each trial. Our computational approach uses the 2D model of Paas [8, 9], where the global score (performance) and ΔHbO (cognitive effort) are standardized into z-scores for each transfer task.

$$P_z = \frac{G_i - G_{GM}}{G_{SD}} \qquad CE_z = \frac{\Delta HbO_i - \Delta HbO_{GM}}{\Delta HbO_{SD}}. \qquad (1)$$

Where P_z is the standardized performance score in standard deviation units, G_i is the Global Score for each subject for each trial for each transfer task. G_{GM} is the grand mean Global Score for each transfer task and G_{SD} is the overall standard deviation for each transfer task. CE_z is the standardized cognitive effort in standard deviation units, HbO_i is the ΔHbO for each subject, trial, transfer task and left or right PFC, ΔHbO_{GM} is the grand mean for the ΔHbO for each transfer task and left or right

PFC while ΔHbO_{SD} is the overall standard deviation for each transfer task and left or right PFC.

This equation is based on calculating the perpendicular distance of a point (CE_z, P_z) defined by the cognitive effort and performance for each practice schedule for each transfer task on the CE_z - P_z axis to a zero relative neural efficiency line (EFF = 0) where $CE_z = P_z$. Given the line is $P_z - CE_z = 0$, to determine the distance from the zero relative neural efficiency line (E = 0) to the point with coordinates (e.g., CE_z -RA-Coordination- LPFC, P_z -RA-Coordination), the equation for the distance for the relative neural efficiency score, $EFF_{rel\text{-}neural}$ is then computed for each participant:

$$EFF_{rel-neural} = \frac{P_z - CE_z(2)}{\sqrt{2}} \tag{2}$$

2.6 Data Analysis

Dependent measures included relative changes in mean ΔHbO and $EFF_{rel\text{-}neural}$ for the left and right PFCs; and a behavioral performance metric of a global score (percentage reflecting the time, instrument path length and accuracy of performance of the task) during transfer for the *coordination* and *cholecystectomy* surgical VR tasks. We assessed if the data met the assumptions of normality and homogeneity of variance for all dependent measures. Non-parametric randomization tests with 10,000 Monte Carlo samples were used to determine if there were differences between BLK vs RND practice orders for each task separately. If the data were non-normally distributed, we used a Mann-Whitney U non-parametric test. Effect sizes were calculated and used to aid in interpretation of the data. The significance criterion for all tests was set at $\alpha = 0.05$. Number Cruncher Statistical Software (NCSS; www.ncss.com) was used for the analyses.

3 Results

We hypothesized that during transfer there will be higher relative neural efficiency, higher behavioral performance metrics, and lower HbO hemodynamic responses with RND practice compared to BLK. For the *coordination* and *cholecystectomy* VR tasks, the behavioral, ΔHbO and $Eff_{rel\text{-}neural}$ measures descriptive statistics, confidence intervals and effect sizes are reported in Table 2.

3.1 Behavioral Results

For both tasks, the behavioral measure descriptive statistics, confidence intervals and effect sizes are reported in Table 2. The *coordination* task Global Score (%) approached significance [$t_{(31)} = -1.89$, p = 0.068] with RND averaging better than the passing score (80 %) relative to BLK. For the *cholecystectomy* task, there were no practice schedule differences for the Global Score (%) [$t_{(31)} = 0.237$, p = 0.827] .

Table 2. Descriptive statistics of the *coordination* and *cholecystectomy* simulated laparoscopic virtual reality (VR) transfer tasks for changes in hemodynamics (oxygenated hemoglobin (ΔHbO) (μm), behavioral (global scores (%)) and relative neural efficiency (Effrel-neural) measures across practice schedules.

Coordination VR Task						
Dependent Variable	Practice Schedule	Mean	± SD	CI[1] (LL	UL)	ES[2]
Global Score (%)	BLK	77.333	12.585	70.341	84.302	0.73
	RND	84.944	10.563	79.693	90.202	
ΔHbO (left)	BLK	0.235	1.320	-0.495	0.966	1.31
	RND	-1.578	1.680	-2.129,	-1.027	
ΔHbO (right)	BLK	0.610	0.945	0.087	1.134	2.55
	RND	-1.391	0.802	-1.790	-0.992	
Effrel-neural (left)	BLK	-0.686	0.701	-1.074	-0.292	-1.86
	RND	0.571	0.785	0.181	0.962	
Effrel-neural (right)	BLK	-0.802	0.719	-1.201	-0.404	-2.04
	RND	0.669	0.855	0.244	1.094	

Cholecystectomy VR Task						
Dependent Variable	Practice Schedule	Mean	± SD	CI[1] (LL	UL)	ES[2]
Global Score (%)	BLK	76.600	14.272	68.702	84.504	0.09
	RND	74.944	23.740	63.141	86.750	
ΔHbO (left)	BLK	1.178	1.820	0.776	2.726	0.79
	RND	-0.061	1.671	-0.920	0.798	
ΔHbO (right)	BLK	1.198	2.234	0.751	3.225	0.61
	RND	0.127	1.700	-0.747	1.001	
Effrel-neural (left)	BLK	-0.313	0.954	-0.841	0.215	-0.59
	RND	0.276	1.199	-0.320	0.873	
Effrel-neural (right)	BLK	-0.292	0.977	-0.834	0.249	-0.55
	RND	0.266	1.211	-0.357	0.888	

KEY: BLK- Blocked; RND-Random; ΔHbO – change in mean oxygenated hemoglobin (μmolar);   Effrel-neural -relative neural efficiency.   [1] Confidence Intervals (95%) with the lower limit (LL) and upper limit (UL) for each practice schedule and variable. [2]Effect sizes (ES) reflects RND-BLK differences/pooled SD. A positive value indicates an advantage for RND for the Global Score and ΔHbO while positive values for the relative neural efficiency measures (Effrel-neural) indicate a disadvantage for RND relative to BLK.

3.2 fNIR Measures

In this paper, the optodes of the PFC are averaged across the left (average of optodes #1-#8) and right (average of optodes #9-#16 – see Fig. #1) regions with mean (μmolar) values assessed for all transfer trials for the *coordination* and *cholecystectomy* tasks. The mean ΔHbO was significant for both the left and right PFCs [$t_{(31)} = 4.29$, $p < 0.001$ and $t_{(31)} = 6.98$, $p < 0.001$] for the *coordination* VR task with RND having substantially lower HbO values than BLK. In addition, for the *cholecystectomy* VR task, there were significant differences between the RND and BLK practice orders for both the left and right PFCs [$t_{(31)}$ = 2.88, p = 0.007 and $t_{(30)}$ = 2.67, p = 0.012], respectively.

Depicted in Fig. 2 are the mean ΔHbO differences for BLK-RND plotted as a function of the two tasks for the left and right PFCs. During transfer of the *coordination* task, RND practice exhibited large effects (see Table 2) and lower means HbO values than BLK practice for the left and right PFCs. For the more difficult *cholecystectomy* task RND and BLK practice differences were detected however the magnitude of the differences were smaller.

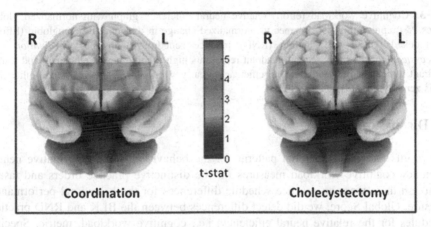

Fig. 2. Topographical map [20] of contrast t-tests ($t_{(25)}$ ≤ 2.206, p ≤ 0.05, 2-tailed) of the mean change in oxygenated hemoglobin (μmolar) for the *coordination* and *cholecystectomy* tasks. Contrasts represent average blocked (BLK) – random (RND) differences.

3.3   Cognitive Workload: Relative Neural Efficiency Analyses

The mean EFF$_{rel-neural}$ was significant for both the left and right PFCs [$t_{(31)}$ = 4.81, p < 0.001 and $t_{(31)}$ = −5.28, p < 0.001] for the *coordination* VR task with RND having very large effects and high relative neural efficiency compared to the low relative neural efficiency for the BLK practice order (see Table 2). In addition, for the *cholecystectomy* VR task, there were significant differences between the RND and BLK practice orders for the left PFC [Z = −1.97, p = 0.049] while the right PFC was just below significance [Z = −1.95, p = 0.054].

In the relative neural efficiency graphs, the fourth quadrant represents low efficiency, where low performance is achieved with high cognitive effort. The second quadrant represents high efficiency where high performance is attained with low cognitive effort. The diagonal y = x is the neutral axis, where relative neural efficiency (Eff$_{rel-neural}$ = 0) representing equal cognitive effort and performance. To determine if there are significant differences in Eff$_{rel-neural}$, we tested the Euclidian distance differences between practice schedules for each transfer task within each PFC. The EFF$_{rel-neural}$ for each task and practice schedule within each PFC are depicted in Fig. 3.

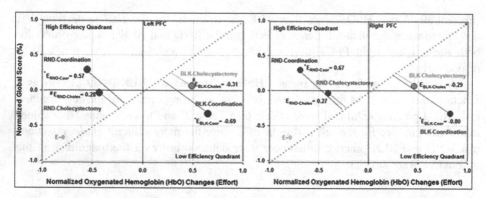

Fig. 3. Cognitive workload (effort) relative neural efficiency graph with normalized global scores (%) representing performance vs. normalized change in oxygenated hemoglobin (Effort) for blocked (BLK) and random (RND) practice schedules with the *coordination* and *cholecystectomy* tasks. the second quadrant represents high relative neural efficiency and fourth quadrant indicates low relative neural efficiency area. y = x is where relative neural efficiency (E) is zero. *(p < 0.001), # (p < 0.05).

4 Discussion

Our results indicate differential patterns for the behavioral, fNIR and relative neural efficiency cognitive workload measures for the distinctive practice orders and tasks. Although there were no practice schedule differences for the behavioral performance measure, Global Score, we did detect differences between the BLK and RND practice schedules for the relative neural efficiency, i.e., cognitive workload, metric. Specifically, in the *coordination* VR surgical task, for the left and right PFCs, RND had higher relative neural efficiency, which means that the learners performed the task with less cognitive load (minimum effort) and with a better performance score (maximum performance) than those learners who acquired the tasks in a BLK practice order (Fig. 3). For the *cholecystectomy* VR surgical task, RND practice had high relative neural efficiency relative to the BLK practice only in the left PFC. These results assist us in understanding the process of learning as mediated by task difficulty, behavioral performance and neurophysiological measures. The *coordination* VR task (see Table 1) can be thought of as a task that represents **interpolation** of the tasks and subtasks that were acquired during acquisition while the *cholecystectomy* VR task represents **extrapolation** of the acquisition tasks and subtasks. Acquiring tasks (*camera navigation, grasp and lift, fine dissection* – see Table 1) under a RND practice order facilitated the same cognitive and behavioral processes that were needed to perform the *coordination* and *cholecystectomy* tasks in transfer, which resulted in higher performance and lower cognitive effort relative to the BLK practice order. Our findings support our hypothesis that RND practice facilitates generalization by better performance and lower neural demands (i.e., cognitive effort) during transfer of simulated laparoscopic surgical tasks.

Our results provide preliminary information about fNIR measures of the anterior PFC hemodynamic response and its relationship to generalizations of skill learning or transfer of surgical laparoscopic tasks in a VR environment. These findings are comparable to those noted by Shewokis and colleagues [5, 18, 26] using fNIR and 3-D spatial navigation tasks and 3-D UAV piloting tasks [22]. In addition, using fMRI, Wymbs and Grafton [23] reported that the left inferior frontal gyrus was differentially activated during late learning as a function of practice schedule for the sequence execution of a go/no-go task. Shewokis et al. [26] showed transfer results illustrating that there is a differential relative mean oxygenation of the left inferior frontal gyrus region (optode #2) for RND and BLK practice orders for spatial navigation tasks. These results help to extend our understanding of the contextual interference effect regarding the influences of the practice order and task type on neural function [5, 17, 18, 23–26].

Since fNIR technology allows the development of mobile, non-intrusive and miniaturized devices, it has the potential to be used in future learning/training environments to provide objective, task related brain-based measures for assessing cognitive workload and neural processing efficiency via different tasks, practice and feedback variables and allow for optimization of the learning process [27]. More importantly, we can observe the impact of positive transfer for tasks (i.e., *coordination* and *cholecystectomy* VR laparoscopy tasks) which illustrate the how learners integrate the processes they used as they learned multiple skills in a novel environment. Our findings support Stephanidis [15] and set the stage for additional learning scenarios within surgery training and medical education [12].

Incorporating brain-in-the loop learning during practice and testing assessments can lead to developing highly efficient and targeted learning/training programs that can adapt based on the learners' state. Preliminary results indicate that fNIR can be used to capture practice effects on performers. Moreover, given fNIR's qualities of portability and safety, this optical imaging modality is well suited for constructing learning assessments and protocols that meet the demands of 21st century learning environments (e.g., simulators, VR, online models, brain computer interfaces and so forth).

Acknowledgement. This study was funded in part under a Drexel University College of Medicine and International Blue Cross Seed Grant #1312002473 (Panait, PI) and National Science Foundation (NSF) grant IIS: 1064871 (Shewokis, PI).

References

1. Chance, B., Zhuang, Z., UnAh, C., Alter, C., Lipton, L.: Cognition-activated low-frequency modulation of light absorption in human brain. Proc. Natl. Acad. Sci. USA **90**, 3770–3774 (1993)
2. Strangman, G., Boas, D.A., Sutton, P.J.: Non-invasive neuroimaging using near-infrared light. Biol. Psychiatry **52**, 679–693 (2002)
3. Chance, B., Villringer, A.: Non-invasive optical spectroscopy and imaging of human brain function. Trends Neurosci. **20**, 435–442 (1997)
4. Ayaz, H., Shewokis, P.A., Bunce, S., Izzetoglu, K., Willems, B., Onaral, B.: Optical brain monitoring for operator training and mental workload assessment. Neuroimage **59**, 36–47 (2012)

5. Shewokis, P.A., Ayaz, H., Izzetoglu, M., Bunce, S., Gentili, R.J., Sela, I., Izzetoglu, K., Onaral, B.: Brain in the loop: assessing learning using fnir in cognitive and motor tasks. In: Schmorrow, D.D., Fidopiastis, C.M. (eds.) FAC 2011. LNCS, vol. 6780, pp. 240–249. Springer, Heidelberg (2011)
6. Gentili, R.J., Shewokis, P.A., Ayaz, H., Contreras-Vidal, J.L.: Functional near-infrared spectroscopy-based correlates of prefrontal cortical dynamics during a cognitive-motor executive adaptation task. Front. Hum. Neurosci. 7, 1–13 (2013). doi:10.3389/fnhum.2013. 00277
7. Procyk, E., Goldman-Rakic, P.S.: Modulation of dorsolateral prefrontal delay activity during self-organized behavior. J. Neurosci. 26, 11313–11323 (2006)
8. Paas, F., Tuovinen, J., Tabbers, H., Van Gerven, P.W.: Cognitive load measurement as a means to advance cognitive load theory. Educ. Psychol. 38, 63–71 (2003)
9. Paas, F., van Merrienboer, J.J.G.: The efficiency of instructional conditions: an approach to combine mental effort and performance measures. Hum. Factors 35, 737–743 (1993)
10. Sweller, J., van Merrienboer, J.J.G., Paas, F.: Cognitive architecture and instructional design. Educ. Psychol. Rev. 10, 251–296 (1998)
11. Osborne, M.P.: William Stewart Halsted: his life and contributions to surgery. Lancet Oncol. 8, 256–265 (2007)
12. Cox, M., Irby, D.M., Reznick, R.K., MacRae, H.: Medical education: teaching surgical skills – changes in the wind. N. Engl. J. Med. 355, 2664–2669 (2006)
13. Lossing, A.G., Hatswell, E.M., Gilas, T., Reznick, R.K., Smith, L.C.: A technical-skills course for 1st-year residents in general surgery: a descriptive study. Can. J. Surg. 35(5), 536–540 (1992)
14. Bridges, M., Diamond, D.L.: The financial impact of teaching surgical residents in the operating room. Am. J. Surg. 177, 28–32 (1999)
15. Stefanidis, D., Sevdalis, N., Paige, J., Zevin, B., Aggarwal, R., Grantcharov, T., Jones, D.B.: Simulation in surgery: what's needed next? Ann. Surg. 261, 1–8 (2014)
16. Magill, R.A., Hall, K.G.: A review of the contextual interference effect in motor skill acquisition. Hum. Mov. Sci. 9, 241–289 (1990)
17. Shewokis, P.A.: Memory consolidation and contextual interference effects with computer games. Percept. Mot. Skills 97, 581–589 (2003)
18. Ayaz, H., Shewokis, P.A., Curtin, A., Izzetoglu, M., Izzetoglu, K., Onaral, B.: Using MazeSuite and functional near infrared spectroscopy to study learning in spatial navigation. J. Vis. Exp. 56, 1–12 (2011)
19. Palter, V.N., Orzech, N., Reznick, R.K., Grantcharov, T.P.: Validation of a structured training and assessment curriculum for technical skill acquisition in minimally invasive surgery a randomized controlled trial. Ann. Surg. 257, 224–230 (2013)
20. Ayaz, H., Izzetoglu, M., Platek, S.M., Bunce, S., Izzetoglu, K., Pourezaei, K., Onaral, B.: Registering fNIR data to brain surface image using MRI templates. In: 28th IEEE EMBS Annual International Conference, pp. 2671–2674, New York City (2006)
21. Ayaz, H., Izzetoglu, M., Shewokis, P.A., Onaral, B.: Sliding-window motion artifact rejection for functional near-infrared spectroscopy. In: 32nd Annual International Conference of the IEEE EMBS, pp. 6567–6570, Buenos Aires, Argentina (2010)
22. Ayaz, H., Çakır, M.P., Izzetoglu, K., Curtin, A., Shewokis, P.A., Bunce, S., Onaral, B.: Monitoring Expertise Development during Simulated UAV Piloting Tasks using Optical Brain Imaging. In: 2012 IEEE Aerosp Conference, pp. 1–11, Big Sky, Montana (2012)
23. Wymbs, N.F., Grafton, S.T.: Neural substrates of practice structure that support future off-line learning. J. Neurophysiol. 102, 2462–2476 (2009)
24. Hatakenaka, M., Miyai, I., Mihara, M., Sakoda, S., Kubota, K.: Frontal regions involved in learning of motor skill - A functional NIRS study. Neuroimage 34, 109–116 (2007)

25. Leff, D.R., Elwell, C.E., Orihuela-Espina, F., Atallah, L., Delpy, D.T., Darzi, A.W., Yang, G.Z.: Changes in prefrontal cortical behaviour depend upon familiarity on a bimanual co-ordination task: An fNIRS study. Neuroimage **39**, 805–813 (2008)
26. Shewokis, P.A., Ayaz, H., Curtin, A., Izzetoglu, K., Onaral, B.: Brain in the loop learning using functional near infrared spectroscopy. In: Schmorrow, D.D., Fidopiastis, C.M. (eds.) AC 2013. LNCS, vol. 8027, pp. 381–389. Springer, Heidelberg (2013)
27. Ayaz, H., Onaral, B., Izzetoglu, K., Shewokis, P.A., McKendrick, R., Parasuraman, R.: Continuous monitoring of brain dynamics with functional near infrared spectroscopy as a tool for neuroergonomic research: empirical examples and a technological development. Front. Hum. Neurosci. **7**, 1–13 (2013)

Team Resilience: A Neurodynamic Perspective

Ronald Stevens[1,2(✉)], Trysha Galloway[2], Jerry Lamb[3],
Ronald Steed[4], and Cynthia Lamb[5]

[1] IMMEX/UCLA, Los Angeles, CA, USA
immex_ron@hotmail.com
[2] The Learning Chameleon, Inc., Los Angeles, CA, USA
trysha@teamneurodynamics.com
[3] Naval Submarine Medical Research Laboratory, Groton, CT, USA
jerry.lamb@med.navy.mil
[4] UpScope Consulting, Inc., Mystic, CT, USA
ronaldsteed@gmail.com
[5] URS Federal Services, Inc., San Francisco, CA, USA
cynthia.lamb@urs.com

Abstract. Neurophysiologic models were created from US Navy navigation teams performing required simulations that captured their dynamic responses to the changing task environment. Their performances were simultaneously rated by two expert observers for team resilience using a team process rubric adopted by the US Navy Submarine Force. Symbolic neurodynamic (NS) representations of the 1–40 Hz EEG amplitude fluctuations of the crew were created each second displaying the EEG levels of each team member in the context of the other crew members and in the context of the task. Quantitative estimates of the NS fluctuations were made using a moving window of entropy. Periods of decreased entropy were considered times of increased team neurodynamic organization; e.g. when there were prolonged and restricted relationships between the EEG- PSD levels of the crew. Resilient teams showed significantly *greater* neurodynamic organization in the pre-simulation Briefing than the less resilient teams. Most of these neurodynamic organizations occurred in the 25 –40 Hz PSD bins. In contrast, the more resilient teams showed significantly *lower* neurodynamic organization during the Scenario than the less resilient teams with the greatest differences in the 12–20 Hz PSD bins. The results indicate that the degree of neurodynamic organization reflects the performance dynamics of the team with more organization being important during the pre-mission briefing while less organization (i.e. more flexibility) important while performing the task.

Keywords: Team neurodynamics · Resilience · EEG · Submarine

1 Introduction

Resilience is a construct that is not well understood in individuals and teams. As a phenomena, resilience is closely tied to the cognitive concepts of attention, memory and decision making, all of which show decrements during stressful conditions [1]. Estimates of the level of team resilience can be made from the short-term decisions and

© Springer International Publishing Switzerland 2015
D.D. Schmorrow and C.M. Fidopiastis (Eds.): AC 2015, LNAI 9183, pp. 336–347, 2015.
DOI: 10.1007/978-3-319-20816-9_32

communications that a team makes, and in time these accumulate into more accurate estimates. What is needed however, are more prospective explanations of teams' responses to disruptions of their rhythm that can illuminate new paths for team assessment and training. These explanations will likely come from descriptions of resilience that are linked to physiologic understandings of individual and team responses to stress.

One way to search for these explanations would be to focus on fundamental biologic and physical principles and computations that dynamically expand into cognitive and behavioral processes that guide teamwork across large scales of training and performance [2]. Rhythm may be one such principle for teams. Scientifically, over shorter periods of time the fluctuating rhythms of teams manifest as a fractal structuring of communication [3], or as the multifractal structure of team neurodynamic rhythms [4]. Disruptions to ongoing team rhythms often occur at major task junctions or when the resilience of a team is challenged [5]. These events force teams to adapt by changing their 'normal' operating rhythm. These changes in team rhythms following adaptive behavior are often nonlinear and punctuated by the emergence of new organizational structures and the establishment of new rhythms [5]. The important point is that rhythms do not arise de novo in a team, i.e. the initiation of a team rhythm requires interaction with both a task as well as other team members.

For several years we have focused on developing team-wide temporal data streams using symbolic representations of various neurodynamic measures. These studies have shown that (1) the neurodynamic rhythms of six-person US Navy submarine navigation teams are measurable and entrained by the task [6], (2) the structure of these rhythms is multifractal, resulting from the meso and micro responses of teams to changes in the task and the sharing of information across the crew [4], and (3) quantitative differences in team's neurodynamic rhythms may be linked with team expertise. Consistent with the nonlinear dynamical systems concepts of elasticity and rigidity in complex adaptive systems [7], the expert navigation teams were positioned at a neurodynamic point midway between rigid and elastic organization [5, 8]. These findings suggest the existence of fundamental processes related to neurodynamical rhythm and organization that quantitatively track across the novice-expert continuum.

In this study we take advantage of naturally occurring perturbations to team function to link neurodynamic measures of within and across-brain team activities with observational measures of team performance. This study became possible when the Naval Submarine Medical Research Laboratory (NSMRL) began an extensive effort to provide the Submarine Force with a way to improve operational performance by not focusing on human error per se, but on human variability which not only considers the action, but also the context within that action occurred [9, 10]. The result was the development of the Submarine Team Behaviors Tool (STBT) which provides an observational means for measuring team performance (Submarine Team Behaviors Tool Instruction Manual, COMSUBLANT / COMSUBPAC N7, December 6, 2013). Our goal was to link the information / organization structures in neurodynamic data streams with expert observational ratings as a way for understanding the neurophysiologic basis of team resilience.

2 Methods

2.1 Submarine Piloting and Navigation Simulations (SPAN)

Each SPAN session contains three segments. First there is a Briefing ($\sim$ 10–30 min) where the training goals of the mission are presented along with the ship's position, other contacts in the area, weather, sea state and the Captain's orders for safe operation. The Scenario ($\sim$ 50–120 min) follows and is a more dynamic task containing easily identified processes of teamwork along with other processes less well defined. The Debrief section ($\sim$ 20–30 min) is an open discussion of what worked, what other options were available and long and short term lessons. The Debrief is the most structured training with individual team member reports. The task for the team was to safely pilot the submarine to /from a harbor while avoiding collisions and groundings. While functioning as a team, officers also had individual task responsibilities that helped determine the position of the ship and possible hazards; for instance the radar operator continually adjusted the radar scope, identified and tracked ships and hazards, and maintained a mental model of the situation.

2.2 Submarine Team Behaviors Tool (STBT)

Development of the STBT originated as a study of submarine mishaps to understand the impacts of emerging complexity on human performance. During the study, certain team performance factors were found that degraded the performance of submarine tactical watch teams. Research at the Naval Submarine Medical Research Laboratory (NSMRL) in Groton, CT indicated that, in addition to technical skills, deliberate and effective team practices are necessary to manage the wide variety of increasingly complex problems that occur during tactical operations. The intent was to go beyond the typical lessons learned about human error and provide the Submarine Force with a way to improve operational performance going forward by not focusing on human error per se, but on human variability which not only considers the action, but also the context within that action occurred [9]. The result was the development of the Submarine Training Behaviors Tool (STBT) which provides an observational means for measuring team performance.

The STBT was accepted by the Submarine Force in late 2013; the near-term objectives for this initiative included improving the quality and consistency of feedback provided to submarine Commanding Officers regarding their teams' performance, providing a model of what 'good' looks like for crews to aspire to, and defining an end state to guide additions to the existing training continuum.

In developing an overall behavioral rating of team resilience, the STBT observers evaluated teams across a set of five practices that have provided new insights into how submarine tactical teams need to operate at sea. When one or more of these practices were absent, team problem solving suffered in some important way. These practices included Dialogue, Decision Making, Critical Thinking, Bench Strength and Problem-Solving Capacity. Each practice contained multiple behavior threads. For Decision Making these were Decisiveness & Leader Detachment while for Critical

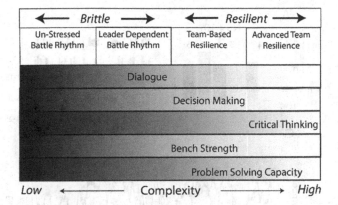

Fig. 1. Overview of STBT ratings. The levels of team resilience (in descending order) were (1) Advanced Team Resilience where the teams could manage multiple dynamic problems; (2) Team-based Resilience where routine activities can be managed even during stress; (3) Leader-dependent battle rhythm where the teams retain their rhythm even under stress, but only because someone takes charge, and; (4) Unstressed battle rhythm where teams exhibit a rhythm, but only in the absence of disruptions. Evaluator rankings were made on a scale from 0 (low) to 4 (high) and the reliability between the two evaluators was 0.89.

Thinking these were Planning & Time Horizon, Setting Context, Managing Complexity, and Forceful Backup, etc. The presence / absence of these practices were linked to four Resilience Levels describing how teams of different experience perform in environments of different complexities (Fig. 1).

2.3 Electroencephalography (EEG)

The X-10 wireless headset from Advanced Brain Monitoring, Inc. (ABM) was used for data collection. This wireless EEG headset system included sensor site locations: F3, F4, C3, C4, P3, P4, Fz, Cz, POz in a monopolar configuration referenced to linked mastoids; bipolar derivations were included which have been reported to reflect sensorimotor activity (FzC3) [11], workload (F3Cz, C3C4) [12], and alpha wave components of the human mirror neuron system [13]. Embedded within the EEG data stream from each team member were eye blinks which were automatically detected and decontaminated using interpolation algorithms contained in the EEG acquisition software [14]. The EEG power spectral density (PSD) values were computed each second at each sensor for the 1–40 Hz frequency bins by the B-Alert Lab PSD Analysis software.

2.4 Modeling Neurodynamic Symbol Streams

Our goal was to develop neurodynamic data streams that had internal structure(s) with temporal information about the present and past organization, function and performance of the teams. Treating data from multiple time series as symbols is one approach

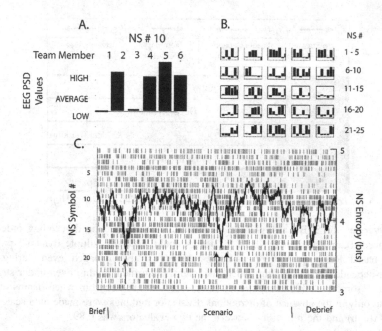

Fig. 2. Steps for extracting low-dimensional, single-trial neurodynamic organization information from the 10 Hz EEG levels of a six-member submarine navigation teams. (a) This symbol represents times when crew members 1 & 3 had below average 10 Hz EEG levels and the remaining crew had above average levels. For this example the 10 Hz PSD values was chosen. (b) The twenty-five-symbol state space is shown with the symbols assigned numbers in rows. (c) Each row represents the expression of the twenty-five NS from the 10 Hz frequency bin. These patterns are overlaid with a trace of the Shannon entropy of the NS symbol stream.

that has been useful for discovering data patterns in temporal data streams [15, 16]. For team dynamics, the state of the team can be represented by a symbol showing the relative EEG marker levels for each person (Fig. 2a). The importance of a symbolic team representation is that it shows the marker levels for each team member, the level in the context of the levels of other team members being studied, and associates it with the changing context of the task.

The temporal expression of these symbols for a SPAN performance is shown in Fig. 2c where each row shows the temporal expression of the twenty-five NS symbols; the expression of was not uniform. The first large NS entropy fluctuation (single arrow) was linked with an increased expression of NS #15-16 and the near absence of NS #11−12. Referring to Fig. 2b NS #11−12 represented periods when many crew members had high 10 Hz EEG levels while NS #15−16 represented times when 10 Hz EEG power levels were low across the team. The second fluctuation (double arrows) showed a reciprocal expression with increased NS #9−11 and decreased NS #15−16. Quantitative estimates of the changing symbol dynamics are shown by the trace in Fig. 2c; these estimates were calculated and quantitated by measuring the Shannon entropy over a sliding window of 100 s [5, 17]. Performance segments with restricted symbol expression had lower entropy levels, while segments with greater symbol diversity had higher entropy. As reference points, the maximum entropy for 25 symbols is 4.64, which decreases to 4.0 when only 16 symbols are expressed. Periods of decreased entropy were operationally considered as times of increased neurodynamic organization across the team.

3 Results

3.1 NS Entropy /Frequency Profiles for SPAN Segments

The NS entropy levels for twelve SPAN teams were determined for the Briefing, Scenario and Debriefing segments across the 1-40 Hz EEG frequency bands (Fig. 3). The highest average NS entropy (i.e. the least team neurodynamic organization) occurred in the Scenario segments while significantly lower entropy levels (i.e. more team neurodynamic organization) were observed in the Brief and Debrief segments $(F = 3.52, df = 2, p = 0.04)$.

The NS entropy profiles were the highest at the lower (3-7 Hz) frequencies and progressively decreased towards the 40 Hz band. In each of the three training segments there was also a significant NS entropy decrease associated with the 8-13 Hz frequency region (i.e. the α band) with the NS entropy in the 10 Hz PSD bin being significantly less in the Debriefings than in the Briefings or Scenarios (F = 7.88, df = 2, p = 0.002). Surrogate data testing was performed in all experiments. In this process the symbols in the NS data streams were randomized before calculating the entropy; as expected, this uniformly removed the NS entropy fluctuations.

3.2 Correlations Between NS Entropy and STBT Ratings

The combined data from the twelve STBT teams in Fig. 3 suggested that neurodynamic organizations were frequent during SPAN teamwork, raising the question of whether

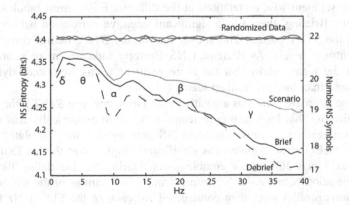

Fig. 3. EEG frequency profiles team NS entropy and averaged PSD levels. The NS entropy streams from twelve SPAN performances were separated into the Brief, Scenario and Debrief segments and the frequency-entropy profiles were generated.

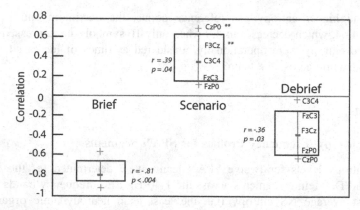

Fig. 4. Correlations between STBT ratings and NS entropy levels. The NS entropy levels for the C3C4, FzP0, FzC3, CzP0, F3Cz sensor pairs for the Brief, Scenario and Debrief segments were correlated with the STBT ratings ($n = 7$). The scenario correlations at the CzP0 and F3Cz were significantly ($p < 0.05$) greater than the correlations at the C3C4, FzC3 and FzP0 sensors.

these organizations had significance in the context of team performance. Seven of the twelve SPAN teams in this study met the criteria of (1) having two independent STBT evaluator ratings, (2) the EEG data from the complete performance (i.e. the Briefing, Scenario and Debriefing segments) was available for modeling, (3) EEG was collected from at least five crew members, and, 4) each of the training segments was at least 500 s long.

The correlation between the NS entropy levels of the entire performance and the STBT evaluation scores was not significant ($r = -.28$, $p = .53$). Correlations were then conducted using the NS Entropy levels of the Briefing, Scenario and Debriefing segments. Between group ANOVA comparisons were significantly different ($F = 17.4$; $df = 2$, $p < 0.001$), and a multiple comparisons analysis by LSD indicated that the Brief, Scenario and Debrief segments differed at the 0.05 level. (Figure 4). Also shown in this figure are the segment-wise correlations at the different EEG sensor bipoles.

During the Briefing, there was a significant negative correlation between the NS entropy and the STBT ratings. This means that higher STBT ratings correlated with lower NS entropy levels. As decreased NS Entropy indicates more neurodynamic organization the results show that the more resilient teams were neurodynamically more organized than the less resilient teams (Fig. 4).

During the Scenario there was a positive correlation between STBT ratings and NS Entropy indicating that high resilience teams were neurodynamically less organized than the lower resilience teams. The team NS entropy that was calculated from the CzP0 or F3Cz EEG sensor bipoles was significantly higher than the NS Entropy from the FzP0, FzC3 or C3C4 sensor combinations. During the Debriefing there was a negative correlation between the NS entropy and STBT ratings of the teams.

Correlations profiles were then constructed for each of the EEG 1 Hz frequency bins for the Briefing, Scenario and Debriefing performance segments to better situate the correlations in the EEG frequency spectrum. With the CzP0 EEG sensor combination, the most significant correlations with the STBT ratings were the negative

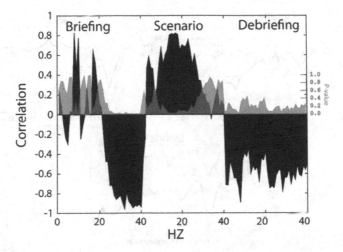

Fig. 5. Correlations between the STBT evaluation scores and the EEG PSD levels for the 1 Hz frequency bins from CzPO (n = 7). The *p*-values for each correlation are shown in light gray. The Briefing, Scenario and Debriefing segments are labeled for each of the forty 1 Hz bins.

correlations in the ~ 20-40 Hz bins of the Briefing segment (Fig. 5). Most of the correlations between 27 – 34 Hz bands were significant at the p < 0.05 level. Similar negative correlations were also seen in the Debriefing. During the Scenario segment the NS entropy / STBT rating correlations were high with the most significant correlations between ~ 10 and 20 Hz.

Figure 6 plots the average NS entropy levels for resilient and less resilient teams as a function of frequency bins. In the Briefing segment there were significant negative correlations (r > 0.5) particularly in the 25–40 Hz region (p ranged from .003 to .05). The positive correlations in the Scenario were most significant (r > 0.7) in the 12-17 Hz frequency range with p values ranging from 0.03 to 0.05.

4 Discussion

In this study the linkages between the behavioral observations of evaluators and neurodynamic measures of teams performing submarine navigation tasks were explored. Neurodynamic organization is used in the sense of persistent temporal relationships in the quantitative expression of EEG rhythms across members of a team. These relationships are captured symbolically as team cognition evolves in parallel with the task. Data streams of these symbolic neurodynamic relationships provide a temporal view of how the team and its members responded to periodic routines and unexpected challenges.

Most teams had characteristic NS Entropy features, the first being the periods of lower NS Entropy during the Briefing and Debriefing segments. This was not surprising as the teams are behaviorally the most organized during the Debriefing when all team members actively participate in the performance critique. The Briefing segment is

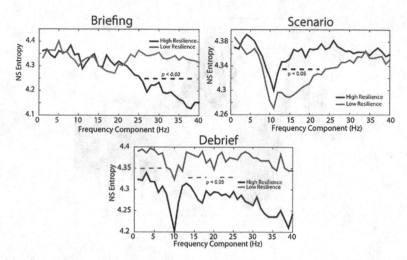

Fig. 6. Correlations between the STBT evaluation scores and the EEG PSD levels are plotted (dark gray) for four high and three low resilience team performances. The p-values for each of the correlations are shown in light gray. The EEG power levels are from the CzP0 bipolar combination and correlations were performed for each 1 Hz bin in the Briefing, Scenario and Debriefing segments of the seven teams. the dotted lines indicate significant differences.

more a hybrid of the Scenario and Debriefing segments with periods of common discussions intermixed with individual instrument calibrations and small group activities.

The neurodynamic organizations (i.e. periods of decreased NS Entropy) of teams were observed in all EEG frequency bands but were least in the theta (θ) and delta (δ) regions. Theta oscillations are important for processing spatial information and for memory encoding and retrieval, and intuitively these activities seem more within brain rather than across-brain cognitive functions. Delta oscillations are primarily seen during sleep, although recently a role in suppression of external distracting information has been suggested [18]. The neurodynamic organizations in the alpha (α) region dominated the NS entropy spectral profile for SPAN teams. This dominance of alpha may in part be due to the task, as prior studies of teams performing more action-oriented tasks showed little neurodynamic organizations in the alpha region, and more in the beta region (Stevens & Galloway, under review). The alpha band oscillations have known heterogeneity with regard to social coordination markers. The μ medial, the phi complex and occipital α rhythms exist in the small frequency range of 9.5 to 13 Hz, with their amplitudes depending on whether the social coordination is intentional or incidental and whether the tasks are synchronic or diachronic [19]. Both of these interactions would be expected in the SPAN task. Synchronic interactions dominate during the Scenario where information flows multi-directionally across all members of the crew, while during the Debriefing segment only one person generally speaks at a given time (i.e. diachronic interaction). The Scenario-Debriefing differences in NS Entropy in the alpha region might also result from increased / prolonged periods of alpha suppression resulting from the increased task requirements of the Scenario [20].

While decreases in the alpha NS Entropy dominated the NS EEG spectral profile, they seemed less important for distinguishing between high and low resilience teams. This may in part be due to the central role of alpha NS organizations during the taking of 'Rounds' which is a periodic and routine activity. As the subjects studied were candidates in advanced training, they had several years of practice performing the 'Rounds' routines, and at least one of the social coordination markers in the alpha region (right mu) decreases when people memorize routine behaviors of others [19].

The beta region of the EEG spectrum is often linked with motor and pre-motor activity and Mu oscillations which are believed to be part of a human mirror neuron system [13, 21]. Mu oscillations are characterized by an α component of $\sim 8 - 13$ Hz attributed to sensory-motor areas (S1 M1), and a beta component of $\sim 15 - 20$ Hz which may link to anticipatory motor activity These rhythms are modulated by the direct observation and imagination of movement. Planning, as well as the execution of hand movements desynchronize (i.e. suppress) these rhythms, while inhibition of motor behavior enhances their activity [22, 23]. The neurodynamic organizations of resilient and less resilient teams showed beta region differences during the Scenario with less resilient teams showing significantly ($p < 0.05$) lower NS Entropy levels. These correlations were mainly seen with the CzP0 and F3Cz sensor combinations.

The synchronizations in the γ region are more enigmatic as social coordination markers have not yet been described in this region. In individuals however, α β and γoscillations interact during working memory manipulations [12]. In this regard it is interesting that periods of γ synchronization were often observed in association with oscillations in α & β bands as well. These periods of increased team neurodynamic organizations in the γ region during the Scenarios were concurrent with 'periods of interest' for the team [5]. This suggests a process whereby a team gradually matched its cognitive organization to changes in the task, and once the team successfully adapted to, or changed the structure of the task, the team developed a new operating rhythm. Neurodynamic measures of the team's rhythm might help evaluators detect when that rhythm is more subtlety disrupted than in the simulation pause above, perhaps enabling a timely instructor intervention, such as real-time coaching, to help the team reorganize cognitively and re-establish its rhythm. A more ambitious aim would be for teams to become self-aware enough to detect these disruptions themselves with behavior clues and to self-correct. Thus, the correlation of NS Entropy levels with related behavior clues is a possible future outcome. Generally, the higher performing teams had fewer periods of decreased NS Entropy (i.e. increased neurodynamic organization) and / or periods of smaller duration or magnitude during the Scenario. This observation was confirmed by correlation analysis between team synchrony and STBT ratings. This fact may complement observer-based measures as a way to quantify the proficiency and resilience of teams; a very useful outcome for developing teams over time in preparation for challenging real-world missions.

What was unexpected from these analyses was the negative correlation between team synchronization and evaluator ratings in the Briefing segment. This relationship suggests that the more cognitively organized a team is during the Briefing, the better they will perform on the task. If larger scale fluctuations indeed relate to the need for increased team organization then by identifying significant periods of team reorganization, instructors could advantageously target discussions and future training activities to develop team skills in these areas, as well as objectively follow team improvement over time. Additionally, a cognitively dis-organized team Brief might provide an early signal to instructors regarding the team's brittleness, and that the team might need more interventions (such as coaching) during the training event.

Neurodynamic measures may also have utility for determining when a team is becoming brittle or 'drifting into danger'. Detection of team breakdowns can be difficult due to the subtle onset and multiplicity of causes before a critical transition towards failure [24]. Team breakdown can be perceived as a sudden event with a dramatic loss of effectiveness, and more often than not, this decrease in performance is a gradual or incremental process [25]. More insight about when teams begin reorganizing would be a step forward toward understanding the antecedent behaviors and developing strategies against them in the future, perhaps in real-time, if teams can be identified as tending toward breakdown.

Acknowledgements. This work was supported in part by The Defense Advanced Research Projects Agency under contract number(s) W31P4Q12C0166, and NSF SBIR grants IIP 0822020 and IIP 1215327. The views, opinions, and/or findings contained are those of the authors and should not be interpreted as representing the official views or policies, either expressed or implied, of the Defense Advanced Research Projects Agency or the Department of Defense. This work was supported by work unit number F1214. JL is an employee of the U.S. Government. This work was prepared as part of my official duties. Title 17 U.S.C. 105 provides that 'copyright protection under this title is not available for any work of the United States Government.' Title 17 U.S.C. 101 defines U.S. Government work as work prepared by a military service member or employee of the U.S. Government as part of that person's official duties

References

1. Staal, M.E., Bolton, A., Yaroush, L.E., Bourne Jr, R.A.: Cognitive performance and resilience to stress. In: Lukey, B.J., Tepe, V. (eds.) Bio-behavioral Resilience to Stress, vol. 2. CRC Press, Taylor & Francis Group, London, UK (2009)
2. Carandini, M., Heeger, D.J.: Normalization as a canonical neural computation. Nat. Rev. Neurosci. **13**, 51–62 (2011). doi:10.1038/nrn3136
3. Butner, J., Pasupathi, M., Vallejos, V.: When the facts just don't add up: the fractal nature of conversational stories. Soc. Cognition **26**, 670–699 (2008)
4. Likens, A., Amazeen, P., Stevens, R., Galloway, T., Gorman, J.C.: Neural signatures of team coordination are revealed by multifractal analysis. Soc. Neurosci. **9**(3), 219–234 (2014)
5. Stevens, R.H., Gorman, J.C., Amazeen, P., Likens, A., Galloway, T.: The organizational dynamics of teams. Nonlinear Dyn. Psychol. Life Sci. **17**(1), 67–86 (2013)
6. Stevens, R., Galloway, T., Wang, P., Berka, C.: Cognitive neurophysiologic synchronies: What can they contribute to the study of teamwork? Hum. Factors **54**, 489–502 (2012)
7. Bak, P., Tang, C., Wiesenfeld, K.: Self-organized criticality: an explanation of 1/f noise. Physical **59**(4), 381–384 (1987)
8. Stevens, R.H., Galloway, T.: Toward a quantitative description of the neurodynamics organizations of teams. Soc. Neurosci. **9**(2), 160–173 (2014)

9. Hollnagel, E.: The four cornerstones of resilience engineering. In: Hollnagel, E., Dekker, S. (eds.) Resilience Engineering Perspectives. Preparation and Restoration, vol. 2, pp. 117–133. Ashgate, Farnham, UK (2009)

10. Hollnagel, E.: FRAM: The Functional Resonance Analysis Method. Modeling Complex Socio-Technical Systems. Ashgate, Aldershot (2012)

11. Wang, Y., Hong, B., Gao, X., Gao, S.: Design of electrode layout for motor imagery based brain-computer interface. Electron. Lett. **43**(10), 557–558 (2007)

12. Roux, F., Uhlhaas, P.: Working memory and neural oscillations: alpha-gamma versus theta-gamma codes for distinct WM information? Trends Cogn. Sci. **18**, 16–25 (2014)

13. Oberman, L.M., Pineda, J.A., Ramachandran, V.S.: The human mirror neuron system A link between action observation and social skills. Soc. Cogn. Affect. Neurosci. **2**, 62–66 (2007)

14. Berka, C., Levendowski, D.J., Cvetinovic, M.M., Petrovic, M.M., Davis, G., et al.: Real-time analysis of EEG indexes of alertness, cognition, and memory acquired with a wireless EEG headset. Int. J. Hum. Comput. Interact. **17**(2), 151–170 (2004)

15. Daw, C.S., Finney, C.E.A., Tracy, E.R.: A review of symbolic analysis of experimental data. Rev. Sci. Instrum. **74**, 915 (2003)

16. Lin, J., Keogh, E., Lonardi, S., Chiu, B.: A symbolic representation of time series with implications for streaming algorithms. In: Proceedings of the 8th Data Mining and Knowledge Discovery, San Diego, CA (2003)

17. Shannon, C., Weaver, W.: The Mathematical Theory of Communication. University of Illinois Press, Urbana (1949)

18. Harmony, T.: The functional significance of delta oscillations in cognitive processing. Front. Integr. Neurosci. **7**(83) (2013). doi:10.3389/fnint.2013.00083

19. Tognoli, E., Kelso, J.A.: The coordination dynamics of social neuromarkers (2013). Bibliographic Code: 2013arXiv1310.7275T

20. Klimesch, W., Sauseng, P., Hanslmayr, S.: EEG alpha oscillations: the inhibition-timing hypothesis. Brain Res. Rev. **53**, 63–88 (2007)

21. Pineda, J.A.: Sensorimotor cortex as a critical component of an 'extended' mirror neuron system: does it solve the development, correspondence, and control problems in mirroring? Behav. Brain Funct. **4**, 47–63 (2008)

22. Menoret, M., Varnet, L., Fargier, R., Cheylus, A., Curie, A., desPortes, V., Nazir, T.A., Paulignan, U.: Neural correlates of non-verbal social interactions: a dual-EEG study. Neurophyschologia **55**, 85–91 (2014)

23. Caetano, G., Jousmaki, V., Hari, R.: Actor's and observers primary motor cortices stabilize similarly after seen or heard motor actions. Proc. Nat. Acad. Sci. **104**, 9058–9062 (2007)

24. Woods, D., Hollnagel, E.: Resilience engineering concepts and Precepts. Ashgate Publishing, Burlington, VT, USA (2006)

25. Rankin, A., Lunderg, J., Woltjer, R., Rollenhagen, C., Hollnagel, E.: Resilience in everyday operations: a framework for analyzing adaptations in high-risk work. J. Cogn. Eng. Decis. Making **8**(1), 78–97 (2014)

Through a Scanner Quickly: Elicitation of P3 in Transportation Security Officers Following Rapid Image Presentation and Categorization

Michael C. Trumbo[✉], Laura E. Matzen, Austin Silva,
Michael J. Haass, Kristin Divis, and Ann Speed

Sandia National Laboratories, Albuquerque, USA
{mctrumb, lematze, aussilv, mjhaass, kmdivis,
aespeed}@sandia.gov

Abstract. Numerous domains, ranging from medical diagnostics to intelligence analysis, involve visual search tasks in which people must find and identify specific items within large sets of imagery. These tasks rely heavily on human judgment, making fully automated systems infeasible in many cases. Researchers have investigated methods for combining human judgment with computational processing to increase the speed at which humans can triage large image sets. One such method is rapid serial visual presentation (RSVP), in which images are presented in rapid succession to a human viewer. While viewing the images and looking for targets of interest, the participant's brain activity is recorded using electroencephalography (EEG). The EEG signals can be time-locked to the presentation of each image, producing event-related potentials (ERPs) that provide information about the brain's response to those stimuli. The participants' judgments about whether or not each set of images contained a target and the ERPs elicited by target and non-target images are used to identify subsets of images that merit close expert scrutiny [1]. Although the RSVP/EEG paradigm holds promise for helping professional visual searchers to triage imagery rapidly, it may be limited by the nature of the target items. Targets that do not vary a great deal in appearance are likely to elicit useable ERPs, but more variable targets may not. In the present study, we sought to extend the RSVP/EEG paradigm to the domain of aviation security screening, and in doing so to explore the limitations of the technique for different types of targets. Professional Transportation Security Officers (TSOs) viewed bag X-rays that were presented using an RSVP paradigm. The TSOs viewed bursts of images containing 50 segments of bag X-rays that were presented for 100 ms each. Following each burst of images, the TSOs indicated whether or not they thought there was a threat item in any of the images in that set. EEG was recorded during each burst of images and ERPs were calculated by time-locking the EEG signal to the presentation of images containing threats and matched images that were identical except for the presence of the threat item. Half of the threat items had a prototypical appearance and half did not. We found that the bag images containing threat items with a prototypical appearance reliably elicited a P300 ERP component, while those without a prototypical appearance did not. These findings have implications for the application of the RSVP/EEG technique to real-world visual search domains.

© Springer International Publishing Switzerland 2015
D.D. Schmorrow and C.M. Fidopiastis (Eds.): AC 2015, LNAI 9183, pp. 348–360, 2015.
DOI: 10.1007/978-3-319-20816-9_33

Keywords: Rapid serial visual presentation · Visual search · EEG · P300

1 Introduction

A wide variety of domains, ranging from medical diagnostics to intelligence analysis, involve searching through large sets of imagery to find and identify specific items. These domains rely on people's ability to discriminate between relevant and irrelevant images as accurately and efficiently as possible. While computer vision systems have been employed in image classification [2], purely computerized systems may lack the sensitivity, specificity and ability to generalize possessed by humans [1, 3], making fully automated systems infeasible in these complex domains. Since visual search and inspection tasks rely primarily on human judgment, researchers have sought other methods for increasing the speed at which humans can triage large sets of imagery. In one such method, termed rapid serial visual presentation (RSVP), images are presented serially in a fixed location, typically at a rate of 3–20 items per second [4]. Intraub [5] demonstrated that participants can accurately identify targets within a rapid stream of images. The RSVP technique has subsequently been employed to study phenomena ranging from language processing [6], to emotion [7], to attention [8].

Recently, researchers have investigated combining the RSVP technique with brain-computer interface (BCI) technology. In this approach, participants typically view image chips in which a larger image is segmented into many small parts. The chips are presented rapidly, in short bursts, and the participants judge whether or not there was a target present in any of the images in that group. Meanwhile, participants' brain activity is recorded using electroencephalography (EEG), a neuroimaging technique that provides temporal resolution on the order of milliseconds [9]. EEG signals can be time-locked to the presentation of stimuli, producing event-related potentials (ERPs) that provide information about the brain's response to those stimuli. The participants' judgments about whether or not each set of images contained a target and the ERPs elicited by target and non-target images are used to identify subsets of images that merit close expert scrutiny [1]. This approach can allow imagery analysts to hone in on the relevant information very rapidly. The ERP signals can also be combined with machine learning techniques to develop classifiers, which can then be used to process additional data and identify blocks of images that are likely to contain a target based on the degree of similarity to trained data [1, 3, 10–12].

Thorpe and colleagues [13] demonstrated the feasibility of pairing EEG with rapid image presentation by asking participants to classify nature scenes presented for 20 ms under a go/no-go paradigm. They found a frontal negativity specific to no-go trails that developed approximately 150 ms following stimulus onset. In the domain of intelligence analysis, Mathan and colleagues [3] used an EEG/RSVP approach with analysts examining satellite imagery. They showed that neurophysiologically driven image classification with rapid image presentation exhibits roughly a five-fold reduction in time required to identify targets relative to conventional image analysis, while retaining a high degree of accuracy. This technique has also been demonstrated using experts searching for masses in mammogram images [12].

The EEG signals used in these imagery triage applications are typically event-related potentials (ERPs). ERPs are obtained when an EEG signal is time-locked to a relevant stimulus [14]. In research settings, ERPs are often averaged across many trials in order to wash out noise (from sources such as eye blinks and facial muscle activity) that can overwhelm the ERP signals. However, the method of averaging across repeated trials is impractical for triage implementations where efficiency is of critical value. In such domains, promise lies in single-trial ERP detection which incorporates spatial information across EEG sensors [15, 16]. Such spatiotemporal EEG activity has revealed distinct patterns for target-present and target-absent images following stimulus presentation that could be exploited for purposes of constructing a single-trial ERP classifier [17].

One of the most useful ERPs for single-trial applications is the P300, or P3. The P3 refers to a positive deflection in voltage that occurs in the latency range of 250–500 ms, typically evoked using an oddball task in which an infrequent "oddball" target (e.g., an image containing a threat) is displayed within a series of frequent distractor stimuli (e.g., innocuous images), and the participant is asked to discriminate between target and non-target stimuli [18, 19]. P3 amplitudes are significantly larger in response to infrequent target items, though in order to evoke a P3 the task must force attention and categorization of stimuli [19]. There are thought to be two subcomponents of the P3, referred to as P3a and P3b, which have distinct neural generators that present as particular scalp topography in the EEG signal. The P3a subcomponent is thought to reflect stimuli-driven frontal attention mechanisms and is therefore maximal over frontal and central electrode locations, while the P3b subcomponent is associated with temporal and parietal lobe activity reflective of memory processing [18]. Therefore, one potential mechanism for the P3 wave as a whole is stimulus detection that engages memory processes [18].

Although the RSVP/EEG paradigm holds promise for helping professional visual searchers to triage imagery rapidly, it may be limited by the nature of the target items. Targets that do not vary a great deal in appearance are likely to elicit ERPs that can be classified by brain-computer interfaces, but more variable targets may not. In the present study, we sought to extend the RSVP/EEG paradigm to the domain of aviation security screening, and in doing so to explore the limitations of the technique for different types of targets. Airport screeners typically inspect X-ray images of baggage in search of threats, such as guns or explosive devices, and other prohibited items, such as flammable materials. As in the other domains in which the RSVP/EEG technique has been applied, the screeners must contend with large sets of imagery and time pressure while making high-consequence decisions. However, unlike domains such as mammography and satellite imagery analysis, the targets that are of interest to an aviation security screener can vary quite drastically in appearance and are sometimes deliberately concealed. In this study, we presented professional Transportation Security Officers (TSOs) with rapid successions of image chips taken from false color baggage X-rays in order to determine if various types of threat items could elicit P3 ERPs. We hypothesized that targets that have a prototypical appearance would elicit a useable P3 signal, but concealed targets or targets that do not have a prototypical appearance would not.

2 Method

2.1 Participants

Twelve individuals (3 female; mean age 32.7, range 21–63), currently working as TSOs with duties that include baggage screening, participated in this experiment and were paid for their time. All participants provided written informed consent and were right-handed, had no early exposure to languages other than English, had no history of neurological disease or defect, and possessed normal or corrected-to-normal vision and hearing.

2.2 Stimuli

False color X-ray images, created using the same types of scanners that are used in airport security checkpoints, were supplied by the Transportation Security Administration (TSA). These images were created by scanning actual pieces of luggage and were representative of the types of bags that are typically seen by TSOs at the airports. Each image presented a single piece of luggage (e.g., a briefcase, a duffle bag). For every piece of luggage there were two images, one showing a top view and one showing a side view. Some of the bags contained a prohibited item (threat bags), some contained no prohibited items (clear bags), and some threat bags were imaged again with the threat item removed (cleared threat bags). The threat bags contained one of two types of weapons, one of which is generally easier to detect than the other. We will refer to the two types of weapons as Threat A (easier to detect) and Threat B (more difficult to detect). The cleared threat bags were identical to the threat bags in all respects other than the absence of the threat item. The difficulty of the bags was rated by the TSA as easy, medium or hard, based on the amount of clutter in the bags and the types of concealment used for the threat items. Only bags rated as easy by TSA were used for this study.

Each of the false color X-ray images was decomposed into image chips and grouped into blocks of 50, with all images in a given group consisting of either 400 × 400 pixel chips (generated from images depicting the top view of luggage) or 400 × 250 pixel chips (generated from images depicting the side view of luggage). Within each block of 50 image chips, there were 49 distractor images taken from clear bags and one target item. The target image chip either contained a threat or the equivalent section of a cleared threat bag. For target images that contained a threat, the entirety of the prohibited item was presented in the image. Within each block of 50 images, all of the images were of the same type and were taken from the same quadrant of a bag. In other words, if the target image showed the top left corner of the top view of a suitcase, all of the distractors within that same block also showed the top left corner of the top view of a suitcase. If the target image was the bottom right corner of the side view of a backpack, all of the distractors showed the same quadrant and same view of other images of backpacks, and so forth.

A total of 10 blocks of images were used for training and 100 blocks of images were used in the main experiment. Of the 100 trials in the experiment, the target image chip was a threat in 60 trials and a cleared threat in 40 trials. Given the finite number of images provided by TSA and the high number of image chips that were required to generate all of the trials, some of the distractor images were used more than once in different trials. Among the 5,500 image chips that were used (5,000 for the task trials and 500 for the 10 trials in the training block), there were 1,653 distractor image chips that appeared more than once. No target images were repeated, and the order of distractor repetition was balanced across participants.

2.3   Procedure for EEG Recording

The EEG was recorded from 128 silver/silver-chloride electrodes embedded in an elastic cap (ANT WaveGuard, "Duke" layout) using a high-impedance amplifier with active shielding. The electrodes were referenced on-line to the average of all electrodes. Following the experiment, the electrodes were re-referenced off-line to the average of the left and right mastoids. All of the electrodes were tested prior to recording in order to ensure that their impedance was below 50 KOhms. The EEG was digitized with a sampling rate of 256 Hz.

ERPs were computed at each electrode for each experimental condition by averaging the EEG data from 100 ms before the onset of an image chip until 920 ms after onset. Trials containing blinks, eye movement or muscle activity were excluded from the averages. The mean amplitude of the ERPs within time windows of interest was calculated using data digitally filtered off-line using a bandpass filter of 0.2 to 20 Hz.

2.4   Rapid Serial Visual Presentation (RSVP) Task

Participants were seated in a dimly-lit, sound-attenuating booth at a viewing distance of approximately 92 cm from a computer monitor with a refresh rate of 60 Hz. Trial presentation was consistent with similar RSVP studies [3, 10]. Each trial began with a fixation cross that was presented in the center of the screen for 1000 ms. Participants were instructed to keep their eyes on the fixation cross for the duration of its presentation, and to avoid blinking or moving their eyes during the subsequent presentation of images. The stimuli within each trial consisted of a group of 50 images that were presented serially against a white background in rapid succession. Following each set of images, participants were asked to indicate via a button press whether or not they believed a threat to be present in any of the images in that set. The participants were given 5 s to make their response. See Fig. 1 for an illustration of the trial structure.

During an initial training period of 10 trials, images were presented at the rate of 5 images/second (200 ms/image) and participants were given feedback following each trial regarding the accuracy of their response. Following training, presentation rate was set to 10 images/second (100 ms/image) and feedback was no longer provided. 100 trials were presented in this fashion; 60 trials contained a threat and 40 trials did not. Within each trial, image chips presented a consistent view and resolution; 50 trials consisted entirely of 400 × 400 pixel image chips displaying the front view of a bag, while 50 trials consisted of 400 × 250 pixel image chips displaying the side view

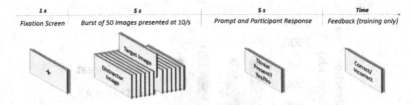

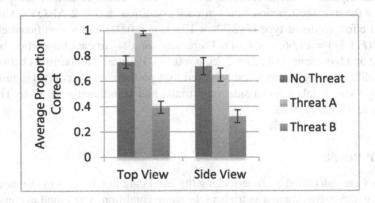

Fig. 1. Time-line of each RSVP trial. Note that response feedback was only provided during the training session.

of a bag. All target image chips were quasi-randomly inserted among the distractor stimuli, with the constraint that target chips were never presented within the first or last 500 ms (5 images) of a trial in order to prevent overlap with ERP signals related to the onset or offset of trials. Participants were given a self-paced break of up to one minute after every 10 trials in order to minimize potential eye strain and fatigue.

3 Results

3.1 Behavioral Results

The participants' average accuracy for each threat condition is shown in Fig. 2.

Fig. 2. Average proportion of correct answers for each threat condition

For Threat A, the threat with a stereotypical appearance, the participants responded correctly to an average of 98 % (SD = 3 %) of top-view trials and 65 % (SD = 20 %) of side-view trials. For Threat B, the threat without a stereotypical appearance, the participants responded correctly to an average of 39 % (SD = 18 %) of top-view trials and 32 % (SD = 19 %) of side-view trials. For the trials containing cleared threat bags (i.e. no threat), participants responded correctly to 75 % (SD = 16 %) of the top-view trials and 72 % (SD = 21 %) of the side-view trials. For the participants' average accuracy in each condition, 3 × 2 ANOVA (threat type by bag view) showed a significant main effect of threat type ($F(2, 22) = 26.04$, $p < 0.01$), a significant main effect of bag view ($F(1,11) = 51.58$, $p < 0.01$), and a significant interaction between threat type and bag

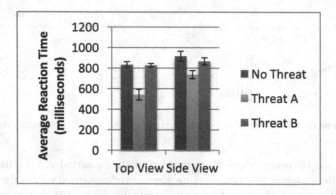

Fig. 3. Average reaction time for responses to each threat condition

view ($F(2,22) = 9.24$, $p < 0.01$). Pairwise comparisons between the threat conditions using paired t-tests showed that participants were significantly more accurate for Threat A trials than for Threat B trials, in both the top-view ($t(11) = 11.36$, $p < 0.001$) and side view ($t(11) = 5.92$, $p < 0.001$) conditions. In addition, participants were significantly more accurate for top-view than for side-view trials for both Threat A ($t(11) = 5.51$, $p < 0.001$) and Threat B ($t(11) = 2.00$, $p < 0.05$).

The participants' average reaction times for each threat condition are shown in Fig. 3. For the average reaction times in each condition, a 3×2 ANOVA showed a significant effect to threat type ($F(2,22) = 17.63$, $p < 0.01$) and a significant effect of bag view ($F(1,11) = 19.66$, $p < 0.01$). There was not a significant interaction between threat type and bag view ($F(2,22) = 2.25$, $p = 0.13$). Pairwise comparisons between the threat conditions using paired t-tests showed that participants responded significantly faster to top-view trials than to side view trials, and significantly faster to Threat A trials than to Threat B trials.

3.2   ERP Results

The ERPs were calculated by time-locking the EEG data to the onset of the target chip in each trial and averaging across trials in the same condition. The grand average ERPs were calculated by averaging across all trials in each condition for each participant. One participant's ERPs were excluded due to a large number of trials contaminated by blinks. For each threat type, the ERPs were compared for the threat and cleared threat bags. These stimuli were identical apart from the presence or absence of the threat in the bag. Representative ERPs from each scalp region are shown in Fig. 4 for Threat A and Fig. 6 for Threat B. Scalp maps showing all electrodes are shown in Figs. 5 and 7. For Threat A, the threat with a prototypical appearance, there were two ERP components that differed between the threat and cleared threat bags. The first was a positive peak over the front of the scalp, peaking at approximately 400 ms. The second was a positive peak over the central electrodes with a corresponding negative peak over the frontal electrodes, peaking at approximately 700 ms. For Threat B, the threat that does

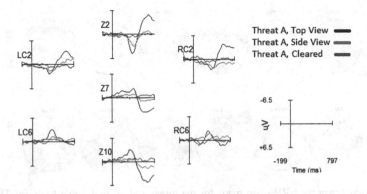

Fig. 4. Representative ERPs from electrodes in each of the seven scalp regions used in the analysis of Threat A.

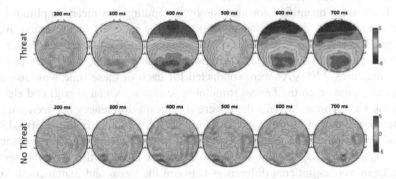

Fig. 5. Grand average ERP scalp maps for the threat and cleared threat trials for Threat A

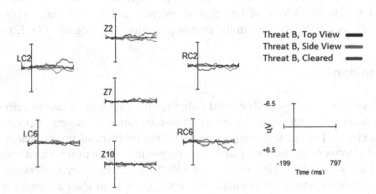

Fig. 6. Representative ERPs from electrodes in each of the seven scalp regions used in the analysis of Threat B.

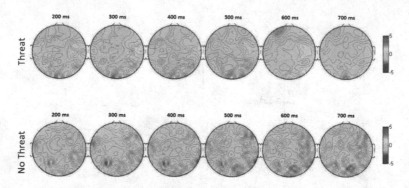

Fig. 7. Grand average ERP scalp maps for the threat and cleared threat trials for Threat B

not have a prototypical appearance, there were no ERP components that differed between the threat and cleared threat bags.

The ERPs were quantified for analysis by computing the mean amplitudes, post baseline correction, of the 300–450 and 600–800 ms intervals in the grand average waveforms. The electrodes were divided into seven scalp regions: left anterior, central anterior, right anterior, central, left posterior, central posterior, and right posterior. Repeated-measures ANOVAs were conducted for each of these time windows in the three central regions with the factors stimulus type (threat or match bag) and electrode site. For top-view Threat A trials, there were significant differences between the threat and match conditions in all three of the central scalp regions in both the 300–450 ms time window (all $Fs > 52.28$, all $ps < 0.001$) and in the 600–800 ms time window (all $Fs > 24.94$, all $ps < 0.001$). For side-view Threat A trials in the 300–450 ms time window, there were significant differences between the threat and match conditions in the central anterior and central posterior scalp regions (all $Fs > 18.77$, all $ps < 0.001$), but not in the central scalp region ($F(1,24) = 2.72$, $p = 0.11$). For side-view Threat A trials in the 600–800 ms time window, there were significant differences between the threat and match conditions in the central anterior and central scalp regions (all $Fs > 8.29$, all $ps < 0.01$), but not in the central posterior scalp region ($F(1,22) = 0.95$).

4   Discussion

Similar to satellite imagery analysts and radiologists, TSO bag screeners operate in a domain concerned with low-frequency, high-consequence targets buried among innocuous clutter. For satellite imagery analysts, the problem of image search centers on the vast number of continuously updating images in conjunction with an insufficient number of trained analysis [20] such that RSVP/EEG driven search offers the opportunity for otherwise un-reviewed images to be subjected to at least a cursory analysis. TSOs are not confronted with a vast image database in the same way that satellite imagery analysts are, in that every single item of luggage is screened. However, unless an item is flagged for further investigation, it is only viewed once by a single screener, making this a domain that stands to benefit from a triage technique which would allow for an efficient double-checking scheme.

The aim of the current study was to examine the viability of constructing a neurophysiologically driven classifier within the domain of TSO baggage screening by determining if the basis for constructing such a classifier exists within an RSVP paradigm. A P300 effect was observed for threats with a stereotyped appearance (Threat A), while for trials containing a threat with a highly variable instantiation (Threat B) we did not observe a P300. Additionally, behavioral performance indicated that participants experienced difficulty detecting this more variable class of threats under RSVP conditions. Responses were more accurate when threats were of a stereotyped nature and when presented via top-down (as opposed to side) view. Even when participants correctly indicated the presence of a threat for a given trial, they may not have been basing their response on the critical image in the trial burst, such that a P300 is not timelocked to the chips of interest.

Currently, fully-automated systems are not viable within complex domains due to issues regarding specificity, sensitivity and ability to generalize [1, 3]. Leveraging the human perceptual system may facilitate generalization since brain responses may be specific to detection of attended targets independent of specific target features, thereby obviating the need to train a classifier that is sensitive to each individual target type. In a domain such as luggage screening in which the size, shape, orientation, and nature of targets may vary substantially and change over time, the flexibility of the human brain may continue to prove superior to fully automated methods of image classification. This is evidenced by research demonstrating that variability between images classes (i.e., target vs. distractor) may be low relative to variability within a class (i.e., target-to-target variability; [3]). It is worth noting that participants in the current study were not informed which types of prohibited items could be present in image blocks, but were simply asked to follow their standard operating procedure for identification of threats.

Our results suggest the possibility of implementing a triage technique within the domain of luggage screening. However, there are a number of important limitations to consider. Presentation of cropped or compressed images is typical of this body of research (e.g., [1, 3, 11, 12]), and the current study is no exception, utilizing cropped images (chips) rather than compressing the visually dense broad images in order to retain discriminability of image components. Rapid presentation rate is a necessity for triage techniques to maintain efficiency, but combination with image chips represents a double-edge sword. The pace of image presentation does not afford time for saccadic search of individual stimuli, which improves EEG signal to noise by minimizing artifactual eye movements. However, as targets become distal from the fixation point, detection rate may decrease [11, 17].

In addition, under RSVP conditions, participants have been shown to exhibit difficulty detecting targets that lay in the boundary between chips [3]. In the current study, each target was entirely contained within a particular image chip. This was intentional given the preliminary nature of the study, but in a real world setting, automatic image decomposition is highly unlikely to result in target items entirely falling within the boundary of the generated image chips. It is possible that overlapping image chips, as used in prior RSVP/EEG research [10] would enhance spatial context, thereby mitigating the issue of boundary items, though such overlap results in an overall decrease in the efficiency of the triage system given that a greater number of images are needed to cover the same amount of image space. Efficiency may be further compromised by the need for frequent breaks to avoid mental fatigue or eye-strain. The current study offered a self-paced break of up to 1 min after every ten trials (500 images); additional work is necessary to determine at what point physical or mental fatigue becomes a factor.

The advantage to EEG provided by limiting eye movement is only valuable if the EEG signal itself is valuable. Recent research suggests that within an RSVP/EEG paradigm, the behavioral performance of participants tracks the detection of evoked response in the EEG signal [11]. In other words, image blocks that contain a target only elicit a distinct EEG signal when the participant is consciously aware that the image block contains a target, such that neuroimaging adds little value beyond overt behavioral information. This stands in contrast to Hope et al. [12] who demonstrated that receiver operating characteristic area under the curve increased from .62–86 to .75–94 when moving from a single electrode to multiple electrodes in an RSVP image triage paradigm. Likewise, Healy and Smeaton [21] demonstrated that using a mere 4 channels of EEG increases image classification accuracy by nearly 50 % beyond using only overt behavioral response. The current study did not attempt construction of a classifier or implementation of modeling for automatic detection of P300 s. Instances in which participants responded incorrectly (e.g., threat present to a threat absent trial) are grouped by response and grand averaged such that instances in which a threat is subconsciously detected may have washed out. Behaviorally, there were not enough instances of false negatives to allow for analysis of a potential subconscious P300. Although the current work was unable to evaluate brain responses on a single-trial basis, it does suggest that for certain items a neural response is elicited which may allow for future construction of a classifier capable of automatic peak identification, thereby allowing neurophysiology to identify the presence of threats in a way not captured by behavioral responses. It is also important to note that such a classifier may provide a better basis for localization of target-containing images within a sequence due to the high temporal resolution associated with ERPs relative to the substantial latency inherent in motor responses [3].

It is currently unknown if task familiarity plays a role in image triage performance within this domain. In the current study, we tracked the amount of time each TSO had spent working in the capacity of a baggage screener in order to determine if job experience related to ability to accurately identify targets in a domain-specific RSVP paradigm. However, all participants were naïve to high throughput analysis of images as experienced in this study, and it is possible that training within this paradigm would result in enhanced ability to discriminate between target and non-target blocks of images. Individual differences may also play a role, as previous investigation has demonstrated that a slower rate of presentation may be necessary in order to attain an acceptable level of accuracy for some individuals [17].

Given the equipment expense and time cost of setup and analysis of EEG data, it is important to determine the extent to which EEG provides a benefit above and beyond overt behavioral data, and if task practice and/or identification of individuals adept at high throughput screening may obviate the need for neurophysiological data. While the current study utilized a 128 channel EEG system, other work has found a small number of electrodes to be sufficient for substantial increases in classification accuracy [12, 21] such that low cost consumer-grade EEG systems may prove a viable option.

References

1. Huang, Y., Erdogmus, D., Mathan, S., Pavel, M.: Large-scale image database triage via EEG evoked responses. In: IEEE International Conference on Acoustics, Speech, and Signal Processing, pp. 429–432 (2008)
2. Collins, R.T., Lipoton, A.J., Kanade, T., Fujiyoshi, H., Duggins, D., Tsin, Y., Wixon, L.: A system for video surveillance and monitoring: VSAM final report (CMU-RI-TR-00-12). Carnegie Mellon University, Robotics Institute. (2000). http://www.ri.cmu.edu/pub_files/pub2/collins_robert_2000_1/collins_robert_2000_1.pdf
3. Mathan, S., Whitlow, S., Dorneich, M., Ververs, P., Davis, G.: Neurophysiological estimation of interruptibility: demonstrating feasibility in a field context. In: Schmorrow, D. D., Nicholson, D.M., Dexler, J.M., Reeves, L.M. (eds.) Foundations of Augmented Cognition, 4th edn, pp. 51 58. Strategic Analysis, Arlington (2007)
4. Kranczioch, C., Debener, S., Herrmann, C.S., Engel, A.K.: EEG gamma-band activity in rapid serial visual presentation. Exp. Brain Res. **169**, 246–254 (2006)
5. Intraub, H.: Rapid conceptual identification of sequentially presented pictures. J. Exp. Psychol. Hum. Percept. Perform. **7**(3), 604–610 (1981)
6. Harris, C.L., Morris, A.L.: Illusory words created by repetition blindness: a technique for probing sublexical representations. Psychon. Bull. Rev. **8**(1), 118–126 (2001)
7. Vroomen, J., Driver, J., de Gelder, B.: Is cross-modal integration of emotional expressions independent of attentional resources? Cogn. Affect. Behav. Neurosci. **1**(4), 382–387 (2001)
8. Chun, M.M., Potter, M.C.: A two-stage model for multiple target detection in rapid serial visual presentation. J. Exp. Psychol. Hum. Percept. Perform. **21**(1), 109–127 (1995)
9. Mantini, D., Marzetti, L., Corbetta, M., Romani, G.L., Del Gratta, C.: Multimodal integration of fMRI and EEG data for high spatial and temporal resolution analysis of brain networks. Brain Topogr. **23**(2), 150–158 (2010)
10. Bigdely-Shamlo, N., Vankov, A., Ramirez, R.R., Makeig, S.: Brain activity-based image classification from rapid serial visual presentation. IEEE Trans. Neural Syst. Rehabil. Eng. **16**(5), 432–441 (2008)
11. Dias, J.C., Parra, L.C.: No EEG evidence for subconscious detection during rapid serial visual presentation. IEEE Signal Process. Med. Biol. Symp. 1–4 (2011)
12. Hope, C., Sterr, A., Elangovan, P., Geades, N., Windridge, D., Young, K., Wells, K.: High throughput screening for mammography using a human-computer interface with rapid serial visual presentation (RSVP). In: Proceedings SPIE Medical Imaging 2013: Image Perception, Observer Performance, and Technology Assessment, vol. 8673, (2013). doi:10.1117/12. 2007557
13. Thorpe, S., Fize, D., Marlot, C.: Speed of processing in the human visual system. Nature **381**, 520–522 (1996)
14. Luck, S.J.: An introduction to the event-related potential technique. MIT press, Cambridge (2014)
15. Gerson, A.D., Parra, L.C., Sajda, P.: Cortical origins of response time variability during rapid discrimination of visual objects. Neuroimage **28**(2), 342–353 (2005)

16. Parra, L., Alvino, C., Tang, A., Pearlmutter, B., Yeung, N., Osman, A., Sajda, P.: Single-trial detection in EEG and MEG: keeping it linear. Neurocomputing **52**, 177–183 (2003)
17. Mathan, S., Whitlow, S., Erdogmus, D., Pavel, M., Ververs, P., Dorneich, M.: Neurophysiologically driven image triage. In: Proceedings of the 2006 Conference on Human Factors in Computing Systems, pp. 1085–1090 (2006)
18. Polich, J.: Updating P300: an integrative theory of P3a and P3b. Clin. Neurophysiol. **118**, 2128–2148 (2007)
19. Luck, S.J., Kappenman, E.S. (eds.): The Oxford handbook of event-related potential components. Oxford University Press, Oxford (2011)
20. Kenyon, H.S.: Unconventional information operations shorten wars. Signal Mag. Armed Forces Commun. Electron. Assoc. **57**, 33–36 (2003). http://www.afcea.org/content/?q=node/167
21. Healy, G., Smeaton, A.F.: Optimising the number of channels in EEG-augmented image search. In: Proceedings of the 25th BCS Conference on Human-Computer Interaction, pp. 157–162 (2011)

Constrained Tensor Decomposition via Guidance: Increased Inter and Intra-Group Reliability in fMRI Analyses

Peter B. Walker[1(✉)], Sean Gilpin[2], Sidney Fooshee[3],
and Ian Davidson[2]

[1] Naval Medical Research Center, Silver Spring, MD, USA
peter.b.walker.mil@mail.mil
[2] University of California – Davis, Davis, CA, USA
sagilpin@davis.edu, davidson@cs.davis.edu
[3] United States Navy – Aerospace Experimental Psychology,
Ann Arbor, MI, USA
sidney.fooshee@navy.mil

Abstract. Recently, Davidson and his colleagues introduced a promising new approach to analyzing functional Magnetic Resonance Imaging (fMRI) that suggested a more appropriate analytic approach is one that views the spatial and temporal activation as a multi-way tensor [1]. In this paper, we illustrate how the use of prior domain knowledge might be incorporated into the deconstruction of the tensor so as to increase analytical reliability. These results will be discussed in reference to implications towards military selection and classification.

Keywords: Tensor decomposition · Functional magnetic resonance imaging · Reliability

1 Introduction

In a series of papers, Davidson and his colleagues [1–4] recently introduced a promising new approach to analyzing functional connectivity that views the spatial and temporal activation as a multi-way tensor. The authors argued that such approaches may pave the way for new and innovative improvements across military domains. For example, the graph analytic approaches were applied to problems ranging from analyzing neuroimaging data to exploring the cause and effect relationships behind event networks.

Similarly, their approach to viewing multi-way data as a tensor, promises a number of different innovative opportunities across military domains. For example, many of the DoD services have begun to investigate the use of neuroimaging modalities for selection and classification [5, 6]. In addition, there has been tremendous interest in the use of using specific neuroimaging techniques to examine mental health issues including Traumatic Brain Injury (TBI) and Post-Traumatic Stress Disorder (PTSD) [7]. One such technique, functional Magnetic Resonance Imaging (fMRI), will be discussed in this paper.

© Springer International Publishing Switzerland 2015
D.D. Schmorrow and C.M. Fidopiastis (Eds.): AC 2015, LNAI 9183, pp. 361–369, 2015.
DOI: 10.1007/978-3-319-20816-9_34

fMRI provides the unique opportunity to visualize neural activity in the brain in real time. Perhaps one of the most promising applications of fMRI data has been on the analysis of functional connectivity [8]. The term functional connectivity has come to be understood as the temporal correlation of neuronal activation for spatially discrete locations. The excitement over this analytic approach is due, in part, to the applicability of these findings in both clinical and diagnostic settings [9].

The theoretical and practical advantages of several of the benchmark analytic approaches are well known [10]. For example, innovations in clustering such as spectral partitioning (SP) allows for the aggregation of several images to form a composite pattern with a single global minimum which can be approximated efficiently via a generalized eigenvalue problem and has been applied to fMRI clustering with promising results [11].

However, limitations in the applicability and interpretability of the results from fMRI following SP have been largely ignored. Specifically, SP and its specific use toward fMRI have been challenged with respect to test/retest reliability. For example, a review by Bennett and Miller [12] reported a mean Intra-class Correlation Coefficient (ICC) from 13 separate studies to be ICC = .50. However, the ICC appeared to vary widely depending on a number of different factors including scanner characteristics (magnet strength; signal-to-noise ratio), subject-specific (cognitive state), and/or task-specific (training effects). Depending on any number of these factors, the ICC ranged between .88 and .16.

The primary aim of this paper is to outline an approach to analyzing functional connectivity that overcomes many of the limitations of current data analytic approaches. Specifically, this paper demonstrates an increase in reliability over and above benchmark analytic approaches through the use of a technique we have termed *Constrained Tensor Decomposition* (hereafter, CTD). CTD attempts to transfer knowledge from existing domain knowledge (i.e., anatomical regions) to assist in the clustering/segmentation process thereby creating more stable fMRI images. In doing so, we show that we are more readily able to dissociate findings from different populations of scans. To accomplish this, we apply a form of spectral clustering to two separate fMRI scans. Unlike traditional clustering algorithms such as Independent Components Analysis, and/or Principle Components Analysis that attempt to segment a graph based on a single image, our approach incorporates knowledge from multiple graphs that might share the same set of nodes with the first graph, but have a different set of edges. Intuitively, the extra knowledge from the second graph may help to find a better partition than the one we can find with the first graph alone.

The lack of test/retest reliability through the use of SP is illustrated in Fig. 1. This figure shows SP results for two resting state fMRI data sets of the same healthy young individual, acquired in short succession on an MRI machine. Barring a major medical event between the two scans, the spatial and temporal patterns of resting state activity should largely be the same. Yet, the spectral partitioning of the two data sets has little in common despite the algorithm finding the global minimum of its objective function. This suggests that the clustering resulting from spectral partitioning are strongly influenced by random "noise" (i.e., MRI scanner noise) that have little to do with the true similarity of the time course of brain activity.

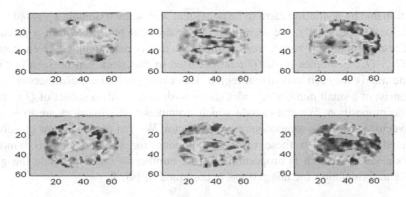

Fig. 1 Lack of test-retest reliability of spectral partitioning. A healthy young individual received two fMRI scans in rapid succession. The top and bottom rows show the three top-ranked spectral partitions of a corresponding slice from the first and second scans. Voxels more strongly associated with one partition, vs. the other, are shown in lighter vs. darker shades, respectively.

Our approach, CTD, offers significant improvements over previous attempts at measuring brain connectivity [13]. The aim of our work was the design of algorithms that can take event data in the form of activations over a three-dimensional spatial region x, y, z, over time t and simplify that data into a network [14]. This involves both aggregation so that the active cohesive regions (nodes) are identified and the formation of relationships (edges) between these regions. The edges and their weights can then be used to indicate properties such as information flow, excitation/inhibition or probabilistic relationships.

2 Constrained Tensor Decomposition

We view fMRI data as containing a complex interaction of signals and noise [14, 15] with a natural question being how to simplify the activity into the underlying cognitive network being used. Let χ (*2D space x time*) be a three-mode tensor representing the fMRI data for a mid-level slice of the brain. The aim of CTD is to decompose (simplify) this tensor into f factors ($\widehat{\chi} = \chi_1 + \chi_2 \ldots + \chi_f$) using a PARAFAC model (though more complex decompositions could be used). Let factor i be defined by the outer product of three factor vectors ($\chi_i = a_i \circ b_i \circ t_i$) and for brevity we write ($\chi_i = A \circ B \circ T$) with the factor vectors being stacked column-wise so that each factor matrix has f columns. Then χ_i can potentially represent a region of the brain with the outer product of a_i and b_i being the active region and t_i their activations over time. However, with unconstrained tensor decomposition χ_i is typically not a spatially contiguous region nor does it necessarily match an anatomical region. To achieve this, guidance is introduced.

In the case of CTD, the objective function is complemented by adding constraints (guidance) as shown in Eq. 1. The addition of guidance helps rule out solutions that are non-actionable by restricting them to be consistent with known domain knowledge and expectations.[1] Specifically, we identified 116 anatomical regions within a prototype scan. These groupings of voxels were defined by a matrix/mask with all given matrices being $Q_1 \ldots Q_m$. Examples of the Q matrices used in this work can be seen in Fig. 2 with one matrix for each anatomical region. However, most anatomical networks will only consist of a small number of nodes so we wish to use only a subset of Q matrices in the decomposition. We can encode which structures/nodes/matrices are to be used with a vector $\mathbf{w}$ with one component/entry per factor. We can represent how closely the discovered factors match these matrices (allowing for some deviation) which is upper-bounded by which is proportional to the number of voxels outside the given group. The formulation for this process is presented in Eq. 1.

$$\underset{w,A,B,T}{\arg\min} \quad \left\| \chi - \sum_i w_i, a_i \circ b_i \circ t_i \right\| F + \|w\|$$
$$\text{subject to} \qquad w_1 a_1 b_1^T - Q_1 \| \leq \in_1$$
$$\vdots$$
$$w_m \| a_m b_m^T - Q_m \| \leq \in_m$$

(1)

The output of this computation will be the smallest set of groups/nodes (defined by $\mathbf{a_i} \circ \mathbf{b_i}$) that best summarize the fMRI scan with $\mathbf{t_i}$ stating the activations over time. The penalty term $\|\mathbf{w}\|$ introduces a sparsity constraint to enforce that the simplest structure is discovered. Furthermore, by rank ordering the factors by their entry in $\mathbf{w}$ we can determine the most important nodes in the network. Figure 2 shows an example of our work where the Q matrices are just of the cores of a pre-defined anatomical network. The top four most important nodes as per the $\mathbf{w}$ matrix and the corresponding Q matrices are shown.

To illustrate the applicability of CTD over and above the benchmark analytic techniques for network segmentation, we applied CTD to a series of scans from resting-state fMRI. Typically, clustering from resting-state fMRI results in the segmentation of a particular set of voxels known as the default mode network (DMN) [16–18]. Further, this clustering, while reliably found in healthy populations, has has been shown to be less clearly differentiated elderly populations, especially those with Alzheimer's Disease.

For the present work, we identified an exemplar scan whose clustering clearly indicated the DMN as one of its clusters. We then applied CTD, using the exemplar scan to demarcate regions of interest, to partition groups of scans including young and elderly individuals. Using this technique, we will illustrate a boost in intra-individual reliability (clustering across scans), by showing greater differentiation between different populations.

---

[1] Unconstrained tensor decomposition results have been shown to be relatively poor for fMRI data since, many spatially adjacent voxels in the same structure are not always active in the same factor. Pre-processing the tensor by applying wavelets can alleviate this and could complement our work, though in practice this pre-processing was time intensive and yielded only marginally better results.

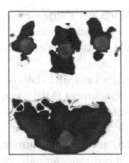

Fig. 2. Q matrices identified (a priori) as the top four nodes of the DMN amongst a possible 116 anatomical regions.

3 Empirical Results

Here, we used CTD to boost the reliability of intra-individual fMRI clustering and provide a new approach for assessing inter-individual clustering commonalities at a population level [3]. CTD uses an efficient generalized eigenvalue formulation to find a 2-category clustering of voxels such that voxels within the one cluster have highly similar time series. But at the same time, CTD attempts to satisfy user-provided guidance about which voxels should and should not cluster together. In this case, guidance took the form of the identification of 116 known anatomical regions used to constrain CTD to cluster a target scan. CTD provides a cluster quality metric that quantifies how difficult it was to provide a high-quality clustering of the target that is similar to that of the exemplar; we use this metric as a *clustering metric* between the groups. In our experiments, we summarize an entire population of fMRI scans in terms of clustering distance from an exemplar; however, we note that the clustering distance between any pair of scans can be quantified by applying CTD, thus providing a fine-grained assessment of the clustering quality between populations.

To illustrate the robustness of our approach, CTD was compared directly to the results of clustering using one of the benchmark analytic approaches, Independent Components Analysis (ICA) [19, 20]. ICA has widely been used across several resting and functional imaging paradigms. Independent component analysis attempts to separate independent "sources" of data by identifying different factors. These factors then, can be used to assess different levels of functional connectivity across populations.

In contrast, CTD attempts to take imaging data in the form of activations over a three dimensional spatial region, x, y, z over time t and simplify that activation into a network. Previously, we illustrated how this can be accomplished so that active cohesive regions (nodes) can be identified along with the formation of relationships (edges) between those regions [2]. Here, we focus more on the use of CTD to boost intra-individual clustering across scans.

We used real resting-state fMRI scans of normal and demented elderly individuals to demonstrate the advantages of CTD over ICA. A particular set of voxels, referred to as the default mode network (DMN), is known to generate highly similar time series in fMRI scans of healthy individuals, and the tightness of this clustering is known to be decreased in individuals with Alzheimer's disease [16]. Therefore, we analyzed the functional scans of 8 normal elderly and 8 demented participants. We used CTD to partition target scans including elderly and demented individuals based on constraints derived from the anatomical boundaries.

We present experimental results on fMRI data of eight healthy (Elderly), eight individuals with Mild Cognitive Impairment (MCI), and eight demented (Alzheimer's) individuals at rest. Each individual had been interviewed and measured using a series of cognitive tests to measure Episodic, Executive, Semantic and Spatial scores (whose range is from -2.5 to +2.5) and were categorized as Normal or having full-set Alzheimer's (Demented). When at rest state, an individual's brain activity exhibits the DMN in some form and in various degrees in all people. In normal individuals, the DMN is expected to be fully intact and well exhibited. However, for demented individuals the DMN may be only partially formed and the signal may be ery weak. These insights are well known and extensively published in the literature [16, 17] and we expect our method to be able to verify these results. The ability to determine the strength of the DMN from the scan is then akin to being able to predict the progression of Alzheimer's which we show is possible by predicting the cognitive scores (see below).

As can be clearly seen in Fig. 3 above, the use of SP was not sufficient in differentiating between the three populations of scans. However, through the use of CTD, we showed a differentiation in network quality between Elderly, MCI, and Demented. In other words, we show that the intra-individual reliability of CTD is greater than that of ICA. We also show that, as expected, the clustering metric (quality of cuts) between the healthy elderly individuals is less than that between the exemplar and demented elderly individuals, while there is no such significant difference for the analogous SP cluster quality metric. Finally, we show that this group difference between healthy and demented elders is robust across a range of constraint set sizes.

To provide convergence with the results presented above, we provided our algorithm with all 116 anatomical regions/masks of the brain encoded each in its own

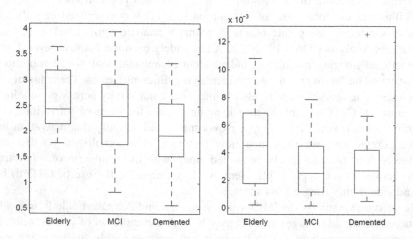

Fig. 3. SP and CTD partition cost differences. As can be seen, ICA (left) fails to differentiate clustering between different populations. However, the use of CTD (right) allows for clearer differentiation between Elderly and MCI and Demented.

Q matrix and performed a tensor decomposition and selected the top four factors (according to the w vector) to determine which nodes/structures were active in the brain during the scan. Table 1 (columns 2 and 3) shows the fraction of the various nodes/parts of the DMN found for Normal and Demented people in the top four factors.

Here, we clearly see that the DMN is completely discovered in seven out of the eight Elderly individuals with the eighth individual's prefrontal region being ranked fifth according to w. However, for the Demented group, the DMN is found in its entirety in only two of the eight patients. In other words, our approach clearly differentiated the signal strength between Elderly and Demented in terms of identifying specific brain regions associated with the DMN.

Figure 4 (top) shows the actual network reconstructed from the top four factors for the majority of the Elderly group. However, as can be seen in Fig. 4 (bottom), CTD was not able to recover the DMN for the majority of participants in the Demented group. This finding suggests, consistent with previous findings, that dementia has resulted in network activation that is less clearly organized and therefore does not preserve the DMN.

Table 1. Mean Pearson correlation for demented individuals for top four nodes of a network discovered for each individual. The nodes/structures denoted by * are part of the DMN.

	Elderly	Demented
Prefrontal Region	88 %	50 %
Posterior Cingulate	100 %	63 %
Inferior Parietal	100 %	38 %
Medial Temporal	100 %	25 %

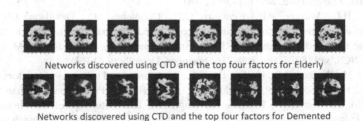

Networks discovered using CTD and the top four factors for Elderly

Networks discovered using CTD and the top four factors for Demented

Fig. 4. Networks reconstructed using the top four factors from Elderly (top) and Demented individuals.

4 Discussion

The primary aim of this paper was to introduce a new method for image segmentation of fMRI data. Specifically, we showed how the use of Constrained Tensor Decomposition could be used to better differentiate three different populations of scans. Here, we showed how this data-driven approach can utilize previous domain knowledge to increase the overall validity of the results.

The widespread use of neuroimaging data has warranted the need for the development of new and innovative techniques that analyze the data with a specific focus towards incorporating domain knowledge. Here, we showed how the use of CTD can be used by incorporating domain knowledge on an a priori basis to drive the data towards answering specific questions. Using this type of technique, we believe new opportunities in areas such as military selection and classification will develop.

Acknowledgments. This research is supported by Office of Naval Research grant NAVY 00014-09-1-0712. The opinions of the authors do not necessarily reflect those of the United States Navy or the University of California - Davis.

Peter B Walker and Sidney Fooshee are military service members. This work was prepared as part of their official duties. Title 17 U.S.C. 101 defines U.S. Government work as a work prepared by a military service member or employee of the U.S. Government as part of that person's official duties.

References

1. Walker, P.B., Davidson, I.: Exploring new methodologies for the analysis of functional magnetic resonance imaging (fMRI) following closed-head injuries. In: Schmorrow, D.D., Fidopiastis, C.M. (eds.) FAC 2011. LNCS, vol. 6780, pp. 120–128. Springer, Heidelberg (2011)
2. Davidson, I., Gilpin, S., Carmichael, O., Walker, P.: Guided network discovery via constrained tensor analysis of fMRI data. In: KDD 2013 Proceedings of the 19th ACM SIGKDD International Conference on Knowledge Discovery and Data Mining, pp. 194–202. ACM, New York (2013)
3. Wang, X., Qian, B., Davidson, I.: On constrained spectral clustering and its applications. Data Min. Knowl. Disc. **28**(1), 1–30 (2014)
4. Phillips, H.L., Walker, P.B., Kennedy, C.H., Carmichael, O., Davidson, I.N.: Guided learning algorithms: an application of constrained spectral partitioning to functional magnetic resonance imaging (fMRI). In: Schmorrow, D.D., Fidopiastis, C.M. (eds.) AC 2013. LNCS, vol. 8027, pp. 709–716. Springer, Heidelberg (2013)
5. Olson, T.M., Walker, P.B., Phillips IV, H.L.: Assessment and selection of aviators in the US military. In: O'Connor, P.E., Cohn, J.V. (eds.) Human Performance Enhancement in High-Risk Environments: Insights, Developments, and Future Directions from Military Research: Insights, Developments, and Future Directions from Military Research, pp. 37–57. ABC-CLIO, Santa Barbara (2009)
6. Gordon, H.W., Leighty, R.: Importance of specialized cognitive function in the selection of military pilots. J. Appl. Psychol. **73**(1), 38 (1988)
7. Graner, J., Oakes, T. R., French, L. M., Riedy, G.: Functional MRI in the investigation of blast-related traumatic brain injury. Front. Neurol. **4** (2013)
8. Friston, K.J., Frith, C.D., Liddle, P.F., Frackowiak, R.S.J.: Functional connectivity: the principal-component analysis of large (PET) data sets. J. Cerebr. Blood Flow Metab. **13**, 5 (1993)
9. Hoge, C.W., Castro, C.A., Messer, S.C., McGurk, D., Cotting, D.I., Koffman, R.L.: Combat duty in Iraq and Afghanistan, mental health problems, and barriers to care. N. Engl. J. Med. **351**(1), 13–22 (2004)

10. Tan, P.N., Steinbach, M., Kumar, V.: Introduction to Data Mining, 1st edn. Addison-Wesley Longman Publishing Co. Inc., Redwood City (2005)
11. Liu, Y., Wang, K., Yu, C., He, Y., Zhou, Y., Liang, M., Jiang, T.: Regional homogeneity, functional connectivity and imaging markers of Alzheimer's disease: a review of resting-state fMRI studies. Neuropsychologia **46**(6), 1648–1656 (2008)
12. Bennett, C.M., Miller, M.B.: How reliable are the results from functional magnetic resonance imaging? Ann. N. Y. Acad. Sci. **1191**(1), 133–155 (2010)
13. Rubinov, M., Sporns, O.: Complex network measures of brain connectivity: uses and interpretations. Neuroimage **52**(3), 1059–1069 (2010)
14. Davidson, I., Gilpin, S., Walker, P.B.: Behavioral event data and their analysis. J. Knowl. Disc. Data Min. **25**, 635–653 (2012). Springer, Special Issue on Human Behavioral Modeling
15. Genovese, C.R., Lazar, N.A., Nichols, T.: Thresholding of statistical maps in functional neuroimaging using the false discovery rate. Neuroimage **15**(4), 870–878 (2002)
16. Greicius, M.: Resting-state functional connectivity in neuropsychiatric disorders. Curr. Opin. Neurol. **21**(4), 424–430 (2008)
17. Greicius, M.D., Srivastava, G., Reiss, A.L., Menon, V.: Default-mode network activity distinguishes Alzheimer's disease from healthy aging: evidence from functional MRI. Proc. Natl. Acad. Sci. U.S.A. **101**(13), 4637–4642 (2004)
18. Raichle, M.E., Snyder, A.Z.: A default mode of brain function: a brief history of an evolving idea. Neuroimage **37**(4), 1083–1090 (2007)
19. Calhoun, V.D., Adali, T., Pearlson, G.D., Pekar, J.J.: A method for making group inferences from functional MRI data using independent component analysis. Hum. Brain Mapp. **14**(3), 140–151 (2001)
20. Ma, L., Wang, B., Chen, X., Xiong, J.: Detecting functional connectivity in the resting brain: a comparison between ICA and CCA. Magn. Reson. Imaging **25**(1), 47–56 (2007)

Cognition, Perception and Emotion Measurement

A Quantitative Methodology for Identifying Attributes Which Contribute to Performance for Officers at the Transportation Security Administration

Glory Emmanuel[1(✉)], Robert Kittinger[2], and Ann Speed[2]

[1] Sandia National Laboratories, Albuquerque, NM, USA
gremman@sandia.gov
[2] Principal Investigator, Sandia National Laboratories, Albuquerque, NM, USA
aespeed@sandia.gov

Abstract. Performance at Transportation Security Administration (TSA) airport checkpoints must be consistently high to skillfully mitigate national security threats and incidents. To accomplish this, Transportation Security Officers (TSOs) must exceptionally perform in threat detection, interaction with passengers, and efficiency. It is difficult to measure the human attributes that contribute to high performing TSOs because cognitive ability such as memory, personality, and competence are inherently latent variables. Cognitive scientists at Sandia National Laboratories have developed a methodology that links TSOs' cognitive ability to their performance. This paper discusses how the methodology was developed using a strict quantitative process, the strengths and weaknesses, as well as how this could be generalized to other non-TSA contexts. The scope of this project is to identify attributes that distinguished high and low TSO performance for the duties at the checkpoint that involved direct interaction with people going through the checkpoint.

Keywords: Measuring and adapting to individual differences · Cognitive modeling · Perception · Emotion and interaction · Quantifying latent variables

1 Introduction

Performance at Transportation Security Administration (TSA) airport checkpoints must be consistent, efficient, and exception to skillfully alleviate and ultimately prevent national security threats and incidents. Security checkpoints are primarily maintained by Transportation Security Officers (TSOs). They are responsible for providing exceptional performance in three primary areas: consistent vigilance of potential threats, ethics to ensure that travelers are respected as their personal property is searched, and efficiency to handle the volume of people who go through each checkpoint. Although high performing TSOs are critical for the TSA to meet its corporate vision and national security goals, it is difficult to measure the human attributes that contribute to performance. Attributes such as cognitive ability (e.g., memory, critical thinking, and competence), personality (e.g., conscientiousness), and social skills (e.g.,

D.D. Schmorrow and C.M. Fidopiastis (Eds.): AC 2015, LNAI 9183, pp. 373–380, 2015.
DOI: 10.1007/978-3-319-20816-9_35

command presence, leadership) are latent variables that are not easily observed, measured, or quantified. Moreover, performance is a challenging variable to measure because it is difficult to quantify threat detection, travelers' reactions, and efficiency in a dynamic operational environment like the airport security checkpoint.

Cognitive scientists at Sandia National Laboratories have developed a methodology to quantitatively link TSOs' cognitive ability to their performance. The scope of this project was to identify attributes that distinguished high and low TSO performance for the duties at the checkpoint that involved direct interaction with people going through the checkpoint. This paper first discusses how the methodology was developed using a strict empirical process. For proprietary purposes, the fine details and results are not presented. We then discuss some of the strengths and weaknesses of the experimental design. Finally, a set of ideas for how this could be generalized to other non-TSA contexts are offered.

The TSOs' job duties, specifically those interacting with passengers at the checkpoint, are challenging and require specific traits, skills, and attributes. Literature has supported the relationship between vocational interests and performance. Researchers conducted a meta-analysis, providing a quantitative summary of over 60 years of research [1]. Their meta-analysis indicates that vocational interests can be as predictive of job performance, tenure, and citizenship behaviors as can personality measures. It was concluded that it is important for an organization to understand the interest profile of the jobs for which they are hiring. Personality has also been linked to job performance. Another meta-analysis explored the predictive ability of personality inventories based on the Big Five personality traits for job performance. It was found that conscientiousness, agreeableness, and openness to experience were all positively correlated with performance.

There has been no study to date that investigates the knowledge, skills, and abilities (KSAs) and attitudes, aptitudes, and attributes (AAAs) that TSOs should have to optimally perform. Findings from a study of this nature would be highly valuable because it would inform how to manage TSOs at the checkpoint and may even influence how TSA hires personnel. The overall goal is to investigate how a TSO's KSAs and AAAs may distinguish high and low performance.

Ultimately, the TSA headquarters research team is highly interested in moving past basic employee requirements and desires to better understand the cognitive and psychosocial factors that may help to improve TSO performance. The current study, designed and executed by the Sandia researchers, aims to examine the following questions:

- How valid are measures shown to successfully predict TSO performance?
- Are we able to use a battery of cognitive assessments to help TSA identify high performing TSOs?

2 Experimental Design

The overall goal of this study is to identify relationships between predictor variables and performance variables. Sandia researchers first started with identifying the performance variables in the TSA context. Through iterative conversations and trips to TSA locations, a number of performance variables were identified. These included, to name a few, annual test scores, human resources data such as attendance and awards, and performance review ratings. Note that the focus was on numerical data. Qualitative data such as supervisor comments and customer feedback were identified but were not used in this study due to their subjective nature. The performance data would ultimately need to be connected to the data we collected from TSOs so it was equally important to understand the identifiers in the performance dataset(s) in order to create a solid link between our collected data (predictor variables) to the TSA performance variables.

Once we established TSA performance metrics that were eligible for quantitative analyses as well as the needed identifiers, we turned our attention to the predictor variables. We classified predictor variables into two categories: (1) competencies and critical knowledge, skills, and abilities (KSAs), and (2) attributes, aptitudes, and attitudes (AAAs). Competencies and KSAs are defined in industrial-organization (I/O) psychology: "A competency refers to an individual's demonstrated knowledge, skills, or abilities [3]. Note, however, that competencies go beyond the more traditional KSAs; they are KSAs that are demonstrated in a job context influenced by the organizational culture and business environment. for the job of interest [4]. These are usually defined by the organization, in this case, TSA. The next category of predictor variables, AAAs, is a concept defined by Sandia and TSA as the cognitive, social, and personality skills that can be measured and quantified and represent the latent, non-tangible KSAs. The process for identifying KSAs and AAAs is presented.

2.1 Knowledges, Skills, and Abilities (KSAs)

To identify KSAs, we used the standard I/O method, which is to utilize job task analyses. Commonly accepted best practices and industry standards call for a job analysis to be completed prior to modifying or developing job candidate selection criteria [4]. This process also fulfills the legal requirements in accord with the Uniform Guidelines on Employee Selection [5]. A Job Task Analysis (JTA) is the process of defining all the elements and work activities required for successful performance of a job and serves as the foundation for determining which assessments are appropriate for administration on TSOs. This includes all job duties, roles, and job tasks, as well as the Equipment, Machines, Tools and Technology (EMTTs) used to accomplish each job task. It also identifies at the employee level all of the knowledge, skills, abilities and other variables (KSA-Os) necessary to successfully complete each job task. Finally, a task analysis can come out of a job analysis providing a detailed explanation each job task's relative importance, frequency of completion, and criticality. This type of task analysis is similar to the DIF (difficulty, importance, and frequency) analysis commonly utilized by HR and Training & Development departments. Fortunately, TSA's Human Capital program had already conducted multiple JTAs which Sandia was able to leverage. However, to specifically address the aims and hypotheses we are interested in, which is connecting TSOs performance at the checkpoint, specifically related to TSOs interaction with the passengers, additional work was needed to connect the different JTAs.

Workshops using subject matter experts (SMEs) were organized. The workshops were used to get a group of SMEs to vote on the most critical KSAs and competencies TSA valued for each job task at the checkpoint. Multiple workshops were held across a variety of airports to get a diversity of opinions. After all the SME workshops were completed, the data was aggregated and analyzed until a SME-based ranking of valued KSAs and competencies was developed. The rankings represented what SMEs collectively reported as the most critical and influential KSAs for high performance on passenger-related (non-X-ray) job tasks.

2.2   Attitudes, Attributes, and Aptitudes (AAAs)

This ranked list of KSAs and competencies created categories that then enabled the Sandia researchers to link to AAAs. The difference between the KSAs and AAAs was that the KSAs were specific to the TSA tasks and duties whereas the AAAs were overarching group of attributes connected to self-report measures or tasks found in the empirical open literature. For example, command presence, independence, accountability, and assertiveness were ranked by SMEs to be important KSAs and competencies related to a number of passenger related tasks at the checkpoint. For the AAAs, these attributes were grouped into one category, "Strong Presence" and quantified using difference subscales from the Personality and Preference Inventory [5]. The purpose of grouping similar AAAs into a single category was to limit the number of hypotheses tested and therefore not inflate alpha levels during statistical analyses. Once the AAA categories were established, a "priority score" was calculated for each group. The priority score number represented how many times six or more SMEs ranked one of the KSAs as an essential ingredient for completing a critical task listed in the JTA.

Overall, the KSAs enabled us to understand what the most important AAAs were to the TSA environment and create a battery of cognitive, social, and personality measures that were either established in open, empirical literature or developed specifically for this study. Established measures in the battery were found to be validated and reliable with high internal consistency; those that were developed will be checked for their internal validity before use in data analyses.

2.3   Participants

This study aimed to collect data from a minimum of 200 existing TSOs across a minimum of eight TSA airports. A power analysis was conducted prior to data collection an estimated 200 TSOs to achieve a power of at least .80. Employees who participated in this study were required to meet the following criteria prior to data collection:

1. Currently hold the job title of TSO, Lead TSO (LTSO), or Supervisor TSO (STSO)
2. They must have had the job as an officer for over one year
3. They must be either passenger (PAX) or DUAL certified
4. Be at least 18 years old

2.4 Data Collection

Once the battery of measures was compiled, the study design went through a human subjects' board (HSB) approval process at Sandia Labs and TSA Headquarters to obtain institutional review and approval. Then, permissions were obtained for the use of each measure. Finally, each measure was loaded onto SurveyMonkey. Survey-Monkey is an online platform designed for web-based data collection. Cellular connected tablets (version 6) were deployed to each airport so that participants could complete the online battery of assessments. Although this led to limited connectivity and data load time issues, the use of tablets was a safer method of protecting participant data because it utilized a cellular internet connection rather than a less protected network such as Wi-Fi.

Proctors were trained at each airport so that the Sandia researchers would only have to be onsite at each airport for 2 to 3 days but data collection could continue for up to two weeks to obtain a large sample from each airport. When participants arrived, a TSA research proctor trained by the Sandia researchers distributed all of the materials (an iPad and a red folder containing a consent form, a checklist, and participant instructions). The proctor directed the participants to read over an HSB stamped and approved informed consent form that detailed the study process and metrics. It stated that participation was voluntary and withdrawal was permitted at any time. If the TSO decided to participate in the study, they signed and dated the consent form and returned it to the proctor. All participants were offered a copy of the informed consent for their records.

Once all signed informed consent documents were collected, the proctor read a formal script addressing the participants, providing instructions on how to begin the battery of assessments, and offering to answer questions or provide other help. Once the script was concluded, the proctor provided additional help to the group (and one-on-one as needed) to help the participants create their unique identifiers and to start the first assessment. Proctors walked participants through the process of how to complete the online assessment on the tablets. The whole battery took approximately 4 to 6 h to complete. The battery was split into seven blocks to encourage breaks and help participants keep their place in the battery. Because participants completed the assessments at their own pace, breaks were taken individually, not as a group. To minimize the effect of cognitive fatigue on the final results the most important assessments were placed earlier in the battery order.

3 Data Analyses

Once data collection is completed at all the airports, all the raw data will be compiled and screened prior to analyses. The screening process will allow the researchers to check for any inaccuracies or issues that may have occurred during data collection. Data collected will also be scored according to the calculations instructed for the subscales prescribed each measure.

3.1 Data Characteristics

Data will be checked for missing data, assumptions of normality of distributions, linearity, homogeneity of variance, homogeneity of regression, and reliability of covariates. Each measure has been validated in the public domain. However, since TSOs is a new sample demographic for many of the measures used in this study, factor analyses will also be conducted for each measure and its corresponding subscales to examine internal consistency and construct validity.

3.2 Hypothesis Testing

Averages for each participant's AAA subscales will be correlated with TSA performance data. It is expected that positive AAAs such as empathy and perspective taking, command presence, and emotional intelligence will positively relate to higher levels of performance. It is also expected that negative AAAs such as indecisiveness, the dark triad of personality, and touch avoidance will relate positively relate to lower levels of performance. Many of the measures have multiple subscales which will also be used to test hypotheses. Statistical analyses such as a profile analysis will be conducted to understand how AAA responses differ based on TSA performance ratings.

3.3 Demographics

Demographic data on age, gender, years of TSO experience, TSO level (TSO, LTSO, STSO) past military experience, education level, entry data, time in TSO position, airport/area, veteran (type) were also collected. Exploratory analyses will be conducted to how both AAAs and performance relate to demographics.

4 Strengths and Weaknesses

This methodology has enabled us to collect data across multiple airports and have large participation rates from a number of TSOs. The major strength is that this study provides a method to take latent variables important to the TSA checkpoint, such as command presence, visual acuity, and intuition, and quantify them so the relationship they have with performance variables can be statistically tested. This enables TSA to make rational, informed decisions on how to structure TSOs' roles and responsibilities at the checkpoint and overall nurture high performance. Another strength is the portability of data collection. Through the deployment of tablets, the utilization of online assessments, and the partnership with TSA headquarters, data was able to be collected across airports to obtain a diverse sample. The large sample size will help both with looking at group differences within the sample (for example, low versus high levels of experience) and for increasing effect sizes to determine if statistical findings are robust.

One major weakness of this study is the limited metric we have of performance. Ideally, performance would be determined by comparing the number of threats identified with the number of threats unidentified. This ground truth is nearly impossible to obtain. Our performance variables were thus limited to how TSA as an employer rates its employees through annual performance review and employee behaviors such as attendance. Data included in statistical models were also required to be quantitative and on a numerical scale. We did not include qualitative data. Future research could utilize techniques such as text analytics to obtain data on TSOs' cognitive processes and performance. For example, if performance records have comments for each TSO on file, the comments could be analyzed using text-based algorithms. One final weakness is the dynamic nature of TSA as a growing, maturing organization. The AAAs were based on the JTAs that listed out the tasks critical to the TSO job. The TSO job and its related standards of practice are occasionally updated to accommodate the changing security checkpoint environment (such as the introduction of the electronic boarding passengers and new screening equipment Research in this area should be updated every few years to maintain the relevance of its findings to the airport security checkpoint environment.

5 Additional Contexts

A major benefit of this research is the insight it provides to the Transportation Security Administration. However, this methodology contains elements that are applicable to many organizations. Most organizations have a set of performance metrics used to understand where employees are on a performance spectrum. Job Task Analyses and the use of I/O psychology in business settings are becoming a more widely used practice. Already existing JTAs can be leveraged or JTAs can be developed from scratch by I/O psychologists to understand what the critical KSAs are. At a minimum, SME workshops can be held to identify and rank the most important tasks and their respective KSAs/competencies. Once a list of predictor variables and performance variables as well as the identifiers that link the two have been established, researchers can utilize the open, empirical literature to locate measures that will quantify the predictor variables. The Sandia researchers have used similar processes to research domains to expand research into other relevant areas of TSA. These methodological principles have also been applied by Sandia researchers to different domains such as cyber security, the impact of the working environment on creativity and collaboration, analysts in military contexts, and other national security contexts.

6 Summary and Conclusion

In summary, this study applies a strict, quantitative methodology to empirically understand the relationship between AAAs and performance in the TSA security checkpoint context. The methodology we developed enables us to investigate how latent, human dimension variables such as memory, personality, and competence specific to a target population's roles and responsibilities, such as TSOs, influence performance in that domain. This methodology is beneficial but not limited to TSA. Researchers that have access to performance metrics and Job Task Analyses could utilize a comparable methodology to accomplish similar goals.

Acknowledgements. Sandia National Laboratories is a multi-program laboratory managed and operated by Sandia Corporation, a wholly owned subsidiary of Lockheed Martin Corporation, for the U.S. Department of Energy's National Nuclear Security Administration under contract DE-AC04-94AL85000, Sandia Report 2015-1424C. Approved for public release; further dissemination unlimited. This research was funded in part or whole by an Interagency Agreement between the Transportation Security Administration and the Department of Energy.

References

1. Nye, C.D., Su, R., Rounds, J., Drasgow, F.: Vocational interests and performance a quantitative summary of over 60 years of research. Perspect. Psychol. Sci. **7**(4), 384–403 (2012)
2. Hurtz, G.M., Donovan, J.J.: Personality and job performance: the big five revisited. J. Applied Psych. **85**(6), 869–879 (2000)
3. Ulrich, D., Brockbank, W., Yeung, A.K., Lake, D.G.: Human resource competencies: an empirical assessment. Human Resource Manage. **34**(4), 473–495 (1995)
4. Society of Industrial-Organizational Psychology (SIOP) official website, http://www.siop.org
5. Equal Employment Opportunity Commission. http://www.eeoc.gov/
6. Personality and Preference Inventory, http://www.cubiks.org

Cognitive-Motor Processes During Arm Reaching Performance Through a Human Body-Machine Interface

Rodolphe J. Gentili[1,2,3]($\boxtimes$), Isabelle M. Shuggi[1], Kristen M. King[1],
Hyuk Oh[1,2], and Patricia A. Shewokis[4,5,6]

[1] Department of Kinesiology, Cognitive Motor Neuroscience Laboratory,
University of Maryland, College Park, MD 20742, USA
rodolphe@umd.edu
[2] Neuroscience and Cognitive Science Program, University of Maryland,
College Park, MD 20742, USA
[3] Maryland Robotics Center, University of Maryland, College Park
MD 20742, USA
[4] School of Biomedical Engineering, Science, and Health Systems,
Drexel University, Philadelphia, PA 19102, USA
[5] Nutrition Sciences Department, College of Nursing and Health Professions,
Drexel University, Philadelphia, PA 19102, USA
[6] College of Medicine, Department of Surgery, Surgical Education,
Drexel University, Philadelphia, PA 19102, USA

Abstract. Head controlled based systems represent a class of human body-machine interfaces that employ head motion to control an external device. Overall, the related work has focused on technical developments with limited user performance assessments while generally ignoring the underlying motor learning and cognitive processes. Thus, this study examined, during and after practice, the cognitive-motor states of users when controlling a robotic arm with limited head motion under various control modalities. As a first step, two groups having a different degree of control of the arm directions were considered. The preliminary results revealed that both groups: (i) similarly improved their reaching performance during practice; (ii) provided, after practice, a similar performance generalization while still relying on visual feedback and (iii) exhibited similar cognitive workload. This work can inform the human cognitive-motor processes during learning and performance of arm reaching movements as well as develop rehabilitation systems for disabled individuals.

Keywords: Cognitive-motor performance · Arm reaching movements · Motor practice and learning · Cognitive workload · Human body-machine interface · Robotic arm · Motor rehabilitation

1 Introduction

Over the last three decades a large body of work has focused on developing assistive technology devices for people having various severe motor disabilities (e.g. locked-in-syndrome, amyotrophic lateral sclerosis, spinal cord injury, quadriplegia,

© Springer International Publishing Switzerland 2015
D.D. Schmorrow and C.M. Fidopiastis (Eds.): AC 2015, LNAI 9183, pp. 381–392, 2015.
DOI: 10.1007/978-3-319-20816-9_36

muscular dystrophy, cerebral palsy) to allow them to regain motor functions for recovering some degree of interaction capabilities with their environment. Numerous studies have proposed and assessed these types of assistive technologies which apply the general underlying principles which are based on human-machine interfaces that record and transform the available biosignals (e.g., muscle, brain activity; eye, head, tongue movements) into control signals to guide an external device (e.g., [1–9])

A particular class of assistive systems is based on human-machine interfaces which relate body motions with their sensory consequences through an external device. Such human body-machine interfaces allow the users to implement full or shared control of the assistive device by employing motion signals recorded from the user's body (e.g., eye, head, shoulder, tongue movements) [10–12]. Independently of the interface and of the type of control signals considered, the user must learn a mapping between the movements of the body segments that remain functional into the corresponding sensory consequences such as the spatial displacement of an external device that often takes the form of a cursor displayed on a computer screen. However, learning the control of an external device is generally a challenging task since the user employs body segments or portions of body segments that are still functional but that would not necessarily be used to perform the same task under normal conditions [10–12].

A particular instance of this class of assistive systems are the devices controlled through head motion to regain navigation (e.g., wheelchairs) or reaching (e.g., computer cursors) capabilities (e.g., [4, 5, 13–15]). In the case of head controlled devices, the execution of reaching tasks which would be usually performed with the upper extremity are now executed with limited head motions which is rather unnatural [16]. Thus, becoming skillful with head reaching controlled devices depends on the learning of sensorimotor mapping between relatively limited head movements and spatial displacements of the external device to control [10–12]. The challenge associated with these types of motor learning and performance tasks can result in an increase in a user's fatigue, motivation, frustration and cognitive workload which can affect the motor performance and/or the capability to perform other tasks [17–20].

However, this particular body of work generally has primarily focused on developing reliable, easy-to-use and low cost head-controlled devices while conducting a relatively limited assessment of the cognitive-motor performance and in particular the motor learning processes underlying the reaching skill with such devices [4, 5, 8, 15, 21–26]. First, although it was previously reported that the mastery of head-controlled pointing systems generally requires practice, the assessment of motor performance throughout the practice period with those devices is relatively limited [8, 15, 23–25, 27–33]. Among the few studies that examined practice of head-controlled pointing devices, analyses are generally limited (e.g., mainly use movement time) and the results are relatively heterogeneous. Such heterogeneity may be attributed to the differences between the various types of head-controlled systems [30]. However, although heterogeneous, as a whole these findings revealed that to reach a certain degree of skillfulness, a practice period is needed and can range from about 60 to almost 800 trials, depending on the device itself [25, 28, 30–32]. Next, the assessment of motor performance after the practice period was generally not assessed by requiring the individual to perform the task under different conditions to inform the state of the acquired mapping (e.g., transfer, reduced visual feedback). Lastly, besides the motor aspect of the performance, the consideration of a user's cognitive states such as cognitive workload was generally overlooked by previous studies [15, 23–25, 28–32]. Moreover, it is important to assess cognitive workload while individuals perform during/after practice since it can: (i) inform about the relationship between the attentional and motor processes (e.g., [18–20, 34]); (ii) impact the capability of the user to perform other tasks and/or to be unable to handle unexpected event (e.g., [18–20, 34]); and (iii) contribute to develop better assistive systems [35, 36]. For instance, it was shown that when individuals perform a motor task under various conditions of challenges and/or while learning a new mapping while executing arm reaching movements, the performer's cognitive workload and allocation of attentional resources can be impacted (e.g., [18–20, 34, 37]). Thus, our aim was to examine the effects of practice on cognitive-motor performance while users control a virtual robotic arm with limited head movements by employing various control modalities (e.g., various directions, velocity control). Theoretically, we posit that work in this area can provide information about the cognitive-motor processes during the learning of sensorimotor maps during performance of reaching tasks while mitigating biases due to previous motor experiences [10–12]. From an applied perspective, our work could contribute to the enhancement of the design, training and assessment of head-controlled reaching devices.

Therefore, as an initial step, by considering two simple directional control modalities through which individuals employed limited head motion to learn control of a virtual robotic arm, we examined their reaching performance: (i) throughout the practice period while subsequently assessing the corresponding cognitive workload and (ii) after the practice period by assessing transfer to untrained targets and reliance on visual feedback while performing the newly acquired reaching skills.

2 Materials and Methods

2.1 The Human-Robot Interface

Signals from two infrared sensors placed on the forehead and chin of the participants were acquired with a motion capture camera-based system (Optotrak™) and were sent to the human body-machine interface to track a user's rotation movements of the head. Then, this information was used to compute the desired directional displacements of a virtual robotic arm in a two dimensional (2D) workspace. A chin sensor was employed for selecting/confirming the acquisition of the target by opening the mouth. Once the target was selected, the participant moved his/her head to reach this target with the robotic arm.

2.2 Participants and Reaching Task

Twelve healthy individuals (N = 12), with normal or corrected-to-normal vision, participated in this study. The participants were randomly assigned into two groups either a four directional (up, down, left and right) or eight directional (up, down, left, right and the four diagonals) limited head motions to move the end-effector of the robotic arm. The head controlled device worked in a similar way to a regular joystick. Namely, in the resting position, the sensor position placed on the forehead was in the neutral region (or *deadband*) and thus the robotic arm stayed motionless. However, when a movement of head rotation in a particular direction was executed, the forehead sensor moved out from the *deadband* and thus resulted in a spatial displacement of the arm in the selected direction. As such, participants were able to stop and drive the robotic arm at a constant velocity throughout the 2D workspace until the end-effector reached a given target. The participants were also able to select the presented target to reach by opening their mouth beyond a certain threshold. For consistency, both groups followed exactly the same experimental protocol, the only difference being the number of directions in which they could move the robotic arm to learn a very simple sensorimotor map between head movements and the spatial displacements of the virtual robotic end-effector.

To familiarize participants of both groups with the interface of the head-controlled system, they performed head movements in any of the four (first group) or eight (second group) directions, which once decoded, were displayed in the form of a corresponding label (e.g., "Up"; "Up and left") on a blank display to allow participants to understand the range of motion required to control the device while minimizing any learning processes. The participants performed this familiarization stage until they felt comfortable to generate appropriate head movements for all the directions their interface allowed.

Next, the experiment was divided into two main stages which were the practice and post-practice periods. During both periods, the target (red diamond) to be reached was displayed on the computer screen to the participants who had to select the target (which turned green when selected) and then reach this target with the robotic arm. Once the target was touched by the robotic end-effector, the next target was presented and the information related to the previous trial was erased.

During the practice period, participants of both groups performed reaching movements toward targets that were randomly presented and spatially distributed to cover the entire workspace (for consistency, the random sequence was the same for every participant).

After completion of the practice period, a rest (>20 min) was provided to the participant during which time they completed two surveys that included a visual analog scale (VAS) and the NASA TLX [38] questionnaires to assess their cognitive workload as well as the level of task difficulty and effort of the participants who just performed the reaching task. Then, after the rest period, two post-practice tests were presented to the participants to assess immediate retention as well as transfer of motor performance to targets that were not experienced before with full and partial visual feedback. The first and second post-practice tests allowed for the performance of reaching movements with full and partial visual feedback where half of the trials (n = 10) included known targets whereas the other half (n = 10) included new targets. Partial visual feedback was defined as the user was unable to see the entire forearm during the spatial region defined as the distance between the robotic end-effector and the target to reach between 1/3 and 2/3 of its radius. The order of the presentation of the two post-practice tests was counterbalanced to avoid any order effects and the presentation of the targets followed a random sequence (but the same random sequence for all participants).

Motor performance was quantified during the practice period as well as the two post-practice periods by computing the number of control signals (CS, defined as the number of changes in direction) sent to the robotic arm, movement time (MT), movement length (ML), and normalized jerk (NJ) for each participant and each trial [29, 35, 39, 40]. Since the distance between the random targets were different, each metric computed for a particular movement executed between two successive targets was normalized to the corresponding Euclidian distance. Then, for the practice period, these normalized metrics were tested using 2 Group (four, eight directions) × 20 Blocks repeated measures ANOVAs with repeated measures on the last factor where one practice block included 10 trials. In addition, the early (the four first trial blocks), middle (trial blocks 9, 10, 11, 12) and late (the four last trial blocks) practice periods were analyzed by employing 2 Group (four, eight directions) × 3 Period (early, middle, late) repeated measures ANOVAs, with repeated measures on the last factor. For the post-practice periods, these metrics were tested using 2 Group (four, eight directions) × 2 Modalities (full, partial visual feedback) × 2 Targets (trained, untrained) repeated measures ANOVAs with repeated measures on the last two factors. A Greenhouse-Geisser correction was applied when sphericity was violated for all repeated measures analyses. Tukey-Kramer multiple comparison tests were used to assess significant interactions and Blocks and Phases main effects. The scores from the VAS and NASA TLX questionnaires were contrasted using either an independent samples *t-test* or *Mann-Whitney* test depending on whether the assumption of normality was met or not. A significance criterion of $\alpha = 0.05$ was used for all tests.

3   Results

3.1   Reaching Performance

Generally, the findings revealed that both groups: (i) performed similarly during practice as well as during the post-test sessions; (ii) were able to transfer their reaching skills to targets that were not experienced before but also exhibited reduced performance with partial visual feedback while still able to reach the targets.

Specifically, the practice period revealed a main effect of the trial blocks for CS, MT and ML $(F(1,19) = 5.05; p < 0.001;$ all conditions considered). The post hoc analysis revealed that the values of CS, MT and ML obtained for the blocks 2, 3 and 7 were significantly higher compared to those for the block 11, 13, 15 and 19 $(p < 0.05,$ all comparisons considered). Moreover, compared to block 17, the values of CS and MT were significantly larger than those obtained for the block 7 while ML were significantly higher for the blocks 2 and 3 $(p < 0.05,$ all comparisons considered) (Fig. 1). Also, the values of CS and ML for block 14 were larger than those of the blocks 13 and 19 $(p < 0.05)$. No effect was observed for NJ $(p > 0.05)$ (Figs. 2 and 3).

When contrasting the value of CS, MT, ML and NJ during the early, middle and late practice periods, the results revealed a main effect for the factor Period for all four metrics $(F(2,20) = 6.03, p < 0.009;$ all conditions considered). The post hoc analysis revealed that the values for MT and ML were significantly higher during the early compared to the middle and late practice $p < 0.04;$ all conditions considered). The same comparison for the values for the CS and NJ during early compared to the middle

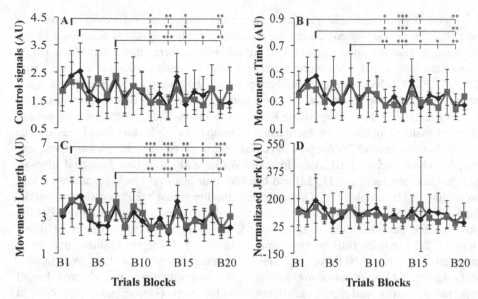

Fig. 1. Performance across the practice blocks considering the number of control signals provided to the robotic arm (A), the movement time (B), movement length (C) and normalized jerk (D) during reaching movements (mean ± SD). AU: Arbitrary unit; Bi: Trial block i. The forks indicate the statistical difference between the blocks 2, 3, 7 (thick ticks) versus the blocks 11, 13, 15, 17 and 19 (thin ticks). The black diamond and gray square represent the first (i.e., using the control modality that includes four directions) and second (i.e., using the control modality that includes eight directions) group, respectively. *:p < 0.05; **: p < 0.01; ***: p < 0.001.

practice revealed a significant difference (p = 0.05) and an absence of significant effect, respectively. However, the values of these two metrics revealed that they were significantly higher during the early compared to late practice period (p < 0.01; all conditions considered). No difference between middle and late period was observed (p > 0.05).

Finally, when analyzing the values for the post-test sessions, the results revealed a main effect of the feedback modality (F(1,10) = 16.51, p < 0.003; all conditions considered). The post hoc analysis, revealed that the CS, MT, ML and NJ were significantly larger for the performance with full compared to partial visual feedback (p < 0.003). No main or interaction effects for the factor groups and targets were observed (p > 0.05; all conditions considered). No main or interaction effects for the factor groups and targets reached significance (p > 0.05; all conditions considered).

3.2 Questionnaires

For both groups none of the components of the VAS and NASA TLX revealed any statistical differences (p > 0.19, all questions considered). It must be noted that the mental demand dimension assessed with both the VAS and NASA TLX provided convergent results.

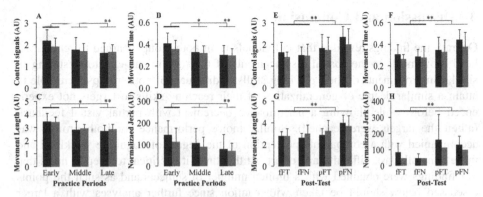

Fig. 2. Reaching performances summarized throughout various practice periods (A-D) and during the post-practice sessions (E-H) (mean ± SD). (A-D) Kinematic performance indexed by the CS, MT, ML and NJ during early, middle and late practice periods. (E-H) Kinematic performance indexed by the same four metrics during post-practice for previously experienced and novel targets with full and partial visual feedback. fFT: Previously experienced targets with full visual feedback; fFN: Novel targets with full visual feedback; pFT: Previously experienced targets with partial visual feedback; fFN: Novel targets with partial visual feedback. The black and gray bars represent the first (i.e., using the control modality that includes four directions) and second (i.e., using the control modality that includes eight directions) group, respectively. The forks represent the comparison between the early (thick lines) and middle/late (thin lines) period. *: $p < 0.05$; **: $p < 0.01$; ***: $p < 0.001$.

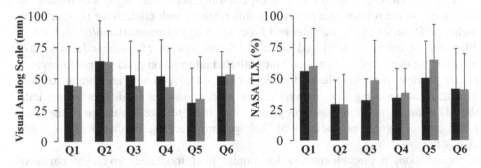

Fig. 3. Questionnaires results to assess the cognitive load, task difficulty and effort during of the performed reaching task. Left panel: results for the visual analog scale for both groups. Q1: "how hard it was to perform the reaching task?"; Q2: "how much did I have to concentrate to perform the reaching task?"; Q3: "how mentally loaded did I feel while performing the reaching task?"; Q4: "how effortful it was to perform the reaching task?"; Q5: "how tired was I after the reaching task?"; Q6: "how do you feel the arm velocity was" (the anchors were too slow, appropriate, too fast). Right panel: result for the NASA TLX for both groups. Qi: score reported for the question #i. The black and gray bars represent the first (i.e., using the control modality that includes four directions) and second (i.e., using the control modality that includes eight directions) group, respectively.

4 Discussion and Conclusion

Overall, the findings revealed that individuals from both groups learned to relate their head movements to the spatial displacements of the robotic end-effector resulting in similar improvements of their reaching skills. Individuals of both groups were able to attain a similar degree of generalization of their reaching skills to targets not experienced before while showing a performance decrement with partial visual feedback (albeit the targets were reached). Similar motor performance for both groups was accompanied with a comparable perception of the degree of cognitive workload and more generally task difficulty and effort. At this time, it is critical to keep in mind that our findings were obtained with a limited number of subjects and as such the points discussed below should be taken with caution since further analyses with a larger sample and increased statistical power must be conducted.

First, it was observed that, compared to the four directional group, individuals of the eight directional group presented a similar cognitive-motor performance (cognitive workload, CS, MT, ML and NJ) whereas the latter had the possibility to employ the four diagonals as additional control signals to move the robotic end-effector. Thus, participants of the eight directional group do not seem to take advantage of these additional control signals to perform better considering the practice period allotted in this study. This finding expands and confirms those from previous studies that proposed and assessed head controlled pointing device with diagonal control directions. Namely, it was reported that some users used the diagonal directions only rarely or that the single-direction movements were more efficient compared to diagonal movements [4, 8, 33].

This is interesting since it could be expected that additional degrees of freedom in the control of the robotic arm to perform this reaching task could have (i) resulted in higher performance (e.g., straighter and faster reaching movements) and/or (ii) have an effect on the cognitive workload since a different system of commands may have modified the degree of challenge and thus affected information processing. However, it is also possible that while the performance metrics analyzed here are similar for both groups, additional long term training and/or specific training conditions for the individuals of the eight directional group may allow them to take advantage of the additional control signals enhancing thus their performance [8]. Further analyses could clarify this point.

In addition, a possible reason for similar (and moderate) levels of cognitive workload for both groups would be that the velocity at which the robotic end-effector was operated was perceived by individuals of both groups as appropriate (see VAS, question 6). The velocity at which the arm moves is important since any substantial augmentation of the velocity could result in an increase of the challenge and thus would likely increase the cognitive workload as shown on other tasks [18, 19]. Thus, the use of an appropriate end-effector velocity to perform the task may possibly place the individuals in the neighborhood of a reasonable level of challenge to learn the reaching movements. Although likely not optimal for some individuals, a reasonable level of challenge would place participants of both groups in a relatively suitable functional task difficulty which would not overwhelm their information processing system resulting in similar (and rather moderate) levels of cognitive workload [41].

The use of an appropriate end-effector velocity may also have contributed to enhanced transfer of performance to novel targets since it was previously suggested that the closer the level of challenge is to optimal, the greater learning benefit as transfer performance improves [41, 42]. Also, the relatively positive transfer of reaching performance to novel targets may also have been a result of how the targets were presented (i.e., which spatially covered the entire workspace). From a computational standpoint, to reach the novel targets, the human motor control system would perform neural computations that may be functionally similar to interpolations. It must be noted that in our case the practice paradigm required the participants to explore the entire workspace while executing reaching movements with the robotic arm. This type of practice method is more ecologically valid in comparison to restraining the individuals to reach specific and limited regions of the workspace using fewer targets as it is the case in classic paradigms that employ center-out reaching movements or standardized ISO (International Organization for Standardization) 9241-9 tasks. Although these laboratory tasks may provide a direct way to assess motor performance and learning processes, they have limited ecological validity.

While the targets were reached in the presence of limited visual feedback of the upper arm, the reduced performance indicates that, after practice, the participants still rely on visual inputs to control the robotic arm. A possible explanation about this reliance on visual feedback may be due to the nature of the control which results into some reduced association between sensorimotor signals related to head commands and the end-effector displacements which are discrete and continuous, respectively [43, 44]. Further analyses with a larger pool of participants should help to further inform this particular aspect of sensorimotor feedback and control.

Future work will include other conditions to examine how the manipulation of the end-effector velocity can influence the cognitive-motor performance of the participants. The long term goal of this work is to inform: (i) the human cognitive-motor processes underlying learning and performance during arm reaching movements executed through human-machine interface when humans perform alone or when teaming with an adaptive system, as well as (ii) develop intelligent human-robotic interfaces and rehabilitation systems for individuals with severe motor disabilities.

References

1. Pinheiro Jr., C.G., Naves, E.L., Pino, P., Losson, E., Andrade, A.O., Bourhis, G.: Alternative communication systems for people with severe motor disabilities: a survey. Biomed. Eng. Online **10**, 31 (2011)
2. Chin, C.A., Barreto, A.: Enhanced hybrid electromyogram/eye gaze tracking cursor control system for hands-free computer interaction. In: 28th IEEE International Conference of the Engineering in Medicine and Biology Society, pp. 2296–2299. IEEE Press, New York (2006)
3. Chen, Y.L., Kuo, T.S., Chang, W.H., Lai, J.S.: A novel position sensors-controlled computer mouse for the disabled. In: 22th IEEE International Conference of the Engineering in Medicine and Biology Society, pp. 2263–2266. IEEE Press, New York (2000)

4. Evans G., Blenkhorn, P.: A head operated joystick-experience with use. In: CSUN 14th Annual International conference on Technology and Persons with Disabilities, Los Angeles (1999)
5. Evans, D.G., Drew, R., Blenkon, P.: Controlling mouse pointer position using an infrared head-operated joystick. IEEE Trans. Rehabil. Eng. **8**(1), 107–117 (2000)
6. Huo, X., Wang, J., Ghovanloo, M.: A magneto-inductive sensor based wireless tongue-computer interface. IEEE Trans. Neural Syst. Rehabil. **16**, 497–503 (2008)
7. Curtin, A., Ayaz, H., Liu, Y., Shewokis, P.A., Onaral, B.: A P300-based EEG-BCI for spatial navigation control. In: 34th IEEE International Conference of the Engineering in Medicine and Biology Society, pp. 3841–3844. IEEE Press, New York (2012)
8. Williams, M.R., Kirsch, R.F.: Evaluation of head orientation and neck muscle EMG signals as command inputs to a human-computer interface for individuals with high tetraplegia. IEEE Trans. Neural Syst. Rehabil. Eng. **16**, 485–496 (2008)
9. Wolpaw, J.: Brain-computer interfaces as new brain output pathways. J. Physiol. **579**(3), 613–619 (2007)
10. Casadio, M., Ranganathan, R., Mussa-Ivaldi, F.A.: The body-machine interface: a new perspective on an old theme. J. Mot. Behav. **44**(6), 419–433 (2012)
11. Mussa-Ivaldi, F.A., Casadio, M., Danziger, Z.C., Mosier, K.M., Scheidt, R.A.: Sensory motor remapping of space in human-machine interfaces. Prog. Brain Res. **191**, 45–64 (2011)
12. Mussa-Ivaldi, F.A., Casadio, M., Ranganathan, R.: The body-machine interface: a pathway for rehabilitation and assistance in people with movement disorders. Expert Rev. Med. Devices **10**(2), 145–147 (2013)
13. Mandel, C., Rofer, T., Frese, U.: Applying a 3DOF orientation tracker as a human-robot interface for autonomous wheelchairs. In: 10th IEEE International Conference on Rehabilitation Robotics, pp. 52–59. IEEE Press, New York (2007)
14. Mandel, C., Frese, U., Röfer, T.: Design improvements for proportional control of autonomous wheelchairs via 3DOF orientation tracker. In: Sandoval, F., Prieto, A.G., Cabestany, J., Graña, M. (eds.) IWANN 2007. LNCS, vol. 4507, pp. 1052–1059. Springer, Heidelberg (2007)
15. LoPresti, E.F., Brienza, D.M., Angelo, J.: Head-operated computer controls: effect of control method on performance for subjects with and without disability. Interact. Comput. **14**, 359–377 (2002)
16. Card, S.K., MacKinlay, J.D., Robertson, G.G.: A morphological analysis of the design. ACM Trans. Inf. Syst. **9**, 99–122 (1991)
17. Abascal, J.: Users with disabilities: maximum control with minimum effort. In: Perales, F.J., Fisher, R.B. (eds.) AMDO 2008. LNCS, vol. 5098, pp. 449–456. Springer, Heidelberg (2008)
18. Miller, M.W., Rietschel, J.C., McDonald, C.G., Hatfield, B.D.: A novel approach to the physiological measurement of mental workload. Int. J. Psychophysiol. **80**(1), 75–78 (2011)
19. Rietschel, J.C., Miller, M.W., Gentili, R.J., Goodman, R.N., McDonald, C.G., Hatfield, B.D.: Cerebral-cortical networking and activation increase as a function of cognitive-motor task difficulty. Biol. Psychol. **90**(2), 127–133 (2012)
20. Rietschel, J.C., McDonald, C.G., Goodman, R.N., Miller, M.W., Jones-Lush, L.M., Wittenberg, G.F., Hatfield, B.D.: Psychophysiological support of increasing attentional reserve during the development of a motor skill. Biol. Psychol. **103**, 349–356 (2014)
21. Betke, M., Gips, J., Fleming, P.: the camera mouse: visual tracking of body features to provide computer access for people with severe disabilities. IEEE Trans. Neural Syst. Rehabil. Eng. **10**(1), 1–10 (2002)

22. Cook, A.M., Dobbs, B.M., Warren, S., McKeever, R.: Measuring target acquisition utilizing Madentecs Tracker system in individuals with Cerebral Palsy. Technol. Disabil. **17**, 155–163 (2005)
23. LoPresti, E.F., Brienza, D.M., Angelo, J., Gilbertson, L.: Neck range of motion and use of computer head controls. J. Rehabil. Res. Dev. **40**(3), 199–211 (2003)
24. LoPresti, E.F., Brienza, D.M.: Adaptive software for head-operated computer controls. IEEE Trans. Neural Syst. Rehabil. Eng. **12**(1), 102–111 (2004)
25. Radwin, R.G., Vanderheiden, G.C., Lin, M.: A method for evaluating head-controlled computer input devices using Fitts Law. Hum. Factors **32**(4), 423–438 (1990)
26. Takami, O., Ire, N., Kang, C., Ishimatu, T., Ochiai T.: Computer interface to use head movement for handicapped people. In: IEEE TENCON Digital Signal Processing Applications, pp. 468–472. IEEE Press New York (1996)
27. Bates, R., Istance, H.O.: Why are eyemice unpopular? a detailed comparison of head and eye controlled assistive technology pointing devices. Univ. Access Inf. Soc. **2**, 80–290 (2003)
28. De Silva, G.C., Lyons, M.J., Kawato, S., Tetsutani, N.: Human factors evaluation of a vision-based facial gesture interface. In: Conference on Computer Vision and Pattern Recognition Workshop, pp. 52–59. IEEE Press New York (2003)
29. Javanovic, R., MacKenzie, I.S.: Markermouse: mouse cursor control using a head-mounted marker. In: Miesenberger, K., Klaus, J., Zagler, W., Karshmer, A. (eds.) ICCHP 2010, Part II. LNCS, vol. 6180, pp. 49–56. Springer, Heidelberg (2010)
30. Pereira, C.A., Neto, B.R., Reynaldo, A.C., Luzo, M.C., Oliveira, R.P.: Development and evaluation of a head-controlled human-computer interface with mouse-like functions for physically disabled users. Clin. (Sao Paulo) **64**(10), 975–981 (2009)
31. Schaab, J.A., Radwin, R.G., Vanderheiden, G.C., Hansen, P.K.: A comparison of two control-display gain measures for head-controlled computer input devices. Hum. Factors **38**(3), 390–403 (1996)
32. Lin, M., Radwin, R.G., Vanderheiden, G.C.: Gain effects on performance using a head-controlled computer input device. Ergonomics **35**(2), 159–175 (1992)
33. Jagacinski, R.J., Monk, D.L.: Fitts law in two dimensions with hand and head movements. J. Mot. Behav. **17**, 77–95 (1985)
34. Gentili, R.J., Rietschel, J.C., Jaquess, K.J., Lo, L.-C., Prevost, C.M., Miller, M.W., Mohler, J.M., Oh, H., Tan, Y.Y., Hatfield, B.D.: Brain biomarkers based assessment of cognitive workload in pilots under various task demands. In: 36th IEEE International Conference of the Engineering in Medicine and Biology Society, pp. 5860–5863. IEEE Press, New York (2014)
35. Gentili, R.J., Oh, H., Shuggi, I.M., Goodman, R.N., Rietschel, J.C., Hatfield, B.D., Reggia, J.A.: Human-robotic collaborative intelligent control for reaching performance. In: Schmorrow, D.D., Fidopiastis, C.M. (eds.) AC 2013. LNCS, vol. 8027, pp. 666–675. Springer, Heidelberg (2013)
36. Deeny, S., Chicoine, C., Hargrove, L., Parrish, T., Jayaraman, A., Onaral, B.: A simple ERP method for quantitative analysis of cognitive workload in myoelectric prosthesis control and human-machine interaction. PLoS One **17**(9(11)), e112091 (2014)
37. Ayaz, H., Shewokis, P.A., Bunce, S., Izzetoglu, K., Willems, B., Onaral, B.: Optical brain monitoring for operator training and mental workload assessment. Neuroimage **59**(1), 36–47 (2012)
38. Hart, S.G., Staveland, L.E.: Development of NASA-TLX (task load index): results of empirical and theoretical research. Hum. Ment. Workload **1**, 139–183 (1988)
39. Kitazawa, S., Goto, T., Urushihara, Y.: Quantitative evaluation of reaching movements in cats with and without cerebellar lesions using normalized integral of jerk. In: Mano, N., Hamada, I., DeLong, M.R. (eds.) Role of the cerebellum and basal ganglia in voluntary movement, pp. 11–19. Elsevier, Amsterdam (1993)

40. Gentili, R.J., Bradberry, T.J., Oh, H., Costanzo, M.E., Kerick, S.E., Contreras-Vidal, J.L., Hatfield, B.D.: Evolution of cerebral cortico-cortical communication during visuomotor adaptation to a cognitive-motor executive challenge. Biol. Psychol. **105C**, 51–65 (2014)
41. Guadagnoli, M.A., Lee, T.D.: Challenge point: a framework for conceptualizing the effects of various practice conditions in motor learning. J. Mot. Behav. **36**(2), 212–224 (2004)
42. Sanli, E.A., Patterson, J.T., Bray, S.R., Lee, T.D.: Understanding self-controlled motor learning protocols through the self-determination theory. Front. Psychol. **11**(3), 611 (2013)
43. Balakrishnan, R., Hinckley, K.: The role of kinesthetic reference frames in two-handed input performance. In: 12th Annual ACM Symposium on User Interface Software and Technology, pp. 171–178 (1999)
44. Hinckley, K., Jacob, R.J.K., Ware, C.: Input/ouput devices and interaction techniques. In: Tucker, A.B. (ed.) Computer Science Handbook, 2nd edn. CRC Press, Boca Raton (2004)

How Mobile Phones Affect the Sustainability of the Work/Life Balance of Their Users

Edward Peter Greenwood White[1,2] and Andrew Thatcher[3(✉)]

[1] School of Computing, College of Science, Engineering and Technology,
University of South Africa, Pretoria, South Africa
[2] Department of Information Technology, Visual Information and Interaction
Technology, Uppsala University, Box 337, 751 05 Uppsala, Sweden
whiteepg@unisa.ac.za
[3] Psychology Department, Witwatersrand University,
Private Bag X3, Johannesburg WITS, 2050, Gauteng, South Africa
Andrew.Thatcher@wits.ac.za

Abstract. This study examined the relationship between sustainability of mobile phone users and work-life balance. Twenty-seven interviews were performed on managerial level mobile phone owners over the duration of a month and half. The study extends Clark's [1] original Border theory that fails to mention how mobile phones (or indeed any other information and communication technology) influence the borders between the two domains. This study found technology has a definitive impact with separate users groups emerging from the data; border-extenders, border-adapters and border-enforcers.

Keywords: Border theory · Mobile phone usage · Mobile phone usage patterns · Work sustainability · Home-work balance · Work-home interface · Mobile phone after-hours work · After-hours work

1 Introduction

Sustainability is the ability to self-sustain while utilising resources without depleting those same resources; providing the ability to allow further sustenance and continuing sustainability [2]. Organisational sustainability is the ability of an organisational system to create balance for human, social and natural resources needs without depleting those resources. A sustainable work system on the other hand, is a work system enabling the sustainability of those in it, ensuring that workers can sustain themselves and the environment without compromising the surrounding system [3]. Therefore a work system is only sustainable when it ensures it does not deplete the resources it requires to function optimally [4] while ensuring a system and a future for it and the workers it requires.

Mobile phones have provided the ultimate tool and availability to work anywhere and anytime. However, this "digital leash" provides limited opportunities for the employee to have downtime as it is becoming more accepted that the phone and the user will always be available and therefore contactable anywhere and anytime. This therefore results in a perpetual state of work engagement. Research indicates that

© Springer International Publishing Switzerland 2015
D.D. Schmorrow and C.M. Fidopiastis (Eds.): AC 2015, LNAI 9183, pp. 393–400, 2015.
DOI: 10.1007/978-3-319-20816-9_37

mobile devices increase work-life conflict [5]. This adaptation has sometimes been framed as an "addiction" or the popular renaming of BlackBerry to CrackBerry [6–11]. Moore and Wen's study [12] found that respondents had little or no work-life balance, with business executives reporting that challenges for balancing their professional and personal life were enormous resulting in clear emerging areas of concern in relation to parenting and elderly care responsibilities [12]. Rationally, the usage of such devices leads to lengthening of work days as there is a potential constant channel for communication all day, every day [13].

Mobile phones can be utilised by the employers as a technological-tether further extending the work day culminating in prolonged connectivity of the employees. In response, German Labour Minister, Andrea Nahles, states that there is an "undeniable relationship between constant availability and the increase of mental illness" [14]. To better understand the conditions and the effects, Minster Nahles has commissioned the German Federal Institute for Occupational Safety and Health to scientifically determine the effects on the workers.

One plausible explanation as to why, traditional office workers work less than their mobile colleagues, is that in an office setting the workers' peers will inform them that it is time to go home, constraining overzealous work behaviour [15]. This is referred to as border-keepers within Border theory (Clark, [1]. Thomée et al.'s [16] study found that women who had a high rate of mobile phone calls and (SMS)ing/texting had prolonged stress and depression, while the men experienced sleep disturbances and symptoms of depression. Stress and depression were similarly found to culminate from blurring of the work-family border in Border theory [17]. Employees who work overtime in the evening are less likely to fully recover as they are using work-related effort during the time that they would usually recover and this therefore increases the effects of negative Work-Home Interference (WHI) [18]. Similarly, Van Hooff et al. [18] found a relationship between fatigue, sleep complaints and work-home interference (WHI) further indicating a lack of recovery due to the extension of the work day. Geurts et al. [19] found that the negative influences predominantly originated from the work domain, while positive influences predominantly originated from the home domain through the provision of recovery time that could counter balance the negative effects limiting further spill over, as seen by Border-crossers. This study looks at how mobile phones affect the sustainability of the work/life balance of their users using Border Theory as an explanatory lens.

1.1   Border Theory

Border theory is a relatively new theory on work/family balance. The theory explains how "border-crossers" move between the domains of home and work while maintaining satisfaction in each domain and controlling role conflict to ensure balance [1, 20]. To create the domain borders and maintain balance, members of the domain utilise proactive or enactive controls to solidify the domain borders [1]. Clark [1] defines balance as "satisfaction and good functioning at work and at home, with a minimum of role conflict". Clark [1], however, fails to define what a proactive domain mechanism is, stating it only twice in her study and then disregarding it. This study looks specifically at these proactive controls.

Clark [1] determines that the enactive control mechanism is created psychologically by borrowing from Kurt Lewin's 'life space' idea [Rychlak, 1981 cited in 1], and used in the creation of separate psychological family and work domains. The interaction between the two domains depends on the border strength. According to Clark [1], enactment, as defined by Weick [21], is the "process in which individuals take elements given in their environments and organise them in a way that makes sense". Weick [21] utilises enactment, as a component of his Sense-making theory.

Borders. Central to border theory is that work and family are separate domains with the ability to influence the opposing domains [1]. There are three planes which borders operate upon namely; physical (e.g. the actual walls of work or home), temporal (e.g. set working time), and psychological (e.g. thinking patterns which are suitable for that domain, usually created through enactment) [1].

Domains. In the industrialization period, work and home were segmented into two domains, one for work and one for family, each with its own unique responsibilities, cultures, rules and purposes, which existed at different times and places [1]. The only shared factor was the participant who was a "member" in both spheres. It is likely therefore, that a member of each domain expects unique duties, rules, thought patterns and behaviours to be performed by its members. Clark's [1] view is that there are only two domains (home and work) to transition between. This is arguably a narrow interpretation as there are likely to be more domains, such as for friends, clubs, and societies.

Study Aim. This study aims to provide a deeper understanding of the following two research questions using Border Theory as the lens:

- RQ1: How does smartphone technology allow work sustainability after-hours?
- RQ2: What is the long term impact of being able to sustainably work after hours?

2 Methods

2.1 Sample

To better understand the complexity of after-hours usage on the user's sustainability a sample of 27 participants were interviewed, the sample consisted of 7 participants and their partners and 13 additional individuals without their partners. Participants were required to own a smart phone and be in a managerial role within their work-place.

2.2 Procedure

The participants for this study had previously consented to be contacted in a related prior study which looked at mobile online usage patterns. To recruit the largest sample possible an Amazon Kindle was offered as a prize for one random participant. The interviews took on average of half an hour to forty-five minutes of their time.

A recording device was utilised to capture the participants input, which was transcribed for further analysis.

2.3 Research Measures Used

The demographics used in the study were the following; age, race, gender, educational level, marital or partner status, partner's occupation, career position, primary income earner, number of children, age of children, working hours, Internet usage time, mobile Internet time, number of phone calls a day, number of hours and minutes on the phone per month. All of the aforementioned biographical and mobile phone use measures were collected through a self-report questionnaire. The questions asked to both the participant and the partner focused on the following areas: general usage of the mobile phone, which domain the communications occurred more frequently, the times and effects of the communication, if it provided facilitation or disruption in the domains and who regulates their usage.

2.4 Analysis

The transcripts were analysed using thematic content analysis on Atlas TI. Thematic content analysis was used to determine common themes in the text according to the areas of interest. Thematic content analysis is known for its epistemological stance and is objective or at least is objectivistic [22].

3 Results

3.1 Border-Expanders

12 of the participants were categorized as border-expanders. The gender distribution of the 12 participants in this group consisted of 9 males and 3 females. 10 of participants were in a domestic relationship or marriage the remaining 2 were single. Finally, 6 of the participants in this group were made up 3 couples, 2 heterosexual couples and 1 homosexual partnership, with the remaining 6 participants consisting of 5 individual male and 1 individual female. Border-expanders were found to be smartphone users who have the inability to delineate the home-work border, frequently allowing after-hour communications to overrun into the home domain ubiquitously thereby not keeping the domains separate. They legitimized their lack of border enforcement needed for career advancement, which is conditioned and encouraged by employers, management and colleagues (which could be considered a form of conditioning so as to blur the borders). Upon further in-depth questioning it became apparent that it seems to be an organisationally conditioned and sanctioned need to respond to all communications, which could be legitimised with a forthcoming deadline, but according to all border-expanders interviewed, all communications require an "urgent" response. When border-expanders were further interrogated they responded that this was a working conditions norm in a client-facing market. The frequent work over-flow into the home

domain, resulted in border-expanders' inability to define or redefine the home-work border, dividing the two thereby resulting in the domains being merged into one domain. Obviously over a period of time the border-expander would no longer able to re-establish the border or determine where it should exist.

A number of border-expanders interviewed legitimised their usage even when their partners complained, culminating in arguments and, in a few cases, the breakdown of the entire relationship. Primarily the leading cause of arguments and general discontent felt by the border-expander and their partner was the border-expander's general inability to delineate the home-work borders so that there was a domain space and time for the partner and family to have their needs met. It was also found that a predominant influencer of border-expanders was if they were client-facing and working in a high-stress related industry such as finance or telecommunications.

Interestingly, 83 % of the border-expanders had partners. Border-expanders extended the border in order to ensure their families financial wellbeing concurrently with their own career advancement. A counter to this of course is that most of the partners of the participants interviewed in this group, frequently fought or disagreed with their partner's usage of their phones after-hours in family time. Therefore, due to the extension of the working hours into the home domain the border-expanders sustainability becomes questionable. Finally the border-expanders do not define the two domains, which imply that the two domains meld into one, meaning redefining the border between the two would be difficult.

3.2   Border-Adapters

10 of the participants were categorized as border-adapters. The gender distribution of the 10 participants consisted of 7 males and 3 females. 7 of participants were in a domestic relationship or marriage the remaining 3 were single. Finally, 4 of the participants interviewed were made up of 2 couples, 1 heterosexual couples and 1 homosexual partnership, with the remaining 6 consisting of 4 participants individual male and 2 individual female.

Border-adapters are those users who arbitrate all incoming communications determining to accept or reject the incoming communication into the home domain from work. Border-adapters juxtapose their family and own needs against their employer's needs culminating in fluctuating domain borders which are used to adapt to the relevant needs in order to keep all groups happy. But, upon completion of the domain transition, the participant reinitiates the border to separate domains once again. The border-adapters make their decisions based on the permeability of the border between home and work which is related to who is contacting them, the higher the seniority of the initiator of the communication the more likely they were to answer, at the time of the communication.

Participants in this group used mechanisms such as refusing to install or enable email facilities on their work or personnel phones. A good example of this is noted in a participant's explanation of why he limits his accessibility as "If you're contactable all the time, people will phone you up all the time." However, the participants are quick to point out that, depending on who contacts them and the urgency of the communication, they will respond in due course. Participant 1 when asked to define urgency and the need to answer the phone, stated "Well, I'll answer the phone and find out what the issue is and then, decide for myself, once I've heard what it is, whether I want to deal with it or not". Thereby creating a self-regulating mechanism to control who contacts them and to see if they see fit to attend to the relevant communication and create an interruption in the home domain.

The predominant difference between group two and one, is that group two determines the validity of the communications by looking at who is making the communication, when the communication is being made and the "urgency" of such, which they determine as beings important and requiring swift action. Group one; however is constantly available to communicate as and when the need arises. 70 % of the border-adapters had partners, but a noticeable difference is that the individuals in this group were not as client-facing as the border-expander group.

3.3 Border-Enforcer

5 of the participants were categorized as border-enforcers. The gender distribution of the 5 participants consisted of 3 males and 2 female, 5 of participants were in a domestic relationship. Finally, 4 of the participants interviewed were made up 2 couples, 2 heterosexual, with the remaining 1 participant being an individual male.

The border-enforcers, as with border-adapters, arbitrate all incoming communication. The major disparity between border-enforcers and border-adapters is that their domain borders are rigid and considerably less malleable than those of border-adapters. 2 of the 3 border-adapters indicated that there is time and place for each domain and emphasised the distinction of the two domains, to all involved. This is re-echoed by participant 14 "I don't believe in receiving any sorts of mail, work related on my cell phone...? For me, I would use my work laptop. Once I leave work, I do not want to be distracted by any work-related issues... There's a very clear defined segregation."

The border-enforcers' definitive border distinction was found to be related to the following; border-enforcers have a clear distinction from the beginning and insist on it or alternatively it was developed due to previous working scenarios where they previously extended the borders or allowed for border blurring. Domain delineation was developed as a coping mechanism. However, border-enforcers as with border-enforcers, will allow for the facilitation of restricted communications beyond the standard work hours into the home domain depending on the urgency but the occurrence of which is far less frequent or none at all.

3.4 Work as an Enforcer of Domain Transitions

All three groups defined by this study allow for the crossing of the border between work and home domain. However the differences come from the way in which the groups will accept all communications at all hours allowing for the merging of the domains. The border-adapters and border-enforcers will screen the communication by seniority of the communicator and the time at which they are being contacted and then redefine the border thereafter. Border-enforcers communicate to their employees their displeasure of the blurring the domains and that if it is only acceptable if it is an emergency and feel that they have provided work the required their time and deserve their own time. The concept of urgency was used by all three groups to necessitate allowing for communications into the home domain after-hours. Urgency is the most frequent validation for blurring the borders, as it necessitates the continuity of business and career development.

In order to prevent the constant barrage of all communications users have opted to change there working scenarios in order to better control their life and lessen the effects on their lives. A good example of which is shown by Participant 7 who moved from her previous company to a new company to obtain a better position "Because I used to work at another company where you know clients thought that they could call you willy-nilly and all of that, and I used to be a very "Yes, yes, I will do it," until I burned out and got – it aggravated my depression and I did not need that. And that's when I decided that's it, you know." A frequent border-expander validation for urgency is that they are client-facing and therefor it is a requirement of the role.

4 Areas for Further Research

The flexibility of the domains will allow for work to facilitate the home domain; however this was not explored in this study. This will impact the sustainability of workers forced or conditioned to work in the home domain.

The participants of the study reported that they were less stressed in the home domain, while stress was more frequently felt in the work domain. What will happen if there is no longer a border between the two, which domain would the user use to de-stress? What would be the long-term effects of domain stress be without relief?

Some new questions emerge such as: Do mobile phone user's border-roles evolve from border-enforcer to border-adapter and finally to border-expander? Are they able to develop a better understanding of the ability to regulate their usage and the border moving from border-expander to border-enforcer?

References

1. Clark, S.C.: Work/family border theory: a new theory of work/family balance. Hum. Relat. 53, 747–770 (2000)
2. World Commission on Environment and Development: Our Common Future. Oxford University Press (1987)
3. Lifvergren, S., Huzzard, T., Docherty, P.: A development coalition for sustainability in healthcare. In: Docherty, P. (ed.) Creating Sustainable Work Systems, pp. 167–185. Routledge, London (2009)
4. Kira, M., van Eijnatten, F.M.: Sustained by work: individual and social sustainability in work organizations. In: Docherty, P., Kira, M., Shani, A.B. (eds.) Creating Sustainable Work Systems: Developing Social Sustainability, pp. 233–246. Routledge, London (2009)

5. Middleton, C.A.: Illusions of balance and control in an always-on environment: a case study of Blackberry users. J. Media Cult. Stud. **21**, 165–178 (2007)
6. Aldoory, L., Hua, J., Elizabeth, L.T., Bey-Ling, S.: A study of work-life balance among men and women in public relations. Public Relat. Soc. Am. **2**, 20 (2008)
7. Dery, K., MacCormick, J.: Who takes the lead?: a study of the impact of Blackberrys on the organisational dancefloor. In: 23rd European Group for Organizational Studies Colloquium, 5-7 July 2007
8. ITS: ITS Salutes CIO Diane Barbour, Selected to Help Build Research Computing Capabilities at RIT. Information and Technology Services at the Rochester Institute of Technology (2006)
9. Mazmanian, M., Yates, J., Orlikowski, W.: Crackberrys: exploring the social implications of ubiquitous wireless email devices. In: European Group for Organisational Studies: Sub-theme 14. Technology, Organization and Society: Recursive Perspectives (2006)
10. Mazmanian, M., Yates, J., Orlikowski, W.: Ubiquitous email: individual experiences and organisational consequences of Blackberry use. In: 65th Annual Meeting of the Academy of Management. (2006)
11. Rosen, C.: Our cell phones, ourselves. N. Atlantis: J. Technol. Soc. **6**, 26–45 (2004)
12. Moore, J.E.: One road to turnover: an examination of work exhaustion in technology professionals. MIS Q. **24**, 141–168 (2000)
13. Wajcman, J., Bittman, M., Brown, J.E.: Families without borders: mobile phones connectedness and work-home divisions. Sociology **42**, 635–652 (2008)
14. Kaufman, A.C.: Germany to Consider Ban on Late-Night Work Emails. The Huffington Post (2014). http://www.huffingtonpost.com/2014/09/29/germany-work-email_n_5883924.html
15. Hill, E.J., Hawkins, A.J., Miller, B.C.: Work and family in the virtual office: perceived influences of mobile telework. Fam. Relat. **45**, 293–301 (1996)
16. Thomée, S., Eklof, M., Gustafsson, E., Nilsson, R., Hagberg, M.: Prevalence of perceived stress, symptoms of depression and sleep disturbances in relation to information and communication technology (ICT) use among young adults - an explorative prospective study. Comput. Hum. Behav. **23**, 1300–1321 (2007)
17. Desrochers, S., Sargent, L.D.: Boundary/Border theory and work-family. Organ. Manage. J. Bibliography **1**, 40–48 (2004)
18. Van Hooff, M.L.M., Geurts, S.A.E., Kompier, M.A.J., Taris, T.W.: Work-home interference: how does it manifest itself from day to day? Work Stress **20**, 145–162 (2006)
19. Geurts, S.A.E., Taris, T.W., Kompier, M.A.J., Dikkers, J.S.E., Van Hooff, M.L.M., Kinnunen, U.M.: Work-home interaction from a work psychological perspective: development and validation of a new questionnaire, the SWING. Work Stress **19**, 319–339 (2005)
20. Podsakoff, P.M., MacKenzie, S.B., Lee, J., Podsakoff, N.P.: Common method biases in behavioral research: a critical review of the literature and recommended remedies. J. Appl. Psychol. **88**, 879 (2003)
21. Weick, K.E.: The Social Psychology of Organising. Addison-Wesley, Boston (1979)
22. Anderson, R.: Thematic Content Analysis (TCA): Descriptive Presentation of Qualitative Data (2007). http://www.wellknowingconsulting.org/publications/pdfs/ThematicContentAnalysis.pdf

Methodology for Knowledge Elicitation in Visual Abductive Reasoning Tasks

Michael J. Haass[✉], Laura E. Matzen, Susan M. Stevens-Adams,
and Allen R. Roach

Sandia National Laboratories, Albuquerque, NM, USA
{mjhaass, lematze, smsteve, raroach}@sandia.gov

Abstract. The potential for bias to affect the results of knowledge elicitation studies is well recognized. Researchers and knowledge engineers attempt to control for bias through careful selection of elicitation and analysis methods. Recently, the development of a wide range of physiological sensors, coupled with fast, portable and inexpensive computing platforms, has added an additional dimension of objective measurement that can reduce bias effects. In the case of an abductive reasoning task, bias can be introduced through design of the stimuli, cues from researchers, or omissions by the experts. We describe a knowledge elicitation methodology robust to various sources of bias, incorporating objective and cross-referenced measurements. The methodology was applied in a study of engineers who use multivariate time series data to diagnose the performance of devices throughout the production lifecycle. For visual reasoning tasks, eye tracking is particularly effective at controlling for biases of omission by providing a record of the subject's attention allocation.

Keywords: Knowledge elicitation · Eye tracking · Abductive reasoning

1 Introduction

Knowledge elicitation, the process of understanding an individual's or group's tacit knowledge so that it can be preserved and disseminated as explicit knowledge, is used in a wide range of research and development fields including psychology, decision analysis and artificial intelligence. Application of knowledge elicitation methods can provide important information about expert judgment and decision making. This information can then be used in the design of expert systems to automate or augment human decision making. The potential for bias to affect the results of knowledge elicitation studies, on the part of both researchers and subjects, is well recognized. Researchers and knowledge engineers commonly attempt to prevent, or at least control for, sources of bias through careful selection of elicitation and analysis methods [1]. However, the development of a wide range of physiological sensors, coupled with fast, portable and inexpensive computing platforms, has added an additional dimension of objective measurement that can reduce effects of unanticipated bias. Incorporating these technologies into knowledge elicitation methodologies can also reinforce the validity of qualitative findings and highlight previously undetected biases.

© Springer International Publishing Switzerland 2015
D.D. Schmorrow and C.M. Fidopiastis (Eds.): AC 2015, LNAI 9183, pp. 401–409, 2015.
DOI: 10.1007/978-3-319-20816-9_38

Abductive reasoning is the process of forming a conclusion that best explains observed facts. This type of reasoning plays an important role in the development and application of expertise in many fields such as scientific research, economics and medicine. A common example of abductive reasoning is medical diagnosis. Given a set of symptoms, a doctor determines a diagnosis that best explains the combination of symptoms. Abductive reasoning has been studied in the fields of logic [2], medicine [3], logistics [4] and artificial intelligence [5], however, little work is available on human visual information processing and reasoning during abductive reasoning tasks. We begin to address this research gap using a knowledge elicitation approach. In the case of an abductive reasoning task, biases during knowledge elicitation can be introduced through design of the stimuli, cues from researchers, or omissions by the experts. Bias introduced through design of the stimuli can arise from the designer's choices for spatial layout of information, or even what information is included or excluded from the stimuli set. Biases of omission, or actual-ideal discrepancies,[1] by the expert may be conscious or unconscious.

This paper describes a methodology for knowledge elicitation from experts for a complex visual abductive reasoning task. The methodology is designed to be robust to various sources of bias by incorporating both objective and cross-referenced measurements. We have applied this methodology in a study of engineers who use multivariate time series data to diagnose the performance of devices throughout the production lifecycle. This study will be used to demonstrate the application of the methodology and to illustrate key findings enabled by this approach.

2 Knowledge Elicitation Methodology

To create a knowledge elicitation method robust to unanticipated biases, we incorporate objective, physiological measures during domain-specific tasks that provide cross referencing information for a verbal walkthrough protocol. We also design the study instruments to include elements that could be cross-referenced during analysis to highlight both consistencies and discrepancies in the raw data. Figure 1 illustrates the process used to design the knowledge elicitation session and instruments.

When knowledge elicitation researchers encounter a new work domain, as was the case with this study, it is advisable to design the elicitation methodology to include multiple opportunities to engage with subject matter experts. Therefore, the first step in the process, which can be omitted if the design team already has a wealth of experience in the work domain, is to interview one subject matter expert (expert point of contact, ePOC) and produce a document describing the work domain and culture (outputs and work products of each step are listed in the right hand column of Fig. 1). This step helps ensure that the elicitation methodology will be compatible with the work culture and the availability of the work domain experts. The second step is to conduct observations of a small set of work domain experts as they perform the work tasks to be studied. The output

---

[1] We use the terminology "actual-idea discrepancies" to describe instances where there are differences between and expert's verbal description of a work process and the actual process followed during completion of the work task.

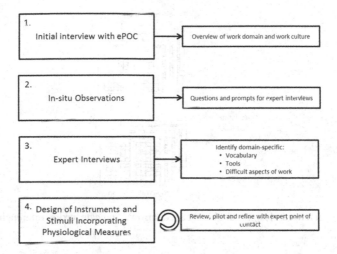

Fig. 1. Process used to design the knowledge elicitation session and instruments.

of this step is a document listing specific questions and more general talking points to facilitate the detailed interviews in Step 3. The third step is detailed interviews with as many work domain experts that time, staffing, or budget will allow. The outputs of this stage are detailed lists of domain-specific vocabulary, tools and difficult aspects of the work. This information is then used in Step 4 to design the instruments and stimuli for the knowledge elicitation sessions. During Step 4, designer should take care to identify opportunities to cross reference information across instruments and incorporate as many cross reference points as possible. At this point, careful consideration is also given to physiological measures that can provide objective measurements of activity during the chosen tasks. Brookings, Wilson & Swain provide one assessment of psychophysiological variables that can be used to assess workload during complex tasks such as air traffic control [6]. Marshall shows that eye metrics (information from pupil size and point-of-gaze) can be used to discriminate between two cognitive states during complex tasks [7]. Matzen, Haass & McNamara suggest eye tracking to be particularly useful for investigating cognitive biases within visual search domains [8]. Figure 2 illustrates the cross referenced methodology incorporating eye tracking as a physiological measure of allocation of attention during a domain-specific task.

3 Physiological Sensors

Modern manufacturing technologies and increasing consumer interest in self-tracking are providing researches with an increasingly wide range of physiological sensors. For example, consumer-grade devices are now available to monitor and record an individual's physical activity level, sleep patterns and even brain electrical activity.[2]

---

[2] For example, Nike's Fuelband, Fitbit's One, Emotiv's EPOC.

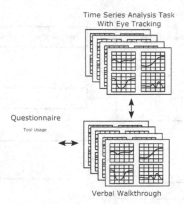

Fig. 2. Cross referenced design: double headed arrows indicate cross referencing between instruments.

Research-grade devices that measure more traditional physiological parameters such as heart and respiration rates have also become more compact and portable and at the same time provide data with increased temporal and measurement resolution.[3] Eye tracking is a prime example of these improvements. Modern systems incorporate small, single mount-point camera modules that are easy to transport and can operate from a single USB connection to a laptop computer. These systems record not only gaze point information, but also provide a wealth of information about the subject's head position and orientation. Many systems also provide information derived from eye lid position, such as blinks or eye closures due to fatigue, along with measurement of the pupil diameter for each eye, all at data rates 60 Hz or 120 Hz.

4 Example Application: Visual Abductive Reasoning Study

We applied the methodology in a study of engineers who use multivariate time series data to diagnose the performance of devices throughout the production lifecycle. The goal of the study was to understand the expert's abductive reasoning processes and the key features of the time series data used in these processes. This information can then be used to create and select input features used by advanced data analytics to model and predict certain response variables.

In the work domain studied, access to experts was limited due to their senior roles spanning multiple engineering teams. Therefore, knowledge elicitation sessions had to be as brief as possible, while still being thorough enough to acquire all data relevant to the work and the expert's reasoning processes.

To design the knowledge elicitation sessions, we followed the multi-stage approach described in Sect. 2. In Step 1, we collaborated extensively with the ePOC to gain an overview of the entire work domain and to develop an elicitation methodology that

---

[3] For example, Seeing Machine's FOVIO, BIOPAC's BioHarness, ANT Neuro's eegoSports.

would be compatible with the work culture and the availability of the expert engineers. In Step 2 we conducted observations of a subset of experienced engineers performing their day-to-day time series analysis work. From these observation sessions, we developed a list of specific questions and general talking points to use in subsequent interviews. In Step 3, we conducted one hour interviews with the each of the three most experienced engineers. After completing the interviews, we analyzed our notes and developed lists of commonly used, domain-specific vocabulary, tools used to complete the time series analysis work, and common difficulties encountered during the analysis work. In Step 4, we used the information from Step 3 to design the instruments to be used in the knowledge elicitation study. We chose to include eye tracking as an objective measure of attention allocation during a domain-specific task. We also chose to create study instruments that could be cross-referenced during analysis to highlight both consistencies and discrepancies in the raw data. This design allows for comparisons across objective measures of attention and subject measures of information collection and reasoning processes that will help guide subsequent studies in this work domain.

Four instruments were developed, (1) a general demographics questionnaire, (2) a work domain-specific questionnaire, (3) a simplified, domain-specific, abductive reasoning task, equipped with eye tracking, and (4) a verbal walkthrough protocol (see Sect. 4.2 for a detailed description of each instrument). For each instrument, we created an initial draft and then reviewed and revised the content and instructions in collaboration with the ePOC. The ePOC also provided technical content (time series) to use as stimuli for the time series analysis task.

4.1 Participants

Thirteen employees at Sandia National Laboratories volunteered to participate in the study. Three of the participants in the study were classified as experts; that is, they diagnosed device performance using the multivariate time series data as part of their daily job. These experts had an average of 15.5 years' experience performing this type of activity. Four participants were categorized as practitioners; that is, they were familiar with the multivariate time series data but did not use it to diagnose device performance. These practitioners had an average of 5.5 years' experience interacting with the multivariate time series data. Six participants were classified as novices who had no experience with the multivariate time series data. This novice cohort was included to provide comparative performance baselines.

4.2 Procedure

The participants completed the study individually. The participant first read through and signed the study consent form and asked any questions he/she had about the study. Next, the participant filled out a demographic questionnaire which assessed the participant's age, gender, years of experience, etc. The experts and practitioners then filled out a questionnaire which asked specific questions about their work with the multivariate time series data. The novices did not fill out this second questionnaire since they did not have any experience with this type of data.

Multivariate Time Series Task. A PowerPoint presentation was displayed to the participant which explained the study and described what the participant would be asked to do. The novices were given very detailed instructions since they did not have experience with the multivariate time series data. The experimenter calibrated the eye tracker[4]and then the participant completed two blocks of trials; the first block consisted of 10 trials and the second block consisted of 5 trials. Each trial consisted of four images displayed on the screen that contained multivariate time series data from a single device test. The participant was asked to classify the images as anomalous or normal. If the participant indicated that the image was anomalous, another screen was displayed which asked the participant to indicate the type of anomaly. Eye tracking data[5] and response times were recorded while the subject inspected the time series stimuli.

Verbal Walkthrough. Finally, the experts and practitioners provided a Verbal walkthrough of the 15 trials. The experimenter opened a PowerPoint presentation that contained the 15 trials and asked the participant to explain their thought processes as they examined the time series data, how he/she reached their decision and what aspects of the images "popped out" or caught his/her eye for each trial. A second experimenter took notes while this discussion was taking place. The novices did not perform this task since they made decisions based on the detailed instructions that were given to them.

5 Analysis and Results

Subject response times were recorded by custom software written in Java and represent the amount of time a subject spent inspecting the time series data in each trial. Subject responses for both the anomaly/normal decision and anomaly type were also recorded by this software. Time series analysis response times trended inversely with level of experience (Fig. 3a). Experts performed best at identifying and categorizing anomalous device performance. Practitioners and novices identified anomalous device performance equally well, however practitioners performed better at anomaly categorization than did novices. Both practitioners and novices performed worse than experts at anomaly categorization (Fig. 3b).

Eye tracking fixation points and durations were calculated in the EyeWorks Analyze software by setting the pixel threshold to 45 pixels and the fixation minimum duration to 0.075 s. Given the display resolution, display size, and typical subject viewing distance (64 cm), these settings define the maximum angular velocity for fixations to be 14.4 °/s, which is consistent with previously published values [9]. An example of the screen layout and a fixation pattern are shown in Fig. 4.

---

[4] FaceLAB 5 Standard System with two miniature digital cameras and one infrared illumination pod.

[5] Eye tracking data were collected and analyzed using EyeWorks software, Eye Tracking Inc., Solana Beach, CA.

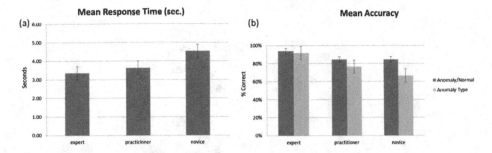

Fig. 3. Response time (a) and accuracy (b) by subject experience level for the multivariate time series task.

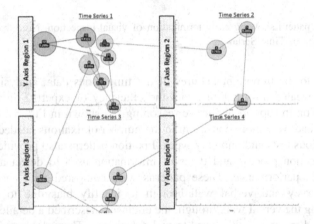

Fig. 4. Example screen layout and fixation pattern for multivariate time series task. The shaded regions, indicating the areas containing y-axis magnitude values, were used to calculate the number of times subjects fixated on the magnitude information for each axis.

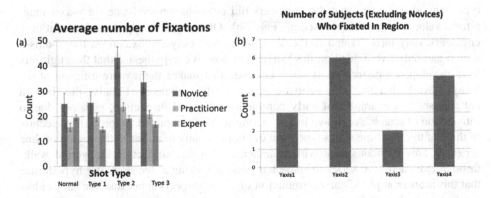

Fig. 5. Average number of fixations per trial by subject level of experience (a), and number of subjects who fixated in each Y-axis magnitude region (b).

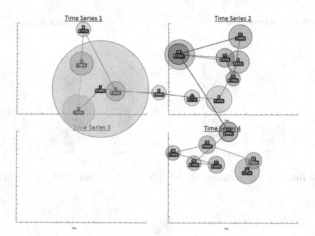

Fig. 6. Fixation pattern showing early termination of visual inspection. Note that no fixations occur in the region of Time Series 3.

In addition to the important features of the time series data, analysis of the eye tracking data revealed information about the efficiency of expertise in visual information acquisition to support abductive reasoning. As shown in Fig. 5a, experts used fewer fixations and were more consistent in the number of fixations needed to correctly identify anomalous tests and anomaly types. Fixation patterns also provide insight into the actual inspection process and types of information used to detect and diagnose abnormal device performance. These patterns were compared with analyses of the task-specific survey and verbal walkthrough to identify bias due to unconscious omission. During the verbal walkthrough, the engineers described a detailed set of time series shapes and thresholds they used to make decisions. They also provided detailed descriptions of how they reasoned about relationships across the different time series. In particular, they described their process as always inspecting each time series type and always checking certain quantitative thresholds for time series types 1, 2 and 4. While the fixation patterns corroborate the use of information from each time series type, they also showed that the engineers did not consistently fixate on y-axis magnitude values for these time series (Fig. 5b). Of the seven expert and practitioner engineers, only three fixated in the Y-axis-1 region, only six fixated on the Y-axis-2 region and only five fixated on the Y-axis-4 region. We hypothesize that the engineers have developed a pattern recognition heuristic that makes them more efficient at the analysis work, but that this heuristic is not easily verbalized. Finally, the fixation patterns showed examples of early completion of visual inspection, possibly due to satisfaction of search. As shown in Fig. 6, one subject completed a thorough inspection of three of the four time series types, but did not have any fixations in the region of time series 3. This is inconsistent with statements from this subject in the verbal walkthrough that each time series is inspected prior to making a decision. We hypothesize that this is an example of early termination of visual inspection because the subject had reached an early conclusion.

6 Summary and Conclusion

We have described a methodology for knowledge elicitation that is robust to many sources of bias. Robustness is achieved through incorporation of one or more physiological sensors to provide cross referencing information for more traditional knowledge elicitation instruments. The example application shows that eye tracking is effective at highlighting actual-ideal discrepancies that would not have been discovered by following a traditional verbal walkthrough protocol. Future work applying this methodology to additional work domains and tasks would provide the experience necessary to develop detailed guidelines for selecting physiological sensors and metrics most appropriate for a given type of task or knowledge elicitation goal.

Acknowledgements. We wish to acknowledge James D. Morrow of Sandia National Laboratories, Albuquerque New Mexico for creating the software used in our study to display the time series stimuli and record subject response times. Sandia National Laboratories is a multi-program laboratory managed and operated by Sandia Corporation, a wholly owned subsidiary of Lockheed Martin Corporation, for the U.S. Department of Energy's National Nuclear Security Administration under contract DE-AC04-94AL85000.

References

1. Booker, J.M., Meyer, M.A.: Eliciting and Analyzing Expert Judgment: A Practical Guide. ASA, pp. 3–16. SIAM, Philadelphia (2001)
2. Thagard, P., Shelley, C.: Abductive reasoning: logic, visual thinking, and coherence. In: DallaChiara, M.L., et al. (eds.) Logic and Scientific Methods: Volume One of the Tenth International Congress of Logic, Methodology and Philosophy of Science, Florence, August 1995, vol. 259, pp. 413–427. Springer, Netherlands (1997)
3. Console, L., Torasso, P.: On the co-operation between abductive and temporal reasoning in medical diagnosis. Artif. Intell. Med. 3(6), 291–311 (1991)
4. Kovacs, G., Spens, K.M.: Abductive reasoning in logistics research. Int. J. Phys. Distrib. Logistics Manage. 35(2), 132–144 (2005)
5. Gelsema, E.S.: Abductive reasoning in bayesian belief networks using a genetic algorithm. Pattern Recogn. Lett. 16(8), 865–871 (1995)
6. Brookings, J.B., Wilson, G.F., Swain, C.R.: Psychophysiological responses to changes in workload during simulated air traffic control. Biol. Psychol. 42(3), 361–377 (1996)
7. Marshall, S.P.: Identifying cognitive state from eye metrics. Aviat. Space Environ. Med. 78 (5), B165–B175 (2007)
8. Matzen, L.E., Haass, M.J., McNamara, L.A.: Using eye tracking to asseess cognitve biasses: a position paper. In: DECISIVe Workshop, IEEE Vis 2014 (2014)
9. Erkelens, C.J., Sloot, O.B.: Initial directions and landing positions of binocular saccades. Vision. Res. 35(23–24), 3297–3303 (1995)

Stability of a Type of Cross-Cultural Emotion Modeling in Social Media

Monte Hancock[1(✉)], Chad Sessions[2], Chloe Lo[2], Shakeel Rajwani[2], Elijah Kresses[2], Cheryl Bleasdale[2], and Dan Strohschein[3]

[1] 4Digital, London, UK
practicaldatamining@gmail.com
[2] Sirius15, Washington, DC, USA
[3] National Aeronautics and Space Administration, Washington, DC, USA

Abstract. Humankind has thousands of years of experience in assessing the emotional context of face-to-face interaction. Written communication has been refined over centuries, and imme-diate voice communication over decades. However, online communication, which tends to be asynchronous and largely empty of conventional social cues, is still emerging as a cultural and cognitive venue. In this paper we present the earliest results of applying our field-theory of "emotional context" to the problem of the cross-cultural online emotion modeling:

Can a field-theoretic model developed using data from one culture be applied to online interaction in another?

We also present the results of a small empirical study focusing on the methods we used to visualize and model the "emotional context" of a social media corpus.

1 Introduction

The history of science provides many instances of rapid advancement when unifying principles are formulated that bring together seemingly unrelated lines of research. In physics and chemistry, this has often taken the form of mathematical field-theoretic models that both generalize and unify a subject. Notable examples are Newton's work on Universal Gravitation, Maxwell's work in Electromagnetism, Einstein's work in General Relativity, and the extended, ongoing developments in Quantum Theory.

We present a general mathematical model for online emotional context as a set of field equations. These equations can be solved, using collected social media text as boundary conditions, to objectively characterize the medium's constantly changing emotional context using a minimum of a priori assumptions (e.g., probabilities, dimensionality, and/or structure). This method has served the physical sciences well, and so far as can be determined, has not been applied to emotion mining of social media.

Just as masses and charges give rise to gravitational and electric fields, the online behaviors of individuals engaged in electronic social discourse give rise to an "emotional context" that conditions, and is conditioned by, these behaviors.

© Springer International Publishing Switzerland 2015
D.D. Schmorrow and C.M. Fidopiastis (Eds.): AC 2015, LNAI 9183, pp. 410–417, 2015.
DOI: 10.1007/978-3-319-20816-9_39

Following this lead, we have formulated a field-theoretic model, and the corresponding field equations, as a unifying principle for the mining of text in social media. The underlying motivating principles are:

1. By the term "emotional context" we mean a vector field generated by documents posted on a specific social medium. Vectors derived from document metrics are themselves within this attribute space.
2. Text sources (i.e., persons) can be regarded as short-memory text generators having goals and a partially-observable history.
3. The output text (forum posts on social media) is purposeful and sequential in time.
4. The output text is constrained by the medium and the medium's linguistics.
5. The text is generated within a "culture" that both informs, and is informed by, each generator.

We take 4 above as our guiding principle, since all field theories are ultimately based upon the idea that,

"The entities whose actions are conditioned by a field are themselves its sources and sustainers."

We begin by assuming that this is just as true of the culture that drives social behaviors as it is of the masses that drive gravitational behaviors. The field can then be viewed as a mathematical device for explaining how entities influence one another without directly interacting.

No assessment is made viz. the reduction of apparently "free" human behaviors to mere outputs of deterministic automata. All that is required is sufficient consistency of stimulus and response to support the formulation of a general and useful field model.

2 Background

The methods described here are used to objectively characterize the "emotional context" that arises from the interaction of humans using social media. The ultimate goal is to inform practical action, either in the real-world, or in the social medium itself.

Mining information about social interaction using text analysis is hard for all the reasons that text mining is hard. Text is an imprecise, coordinate-free, non-geometric way of expressing information. This problem is compounded in social media, where the object of analysis, the "emotional context", both affects and is affected in real-time by the dynamic, asynchronous interaction of the text sources (people) [1].

The goals of this research are three-fold:

1. Automate the mathematically complex portions of text feature extraction using conventional text processing methods (e.g., Tf.idf, table of semantically tagged reference terms if available)
2. Use the field-theoretic method to geometrize and visualize the attribute space
3. Use data mining methods to assess the cross-cultural stability of context assessment

Our method makes liberal use of High-Dimensional graphics technology to depict the data and support its analysis in a natural N-dimensional Euclidean Space.

3 The Data

Data were obtained from an internet forum and reduced to a coordinate-free term set. The corpus consisted of 4,487 multi-post threads covering two years of colloquial interaction among 229 members, in 87,000 + posts. The data were provided by the forum owner as single, lightly annotated text file. Each post was a logical record, with post number, thread number, and poster id (anonymized). The file is essentially a "raw dump" of the forum posts as entered by interacting forum members.

Post #	Thread #	Post_in_thread	Poster ID	Post
85526	4344	17	13	Ray Small is IN THE HOUSE!!!!!!!!!!
85527	4344	18	297	Damn it Small, how the hell do you get tackled by the Punter!! !? !? !? !
85528	4344	19	377	That's alright... He's smaller than the punter!
85529	4344	20	297	Well, 3rd and 11... let's see what they do...
85562	4345	1	0	Ricky Dobbs back at it Out the past 2 weeks and Navy felt it. Winning against Wake 13-10 and l
85563	4345	2	181	Sorry Vespula, take out Nesbitt and put Ricky Dobbs in GA Tech's option. forget about it.
85564	4345	3	13	Uh oh, Navy up 14-0
85566	4345	5	297	GO NAVY!!
85567	4345	6	13	Now he throws a 50+ yard TD. Dobbs for Heisman.
85568	4345	7	297	GO NAVY GO!
85569	4345	8	372	Where is Bks for this?
85570	4345	9	6	Go Midshipmen!!
85572	4345	11	128	GO NAVY!!
85574	4345	13	13	Yes, but he isn't Ricky Dobbs.
85575	4345	14	415	and Navy wins!!!!!!!!
85576	4345	15	20	Uhh I wasn't aware that you could onside kick after a safety. I thought you had to punt/kick it de
85577	4345	16	20	So Navy gets the safety to make it 23-14 and Notre Dame onside kicks the safety kick? ? and rec
85578	4345	17	128	YEAH,BABY! GO NAVY!
85579	4345	18	20	Navy recovers the onside kick and runs out the clock. Game = Navy2 times in 3 years for the Mi
85580	4346	1	0	OH MY GOSH MY HEAD IS GOING TO EXPLODE I hate living in Oklahoma. The newspaper says
85581	4346	2	111	Get DirectTV. lots of options there...
85582	4346	3	377	'Stro, I'm having the same problem. Thank goodness Comcast settled finally with ESPN360 and
85583	4346	4	420	try justin tv. . I love that site now. . NO HD quality but it's better than nothing. .
85584	4346	5	181	TG for AT&T, they are an affiliate of ESPN360.
85585	4346	6	297	Watching it on ABC with me Mum sorry Stro

As raw text, the data are a coordinate-free representation of user interaction. Abstract attributes such as "mood", "tone", "erudition", "anger" as they occur in social media are usually described subjectively, and in nominal terms: e.g., High/Medium/Low. This is because there is not a general principled method for assigning absolute numeric values to abstract attributes.

There are, however, relatively natural ways of assessing differences in abstract attributes (even if only in nominal terms: greater/lesser). Defining differences between explicit exemplars of an attribute can often be done without reference to any absolute scale. Rather than relying on an arbitrary catalog of codes for abstract attributes, the field equations use the data to determine a natural coordinate system for the attribute space.

The derived attribute space is a Hilbert Space of low-dimension (generally < 10) that creates coordinates in a natural way using unsupervised machine learning. The method was discovered independently by our team, but was first described in [2].

4 The Mathematical Underpinnings of the Field Equations

The field-theoretic approach gives a unifying mathematical framework for applications of computational linguistics to emotion mining akin to the framework Maxwell's Equations provide for Electromagnetism: a set of field equations that provide a rigorous mathematical framework for automating aspects of currently man-intensive characterization of the "emotional context" of online social behavior. The mathematics is relatively straightforward:

Let $\mathcal{F}$ be a collection of finite length character strings ("threads"):

$$\mathcal{F} = \{A_j\} = \{A_1, A_2, \cdots, A_M\}$$

Let $d_{ij}(A_i, A_j) = d_{ij}$ be a metric on $\mathcal{F}$. Form the distance matrix:

$$D(A_i, A_j) = [d_{ij}], \quad i, j = 1, 2, \dots M$$

This matrix will be symmetric, zero diagonal, and non $-$ negative.

Let: $$S = \{\vec{a_j}\} = \{\vec{a_1}, \vec{a_2}, \cdots, \vec{a_M}\} \in \mathbb{R}^N$$

be a (hypothetical) set of vectors having distance matrix D. Regarding the $\vec{a_j}$ as
<u>field sources</u>, we define a discrete scalar potential $\wp$ on S by:

$$\wp(\vec{a_i}) = \mathscr{g} \sum_{j=1}^{M} \left(\|\vec{a_i} - \vec{a_j}\| - d_{ij} \right)^2 \quad (*)$$

Here $\mathscr{g}$ is a non-negative constant that can be chosen arbitrarily to facilitate
specific anticipated applications of the theory (e.g., sensitivity analysis).

In general, the existence of such an S for a given D is not guaranteed; in
particular, D might not exist for N=1, but exist for N=2. Also, because S is
informed only by the distances between the $\vec{a_j}$, any rigid placement of a solution
is also a solution. Therefore, a solution can be registered in $\mathbb{R}^N$ for convenience.

An approximate solution S for (*) can be found by various methods (e.g., SVD,
Gradient Descent, Monte-Carlo).

It is laborious, but neither difficult nor particularly instructive to show that the
formal gradient:

$$\nabla \wp(\vec{a_i}) = C(\vec{a_i})$$

Is a vector field on S, and that S is precisely the set of zeros of the
Laplacian of $\wp$ (which is to be expected).

5   Software Instantiation of Sirius15

We call our emotional context field-modeling application **Sirius15**. The field model is
the foundation of **Sirius15**, actualizing a mining and modeling:

- Parse internet forum data to create a document space and a term space (136 threads
  covering several months of colloquial interaction among 152 members, using 4,187
  terms)
- Apply information gain (viz. Tf.idf) and a metric to extract features
- Solve the field equations to coordinatize attribute space (an 8-dimensional Hilbert
  Space)
- Use data mining tools to segment the entities into cliques
- Explore the resulting patterns using special-purpose mining and visualization
  tools [3]

The field equations are recursively solved using the term space as the field constraints; in keeping with our guiding principle, the posts to be mined determine the structure of the field. The synthesis of a natural coordinate system is a spectral decomposition of attribute space.

The process architecture operates according to a 6-phase sequence:

The Six Phase Processing Sequence

Phase_0_exe
(Ingest and conform raw forum post set, create initial word list)
input: Forum.csv
output: Phase_I_In.csv

Phase_I.exe
(Ingests original word list with repetitions, annotates with idf scores)
input: Phase_I_In.csv
output: Phase_I_Out.csv
        Wordstring_I.txt

Phase_II.exe
(filter out misspelled words, renumber threads in annotated word list and forum text)
input: validwords.csv
         Phase_I_Out.csv
         Forum.txt
output: Phase_II_Out.csv
         Forum_II.txt

Phase_III.exe
(Create idf-weighted angles-only distance matrix, check metric consistency)
input: Phase_II_out.csv
         validwords.csv
output: Phase_III_out.csv
         dmFAIL.csv
         trifail.csv

Phase_IV.exe
(Generate a Torgerson Coordinate feature vector file having selected dimension)
input: Phase_III_out.csv
output: Phase_IV_out.csv
        Rowrand_IV.csv

Phase_V.exe
(Cluster the Torgerson Coordinate feature vector file, produce C45 file and summaries)
input: Phase_IV_out.csv
output: Phase_V.hOT
        Phase_V_cl.csv
        P5_"clus#".csv (if selected; could be up to 999 files)

All Phases of the application run under Microsoft Windows on a 1-core processor. The prototype operates in a "batch" mode.

The application does not need to operate on all the data at once. During learning, the computational complexity is $O(N^2)$ in the number of threads (a thread is a topically heterogeneous collection of posts). Our benchmark data set contained 4,487 threads. The experiment reported below is based upon a subset of 136 threads, consisting of a total of 2,847 posts.

A large-scale processing-complexity experiment gave the following performance information:

**Torgerson Coordinates inferred using
the Laplacian of the Field Potential**

Thread / Feature 1	Feature 2	Feature 3	Feature 4	Feature 5	Feature 6	Cluster #
1	1.132851	-0.7324935	-2.807379	-0.3270132	-1.127138	0.4688708	1
2	1.713233	-0.7147069	-3.061881	-0.6393204	-1.826719	0.4107876	17
3	0.7090647	-1.19348	-2.330333	-0.6497642	-1.06594	0.7433085	1
4	1.510779	-1.410487	-2.479628	-0.501007	-1.247656	0.603342	1
5	1.507237	-1.195071	-2.303251	-0.1950196	-1.16112	0.7606344	1
6	1.328545	-1.361132	-2.976217	-0.4625052	-1.259196	0.413531	1
7	1.234295	-1.261456	-2.197749	-0.547074	-1.170727	4.41E-02	1
8	-0.3268293	0.5176432	4.71E-02	0.9533091	0.1505481	1.71E-02	32
9	-0.8928862	0.7833326	-0.3112981	0.4345004	0.3846253	-0.1534715	32
10	-1.340502	-0.2307369	-0.4626657	-1.561791	1.752655	0.7273926	67
11	-1.590019	-0.3873197	-0.6369065	-1.117083	1.774765	0.8706808	67
12	-1.511013	-0.6160021	-0.4751602	-1.668562	1.521265	0.3149354	67
13	-1.366065	0.12779	-0.1892876	-1.577721	1.500369	0.5746704	67
14	-1.6567	-0.4571404	-0.5007457	-1.743836	1.283633	0.8670825	67
15	-1.308596	-3.09E-02	-0.2335659	-1.30887	1.754491	0.34057	67
16	-1.59445	0.1800286	-1.094328	-1.371261	2.16339	0.5787393	67
17	-1.674331	-0.3219829	-0.6503383	-1.427543	1.829624	1.084335	67
18	0.4031281	1.543705	-0.8230213	-1.761889	1.7895	1.277841	49
19	0.2925319	1.633054	-0.294793	-1.6646	2.074924	1.346127	49

Prototype Performance

Corpus: ~10 million words
Duration: 2 years
Posts: 87,983
Threads: 4,487
Members: 224
Machine: Intel i7 920 @ 2.67 GHz CPU (Windows XP)

Function Execution times

Phase_0:   6 seconds
Phase_I.exe: 22 seconds
Phase_II.exe: 1 hour and 28 minutes
Phase_III.exe: 2 hours, 59 minutes, and 13 seconds
Phase_IV.exe: 12 hours, 35 minutes, and 53 seconds (*)
Phase_IV_NCC.exe: 13 minutes, and 1 second
Phase_V.exe: 27 seconds

Tfidf_II.exe: 2 minutes and 29 seconds

(*) Operator discretion. Time is $O(n^2)$ in number of threads.

6   The Cross-Cultural Modeling Experiment

We assembled two teams, one consisting of native English speakers, and one consisting of Cantonese speakers having English as a second language. Each team member was assigned a set of English posts taken from an English-language online sports blog; the members rated these posts for "emotional impact" from 0 (emotionless) to 10 (rant/rave). No distinction was made between expressions of "positive" or "negative" emotion; only emotional intensity. In keeping with our goal of assessing this question "in the wild," team members were told to rely entirely on their personal perception of emotional level, so long as they remained consistent among the posts.

Data from the raters were split into separate groups to determine whether ANOVA analysis could show that any group of rater's means could be considered equal. To prepare for these tests, a subset of data was generated that only contained common scores for all the raters, i.e. only posts that were rated by all of the English and Cantonese speakers were included.

The test subsets were as follow: English speakers, Cantonese speakers, combined English and Cantonese speakers, English speakers based on gender and Cantonese based on gender. Each of these were subject to ANOVA ($p = 0.05$) analysis. In each case, the F score > F critical. That is, the raters were concluded not to belong to the same underlying population, either within the rater's first language, or across it.

This isn't too surprising, given the small number of raters (8 English and 4 Cantonese). Future studies should use larger samples, and a more balanced gender split. Further analysis could look at patterns of the ratings, not just raw base score (such as location of the peaks and valleys of the ratings).

While the statistical analysis was not able to draw conclusions about the cross-cultural stability of the rating methodology, the visualization contained a striking artifact. An experiment was performed to see whether a supervised learning model could learn from one of the languages to recognize high-emotion posts in the other. In visualizing the data in 8-dimensional space, it was found that, with one exception, the

English and Cantonese speakers only agreed that a post was highly emotional if that post was part of a particular clique structure in the Euclidean space, seen below:

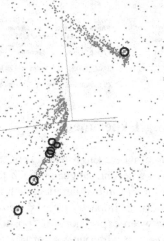

When both English and Cantonese agree that a post is highly emotional, it lies on a particular clique structure (with 1 exception)

This suggests that there is a specific set of semantic producing agreement between the two cultural groups.

Here are most of the posts that both groups agreed had high emotional content (< # > denotes a coded vulgarism):

```
Welcom King...you old grouchy goober! or i could call you grumpy <30> er....cuz we
can do that here...or I could just put this up-- It makes the same point!!\Good to
have you here!!! Looking forward to trading paint with you....
```

```
Hey Geek....that was funny...kinda reminded me of one of you SEC boys engaged in
foreplay
```

```
You'll have to speak up a little lad because you know us old dudes can't hear real
well when you young whipper snappers start mouthing off.Tell you what son the truth
of the matter is that ole King has given KU loads of props over their recent
success but my point here is that I ain't taking a lot of <18> off of a cow milking
tow-headed goober head just because his team has had a couple of good years for a
change.
```

```
Au contraire my friend those barely beats are relative to a certain extent when
there are several of them and you should know that. Just like ranking recruiting it
is not an exact science and there are always if's and's and buts. Just the same and
just like I said there is a mound of proof out there to show that the South is way
deeper and tougher than the Big XII North. Regardless you say you aren't debating
that premise anyhow so why press the issue any further?
```

```
Nice Job Guys! (and Girl) Pretty cool stuff.1 Real complaint: The pages are wider
than my screen had trouble finding the Register button cause all that I seen was
reg. No biggie though. 1 Homer complaint: An OU background? Are you trying to
attract horseflies?Very nice website I still need to look around some more but very
professional. Those are also some major editing tools for this forum.
```

```
BTW Oregon is on list # 2 I guess this just supports your narrow mindedness
```

7 Future Work

The field-theoretic approach suggests a unifying mathematical framework for text processing akin to the framework Maxwell's Equations provide for Electromagnetism: a set of field equations that can be rigorously solved to characterize and exploit the otherwise intangible cultural elements of online social behavior.

Our presentation shows how this theory supports emotion mining, e.g., the development of predictive analytics. Perhaps more interesting is the factor analysis it provides, which might be used to determine which members of a forum are most likely to engage in displays of emotive language. This is a type of "Emotion Terrain-Forming."

We have used this characterization to construct both unsupervised and supervised models of the behaviors of media participants; in particular, during Phase V, an "emotion clique" structure is inferred, along with a topical decomposition and logging of the media discourse. If the discourse is in English, a keyword list might be used to denote the topic, a type of "semantic tagging."

In looking at the details of the benchmarked data set, the techniques discussed above are able to identify cliques of "emotionally similar" posts. More importantly, the "emotional distance" between cliques can be quantified, supporting assessment of the "emotional separation" of cliques, and possible individuals within cliques. Further, the level of emotional impact of certain "hot-button" terms might be numerically estimated.

References

1. Lee, S., Song, J., Kim, Y.: An empirical comparison of four text mining methods (2010)
2. Torgerson, W.S.: Theory & Methods of Scaling. Wiley, New York (1958). ISBN 0-89874-722-8
3. Hancock, M.: Practical Data Mining. CRC Press, Boca Raton (2011). ISBN 978-1-4398-6836-2

Field-Theoretic Modeling Method
for Emotional Context in Social Media:
Theory and Case Study

Monte Hancock[1]([⊠]), Shakeel Rajwani[2], Chloe Lo[2], Suraj Sood[2],
Elijah Kresses[2], Cheryl Bleasdale[2], Nathan Dunkel[2], Elise Do[2],
Gareth Rees[2], Jared Steirs[2], Christopher Romero[2], Dan Strohschein[3],
Keith Powell[2], Rob French[2], Nicholas Fedosenko[2],
and Chris Casimir[2]

[1] 4Digital, National Aeronautics and Space Administration,
Washington, DC, USA
mfhancock@aol.com
[2] Sirius15, National Aeronautics and Space Administration,
Washington, DC, USA
[3] National Aeronautics and Space Administration,
Washington, DC, USA

Abstract. Just as masses and charges give rise to gravitational and electric
fields, the online behaviors of individuals engaged in online social discourse
give rise to an "emotional context" that conditions, and is conditioned by, these
behaviors. Using Information Geometry and Unsupervised Learning, we have
formulated a mathematical field theory for modeling online emotional context.
This theory has been used to create a soft-ware application, **Sirius15**, that infers,
characterizes, and visualizes the field structure ("emotional context") arising
from this discourse. A mathematical approach is presented to social media
modeling that enables automated characterization and analysis of the emotional
context associated with social media interactions. The results of a small, preliminary case study carried out by our team are presented.

1 Background

Human collaborative processes are being revolutionized by the emergence of ubiquitous, completely portable social media. Group decision-making, social interaction,
educational instruction, and many other directed and undirected cognitive interactions
are now conducted without a single spoken word being exchanged.

Augmented cognition is a form of human-systems interaction in which a tight
coupling between user and computer is achieved via physiological and neurophysiological sensing of a user's cognitive state. An essential, sometimes determinative
component of this state is the user's emotional state; this not only affects his or her
cognition, but the cognition of others by means of the way individual online behaviors
condition the emotional context within which interactions take place.

© Springer International Publishing Switzerland 2015
D.D. Schmorrow and C.M. Fidopiastis (Eds.): AC 2015, LNAI 9183, pp. 418–425, 2015.
DOI: 10.1007/978-3-319-20816-9_40

The underlying motivating principles are:

1. By the term "emotional context" we mean a vector field generated by documents posted on a specific social medium. The documents are themselves within this attribute space.
2. Text sources (i.e., persons) can be regarded as short-memory text generators having goals and a partially-observable history.
3. The output text (forum posts on social media) is purposeful and sequential in time.
4. The output text is constrained by the medium and the medium's linguistics.
5. The text is generated within an "emotional context" that both informs, and is informed by, each generator.

We take 4 above as our guiding principle, since all field theories are ultimately based upon the idea that,

"The entities whose actions are conditioned by a field are themselves its sources and sustainers."

We begin by assuming that this is just as true of the emotion that drives social behaviors as it is of the massive objects that drive gravitational behaviors. The field can then be viewed as a mathematical device for explaining how entities influence one another without directly interacting.

2 The Data

Sirius15 has been benchmarked using two years of colloquial, natural-language discourse from an English-language blog site. No prior domain assumptions are made (e.g., the method is language independent and does not require "translation" in order to operate). Results from the benchmark indicate that content-clustering is supported, and that "social signatures" of individual posters can be characterized.

The figure below shows a short sequence of blog posts from the data used to create the benchmark.

Post #	Thread #	Post_in_thread	Poster ID	Post
85526	4344	17	13	Roy Small is in THE HOUSE! ! ! ! ! ! ! ! !
85527	4344	18	297	Damn it Small, how the hell do you get tackled by the Punter! ! !? !? !? !
85528	4344	19	377	That's alright... He's smaller than the punter!
85529	4344	20	297	Well, 3rd and 11... let's see what they do...
85562	4345	1	0	Ricky Dobbs back at it Out the past 2 weeks and Navy felt it. Winning against Wake 13-10 and l(
85563	4345	2	181	Sorry Vespula, take out Nesbitt and put Ricky Dobbs in GA Tech's option. forget about it.
85564	4345	3	13	Uh oh, Navy up 14-0
85566	4345	5	297	GO NAVY! !
85567	4345	6	13	Now he throws a 50+ yard TD. Dobbs for Heisman.
85568	4345	7	297	GO NAVY GO!
85569	4345	8	372	Where is Bks for this?
85570	4345	9	6	Go Midshipmen! !
85572	4345	11	128	GO NAVY! !
85574	4345	13	13	Yes, but he isn't Ricky Dobbs.
85575	4345	14	415	and Navy wins! ! ! ! ! ! ! !
85576	4345	15	20	Uhh I wasn't aware that you could onside kick after a safety. I thought you had to punt/kick it de
85577	4345	16	20	So Navy gets the safety to make it 23-14 and Notre Dame onside kicks the safety kick? ? and rec
85578	4345	17	128	YEAH, BABY! GO NAVY!
85579	4345	18	20	Navy recovers the onside kick and runs out the clock. Game = Navy2 times in 3 years for the Mi(
85580	4346	1	0	OH MY GOSH MY HEAD IS GOING TO EXPLODE I hate living in Oklahoma. The newspaper says
85581	4346	2	111	Get DirectTV, lots of options there...
85582	4346	3	377	'Stro, I'm having the same problem. Thank goodness Comcast settled finally with ESPN360 and
85583	4346	4	420	try justin tv. . I love that site now. . NO HD quality but It's better than nothing. .
85584	4346	5	181	TG for AT&T, they are an affiliate of ESPN360.
85585	4346	6	297	Watching it on ABC with me Mum sorry Stro

3 Approach

The ultimate goal of this work is to extend and mature emotion-mining applications that will inform practical action, either in the real-world, or in the social medium itself.

While much work has been done (and remains to be done) in machine translation of colloquial text, relatively little formal mathematical analysis of the ambient emotional context that emerges from the interaction of humans using social media has been published. The **Sirius15** application ingests bulk social media data and, by means of a six-phase procedure, infers an empirical vector field structure characterizing the emotional attributes of the discourse. This we call the media's "Emotion Field".

The Six Phase Processing Sequence

```
Phase_0_exe
(Ingest and conform raw forum post set, create initial word list)
input:   Forum.csv
output: Phase_I_In.csv


Phase_I.exe
(Ingests original word list with repetitions, annotates with idf scores)
input:   Phase_I_In.csv
output: Phase_I_Out.csv
         Wordstring_I.txt


Phase_II.exe
(filter out misspelled words, renumber threads in annotated word list and forum text)
input:   validwords.csv
         Phase_I_Out.csv
         Forum.txt
output: Phase_II_Out.csv
         Forum_II.txt


Phase_III.exe
(Create idf-weighted angles-only distance matrix, check metric consistency)
input:   Phase_II_out.csv
         validwords.csv
output: Phase_III_out.csv
         dmFAIL.csv
         trifail.csv


Phase_IV.exe
(Generate a Torgerson Coordinate feature vector file having selected dimension)
input:   Phase_III_out.csv
output: Phase_IV_out.csv
         Rowrand_IV.csv


Phase_V.exe
(Cluster the Torgerson Coordinate feature vector file, produce C45 file and summaries)
input:   Phase_IV_out.csv
output: Phase_V.hOT
         Phase_V_cl.csv
         P5_"clus#".csv  (if selected; could be up to 999 files)
```

Modern text mining methods generally rely on a combination of statistical and graph-theoretic schemas for representing information. These schemas are parsed and quantified to obtain information about associations, processes, and conditional probabilities for variables of interest. While some automation exists, the semantic characterization of corpora is largely manual and ad hoc. The state of the art is described in detail in [1].

The shortcomings of current approaches arise largely because each was designed fairly specifically to overcome failures observed in others. Because a "trouble-shooting" mentality is inherently ad hoc, none of the current methods is founded upon a mathematical formalism intended to cover the entire problem space. Each of these proposed solutions has given rise to new problems. Our work re-addresses this space by employing a broader and more mature mathematical foundation.

The six-phase **Sirius15** processing sequence begins by fusing a collection of document metrics to create a matrix of pair wise distances between social media posts. This can be done in a coordinate-free way, since many document metrics are statistical rather than "vectorial" in nature (e.g., Tf.idf, term histograms). The combined differences between the selected metrics are taken as a similarity measure, where greater differences imply a greater distance between the underlying documents.

From this document distance matrix is inferred a set of points in an N-dimensional Euclidean space, with each point representing a single document in the corpus. The points are developed as a set to have the same distance matrix as the corpus of documents. This embedding geometrizes the document analysis problem, facilitating the use of many mature data mining tools that require numerical (rather than nominal) input features.

The figures immediately below are snippets collected during the model building process:

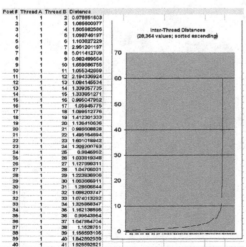

Bag-Of-Words for Thread 4345

[RICKY] [DOBBS] [PAST] [2] [WEEKS] [NAVY] [WINNING] [WAKE] [LOSING] [GUESS] [SCORED] [SEASON] [QUARTER] [NOTRE] [KID] [RICKY] [DOBBS] [FORGET] [TH] [NAVY] [NAVY] [DAME] [OUTSCORE] [STOP] [THROWS] [YARD] [DOBBS] [NAVY] [BKS] [NAVY] [NAVY] [PAST] [2] [WEEKS] [NAVY] [WINNING] [WAKE] [LOSING] [GUESS] [SCORED] [SEASON] [QUARTER] [NOTRE] [KID] [BACKUP] [PROCTOR] [DECENT] [MENTION] [DAUGHTER] [KID] [RICKY] [NAVY] [AWARE] [KICK] [NAVY] [SAFETY] [NOTRE] [DAME] [KICKS] [SAFETY] [RECOVERS] [DRIVE] [NAVY] [SECS] [KICK] [NAVY] [RECOVERS] [KICK] [RUNS] [GAME] [3] [CONGRATS] [NAVY] [WINNING] [RECORD] [RECORD] [WINNING] [TEAMS] [RIDICULOUS] [RUN] [BKS] [CROW] [BOARD]

```
4344,SAFETY, 3.090218
4344,SAFETY, 3.690218
4344,SAFETY, 3.690218
4344,RECORD, 2.432366
4344,RECORD, 2.432366
4345,OKLAHOMA, 2.759742
4345,GEORGIA, 2.489823
4346,SOUTHERN, 3.095511
4346,ILLINOIS, 3.384836
4346,VILLANOVA, 4.882356
4346,RICHMOND, 4.797799
4346,RICHMOND, 4.797799
4346,RICHMOND, 4.797799
4347,OREGON, 2.745756
4347,ARIZONA, 3.418284
4347,STANFORD, 3.793596
4347,STANFORD, 3.793596
4347,THREAD, 1.975777
```

idf (inverse document frequency) scores indicate the corpus-wide significance of individual terms.

The snippet depicted here is from an experiment where only terms having at least six symbols were allowed.

Post #	Thread A	Thread B	Distance
1	1	2	0.979551603
2	1	3	1.065600077
3	1	4	1.505562595
4	1	5	1.098746197
5	1	6	1.103827229
6	1	7	2.951201197
7	1	8	5.011412709
8	1	9	0.982469654
9	1	10	1.659686755
10	1	11	1.055342869
11	1	12	2.194336924
12	1	13	1.084146534
13	1	14	1.339357735
14	1	15	1.333951271
15	1	16	0.996047962
16	1	17	1.05945775
17	1	18	1.099512776
18	1	19	1.412301333
19	1	20	1.136410636
20	1	21	0.988608828
21	1	22	1.485164694
22	1	23	1.601018942
23	1	24	1.209200763
24	1	25	0.9846962
26	1	26	1.033819348
26	1	27	1.127896311
27	1	28	1.04706031
28	1	29	1.223536906
29	1	30	1.003666911
30	1	31	1.28606844
31	1	32	1.098203747
33	1	33	1.074013292
33	1	34	1.325868347
34	1	35	1.162138696
35	1	36	0.99643964
36	1	37	1.047864704
37	1	38	1.1628761
38	1	39	1.156593195
39	1	40	1.842862929
40	1	41	1.928592621

Inter-Thread Distances
(28,364 values; sorted ascending)

```
VECTOR # =   2401    id =   2401   ground truth class =  1
VECTOR # =   3408    id =   3408   ground truth class =  1
VECTOR # =   2412    id =   2412   ground truth class =  1

VECTORS ASSIGNED TO CLUSTER  316 BY THE MACHINE:
(The majority ground truth class for this cluster is  1)

VECTOR # =   4339    id =   4339   ground truth class =  1
VECTOR # =   4344    id =   4344   ground truth class =  1
VECTOR # =   4345    id =   4345   ground truth class =  1
VECTOR # =   4346    id =   4346   ground truth class =  1
VECTOR # =   4348    id =   4348   ground truth class =  1
VECTOR # =   4351    id =   4351   ground truth class =  1
VECTOR # =   4358    id =   4358   ground truth class =  1
VECTOR # =   4361    id =   4361   ground truth class =  1
```

The distances derived between "threads" in the social medium were used to infer Euclidean coordinates for for threads. The resulting vectors were then clustered to determine Blog "Clique Structure".

All Phases of the application run under Microsoft Windows on a 1-core processor. The **Sirius15** prototype operates in a "batch" mode; all posts are assumed to be present when modeling is performed.

During model construction, computational complexity is $O(N^2)$ in the number of threads (a thread is a topically heterogeneous collection of posts). Our benchmark data set contained 4,487 threads. The experiment reported below is based upon a subset of 136 threads, consisting of a total of 2,847 posts.

A large-scale processing-complexity experiment had the following results:

Torgerson Coordinates inferred using the Laplacian of the Field Potential

Thread #	Feature 1	Feature 2	Feature 3	Feature 4	Feature 5	Feature 6	Cluster #
1	1.132851	-0.7324935	-2.807379	-0.3270132	-1.127138	0.4688708	1
2	1.713233	-0.7147069	-3.051881	-0.6393204	-1.826719	0.4107876	17
3	0.7090647	-1.19348	-2.330333	-0.6497642	-1.06694	0.7433085	1
4	1.510779	-1.410487	-2.479628	-0.501007	-1.247656	0.603342	1
5	1.507237	-1.195071	-2.303261	-0.1950196	-1.16112	0.7606344	1
6	1.328545	-1.361132	-2.976217	-0.4525062	-1.259198	0.413531	1
7	1.234295	-1.261456	-2.197749	-0.547074	-1.170727	4.41E-02	1
8	-0.3268293	0.5176432	4.71E-02	0.9533091	0.1505481	1.71E-02	32
9	-0.8928862	0.7833325	-0.3112981	0.4346004	0.3846253	-0.1534715	32
10	-1.340502	-0.2307369	-0.4626657	-1.561791	1.762655	0.7273825	67
11	-1.590019	-0.3873197	-0.6359065	-1.117083	1.774766	0.8708808	67
12	-1.511013	-0.6160021	-0.4751602	-1.668562	1.521265	0.3149354	67
13	-1.366065	0.12779	-0.1892876	-1.577721	1.500369	0.6746704	67
14	-1.6567	-0.4571404	-0.5007457	-1.743836	1.283633	0.8670825	67
15	-1.308586	3.09E-02	-0.2335659	-1.30887	1.754491	0.34057	67
16	-1.59445	0.1800286	-1.094328	-1.371261	2.15339	0.5787393	67
17	-1.674331	-0.3219829	-0.6503383	-1.427543	1.829624	1.084335	67
18	0.4031281	1.543705	-0.8230213	-1.761989	1.7895	1.277841	49
19	0.2925319	1.633054	-0.294793	-1.6646	2.074924	1.346127	49

Prototype Performance

Corpus: ~10 million words
Duration: 2 years
Posts: 87,983
Threads: 4,487
Members: 224
Machine: Intel i7 920 @ 2.67 GHz CPU (Windows XP)

Function Execution times

Phase_0:   6 seconds
Phase_I.exe: 22 seconds
Phase_II.exe: 1 hour and 28 minutes
Phase_III.exe: 2 hours, 59 minutes, and 13 seconds
Phase_IV.exe: 12 hours, 35 minutes, and 53 seconds (*)
Phase_IV_NCC.exe: 13 minutes, and 1 second
Phase_V.exe: 27 seconds

Tfidf__II.exe: 2 minutes and 29 seconds

(*) Operator discretion. Time is $O(n^2)$ in number of threads.

4   The Mathematics of the Approach

The field-theoretic approach gives a unifying mathematical framework for applications of computational linguistics to emotion mining akin to the framework Maxwell's Equations provide for Electromagnetism: a set of field equations that provide a rigorous mathematical framework for automating aspects of currently man-intensive characterization of the "emotional context" of online social behavior. The mathematics is relatively straightforward:

Let $\mathcal{F}$ be a collection of finite length character strings ("threads"):

$$\mathcal{F} = \{A_j\} = \{A_1, A_2, \cdots, A_M\}$$

Let $d_{ij}(A_i, A_j) = d_{ij}$ be a metric on $\mathcal{F}$. Form the distance matrix:

$$D(A_i, A_j) = [d_{ij}], \qquad i, j = 1, 2, \ldots M$$

This matrix will be symmetric, zero diagonal, and non $-$ negative.

Let: $\qquad S = \{\vec{a_j}\} = \{\vec{a_1}, \vec{a_2}, \cdots, \vec{a_M}\} \in \mathbb{R}^N$

be a (hypothetical) set of vectors having distance matrix D. Regarding the $\vec{a_j}$ as <u>field sources</u>, we define a discrete scalar potential $\wp$ on S by:

$$\wp(\vec{a_i}) = g \sum_{j=1}^{M} \left(\|\vec{a_i} - \vec{a_j}\| - d_{ij} \right)^2 \quad (*)$$

Here g is a non-negative constant that can be chosen arbitrarily to facilitate specific anticipated applications of the theory (e.g., sensitivity analysis).

In general, the existence of such an S for a given D is not guaranteed; in particular, D might not exist for N=1, but exist for N=2. Also, because S is informed only by the distances between the $\vec{a_j}$, any rigid placement of a solution is also a solution. Therefore, a solution can be registered in $\mathbb{R}^N$ for convenience.

An approximate solution S for (*) can be found by various methods (e.g., SVD, Gradient Descent, Monte-Carlo).

It is laborious, but neither difficult nor particularly instructive to show that the formal gradient:

$$\nabla \wp(\vec{a_i}) = C(\vec{a_i})$$

Is a vector field on S, and that S is precisely the set of zeros of the Laplacian of $\wp$ (which is to be expected).

The field equations give rise to a radially symmetric scalar potential, depicted in the figure on the left below. The field source is the center, which is a blog post that establishes an "energy well" that can be occupied by another document (at "7 o'clock").

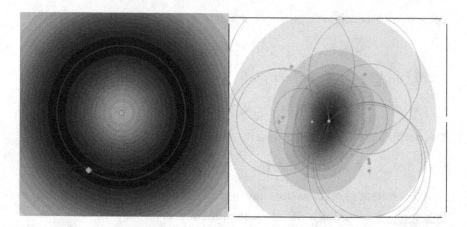

The field satisfies the superposition principle, so as additional blog posts are generated, they can just be directly added in (the figure on the right above). Further, by the methods of Differential Geometry, it can be shown that the "emotion" field is conservative. In particular, it is path-independent, which implies that we need not retain the history of a post to understand its immediate effect on the emotion field. This "statelessness" is potentially important for future work, though we have not exploited it.

The derived attribute space is a Hilbert Space of appropriate dimension that creates coordinates in a natural way using unsupervised machine learning. The method was discovered independently by our team, but was first described by [2].

The dimension of the Euclidean Space can be chosen at will (though poor choices cause convergence problems; see below). We use a variation of the Delta Rule from machine-learning for inferring the embedding.

The Delta Rule is a first-order gradient descent method. When it is written as a distance minimization expression, it can be interpreted as a differential equation describing a vector field; a solution (to coordinatize the document data) is then a set of Lagrangian Points for this differential equation. In this way, the field is an emergent property of the points it positions, and the positions are constrained by the field. Specifics are given below.

Other methods can be used to coordinatize the data from the distance matrix (e.g., Singular Value Decomposition, Lagrange Multipliers, Newton's Method). We have found that convergence by gradient descent is usually not complete, owing largely to the fact that natural text metrics might not result in a fused distance function that is a metric (e.g., Triangle Inequality is satisfied only approximately). This is sometimes overcome by increasing the dimension of the Euclidean Space. We also use an adaptive convergence rate and an annealing schedule to speed up convergence.

Once the data are geometrized, data mining methods for data visualization, signature extraction, clustering, building classifiers, etc., can be used to complete the emotional context modeling process [3].

5   Future Work

The field-equations can be used to impose an inherent, a priori clustering of entities in the space. This clustering determines, and is determined by, the terrain geometry; these are in dynamic tension. Clusters, or cliques, correspond to "emotion plateaus" in the original feature space.

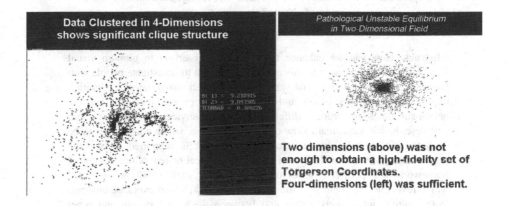

Data Clustered in 4-Dimensions shows significant clique structure

Pathological Unstable Equilibrium in Two-Dimensional Field

Two dimensions (above) was not enough to obtain a high-fidelity set of Torgerson Coordinates. Four-dimensions (left) was sufficient.

We have performed some preliminary work on the development of predictive analytics. Perhaps more interesting is the "domain segmentation" clustering provides, which might be used to identify those members of a forum most likely to engage in displays of emotive language. This is a type of Signaturing; done across the entire problem space, it constitutes a type of "Emotion Terrain-Forming."

In looking at the details of the benchmarked data set, the techniques discussed above are able to identify cliques of posters. More importantly, the "emotional distance" between cliques might be quantified, supporting assessment of the "emotional separation" of cliques, and individuals within cliques. Further, the level of emotional impact of certain terms might be numerically estimated.

References

1. Lee, S., Song, J., Kim, Y.: An empirical comparison of four text mining methods (2010)
2. Torgerson, Warren S.: Theory & Methods of Scaling. Wiley, New York (1958). ISBN 0-89874-722-8
3. Hancock, M.: Practical Data Mining. CRC Press, Boca Raton (2011). ISBN-13: 978-1439868362

A Neurocognitive Approach to Expertise in Visual Object Recognition

Assaf Harel[(⊠)]

Department of Psychology, Wright State University, Dayton, OH, USA
assaf.harel@wright.edu

Abstract. How can we enhance the ability of observers to pick-up visual information? One approach to this question has been to investigate people who naturally develop an exceptional skill, or expertise, in visual object recognition (e.g. bird watchers, car buffs), and determine how expert processing and the neural substrates supporting it differ from those in novices. The present paper will describe the mainstream view of visual expertise, which considers it to be an automatic, stimulus-driven perceptual skill that is supported by specific regions in high-level visual cortex. Following a critical review of the perceptual framework of expertise, a series of neuroimaging studies will be presented which reveal that in contrast to the mainstream view, visual expertise emerges from multiple interactions within and between the visual system and other cognitive systems (e.g. top-down attention and conceptual memory). These interactions are manifest in widespread distributed patterns of activity across the entire cortex, and are highly susceptible to high-level factors, such as task relevance and prior knowledge. Lastly, the applied and theoretical implications of the interactive framework to performance enhancement and neuroplasticity will be discussed.

Keywords: Expertise · Object recognition · Vision · Top-down control · fMRI

1 Introduction

What is common to architecture, basketball, bird watching, and chess? All of these seemingly disparate activities contain a central visual component, which is essential for mastering these activities and developing expertise with them. But, how do people become experts in a given domain? What processes change following the acquisition of expertise, how and are the neural substrates supporting expertise differ from those in novices? Most broadly, expertise is defined as consistently superior performance within a specific domain relative to novices and relative to other domains [1]. The current article focuses on expertise in visual object recognition, which is an acquired skill certain people show in discriminating between similar members of a homogenous object category, a particularly demanding perceptual task. For example, car experts can distinguish between different car models [2] or make ad hoc distinctions, such as between Japanese and European cars [3], but this expertise does not generalize to other similar domains, including airplanes [2] or antique cars [4].

© Springer International Publishing Switzerland 2015
D.D. Schmorrow and C.M. Fidopiastis (Eds.): AC 2015, LNAI 9183, pp. 426–436, 2015.
DOI: 10.1007/978-3-319-20816-9_41

This article presents a neurocognitive approach to the study of visual expertise, the aim of which is to explain the superior performance displayed by experts, often marked by unique behavioral signatures, by specifying the neural mechanisms underlying expertise, and how they pertain to these unique signatures. Recent neuroimaging studies suggest that the neural substrates of expert object recognition are distributed and highly interactive, with the specific regions engaged defined by the domain of expertise and the particular information utilized by the expert. Through experience, this information comes to be extracted and processed through specific observer-based interactions both within the visual system and between visual regions and extrinsic systems, key amongst which are those supporting long-term conceptual knowledge and top-down attention. Such an interactive framework contrasts with the view of expertise as a predominantly sensory or perceptual skill supported by automatic stimulus-driven processes, often localized to discrete category-selective visual regions in occipito-temporal cortex (OTC) [5, 6]. I will start by describing the perceptual view of visual object expertise, as it had a pronounced and long-lasting influence the field of object expertise. I will then highlight its major theoretical and empirical limitations, and present evidence in favor of an alternative, interactive account of expertise. I will conclude by suggesting how this account can be generalized to explain other forms of expertise and used to guide the enhancement of perceptual-cognitive performance.

2   The Perceptual View of Expertise

The hallmark of expert object recognition is the ability of experts to categorize quickly, effortlessly and accurately specific exemplars from a homogenous object category [7]. The remarkable skill that experts display in within-category discrimination (also known as subordinate categorization) manifests in increased sensitivity to fine differences between highly similar stimuli. Thus, one intuitive possibility is that expert object recognition involves primarily changes to sensory or perceptual processing [5]. I refer to this view as the perceptual view of expertise. According to the perceptual view of expertise, in order to overcome the inherent difficulty of within-category discrimination, new modes of processing emerge following the acquisition of expertise. In expertise with natural objects, such as cars or birds, this was suggested to entail changes from local part-based representations to holistic representations [8]. These perceptual processes become automatic over time, to the extent that the expert is assumed to recognize objects in their most specific identity ("Lassie") as fast they would recognize the at their basic-level ("dog") [9]. Such automatic stimulus-driven perceptual processing separates expert performance from the novice.

Given its stress on perceptual processing, the perceptual view of expertise suggests that expertise is accompanied by local changes to neural activation in specific regions of visual cortex [10–12]. This view is supported by the experience-dependent changes in neural tuning in areas of visual cortex reported in perceptual learning. For example, extensive training on orientation discrimination tasks results in stronger responses and narrower orientation tuning curves in early visual areas [13]. Similarly, long-term training with artificial objects is associated with specific changes in the response of high-level visual cortex [14].

One domain of visual expertise extensively investigated by the perceptual view of expertise is face perception. In terms of natural experience, recognizing faces is arguably the quintessential example of visual expertise [15]. Faces form a highly homogenous set of stimuli with a very similar spatial configuration of parts and therefore, discriminating between individual faces should be, in theory, a difficult perceptual task. Nonetheless, humans are extremely adept in recognizing individual faces and categorizing faces along many other subordinate dimensions (e.g. race, gender). Face perception displays many unique characteristics that differentiate it from recognition of everyday objects. Face processing is holistic [16] and automatic: faces are recognized pre-attentively, and they capture attention exogenously [17]. Accordingly, the perceptual view contends that face recognition can be considered as a general manifestation of perceptual expertise. Consequently, face processing and object expertise were suggested to share common cognitive and neural mechanisms. Expert object processing under this perceptual view is automatic and stimulus-driven, with little impact of attentional, task demands or other higher-level cognitive factors [6]. In line with this view, numerous works examined long-term visual expertise in object recognition using the face perception analogy (for a critical review of these works, see [29]). Like in face perception, experts were shown to automatically process objects of expertise at their individual level relying on holistic information. This was observed in a variety of object categories, including birds, cars, dogs, fingerprints, and chess displays (for a review see [5]). Similarly, the face-selective N170 ERP component was reported to be modulated by visual expertise [19], indicating that expertise impacts early, perceptual stages of processing. Objects of expertise were suggested to be processed by face/category-selective regions in OTC, and particularly by the Fusiform Face Area (FFA: [20]) [6, 21–24]. FFA was suggested to support the subordinate categorization of objects (any objects, regardless of category), as long as they share a prototypical configuration of features requiring experience to discriminate between the category members. However, the extent to which FFA supports expert object recognition is highly debated, with several studies failing to find an increase in response magnitude in FFA as a function of expertise [2, 25–27].

Regardless of the controversy concerning the reproducibility of expertise effects in FFA, two issues arise when discussing the neural correlates of visual expertise. The first issue is whether the enhanced response in FFA may in actuality reflect the involvement of extraneous top-down factors, which are associated with the expertise of the observers but are not perceptual per se. For example, objects of expertise are more salient and engaging for the expert than for the novice [28], and such enhanced engagement of the expert with objects from his domain of expertise may enhance the magnitude of response in FFA. Enhanced engagement may denote many observer-based factors, such as specific recognition goals, depth of processing, arousal and in particular task-based attention, which has been shown to modulate FFA's magnitude of response [29]. This is an inherent concern when studying real world expertise, since the experts are selected based on their particular skill, so there is no random assignment to the experimental conditions. Thus, expertise-related modulation of neural activity might reflect controlled top-down modulation of activity in object-selective regions rather than reflecting the operation of a stimulus-driven automatic expert perceptual mechanism [18]. Also pertinent to the question of top-down attention impacting expert-related activity, the second issue with the neuroimaging studies mentioned above, is that these studies focused primarily on the FFA (or other functionally-defined regions in visual cortex), ignoring the possibility that expertise effects may be expressed across the entire cortex, reflecting the operation of wider large-scale cortical networks. If expertise involves top-down controlled processing, one network in particular which might be employed is the fronto-parietal dorsal attentional network [30]; observing widespread patterns of activations characteristic of the dorsal attentional network which are nonetheless specific to category and level of expertise would provide a strong indication that visual expertise recruits additional processes and is not a strictly perceptual skill. Hence, it stands to reason that a full account of the neural correlates of visual expertise, the extent to which they spread beyond visual cortex, and critically, their susceptibility top-down modulations, will provide important insights into the nature of processing in visual expertise. Such studies are described next.

3 The Interactive View of Expertise

Clues regarding the full extent of expertise-related activity comes from fMRI object training studies that reported changes following training outside of FFA, both in additional areas of OTC and outside of OTC, including superior temporal sulcus, posterior parietal cortex and prefrontal cortex (for a review, see [31]). However, while these training studies demonstrate changes following experience, this type of visual-perceptual experience is only one aspect of real world object expertise. Real-world natural objects embody rich information not only in terms of their appearance, but also in their function, motor affordances, and other semantic properties. Given these extended properties, the cortical representations of objects can be considered conceptual and distributed rather than sensory and localized [32]. Critically, it is these differences in conceptual associations, which distinguish experts from novices since long-term real world expert object recognition is not only characterized by perceptual changes, but also by the ability to access relevant and meaningful conceptual information that is not available to non-experts [33–35]. In the acquisition of expertise, conceptual knowledge develops, along with other observer-based high-level factors (e.g. autobiographical memories, emotional associations) in conjunction with experience-dependent changes in perceptual processing. However, the conceptual properties of objects have not typically been manipulated in training studies such as those described above (but see [36]). Indeed, a complete account of real world expert object recognition cannot ignore observer-based high-level factors, and must specify how stimulus-based sensory-driven processing interacts with high-level factors. For example, the expert's increased knowledge and engagement may guide the extraction of diagnostic visual information, which in turn, may be used to expand existing conceptual knowledge [34]. This experience-based interplay between conceptual and perceptual processing is at the core of the interactive view of expertise. This interactive view of expertise contrasts with the perceptual view of expertise (i.e. as automatic, domain-specific, and attention-invariant) and echoes a more general view of visual recognition as an interaction between stimulus information ("bottom-up") and observer-based cognitive ("top-down") factors such as goals, expectations, and prior knowledge [37–39]. It is important to note that while the interactive view does not support a strict stimulus-driven view of expert processing, it also does not suggest that the effects of experience are driven solely by top-down factors that operate independently of the perceptual processing in sensory cortex. Rather, the interactive view proposes that expert object recognition depends on both sensory stimulus-driven processing as well as more high-level cognitive factors with a critical interaction between these processes, whereby the expert's increased knowledge and attention guides the extraction of diagnostic visual information.

One of the first neuroimaging studies to explicitly test the role of task-based attentional engagement in visual expertise was Harel et al. (2010) [2]. They assessed the full extent of the neural substrates of visual expertise across the entire brain by presenting car experts and novices with images of cars, faces, and airplanes while they were performing a standard one-back task, requiring detection of image repeats [11]. Directly contrasting the car-selective activation (cars vs. airplanes) of car experts with that of novices culminated in widespread effects of expertise, which encompassed not only category-selective regions in OTC, but also retinotopic early visual cortex as well as areas outside of visual cortex including the precuneus, intraparietal sulcus, and lateral prefrontal cortex. This widespread distributed effect of expertise overlaps with the fronto-parietal dorsal attentional network, and accordingly was suggested to reflect the increased level of top-down engagement that the experts have with their objects of expertise. This hypothesis was tested in a second experiment, which controlled the attentional engagement of experts by manipulating the task relevance of their objects of expertise [11]. Car experts and novices were presented with interleaved images of cars and airplanes but were instructed to attend to cars in one half of the trials (making cars task-relevant), and to attend to airplanes the other half of the trials (deeming cars task-irrelevant), responding whenever they saw an immediate image repeat in the attended category. A view of expertise as an automatic stimulus-driven process would predict a similar pattern of activation irrespective of the task relevance of the cars [6]. Contrary to this prediction, experts showed widespread selectivity for cars only when they were task-relevant (i.e. when they were actively attended to). When the same car images were presented, but were task-irrelevant, the car selectivity in experts diminished considerably, to the extent that there were almost no differences between the experts and novices. In other words, the neural activity characteristic of visual object expertise reflects the enhanced attentional engagement of the experts rather than the mandatory operation of perceptual, stimulus-driven recognition mechanisms. The neural correlates of expertise are not limited to a number of "hot spots" in visual cortex, but rather constitute a large-scale distributed network operating when experts are highly engaged in the recognition of objects from their domain of expertise. This raises the possibility that the preferential activation associated with object expertise is elicited only if the expert is voluntarily engaged in processing of diagnostic visual information - either because it is task relevant or because there are no task constraints limiting this process. This would explain why experimentally reducing the engagement level of the expert reduces the selective cortical activity underlying the visual expertise. Subsequent fMRI studies with car experts supported this conjecture, both in terms of the extent of activation, and its modulation by attentional engagement [24, 40, 41].

Widespread distributed effects were reported in car experts both within visual cortex and outside of it. Visual experience with cars was found to predict neural activity not only in the functionally-defined FFA, but also medial fusiform gyrus, lingual gyrus, and precuneus [24], as well as in early visual cortex, parahippocampal gyrus, hippocampus, middle and superior temporal gyrus, intraparietal sulcus, inferior frontal gyrus, and cingulate gyrus [40]. Such extensive activation as reported in [40] clearly indicates that even when experts are engaged with a very simple visual task, a host of cognitive processes are at play, and many of them, are arguably non-visual. This further demonstrates how visual expertise is intrinsically linked to multiple top-down factors, which interact and modulate "pure" visual processing of the stimulus. Importantly, the attentional modulation by engagement was also addressed in [40]. Visual selective attention was manipulated by including conditions in which cars were always presented in a pair with another object. Distributed patterns of activation were manifest when the cars were attended and the other object ignored (albeit reduced relative to the isolated condition due to the more taxing nature of this task), and critically, when the car images in the pairs were ignored, the extent of activation decreased dramatically. A univariate region of interest analysis further revealed that manipulating the engagement of the experts with their objects of expertise almost entirely abolished car expertise effects in functionally defined regions in OTC.

It is important to note that experts not only direct more attention to objects of expertise, they engage in a multitude of other unique cognitive and affective processes. For example, chess experts utilize multiple cognitive functions, including object recognition, conceptual knowledge, memory, and the processing of spatial configurations [42]. Accordingly, several cortical regions were reported to be active in chess experts when they observe chessboards [25, 42]. Expert-related activity during visual recognition was found to be widespread, extending beyond visual cortex to include activations in collateral sulcus, posterior middle temporal gyrus, occipitotemporal junction, supplementary motor area, primary motor cortex, and left anterior insula. These regions have been suggested to support pattern recognition, perception of complex relations, and action-related functional knowledge of chess objects [42]. Critically, task context and prior knowledge have been shown to play an essential role in driving cortical activations in chess experts [23, 42]. Expert-specific patterns of activation manifested only when the task was specific to the domain of expertise (e.g., searching for particular chess pieces), and not when comparable control tasks with identical visual input were used (i.e., a task that did not require the recognition of particular chess pieces). In essence, when the chess experts were not engaged there was little activity that distinguished them from novices, directly echoing the findings of Harel et al. (2010). Further research is required to determine the exact nature of the interaction between the different cognitive processes involved in chess expertise and actual visual processing (i.e. how visual information is utilized and accessed by higher-level cognitive processes ubiquitous to chess). One chess expertise study pointing at this direction has highlighted the importance of characterizing the functions of different prefrontal and parietal regions as they relate to expertise [43]. Specifically, experts' processing of random chess displays, as compared to normal displays was linked to activation in prefrontal and lateral parietal brain regions. This was interpreted as support for the idea that expert chess players perform a working memory task when they respond to random boards by engaging an active search for novel chunks involving the dorsal fronto-parietal network.

A complementary approach to study the neural manifestations of expertise is to measure how brain structure differs with expertise as opposed to measuring differences in brain activation. Expertise-related structural changes in the brain allow assessment of consequences of long-term expertise on gray matter structure across the entire brain, independently of the context set by a particular experimental task. Using the structural data from the set of experiments by Harel and colleagues reported above, a recent voxel-based morphometry (VBM) [44] study investigated whether inter-individual differences in behavioral performance with cars would predict differences in gray matter density [35]. According to the interactive view of expertise, one should predict structural changes to be outside of visual cortex, reflecting the involvement of higher-level cognitive processes, rather than visual processing per se. Consistent with this prediction, although the skill demonstrated by the experts was in recognizing and visually matching the models of cars, changes in neural structure associated with their expertise were found outside the of visual cortex. Long-term experience in car recognition positively correlated with increasing gray matter density in local prefrontal cortex structures, and not in OTC. In sum, long-term expertise for real-world objects does not necessarily entail structural changes in regions associated with visual processing per se, but rather in more anterior regions in prefrontal cortex associated with retrieving of goal-relevant knowledge from semantic memory [45]. Experts are more knowledgeable about both shape and function of their objects of expertise and this domain-specific conceptual knowledge interacts with and guides the extraction of visual information [33, 46].

4   Implications of the Interactive View of Expertise

The current paper focused primarily on expertise in visual object recognition, reassessing its common view as a predominantly automatic stimulus-driven perceptual skill that is supported by category-selective areas in high-level visual cortex. However, the interactive view of visual expertise can be expanded to account for the neural manifestations of other types of expertise that involve the extraction of visual information. The interactive framework posits that visual expertise emerges from multiple interactions within and between the visual system and other cognitive systems, such as top-down attention and conceptual memory. These interactions are manifest in widespread distributed patterns of activity across the entire cortex, and are highly susceptible to high-level factors. Importantly, which brain networks will be engaged by different types of expertise is determined by the informational demands imposed by the particular domain of expertise, that is, based on the totality of the cognitive processes invoked by the particular domain [31].

While the current paper concentrated on task relevance and prior knowledge, other mental operations are certain to interact with and constrain visual processing. For example, professional basketball players have been shown to excel at anticipating the consequences of the actions of other players (i.e. success of free shots at a basket). This visual skill has been associated with activations in a body-selective region in OTC as well as in frontal and parietal areas. Whereas the former reflects expert reading of the observed action kinematics, the latter traditionally has been involved in action observation [47]. Extensive and varied activations have been observed in many additional domains of expertise, including architecture, musical notation reading, archery, taxi driving, and reading (for a review, see [31]). This demonstrates that the neural substrates of visual expertise extend well beyond visual cortex, and are manifest in regions supporting attention, memory, spatial cognition, language, and action observation. Importantly, the involvement of these systems is predictable from their general functions, suggesting that expertise evolves largely within the same systems that initially process the stimuli. Overall, it is clear that more complex forms of visual expertise recruit broad and diverse arrays of cortical and subcortical regions. This, in fact, may be the key feature of the neural architecture of expertise: visual expertise, in its broadest sense, engages multiple cognitive processes in addition to perception, and the interplay between these different cognitive systems unites what seems to be very different domains of expertise. Studying the different networks that form the neural correlates of expertise can inform us of the diverse cognitive processes involved in particular domains of expertise. Uncovering the involvement of specific cortical networks in a particular domain of expertise has the potential to reveal the involvement of cognitive processes, which hitherto were not thought to be involved in that domain. This has the potential to transform not only our theoretical understanding of visual expertise, but also can change the way specialized training regimens are developed for expertise. Put simply, processes that were not traditionally considered part of visual expertise would be further addressed and incorporated to newer, neurally feasible models of expertise. These neurally feasible non-visual processes of expertise will be operationalized and used to form specific training programs. The interactive framework to visual expertise implies that training people to become experts in visual recognition has to involve additional non-visual forms of information. Moreover, special consideration needs to be given to the question of how to train observers to become more engaged in their domain, and critically, how to exert control over this enhanced engagement, so it will be applied in the right situation at the right time. In that respect, to guarantee enhanced performance of visual experts would ultimately require integrative multi-faceted training programs, which address basic perceptual processing as well as high-level cognitive, and even motivational or affective factors.

5   Summary

The interactive view of visual expertise suggests that superior performance in recognizing objects is an interactive process, which emerges from multiple interactions within and between the visual system and other cognitive systems, such as top-down attention and conceptual memory. These interactions are manifest in widespread distributed patterns of activity across the entire cortex, and are highly susceptible to high-level factors, such as task relevance and prior knowledge. Notably, which cortical areas and the extent to which they are involved, is determined by the informational demands imposed by the particular domain of expertise. Moreover, the different brain areas implicated in a certain type of expertise do not operate independently, as activity in one area is mutually constrained by activity in the others, reflecting the interactive nature of visual processing in general, and expertise in particular. These insights into the nature processing in visual expertise provide a basis for future cognitive-perceptual training programs, which will capitalize on the multi-process nature of visual expertise.

References

1. Ericsson, K.A., Lehmann, A.C.: Expert and exceptional performance: evidence of maximal adaptation to task constraints. Annu. Rev. Psychol. **47**, 273–305 (1996)
2. Harel, A., Gilaie-Dotan, S., Malach, R., Bentin, S.: Top-Down engagement modulates the neural expressions of visual expertise. Cereb. Cortex **20**, 2304–2318 (2010)
3. Harel, A., Bentin, S.: Are all types of expertise created equal? Car experts use different spatial frequency scales for subordinate categorization of cars and faces. PLoS ONE **8**, e67024 (2013)
4. Bukach, C.M., Phillips, W.S., Gauthier, I.: Limits of generalization between categories and implications for theories of category specificity. Atten. Percept. Psychophys. **72**, 1865–1874 (2010)
5. Bukach, C.M., Gauthier, I., Tarr, M.J.: Beyond faces and modularity: the power of an expertise framework. Trends Cogn. Sci. **10**, 159–166 (2006)
6. Gauthier, I., Skudlarski, P., Gore, J.C., Anderson, A.W.: Expertise for cars and birds recruits brain areas involved in face recognition. Nat. Neurosci. **3**, 191–197 (2000)
7. Tanaka, J.W., Gauthier, I.: Expertise in object and face recognition. Psychol. Learn. Motiv. **36**, 83–125 (1997)
8. Diamond, R., Carey, S.: Why faces are and are not special. an effect of expertise. J. Exp. Psychol. Gen. **115**, 107–117 (1986)
9. Tanaka, J.W., Taylor, M.: Object categories and expertise - is the basic level in the eye of the beholder. Cogn. Psychol. **23**, 457–482 (1991)
10. Logothetis, I.G.N.K., Gauthier, I.: Is face recognition not so unique after all? Cogn. Neuropsychol. **17**, 125–142 (2000)
11. Sigala, N., Logothetis, N.K.: Visual categorization shapes feature selectivity in the primate temporal cortex. Nature **415**, 318–320 (2002)
12. Baker, C.I., Behrmann, M., Olson, C.R.: Impact of learning on representation of parts and wholes in monkey inferotemporal cortex. Nat. Neurosci. **5**, 1210–1216 (2002)
13. Lu, Z.L., Hua, T., Huang, C.B., et al.: Visual perceptual learning. Neurobiol. Learn. Mem. **95**, 145–151 (2011)
14. Op de Beeck, H.P., Baker, C.I.: The neural basis of visual object learning. Trends Cogn. Sci. **14**, 22–30 (2010)
15. Tanaka, J.W.: The entry point of face recognition: Evidence for face expertise. J. Exp. Psychol. Gen. **130**, 534–543 (2001)
16. Maurer, D., Grand, R.L., Mondloch, C.J.: The many faces of configural processing. Trends Cogn. Sci. **6**, 255–260 (2002). doi:10.1016/S1364661302019034 [pii]
17. Palermo, R., Rhodes, G.: Are you always on my mind? A review of how face perception and attention interact. Neuropsychologia **45**, 75–92 (2007)
18. McKone, E., Kanwisher, N., Duchaine, B.C.: Can generic expertise explain special processing for faces? Trends Cogn. Sci. **11**, 8–15 (2007)
19. Tanaka, J.W., Curran, T.: A neural basis for expert object recognition. Psychol. Sci. **12**, 43–47 (2001)

20. Kanwisher, N., McDermott, J., Chun, M.M.: The fusiform face area: a module in human extrastriate cortex specialized for face perception. J. Neurosci. **17**, 4302–4311 (1997)
21. Gauthier, I., Tarr, M.J., Anderson, A.W., et al.: Activation of the middle fusiform "face area" increases with expertise in recognizing novel objects. Nat. Neurosci. **2**, 568–573 (1999)
22. Xu, Y.: Revisiting the role of the fusiform face area in visual expertise. Cereb. Cortex **15**, 1234–1242 (2005)
23. Bilalić, M., Langner, R., Ulrich, R., Grodd, W.: Many faces of expertise: fusiform face area in chess experts and novices. J. Neurosci. **31**, 10206–10214 (2011)
24. McGugin, R.W., Gatenby, J.C., Gore, J.C., Gauthier, I.: High-resolution imaging of expertise reveals reliable object selectivity in the fusiform face area related to perceptual performance. Proc. Natl. Acad. Sci. USA **109**, 17063–17068 (2012)
25. Krawczyk, D.C., Boggan, A.L., McClelland, M.M., Bartlett, J.C.: The neural organization of perception in chess experts. Neurosci. Lett. **499**, 64–69 (2011)
26. Rhodes, G., Byatt, G., Michie, P.T., Puce, A.: Is the fusiform face area specialized for faces, individuation, or expert individuation? J. Cogn. Neurosci. **16**, 189–203 (2004)
27. Brants, M., Wagemans, J., Op de Beeck, H.P.: Activation of fusiform face area by Greebles is related to face similarity but not expertise. J. Cogn. Neurosci. **23**, 3949–3958 (2011)
28. Golan, T., Bentin, S., DeGutis, J., et al.: Association and dissociation between detection and discrimination of objects of expertise: evidence from visual search. Atten. Percept. Psychophys. **76**, 1–16 (2013)
29. Reddy, L., Moradi, F., Koch, C.: Top-down biases win against focal attention in the fusiform face area. Neuroimage **38**, 730–739 (2007)
30. Corbetta, M., Shulman, G.L.: Control of goal-directed and stimulus-driven attention in the brain. Nat. Rev. Neurosci. **3**, 201–215 (2002)
31. Harel, A., Kravitz, D., Baker, C.I.: Beyond perceptual expertise: revisiting the neural substrates of expert object recognition. Front Hum. Neurosci. **7**, 885 (2013)
32. Martin, A.: The representation of object concepts in the brain. Annu. Rev. Psychol. **58**, 25–45 (2007)
33. Barton, J.J.S., Hanif, H., Ashraf, S.: Relating visual to verbal semantic knowledge: the evaluation of object recognition in prosopagnosia. Brain **132**, 3456–3466 (2009)
34. Harel, A., Bentin, S.: Stimulus type, level of categorization, and spatial-frequencies utilization: implications for perceptual categorization hierarchies. J. Exp. Psychol. Hum. Percept. Perform. **35**, 1264 (2009)
35. Gilaie-Dotan, S., Harel, A., Bentin, S., et al.: Neuroanatomical correlates of visual car expertise. Neuroimage **62**, 147–153 (2012)
36. Gauthier, I., James, T.W., Curby, K.M., Tarr, M.J.: The influence of conceptual knowledge on visual discrimination. Cogn. Neuropsychol. **20**, 507–523 (2003)
37. Schyns, P.G.: Diagnostic recognition: task constraints, object information, and their interactions. Cognition **67**, 147–179 (1998)
38. Schyns, P.G., Goldstone, R.L., Thibaut, J.P.: The development of features in object concepts. Behav. Brain Sci. **21**, 1–54 (1998)
39. Harel, A., Kravitz, D.J., Baker, C.I.: Task context impacts visual object processing differentially across the cortex. Proc. Natl. Acad. Sci. USA **111**, E962–E971 (2014)
40. McGugin, R.W., Van Gulick, A.E., Tamber-Rosenau, B.J., et al.: Expertise effects in face-selective areas are robust to clutter and diverted attention, but not to competition. Cereb. Cortex (2014). doi:10.1093/cercor/bhu060
41. McGugin, R.W., Newton, A.T., Gore, J.C., Gauthier, I.: Robust expertise effects in right FFA. Neuropsychologia **63**, 135–144 (2014)
42. Bilalić, M., Langner, R., Erb, M., Grodd, W.: Mechanisms and neural basis of object and pattern recognition: a study with chess experts. J. Exp. Psychol. Gen. **139**, 728–742 (2010)

43. Bartlett, J.C., Boggan, A.L., Krawczyk, D.C.: Expertise and processing distorted structure in chess. Front Hum. Neurosci. **7**, 825 (2013)
44. Ashburner, J., Friston, K.J.: Voxel-based morphometry—the methods. Neuroimage **11**, 805–821 (2000)
45. Wagner, A.D., Bunge, S.A., Badre, D.: Cognitive control, semantic memory, and priming: contributions from prefrontal cortex. Cogn. Neurosci. **III**, 709–726 (2004)
46. Dennett, H.W., McKone, E., Tavashmi, R., et al.: The Cambridge Car Memory Test: a task matched in format to the Cambridge Face Memory Test, with norms, reliability, sex differences, dissociations from face memory, and expertise effects. Behav. Res. Methods **44**, 587–605 (2012)
47. Abreu, A.M., Macaluso, E., Azevedo, R.T., et al.: Action anticipation beyond the action observation network: a functional magnetic resonance imaging study in expert basketball players. Eur. J. Neurosci. **35**, 1646–1654 (2012)

Augmenting Bioacoustic Cognition
with Tangible User Interfaces

Isak Herman[1]([✉]), Leonardo Impett[2], Patrick K. A. Wollner[2],
and Alan F. Blackwell[1]

[1] Computer Laboratory, University of Cambridge, 15 J. J. Thompson Ave.,
Cambridge CB3 0FD, UK
isak.herman@cl.cam.ac.uk
[2] Department of Engineering, University of Cambridge, Cambridge, UK

Abstract. Using a novel visualization and control interface – the
Mephistophone – we explore the development of a user interface for
acoustic visualization and analysis of bird calls. Our intention is to
utilize embodied computation as an aid to acoustic cognition. The
Mephistophone demonstrates 'mixed initiative' design, where humans
and systems collaborate toward creative and purposeful goals. The interaction modes of our prototype allow the dextral manipulation of abstract
acoustic structure. Combining information visualization, timbre-space
exploration, collaborative filtering, feature learning, and human inference tasks, we examine the haptic and visual affordances of a 2.5D tangible user interface (TUI). We explore novel representations in the audial
representation-space and how a transition from spectral to timbral visualization can enhance user cognition.

Keywords: Tangible user interfaces · Embodied interaction ·
Bioacoustics · Information visualization · Collaborative filtering

1 Introduction

Initially devised for a case-study exploring the dynamics of modern music production and performance, we have now designed and built a generalized device
capable of a novel set of modes for human and computer interaction with sound,
space, and light. The Mephistophone is a haptic interaction device combining
sensors for surface-depth data and local illumination levels along with controlling
actuators which deform the shape of its latex surface. The computational architecture supports real-time algorithms capable of generating novel and familiar
mappings of movement and light from sound features and vice versa. In this
paper, we briefly outline the design concept and introduce a specific application of this novel device as a mechanism for enhancing user cognition of bird
calls through high dimensionality information visualization. We have described
the low-cost design and development of the initial prototype and specified the
technical challenges in creating a novel, large-scale interaction controller from
scratch [24]. We have classified potential interactions with the tangible user

D.D. Schmorrow and C.M. Fidopiastis (Eds.): AC 2015, LNAI 9183, pp. 437–448, 2015.
DOI: 10.1007/978-3-319-20816-9_42

interface (TUI) as the triggering, controlling, editing, and manipulation of sounds with varying temporal scope and structure. The system allows the incorporation of collaboratively filtered end-user gesture behavior performed in reaction to sound samples to inform the behavior of the physical and visual representation presented to subsequent users. The design is premised on the concept of a TUI which satisfies the metaphor of instrument-as-participant, rather than instrument-as-tool. As a user interacts with the device, it becomes aware of correlates between perception of sound and shape; with time the Mephistophone comes to augment the users intentions, guiding them towards learned pathways reflecting prior users' interactions.

We are exploring the future development of haptic TUIs and embodied computation. Our goal with the Mephistophone is to question the dynamics of acoustic visualization and analysis through a technically advanced prototype that demonstrates "mixed initiative" design, where humans and algorithms together collaborate toward creative and purposeful goals and where the interaction modes allow direct manipulation of abstract structure [5]. For this case-study, we selected the bioacoustic domain for bird calls express high timbral variation which is not captured using current information visualization techniques. Using a set of training gestures from prior research that were generated in response to timbre based samples, we explore physical mappings from extracted acoustic features and have augmented the system with new dimensions of visual feedback. In ongoing research we are comparing the efficacy of standard acoustic features with learned feature sets extracted from environmental audio for user cognition in the physical and visual domains.

2   Prior Work

Our investigation arrives at a confluence of research paths which treat the visual and auditory domains in analogous fashion. Through this research, we explore how connections made by both the system and the user from one domain or with one sense may inform interpretation of the other demonstrating mixed-initiative design.

2.1   Timbre Spaces

Timbre refers broadly to those features of sound which cannot be summarized by frequency and amplitude. With such an opaque definition, timbre does not easily lend itself to visual representation. In the iterative design of the device, we realized that the affordances of the haptic tangible interface, whilst novel as an interaction mechanism, provided similar dimensionality reduction requirements as with information visualized on a conventional 2D color display. This led to the current design which can overlay an equivalent 2D visual interface on our physical surface decreasing the need for such dimensionality reduction.

The majority of bioacoustic research into the analysis of audio data has been performed using temporal and spectral information, visualized as spectrograms. The time/frequency resolution trade-offs implicit to such models, as well as the limitations of augmenting user cognition of audio signals given only time-series frequency and amplitude data, left us considering the role of timbre in audio cognition and means by which temporally relevant timbral feature patterns could be visually depicted simultaneously with familiar spectral features. In attempting to augment novice users' bioacoustic cognition based on visual representation of timbral information, we explore means to offer 'implicit learning processes [which] enable the acquisition of highly complex information in an incidental manner and without complete verbaliz[able] knowledge of what has been learned' [23].

Timbre remains the audio component least quantified across a variety of research approaches; in various works it has been proposed to comprise a combination of attack time, spectral centroid, spectral flux, and spectrum fine structures [1]. It is this information which we endeavor to visualize as an augmentation to spectral representations of audio data. Researchers from Institut de Recherche et Coordination Acoustique/Musique (IRCAM) have proposed various means to visualize 'the structure of the multidimensional perceptual representation of timbre (the so-called timbre-space) ... and then attempt to define the acoustic and psychoacoustic factors that underlie this representation' [11]. Early psychoacoustic modeling work pursued the use of multidimensional scaling (MDS) to obtain a timbre-space from which acoustic correlates of the dimensions could be identified and predictive models built. They state that 'timbre spaces represent the organization of perceptual distances, as measured with dissimilarity ratings, among tones equated for pitch, loudness and perceived duration' along with spatial location and the environmental reverberance [1]. They further resolved the statistical problems arising from the fact that such models were defined so that each listener added to their data set increased the number of parameters in the model by proposing that listeners' perceptions of timbre would fall into a pre-defined, comparatively small, number of latent classes [11]. These models have shown promise, insofar as they offer replicable dissimilarity judgments between classes. Experiments based on finding associations between these acoustic correlates of timbre (flux, centroid and attack) and proposed neural correlates of timbre have seen support in fMRI studies showing greater activation in response to increases in flux and centroid combined with a decreased attack time [12]. For our novel visualization interface, we considered not only the need to augment the traditional spectral representations of audio with timbral information, but the likelihood that users, whilst not initially cognoscente of our timbral visualization mapping, would through exploration be able to build a mental model between the visual representation of our timbral model and a set of latent timbral class representations which could show correlation to the timbral attributes of attack time, spectral centroid, and spectrum fine structure.

2.2 Information Visualization

The instrument-as-participant characterization of the Mephistophone from its earliest design encouraged us to explore mechanisms by which information visualized, as well as informed as gestures, on its surface could map to known acoustic features. With the augmentation of illumination we maintain the capacity for replicating familiar acoustic information visualization metaphors whilst retaining additional degrees of freedom. Recent frameworks for information visualization theory have proposed that 'a model of data embodied in a visualization must be explored, manipulated and adapted ... [and w]hen there are two processing agents in a human-computer interaction context ... either or both can perform this processing.' We research the 'interpretation of a visualization through its physical form' as collaboratively filtered by the user, as well as the 'exploration and manipulation of the internal data model by the system in order to discover interrelationships, trends and patterns' [17] in our acoustic datasets. Purchase et al. further note that 'a prediction that a dataset may contain groups (clusters) of objects with similar characteristics does not define what specific clusters there are ... [but] orients tool designers who will know that the tool must help the users to detect clusters.' Although we consider the Mephistophone a participant in the interaction rather than a tool, these ideas guide our design in selecting a space of exploration in which latent timbral and gestural classes are modeled to arise. Early representations of acoustic data on 2D interfaces began mitigating the limitations of such displays to convey high dimensionality feature data by taking advantage of multi-dimensional color features such as the RGB *tristimulus equivalent* forming a *chromaticity vector* as augmentations to the physical axes of the display [9]. Spectrograms, which have formed the primary mode of visualization for the features of an acoustic signal both in bioacoustic informatics and other audio domains, are limited to the spectral to the detriment of conveying timbral information.

Acoustic Visualization. Visualizations of acoustic data have predominantly been used to describe spectral information over time, from early grayscale implementations, to those using the RGB tristimulus dimensions of color as previously noted. With the Mephistophone, we have the capacity to retain all such spectrotemporal features and convey further information on the unused tangible dimensions or map those features to the tangible interface retaining the illumination space for a novel mapping. Within bioacoustics, be it research into general biodiversity metrics, or single species identification, spectral representations remain the most investigated. This is a result of researchers' familiarity with the spectrogram visual representation rather than an implicit result of such representations being superior. Recent research into the efficacy of temporally brief sound event (as opposed to speech) classification, which better reflects our target audio when working with bird calls, has identified 'distinctive time-frequency representations ... motivated by the visual perception of the spectrogram image' which work with grayscale spectrograms to reduce noise [3]. While noise reduction remains important, such methods eliminate significant information contained within the original audio signal.

We propose that methods of timbral visualization, used previously in musical analysis to supplant rather than augment standard spectral visualizations, offer valuable additional information of use to a novice user or automated recognition system. The additional dimensions available with the Mephistophone, allow us to map timbral information as well as spectral onto the same interface. Early work from the Center for Computer Research in Music and Acoustics (CCRMA) at Stanford University has proposed mapping the physical parameters of timbre to a constrained feature set derived from Fourier output including power, bandwidth, centroid, harmonicity, skew, roll-off and flux [19]. Subsequent work by those researchers found support for a visual representation of a tristimulus based timbre descriptor "based on a division of the frequency spectrum in three bands [which] like its homonymous model for color description ... provides an approximation to a perceptual value through parametric control of physical measurements" overcoming the time-frequency trade-off inherent to spectrogram visualizations [20]. Their multi-timescale aggregation 'maps features to objects with different shapes, textures and color in a 2D or 3D virtual space' [19]. We have taken this mapping from a virtual to tangible interface, concurrently maintaining the multi-scale temporal representations of their visualization, with additional dimensions available to visualize conventional time-series information. Several alternative multi-timescale aggregation visualizations have been developed which animate characteristics of timbral space including but not limited to centroid width and spread, skewness, flux, bark-flux, and centroid-flux, as well as roll-off [21]. As we are less constrained in dimensionality reduction when working with projection and animation on a 2.5D tangible interface, the Mephistophone allows us to overcome some of the temporal and dimensionality reduction limitations of a standard screen when simultaneously visualizing spectral and timbral information.

2.3 Tangible User Interfaces

Haptic, tangible interfaces have been devised for a variety of purposes, from physical modeling of landscapes to musical collaboration environments. The Mephistophone was designed to simultaneously display a representation of audio and allow the user to haptically interact with the surface for tangible real-time audio manipulation. Various projects have designed reconfigurable, haptic, input devices with the capacity to sense objects placed within, on, or near a device, using techniques ranging from capacitive sensing to optical approaches [7]. Our 2.5D display technology incorporates a number of features of previous work, albeit at significantly reduced cost, but, given our sensing and display techniques, without the issue of occlusion of information on the surface by the user.

Early work from the MIT Media Lab explored the 'benefits of [a] system combining the tangible immediacy of physical models, with the dynamic capabilities of computation simulations' where the user alters a model's physical topography in a feedback loop with a computational system capable of assessing the changes brought about by the interaction [16]. Prior research in the domain of acoustic interaction explored the use of projection from beneath onto a surface, thus avoiding the issue of occlusion, whilst providing dynamic visual feedback to the users regarding the state of the device. As an extension of this model with our current design, we combine projection with embedded illumination on the physical surface [8]. Another project informing our system 'is both able to render shapes and sense user input through a malleable surface' although they achieved actuation using electric slide potentiometers requiring significantly more embedded computational power than our construction for roughly equivalent rates of surface animation [10]. Most recently, another group from the MIT Media Lab constructed a shape display which 'provide[s] multiple affordances over traditional displays namely graspable deformable screens and tangible output ... giving [the] functionality of linear actuator displays with the freeform interaction afforded by elastic surfaces to create a hybrid 2.5D display' [2]. As an extension in their work, "a grammar of gestures has been implemented illustrating different data manipulation techniques" [2]. We propose instead a model where gesture classes are learned by the device through collaboratively filtered user interactions. We are exploring extensions to the acoustic spaces we can represent compared to those on a 2D display, such as traditional spectrograms, given the affordances of haptic over visual representations as well as intuitive 3D analysis with physical models.

2.4   Bioacoustics

Bioacoustics, research into the acoustic emissions of animals, offers an accessible method for performing semi-automated biodiversity monitoring offering 'reproducible identification and documentation of species' occurrences' [14]. Rapid analysis of extensive recordings requires efficient methods of target identification and noise reduction. We propose that the simultaneous spectral and timbral display capabilities of the Mephistophone diminishes the expertise necessary for novice users to isolate regions of interest in a visual representation of sound when combined without our haptic filtering model.

Effective bioacoustic monitoring, combining autonomous static or mobile user-centric sensor networks for data collection with interfaces whereby novice users can participate in data assessment, requires less user training than current visual monitoring techniques although a role for experts in validation remains. In our research we consider avian species which are frequently acoustically conspicuous whilst visibly camouflaged. However, 'comparatively high song variability within and between individuals makes species identification challenging for observers and even more so for automated systems' [14]. This has guided us to the following approach:

1. As avian calls are less temporally diverse than songs, we focus on short, timbrally variable utterances. These are best suited to generating community rather than species specific information.
2. As automated systems benefit from the results of human inference, we propose a collaborative filtering model.
3. As validated user feedback in a collaborative learning framework is necessary, we propose the training phase incorporate expert, if avocational, users.

Acoustic biodiversity surveyors have proposed indices measuring acoustic entropy (α), correlated with number of species in a community, and temporal and spectral dissimilarity (β), correlated with variation across communities. 'Total species diversity in a set of communities has been traditionally seen as the product of the average diversity within communities (α) and the diversity between communities (β)' [22]. Extensions to this model have demonstrated that these indices yield results equivalent to visual approaches to biodiversity assessment with increased efficiency [4]. Avian research has explored 'the suitability of the acoustic complexity index (ACI) ... an algorithm created to produce a direct quantification of the complex biotic songs by computing the variability of the intensities registered in audio-recordings, despite the presence of constant human-generated noise' and note that:

> 'The ACI formula is based on the assumption that biotic sounds ... have a great variability of intensity modulation, even in small fractions of time and in a single frequency bin [and propose that] this new methodology could be efficiently used in hi-fi soundscape investigation to provide an indirect and immediate measure of avian vocalization dynamics, both in time and space, even when conducted by observers with limited skills identifying bird song' [6,15].

Acoustic indices reinforce the validity of short time event analysis as a means of noise reduction but only propose clustering by spectral similarity. We propose that timbral similarity distance functions might be learned on a device such as the Mephistophone and provide a useful extension to classification from clusters.

3   The Mephistophone

The underlying mechanical structure and computational architecture of the Mephistophone have been described previously and outline our modular arrangement of actuators, sensors, and micro-controllers as well as an early model of information flow [24]. In initial experiments, audio features including pitch classes and mel-frequency cepstral coefficient (MFCCs) were time synced with physical measures of static gestures informed on the surface (see Fig. 1). A preliminary machine learning model applied principal component analysis (PCA) to the extracted audio feature space and inferred a mapping to the tangible gesture space. Due to the computational complexity of audio feature extraction in previous experiments exceeding the capacity of the on-board micro-controllers, the analysis has been performed off-line using prerecorded samples. Subsequently we have implemented a number of extensions to the 2.5D haptic tangible display previously described as well as refined multiple computational architectures specific to various tasks.

In the current prototype an efficient, albeit low resolution, Fourier analysis program provides real-time spectral feature extraction from microphone input and runs on one of the micro-controllers allowing the the Mephistophone to dynamically depict local soundscapes. For more complex interaction, a small

Fig. 1. Preliminary training where static gestures informed on the surface in response to audio cues are sensed.

computer mounted on the chassis provides augmented feature extraction capabilities. Incorporating further dimensions for feature representation on the device allows us to reduce the constraints on dimensionality reduction of sensed and analyzed features. In this iteration of the design, we have augmented the device with two mechanisms for displaying color allowing the mapping of more information from the acoustic feature space to the tangible and visual feature spaces. Base mounted projection capabilities allow color mapped representations to be displayed across the surface without occlusions, and surface mounted illuminated nodes allow fine-grained color-based representations of state to exist uniformly spaced across the surface (see Fig. 2. Upon incorporating both coarse and fine-grained illumination capabilities into the visual representation of the physical model, we retain the original 2.5D tangible space initially for depicting familiar features, and use the visual overlay on the surface to depict additional information. In our initial experiments, visual representation of analyzed audio features, including spectral bands and MFCCs, have been partitioned to be depicted on the device as physical and visual components; we treat illumination as a space for mapping timbral features overlaid on the physical representation of spectral features. In future work, we are developing a model whereby learned features are extracted from raw audio and mapped across both the physical and visual dimensions of the Mephistophone.

We use the Mephistophone to examine the potential of a novel 2.5D haptic representation of avian vocalizations amidst environmental soundscapes as a tool for bioacoustic analysis and biodiversity assessment; additionally we explore motivating novice user interaction with representations of various feature sets. The mechanical characteristics of the device allow more features extracted from the raw audio to be mapped than with a standard 2D color display extending bioacousticians current data visualization frameworks. As a visualizer, the Mephistophone can depict temporal patterns in the timbre-space of a soundscape,

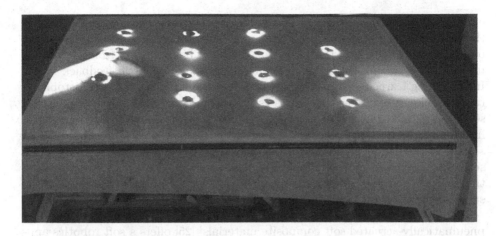

Fig. 2. Coarse and fine-grained illumination of the tangible interface

subsuming, supplanting, or combining with spectral patterns to provide multi-timescale representations unavailable with traditional displays. As we augmented the design with illumination and projection capabilities designed to reactively change the visual information presented on the physical surface, we augment standard bioacoustic visualizations and offer more simultaneous output dimensions. By removing the user from the familiar metaphor of 2D spectral representations of sound, the surface contains information about the original signal not available in traditional visualizations and elicits motivating curiosity in avocational users. With this design, dimensionality reduction algorithms need not be as constrained in output as would normally be the case in bioacoustics research where the spectrogram visualization metaphor remains the status quo. Instead, users assimilate collaboratively filtered interpretations from previous interactions, mediated by a feature learning model, allowing the information content depicted on the device to identify novel clusters of information associated with the original input.

4   Continuing Research

Our iterative design of the Mephistophone is ongoing, with subsequent versions informed by the efficacy of our sensing, actuating, illuminating and mapping models. As bioacoustic source material we have been using a subset of an open source database of bird calls available from xeno-canto[1] released as part of the BirdCLEF2014 competition[2]. Two autonomous embedded micro-controllers interact with various features from the audio: the first extracting the spectrum of the signal and passing the output to the actuators informing the resultant spectrogram on the physical model of the surface; the second receiving the output of a timbral analysis of the audio and passing it to both projection and

---

[1] http://www.xeno-canto.org.
[2] http://www.imageclef.org/2014/lifeclef/bird.

embedded illumination sources. This mode is sufficiently fast and robust to run the analysis either on prerecorded audio, as currently described, or in real-time on the local soundscape; the latter for the time being suffers from significant internal noise within the machine, generating haptic/acoustic feedback loops. In informing learned gestures mapped to acoustic features, the Mephistophone takes previous users' sensed gestures as input, building a collaboratively filtered set of gestures correlated to a training set of acoustic samples. Users' gestural interactions with the system are collected in response to a prerecorded set of sounds and subsequent actuation on the surface as a result of a given audio seed are a composite of a mapping of the raw audio features extracted from the sample, and the collaboratively filtered behavior of prior users given the same seed.

'An enabling technology to build shape changing interfaces through pneumatically-actuated soft composite materials' [25] offers a soft robotics approach to shape change without the limitations of our arrangement of actuators thus allowing more complex shape and gesture dynamics. These types of changes are enumerated as 'orientation, form, volume, texture, viscosity, spatiality, adding/subtracting, and permeability' [18,25]. Within this space, the Mephistophone currently offers interaction in the first three instances. Additionally, we are exploring the potential of comparing the mapping of conventional spectral and timbral feature versus a learned set of acoustic features to the physical and illuminated display surface. Using feature learning approaches on the audio alone, the mapping of the raw signal to the TUI can reflect a higher dimensional representation than afforded by traditional displays and perhaps a more intuitive mapping than afforded by conventional acoustic features optimized for 2D displays [13]. In our next implementation, we are exploring the use deep belief models for generating learned features from a composite of audio and collaboratively filtered prior gestures. This will be used to construct a system wherein subsequent information from environmental soundscapes is augmented by inference from past interactions.

5   Discussion

Through ongoing research combining collaborative filtering, feature learning and human inference tasks we are exploring the haptic and visual affordances of a 2.5D TUI for bioacoustics using collaborative inference models. We are exploring novel representations in the audio representation-space and how a transition from spectral to timbral visualization can enhance user cognition. Despite the varied information, be it timbral, spectral or learned, available when treating the Mephistophone as a visualizer, preliminary user testing has proposed that users maintain sufficient familiarity with the information mapped to the surface of the Mephistophone to consistently, if arbitrarily, define regions of interest for given pre-recorded sounds or *pathways of interest* across soundscapes [24]. In further mixed-initiative development, users will tangibly interact with regions or pathways of interest collaboratively filtered by past users mediated by the

Mephistophone, yielding filtered output represented by the selection. As an installation piece, the Mephistophone collects users? literal impressions delineating perceived regions and pathways of interest informed on the surface. Through analysis of deep belief outputs from collaboratively filtered behaviors a learned mapping from a data set of prerecorded environmental soundscapes can be used as the basis for a generative model of subsequent user interactions. This in turn provides feedback to the algorithms refining the boundaries of regions of interest in a given signal resulting from learned latent interaction classes. As subsequent users define regions or pathways of interest, the embodied cognition of the Mephistophone can haptically reinforce learned timbre-space pathways. By training algorithms to reflect prior users decision regarding regions and pathways of interest we provide a novel mechanism for subsequent users to be trained by, rather than on, the Mephistophone, augmenting their understanding of soundscapes old and new and further simplifying the task of training novice users to assess new recordings.

References

1. Caclin, A., McAdams, S., Smith, B.K., Winsberg, S.: Acoustic correlates of timbre space dimensions: a confirmatory study using synthetic tonesa). J. Acoust. Soc. Am. 118(1), 471–482 (2005)
2. Dand, D., Hemsley, R.: Obake: interactions on a 2.5d elastic display. In: Proceedings of the Adjunct Publication of the 26th Annual ACM Symposium on User Interface Software and Technology, pp. 109–110. UIST 2013 Adjunct. ACM, New York, NY, USA (2013). http://doi.acm.org/10.1145/2508468.2514734
3. Dennis, J., Tran, H.D., Li, H.: Spectrogram image feature for sound event classification in mismatched conditions. IEEE Sig. Process. Lett. 18(2), 130–133 (2011)
4. Depraetere, M., Pavoine, S., Jiguet, F., Gasc, A., Duvail, S., Sueur, J.: Monitoring animal diversity using acoustic indices: implementation in a temperate woodland. Ecol. Ind. 13(1), 46–54 (2012)
5. Edge, D., Blackwell, A.: Correlates of the cognitive dimensions for tangible user interface. J. Vis. Lang. & Comput. 17(4), 366–394 (2006)
6. Farina, A., Pieretti, N., Piccioli, L.: The soundscape methodology for long-term bird monitoring: a mediterranean europe case-study. Ecol. Inform. 6(6), 354–363 (2011)
7. Hook, J., Taylor, S., Butler, A., Villar, N., Izadi, S.: A reconfigurable ferromagnetic input device. In: Proceedings of the 22nd Annual ACM Symposium on User Interface Software and Technology, pp. 51–54. ACM (2009)
8. Jorda, S., Kaltenbrunner, M., Geiger, G., Bencina, R.: The reactable*. In: Proceedings of the International Computer Music Conference (ICMC 2005), Barcelona, Spain, pp. 579–582 (2005)
9. Kuhn, G.: Description of a color spectrogram. J. Acoust. Soc. Am. 76(3), 682–685 (1984)
10. Leithinger, D., Ishii, H.: Relief: a scalable actuated shape display. In: Proceedings of the Fourth International Conference on Tangible, Embedded, and Embodied Interaction, pp. 221–222. ACM (2010)
11. McAdams, S.: Perspectives on the contribution of timbre to musical structure. Comput. Music J. 23(3), 85–102 (1999)

12. Menon, V., Levitin, D., Smith, B.K., Lembke, A., Krasnow, B., Glazer, D., Glover, G., McAdams, S.: Neural correlates of timbre change in harmonic sounds. Neuroimage **17**(4), 1742–1754 (2002)
13. Mohamed, A.R., Dahl, G.E., Hinton, G.: Acoustic modeling using deep belief networks. IEEE Trans. Audio, Speech, Lang. Process. **20**(1), 14–22 (2012)
14. Obrist, M.K., Pavan, G., Sueur, J., Riede, K., Llusia, D., Márquez, R.: Bioacoustics approaches in biodiversity inventories. Abc Taxa **8**, 68–99 (2010)
15. Pieretti, N., Farina, A., Morri, D.: A new methodology to infer the singing activity of an avian community: the acoustic complexity index (aci). Ecol. Indic. **11**(3), 868–873 (2011)
16. Piper, B., Ratti, C., Ishii, H.: Illuminating clay: a 3-d tangible interface for landscape analysis. In: Proceedings of the SIGCHI conference on Human factors in computing systems, pp. 355–362. ACM (2002)
17. Purchase, H.C., Andrienko, N., Jankun-Kelly, T.J., Ward, M.: Theoretical foundations of information visualization. In: Kerren, A., Stasko, J.T., Fekete, J.-D., North, C. (eds.) Information Visualization. LNCS, vol. 4950, pp. 46–64. Springer, Heidelberg (2008)
18. Rasmussen, M.K., Pedersen, E.W., Petersen, M.G., Hornbæk, K.: Shape-changing interfaces: a review of the design space and open research questions. In: Proceedings of the SIGCHI Conference on Human Factors in Computing Systems, pp. 735–744. ACM (2012)
19. Segnini, R., Sapp, C.: Scoregram: displaying gross timbre information from a score. In: Kronland-Martinet, R., Voinier, T., Ystad, S. (eds.) CMMR 2005. LNCS, vol. 3902, pp. 54–59. Springer, Heidelberg (2006)
20. Sequera, R.S.: Timbrescape: a musical timbre and structure visualization method using tristimulus data. In: Proceedings of the 9th International Conference on Music Perception and Cognition (ICMPC), Bologna (2006)
21. Siedenburg, K.: An exploration of real-time visualizations of musical timbre. In: Welcome to the 3rd International Workshop on Learning Semantics of Audio Signals, p. 17 (2009)
22. Sueur, J., Pavoine, S., Hamerlynck, O., Duvail, S.: Rapid acoustic survey for biodiversity appraisal. PLoS One **3**(12), e4065 (2008)
23. Tillmann, B., McAdams, S.: Implicit learning of musical timbre sequences: statistical regularities confronted with acoustical (dis) similarities. J. Exp. Psychol. Learn. Mem. Cogn. **30**(5), 1131 (2004)
24. Wollner, P.K.A., Herman, I., Pribadi, H., Impett, L., Blackwell, A.F.: Mephistophone. Technical Report UCAM-CL-TR-855, University of Cambridge, Computer Laboratory, June 2014. http://www.cl.cam.ac.uk/techreports/UCAM-CL-TR-855.pdf
25. Yao, L., Niiyama, R., Ou, J., Follmer, S., Della Silva, C., Ishii, H.: Pneui: pneumatically actuated soft composite materials for shape changing interfaces. In: Proceedings of the 26th Annual ACM Symposium on User Interface Software and Technology, pp. 13–22. ACM (2013)

Predicting Learner Performance Using a Paired Associate Task in a Team-Based Learning Environment

Othalia Larue[✉], Ion Juvina, Gary Douglas, and Albert Simmons

Adaptive Strategic Thinking and Executive Control of Cognition and Affect (ASTECCA) Laboratory, Wright State University, 3640 Colonel Glenn Hwy, Dayton, OH 45435, USA
{Othalia.larue,ion.juvina,douglas.45, simmons.106}@wright.edu

Abstract. In this paper, we use a computational cognitive model to make a priori predictions for an upcoming human study. Model predictions are generated in conditions identical to those that human participants will be placed in. Models were built in a computational cognitive architecture, which implements a theory of human cognition, ACT-R (Adaptive Control of Thought - Rational) (Anderson, 2007). The experiment contains three conditions: lecture, interactive lecture, and team-based learning (TBL). Team-based learning has been shown to improve performance compared to the classical non-interactive lecture. Our model predicted the same outcome. It also predicted that players in the TBL condition would perform better than players in the interactive lecture condition.

Keywords: Cognitive modeling · Team-based learning · A priori model prediction

1 Introduction

The Paired Associate Task [1] is a learning task in which participants have to study and recall a list of paired associates (a noun and a digit). Response time and accuracy are measured as a function of the number of exposures to each pair. Over time, accuracy increases while response time for correct answers decreases.

Variants of this task have been simulated in the ACT-R cognitive architecture to create fMRI predictions [2], study the involvement of visual search and associative memory [3], study the fan effect, and the effect of practice [4].

The current study uses variants of this task and an ACT-R model to investigate the benefits of a teaching method: team-based learning (TBL) compared to other more classical teaching methods (lecture and interactive lecture conditions).

Team-based learning [5] is an instructional strategy in which students learn in groups and which has been shown to enhance participants' performance in certain conditions [6] and increase student engagement [7]. TBL has also been shown to improve the speed of learning [8] with the TBL group scoring higher in early stages of a learning task. Sharing answers and discussing among their group has shown to be

© Springer International Publishing Switzerland 2015
D.D. Schmorrow and C.M. Fidopiastis (Eds.): AC 2015, LNAI 9183, pp. 449–460, 2015.
DOI: 10.1007/978-3-319-20816-9_43

beneficial to participants involved in a TBL setting [9]. The cognitive mechanisms that underlie those effects are however yet poorly understood. In an upcoming study, we will try to elucidate the different cognitive mechanisms that are at play in TBL and that might explain the improvement of learning and retention in this condition. In this paper, we use a computational cognitive model to make a priori predictions for an upcoming human study on the performance of human participants to a Paired Associate task in lecture, interactive lecture (IL), and TBL condition.

2   Related Work

In the Paired Associates Task [1], subjects have to study and recall a list of 20-paired associates (a noun and a digit). Response time and accuracy are measured as a function of the number of exposures to each pair. The paired associates task has been used to study the relationship between response latency and accuracy. Over time, accuracy increases while response time for correct answers decreases. In its original version, two experiments using classic paired-associate paradigms were performed. The first experiment was a recall task, the second a recognition test. The two experiments illustrated an interesting result: even, when recall accuracy in interference conditions were raised to the level of control conditions by extra study trials, the deficit in response time in the interference condition didn't change. Response time was thus not varying in the same way as recall, a result that can only be accounted for by theories postulating a difference in encoding and retrieval mechanisms. ACT theory [10] is such a theory, and, in his 1981 paper [1], Anderson demonstrated that its predictions reproduced the human results pattern. While the theory postulates that memory items are encoded completely or not at all, their retrieval relies on continuous quantities that are subject to interference, thus explaining the still affected response time (an indicator of interference), even when the accuracy is not affected. Interference has an effect on retrieval but not encoding.

Variants of this task have since been simulated in the computational cognitive architecture, which implements a theory of human cognition, ACT-R [11]. Borst [2] used a classical paired associate task and a variant, a generated condition to create fMRI predictions. In the generated condition, representational manipulations were involved. Instead of showing the paired-associate directly, a word phrase was given: 'b-nd –id = adhesive strip'. While manipulation of delay led to a clear difference in response times, there was no great difference in response time between the two conditions. There was also no effect on accuracy. In this specific setting, behavioral data (accuracies and response times) didn't provide the information necessary to define and restrict the model. fMRI predictions made by ACT-R, however, in accordance with human results showed a clear difference between these two conditions. The improvement of the model with fMRI predictions allowed to improve its significance. The classical condition led to the activation of the prefrontal region (reflecting declarative memory retrievals). The generated condition (involving representational manipulation) led to the activation of posterior parietal cortex (reflecting the update of problem representation). Those two predictions were in agreement with the existing data.

In Halverson and Gunzelman's work [3], a different type of paired associate task is used: the Digit Symbol Substitution Test (DSST) where a symbol and digit are used (instead of a noun and a digit in the original task), to study the involvement of visual search and associative memory in the task. Two conditions with static (pair-memory variant) and moving pairs further allow the study of the tradeoff between complementary perceptual and cognitive processes and its evolution with learning. Results of the cognitive model here showed that the pair-memory variant relied mainly on "explicit" learning whereas the moving-pair variant relied more on "implicit" learning.

Finally, Pavlick and Anderson [4] used a paired associate to study the fan effect, and the effect of practice. The experiment they performed allowed to investigate the effects of practice and spacing on retention of Japanese–English vocabulary paired associates. Results showed that wide spacing of practice proved increasingly beneficial as the subject accumulated more practice. Different models of practice, forgetting, and the spacing effect were produced and compared to the data. The ACT–R's activation equation was augmented to make the forgetting rate of a memory chunk be a function of its activation at the time of the presentation. The produced model was compared to existing model of the literature [12] and fitted to existing results. The model required less parameters manipulation to fit the data than other existing models.

In this paper, we also use variants of this task and an ACT-R model. But, on top of an individual Paired Associate task (in lecture and IL condition), we investigate a team version of the task (the TBL condition). We are thus able to compare the benefits of TBL against those other teaching methods (simple and interactive lectures) and study the cognitive mechanisms underlying the performance in TBL and more generally a team setting.

Team-based learning [5] is an instructional strategy in which students learn in groups. In TBL, a high amount of class time is spent in teams, completing team assignments. Students are organized in small groups (that remain permanent during the length of the semester of the course) and the course is organized in major units (five to seven).

TBL occurs in three sequences of learning activities: a preparation phase, an application phase, and an assessment phase. In the preparation phase, students have to study on their own the unit before class. A short test (readiness assessment test) assesses their retention of the key concepts. Application phase has the students apply the course content to solve problems that get increasingly complex. The instructor provides feedback about their responses. Finally, in the assessment phase, the instructor gives a score.

TBL courses are structured around four principles: immediate feedback, accountability, simultaneous reporting, and team development promotion. Immediate feedback is necessary for learning and retention. This aspect is not unique to TBL, it is well documented in the literature of learning in education [13]. Students must be accountable for the quality of their work. Answers have to be reported simultaneously, to avoid the potential impact of a first response in a sequential report, "answer drift", [14] on all the others students. The chosen assignment must promote both learning and team development.

TBL has been shown to enhance participants' performance on four aspects: engagement, retention, critical thinking and general performance increase (increased retention for students who usually have lower performance).

Kelly et al. [7] reported student engagement in a seven lectures medical course in which four of the lectures were problem-based learning (PBL) and three were TBL. Student engagement was assessed with the STROBE [15], a test that relies on observational data. Learner to learner engagement was similar in PBL and TBL conditions (but still greater than in classical lectures). Similarly, Clark et al. [16] reported the attitudes of student during a course using traditional lectures and a course using TBL. According to the classroom engagement survey (FIPSE, 2003), student participation was higher in TBL conditions. Dinan and Frydrchowski [17] also reported that students participated more during the courses. And also, that preparation, participation, and attendance all increased in a TBL environment.

Retention is also improved by TBL. McInerney [6] used TBL to improve retention in an undergraduate biology course. The performance of students at the final examination in a TBL condition was compared to a control group results obtained in previous years for the same course content but using classical lectures. TBL condition students performed better in the final exam. In a biology class, observed with two groups (one with TBL one with normal lecture), while not observing the same results in final examination, Carmichael [8] noticed that TBL class scored higher on all tests during the semester than the traditional class, except the final exam where students performed equally well. Kreie, Headrick, and Steiner [18] applied TBL to introductory Information Systems (IS) course (2 groups traditional lecture-based instruction and TBL). Retention and attendance of the course was significantly higher in TBL, and the drop out lower.

Courses given with TBL also seem to improve critical thinking and higher order reasoning in students. Students self-reported that sharing their answers and discussing them among their group has shown to be beneficial to participants involved in a TBL setting [9]. In McInerney's study [6], notably, a large number of teams offered creative solutions to the problem, and found a solution to solve problem that was neither discussed in lecture nor in the text of the problem indicating deeper learning. Students who usually perform well also reported that they gained new problem solving skills discussing with their teammates.

Similarly, Drummond [19] found that students enrolled in an engineering entrepreneurship course for two semesters (one with classical lectures and one in TBL) had improved critical skills (according to the Critical Thinking Skills (CTS) -Washington State University). And, Carmichael [8] observed that in TBL condition students got better at data interpretations (which rely on critical thinking).

A final benefit of TBL is to reduce performance gap between the students who usually perform well and students who usually have a lower performance [6]. The authors reported that the grade distribution had changed, fewer students had scored under 70 % and more students had scored between 70 % and 90 % than in the control group (course given in the previous year without TBL).

In this paper, we use a computational cognitive model to make a priori predictions for an upcoming human study. Model predictions are generated in conditions identical to those that human participants will be placed in: a classical lecture condition, an IL condition, and a TBL condition. As reported in the literature [6, 8, 18], we expect that the more interactive the lecture setting is the better the performance should be. IL leading to better performance in retention than classical lecture, and TBL leading to better performance than IL (TBL > IL > L). Similarly to what is seen in the literature [6], we also expect our TBL condition to reduce the gap between our distinctly simulated players (differing in the time they allocate to practicing the task at home). Finally, we wish to propose, through our models, hypotheses as to which cognitive mechanisms might explain the differences in performance in the different condition.

3 Model

The model was built in the computational cognitive architecture, which implements a theory of human cognition, ACT-R (Adaptive Control of Thought - Rational) [11]. In ACT-R, different modules, including two memory modules (procedural and declarative) interact to complete a cognitive task. The modules are accessed via their associated buffers. ACT-R has been used to model several tasks (see [20] for a review).

Declarative memory stores facts about the environment (know what). The procedural memory, thanks to procedural rules (know how) allows for action selection. ACT-R is a hybrid cognitive architecture. Symbolic components are combined to subsymbolic components: the retrieval of a fact from declarative memory depends on subsymbolic retrieval equations (pondering the context and history of retrieval of the fact), and, the selection of a rule depends on utility subsymbolic equations (which computes costs and benefits associated to the rule). The memory elements (chunks) are reinforced through reward patterns that occur within the environment. Learning processes act at both subsymbolic and symbolic levels.

In our model, in the lecture condition, when the model attempts to read an element on the screen during "school time", its value is held in a chunk pair in the imaginal buffer of the imaginal module. The pair with the value read on screen is held, and, an answer that is later presented will be associated to the value in the pair. The rule that guided this behavior will thus clear the imaginal buffer, leading the pair to enter the declarative memory. If a pair chunk that had the same values associated with is already present in the declarative memory, then it will merge with the existing chunk: its base-level activation will increase. The base level-activation will decrease during the task as a function of time since the last merge.

In the IL condition, the model has the opportunity to attempt to generate a response before being given the right answer. When the pair is stored in the imaginal buffer (as described in the lecture condition), a request will be made to retrieve that pair from declarative memory and eventually give an answer. When the right answer is thus displayed, as in the lecture condition, activation of that pair will increase (due to its merging with an existing pair in declarative memory). But, an additional mechanism is involved: retrieval. Recall that retrieval of an element from declarative memory depends on the subsymbolic components. Every chunk from the declarative memory is associated with an activation, which reflects past experiences. When a retrieval request is made, the chunk that matches the requirement of the rule and has the highest activation will be retrieved. The retrieval of a chunk pair will increase its activation.

Therefore, the probability of recall of this pair will increase with every retrieval and merging. Because of retrieval, it should be easier to recall a pair that has been presented in the IL condition than in the lecture condition thanks to the additional retrieval that the model had to perform.

Performance in the TBL condition is supported by one additional mechanism: utility learning. Utility learning in ACT-R supports the choice of the strategy with the best probability of success. While there might initially be a set of competing strategies, as the task goes and the model gains more experience, the utility of the competing strategies will change. For the TBL condition we initiated a set of additional eight rules to govern the reading of another player's answer and the selection of another player's answer (one of each of those rules per player, e.g., 'attend-first-answer-of-player1' and 'select-response-of-player1). 'attend-first-answer-of-player-X' enables a player to attend the screen location of the answer of a specific player. 'select-response-of-player-X' allows the player to chose the answer of that specific player as its own. Initially, those rules were given an equal utility value, thus indicating no initial preferences. But, when the player select an answer which is the correct answer a reward is propagated. As the experiment goes on, since the model will adjust its behavior depending on the success of him following the choice of another player, we expect the utility values to adjust and reflect a preference towards the selection of the answer of the player who usually perform the best. While this mechanism will improve the performance of all players during the lecture phase, it does not account for a better performance in the final session (i.e., exam). A mechanism that was already at play in the two previous conditions will account for the increased performance in the final session. When the player selects the solution of another player, this solution is associated to the word that was placed in the imaginal module. When the imaginal module is cleared, similarly than we previously described, the pair will either enter the declarative memory if it was not already learned by the player or be merged with an existing pair in declarative memory, thus increasing its current activation. Afterwards, similarly than in the lecture and IL condition, the player sees the correct answer which he similarly will place in the imaginal module that will be cleared later on and again the correct answer entered in the declarative memory. In lecture condition and IL condition, this also occurs when the player sees the correct answer but since the player doesn't look at the answer of other players beforehand, there is one less addition to the declarative memory.

The chunk pair is potentially reinforced in three different ways during lecture in the TBL condition: when the pair is displayed, when the model has to provide a first answer and thus retrieve the pair, and when the model can see and select the answer of another player before he provides a second answer. Utility learning ensures that, over time, the player will select the answer of the better player, who is most often the correct answer. As the player has had one more chance to memorize the correct answer, we expect performance to be better in the TBL condition than in the IL condition.

4 Experimental Procedure

The TBL condition necessitates that we run the simulations in parallels to allow the models to interact. The procedure used was the one defined by Bütner [21], which allows communication between the ACT-R model in LISP and the Java program that administrates the test over a network using the TCP/IP connection. In each of the three variants (lecture, IL, and TBL) of the Paired Associate task, four ACT-R models run simultaneously (but interacted only in the third variant).

The 40 words used in the paired associate task are selected from the study of Paivio, Yuille, and Madigan [22]. Responses assigned to the nouns were the digits 0-9. The digits are randomly assigned to the 40 words stimuli. Equal duration time is spent in front of the word stimuli during "school time" in all conditions. Each player in each condition has 10 "school time" sessions to test and acquire its knowledge. Models are given the opportunity to practice the task on their own during "home time" sessions. During "home time", participants can choose to study or play. During "school time", participants can only study and take tests. Individual differences in the time they allocate to study the task individually were assigned to the models. We assigned 4 different profiles to the players, which determined the amount of time they could study at home. Players 1 to 4 practice the task 100 %, 80 %, 60 % and 40 % of the home time, respectively. Thus, player 1 practices more than twice as much as player 4. This variety of profiles allowed us to emulate the different types of students in a classroom: from students who study more during "home time" to those who study less.

In the lecture condition the four players only receive pairs of words and numbers without the opportunity to give answers. Afterwards, they take a test during which their recall of the pairs is evaluated (final test session).

The IL condition allows the model to test its past learning while learning new pairs in an interactive setting (giving a tentative answer and getting the correct answer immediately).

In the third condition (TBL), an additional stage allows the models to work in teams by interacting with each other. At each round, each model answers and then has the opportunity to see the answers of the other players and change its answer. As in classical TBL, the first answers of the other players are displayed simultaneously. The most frequent second response is automatically chosen as the group response, and feedback (i.e., correct response) is displayed. Players are thus rewarded for picking the right answer and eventually picking the answer of the players who gets the right answer most often. An individual final test is also administered.

5 Results and Discussion

We computed the mean accuracy of the players during each round in every condition over 32 artificial players. Figure 1 shows the IL and TBL (first answers and second answers) conditions and the 95 % confidence intervals during "school time" (10 lecture sessions). Figure 2 shows results for final evaluation session (session 11).

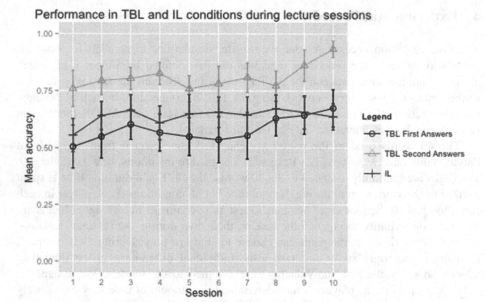

Fig. 1. Mean accuracy by session for IL and TBL conditions with confidence intervals of 95 %

We were able to confirm our two hypotheses in regards to TBL: final performance was better in this condition and the gap in performance between players was reduced.

As we predicted the model performed the best in TBL condition. Performance of players, as measured by the mean accuracies, was significantly lower during the IL condition than during the TBL condition for the second answer ($p < 0.001$), the difference was also significant between TBL condition for first answer and IL condition ($p < 0.05$). Also, during the final session, performance of the players at lecture condition (as measured by mean accuracy) was lower than performance at IL condition, with the difference between the accuracies in final session in the two conditions being significant ($p < 0.05$). Performance at IL was itself lower than performance at the TBL condition with the difference between the accuracies in final session in the two conditions being highly significant ($p < 0.001$). With this, we also confirmed that the more interactive the lecture was (TBL and IL condition), the better the final results were, a result that has been similarly observed in literature [13]. Players during lecture condition had lower performance at the final session than during both IL and TBL conditions. This may be attributed to the immediate feedback, which is present in both conditions.

The accuracies in the TBL condition - second answers (Fig. 1) were the highest. It illustrates the player's increasing ability to pick the answer of another player who usually succeeds as second answer as the experiment goes on. Accuracy in the final session for TBL being higher than IL condition also demonstrates that the player not only does learn to pick the player that has the better performance but also that through this process he reinforces his knowledge (the pair) in the declarative memory of the model. This reinforcement occurs when the player selects the answer of another player, places it in the buffer of its imaginal module. The imaginal module is cleared before the player observes the correct answer, the pair selected is then either entered or reinforced in declarative memory.

Players perform initially lower at lecture sessions in TBL condition than IL condition. There are two explanations for this result. While players in IL have a specific amount of time to provide an answer, players in TBL have this same amount of time to provide a first answer, and select the answer of another player. Players in TBL have thus less time to retrieve their answer. Additionally, players don't select initially the answers of the better player, they have to learn which player is the better one. In the model, players are rewarded in TBL when they pick the correct answer, this ensures that slowly the model will learn to pick the player that lead him to answer correctly the most. That's why, it takes them more sessions to perform as well, and even perform a bit higher than players in IL in the 10th lecture session. In the final, evaluation, session however TBL players perform better, indicating a better retention than IL players, a result similar to what has been observed in [6].

Standard deviation was the lowest in the TBL condition. TBL condition is the one where there are the less differences in performance between players of different profile. This is also another result from the literature: TBL reduces the performance gap between the lowest player and the better one.

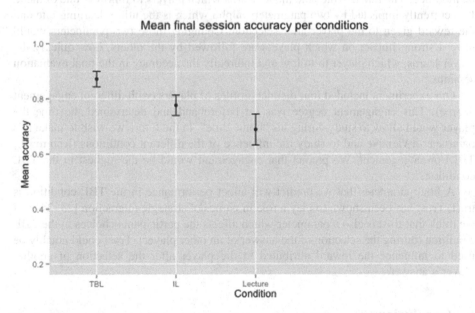

Fig. 2. Mean accuracy in final session for lecture, IL and TBL conditions with confidence intervals of 95 %.

Through this model we were also able to formulate some preliminary hypothesis concerning the cognitive mechanisms that are involved in the difference of performances in simple lecture courses and TBL courses.

Immediate feedback, which we described earlier, is one of the principles of TBL. The students get frequent and immediate feedback during courses. Similarly, our player gets an immediate display of the correct answer. Our model shows how immediate feedback can support learning and recall by either inserting or reinforcing the knowledge in memory. Another aspect of TBL, simultaneous report of answer forces the student and in this paper our player to recall the knowledge and either create or reinforce its knowledge by eventually afterwards looking at the answer of other players.

Having to recall the answer to produce its own answer before he sees the answer of others also trains the student to develop its own knowledge rather than just apply the strategy of picking the answer of the "better student". This explains notably why our model did not just learn to always pick the answer of the better player but was also able to perform better than all the other conditions in the final session in which interacting with other players was not permitted.

With this model we were able to make a priori predictions. However, several elements need to be taken into account to make it a complete model of the different cognitive phenomena underlying TBL.

This model provides a gross simulation of the patterns of human results we could observe in our upcoming study. And, we already have some hypotheses on which parameters we will have to work on to fit our model to data. Several parameters could be modified. The rate at which the model learns which players to follow is one of them. It is currently impacted by two parameters, alpha which is the utility learning rate and the reward given to the player after selection. Changing those two parameters would have a strong impact on which players are followed by the others, how quickly the player learns, which player to follow and indirectly the accuracy in the final evaluation session.

Our experiment included four distinct profiles of players (with different engagement degree). This engagement degree was set beforehand and determined the time the player would allow to study during his "home time". In the future we wish to make this parameter a variable and to study the influence of the different conditions (lecture, IL, TBL) on engagement. We predict that engagement would be the highest in the TBL condition.

A final parameter that we predict will affect performance in the TBL condition is trust. Trust has been shown to play a role in games of strategic interaction [23, 24] and we think that trust is also a parameter which affects the participants choices in the TBL condition (during the selection of the answer of an other player). Trust could notably be used to influence the reward attributed to the player after the selection of another player's answer.

6   Conclusion

The Paired Associates Task [1] is a task in which subjects have to study and recall a list of paired associates of a noun and a digit. Response time and accuracy in this task are a function of the number of exposures to each pair and the task has been used to study the relationship between response latency and accuracy.

TBL is an instructional strategy in which students spend a significant amount of class time in teams. Enhancing motivation and engagement, TBL has been shown to lead to better student performance than classical non-IL.

A computational cognitive model was built to test those three conditions and predict results of an upcoming study with human participants. Our model reproduced the results from the existing literature comparing classical lectures and TBL. Performance of players was significantly lower during the IL condition than during the TBL condition throughout the course. And, in final session, performance of the players at lecture condition was lower than performance at IL condition which itself was lower than performance at the TBL condition. TBL also reduced the standard deviation in accuracies between players of different profiles (difference in the times allocated to work during "home time").

Simulating TBL allowed us to observe interactions at the intra group level and their effect on accuracy during the course and in the final test session. In the future, it will also allow us to make predictions with regard to strategic interactions and the effect of interpersonal dynamics (e.g., trust) in this setting and its influence on student's engagement.

References

1. Anderson, J.R.: Interference: the relationship between response latency and response accuracy. J. Exp. Psychol. Hum. Learn. Mem. **7**, 326 (1981)
2. Borst, J.P., Anderson, J.R.: Using the ACT-R cognitive architecture in combination with fMRI data. In: Forstmann, B.U., Wagenmaker, E.-I. (eds.) An Introduction to Model-Based Cognitive Neuroscience. Springer, New York (2014)
3. Halverson, T., Gunzelmann, G.: Visual search versus memory in a paired associate task. In: Proceedings of the Human Factors and Ergonomics Society Annual Meeting, pp. 875–879. SAGE Publications (2011)
4. Pavlik, P.I., Anderson, J.R.: Practice and forgetting effects on vocabulary memory: an activation-based model of the spacing effect. Cogn. Sci. **29**, 559–586 (2005)
5. Michaelsen, L.K., Knight, A.B., Fink, L.D.: Team-based Learning: A Transformative Use of Small Groups. Greenwood Publishing Group, Westport (2004)
6. McInerney, M.J., Fink, L.D.: Team-based learning enhances long-term retention and critical thinking in an undergraduate microbial physiology course. Microbiol. Educ, **4**, 3 (2003)
7. Kelly, P.A., Haidet, P., Schneider, V., Searle, N., Seidel, C.L., Richards, B.F.: A comparison of in-class learner engagement across lecture, problem-based learning, and team learning using the STROBE classroom observation tool. Teach. Learn. Med. **17**, 112–118 (2005)
8. Carmichael, J.: Team-based learning enhances performance in introductory biology. J. Coll. Sci. Teach. **38**, 54–61 (2009)
9. Kühne-Eversmann, L., Eversmann, T., Fischer, M.R.: Team-and case-based learning to activate participants and enhance knowledge: an evaluation of seminars in Germany. J. Continuing Educ. Health Prof. **28**, 165–171 (2008)
10. Anderson, J.R.: The Architecture of Cognition. Psychology Press, Philadelphia (2013)
11. Anderson, J.R.: How Can the Human Mind Occur in the Physical Universe?. Oxford University Press, New York (2007)

12. Raaijmakers, J.G.: Spacing and repetition effects in human memory: application of the SAM model. Cogn. Sci. **27**, 431–452 (2003)
13. Hattie, J., Timperley, H.: The power of feedback. Rev. Educ. Res. **77**, 81–112 (2007)
14. Michaelsen, L.K., Sweet, M.: Team-based learning. New directions for teaching and learning 2011, pp. 41-51 (2011)
15. O'Malley, K.J., Moran, B.J., Haidet, P., Seidel, C.L., Schneider, V., Morgan, R.O., Kelly, P.A., Richards, B.: Validation of an observation instrument for measuring student engagement in health professions settings. Eval. Health Prof. **26**, 86–103 (2003)
16. Clark, M.C., Nguyen, H.T., Bray, C., Levine, R.E.: Team-based learning in an undergraduate nursing course. J. Nurs. Educ. **47**, 111–117 (2008)
17. Dinan, F.J., Frydrychowski, V.A.: A team learning method for organic chemistry. J. Chem. Educ. **72**, 429 (1995)
18. Kreie, J., Headrick, R.W., Steiner, R.: Using team learning to improve student retention. Coll. Teach. **55**, 51–56 (2007)
19. Drummond, C.K.: Team-based learning to enhance critical thinking skills in entrepreneurship education. J. Entrepreneurship Educ. **15**, 57–60 (2012)
20. ACT-R. http://act-r.psy.cmu.edu/publication/
21. Büttner, P.: "Hello Java!" Linking ACT-R 6 with a Java simulation. In: Proceedings of the 10th International Conference on Cognitive Modeling, pp. 289–290. Citeseer (2010)
22. Paivio, A., Yuille, J.C., Madigan, S.A.: Concreteness, imagery, and meaningfulness values for 925 nouns. J. Exp. Psychol. **76**, 1 (1968)
23. Camerer, C.: Behavioral Game Theory: Experiments in Strategic Interaction. Princeton University Press, Princeton (2003)
24. Juvina, I., Lebiere, C., Gonzalez, C.: Modeling trust dynamics in strategic interaction. J. Appl. Res. Mem. Cogn. 1–31 (2014)

Exploring Day-to-Day Variability in the Relations Between Emotion and EEG Signals

Yuan-Pin Lin$^{(\boxtimes)}$, Sheng-Hsiou Hsu, and Tzyy-Ping Jung

Swartz Center for Computational Neuroscience, Institute for Neural
Computation, University of California, San Diego, USA
{yplin,goodshawnl2,jung}@sccn.ucsd.edu

Abstract. Electroencephalography (EEG)-based emotion classification has drawn increasing attention over the last few years and become an emerging direction in brain-computer interfaces (BCI), namely affective BCI (ABCI). Many prior studies devoted to improve emotion-classification models using the data collected within a single session or day. Less attention has been directed to the day-to-day EEG variability associated with emotional responses. This study recorded EEG signals of 12 subjects, each underwent the music-listening experiment on five different days, to assess the day-to-day variability from the perspectives of inter-day data distributions and cross-day emotion classification. The empirical results of this study demonstrated that the clusters of the same emotion across days tended to scatter wider than the clusters of different emotions within a day. Such inter-day variability poses a severe challenge for building an accurate cross-day emotion-classification model in real-life ABCI applications.

Keywords: EEG-based emotion classification · Day-to-day variability

1 Introduction

Electroencephalography (EEG)-based emotion classification has drawn increasing attention over the last few years and become an emerging direction in brain-computer interfaces (BCI), namely affective BCI (ABCI) [1]. Researchers continue to develop advanced computational frameworks by leveraging the domain knowledge of brain functions, computational neuroscience, and machine learning. Prior to the deployment of real-life ABCI applications, a practical challenge to the emotion-aware model is its ability to adapt to the EEG variability associated with emotional responses over time.

Referring to the literature, many prior studies endeavored to the analyses focusing on EEG feature extraction/selection [2], EEG electrode optimization [3], machine-learning framework [4, 5], and multidisciplinary information sources [6]. All these empirical results contributed to the understanding of how to develop an accurate emotion-aware model. However, nearly all of the previous works accessed the data collected within a single-day session and ignored the day-to-day variability. To the best of our knowledge, only few studies have examined the inter-day physiological-signal

© Springer International Publishing Switzerland 2015
D.D. Schmorrow and C.M. Fidopiastis (Eds.): AC 2015, LNAI 9183, pp. 461–469, 2015.
DOI: 10.1007/978-3-319-20816-9_44

variability related to emotional responses. Picard et al. [7] assessed inter-day variations based on a single-subject multiple-day dataset, in which the peripheral signals, such as facial muscle, blood volume pressure, skin conductance, and reparation, were measured. Their results showed that the features of the same emotion across days tended to cluster looser than those of different emotions within a single day. Our recent study [8] also reported that the inter-day variability in the EEG recordings in two subjects; each performed music-listening experiments on four different days. In principle, incorporating more training data for building an individualized model should improve the classification performance. However, pilot results only showed a very subtle improvement when the classification model was trained with data from multiple days. It is worth noting that if the inter-day variability can somehow be alleviated, a multiple-day data recording should be more desirable than a conventional single-day experiment. Presumably, multiple-day EEG data can better encompass EEG dynamics about implicit emotional responses.

This study extended our previous pilot study [8] to collect more longitudinal data from a larger population, *i.e.*, a 12-subject five-day dataset, for assessing the inter-day EEG variability. The goal of this study was to better understand the complications of inter-day variability so that an affective BCI can be appropriately modeled and/or accounted for in the design toward real-world applications.

2 Material and Method

2.1 Participants

Twelve non-musician subjects (9 males and 3 females; age: 21.83 ± 3.76 years; all right handed) participated in a 5-day music-listening experiment with an averaged time interval of 7 ± 1.13 days (min: 5 days, max: 11 days). Each subject read and signed a consent form before the experiment, which was approved by the Human Research Protections Program of University of California, San Diego.

2.2 Music-Listening Experiment Setup

This study selected 24 music excerpts from an emotion-tagged music database [9] to induce two emotions (happiness and sadness). Each of the selected excerpts was associated with a consensus label of happiness (001 $\sim$ 012.wav from Set 1) or sadness (031 $\sim$ 042.wav from Set 1). Interested readers are referred to [9] for more details about the music excerpts and the collection of consensus labels. All selected excerpts were repeated once to make each trial last around 37 s. The 24 excerpts were randomly separated into three four-block sessions for each subject and for each day. Each block comprised both happy and sad trials in random order. Each trial began with a 15-s rest and ended with a self-emotion-assessment task, in which the subjects required to report one of the target emotions (happiness or sadness) or neutral (no feelings) based on what they had experienced. The experiment is completely self-paced so that each subject can decide the time lapse of rest (typically a few tens of seconds) before proceeding to next trial. The protocol was designed to avoid possible auditory fatigue and/or distraction.

The music-listening experiment took place in a dimly lit room. All subjects wore an in-ear earphone and were instructed to keep seated with eyes closed during music listening.

2.3   EEG Data Acquisition

This study used a 14-channel Emotiv EEG headset (Emotiv, Inc.) to sample EEG signals at 128 Hz and in a bandwidth of 0.16 and 43 Hz. Twelve channels (AF3, AF4, F3, F4, FC5, FC6, F7, F8, P7, P8, O1, and O2) were included for measuring EEG signals referentially against left and right mastoids in accordance to the international 10-20 system. The electrode impedance was checked before each session via the Emotiv Control Panel. During rest, to ensure the recording of best-quality EEG signals for analysis, a syringe was used to inject a small amount of saline solution to the sponge of poorly contacted electrodes (if any) without uncapping the headset.

2.4   EEG Feature Extraction, Selection, and Classification

Each subject performed the music-listening experiment on five different days and each experiment comprised 24 EEG trials. Each of the trails corresponded to a self-reported emotion label (either happiness, sadness or neutral). The recorded EEG data were first processed by a 1-Hz high-pass finite impulse response filter to remove low-frequency drift. The short-time Fourier transform with a 1-second non-overlapping Hamming window was then employed to estimate the power spectral density in five frequency bands for each of the 12 channels, including delta (1-3 Hz), theta (4-7 Hz), alpha (8-13 Hz), beta (14-30 Hz), and gamma (31-43 Hz).

This study adopted an EEG feature type namely differential laterality (DLAT) [6] to associate the EEG spatio-spectral patterns with implicit emotional states. The DLAT calculates the differential band power asymmetry between left-right symmetric electrode pairs in order to reflect the extent of hemispheric lateralization over the scalp. Previous studies have demonstrated the efficacy of DLAT for emotion classification [3, 6]. Upon the 12-channel montage, the DLAT formed a feature dimension of 30 for six left-right electrodes pairs (AF3-AF4, F7-F8, F3-F4, FC5-FC6, P7-P8, and O1-O2) across five frequency bands.

In addition, this study adopted a computationally efficient feature-selection method, namely F-score, to exclude the features that were relatively irrelevant to the emotion classification from the entire DLAT space. The F-score first calculates the ratio of between-class and within-class variance upon the data distribution formed by each feature individually, and then to sort the contributions of the features according to the F-score values. The larger the F-score value is, the more contributions the feature makes. The F-score index has been proven effective in improving emotion-classification performance by selecting emotion-relevant features [3, 6].

Lastly, a Gaussian Naïve Bayes (GNB) classifier was employed to model the data distributions associated with the emotional states in the F-score trimmed feature space for each subject. Note that this study discarded the EEG trials labeled as neutral and performed a two-class emotion (happiness versus sadness) classification task.

2.5   EEG Feature Validation and Visualization

This study aimed to explore the day-to-day EEG variability associated with emotional responses and its impacts on multiple-day, *i.e.*, cross-day, emotion-classification accuracy. To this end, two validation methods were performed on the five-day dataset for each subject individually: leave-day-out (LDO) and leave-trial-out (LTO) validation methods. First, the LDO method used data from D training days ($D = 1, 2, 3,$ and 4) to build an emotion classifier and to test it against data from a separate day to evaluate the multiple-day, *i.e.*, cross-day, classification accuracy. Specifically, the EEG data from D training day(s) were concatenated to explore the optimal feature set, *i.e.*, features with high F-score values, to train the GNB model, and then to test against the data from a separate day. Given $D = 4$, for example, the LDO returned a subject-dependent 5-day classification performance by averaging the results of five training-testing day pairs with each of five days being the testing data once. Such validation accounting for heuristic training-testing day pairs presumably led to a fairly reliable cross-day classification result. Second, the LTO method calculated single-day, *i.e.*, within-day, classification accuracy based on the data from each single day, which was not affected by inter-day variability and considered to be the benchmark for the multiple-day scenario. The LTO calculated the averaged performance of T classification repetitions ($T = 24$, trials in this study) with each of T trials being equally tested using T-1 training trials. Note that the LTO performed F-score feature selection on the entire data of a single day rather than on the training trials in order to comply with the LDO condition.

In addition, this study explored the distributions of EEG features across different emotions and days to better interpret the empirical cross-day classification results. The linear discriminative analysis (LDA) was employed to reduce the dimension of the DLAT feature space (30) to a comprehensible space spanned by first two LDA components (corresponding to the two largest eigenvalues) with the maximization of discriminatory information between classes. Prior to the LDA projection, the features from each day were normalized, making the input samples varied between 0 and 1. Note the LDA was not involved in the aforementioned classification framework. In addition to the 2D informative feature space, this study further superimposed a linear decision boundary that was calculated from the data distributions of D training days. The normal vector and intercept of the decision boundary were defined as $\vec{v} = \vec{u}_1 - \vec{u}_2$ and $\vec{c} = (N_1\vec{u}_1 + N_2\vec{u}_2)/(N_1 + N_2)$ respectively, where $\vec{u}_1$ and $\vec{u}_2$ are the means of the class distributions, and N_1 and N_2 are the numbers of samples in each class. It is worth mentioning that although such boundary was not the high-dimensional hyperplane appeared in the actual GNB classifier, it remained effective to conceptually reveal the interrelationship among training-testing data distributions and their corresponding actual classification accuracy.

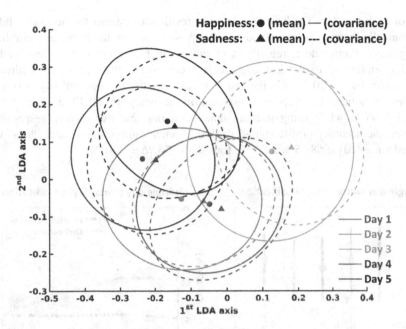

Fig. 1. EEG features' distributions of happiness and sadness across five days from a representative subject. X and Y axes represent the first two LDA components corresponding to the largest eigenvalues of the data variance in the original 30-dimensional DLAT feature space. Filled circles and triangles represent the mean values of the data distributions of happiness and sadness, respectively, whereas solid and dotted lines indicate their covariance ellipses.

3 Results

Figure 1 shows the EEG features' distributions of two emotion classes for five different days from a representative subject. The data distributions of emotional classes (solid vs. dotted ellipses) projected onto the two most discriminative LDA axes exhibited considerable overlap between the covariance ellipses within any given day. These class distributions scattered widely across different days (ellipses in different colors). These results provided insights into the day-to-day variability in EEG, which makes inter-day EEG-based emotion classification extremely difficult. It is also worth mentioning that even though the EEG features varied widely, the EEG features in some of days had relatively comparable distributions, *e.g.*, Days 4 and 5.

Figure 2 shows the results of the within- and cross-day two-class (happiness versus sadness) emotion classification. As shown in Fig. 2(A), the within-day classification obtained by the LTO validation returned the averaged accuracy of 65.49 ± 5.20 %, which exceeded chance level (50 %). There was no trend on the classification accuracy versus the recording days. Figure 2(B) shows the cross-day classification results using two scenarios namely 'heuristic-day-pair' and 'optimal-day-pair'. The heuristic-day-pair (black dashed line) profile showed the averages of all training-testing day pairs, which presumably suffered more from inter-day variability than the optimal- day-pair (red solid line) profile that reflected the best performance among all the training-day pairs for each test day. The heuristic-day-pair result showed that the accuracy did not monotonically increase but remained around 55 ~ 56 % with the increasing number of training days. Furthermore, regardless of the number of training days involved, all cross-day emotion-classification accuracies were worse than those of within-day classification by ~ 10 %. Unlike the heuristic results, the optimal-day-pair result exhibited a noticeable jump in classification accuracy to 60.43 ± 2.55 % and 60.58 ± 3.05 % while using training data from one and two day(s), respectively. However, the accuracy profile started declining when more training data (days) were included (three days: 58.75 ± 2.80 %, four days: 55.76 ± 3.81 %).

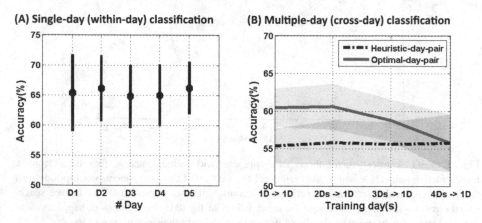

Fig. 2. Averaged results of within- and cross-day two-class emotion classification in this study. (A) Within-day classification obtained by the LTO validation was regarded as a benchmark for evaluating (B) the cross-day scenario obtained by LDO validation that accounted for inter-day EEG variability. In the cross-day plot, the heuristic-day-pair (black dashed line) shows the averaged results of all combinations of training-testing day pairs, whereas the optimal-day-pair result (red solid line) shows the best performance among all D training-day conditions ($D = 1, 2, 3$, and 4) for each of testing days. The shaded areas indicate the standard deviation (Color figure online).

Figure 3 further illustrates the effects of the selection of training days on the classification accuracies from the same sample subject shown in Fig. 1. In general, given the inter-day variability, the trained decision boundary worked well to a certain extent on estimating emotional responses in a separate day whose EEG feature distributions were compatible to those of the training day(s). Otherwise, it could fail and only return accuracy close to chance level. As shown in Fig. 1, Days 4 and 5 exhibited most comparable class distributions among five different days. The model used to test against Day 5 provided better classification performance as long as the data from Day 4 were included in the training data (see the left column of Fig. 3). In contrast, the class distributions of Days 1, 2, and 3 largely differed from those of Day 4, and thereby built a useless decision boundary for estimating emotional responses in Day 4 (see the right column of Fig. 3). Furthermore, as comparing the best 1 ~ 4-day models, the classification accuracy did not improve progressively as adding more data from more days.

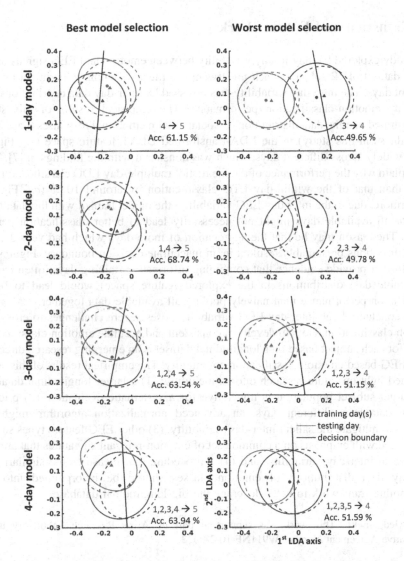

Fig. 3. The impacts of the selection of training days on the emotion-classification performance from the same sample subject shown in Fig. 1. Blue and red ellipses show the distributions of training and testing data along the first two discriminative LDA-transformed DLAT space, respectively, whereas black lines represent the linear decision boundaries calculated from the training-data distribution. Filled circles and triangles show the mean values of the data distributions of happiness and sadness, respectively, whereas solid and dotted lines indicate their covariance ellipses. Numbers in blue and red represent the day(s) for training and testing, respectively, whereas Acc. represents the classification accuracy (Color figure online).

The 2-day model that leveraged Days 1 and 4 showed the highest accuracy of 68.74 % in predicting emotions in Day 5, especially as compared to the 4-day model (63.94 %).

4 Discussion and Future Work

This study explored the day-to-day variability between emotion and EEG signals based on the dataset of 12 subjects, each underwent the music-listening experiment on five different days. The inter-day variability was assessed by inter-day data distributions and cross-day emotion-classification performance. The empirical results of this study demonstrated that the data distributions associated with emotional responses (happiness and sadness in this study) in the LDA-transformed DLAT feature space (*c.f.* Fig. 1) varied widely across different days, which was consistent with the findings in [7]. This can explain why the performance of the 'heuristic' multiple-day LDO classification was worse than that of the within-day LTO classification by around 10 % (*c.f.* Fig. 2). Furthermore, due to the inter-day EEG variability, the model trained with the data from more or all available days might not necessarily lead to better classification performance. The reason may be that the aggregation of more days which had very distinct data distributions presumably resulted in an inaccurate decision boundary. Figures 2B and 3 further provide evidence that combining informative training days (often having comparable data distributions in the explored feature space) would lead to better classification performance than naively pooling all available data together.

To conclude, large inter-day EEG variability poses severe challenges to cross-day emotion classification. How to develop a consistent and accurate emotion-classification model for each subject based on a longitudinal dataset is an emerging research direction in the EEG-based emotion classification community. The empirical results of this study may shed light on future research efforts, including: (1) a larger longitudinal database on a larger subject population is imperative for a systematic evaluation, (2) prior to pooling data from different days, an advanced normalization algorithm might be required to mitigate the salient inter-day variability, (3) other EEG feature types should be explored with emphasis on a common set of emotion-relevant signatures that are less sensitive to inter-day variability, and (4) a procedure that measures the similarity of inter-day data distributions of emotion classes should be incorporated into the data-pooling framework to better leverage the big longitudinal database.

Acknowledgement. This work was support in part by Army Research Laboratory under Cooperative Agreement Number W911NF-10-2-0022.

References

1. Mühl, C., Allison, B., Nijholt, A., Chanel, G.: A survey of affective brain computer interfaces: principles, state-of-the-art, and challenges. Brain-Comput. Interfaces **1**, 66–84 (2014)
2. Jenke, R., Peer, A., Buss, M.: Feature extraction and selection for emotion recognition from EEG. IEEE Trans. Affect. Comput. **5**, 327–339 (2014)
3. Lin, Y.P., Wang, C.H., Jung, T.P., Wu, T.L., Jeng, S.K., Duann, J.R., Chen, J.H.: EEG-based emotion recognition in music listening. IEEE Trans. Bio-Med. Eng. **57**, 1798–1806 (2010)
4. Koelstra, S., Patras, I.: Fusion of facial expressions and EEG for implicit affective tagging. Image Vis. Comput. **31**, 164–174 (2013)

5. Chanel, G., Kierkels, J.J.M., Soleymani, M., Pun, T.: Short-term emotion assessment in a recall paradigm. In.t J. Hum. Comput. Stud. **67**, 607–627 (2009)
6. Lin, Y.P., Yang, Y.H., Jung, T.P.: Fusion of electroencephalogram dynamics and musical contents for estimating emotional responses in music listening. Front. Neurosci. **8**, 94 (2014)
7. Picard, R.W., Vyzas, E., Healey, J.: Toward machine emotional intelligence: analysis of affective physiological state. IEEE Trans. Pattern Anal. **23**, 1175–1191 (2001)
8. Lin, Y.P., Jung, T.P.: Exploring day-to-day variability in EEG-based emotion classification. In: IEEE International Conference on Systems, Man and Cybernetics (SMC), pp. 2226–2229 (2014)
9. Eerola, T., Vuoskoski, J.K.: A comparison of the discrete and dimensional models of emotion in music. Psychol. Music **39**, 18–49 (2011)

Integration and Disintegration of Auditory Images Perception

Sergei Lytaev[1,2(✉)] and Ksenia Belskaya[1]

[1] Saint Petersburg State Pediatric Medical University, Saint Petersburg, Russia
slytaev@spiiras.nw.ru, belskaya.k.a@gmail.com
[2] North-Western Federal Medical Research Center, Saint Petersburg, Russia

Abstract. Defects of sensory perception are one of essential features in structure of psychopathological frustration. The conscious mental activity includes components of perception, construction of an image, memory and thought processes. The perception is formed on the basis of synthesis of three kinds of the information flows: sensory, taken from memory and coming from the centers of motivation. The sensory information defines communication of cognition with an external world. Purpose of present research was aimed for studying character and a degree of disorders of mechanisms of perception and integration of auditory figurative information at depressive psychopathological states. Outcomes of present research, including EEG coherent analysis, represent convincing acknowledgement of brain decomposition at perception of the auditory information at patients with psychopathological frustration.

Keywords: Sensory perception · Auditory images (AI) · EEG · Decision-making

1 Introduction

We are surrounded by world of our sensations, but we live in world of our consciousness, our sensations, ideas and feelings. The real world and perceived by us world not always completely correspond. Our life is a life of our consciousness. Therefore so problem of consciousness' research is important. For neurosciences it is necessary to understand a problem how on basis of movement of nervous impulses there is that we feel inside of ourselves – world of our ideas and feelings [6].

Interest for analysis of information – substantial side of brain work on basis of its physiological parameters sometimes has explosive character. Irrespective from the purposes and tasks in many laboratories brain bioelectric activity is used. Quite often this problem is designated as "reading of a brain" by analogy to how human comprehends the text on alphabetic symbols. It is a new stage in the decision of a global problem "a brain and mentality" as such investigations integrate technology of brain processes and their results in form of mental functions [7].

Besides theoretical value this problem has also practical outputs – at creation of more perfect generation of interfaces between brain and computer. The understanding

© Springer International Publishing Switzerland 2015
D.D. Schmorrow and C.M. Fidopiastis (Eds.): AC 2015, LNAI 9183, pp. 470–480, 2015.
DOI: 10.1007/978-3-319-20816-9_45

of a thinking brain is solving at creation of devices of an artificial intellect and new generations of computers [11].

There is a representation [3] that problem "consciousness and a brain" includes two main tasks. The first problem – to find out how on basis brain work, or on basis of movement of electric nervous impulses a subjective experience, a private person world are formed. The second problem is to specify what brain mechanisms underlie certain cognitive actions [1, 6].

One of explanations of how on basis of brain processes there is a subjective experience belongs to I.P.Pavlov who has assumed, that "consciousness is a result of activity of that cortex area which is in a condition of optimum excitability" [12]. I.P.Pavlov wrote, "if we could see through a cranium would observe the freakish form a light spot moving on a cortex which reflects the area connected with consciousness". Modern methods of brain research allow looking very similar – EEG-mapping, ERPs-mapping, MEG-mapping, fMRI, PET-scan, near infrared sources, etc. [8, 14, 16].

One of key brain structure responsible for support of status "consciousness – wakefulness" formation reticular has acts [11]. It receives collaterals from sensory and from motor paths of a brainstem. This approach by the theory of centrencephalic Penfild's system is presented [13].

Purpose of present research was aimed for studying character and a degree of disorders of mechanisms of perception and integration of auditory figurative information at depressive psychopathological states.

2 Methods

Healthy examinees (40 persons) and 72 patients with homogeneous psychopathological frustration of depressive character (middle age 34 ± 3.4 years) by means of standard and original techniques have been surveyed. Individually-psychological characteristics and a degree of expressiveness for cognitive defect estimated according to clinical interview, research of the auditory-speech memory, traditional techniques of an estimation of situational and personal uneasiness, differential diagnostics of depressions.

Auditory cognitive system by means of original technique "recognition of auditory images (AI)" was investigated. Examinces have listened and identified a continuous series of AI. Further a level of an identification of AI, speed of perception and accuracy of a semantic estimation of the acoustical nonverbal information were defined. Multichannel EEG until stimulation and also synchronously with AI perception was registered.

The instruction and tasks for all patients were clear. For patients AI were offered to listen and identify. For strengthening intensity of process of listening AI not separated were showed. The images a uniform continuous series by general duration of 10 min have represented (20 AI for 30 s) (Table 1).

The interval between AI has made 3 s. AI have been saved on the digital memory and have submitted binaural. The level of sound pressure was comfortable and made 80 dB above a threshold of audibility.

Table 1. EEG registration with presentation of auditory images

Background EEG	Awake rest
EEG with AI presentation	Acoustical images
Presentation of pure AI	Call of phone
	Shout of the cock
	Crying of the child
	Sound of a moving train
	Shooting from a gun
Presentation of noise AI	Noise of a thunder-storm
	Noise of a sea surf
	Noise of a mountain stream with singing birds
	Roar of the engine of the take off plane
	Noise of city

For EEG analysis software WIN-EEG from N.Bechtereva Institute of Human Brain was applied. Also coherent EEG analysis was applied, chose non artifact epochs which duration was established experimentally. Reliability of the received results was estimated by t-criterion. EEG data in the form of individual coherent-grams and diagrams were represented.

The present investigation by local ethical committee is approved.

3 Results

Base coherence for persons with psychopathology before stimulation is characterized by impoverished functional communications (Table 2) by comparison with healthy examinees. The difference varies within the limits of 18.8–42.7 % (Fig. 1).

Inside of each hemisphere at healthy examinees in a condition of rest all cortex zones – occipital, parietal, central and frontal were characterized by precise communications. Besides, each of these zones in one hemisphere in pairs with symmetric area in other hemisphere is connected.

At schizophrenia generalized decomposition inter-and-intra hemispheric coherent communications was registered. Infringements of intercentral attitudes complicate carrying out of nervous impulses on inter- and intra- hemispheric brain communications. It promotes infringement of perception and AI identification, difficulty of integration of the information and formation of the cognitive decrease. At patients impoverished intra- hemispheric communications were registered. However, inter hemispheric interaction almost completely was absent or has been weakened.

During task performance at healthy examinees the set inter- and intra- hemispheric communications is registered. The pattern, characteristic for a condition of rest, at thinking varies. Communications start to converge to the certain fields of an associative cortex. Such centers of communication have been named by "focuses of interaction" which were formed at healthy examinees (Fig. 2).

Table 2. Variants of perception of auditory images

NN п\п	Variants of perception	Recognition, n (%)	
		Patients	Healthy
1	Correct recognition	0 (0)[d]	30 (75)[d]
2	Unreasonably certain character and-or occurrence of affective illusions	6 (8.3)[a]	0 (0)[a]
3	Absence of associations (guessing)	6 (8.3)[a]	0 (0)[a]
4	Prolonged recognition of acoustical image	11 (15.3)[b]	2 (5)[a]
5	Splitting of perception	9 (12.5)[c]	0 (0)[c]
6	Late recognition	10 (13.8)[c]	1 (2.5)[c]
7	Propensity to jamming the same images	6 (8.3)[a]	0 (0)[a]
8	False recognition	16 (22.2)[b]	2 (5)[b]
9	Easy illegibility of an identification, scarcity and monotony of hypotheses	8 (11.1)[a]	5 (12.5 %)[a]

Note. [a]– $p > 0.05$; [b]– $p < 0.005$; [c] – $p < 0.05$; [d] $p < 0.001$.

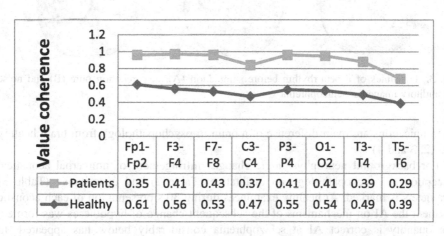

Fig. 1. Parameters of coherence before auditory stimulation at healthy and at psychopathology

The tasks of brain are perceive, processing and transfer the information by excitation of the certain structures and establishment of communications, including cortex. Transfer of the information is possible only at occurrence of interrelations between participating structures.

At psychopathology number of communications (Fig. 3) considerably below was registered. Inside of hemispheres their quantity increased in comparison with a condition of rest. But main mechanism testifies that hemispheres have been completely "separated". Thus, disintegration and breakage neural networks forming inter- hemispheric

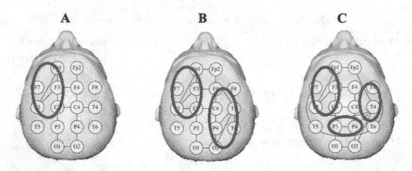

Fig. 2. Dynamics of a beta-rhythm before stimulation (A), at perception pure (B) and noise (C) acoustic images at healthy examinees.

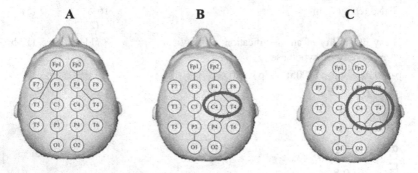

Fig. 3. Dynamics of a beta-rhythm before stimulation (A), at perception pure (B) and noise (C) auditory images at schizophrenia.

communications are main difference of a brain in psychopathology from brain healthy (Fig. 2, 3 and 4).

For background neurophysiologic changes infringement of nonverbal acoustical perception at psychopathology on qualitative (Table 2) and quantitative (Table 3) parameters is marked. At healthy examinees during 30 s presentation of each acoustic fragment the AI on mechanisms of the subsequent change of hypotheses was formed. The quantity is correct AI at schizophrenia considerably below has appeared. In comparison with control group high reliability of distinctions (p < 0.001) is marked (Table 2).

At patients more often tendency of association with professionally habitual or actual sounds in personal interests is observed. Perception in this case has unreasonably concrete and/or affective-illusory character. The person hears "crying of familiar human", instead of crying of person in general, "noise of a familiar place", instead of abstract noise of street, etc. Instead of habitual sounds patients hear flick a shutter of a gun, shots, steps and breath of persecutors, dying groans and shouts of people familiar to them. Such frustration of perception is noted in 8.3 % of cases at patients and was absent at healthy (Table 2).

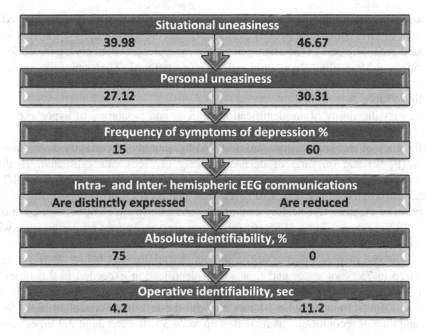

Situational uneasiness	
39.98	46.67

Personal uneasiness	
27.12	30.31

Frequency of symptoms of depression %	
15	60

Intra- and Inter- hemispheric EEG communications	
Are distinctly expressed	Are reduced

Absolute identifiability, %	
75	0

Operative identifiability, sec	
4.2	11.2

Fig. 4. Parameters of healthy examinees (left) and persons with psychopathology (right) at identification of acoustical images.

In 8.3 % of cases at schizophrenia associations did not arise. The identification had guessing character. At healthy such features of perception AI did not registered (Table 2).

Long identification of AI in 15.3 % of cases at mentally sick was marked. In control group such feature only in 5 % of cases was observed. At patients it was quite often observed "prolonged identification of AI". "Ideal standards" already are stored in memory of images and examinees are capable to find conformity between them and the acting deformed images (Table 2).

Splitting of perception (loss of ability to form a complete image) in 12.5 % of cases at schizophrenia was registered. Patients could perceive correctly separate details of AI, but could not connect them in uniform structure. They heard sounds, marked their start and finish, gave them the characteristic, but could not recognize AI as a whole. The perception in such cases was characterized by "the split identification". The patient speaks: "something turns", but during 30 s does not identify AI (for example, a sound of "helicopter' helicopter take off"). Other patient speaks: "it is clear such sound with shine", but does not learn a sound of a mountain stream (Table 2).

Late recognition at schizophrenia marked in 13.8 % of cases (2.5 % in control group, $p < 0.05$). To speak about full loss of subject perception it is impossible. Patients could not during the necessary moment recognize AI, but in further the braked association as reaction to another stimulus was formed (Table 2).

Typical feature of acoustical perception for patients is the expressed inertness, propensity to "jamming of the same images" (Table 2).

False recognition AI on a background agnosia of subject sounds it is established in 22.2 % of cases at patients (at healthy persons of cases of 5 %, p < 0.005). Patients have supposed gross blunders in the assumptions (for example, accepted crying the child for cat's miaow). More often they could not associate with AI. They painfully searched "with what for it to compare", but did not find, though is thin enough caught shades of sounding (Table 2).

The easy illegibility of an identification, scarcity and monotony of hypotheses met in 11.1 % at patients (12. 5 % at healthy) (Table 3).

Efficiency of recognition pure and noise AI by quantity of correctly distinguished images (P, %) and on time of decision-making (T, sec) was estimated. Healthy examinees successfully coped put with cognitive task (95 %) on average for 4.2 s. Difficulties have fixed only in 5 % of cases at an identification of AI "noise of city". At perception of the noise AI healthy examinees successfully have coped with cognitive task in 80 % of cases. Time of identification has risen in 2 times by comparison with pure AI (Table 3).

An outcome of perception at schizophrenia essentially was below. Pure AI have recognized in 75 % of cases and time of an identification exceeded in 2.6 times of healthy examinees.

At an identification of noise AI patients with the task have consulted in 40 % of cases and time of recognition has increased up to 24.3 s. It exceeds in 2.9 times period of identification in comparison with healthy examinees. Time of a correct identification of noise AI at patients has increased in 2 times by comparison with an identification pure AI (Table 3).

Thus, level of AI identification on qualitative and to quantity indicators is lowered in patients with psychopathology by comparison with identification in control group of healthy people. From presented data (Fig. 4) it is visible that healthy examinees successfully coped with AI identification on average for 4.2 s. Patients have identified AI in 2.7 times more slowly (aver. for 11.2 s). Quality indicators of recognition also were much worse at patients with psychopathology. Absolutely correct identification of AI in patients did not meet.

At successful perception of AI by healthy examinees on EEG data coherence focus was formed. At patients with psychopathology coherence focuses either were not formed or have been weakened.

Depression at healthy met much less often (in 15 % of cases) unlike patients (in 60 % of cases). Parameters of situational and personal uneasiness were below in group healthy, unlike patients with psychopathology.

Table 3. Pure and noise auditory images recognition

Acoustic Images	Healthy		Patients	
	P	T	P	T
Pure AI	38 (95 %)	4.2	54 (75 %)	11.2
Noise AI	32 (80 %)	8.4	29 (40 %)	24.3

Note. P – quantity of correctly identified images, T – time of decision-making.

4 Discussion

Transition of physiological process to psychic level is provided by ring movement of impulses (Fig. 5) with activation of memory centers, including hippocampus and motivational structures with subsequent return of excitation to a projective cortex. Such mechanism has provides an opportunity of comparison and synthesis of the information on physical and signal properties of stimulus that underlies sensations [2, 15].

Return of sensory impulses to points of initial projections after inquiry in other structures allows comparing the new information with last experience. It allows a basis to lead its updating [4].

Human consciousness consists not only of consecutive images. It also is capable to manipulate these images and symbols forming thought process. These points of view are close to "cinema theory of perception" [5].

Focus consists from neuron's groups, each of which is connected by flexible communications with peripheral neurons (Fig. 6). Neuron' groups work on same frequency and are incorporated in uniform neural network on the basis of isosynchronous principle. Inside of the focus neurons are incorporated by rigid communications. It enables to integrate information circulating in separate neural networks. Thus, information synthesis includes three basic components: the sensory information, the data from long term memory and data from the motivation centers. At psychopathology in all components deficiency (Fig. 7) is marked that leads to infringement of perception of AI [1, 6].

Processes of perception and integration of the auditory information in norm occur instantly and are accompanied by increase both intra- and inter- hemispheric coherent communications. It is marked precise lateralization of the focus coherence in a temporal-frontal cortex over again in the right hemisphere, responsible for an identification of physical, spatial and semantic AI characteristics, and then in a

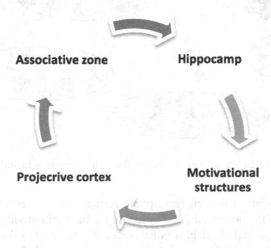

Associative zone   **Hippocamp**

Projecrive cortex   **Motivational structures**

Fig. 5. Cyclic movement of impulses and information synthesis at an identification of auditory images.

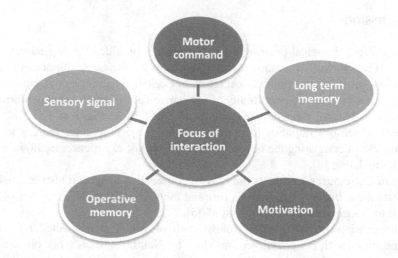

Fig. 6. The scheme of focus of interaction which is carrying out synthesis of the information during perception of auditory image.

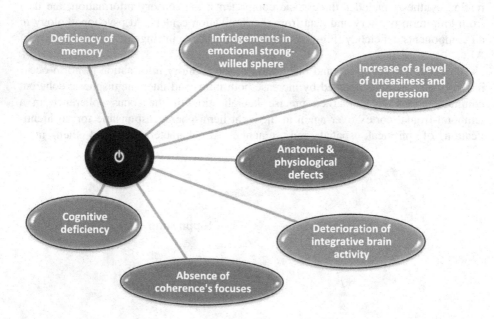

Fig. 7. Deficiency of basic segments for auditory images identification

frontal-temporal region of the left hemisphere responsible for verbalization and conceptual judgment of the perceived information on the basis of individual experience. At successful perception of the AI in a brain cortex the behavioral dominant that finds reflection in dynamics of coherent communications is formed. Inter central attitudes undergo respective alterations. The pattern of coherent communications in the form of the strengthened combination of potentials of frontal and temporal areas of the right hemisphere in a high-frequency range is formed. Bioelectric activity has correlates with cognition dominant at a behavioral level [1, 6, 9, 10].

At psychopathology before stimulation comes to light essential decrease inter- and intra- hemispheric EEG synchronization. It is the objective certificate of infringement of the inter central attitudes, decrease in a degree of functional coherence between temporal, frontal and parietal structures of the left and right and left hemispheres of a brain.

Remedial changes of initially lowered level of integration processes at audio-cognitive activity carry at schizophrenia torpid character. Characteristic for norm asymmetry of the coherence focuses at perception of integration of the mono- modal information, at schizophrenia or completely was absent, or in separate supervision had the expressed tendency.

5 Conclusion

1. In norm the perception pure and noise AI has high recognition (up to 95 %) and efficiency with the latent period 4.2–8.4 s. In view of time for verbalization and decision-making on biologically significant action such time interval corresponds to physiological norm. Productivity of AI perception at psychopathology is within the limits of 40–75 %, and the latent period – within the limits of 11.2–24.3 s, that in 2.6–2.9 times exceeds a standard time of identification.

2. At psychopathology before stimulation reveal essential decrease of inter- and intra- hemispheric EEG synchronization. It is the objective certificate of infringement of the intercentral attitudes, decrease in a degree of functional coherence between temporal, frontal and parietal structures of left and right and left hemispheres of brain.

An infringement of functional interaction in basic frequency EEG ranges at psychopathology specifies steady infringements of neurons functioning. Infringement of synchronization of the basic rhythms shows, that this mechanism can define infringement of AI recognition.

3. At successful AI perception in a brain cortex the behavioral dominant that finds reflection in dynamics of coherent communications is formed. The intercentral attitudes undergo respective alterations; the pattern of coherent communications in the form of the strengthened combination of potentials of frontal and temporal areas of the right hemisphere in a high-frequency range is formed. Bioelectric activity has correlates with recognition dominant at a behavioral level.

4. At psychopathology authentic infringement of a holistic and segmental way of processing of the acoustical information is marked. In the first case synthesis of the acting information with the ready standards stored memory, and in the second is carried out, on the basis of a principle of likelihood forecasting – from separate fragments of a signal the person on the basis of the experience hypotheses about a possible subject accessory of an image has builds.

References

1. Belskaya, K.A., Lytaev, S.A.: Features of perception of acoustical images and maintenance of noise stability in acoustical system with a various level of uneasiness at patients with psychopathology. Vestn. Saint Petersburg State Univ. 11(3), 56–67 (2010)
2. Belskaya, K.A., Lytaev, S.A.: Psychological features of audio cognitive defect at psychopathology. Pediatric 5(1), 37–44 (2014)
3. Chalmers, D.J.: Facing up to the problem of consciousness. J. Conscious. Stud. 2(3), 200–219 (1995)
4. Freeman, W.J.: A cinematographic hypothesis of cortical dynamics in perceptions. J. Int. Psychophysiol. 60, 149–161 (2006)
5. Gur, R.E.: Disturbances in the Normal Asymmetry of Brain Structure and Function are a Hallmark of Schizophrenia and May Relate to Sex Differences and Age Effects on Disease Course. Abstr. 4. Laterality and Psychopathology Conference "Applied and Basic Research". London, p. 25, 19–21 June 1997
6. Ivanitsky, A.M.: Science about a brain on a way to the decision of a problem of consciousness. Vestnik Rus. Acad. Sci. 80(5–6), 447–455 (2010)
7. Ivanitsky, A.M.: Reading of a brain: achievements, prospects and ethical problems. J. High. Nerv. Act. 62(2), 133–142 (2012)
8. Lytaev, S.: Brain topography of perception of target and non-target acoustic signals. In: Tolstoy, A., Teng, Y.-C., Shang, E.C. (eds.) Theoretical and Computational Acoustics 2003. Honolulu, Hawaii, USA, 11–15 August 2003. New Jersey, London, Singapore, pp. 291–297. World Scientific, Beijing (2004)
9. Lytaev, S., Belskaya, K., Denisov, V.: Modeling of the Frustration Status and Noiseproof Feature during Perception of the Auditory Images. Undersea Human System Interaction Symposium. Providence, RI, 27–29 July (2010)
10. Lopes de Silva, F.N.: The cortical source of the alpha rhythm. Neurosci. Lett. 6(5), 237–241 (1977)
11. Lopes de Silva, F.N.: Anatomical organization and physiology of the limbic cortex. Physiol. Revs. 70, 453–511 (1990)
12. Pavlov, I.P.: Objective studying of the higher nervous activity of animals. In: Twenty Years' Experience of Objective Studying of the Higher Nervous Activity of Animals, pp. 236–250. USSR Acad. Sci., Moscow, Leningrad (1951)
13. Penfield, W.: The Mystery of the Mind: A Critical Study of Consciousness and the Human Brain. Princeton Univ. Press, Princeton (1975)
14. Schmorrow, D., Reeves, L.: 21th century human-system computing: augmented cognition for improved human performance. Aviat. Space Environ. Med. 78(5), B7–B11 (2007). Sect. II
15. Teder-Sälejärvi, W.A., Hillyard, S.A., Röder, B., Neville, H.J.: Spatial attention to central and peripheral auditory stimuli as indexed by event-related potentials. Brain Res. Cogn. Brain Res. 25(8), 213–227 (1999)
16. Teder-Sälejärvi, W.A., Pierce, K.L., Courchesne, E., Hillyard, S.A.: Auditory spatial localization and attention deficits in autistic adults. Brain Res. Cogn. Brain Res. 23(2–3), 221–234 (2005)

Effects of Professional Visual Search Experience on Domain-General and Domain-Specific Visual Cognition

Laura E. Matzen[✉], Michael J. Haass, Laura A. McNamara,
Susan M. Stevens-Adams, and Stephanie N. McMichael

Sandia National Laboratories, Albuquerque, USA
lematze@sandia.gov

Abstract. Vision is one of the dominant human senses and most human-computer interfaces rely heavily on the capabilities of the human visual system. An enormous amount of effort is devoted to finding ways to visualize information so that humans can understand and make sense of it. By studying how professionals engage in these visual search tasks, we can develop insights into their cognitive processes and the influence of experience on those processes. This can advance our understanding of visual cognition in addition to providing information that can be applied to designing improved data visualizations or training new analysts.

In this study, we investigated the role of expertise on performance in a Synthetic Aperture Radar (SAR) target detection task. SAR imagery differs substantially from optical imagery, making it a useful domain for investigating expert-novice differences. The participants in this study included professional SAR imagery analysts, radar engineers with experience working with SAR imagery, and novices who had little or no prior exposure to SAR imagery. Participants from all three groups completed a domain-specific visual search task in which they searched for targets within pairs of SAR images. They also completed a battery of domain-general visual search and cognitive tasks that measured factors such as mental rotation ability, spatial working memory, and useful field of view. The results revealed marked differences between the professional imagery analysts and the other groups, both for the domain-specific task and for some domain-general tasks. These results indicate that experience with visual search in non-optical imagery can influence performance on other domains.

Keywords: Visual search · Expertise

1 Introduction

There are numerous domains in which professionals must search through visual displays of information to identify key features and make decisions about them. From radiologists looking for evidence of cancer to radar analysts searching for unusual radar signatures, many high-consequence decisions rely on visual cognition. Despite the importance on these tasks, few studies have investigated the relationships between

© Springer International Publishing Switzerland 2015
D.D. Schmorrow and C.M. Fidopiastis (Eds.): AC 2015, LNAI 9183, pp. 481–491, 2015.
DOI: 10.1007/978-3-319-20816-9_46

professional visual search experience and visual cognition. Although a great deal of research has focused on characterizing visual search performance in humans, most studies have used college students with no particular expertise in visual search tasks beyond those encountered in daily life [1–3].

Only a handful of studies have investigated the performance of people with professional experience in high-consequence visual search tasks. Work by Mitroff and colleagues has investigated the visual search performance of Transportation Security Officers (TSOs) who have experience with searching X-ray images of luggage for prohibited items [4]. However, in most of these studies, the TSOs completed domain-general visual search tasks rather than tasks from within their area of expertise [4, 5]. Other researchers have focused on radiologists who have experience with searching images for evidence of cancer or other abnormalities [6–9]. In that domain, participants typically view images from within their area of expertise, such as mammograms. Very few studies have tested radiologists using domain-general tasks.

There are even fewer studies that compare professional visual searchers to novices [4, 10, 11]. The lack of research in this area represents a substantial gap in the literature. A deeper understanding of the interplay between experience and visual cognitive processes would benefit numerous areas, including training, assessment, and system design. Further research in this area could also help to address fundamental questions about learning. While some researchers argue that professional visual search experience does not alter visual cognition [12], there is evidence from other domains suggesting that domain-specific experience can influence visual processing, even on a neural level [13].

To add to the existing research on the effects of professional visual search experience on basic cognitive processes, we sought to test the visual search performance of participants with varying levels of experience in a previously unstudied domain. In the present study, participants completed a battery of visual search and general visual cognition tasks. One of the visual search tasks used Synthetic Aperture Radar (SAR) imagery. SAR is used in a variety of surveillance and mapping applications. The imagery is superficially similar to optical imagery, but extensive training is required for analysts to learn to interpret SAR phenomenology correctly This makes it particularly useful for investigating differences in visual search between experts and novices. In addition, unlike X-rays and other more common forms of imagery, most people have never seen a SAR image and are true novices in this domain (Fig. 1).

There were three groups of participants in this experiment. The first group consisted of professional SAR imagery analysts who conduct visual search tasks using SAR imagery in their daily jobs. They have had extensive training and experience working with SAR imagery. The second group consisted of professionals who work with SAR images regularly, typically on a weekly basis. They had extensive knowledge of the domain, but do not typically engage in visual search tasks using the imagery. Most of the participants in this group were radar engineers who design and test the SAR systems. The third group consisted of novices who had no prior exposure to SAR imagery. All three groups completed three behavioral tasks and three eye tracking tasks. The behavioral tasks tested basic aspects of visual cognition, including visual attention, mental rotation, and spatial working memory. The eye tracking tasks

Fig. 1. SAR image of a baseball diamond. Image courtesy of Sandia National Laboratories, Airborne ISR.

included two domain-general visual search tasks and the domain-specific visual search task using SAR imagery.

2   Method

2.1   Participants

Twenty-four people participated in the study. Eight were professional SAR analysts (1 female; mean age 42), eight were employees of Sandia National Laboratories who work with SAR images regularly but are not trained as imagery analysts (3 female; mean age 41), and eight were Sandia employees with no prior experience with SAR imagery (4 female; mean age 32). In the analysis, we will refer to these groups as the analysts, experienced non-analysts, and novices, respectively. All participants gave their written informed consent before participating in the study.

2.2   Domain-Specific Visual Search Task

In the domain-specific visual search task, participants were presented with two SAR images presented side-by-side. The left side of the screen showed a SAR image of a scene and the right side of the screen showed a Coherent Change Detection (CCD) image of the same scene. The CCD image is created by co-registering SAR images of the same scene and measuring changes in coherence that can reveal temporal changes [14]. Essentially, the left image provided viewers with contextual information about the scene and the right image provided viewers with information about the presence or absence of targets in the scene. There were 20 pairs of images, half of which contained a target and half of which did not. The targets were the same types of targets that the professional SAR analysts look for in their daily work. The experienced non-analysts were also familiar with the nature of the targets. The novices received instructions about what to look for to determine whether or not a target was present in the scene. Each stimulus was preceded by a fixation cross that appeared on the screen for one second. When the stimulus appeared, participants were asked to search for any targets and to use a 1–4 scale to indicate whether or not they thought a target was present. A response of "1" indicated that they were sure that there was not a target in the scene. A response of "2" indicated that they thought there was no target, but they were unsure. A response of "3" indicated that they thought there was a target present, but were unsure. A response of "4" indicated that they were sure that there was a target present. The participants were asked to respond as quickly and accurately as possible. They had a maximum of 45 s to respond to each stimulus and they did not receive feedback about their answers.

2.3   Domain-General Visual Search Tasks

Participants completed two domain-general eye tracking tasks. The first, the O and Q task, was based on classic visual perception studies [15]. The O and Q task consisted of 120 trials, 60 in which participants were asked to search for the letter O hidden among a field of Qs and 60 in which participants were asked to search for the letter Q hidden among a field of Os. The order of the O block and the Q block was counterbalanced across participants. In both blocks, each stimulus contained 1, 4, 8, 16 or 24 letters. Examples of stimuli from each block are shown in Fig. 2. One letter was always the target and the remainder were distractors. The target appeared equally often in each quadrant of the screen and the stimuli were presented in a pseudorandom order so that

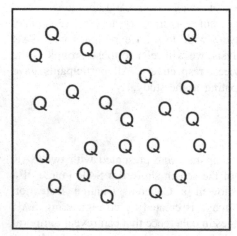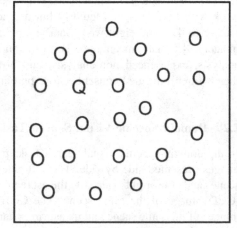

Fig. 2. Examples of the stimuli used in the O Task (left) and the Q Task (right), both with a set size of 24.

Fig. 3. Examples of the stimuli from the T and L task, showing set sizes 4, 8, and 16

no more than two stimuli of the same set size appeared in a row. Each stimulus was preceded by a fixation cross that appeared on the screen for one second. When the stimulus appeared, participants were asked to find the target as quickly as possible and to press the space bar when they had found it.

The second domain-general task was the T and L task, which has been used in prior studies of professional visual searchers [4]. In the T and L task, participants were tasked with determining whether or not there was a perfect T, with a centered crossbar, in the image. The distractors were offset Ts that looked more like Ls. The targets and distractors appeared in grey against a mottled grey background and could be oriented in any of four directions (0°, 90°, 180°, 270°). Each image contained 4, 8 or 16 letters. Examples of stimuli from each set size are shown in Fig. 3. There were 48 trails, half of which contained a target. The targets appeared equally often in each quadrant of the screen. As in the other eye tracking tasks, each stimulus was preceded by a fixation cross that appeared on the screen for one second. When the stimulus appeared, participants were asked to respond as quickly and accurately as possible by pressing the "z" key on the keyboard if a target was present and the "m" key if the target was absent.

Behavioral (accuracy and reaction time) and eye tracking data were recorded for both tasks.

2.4   Domain-General Visual Cognition Tasks

The participants completed three visual cognition tasks that tested mental rotation, visual attention, and spatial working memory. In the mental rotation task, participants saw pairs of line drawings representing three-dimensional figures. They were asked to mentally rotate the figures to determine whether or not the two figures were the same. They responded by clicking the left or right mouse button. Participants were asked to complete as many trials as possible in 60 s. Their scores were calculated by subtracting the number of incorrect responses from the number of correct responses (Fig. 4).

In the visual attention task, participants fixated on a point in the center of the screen. An array of squares, radiating away from the fixation point along eight arms, was presented for 30 ms. All of the squares were white, except for one that was black. The stimulus was followed by a visual mask. Then participants were asked to indicate which of the eight arms contained the black square. There were a total of 24 trials, 8 at each of three distances from the fixation point (close, middle and far). Participants were scored based on how many trials they answered correctly at each distance (Fig. 5).

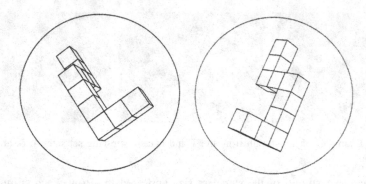

Fig. 4. Example stimulus from the mental rotation task

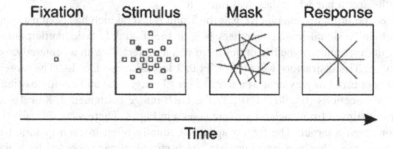

Fig. 5. Timeline for the visual attention task

The spatial working memory task was a rotation span task based on work by Shah and Miyake [16]. There were two interleaved tasks. In the memory task, participants saw arrows that were one of two lengths (long or short), pointing in one of eight directions (0°, 45°, 90°, 135°, 180°, 225°, 270°, 315°). In the secondary task, participants saw one of five letters (R, L, J, G, and F) that was either normal or backwards (flipped across the vertical axis) and were rotated in one of eight different orientations (0°, 45°, 90°, 135°, 180°, 225°, 270°, 315°). On each trial, participants saw a sequence of letters, each of which was followed by an arrow. For each letter, the participants had to press a key on the keyboard to indicate whether the letter was presented normally or backwards. The letter remained on the screen until the participant made a response. Then an arrow was presented for 1000 ms. The trials varied in length and contained between two and five arrows. After the last arrow was presented, participants were asked to recall the sequence of arrows that they had seen in that trial. The recall screen showed all 16 possible arrows (long or short arrows at each of eight orientations). Participants clicked on the arrows to indicate which arrows had appeared in the previous sequence, in the order that they appeared. Participants were scored based on the number of arrows that they recalled correctly (Fig. 6).

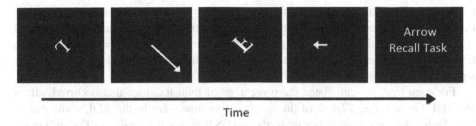

Time

Fig. 6. Timeline for the spatial working memory task

2.5 Eye Tracking Methods

The eye tracking data was collected using the FaceLab 5 Standard System and Eye-Works software. The eye tracker was mounted below the computer monitor and consisted of two miniature digital cameras and one infrared illumination pod. The system was calibrated for each participant by having the participants look at each point of a 9-point grid displayed on the monitor. After calibration, observers were free to move their heads while completing eye tracking tasks.

3 Results

3.1 Domain-Specific Visual Search Task

Behavioral Results. On the SAR imagery search task, the novice participants responded correctly to 56.9 % of the trials, the experienced non-analysts responded correctly to 70.0 % of the trials, and the analysts responded correctly to 74.4 % of the trials, on average. A one-way ANOVA showed that the average accuracy differed significantly between groups ($F(2,21) = 4.62$, $p < 0.03$). Post hoc t-tests showed that the analysts had significantly higher accuracy than the novices ($t(14) = 2.95$, $p < 0.01$), as did the experienced non-analysts ($t(14) = 2.14$, $p < 0.03$). The performance of the analysts and experienced non-analysts did not differ significantly ($t(14) = 0.73$).

The average reaction times were 22.4 s for the novices, 14.5 s for the experienced non-analysts, and 9.5 s for the analysts. A one-way ANOVA showed that the groups differed significantly in their reaction times ($F(2,21) = 11.98$, $p < 0.001$). Post hoc t-tests showed that the analysts were significantly faster than the experienced non-analysts ($t(14) = 2.93$, $p < 0.01$) and the novices ($t(14) = 4.34$, $p < 0.001$), and the experienced non-analysts were significantly faster than the novices ($t(14) = 2.57$, $p < 0.02$).

Eye Tracking Results. Two participants, one from the novice group and one from the experienced group, were excluded from the eye tracking data analysis due to noisy data. A region of interest (ROI) was demarcated around each target and contained the target itself plus a buffer intended to represent a person's useful field of view (approximately 90 pixels on each side of the target). Time to first fixation in the ROI was calculated for each trial in which a target was present. The average time to the first fixation in the ROI was 5.3 s for novices, 3.0 s for experienced non-analysts, and 2.1 s for analysts. The difference between groups was significant ($F(2,19) = 9.21, p < 0.01$). Post hoc t-tests showed that the experienced non-analysts and the analysts were both significantly faster than the novices ($t(12) = 2.41, p < 0.02$ and $t(13) = 4.36, p < 0.001$, respectively). However, the experienced non-analysts and the analysts did not differ significantly from one another ($t(13) = 1.53, p = 0.08$).

For each trial, we calculated the percentage of total fixations that occurred within the ROI. On average, 17.4 % of the novice's fixations were in the ROI, compared to 25.3 % for the experienced non-analysts and 38.9 % for the analysts. The difference between groups was significant ($F(2, 19) = 8.08, p < 0.01$). Post hoc t-test showed that the experienced non-analysts had a significantly higher percentage of fixations in the ROI than the novices ($t(12) = 2.47, p < 0.02$) and the analysts had a significantly higher percentage of fixations in the ROI than the experienced non-analysts ($t(13) = 2.13$, $p < 0.03$).

3.2   Domain-General Visual Search Tasks

The participants' average response times for each target type and set size in the O and Q task are shown in Fig. 7. A one-way ANOVA showed that the three groups' average reaction times on the O block did not differ significantly ($F(2, 14) = 0.31$). However, the average reaction times of the three groups did differ significantly on the Q block (F $(2,14) = 4.10, p = 0.04$). Post hoc t-tests showed that the reaction times of the participants in the novice group were significantly slower than those of the experienced non-analysts ($t(8) = 2.56, p = 0.02$) and those of the analysts ($t(8) = 2.15, p = 0.03$). The

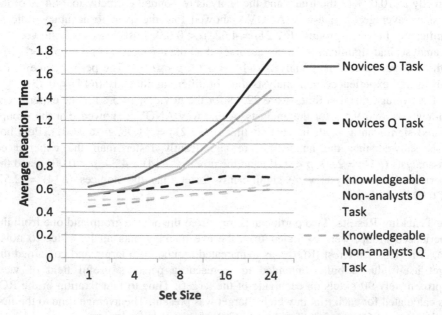

Fig. 7. Average reaction times for the O and Q tasks

analysts and experienced non-analysts did not differ significantly from one another (t (8) = 0.59).

On the T and L task, novice participants responded correctly to 83.3 % of the trials, experienced non-analysts responded correctly to 85.4 %, and analysts responded correctly to 83.0 %, on average. The differences in accuracy between the groups were not significant ($F(2, 19) = 0.28$). The average reaction times for the groups were 4.7 s for the novices, 4.1 s for the experienced non-analysts, and 3.5 s for the analysts. A one-way ANOVA showed that there was a significant difference in average reaction times between the groups ($F(2,19) = 3.61, p < 0.05$). Post hoc t-tests showed that the analysts were significantly faster than the novices ($t(12) = 4.49, p < 0.001$).

3.3 Domain-General Visual Cognition Tasks

Due to time constraints, only five of the eight participants in the analyst group completed the visual attention task. The novice participants averaged 6.5 correct for the close trials, 7.25 correct for the middle trials, and 7 correct for the far trials. The experienced non-analysts averaged 7.25 correct for the close trials, 8 correct for the middle trials, and 7.88 correct for the far trials. The analysts averaged 6.8 correct for the close trials, 7.2 correct for the middle trials, and 7.6 correct for the far trials. One-way ANOVAs were used to compare the scores of the three groups for each trial type. These showed that the performance of the three groups did not differ significantly for any of the trial types (all $Fs < 2.83$, all $ps > 0.09$).

On the mental rotation task, the novices completed an average of 6.75 trials with an average score of 3 (the number of correct trials minus the number of incorrect trials). The experienced non-analysts completed an average of 10.25 trials with an average score of 5.5. The analysts completed an average of 12 trials with an average score of 5.5. One-way ANOVAs showed that there were no significant differences between groups in the number of trials completed ($F(2,21) = 2.24, p = 0.13$) or in score ($F(2,21) = 1.43, p = 0.26$).

On the rotation span task, the novices correctly recalled 54.8 % of the arrows, the experienced non-analysts correctly recalled 49.7 % of the arrows, and the analysts correctly recalled 50.4 % of the arrows, on average. Two of the analysts and one of the experienced non-analysts did not complete the rotation span task due to time constraints. A one-way ANOVA showed that the three groups did not differ significantly in performance ($F(2,18) = 0.19$).

4 Discussion

The results of this study indicate that professional experience in a specific visual search domain corresponds with improved performance on domain-general visual search tasks. Working within their domain of expertise, the SAR imagery analysts and experienced non-analysts were both more accurate in their responses than the novices, who had not viewed SAR imagery before taking part in the experiment. In addition to their high accuracy, the analysts were faster than experienced non-analysts and novices, both in terms of overall task reaction time and in terms of the time to first fixation in the ROI. The analysts were highly efficient in their ability to identify the ROI, typically fixating in the ROI within two seconds of stimulus onset. They devoted a higher proportion of fixations to the ROI than either of the other groups.

The analysts and experienced non-analysts also out-performed the novices on the domain-general visual search tasks. The analysts had significantly faster reaction times than the novices on the T and L task, and both the analysts and experienced non-analysts were significantly faster than the novices on the parallel visual search component of the O and Q task. However, on the domain-general visual cognition tasks that were not directly related to visual search, the performance of the three groups did not differ.

Our finding that that professional imagery analysts were faster than novices on domain-general visual search tasks stands in contrast to some prior literature. One of the few prior studies to compare professional visual searchers to novices [4] found that the professionals were more accurate than the novices, but significantly slower. However, these studies differ in several important respects, most notably with regard to the groups of professionals used. The present study indicates that experience with non-optical imagery may improve visual search capabilities in ways that benefit performance on general visual search tasks, but the differences between this study and the work by Biggs and Mitroff suggest that the effects of experience may depend on the domain. Different professional domains are likely to draw on slightly different cognitive processes or skills, leading to different effects on domain-general tasks. More research is needed to tease apart the influences of various kinds of visual search experience on specific aspects of visual cognition.

The work described in this paper is part of a broader set of research activities at Sandia National Laboratories related to real-world visual search. We are developing a cross-domain research program, focused on populations of professionals with varying levels of experience who spend a predominant amount of their work time searching for anomalies and/or known signatures in imagery or other visual representations of data. As discussed in McNamara et al. (this volume), our team is exploring integrated qualitative and quantitative methodological frameworks that will enable us to balance experimental rigor with work domain realism. The goal of this research is to inform the design and implementation of real-world work tools, training, and processes to best support the complex, often stressful work of rapid visual anomaly detection in high-pressure work situations. In doing so, we also aim to generate richer empirical data about the role of visual perception and cognition in complex decision-making environments.

References

1. Fleck, M.S., Mitroff, S.R.: Rare targets are rarely missed in correctable search. Psychol. Sci. **18**(11), 943–947 (2007)
2. Goh, J., Wiegmann, D.A., Madhavan, P.: Effects of automation failure in a luggage screening task: a comparison between direct and indirect cueing. In: Proceedings of the Human Factors and Ergonomics Society Annual Meeting, vol. 49, no. 3, pp. 492–496. SAGE Publications, September 2005

3. McCarley, J.S., Kramer, A.F., Wickens, C.D., Vidoni, E.D., Boot, W.R.: Visual skills in airport-security screening. Psychol. Sci. **15**(5), 302–306 (2004)
4. Biggs, A.T., Mitroff, S.R.: Different predictors of multiple-target search accuracy between nonprofessional and professional visual searchers. Q. J. Exp. Psychol., 1–14 (2013)
5. Biggs, A.T., Cain, M.S., Clark, K., Darling, E.F., Mitroff, S.R.: Assessing visual search performance differences between transportation security administration officers and nonprofessional visual searchers. Vis. Cogn. **21**(3), 330–352 (2013)
6. Cooper, L., Gale, A., Darker, I., Toms, A., Saada, J.: Radiology image perception and observer performance: How does expertise and clinical information alter interpretation? Stroke detection explored through eye-tracking. In: SPIE Medical Imaging, pp. 72630 K–72630 K. International Society for Optics and Photonics, February 2009
7. Kok, E.M., Bruin, A.B., Robben, S.G., Merriënboer, J.J.: Looking in the same manner but seeing it differently: bottom-up and expertise effects in radiology. Appl. Cogn. Psychol. **26** (6), 854–862 (2012)
8. Leong, J.J.H., Nicolaou, M., Emery, R.J., Darzi, A.W., Yang, G.Z.: Visual search behavior in skeletal radiographs: a cross-specialty study. Clin. Radiol. **62**(11), 1069–1077 (2007)
9. Mello-Thoms, C., Nodine, C.F., Kundel, H.L.: What attracts the eye to the location of missed and reported breast cancers? In: Proceedings of the 2002 symposium on Eye tracking research & applications, pp. 111–117. ACM, March 2002
10. Beck, M.R., Martin, B.A., Smitherman, E., Gaschen, L.: Eyes-on training and radiological expertise an examination of expertise development and its effects on visual working memory. Human Factors: J. Human Factors Ergon. Soc. **55**(4), 747–763 (2013)
11. Lansdale, M., Underwood, G., Davies, C.: Something overlooked? how experts in change detection use visual saliency. Appl. Cogn. Psychol. **24**, 213–225 (2010)
12. Reingold, E.M., Charness, N., Pomplun, M., Stampe, D.M.: Visual span in expert chess players: evidence from eye movements. Psychol. Sci. **12**(1), 48–55 (2001)
13. Tanaka, J.W., Curran, T.: A neural basis for expert object recognition. Psychol. Sci. **12**, 43–47 (2001)
14. Doerry, A.W.: SAR data collection and processing requirements for high quality coherent change detection. In: Proceedings of SPIE, the International Society for Optical Engineering. Society of Photo-Optical Instrumentation Engineers (2008)
15. Treisman, A., Souther, J.: Search asymmetry: a diagnostic for preattentive processing of separable features. J. Exp. Psychol. Gen. **114**, 285–310 (1985)
16. Shah, P., Miyake, A.: The separability of working memory resources for spatial thinking and language processing: An individual differences approach. J. Exp. Psychol. Gen. **125**, 4–27 (1996)

Ethnographic Methods for Experimental Design: Case Studies in Visual Search

Laura A. McNamara[✉], Kerstan Cole, Michael J. Haass,
Laura E. Matzen, J. Daniel Morrow, Susan M. Stevens-Adams,
and Stephanie McMichael

Sandia National Laboratories, Albuquerque, USA
lamcnam@sandia.gov

Abstract. Researchers at Sandia National Laboratories are integrating qualitative and quantitative methods from anthropology, human factors and cognitive psychology in the study of military and civilian intelligence analyst workflows in the United States' national security community. Researchers who study human work processes often use qualitative theory and methods, including grounded theory, cognitive work analysis, and ethnography, to generate rich descriptive models of human behavior in context. In contrast, experimental psychologists typically do not receive training in qualitative induction, nor are they likely to practice ethnographic methods in their work, since experimental psychology tends to emphasize generalizability and quantitative hypothesis testing over qualitative description. However, qualitative frameworks and methods from anthropology, sociology, and human factors can play an important role in enhancing the ecological validity of experimental research designs.

Keywords: Visual search · Qualitative methods · Experimental design · Synthetic aperture radar · Imagery analysis

1 Introduction

Researchers who study human work processes often use qualitative theory and methods, including grounded theory, cognitive work analysis, and ethnography, to generate rich descriptive models of human behavior in context (e.g., Vicente 1999). In contrast, experimental psychologists typically do not receive training in qualitative induction, nor are they likely to practice ethnographic methods in their work, since experimental psychology tends to emphasize generalizability and quantitative hypothesis testing over qualitative description. However, qualitative frameworks and methods from anthropology, sociology, and human factors can play an important role in enhancing the ecological validity of experimental research designs.

This paper describes elements of work domain field research conducted as part of Sandia National Laboratories' Pattern ANalytics for High Performance Exploitation and Reasoning (PANTHER) project, an internally-funded effort to develop algorithms, software and visualization environments that will enable national security analysts to detect, characterize and communicate meaningful geospatial and temporal patterns in large, complicated remote sensing data. A key PANTHER goal is empirical

© Springer International Publishing Switzerland 2015
D.D. Schmorrow and C.M. Fidopiastis (Eds.): AC 2015, LNAI 9183, pp. 492–503, 2015.
DOI: 10.1007/978-3-319-20816-9_47

identification and experimental validation of the perceptual and cognitive skills that characterize effective geospatial pattern analysis in high-throughput work environments. This information is considered a critical source of requirements for developing, implementing and evaluating new visual analytics technologies aimed at balancing human detection skill with automated analysis of threat patterns over greater geospatial and temporal domains (see discussion in Jian et al. 2000).

Given the significance of visual inspection in a wide variety of national security work domains, experimental studies examining visual search strategies, skill acquisition and factors influencing performance are quite important in realizing this larger project goal. However, such research should replicate key parameters of the work environment to optimize the ecological validity and applicability of findings. Experimental, laboratory-based studies of human visual attention tend to rely on batteries of detection tasks that use standardized stimulus sets (i.e., identifying a unique Q in a field of distractor Os), which bear little resemblance to the real-world work of visual inspectors. This lack of conformity challenges the ecological validity of experimental findings; for example, by failing to account for the importance of human memory in visual search strategy and target detection; or by underestimating the complexity of the perceptual environment when designing information displays (Shore and Klein 2000; Burke et al. 2005). In contrast, human factors and industrial engineering researchers who study visual inspection often collect data using study designs that mirror real-world work contexts; for example, observing and evaluating the performance of industrial inspectors as they examine an aircraft for anomalies associated with structural defects (Drury et al. 1997, Hong et al. 2002; Wenner et al. 2003; Drury et al. 2004). Yet developing realistic models of work environments to inform experimental designs that also meet the standards required high experimental validity is both methodologically and conceptually challenging.

2 Field Studies in the Analytic Workplace

Over the past decade, Sandia National Laboratories has expanded capabilities in the study of perception and cognition among professionals whose work predominantly consists of visual search and anomaly detection. As Matzen et al. (2015) point out, studies that examine issues such as variability in search performance using real world stimuli, or the acquisition of search skills among "professional searchers," are surprisingly rare. This is despite the fact that visual anomaly detection is critical for detecting, characterizing, and taking action against a broad range of problems, from evidence of persistent threat activity on corporate information networks, to recognizing evidence of emerging neoplasms in radiological scans. The complex cognitive and perceptual activities of visual search comprise a socially, economically, and even politically critical skill domain that deserves attention, if only to ensure the design of work environments that minimize unnecessary sources of load and stress that could induce error. In addition, studying visual search in context presents new opportunities to appreciate the role of environment and experience in the acquisition, maintenance, and evolution of perceptual and cognitive skill.

Yet developing domain-faithful study designs that allow at least some generalization of research findings is not an easy task. Work domains can be difficult to identify and access, which is not surprising considering how sensitive some of the information may be. In addition, measures of human performance on a visual inspection task may themselves constitute sensitive information for the company or government agency. Thirdly, real-world visual search and analysis workflows tend to be highly idiosyncratic, even when inspection goals are nominally identical. For example, academic, industrial and government institutions in the United States employ many research and analysis teams in which people scan remote sensing imagery for evidence of landcover changes. However, across these institutions, the tools, methods, training, physical environment, and products vary in ways that make comparative studies quite challenging.

To address this gap, we have explored the use of qualitative field methods, particularly ethnographic methods from cultural anthropology, to understand how people accomplish visual search-related work tasks. During the past three years, we have been focusing on imagery analysts who work with SAR image products in a high-pressure, high-throughput national security work environment. Our work was motivated by the need to determine if new electronic image products, interaction models, and graphical representations being developed by our PANTHER counterparts could be effective in helping imagery analysts detect and characterize a greater range of signature types using larger collections of electronic imagery. Doing so required empirical characterization of the existing workflow, including individual strategies for detecting, identifying, and making decisions about the meaning of anomalous artifacts in SAR image products. To ensure that our experimental studies captured relevant elements of the real-world analytic workflow, we invested roughly 18 months of work characterizing the SAR image analysis process; a year of this work was completed before designing and implementing the experimental studies described in Matzen et al. (2015).

2.1 Ethnographic Field Methods: From the Village to the Corporation

Ethnography, literally the "writing of culture", is the hallmark methodology of cultural anthropology. This methodology comprises a number of methods, including participant-observation, interviews, and the collection and documentation of domain-relevant artifacts that inform a holistic account of collective ways of knowing that knit a group of individuals into a socioculturally coherent whole.

At first blush, the relevance of ethnography for design of perceptual and/or cognitive experimental studies may not be obvious. However, since the late 1980s, a number of fields have embraced qualitative research, including approaches associated with ethnography, to address the knowledge gaps associated with quantitative paradigms, including the design of quantitative data collection strategies. This trend is particularly apparent in applied research domains where research findings are being used to influence program, technology, policy, or organizational design decisions. For example, healthcare evaluation researchers now commonly use a blend of quantitative and qualitative methods, both serially and in parallel, when examining how variations in organizational structure, hospital service delivery models, and staff-patient interactions influence health outcomes (Ostlund et al. 2010; see also Bastien 2008).

Arguably, however, the vanguard of mixed-approach methodological innovation is located in the consumer technology industry, where since the late 1980s qualitative inquiry has become core element of design practice. The work of anthropologist Lucy Suchman is often cited as inspiration for the emergence of user-focused design paradigms. As Suchman's work emphasizes, technological artifacts reify tasks and goals in ways that are intended to support or facilitate human enactment of those activities (Suchman 1987). Ball and Ormerod (2000) locate Suchman's theories of artifacts in the earlier work of psychologist Herbert Simon, who described the design of physical artifacts as the archetypical externalization of human cognitive work and problem-solving. When people are creating artifacts for themselves, the reification of tasks, processes and goals is a relatively straightforward matter: we are creating things that meet needs we understand intimately and implicitly. However, technology designers often work at a distance from the activities they intend to influence. This distance puts them at a disadvantage when it comes to creating artifacts that are "ready to hand," to use Martin Heidegger's phrase (Macaulay et al. 2000).

Ethnographic field methods, which emphasize close attention to the particularities of human practice in place – that is, in historically, organizationally, and geographically bounded contexts - are widely understood to offer a framework that can help designers gain insight into the implicit characteristics of the human activity they seek to influence. But what research practices constitute "ethnography," and how they are properly exercised, has long been a matter of methodological debate within anthropology. These days, ethnographic practice is also an active topic of debate among practitioners who are extending anthropology's theory and methods beyond the discipline's traditional focus on the social life of the non-Western others.

Ethnography can feel like a frustratingly open-ended, perhaps unending process of iterative observation, note-taking, memo-writing, and qualitative coding, punctuated by rounds of semi-structured interviews with domain natives. Cultural anthropologists are trained to engage in long periods (typically a one-year cycle of activity) of inductive, iterative exploration and documentation within a community. Deep engagement with the lived experience and subjective accounts of field interlocutors enable the anthropologist to identify critical events, issues and topics. However, this relatively open ended commitment to data collection does not translate well to the project-and-product oriented organizational culture of Western industrial and government work environments. Applied, collaborative research typically requires the anthropologist/fieldworker to provide team members with regular data and information projects to inform other project activities, such as experimental data collection.

At Sandia, to ensure that our ethnographic techniques yield relevant and timely observations about the work environment under study, our team structures observational activities using elements from two well-documented methodological frameworks, namely *Cognitive Work Analysis* (CWA) and *Cognitive Task Analysis* (CTA). We discuss each of these below, specifying how we have incorporated elements of both CWA and CTA into the planning, implementation and documentation of observational research in high-throughput work domains. Before doing so, however, we provide a brief overview of the SAR technologies so the reader can appreciate the challenges of studying visual cognition in this domain.

3   Synthetic Aperture Radar and Imagery Analysis

Synthetic Aperture Radar, or SAR, is a type of active remote sensing that uses pulses of energy to create complex, two-dimensional electronic images of a scene. Because SAR is an active sensing system – i.e., the radar provides its own source of illumination – SAR systems complement established passive sensing systems, such as those operating in the near-infrared or optical range of the electromagnetic spectrum. SAR is excellent for generating broad-area, high-resolution images of terrain features under a wide range of weather conditions. They are also highly sensitive to changes in terrain features and can be used to generate detailed information about trends and events associated with weather, animal, or human activity (more information on SAR systems is available at Sandia National Laboratories' public website on SAR systems, www.sandia.gov/radar/what_is_sar/index.html). SAR images are formed using sophisticated image formation algorithms that extract and represent different types of information in electronic format, usually on high-resolution optical displays, for human inspection.

Although SAR technologies are among the most sophisticated of today's electronic imaging systems, analysis of SAR imagery still relies heavily on human perceptual and cognitive engagement to detect, recognize and characterize signatures of interest in rendered scenes. Organizations that use SAR imagery in their work typically employ teams of SAR analysts who are specially trained to read SAR image products, which have unique visual artifacts due to the way that SAR systems are configured and flown. At first glance, SAR imagery looks a lot like a black-and-white optical photograph, but closer inspection will reveal (among other things) oddities in spatial relationships and dark shadows that may seem to be cast by the sun, but are actually aligned with the position of the radar.

Understanding how SAR imagery analysts become skilled in reading and interpreting these features is important if projects such as PANTHER are to augment human visual skill with automated systems that enhance key features while minimizing sources of clutter and noise. What elements should be enhanced, however, depends on the problems that people are actually trying to solve using SAR image products. Even SAR analysts working in the same organization may approach their inspection tasks very differently, depending on the mission and context for which the imagery is being collected. Environmental monitoring, for example, may require an analyst to look for subtle changes in ground elevation using imagery collected over hundreds of square miles of terrain, on a monthly basis. In contrast, an analyst looking for evidence of illicit human or drug trafficking along a contested border in the very same region might search for activity signatures generated on a much shorter timescale, perhaps over a few tens of square miles. To complicate matters, SAR waveforms are data-rich and can be processed into a portfolio of image products that highlight and/or minimize different types of scene features, which are variably useful depending on the analyst's goals.

In summary, SAR imagery analysts have access to wide range of image products that can be accessed in different order and/or resolution to support the detection and characterization of a wide range of mission-relevant information signatures. Factors related to the context of SAR imagery analysis work can therefore introduce a significant source of variability in the design of empirical data collection activities aimed at understanding how SAR professionals learn to navigate the unique, often confusing visual artifacts in SAR imagery.

4 Structuring Ethnography Using Cognitive Work and Task Analysis

Approximately four years ago, a research colleague at Sandia National Laboratories approached our team with a question: could we help her evaluate the usefulness of a new image product for a SAR image analysis task? At the time, our small team consisted of a cognitive neuroscientist, a physicist, and an anthropologist (the author). We had no experience with SAR image products; and although the anthropologist had recently completed a year of field research among professional imagery analysts, the project in question was on a much tighter timeline. We needed to quickly develop familiarity with the technology, the mission space, and the professionals doing the work. To do so, we turned to CWA and CTA for guidance in bootstrapping ourselves to a necessary-and-sufficient understanding of the SAR work domain, and we have been incorporating elements of these frameworks into our research activities ever since.

CWA and CTA are complementary frameworks for studying, respectively, a *domain* of work activity, as well as individual workers' *strategies for accomplishing key tasks* within that domain. CWA has its origins in the ecological approaches to work first articulated by Jens Rasmussen and colleagues in Denmark in the late 1980s, and later elaborated by design researchers including Vicente (1999), Bisantz and Burns (2008) and Naikar (2011). What these practitioners share is an emphasis on holistic study of human problem-solving activities within the constraints of a work domain. These constraints span the material, ideational, purposive, communicative, organizational, and skill/knowledge elements that collectively constitute meaningful activity within the domain. CTA, in contrast, aims at detailing how an individual or team of individuals access and deploy knowledge, skill, and external resources and artifacts to accomplish critical elements of work within the domain under study (Clark and Estes 1996; Crandall et al. 2006). Used together, these frameworks can guide the collection of behavioral data to document individual, team, and organizational approaches to problem-solving in the context under study.

A deeper discussion of the theories, methods, and impact of both CWA and CTA is beyond the scope of this paper. Instead, we are interested in discussing how we adapted elements of these frameworks to inform the design of the visual search studies described in Matzen et al. (2015). In point of fact, application is one of the biggest challenges for both CTA and CWA, whose advocates prescribe implementation with significant rigor and detail. Holism is neither cheap nor easy, and as Naikar has pointed out, even experienced social, cognitive and behavioral scientists can be put off by CWA's conceptual complexity, jargon, detailed representations, and required depth of inquiry. In a very real sense, CWA and CTA are burdened by the very prescriptive detail that ethnography lacks, and therein lies an opportunity: we assert that CWA and CTA frameworks may be selectively applied to bring structure, efficiency, and closure to ethnographic observation.

4.1 A Quick Explanation of Work Domain Analysis

Our field studies over the past four years have examined visual search among SAR imagery analysts working in two different domains. Both groups support similar missions, but each group uses different image display tools, auxiliary sources of data, and relies on different SAR image products in their work. Characterizing both domains was necessary to support PANTHER goals, as the analytic algorithms under development are intended to support the work done in each domain. However, we did not have much time: in total, we spent approximately 18 months doing observational work with workers employed by the SAR mission that we were studying, but we had to provide updated observations to our team counterparts on a monthly basis.

To structure our work, we relied heavily on two of the five core research activities prescribed under CWA: *Work Domain Analysis* and the *Decision Ladder*. In this paper, we focus on Work Domain Analysis, which systematically decomposes work into five interwoven layers of detail, starting with the artifacts that comprise the domain's material resource base and hierarchically linking these *artifacts* through the *processes, functions, values and priority measures*, and *functional purpose of the domain*. Figure One is a conceptual sketch of the hierarchical representation that this line of inquiry creates. The base of the pyramid, Level One, consists of all the artifacts that the domain professionals need to do their work. The top of the pyramid, Level Five, succinctly states the domain's *raison d'etre;* that is, why people created it and what purpose it fulfills in the world. In our experience, these levels are relatively straightforward to elaborate. The middle levels are a bit more challenging to understand, which is why we have labeled them with illustrative questions in Fig. 1, instead of the conceptual labels that CWA texts use.

To motivate explanation of this framework, consider a SAR work domain that we will call "Landcover Change Monitoring," or LCM, whose analysts are responsible for characterizing changes in land cover associated with agricultural activities and weather. We may begin our inquiry by elaborating Level One of the hierarchy by seeking information about the tools, technologies, data, information and other material/information resources used in the work. Good sources for this information include training materials, software documentation, interviews, and observation sessions. As we populate Level One with artifacts, we will be learning how people use these things. This information is represented in Level Two of the hierarchy, which captures the *processes* that rely on Level One's artifacts. Level Two answers the question, "In what activities do people actually use artifacts?" For example, an LCM imagery analyst may have a desktop computer, a display monitor, a mouse, a keyboard, a server connection, image viewing software, and a file of SAR images on her local drive. The hypothetical process "Open this week's SAR images from C:" requires all these artifacts, except the server connection; i.e., her local computer, monitor, mouse,

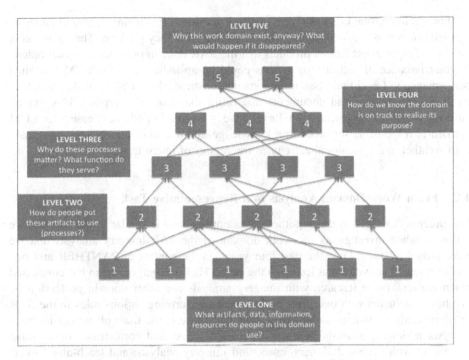

Fig. 1. Simplified nominal work domain analysis hierarchy

keyboard software, and locally stored images are *necessary and sufficient* to perform this process. Thus *artifacts define a process*, while a *process endows artifacts with value*.

In a similar fashion, the *processes* in Level Two are executed in service of the functions comprising Level Three. To elaborate Level Three, we ask, "Why do these processes matter? What purpose do they serve?" In our hypothetical LCM work domain, we might find that the simple process of retrieving images from a local store is one of three processes that our landcover analyst performs as part of the function, "Evaluate recent changes in agricultural activity." Note that the functions of Level Three can be described to a necessary and sufficient approximation in terms of the processes comprising those functions. Similarly, our LCM imagery analyst only performs those processes because they enable her to complete a key function of the domain; *functions endow processes, and therefore artifacts, with value*.

It is between Levels Three and Four that the Work Domain Analysis hierarchy conceptually links the internal activities of the domain – the regular, mundane analysis tasks described above – to the larger world in which the domain is embedded. To wit, Level Four asks the researcher to consider *indicators of the state of the domain with regard to its raison d'etre*. The functions of Level Three generate products, outcomes, knowledge, data, information, communications, etcetera. These products contribute to outward evidence that the domain is working (so to speak) as intended. The nature of this evidence is summarized in Level Four.

For example, our LCM analysts may tell us that, "Evaluating recent changes in agricultural activity" is one of the critical functions that they perform. They generate a number of reports and written products that the SAR domain provides its stakeholders. Regular issuance of high-quality reports could be an indicator of the LCM domain's performance in Level Four. Issuing reports demonstrates that LCM analysts are indeed producing knowledge and documents that fulfill the domain's purpose. This overall purpose would be represented on Level Five – in this hypothetical case, our LCM domain is responsible for producing knowledge about land cover changes associated with weather and agricultural activity in the region of interest.

4.2   From Work Domain Analysis to a Representative Task

The process described in the hypothetical example above is similar to the one that we followed when investigating the work domain of the SAR imagery analysts that we were tasked to study. Over the past four years, in the context of PANTHER and two earlier research activities that led up to the PANTHER project, our team has conducted extensive qualitative research with imagery analysts and other domain professionals. We have interacted with over fifty professionals performing various roles in the SAR imagery analysis domain under study. Our data have come from observing imagery analysts reviewing analysis products for completeness and correctness; open-ended interviews with system designers, users, and imagery analysts; and teach-aloud interviews with imagery analysts in both domains. In addition, we attended the SAR program's introductory classes and practice activities, attended approximately one year's worth of program team meetings, and observed imagery analysts participating in expert/novice paired training sessions in the program's training center.

The prescriptive mapping of CWA's Work Domain Analysis was extremely useful in helping us organize and summarize our research findings into a structured representation of the domain. Importantly, it also provided a starting point for our data collection interactions with the domain's professionals, insofar as we began by asking them for assistance in creating a comprehensive inventory of the software tools, hardcopy/paper resources, electronic databases, and hardware they needed to do their jobs. Most people can understand the need to create an inventory, so this activity was a good icebreaker. Moreover, in the process of identifying an artifact, people often describe how the artifact is used and why it is important – generating information that populates other layers in the CWA hierarchy illustrated in Figure One (Fig. 2).

The process of developing our WDA mapping also enabled us to identify key tasks and the artifacts and processes associated with those, which is very useful in developing a protocol for Cognitive Task to focus on the details of individual strategies for completing a particular element of domain work. In our experience, tasks can be derived from Level Four's functional elaboration of the work domain. The artifacts and processes that support the function should be necessary and sufficient for a knowledgeable domain professional to perform the task. For example, in Figure Two, we have highlighted a function at Level Three, along with the processes and artifacts on Levels Two and One that are required for the function to be performed. Level Four tells us about what the task generates and why it is important for demonstrating domain

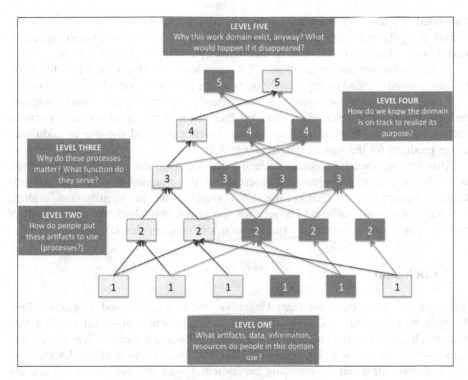

Fig. 2. Task elements extracted from WDA representation

performance. Extracted from the WDA framework, these elements form the basis for a CTA.

4.3   From Cognitive Task Analysis to Experimental Design

Cognitive Task Analysis, which is quite thoroughly described in Crandall et al. (2006), has emerged as a bridge research activity in the conceptualization of more formal experimental data collection. We design our CTA activities using information collected as we are developing the domain representations described above. In our experience, the two activities can be conducted in parallel, as long as there is continuous iterative comparision between the two. In that case, CTA and Work Domain Analysis are complementary, as the former supports validation of the domain description emerging from the latter.

In the case of the SAR imagery analysts we engaged for the PANTHER project, we developed a CTA protocol in which approximately twelve participant analysts reviewed several dozen images for particular classes of objects and signatures, similar to those they seek while on station in the SAR analysis environment. We used screen capture software to record their interactions with the imagery and developed a logging suite that captured which images the analyst was using and some of their interactions with those images (panning, zooming, switching between scenes). Once the analyst had completed the task, we immediately performed a cognitive walk through with the analyst using the video to guide the discussion, using both voice and video capture to record their subjective description of their strategy as they explained it to us.

In reviewing the data from these CTA interviews, we discovered that the SAR imagery analysts tended to rely heavily on two types of imagery made available by the SAR program's image display software. Importantly, this finding somewhat countered the analysis process descriptions that we had documented in interviews, program documentation, and training sessions, all of which prescribed the use of additional image products for the signature detection task.

This finding played a crucial role in the development and implementation of the experimental eye tracking protocol described in the companion paper by our colleagues Matzen et al. (2015): the CTA enabled us to identify the critical, necessary-and-mostly-sufficient imagery for use in a highly abstracted task to collect data for comparing novice and expert search strategies in this domain.

5   Conclusion

Our team has used concepts from Cognitive Work Analysis and Cognitive Task Analysis to inform the collection, analysis, and representation of information that describes human activity in a complex, high-throughput work domain. We suggest that frameworks such as these help researchers balance internal and ecological validity in their experimental designs. Grounding experimental work in qualitative work domain analysis enables researchers to generate data and information that constitute valid input toward the design and evaluation of technologies intended to enhancing key elements of the perceptual and cognitive work of national security imagery analysts.

Acknowledgement. This research was funded under the PANTHER Laboratory Directed Research and Development Project through Sandia National Laboratories' Laboratory Research and Development Program. Sandia National Laboratories is a multiprogram laboratory managed and operated by the Sandia Corporation, a wholly owned subsidiary of the Lockheed Martin Corporation, for the U.S. Department of Energy's National Nuclear Security Administration under contract DE-AC04-94AL85000.

References

Vicente, K.: Cognitive Work Analysis: Toward Safe, Health and Productive Computer-Based Work. Lawrence Earlbaum Associates, Mahwah (1999)

Jian, J.Y., Bisantz, A.M., Drury, C.G.: Foundations for an empirically determined scale of trust in automated systems. Int. J. Cogn. Ergon. 4(1), 53–71 (2000)

Shore, D.I., Klein, R.M.: On the manifestations of memory in visual search. Spat. Vis. 14(1), 59–75 (2000)

Burke, M., Hornof, A., Nilsen, E., Gorman, N.: High-cost banner blindness: Ads increase perceived workload, hinder visual search, and are forgotten. ACM Trans. Comput.-Human Interact. 12(4), 423–445 (2005)

Matzen., L., Haass, M., McNamara, L., Stevens-Adams, S., McMichael, S.: Effects of professional visual search experience on domain-general and domain-specific visual cognition. In: Schmorrow, D.D., Fidopiastis, C.M. (eds.) Human Computer Interaction International. LNCS, vol. 9183, pp. 481–492, Springer, Heidelberg, 2–7 August 2015

Ostlund, U., Kidd, L., Engestrom, Y., Rowa-Dewar, N.: Combining qualitative and quantitative research within mixed method research designs: a methodological review. Int. J. Nurs. Stud. **48**, 369–383 (2010)

Bastien, J.M.C.: Usability testing: a review of some methodological and technical aspects of the method. Int. J. Med. Inform. **79**, e18–e23 (2008)

Suchman, L.: Plans and Situated Actions: The Problem of Human-Machine Communication. Cambridge University Press, New York (1987)

Ball, L.J., Ormerod, T.C.: Putting ethnography to work: the case for a cognitive ethnography of design. Int. J. Hum Comput Stud. **53**, 147–168 (2000)

Macaulay, C., Benyon, D., Crerar, A.: Ethnography, theory and systems design: from intuition to insight. Int. J. Hum Comput Stud. **53**, 35–60 (2000)

Bisantz, A., Burns, C.: Applications of Cognitive Work Analysis. CRC Press, Boca Raton, FL (2008)

Naikar, N.: Cognitive Work Analysis: Foundations, Extensions and Challenges. Defence Science and Technology Organization, Victoria (2011)

Clark, R.E., Estes, F.: Cognitive task analysis. Int. J. Educ. Res. **25**(5), 403–417 (1996)

Crandall, B., Klein, G., Hoffman, R.: Working Minds: A Practitioner's Guide to Cognitive Task Analysis. MIT Press, Cambridge (2006)

Removal of Ocular Artifacts
with the Utilization of Filter Banks

Umut Orhan[1,2(✉)] and Santosh Mathan[1]

[1] Honeywell Laboratories, Redmond, WA, USA
[2] Cortech LLC, Atlanta, GA, USA
umut.orhan@honeywell.com

Abstract. Eye blinks and other ocular artifacts represent a dominant source of EEG signal interference, especially in frontal EEG electrodes. Even though there are several widely accepted methods for the removal eye-blinks, (e.g. linear filtering and ICA), it is still a difficult problem to address when the number of EEG electrodes are limited (as is the case for EEG systems designed for everyday application contexts), and dedicating a subset of these for monitoring eye activity is impractical. In this paper, we propose a novel and general method to eliminate the ocular artifacts based on a combination of filter banks and an eye tracker. This approach offers the promise of making non-intrusive, efficient, and robust ocular artifact detection and correction a tractable prospect.

Keywords: Artifacts · EEG · Ocular · Filter banks · Filtering

1 Introduction

Accurate estimation of mental workload is a capability of considerable theoretical and practical interest. Applications include estimating learning efficiency, assessing cognitive deficiencies, and serving as the basis for adapting human computer interfaces [1,2]. Inferences of cognitive load are typically made by assessing task performance related metrics, behavioral actions and measurement of various physiological signals like eye activity, heart rate or electroencephalography (EEG). EEG, as a measure of ongoing cortical activity, offers the prospect of direct, quantitative assessment of workload. However these signals can be compromised by artifacts and interferences, consequently decreasing the robustness and reliability of the estimation of the cognitive state. In particular, cognitive tasks requiring eye movements increase the likelihood of ocular artifacts. Eye blinks constitute one of the most prominent artifact sources due to their relatively large amplitude in EEG compared to the neural activity. Even though the removal of ocular artifacts has been widely addressed [3–7], effective filtering when only a low number of EEG electrodes are available, and when a dedicated electrooculogram (EOG) impractical, is still an important and interesting problem.

In this paper, we address the problem of the correction of ocular artifacts in EEG using filter banks, with the joint utilization of an eye tracker as the

© Springer International Publishing Switzerland 2015
D.D. Schmorrow and C.M. Fidopiastis (Eds.): AC 2015, LNAI 9183, pp. 504–513, 2015.
DOI: 10.1007/978-3-319-20816-9_48

basis for accurate and robust correction of eye artifacts. Reliance on a combination of EEG, and eye tracker data requires an additional consideration of the synchronization of the signals, which is typically underestimated or ignored in the literature. Therefore, we first illustrate the importance of the signal synchronization and demonstrate a procedure to achieve event matching and signal resampling. Consequently, we introduce a filter bank based artifact removal, which is the main novelty of this paper. Even though the proposed methodology is specifically designed for the removal of (EOG) artifacts, these methods are generalizable to other artifact sources with sufficient ease.

2   Methods

2.1   Signal Synchronization

For the joint utilization of two or more independently recorded discrete signal sources, it is imperative to synchronize the corresponding sample times. This importance is primarily a consequence of the slight differences between actual sampling rates and nominal sampling rates. These small discrepencies stem from the practicality of the recording hardware or rounded reporting of the nominal sampling rates. For example, the characteristics of oscillators used for analog to digital conversion in most recording equipment depends on temperature, causing slight deviations from the tuning frequency. Even the slightest difference between the nominal and actual sampling rates might become relatively significant over the span of minutes. To illustrate this phenomenon, let T, f_n and f_s be the recording duration, nominal sampling rate and actual sampling rate, respectively. Corresponding time difference introduced at the end of the recording due to the sampling rate difference becomes,

$$\Delta t = T \left| 1 - \frac{f_s}{f_n} \right|.$$

For $T = 20\,\text{min}$, $f_s = 59.99\,\text{Hz}$ and $f_n = 60\,\text{Hz}$, Δt becomes $200\,\text{ms}$, which might be extremely significant for a psychological experiment or for time-locked EEG analysis. Additionally, some of the recording equipment might contain discontinuities due to data losses or exclusions, which contributes further to signal synchronization problems. For example, an eye tracker may stop recording after prolonged durations of looking away.

Event Matching. Event synchronization between the recording equipments can be addressed by utilization of shared hardware triggers. The experimental stimulus or task computer may send simultaneous trigger events to all devices. To align the independently recorded triggers, common event sequences may be matched iteratively, starting from the longest one and removing the matched event sequences. This longest event sequence matching may be solved by the longest common substring problem [8,9], which can be solved in linear time.

Such an event matching approach is only applicable when the event triggers do not contain many repeated sequences.

Following is a high-level operational overview of the simple event matching algorithm, which separates events to blocks according to the matching of the event sequences. Let $e_{k,m}, n_{k,m}$ represent the event label and position pair corresponding to m^{th} event for recording device k,

1. For block v, starting from $v = 0$
2. Find the longest common sequence $s_{v,0}, s_{v,1}, s_{v,2}, \cdots, s_{v,L_v-1}$ over the event labels, where $s_{v,0}$ corresponds to the event pair of $e_{k,m_{k,v}}, n_{k,m_{k,v}}$ for each device k.
3. Remove the event sequence block from the event sequences corresponding to each device.
4. $v = v + 1$

It is worthwhile to note that if there are no event or data losses, the longest common sequence would correspond to the sequence of all the events.

Resampling. Bringing signals to a common sampling rate might be necessary for some signal processing applications. In particular, most adaptive filtering algorithms, e.g. least mean squares (LMS), recursive least squares (RLS) [10], typically expect signals to have identical sampling rates. Even though sample-rate conversion is well-known in discrete time signal processing [11,12], the consideration of the variations from the nominal sampling rates, as indicated in Sect. 2.1, requires additional consideration for their match. Changing the sampling rate by a rational factor, $R = \frac{L}{M}$, may be achieved using the system depicted in Fig. 1, where $\uparrow K$ and $\downarrow K$ represents upsampling and downsampling by a factor of K, respectively.

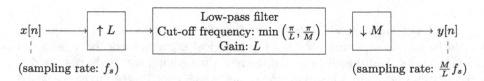

Fig. 1. The system for changing the sampling rate by a factor of $R = \frac{L}{M}$

One of the recording devices is designated as the master device for the purpose of resampling. Correspondingly, a rational common sampling rate is selected relative to the nominal sampling rate of the master device.

For the sake of simplicity, let device 0 be selected as the master device with $f_{n,0}$ as the corresponding nominal sampling rate, and f_c be the common target nominal sampling rate. Subsequently, the sampling rate of device k relative to the master device in block v may be estimated utilizing the matched events according to

$$Rf_{k,v} = \frac{n_{k,m_{k,v}+L_v-1} - n_{k,m_{k,v}}}{n_{0,m_{0,v}+L_v-1} - n_{0,m_{0,v}}}.$$ (1)

Consequently, the corresponding resampling rate becomes,

$$R_{k,v} = Rf_{k,v} \times \frac{f_c}{f_{n,0}}.$$ (2)

Accordingly, the signals from device k are resampled by a factor of $R_{k,v}$ for block v (using the resampling system depicted in Fig. 1) to obtain signals synchronized across devices with a nominal sampling rate of f_c. In the following sections, the signals are going to be assumed to have been synchronized.

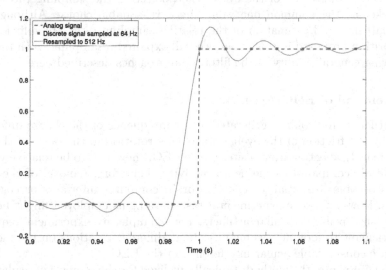

Fig. 2. A demonstration of the ambiguity of the high frequency components. An analog step signal, discrete signal obtained by sampling at 64 Hz and resampled signal obtained by resampling the discrete signal to 512 Hz are all equal at the sampling points.

It is worth noting that the signal synchronization process depicted in this section might have some limitations depending on the content of the signals and events. Expectedly, decreasing the sampling rate would cause high frequency components to be lost. Therefore, if there are signals of interest at high frequencies relative to the corresponding Nyquist rate, the nominal common sampling rate should be set to be sufficiently high. As further consideration, discrete signals do not contain any additional information on their analog counterparts. Typically an anti-aliasing filter is applied prior to analog-to-digital conversion, removing the high frequency components in the analog signal enabling a perfect reconstruction. However, in some contexts, the analog signal might be discontinuous, e.g. step function, correspondingly the resampled signal would be distorted, since signal is assumed to have zero power beyond the Nyquist frequency. An example of this phenomenon is given in Fig. 2. If this is not the intended behavior for the signals from one of the recording devices, common sampling rate may be selected to be equal to the nominal sampling rate of the corresponding recording device to prevent resampling. Alternatively, if there is more than one such pieces of recording equipment, a specialized resampling method utilizing additional information on the nature of the analog counterpart may be implemented to mitigate the ambiguity of the content beyond the Nyquist frequency.

For the joint utilization of EEG and eye-tracker, the discontinuity mentioned above becomes a matter of concern. When the eye is closed, e.g. during eye blinks, the gaze position or the pupil diameter become untracked for a brief duration. Consequently, the signal is expected to be discontinuous at the time of eye closure or opening. Therefore if the signal of interest in the EEG is negligible beyond the Nyquist rate of the eye tracker, selecting the sampling rate of the eye tracker as the common one would be a reasonable choice. Although the event matching and estimation of the relative sampling rates are sufficient for the algorithm proposed in this paper, we still explored resampling, with the goal of fostering generalizability of the filtering approaches described here.

2.2   Removal of EOG Artifacts

EOG artifacts are typically generated as a consequence of the charge difference caused by the friction of the eyeball during its rotation in the orbit of the eye. Predominantly affecting frontal sites in the EEG, they tend to be relatively large in amplitude compared to the neural activity. Therefore, removal of the EOG artifacts becomes essential for effective brain computer interfaces or cognitive analyses. However, some experimental task paradigms employed might be particularly susceptible to ocular artifacts. For example, an experiment requiring the participant to look at flashing objects at different positions on the monitor may cause considerable ocular interference in the EEG.

In the literature, the methods typically utilized for the removal of ocular artifacts are band-pass filtering, independent component analysis (ICA), principal component analysis (PCA), linear regression and adaptive filtering [4]. These approaches have limitations. For example, since most ocular artifacts tend to be in the lower frequencies, applying a high pass filter may be a useful approach for filtering out artifacts with low impact on the broader EEG spectrum. The main limitation of such a filtering approach is that it is relatively coarse, introducing the possibility of filtering our cortical signals, and leaving residual artifact activity. ICA has been used as a filtering approach as a response to shortcomings associated with high pass filters. Even though ICA or other blind source separation methods are usually effective on identifying eye blinks as an independent source in the EEG without requiring any EOG electrodes or any other external source of indicators, they typically require a high number of EEG channels and manual identification of the interference sources. Moreover, the assumptions of independence and non-Gaussianity in ICA might possibly conflict with the signals of interest or need a substantially large amount of data to be able to identify the sources [5]. PCA based approaches to artifact corrections have limitations as well. In its characteristic application, PCA maps EEG channels to spatially uncorrelated components. Therefore, PCA inevitably fails to preserve signals of interest occurring in frontal lobes. Linear regression analysis, another commonly used approach to artifact reduction, is typically applied either assuming a proportional propagation of eye activity (measured using EOG sensors placed close to the eye) to EEG channels or matching pre-built templates representing the form of eye blinks. However the variations in the eyeblink shape and possibility of nonlinear progression of eye blinks through scalp limits the effectiveness of regression approaches. Moreover, EOG sensors also pick up neurological activity from frontal lobe. Finally, linear adaptive filters are typically applied with the cost function of minimization of EEG activity, causing possible removal of signal of interest. Additionally, most of the limitations noted for linear regression also apply to linear adaptive filtering.

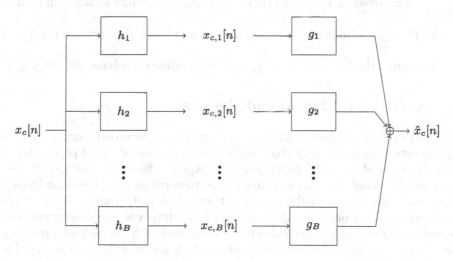

Fig. 3. The representation of filter bank analysis and synthesis. h_b and g_b represent the FIR filter to extract b^{th} frequency sub-band and the corresponding perfect reconstruction filter, respectively.

In this paper, we describe an alternative approach for artifact removal utilizing filter banks and a gating mechanism. Filter banks are an array of filters designed to decompose the signal into different components [12–14]. Although it is possible to utilize the filter banks with various types of systems, each bank is an FIR filter decomposing the signal into frequency sub-bands in the typical application, e.g. graphical equalizers. With a careful consideration on the design of the decomposition and reconstruction filters, it is possible to achieve perfect reconstruction [15]. Correspondingly, we decompose each EEG channel, $x_c[n]$ to their frequency sub-bands using filter banks with the perfect reconstruction property as in Fig. 3. As a special selection of such filters, we select h_1 to correspond to a low pass filter designed in the least square sense [16] and h_b to correspond to frequency shifts of h_1.

Following the decomposition (analysis) step of the filter bank, $x_{c,b}[n]$ representing the EEG component for channel c and frequency sub-band b is obtained. Using an independent measure of artifact contamination, the temporal sections of artifacts are identified. In this paper, artifact indicator signal corresponds to eye blinks detected from an eye tracker. In non-contaminated sections, the statistics for each channel and band are learned, and in contaminated sections, the samples outside the tolerance interval of the learned statistics are removed.

The learning procedure for a single sub-band is as the following, where $o[n]$ represents a binary signal indicating the existence of artifacts:

1. Decompose each EEG channel into frequency sub-bands with a filter bank
2. $\forall$ sub-band signal $x_{c,b}[n]$ for channel c and band b and $\forall n$
   (a) If $o[n] = 0$, indicating non-contamination by artifacts, use $x_{c,b}[n]$ to estimate second order statistics of the corresponding channel and band, $\sigma_{c,b}$.
   (b) If $o[n] = 1$, indicating contamination, and $|x_{c,b}[n]| > \tau\sigma_{c,b}$, set $x_{c,b} = 0$ ($\tau = 3$)
3. Reconstruct the EEG channels, $\hat{x}_c[n]$, from modified sub-band signals, $x_{c,b}[n]$

3   Experimental Setup and Results

EEG and eye-tracker data utilized in this paper were recorded from a series of experiments designed to vary cognitive load during a set of visual psychological tasks. For most of the tasks, participants are expected to direct their gaze to various spatial elements in order to match colors, perform an n-back task and follow directional cues. Correspondingly, the nature of the tasks require frequent eye movements causing ocular artifacts in the EEG. Moreover, the most prominent components of neurophysiological activity associated with the task manipulation is expected to occur in the prefrontal cortex, which is one of the most susceptible regions to ocular artifacts.

During the sessions, EEG is acquired from a 64 channel Biosemi ActiveTwo system with the sampling rate of 256 Hz. Concurrently, pupil diameter, horizontal and vertical eye positions are recorded using an ASL EYE-TRAC 6 Series eye tracker (sampling rate: 120 Hz). Event triggers are sent to both devices through parallel port. Following an application of a linear phase high pass filter (cut-off: 1 Hz, length: 480) on the EEG to remove the low frequency drifts, the signals are synchronized and resampled to 120 Hz (sampling rate of the eye tracker). Eye tracker signals contain discontinuities due to the loss of tracking during the closure of eyes, and the selection of 120 Hz as the common sampling rate prevents distortions in the signals caused by the antialiasing filters in the resampling operation.

Using the vertical eye position from the eye tracker, eye blinks are detected via a simple thresholding on the vertical speed. A filter bank, consisting of 30 FIR filters (length 480) with 4 Hz intervals, is designed with the perfect reconstruction property. Consequently, each EEG channel is passed through the filter bank and ocular artifacts are removed utilizing the proposed algorithm. Examples of the artifact removal for channel Fp1 are given in Fig. 4.

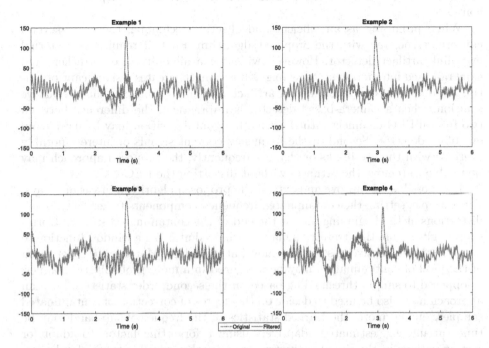

Fig. 4. Examples of artifact removal for Fp1. Proposed algorithm was also successful on effectively eliminating ocular artifacts with sporadic waveforms as in Example 4.

4 Discussion

In this paper, we demonstrated a novel methodology to filter ocular artifacts from EEG. Our approach employed filter banks in conjunction with an eye tracker based eye activity detector. The frequency sub-bands which change significantly compared to typical signal levels are removed from the temporal sections detected to be contaminated. Even though we have focused on the eye blinks in this paper, a similar methodology is applicable for other artifact sources or detectors with minor changes to this approach. For example, an accelerometer based detector may be used to remove artifacts caused by extraneous movements, or a dedicated EOG channel may be utilized for ocular artifacts. However, if different pieces of recording equipment are used as artifact detectors, a signal synchronization step, as described in Sect. 2.1, becomes imperative for alignment with EEG signals.

One of the advantages of the artifact filtering algorithm presented in this paper is that it works with a very low number of EEG channels. EEG systems with a small number of electrodes are becoming increasingly popular, as researchers begin to apply EEG-based solutions in a variety of practical tasks contexts.

While promising as an efficient and effective technique, there are several concerns associated with the proposed algorithm. First, it requires an external eye blink/artifact detector. However, widening availability of eye trackers and camera-based interaction systems (e.g. Xbox Kinect) creates a significant potential for detection of eye blink and artifact inducing events. As an alternative solution, when a camera-based detector is impractical, the difference between two frontal EEG channels with the same horizontal position may be used as an eye blink detector. Second, if the frequency content signals of interest notably overlaps with the eye blinks or changes frequently, the proposed approach may be unable to remove the artifacts without distorting the EEG.

It is possible to improve and extend the proposed algorithm in various ways. For example, setting the contaminated frequency components to zero introduces distortions at the beginning and at the end of the contaminated section. Correspondingly, a smoother transition may be achieved utilizing a window function to decrease the aggressiveness of the removal at the edges. Moreover, the detection of the level of contamination may be measured in a more probabilistic manner, as opposed to simply thresholding based on the second order statistics. Such an approach may also be used to decide on the degree of correction of contaminated samples. Furthermore, the learned statistics of the frequency sub-band may be time variant, e.g. estimated adaptively using a forgetting factor, to adapt for slow variations in the signal characteristics. Another possible track of enhancement is to utilize filter banks in a multidimensional manner with multiple EEG channels.

References

1. Mathan, S., Smart, A., Ververs, T., Feuerstein, M.: Towards an index of cognitive efficacy. In: Engineering in Medicine and Biology (2010)
2. Turner, G.R., Levine, B.: Augmented neural activity during executive control processing following diffuse axonal injury. Neurology **71**(11), 812–818 (2008)
3. Quinn, M., Mathan, S., Pavel, M.: Removal of ocular artifacts from EEG using learned templates. In: Schmorrow, D.D., Fidopiastis, C.M. (eds.) AC 2013. LNCS, vol. 8027, pp. 371–380. Springer, Heidelberg (2013)
4. Fatourechi, M., Bashashati, A., Ward, R.K., Birch, G.E.: Emg and eog artifacts in brain computer interface systems: a survey. Clin. Neurophysiol. **118**(3), 480–494 (2007)
5. Jung, T.P., Makeig, S., Westerfield, M., Townsend, J., Courchesne, E., Sejnowski, T.J.: Removal of eye activity artifacts from visual event-related potentials in normal and clinical subjects. Clin. Neurophysiol. **111**(10), 1745–1758 (2000)
6. Croft, R., Barry, R.: Removal of ocular artifact from the eeg: a review. Neurophysiol. Clin./Clin. Neurophysiol. **30**(1), 5–19 (2000)

7. Castellanos, N.P., Makarov, V.A.: Recovering eeg brain signals: artifact suppression with wavelet enhanced independent component analysis. J. Neurosci. Methods **158**(2), 300–312 (2006)
8. Gusfield, D.: Algorithms on Strings, Trees and Sequences: Computer Science and Computational Biology. Cambridge University Press, Cambridge (1997)
9. Hirschberg, D.S.: A linear space algorithm for computing maximal common subsequences. Commun. ACM **18**(6), 341–343 (1975)
10. Haykin, S.: Adaptive Filter Theory. Prentice-Hall Information and System Sciences Series. Prentice Hall, Upper Saddle River (2002)
11. Oppenheim, A., Schafer, R., Buck, J.: Discrete-Time Signal Processing. Prentice Hall International Editions. Prentice Hall, Upper Saddle River (1999)
12. Crochiere, R., Rabiner, L.: Multirate Digital Signal Processing. Prentice-Hall Signal Processing Series Advanced monographs. Prentice-Hall, Upper Saddle River (1983)
13. Cristi, R.: Modern Digital Signal Processing. Thomson/Brooks/Cole, Pacific Grove (2004)
14. Cvetkovic, Z., Vetterli, M.: Oversampled filter banks. IEEE Trans. Signal Process. **46**(5), 1245–1255 (1998)
15. Vetterli, M.: Filter banks allowing perfect reconstruction. Signal Process. **10**(3), 219–244 (1986)
16. Lim, J., Oppenheim, A.: Advanced Topics in Signal Processing. Prentice-Hall Signal Processing Series. Prentice-Hall, Upper Saddle River (1988)

The Quantified Self

Celementina R. Russo(⊠)

AnthroTronix Inc., Silver Spring, USA
crusso@atinc.com

Abstract. Over the course of this decade, both mobile devices and mobile device applications designed for the express purpose of tracking physiological and cognitive performance metrics are nearly ubiquitous in our everyday endeavors. Though the idea of tracking our own various daily metrics is nothing new, the advent of technological innovations that carry the capacity to store, sort and share these ever-accruing amounts of data presents to us unchartered territory regarding our relationship to and understanding and interpretation of these metrics both singularly (as snapshots) and in the aggregate (over time). This work explores the form and function of the Quantified Self Movement. It discusses the current state of analyzing and interpreting information accrued from various metrics, specifically the issues that arise in synchronizing heterogeneous metrics, and in the context of an AugCog framework, proposes a method of approach to analyze multivariate data by curation based on the simultaneity of measured events.

1 The Concept of Self-Quantification

First coined in 2007 by the editors of Wired, "The Quantified Self" is a movement that by 2012 had accrued countless online social networking forums and more than 70 meetup groups worldwide. Though the notion of self-tracking information may arguably pre-date history, in our modern era the sheer quantity of available metrics to track, continuously, is unparalleled. Benjamin Franklin famously recorded his "13 Virtues" in a daily journal, Buckminster Fuller maintained a diary of his daily life and ideas in which he referred to himself as, "Guinea Pig B," but not until Stephen Wolfram recently stated that, "[o]ne day I'm sure everyone will routinely collect all sorts of data about themselves," (as does he on his own self) has it become apparent that the level of self-tracking various and heterogeneous information has reached near-ubiquity.

With the advent of wearable technologies that possess the ability to communicate, we have the capability of not only recording our information but of transmitting it to: linked devices and cloud databases as well as social networks and other interested parties. Biosensing applications are one of the largest arenas for growth with regard to the Internet of Things [19], and expounding upon the IoT concept, Wolfram Research is now developing algorithms for linking and analyzing multiply tracked physiological metrics for the creation of wholistic diagnostics and assessments for healthcare applications [22].

© Springer International Publishing Switzerland 2015
D.D. Schmorrow and C.M. Fidopiastis (Eds.): AC 2015, LNAI 9183, pp. 514–520, 2015.
DOI: 10.1007/978-3-319-20816-9_49

A previous work described a method approach to instantiate a ubiquitous AugCog framework, specifically one that addresses: how to meaningfully interpret combined objective and subjective metrics (e.g., physiological data and mood), how to efficiently and intelligently utilize heterogeneous measurements made in real-time and over time, and how to determine the limits of cognitive load to assist in the delegation of task work functions in human-computer interactions [18]. With regard to commercially obtainable devices, this work discusses the current state of the Quantified Self movement for both personal and research applications, and proposes the instantiation of the Quantified Self in an AugCog framework.

2   Quantification: Have Device, Will Take Data

2.1   The Quantified Persona

With wearable technologies, the movement of the Quantified Self is purposed for the measurement of all aspects of daily life. Recent polls show that 45 % of US adults manage at least 1 chronic condition, and 69 % of US adults track at least one health indicator either for themselves or for someone else [3]. Of those managing two or more chronic conditions, 56 % say that self-tracking has affected their overall approach to maintaining their health status [3].

On a wearable or mobile device platform, some common daily metrics to track may be blood pressure, heart rate, hours slept and to some degree by actigraphy, *quality* of sleep; dietary and caloric intake, and the number of steps walked (or run); for example, the iPhone 6 and the Galaxy S5 each carry a suite of health-tracking apps, and the panoply of wearables such as the Fitbit, Jawbone Up, and Nike Fuelband all utilize similar sensors that result with similar metrics. Though the variables measured are essentially the same, each device platform implements its own unique calculation algorithm, and each platform plus each embedded sensor array carry their own set of latency and measurement error parameters. None of these parameters are described to the consumer such that the consumer is left with a deficient understanding of how to interpret a measurement within realistic error bounds and specificity. A recent BBC investigative report lamented the measurement discrepancy betwixt each of four popular trackers, the response to which by a developer of one of the four in question underlined that there is both a communication gap between the manufacturer and the consumer as well as an inherent misunderstanding on the part of the consumer in terms of how to best utilize the technology and interpret the resulting data [6].

The resulting data itself presents what is heretofore referred to as *The Quantified Conundrum*. Tracking multiple variables that each likely relate to only singular applications presents a quandary: how does one visualize the time-aggregated and time-specific data from one application, let alone across multiple applications and/or devices? And, perhaps more importantly in the context of commercial devices, who owns the data that's been collected? A community of biohackers are beginning to answer these questions, for both ordinary and medical devices. For example, FluxStream is an open-source framework with many

APIs available to visualize personal data across different applications, the code for which is freely posted on GitHub [20]. Though it seems the obvious solution, an app to manage and visualize data from various devices and applications is a nontrivial idea: a consumer actually has little to no control over the storage and usage of the data accrued on and across apps, devices and services, and though a multitude of developers have attempted to alleviate this problem, not many have succeeded. As of the time of this manuscript, there is still no one-stop-shop app for aggregating and visualizing the myriad metrics a consumer may collect on his or herself, but a laundry list of both live and now-defunct apps and APIs is available on a blog popular to Quantified Selfers, called LifeStream [7].

The concept of The Quantified Conundrum is thrust into deeper and darker waters in the context of mobile medical devices. Type 1 diabetics must monitor their blood sugar frequently through the course of the day, and for a parent of a diabetic child, that once meant round-the-clock testing, during both waking and resting hours (nighttime hypoglycemia is a serious problem for Type 1 adolescents). With the advent of the Continuous Glucose Monitor (CGM), a hair-width sensor placed under the skin logs and reports blood sugar levels every few minutes, via a short-range connection to an external monitor. Should the levels plummet somewhere perilous, the monitor sounds an alarm. This technology was revolutionary in 2012, but owing to the short-range connection, the external monitor had to be within 100 ft of the patient such that outside of resting hours, this technological solution became less useful for a primary caregiver.

When managing the logistics of this monitor became another job, one tech-savvy parent of a diabetic child coded an Android app that allowed him to monitor from afar on his mobile phone his child's CGM data that had been subsequently transmitted to the cloud. After the app had proven to work, he tweeted a screenshot of the CGM results and other frustrated, medical device owning, biohacking parents, patients, and caregivers followed suit as comrades-in-arms (included in this proclaimed "revolution" was the very real development of a bionic pancreas) [2]. Interestingly, the response to this revolution came from the manufacturer of that particular CGM, in the form of an FDA cleared (January, 2015) docking station that transmits a patient's CGM data via bluetooth to up to five telephones residing anywhere in the world [8]. Though this new product is a fortuitous uprgrade from the original setup, the new design implies that while the data should be easily shared amongst guardian/caregiving parties, it is still ultimately owned by the manufacturer and not by the data provider.

2.2   The Quantified Task Force

Relating together physiological and cognitive informatics has been of interest across research communities to assess, for example: the neurocognitive and physiological interplay in human sexuality, [24,25], the dynamics of human cognition in psychosomatic and interoceptive processes [16,21,23,26], and cognitive load resulting from delegated tasks in complex operational environments [4,14,17]. Though the results of such measurements are intended for different purposes, the metrics themselves are similar if not identical and when the level of complexity in assessment increases, the same resulting data problems arise, irrespective of origin.

The appropriate synchronization and combination of time-sensitive physiological and cognitive measurements requires a well-executed experimental design and a subsequent visualization scheme for analyzing the data that may potentially also include with it observational meta-data recorded over the course of the experiment; this is an inherently difficult task. Within complex operational environments, the capability to assess cognitive workload is imperative to an efficient and successful outcome of the operation but is often logistically problematic to conduct. In a paper from 2003, Gevins and Smith stated that, "perhaps the most basic issue in the study of cognitive workload is the problem of how to measure it," [4]. Electroencephalogram (EEG), functional near-infrared (fNIR), electrocardiogram (ECG), electrooculogram (EOG), skin conductance, plethysmography, heart rate variability, eye-tracking, pressure sensing and haptic feedback are some of the many various measures commonly acquired in cognitive workload research, though a systematic approach to interpreting these data in concert has yet to be developed.

A performer on DARPA's AugCog program described in 2002 a method to define an Index of Cognitive Activity with eye-tracking measurements, but when eye-tracking was combined with EEG there was no immediately understandable way to relate the two, and it was acknowledged that the study design should be simplified in order to unveil a discernible relationship between them [9]. The intended purpose of AugCog was to, "develop technologies to mitigate sensory or cognitive overload and restore operational effectiveness by extending the information management capacity of the warfighter," and over the course of the program various methods were developed to corroborate heterogeneous physiological metrics, such as eye tracking, skin conductance, and blood flow [5], but combining these with cognitive assessment via EEG or fNIR presented engineering obstacles then and continues to do so now [1]. While progress has been made on the fronts of dry-use EEG monitors [13] and compact arrays of singular physiological sensors as well as combined cognitive and physiological sensors [12,15], there still remain technological and analytical grounds to break. With no packaged, single-solution sensor suite and no patented synchronization algorithm, we thus find ourselves immersed in another layer of The Quantified Conundrum.

3 Conundrum: Have Data, Will Infer Meaning

Whether the data-gathering expedition originated from either a commercial or research prospectus, the data-gatherer is ultimately directed towards data analysis. In both cases, there is prolific difficulty in the foundational matching of various metrics in time and sampling frequency in a manner that will foster meaningfully sensical results. The difficulties partly reside in the fact that these metrics are separately recorded, but moreover, such issues are also products of the magnitude of data processing that frequently occurs at the level of either the device or the application interface. With little to no control over the basic parameters of the measurements to be made, the subsequent interpretation of the results may be cursory only, owing to the lack of available analytical details. For example, because the calculating algorithms of and the error bounds on the measurements are both unknown in commercial health trackers, the tracked data can be only be meaningfully interpreted by changes in trends. Similarly problematic with research tools, the investigator is largely limited by the level of processing imposed upon the data before it is output or reported. Of greater importance are both the underlying intention set to collect the information as well as an a priori understanding of the various measurements individually, i.e., if different measurements result in redundancy, is the redundancy itself intentional, perhaps to speak ground truth against comparative measurands, or is it not intentional, in which case what version of the measurement provides the best option?

In an AugCog framework, we consider intentionally curated information to divulge relationships between measured factors such that those relationships exhibit a profile of the experimental state, in time. In particular, any one given measurement may vary with any number of stimuli, and some variables may be interdependently linked such that the relationships betwixt them are not obvious until the confounding factors are removed. For example, heart rate variability may temporally increase with every other cognitive and physiological metric and thus to remove the effects on other variables driven by heart rate variability, we normalize each by heart rate variability to find potential second-order effects. Second order effects may elucidate response characteristics that are unique to particular stressors, whether environmental or internal in origin, but are only discovered in the analysis post-process.

With respect to data from self-tracking devices, an instantiated AugCog method approach could entail importing multiple variables into an API that aggregates data across various platforms and visualizes the variables in a time series analysis to determine with what factors the variables dynamically change. In a complex operational environment, the challenge is to determine what suite of sensors delivers the most relevant combination of information while minimally encumbering the humans-in-the-loop. For example, sopite syndrome is a complex that arises from exposure to real or apparent motion, defined by a number of nonspecific symptoms such as yawning and skin pallor without nauseagenic stimulus, and that results in a reduced ability to focus on an assigned task [10,11], and hence, the human subject experiencing the distress is already physically and cognitively taxed such that surpassing a critical number of sensors in the array could prove to be analytically superfluous at best and deleterious at worst. In both cases, the garnered understanding of the first and second-order relationships between various metrics gives rise to a further understanding of how to approach the development of learning algorithms that could provide real-time predictions of events that may be informative of impending physiological and/or cognitive distress. This type of information is exceptional and unique to our modern, quantifying era, and as such it is ultimately important to concerned parties, whether self-trackers, caregivers and medical providers, or assignment-delegating computers and thus worthy of future work and inquiry.

References

1. Cummings, M.: Technology impedances to augmented cognition. Ergonomics in Design (Views & Provocations), 25–27 (2010)
2. Hurley, D.: Wired: Diabetes patients are hacking their way toward a bionic pancreas (2014). http://www.wired.com/2014/12/diabetes-patients-hacking-together-diy-bionic-pancreases/
3. Fox, S., Duggan, M.: Tracking for health (2013). http://www.pewinternet.org/2013/01/28/tracking-for-health/
4. Gevins, A., Smith, M.: Neurophysiological measures of cognitive workload during human-computer interaction. Theor. Issues in Ergon. Sci. **4**, 113–131 (2003)
5. Ikehara, C., Crosby, M.: Assessing cognitive load with physiological sensors. In: Proceedings of the 38th Hawaii International Conference on System Sciences - 2005 (2005)
6. Lewington, L.: BBC: Why activity trackers deliver mismatched fitness data (2015). http://www.bbc.com/news/technology-31113602
7. Life Stream (2013). http://lifestreamblog.com/lifelogging
8. Hoskins, M.: Healthline: newsflash: Dexcom SHARE gets FDA clearance! (2015). http://www.healthline.com/diabetesmine/newsflash-dexcom-share-gets-fda-clearance/
9. Marshall, S.P.: The index of cognitive activity: measuring cognitive workload. In: IEEE 7 Human Factors Meeting, Scottsdale, Arizona, pp. 7-5-7-9, August 2002
10. Matsangas, P., McCauley, M.: Sopite syndrome: a revised definition. Aviati. Space Environ. Med. **85**, 672–673 (2014)
11. Matsangas, P., McCauley, M.: Yawning as a behavioral marker of mild motion sickness and sopite syndrome. Aviati. Space Environ. Med. **85**, 658–661 (2014)
12. Matthews, R., McDonald, N., Hervieux, P., Turner, P., Steindorf, M.: A wearable physiological sensor suite for unobtrusive monitoring of physiological and cognitive state. In: 29th Annual International Conference of the IEEE Engineering in Medicine and Biology Society, EMBS 2007, pp. 5276–5281, August 2007
13. Matthews, R., Turner, P., McDonald, N., Ermolaev, K., Manus, T., Shelby, R., Steindorf, M.: Real time workload classification from an ambulatory wireless eeg system using hybrid eeg electrodes. In: 30th Annual International Conference of the IEEE Engineering in Medicine and Biology Society, EMBS 2008, pp. 5871–5875, August 2008
14. Mehler, B., Reimer, B., Coughlin, J.: Sensitivity of physiological measures for detecting systematic variations in cognitive demand from a working memory task: An on-road study across three age groups. Hum. Factors **54**, 396–412 (2012)
15. Orbach, T.: Methods and systems for physiological and psycho-physiological monitoring and uses thereof, U.S. Patent App. 11/884,775, 4 September 2008. http://www.google.com/patents/US20080214903
16. Paulus, M., Stein, M.: Interoception in anxiety and depression. Brain Struct. Funct. **214**, 451–463 (2010)
17. Ryu, K., Ayung, M.: Evaluation of mental workload with a combined measure based on physiological indices during a dual task of tracking and mental arithmetic. Int. J. Industr. Ergon. **35**, 991–1009 (2005)

18. Skinner, A., Russo, C., Baraniecki, L., Maloof, M.: Ubiquitous augmented cognition (2014). http://2014.hci.international/index.php
19. Swan, M.: Sensor mania! the internet of things, wearable computing, objective metrics, and the quantified self 2.0. J. Sensor. Actuator Netw. **1**, 217–253 (2012)
20. The BodyTrack Team (2015). http://fluxstream.org
21. Tomaka, J., Blascovitch, J., KIbler, J., Earnst, J.: Cognitive and physiological antecedents of of threat and challenge appraisal. J. Personailty Soc. Psychol. **1**, 63–72 (1997)
22. Weintraub, K.: Quantified self: The tech based route to a better life? (2013). http://www.bbc.com/future/story/20130102-self-track-route-to-a-better-life
23. Widerhiold, B., Jang, D., Kim, S., Wiederhold, M.D.: Physiological monitoring as an objective tool in virtual reality therapy. Cyberpychology Behav. **5**, 77–82 (2002)
24. Winzce, J., Hoon, P., Soon, E.: Sexual arousal in women: a comparison of cognitive and physiological responses by continuous measurement. Arch. Sex Behav. **2**, 121–133 (1977)
25. Winzce, J., Vendetti, E., Barlow, D., Mavissakalian, M.: The effects of a subjective monitoring task in the physiological measure of genital response to erotic stimulation. Arch. Sex Behav. **9**, 533–545 (1980)
26. Zaki, J., Davis, J., Ochsner, K.: Overlapping activity in anterior insult during interoception and emotional experience. NeuroImage **62**, 493–499 (2012)

Adapting Ethics for Future Technologies

Todd Seech[(⊠)]

Operational Psychology Department, Naval Aerospace Medical Institute,
340 Hulse Road, Pensacola, FL 32508, USA
todd.seech@dominican.edu

Abstract. From the handheld tools of the first humans to the latest computer interfaces, technology has augmented our perceptions and interactions with each other and the world around us. Each new generation is born into its own evolution of technological advancements with seemingly preprogrammed literacy in the scientific innovation of the day. These novel technologies are examples of science's fluid nature and linear progression, which drive researchers to produce the next life-changing advancement as quickly as possible. However, rapid and unbridled scientific advancement can veil unacceptable ethical pitfalls. Therefore, the speed with which technology advances must be matched with complementary development of ethical principles. The present paper applies this concept to a handful of modern and near-future technologies that represent paradigm changes to science as well as to everyday life. The paper then explores ethical issues that may arise from these technologies and presents an outline for a new ethical framework.

Keywords: Ethics · Cognitive augmentation · Genetics

1 Introduction

The 21st Century has already delivered a slew of advancements that were virtually inconceivable in preceding decades. Today, concrete can curb pollution [1], drinking water can be produced out of thin air [2], and cars have been given license to drive themselves [3]. The following sections explore current and upcoming advancements specific to the areas of human biology, sensation, perception, and communication to predict the necessary changes in ethical procedures that will mitigate risk in the research required to make these technologies safe and reliable.

Although a detailed review of future technologies is not within the scope of this paper, general overviews of future technologies are included to demonstrate the imminent changes to science and everyday life that are awaiting us.

1.1 Neurointerfaces and Implantable Technology

Humans and computers have been working together for decades. With the advent of the personal mobile device, which now takes on tasks previously allocated to brain power and/or diligent note taking (e.g., managing calendars, calculating tips, composing letters), the cooperative relationship between people and their computers has never

© Springer International Publishing Switzerland 2015
D.D. Schmorrow and C.M. Fidopiastis (Eds.): AC 2015, LNAI 9183, pp. 521–527, 2015.
DOI: 10.1007/978-3-319-20816-9_50

been more apparent. In fact, the paths of the human brain and the computer have become increasingly harmonious and all signs point to this trend continuing. With this pattern recognized, the topic of human-computer collaboration becomes particularly relevant to the discussion of future technologies and their related ethical dilemmas.

Hints of future biotechnology can be gathered from companies like Google, which have introduced an array of programs intended to assist human cognition. For example, Google's programs *Google Goggles* and *Google Translate* use image recognition software to analyze pictures and video on a mobile device to give users information about an image's location, history, and meaning in real-time. The latter of the two programs even translates written words on-screen, which gives the user the visual experience of reading foreign language in his or her native tongue. Other commercially available programs like Microsoft's *Xbox Kinect* and Nuance's *Dragon* allow users to communicate with their computers through natural human movement and speech, thereby moving us closer to truly seamless human-computer interface.

As computers continue to adapt to our brains, it becomes easier to imagine science fiction plots like those of the *Matrix* or *Terminator* films becoming reality, but how close are we to implanting hardware into the human nervous system? In many cases, this feat has already been achieved. Examples of neural implants can be found in the health sciences, which have successfully used neural prosthesis for years. Individuals with auditory or visual impairments can now receive implants that bypass primary sensory organs (e.g., eyes, ears) and instead interface with cranial nerves (i.e., nerves projecting directly from the brain) [4, 5]. Scientists are also perfecting robotic limbs that have both afferent (i.e., sent *to* the brain) and efferent (i.e., sent *from* the brain) signals, which allow a person to receive sensory input and send motor commands by only communicating with an implanted device (e.g., controlling a robotic hand to grasp and release a ball without visual assistance) [6], which thereby mimics natural processes of the healthy nervous system.

The perfection of "two-way" neural communication will undoubtedly be the foundation from which future health and experimental sciences discover paradigm-changing innovation. Organizations like the Defense Advanced Research Projects Agency (DARPA) have acknowledged this fact by prioritizing projects like the Reliable Neural-Interface Technology (RE-NET) and the Revolutionizing Prosthetics Programs. DARPA programs like these have goals of refining hardware and software interfaces with the central and peripheral nervous systems as well as to advance robotic prosthesis [7, 8]. Currently, these programs have clinical aims (e.g., limb replacement for veterans), but the potential to achieve other ends is undeniable.

With these advances in human-computer interface and the existence of software frameworks that alter and improve perception (e.g., Google Goggles/Translate), the application of these technologies to human performance enhancement is a next logical step. The potential of this endeavor seems endless. One human brain could be seamlessly linked to an aircraft, squadron, air wing, or regional command—not unlike he/she is connected to his/her arms and legs. The free flowing information *to* and *from* this individual's brain could make coordination of massive amounts of information possible through intrinsic proprioceptive control. Although futuristic applications of this sort of technology are difficult to predict, it is foreseeable that it would have invaluable use in government, military, commercial, and private sectors. With such amazing possibilities on the horizon, it is our duty as a society to ensure the cost of such technology is not too great. The research path that will bring these technologies into operational status will have many ethical dilemmas, including challenges to individuals' autonomy as well as difficult comparisons of risks and rewards.

1.2   Genomics and Genetic Manipulation

Most scientists agree that the study of genetics began with a Monrovian friar and his peas—little could Gregor Johann Mendel have known that his work would serve as the foundation for today's genetic sciences. As much as gene research has changed in the 150 years since Mendel's work was presented, many of today's researchers have a similar goal—to predict—and have had remarkable success at achieving this end.

Today, testing allows geneticists to predict the likelihood of developing a number of diseases with near certainty, including Huntington's Disease [9], Sickle Cell Anemia [10], and Cystic Fibrosis [11]. Unfortunately, the predictions of many phenotypes (including disease manifestation) do not follow Mendelian (i.e., corresponding to a single-gene) models and have required researchers to look to larger scale models. The result has been that researchers studied the genome, which encompasses the entirety of genes in an organism.

In 2003, the 13-year-long, publicly-funded National Human Genome Research Institute (NHGRI) completed its goal, which was to provide a map of the complete human genome [12]. Of this truly paradigm-changing achievement, then Director of NHGRI Francis Collins described it as follows:

> It's a history book - a narrative of the journey of our species through time. It's a shop manual, with an incredibly detailed blueprint for building every human cell. And it's a transformative textbook of medicine, with insights that will give health care providers immense new powers to treat, prevent and cure disease. [13]

In the years since the completion of the Human Genome Project, a surge of research exploring the complex interplay of multiple genes in developing disease has come forth. Our understanding of disease development has grown markedly and a movement toward using genetic testing to inform individualized medical care has gained great support. Researchers have even begun to alter genetic codes by introducing a 47th chromosome or by augmenting the existing chromosomes; this progress is a promising sign for manipulating human antibodies, treating monogenic diseases, and optimizing medication response [14]. However, genetic research in this vein has not been limited to disease prediction and treatment. Human performance enhancement researchers have also shown interest in the genetic influences of elite performance in the areas of athletics [15] and cognition [16]. It is not unreasonable to expect that research of the near future will involve genetic prediction and manipulation with the goal of creating superior cognitive and/or athletic performers.

Advances in genetics provide researchers and healthcare professionals an unprecedented ability to predict and control human trait expression. Current and future research in this area will therefore introduce new ethical dilemmas, especially in the areas of assent/consent and secondary research findings.

2   Ethics in Future Research

As research and technology advance, ethical principles must adapt to keep pace. One of the greatest examples of this notion was the Belmont Report [17] issued by the United States Department of Health and Human Services. With references to Nazi experiments and the Tuskegee clinical trials and following other studies of questionable ethics (e.g., Zimbardo's prison study, Milgram's obedience study), this document provided specific guidelines for conducting ethical human research.

Today, it is science's prerogative to evolve again. Through implementation of a new approach to ethics, described here as the Personalized Participant Protocol (3-P) approach, future studies can mitigate risk to participants by using the most up-to-date research methods to tailor ethical procedures to each individual participant.

The following sections describe the 3-P approach and apply it to specific areas of research, using the previously described new technologies as examples. It should be noted that the goal of the current paper is not to dictate a complete, research-ready guide to future ethics, but instead is to begin a conversation regarding new ethical principles that might improve future research efforts and their protection of human participants.

2.1   Principles of the 3-P Approach

The 3-P approach was formed in response to the "boiler-plate" quality of many ethical procedures used in today's research. Methods of assessing risk, determining inclusion/exclusion, and gathering consent often have binary or oversimplified categories (e.g., sex, age, ethnicity, clinical diagnosis) that run are in danger of securing poor measurement of risk and/or excluding valuable participants unnecessarily. The 3-P approach attempts to address these issues through two central principles that are intended to aid researchers in designing ethically responsible modern research studies.

The first principle in the 3-P approach is that it is *individualized*, which can be described as a tailoring of ethical plans to fit each participant's personal level of eligibility for inclusion, likelihood of risk and benefit, and desires regarding incidental findings.

The second principle of the 3-P approach that it is *hierarchical*, which means that it has graded levels of study participation, to include additional levels of consent/participation prior to official study enrollment that allow for more accurate assessment (to include providing physiological samples).

These principles are intended to be flexible and somewhat broad.

2.2   Applying 3-P Principles

Designing a research study is often a difficult and time-consuming activity that requires numerous iterations. A great deal of energy goes into identifying research questions, making hypotheses, and choosing populations, among other tasks. However, less effort appears to be put forth related to dynamically assessing risk or implementing new consent procedures, as evidenced by static inclusion/exclusion criteria and a single consent form. The 3-P approach suggests that hierarchical or graded advancement through study participation starts well before traditional enrollment stages and adapts to the individual as he/she progresses through the study.

Consider the example of study that would involve the implantation of a human-computer interface device on the sensory and motor cortical areas with the goal of controlling a set of artificial hands. Initial screening could involve minimal physiological, psychological, and social information (e.g., blood pressure, history of substance abuse, family health history) to predict risk of adverse events to the individual participant based on the extant literature. Heightened risk to the individual participant might require additional pre-procedure or aftercare measures, which is information that would be shared following this first screening and would allow the participant to make a more informed decision regarding study participation. If the participant consents, further assessment would be conducted to allow more in-depth understanding of the participant's fitness for inclusion, potential for additional safety needs, and even likelihood of retention for the duration of the study. The individually-tailored risk-benefit analysis would be presented to the participant at the time of official study enrollment, which would allow him/her to make a more informed decision regarding participation as well as to allow study personnel to understand each individual's appropriateness for the study (potentially saving resources by thoroughly screening out individuals whose level of risk was unacceptable).

The above example of 3-P principles requires some changes to the current expectations for ethics in human research. First, informed consent and official study participation would have to move from the current binary "included versus excluded" framework to a process of information gathering and dissemination to the participant. Investigators and Institutional Review Boards would have to accept that traditional consent forms would be broken down into segments, which allowed study personnel access to specific information of increasing sensitivity at clearly delineated points of study enrollment to achieve specific tasks. This annotated version of consent forms would be in the interest of both the investigator and the participant to ensure to prevent adverse events, improve participants' understandings of risk, and allow studies early (yet minimal) data collection. Of course, special rules would have to be in place to safeguard this "early" information, but their implementation would be a minor burden given the potential rewards noted above.

"Custom" consent forms would not have to be lengthy personal essays, but could contain a few specific details that would carry great weight with participants. The 3-P *individualized* concept would also allow participants to choose options if undesirable outcomes arose.

For example, consider the hypothetical study in which gene therapy was being used to improve outcomes in patients who are expected to develop Huntington's disease in later life. In this case, initial screening phases could include full genome mapping (assuming such testing will be economically feasible in a screening phase), but would be preceded by an explicit consent document that provided the participant with detailed information regarding what information would be collected and how it would be presented to him/her thereafter. This consent would allow the participant to elect to be told or not told about specific types of incidental findings (e.g., information about other morbidities).

Considered together, the individualized and hierarchical nature of this new approach would make ethics adaptable to future research findings by providing participants with the most up-to-date information regarding their risk through the least invasive procedures. Through this framework, scientists can retain the Belmont Report principles of "Respect for Persons" and "Beneficence" in a new era of research.

3   Conclusion

The current paper explored current and near-future technologies in an effort to predict directions of future research and their related ethical considerations. Two areas of notable recent advancement were discussed—human-computer interfaces and genetics—and the disparity between these areas' progress and the static state of ethics in human research were observed. To address this problem, the broad notion of a person-based form of ethics in human research was described. Referred to as the Personalized Participant Protocol (3-P) approach, this paper described the loose framework for an updated method of addressing ethics in a new age of research.

This new 3-P approach focused on two principles that differed from previous ethical systems. These two principles were (1) individualization of risk/benefit analysis, consent processes, and issues of incidental findings and (2) hierarchical grouping of screening/consent processes that allow investigators and participants to collect/provide information on a gradual scale of increasing sensitivity to better understand relative risk of participating as well as the effect of including each participant in a study.

It is the hope of this author that ethics in human research continues to evolve alongside the exciting research that lies on the horizon and that this new approach can spur conversations necessary for protecting human subjects as well as improving research.

References

1. Cassar, L.: Photocatalysis of cementitious materials: clean buildings and clean air. Mater. Res. Soc. Bull. **29**, 328–331 (2004)
2. Sher, A.M.: U.S. Patent No. 20080135495A1. Washington, D.C.: U.S. Patent and Trademark Office (2008)
3. Smith, B.W.: Automated Vehicles Are Probably Legal in the United States. Texas A&M Law Review, 441 (2012). http://www.cyberlaw.stanford.edu/publications/automated-vehicles-are-probably-legal-united-states
4. House, W.F., Berliner, K.I.: Safety and efficacy of the house/3M cochlear implant in profoundly deaf adults. Otolaryngol. Clin. North Am. **19**, 275–286 (1986)
5. Humayun, M.S., Dorn, J.D., da Cruz, L., Dagnelie, G., et al.: Interim results from the international trial of second sight's visual prosthesis. Ophthalmology **119**, 779–788 (2012)
6. Warwick, K., Gasson, M., Hutt, B., Goodhew, I., et al.: The application of implant technology for cybernetic systems. JAMA Neurol. **60**, 1369–1373 (2003)

7. Defense Advanced Research Projects Agency: Biological Technologies Office: Reliable Neural-Interface Technology (RE-NET) (2015). http://www.darpa.mil/Our_Work/BTO/Programs/Reliable_Neural-Interface_Technology_RE_NET.aspx

8. Defense Advanced Research Projects Agency: Biological Technologies Office: Revolutionizing Prosthetics (2015). http://www.darpa.mil/Our_Work/BTO/Programs/Revolutionizing_Prosthetics.aspx

9. Rubinsztein, D.C., Leggo, J., Coles, R., Almqvist, E., et al.: Phenotypic characterization of individuals with 30–40 CAG repeats in the Huntington disease (HD) gene reveals HD cases with 36 repeats and apparently normal elderly individuals with 36–39 repeats. Am. J. Hum. Genet. **59**, 16–22 (1996)

10. Saiki, R.K., Scharf, S., Faloona, F., Mullis, K.B., et al.: Enzymatic amplification of beta-globin genomic sequences and restriction site analysis for diagnosis of sickle cell anemia. Science **230**, 1350–1354 (1985)

11. Kerem, B., Rommens, J.M., Buchanan, J.A., Markiewicz, D., et al.: Identification of the cystic fibrosis gene: genetic analysis. Science **245**, 1073–1080 (1989)

12. Chial, H.: DNA sequencing technologies key to the human genome project. Nat. Educ. **1**, 219 (2008)

13. National Human Genome Research Institute: An Overview of the Human Genome Project (2012). http://www.genome.gov/12011238

14. Kouprina, N., Earnshaw, W.C., Masumoto, H., Larionov, V.: A new generation of human artificial chromosomes for functional genomics and gene therapy. Cell. Mol. Life Sci. **70**, 1135–1148 (2013)

15. Yang, N., MacArthur, D.G., Gulbin, J.P., Hahn, A.G., et al.: ACTN3 genotype is associated with human elite athlete performance. Am. J. Hum. Genet. **73**, 627–631 (2003)

16. Meyer-Lindenberg, A., Straub, R.E., Lipska, B.K., Verchinski, B.A., et al.: Genetic evidence implicating DARPP-32 in human frontostriatal structure, function, and cognition. J. Clin. Invest. **117**, 672–682 (2007)

17. National Commission for the Protection of Human Subjects of Biomedical and Behavioral Research.: The Belmont Report: Ethical Principles and Guidelines for the Protection of Human Subjects of Research (1978)

Visual Search in Operational Environments

Balancing Operational Constraints with Experimental Control

Ann Speed[✉]

Sandia National Laboratories, Albuquerque, NM 87185, USA
aespeed@sandia.gov

Abstract. Visual search has been an active area of research – empirically and theoretically – for a number of decades, however much of that work is based on novice searchers performing basic tasks in a laboratory. This paper summarizes some of the issues associated with quantifying expert, domain-specific visual search behavior in operationally realistic environments.

Keywords: Visual search · Expertise · Domain specific tasks · Ecological validity · Operational environments

1 Introduction

Visual search has been a very active area of research for a number of decades, and many theories of different aspects of visual search and visual cognition exist to explain any number of behavioral and neural phenomena. This particular paper, and associated conference session, is not intended to re-tread this ground. Rather, the intent is to highlight a program of research at Sandia National Laboratories in domain specific visual search by experts and novices in a variety of high-consequence, real-world, national security problems. This program of research is relatively new at the Laboratory, with human subjects research going back to ~2009. However visual search spans a large number of problems within the mission space of the Laboratories, thus the area has rapidly grown to comprise 15–20 researchers who explore the human cognition aspect of the problem (as opposed to focusing on algorithm or visualization development) using both qualitative and quantitative empirical methods.

This paper discusses what we believe are important task differences between domain-specific search in national security environments and the domain–general tasks typically used to develop the extant theoretical literature. Then, summaries of several key themes in each of the papers appearing in this session are presented.

© Springer International Publishing Switzerland 2015
D.D. Schmorrow and C.M. Fidopiastis (Eds.): AC 2015, LNAI 9183, pp. 528–536, 2015.
DOI: 10.1007/978-3-319-20816-9_51

1.1   Comparing Visual Search Tasks in the Laboratory and the Field

Visual search in the typical laboratory setting involves stimuli that the vast majority of subjects have experience seeing, such as letters or natural scenes. Of course, the actual construction of the stimuli depends on the specific question being asked (e.g., Figures 1 and 2).

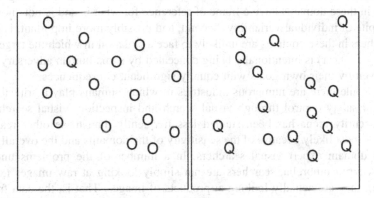

Fig. 1. Stimuli to investigate parallel (left side) versus serial (right side) visual search. Because of the differences in ratios of Os to Qs in each of these stimuli, they appear to elicit different search strategies, revealing something about how the visual system processes information.

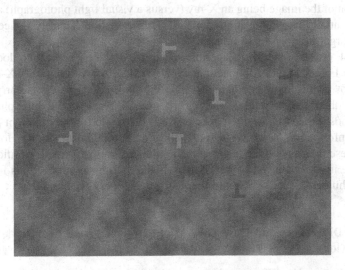

Fig. 2. A sparsely populated visual search task involving the search for perfect Ts amidst a field of Ls.

By way of comparison, stimuli in real world visual search tasks include stimuli such as X-ray or MRI imagery in medical or quality inspection environments. While the consequences of incorrect interpretations of these images are certainly high, there are a couple of critical difference between these real-world tasks and the national security domains in which this group of researchers has been working. First is the fact that visual search in radiography (or fuselage inspection, or quality control of manufactured items) is constrained by the anatomy of the patient, airplane, or widget. Thus, searchers in these domains have a frame of reference for what is and is not "normal" – even in spite of individual variability. Second, and possibly more important, is the fact that searchers in these contexts are unlikely to face a situation in which the target of the search (e.g., cancer) is intentionally being concealed by some human adversary who is being driven by their own goals with equally significant consequences.

Thus, while there are numerous industries in which humans play a critical role in quality and safety control through visual search and inspection, visual search in the national security arena has been studied less frequently than these other real-world problems – most likely because of the sensitivity of the domains and the overall lack of access to domain expert visual searchers. In a number of the problems under the national security umbrella, searchers are not simply looking at raw images (x-ray or otherwise), they are actually looking at products of images. That is, the data from the sensors is subjected to post-processing that is intended to highlight aspects of the image that might be particularly useful to the image analyst. One might think of the results of this post-processing to be automatic methods for creating a cued visual search environment [1]. For example, Fig. 3 displays an X-ray image of a carryon bag with a gun in it. While the image is a veridical representation of the contents of the bag, the dual manipulation of the image being an X-ray (versus a visual light photograph) and falsely colored potentially has implications for how Transportation Security Officers (TSOs) search for target items in these images.

Figure 4 presents synthetic aperture radar (SAR) images of two locations on Kirtland Air Force Base in Albuquerque, New Mexico. As with the TSA X-ray image, these are not visible light photographs, thus the dark and light spots carry different information than they would if they were normal black and white photographs. Additional post-processing is often done on SAR images to further highlight potentially interesting information (see Matzen et al. [2] for additional information). However, the nature of these images and the fact that manipulations are performed specifically to try and enhance imagery analyst search of them is likely to have implications for how we understand human visual search and the neural machinery enabling it.

1.2   Task Differences and How They Might Impact Visual Search Behavior

In addition to stimulus differences between domain general and domain specific tasks, operationally-oriented research also has procedures that are constrained by the operational environment in which they occur. For example, one effect that creates a stir in operational environments is Wolfe's prevalence effect [3, 4] in which subjects are more likely to miss targets when they occur infrequently. Interestingly, this effect seems to be

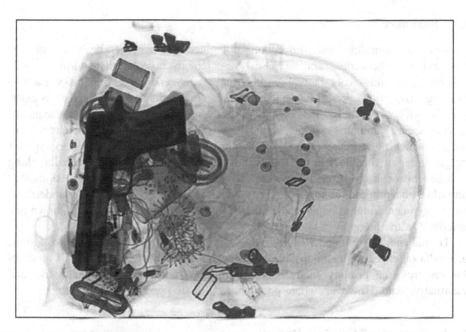

Fig. 3. TSA passenger checkpoint x-ray image (taken from the TSA Media Twitter Feed: https://twitter.com/TSAmedia_RossF/status/530756668154728448/photo/1).

Fig. 4. Synthetic Aperture Radar (SAR) images of a static display of a helicopter and plane (left) and of the Kirtland Air Force Base golf course clubhouse (right). Images are courtesy of Sandia National Laboratories, Airborne ISR (http://www.sandia.gov/radar/imagery/index.html).

partially mediated by the trial-by-trial feedback provided to subjects in the lab [5, 6] – a luxury rarely afforded to real-world analysts in their everyday jobs. Thus, research attempting to understand performance in that everyday world will often include procedures that mimic standard operating procedures (SOPs) that are in use on the job, rather than using procedures directly out of the peer-reviewed literature. Of course, the comparison between performance in a domain-specific task under SOPs versus lab-based procedures can help to highlight differences in search behavior that are not due solely to the stimuli or to the neural machinery of the visual system.

1.3   Summary

Because of stimulus and procedural differences, the generalizability of the peer-reviewed theoretical and empirical research to operational environments is unknown. Certainly work in real-world visual search and inspection tasks, such as radiology inspection, aircraft fuselage inspections, inspections of machined parts exists [e.g., 7–14], but it is unclear that even these results generalize well to high-consequence national security domains in which there is an adversary attempting to hide target items and for which there has been a large amount of work done on post-processing raw images in an attempt to help the analyst better search the space. Thus, Sandia, along with several other government agencies tasked with national security missions, has embarked on a program of human subjects studies and experiments to better understand where high-consequence expert visual search departs from what is already known and described in the literature.

To that end, the remainder of this paper summarizes some of the recent work done at Sandia on expert, domain-specific visual search. Due to the sensitivity of much of this research, the primary focus is on methods for collecting both qualitative and quantitative data. However, where possible, results are presented.

2   Summary of Session Papers

The papers in this session describe a number of different methods – both qualitative and quantitative – aimed at better understanding the nature and complexity of visual search in an adversarial environment. To set a larger context in which these methods have been developed, each of the projects involved has collected (or is currently collecting) data on the relevant experts' domain-specific visual search task (e.g., SAR analysis, X-ray analysis) and each has collected data on a common battery of domain-general visual cognition tasks (described in more detail in Matzen et al. [2]) including:

- Parallel versus serial visual search (the O/Q task in Fig. 1)
- A visual inspection task (the T/L task in Fig. 2)
- Spatial working memory, mental rotation, attention beam, and Raven's-like matrix reasoning problems

As of the date of the writing of this paper, an insufficient amount of data on these tasks had been collected to be presented (with the exception of Matzen et al. [2] and Trumbo et al. [15]). However, we anticipate future publications covering these results.

Methods used in the following papers include qualitative approaches from cultural anthropology to perform workflow and cognitive task analysis and more quantitative methods of eliciting knowledge from these experts. Additional work describes domain experts performing laboratory-based tasks (e.g., a rapid serial visual presentation (RSVP) paradigm) using real-world stimuli and methods for collecting data on experts performing their domain-specific visual search task in a near-real operational environment. Finally, some exploratory data analysis methods are presented for dealing with data that has high temporal and spatial fidelity, which characterizes the data that many of these projects will generate.

2.1   Understanding the Nature of Visual Search Work: Knowledge Elicitation and Workflow Analysis

One of the issues with experimentally studying domain experts performing their domain task in a national security environment is that disruption of the analysts' workflow to instrument their workstation in a way that allows for quantifying their behavior can be very disruptive to the mission. Furthermore, there can be a very strong push against any modifications of their systems when the stakes are what they tend to be in these situations and because such modifications can be quite costly. Thus, insight into how these analysts perform their jobs is often limited to observation, interviews of various sorts, and examination of work documents like standard operating procedures.

McNamara and colleagues [16] describe a nice combination of a number of methods from cultural anthropology and psychology for exploring the way analysts conduct their work including ethnographic approaches, work analysis and hierarchical cognitive task analysis. They demonstrate that this "hybrid" approach yields understanding of analysts' methods that would not have been identified otherwise.

Haass and colleagues [17] take this approach a step further, incorporating eye tracking into their study of analysts performing abductive reasoning on data analogous to spectroscopic waveforms. Fortunately, despite their small sample of analysts, Haass et al., were able to collect data from highly experience ($\sim$ 15 years), "practitioners" who had about 5.5 years of experience and novices who had no experience with the task, but who were technically qualified and cleared to perform the task. As with McNamara, et al., Haass and colleagues demonstrated the ability to detect differences in analyst behaviors and their narrative about how they were making decisions.

2.2   Stimuli – Creation and Validation

ough they can be collected. In the case of the TSA, ground truth about the bag contents is not known. Similarly, for the SAR tasks, ground truth is often not known – specifically for target events that are not detected by analysts. In addition, if a stimulus-specific independent variable is of interest (e.g., threat prevalence rates) using real stimuli often prevents this because of the lack of control of other variables that could function as confounds. Thus, stimuli need to be created that mimic the operational environment as closely as possible. Several of the papers in this session include methods for creating realistic stimuli, but the most detailed description of this process is in Speed et al. [18].

For that project, the goal was to have Transportation Security Officers (TSOs) interrogate X-ray images of mock passenger bags for two hours in order to determine if there are significant decrements in threat detection performance over that timescale. Because the task was self-paced, based on prior research with TSOs, it was estimated that in order to ensure every TSO performed the task for two hours, there would need to be 1,000 different passenger items for each TSO to interrogate. In order to replicate the image manipulation capabilities TSOs have access to at the checkpoint X-ray, more than 83,000 unique images were loaded into a custom-built software X-ray emulator. Thus, validating that there were, indeed, unique images for each requested image product, and that there were the right number of image products for each passenger item, became a very important task.

2.3 Expert Performance on Basic Visual Search Tasks

As mentioned previously, many of the projects presented include collection of data from expert visual searchers on a common battery of basic visual search tasks. Trumbo et al. [15] and Matzen et al. [2] describe in more detail the performance of domain experts on an RSVP task that uses chips of X-ray images and on that general visual search battery, respectively.

Trumbo et al. [15] describe a variation of an approach initially developed by DARPA for the Neurotechnology for Intelligence Analysts (NIA) program. Specifically, that program utilized event-related potentials (ERPs) in electroencephalography (EEG) to enable satellite imagery analysts to triage large numbers of images. Specifically, researchers presented "chips" of large satellite images to analysts using a rapid serial visual presentation (RSVP) paradigm and utilized the presence of specific ERPs to determine if those image chips, and their associated whole images, needed to be looked at more closely. Trumbo et al., apply this method to TSOs, using chips of actual false-color X-ray images. The researchers demonstrated that TSOs were able to identify threats in the chips despite the speed at which they were presented (100 ms per image chip) and that there was a positive waveform appearing approximately 300 ms after chip onset for stereotypically presented threat items, thus demonstrating the applicability of the EEG-based triage approach to X-ray baggage screening.

Matzen et al. [2] present data for expert and novice visual searchers on both their domain-specific task (SAR imagery) and on the aforementioned domain-general cognitive battery. They find important differences between experts and novices on both tasks, thus demonstrating that expertise in visual search does correlate with changes in performance in other visual cognition domains. This finding replicates other similar research (e.g., Biggs et al. [19]).

Silva et al. [20] describe measuring visual search in a slightly different domain: cyber incident responders (IRs). Interestingly, IRs are sometimes faced with a difficult visual search task in searching log files for malware. This task is driven much less by the characteristics of the stimulus and more by the individual IR's knowledge of malware code structure.

2.4 Data Analysis

Several of the projects described in this session involve collection not only of behavioral data (e.g., classifying a stimulus as either "normal" or "abnormal"), they also include eye tracking data and, in some cases, very temporally detailed information about how the analysts interact with the stimulus presentation system to make their decisions. Thus, analyses of the resulting data necessarily go beyond traditional parametric statistical tests and branch into machine learning and, in some cases, text analysis-based methods. Stracuzzi et al. [21] describe a framework for analyzing data that have both temporal and spatial aspects to them. This framework will likely be applied to many of the datasets being generated by the projects described in this session.

3 Conclusion

As Matzen et al. [2] point out, there is a lack of research on domain expertise in visual search and how that expertise both impacts performance on domain-general tasks and how performance on both domain-specific and domain-general tasks differs between novices and experts. While much of the data being collected for the projects described in this session is yet to be analyzed as of the writing of this paper, hopefully many of the methodological issues surrounding collecting such data can inform others' efforts such that this gap in the literature can be more quickly closed. Understanding the nature of expertise in various real-world, high-consequence visual search domains, how that differs from the behavior of domain novices, and how that might impact (or be predicted by) performance on domain-general tasks potentially has significant implications for theories of visual search, including understanding the neural machinery underlying visual search behavior.

For additional examples of this kind of research, the reader is referred to another session in these same Proceedings entitled "Applying Science to Complex Operational Environments: Methodological Case Studies from the Transportation Security Administration's Human Factors Group."

Acknowledgements. Sandia National Laboratories is a multi-program laboratory managed and operated by Sandia Corporation, a wholly owned subsidiary of Lockheed Martin Corporation, for the U.S. Department of Energy's National Nuclear Security Administration under Contract DE-AC04-94AL85000. This research was funded in part by an Interagency Agreement between the Transportation Security Administration and the Department of Energy.

References

1. Eckstein, M.P.: Visual search: a retrospective. J. Vis. **11**, 1–36 (2011)
2. Matzen, L.E., Haass, M.J., McNamara, L.A., Stevens-Adams, S.M., McMichael, S.N.: Effects of professional visual search experience on domain-general and domain-specific visual cognition. In: 17th International Conference on Human-Computer Interaction. Springer (2015)
3. Wolfe, J.M., Horowitz, T.S., Van Wert, M.J., Kenner, N.M.: Low target prevalence is a stubborn source of errors in visual search tasks. J. Exp. Psychol. Gen. **136**, 623–638 (2007)
4. Wolfe, J.M., Van Wert, M.J.: Varying target prevalence reveals two dissociable decision criteria in visual search. Curr. Biol. **20**, 121–124 (2010)
5. Fiedler, K.: Beware of samples! a cognitive-ecological sampling approach to judgment biases. Psychol. Rev. **107**, 659–676 (2000)
6. Fiedler, K., Brinkmann, B., Tilmann, B., Wild, B.: A sampling approach to biases in conditional probability judgments: beyond base rate neglect and statistical format. J. Exp. Psychol. Gen. **129**, 399–418 (2000)

7. Drury, C.G., Saran, M., Schultz, J.: Effect of fatigue/vigilance/environment on inspectors performing floursecent penetrant and/or magnetic particle inspection: Year 1 interim report (2004)
8. Drury, C.G., Watson, J.: Good practices in visual inspection
9. Gallwey, T.J., Drury, C.G.: Task complexity in visual inspection. Hum. Factors 28, 595–606 (1986)
10. Lansdale, M., Underwood, G., Davies, C.: Something overlooked? How experts in change detection use visual saliency. Appl. Cogn. Psychol. 24, 213–225 (2010)
11. Panjwani, G., Drury, C.G.: Effective interventions in rare event inspection. In: Proceedings of the Human Factors and Ergonomics Society 47th Annual Meeting (2003)
12. See, J.E.: Visual inspection: A review of the literature. Sandia Technical Report, SAND2012-8590 (2012)
13. Spencer, F., Schurman, D.: Reliabiity assessment at airline inspection facilities, vol. III. Results of an eddy current inspection reliability experiment. Technical report for the Federal Aviation Administration, DOT/FAA/CT-92-12, III (1995)
14. Spitz, G., Drury, C.G.: Inspection of sheet materials: test of model predictions. Hum. Factors J. Hum. Factors Ergon. Soc. 20, 521–528 (1978)
15. Trumbo, M.C., Matzen, L.E., Silva, A., Haass, M.J., Divis, K., Speed, A.: Through a scanner quickly: elicitation of event-related potentials in transportation security officers following rapid image presentation and categorization. In: 17th International Conference on Human-Computer Interaction. Springer (2015)
16. McNamara, L.A., Cole, K., Haass, M.J., Matzen, L.E., Morrow, J.D., Stevens-Adams, S.M., McMichael, S.: Ethnographic method for experimental design: case studies in visual search. In: 17th International Conference on Human-Computer Interaction. Springer (2015)
17. Haass, M.J., Matzen, L.E., Stevens-Adams, S.M., Roach, A.R.: Methodology for knowledge elicitation in visual abductive reasoning tasks. In: 17th International Conference on Human-Computer Interaction. Springer (2015)
18. Speed, A., Silva, A., Trumbo, D., Stracuzzi, D.J., Warrender, C., Trumbo, M.C., Divis, K.: Determining the optimal time on X-ray analysis for transportation security officers. In: 17th International Conference on Human-Computer Interaction. Springer (2015)
19. Biggs, A.T., Cain, M.S., Clark, K., Darling, E.F., Mitroff, S.F.: Assessing visual search performance differences between transportation security administration officers and non-professional visual searchers. Vis. Cogn. 21, 330–352 (2013)
20. Silva, A.R., Emmanuel, G., McClain, J.T., Forsythe, J.C., Matzen, L.E.: Measuring expert and novice performance within computer security incident response teams. In: 17th International Conference on Human-Computer Interaction. Springer (2015)
21. Stracuzzi, D.J., Speed, A., Silva, A., Haass, M.J., Trumbo, D.: Exploratory analysis of visual search data. In: 17th International Conference on Human-Computer Interaction. Springer (2015)

Exploratory Analysis of Visual Search Data

David J. Stracuzzi[✉], Ann Speed, Austin Silva,
Michael Haass, and Derek Trumbo

Sandia National Laboratories, Albuquerque, NM 87185, USA
{djstrac,aespeed,aussilv,mjhaass,dtrumbo}@sandia.gov

Abstract. Visual search data describe people's performance on the
common perceptual problem of identifying target objects in a complex
scene. Technological advances in areas such as eye tracking now provide
researchers with a wealth of data not previously available. The goal of
this work is to support researchers in analyzing this complex and multimodal data and in developing new insights into visual search techniques.
We discuss several methods drawn from the statistics and machine learning literature for integrating visual search data derived from multiple
sources and performing exploratory data analysis. We ground our discussion in a specific task performed by officers at the Transportation
Security Administration and consider the applicability, likely issues, and
possible adaptations of several candidate analysis methods.

Keywords: Visual search · Eye tracking · Data analysis · Transportation Security Administration

1 Introduction

Visual search research considers the perceptual problem of actively scanning a
scene to locate target objects embedded in a complex visual scene. Examples range
from everyday activities such as finding a friend among a crowd to detail-oriented
activities such as radiologists reading X-ray or MRI images. Methods by which
people engage in visual search have been studied for several decades. However,
recent advances in eye tracking systems enable collection of fine-grained data in
visual search domains under realistic conditions. For example, eye tracking systems can now be embedded into operational environments that include multiple
monitors and a variety of display manipulation tools. As a result, visual search
studies now produce increasingly rich data in increasingly large volumes. These
data may include the eye tracking observations, participant interactions with the
environment (such as image manipulation software), performance results with
respect to the given task, and the stimulus itself (such as images).

Such rich data requires increasingly sophisticated analysis techniques. Traditional statistical analysis remains an appropriate choice for characterizing variables such as overall performance, changes in performance over time, participant
usage of available image manipulation tools, and so on. Importantly, tools for
viewing and analyzing the eye tracking results have improved in step with hardware advances. For example, researchers can easily generate and compare heat

© Springer International Publishing Switzerland 2015
D.D. Schmorrow and C.M. Fidopiastis (Eds.): AC 2015, LNAI 9183, pp. 537–547, 2015.
DOI: 10.1007/978-3-319-20816-9_52

maps and temporally annotated gaze patterns among both individuals and selected groups. They can also identify specific regions of interest and analyze the participants' search with respect to those regions. The available tools support analysis of visual search patterns, differences in search patterns among selected populations, and visual salience of specific image features.

Nevertheless, important limitations remain for the analysis and modeling of visual search data. In particular, data from different sources, such as eye tracking and user software interactions, are typically analyzed separately. Methods for integrating all data sources into a single analysis that can provide deep insights into visual search processes remain elusive. In this paper, we discuss an ongoing effort to apply state of the art machine learning and statistical modeling methods to perform exploratory analysis of complex and multimodal visual search data. We hypothesize that querying and comparing the resulting models will provide deeper insights into the methods and performance of the study participants than otherwise possible. We ground the discussion of our proposed approach with an ongoing study of Transportation Security Administration (TSA) officers who are tasked with interrogating X-ray images of carry-on luggage for threats at airport security checkpoints. Our discussion then focuses on the proposed analysis algorithms, their justification, and anticipated adaptations as the data for this study is still being collected as of this writing.

2   The TSA Task and Data Collection

One of the primary features of airport security is the passenger checkpoint at which both the passengers and their carry-on luggage are checked for items that may pose a threat. The task of reading the X-ray imagery of the carry-on luggage is a perfect example of a visual search task. The Transportation Safety Officers (TSOs) must scan the imagery associated with each bag to determine whether it contains any potential threats.

The TSO's task is difficult for several reasons. For example, the X-ray image converts a three-dimensional collection of objects (the bag and its contents) into a two-dimensional image, thereby superimposing many objects onto one another and obscuring the defining features of many objects. Also challenging is that the class of threat objects is fairly large and varied (consider all of the different items that are not allowed in carry-on luggage). Finally, TSOs must perform their analysis under time pressure, as checkpoint throughput is a significant concern.

Given these issues, the goal of studying the visual search performance of TSOs is to develop insight into how they interrogate the bags, how they identify threat objects, and what changes might be made to the X-ray display system to improve overall performance with respect to measures such as throughput, probability of detection, and probability of false alarms. The exploratory analysis methods that we discuss below focus on identifying features that are predictive of conditions of interest, and identifying specific, testable hypotheses. Sample questions of interest might consider differences among common and anomalous image interrogation patterns, differences between high- and low-performing analysts, differences between easy and hard to interrogate objects, and predictors of impending analyst errors.

Data collection focuses on TSOs reading imagery in a high-fidelity, simulated setting. Each TSO reads a sequence of X-ray images for two hours or a maximum of 1,000 luggage items. The luggage contents generally mirror the stream of commerce at a typical airport security checkpoint as determined by the TSA, except that 10 percent of the items include simulated threats. Limited ground truth information is available for each luggage item, including the presence and location of any threat items, the presence of prohibited items such as toothpaste tubes and full water bottles, and the presence of other items of interest such as laptops. Each luggage item includes a set of 31 image products that the TSOs can toggle on and off. Each image product is derived from the X-ray scan and highlights different aspects of the scanned item. These images are identical to those used at the checkpoint and represent the most commonly used subset of all available image products.

We used a simulator to collect data because the scanners used at the checkpoint are closed, proprietary systems. It provides the same viewing environment and most of the same controls as the checkpoint scanners. TSOs view the imagery on two, side-by-side monitors showing a top and side view of the luggage items. The images scroll right-to-left across the monitors until either stopping automatically, or the officer stops them with a key press (depending on which operating procedure is in force). An important side effect of the scrolling is that a signification portion of the eye tracking occurs with respect to a moving image. See Speed et al. [13] for an in depth discussion of the stimulus creation, experimental design, and data collection procedures.

The collected data are illustrated in Fig. 1 includes gaze locations and durations from an integrated SmartEye Pro 6.0 three camera eye tracking system. The data also includes user keystroke information such as image product selections, and TSO judgments such as threat versus no threat for each luggage item. All of the data sources include time stamps. The 31 X-ray image products presented to the TSOs are also available to the analysis algorithms.

3   Data Preparation

Before we can apply the selected statistical and machine learning algorithms to the data, we first need to encode the data in an appropriate format. Given the sequential nature of visual search in general, and the eye tracking data in particular, we elect to represent the data as a time series and apply analysis methods that assume a temporal component. Preparing the data entails several steps. For example, the eye trackers produce data at a high sampling rate that requires significant aggregation before it can be combined with the viewed imagery. Likewise, the raw image pixel values may be less useful during analysis than aggregate image properties such as edges or regions of uniform color.

Also important will be efforts to establish relationships between the different data streams. For example, associations of gaze locations with properties of the

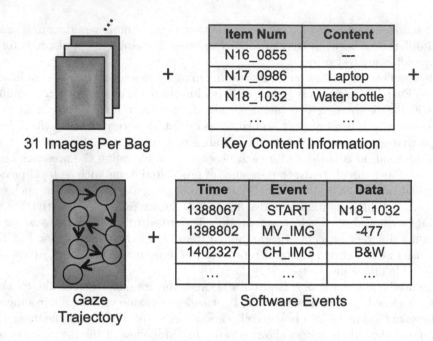

Item Num	Content
N16_0855	---
N17_0986	Laptop
N18_1032	Water bottle
...	...

31 Images Per Bag   Key Content Information

Time	Event	Data
1388067	START	N18_1032
1398802	MV_IMG	-477
1402327	CH_IMG	B&W
...	...	...

Gaze
Trajectory   Software Events

Fig. 1. Illustration of the stimulus imagery, associated ground truth, eye tracking and software event data collected by the checkpoint simulator.

underlying image may together relate to the TSOs decision to switch image products. Identifying these associations, known as feature extraction, plays a critical role in data analysis. In the remainder of this section, we discuss the steps necessary to transform the raw data into a form that facilitates the learning, modeling, and generalization steps that follow.

3.1 Preprocessing of Eye Tracking Data

The SmartEye eye tracking system records raw gaze and head orientation samples at a rate of 60 Hz. These samples are time-synchronized with the stimulus display and user actions (such as keyboard events) using the MAPPS[1] analysis software package. The MAPPS algorithms are used to calculate fixation points and durations from the eye tracking data stream.

For the TSA data, we set the *fixation minimum duration* parameter to 0.13 seconds and the *size of point cloud* parameter to 71 pixels. Importantly, the point cloud parameter controls the trade-off between fixation size and noise tolerance. Larger values group more gaze locations into a single fixation (possibly combining multiple fixations) while smaller values provide a more fine-grained separation of fixations at the expense of adding noise to the preprocessing results.

Given the display resolution, display size, and typical subject viewing distance (66 cm), these settings define the maximum angular velocity for fixations

---

[1] http://www.eyesdx.com/products/mapps/.

to be 15.25 degrees/second, which is consistent with published values [3]. As an additional sanity check, we also compared the maximum angular velocity for fixations to the angular velocity (from the participant's viewing position) of the image as it scrolls across the screen. We found that the velocity of the scrolling images was three orders of magnitude slower than that allowable within a fixation. This implies that our preprocessing methods should recognize any visual tracking of the scrolling image as a single fixation and not a sequence.

3.2   Feature Extraction

In the context of data analysis, features are variables derived from the raw data that are more informative and discriminating than the constituent variables. The objective of feature extraction is to simultaneously reduce the size of a data set while highlighting properties of the data that will improve both the accuracy and structure of classifiers and probabilistic models. Feature extraction is therefore a process of both discovery and relevance evaluation. Exploring the space of candidate features requires consideration of a variety of methods and algorithms.

The visual search literature provides extensive discussion of possible image features. For example, Wolfe [15] discusses asymmetry in visual search, which is the notion that detecting the absence of a feature is much more difficult than detecting its presence. This implies that having variables that indicate the absence of a pattern in the imagery may be of value. Itti [7] has conducted extensive research on visual salience, including algorithms for computing heat maps that indicate the bottom-up salience of imagery.

The computer vision literature focuses on identifying objects and relationships in images, irrespective of how the human visual system processes the imagery. Yu and Ng's tutorial [16] introduces a variety of established methods for identifying features such as object boundaries and classes, and for estimating the relative contributions of all features. Recent work on statistical relational learning (see Getoor and Taskar [5] for an extensive overview) is particularly relevant because it focuses on modeling relationships among objects and events. Nowozin and Lampert [9] provide an extensive review of how such methods have been applied to a variety of problems in image processing.

A third class of relevant features derives from the literature on trajectory analysis, of which the eye tracking data sequences are an example. For example, recent work by Raschke et al. [11] considers how to identify and compare scan path structures. More generally, Rintoul and Wilson [12] discuss domain agnostic methods for extracting geometric features from trajectories which they then use to characterize and compare them. The approach has shown success both as a similarity metric among trajectories and as an outlier detector.

3.3   Representing Visual Search Data as a Time Series

The goal of this work, which is to develop deep insights into visual search processes through exploratory data analysis, requires that we identify features that relate the different data streams to each other. Thus, we need to extend the above image and trajectory analysis methods to identify relationships between the trajectories and the underlying image content. Designing a data representation that facilitates this type of multi-source analysis is therefore critical. For the visual search data, a time series may be the most appropriate choice. This entails representing all of the data as a sequence of observations based on the features identified in the previous step.

The primary issue in constructing the time series relates to encoding features of the static stimulus images into a sequential format. In practice, this requires a two step process. First, we process the images separately from the eye trajectories to identify edges, regions of uniform color, or other identifiable object (laptops, for example). Given these, we can then encode the specific content of the images associated with each fixation area. Thus, the time series represents the sequence of observations made by the participant, as opposed to the entire image.

Traditional time series analysis focuses on sequences of uniformly-spaced, typically univariate measurements [4]. In the context of eye tracking applications, the measurements correspond to both eye events (fixations in particular) and user interactions with the software (such as key presses), which are neither uniformly spaced nor of uniform duration. This raises several issues related to the time series representation, such as whether to explicitly represent event time and duration, or interpolate between individual eye events. The former approach is relevant in the context of trajectory analysis, while the latter may be sufficient for relating fixation locations to features of the underlying image.

Encoding the data as a single time series also raises a variety of other questions. For example, calculating and encoding features of the image content under the participant's gaze becomes tricky when the image moves or the participant changes image products during a fixation. Likewise, the data contains a variety of non-events, such as when the participant looks away from the monitors during their analysis. There is also the question of whether saccades provide any valuable information beyond the fixations. In practice all of these are empirical questions that we will answer as a part of the exploratory analysis. Nevertheless, these questions illustrate the scope of research remaining to be done with respect to visual search data analysis.

4   Visual Search Data Analysis

Having constructed the time series data representation that will support the remainder of the proposed analyses, we now consider specific analytic methods. Given the complexity of the visual search data, the exploratory data analysis process will necessarily be both incremental and iterative. The process is incremental in the sense that identifying and extracting useful patterns and features of the data may require sequential application of several different algorithms and techniques. The process is also iterative in that both individual algorithms and subsequences of them may need to be revisited to achieve the desired results, particularly in light of results achieved later in the process.

Figure 2 summarizes the analysis process (single line) and data flow (double line). The numbers in the figure identify the sections of the paper that provide

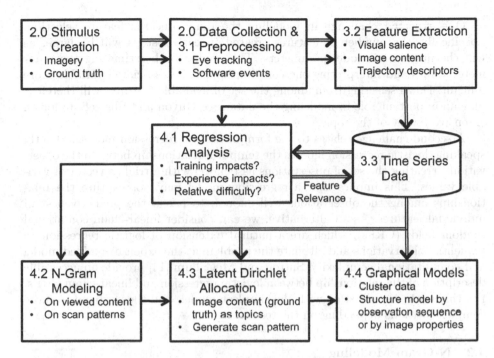

Fig. 2. Process flow (single line) and data flow (double line) for the envisioned visual search data analysis. Numbers indicate the sections of the paper in which we discuss the details of each step.

details for each step. Many of the analytic steps may identify new features that can be added into the time series description of the data. We highlight some of these opportunities in the discussion below. Finally, note that for the remainder of the paper, we use the word *trial* to indicate the interrogation of and decision for a single luggage item by a single TSO.

4.1   Bayesian Logistic Regression

Our first pass at analysis will gain domain insight by modeling questions of interest and by determining feature relevancies based on their contributions to models. Although the models themselves may prove useful, we are most interested in understanding the extent to which various features predict classes of interest, such as participant experience level or the difficulty of a given luggage item. Logistic regression predicts the probability that a trial belongs to a given class by optimizing the distribution over the parameters for a linear combination of predictor variables (features). Though similar in form to traditional regression analysis, the Bayesian approach offers several benefits such as a reduced chance of overfitting and information about the uncertainty associated with both parameter values and predictions [1]. In many cases, this uncertainty can say more about the predictiveness of a feature than the feature's weight.

One expected challenge in modeling the data concerns feature selection. Specifically, the number of features created in earlier steps will be large, as will the number of model parameters. This makes both estimating the parameter values and interpreting the contribution of the associated variable more difficult. Down selecting from among the set of available features, will therefore play an important role in modeling the data. See Guyon and Elisseeff [6] for an extensive review of the topic.

A second challenge relates to the form of logistic regression models. Strictly speaking, logistic regression ignores the temporal relationship between the observations, treating the set of observations associated with a trial as vector of variable values. This implies that a regression model may not capture the relationships among the observations well enough to reveal the predictiveness of individual features. As an alternative, we can consider linear-chain conditional random fields (CRFs), which are a natural extension of logistic regression to sequential observations and alleviate the problem at the expense of added model and computational complexity. Sutton and McCallum [14] provide an accessible description of the relationship between logistic regression and linear-chain CRFs. For this work, we will start with the simplest model, and then expand to more complex methods depending on the results.

4.2   N-Gram Modeling

The remaining three analysis methods draw substantial inspiration from the text analysis literature. We hypothesize that, although text analysis is more constrained than image analysis — English must be read left-to-right and top-to-bottom while images features can be considered in any order — a number of similarities remain. For example, local structures and relationships play a major role in determining meaning. N-gram models exploit combinations of temporally adjacent features to predict larger patterns, such as "political news article" or "luggage containing water bottle".

N-gram models estimate the probability of the next observation in a sequence based on the previous $n - 1$ observations by counting the number of times the same combination appears in training data. For text analysis, this corresponds to the probability of observing a word given a small number of words that precede it in the sentence. By extension, we can use n-grams to estimate the probability of observing certain image features given the previous few observations (fixations).

This provides a simple mechanism for finding local structure and relationships in sequences, and then using them to evaluate much longer sequences. For example, the presence of certain fixation sequences may predict whether a TSO will mark a bag as a threat. Discovery of such sequences would provide substantial insight into what image features trigger officers to recognize threats, whether correctly or incorrectly. This information can then be used to improve the algorithms that process the raw X-ray data into images.

Extending n-grams to the visual search domains requires a few key extensions to the method. For example, no two fixation descriptors (points in the time series) will be exactly the same. In order to calculate the probability of observing a given sequence of observations, we will need to develop a notion of similarity. Similarly, only a few of the possible fixation sequences will be observed in the collected data, so we need a way to account for the sequences that we didn't observe (or make the unreasonable assumption that they never occur). Jurafsky and Manning [8] provide an accessible introduction to this issue and possible solutions. Also consider that, like language analysis, image analysis may have long-distance dependencies. Although in practice local dependencies are sufficient to produce useful models, we still need determine a reasonable value for n in the context of visual search. Finally, note that the n-gram features may be added into the time series representation for use by other models.

4.3   Latent Dirichlet Allocation

Continuing with the text-processing analogy, latent Dirichlet allocation (LDA) treats each example as a mixture of *topics*. Traditionally used to classify documents, each topic is considered responsible for generating portions of the document text. Thus, by identifying the topics associated with a document, we can draw conclusions about the document's content. Blei [2] provides an extensive introduction to LDA and its relatives.

We can apply the same method to visual search data by viewing the sequence of fixations with associated image features as the document text. The goal then is to cluster the fixations from the trials, such that the clusters represent the key features of the image and the TSO's analysis of it. When finished, we can identify the set of topics that governs any observation sequence based on the available ground truth data. Given that we know the contents of the image (such as laptop, water bottle, or threat item) and the outcome of the analysis (false positive, false negative, and so on), we can identify descriptive features for each topic and use them for insight into the visual search process. For example, we may find that experienced TSOs consistently focus on a different set of image features than novices.

As with the n-gram models, LDA will rely heavily on defining a notion of similarity between two fixation descriptors. Likewise, we also need to account for the many possible fixation descriptors that will not appear in the collected data. Although not strictly required, providing meaningful names for the identified topics may require a significant visualization effort. Topic names ultimately derive from the content of the fixation clusters, which will not be easy to interpret. Finally, LDA assumes that the ordering of the observations does not matter (equivalent to bag-of-words in text analysis). More sophisticated variants of LDA can take this ordering into account, but as with the regression analysis, we will begin with the simplest models first.

4.4   Discriminative Graphical Models

Extending now beyond models designed for text classification, discriminative graphical models represent a generalization of the linear-chain CRFs noted above [14]. The method treats the trials as a sequence of interdependent variables. The structure of the graph indicates how the individual observations depend on each other, and many structures are possible. In particular, features of the underlying imagery that are independent of the TSO's fixations can be incorporated into the model. This allows the model to incorporate more context from the underlying imagery than was possible with the previously described methods.

Applying graphical models to the visual search domain will require finding an appropriate division of the trials. The TSOs can search an image in a variety of ways, and combining data from trials that differ wildly in interrogation style will likely have a dissonant effect on parameter estimation. The same may hold for images that do not share similar content or visual properties. The ground truth associated with the images and trials, such as luggage content, analyst performance, and analyst experience level, can inform these, but may not be sufficient. An alternative is to first cluster the trials (or images), and then model each cluster separately, as demonstrated by Oates et al. [10].

We can use the cluster-based graphical models to derive insights into visual search processes in multiple ways. One option is to consider the set of trials contained in each cluster and identify similarities. This is similar in spirit to identifying topics in LDA and serves to highlight the distinguishing properties of each trial. A second option is to evaluate trials held separate from those used during clustering for goodness of fit to each cluster. This type of trial classifier can also help to identify the key properties of trials in each cluster.

5   Summary and Conclusion

Insight into visual search processes can impact a variety of research and development areas. Just in the context of TSA domain considered in this paper, deeper insights into how the checkpoint officers read the imagery to recognize and identify threats could impact how the X-ray data is collected, how it is processed, and how it is displayed to the user. In this paper, we outlined an extensive process for collecting and analyzing visual search data from the TSA domain. Our proposed analysis focuses on identifying a broad variety of features in the data and on integrating the different data sources into a single analysis.

Integrating sources such as eye tracking, software interactions, stimulus imagery, and its associated ground truth information makes the analysis process very complex, as illustrated by the large number of steps and open issues described above. Nevertheless, we assert that combining all of the data as described offers the best opportunity to answer important questions such as what predicts how difficult a luggage item will be to assess, or what might indicate an impending TSO error. Progress on these questions will help to improve security at airport checkpoints.

Acknowledgements. The authors thank David Robinson and Travis Bauer for helpful discussions on the data analysis methodologies. This research was funded in part or whole by an interagency agreement between the Transportation Security Administration and Sandia. Sandia National Laboratories is a multi-program laboratory managed and operated by Sandia Corporation, a wholly owned subsidiary of Lockheed Martin Corporation, for the U.S. Department of Energy National Nuclear Security Administration under contract DE-AC04-94AL85000.

References

1. Bishop, C.M., Tipping, M.E.: Bayesian regression and classification. In: Suykens, J., Horvath, I., Basu, S., Micchelli, C., Vandewalle, J. (eds.) Advances in Learning Theory: Methods, Models and Applications. NATO Science Series III: Computer and Systems Sciences, vol. 190. IOS Press, Amsterdam (2003)
2. Blei, D.M.: Probabilistic topic models. Commun. ACM **55**(4), 77–84 (2012)
3. Erkelens, C.J., Sloot, O.B.: Initial directions and landing positions of binocular saccades. Vis. Res. **35**(23–24), 3297–3303 (1995)
4. Fu, T.: A review on time series data mining. Eng. Appl. Artif. Intell. **24**, 164–181 (2011)
5. Getoor, L., Taskar, B.: Introduction to Statistical Relational Learning. MIT Press, Cambridge (2007)
6. Guyon, I., Elisseef, A.: An introduction to variable and feature selection. J. Mach. Learn. Res. **3**, 1157–1182 (2003)
7. Itti, L.: Visual salience. Scholarpedia **2**(9), 3327 (2007). http://www.scholarpedia.org/article/Visual_salience
8. Jurafsky, D., Manning, C.: Natural language processing, January 2012. https://www.coursera.org/course/nlp
9. Nowozin, S., Lampert, C.H.: Structured learning and prediction in computer vision. Found. Trends Comput. Graph. Vis. **6**(3–4), 185–365 (2010)
10. Oates, T., Firoiu, L., Cohen, P.R.: Clustering time series with hidden markov models and dynamic time warping. In: Proceedings of the IJCAI 1999 Workshop on Neural, Symbolic and Reinforcement Learning Methods for Sequence Learning, pp. 17–21 (1999)
11. Raschke, M., Herr, D., Blascheck, T., Ertl, T., Burch, M., Willmann, S., Schrauf, M.: A visual approach for scan path comparison. In: 2014 Symposium on Eye Tracking Research and Applications. ACM, Safety Harbor (2014)
12. Rintoul, M.D., Wilson, A.T.: Trajectory analysis via a geometric feature space approach (2014) (unpublished, in preparation)
13. Speed, A.E., Silva, A., Trumbo, D., Stracuzzi, D.J., Warrender, C., Trumbo, M., Divis, K.: Determining the optimal time on X-ray analysis for transportation security officers. In: Proceedings of the 9th International Conference on Augmented Cognition. Springer, Los Angeles (2015)
14. Sutton, C., McCallum, A.K.: An introduction to conditional random fields. Found. Trends Mach. Learn. **4**(4), 267–373 (2011)
15. Wolfe, J.M.: Asymmetries in visual search: an introduction. Percept. Psychophys. **63**(3), 381–389 (2001)
16. Yu, K., Ng, A.: ECCV-2010 tutorial: feature learning for image classification, September 2010. http://ufldl.stanford.edu/eccv10-tutorial/

Adaptive Tutoring and Training

Transitioning from Human to Agent-Based Role-Players for Simulation-Based Training

Robert G. Abbott$^{(\boxtimes)}$, Christina Warrender, and Kiran Lakkaraju

Sandia National Laboratories, Albuquerque, NM 87111, USA
rgabbot@sandia.gov

Abstract. In the context of military training simulation, "semi-automated for-ces" are software agents that serve as role players. The term implies a degree of shared control – increased automation allows one operator to control a larger number of agents, but too much automation removes control from the instructor. The desired amount of control depends on the situation, so there is no single "best" level of automation. This paper describes the rationale and design for Trainable Automated Forces (TAF), which is based on training by example in order to reduce the development time for automated agents. A central issue is how TAF interprets demonstrated behaviors either as an example to follow specifically, or as contingencies to be executed as the situation permits. We describe the behavior recognizers that allow TAF to produce a high-level model of behaviors. We assess the accuracy of a recognizer for a simple airplane maneuver, showing that it can accurately recognize the maneuver from just a few examples.

Keywords: Learning by example · Training by demonstration · Software agents

1 Introduction

When automating a task that has previously been performed by a person, recordings of human performance data can provide examples of desired behaviors. Our current domain is fighter combat, where student pilots fly against "enemy" role-players who emulate anticipated threat tactics. The tactics can be recorded in an airplane instrumented with position tracking equipment, or from a flight simulator. This paper presents our recent work on Trainable Automated Forces (TAF), which is a system to simulate tactical behavior based on recorded examples.

In the context of Live/Virtual/Constructive training [1], TAF is designed to create a Constructive entity from a Live or Virtual (i.e. human in the loop) example. The output of TAF is a set of inputs for the Next Generation Threat System (NGTS), which is a constructive entity simulator that focuses on fighter tactics [2] (Fig. 1). NGTS simulates both the physics and behaviors of entities, but TAF focuses exclusively on the behaviors. The design of TAF assumes that NGTS is capable of producing the desired

© Springer International Publishing Switzerland 2015
D.D. Schmorrow and C.M. Fidopiastis (Eds.): AC 2015, LNAI 9183, pp. 551–561, 2015.
DOI: 10.1007/978-3-319-20816-9_53

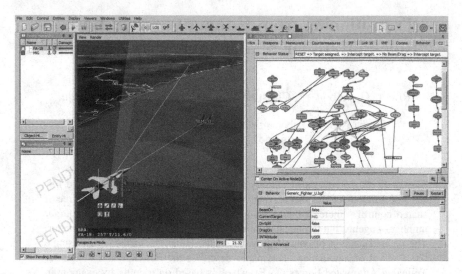

Fig. 1. The next-generation threat system (NGTS) simulates fighter tactics. On the right is a portion of the decision logic for the white aircraft on the left. TAF addresses the difficulty of developing this logic.

tactics if it is programmed correctly, but programming the tactics can be difficult and time-consuming. The objectives of TAF are:

1. Minimize the time and cost of creating new behavior models.
2. Create a fully realized, executable NGTS entity from recordings that do not explicitly capture the goals of the pilot or details non-visible behavior such as turning on sensors or jammers and making radio calls.
3. Interpret the example behavior literally or generally as desired by the user, inferring which actions are to be replicated, and which arose by chance and should only be executed if necessary.
4. Strike a balance between open-ended behaviors that respond realistically to a wide range of situations and aren't overly predictable, yet don't distract from the training objectives by being erratic.
5. Fall back to a reasonable general-purpose behavior model when there are no relevant examples in the set of scenario recordings.
6. Learn from a small number of training examples; flight recordings are expensive to obtain.
7. Produce behavior models that are human-readable, allowing the model to be manually corrected or tailored if necessary.

The key to balancing these goals is leveraging the subject matter expertise that is built into NGTS, re-combining and parameterizing the provided behaviors. The alternative would be to build models based completely on flight recordings, ignoring the existing physics and behavior models in NGTS. However, unless vast amounts of example behavior data are available, a software agent based solely on observed behaviors will be limited. The range of agent behaviors will be limited to behaviors that occurred within the training data, and the agent will take inappropriate actions, because a large number of examples are required to distinguish casual effects from spurious correlations. Moreover, some aspects of the behavior cannot be learned by observation because they are not observable to the system, e.g. the employment of sensors and emitters by a fighter pilot.

2 Related Work

Programming by demonstration (PBD) is the approach of programming an agent by replicating the actions of a person, whose actions are recorded in a simulator or instrumented environment (e.g. an airplane that records its position over time). PBD is a natural approach to progressively automating a task that was formerly performed by a person, such as role-playing for training scenarios. PBD was originally used for tasks such as assembly-line robotics in which the robot would carry out the same sequence of steps each time. Most of this research has been done in the field of robotics and targets low-level sensor/motor actions [3]. As more complex tasks were undertaken, generalizing the behavior to accommodate different situations became increasingly important. Rather than replicating actions specifically, the agent must infer the goals implied by the example, and select and refine actions as necessary to accomplish those goals.

Goals are necessarily domain-specific, so PBM must be adapted to each new domain with a set of possible goals and means to attain them. Specifying a set of goals compromises the original intent of PBD to reduce manual programming, but ensures that the set of goals are consistent with how human experts understand the domain. This is crucial if humans are to monitor to agent's actions and sometimes influence them for reasons external to the system, such as instructors using TAF to train students.

3 TAF Design and Rationale

This section describes the design of TAF, and how the design supports the objectives listed in the introduction (Fig. 2).

3.1 TAF Knowledge Base

The TAF Knowledge Base (KB) is the key to mapping desired agent behaviors to the NGTS inputs that elicit that behavior. It contains numerous examples of

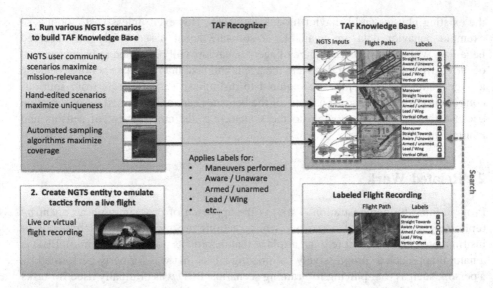

Fig. 2. TAF. During development, the knowledge base is populated with NGTS scenario executions that establish the entity behaviors resulting from various NGTS inputs. Then TAF can generate NGTS entities whose behaviors match those found in a flight recording. The TAF recognizer is the basis for this matching.

scenarios executed in NGTS that include agents using various settings. These include the behavior rules assigned to the agent, parameters for the behavior rules, and the scenario in which the agent was embedded. The KB is analogous to the experience accumulated by a human user of NGTS who experiments with various settings and observes the results to develop an understanding of what to expect from the software.

The mapping from NGTS inputs to agent behaviors may change as the NGTS software is revised, so it is important that TAF be able to re-learn this association in an efficient manner. We have developed TAF training software that automatically executes an NGTS run for each of a set of inputs which may be very large, so TAF can re-learn each new version of NGTS.

The behavioral repertoire of TAF is constrained by the KB examples – it can only take actions contained in its knowledge base. A benefit of the KB-limited approach (vs. generating inputs before or during scenario execution) is that the KB can be audited to remove unwanted examples. However, the parameter space of NGTS is practically infinite - far too large to explore exhaustively. Therefore the selection of scenarios for the KB is very important. To date we have used three sources. **NGTS user community scenarios** are developed manually by NGTS users to meet specific end-user needs, so they are full of realistic situations and behaviors of great use to TAF. On the other hand, re-combining elements from them will not allow TAF to author scenarios much different than users already have, so additional sources are needed. We have developed a number of **hand-edited** scenarios that each differ significantly from each other, and from previously existing scenarios. Scenarios from **automated sampling algorithms** allow TAF to explore beyond human-specified entities. These are easy to generate in large numbers and can potentially allow TAF to output any type of behavior of which NGTS is capable, including behaviors not envisioned by NGTS developers. The risk is of generating large numbers of behaviors that are unrealistic, irrelevant, or redundant. Our approach is to use scenarios from the user community and our own hand-edited scenarios as the basis for subsequent modification by the sampling algorithm.

Once each scenario is run, it is inserted into the KB. The KB example includes the paths of all entities and the NGTS inputs used to produce them, such as the version of the NGTS software used and the behavior rules and settings assigned to the entity. Then the TAF Recognizer is applied to recognize actions in the example scenario execution.

3.2   TAF Recognizer

The TAF Recognizer applies semantic labels to traces in the KB, and in flight recordings. The granularity of the labels determines how much TAF will abstract the example scenarios when matching them to flight recordings. For example, a trajectory could be recognized either as a series of specific maneuvers (e.g. "turn left 30°, proceed ahead for 25 NM, then turn left 15°...") or at a more abstract, goal-oriented level ("e.g. Lead Pursuit on target aircraft"). Labels are tested from general to specific, and processing of mutually exclusive labels stops with the first match. However, not all labels are mutually exclusive, and some recognizers use the output of those applied beforehand. For example, several recognizers look at the position of the aircraft relative to each of enemies, where groups are identified by one of the early recognizers.

TAF recognizers are implemented as feature extractors in the RBBML framework [1]. In the RBBML framework, a *model* is a Java class that defines methods to derive a set of features to derive and store in the database. For example the Intercept Geometry model samples the positions of two entities at regular distance intervals and then computes their turn rates, and the range and aspect angle from each to the other. This model also has receptors for range categories Near/Medium/Far, which are not used in matching, but are consulted after a match is found to determine the range at which the entity will maneuver. A *model instance* is a model populated with examples that exemplify a particular behavior, and specifies which model features are relevant to identifying the behavior. For example the Beam Maneuver model instance contains examples of that maneuver flown by a human pilot and by an NGTS entity and selects the features *target aspect* and *threat turn rate*. The Intercept Geometry model can be trained with different examples to recognize different maneuvers.

Recognizing Groups of Entities. Fighters normally work together, often flying in formation. The basic unit of organization is a *group* of two or more fighters. A constructive simulation of fighter tactics must capture this organizational structure because the roles of two aircraft (*lead* and *wing*) are somewhat different. The roles must be made explicit for NGTS, since otherwise the lead and wing would not stay in formation. However, flight recordings do not specify the formation hierarchy; it must be recognized from spatial information.

The TAF algorithm for recognizing groups is based on two aircraft being "usually near" each other. This is complicated by the fact that aircraft have separate lifetimes (either may exist while the other does not), and that aircraft in the same group may occasionally separate for a period of time. For each pair of aircraft, TAF samples the positions at a regular interval (1 s), and tallies the samples in which the pair of aircraft are near (the distance is less than a threshold of 5 nautical miles using the Haversine formula) vs. far (the distance exceeds the threshold, or only one of the two aircraft currently exist). The two aircraft are considered "usually near" if the ratio of near to far instances exceeds a threshold (at least 80 % of all samples are near). Next, each aircraft is placed into a separate group. Two groups are considered near if any aircraft in one group is "usually near" any aircraft in the other group. The groups, which initially contain a single aircraft each, are merged with all other near groups, until no group is near any other (Fig. 3).

Fig. 3. Six aircraft are assigned to three groups. Note that the grouping does not correspond precisely to the groups implied by the manually-designated callsigns, because victory 33 deviates from victory 31 later in the scenario. Formation-flying is typical in tactical flight, and grouping them reduces the combinatorial complexity of identifying interactions among aircraft.

The leader of each group is recognized by computing the mean velocity vector of members of the group at each timestep. The position of each group member is projected onto the velocity vector, and the member with the highest median projected value is designated the leader.

A limitation of this approach is that group membership and leadership are static – each aircraft belongs to only a single group over time. The advantage of this approach is that it avoids discontinuities in the spatial relations between groups that would occur from re-assigning an aircraft from one group to another. However the results at a point in time may appear incorrect because the group assignment is dominated by the rest of the scenario.

Recognizing Maneuvers. A simple maneuver (e.g. a flying a loop) is a relatively fixed path through space over time relative to a starting position. In combat, maneuvers are

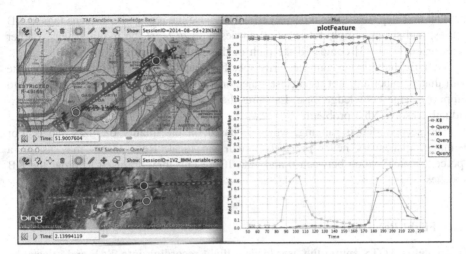

Fig. 4. A recognizer for the beam maneuver. Flight recordings (bottom) are searched for an example of the maneuver (top) on the basis of time-varying spatial features such as range, aspect, and turn rate.

generally executed relative to other aircraft, and the maneuver is characterized by a prescribed path through the state space of relative positions and angles. For example, in a beam maneuver the pilot flies perpendicular to the attacker so as to avoid moving either towards or away from the attacker. If the attacking aircraft or missile has a relatively simple Doppler radar, this maneuver may cause the radar difficulty in distinguishing the aircraft from stationary objects on the ground.

In TAF, maneuvers are sampled from KB examples or flight recordings. For the beam maneuver (Fig. 4), the aspect transitions from 1 (towards) to 0 (perpendicular) then back to 1. The turn rate of the aircraft is also matched to ensure that it, and not its target, is performing the maneuver.

TAF searches for maneuvers by computing the time-varying spatial relations between each group of fighters. The position of a group is defined as the position of the lead aircraft in the group. The rate of execution of a maneuver may vary somewhat, so TAF uses the dynamic time warping algorithm [2] to match spatio-temporal trajectories that vary only in rate of execution.

Spatio-temporal matching always yields approximate matches, so the quality of match is also recorded on a scale from 100 (perfect match) to 0 (not considered a match). The percentage is used to place different recognizers on a comparable scale.

3.3 TAF Search

In TAF the goal of search is to find examples of NGTS inputs that resulted in an entity exhibiting the desired behaviors, and secondly to rank the results order of match quality.

The first step (search) is relatively trivial because the recognizer assigns tags to KB entries, and search simply retrieves all entries with *at least* the required tags. Earlier iterations of TAF [3] compared the path of the flight recording to each KB example individually, but this was unnecessarily specific (since it is the *meaning* or label of the path that is important, not its precise trajectory) and too computationally intensive to support a large knowledge base. Labeling the KB examples and the flight path individually resolves this problem.

The second step is ranking, which is based on the quality of fuzzy labels. For example, maneuvers never *precisely* match the ideal. Recognizers may assign a "percent match" value between 0 and 100. If present, they are used to order the KB matches.

3.4   Flight Recording

To create an NGTS entity, the user loads a flight recording into TAF and selects the example entity. When the flight recording is read in, TAF applies the recognizer to it. A user interface is supplied so the user can correct the recognized behaviors, or change the labels used in the search so the resulting NGTS entity differs from the example in some aspects.

The set of TAF behavior labels must be compatible with richness or sparsity of the source of the flight recording. For example, a manually-controlled entity in NGTS will result in a highly detailed flight recording without any sensor noise. A virtually-piloted entity recorded from a network simulation (commonly the HLA protocol [4]) will also be noise-free, but will generally only have information about the externally-visible attributes of the aircraft and pilot behavior, with no explicit information about goals. A flight recording from a live source will have sensor noise and dropouts, but (depending on the source) may have detailed information about onboard systems. However, the 'black box' from a single aircraft is not sufficiently informative to model tactics, since tactical flight is generally performed relative to other aircraft, ground targets, etc.

4   Evaluation of TAF Behavior Recognition

This section describes an assessment we performed on the TAF Behavior Recognizer for the beam maneuver that was described in the previous section. The behavior recognizer is a key element of TAF, because it determines the similarity between a flight recording to be emulated and the repertoire of behaviors in the TAF Knowledge Base. We collected flight recordings, identified beam maneuvers independently both manually and with the TAF Recognizer, and then compared the results.

We collected a set of examples of the beam maneuver in the context of a larger mission that was executed repeatedly. This data set included executions of the maneuver both by human pilots, and by NGTS entities. In the case of NGTS entities, we performed recognition on the maneuver using only positional information, disregarding whether the maneuver had been triggered by the NGTS Beam Maneuver

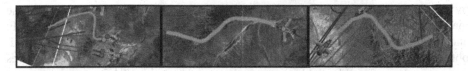

Fig. 5. Sections of flight paths that, to varying degrees, resemble an ideal beam maneuver in which the aircraft turns to place an oncoming threat directly to the left or right. TAF assigned a match quality of 99 % (left), 55 % (middle), and 34 % (right).

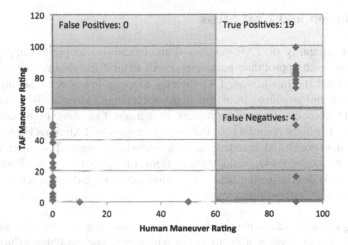

Fig. 6. Ratings of 23 candidate instances of the beam maneuver in a set of flight recordings

command. (Modeling NGTS behaviors is of interest because they may be controlled by a human operator manually issuing commands, and these operators are to be modeled in addition to actual pilots.) We examined 77 scenario executions, each of which included 32 airplanes, for a total of 2,464 trajectories.

By examining these trajectories the human rater identified 36 candidate examples of the beam maneuver. Each candidate maneuver was assigned a quality score between 1 and 100, with 100 being ideal, and 1 deemed only marginally similar to the ideal. Note that there is no "ground truth" (beyond the human rater) of whether a beam maneuver was performed – a pilot might try to perform the maneuver and be interrupted, or simply make a mistake. Textbook definitions of maneuvers [7] *may* include tolerances for relevant angles etc. but human raters, and TAF, recognize degrees of success (Fig. 5).

We then ran the TAF recognizer on the same data set. TAF also assigns a quality score, and identified 41 candidate matches. Matches identified by the human and TAF were considered to refer to the same event if they were performed by the same aircraft during time windows that coincided. The probability of matching by chance was low, since fewer than 1 in 60 trajectories contained a candidate example, and a typical example covered less than 10 % of the duration of a single trajectory (80 s vs. 900 s).

The human and TAF ratings of maneuvers identified are shown in Fig. 6. The correlation between human and TAF ratings is 0.63. The correlation is brought down by several possible matches identified by TAF (in the lower-left of the figure). These matches are not necessarily a problem since they are assigned a low quality by TAF, and could be automatically suppressed. With a decision boundary of 60 % quality, TAF obtains 19 true positives, 0 false positives, and 4 false negatives. Of the false negatives (maneuvers recognized by the human rater but not detected by TAF), some are corner cases such as a maneuver performed against a threat that was destroyed before the maneuver was completed. It should be noted that a group of human raters would not have 100 % agreement, although we do not have data on inter-rater reliability.

5 Conclusion and Next Steps

The current capability of TAF matches flight recordings to pre-existing models of behavior that (with appropriate parameters) will exhibit the desired behaviors in the appropriate contexts. In addition, TAF directly adopts a few specific settings (such as initial aircraft and heading) from the flight recording. Our plan is to expand this capability to combining novel sequences of actions that directly model observed behaviors from a flight recording. In the current version of TAF, novel behaviors must be generated a priori and inserted into the knowledge base. This approach is not scalable to all conceivable, valid combinations of behaviors. Our efforts are now directed towards discriminating between planned actions (goals) and actions that arose due to happenstance (contingencies).

Acknowledgement. Sandia National Laboratories is a multi-program laboratory managed and operated by Sandia Corporation, a wholly owned subsidiary of Lockheed Martin Corporation, for the U.S. Department of Energy's National Nuclear Security Administration under contract DE-AC04-94AL85000.

References

1. Schnell, T., Postnikov, A., Hamel, N.: Neuroergonomic assessment of simulator fidelity in an aviation centric live virtual constructive (LVC) application. In: Schmorrow, D.D., Fidopiastis, C.M. (eds.) FAC 2011. LNCS, vol. 6780, pp. 221–230. Springer, Heidelberg (2011)
2. Hildreth, B., Linse, D.J., Dicola, J.: Pseudo six degree of freedom (DOF) models for higher fidelity constructive simulations. In: AIAA Modeling and Simulation Technologies Conference and Exhibit, Hohololu, Hawaii (2008)
3. Abbott, R.G.: The relational blackboard. In: Behavior Representation in Modeling and Simulation, Ottawa, Ontario, Canada (2013)
4. Rakthanmanon, T., Campana, B., Mueen, A., Batista, G., Westover, B., Zhu, Q., Zakaria, J., Keogh, E.: Searching and mining trillions of time series subsequences under dynamic time warping. In: Proceedings of the 18th ACM SIGKDD international conference on Knowledge discovery and data mining (KDD 2012), New York, USA (2012)
5. Abbott, R.G., Lakkaraju, K., Warrender, C.: Semi-automated construction of adversarial agents for trainable automated forces. In: AAMAS, Paris (2014)
6. Kuhl, F., Weatherly, R., Dahmann, J.: Creating Computer Simulation Systems: An Introduction to The High Level Architecture. Prentice Hall, Upper Saddle River (1999)

7. Naval Air Training Command, Flight Training Instruction: Air to Air Intercept Procedures Workbook (CNATRA P-825), Department of the Navy, NAS Corpus Christi, TX, USA (2010)
8. Sigaud, O., Peters, J.: Abstraction levels for robotic imitation: overview and computational approaches. In: Sigaud, O., Peters, J. (eds.) From Motor Learning to Interaction Learning in Robots. SCI, vol. 264, pp. 1–12. Springer, Heidelberg (2010)

Authoring Tools for Adaptive Training – An Overview of System Types and Taxonomy for Classification

Keith Brawner[✉]

Army Research Laboratory, Orlando, FL, USA
keith.w.brawner.civ@mail.mil

1 Introduction

The Intelligent Tutoring Systems (ITS) community has recently renewed its interest in authoring tools, as evidenced in recent workshops, publications, and developments. Part of this renewal of effort has been in the development of authoring tools systems for maturing products and processes. As an example, the Cognitive Tutor Authoring Tools (CTAT), AutoTutor Script Authoring Tools (ASAT), and Generalized Intelligent Framework for Tutoring (GIFT) Authoring Tool (GAT) are all available for community use and feedback through their various portals. As these authoring tools come available, it is helpful to classify them into groups, for the purpose of study, based upon their similarities and differences .

As part of these recent activities, conversations and discussions from authoring tools experts naturally align themselves to a few basic categories. The research presented in this paper attempts to condense and summarize the state of art, practice, and future along its natural dividing lines. The basic categories of division are the intended users, the intended training environment, the type of content authored, and the level of automation.

The first part of this ontology divides itself according to the intended author. Authors of the various authoring tools range from "super user", to "content developer", to "end user". Each of these users fits a different profile, with different expertise, and different demands. Several tools involved the collaboration between one of more of these categories, such as a tool developed by Carnegie Mellon University, Cognitive Tutor SDK, which uses programmer support and SME authored instruction in order to automatically generated rules for use in student diagnostics. The section of this paper dedicated to various user categories goes into detail about the expected and required expertise for each user category, elaborates on examples of tools constructed for each group, and attempts to predict the direction of future research in each of the categories.

The second part of the ontology divides itself according to the nature of the intended student environment. Student environments can include text-based and plain HTML-delivered websites, simulated environments for skill practice, or fully inter-actable 3-dimensional game worlds. Unlike the intended author classification, few tools fall into a category where they target multiple environments. The functions of the authoring tools for each environment varies significantly, and the section of this paper

© Springer International Publishing Switzerland 2015
D.D. Schmorrow and C.M. Fidopiastis (Eds.): AC 2015, LNAI 9183, pp. 562–569, 2015.
DOI: 10.1007/978-3-319-20816-9_54

dedicated to details about the expected and required expertise for each environment category elaborates on examples of the tools constructed for each broad group category and gives basic predictions about the near-term tracks for this research.

The third part of the ontology is divided according to the type of content which requires authoring. Typically, the components of intelligent tutoring which require authoring involve content, assessments, feedback, or within-game adjustments. However, there are fringe areas of authoring which perform these functions in novel manners, such as the use of demonstration by practice for user-authored assessments, or automated feedback generation. Past areas of this technology, such as automatic content reuse for remediation, may now leverage the large body of Internet-accessible content. These novel applications still fit within the overall ontological classification but are noteworthy for their interactions with other portions of this grouping scheme. The section of this paper dedicated to the discussion of the relative difficulties and conflicting goals among the various types of content authoring.

The last component of the ontology is the portion which is centered on automation of the authoring process. Tools in this category are not intended for direct human use, but make use of either machine processes or crowdsourcing to create components of intelligent tutoring systems. The design of such tools is fundamentally different from the other groups of users to warrant further overall discussion.

A single authoring tool may fit in one or more of these categories, but these categories are functionally useful for describing the purpose, construction, and users of modern ITS tools. As an example, a tool which allows content developers to create assessments of student performance within a game world and automatically suggests feedback based on those items fits three categories of tool: one for its user group, one for its purpose, and one for the automaticity of one of its functions. Describing a tool in this detail, however, provides a working definition and taxonomy by which to classify, fairly evaluate, and discuss future authoring tools.

Each ITS development tool logical falls into one of more of these categories. Particular authoring tools will be presented throughout this paper as examples of tools within specific categories.

2   User Category

The first fundamental category from which authoring tools diverge for classification purposes is the category of user which they are built for. Generally, an authoring tool user requires familiarity of a few basic categories: either familiarity of a tool, tutoring/learning theory, the representation of knowledge, or of the actual job/domain/task that the student is supposed to be learning [1]. Each of the authoring tools developed for adaptive training attempts to automate or supplement some part of this functionality in an effort to save time or produce better training.

2.1 Super User

Tools intended for 'super user' consumption is categorized by programmatic or system assembly ability. Generally speaking, any tool which involves programming, editing of XML documents, manipulations of agent actions, or the creation of objects within a virtual world becomes a 'super user' tool requiring specific expertise. The primary differentiation for a super user tool is that it is one step removed from programming or configuration (e.g. XML editor is a tool, but Notepad is not).

Carnegie Learning, in the form of the Cognitve Tutor Software Development Kit (CT-SDK) has an example of a tool which is intended for the use of super users to create tutoring systems [2]. The process involves a knowledge engineer, who is familiar with the process of writing Cognitive Tutor rules, to work in conjunction with a domain expert, who is familiar with the processes of novices and experts, and a programmer, who is capable of creating interfaces and systems which work appropriately. This toolset allows the domain expert to articulate knowledge, the knowledge engineer to capture it in the form of Cognitive Tutor processes in procedural software windows, and the programmer to create an environment to execute the knowledge. While this process requires significant expertise, it is speeded enough that it is commercially viable and successful to create tutors.

2.2 Content Developer

Tools intended for content developers primarily revolve around the expertise categories of either a) instructional system design or b) subject matter expertise with a domain. Automated examples such as the content-augmentation process described later, in Sect. 4.1, or the system which uses subject matter expertise and training materials to craft a dialogue tutor, described in Sect. 5.2, can be seen as tools for such individuals.

2.3 End User

There are few existing systems which rely upon the end user to help in the creation of the system. However, the recent trend towards crowd-sourcing includes tools that the students can use, while interacting with the system, to create content for consumption of other students. It is expected that more 'social' tools will be available in the future, as part of the ongoing process of improving tutoring systems.

3 Student Environment

The second fundamental category to distinguish authoring tools is the intended environment for consumption. Student environments can range from multiplayer 3D worlds to simple "page turner" book replacement content, with several types of environments in between.

3.1   Basic Consumption

A basic consumption environment is nothing more than a "page turner", webpage, PowerPoint slide set, video, or other form of static content. While there is little doubt that the presentation of content is part of tutoring, there generally exist few adaptive authoring tools to create this content. There are many tools to create content of this nature, many environments in which to consume it, and the listing of them is beyond the scope of this paper.

3.2   Enhanced Consumption

Adaptive training tools have the capability to apply enhanced value to existing pieces of training content. Systems such as the Generalized Intelligent Framework for Tutoring (GIFT) [3] and REDEEM [4] operate as "shell tutors" to provide a framework for the import and use of previously existing materials, the addition of feedback, and the embedding of pedagogical practices..

An example of an enhanced consumption authoring tools is the eXtensible Problem-Specific Tutor [5]. This system allows for content authors to highlight certain interactable portions of content on a webpage in order to provide a "tutoring layer" overtop of the existing content. In this manner, an author can use familiar tools for the creation of basic content while creating an overlay of instructional interactions. Later, when the student takes predefined actions, they can receive feedback, additional content, or other information.

3.3   Practice Environment

An example of an authoring tool which is intended for the student practice environment is SimStudent [6]. SimStudent watches expert actions within the environment in order to attempt to generalize rules of human behavior through the creation and population of behavior graphs. Later, these behavior graphs are applied to the assessment of novices. This works very well in procedural domains such as stoichiometry and algebra, as it can easily spot novice mistakes in problem solving order. This can effectively bridge the gap between maximally general Cognitive Tutors and maximally specific example tracing tutors for domains of instruction which involve step-by-step problem solving.

3.4   Virtual Environment

The VECTOR project is an example of an authoring tool designed around the principle of scenario-based training and the incorporation of instructional design workflow into virtual environments. It does this through anchoring instruction explicitly to objects within the game world. It has been applied to ill-defined tasks such as cross-cultural awareness, clinical communication, and negotiation skills [1]. Another example of a system which operates under similar constraints is the Situated Pedagogy (SitPed) authoring tool developed by the Institute of Creative Technologies, which offers the authoring of characters and events from the student's perspective, within a game environment.

4 Content Authoring

4.1 Content

The majority of content which is consumed in an adaptive training system is created in systems external to the system itself. PowerPoint and HTML-based training is a prime example of where intelligent tutoring technologies can serve to enhance training value.

An example of a tool created for the modification of content in adaptive training systems, instead of a content creation tool (e.g. PowerPoint™), is the Metadata Authoring Tool (MAT). The MAT is a part of the GIFT standard package of publicly available tools [7]. The purpose of the tool is to enable authors to describe the attributes of created content in a machine-consumable fashion. Authors essentially check boxes which content attributes. During the tutoring process, the Engine for Management of Adaptive Pedagogy (EMAP) matches learner traits and content attributes in a manner which has been validated in the literature to produce learning gains. An automated version of this tool is currently under development from Advanced Distributed Learning [8].

4.2 Assessments

A critical part of any adaptive training system is the ability to assess student competency, either for the purpose of giving feedback, selecting the next scenario, or assigning remediation. The authoring of assessments is usually dependent on the domain of the system which is attempting to assess, but recent efforts have attempted to perform domain-independent assessments. The creation of such domain-independent assessments is usually highly dependent on templates, such as with the AutoTutor Script Authoring Tool (ASAT) [9], or the GIFT Student Information Models for Intelligent Learning Environments (SIMILE) Workbench tool [7]. Each assessment in an intelligent tutoring system ties to a learning objective or cognitive tracking variable.

4.3 Feedback

Most intelligent tutoring systems authoring tools couple the authoring of assessment and feedback, simultaneously creating the way to assess student misconception or poor performance with the actions that the system has available to it. Systems such as SitPed, GIFT Authoring Tool (GAT), and ASAT all allow the authoring of feedback and interactions within the same user interaction.

5   Authoring Process

Lastly, the functionality that divides authoring tools is the process by which they are used. Super user intended tools are primarily human-oriented in nature, while most tools use some combination of machine processes and templates to create interactions. Finally, there is the potential for highly automated tools to use a wide availability of data to construct interactions without human intervention.

5.1   Primarily Human

The majority of authoring processes are primarily human in nature, utilizing tools to supplement either author knowledge, steps in the authoring process, or as supplemental information. Tools for highly knowledgeable users have a tendency to be especially manual, while tools for content developers have a tendency to be dependent on templates, leaving user tools to be with highly automatic or non-existent. The GIFT architecture has a number of primarily human configuration tools, and is hardly unique in this respect, as most systems involve some amount of system-specific tool for configuration of various variables, assessments, content, and feedback.

5.2   Machine-Assisted

Machine-assisted authoring is the standard for non-super user authoring tools, using the function of the computer to supplement or augment some level of expertise of the author. Tools such as SimStudent [6], once developed for a specific domain, are intended to be used in conjunction with a domain expert in order to create interactive tutoring events. Another example of a adaptive training authoring tool which depends on both automated and human authoring is the Tool for Rapid Automated Development of Expert Models (TRADEM) available at http://tradem.gifttutoring.org [10]. This tool takes a number of pieces of training content, performs a text analysis to determine the key text items, creates a topic map of the core concepts, and requires a content author to fine-tune the results and assessments before exporting to a digital agent. In each of these cases fashion, a framework for the content delivery can be rapidly created and augmented through human use.

5.3   Primarily Automated

Although systems such as TRADEM and automatically constructed concept maps work better with human intervention, they have the potential to ignore human intervention. There is the potential for fully automated intelligent tutoring systems which construct themselves from data, such as the data in DataShop [11]. Technologies such as automatically-created student models from small samples of learner interaction data, or from systems which measure learning gains in order to select the optimal instructional interventions [12] may provide a future path for the creation of adaptive learning content and interactions.

6 Ontology Use and Example Classifications

The Generalized Intelligent Framework for Tutoring (GIFT) has a number of authoring tools available, each of which has its own purpose and is intended for a variety of audiences and environments. As an example, the GAT is a single, web-based, instance where an entire tutoring experience can be created. A GAT-authored course may consist of embedded content assessments, nodes within a course flow, or adaptive branching based on learner experiences.

	GAT	MAT	TRADEM	CT-SDK	Sim-Student	xPST	VECTOR	SitPed
User								
Super User				X	X	X	X	
Content Developer	X	X	X	X		X	X	X
End User								X
Environment								
Basic Consumption	X	X	X			X		
Enhanced Consumption	X			X				
Practice Environment	X	X		X	X			X
Virtual Environment	X	X					X	X
Content								
Content	X	X	X	X	X	X	X	X
Assessments	X		X	X	X	X	X	X
Feedback	X			X	X	X	X	X
Process								
Human	X	X		X		X	X	X
Automated					X			
Both			X		X			

7 Conclusion and Future Research

The reuse of ITS systems for learning research reduces the overall need for authoring tools and enables the field to continue to develop system-specific systems. ITS authoring tools generally do not exist in large enough numbers to be considered a subfield, but general software engineering design principles are emerging. These principles, such as the division of tool and function, a tool for each function, the limitation of complexity per user allow the field to be categorized by function. The most recent work on the subject catalogues these items in great detail [13].

A set of general-purpose authoring tools for a general-purpose intelligent tutoring system remains a difficult goal, but the GIFT GAT, AutoTutor ASAT, and xPST are all now publicly available. In addition to these tools, increasing automation, such as from TRADEM and SimStudent, is removing the task of authoring from the user. The author believes that these trends of traditional design, domain generality, system generality, and increased automation, will dominate the ITS authoring tools field in the coming years.

References

1. Zachary, W., Santarello, T., Engimann, J., Hu, X.: Authoring by whom? Two perspectives on its authoring tools. In: Intelligent Tutoring Systems 2014, Honolulu, Hawaii (2014)
2. Brawner, K., Sinatra, A.: intelligent tutoring system authoring tools: harvesting the current crop and planting the seeds for the future. In: Intelligent Tutoring Systems. Springer (2014)
3. Sottilare, R.A., Brawner, K.W., Goldberg, B.S., Holden, H.K.: The Generalized Intelligent Framework for Tutoring (Gift) (2012)
4. Ainsworth, S., Major, N., Grimshaw, S., Hayes, M., Underwood, J., Williams, B., Wood, D.: REDEEM: simple intelligent tutoring systems from usable tools. In: Murray, T., Blessing, S.B., Ainsworth, S. (eds.) Authoring Tools for Advanced Technology Learning Environments, pp. 205–232. Springer, Heidelberg (2003)
5. Gilbert, S., Blessing, S.B., Kodavali, S.: The Extensible Problem-Specific Tutor (Xpst): evaluation of an API for tutoring on existing interfaces. In: Dimitrova, V., Mizoguchi, R., du Boulay, B., Graesser, A. (eds.) Proceedings of the 14th International Conference on Artificial Intelligence in Education, pp. 707–709. IOS Press, Amsterdam (2009)
6. MacLellan, C.J., Koedinger, K.R., Matsuda, N.: Authoring tutors with simstudent: an evaluation of efficiency and model quality. In: Trausan-Matu, S., Boyer, K.E., Crosby, M., Panourgia, K. (eds.) ITS 2014. LNCS, vol. 8474, pp. 551–560. Springer, Heidelberg (2014)
7. Army Research Laboratory: Gift 2014-1x, Generalized Intelligent Framework for Tutoring Release Page (2014). http://www.gifttutoring.org
8. https://github.com/adlnet/DECALS
9. Susarla, S., Adcock, A., Van Eck, R., Moreno, K., Graesser, A., Group, T.R.: Development and evaluation of a lesson authoring tool for autotutor. In: AIED2003 Supplemental Proceedings, pp. 378–387 (2003)
10. Ray, F., Brawner, K., Robson, R.: Using data mining to automate addie. In: Educational Data Mining 2014 (2014)
11. Koedinger, K.R., Brunskill, E., de Baker, R.S.J., McLaughlin, E.A., Stamper, J.C.: New potentials for data-driven intelligent tutoring system development and optimization. AI Mag. 34, 27–41 (2013)
12. Liu, Y.-E., Mandel, T., Brunskill, E., Popovic, Z.: Trading off scientific knowledge and user learning with multi-armed bandits
13. Sottilare, R., Graesser, A., Hu, X., Brawner, K.: Design Recommendations for Intelligent Tutoring Systems: Authoring Tools (2015) (in press). www.gifttutoring.org

Prolonged Physical Effort Affects Cognitive Processes During Special Forces Training

Clayton A. Domingues[1,2,3(✉)], Esmaela C.P. Domingues[2],
Osvaldo J. Nascimento[2], Nilton G. Rolim Filho[3],
Jorge T. Annunziato[3], Jorge L.C. Rebelo[3], Seth R. Nieman[1],
Kyle J. Jaquess[1], Rodolphe J. Gentili[1,4], and Bradley D. Hatfield[1]

[1] Department of Kinesiology, University of Maryland,
College Park, USA
kkamaral2002@hotmail.com
[2] Departament of Neurology, Federal Fluminense University,
Niterói, Brazil
[3] Special Operations Instruction Center, Niterói, Brazil
[4] Maryland Robotics Center, University of Maryland,
College Park, USA

Abstract. This study aimed to investigate the effects of strenuous physical exertion on biomarkers of muscle damage, on physical and mental fatigue, and on cognitive processes. Seventeen military (males 24–40 years old) were tested cognitively at six time points, while they were progressively exhausted over the course of 102 h of continued operations. Three types of variables were analyzed: biomarkers of muscle damage [serum levels of creatine kinase (CK) and lactate dehydrogenase (LDH)], reported physical fatigue (PF) and mental fatigue (MF), and cognitive processes [(verbal reasoning (VR), numerical reasoning (NR) and spatial reasoning (SR) and short-term memory (STM)]. The results revealed significant increases in CK, LDH, PF and MF. On the other hand, we found significant decreases in VR, NR, SR and STM, which were negatively correlated MF. Our results show additional evidences about the impact of strenuous physical exertion on muscle damage, physical and mental fatigue, and cognitive processes.

Keywords: Strenuous physical exertion · Physical fatigue · Mental fatigue · Cognitive processes · Continued operations

1 Introduction

Continued operations is a common type of military operation prevalent in ground warfare involving continuous individual performance for periods longer than twenty-four hours. The soldiers must work steadily for long periods without rest, and are typically unaware of their next opportunity for sleep, feed and hydration, working instead until an objective is reached [1–3]. This type of operation entails continuous physical and mental workload that result in fatigue, which may collectively lead to poor performance, accidents, and decrease of mission effectiveness [4–7].

© Springer International Publishing Switzerland 2015
D.D. Schmorrow and C.M. Fidopiastis (Eds.): AC 2015, LNAI 9183, pp. 570–582, 2015.
DOI: 10.1007/978-3-319-20816-9_55

A critical issue for military authorities in Brazil is the identification of parameters that indicate the intensity of military training and how physical exertion can interfere with the cognitive performance of military enrolled in training with high physical and psychological demands [8–10]. In order to accomplish this goal, since 2012 the Special Operations Instruction Center has developed the project entitled Biomedical Research in Commandos Actions, which aims, among other objectives, to evaluate the impact of strenuous physical exertion on muscle damage, how it is related with physical and mental fatigue, and how the fatigue can affect cognitive processes [7].

Strenuous physical exertion can cause muscle damage that is a dysfunction in the cell membrane, which allows the migration of the intracellular content into the extracellular environment and into the systemic circulation [11–15]. Muscle damage can be identified from apparent histological changes and from quantification of specific serum levels of muscle enzymes such as creatine kinase (CK) and lactate dehydrogenase (LDH), which serve as indicators of increased of permeability or destruction of muscle cells. Thus, biomarkers of muscle damage have been used to screen overtraining and fatigue [12, 16–19].

It is well known that high levels of fatigue and stress can negatively affect cognitive functions needed for decision-making [20–24]. For example, errors are likely to occur in cognitive functions such as: attention, memory formation and memory recall [23, 25–28], in decision processes that underlie perception, attention such as signal detection and executive functioning [29, 30] such as set shifting and categorization [30] or operant conditioning [31].

In such a context, by employing biomarkers of skeletal muscle damage, this study aims to examine the effects of strenuous physical exertion on physical and mental fatigue, which can in turn affect the cognitive processes during 102 h of Special Forces training. We hypothesized that during continued operations there would be an increase in biomarkers of muscle damage, which would be positively associated with the levels of physical and mental fatigue. On the other hand, we also hypothesized that cognitive performance would significantly decrease, and would be negatively correlated with biomarkers of muscle damage, physical fatigue and mental fatigue.

2 Methods

Participants were requested to complete 102 h of the Leadership Development Exercise (LDE), while variables of interest (biomarkers of muscle damage, subjective perceptions of physical and mental fatigue, and performances on cognitive tests) were recorded. All variables of interest were collected in six different time points: Baseline (BL) - 6:00 am first activity of the LDE, 24 h (24 h), 48 h (48 h), 72 h (72 h), 96 h (96 h), and 102 h after LDE had begun (102 h). The data collection procedures included taking a blood sample and filling out the Clinical Subjective Parameters Questionnaire (CSPQ), followed by the completion of a cognitive test. Each data collection at each time point lasted approximately 45 min. The first five collections were performed at the beginning of each day at 6:00 am. The sixth test routine was conducted at 12:00 am at the end of LDE. Subjects were not permitted unallowed to rest, sleep, eat or hydrate themselves over the course of the LDE.

Subjects. Seventeen subjects (all men, age range = 24–40 years, mean = 28.7 and standard deviation = 4.19), enrolled in the 2013 Command Actions Course of the Brazilian Army, participated in the present study. All subjects were right-hand dominant and right-eye dominant without a history of neurological or psychiatric disorders or psychotropic medications at the time of their participation in the study. Prior to testing, all participants gave their written informed consent in accordance with the protocol approved by Special Operations Instruction Center Institutional Review Board, and were also informed that they were free to withdraw from the study at any time. Before beginning the LDE, all participants were evaluated by a medical committee.

Leadership Development Exercise. The LDE is a field military exercise conducted in the context of 102 h of continued operations, which was developed with the purpose of enabling military performance evaluation over the course of one week of intense physical and mental activity. The LDE is divided into three stages: 48 h Rest Time (RT), Leader Reaction Test Preparation (LRTP - 96 h) and Leader Reaction Test (LRT - 6 h) [8]. The participants were instructed to eat, hydrate, prepare their equipment, and rest as must as possible (at least 7 h of sleep) per evening 48 h prior to base line (BL). During LRTP, the participants performed patrols and typical military activities in a continued operations context during four cycles of 24 h, which involve studies of tactical situations, planning tactical missions, an approach march (about 20 km), mission performance, orientation, transposition of watercourses, shooting and obstacle courses, and a return march to base (about 20 km). During the LRT, subjects must perform 12 workshops that simulate combat, which requires them to demonstrate effective attributes of leadership, selflessness, courage, adaptability, self-confidence, cooperation, decision, emotional balance, objectivity, persistence and resistance. While the activities were performed, combat stressors were progressively applied, according Table 1.

Blood Sampling. Blood samples were collected by qualified professionals linked to the Clinical Analysis Laboratory of the Doctrine and Research Division (DRD) of the Especial Operations Instruction Center. An 8-ml blood sample was collected from the antecubital vein at each sample time, using a winged cannula attached to a

Table 1. Combat Stressors applied during Leadership Development Exercise.

Combat Stressors	Time Points					
	BL	**24 h**	**48 h**	**72 h**	**96 h**	**102 h**
Water restriction (l)	Free	2.0	1.0	0.5	0.0	0.0
Food restriction (cal)	Free	2,500.0	1,000.0	500.0	0.0	0.0
Sleep allowed (hr)	Free	2.0	1.0	0.5	0.0	0.0
Weight carried (kg)	0.0	30.0	35.0	40.0	45.0	0.0
Physical effort**	Rest	4	5	6	7	8
Mental effort**	Rest	4	5	6	7	8

*48 h to rest from 6:00am on Saturday until 6:00am on Monday (Base line day).
**Adapted from 0-10 Borg Rating of Perceived Exertion Scale [32]. The numbers mean:
   Somewhat strong (4), Strong (5, 6), Very strong (7, 8).

vacutainer (Becton Dickinson Rutherford, N. J.). A fresh venous puncture was used for each sample. The blood sample was collected into 8 ml Serum Clot Activator with gel Separator Blood Collection Tube clotting tubes with separator gel (VACUETTE®). After clot retraction, the gel tubes were centrifuged at 3000 rpm for 15 min to separate the serum for determination of the measures of interest. Serum levels of CK and LDH were determined by using the automated analyzer Vitros250® (Ortho Clinical Diagnostics - Johnson & Johnson), using Johnson & Johnson kits by dry-chemistry method.

Subjective Measures. We investigated the subjective clinical parameters using the Clinical Subjective Parameters Questionnaire (CSPQ) developed by the DRD. The CSPQ is divided into seven (7) parts, which had to be answered in 5 min. In order to assess the levels of physical fatigue (PF) and mental fatigue (MF) accumulated in the preceding 24 h, we used the fourth part of CSPQ (P4). The measurement scale was adapted from 1-10 Borg Rating of Perceived Exertion Scale [32] and the subjects were required to indicate their levels of PF and MF checking one value that could vary between: Nothing at all (0), Very, very weak (0.5), Very weak (1), Weak (2), Moderate (3), Somewhat strong (4), Strong (5, 6), Very strong (7, 8, 9), Very, very strong (10). The different verbal expressions were then placed where they belonged according to their ratio properties. When using this scale, subjects were allowed to use decimals but they could not go beyond 10.

Cognitive Test. Cognitive processes were investigated using the Cognitive Tests (CT) developed by DRD. The CT is divided into seven questions (Q) in a total of 80 scores: two for verbal reasoning (VR - 20 scores), two for numerical reasoning (NR - 20 scores), two for spatial reasoning (SR - 20 scores) and a for short-term memory (STM - 20 scores). VR was evaluated in questions 1 and 4 (Q1 and Q4). In Q1, VR was tested by analysis of four words, which had to be compared to one another. The subject was asked to indicate the different word among the four according to the following criteria: spelling, size, context or meaning. In Q4, the subjects were told to read a sentence and evaluate ten claims about the sentence, stating whether these claims were true or false depending on the statement in the sentence. NR was evaluated in questions 2 and 3 (Q2 and Q3). In Q2 the subject had to fill two gaps, one related to an arithmetic progression and another referring to a geometric progression. In Q3, the participants filled gaps related to mathematical operations in the following order: addition, multiplication, division and subtraction. Questions 5 and 6 (Q5 and Q6) evaluated SR. In Q5, the object was to understand the logical sequence in which black squares were presented on a 10×10 white square board, while the black squares changed their positions from the first board to the second board. The subjects were asked to fill the gaps into a third board on their respective logical future positions. In Q6, the participants marked with a circle the different crosses symbols on a 30×30 crosses board. Question 7 (Q7) assessed STM. In Q7, the subjects were required to memorize a sequence of 20 characters (12 numbers and 8 letters) for one minute, turn the page, and wait for one minute until the command was given to fill in the answer sheet. The CT took 15 min to complete.

Statistical analysis. The Shapiro-Wilk test was employed to verify the hypothesis of normal distribution of frequencies. Since the data were not normally distributed, we used the Friedman ANOVA test to determine whether there were significant differences among the measures of interest (serum levels of CK and LDH, PF and MF, VR, NR, SR and STM) as a function of the severity of military training conditions imposed by the LDE. The Wilcoxon tests were applied post hoc to determine nature of the significant differences. The Spearman Rank Correlation Coefficient tests were applied to determine correlations among biomarkers of muscle damage physical and mental fatigue, as well as among cognitive performances and physical and mental fatigue. Significance was established at the $p < 0.05$ level. Analysis of all data was conducted using the SPSS for Windows (version 20).

3 Results

Muscle damage and physical and mental fatigue. We found significant differences in serum levels of CK ($\chi^2 = 66.714$, $p < 0.001$) and LDH ($\chi^2 = 76.529$, $p < 0.001$) as well as PF ($\chi^2 = 79.288$, $p < 0.001$), MF ($\chi^2 = 81.096$, $p < 0.001$) among the six time points of test. The descriptive measures of CK, LDH, PF and MP are shown respectively in the Figs. 1 and 2.

In order to evaluate which time point were different from each other, we applied the Wilcoxon test (see Table 2).

Serum levels of CK were different among all time points of test compared to baseline (BL < 24 h, BL < 48 h, BL < 72 h, BL < 96 h, BL < 102 h). CK increased on

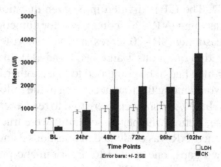

Fig. 1. Serum levels of CK and LDH during 102 h of strenuous physical exertion.

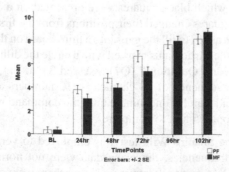

Fig. 2. Reported physical and mental fatigue during 102 h of strenuous physical exertion.

Table 2. Differences in serum levels of creatine kinase, lactate dehydrogenase, physical and mental fatigue as a function of time points of test.

Time points		CK Dif	Z	p	LDH Dif	Z	p	PF Dif	Z	p	MP Dif	Z	p
24 h	BL	731.41	-3.621	<0.001**	287.88	-3.622	<0.001**	3.47	-3.729	<0.001**	2.71	-3.671	<0.001**
48 h	BL	1,637.24	-3.621	<0.001**	425.53	-3.621	<0.001**	4.47	-3.647	<0.001**	3.65	-3.671	<0.001**
72 h	BL	1,773.53	-3.621	<0.001**	473.18	-3.621	<0.001**	6.35	-3.690	<0.001**	5.06	-3.695	<0.001**
96 h	BL	1,747.76	-3.621	<0.001**	577.65	-3.621	<0.001**	7.35	-3.782	<0.001**	7.65	-3.716	<0.001**
102 h	BL	3,208.76	-3.621	<0.001**	825.24	-3.574	<0.001**	7.82	-3.684	<0.001**	8.41	-3.779	<0.001**
48 h	24 h	905.82	-3.479	0.001**	137.65	-3.574	<0.001**	1.00	-2.506	0.012*	0.94	-2.388	0.017*
72 h	24 h	1,042.12	-3.621	<0.001**	185.29	-3.574	<0.01**	2.88	-3.697	<0.001**	2.35	-3.714	<0.001**
96 h	24 h	1,016.35	-3.290	0.001**	289.76	-3.574	<0.001**	3.88	-3.782	<0.001**	4.94	-3.711	<0.001**
102 h	24 h	2,477.35	-3.621	<0.001**	537.35	-3.621	<0.001**	4.35	-3.687	<0.001**	5.71	-3.649	<0.001**
72 h	48 h	136.29	-1.207	0.227	47.65	-2.817	0.005*	1.88	-3.231	0.001**	1.41	-3.096	0.002**
96 h	48 h	110.53	-1.112	0.266	152.12	-2.817	0.005*	2.88	-3.648	<0.001**	4.00	-3.656	<0.001**
102 h	48 h	1,571.53	-2.627	0.009**	399.71	-3.621	<0.001**	3.35	-3.646	<0.001**	4.76	-3.666	<0.001**
96 h	72 h	-25.76	-1.538	0.124	104.47	-2.485	0.013*	1.00	-3.314	0.001**	2.59	-3.703	<0.001**
102 h	72 h	1,435.24	-2.059	0.039*	352.06	-3.621	<0.001**	1.47	-3.119	0.002**	3.35	-3.652	<0.001**
102 h	96 h	1,461.00	-3.006	0.003**	247.59	-3.622	<0.001**	0.47	-1.730	0.084	0.76	-2.517	0.012*

* Differences are significant at the 0.05 level (2-tailed).
** Differences are significant at the 0.01 level (2-tailed).

average of 1,085.84 % among the time point. CK increased significantly until the first 48 h of the LDE, remained relatively stable up to 96 h (48 h = 72 h = 96 h) and increased again by the end of the LDE (102 h > 96 h, 102 h > 72 h, 102 h > 48 h, 102 h > 24 h, 102 h > BL). CK was positively correlated with PF ($r_s = 0.726$, p < 0.001) and with MF ($r_s = 0.687$, p < 0.001). Serum levels of LDH were also different among all time points of test compared to baseline (BL < 24 h, BL < 48 h, BL < 72 h, BL < 96 h, BL < 102 h). LDH increased on average of 94.17 % among the time points and were different from each other in all time points of test (BL < 24 h < 48 h < 72 h < 96 h, < 102 h). LDH was positively correlated with PF ($r_s = 0.761$, p < 0.001) and with MF ($r_s = 0.725$, p < 0.001).

Reported physical fatigue levels were different in all time points compared to baseline (BL < 24 h, BL < 48 h, BL < 72 h, BL < 96 h, BL < 102 h). As expected, physical fatigue levels increased progressively until the first 96 h remaining high until the end of the LDE (BL < 24 h < 48 h < 72 h < 96 h = 102 h). Similarly, mental fatigue levels were different in all time points compared to baseline (BL < 24 h, BL < 48 h, BL < 72 h, BL < 96 h, BL < 102 h), increasing progressively until the end of the LDE (BL < 24 h < 48 h < 72 h < 96 h < 102 h). PF was positively correlated with MF ($r_s = 0.969$, p < 0.001).

Cognitive processes. As expected, we found significant differences in all subcomponents of the cognitive tests [VR ($\chi^2 = 82.728$, $p < 0.001$), NR ($\chi^2 = 82.072$, $p < 0.001$), NR ($\chi^2 = 81.955$, $p < 0.001$), e STM ($\chi^2 = 84.019$, $p < 0.001$)] among the six time points of test (Fig. 3).

In order to evaluate which time point were different from each other, we applied the Wilcoxon test (see Table 3).

VR performances were different in all time points of test compared to baseline (BL < 24 h, BL < 48 h, BL < 72 h, BL < 96 h, BL < 102 h), decreasing progressively until the end of the LDE (BL < 24 h < 48 h < 72 h < 96 h < 102 h). RV decreased on

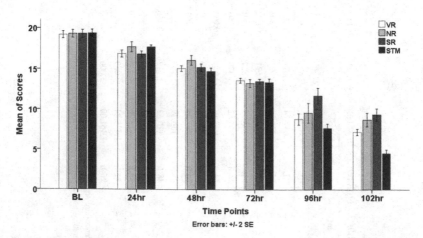

Fig. 3. Performance on verbal reasoning, numerical reasoning, spatial reasoning and short-term memory tasks during 102 h of strenuous physical exertion.

Table 3. Differences in cognitive processes as a function of time points of test

Time points			VR			NR			SR			STM		
			Dif	Z	p	Dif	Z	p	Dif	Z	p	Dif	Z	p
24 h	–	BL	2,35	-3,695	<0.001**	1,65	-3,742	<0.001**	2,53	-3,654	<0.001**	1,71	-3,624	<0.001**
48 h	–	BL	4,18	-3,672	<0.001**	3,29	-3,714	<0.001**	4,18	-3,641	<0.001**	4,71	-3,644	<0.001**
72 h	–	BL	5,65	-3,655	<0.001**	6,12	-3,779	<0.001**	5,88	-3,695	<0.001**	6,06	-3,651	<0.001**
96 h	–	BL	10,41	-3,632	<0.001**	9,76	-3,641	<0.001**	7,65	-3,646	<0.001**	11,71	-3,652	<0.001**
102 h	–	BL	12,00	-3,652	<0.001**	10,59	-3,688	<0.001**	9,94	-3,638	<0.001**	14,82	-3,671	<0.001**
48 h	–	24 h	1,82	-3,453	0.001**	1,65	-3,276	0.001**	1,65	-3,223	0.001**	3,00	-3,650	<0.001**
72 h	–	24 h	3,29	-3,689	<0.001**	4,47	-3,703	<0.001**	3,35	-3,676	<0.001**	4,35	-3,658	<0.001**
96 h	–	24 h	8,06	-3,642	<0.001**	8,12	-3,644	<0.001**	5,12	-3,634	<0.001**	10,00	-3,652	<0.001**
102 h	–	24 h	9,65	-3,649	<0.001**	8,94	-3,658	<0.001**	7,41	-3,647	<0.001**	13,12	-3,658	<0.001**
72 h	–	48 h	1,47	-3,473	0.001**	2,82	-3,487	<0.001**	1,71	-3,568	<0.001**	1,35	-3,289	0.001**
96 h	–	48 h	6,24	-3,650	<0.001**	6,47	-3,650	<0.001**	3,47	-3,421	0.001**	7,00	-3,640	<0.001**
102 h	–	48 h	7,82	-3,651	<0.001**	7,29	-3,703	<0.001**	5,76	-3,633	<0.001**	10,12	-3,657	<0.001**
96 h	–	72 h	4,76	-3,647	<0.001**	3,65	-3,324	0.001**	1,76	-2,834	0,005**	5,65	-3,652	<0.001**
102 h	–	72 h	6,35	-3,711	<0.001**	4,47	-3,711	<0.001**	4,06	-3,640	<0.001**	8,76	-3,654	<0.001**
102 h	–	96 h	1,59	-3,119	0,002**	0,82	-1,474	0,140	2,29	-3,482	<0.001**	3,12	-3,658	<0.001**

* Differences are significant at the 0.05 level (2-tailed).
** Differences are significant at the 0.01 level (2-tailed).

average of 17.25 % among the time points, being more evident in 102 h (62.58 % lower than BL). VR was negatively correlated with MF (r_s = -0.919, p < 0.001).

NR performances were different in all time points of test compared to baseline (BL < 24 h, BL < 48 h, BL < 72 h, BL < 96 h, BL < 102 h). NR decreased progressively until 96 h, remaining low until the end of the LDE (BL < 24 h < 48 h < 72 h < 96 h = 102 h). NR decreased on average of 14.37 % among the time points of test, being more evident in 102 h (54.88 % lower than BL). NR was negatively correlated with MF (r_s = -0.903, p < 0.001).

SR performances were also different in all time points of test compared to baseline (BL < 24 h, BL < 48 h, BL < 72 h, BL < 96 h, BL < 102 h), decreasing on average of 13.41 % until the end of the LDE (BL < 24 h < 48 h < 72 h < 96 h < 102 h), being also more evident in 102 h (51.52 % lower than BL). SR was negatively correlated with MF (r_s = -0.919, p < 0.001).

STM performances were also different in all time points of test compared to baseline (BL < 24 h, BL < 48 h, BL < 72 h, BL < 96 h, BL < 102 h), decreasing progressively until the end of the LDE (BL < 24 h < 48 h < 72 h < 96 h < 102 h). STM was the most affected by LDE, decreasing on average of 23.66 % among the time points, being also more evident in 102 h (76.60 % lower than the BL). STM also was negatively correlated with MF (r_s = -0.930, p < 0.001).

4 Discussion

The aim of this study was, through biomarkers of skeletal muscle damage, to evaluate the effects of 102 h of strenuous physical exertion on subjective perceptions of physical and mental fatigue, and on important cognitive processes that may affect decision-making such as verbal reasoning, numerical reasoning, spatial reasoning and short-term memory.

Biomarkers of muscle damage were assessed in order to describe the impact of strenuous physical activity on skeletal muscles and to investigate the relationship of such measure with the subjective perception of physical and mental fatigue of the subjects over the military training days. The post exercise increase of CK and LDH activity is widely documented and regarded by many researchers as a specific bio-marker of muscle damage [12, 16–19, 33]. Analyses of serum levels CK and LDH showed a significant and gradual increase in the muscle damage during all time points of the LDE. The type of physical activity performed during the LDE (long marches on land with great variability of elevations, transposition of obstacles and watercourses) makes the military to perform concentric and eccentric contractions against a constant resistance. This exhaustive physical exercise combined with excess weight transported (backpacks, weapons and ammunition), lack of rest and impossibility of post-exercise recovery, increase the intensity of the extravasation of enzymes from skeletal muscle into blood circulation. Considering the normal serum levels of CK on plasma (55–170 U/l) is important to report that after 48 h serum levels of CK reached 10 times the reference levels and by the end of the LDE 19 times. It means that after 48 h all subjects were affected by rhabdomyolysis [34–36]. It is a fact that the combination and accumulation of lack of hydration, nutrition and rest, combined with strenuous physical exercise intensified muscle damage, but analysis of the collaboration of each type of stressor for onset of rhabdomyolysis still need to be performed. The serum levels CK and LDH also were positively correlated with PF and MF. It reinforces the value of this type of screening to have better adjusts in the levels of physical and mental effort in order to improve the learning during the military training.

The levels of PF and MF were partly consistent with the levels of planned physical and mental effort. During the first 72 h, the levels of PF and MF were in accordance with the planning, but the reported PF and MF at 96 h were a point higher than expected. At the end of LDE (102 h), the levels of PF were in accordance with the requirements, but the MF levels were still a point higher than expected. This probably occurred because after 72 h the participants were not allowed to sleep and the cumulative effect of sleep deprivation may have emphasized even more the perception of fatigue. Fatigue is known to result in less accurate performance, increased error rates, and to significant alter judgment capabilities [37, 38]. Due to these high levels of mental fatigue, the subject is affected by the decrease in attention, concentration and short term memory, planning and organizing of ideals, which negatively impact the performance on cognitive tasks with high demands [39, 40].

In order to evaluate the effects of mental fatigue caused by strenuous physical effort in decision-making processes in combat, we use questions related to cognitive processes that are typically used in military tactical planning, such as VR, NR, SR and STM. Our results show that both VR, NR, SR and STM decreased during de all time points and also were negatively correlated with the reported MF. MF can cause lapses of attention and decrease the focus of attention, which directly affects the cognitive load to the extent that the perception, concentration and working memory will be negatively affected [6, 20–22, 24, 41–44]. We assume that the workload is a result of the proportion of time required to process the information available for the resolution of questions in relation to the time available for decision-making. With less information available (perceived or processed), the subjects take longer to evaluate and decide. With less time to decide increases the possibility of making mistakes or even not answer the question (by not having enough time to analyze and answer the question or simply disengage).

Our results indicate that the participants showed poor performances in complex questions compared with simple questions. For instance, in the VR questions the subjects revealed a high difficulty to decide whether a statement was true or false in relation to the sentences (as in Q4), suggesting that some important information may have been lost throughout the process that includes reading the sentences, understand them and compare the statements with the preestablished rule. On the other hand, when the important information to answer the question remained visually available (as in Q1) they were able to identify a different word in the group, but faced high difficulty to justify their choices. The more complex mathematical operations (multiplication, division, arithmetic and geometric progressions) also showed more response errors than simple mathematical operations (addition, and subtraction).

Regarding the SR, the subjects showed worse performance on questions related with spatial logic reasoning (as Q5) than questions of simple visuo-spatial localization (such as Q6). This may indicate that the visuo-spatial localization process and visual discrimination seems to be less affected by fatigue than the processing of the visuo-spatial information. It may occur because spatial logic tasks require the maintenance of relevant information in working memory, while the simple spatial localization tasks do not so much require working memory [43, 44].

The STM was the most affected by fatigue among other cognitive processes. At the end of LDE, subjects were able to remember only 13.40 % of the sequence of letters and numbers. When they could remember two or three letters and numbers in sequence, generally they were in the first positions of the answer sheet. This probably occurred since the subjects were progressively fatigued and it took them longer to memorize the sequences. Due to their state of fatigue, letters and numbers were forgotten while as the time elapsed. Thus, the subjects had to return to the beginning of the sequence in order to recall them, which further decreased the time to memorize the other parts of the sequence. In fact, when the letters and numbers placed in the middle and the end of the sequence were recalled, the subjects could rarely fill them in their respective positions. It also should not be denied that the subjects simply disengaged from the task due to fatigue.

In summary, the results revealed additional evidences about the impact of strenuous physical activity on biomarkers of muscle damage and on physical and mental fatigue. Such biomarkers could be used as screening to better estimate the physical and mental states of military while conducting military training with high physical demands. In the same direction, we present additional evidence on the impact of mental fatigue on important cognitive processes related to decision-making. Specifically for the Special Forces training, this type of screening can provide accurate feedback about the physical and mental fatigue states, in real time, to assist in adjusting levels of physical effort required during military training in order to improve learning conditions and also prevent the occurrence of accidents. In future studies we propose the performance of logistic regression and multifactorial analysis to check how much each of the independent variables contributes to the variability in cognitive performance. In addition, we propose to evaluate the specificity of combat stressors such as lack of nutrition, hydration, sleep deprivation and level of physical exertion in order to predict the mental fatigue levels and cognitive performance.

References

1. Krueger, G.P.: Sustained work, fatigue, sleep loss and performance: a review of the issues. Work Stress 3(2), 129–141 (1989)
2. Krueger, G.P.: Sustained military performance in continuous operations: combatant fatigue, rest and sleep needs. In: Gal, R., Mangelsdorff, A.D. (eds.) Handbook of Military Psychology, pp. 244–277. Wiley, Chichester (1990)
3. United States of America. Headquarters, Departament of the US Army. Combat and Operational Stress Control Manual for Leaders and Soldiers. FM 2-22.5 (2009)
4. Banks, J.H., Sternberg, J.J., Farrell, J.P., Debow, C.H., Dalhamer. W.A.: Effects of continuous military operations on selected military tasks. Technical research report 1166. AD718253. Behavior and Systems Research Laboratory, United States Army, pp. 1–25 December 1970

5. Wimmer, F., Hoffmann, R.F., Bonato, R.A., Moffitt, A.: The effects of sleep deprivation on divergent thinking and attention processes. J. Sleep Res. 1(4), 223–230 (1992)
6. Dolan, C.A., Adler, A.B., Thomas, J.L., Castro, C.A.: Operations tempo and soldier health: the moderating effect of wellness behavior. Mil. Psychol. 17, 157–174 (2005)
7. Domingues, C.A.: Projeto Pesquisas Biomédicas nas Ações de Comandos: Resultados do Curso de Ações de Comandos 2012 (in Portuguese). Reunião Anual dos Estabelecimentos de Ensino do Sistema Departamento de Educação e Cultura do Exército. Itaipava (2012)
8. Brasil. Ministério da Defesa. Exército Brasileiro. Comando de Operações Terrestres. Caderno de Instrução. Exercícios de Desenvolvimento da Liderança (EDL) (in Portuguese). Brasília (2006)
9. Brasil. Exército Brasileiro. Comandante do Exército. Diretriz para a Implantação do Programa de Prevenção e Controle da Rabdomiólise Induzida por Esforço Físico e pelo Calor, no âmbito do Exército (in Portuguese). Portaria N° 129, de 11 de março de 2010. Brasília (2010)
10. Brasil. Exército Brasileiro. Departamento de Educação e Cultura do Exército. Diretrizes do Chefe do Departamento de Educação e Cultura / 2012 (in Portuguese). Rio de Janeiro (2012)
11. Vincent, H.K., Vincent, K.R.: The effect of training status on the serum creatine kinase response, soreness and muscle function following resistance exercise. Int. J. Sports Med. 18, 431–437 (1997)
12. Lu, S.S., Wu, S.K., Chen, J.J.: The effects of heavy eccentric contractions on serum creatine kinase levels. Clin. J. Physiol. 35, 35–44 (1992)
13. Clarkson, P.M., Byrnes, W.C., McCormik, K.M., Turcotte, L.P., White, J.S.: Muscle soreness and serum creatine kinase activity following isometric, eccentric and concentric exercise. Int. J. Sports Med. 7, 152–155 (1986)
14. Clarkson, P.M.: Eccentric exercise and muscle damage. Int. J. Sports Med. 18(4), 314–317 (1997)
15. Chen, T.C., Hsieh, S.S.: The effects of repeated maximal voluntary isokinetic eccentric exercise on recovery from muscle damage. Res. Q. Exerc. Sport 71(3), 260–266 (2000)
16. Mougios, V.: Reference intervals for serum creatine kinase in athletes. Br. J. Sports Med. 41, 674–678 (2007)
17. Noakes, T.D.: Effect of exercise on serum enzyme activities in humans. Sports Medicine 4 (4), 245–267 (1987)
18. Fallon, K.E., Sivyer, G., Sivyer, K., Dare, A.: The biochemistry of runners in a 1600 km ultramarathon. Br. J. Sports Med. 33, 264–269 (1999)
19. Brancaccio, P., Limongelli, F.M., Maffulli, N.: Monitoring of serum enzymes in sport. Br. J. Sports Med. 40, 96–97 (2006)
20. Keinan, G., Friedland, N., Ben-Porath, Y.: Decision making under stress: scanning of alternatives under physical threat. Acta Psychol. 64, 219–228 (1987)
21. Kerstholt, J.H.: The effect of time pressure on decision-making behavior in a dynamic task environment. Acta Psychol. 86, 89–104 (1994)
22. Féry, Y.-A., Ferry, A., Vom Hofe, A.: Effect of physical exhaustion on cognitive functioning. Percept. Mot. Skills 84, 291–298 (1997)
23. Mendl, M.: Performing under pressure: stress and cognitive function. Appl. Anim. Behav. Sci. 65, 221–244 (1999)
24. Starcke, K., Brand, M.: Decision making under stress: a selective review. Neurosci. Biobehav. Rev. 36, 1228–1248 (2012)
25. Orasanu, J.M., Backer, P.: Stress and military performance. In: Driskell, J.E., Salas, E. (eds.) Stress and Human Performance, pp. 89–125. Lawrence Erlbaum Associates Inc., Mahwas (1996)

26. Lupien, S.J., Maheu, F., Tu, M., Fiocco, A., Schramek, T.E.: The effects of stress and stress hormones on human cognition: implications for the field of brain and cognition. Brain Cogn. **65**, 209–237 (2007)
27. Wolf, O.T.: Stress and memory in humans: twelve years of progress? Brain Res. **1293**, 142–154 (2009)
28. Kleider, H.M., Parrott, D.J., King, T.Z.: Shooting behaviour: how working memory and negative emotionality influence police officer shoot decisions. Appl. Cogn. Psychol. **24**, 707–717 (2010)
29. Hsu, F.C., Garside, M.J., Massey, A.E., McAllister-Williams, R.H.: Effects of a single dose of cortisol on the neural correlates of episodic memory and error processing in healthy volunteers. Psychopharmacol. **167**, 431–442 (2003)
30. McCormick, C.M., Lewis, E., Somley, B., Kahan, T.A.: Individual differences in cortisol levels and performance on a test of executive function in men and women. Physiol. Behav. **91**, 87–94 (2007)
31. Schwabe, L., Wolf, O.T.: Stress prompts habit behavior in humans. J. Neurosci. **29**, 7191–7198 (2009)
32. Borg, G.A.V.: Psychophysical bases of perceived exertion. Med. Sci. Sports Exerc. **14**(5), 377–381 (1982)
33. Poprzecki, S., Staszkiewicz, A., Hübner-Wozniak, E.: Effect of eccentric and concentric exercise on plasma Creatine Kinase (CK) and Lactate Dehydrogenase (LDH) activity in healthy adults. Biol. Sport **21**, 193–203 (2004)
34. Skenderi, K.P., Kavouras, S.A., Anastasiou, C.A., Yiannakouris, N., Matalas, A.L.: Exertional Rhabdomolysis during a 246-km continuous running race. Med. Sci. Sports Exerc. **38**(6), 1054–1057 (2006)
35. Clarkson, P.M., Kearns, A.K., Rouzier, P., Rubin, R., Thompson, P.D.: Serum creatine kinase levels and renal function measures in exertional muscle damage. Med. Sci. Sports Exerc. **38**(4), 623–627 (2006)
36. Lee, G.: Exercise-induced Rhabdomyolysis. R. I. Med. J. (2013) **97**(11), 22–24 (2014)
37. Abbiss, C.R., Laursen, P.B.: Is part of the mystery surrounding fatigue complicated by context? J Sci Med Sport **10**(5), 277–279 (2007)
38. Moreira, P.V.S., Teodoro, B.G., Magalhães Neto, A.M.: Bases Neurais e Metabólicas da Fadiga Durante o Exercício (in Portuguese). Biosci. J. **24**(1), 81–90 (2008)
39. Hogervost, E., Riedel, W., Jeukendrup, A.: Cognitive performance after strenuous physical exercise. Percept. Mot. Skills **83**, 479–488 (1996)
40. Trejo, L.J., Kochavi, R., Kubitz, K., Montgomery, L.D., Rosipal, R., Matthews, B.: Measures and Models for Estimating and Predicting Cognitive Fatigue. 44th Society for Psychophysiological Research Annual Meeting. Society for Psychophysiological Research, Santa Fé, Out (2004)
41. Killgore, W.D.S., Balkin, T.J., Wesensten, N.J.: Impaired decision making following 49 h of sleep deprivation. J. Sleep Res. **15**(1), 7–13 (2006)
42. Abd-Elfattah, H.M., Abdelazeim, F.H., El Shennawy, S.A.W.: Physical and cognitive consequences of fatigue: a review. J. Adv. Res. (2015), In press
43. Constantinidis, C., Wang, X.J.: A neural circuit basis for spatial working memory. Neuroscientist **10**(6), 553–565 (2004)
44. Oberauer, K.: Access to information in working memory: exploring the focus of attention. J. Exp. Psychol. Learn. Mem. Cogn. **28**, 411–421 (2002)

Development of a Smart Tutor
for a Visual-Aircraft Recognition Task

Priya Ganapathy[1]([⊠]), Ion Juvina[2], Tejaswi Tamminedi[1],
Gautam Kunapuli[1], Matt Sherwood[2], and Mohd Saif Usmani[2]

[1] Utopia Compresion Corporation, Los Angeles, USA
priya@utopiacompression.com
[2] Wright State University, Dayton, USA

Abstract. The goal of this project is to design an intelligent tutor to teach visual aircraft recognition (VACR) skills to military population. Under extreme cognitive demand, soldiers must learn to rapidly recognize and identify the aircraft prior to engagement. The goal of the smart tutor is to train the trainees to look at specific features (called Wings, Engine, Fuselage and Tail- WEFT) of the aircraft that will help them proceduralize the skill of aircraft recognition.

We have conducted an empirical (fMRI, eye-tracking, behavior) study and developed a cognitive model based on ACT-R architecture that emulates trainee performance. In this paper, we present insights gained from ACT-R modeling which, in turn, will be used to develop a VACR smart tutor.

Keywords: Visual aircraft recognition · Smart tutor · ACT-R models · Dynamic bayesian networks · Intelligent tutoring systems

1 Introduction

1.1 Current Limitation of VACR Training

Visual Aircraft Recognition (VACR) task is a military-relevant training procedure (Pliler, 1996) to visually recognize aircraft and categorize them as friendly, neutral, or hostile prior to engagement. Typically, VACR training involves a two step-procedure: Step (1) involves an instructor-led classroom session where VACR and the concept of breaking down an aircraft in terms of wings, engine, fuselage and tail (WEFT) components are introduced; Step (2) is a computer-based training (CBT) where trainees learn to recognize 50-75 aircraft in 2 days. Research on VACR training efficacy was performed in the early 80 s where the technique resulted in a poor outcome with only 30 % of 900 trainees achieving a minimum pass accuracy of 90 % (Tubbs, Deason, Evertt, & Hansen, 1981).

1.2 Motivation to Use ITS for VACR

Research on ways to improve VACR training is once again gaining prominence with increase in unmanned air systems (UASs) and the rate of fratricide reported in recent wars. With the increased rate of adoption of learning management systems (LMS) and

© Springer International Publishing Switzerland 2015
D.D. Schmorrow and C.M. Fidopiastis (Eds.): AC 2015, LNAI 9183, pp. 583–594, 2015.
DOI: 10.1007/978-3-319-20816-9_56

personalized tutoring across all three DoD agencies there is a strong emphasis on building an upgraded VACR training system with a smart tutor. The goal of this smart tutor is in general to minimize the training time by accelerating learning, facilitating better retention and transfer. Intelligent tutoring systems (ITS) developed based on insights gained from learning science and cognitive theory have shown significant learning gains over traditional CBT methods (Anderson, Corbett, Koedinger, & Pelletier, 1995).

1.3   Structure of the Tutor

An ITS mainly consists of the following modules: A student assessment model, a domain (or an expert) module, a pedagogic (tutor) module and the front-end interface that the trainee interacts with (Corbett & Anderson, 2004). The student model infers student's skill level and knowledge gaps using knowledge-tracing approaches (Corbett & Anderson, 2004). The domain module contains the domain knowledge and the expert model to solve the problems the tutor module presents to the students. The tutor module controls the interaction with the student, based on its teaching knowledge and comparisons between the student and the expert models. Depending on the domain, complexity involved in modeling of the expert and student models may vary. For example, in this particular application the expert model would simply be the correct answer to the aircraft. The tutor model is essentially to teach the subjects to learn around 50-75 aircraft as is typically done for military trainees. The tutoring (or pedagogic) material includes the WEFT procedure to help trainees recognize aircraft and distinguish them from confounding ones. Due to the relative simplicity of the pedagogic content generation compared to more complex domains such as Math problem solving (Koedinger & Anderson, 1993) or dermatology-based problem diagnosis (Crowley & Medvedeva, 2006) the central component of our ITS is the student model.

1.4   Development of Student Model

There are various methods to model the student behavior in an ITS. Once modeled, the tutor can track the student behavior and compare with that of the expert. Popular tutors are generally based in cognitive science of learning and leverage adaptive control of thought-rational (ACT-R) architecture to model and track student behavior. These rule-based cognitive models form the core component of the tutor and simulate student thinking and how students can solve a given problem in multiple ways. These models also contain rules that represent incorrect behavior enabling the tutor to track errors and provide timely hints by means of a knowledge tracing algorithm. By tracking individual student behavior over time it is possible to infer the mastery of students across different skills.

Skill mastery tracking is generally performed using a Bayesian knowledge tracing (BKT) algorithm, developed originally by Corbett and Anderson (Corbett & Anderson, 2004). The BKT algorithm has been used to predict the likelihood that an individual student will get the next question correct and the updated probability that the student has mastered the skill based on the actual answer. A traditional ITS, such as the Cognitive Tutors for Algebra, have both the cognitive models and the BKT algorithms to fully infer the student state. In this proposed effort, we use cognitive-models based on ACT-R architecture to model the VACR task. These models were then used to predict student behavior and thereby aid in modeling the attributes of the tutor. Our motivation to build an ACT-R student model was to overcome the limitation of collecting large amounts of data for testing various attributes of the tutor that can cause or accelerate learning. The ACT-R model allowed us to test the different ways to present the training/tutoring material and optimize the tutor to maximally benefit the student. We present the ACT-R model development effort, validation of these models based on a small study and the simulation results of the models under different tutoring scenarios.

The preliminary data to refine the ACT-R based model was collected during a 10-week behavior and interspersed fMRI study of subjects undergoing VACR training at Wright State University (WSU), Dayton, OH. The data collection protocol and analysis of results is presented in Juvina et al. (Juvina, et al., 2015).

2   Methods

We begin this section by briefly describing a study that was performed at WSU. The 10-week study was designed to collect behavior (accuracy and response time and eye tracking measures) and neuroimaging data from n = 15 participants (age: 18–35) learning to recognize 75 military aircraft. In Fig. 1, a pictorial description of the sequence in which the data gathering sessions (in lab OR in the fMRI scanner) were performed is shown. Each in-lab session consisted of 3 training (TR) rounds and 1 test (TE) round (sequence: TR, TR, TR, and TE). In each round, 75 aircraft where randomly shown just once to the user. The participants had to choose the correct aircraft name from three other random aircraft names from the list. In TR rounds, after participants provide an answer, they were given feedback if they answered correctly and what the correct aircraft name is. Only in TR rounds the participants were expected to learn from the feedback provided (Fig. 2). In TE rounds, no feedback was provided. This was a fixed-paced study with subjects given 4 s to give an answer and learn from feedback. Each fMRI session had around 2 TE rounds. To refine the ACT-R model only the in-lab session data (behavior measures only) was used.

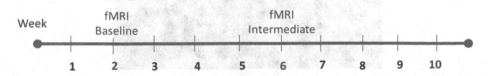

Fig. 1. The study was designed for 10 weeks with 7 in-lab sessions and 3 fMRI sessions. Each in-lab sessions included 3 training (TR) and 1 test (TE) round.

2.1   ACT-R Architecture

Adaptive control of thought-rational (ACT-R) is a cognitive architecture based on the rational analysis theory developed by Anderson et al. (Anderson, Bothell, Byrne, Douglass, Lebiere, & Qin, 2004). ACT-R provides us a mechanism to study how different aspects of cognition take place in humans. The architecture provides us with two main memory modules: 1) declarative memory (DM) – to code knowledge of the world, facts and domain-specific information and 2) procedural memory contains knowledge of how to do things (skill-based). There are perceptual modules (visual, auditory) and motor modules to take inputs from or send response to environment. The other modules are the goal, retrieval and imaginal modules which co-ordinate with other modules via a production system to complete or learn a given task. The production system fires a list of productions (series of condition-action, "if-then", rules) to complete a given goal. The knowledge, current state of the modules (via corresponding buffers), and actions of the model are represented symbolically. However, rather than performing as a deterministic system given the pre-coded productions and DM, the ACT-R performs more human-like due to underlying sub-symbolic knowledge which come into play when productions are fired and the model learns from the outcome of those productions. Thus it is possible for us to simulate real-world outcomes by modeling incomplete knowledge of the world, introducing random noise, decay of given fact if not used often and proceduralization (i.e., forming new implicit rules).

2.2   ACT-R Model for VACR

In this effort, we have modeled the ACT-R environment to match the experimental conditions of the study. Similar to the study, the model is presented with 75 aircraft (symbolic representation and not an image, see Fig. 3) in random order each round. For

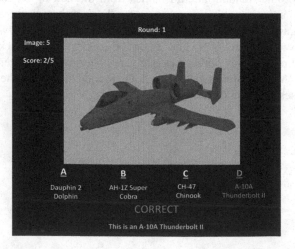

Fig. 2.   The interface used for collecting data from n = 15 participants. Same interface was used for fMRI data collection.

Fig. 3. Aircraft (EC)'s notional image representation (as 'ec1') is shown to the model. The four options similar to VACR UI in **Fig.** 2. Here, aircraft names EC, CB, ID and GF) are attended by the visual module. The model here is currently attending to option GF.

each of the corresponding aircraft image four corresponding options (one option is the correct aircraft name) is provided to the model. The model learns to recognize the correct option based on reinforcement learning. ACT-R implements a special category of reinforcement learning where the estimated reward received by the model depends on the behavior reward (provided by the environment) and the time when the correct or wrong rules were fired (temporal difference) during the whole trial (Gray, Schoelles, & Sims, 2005). As a result, a good ACT-R model can emulate human learning within almost comparable number of training sessions (Janssen & Gray, 2012). The modeling of the positive and negative reinforcement (reward) may not match in magnitude with the reward given in the actual environment. The reward (modeled in ACT-R as "Trigger Reward") is largely determined by the number of rules that were fired during a single production cycle. With smaller reward, not all the correct rules at beginning of production cycle will receive enough weight to propagate further as good rules.

Here, our focus in building the model is to capture higher-order cognitive processes associated with learning and retention and therefore, there is less emphasis at this point to develop an environment where actual visual aircraft features are provided to the model (Vinokurov, Lebiere, Herd, & O'Reilly, 2011) (Hiatt & Trafton, 2013). We therefore use generalized functions in the ACT-R framework for retrieval/chunk activation and production utility compilation to show the proceduralization of the VACR skill (Gray, Schoelles, & Sims, 2005) (Bothell, 2007) (Janssen & Gray, 2012).

We have built this model based on our assumption of how VACR task will be learnt by subjects and then explore various teaching/pedagogic strategies of presenting these aircraft stimuli that can potentially accelerate learning.

To model the TR rounds similar to the experimental interface (Figs. 2 and 3) the model is given the actual correct answer after trial is complete. Additionally, the model is allowed to rehearse the recent trial with the correct answer put in the goal buffer (to increase strength of the correct chunk). This simulates the two-level (correct/incorrect and the correct aircraft name) learning in subject during training rounds. Consequently, in the TE rounds, there is no reward provided to the model for giving correct answers (i.e., there is no feedback of any kind). This is similar to the experimental UI where TE rounds are only to test how much of learning has actually occurred in subjects.

The primary set of production rules developed by the modeler is as follows:

- FindStimulus: Find the stimulus ('notional aircraft image') on the screen and place it in the visual buffer,
- RetrieveAircraftContent: retrieve the aircraft content (i.e., an internal representation of the aircraft image),
- RetrieveAircraftName: retrieve the appropriate aircraft name
- FindOption1, FindOption2, FindOption3, FindOption4: find the options shown in the user interface and place the options in the imaginal buffer
- CompareWithOption1, CompareWithOption2, CompareWithOption3, Compare-WithOption4: compare the retrieved aircraft name with existing options list in the imaginal buffer.

Parameter Optimization: Once developed, we try to match the model performance trace (for same number of TR and TE rounds) with subject performance by adjusting relevant ACT-R parameters (discussed below). Optimization is crucial as the teaching strategies will be derived by testing them in the performance-matched ACT-R model.
Trigger Reward: Combines the objective feedback provided by the environment and the reward required by the model to discount utilities.
Alpha: Controls the rate of learning the rule utilities. With very high learning rate, the model reaches a local optimum solution faster. A slow learning rate will result in slower elimination of bad rules and strengthening of good rules thereby converging at a slower rate.
Egs: Accounts for variation in noise associated with utility values. A low Egs would mean less noise in utilities and therefore restricting the model to exploit as opposed to explore and find new strategies. A high Egs value will result in too many explorations and never settling on any strategies.
Set-Similarities: Allows controlling the degree of similarities between chunks placed in the declarative knowledge. The objective knowledge of aircrafts "knowledge of world" can be encoded using set-similarities command.
Initial utility (iu) and new utility (nu): The initial rules encoded by the modeler are given more chances to fire as opposed to new utilities created by ACT-R's production compilation module. The new utility parameter is set to zero to allow for new rules to prove themselves before they fire.
Goal activation (GA) and Maximum associative strength (MAS): The parameters control how quickly declarative chunks can be retrieved and increase the activation of retrieved chunks placed in the goal buffer.
Mismatch penalty (mp): Controls whether the partial matching of the DM chunks is enabled. To model the errors in aircraft recognition due to confusion between similar aircraft, "mp" was not set to nil (i.e., partial matching is enabled).

The initial values for these parameters were set based on literature (Hiatt & Trafton, 2013) (Vinokurov, Lebiere, Herd, & O'Reilly, 2011) and further fine-tuned in a trial and error fashion. Once the model behavior matches reasonably well with the subject traces we then use the model to predict student performance when number of training aircraft are increased, increase in level of confusion between aircraft, changes in the aircraft presentation method.

3   Results

In this section, we present the results of the ACT-R model behavior with parameter optimization and the model performance on changes to aircraft presentation method. The performance data from the study was clustered to identify two groups of learners, named "fast" and "slow" learners. By varying the following parameters, Alpha, egs, GA and mp values we could obtain a good match for the "fast" and "slow" learners, respectively (See Sect. 3.1). We choose the "Fast" learner-based model to run the additional simulations on testing different teaching strategies (See Sect. 3.2). The "Fast" learner category reaches a minimum acceptable accuracy of 90-92 % for VACR by the 6th session (end of 24 rounds including TE rounds) (Fig. 4). Therefore, the goal is to identify which aircraft presentation strategy can result in even faster learning to minimize overall training time from 2 h (75 aircraft × 24 rounds × 4 s presentation time = 1.9 h). Subsequently, once identified, the next step (not covered in this paper) is to develop the second piece of the tutoring component which is presenting aircraft-specific hints in terms of WEFT. We hypothesize that presentation of hints to help recognize aircraft will benefit the "Slow" learners compared to "Fast" learners. Consequently, a simulation to see if further reinforcement of aircraft knowledge results in improving learning in the "Slow" learner-based model (See Sect. 3.2) was performed.

3.1   ACT-R Parameter-Optimized Results

In Fig. 4 we show the model-optimized result for both "Slow" and "Fast" learner category.

3.2   Optimized ACT-R Model Simulation Results

Changing aircraft presentation rate The goal was to manipulate the presentation of aircraft images to reduce training time and/or improve learning performance. The true learning accuracy was assessed by showing all 75 aircraft once during the test rounds (TE). Every 4th round is a test round. It was observed (Fig. 5) that by showing only incorrect aircraft after Round 16 yielded similar performance to showing all 75 aircraft once during each round (for total 24 rounds) (refers to default case- Fig. 4). This result shows that a sufficient degree of proceduralization occurs by Round 16 and consequently, showing only those aircraft that were incorrect previously in the next TR rounds (Rounds 17-24) does not impact the accuracy of learnt aircraft (TE round accuracy remains at 90 %).

Subset training. We group subsets of aircraft based on their level of similarity. We created 3 different clusters with 25 aircraft. We presented the first cluster in the 1-10 rounds and then sequentially added the second and third cluster for rounds 10-20 and

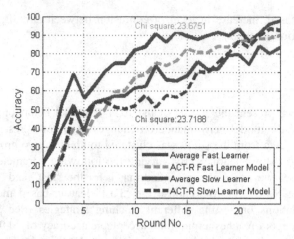

Fig. 4. ACT-R model predictions for 'fast learner' and 'slow learner' groups

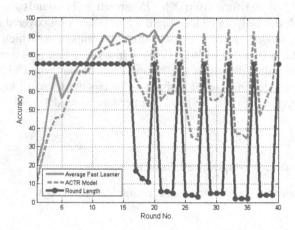

Fig. 5. After Round 16, there is sufficient proceduralization as a result we can increase presentation of aircraft that are harder to learn and decrease presentation of learnt aircraft. Here, after 16 training rounds, each round only consisted of 7-8 aircraft that subjects had to learn.

then 20-30. We observe a clear dip in performance when model training is performed in subsets than a random presentation (Fig. 6).

Presentation of additional hints. We ran a simulation where additional hint was presented to the model to reinforce the aircraft. The simulation shows that by presenting additional hint in terms of aircraft feature the model learning rate is accelerated. The simulation was performed for the slow learner model (Fig. 7).

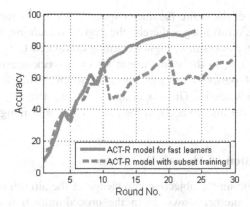

Fig. 6. Introducing aircraft in subsets (grouped by their level of similarity) for the model to learn ('dashed' plot).

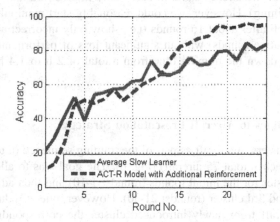

Fig. 7. Improvement in ACT-R model ('dashed' line) after additional reinforcement (20 % increase in accuracy post-round 16).

4 Discussion

4.1 ACT-R Model's Performance Optimization

By adjusting the learning rate parameter 'alpha' the initial increase in learning (from round 1 to 3) seen in the study data could not be achieved in the model (Fig. 4). The increase in learning during the initial few rounds (1-3 training rounds) could be achieved only by updating the mismatch penalty parameter (MP) incrementally after each round up to round 3 and then keeping it constant. This in real-world context would mean that as the trainees receive feedback they quickly resolve the aircraft with obvious discriminant features. The model does however underperform compared to subjects, mainly the fast learners (Fig. 4). From an ITS standpoint, this would mean the model-predicted performance end point (may occur sooner in trainees). We did not do an exhaustive search of the entire parameter space as we know for a fact that trainees where shown actual aircraft images thereby the degree of learning due to visual stimuli and feedback will always result in higher learning compared to that in our model.

The training sessions in the study where set up a week apart. However, no significant degrading of performance was observed when participants played the first round of a new week's session (Juvina, et al., 2015). As a result, there was no decay introduced in the model also to account for gaps in actual training sessions.

4.2   Procedularization of Aircraft Knowledge

The impact of introducing the objective knowledge of the aircraft and their differences with respect to one another slows down the proceduralization of aircraft. This is reflected in the fact that only after around 16-20 rounds, does the learning curve starts to plateau. The fMRI results (Juvina, et al., 2015) further confirms our finding that proceduralization of the aircraft starts to occur only after 20 training rounds (approximately 2 h of training). However, we could reasonably start manipulating the aircraft presentation stimuli after about 16 rounds (i.e., show only incorrect aircraft tracked in the past 4 consecutive rounds) without significant loss of performance (Fig. 5). This will further bring down the training time from a total of 2 h to 1.4 h without loss in accuracy.

4.3   Other Changes to Aircraft Presentation Strategy

We introduced clusters of aircraft as part of the training sequence (a total of 3 clusters with 25 aircraft each – total 75 aircraft) (Fig. 6). The goal was to allow the model to only learn 1st cluster for the initial rounds (rounds: 1-10) and then add the 2nd cluster (rounds: 11-20) and 3rd cluster (rounds: 21-30). However, due to reduced presentation time of each aircraft from newly introduced cluster the corresponding correct rules were not given sufficient time to be reinforced in the model. Rather the random presentation of aircraft from all the 3 clusters such that all 75 aircraft where shown at least once in each round (although slightly longer overall time $\sim$ 20 min) showed higher end accuracy.

4.4   Performance Boost with Additional Reinforcement

The eye tracking results from the behavior study shows that slow learners spent very less time looking at the aircraft (both before response and after they receive feedback) (Juvina, et al., 2015). In general, the behavior profile shows that slow learners are low on motivation compared to fast learners. The subjects seem to be less mindful of the task and need extra help/hints to remember the aircraft. We obtained a performance boost (about 20 % increase post round 15) in the slow learner-based model (Fig. 7) by providing an additional 'notional hint' (a distinct aircraft feature) to remember the aircraft. Therefore, in the actual ITS as well we will introduce the pedagogic component in the form of hints based on student performance.

The simulations presented here are not exhaustive; as we continue to develop the ITS design, we will test different training hypotheses using this ACT-R model.

5   Conclusion and Future Work

Our choice of VACR as the candidate task is strongly tied to its utility in operation and its wide-spread requirement for operation of Stinger missiles by ground troops. The lessons learnt from the ACT-R modeling experiment will be implemented as part of the ITS tutor design. We have also developed a BKT based algorithm (integrated with ITS) for real-time tracking of student performance. Our next study will use the Amazon Mechanical Turk platform to recruit participants to validate the findings from the model simulation and also test the overall efficacy of our ITS.

Acknowledgment. The authors thank the Office of Naval Research (SBIR Phase II, Navy Contract # N00014-13-C-0138) for funding this project.

Bibliography

Anderson, J., Bothell, D., Byrne, M., Douglass, S., Lebiere, C., Qin, Y.: An integrated theory of the mind. Psychol. Review **111**, 1036–1060 (2004)

Anderson, J., Corbett, A., Koedinger, K., Pelletier, R.: Cognitive tutors: lessons learned. J. Learn. Sci. **4**(2), 167–207 (1995)

Bothell, D.: ACT-R 6.0 Reference Manual (2007). Accessed 20 February 2015. ACT-R Web site: http://act-r.psy.cmu.edu/wordpress/wp-content/themes/ACT-R/actr6/reference-manual. pdf

Corbett, A., Anderson, J.: Knowledge tracing: modeling the acquisition of procedural knowledge. User Model. User-Adap. Inter. **4**(4), 253–278 (2004)

Crowley, R., Medvedeva, O.: An intelligent tutoring system for visual classification problem solving. Artif. Intell. Med. **36**(1), 85–117 (2006)

Gray, W., Schoelles, J., Sims, R.: Adapting to the task environment: explorations in expected value. Cogn. Syst. Res. **6**, 27–40 (2005)

Hiatt, L., Trafton, J.: The role of familiarity, priming and perception in similarity judgments. In: Proceedings of the 35th Annual Meeting of the Cognitive Science Society, pp. 573–578. Cognitive Science Society, Berlin (2013)

Janssen, C., Gray, W.: When, what, and how much to reward in reinforcement learning based models of cognition. Cogn. Sci. **36**(2), 333–358 (2012)

Juvina, I., Ganapathy, P., Sherwood, M., Usmani, S., Kunapuli, G., Tamminedi, T., et al.: Neurocognitive correlates of learning in a visual object recognition task. Human Computer Interaction. Los Angeles (2015)

Koedinger, K., Anderson, J.: Effective use of intelligent soft-ware in high school math classrooms. In: Brna P, Ohlsson S, Pan H, (eds.) Proceedings of the World Conference on Artificial Intelligence in Education, AACE, pp. 241–8 (1993)

Pliler, J.: Aircraft Recognition Training: A Continuing Process. Air Defense Artillery (1996)

Tubbs, J., Deason, P., Evertt, E., Hansen, A.: CHAPARRAL training subsystem effectiveness analysis (TSEA). In: Proceedings 23rd Annual Conference of the Military Testing Association (1981)

Vinokurov, Y., Lebiere, C., Herd, S., O'Reilly, R.: A Metacognitive Classifier Using a Hybrid ACT-R/Leabra Architecture. In: AAAI Workshop, pp. 50–55, San Francisco (2011)

Augmenting Instructional Practice in GIFT Using the Engine for Management of Adaptive Pedagogy (EMAP)

Benjamin Goldberg[✉]

U.S. Army Research Laboratory-Human Research and Engineering Directorate,
Orlando, FL, USA
Benjamin.s.goldberg.civ@mail.mil

Abstract. Authoring adaptation in the Generalized Intelligent Framework for Tutoring (GIFT) is dependent on the functions made available in the pedagogical module. The Engine for Management of Adaptive Pedagogy (eMAP) has been constructed as an instructional management framework that guides pedagogical authoring and implementation within GIFT. The eMAP is structured around David Merrill's Component Display Theory (CDT) and is designed to support adaptive instruction based on the tenets of knowledge and skill acquisition. The framework is designed to assist with two facets of lesson creation. First, it is designed to serve as a guiding template for Subject Matter Experts when constructing intelligent and adaptive course materials that adhere to sound instructional design principles. And second, it serves as a framework to support instructional strategy focused research to examine pedagogical practices and the influence of individual differences on learning outcomes. In this chapter we will describe the fundamental components that make up the eMAP, followed by the authoring workflow associated with its implementation as described above. This includes an overview of the dependencies associated with the eMAP, which runs on relevant data stored in the learner model informing content selection and metadata used to describe course materials and pedagogical practices.

Keywords: Intelligent tutoring systems · Adaptive pedagogy · Instructional management · Individual differences · Personalized instruction

1 Introduction

Augmented Cognition (AugCog) focuses on the use of technology to enhance cognitive function across a set of users during the execution of a particular problem or task. From the perspective of building Intelligent Tutoring Systems (ITS) to support personalized instruction, AugCog is focused on the use of technology to enhance computer-based learning experiences by augmenting instruction to optimize outcomes. These instructional augmentations are based on principles established within the tutoring literature on how people learn and the human computer-interaction literature on how people apply technology to perform tasks and solve problems. These principles

© Springer International Publishing Switzerland 2015
D.D. Schmorrow and C.M. Fidopiastis (Eds.): AC 2015, LNAI 9183, pp. 595–604, 2015.
DOI: 10.1007/978-3-319-20816-9_57

are then used to inform strategies that adapt learning experiences around defined state representations of a given learner.

The state representations of interest are based on both historical and realtime captured data, including but not limited to: (1) performance-based metrics inferred upon through user inputs and actions in a learning environment; (2) affective and cognitive state-based metrics derived from interaction sequences and the use of physiological and behavioral sensors; (3) and trait-based metrics linked with historical data found to be more persistent in terms of its effect on learning, such as an individual's prior knowledge, motivation, and grit [1, 2]. While a large portion of the research and development across ITSs is dedicated to assessment techniques for measuring the state spaces listed above, an area of research that requires considerably more attention to optimize ITS development is the field of pedagogical modeling and instructional management.

In this paper, we will discuss the tools and methods constructed by the U.S. Army Research Laboratory's Human Research and Engineering Directorate to support instructional management focused research within the ITS and adaptive training communities of practice. The specific tools of interest are the Generalized Intelligent Framework for Tutoring (GIFT) and the Engine for Management of Adaptive Pedagogy (EMAP). An in-depth review of the EMAP and how it supports pedagogical principles grounded in AugCog theory and practice will be provided. The types of augmentations supported by the EMAP will be presented along with the authoring tools developed to enable the implementation of adaptive instruction for any technology-driven educational product.

2 Adaptation in the Generalized Intelligent Framework for Tutoring

In an effort to promote the advancement of building and researching ITSs and educational technologies, GIFT was developed as a modular, service-oriented architecture built upon standardized tools and methods to support personalized instruction across an array of computer-based training applications [3]. With an emphasis on personalization, GIFT requires a domain-agnostic pedagogical structure to support the authoring and delivery of varying instructional techniques that can be executed within any learning environment [4]. From an implementation standpoint, this pedagogical framework requires authoring functions that enable a system developer to configure strategy types to specific domain calls and a runtime component that supports strategy execution in real-time based on learner model inputs. During an initial market survey to address this requirement, it was recognized that there is no open-source solution that provides adaptive course-flow capabilities based on both individual differences and historical and real-time performance metrics.

To facilitate the recognized need, we developed the EMAP. The EMAP is composed of a set of tools and methods housed within GIFT. It is designed to enhance the architecture by extending the authoring capabilities to support highly adaptive courseware materials. In the following sections we will review the multiple components that make up the EMAP and how the various tools are used to build customized learning experiences based on learner data linked with the varying state spaces described above. Further, we will explore how the EMAP can be leveraged by the Human Computer Interaction (HCI) community to support robust research associated with education and training with technology.

2.1 Augmenting Instructional Practice in GIFT Using the EMAP

The primary functions made available in the EMAP to support AugCog based practices are focused on the implementation of sound instructional design principles that account for individual differences related with learning, retention, and transfer [5]. The goal is to select and adapt strategies so as to optimize a learning experience to promote efficient training outcomes. The variables of interest are defined in terms of an individual's knowledge, skills, and abilities (KSAs) associated with a domain. The established KSAs serve as moderators in determining what information to deliver and how best to guide the learning event in relation to sequence of instruction and feedback [2].

The pedagogical framework is intended to support the various interactions that occur when an individual is learning a new topic or skill. This includes the design of actionable logic that determines for every domain of instruction (1) what material to present, (2) how best to assess knowledge and skill linked to a task and set of competencies, and (3) what guidance and feedback practices most reliably impact subsequent performance outcomes. The goal is to establish a data-driven pedagogical model that adapts strategy execution based on the type of learner the interventions moderate most appropriately. To make this a manageable problem space, the first steps associated with the EMAP design was identifying a generalized framework to support its function that is grounded in sound instructional system design (ISD) theory.

Following an extensive review of literature focused on ISD and pedagogical strategy implementations within computer-based learning environments, we selected David Merrill's Component Display Theory (CDT) to serve as the guiding framework to formalize the EMAP requirements around [4]. The CDT was originally constructed as a way to simplify theories and models of instruction around a set of core interactions a learner engages in when mastering a new domain [7]. For our efforts, the CDT served as a simplistic framework to organize instructional strategy research that ultimately informs the development of the EMAP's domain independent structure.

The CDT breaks learning down into four fundamental forms of instruction that focus on content and presentation modes. These instructional conditions, known as CDT's Presentation Forms, provide the basic building blocks for the instructional strategies present in the EMAP. CDT indicates two paths when it comes to content: it can be presented (expository) or the instructor asks the student to remember or use the content (inquisitory). The content can represent a general case (generality) or it can represent a specific case (instance). Therefore, instruction can be divided into four categories: Expository generality – present a general case (Rule); Expository instance – present a specific case (Example); Inquisitory generality – ask the student to remember or apply the general case (Recall); and Inquisitory instance – ask the student to remember or apply the specific case (Practice).

These four categories can be used as high-level descriptors to associate training content with, assuming each category applies different pedagogical practices inherent to the learning process. Therefore, instructional strategies can be explicitly defined and categorized within each component of the CDT. This association allows an instructional designer to understand what a piece of content is intended to provide in a lesson context (i.e., this video provides an example for enabling objective x), and further instructional strategies can be defined to inform when this piece of material is most suitable for use.

With the CDT serving as a generalized pedagogical framework for course construction, the next task was building empirically driven condition statements for the delivery of instructional materials that account for individual differences across a set of learners. The initial construction was facilitated through the creation of an algorithm in the form of a decision tree that informs adaptation based on general learner characteristics [4]. Specifically, the decision tree informs the selection of instructional strategies based on known information about the learner (e.g., learner motivation, learning style, previous experience, etc.) and the logic is established using GIFT's Pedagogical Configuration Authoring Tool (PCAT), which will be described in detail below. The resulting strategies were identified through an extensive literature review of empirically based research in an attempt to produce a list of commonly applied techniques found to reliably impact learning outcomes.

While many strategies were investigated across the learning sciences community, and many themes recognized, the studies often were limited to single domains and learning environments. The summary of this work can be seen across two publications [2, 4]. As a result, establishing a truly generalized pedagogical manager requires future research in an attempt to study the effect of strategies on outcomes and how those specific instructional techniques transfer to different learning environments. In this vein, the EMAP was designed to support both the creation of customized learning applications in addition to providing tools to support robust instructional strategy focused research. In the next section, we highlight the various authoring tools developed to support EMAP functions and how the tools are applied in AugCog based research formats.

3   GIFT's Engine for Management of Adaptive Pedagogy

The goal of the EMAP is to provide a means for instructors and course developers to build highly individualized lesson interactions that manage the student experience based on configured learning paths and real-time performance. It is intended to serve as an automated lesson manager when a learning event is executed in a self-regulated environment. It is currently being built to manage the delivery of information and course materials, perform assessment related practices to determine an individual's knowledge and skill for a set of concepts linked with a domain, manage the delivery of real-time guidance and interventions found to support learning outcomes, and directs remediation paths based on reported outcomes.

Identified augcog based instructional principles managed by the EMAP are configured by two levels of operational data: (1) enumerated metadata values used to describe content and interaction characteristics on a domain-agnostic level and (2) learner attribute data that categorizes education-centric individual differences on KSAs across a sample of learners. The learner attribute data is used as a moderator in selecting appropriate metadata values when adapting a lesson for a given learners knowledge and abilities. This structure is critical for maintaining GIFT's generalizability across disparate domains, while providing a means to effectively support adaptive practices through descriptive tags that characterize lesson materials and pedagogical strategy instantiations. To further enhance standardization, our current enumerated metadata values are mapped with standards outlined in IEEE's Learning Object Metadata [8]. This is intended to support reuse of existing content and for easy integration of external materials never implemented using GIFT. Next, we present the authoring tools and processes associated with building an EMAP driven lesson.

3.1 Configuring the EMAP Using GIFT Authoring Tools

A number of authoring processes have been established to support the various pedagogical functions made available by the EMAP. In this subsection we will introduce the environments currently in place to implement specific configurations that the EMAP operates on. While work is underway to create an intuitive web-based interface to guide the authoring process of EMAP functions, it is important to understand the underlying tools and methods created and how they impact course construction and delivery. The tools to be reviewed include (1) the Pedagogical Configuration Authoring Tool, (2) the Metadata Authoring Tool, (3) the Survey Authoring System, and (4) the Course Authoring Tool. Each tool serves a different function in building out the adaptive logic associated with a lesson using Merrill's CDT to structure interaction and assessment types.

Pedagogical Configuration Authoring Tool. The Pedagogical Configuration Authoring Tool (PCAT) is an interface component designed for linking learner relevant information with metadata that drives pedagogical decisions in GIFT. One important note to mention is the domain-independent nature of what is authored in the PCAT. More often than not, systems tightly couple pedagogy with the domain, providing little reuse for future developmental efforts. The EMAP differs from this description in that the authoring process is based on generalized tools and methods that translate across domain applications, including the pedagogical strategies the system acts upon [2]. A developer interacting with the PCAT defines learner model attributes they want GIFT to use for moderating adaptive practices. This is accomplished by linking a set of content descriptors with a given attribute across each of the established CDT quadrants represented in GIFT. These descriptors are a collection of metadata tags that are machine actionable and provide generalized information associated with content and guidance that can be used to configure system interactions in real-time. The metadata currently in use is based on the LOM standards put in place by the Institute for Electrical and Electronics Engineers (IEEE) [8]. This provides a set of high level categories (e.g., interactivity type, difficulty, skill level, coverage, etc.) and value ranges (i.e., skill level is broken down into novice, journeyman, and expert) that inform characteristics for a type of interaction.

While 'Rules' and 'Examples' primarily focus on information delivery, the 'Recall' and 'Practice' quadrants are focused on assessment, guidance, and remediation. The 'Recall' quadrant is unique because it focuses on knowledge elicitation through an automatically generated quiz that serves as a 'check on learning' function. To enable this capability, there are two additional authoring processes that take place. First, in the Survey Authoring System (SAS) you build a bank of concept questions to generate a recall assessment from and second, you use the Course Authoring Tool (CAT) to configure assessment scoring outcomes that determine if you advance to practice or if a remediation loop is triggered. Each process will be covered in more detail below.

In the 'Practice' quadrant, an author establishes adaptive configurations associated with the difficulty and complexity of a scenario, along with timing and specificity configurations linked to strategies executed as the result of concept assessments being managed during run-time. These specific 'Practice' pedagogical capabilities are still being addressed in the EMAP baseline. Much of this work is being based around Vygotsky's Zone of Proximal Development [6]. This theory of instruction focuses on the use of guidance to assist a learner in attaining knowledge and skills to complete a task outside of their ability level in conjunction with adapting the complexity of a problem to maintain an appropriate challenge level of a given learner. These tradeoffs must be fully understood to implement sound pedagogical structure when handling practice events in a generalized fashion. The initial configurations will require numerous studies to determine their efficacy.

Metadata Authoring Tool. The Metadata Authoring Tool (MAT) is an interface component in GIFT that provides a simple function; it allows you to tag existing training content with concept-dependent metadata that is acted upon by the EMAP. While the PCAT enables an ITS developer to build configurations between learner model data and metadata descriptors linked with pedagogical techniques, the MAT is established to build files that link metadata with actual content that can be delivered for learning purposes. When in an EMAP managed lesson, a learner is directed through defined branch points, called Merrill's Branching, that associate with the four quadrants of the CDT. When a learner starts instruction in the 'Rules' quadrant, the PCAT produced file is referenced for determining the type of content to search for based on a learner's individual profile and the type of metadata their models inform. Next, the EMAP searches through the various files generated in the MAT, for a given lesson, and looks for the closest match with respect to the number of descriptors for a tagged learning content and the ideal match informed by the PCAT (see GIFT documentation provided with software download for algorithm that manages content selection based on metadata attributes). As such, the MAT is a very important tool that allows an author and system developer to label their content in a controlled fashion that is then moderated autonomously by the EMAP during run-time.

Survey Authoring System. The Survey Authoring System (SAS) was developed for two primary purposes; (1) to collect learner relevant information through surveys that are used to update learner model attributes for the purpose of adaptation and (2) to deliver knowledge assessments in the form of questions that can be automatically scored for updating competency states and reporting performance across a set of learning objectives and concepts. In terms of the EMAP, both functions are highly relevant. Firstly, if you define configurations in the PCAT that act on learner trait information such as motivation or grit, the SAS allows a developer to present validated questionnaires and surveys that can be used to classify that individual learner.

For the purpose of this paper, we will focus on how the SAS is used to support the 'Recall' quadrant in the EMAP by assembling and delivering a set of questions for determining competency and informing remediation paths if required. The SAS was modified to support the EMAP by providing a 'check on learning' function through the assessment of knowledge states. A course developer would start interaction in the SAS by building out a bank of questions that are of relevance to the topic of instruction. GIFT's SAS provides a web interface to author the question, the answer type, and scoring weights that are used in determining knowledge states. A new field added to the question building process is defining a set of associated concepts the specific item informs. For EMAP purposes, this field is very important as it is used in defining the specific concept question bank that will be referenced within the 'Recall' quadrant interactions. You can also define the difficulty level of a question in the properties field, as a course developer can configure the number of questions to be administered for a difficulty level across a specified concept.

Following question generation, a course developer is then required to build the context for which the generated items will be acted upon. This is achieved by establishing the specified concept question bank the EMAP will operate on within the SAS's Survey Context interface window. The survey context is referenced by GIFT's Course Authoring Tool, which will be described next, and is used to identify the questionnaires in the database that are referenced during course construction, as well as establishing question banks that are used for 'Recall' assessment purposes. In the SAS survey context interface, the author has the ability to add concept question banks by selecting a specific concept that was established during question generation. If you are using the EMAP to deliver a lesson on three concepts, this is where you organize separate questions banks for each concept, thus providing a granular approach to assessment that directs personalized and performance driven remediation.

Course Authoring Tool. The GIFT Course Authoring Tool (CAT) is the final authoring interface a researcher interacts with once all of their materials and assessments have been appropriately configured for EMAP run-time. It is in this environment that an author designates the sequence of interaction a learner will experience for a specific lesson. The lesson is composed of defined transitions that dictate what will be presented next (See GIFT documentation for a full list of available transitions and their associated descriptions). The transitions of interest for the EMAP are 'Present Survey' and 'Merrills Branch Point'. The 'Present Survey' transition enables an author to select a questionnaire present in the SAS that will be delivered to a learner at any point in the course flow. For EMAP purposes, a course developer might call for surveys upfront to collect information on learner model attributes, such as measuring an individual's motivation for a topic. This requires an author to designate a survey context present within the SAS that determines what surveys are made available.

With defined surveys used to inform learner attributes, the next step for an author is establishing Merrill Branch Points. These branch point transitions are managed by the configurations established in the PCAT and MAT, as described above. Within the CAT, the author selects specific concepts used to build the quadrants of the CDT for a given branch point. Within a single course you can define multiple branch point transitions. Once you select the concepts a branch point associates with, the author then has the opportunity to configure interactions across the quadrants of the CDT. The CAT configurations allow a user to deselect certain quadrants that would be bypassed when a learner enters that branch transition.

The last configurations an author can make within the CAT is specifying what will be delivered to a learner within the Recall quadrant of the CDT. Once a user specifies the survey context referenced in the SAS and the concepts a Merrills Branch Point is used to manage, the next step is defining the number of questions to deliver for knowledge state assessment purposes and the scoring rules that determine the state value to communicate out to the learner module. When defining the number of questions to deliver, the inputs are used to identify matches within the established question banks that are built in the survey context interface within the SAS. It first looks for questions linked to a concept and then it looks for metadata values used to classify a difficulty ranking.

With the 'Recall' quadrant specified, an author then configures what is to be experienced with the 'Practice' quadrant. This interaction takes the form of a traditional 'Training Application' transition in the CAT where the user designates what application is being used and what Gateway is being applied for communication purposes. In addition, the author also defines specific scenario files to load based on metadata and the associated Domain Knowledge Files (DKFs) built for assessment purposes. These DKFs are essential components of all GIFT practice-based interactions. It is in the DKF where conditions are created for real-time assessment purposes, as well as where specific feedback strategies are translated into tactics that are delivered to a learner in real-time. The DKF is being modified to support the personalized strategy configurations that link to timing and specificity of feedback along with available scenario adaptations. See the GIFT documentation for all materials related to the DKF. With these final touches in place, an author is now ready to deliver an EMAP driven course. While the tools were established to build courses and lessons to be managed by GIFT, their intended function may differ. Depending on how a developed lesson is used will determine the specific authoring interfaces a user needs to interact within.

4   AugCog Research Using GIFT and the EMAP

When designing the EMAP, two primary end users were considered. These included traditional educators and training developers that would use the EMAP toolsets to author adaptive courseware materials they could distribute across classes and training organizations, and it included researchers and scientists within an AugCog focused research community that has interest in adaptive instruction, individual differences, and pedagogical heuristics. Making the distinctions between these two user groups is important because it will dictate the primary authoring tools they will interact with.

When considering the authoring experience across the EMAP tools for the AugCog community, an assumption is that this user group is interested in the creation of experimental treatments for running studies associated with cognitive intervention based research. The main difference between these individuals and educators/training developers is that the AugCog group will interact heavily with the PCAT to build out specific configurations in support of their research questions. This involves modifying current attributes available in the EMAP as well as adding additional variables in the learner model with the goal of assessing its effectiveness in informing adaptive intervention approaches. Within the PCAT, an author references a learner model attribute as well as metadata descriptors associated with the ideal type of content to deliver to that specific learner. For research purposes, the AugCog user group will be responsible for adding and removing available attribute tags for both the learner model and metadata variables and associated values. Each of the available tags are referenced in an enumeration file in GIFT's source code that can be modified to support the type of learner attribute and metadata a researcher desires the EMAP to act on. These files can be located at the following directory off of GIFT root: GIFT\src\mil\arl\gift\common\enums\MetadataAttributeEnum.java and GIFT \src\mil\arl\gift\common\enums\LearnerStateAttributeNameEnum.java. For each of the attributes represented in the learner state attribute enumerations file, a user will need to author an additional.java file that specifies the available tags made available for that variable when manipulating the PCAT authoring tool. Many examples are available to work from in the GIFT\src\mil\arl\gift\common\enums\ folder.

In implementing the EMAP for support in the AugCog research community, there are a couple assumed dependencies associated with the authoring tools. While an author will be required to modify enumeration files in the source code to introduce variables of interest not currently supported in GIFT's baseline version, an author will also be required to make additions in the SAS for the purpose of collecting individual differences metrics used to inform variables that dictate strategy selection. Further, GIFT also supports tracking and inferring upon affective based data for the purpose of diagnosing cognitive and emotional states experienced during a learning event. None of the current EMAP configurations are built to support acting on this type of assessment. The PCAT needs to be modified for this very purpose, along with establishing classifiers within the learner and sensor modules of GIFT that would inform state.

In addition, the EMAP's current baseline provides an automated lesson manager for a GIFT course with some caveats. For example, the course author has but only one option for a 'check on learning' as part of the Recall quadrant and that is a test composed of questions selected at runtime from a pre-established bank. Other forms of knowledge assessment could be given either with a static pre-authored survey or using AutoTutor which is also integrated with GIFT [9]. Using AutoTutor allows GIFT to hold a conversation in natural language between one or more agents and the learner. This interaction can be used to elicit comprehension of the concepts covered in prior Rule and Example quadrants that goes beyond just recalling information. Implementing this approach allows a learner to explain knowledge in their own words, thus providing evidence of higher order cognitive understanding of the material.

5   Conclusion

The EMAP provides a suite of authoring interfaces to build highly individualized and adaptive courseware materials. In this paper, we review the authoring tools developed in support of the EMAP functions that relate to AugCog based principles associated with training and education. A description of each tool is provided, along with the data used to inform its logic. The AugCog community can leverage these tools to create highly robust testbeds to evaluate intervention techniques, as well as examining new domain of application, such as robotics and human-machine interaction.

References

1. Duckworth, A.L., Peterson, C., Matthews, M.D., Kelly, D.R.: GRIT: perseverance and passion for long-term goals. J. Pers. Soc. Psychol. **92**, 1087–1101 (2007)
2. Goldberg, B., Brawner, K.W., Sottilare, R., Tarr, R., Billings, D.R., Malone, N.: Use of evidence-based strategies to enhance the extensibility of adaptive tutoring technologies. Paper presented at the Interservice/Industry Training, Simulation, and Education Conference (I/ITSEC) 2012, Orlando, FL (2012)
3. Sottilare, R., Brawner, K.W., Goldberg, B., Holden, H.: The generalized intelligent framework for tutoring (GIFT). In: Best, C., Galanis, G., Kerry, J., Sottilare, R. (eds.) Fundamental Issues in Defense Training and Simulation, pp. 223–234. Ashgate Publishing Company, Burlington (2013)
4. Wang-Costello, J., Goldberg, B., Tarr, R.W., Cintron, L.M., Jiang, H.: Creating an advanced pedagogical model to improve intelligent tutoring technologies. Paper presented at the The Interservice/Industry Training, Simulation & Education Conference (I/ITSEC) 2013, Orlando, FL (2013)
5. Sottilare, R., Goldberg, B.: Designing adaptive computer-based tutoring systems to accelerate learning and facilitate retention. J. Cogn. Technol. **17**(1), 19–33 (2012)
6. Vygotsky, L.: Zone of proximal development. In: Cole, M. (ed.) Mind in Society: The Development of Higher Psychological Processes, pp. 52–91. Harvard University Press, Cambridge (1987)
7. Merrill, M.D.: The Descriptive Component Display Theory. Educational Technology Publications, Englewood Cliffs (1994)
8. Mitchell, J.L., Farha, N.: Learning object metadata: use and discovery. In: Harman, K., Koohang, A. (eds.) Learning Objects: Standards, Metadata, Repositories, and LCMS, pp. 1–40. Informing Science Press, Santa Rosa (2007)
9. Graesser, A.C., Chipman, P., Haynes, B.C., Olney, A.: AutoTutor: an intelligent tutoring system with mixed-initiative dialogue. IEEE Trans. Educ. **48**, 612–618 (2005)

Measuring Concentration While Programming with Low-Cost BCI Devices: Differences Between Debugging and Creativity Tasks

Víctor M. González[1(✉)], Romain Robbes[2], Gabriela Góngora[1],
and Salvador Medina[1]

[1] Department of Computer Science, Instituto Tecnológico Autónomo de México,
Mexico City, Mexico
victor.gonzalez@itam.mx
[2] Computer Science Department (DCC), Universidad de Chile, Santiago, Chile

Abstract. Computing devices have become a primary working tool for many professional roles, among them software programmers. In order to enable a more productive interaction between computers and humans for programming purposes it is important to acquire an awareness of human attention/concentration levels. In this work we report on a controlled experiment to determine if a low-cost BCI (Brain Computer Interface) device is capable of classifying whether a user is fully concentrated while programming, during three typical tasks: creativity (writing code), systematic (documenting the code) and debugging (improving or modifying the code to make it work). This study employs EEG (Electroencephalogram) signals, to measure an individual's concentration levels. The chosen BCI device is NeuroSky's Mindwave due to its availability in the market and low cost. The three tasks described are performed in a physical and digital form. A statistically significant difference between debugging and creativity tasks is revealed in our experiments, in both physical and digital tests. This is a good lead for following experiments to focus on these two areas. Systematic tasks might not bring good results due to their nature.

Keywords: BCI · EEG · Concentration levels · Programming tasks · Debugging · Creativity · Systematic

1 Introduction

Computing devices have become a primary working tool for many professional roles, among them software programmers, whose work can be regarded as requiring discipline, creativity, expertise, but, perhaps most importantly, extended periods of sustained concentration. In order to create a more seamless and productive interaction between computers and humans for software programming we believe that it is important to open mechanisms and create new technologies that make computers aware of the level of attention/concentration level of the user.

EEG (Electroencephalogram) devices have a wide range of applications [1], ranging from control of computers, wheelchairs, and videogames or even determine the cognitive state when performing tasks in the real world. All these applications foresee a

© Springer International Publishing Switzerland 2015
D.D. Schmorrow and C.M. Fidopiastis (Eds.): AC 2015, LNAI 9183, pp. 605–615, 2015.
DOI: 10.1007/978-3-319-20816-9_58

positive future for EEG devices; their unfortunate downside is their high cost thereby limiting the research to large laboratories with enough funding. This is why noninvasive, low cost EEG devices such as NeuroSky, Emotiv, Epoc, amongst others, have become so popular in the past years [2, 3]. They have expanded the applications of Brain-Computer Interfaces (BCI), for example controlling day-to-day device such as mobile phones [4].

There are two different types of sensors to capture neurological bio-signals: dry (e.g. used by NeuroSky's [5] products) and wet sensors, used, for instance, by the Biopac equipment [3], popular equipment in the research field, which brings high quality readings but at a great cost [6]. When it comes to electrodes, we also have two types: monopolar and bipolar. The monopolar electrodes collect signals at the active site and compare them to a reference point, which is usually located at the earlobe [2].

A comparison of the of the NeuroSky's single dry electrode against the Biopacs nineteen (19) wet electrodes have been made showing a great similarity in the results demonstrating the reliability of their product at a lower cost [6], therefore our chosen BCI device is NeuroSky's Mindwave. The signal obtained from the EEG by Neuro-Sky's products ranges from 1-100 μV, which are read as signals through time. The signals are classified according to their frequency bands as Alpha, Beta, Gamma, Delta and Theta signals [5], where each class corresponds to different mental and emotional states of the individual.

2   Related Work and Justification of the Study

Studies in this field usually examine interruptions presented to working people, in particular in the information-centric context, either external or self-inflicted [9]. Interruption and workflows can be better understood if we can characterize individual's concentration stages during different types of tasks. This study is focused on user's awareness and concentration, by trying to determine if a low- cost EEG signal reader device befits the task and is able to determine if users are concentrated on their task or not. The chosen BCI device, as already mentioned, is NeuroSky's Mindwave due to its availability in the market and having the lowest cost at the moment of this study. The tasks to be performed by the users are three basic and typical activities in programming workflows: creative (thinking and writing code), debugging (improving or modifying the code to make it work) and systematic tasks (commenting and documenting the code).

As an initial hypothetical scenario we thought of a system that could obtain the user's concentration as a numerical input, enabling the system to aid the user to concentrate in a faster way and for longer periods of time by adapting his or her environment i.e. reducing any possible distraction. Distractions such as: notifications in the GUI on screen, notification sounds, telephone rings and even face-to-face unplanned type of interactions.

Goldberg et al. [7] tried to determine the user's engagement on certain task by using an electroencephalogram (EEG) device and a galvanic skin resistance (GSR) reader. Their results invite to the development of ubiquitous devices. This could also be applied for learning techniques, helping the lecturer with a real-time measurement of their students. Additionally they stated that the interruption analysis is an important issue while trying to determine the attention of the user.

This assumption is confirmed by Mark et al. [9] and derived in a series of studies that determined for how long a person is able to complete a task after being interrupted while trying to achieve a certain task. In that study they determined that information workers in average focus, on a given task for 3 min before switching to another related task, and interrupt themselves or are interrupted by external sources every 11 min. However, studies like that have been made using observational approaches and a quantitative measure is required to extend their results and conclusions.

For this reason we decided to make an experiment as a first step, attempting to measure the concentration of a group of individuals which are aiming to complete programming tasks, both in a digital and a physical contexts. We aimed at exploring a typical programming scenario by studying a digital programming context, but to also a physical programming context as we are seeing more and more physical component programming scenarios emerging (e.g. Little Bits components).

3   Methodology

The experiments conducted in this study were divided into two one-hour sessions, for a total of 24 participants. Each session consists of three different types of tasks: systematic, debugging and creative. In the first session all tasks require a physical action, while in the second session they are done on a computer. The sessions were conducted on different days in order to avoid individuals' fatigue.

At the beginning of each experiment, the individuals were asked to watch a relaxing video in order to set the same starting mental basis on all the users. Afterwards, they were asked to fill out agreement forms and allow the evaluator to place and adjust the NeuroSky Mindwave device on them. The device had to be synchronized with the computer in order to record a total of seven brainwaves from the participant while performing the given tasks. The captured signals were the alpha, beta, gamma, delta, theta and NeuroSky's proprietary compound signals: attention and meditation.

During all tasks a video of the participants' actions on the screen was recorded. For any given task the time established was 10 min, with a 3–5 min interval between tasks in order to give sufficient time for reading instructions and answering doubts that might come up. The tests were conducted mostly on engineering university students (sophomores or older), ranging from specialized on computer engineering, telecommunications engineering, mechatronics engineering or industrial engineering. The requirement was to have passed the basic programming courses offered by the university in which they learn data structures and Java language.

3.1   Physical Tasks

The session where the participants were asked to accomplish physical (programming) tasks started with the systematic task, where the individual was asked to organize a set of Legos by color and size, while filling an inventory sheet with the amount of Legos corresponding to each type. For the creativity task, with the separated Legos from the previous task, the individual had to build a house with certain characteristics. The how, shape and color was for each individual to decide on, as long as it used the provided Legos and fulfilled the given characteristics such as the amount of doors or windows it should have. The third and final task simulated debugging, where the participant was given a tower of Uno-Stacko (similar to Jenga but with colors and numbers) and he or she had to move one piece at a time in order to build the pattern provided to them in a separate piece of paper i.e. physically debug the plastic tower of sticks.

3.2 Digital Tasks

The second session was formed by a set of three programming tasks. During the first task the individual had to debug a certain code in Java (using NetBeans IDE). The requirement was to be able to compile the code and print an expected output, of which each individual was informed of, prior to the test. Afterwards, the individual had to program, in Java language, small problems extracted from Project Euler [11]. The problems obtained vary in difficulty according to what is taught in the required programming course. The participant could choose which ones and in which order to solve the problems given. For the last test the individual was asked to document the code he or she generated in the previous task. With these we again have the same three categories of tasks as in the previous session: debugging, creativity and systematic.

4 Participant's Characterization

The experiment described was conducted on 24 participants, mostly engineering students, sophomores or older, as long as they fulfilled the prerequisites. The initial experiment was re-designed and corrected with the help of an additional 8 participants. From the other 24 individuals, only 20 had useful signals and complete physical and digital tasks. From the total 32 participants, 26 of them were male students and 6 female students. The latter reported consistent problems with the Mindwave, as it kept falling off their heads.

Table 1. Demographics of participants

Measure	Age	Semester	GPA
Min.	20.00	3.000	7.500
1st Qu.	20.00	5.000	8.000
Median	21.00	7.000	8.775
Mean	21.04	6.179	8.679
3rd Qu.	21.25	7.000	9.125
Max.	24.00	11.000	9.900

A more detailed characterization of the students was made in order to understand the population at hand and the results obtained. Table 1 shows the range of age, semester and GPA of all the students that participated in the experiment. The GPA is measured under a 10-point scale, where 5 is a fail, 6 is a passing grade and 10 is the highest grade possible. All our participants have ages 20 to 24 and in average are more than halfway through their bachelor's degree.

Table 2. Participant's area of study (Mayor)

Degree	Number of students
Computer Eng.	21
Mechatronics	6
Telecommunications	1

The majority of the students Computer Engineers, Table 2 shows the distributions of BSc degrees.

Table 3. Participant's with a double degree

Degree	Number of students
None	16
Administration	1
Industrial Eng.	2
Applied Mathematics	2
Mechatronics	2
Telecommunications	5

Some of the individuals study two degrees and Table 3 accounts for them. The variety in the second degree is more than in the first one, although only 16 out of 32 participants have double mayors.

5 Signal Processing

One of the main problems presented while working with the Mindwave headset was its recording resolution. The maximum sample rate of the signals is 1 Hz. This forced the experiment to sample long periods of time in order to obtain relevant results.

The Mindwave device was capable to sample the alpha, beta, gamma, delta and theta waves, as well as two composite signals: attention and meditation. All the signals aforementioned were taken into consideration for the statistical analysis, although our main focus was the Mindwave's attention proprietary signal. This signal brought the most reliable and stable results.

5.1 Cleaning the Results

The cleaning process of the results obtained required the elimination of six individuals due to the loss of recording during their testing period.

The loss of the recording signal can be due to many factors such as: a lousy bluetooth signal from the Mindwave device; the participant's head size where the Mindwave would be too big; the participants forward tilting their heads while making some of the physical tests. This last factor should be taken into consideration in future tests by trying to avoid that the individuals move their head during their test.

The graphic representation of how a signal was lost during the test looks like Fig. 1.

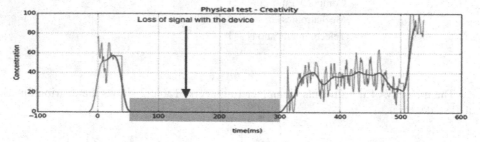

Fig. 1. Loss of signal during session

The next table shows the amount of individuals whose captured data was relevant. All of them participated in each of the three tests: Systematic, Debugging and Creativity, in both of their modalities: Physical and Digital.

Afterwards, the signals' noise was removed based on the work done by Hong Tan [9] we decided to apply a FIR filter to smooth the signals as they are impossible to work with at first instance. The FIR filter had a cutoff of *1/100* a filter order of 30 and a warm-up of 30 s, as the individuals were opening the required software or being explained the tasks during that time (Table 4).

Table 4. Most relevant test subjects

Type of Task	Number of individuals
Systematic	14
Debugging	16
Creativity	16

6 Results

An initial sampling of the signals through a means plot, Fig. 2, lets us evaluate a visual difference between the three types of tasks and in particular between creative and debugging tasks. A resemblance amongst physical and digital tests can also be observed from this figure. Further statistical analysis will provide solid evidence and explanation for this outcome.

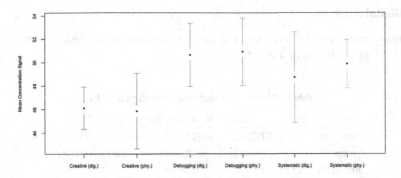

Fig. 2. Means Plot with 95 % Confidence Interval

As a first approach, an ANOVA of means was performed taking into consideration all signals obtained, including composite signals. The analysis was done for the physical tests and the digital tests separately. Then an ANOVA was made to find if a similarity existed among the tasks in the physical world compared to their digital counterparts.

6.1 Physical Analysis

The ANOVA test was applied to the means of each signal obtained through out the whole test of each participant. The hypothesis for this particular test is:

H_0:   means are the same

H_1:   means differ (at least one in the group)

Table 5. Anova test performed on physical tasks

	Df	Sum squares	Mean squares	F value	Pr(> F)
(Intercept)	1	109764.59	109764.59	4105.96	0.0000
groups	2	227.94	113.97	4.26	0.0205
Residuals	43	1149.52	26.73		

The *p-value* for the ANOVA test was *0.0205*, which is less than *0.05*, therefore we can reject H_0 and conclude that at least one mean in our tested population differs from the others. Further testing has to be in order to know which group in particular we are referring to (Table 5).

6.2   Digital Analysis

The already explained ANOVA test was employed to the digital tasks, obtaining a *p-value* of *0.044* as shown in Table 6.

Table 6. Anova test performed on digital tasks

	Df	Sum squares	Mean squares	F value	Pr(> F)
Intercept	1	108182.02	108182.02	4054.37	0.0000
groups	2	166.81	83.41	3.13	0.0440
Residuals	43	1147.36	26.68		

From these tasks we can also reject H_0 and expect to find differences between the type of tasks (debugging, systematic, creative) when using a post hoc analysis.

6.3   Post-Hoc Analysis

When evaluating both physical and digital results the difference between each task becomes even more evident than in previous results shown.

The *p-value* for the ANOVA test for all, physicial and digital tasks, was *0.0158*, as shown in Table 7, which is less than *0.05*, therefore we can reject H_0 and conclude that at least one mean in our tested population differs from the others.

Table 7. Anova test performed on all tasks

	Df	Sum squares	Mean squares	F value	Pr(> F)
Intercept	1	217943.74	217943.74	8160.27	0.0000
groups	5	397.63	79.53	2.98	0.0158
Residuals	86	2296.88	26.71		

The Holm adjustment method, as post hoc for ANOVA analysis, is useful in our case as it contrasts the lowest p-value with a Type I error rate i.e. decreasing it for each subsequent test. The results are shown in Table 8.

The obtained results identify a clear difference between creative and debugging tasks, both in physical and digital tasks. A distinction between creative and systematic tasks can also be established, although such observation is only statistically significant in physical tasks (phy.) and not in digital tasks (dig.).

Another method employed for comparing results is the Tukey Honest Significant Difference (HSD), as it can adjust to correct Type I error rates between multiple comparisons and it is considered as an acceptable statistical technique. The results obtained are shown in Table 9. It can be observed that our results are quite identical (although not mathematically) to the ones using the Holm adjustment method.

Table 8. Pairwise comparisons using t tests with pooled SD - Holm adjustment method

	Creat. (dig.)	Creat (phy.)	Debugg (dig.)	Debugg (phy.)	Syst. (dig.)
Creat. (phy.)	0.89	–	–	–	–
Debugg. (dig.)	0.01	0.01	–	–	–
Debugg. (phy.)	0.01	0.01	0.88	–	–
Sys. (dig.)	0.17	0.13	0.31	0.25	–
Sys. (phy.)	0.05	0.04	0.68	0.58	0.56

Table 9. Tukey multiple comparisons of means test, 95 % family-wise confidence level

Task Compared	Diff. in means	Lower end	Upper end	p-value (after adj.)
Debugging (dig.)-Creative (dig.)	4.55	0.12	8.98	0.04
Systematic (dig.)-Creative (dig.)	2.64	-1.95	7.22	0.35
Systematic (dig.)-Debugging (dig.)	-1.91	-6.50	2.68	0.57
Debugging (phy.)-Creative (phy.)	5.08	0.64	9.51	0.02
Systematic (phy.)-Creative (phy.)	4.03	-0.56	8.63	0.10
Systematic (phy.)-Debugging(phy.)	-1.04	-5.64	3.55	0.85
Debugging (phy.)-Debugging (dig.)	0.27	-5.05	5.60	1.00
Systematic (phy.)-Systematic (dig.)	1.14	-4.55	6.84	0.99
Creative (phy.)-Creative (dig.)	-0.26	-5.58	5.07	1.00
Debugging (phy.)-Creative (dig.)	4.82	-0.50	10.15	0.10
Systematic (phy.)-Creative (dig.)	3.78	-1.74	9.29	0.35
Systematic (phy.)-Debugging(dig.)	-0.77	-6.29	4.74	1.00

Debugging and systematic tasks did not differ much, as shown in light blue in Table 9, they have *p-values* equal or close to 1.0 i.e. their means hardly differ and can be considered as equally demanding tasks in terms of concentration brainwaves. Debugging and creative tasks do show a statistical difference in their means, as can be appreciated in light yellow in Table 9, as their *p-values* are less than 0.05.

7   Conclusions and Future Work

We observed a statistically significant difference between debugging and creativity tasks no matter if the test was physical or digital. This is a good lead for following experiments to focus on these two areas. Systematic tasks might not bring good results due to their nature: a systematic task does not require the participant's entire focus to achieve its completion and as such may lead the individual to a state of complete dispersion. Finally, we observed that the data generated by the BCI was rather noisy; research is being performed to analyze the performance of other higher-end BCI devices in our subsequent studies.

One of the main contributions of this paper is that it gives some insights into the differences between creative, debugging and systematic programming tasks, both in the digital and physical worlds. In the long-term, these results could be used to implement better software development environments.

Nonetheless this study holds some limitations. First of all, the programming tasks given throughout the experiments are very short in time, for example the digital creative tasks usually took between 3-9 min (depending on the programmer's skills). A full-time programmer could spend 8-12 h a day working on the same programming problem, thereby having longer spaces of time to concentrate. This limitation can also be viewed as an advantage, since we could consider that a working programmers is, in many cases, subject to various interruptions throughout the day and has to get back into the work flow as quickly as possible i.e. this limitation is actually an insight into how fast a programmer can get concentrated in each type of task.

Future work could show us if the 3-9 min in creative digital tasks are a true sample of a full-time programmer's awareness level, and the insights could be expanded to cover more situations resulting from this process. Other devices (e.g. heart rate monitors) and camera recordings could be of aid in this.

NeuroSky's MindWave has a proven to be a reasonable device for the experiments performed, as it was easy to use, below a $200 dollar budget and non-intrusive to wear. The only three problems reported throughout the process were the loss of connectivity (computer-device), the interference of other Bluetooth devices around the individual and headband falling off some individuals. Therefore we are currently continuing the study with an Emotiv EPOC device, as to have more data that will backup the MindWave and to obtain further characterizations of programmer's concentration during debugging and creative tasks aside from evaluating how each programmer gets back into its work flow. Future work plans also include the incorporation of interruptions into the study, an in-depth profiling of the programmers participating and longer tasks.

Acknowledgements. This work has been supported by LACCIR (Project ID: RFP1212LAC004) the Asociación Mexicana de la Cultura A.C. and the Consejo Nacional de Ciencia y Tecnologia de México (CONACyT). We thank Frida Rojas and Farid Fajardo Oroz for their help editing and proofreading the document.

References

1. Tan, D., Nijholt, A.: Brain Computer Interaction: Applying our Minds to Human-Computer Interaction, vol. Ch. 1. Springer, London (2010)
2. Stamps, K., Hamam, Y.: Towards inexpensive BCI control for wheelchair navigation in the enabled environment – a hardware survey. In: Yao, Y., Sun, R., Poggio, T., Liu, J., Zhong, N., Huang, J. (eds.) BI 2010. LNCS, vol. 6334, pp. 336–345. Springer, Heidelberg (2010)
3. Duvinage, M., Castermans, T., Petieau, M., Hoellinger, T., Cathy, D.S., Seetharaman, K., Cheron, G.: A P300-based quantitative comparison between the Emotiv Epoc headset and a medical EEG device. In: Proceedings of the 9th IEEE/IASTED International Conference on Biomedical Engineering. Acta press, Innsbruck (2012)

4. Campbell, A.T., Choudhury, T., Shaohan, H., Hong, L., et al.: NeuroPhone: brain- mobile phone interface using a wireless eeg headset. In: Proceedings of the Second ACM SIGCOMM Workshop on Networking, Systems, and Applications on Mobile Handhelds, MobiHeld 2010. ACM, New York (2010)
5. NeuroSky Brain-Computer Interface Technologies. Brain Wave Signal (EEG) of NeuroSky, Inc. NeuroSky, Inc. (2009)
6. Crowley, K., Sliney, A., Pitt, I., Murphy, D.: Evaluating a brain-computer interface to categorize human emotional response. In: 10th IEEE International Conference on Advanced Learning Techniques. Cork, Ireland (2010)
7. Goldberg, B.S., Sottilare, R.A., Brawner, K.W., Holden, H.K.: Predicting learner engagement during well-defined and ill-defined computer-based intercultural interactions. In: D'Mello, S., Graesser, A., Schuller, B., Martin, J.-C. (eds.) ACII 2011, Part I. LNCS, vol. 6974, pp. 538–547. Springer, Heidelberg (2011)
8. Tan, B.H.: Using a Low-cost EEG Sensor to Detect Mental States. Diss. Carnegie Mellon University (2012)
9. Mark, G., Gudith, D., Klocke, U.: The cost of interrupted work: more speed and stress. ACM, Proceedings of the SIGCHI conference on Human Factors in Computing Systems (2008)
10. Project Euler. https://projecteuler.net/
11. Banerjee, A., Kanad B., Aruna C.: Prediction of EEG signal by digital filtering. In: Proceedings of International Conference on Intelligent Systems & Networks, Jagadhri, India (2007)
12. Oikonomou, V.P., Tzallas, A.T., Fotiadis, D.I.: A Kalman filter based methodology for EEG spike enhancement. Comput. Methods Programs Biomed. 85(2), 101–108 (2007)

Adapting Immersive Training Environments to Develop Squad Resilience Skills

Joan H. Johnston[1], Samantha Napier[2], and William A. Ross[3(✉)]

[1] Army Research Laboratory, Human Research Engineering Directorate,
Orlando, FL, USA
joan.h.johnston.civ@mail.mil
[2] Army Research Laboratory, Human Research Engineering Directorate, Aberdeen
Proving Ground, Aberdeen, MD, USA
Samantha.j.napier.civ@mail.mil
[3] Cognitive Performance Group, Orlando, FL, USA
bill@cognitiveperformancegroup.com

Abstract. The United States Army defines readiness and resilience as tactically proficient Soldiers and highly adaptive problem solvers capable of overcoming challenges and making decisions with strategic consequences in ambiguous situations. To address the resilience training gap, the Squad Overmatch study produced recommendations for employing immersive and live training strategies within the Stress Exposure Training (SET) framework. SET is a three-phase training method designed to provide information, skills training, and practice; with the goal of learning how to cope and perform while exposed to combat stressors. The potential for a wide range of Soldier experience levels in the pre-deployment training phase requires structuring and facilitating immersive and live training to develop resilience skills. In this paper we provide recommendations for adapting immersive environments to focus on assessing unit "readiness to train," and employing methods and tools that improve training effectiveness.

Keywords: Stress exposure training · Resilience · Immersive · Battlefield · Squad Overmatch

1 Introduction

Despite their extensive pre-deployment training and preparations, Warfighters must develop resilience on-the-job in an operational setting and struggle to manage the effects of emotional or operational stress as a result. Recognizing the need to overcome this problem, the US Army has been proactively addressing the challenge of improving Soldier performance, resilience, and readiness, and reducing vulnerability to Post-Traumatic Stress (PTS) through the Ready and Resilience Campaign – R2C [1]. R2C requires developing "tactically proficient soldiers and highly adaptive problem solvers capable of overcoming challenges and making decisions with strategic consequences in ambiguous situations." Preventative training for resilience is an R2C key priority; starting in the schoolhouse, and continuing through lifelong learning

© Springer International Publishing Switzerland 2015
D.D. Schmorrow and C.M. Fidopiastis (Eds.): AC 2015, LNAI 9183, pp. 616–627, 2015.
DOI: 10.1007/978-3-319-20816-9_59

experiences. The Army Maneuver Center of Excellence (MCoE) has been aligned with this vision; their concept for Squad Overmatch (SOvM) focuses on making the Squad "the foundation of the decisive force." SOvM training requirements include developing the cognitive, physical, social-cultural, resilient, and moral-ethical components of the human dimension [2].

Solving the resilience training gap was the primary purpose of the Army Study Program's Squad Overmatch (SOvM) Study [3]. The demonstration was a paradigm shift from the current strategy of training warrior skills; an initial prototype was developed first so that Army squads could interact - "kick the tires" - and provide their evaluations of it. The Study was led by the US Army Program Executive Office for Simulation Training and Instrumentation (PEO STRI), and was a collaborative effort with several DOD agencies, including ARL HRED's STTC. The authors were part of the integrated product team leading the study evaluation, and contributed to the final report. The study report provides a detailed description of the evaluation findings and describes requirements for training methods, tools, strategies, and technologies that have the potential for improving individual and squad resilience skills. In this paper we summarize how the Stress Exposure Training (SET) framework was used to structure the SOvM demonstration. Lessons learned and recommendations are provided for increasing training effectiveness by adapting immersive environments, assessments, instruction, and feedback based on a soldier's "readiness to train."

1.1   SOvM Demonstration

Numerous guidelines have recommended SET for pre-deployment dismounted infantry combat training [4–7]. For example, Stanley and Jha recommended that training under more extreme conditions (e.g., injecting stressors such as battle sounds and smells) by exposing Warfighters to more complex tasks (such as having to concurrently manage treatment of casualties, communicate with locals, and provide security), may enhance Soldiers' resilience and performance after adequate physical and psychological preparation [7]. Sponsored by the Office of Naval Research, SET was developed as part of a comprehensive 10-year program of theory development and empirical research focused on improving tactical decision making under stress (TADMUS) in Navy combat teams [8]. The TADMUS program resulted in a detailed set of training requirements and guidelines for developing a "triad" of skills for resilience: decision making (DM), stress management (SM), and teamwork (TW).

The SET approach is counter to the notion that training under only extreme conditions hardens the Warfighter to combat stressors; an approach that neither improves resilience nor performance. It was designed for non-clinical settings as a framework so that instructional content could be adapted based on learning requirements for each of the resilience skills. The goal is for stressors to trigger employment of effective resilience skills instead of yielding to ineffective behaviors [9]. A 3-phase approach is employed that primes learning, sets learner expectations and then exposes learners and their teams to a series of progressively complex problems embedded with common stressors. Guided practice and performance feedback are critical to learning. In the second and third phases, practice takes place under graduated exposure to stressors in simulations and live exercises, with the number and types of stressors gradually increased in successive training scenarios. Literature reviews and empirical studies have reported that self-confidence, stress management, and teamwork are improved with resilience skills training [4, 7, 10–12]. However, the complete 3-phase approach was never fully validated under the TADMUS program, and even today little is known about its effectiveness. Therefore, the SOvM study provided an opportunity to more fully vet the SET concept for operational training environments. Figure 1 depicts the concept of operation for the SOvM demonstration that is based on the SET design guidelines regarding stressor fidelity, training sequencing and content, training delivery, and assessments [9]. Training methods and technologies were selected for the evaluation that focused on DM, SM, and TW skills at the individual and squad level. A two-day demonstration was provided to each squad. Thirty-three Army soldiers participated as four separate squads. Level of soldier expertise ranged from zero to several deployments.

Information Provision. On the morning of day 1, soldiers were introduced to the SOvM concept. The evaluation strategy was explained, which was to provide their opinions on paper-based surveys and provide feedback through interviews following each capability demonstration. During the "Information Provision" phase soldiers were presented with a short instructor-led introduction to the Army's Training for Advanced Situation Awareness (ASA), the Comprehensive Soldier and Family Fitness (CSF2) program for stress management, and the Stress Resilience in Virtual Environments (STRIVE) prototype. A two-week training for ASA is delivered at the MCoE in an instructor-led classroom and through practical field exercises. The objective is to develop pattern recognition, predictive analysis and anticipatory thinking skills for high risk contexts [13].

The CSF2 program is an instructor led in-class course that is available twice during a 24-month training continuum (once during unit training and once during deployment) [14]. It provides cognitive skills training to build confidence, goal-setting, attention control, stress and energy management, visualization and imagery, problem solving, identifying strengths in self and others, and assertive communication. Participants learn that negative thoughts and emotions diminish task performance, and that replacing them with task-focused thoughts and positive emotions reduces stress. Behavioral modeling of appropriate behaviors and thought processes is used to introduce the trainee to how both thoughts and actions can influence stress reduction. STRIVE was developed by the Institute for Creative Technologies, University of Southern California, as an experiential learning prototype for developing stress management techniques and cognitive-behavioral emotional coping strategies [15]. It employs simulations and video-vignettes to present a set of combat scenarios that are part of a multi-episode interactive narrative experience. Users are immersed within challenging combat contexts and interact with virtual characters within these episodes. Videos employ avatars modeling appropriate coping skills behaviors.

Skills Acquisition. On the afternoon of day 1, for the "Skills Acquisition" phase, soldiers were introduced to STRIVE video snippets of typical combat stress scenarios and then had about an hour to play the gaming prototype Stress Resilience Training System (SRTS). Sponsored by DARPA and the US Navy, SRTS is a tablet-based game that collects noninvasive physiological measures for trainee biofeedback. It provides

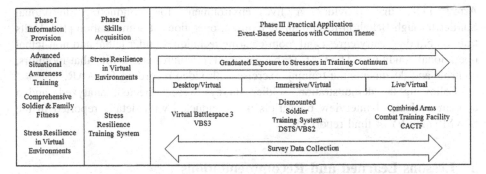

Phase I Information Provision	Phase II Skills Acquisition	Phase III Practical Application Event-Based Scenarios with Common Theme		
Advanced Situational Awareness Training	Stress Resilience in Virtual Environments	Graduated Exposure to Stressors in Training Continuum		
		Desktop/Virtual	Immersive/Virtual	Live/Virtual
Comprehensive Soldier & Family Fitness Stress Resilience in Virtual Environments	Stress Resilience Training System	Virtual Battlespace 3 VBS3	Dismounted Soldier Training System DSTS/VBS2	Combined Arms Combat Training Facility CACTF
		Survey Data Collection		

Fig. 1. Concept of operation for the SOVM stress exposure training demonstration

educational modules and games using the biofeedback data for learning cognitive restructuring and physiological stress management skills [16]. An automated Adaptive Coach monitors trainee progress and self-test results, and provides recommendations on how best to progress through the training program.

Practical Application. For the "Practical Application" phase, the study team used three mission task scenarios (Scenario 1 (S1), S2 and S3) in the context of an Eastern European theme; connecting the gaming, virtual, and live training environments with a common storyline. Following SRTS, squads interacted in the desktop Virtual Battle-space (Version 3) (VBS3) simulator and communicated over simulated radio nets to perform a squad mission in a village using S1 and S2 that were about 25 min each. VBS3 is an Army Program of Record (POR) that provides semi-immersive environments, dynamic terrain, simulated military and civilian entities, and a range of geo-typical (generic) and geo-specific virtual terrains [17]. The study team used the 3-D scenario editor to design and implement event-based scenarios with increasing levels of stressors.

The second day continued with "Practical Application" demonstrations; in the morning, squads participated in the Dismounted Soldier Training System (DSTS) virtual battlefield using S1 for about 25 min. Each Squad participated in an abbreviated planning session and then conducted a combat patrol. Then, for comparison, squads participated in a brief demonstration of DSTS with an enhanced graphics engine. DSTS is an Army POR that provides squad training that can support increasing levels of stressors using VBS (Version 2) [18]. DSTS provides a fully immersive 360-degree virtual view using head-mounted displays and un-tethered rifle simulators. Each DSTS standalone system is designed for an Army squad; it has nine un-tethered, manned modules, with an exercise control/After Action Review (AAR) workstation and one semi-automated forces workstation.

The last demonstration took place on the afternoon of Day 2. It was a combination of virtual and enhanced live simulations embedded at the outdoor Combined Arms Combat Training Facility (CACTF). Squads participated in the one hour S3 that demonstrated how embedding events with virtual targets, interactive dialog with multiple avatars, and enhanced realism (e.g., live role players and fake Improvised Explosive Devices) could be manipulated to increase stressors. CACTF is an

Army POR that provides a live environment for conducting individual Soldier-through-Battalion-level training in urban-operations at home-station [19]. Units train on building-entry/egress and room-clearing techniques under lethal and non-lethal operational conditions. The CACTF has an observer/controllers facility that monitors, controls and documents the training exercise with video recording for AAR.

Following the demonstration, soldier surveys were collected, analyzed, and a content analysis of interview transcripts was conducted with details reported in the SOvM study FY14 final report [3].

2   Lessons Learned and Recommendations

The SET framework afforded a flexible demonstration environment that allowed Soldiers to compare and contrast the desirability of each training capability. In this section, based on lessons learned, we more fully examine how a SET curriculum could be implemented and provide research recommendations in the context of each SET guideline.

2.1   Stressors, Coping Skills, and Fidelity

Conducting a thorough analysis of theory and empirically-based research, and working with Subject Matter Experts (SMEs) and known experts in the field helped to mitigate risk of problems with the final demonstration. Research literature reviews and interviews with SMEs led to identifying the key task stressors and cues that trigger performance problems in terms of psychomotor and cognitive processes. Walter Reed Army Institute for Research (WRAIR) scientists had thoroughly documented the combat stressors known to be related to PTSD [20]. The WRAIR scientists identified stressors and triggers in mission tasks involving searching, clearing, maneuver and engagement that increase risk of injury and death, including: clearing or searching homes or buildings, indirect fire attack from incoming artillery, rocket, or mortar fire, attack by enemy on forward operating base or patrol base perimeter, and engaging enemy with direct fire or returning fire, a close call, was shot or hit, but protective gear saved you; wounded in action, seeing ill or injured women or children whom you were unable to help, being responsible for the death of a noncombatant/enemy combatant, and exposure to human remains.

These findings, coupled with the TADMUS program results, enabled the study team to identify the three major squad coping skills – DM, SM, and TW skills - needed to mitigate mission stressors. Decision making (DM), involves establishing situation awareness (SA) through detecting, observing, and evaluating cues in the physical environment (including the human domain) that are needed to anticipate and effectively react to and make decisions about potential threats [21]. Teams develop shared SA of the common operating picture by passing key information and using proper communication protocols. SM skills involve using attention and concentration skills that manage and reduce distracting negative thoughts and physiological reactions experienced under stress [10]. TW skills help team members adapt to high stress and reduce

Table 1. SOvM case-based scenarios (DM=Decision Making; TW=Teamwork; SM=Stress Management).

Skill type	Event-based tasks	S0 Baseline	S1 Raid	S2 Financier	S3 Hostage
DM	Conduct tactical questioning			X	X
DM	Detain an individual		X		X
DM	Perceive threats		X	X	X
DM	Respond to contact		X	X	X
DM	Direct fire engagement		X		X
TW	Communicate information within squad	X	X	X	X
SM	Seeing ill or injured females or children		X	X	X
SM	Member of patrol wounded in action			X	X
SM	Exposed to dead bodies or human remains		X	X	X
SM	Responsible for death of a non-combatant			X	X
SM	Handle casualties		X	X	X

errors by exchanging critical information in a timely manner, providing priorities to focus DM, proactively monitoring each other for signs of stress, providing backup and support, and taking corrective actions without having to be asked [22].

Next, the study team adopted a previously tested case-based method to establish the link between the combat stressors and scenario triggers for resilience skills [23]. Scenario documentation established the traceability of event features in the storyline to requirements for DM, SM, and TW behaviors. Four case-based scenarios (S0, S1, S2, and S3) were connected through the Eastern European storyline. Table 1 denotes skill type, a sampling of event based tasks, and scenarios in which the tasks are triggered. S0 was designated a "low stress" scenario that was intended to allow the squads to practice establishing a "pattern of life baseline" for DM, but there was not enough time in the demonstration to use it. S1 (Raid), S2 (Financier) and S3 (Hostage) had increasing levels of embedded stressors. Events within each scenario that were expected to increase mental workload were interactions with the local populace, behavioral anomalies, communicating with own forces, and detecting deception by potential hostiles. Stress events were heavily weighted in S2 and S3. An objective of the study was to determine whether the tasks/stressor triggers were noticed by the squad members as an indication that the demonstration was successful in introducing them. Using an event-based scenario checklist, the authors found the soldiers reported or responded to many of the scenario events during the demonstrations with the VBS3, DSTS, and CACTF. Post demonstration most soldiers reported the events were realistic and relevant to developing resilience.

Recommendation 1. The study team learned that relevant stress triggers can be linked to DM, SM, and TW skill requirements and can be implemented in gaming, virtual and live squad training. Research is needed to extend what was learned to determine how training each skill should be fully developed based on dismounted squad mission task requirements. Research should define and test specific skills for each phase of SET. Past research should be leveraged to solve this problem [8].

Recommendation 2. We learned that building scenarios to trigger resilience skills, and adapting the training environments for them was highly labor intensive; it took over six months to plan, design and author scenarios for the stress triggers in VBS3, DSTS, and CACTF. Nevertheless, the scenario development process using the case-based method is crucial to effective training because it sets the learning and performance objectives, and specifies expected performance outcomes for training assessment and AARs. Research should develop instructor training and support tools that automate the scenario design and implementation process to efficiently establish stressor fidelity for training simulations [12, 22].

2.2 Training Sequencing and Content

Recommendation 3. We learned that sequencing - information provision, skill acquisition and application - and training content are important for developing resilience skills. The ASA training and CSF2 curriculums demonstrated the potential to develop them within the SET framework. There was not enough time to introduce the squads to an example of a TW skills training (e.g., Team Dimensional Training), but the demonstration scenarios did include several TW tasks, and TW skills were discussed with Soldiers following each of the scenario runs with VBS3, DSTS, and CACTF.

Research is needed to develop and evaluate the complete curriculum for the information provision and skill acquisition phases, including how to encourage learning outside of class, and using valid learning measures for assessing and tracking progress and training transfer. We recommend that each resilience competency (DM, SM, and TW) have a separate curriculum, including the skills application phase. Scenario design should be used to create events that trigger learning within each competency. Following this, a simulation-based training curriculum with capstone exercises should help squads learn and practice skill integration. The training effectiveness of a complete curriculum for individuals and squads within a reasonable time frame in the pre-deployment training cycle needs to be determined. Research has shown that as little as one-hour of information provision training can significantly increase confidence in managing stress during a tactical scenario [10]. Similar results have been found with DM [8], and TW training [22]. Non-class time should be utilized, encouraging diary keeping, and providing on-line/mobile simulations and games for skill acquisition and practice. For example, research has shown that practicing cognitive coping skills and relaxation at least once per day outside of the training environment and preferably during typical stressful situations enables skills acquisition [9].

2.3   Delivery and Assessment

We observed that the wide range of soldier experience levels influenced the speed of demonstrations at each SET phase. Some Soldiers needed more time to understand the concepts than others. We also observed that squad leaders with more experience were able to help their squad members learn the concepts more quickly with examples and coaching behaviors. Part of the problem could have been solved if there had been more time available for familiarization with the new technologies. But, overall, we concluded that "readiness to train" should be a central factor to implementing SET. We propose that SET could be more effective if the Squad composition (i.e., training, qualifications, and experience levels) were better understood. Assessing Soldier competency and experience levels should be determined prior to implementing SET to tailor the curriculum depending on levels of proficiency. Five recommendations are discussed for adapting SET based on competence and experience levels.

Recommendation 4. Beginners are capable of observing instructors, avatars, or team leaders who model appropriate behaviors, but are not yet ready to acquire skills. SET should begin by focusing on acquiring knowledge, and learning principles and rules. At the intermediate skill level, soldiers can recognize critical cues in behaviors, and SET should move quickly to skill acquisition and application of job knowledge. At higher levels of proficiency, soldiers are able to perceive, think critically, and use adaptive reasoning and reflection, so SET should move quickly to the full application phase. Research is needed to develop measures that can support and evaluate an adaptive SET curriculum.

Recommendation 5. Research is needed to determine how types, not just levels of, stressors might influence Soldier expertise development. For example, the Center for Naval Analyses (CNA) developed a rationale for manipulating task stressors based on a model of expertise development in executing mission based tasks [24]. In a 10-year study of naval strike squadron live training, they developed a systematic method for assessing the development of pilot expertise from beginner (L1), through intermediate (L2) and proficient (L3), to highly expert (i.e., L4: instructor qualified). It involves gradually increasing the type and complexity, and stress, of conducting strike missions. For example, mission training should gradually increase complexity of skills training from "maintaining situation awareness" (L1), to "perform laser designation" (L2), "determine attack tactics" (L3), and then "assess go/no go criteria" (L4). An analytic method similar to the CNA study is needed for decomposing squad mission tasks into types of stressors, and documenting how it would impact developing squad leader expertise. For example, to address DM skills, beginners would focus on learning how to deal with information load and time pressure, whereas intermediate levels of expertise would focus on such stressors as uncertainty and risk management. Higher levels of soldier proficiency would focus on multi-tasking and in-stride planning. Research should apply this approach to developing squad leaders and squad skills within the context of platoon and company level missions.

Recommendation 6. The instructional strategy should be flexible, adapting depending on Soldier and squad expertise levels [25]. Beginners require more time on the orientation and familiarization of SET knowledge and concepts without stress exposure.

A more experienced squad should focus more on procedural knowledge with stress exposure supported by gaming environments, and then skills practice on mission tasks and procedures with stress exposure supported by a virtual simulation of a complex environment. A proficient squad should spend more time on deliberate practice in mission tasks and procedures supported by interaction with a live simulation of a complex environment. Research should focus on methods, tools, and strategies that support development of skills, and technologies that can recommend training to squads based on expertise.

Recommendation 7. The instructional system is the techniques, tools, and procedures that support the instructional strategy. This includes instructor and team leader roles. For the beginner level, a live instructor should spend more time on the information provision phase of SET, engaging trainees using a didactic approach, behavioral modeling, demonstrations, discussions, and out of class assignments using such games as SRTS. If squads have greater expertise, then they are capable of moving more quickly through the information provision phase to the skill acquisition phase. Trainees embedded in their squads should have instructors facilitating practical exercises, with application of job knowledge, and training systems that can provide automated assessment and feedback. At higher levels of proficiency, squads are likely to move through information and provision phases more quickly and can focus on planning and practicing problem solving exercises in distributed simulations. They can quickly develop skills in guided team self-correction, where the team leader engages the squad in their own AAR following simulation based training exercises [22].

We recommend that research is needed to develop an instructor/team leader training curriculum that would enable them to quickly adapt instruction based on level of soldier and squad expertise. It should include learning how to use assessment tools and such AAR methods as guided team self-correction. For example, a team leader prototype instruction was developed by Wilkinson, Holness, and Geisey and demonstrated with Soldiers and Marines [21]. Two instructional methods were adapted: the US Army's Think Like a Commander and the US Navy's Team Dimensional Training (TDT). They were revised to focus on the dismounted warrior and small unit team, and TLAC was renamed Think Like a Leader (TLAL). TLAL training was designed to train team leaders and their squads to: focus on the mission and higher's intent; model a thinking enemy/consider the terrain; use all available assets; see the big picture/visualize the battlefield; and consider contingencies/remain flexible.

TDT was designed for team leaders and their squads to use team self-correction to improve: information exchange; effective communication protocols; backup and error correction; and initiative/leadership. TLAL and TDT were linked together in the AAR and focused on empowering the squad to be proactive in the face of complex decision events. Key decision points were identified in each event-based training scenario and development of specific questioning probes were developed for use by the trainer and/or team leader in the AAR to facilitate self-assessment and reinforce the behavior themes in TLAL and TDT. The structured queries were developed before the AAR that link specific scenario decision events to the training to enable rapid post exercise development of the AAR and provide the trainer with clear, focused probes to ensure the discussion stays on track. The squad leader was trained on the process and was provided the TDT/TLAL probes for his use during the AAR. The squad leader identified those areas of focus for the AAR, selected the TDT/TLAL probes to use, and rehearsed with the materials provided by the support team. The squad leader then conducted the AAR and employed the TDT/TLAL.

Recommendation 8. A main objective of SET is to ensure training effectiveness. Robust learning assessments and checks on learning throughout and beyond training are needed to transfer learning and reduce PTS. Achievement and knowledge tests support the beginner. Performance tests and feedback through AAR support the intermediate level trainee/squad. Team self-correction through AAR, reflection activities, and coaching feedback encourages transfer of what has been learned in the practical application phase. We recommend developing valid and reliable assessment tools that provide appropriate and immediate feedback to the trainees to enhance their coping skill strategies while they are exposed to the stressors. This helps trainees to adapt their behavior and responses in real time. Measures of trainee attitudes and performance to determine SET effects should be used; and multiple measures of performance and attitudes over time should be assessed. Measures of performance and attitudes should be assessed both prior to and after SET in order to determine changes in these factors. Research is needed to develop reliable and valid measures of learning, retention and skills transfer throughout the phases of SET.

3 Summary

Figure 2 translates our recommendations into a concept for adapting immersive training environments to develop squad resilience skills. Research is needed to evaluate this approach. We envision Phase I beginning with individual coursework, in and outside of class using mobile devices. DM, SM, and TW skills training would be implemented simultaneously, but as individual modules. During Phase II, individualized skills acquisition training continues with game-based training inside and outside of class. At the Practical Application phase, graduated exposure to stressors begins with individualized

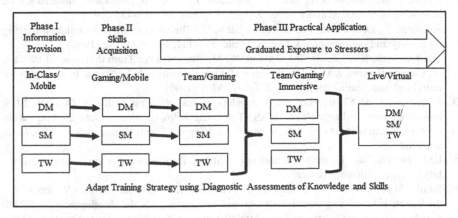

Fig. 2. A concept for adapting immersive training environments to develop Decision Making (DM), Stress Management (SM), and Teamwork (TW) skills for squad resilience.

skill training in a team-based environment. Next would be integrated skills training in gaming and immersive training environments. Capstone exercises with virtual simulations embedded in the live environment would enable team leaders and squads to demonstrate their overmatch capabilities. The training strategy would use diagnostic assessments of knowledge and skills to adapt instruction and training at each phase, enabling instructors and team leaders to tailor training based on level of expertise.

References

1. US Department of the Army. Ready and Resilient Campaign. Arlington (2013)
2. US Department of the Army. The US Army Human Dimension Concept. TRADOC, FT Eustis (2014)
3. US Army PEO STRI. Squad Overmatch Study FY14 Final Report: Training Human Dimension to Enhance Performance, US Army PEO STRI, Orlando (2014)
4. Driskell, J.E., Salas, E., Johnston, J.H.: Decision making and performance under stress. In: Britt, T.W., Castro, C.A., Adler, A.B. (eds.) Military Life: The Psychology of Serving in Peace and Combat 2006, Part IV, Military Performance, vol. 1, pp. 128–154. Praeger, Westport (2006)
5. Helmus, T.C., Glenn, R.W.: Steeling the Mind: Combat Stress Reactions and Their Implications for Urban Warfare. Rand Corporation, Santa Monica (2005)
6. Meredith, L.S., Sherbourne, C.D., Gaillot, S.J., Hansell, L., Ritschard, H.V., Parker, A.M., Wrenn, G.: Promoting Psychological Resilience in the U.S. Military. Rand Center for Military Health Policy Research, Santa Monica (2011)
7. Stanley, E.A., Jha, A.P.: Mind Fitness: Improving Operational Effectiveness and Building Warrior Resilience. Jt. Force Q. **55**, 144–151 (2009)
8. Cannon-Bowers, J.A., Salas, E.: Making Decisions under Stress: Implications for Individuals and Teams. APA, Washington, DC (1998)
9. Johnston, J.H., Cannon-Bowers, J.A.: Training for stress exposure. In: Driskell, J.E., Salas, E. (eds.) Stress and Human Performance 1996, Part II. Applied Psychology, pp. 223-256. Lawrence Erlbaum Associates Inc., Mahwah (1996)
10. Inzana, C.M., Driskell, J.E., Salas, E., Johnston, J.: Effects of preparatory information on enhancing performance under stress. J. Appl. Psychol. **81**, 429–435 (1996)
11. Saunders, T., Driskell, J.E., Johnston, J., Salas, E.: The effect of stress inoculation training on anxiety and performance. J. Occup. Health Psychol. **147**, 170–186 (1996)
12. Smith-Jentsch, K.A., Zeisig, R.L., Acton, B., McPherson, J.A.: Team dimensional training. In: Cannon-Bowers, J.A., Salas, E. (eds.) Making Decisions Under Stress: Implications for Individual and Team Training, pp. 271-297. APA (1998)
13. Holmes, A.: ASAT training helps develop critical thinking skills, 9 October 2013. http://www.army.mil/article/112916/ASAT_training_helps_develop_critical_thinking_skills
14. US Department of the Army. Comprehensive Soldier and Family Fitness (CSF2). http://csf2. army.mil
15. USC Institute for Creative Technologies, Stress Resilience in Virtual Environments. http://ict.usc.edu/prototypes/strive
16. Smith, M.A., Woo, H.J., Parker, J.P., Youmans, R.J., LeGoullon, M., Weltman, G., de Visser, E.J.: . Using iterative design and testing towards the development of SRTS: a mobile, game-based stress resilience training system [CD-ROM]. In: Proceedings of the Human Factors and Ergonomics Society Annual Meeting 57, pp. 2076-2080. SAGE (2013)

17. US Army Stand To! (May 19, 2014). Virtual Battlespace 3 (VBS3). http://www.army.mil/standto/archive_2014-05-19/

18. US Army PEO STRI (2015a). Close Combat Tactical Trainer. http://www.peostri.army.mil/PRODUCTS/CCTT/

19. US Army PEO STRI (2015b). Combined Arms Collective Training Facility (CACTF). http://www.peostri.army.mil/SUSTAINMENT/CACTF/

20. Grieger, T.A., Cozza, S.J., Ursano, R.J., Hoge, C., Martinez, P.E., Engel, C.C., Wain, H.J.: Posttraumatic Stress Disorder and Depression in Battle-Injured Soldiers. Am. J. Psychiatry. **163**, 1777–1783 (2006)

21. Wilkinson, J., Holness, D., Giesey, W.: FITE – Team training for cross cultural decision making. In: Karwowski, W.K., Salvendy, G. (eds.) 2010 Applied Human Factors and Ergonomics International Conference Proceedings [CDROM]. USA Publishing, Louisville (2010)

22. Smith-Jentsch, K.A., Cannon-Bowers, J.A., Tannenbaum, S.I., Salas, E.: Guided Team Self-correction: Impacts on Team Mental Models, Behavior, and Effectiveness. Small Group Res. **39**, 303–327 (2008)

23. Ross, W.A., Kobus, D.A.: Case-Based Next Generation Cognitive Training Solutions. In: The Proceedings of the Interservice/Industry Training, Simulation and Education Conference [CD-ROM]. NTSA, Arlington (2011)

24. Randazzo-Metsel, A.: (2008). USMC Training: A Synthesis of CNA's Work. Technical report. CNA Analyses & Solutions (2008)

25. Kozlowski, S.W.J., Watola, D.J., Jensen, J.M., Kim, B.H., Botero, I.C.: Developing adaptive teams: a theory of dynamic team leadership. In: Salas, E., Goodwin, G.F., Burke, C.S. (eds.) Team Effectiveness in Complex Organizations: Cross-Disciplinary Perspectives and Approaches 2008, Part II. SIOP, pp. 113-155. Routledge, New York (2008)

Authoring Intelligent Tutoring Systems Using Human Computation: Designing for Intrinsic Motivation

Andrew M. Olney[(✉)] and Whitney L. Cade

Institute for Intelligent Systems, University of Memphis,
Memphis, TN 38152, USA
aolney@memphis.edu
http://andrewmolney.name

Abstract. This paper proposes a methodology for authoring of intelligent tutoring systems using human computation. The methodology embeds authoring tasks in existing educational tasks to avoid the need for monetary authoring incentives. Because not all educational tasks are equally motivating, there is a tension between designing the human computation task to be optimally efficient in the short term and optimally motivating to foster participation in the long term. In order to enhance intrinsic motivation for participation, the methodology proposes designing the interaction to promote user autonomy, competence, and relatedness as defined by Self-Determination Theory. This design has implications for learning during authoring.

Keywords: Authoring · Intelligent tutoring system · Human computation · Motivation

1 Introduction

It is commonly believed that it takes several hundred hours of authoring effort to create one hour of instruction for an intelligent tutoring system [3,11]. What is less commonly considered is that those are "expert hours", namely the time spent by highly trained knowledge engineers, instructional designers, and subject matter experts. Typical authoring tools for ITS are intended to reduce this ratio. However these authoring tools do not address the shortage of experts needed to use the tools.

In our current work, we are trying a radically different approach to address this shortage of experts. We address expertise by letting novices do the authoring but then let other novices check the work to ensure quality. We address motivation by disguising the authoring task as another task that novices are already engaged in. We call this system BrainTrust.

The idea is that as students read online, they work with a virtual student on a variety of educational tasks related to the reading. These educational tasks are designed to both improve reading comprehension and contribute to the creation

D.D. Schmorrow and C.M. Fidopiastis (Eds.): AC 2015, LNAI 9183, pp. 628–639, 2015.
DOI: 10.1007/978-3-319-20816-9_60

of an intelligent tutoring system based on the material read. After the human students read a passage, they work with the virtual student to summarize, generate concept maps, reflect on the reading, and predict what will happen next. The tasks and interaction are inspired by reciprocal teaching [30], a well known method of teaching reading comprehension strategies.

The virtual student's performance on these tasks is a mixture of previous student answers and answers dynamically generated using AI and natural language processing techniques. As the human teaches and corrects the virtual student, they in effect improve the answers from previous sessions and author a domain model for the underlying intelligent tutoring system. It should be pointed out that while this process is domain-independent, the domain model that results is specifically designed for a conversational, conceptual style of tutoring, described in detail below.

In developing BrainTrust, several interaction designs were created and evaluated. The early designs were rigidly aligned with intelligent tutoring system authoring tasks. Although early designs were efficient from an authoring standpoint, they were perceived as boring in our focus groups, leading to concerns about the motivation of students to participate. After iterating through many storyboards, we adopted the principles of Self-Determination Theory [14] in order to enhance the intrinsic motivation of users. Designing for intrinsic motivation increases the amount of time users spend in non-authoring activities, which is at odds with the goal of efficient authoring. However, we argue that the same design choices have positive implications for the user's reading comprehension and learning.

2   Background & Motivation

2.1   Tutoring by Humans and Computers

It is well established that human tutoring is a highly effective form of instruction that yields better outcomes that typical classroom instruction. An early meta-analysis of tutoring studies found that even novice human tutors enhanced learning with a medium effect size ($d = .4$) compared to classroom and comparable control conditions, an improvement of approximately half a letter grade [9], and an early study of expert tutors reported a very large effect size ($d = 2$) for mathematics skill training, an improvement of approximately two letter grades [5]. Early studies like these were influential in driving the emerging field of intelligent tutoring systems [36], or ITS.

During the last 30 years, researchers have made some important progress in developing ITSs that have the potential to seriously increase learning gains at deeper levels of comprehension and mastery [18]. The ITSs implement systematic strategies for promoting learning, such as error identification and correction, building on prerequisites, frontier learning (expanding on what the learner already knows), building on the zone of proximal development, student modeling (inferring what the student knows and having that guide tutoring), modeling-scaffolding-fading, and building coherent explanations [37,38]. The defining characteristic of an ITS is that it tracks knowledge and adaptively responds to the learner [43], using computational modeling techniques like production rules, graphical models, and vector spaces. Recent meta-analyses have found that ITS learning gains are indistinguishable from human tutor controls [21,40], suggesting that ITS research has sufficiently matured to make it broadly applicable to K-16 education.

2.2 ITS Authoring with Natural Language

Many ITS have been developed for mathematically well-formed topics, including algebra, geometry, programming languages [33], and physics [41]. Unfortunately, developing mathematically oriented ITS is problematic in terms of development costs, which can be as high as 100 hours of development time for 1 hour of instruction, even with special authoring tools [3]; see [25] for a review of emerging authoring methods. However, a number of ITS have been built over the last decade that tackle knowledge domains with a natural language foundation as opposed to mathematics and subject matters that require precise analytical reasoning [23]. The learning gains on these natural language ITS are consistent with large effects found in ITS meta-analyses [40]. and the development cost for these natural language ITS tends to be very low, the lowest reported time being two hours of development time for one hour of instruction [17].

These conversational ITS based in natural language share two defining attributes (see [27,29] for a review). First, they are based on naturalistic observations and computational modeling of human tutoring strategies embedded in tutorial dialogue. A common strategy is the so-called five-step dialogue frame:

1. Tutor asks a deep reasoning question,
2. Student gives an answer,
3. Tutor gives immediate feedback or pumps the student,
4. Tutor and student collaboratively elaborate an answer, and
5. Tutor assesses the student's understanding.

The five-step dialogue frame illustrates the other defining attribute of natural language ITS, which is their interactive and collaborative nature: the tutor and student are co-constructing an explanation together. According to theories of learning, the interactive and collaborative nature of tutoring is what makes it more effective than activities like individual problem solving [7].

From a computational perspective, the goal of a natural language ITS is to help the student construct an explanation to a given problem. A full explanation is has multiple points, which are commonly called *expectations* because they are the expected parts of the correct answer. A natural language ITS manages the tutoring session by keeping track of the expectations and directing the student's attention to expectations that have not been covered. The ITS directs the student's attention by asking questions, ranging from relatively vague *pumps* like "What else can you say?" to *hints* like "What can you say about the force of gravity?" to very specific *prompts* like "The direction of gravity is?" Authoring a natural language ITS consists of constructing a paragraph length correct answer, generating questions for each expectation in the paragraph, and using text similarity measures like latent semantic analysis [20] to judge the difference between the student's answers and the expectations. The correct answer, expectations, questions, and vector space for latent semantic analysis are collectively referred to as the domain model of the ITS – the key components that must be authored every time a new topic must be covered. Even so, one of the reasons that natural language ITS are relatively easy to author is because the authoring is done in natural language.

2.3   Conversational ITS Authoring and Reading Comprehension

Recent attempts have been made to fully automate the authoring of natural language ITS using natural language processing technologies like semantic parsing, coreference resolution, automated inference, and ontology extraction [26,28,29]. The core aspects of automation were keyword identification, concept map generation, and question generation using manually generated summaries (equivalent to correct answers and expectations) as resources. After the keywords, concept maps, and questions were automatically generated, they were checked manually and corrected for errors. The BrainTrust approach extends this work by using human computation to correct errors.

BrainTrust maps authoring to human computation tasks using the key insight that keyword identification, summarization, concept map extraction, and question generation are not just authoring tasks but also reading comprehension strategies. Several meta-analyses have concluded that strategies like these should be taught explicitly to maximize reading comprehension, particularly for low-achieving students who lack the knowledge and skill to effectively comprehend reading at their grade level [15,22]. A specific program of multiple-strategy instruction is *reciprocal teaching* [30]. In this program, as instructors read the text, they think aloud to model their comprehension process to the student including their reasoning for when to use each strategy. In a classic modeling-scaffolding-fading paradigm, the instructor and student take turns as the student gradually learns the strategies and practices them while the instructor provides feedback. More specifically, students read paragraph by paragraph and generate questions, summarize, clarify terms and concepts, and make predictions about what is coming up in the text. This practice becomes a dialogue as the instructor comments on and contributes to the student's questions, summaries, and other activities, or as other students make similar contributions in small group sessions.

2.4   Human Computation for Knowledge and Language

Recently a new subfield of computer science has emerged, known as *human computation*, that studies how to represent computationally difficult tasks so that humans will be motivated to work on them [1,31,35]. Human computation can be extremely powerful. In a recent example, a human computation game called Foldit was used to find the lowest energy form of a protein causing AIDS, a long-standing problem that had defied solution for nearly 15 years [10,19]. Foldit makes use of humans' spatial reasoning abilities and motivates them to work by presenting the task as a game. However, this simple description belies the complexity involved in representing human computation tasks and executing them to produce a desired result. In essence, a human computation is a step in a larger algorithm that distributes tasks, checks their quality, and aggregates them into a solution. Much of the advantages and challenges of human computation stem from the issue that a human is "in the loop", because while humans are capable of solving complex and difficult problems, they are also autonomous beings with their own motivations and physical limits.

Several human computation games have been proposed to create knowledge representations and language data. FACTory is a human computation game designed to validate the truth of propositions in the Cyc Knowledge Base [12]. Users vote on the correctness of a proposition's natural language interpretation, for example, "Conjunctivitis is a symptom of earache", until enough users agree that FACTory stops asking for confirmation. Verbosity is a human computation game that presents itself as a two-player guessing game where each player has a secret word and a set of sentence template *cards* and chooses the card that will best allow the other player to guess the word, e.g. the word may be "cat" and the played card may be "tiger is a kind of __" [1]. A related game, 1001 Paraphrases, uses a similar template providing strategy, except that its goal is to generate alternative phrasings of statements rather than facts [8]. Human computation systems like these often present previously proposed solutions to new users to improve upon, a process called *iterative improvement* in the human computation literature. Because even simple tasks, such as determining if an image includes the sky, can have non-agreeing "schools of thought" that systematically respond in opposing ways [39], it is preferable to use Bayesian models of agreement jointly to determine the ability of the user (and their trustworthiness as teachers) as well as the difficulty of the items they correct [32].

Currently underway is a human computation project called Duolingo, whose stated purpose is to help people learn a language while simultaneously translating the Web [2,35]. Thus Duolingo appears to make use of two human computation motivators previously described [31]: altruism and implicit work. Altruism stems from helping others by translating the Web. Implicit work means the work achieved as a side-effect of the main task; in this instance the implicit work of learning the language is translation. In Duolingo, users translate sentences from a foreign language into their own language, with some computer support that provides dictionary translations of individual words. As users proceed, Duolingo increases the complexity of the task. A recent review of Duolingo praised its use of hints and feedback in guiding the translation process but also questioned the use of a translation-based approach to learning a language, an educational approach that fell out of fashion about 50 years ago [16].

3   Designing BrainTrust

3.1   Motivating Human Computation with Virtual Students

Designs for human computation include user motivation to participate, typically focusing on pay, enjoyment, altruism, reputation, and implicit work [31]. Psychological theories of motivation contrast intrinsic and extrinsic motivation, such that of the typical motivators used in human computation, only altruism (without recognition) and enjoyment would qualify as intrinsic motivators [14]. This is an important distinction because numerous experiments have found that introducing extrinsic motivators, like pay, can actually diminish intrinsic motivation for an activity [13]. Therefore, if the goal of BrainTrust is to increase learning and the desire for learning, it is important to design for intrinsic motivation rather than extrinsic motivation.

Self-Determination Theory identifies three factors influencing intrinsic motivation: competence, autonomy, and relatedness [34]. Competence is enhanced by maintaining optimal challenge so that participants achieve success and positive feedback. Autonomy interacts with competence, enhancing motivation when the participant feels in control. In contrast, when the participant feels controlled, pressured, or manipulated, autonomy and motivation decrease. Relatedness occurs when the participant is socially connected to others who pay attention to or even care about what the participant is doing. By supporting competence, autonomy, and relatedness, a human computation design should maximize intrinsic motivation.

The BrainTrust approach to maximizing intrinsic motivation is to present the human computation tasks through a virtual student, sometimes called a teachable agent [4], as shown in Fig. 1. The virtual student's performance on these tasks is a mixture of previous student answers and answers dynamically generated using AI and natural language processing techniques. As the human teaches and corrects the virtual student, they in effect improve the answers from previous sessions and author a domain model for the underlying intelligent tutoring system. From the perspective of Self-Determination Theory, users may demonstrate competence if teaching the student presents an optimal level of challenge, experience autonomy if their interaction with the student is loosely directed, and feel relatedness because the student is presented as a animated conversational character. Although previous research has not directly assessed the effects of virtual students on intrinsic motivation, studies have shown that students spend more time with virtual students, attribute mental states to them, and are more likely to acknowledge their own errors [6].

3.2   Designing Motivating Interactions

We do not claim that simply adding a virtual student makes the design intrinsically motivating. If the reading comprehension tasks themselves do not reinforce competence, autonomy, and relatedness, then the design will fail in this regard.

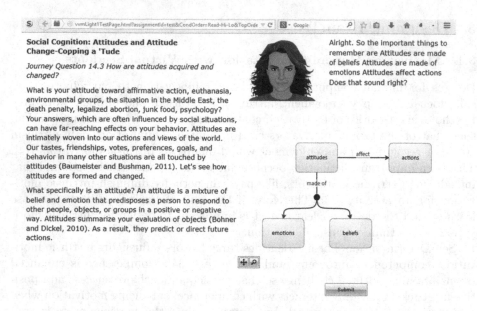

Fig. 1. BrainTrust during a concept mapping activity

And it is these reading comprehension activities that individually represent specific human computation tasks.

As we developed BrainTrust's human computation tasks, we iterated through six different interaction designs before settling on one that best supports intrinsic motivation. Because of space limitations, we will only describe the first and the last designs, as their differences best illustrate how competence, autonomy, and relatedness can be enhanced. The earliest design was rigidly aligned with intelligent tutoring system authoring tasks. The original storyboard proceeded as follows:

1. Virtual student reads the selected paragraph aloud.
2. Virtual student summarizes the material by selecting key sentences.
3. Human corrects the summary.
4. Virtual student generates questions and answers on important facts.
5. Human corrects or adds questions and answers.
6. Virtual student clarifies by identifying key concepts and linking them in a concept map.
7. Human corrects or adds key concepts and links.
8. Next paragraph is selected and process is repeated.

Although this earliest design was efficient from an ITS authoring standpoint, it was perceived as boring in our focus groups, leading to concerns about the intrinsic motivation of students to participate. Using Self-Determination Theory as a lens, we can identify several design weaknesses in this storyboard. First, the interaction is very mechanical, with the virtual student controlling as much of the interaction as possible, leading to low autonomy. For example, summaries involve sentence selection rather than free-response. Likewise questions are generated complete with answers, so again little opportunity for free-response. Second, user competence is diminished because the virtual student is essentially asking the user to do the same kinds of tasks repeatedly: the questions are just rephrased pieces of the summary, and the keywords/concept maps are just rephrased pieces of the questions. Finally, relatedness is reduced because the virtual student gives the user very little opportunity to inject their own ideas, and as a consequence creates fewer opportunities to learn from teaching the virtual student [7]. The first design, perhaps counterintuitively, has low intrinsic motivation precisely because it is closer in spirit to typical human computation tasks like template filling [1,8,12] but without providing a game-like metaphor to make the task more enjoyable.

The final design enhances intrinsic motivation without gamifying the task by rethinking autonomy, competence, and relatedness. To make the task more motivating and useful to the user, we accepted that some of the activities the user performs will have low utility to the end goal of creating an intelligent tutoring system; however those same activities will have high utility to the goals of enhancing intrinsic motivation and helping the user comprehend the text they are reading. The final design is inspired by the methodology of reciprocal teaching [30], which provides a natural interaction paradigm in which these reading comprehension activities can be learned and practiced. The final storyboard proceeds as follows:

1. Human reads the selected paragraph, and, if desired, activates the virtual student.
2. Virtual student voices the gist, or topic, of the paragraph.
3. Human corrects the gist as free-response.
4. Virtual student generates open ended, authentic questions.
5. Human provides their answers as free-response
6. Virtual student clarifies by identifying key concepts and linking them in a concept map.
7. Human corrects or adds key concepts and links.
8. Virtual student predicts the topic of the next paragraph.
9. Human corrects as free-response.
10. Next paragraph is selected and process is repeated.

In this design, autonomy is increased because all tasks are open-ended and are answered using free-response. Open-ended tasks like gists, authentic questions, and predictions allow for interpretations and personalized responses, and free-response options for these tasks further allow for autonomy. Competence is strengthened because the tasks are now decoupled from each other, and the tasks themselves are both more challenging because they require free-response as well as less evaluative because they allow for personalized responses. Related-ness improves through open-ended, authentic questions [24], such as "What are your beliefs about gun control?" which invite the user to contribute their own ideas and interpretations of the text. Both of these features make the tasks less about the *facts* of the text and more about the global meaning of the text – a key aspect of reading comprehension.

Clearly, making the tasks open-ended and free-response makes the corresponding answers more difficult to use for ITS authoring. The tasks of gist, authentic questions, and prediction, do not clearly correspond to ITS authoring tasks like summarization and question generation. Indeed, the core piece of ITS authoring is now largely encapsulated in the concept map. This is not a problem for ITS authoring as concept maps can be used to generate the questions, summaries, and other materials needed for a natural language ITS [26,28,29]. On the other hand, the shift from the earliest interaction design to the final design does illustrate the tension between making the human computation for authoring efficient in the short term and keeping the process viable in the long term by enhancing intrinsic motivation. Similar trade-offs occur when human computation is embedded in actual games with extraneous game play [42].

However, BrainTrust seems to differ from previous human computation systems in the sense that the tasks users engage in have three side effects: the tasks improve the users' understanding of the texts they wish to read, the process of correcting the virtual student improves reading comprehension skills, and the tasks create knowledge representations and content for an intelligent tutoring system. In other words, the tasks help students understand what they read, improve their reading skills for the future, and use their efforts to help other students in the same way.

4   Conclusion

This paper presented a methodology, called BrainTrust, for authoring of intelligent tutoring systems (ITS) using human computation. In BrainTrust, as users read online, they work with a virtual student on reading comprehension tasks that are aligned with authoring tasks in natural language ITS. This approach circumvents the shortage of experts who are typically needed to create ITS by leveraging novice users who are already engaged in reading a text.

Although our earliest design included superficially motivating components like a virtual student and tasks inspired by reciprocal teaching, it did not carefully address the intrinsic motivation of users. Using Self-Determination Theory, we presented an analysis of the earliest design and our final design in light of the core principles of autonomy, competence, and relatedness defined by that theory. To include these principles, the final design included more open-ended tasks with free-response options, many of which are not directly applicable to the task of authoring a natural language ITS. However, the open-ended tasks bring the final design closer to collaborative dialogue that various studies suggest is optimal for learning [7,24,30]. Thus designing BrainTrust for intrinsic motivation may also optimize for student learning, not only by increasing participation in authoring, but by making participation itself a beneficial learning experience.

Acknowledgements. This research was supported by the National Science Foundation (1235958 & 1352207), Institute of Education Sciences (R305C120001 & R305A130030), Office of Naval Research (N00014-12-C-0643), and Army Research Laboratory (W911NF-12-2-0030). Any opinions, findings and conclusions, or recommendations expressed in this paper are those of the author and do not represent the views of these organizations.

References

1. von Ahn, L.: Human Computation. Doctoral thesis, Carnegie Mellon University (2005). uMI Order Number: AAI3205378
2. von Ahn, L.: Three human computation projects. In: Proceedings of the 42nd ACM Technical Symposium on Computer Science Education, pp. 691–692. SIGCSE 2011. ACM, New York, NY (2011). http://doi.acm.org/10.1145/1953163.1953354
3. Aleven, V., Mclaren, B.M., Sewall, J., Koedinger, K.R.: A new paradigm for intelligent tutoring systems: example-tracing tutors. Int. J. Artif. Intell. Educ. **19**(2), 105–154 (2009)
4. Biswas, G., Schwartz, D., Leelawong, K., Vye, N.: Learning by teaching: a new agent paradigm for educational software. Appl. Artif. Intell. **19**, 363–392 (2005)
5. Bloom, B.S.: The 2 sigma problem: the search for methods of group instruction as effective as one-to-one tutoring. Educ. Res. **13**(6), 4–16 (1984)
6. Chase, C.C.: Motivating Persistence in the Face of Failure: The Impact of an Ego-protective Buffer on Learning Choices and Outcomes in a Computer-based Educational Game. Ph.D. thesis (2011). http://books.google.com/books?id=uHsdh6mKHuYC
7. Chi, M.T.H.: Active-constructive-interactive: a conceptual framework for differentiating learning activities. Top. Cogn. Sci. **1**(1), 73–105 (2009). http://dx.doi.org/10.1111/j.1756-8765.2008.01005.x
8. Chklovski, T.: Collecting paraphrase corpora from volunteer contributors. In: Proceedings of the 3rd International Conference on Knowledge Capture, pp. 115–120. K-CAP 2005. ACM, New York, NY (2005). http://doi.acm.org/10.1145/1088622.1088644
9. Cohen, P.A., Kulik, J.A., Kulik, C.L.C.: Educational outcomes of tutoring: a meta analysis of findings. Am. Educ. Res. J. **19**, 237–248 (1982)
10. Cooper, S., Khatib, F., Treuille, A., Barbero, J., Lee, J., Beenen, M., Leaver-Fay, A., Baker, D., Popovic, Z., Players, F.: Predicting protein structures with a multiplayer online game. Nature **466**(7307), 756–760 (2010). http://dx.doi.org/10.1038/nature09304
11. Corbett, A.T.: Cognitive tutor algebra I: adaptive student modeling in widespread classroom use. In: Technology and Assessment: Thinking Ahead. Proceedings from a Workshop, pp. 50–62. National Academy Press, Washington, DC, November 2002
12. Cycorp: FACTory. http://game.cyc.com/ (2005). Accessed 23 July 2012
13. Deci, E.L., Koestner, R., Ryan, R.M.: A meta-analytic review of experiments examining the effects of extrinsic rewards on intrinsic motivation. Psychol. Bull. **125**(6), 627–668 (1999)
14. Deci, E.L., Ryan, R.M.: Handbook of Self-Determination Research. University of Rochester Press, Rochester (2004). http://books.google.com/books?id=DcAe2b7L-RgC

15. Edmonds, M.S., Vaughn, S., Wexler, J., Reutebuch, C., Cable, A., Tackett, K.K., Schnakenberg, J.W.: A synthesis of reading interventions and effects on reading comprehension outcomes for older struggling readers. Rev. Educ. Res. **79**(1), 262–300 (2009). http://rer.sagepub.com/content/79/1/262.abstract

16. Garcia, I.: Learning a language for free while translating the web. does duolingo work? Int. J. Engl. Linguist. **3**(1), 19–25 (2013)

17. Graesser, A., Rus, V., D'Mello, S., Jackson, G.T.: Learning through natural language dialogue that adapts to the cognitive and affective states of the learner. In: Robinson, D.H., Schraw, G. (eds.) Recent Innovations in Educational Technology that Facilitate Student Learning. Current perspectives on cognition, learning, and instruction, pp. 95–125. Information Age Publishing, Greenwich (2008). http://books.google.com/books?id=66sJmAycEcC

18. Graesser, A.C., Conley, M.W., Olney, A.: Intelligent tutoring systems. In: Harris, K.R., Graham, S., Urdan, T., Bus, A.G., Major, S., Swanson, H.L. (eds.) APA Educational Psychology Handbook: Application to Teaching and Learning, vol. 3, pp. 451–473. American Psychological Association, Washington (2011)

19. Khatib, F., DiMaio, F., Cooper, S., Kazmierczyk, M., Gilski, M., Krzywda, S., Zabranska, H., Pichova, I., Thompson, J., Popović, Z., Jaskolski, M., Baker, D.: Crystal structure of a monomeric retroviral protease solved by protein folding game players. Nat. Struct. Mol. Biol. **18**(10), 1175–1177 (2011). http://dx.doi.org/10.1038/nsmb.2119

20. Landauer, T.K., McNamara, D.S., Dennis, S., Kintsch, W. (eds.): Handbook of Latent Semantic Analysis. Lawrence Erlbaum, Mahwah (2007)

21. Ma, W., Adesope, O.O., Nesbit, J.C., Liu, Q.: Intelligent tutoring systems and learning outcomes: a meta-analysis. J. Educ. Psychol. **106**(4), 901–918 (2014)

22. National Institute of Child Health and Human Development: Report of the National Reading Panel. Teaching children to read: An evidence-based assessment of the scientific research literature on reading and its implications for reading instruction. NIH Publication No. 00–4769, U.S. Government Printing Office, Washington, DC (2000)

23. Nye, B.D., Graesser, A.C., Hu, X.: Autotutor and family: a review of 17 years of natural language tutoring. Int. J. Artif. Intell. Educ. **24**(4), 427–469 (2014). http://dx.doi.org/10.1007/s40593-014-0029-5

24. Nystrand, M. (ed.): Opening Dialogue: Understanding the Dynamics of Language and Learning in the English Classroom. Language and Literacy Series. Teachers College Press, New York (1997)

25. Olney, A.M., Brawner, K., Pavlik, P., Keodinger, K.: Emerging trends in automated authoring. In: Sottilare, R., Graesser, A., Hu, X., Brawner, K. (eds.) Design Recommendations for Intelligent Tutoring Systems, Adaptive Tutoring, vol. 3. U.S. Army Research Laboratory, Orlando (2015)

26. Olney, A.M., Cade, W., Williams, C.: Generating concept map exercises from textbooks. In: Proceedings of the Sixth Workshop on Innovative Use of NLP for Building Educational Applications, pp. 111–119. Association for Computational Linguistics, Portland, Oregon, June 2011. http://www.aclweb.org/anthology/W11-1414

27. Olney, A.M., Graesser, A.C., Person, N.K.: Tutorial dialog in natural language. In: Nkambou, R., Bourdeau, J., Mizoguchi, R. (eds.) Advances in Intelligent Tutoring Systems, Studies in Computational Intelligence, vol. 308, pp. 181–206. Springer-Verlag, Berlin (2010)

28. Olney, A.M., Graesser, A.C., Person, N.K.: Question generation from concept maps. Dialogue Discourse **3**(2), 75–99 (2012)

29. Olney, A.M., Person, N.K., Graesser, A.C.: Guru: designing a conversational expert intelligent tutoring system. In: McCarthy, P., Boonthum-Denecke, C., Lamkin, T. (eds.) Cross-Disciplinary Advances in Applied Natural Language Processing: Issues and Approaches, pp. 156–171. IGI Global, Hershey (2012)
30. Palincsar, A.S., Brown, A.L.: Reciprocal teaching of comprehension-fostering and comprehension-monitoring activities. Cogn. Instr. **1**, 117–175 (1984)
31. Quinn, A.J., Bederson, B.B.: Human computation: a survey and taxonomy of a growing field. In: Proceedings of the 2011 Annual Conference on Human Factors in Computing Systems, pp. 1403–1412. CHI 2011. ACM, New York, NY (2011). http://doi.acm.org/10.1145/1978942.1979148
32. Raykar, V.C., Yu, S., Zhao, L.H., Valadez, G.H., Florin, C., Bogoni, L., Moy, L.: Learning from crowds. J. Mach. Learn. Res. **99**, 1297–1322 (2010)
33. Ritter, S., Anderson, J.R., Koedinger, K.R., Corbett, A.: Cognitive tutor: applied research in mathematics education. Psychon. Bull. Rev. **14**(2), 249–255 (2007)
34. Ryan, R.M., Deci, E.L.: Self-determination theory and the facilitation of intrinsic motivation, social development, and well-being. Am. Psychol. **55**(1), 68–78 (2000)
35. Savage, N.: Gaining wisdom from crowds. Commun. ACM **55**(3), 13–15 (2012). http://doi.acm.org/10.1145/2093548.2093553
36. Sleeman, D., Brown, J.S. (eds.): Intelligent Tutoring Systems. Academic Press, New York (1982)
37. Sottilare, R., Graesser, A., Hu, X., Goldberg, B. (eds.): Design Recommendations for Intelligent Tutoring Systems: Instructional Management, Adaptive Tutoring, vol. 2. U.S. Army Research Laboratory, Orlando (2014). ISBN: 978-0-9893923-3-4. https://gifttutoring.org/documents/
38. Sottilare, R., Graesser, A., Hu, X., Holden, H., et al. (eds.): Design Recommendations for Intelligent Tutoring Systems, Adaptive Tutoring, vol. 1. U.S. Army Research Laboratory, Orlando (2013). ISBN: 978-0-9893923-0-3. https://gifttutoring.org/documents/42
39. Tian, Y., Zhu, J.: Learning from crowds in the presence of schools of thought. In: Proceedings of the 18th ACM SIGKDD International Conference on Knowledge Discovery and Data Mining. pp. 226–234. KDD 2012. ACM, New York, NY, USA (2012). http://doi.acm.org/10.1145/2339530.2339571
40. VanLehn, K.: The relative effectiveness of human tutoring, intelligent tutoring systems, and other tutoring systems. Educ. Psychol. **46**(4), 197–221 (2011)
41. VanLehn, K., Graesser, A.C., Jackson, G.T., Jordan, P., Olney, A., Rose, C.: When are tutorial dialogues more effective than reading? Cogn. Sci. **31**, 3–62 (2007)
42. Vannella, D., Jurgens, D., Scarfini, D., Toscani, D., Navigli, R.: Validating and extending semantic knowledge bases using video games with a purpose. In: Proceedings of the 52nd Annual Meeting of the Association for Computational Linguistics (Volume 1: Long Papers), pp. 1294–1304. Association for Computational Linguistics (2014). http://aclweb.org/anthology/P14-1122
43. Woolf, B.P.: Building Intelligent Interactive Tutors: Student-Centered Strategies for Revolutionizing E-Learning. Morgan Kaufmann Publishers/Elsevier, Amsterdam (2008). http://books.google.com/books?id=MnrUj3J_VuEC

Opportunities and Risks for Game-Inspired Design of Adaptive Instructional Systems

Scott Ososky[✉]

U.S. Army Research Laboratory (ARL), Orlando, FL, USA
Scott.j.Ososky.ctr@mail.mil

Abstract. The application of game elements within learning environments takes many forms, including serious games, interactive virtual environments, and the application of game mechanics within non-gaming contexts. Given the breadth of strategies for implementation game-elements into instructional systems, it is important to recognize that each strategy carries its own potential benefits and risks. The purpose of the current paper is to review the relevant interdisciplinary literature regarding the application of games and game-elements to learning contexts, and identify the factors to consider when developing a game-inspired instructional system. Secondly, the current discussion considers the special case of game technology and game design elements in intelligent tutoring, and identifies future research opportunities to meaningfully integrate such features in adaptive tutoring systems.

Keywords: Game-based learning · Intelligent tutoring systems · Adaptive tutoring · Gamification · Mental models · Motivation · Tutor-user interface

1 Introduction

As the prevalence of games continues to increase within popular culture, educators and instructional developers continue to look to games as a model for successful design of interactive media. Games are one of many media-based tools with a number of potential benefits for learners. It stands to reason that, because video games are fun and engaging, applying elements of video games to instructional contexts will therefore make instruction fun and engaging [1–3]. Though, the *game* label is often used as an umbrella term for a variety of implementation strategies; for example, the label might describe the technology used within the instructional program, certain rules that govern instructional activities, the manner in which learner progression is measured/tracked, or collaborative features of the instructional environment.

Indeed, the influence of games within learning environments takes many forms, including serious games, interactive virtual environments, social media frameworks, or the use of game mechanics within non-gaming contexts (sometimes referred to as *gamification*). Given the various strategies for the design of game-inspired instruction, great care must be taken to ensure that the impact of those strategies is positive, such as supporting learner motivation and/or engagement with instructional content. Additionally, it is important to consider the influence of learners' existing knowledge on user-system interaction with different game design elements and technologies. Further,

© Springer International Publishing Switzerland 2015
D.D. Schmorrow and C.M. Fidopiastis (Eds.): AC 2015, LNAI 9183, pp. 640–651, 2015.
DOI: 10.1007/978-3-319-20816-9_61

what considerations must be made in transitioning game-inspired strategies from traditional computer-based training to *adaptive* tutoring systems? The current discussion provides an overview of these topics, through a review of relevant interdisciplinary literature. This paper will offer suggestions for selecting appropriate game-inspired features in instructional design, guidance for avoiding potential pitfalls when working with game elements, and identify vectors for future research and discussion in integrating game-inspired features with adaptive tutoring systems.

2 Games in Learning and Learner Perception of Gameness

Video games are often leveraged in or developed for instructional systems. Though, simply adding game software to an instructional system does not necessarily lead to benefits associated with the playing of a game. Consider the distinction between *games* as software products versus activities characterized as games. Juul [4] proposed a functional definition of a *game* which is sufficient and relevant for the current discussion: "A game is a rule-based formal system with a variable and quantifiable outcome, where different outcomes are assigned different values, the player exerts effort in order to influence the outcome, the player feels attached to the outcome, and the consequences of the activity are optional and negotiable." The criteria are not comprehensive; rather they articulate core characteristics that are common to games. One characteristic, for example, that is conspicuously missing from this list is *narrative* [2]. While narrative is a powerful element of a game's design, it is not central in defining an activity as a game.

These characteristics can also be used to identify edge cases, or activities that meet some of these criteria, but not other criteria. Children's sandboxes, for instance, are intended to be freely explored; there are no rules that govern the activity, and the outcomes of the activity do not have defined values. A children's sandbox might be more accurately described as semi-structured *play*. Even in a structured video game, players can choose to ignore rules to pursue other interests (e.g., exploration, goofing off). Thus, the context surrounding the activity can change its classification. For example, if the game, *Grand Theft Auto* were used as a training environment to teach students about obeying traffic laws and safe driving, then the user experience may be more simulation than game-like. Therefore, *gameness*, as it were, might be more accurately described as an *emergent property* from the interaction between the context (users and environment) and the system (software, physical objects, etc.).

To that end, game characteristics may seem to sometimes be at odds with instructional goals, where consequences of performance outcomes may not be optional or negotiable (e.g., poor grades requiring remediation), or the learner may not feel attached to said outcomes (e.g., lack of interest, non-voluntary participation). Game software can be educational by design, such is the case in serious games [2]. However, traditional games can lose their *gameness* as more of their defining characteristics are altered or eschewed. For instance, game-players build game expertise by learning from failures associated with attempting different strategies (including goofing-off) [5]. If failure tolerance is low within a learning environment, then the potential value added by games, like autonomy or fun, might be compromised. Just as illustrations or slide stacks are used to generate learner interest [6], games are one of many available tools for instructional design. Developers should consider the balance between the playing of a game and achieving instructional objectives, as well as how closely the two align with one another in order to effectively leverage games in instruction.

3   Game Technology in Learning and Learner Mental Models

For instructional contexts in which game-playing is not desired, game-based technology components still provide rich simulation opportunities to encourage scenario-based critical thinking, exploration, and collaboration in serious settings. When leveraging individual game-based technologies outside of traditional gaming contexts, it is important to consider learners' *mental models*, which significantly influence system perception and user interaction.

Rouse and Morris [7] explained that mental models "are the mechanisms whereby humans are able to generate descriptions of purpose and form, explanations of system functioning and observed system states, and predictions of future states" (p. 7). Mental models influence users' expectations regarding a system's functionality and guide user interaction behavior [8]. An individual's mental model regarding a particular system is influenced by past experiences and perceived similarity of other systems to the target system. Further, human mental models do not to be complete or even accurate in order to be applied to a specific system interaction [9].

Mental model theory applies directly to learner understanding of and interaction with instructional systems. Individual mental models make it possible for a learner to perceive a system in a way that was unintended by the designer. For instance, it may prove difficult to instill a sense of seriousness in learners if they have prior experience with the playful aspects of a COTS game that was modified for use with an instructional program. Alternatively, learners can experience similar affect with a system for different reasons (e.g., reward structure, learner autonomy), or can respond the same game-like elements in different ways [10].

Regarding system usability, non-game virtual-world simulation products can choose to evoke specific interaction mental models through utilizing game elements familiar to frequent gamers (e.g., mini-map, health bar), thus potentially reducing the time needed to explain controls or rules regarding certain aspects of instructional systems. Placing heart icons at the top corner of the UI, for example, would indicate to a learner that the number of acceptable errors within a session is limited.

Users with prior game experience will expect game-based elements to function in specific ways; therefore, deviation from expected behavior is undesirable and may lead to unintended user confusion or frustration. Dedicated gamers are believed to have a set of meta-knowledge that transfers between games [5], which might include avatar behaviors (e.g., jump, run, crouch) or properties of objects (e.g., red barrels explode). This meta-knowledge also includes expectations regarding how controller buttons are mapped to user actions in certain game genres, such as pulling the trigger to shoot in first-person shooter (FPS) games. Less-frequent game players may also impose different mental model interaction paradigms, based on their own unique experiences to novel instructional systems, such as touch-based and swipe-input gestures for mobile applications.

Anticipating the way in which learners will perceive and react to certain aspects of game-inspired instructional elements, including non-game simulated environments, requires designers and developers to understand learner's mental models. When a learner interacts with an instructional system, there are likely multiple mental models in play. The learner is working to build a mental model of domain knowledge, while maintaining a mental model to interact with the actual learning system used to facilitate the domain content, in addition to other mental models required to interact with technology systems, including games and simulations, integrated within the learning system. Streitz [11] identified the distinction between domain knowledge mental models and system use mental models as the *content problem* and the *interaction problem*, respectively. System design with consideration for users' multiple mental models, including domain knowledge acquisition, expands upon user-centered design, as described by Quintana et al. [12] as *learner-centered design.*

Meanwhile, developers (engineers, designers, authors, etc.) have their own mental models of how their instructional systems *should* function. However, it is a mistake to assume that end-users have the same skills and expertise as those that designed and developed the instructional game and/or system. Recognizing the differences between developers' and learners' mental models is paramount. When possible, game-inspired instructional designs should align with existing *user* models, in order to reduce the time and resources needed for a learner to understand how to interact with the system. Therefore, in the same way that learner analysis is a critical step in the systematic design of instruction [13], so too is game user research (for an overview, see Isbister and Schaffer [14]) in evaluating the design implementation of instructional systems including games or game-like features.

4   Game Elements in Learning and Learner Motivation

Well-designed and tested games are successful because they are designed to engage players [1]; but, it is usually not the purpose of game-inspired instructional design to generate a commercially successful game. Games can also serve as a means to initially draw users' attention toward a system simply based on interest in games [15]; though, it is important to recognize the difference between gaining initial interest through compelling sensory stimulation, and prolonged sustained engagement. Further, it is also not always practical or appropriate to instantiate a game or fully realized virtual environment within an instructional system. Rather, the impetus for a game-inspired instructional design might be to develop a compelling experience that engages and sustains learner motivation. With those considerations in mind, it is increasingly becoming common to see individual game design elements applied to non-gaming instructional content and systems.

4.1   Design for Motivation

Student motivation is an important driving force behind learning. For instance, motivation has been shown to have a positive relationship with performance outcomes, both in traditional [16] and computer-based training environments [17]. Prior research demonstrated that human instructors positively influence learner motivation [18], but motivating students in computer-based environments has been noted as a challenge to the wide-spread implementation of self-directed e-learning environments [19].

Additionally, the source of learners' motivation is relevant to achieving instructional performance outcomes. Ryan and Deci [20] distinguished between *extrinsic motivation*, "the performance of an activity in order to attain some separable outcome" and *intrinsic motivation*, "which refers to doing an activity for the inherent satisfaction of the activity itself" (p. 71). Prior research indicated that intrinsically motivated students can experience greater engagement in learning [21], engage in more exploratory behaviors within instructional content [22], and can exhibit better learning and performance [23]. Some externally motivating factors can be internalized by students, to a similar or complimentary effect as internally motivating factors, which suggests that the two types of motivation are not mutually exclusive [24].

Intrinsic motivation is at the foundation of self-determination theory (SDT), which highlights the importance of self-motivation in well-being and personal growth [20, 25]. SDT identifies three fundamental psychological needs, which form the basis for self-motivation when met. These needs are: 1. *Competence*, or the need for mastery and accomplishment; 2. *Autonomy*, or the feeling that one's actions are aligned with one's self and made of one's own volition; and 3. *Relatedness*, or the desire to connect and interact with others [20, 26].

Leveraging SDT in the study of games, Rigby and Ryan [27] described the ways in which games stimulate and sustain intrinsic motivation in players, through the psychological need satisfaction of competence, autonomy, and relatedness, respectively. For example, in a role-playing game (RPG), players' need for autonomy is satisfied by the ability to customize the physical appearance of the player-character, and make decisions within the narrative that influence the game world. In a puzzle game, competence needs are satisfied thorough visual and auditory feedback and score bonuses or multipliers that acknowledge player mastery. Finally, player needs for relatedness are met in action games by sophisticated NPC (non-player controlled) agents that interact with the player, as well as through social aspects of gaming that occur with other players in online competitive and cooperative gameplay. Such elements can be integrated into existing instructional systems, without a complete game environment.

4.2 Game Design Elements

Gamification refers to the approach of applying game-elements to non-gaming contexts, with the goals of influencing behavior, improving motivation, and/or sustaining engagement [28]. Elements of gamification include achievements, levels, leaderboards, points, badges, and virtual currency. Gamification is applied in a variety of domains including social networking, web design, business, and learning. From a business perspective, Zichermann and Cuningham [29] described gamification as the use of game mechanics to engage users and solve problems. However, the academic validation of gamification is still in early-stages. A recent literature review revealed mixed results for gamification; the researchers found that gamification has different effects in different settings, can be polarizing to users, can encourage unintended behavior, and may undermine users' intrinsic motivation [30]. (A broad discussion of the state of *gamification* can be found in Fuchs et al. [31]).

Certain game elements are sometimes implemented to capitalize on the psychology of human behavior, and do not necessarily coincide with SDT needs, described earlier. In some free-to-play and social network games, for example, real-world time limitations, carrot dangling, and social notifications serve to artificially delay or diminish reward distribution in order to compel players to return to the game in regular intervals [32]. Alternatively, these systems offer users the ability to spend real-world money to accelerate game progress [33, 34]. While the idea of getting learners addicted to frequent, yet minimal reward-loops within an instructional system may sound appealing, it is more likely students will game the system [35] in search of the next extrinsic reward satisfaction (e.g., achievements or social status on leaderboards), thus becoming disengaged with the actual instructional content [36].

In a meta-analysis conducted by Deci and colleagues [37], the researchers found that extrinsic rewards can undermine intrinsic motivation. However, the specific effects for various types of rewards (verbal, tangible, etc.) tended to vary among men, women, and children, respectively. The authors suggested that the negative impact of rewards on intrinsic motivation may be due to the nature by which rewards control user behavior and thwart user volition under certain conditions [38]. Though, extrinsically motivating features may be necessary when learners are not intrinsically motivated to interact with an instructional system. For instance, Thom and colleagues [39] examined an enterprise social network system, which incentivized participation through points and leaderboards. When those features were removed from the system, participation within the social network significantly decreased.

Of course, games have more to offer instructional systems than badges and micro-transactions. Allowing the learner to customize non-critical elements of the user experience supports the need for autonomy. Customization may take the form of the learners' avatar, or the style and layout of the interface (e.g., backgrounds or themes). Stories and narratives can be used to help learners sequence and organize knowledge [40]. For non-sequential learning modules, allowing learner autonomy in course navigation can encourage self-regulated exploration of the instructional content; though, there is a potential danger of losing the attention of learners due to apathy or off-task exploration in open-ended environments [41].

5   Opportunities and Risks for Games in Adaptive Tutoring

Given the variety of ways in which games and instructional systems can intersect, game technology and game design elements offer both opportunities and risks in the design of adaptive tutoring systems. Adaptive tutoring systems, sometimes referred to as intelligent tutoring systems, have been described as "computer-based learning systems which attempt to adapt to the needs of learners" (p. 350) [42], or a computer system that customizes instruction and/or feedback to learners [43]. The system is composed of a series of models or modules that interact with one another. At the core of the system are four models/modules: the learner/student model, the pedagogical/instructional model, the domain knowledge model, and the user interface/communications model. Compared with traditional computer based training, adaptive tutoring systems possess the unique quality of adapting instruction to meet the idiosyncratic needs of the learner. Similarly, these systems can support the affective and motivational needs of the learner as well [17, 44].

5.1 Adaptive Assistance

Many games are not adaptive by nature. They do not alter or change their presentation or challenge based on the player's performance. Typically, the player adapts to the game (not the other way around) to meet increasingly difficult challenges. For instance, memorizing the patterns of enemies and locations of power-up items are part of a player adaption strategy. Likewise, game-players are typically not given the option to skip levels within a video game based on current performance or pre-test evaluations. Single-player video games often offer a difficulty selection option prior to starting a campaign (i.e., easy, medium, hard), though the selection is made by the player and not adaptively changed over the course of gameplay. Challenge adaptation at the macro-level may not be a practical option when teaching to a criterion; however, it might be useful in the identification of novice, journeymen, and expert performers for intervention strategies and subsequent training effectiveness evaluations.

Recently, Nintendo explored micro-adaptive assistance in games with a feature called *Super Guide* [45]. Within some games, such as *New Super Mario Bros. Wii*, Super Guide offers the opportunity to access assistance after multiple failed attempts at completing a level. The automated guide helps the player in completing the level; however, using the guide prevents the player from obtaining certain achievements related to overall game completion. The logical analog to a *Super Guide* in adaptive tutoring might be a hinting system, where learners can request or receive a guidance after a number of errors [3]. However, less motivated learners may be inclined to *game the system* by intentionally making errors in order to get hints and progress through the content more quickly. Research efforts in adaptive assistance evaluate the content and frequency of challenge-based adaptive solutions in interactive learning environments so that they are not abused by unmotivated learners.

5.2 Adaptive State Management

Game-state management is another commonly employed game technology which might be closely coupled with adaptive assistance in intelligent tutoring systems [46]. Many video games, for instance, provide the ability to create multiple *save* files during play, and then *load* those game states at some point in the future in order in the event that the player fails, or wishes to explore alternate strategies. With respect to adaptive tutoring, game-state management might be leveraged in teachable moments to repeat key learning situations [47]. Archived save state data might also be used to replay critical events as a part of an after action review (AAR) procedure.

There are a number of research challenges in this area. Adaptive tutors need to be able to manage the data associated with saving and loading world-states, and may also need to maintain a meta-awareness of the current world state, which states were accessed, and how often the feature was used. Further, there are user research questions regarding whether learners should be able to save their own world-states, if the system should automatically save world-states based on some set of criteria, or if a hybrid approach is more appropriate.

5.3 Adaptive Gamification

Gamification is the use of game elements in non-gaming situations. Used in this manner, gamification can direct user behavior toward specific goals or actions via extrinsically motivating features. However, some research suggested that gamification features can be perceived as controlling, which undermines users' sense of autonomy, therefore negatively impacting intrinsic motivation [37]. With respect to adaptive tutoring systems, an opportunity exists to implement gamification features within an instructional system in situations only in which they are deemed necessary.

Future work should investigate the impact of various game-inspired features among different types of learners. For example, what is the differential impact of badges and achievements on high-interest and low-interest learners, respectively? External incentives might support students with little interest in the domain content [2]. The results of such studies might be used to augment the types of tactics that could be implemented within an adaptive tutoring system based on learner model data, including learners' interest in the domain content and motivation to learn or interact with the tutoring system.

5.4 Adaptive Team Training

Team training is another area in which game technology can support adaptive tutoring efforts. With the rise of online gaming, particularly in the console gaming space, significant research effort has been placed in *matchmaking*. Matchmaking technology intelligently assists players in finding teams to join and other teams to complete against in matches that will yield a positive experience. Players are believed to have an enjoyable experience if the skill balance between teams is evenly distributed, and the chance of either team winning an online match is considered somewhat even [48]. Scientists at Microsoft Research developed a system called TrueSkill, which is used in competitive matchmaking games on Microsoft's online gaming service, Xbox Live. TrueSkill maintains the skill-rating of individual players over time in team-based or free-for-all matches based on the calculation of an average score and an uncertainty modifier [49]. With respect to adaptive tutoring, a similar approach can be leveraged to construct teams and analyze team/individual performance using data collected and stored within long-term learner models.

Matchmaking is not limited to skill-based metrics. The technique is also used to assemble teams based on the player's team-role preference. Specialized team roles in games are becoming increasingly common. For instance, the military-inspired FPS game, *Battlefield* (EA Games), allows players to assume squad roles such as recon, engineer, or medic. With respect to adaptive tutoring, matchmaking could be used to assemble teams of distributed learners based on team role, or to pair novice learners with journeymen learners to encourage learner collaboration. Such specialization data might also be found within the learner's profile, or long-term learner model.

6 Conclusion

The purpose of the current discussion was twofold. First, a review was provided of relevant, interdisciplinary literature regarding the various means by which games intersect with computer based instructional systems. Games used in learning environments, in part or in whole, can influence users' mental models and affective states, regarding learning. Instructional designers and developers should seek to understand the learners for which the system is designed in order to achieve the desired outcomes resulting from learner-system interaction.

Secondly, the current effort identified potential opportunities for research in implementing game technology and game elements within *adaptive tutoring systems*. Game technologies and design elements have been refined over many years through iterative console development cycles and game releases. However, implementing features such as adaptive assistance, gamification, or matchmaking, requires continued research into areas such as information management, learner modeling, and machine learning, respectively. Research is also needed to examine the differential effects of including specific game features, both isolated and in combination, within adaptive tutoring environments across different groups of learners.

Finally, no matter how game design elements are incorporated into instructional systems, games should not be a panacea for sound instructional design. Games are designed to be *fun* [50], while gamification leverages quantification metrics and social status to incentivize non-game activities and drive user behavior toward specific goals [51]. As such, neither games nor gamification is a substitute for instructional content. As M. David Merrill [52] stated, "a horse led to an empty well will still die of thirst if there is no water in it." With that in mind, adaptive tutoring systems should continue to evaluate the effectiveness of game-based design approaches to ensure a positive learning experience and that system features align with instructional objectives.

Acknowledgments. Research was sponsored by the Army Research Laboratory and was accomplished under Cooperative Agreement Number W911NF-12-2-0019. The views and conclusions contained in this document are those of the authors and should not be interpreted as representing the official policies, either expressed or implied, of the Army Research Laboratory or the U.S. Government. The U.S. Government is authorized to reproduce and distribute reprints for Government purposes notwithstanding and copyright notation herein.

References

1. Dickey, M.D.: Engaging by design: how engagement strategies in popular computer and video games can inform instructional design. Educ. Tech. Res. Dev. **53**, 67–83 (2005)
2. McNamara, D.S., Jackson, G.T.: Intelligent tutoring and games (Itag). In: Workshop on Intelligent Educational Games (AIED 2009), Brighton, England (2010)
3. Peirce, N., Conlan, O., Wade, V.: Adaptive educational games: providing non-invasive personalised learning experiences. In: Second IEEE International Conference on Digital Games and Intelligent Toys Based Education, pp. 28–35. IEEE (2008)
4. Juul, J.: The game, the player, the world: looking for a heart of gameness. In: Copier, M., Raessens, J. (eds.) Level Up: Digital Games Research Conference Proceedings, pp. 30–45. Ulrecht Univeristy, Ulrecht (2003)
5. Fortugno, N.: The strange case of the casual gamer. In: Isbister, K., Schaffer, N. (eds.) Game Usability, p. 143. Elsevier, Burlington, MA (2008)
6. Harp, S.F., Mayer, R.E.: The role of interest in learning from scientific text and illustrations: on the distinction between emotional interest and cognitive interest. J. Educ. Psychol. **89**, 92 (1997)
7. Rouse, W.B., Morris, N.M.: On looking into the black box: prospects and limits in the search for mental models. Psychol. Bull. **100**, 349 (1986)
8. Ososky, S.: Influence of Task-Role Mental Models on Human Interpretation of Robot Motion Behavior. University of Central Florida, Orlando (2013)
9. Norman, D.A.: Cognitive engineering. In: Norman, D.A., Draper, S.W. (eds.) User Centered System Design: New Perspectives on Human-Computer Interaction, pp. 31–61. Lawrence Erlbaum Associates, Hillsdale (1986)
10. Morie, J.F., Tortell, R., Williams, J.: Would you like to play a game? experience and expectation in game-based learning environments. In: O'Neil, H.F., Perez, R.S. (eds.) Computer Games and Team and Individual Learning, pp. 269–286. Elsevier, Amsterdam (2008)
11. Streitz, N.A.: Mental models and metaphors: implications for the design of adaptive user-system interfaces. In: Mandl, H., Lesgold, A. (eds.) Learning Issues for Intelligent Tutoring Systems, pp. 164–186. Springer, New York (1988)
12. Quintana, C., Krajcik, J., Soloway, E.: Exploring a structured definition for learner-centered design. In: Fishman, B., O'Connor-Divelbiss, S. (eds.) Fourth International Conference of the Learning Sciences, pp. 256–263 (2000)
13. Dick, W., Carey, L., Carey, J.O.: The Systematic Design of Instruction. Pearson Allyn and Bacon, Boston (2005)
14. Isbister, K., Schaffer, N.: Game Usability. Elsevier, Burlington
15. Blumenfeld, P.C., Kempler, T.M., Krajcik, J.S.: Motivation and cognitive engagement in learning environments. In: Sawyer, R.K. (ed.) The Cambridge Handbook of the Learning Sciences. Cambridge University Press, Cambridge (2006)
16. Covington, M.V., Omelich, C.L.: Task-Oriented Versus Competitive Learning Structures: Motivational and Performance Consequences. J. Educ. Psychol. **76**, 1038–1050 (1984)
17. Beck, J., Stern, M., Haugsjaa, E.: Applications of AI in education. Crossroads **3**, 11–15 (1996)
18. Lepper, M.R., Hodell, M.: Intrinsic motivation in the classroom. In: Ames, C., Ames, R. (eds.) Research on Motivation in the Classroom, vol. 3, pp. 73–105. Academic Press, San Diego (1989)
19. Keller, J., Suzuki, K.: Learner motivation and e-learning design: a multinationally validated process. J. Educ. Media **29**, 229–239 (2004)

20. Ryan, R.M., Deci, E.L.: Self-determination theory and the facilitation of intrinsic motivation, social development, and well-being. Am. Psychol. **55**, 68 (2000)
21. Cordova, D.I., Lepper, M.R.: Intrinsic motivation and the process of learning: beneficial effects of contextualization, personalization, and choice. J. Educ. Psychol. **88**, 715 (1996)
22. Martens, R.L., Gulikers, J., Bastiaens, T.: The impact of intrinsic motivation on e-learning in authentic computer tasks. J. Comput. Assist. Learn. **20**, 368–376 (2004)
23. Vansteenkiste, M., Simons, J., Lens, W., Sheldon, K.M., Deci, E.L.: Motivating learning, performance, and persistence: the synergistic effects of intrinsic goal contents and autonomy-supportive contexts. J. Pers. Soc. Psychol. **87**, 246 (2004)
24. Rigby, C.S., Deci, E.L., Patrick, B.C., Ryan, R.M.: Beyond the intrinsic-extrinsic dichotomy: self-determination in motivation and learning. Motiv. emot. **16**, 165–185 (1992)
25. Deci, E., Ryan, R.M.: Self-Determination Theory. Handbook of Theories of Social Psychology 1,pp. 416–433 (2011)
26. Niemiec, C.P., Ryan, R.M.: Autonomy, competence, and relatedness in the classroom applying self-determination theory to educational practice. Theory Res. Educ. **7**, 133–144 (2009)
27. Rigby, S., Ryan, R.M.: Glued to Games: How Video Games Draw Us in and Hold Us Spellbound. Praeger, Santa Barbara (2011)
28. Marczewski, A.: Gamification: A Simple Introduction. Lulu Press, Raleigh (2013)
29. Zichermann, G., Cunningham, C.: Gamification by Design: Implementing Game Mechanics in Web and Mobile Apps. O'Reilly Media Inc., Sebastopol (2011)
30. Hamari, J., Koivisto, J., Sarsa, H.: Does gamification work? a literature review of empirical studies on gamification. In: 47th Hawaii International Conference on System Sciences (HICSS), pp. 3025–3034. IEEE, New York (2014)
31. Fuchs, M., Fizek, S., Ruffino, P., Schrape, N.: Rethinking Gamification. Meson Press, Luneburg (2014)
32. Landers, R.N., Callan, R.C.: Casual social games as serious games: the psychology of gamification in undergraduate education and employee training. In: Ma, M., Oikonomou, A., Jain, L.C. (eds.) Serious Games and Edutainment Applications, pp. 399–423. Springer, London (2011)
33. Shokrizade, R.: The Top F2p Monetization Tricks (2013). Gamasutra.com
34. Brown, M.: In Gaming, Free-to-Play Can Pay (2011). Wired.com
35. Baker, R.S., Corbett, A.T., Koedinger, K.R., Evenson, S., Roll, I., Wagner, A.Z., Naim, M., Raspat, J., Baker, D.J., Beck, J.E.: Adapting to when students game an intelligent tutoring system. In: Ikeda, M., Ashley, K.D., Chan, T.-W. (eds.) ITS 2006. LNCS, vol. 4053, pp. 392–401. Springer, Heidelberg (2006)
36. DeFalco, J.A., Baker, R.S., D'Mello, S.K.: Addressing behavioral disengagement in online learning. In: Sottilare, R.A., Graesser, A.C., Hu, X., Goldberg, B.S. (eds.) Design Recommendations for Intelligent Tutoring Systems, vol. 2, pp. 49–70. U.S. Army Research Laboratory, Orlando (2014)
37. Deci, E.L., Koestner, R., Ryan, R.M.: A meta-analytic review of experiments examining the effects of extrinsic rewards on intrinsic motivation. Psychol. Bull. **125**, 627 (1999)
38. Deterding, S.: situated motivational affordances of game elements: a conceptual model. In: Gamification: Using Game Design Elements in Non-Gaming Contexts, a workshop at CHI 2011, Vancouver, BC, Canada (2011)
39. Thom, J., Millen, D., DiMicco, J.: Removing gamification from an enterprise SNS. In: Proceedings of the ACM 2012 conference on Computer Supported Cooperative Work, pp. 1067–1070. ACM (2012)
40. Jonassen, D.H., Hernandez-Serrano, J.: Case-based reasoning and instructional design: using stories to support problem solving. Educ. Tech. Res. Dev. **50**, 65–77 (2002)

41. Lawless, K.A., Brown, S.W.: Multimedia learning environments: issues of learner control and navigation. Instr. Sci. **25**, 117–131 (1997)
42. Self, J.: The defining characteristics of intelligent tutoring systems research. Int. J. Artif. Intell. Educ. (IJAIED) **10**, 350–364 (1998)
43. Psotka, J., Massey, L.D., Mutter, S.A.: Intelligent Tutoring Systems: Lessons Learned. Psychology Press, Hillsdale (1988)
44. Sottilare, R.A., Graesser, A.C., Hu, X., Holden, H.: Design Recommendations for Intelligent Tutoring Systems: Learner Modeling, vol. 1. U.S. Army Research Laboratory, Orlando (2013)
45. Totilo, S.: Kind Code Demo Shows New Super Mario Bros on Auto-Pilot (2009). Kotaku.com
46. Novak, J.: Game Development Essentials: An Introduction. Delmar Cengage Learning, Clifton Park (2008)
47. Havinghurst, R.J.: Human Development and Education. England, Oxford (1953)
48. Graepel, T., Herbrich, R., Magazine, I.G.D.: Ranking and Matchmaking. Game Developer Magazine 25–34 (2006)
49. Herbrich, R., Minka, T., Graepel, T.: Trueskill™: a bayesian skill rating system. In: Advances in Neural Information Processing Systems, pp. 569–576 (2006)
50. Lazzaro, N.: The four fun keys. In: Isbister, K., Schaffer, N. (eds.) Game Usability: Advancing the Player Experience, pp. 315–344. Elsevier, Burlington (2008)
51. Hemley, D.: 26 Elements of a Gamification Marketing Strategy (2012). http://www.socialmediaexaminer.com
52. Merrill, M.D.: Merrill on Instructional Design (2008). http://youtu.be/i_TKaO2-jXA

From Desktop to Cloud: Collaborative Authoring for Intelligent Tutoring

Charlie Ragusa[✉]

Dignitas Technologies, LLC, Orlando, FL, USA
cragusa@dignitastechnologies.com

Abstract. Authoring of computer-based instruction employing intelligent tutoring (IT) presents many challenges. Chief among them is that for non-trivial domains, the knowledge and skills required to author maximally effective instruction often do not reside in a single individual. More often the best outcome is achieved by collaboration among some combination of instructional designers, subject matter experts, psychologists, traditional educators, and in some cases, software engineers. To meet this challenge, well designed collaborative authoring systems are needed. Cloud computing technologies, such as Platform as a Service (PaaS) and Infrastructure as a Service (IaaS), offer new possibilities for the construction of distributed authoring systems. In this paper we discuss several high-level design considerations for developing collaborative IT authoring systems, focusing on extending the capabilities of the existing Generalized Intelligent Framework for Tutoring (GIFT).

Keywords: Collaborative authoring · Intelligent Tutoring Systems · Cloud computing

1 Introduction

In recent years we've witnessed an explosion in the number and variety of eLearning systems. Growth has been driven by demand from educational institutions, corporations, and governments and has been enabled by technological advancements such as cloud computing, Software as a Service (SaaS), and a growing variety of delivery platforms including traditional PC's, mobile devices, and tablets.

Despite the frenetic pace of advancement, when one envisions future possibilities it's easy to imagine that eLearning is still in its infancy. Nevertheless, as a practical matter, much of eLearning has matured to the point of widespread adoption and extensive application and commercialization.

Within this larger context exist Intelligent Tutoring Systems (ITSs) – a subtype of eLearning systems that seeks to improve learning effectiveness by applying algorithms, agents, or other artificial intelligence to effect a tutoring capability which adapts, customizes, or otherwise personalizes the learning experience with the intent of equaling and perhaps even surpassing the value added by a real-life human tutor. ITSs have the potential to increase learning effectiveness, increase access to quality training, and decrease the cost of delivering the learning content.

© Springer International Publishing Switzerland 2015
D.D. Schmorrow and C.M. Fidopiastis (Eds.): AC 2015, LNAI 9183, pp. 652–662, 2015.
DOI: 10.1007/978-3-319-20816-9_62

Compared to their non-ITS eLearning peers, ITSs are fewer in number, less mature, and remain largely in the realm of research and development. Furthermore, while many non-ITS eLearning systems are domain independent, the vast majority of ITSs are tightly coupled to specific domains. The reason is simple: developing ITSs is difficult and development of domain independent ITSs is even more so.

Though development of ITSs is likely to remain challenging for some time, advances in basic research areas, such as learner modeling, domain knowledge representation, instructional strategies, and natural language processing, are expected to make ITSs increasingly viable. As the fundamental precepts of intelligent tutoring emerge and the technology proves itself, a key enabler to the widespread adoption of ITSs will be the existence of robust and easy-to-use tools for authoring.

Though certainly not trivial, the basics of authoring for many non-ITS eLearning systems are relatively straightforward. At their core, they typically include support for authoring (or uploading/linking to existing) content and a means for learner assessment, typically quizzes or exams. At times, this results in little more than a migration of off-line content, such as text books and lecture notes, to an online environment, perhaps with a little multimedia thrown in for good measure. In this case, it is likely that few, if any, improvements were made in the effectiveness of the instruction.

In contrast, authoring for an ITS, especially a domain independent ITS, is significantly more demanding. Authoring of content and knowledge assessment remains essential, but authoring ITS-enabled courses requires much more, including authoring of domain knowledge, learner models, expert models, pedagogical models, meta-data, non-linear flow through the material, etc. For ITSs equipped with physiological sensors, still more authoring is required to factor in affective state to adapt the learner experience. The bottom line is that authoring for ITSs is significantly more complex than it is for basic eLearning systems, and creation of nontrivial ITS applications will likely be best handled via collaborative authoring teams. This paper discusses several design considerations relevant to the development of any new collaborative authoring tools for ITSs.

2 Discussion

A relative newcomer to the ITS world is the Generalized Intelligent Framework for Tutoring (GIFT) [1, 2]. As an intelligent tutoring framework, GIFT is unique in that it is open source, domain independent, includes a sensor framework, and is designed to integrate with external training applications. These characteristics, along with the author's familiarity with GIFT, make it well suited for a discussion on collaborative ITS authoring [3]. Furthermore, since authoring for an ITS is inherently coupled to the underlying capabilities of the ITS, this paper will use the GIFT capabilities as its model. Unless otherwise noted, the term "course" will be used throughout the remainder of this document to reflect a GIFT course as currently implemented by GIFT.

2.1 Authoring in the Cloud

A cloud architecture is ideal for a collaborative authoring system. In addition to supporting concurrent access by multiple users, cloud infrastructure typically includes support for several key elements of a collaborative system such as authentication, storage, versioning, and scalability. For courses that only require a web browser, content can remain in the cloud and be fetched by the browser as needed. For the desktop runtime environment, courses and any resources needed locally can be downloaded (and likely cached) as necessary.

For the remainder of this paper, a cloud-based authoring system is assumed. Given this assumption, GIFT must move all core authoring functions to the cloud, including:

- Authoring, uploading, and management of content
- Authoring, uploading, and management of GIFT configuration elements/files
- Authoring and management of surveys[1]
- Publication of authored courses (i.e. making them available for use)

The objective is for the authored courses, along with all required resources, to be served from the cloud, and fetched or downloaded as needed. Courses requiring only a browser and internet connection are delivered on demand to the browser from the cloud. Courses using sensors, third-party desktop applications, and the like will be downloaded and cached by the local GIFT runtime. It may be that the user will still bear some responsibility for downloading and installing said desktop applications.

The same cloud application responsible for authoring will no doubt include other capabilities such as tools for report generation, etc., but these features are outside the scope of this document.

2.2 Modes of Collaboration

There are various modes of collaboration. Most readers will have some experience with collaborative authoring even if that experience is limited to review or serial editing of documents circulated via email. Certainly, collaborative authoring in GIFT can be performed in the same way using the current tool suite; however, any such collaboration is limited to unsophisticated techniques such as sharing files via email or shared file systems, or using a distributed revision control system such as Git. In the following sections various collaboration modes and related issues are discussed.

2.3 Concurrent Editing

In a concurrent editing environment multiple authors can edit a shared document in real time. Edits made by one author appear immediately in the views of the other authors. Concurrent editing has the advantage of allowing real time collaboration between two

---

[1] GIFT uses "survey" as a catch-all term for quizzes, assessments, exams, as well as traditional surveys (e.g. psychological, biographical, satisfaction, etc.).

or more remote authors, in a way that closely mimics working together side-by-side at a single workstation or whiteboard, especially when paired with a voice or text communication channel to discuss ideas. This is especially useful for authoring when ideas are not fully developed and require some discussion, negotiation, and/or agreement by the authors.

Well known commercial applications supporting concurrent authoring include recent versions of Microsoft Office applications, Microsoft OneNote, Etherpad, and various document types within Google Drive. Aside from a few variations, these applications all work similarly in that all are cloud based, all require sharing of the document with other collaborators, and once a document is shared, all allow updates and edits to be seen by other collaborators in real time.

Another interesting and highly relevant collaborative authoring environment is Stanford University's WebProtégé [4], a free open-source collaborative ontology development environment for the web. WebProtégé is particularly interesting because, in addition to being a cloud-based collaborative authoring environment, it embodies many of the concepts described in this document, including history and revision management, built-in discussion support, and interoperability with a desktop version of the authoring tool. Furthermore, much like GIFT, it's a highly technical editor that outputs XML. Lastly, it appears that WebProtégé is constructed using the Google Web Toolkit (GWT), the same platform use to construct GIFT's current web based authoring tools. Assuming the continued use of GWT by the GIFT team, approaches and techniques used by WebProtégé could be considered for potential reuse in future GIFT collaborative authoring tools.

2.4   Roles

In the context of intelligent tutoring, the term *collaborative authoring* implies a team of two or more individuals working together to create an intelligent tutor. In some cases the team members may be peers, in which case the team may exist for no other reason than to divide the workload or to support peer reviews. However, a more likely scenario is that the team consists of individuals with differing skills and backgrounds that are brought together to leverage their complementary talents. Thus, before considering the nature of role-based collaboration we will first define some common roles of potential collaborators.

Primary roles include:

- **Instructional System Designer** – This is a person with experience and/or formal training in the design and construction of instructional systems. A person in this role is well founded in learning theory and the application of current technology to the learning process.
- **Subject Matter Expert** – Within the context of a given authoring project this is the person with advanced domain knowledge in the area to be trained. The expertise could be from advanced education in the area, life experience, or both.

- **Course Facilitator** – This is the person(s) that will be responsible for delivering the training to the end users (learners). They could be an actual instructor in a blended learning environment or simply a training coordinator.

Additional roles include:

- **Educational Psychologist** – This is a person with an expertise in the science of learning from both a cognitive and behavioral perspective.
- **Software Engineer** – The existence of this role reflects the idea that ITSs are relatively immature and any new collaborative authoring tool will be even less so. Thus the Software Engineer's role is to manage and/or implement any lower-level system requirements or configuration items that are either not handled by the authoring tool's user interface or are beyond the grasp of less technical users.
- **Experimenter** – The Experimenter role exists because ITSs are often used in research environments. Thus, a person in this role comes to the table with an experimental design in mind and is there to ensure that the correct types and quantities of data are captured to satisfy the objectives of an experiment.
- **Reviewer** – This is a catch-all role that may overlap substantially with other roles, especially the Course Facilitator, and exists to identify individuals with responsibility for review and approval during the authoring process. An example would be a training compliance officer within a corporate environment.
- **Administrator** – This is a system-level role. Users with administrative privileges have the ability to configure authoring tool and application-wide settings, perhaps including adding and/or approving new users to the site and assigning roles.

It's worth noting that the composition of authoring teams is likely to vary widely from one organization to another and even from one project to another within an organization. In many cases, a single individual may support multiple roles, and in other cases multiple individuals may potentially serve the same role. Additionally, though the set of roles described above may be sufficient for many authoring environments, the system should not limit users to the roles in this set. Rather, the system should support the arbitrary creation of new roles and customization of their access levels and privileges.

2.5   RoleBased Access Control

In a collaborative ITS authoring system, controlling access to project resources based on role makes sense for several reasons. However, because this is such a ubiquitous concept in multi-user IT systems, the rationale for its use and the basic operational concepts probably requires little explanation. On a per-project basis, collaborators are assigned one or more roles and their access to resources is constrained by their least restrictive role. Independent setting of *read* and *write* privileges for each role may be sufficient for most purposes, though *manage* (i.e., the ability to create and delete) may also be required. Such constraints serve to declutter views and minimize unwanted and potentially costly erroneous operations.

The granularity at which privileges are set is important and deserves some analysis. Coarse granularity is easier to implement but may not provide a sufficient level of control. Fine granularity gives more control, but may be overly burdensome during project configuration. In places where granular control is required, any such burden should be minimized by cascading setting changes on nested resources and resource elements.

Lastly, the system should be configurable at both the organizational level and the project level. Roles and permissions established at the organizational level become defaults for any new project, but can be customized by the project as needed.

2.6 Role-Based Interface Customization

During course development, resources may frequently require input and/or review by more than one user. Collaborators will often bring a diverse set of skills and experiences to the authoring process and may expect to interact with the authoring system in substantially different ways. To accommodate these differences, multiple viewers/editors can be built in to the authoring system and the set of views and editors available to each configured based upon their role(s). Users with a given role will be expected to have similar expectations and technical abilities. For example, many software engineers may prefer editing a raw XML, whereas most subject matter experts might prefer a graphical drag-and-drop interface.

Certainly, not every aspect of the authoring system will require multiple interfaces and there's a clear trade-off in terms of effort required to implement additional interfaces and the expected pay-off in terms of usability of those interfaces. Accordingly, decisions to implement multiple interfaces should be preceded by appropriate analysis informed by input from potential users in each of the target roles.

2.7 Workflow

Role-based access controls constrain access based on who and what, while workflow typically exists on top of access control and imposes additional role-based constraints, as well as constraints based on timing and sequencing. Many readers will have encountered formal document workflow via interaction with an enterprise document management system, such as Microsoft SharePoint.

GIFT authoring is currently unconstrained by workflow. Courses can be authored in a top-down or bottom-up fashion and any and all aspects of a GIFT course can be edited at any time. If workflow is desired it must be agreed upon and managed by the collaborators themselves. Given the extreme flexibility and generalized nature of GIFT, low-level authoring is unlikely to ever be constrained by workflow. Nevertheless, implementing support for workflow for high-level authoring could have several advantages for collaborators, including division of labor, support for review/approval processes, assignments based on expertise, and simply enforcement of authoring best practices.

EasyGenerator [5] is a commercial cloud-based tutoring system that supports both collaborative authoring and workflow. In EasyGenerator, authoring is performed using a didactical approach. Authors first enter learning objectives based on course goals. After goals and objectives are established, authors enter questions used to evaluate the learning goals. Finally, learning content is added/authored. Content can be added separately or it can be tied directly to a question.

For GIFT, assuming some level of workflow is desired; support could be created at one of three different levels. The first and simplest level would be to provide built-in support for one or more pre-defined workflow templates, analogous to the EasyGenerator approach. The second level would integrate a workflow engine into the authoring system and provide a means to upload (or choose from previously uploaded) workflow configurations created outside of the authoring system. The third, and most sophisticated, approach builds on the second but includes support for creating the workflow definition within the authoring tool itself.

2.8 Inline Support For Collaborator Communication

It is helpful for any collaborative authoring system to support inline communication between collaborators. Two primary modes of communication come to mind. The first is a global real-time chat capability allowing real time conversations/discussions between collaborators. Clearly, this sort of capability is widely available for no cost through applications such as Google Chat. For many use cases this may be sufficient; however, there is some advantage to having the capability built in to the collaborative authoring system. One advantage is that the record of the conversation can be persisted as part of the course authoring project and thus available for future reference. Another advantage is that collaborators will more easily be able to reference the current state of the course they are discussing, because it will be readily available on their screen.

The second mode of communication is the ability for authors to make per-element comments on the various aspects of the course. This idea is akin to the familiar *comment* feature available through the review tab in Microsoft Word. Such a feature provides an easy-to-use mechanism for asynchronous communication between authors concerning specific aspects of a course. For example reviewers could use it to make suggestions for improvements during the review process. Should the GIFT team decide to implement support for comments, decisions must be made as to the appropriate level of granularity.

2.9 Course Resource Metadata

A potentially valuable feature for the authoring system would be support for metadata tagging of course resources. Such a capability is probably best described as a *like-to-have* more than a *must-have* feature, but is still worthy of consideration. Such a scheme would be useful for capturing and managing documentation of rationales for key decisions, references for content acquired from third parties, and virtually any other sort of data relevant to the authoring process. Having such data stored and available alongside the corresponding resource could be useful to authors in the same way that in-line code comments are useful to computer programmers. And, as with code comments, their true value is often fully appreciated (either by their presence or their absence) only when the code (or in this case, the course), is revisited for rework at some point in the future.

Managing metadata at the file level could be done as a sub element of the project construct and/or as part of a shared content repository. Approaches for finer grained management will vary depending on the resource. For example metadata for objects housed in a database (e.g. surveys) are probably best handled by extending the database schema appropriately. Given that GIFT already supports metadata tagging of content for pedagogical purposes, there may be some opportunity for synergy or reuse.

2.10 Integration with Third Party Authoring Tools

GIFT is designed to support authoring of intelligent tutoring systems that employ external (third-party) applications to deliver content and user experiences within the context of a course. Indeed, the current version of GIFT includes sample courses that use AutoTutor, Virtual Battlespace 2 (VBS2) [7], Tactical Combat Casualty Care Simulation (TC3Sim) [8], PowerPoint, and others. In each case, scenarios and/or content was developed external to GIFT using the training application's respective authoring capabilities.

Though conceptually appealing, it's highly impractical for GIFT authoring tools to integrate with more than a small subset of possible third-party authoring tools. Many such third-party authoring tools exist only as proprietary desktop applications and very few expose the requisite functionality via an API. Furthermore, even in the absence of these barriers, tool integration carries with it the burden of ongoing testing and maintenance with each new release of either system. Hence, as a general rule, external authoring tools should not be integrated, but rather should remain as independent tools. The output of these external tools should then be used as input to the GIFT authoring system.

Exceptions to this rule should be supported by a compelling use case underpinned by either a unique technical capability and/or substantial user demand. Of course, the extent to which such integration can be made seamless will vary based upon technical feasibility.

To date, GIFT has some level of integration (though none qualify as truly seamless) with four systems having potential for further authoring integration. Those are: AutoTutor [9], SIMILE Workbench [10], TRADEM [11], and RapidMiner [12]. Of these four, AutoTutor, an ITS unto itself, offers the most promise in terms of authoring integration.

AutoTutor's compelling capability is that it provides the ability to engage learners in two-way dialog, based on computational linguistics and latent semantic analysis [13]. Additionally, the AutoTutor runtime has been integrated with GIFT for some time now. More recently the AutoTutor Script Authoring Tool has been released as a web application, and thus is well suited for integration with any web or cloud based authoring system for GIFT.

As GIFT authoring matures and enjoys wider use, there will likely be increased demand and opportunity for integration with additional third-party authoring systems. Each should be considered on its own merit and weighed against competing opportunities. With GIFT as an open-source project, this sort of specialized integration may best be left to third-parties with a vested interest in the success of the respective authoring system.

2.11   Scalability and Cloud Architecture Considerations

Earlier we made the assumption that any collaborative ITS authoring system would be best constructed as a cloud-based web application. However, the discussion thus far has relied very little on cloud technology per se. In fact, the only real assumption has been that an authoring tool should be internet accessible and support multiple concurrent users. Thus, for small scale operations, deployment as a traditional web application is sufficient, and the entire system could reside on a single host, perhaps augmented by a second host to support database operations and the like.

For enterprise-level deployments, more sophisticated architectures are required to take full advantage of the cloud, especially in the area of scalability. Perhaps the greatest scalability challenge would arise from offering GIFT (inclusive of the authoring system) as a Software as a Service platform. In such a case, there would simply be a single GIFT presence in the cloud which would scale to meet demand as new organizations and their users came on board.

To gracefully support this kind of scalability, GIFT must be architected for and implemented on a cloud infrastructure, either Platform as a Service (PaaS) or Infrastructure as a Service (IaaS). A detailed discussion on the implications of these choices is beyond the scope of this document; however, it seems clear that choosing PaaS would allow developers to start at a higher level of abstraction and thereby accelerate development. The trade-off, of course, is that PaaS ties the application to the chosen platform, reducing, and perhaps even eliminating, any hopes for portability. This may be irrelevant for a commercial venture, but may be of some concern for an open source project such as GIFT. Conversely, the choice of IaaS will tend to maintain a higher level of portability at the expense of development time and perhaps increase long term maintenance concerns.

A particularly interesting IaaS option is OpenStack [14], an open source IaaS platform. Ignoring the relative merits of OpenStack vs. other IaaS options, OpenStack has the unique advantage of being available both through commercial in-the-cloud OpenStack service providers, while also being deployable to organization-owned hardware for an internally owned and operated cloud.

Lastly, regulatory and compliance requirements, such as ITAR, must be considered if certain applications within US government agencies and contractors are to be supported. Amazon Web Services, for example, offers AWS GovCloud [15] to address this concern. Certain other service providers may as well.

The IaaS/PaaS choice is just the first of several architectural considerations, all of which require attention, as getting the architecture right is almost certainly the single most important design task, especially with regard to scalability. The bottom line is that development of any cloud based authoring system should be preceded by a thorough analysis of cloud architectures, cloud services/platforms, as well as current and anticipated system requirements.

3 Conclusions and Recommendations

Authoring of quality learning content, expert models, and knowledge assessment is critical to the success of any ITS. Without it, the great potential of ITS technologies will not be realized. Effective collaborative authoring tools are needed to allow contributors with varying expertise and skill sets to work together.

Cloud technologies have made great strides in recent years, and appear to be stable and effective at hosting real time collaborative environments for documents. These technologies should be leveraged to build an authoring tool for GIFT that provides many of the features seen in popular cloud based document editing environments such as chat, comments, real time updating from multiple authors, version control, optional off-line editing, etc. A collaborative authoring tool based on cloud technologies ensures accessibility and compatibility with any modern, internet connected computer.

Development of a collaborative authoring tool for GIFT is a necessary step to even wider acceptance and adoption of the framework for ITS solutions. It will ease the development process and place fewer requirements on the software development team during the learning content authoring phase. To start, analysis needs to be completed to determine the system level requirements for a collaborative authoring tool, to include considering the architectural choices (PaaS/IaaS) and the tradeoffs associated with each. This analysis should include discussion with the GIFT community to provide input into desired features, including assignment of priorities to each requirement. A GIFT collaborative authoring tool should be developed in phases, with iterative improvements being developed and thoroughly tested with a team of authors collaborating to develop actual learning content and assessments. Development will be phased according to the prioritized list of requirements, budget, allocation of resources against other GIFT priorities, and the GIFT release schedule.

A cloud based collaborative authoring tool for a framework such as GIFT brings to life many possibilities for the construction of distributed authoring systems. It will allow the right personnel—whether instructional designers, subject matter experts, psychologists, or traditional educators—to work together efficiently to generate quality training materials.

References

1. Sottilare, R.A., Brawner, K.W., Goldberg, B.S., Holden, H.K.: The Generalized Intelligent Framework for Tutoring (GIFT). US Army Research Laboratory–Human Research & Engineering Directorate (ARL-HRED), Orlando (2012)

2. Sottilare, R.A.: Considerations in the development of an ontology for a generalized intelligent framework for tutoring. In: International Defense & Homeland Security Simulation Workshop (2012)
3. Hoffman, M., Ragusa, C.: Unwrapping GIFT: A Primer on Authoring Tools for the Generalized Intelligent Framework for Tutoring. In: Generalized Intelligent Framework for Tutoring (GIFT) Users Symposium (GIFTSym2), p. 11 (2015)
4. Protégé. http://protege.stanford.edu/
5. EasyGenerator. https://www.easygenerator.com/
6. OpenStack. https://www.openstack.org/
7. Army-Technology.com.   http://www.army-technology.com/contractors/training/bohemia-interactive/
8. Goldberg, B., Cannon-Bowers, J.: Experimentation with the generalized intelligent framework for tutoring (GIFT): a testbed use case. In: AIED 2013 Workshops Proceedings, vol. 7, p. 27 (2013)
9. Nye, B.D.: Integrating GIFT and AutoTutor with sharable knowledge objects (SKO). In: AIED 2013 Workshop on GIFT. CEUR, pp. 54–61 (2013)
10. Mall, H., Goldberg, B.: SIMILE: an authoring and reasoning system for GIFT. In: Generalized Intelligent Framework for Tutoring (GIFT) Users Symposium (GIFTSym2), p. 34 (2015)
11. Eduworks. http://eduworks.wix.com/eduworks#!tradem/cktl
12. RapidMiner. https://rapidminer.com/
13. Graesser, A.C., Penumatsa, P., Ventura, M., Cai, Z., Hu, X.: Using LSA in AutoTutor: learning through mixed initiative dialogue in natural language. In: Handbook of Latent Semantic Analysis, pp. 243–262 (2007)
14. OpenStack. http://www.openstack.org/
15. Amazon Web Services GovCloud. http://aws.amazon.com/govcloud-us/

Designing Representations and Support for Metacognition in the Generalized Intelligent Framework for Tutoring

James R. Segedy[1(✉)], John S. Kinnebrew[1], Benjamin S. Goldberg[2],
Robert A. Sottilare[2], and Gautam Biswas[1]

[1] Institute for Software Integrated Systems, Department of Electrical
Engineering and Computer Science, Vanderbilt University, 1025 16th Avenue
South, Nashville, TN 37212, USA
{james.segedy,john.s.kinnebrew,
gautam.biswas}@vanderbilt.edu
[2] U.S. Army Research Laboratory – Human Research and Engineering
Directorate, Simulation and Training Technology Center, 12423 Research
Parkway, Orlando, FL 32826, USA
{benjamin.s.goldberg.civ,
robert.a.sottilare.civ}@mail.mil

Abstract. An important component of metacognition relates to the understanding and use of strategies. Thus, measuring and supporting students' strategy understanding in complex open-ended learning environments is an important challenge. However, measuring students' strategy use and understanding is a difficult undertaking. In this paper, we present our design for representing and supporting students in their understanding of strategies while working in complex, open-ended learning environments using the Generalized Intelligent Framework for Tutoring (GIFT). Our approach utilizes a wealth of previous research and relies on three primary instructional interventions: contextualized conversational assessments and feedback; reviewing knowledge and strategies; and teaching through analogies. We believe that incorporating these approaches into GIFT will allow for powerful instruction of complex tasks and topics.

Keywords: Metacognition · Strategy instruction · Feedback · Open-ended learning environment

1 Introduction

The Generalized Intelligent Framework for Tutoring (GIFT) is a software platform for designing, developing, and implementing online and in-class educational programs [1, 2]. The goals of GIFT are many, including reducing the high development costs and low reusability of educational applications while also creating engaging and adaptive learning spaces that students can access as needed. A critical aspect of GIFT that makes it different from a number of conventional tutoring systems is its emphasis on accumulating and tracking long-term information about each student. This helps the system

© Springer International Publishing Switzerland 2015
D.D. Schmorrow and C.M. Fidopiastis (Eds.): AC 2015, LNAI 9183, pp. 663–674, 2015.
DOI: 10.1007/978-3-319-20816-9_63

evaluate an individual student's learning progress and behaviors over an extended period of time and then use this information to provide support, recommendations, and tutoring sessions that are specific to the student's experiences and previously-demonstrated understanding of targeted concepts.

In general, collecting and studying long-term data about students' use of learning technologies is not new; learning management systems have been used to study multi-year trends in students' progressions through their degree programs [3, 4]. However, GIFT is designed to collect finer-grained data about students' interactions with a variety of educational technologies. For example, GIFT can collect and evaluate data on students' understanding of doctrinal and tactical concepts of battlefield operations across a variety of pedagogical media that vary from PowerPoint presentations and videos to simulations of offensive and defensive battlefield tactics in the Virtual Battlespace simulator [5]. Integrating information about a student's learning and performance across such disparate formats and contexts over extended periods of time is challenging, but there is promise that this information is the key to providing more effective and individualized adaptive support to learners.

In this paper, we present our design for supporting students in learning to employ metacognition while working in complex, open-ended learning environments [6, 7] through GIFT. We present an overview of metacognition, challenges in assessing students' use of metacognitive processes, and a framework for interactively assessing metacognition and providing students with adaptive support based on their needs.

2 Background

Metacognition [8] describes the ability to reason about and explicitly manage one's own cognitive processes. It is often broken down into two sub-components: knowledge and regulation [9, 10]. Metacognitive knowledge refers to an individual's understanding of their own cognition and strategies for managing that cognition. Metacognitive regulation refers to how metacognitive knowledge is used in order to create plans, monitor and manage the effectiveness of those plans, and then reflect on the outcome of plan execution in order to refine metacognitive knowledge [11].

When applied to learning, metacognition is considered a subset of self-regulated learning (SRL). SRL is an active theory of learning that describes how learners are able to set goals, create plans for achieving those goals, continually monitor their progress, and revise their plans when necessary [12]. In terms of SRL, metacognition deals directly with cognition without explicitly considering its interactions with emotional or motivational constructs [13]. Despite this, models of self-regulation are valuable in depicting key metacognitive processes. For example, [14] describes SRL as containing "multiple and recursive stages incorporating cognitive and metacognitive strategies" (p. 286). This description of SRL involves phases of orientation and planning, enactment and learning, and reflection and self-assessment.

Students may start by orienting themselves to the task and formulating task understanding (*i.e.*, an understanding of what the task is). A student's task understanding is necessarily influenced by her metacognitive knowledge about her own abilities and available strategies for completing the task [15]. Together, these two sources of information, task understanding and metacognitive knowledge, provide a foundation that, in conjunction with other student attributes such as self-efficacy, governs students' subsequent goal-setting and planning processes. Once a plan has been formulated, students begin executing it. As they carry out the activities specified in their plans, students may exercise metacognitive monitoring as they consciously evaluate the effectiveness of their plans and the success of the activities they are engaging in. The result of these monitoring processes may lead students to exercise metacognitive control by evaluating and then modifying or even abandoning their plan as they execute it. Once a plan has been completed or abandoned, students may engage in reflection as they analyze the overall effectiveness of their approach and their planning processes. Such reflection may lead students to add to or revise their meta-cognitive knowledge and task understanding.

In this paper, our focus on metacognition is centered on students' understanding of and use of *strategies*, which have been defined as consciously-controllable processes for completing tasks [16]. Strategies comprise a large portion of metacognitive knowledge; they consist of declarative, procedural, and conditional knowledge that describe the strategy, its purpose, and how and when to employ it [9]. The research community has identified several types of strategies based on the tasks for which they are designed. For example, strategies may be cognitive (*e.g.*, a strategy for applying a particular procedure, or completing an addition problem), metacognitive (*e.g.*, strategies for choosing and monitoring one's own cognitive operations), involve management (*e.g.*, for managing one's environment to promote focused attention), be directed toward learning (*e.g.*, a strategy for memorizing new information), or involve a combination of these [17, 18]. For example, a metacognitive learning strategy might involve *activating prior knowledge* before learning about a topic by consciously bringing to mind information one already knows about the topic [19]. When faced with a complex task, students must either identify a known strategy for completing it or invent one using their metacognitive knowledge.

An important characteristic of a strategy is its *level of generality*. That is, some strategies apply to very specific situations (*e.g.*, an approach to adding two-digit numbers) while other strategies apply to a broader set of situations (*e.g.*, summarizing recently learned information to improve retention). An understanding of more general strategies, as well as their specific implementations for concrete tasks, is important for developing one's ability to adapt existing strategies to new situations or even invent new strategies. Thus, our goal in GIFT is to explicitly teach students general strategies and help students understand how to apply them to complex tasks. In the longer run, as students encounter different situations in which a strategy applies, we hope to make students aware of how strategies, such as those for maintaining situational awareness, monitoring the execution of one's plan, and evaluating the benefits and drawbacks of a previously-executed task, may generalize across tasks and domains [20]. A pre-requisite to achieving this goal in the GIFT framework is to develop the ability to conceptualize and build domain-independent structures for representing metacognitive strategies and processes.

2.1 Measuring Strategy Understanding

Measuring students' understanding of strategies by observing their behavior in real time is a difficult task; it requires determining whether their behaviors are consistent with a strategy. For small tasks the interpretation is straightforward. For example, to assess a student's understanding of an algebraic problem-solving strategy, a learning environment can present multiple problems and observe the steps that a student takes to solve these problems. If the student carries out a sequence of steps that matches the steps prescribed by the strategy, the learning environment can assume that the student understands the strategy. This approach is employed in many step-based intelligent tutoring systems such as Cognitive Tutors [18, 21, 22].

However, for complex tasks, interpretation is more difficult. For example, open-ended learning environments (OELEs; [6, 7]) present students with a learning context and a set of tools for exploring and building solutions to problems. Students are expected to use the environment's resources to learn needed information, construct and test solutions, and manage their own learning and problem solving processes. Succeeding in these tasks involves breaking up the overall task into sub-tasks, setting goals, and applying strategies for completing each sub-task. Thus, learning environments need methods for inferring: (1) the student's chosen task decomposition; (2) the sub-task the student is currently working on; (3) the strategy they are using to complete that sub-task; and (4) whether or not they are executing the strategy correctly. The open-ended nature of OELEs further exacerbates the measurement problem; a student may constantly change her chosen task decomposition, the task she is working on, or the strategies she is utilizing, and the analysis technique must be able to detect these changes. Moreover, incomplete or incorrect metacognitive knowledge may lead the student to employ suboptimal strategies, and detecting and properly interpreting these sub-optimal strategies presents additional analysis challenges.

Researchers have approached this problem from multiple angles. For example, *MetaTutor* [19] adopts a very direct approach with some similarities to self-report; it provides interface features through which students explicitly state the tasks they are working on (called sub-goals) and the strategies they are using to complete those tasks. For example, students can use the interface to indicate that they would like to create a sub-goal or employ a specific learning strategy. This allows the system to directly capture students' strategy use without having to make inferences based solely on their activities in the system. However, this relies on students' accurately communicating their intent to the system.

Another approach avoids measuring specific task decompositions, goals, and strategies entirely and instead defines a *model of desired performance* [23] describing desirable and productive qualities of students' problem-solving behaviors. If students' behaviors conform to this model, then they are assumed to understand effective strategies for solving the problem. For example, previous research with *Betty's Brain* [24] used an approach called *coherence analysis* (CA) [7] to estimate students' strategy understanding. In *Betty's Brain*, students learn about a science topic by reading about it and constructing a causal model that represents the topic as a set of entities connected by directed links.

Instead of measuring students' uses of specific strategies, CA identifies logical relationships in students' behaviors as they view sources of information (typically hypertext pages) and apply the information acquired to constructing and refining their causal models. The model of desired performance underlying CA is as follows: (1) when students encounter information that could help them add to or refine their causal models, they should act on that information by making the indicated changes to their model; and (2) students should not rely on guessing to change their causal model, so changes should usually be motivated by information encountered in the environment (*i.e.*, their model edits should be *supported* by previously-viewed information). Behavior that adheres to these two properties is said to be *coherent*, and the assumption is that as long as students' behaviors are coherent, they understand effective strategies for accomplishing the task.

The CA approach is attractive because it simplifies the analysis and interpretation tasks. The proposed hypothesis is that as long as students' actions are coherent, they are demonstrating an understanding of the task and a set of effective strategies for completing it. It also allows flexibility in interpretation: students can develop behaviors (presumably linked to strategies) that work best for them as long as these behaviors lead to coherent behavior. However, the challenge of applying CA is that observing non-coherent behavior provides little information regarding the *reasons* behind the non-coherence. Students exhibiting non-coherent behavior may be struggling with task decomposition, sub-task selection (*i.e.*, choosing the next sub-task to work on), strategy selection (*i.e.*, choosing a strategy for completing a task), or strategy execution. Alternatively, they may lack domain knowledge understanding that is critical for systematically solving the problem. Thus, the learning environment must rely on (or gather) additional information in order to support students who are struggling.

2.2 Supporting Strategy Understanding

If a learning environment determines that a student does not understand a specific strategy, then it may take steps to support the student in learning about that strategy. This can involve teaching students declarative, procedural, and conditional knowledge about the strategy [9]. Several effective approaches for *strategy instruction* (*i.e.*, directly instructing students on particular strategies) have been developed and tested by researchers (*e.g.*, [25]). These include: (1) providing students with worked examples of the strategy applied to a concrete task (*e.g.*, [26]); (2) engaging students in guided strategy practice with feedback (*e.g.*, [27]); and (3) holding conversations with the student that explain the strategy, its purpose, when it should be used, and its value in helping the student (*e.g.* [28]). These conversations are often contextualized by the student's current learning task and their recent activities in the learning environment.

In developing metacognitive tutoring for GIFT, we seek to leverage this wealth of previous research and incorporate it into GIFT. Our design, presented in the next section, takes advantage of coherence analysis, contextualized conversational feedback, and strategy instruction through guided practice. When students perform sequences of non-coherent or otherwise suboptimal behaviors, our approach employs contextualized conversational assessment to probe the student's metacognitive knowledge further.

When appropriate, these conversations also include feedback of the types (1)-(3) discussed above. The goals are to: (1) more accurately identify the source of students' errors so that we can (2) provide tailored instruction on the strategies (either cognitive or metacognitive) that they are struggling with. Toward this end, we are developing a strategy monitoring approach that will allow GIFT to analyze students' learning behaviors according to an understanding of how strategies are executed. The next section describes our design approach in detail.

3 Designing Metacognitive Tutoring in GIFT

3.1 Representations and Learner Modeling

To represent metacognition in GIFT, we will extend its current learner modeling capabilities. In GIFT, a learner model consists of a set of named *concepts* that are assessed continually while students are interacting with designated course materials. At any time, each concept may be assessed as being below, at, or above expectation, and higher level concepts may be related hierarchically to lower level concepts. Thus, a *basic mathematics* concept may be based on assessments of its component concepts: *addition*, *subtraction*, *multiplication*, and *division*. The data representation is similar to the sampling of a stream: GIFT monitors each student's task performance over time, updating the concept assessments based on his or her most recent performance. Thus, a student may perform above expectation on one addition problem and below expectation on the next. A history of these assessments is maintained for feedback purposes, both during and after learning.

Building from this, we will employ a three-level framework for analyzing and representing students' skill and strategy proficiency, shown in Fig. 1. Analyses will involve making a set of inferences based on students' observed behaviors while using the learning environment. In this framework, direct observations of students' behaviors will serve as assessments of their ability to correctly execute strategies. To accomplish this, we will design tools that allow learning environment designers to specify how actions can be combined to enact a strategy. The resulting strategy model can be used online to interpret students' action sequences in terms of these strategies. The strategy that best matches students' behaviors will be assumed to be the strategy they are applying, and further assessments will examine whether or not they execute the strategy correctly. For example, a student may be using a monitoring strategy in which they check their recently-completed work to make sure it is correct. However, they may erroneously conclude that their work was completed correctly, indicating an ineffective execution of the strategy.

These assessments and interactions, along with continued monitoring of student behavior, will serve as the basis for assessing students' understanding of domain-specific strategies. When GIFT observes a correctly-executed strategy, it will increase its confidence in the student's understanding of the associated procedural knowledge. Similarly, when GIFT observes a strategy executed at an appropriate time, it will increase its confidence in the student's understanding of the associated conditional

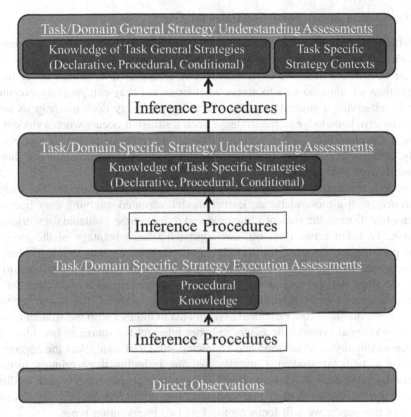

Fig. 1. Metacognitive learner modeling approach

knowledge. To test students' declarative knowledge, GIFT will interact with them directly and ask them questions testing their understanding.

The final level of our framework involves linking students' understanding of task-specific strategies to task-general representations of those strategies. An important aspect of metacognition is that the declarative form of a number of strategies can be expressed in a domain-general form. In other words, many strategies can be applied to multiple tasks, situations, and contexts. Our approach leverages this property by developing new GIFT capabilities for tracking and supporting task-general strategies in multiple contexts. When a student correctly employs a task-specific strategy, GIFT will link this use of the strategy to its task-general representation and the context in which the strategy was applied. This information will be stored in GIFT's long-term learner model and can be referenced during future learning sessions with GIFT. The goal is to integrate information about a student's use of strategies across multiple formats and contexts. This will allow GIFT to provide instruction and guidance that draws connections between a learner's current learning tasks and their previous experiences. For example, GIFT may guide the student through an analogy: *"This task is just like when you had to do [X] in [ENV] back in [MONTH]. The main difference is [Y]"*.

3.2   Developing Instructional Strategies for GIFT

Even with the learner modeling and assessment approach described above, it is difficult to form a complete and accurate model of students' understanding of strategies while using an open-ended learning environment. For example, if a student never uses a strategy, then we have no data to assess whether or not they can properly execute it. Similarly, observing a student correctly executing a strategy does not help us assess their declarative knowledge of the strategy. Such a situation occurs when a student can "*do* but not *explain*" [29]. Thus, accurately modeling students in OELEs may require directly interacting with them in order to obtain additional information not directly revealed through their actions.

However, this interaction represents a trade-off. While it provides the learning environment with a more elaborate learner model, repeated querying may become a distractor that disrupts the student's attention and reduces time available for working on their task. To balance this trade-off, our approach takes advantage of the model of desired performance discussed in Sect. 2.1. For example, we may employ coherence analysis as was done in *Betty's Brain*. As long as a student's behavior conforms to our model, we allow her to proceed and desist from intervening until such time that her behavior becomes clearly suboptimal or non-coherent. At such times, our approach employs contextualized conversational assessments to interact with the student in order to collect additional evidence necessary to better interpret the source of her difficulties.

Once a difficulty is understood and characterized, GIFT can select the appropriate instruction to help the student. Currently, we are designing three primary forms of instructional interventions: contextualized conversational assessments and feedback; reviewing knowledge and strategies; and teaching through analogies (as discussed earlier). In this paper, we will focus on the first two intervention types.

Strategy 1: Collect Evidence through Contextualized Conversational Assessments
When GIFT observes that the student has performed sub-optimal or non-coherent behaviors, it may use its current learner model to generate multiple potential reasons linked to lack of domain and/or strategy knowledge for explaining the student's performance. For example, the student may not have been aware of important details in the environment (perhaps indicating the use of a poor strategy for analyzing the task). Alternatively, she may have been unsure of how to apply the important details she encountered (indicating poor strategy knowledge). Still another possibility is that she understands that the information is important, knows what strategy to use, but makes mistakes when executing the strategy.

To properly assess this student's strategy understanding, GIFT needs to interact with her using conversational assessments. For example, GIFT may decide to ask her about important details in the environment, awareness of which is needed to succeed in her current task(s). GIFT may also choose to probe her understanding of how identified information may be used to perform a chosen task. The student's answers to these questions can provide a better understanding of what she knows and which tasks, strategies, and environmental conditions are causing her trouble.

In holding these conversations with students, GIFT can embed contextualized instructional guidance for the student. For example, the following is a short excerpt of a conversation we envision taking place between GIFT and a student learning about counter-insurgency using UrbanSim, a counter-insurgency command simulation:

GIFT: Uh oh. Take a look at this report. It looks like insurgents took out a gas station in the southwestern section of the city in our area of operation. What is your assessment?

STUDENT: This is bad. We should rebuild it ASAP and then commit forces to protecting it!

GIFT: Why do you think it is such a high priority? What effect will the loss of this gas station have on our operations?

STUDENT: Without this gas station, the local population will struggle to travel throughout the area, prepare their food, and control the temperature of their homes.

GIFT: Agreed. Where will you pull resources from to accomplish this?

STUDENT: I'll recommit the engineering squad from bridge building to repairing the gas station, and I will pull some troops from the central square to provide the protective cover. The central square is pretty secure right now so I do not think that the loss of protection will involve much risk.

GIFT: I have another idea. Did you know there was another gas station in the area?

STUDENT: No, I didn't! Where is it?

GIFT: It is in the north-east. It is actually well supplied and in a less hostile area. If we commit forces to protecting that gas station, we will not have to commit funds to rebuilding the other station and we can continue building the bridge, which will open up a key supply route. This will allow us to meet gasoline demands for the area with the other gas station while continuing to make progress toward improving living conditions for the locals. If we rebuild the gas station, the same insurgents that destroyed it the first time might destroy it a second time; this may bolster their confidence.

STUDENT: That makes a lot of sense! I will follow that, and thanks for the help.

In this conversation, GIFT combines assessment with explanation and instruction. In the first three exchanges, GIFT collects information in order to better understand the student's awareness of critical information and ability to make trade-offs in the counter-insurgency scenario. Once it has collected this information, it presents and justifies an alternative approach to the student based on specific strategies (*e.g.*, gain control of an area before rebuilding its infrastructure and commit resources where there is greatest added benefit). Through these conversations, students will hopefully come to understand the cognitive and metacognitive processes important for success in their learning task. For some students, instruction through conversational assessment and feedback should be sufficient to aid their learning and consequently improve their problem solving behaviors. However, other students may continue to participate in conversational assessments, receive contextualized feedback, but show little improvement on their task performance. For these students, additional, more targeted instruction may be required.

Strategy 2: Review Knowledge and Strategies
As GIFT collects evidence about students' understanding of various strategies, it may determine that a student has continued to struggle with understanding tasks and strategies for completing those tasks despite conversational assessment and feedback. When this happens, GIFT will transition the learner from their current task into a more

targeted training environment. For example, if the student seems to have forgotten key background or pre-requisite information, GIFT may decide that she needs to review a PowerPoint presentation and correctly answer questions about the material she has reviewed before she can come back to work on her primary tasks in the problem scenario. If she seems unaware of an important strategy, GIFT can place the student into a guided-practice environment to instruct her on the use of the strategy [14, 28]. This can help develop and confirm the student's declarative, procedural, and conditional knowledge by practicing the strategy and correctly answering questions about the strategy. The idea here is that a complex open-ended task requires a basic understanding of several different concepts and strategies. If a student does not have this understanding, she may not profit much from attempting to complete the complex tasks. Therefore, it is prudent to help her overcome her lack of understanding in-the-moment, because this can improve both current and future performance.

Another important aspect of this approach is that a student's difficulties in her primary task can serve as motivation to learn needed information. It is possible that the student would not be engaged in relevant PowerPoint slides until she realized the importance of the information for being able to succeed in the primary task. Thus, we would like GIFT to draw explicit connections between the student's experiences in an environment like UrbanSim and the remediation she is about to experience. For example, GIFT might say "*I would like you to take a break from UrbanSim and focus on learning strategies for maintaining situational awareness. This will help you better understand how to manage the large amount of information that is available in this learning environment, and it will help you have more success in defeating the insurgents*".

4   Discussion and Conclusions

In this paper, we have presented the design of our approach to incorporating meta-cognitive instruction in the Generalized Intelligent Framework for Tutoring (GIFT). Our approach focuses on modeling students according to their understanding and use of strategies for completing tasks. Such strategy understanding is a critical aspect of students' metacognitive knowledge, and students who utilize good strategies have been shown to perform better in learning and problem solving tasks ([18]).

In addition to modeling students' understanding of strategies, our approach also helps students develop their understanding of strategies for completing their learning tasks in open-ended learning environments. We plan to utilize contextualized conversations for assessment and feedback and strategy instruction through guided practice with feedback. Further, we plan to extend these approaches by incorporating students' prior experiences in the GIFT platform into conversations. The goal is to use these prior experiences to help provide instruction in the current task through analogies, as described briefly in Sect. 2.2. We believe that incorporating these approaches into GIFT will allow for powerful instruction of complex tasks and topics.

As we implement this design into GIFT, we will develop a suite of authoring tools that allow future GIFT users to design metacognitive strategy instruction for their learning tasks and environments. We will also study the effectiveness of this approach with students from US Army training programs in order to test its usefulness and effect on students. We expect to learn many lessons from these studies, and this will help us refine our design and implementation of the GIFT Meta-tutoring environment.

References

1. Sottilare, R., Graesser, A., Hu, X., Goldberg, B. (eds.): Design Recommendations for Intelligent Tutoring Systems, vol. 2. U.S. Army Research Laboratory, Orlando (2014)
2. Sottilare, R., Graesser, A., Hu, X., Holden, H. (eds.): Design Recommendations for Intelligent Tutoring Systems, vol. 1. U.S. Army Research Laboratory, Orlando (2013)
3. Jayaprakash, S.M., Moody, E.W., Lauria, E.J.M., Regan, M.R., Baron, J.D.: Early alert of academically at-risk students: an open source analytics initiative. J. Learn. Analytics 1(1), 6–47 (2014)
4. Macfadyen, L.P., Dawson, S.: Mining LMS data to develop an "early warning system" for educators: a proof of concept. Comput. Educ. 54(2), 588–599 (2010)
5. Virtual Battlespace 3. http://www.bisimulations.com/virtual-battlespace-3. Accessed 4 March 2015
6. Land, S., Hannafin, M., Oliver, K.: Student-centered learning environments: foundations, assumptions and design. In: Jonassen, D., Land, S. (eds.) Theoretical Foundations of Learning Environments, pp. 3–25. Routledge, New York (2012)
7. Segedy, J.R., Kinnebrew, J.S., Biswas, G.: Using coherence analysis to characterize self-regulated learning behaviours in open-ended learning environments. J. Learn. Analytics (to appear)
8. Flavell, J.: Metacognitive aspects of problem solving. In: Resnick, L. (ed.) The Nature of Intelligence, pp. 231–236. Erlbaum, Hillsdale (1976)
9. Schraw, G., Crippen, K., Hartley, K.: Promoting self-regulation in science education: metacognition as part of a broader perspective on learning. Res. Sci. Educ. 36(1), 111–139 (2006)
10. Young, A., Fry, J.: Metacognitive awareness and academic achievement in college students. J. Sch. Teach. Learn. 8(2), 1–10 (2008)
11. Veenman, M.: Learning to self-monitor and self-regulate. In: Mayer, R., Alexander, P. (eds.) Handbook of Research on Learning and Instruction, pp. 197–218. Routledge, New York (2011)
12. Zimmerman, B., Schunk, D. (eds.): Handbook of Self-Regulation of Learning and Performance. Routledge, New York (2011)
13. Whitebread, D., Cárdenas, V.: Self-regulated learning and conceptual understanding in young children: the development of biological understanding. In: Zohar, A., Dori, Y.J. (eds.) Metacognition in Science Education: Trends in Current Research. Contemporary Trends and Issues in Science Education, vol. 40, pp. 101–132. Springer Science + Business Media, Netherlands (2012)
14. Roscoe, R., Segedy, J.R., Sulcer, B., Jeong, H., Biswas, G.: Shallow strategy development in a teachable agent environment designed to support self-regulated learning. Comput. Educ. 62, 286–297 (2013)
15. Veenman, M.: Assessing metacognitive skills in computerized learning environments. In: Azevedo, R., Aleven, V. (eds.) International Handbook of Metacognition and Learning Technologies. Springer International Handbooks of Education, vol. 26, pp. 157–168. Springer Science + Business Media, New York (2013)

16. Pressley, M., Goodchild, F., Fleet, J., Zajchowski, R., Evansi, E.: The challenges of classroom strategy instruction. Elementary Sch. J. **89**, 301–342 (1989)
17. Donker, A., de Boer, H., Kostons, D., Dignath van Ewijk, C., van der Werf, M.: Effectiveness of learning strategy instruction on academic performance: a meta-analysis. Educ. Res. Rev. **11**, 1–26 (2014)
18. Zhang, L., VanLehn, K., Girard, S., Burleson, W., Chavez-Echeagaray, M.E., Gonzalex-Sanchez, J., Hidalgo-Pontet, Y.: Evaluation of a meta-tutor for constructing models of dynamic systems. Comput. Educ. **75**, 196–217 (2014)
19. Bouchet, F., Harley, J., Trevors, G., Azevedo, R.: Clustering and profiling students according to their interactions with an intelligent tutoring system fostering self-regulated learning. J. Educ. Data Min. **5**(1), 104–146 (2013)
20. Bransford, J., Schwartz, D.: Rethinking transfer: a simple proposal with multiple implications. Rev. Res. Educ. **24**(1), 61–101 (1999)
21. VanLehn, K.: The behavior of tutoring systems. Int. J. Artif. Intell. Educ. **16**(3), 227–265 (2006)
22. Aleven, V., McLaren, B., Roll, I., Koedinger, K.: Toward meta-cognitive tutoring: a model of help seeking with a cognitive tutor. Int. J. Artif. Intell. Educ. **16**(2), 101–128 (2006)
23. Mathan, S.A., Koedinger, K.R.: Fostering the intelligent novice: learning from errors with metacognitive tutoring. Educ. Psychol. **40**(4), 257–265 (2005)
24. Leelawong, K., Biswas, G.: Designing learning by teaching agents: the Betty's brain system. Int. J. Artif. Intell. Educ. **18**(3), 181–208 (2008)
25. Graham, S., Harris, K.R., Mason, L.: Improving the writing performance, knowledge, and self-efficacy of struggling young writers: the effects of self-regulated strategy development. Contemp. Educ. Psychol. **30**, 207–241 (2005)
26. Muldner, K., Conati, C.: Scaffolding meta-cognitive skills for effective analogical problem solving via tailored example selection. Int. J. Artif. Intell. Educ. **20**, 99–136 (2010)
27. Roscoe, R.D., Brandon, R.D., Snow, E.L., McNamara, D.S.: Game-based writing strategy practice with the writing pal. In: Pytash, K.E., Ferdig, R.E. (eds.) Exploring Technology for Writing and Writing Instruction, pp. 1–20. Information Science Reference, Hershey (2013)
28. Segedy, J.R., Kinnebrew, J.S., Biswas, G.: The effect of contextualized conversational feedback in a complex open-ended learning environment. Educ. Technol. Res. Dev. **61**(1), 71–89 (2013)
29. Koedinger, K., Corbett, A., Perfetti, C.: The knowledge-learning-instruction framework: bridging the science-practice chasm to enhance robust student learning. Cogn. Sci. **36**, 757–798 (2012)

A Personalized GIFT: Recommendations for Authoring Personalization in the Generalized Intelligent Framework for Tutoring

Anne M. Sinatra[⊠]

U.S. Army Research Laboratory, Simulation and Training Technology Center,
Orlando, FL, USA
anne.m.sinatra.civ@mail.mil

Abstract. Personalization of learning content can have a positive impact on learning in a computer based environment. Personalization can occur in a number of different ways, such as including an individual's name or entered content throughout the learning materials, or selecting examples based on self-reported preferences. The Generalized Intelligent Framework for Tutoring (GIFT) is an open-source, domain independent intelligent tutoring system framework. GIFT includes a number of different authoring tools (e.g., GIFT Authoring Tool, Survey Authoring System) that can be used to generate adaptive courses. In its current form, GIFT does not have specific mechanisms to support personalization of materials to the individual user based on pre-entered preferences. The current paper describes ways that personalization research has previously been conducted with GIFT. The paper additionally provides recommendations on new features that could be added to GIFT's authoring tools in order to support personalizing learning materials, guidance, and surveys that are provided to the learner.

1 Introduction

Personalization is an instructional strategy that has been shown to have a positive impact on an individual's learning. Depending on the area of research, the term personalization can have different meanings. In some cases, personalization refers to the ability for an adaptive tutor to store information about an individual's skill level or current performance and adapt the level of difficulty of future materials accordingly. However, for the purposes of the current paper, the type of personalization that is being discussed is defined as including information that is important or interesting to an individual learner within the learning materials that they are presented with. Research into this type of personalization has roots in cognitive psychology research in regard to the self-reference effect, as well as in educational psychology research in the area of context personalization [1, 2]. Research into the self-reference effect has consistently shown that if an individual links material to themselves it is easier for them to recall than if it is linked to something unrelated to them [3]. Similarly, there have been positive effects that have been found from linking information to people that the learner knows, or information that is important to them. This concept has been additionally

© Springer International Publishing Switzerland 2015
D.D. Schmorrow and C.M. Fidopiastis (Eds.): AC 2015, LNAI 9183, pp. 675–682, 2015.
DOI: 10.1007/978-3-319-20816-9_64

applied in research that personalizes the context of the materials to be learned to topics that are of interest to the individual. There has been research that suggests that this tailoring of topics can have a positive impact on the retention of the material [4, 5].

2 Personalization as an Instructional Strategy

The impact of personalization as an instructional strategy has been studied in both the classroom [4–6] and computer-based learning environments [7, 8]. While these studies have found fairly consistent results, the strategies they used for collection of information from the students has varied. Further, the way that the materials were personalized in response to the student provided information has also differed. In some cases, materials were adjusted to the most popular items provided by students in the class, as opposed to being unique to the individual [6]. In other cases, personalization and utilization of the self-reference effect was done by phrasing materials generally to include the word "you" and make reference to the self, with the goal of prompting the individual to think of themselves in relationship to the material to be learned [8]. Other studies have included the student-entered information directly in the individual student's learning material and questions to examine its impact on the learning outcomes [7, 9]. The mechanism by which the benefits are provided has not been entirely agreed upon in the literature. It has been hypothesized that personalization takes advantage of the self-reference effect, and the links to the self [8, 9]. Consistent with this hypothesis, this self-reference and interest is lowering the cognitive workload needed to interpret the information, making it easier and more efficient for the individual to learn. Additionally, it has been hypothesized that there may be affect-related benefits to personalization that result from the system taking an interest in the individual, and that the student feels that his or her preferences have been acknowledged [10].

It has been found that there are advantages to changing the context of learned materials to be consistent with individual college majors and that there are better learning outcomes when the examples match the major. Specifically, when nursing students were taught using medical examples (as opposed to education examples) they performed better on achievement measures; conversely, when education students were taught using education examples they performed better on the same tasks [4, 5]. In regard to computer adaptation, Anand and Ross [7] designed a computer program which asked individuals questions such as their names, the names of their friends, their favorite foods, and favorite interests. After entering this information into the program it modified the specific learning materials and questions for the students' interactions. They found that the individuals who received the personalized information performed better than those who did not.

Recent research, has examined the role of personalization in adaptive tutoring systems. Carnegie Learning's MATHia software has begun to examine the impact of providing questions to students that were personalized based on their interest selections [10]. Research has also suggested that by adapting the contexts of math instruction in adaptive systems there are positive learning outcomes [2].

In many studies of personalization, benefits have not been found in all types of assessments that have been given to students. Evaluations regarding a direct interpretation of the learned material, or simple multiple choice questions may not always yield significant differences between personalized and non-personalized instruction. However, it has been consistently found that personalization provides benefits over non-personalization in regard to evaluating transfer performance [2, 8]. This is particularly important, as it is shows that personalization is leading to a deeper understanding of the material by the individual student which results in being able to apply it in new situations. This deeper learning is beneficial as it leads to long term gains and understanding in both similar domains and related tasks [11].

3 The Generalized Intelligent Framework for Tutoring (GIFT) and Personalization

The Generalized Intelligent Framework for Tutoring (GIFT) has been utilized to conduct research into the impact of name personalization on learning in a computer-based environment [9, 12]. GIFT is an open-source domain-independent intelligent tutoring system (ITS) framework [13]. It allows individuals to create their own ITSs, which can include customized surveys, and integration with training applications such as PowerPoint, Virtual Battlespace, or TC3 Sim, which can display interactive materials. GIFT is very useful for different types of users including students, authors/instructors who are designing ITSs, and researchers who are conducting studies.

There are several authoring tools available in the GIFT system to support the creation of courses. Among the relevant tools for experimentation are the Survey Authoring System (SAS), Course Authoring Tool (CAT), Domain Knowledge File Authoring Tool (DAT), and GIFT Authoring Tool (GAT). There are additional tools which allow for further adaptation and options that can be selected when designing experiments or building an ITS.

The tools can be accessed by GIFT authors in the control panel interface, which can be seen in Fig. 1.

In the current configuration of tools, there is the potential to personalize material to the individual user, however much of that personalization is required to be programmed separately into a training application (e.g., PowerPoint). Included in this paper are recommendations for new functionalities or additions that can be made to the current tools which would open up the possibility of personalization. These changes can give instructors and researchers options to provide personalized materials within the adaptive tutor.

3.1 Personalization Research Conducted with GIFT

In the personalization study conducted with GIFT [9, 12], the impact of using different names on tutorial retention and transfer performance was examined. In the first, or self-reference condition, the participant entered his or her own name and the names of

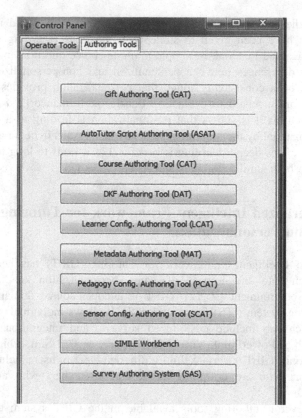

Fig. 1. GIFT's authoring tools control panel (version 2014-3X)

friends. This condition was designed to encourage the individual to relate the learned information to themselves. In the second, or popular culture condition, the names of characters from the *Harry Potter* book series were included in the learning materials to encourage the learner to link the familiar series to the material, which could potentially make the learned information easier to retrieve in a similar way as self-reference. Finally, in a baseline/generic condition, names that were not expected to have meaning to the individuals were included. These names were included as part of the materials that individuals were tutored with as they engaged in a computer-based logic grid puzzle tutorial, which teaches the skill of deductive reasoning. Logic grid puzzles present the learner with a vignette, a series of clues, and a grid. Using the information provided, the learner needs to use both the process of elimination and the clues to determine specific answers/items that go together. The logic grid puzzle tutorial taught learners to successfully complete the puzzles. During the tutorial the names were personalized in the vignette, clues, and grid. An example of the name personalization can be seen in Figs. 2 and 3. Figure 2 demonstrates the popular culture condition, and Fig. 3 demonstrates the baseline/generic condition. Note the differences in the names present throughout the clues and the grid.

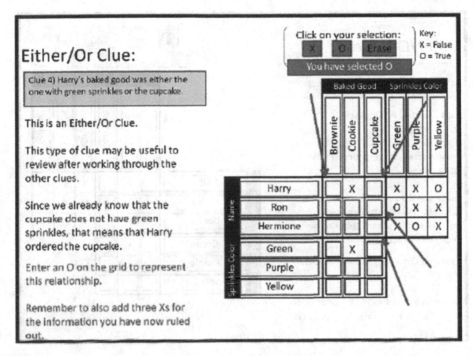

Fig. 2. Screenshot of the logic puzzle tutorial's popular culture condition's personalization

An example of the Logic Puzzle Tutorial baseline condition can be found in the downloadable versions of GIFT, which are available from www.gifttutoring.org. The impact of these materials on student information retention, ability to apply learned knowledge, and ability to transfer performance to a more difficult puzzle were examined.

The tutorial itself was developed in PowerPoint using Visual Basic for Applications (VBA) and the personalization was handled by having participants enter their names into a dialogue box in PowerPoint, which were then stored as a variable in PowerPoint, and inserted into the text of the materials during the tutorial. This entire personalization process was handled in PowerPoint/VBA. While this strategy allowed for personalization research to be conducted with GIFT and could be used in the future to personalize materials based on names or interests, there are features of GIFT that could be further adapted in order to provide more personalization options.

3.2 Recommendations for Providing Personalization Flexibility in GIFT's Authoring Tools

As of GIFT 2014-3X, there are two ways to login to the GIFT software. An individual can login through their gifttutoring.org website account, or use a created system username (simple login) that is local to their computer. In both cases, the system is storing a name for the individual learner. While this name can later be output in log files, it

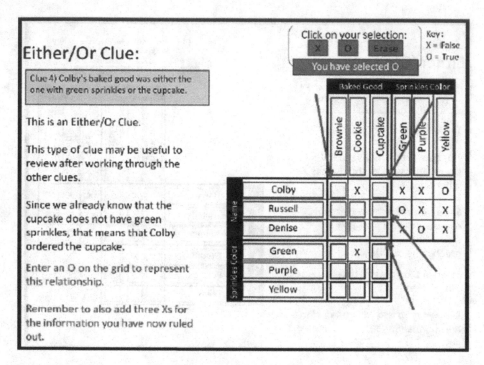

Fig. 3. Screenshot of the logic puzzle tutorial's baseline/generic condition's personalization. Note the difference in the names present in the puzzle and clues in the two versions.

could be useful for the author to have the option of using the individual's name within the training course.

The author creates guidance and messages that are displayed to the learner using either the CAT or GAT. Additionally, they create survey questions and surveys that will be displayed to the user using the SAS. In the case of the guidance and messages, authors are provided with a blank text box in which they can enter the desired text that will be displayed. It would be very helpful if the author had the ability to access the variable of the user's name and have it display within the provided text. This could be done in a similar way as would be required within PowerPoint with VBA. For instance the author could type: "Welcome to the Tutorial, [name]", which could then pull in the stored information about the learner's name, and display it when they see the given information screen (e.g., "Welcome to the Tutorial, Harry"). An additional way to allow authors to interact with this feature would be to include a "name" button next to the font size options with the text editor that can be clicked to enter in the name within the text. A similar method could be integrated within the SAS in order to allow the author to include the individual's names in the directions or directly in the questions when they create surveys. This would give GIFT course authors the ability to directly address the student within the materials, or examine the impact of doing so in research experiments.

It would also be beneficial to provide the author the ability to present surveys to the learner to gather information about their interests. Once these surveys are answered the entered information can be stored by GIFT and later brought into authored questions. This would be a similar method as to the name storage, but could allow the author to create open entry textbox questions that will be presented to the learner, with the answers stored in specified variable names. The defined and stored variable names could then be entered into the guidance in the CAT/GAT and questions in the SAS to provide personalized information and questions. For example the question might be, "[name] and Ron were watching their favorite TV show, [tvshow]. The special episode of the show was 65 min long instead of 44. How many additional minutes were in the show?" The customized version of this question might display as "Harry and Ron were watching their favorite TV show, Once Upon a Time..." There would also need to be an option for the author to provide a default value in the case that the individual decides to skip the question that would write into the variable.

A personalization tool could be designed that would allow the user to write specific questions that would save to specific variables that will later be able to be read into the text. Additionally, the tool would need to provide the author the ability to define the variable names that are to be saved. Rather than creating a whole new tool, this could potentially become a feature of the current SAS that would allow for the creation of specific personalization based surveys.

While name and specific interest personalization in GIFT would be beneficial, there is also the potential for an author creating a set of similar assessment questions that are edited to be in different contexts. For instance, the learner can be asked if he or she is interested in movies, sports, or music. Based on what the learner selects, a specific question will be provided to them which is tailored toward the topic of the interest area. For instance, in one version of the question the text may be about buying tickets to a film. In the second version it might be about buying tickets to a baseball game, and in the third version it might be about buying tickets to a concert. This type of personalization may be able to be achieved through edits to the SAS that would allow for linking questions that are similar together and selecting the one that is appropriate for the student's preferences.

4 Conclusion

The above recommendations and ideas would provide more flexibility in authoring personalized content and questions in GIFT. Personalization has been shown to have a positive impact on learning retention, particularly in the case of transfer performance. Additionally, by personalizing material to the interests of an individual it may result in them having more positive feelings toward the tutoring system. It would be beneficial to create a personalization authoring tool in GIFT, or to make edits to GIFT's existing authoring tools that would provide more opportunities to personalize materials. By providing these options to GIFT authors it will allow for future personalization experimentation, and for the design of courses that include name and context personalization.

References

1. Cordova, D.I., Lepper, M.R.: Intrinsic motivation and the process of learning: beneficial effects of contextualization, personalization, and choice. J. Educ. Psychol. **88**(4), 715–730 (1996)
2. Walkington, C.A.: Using adaptive learning technologies to personalize instruction to student interests: the impact of relevant contexts on performance learning outcomes. J. Educ. Psychol. **105**(4), 932–945 (2013)
3. Symons, C.S., Johnson, B.T.: The self-reference effect in memory: a meta-analysis. Psychol. Bull. **121**(3), 371–394 (1997)
4. Ross, S.M.: Increasing the meaningfulness of quantitative material by adapting context to student background. J. Educ. Psychol. **75**(4), 519–529 (1983)
5. Ross, S.M., McCormick, D., Krisak, N.: Adapting the thematic context of mathematical problems to student interests: individualized versus group-based strategies. J. Educ. Res. **79**, 245–252 (1986)
6. Ku, H.Y., Sullivan, H.J.: Student performance and attitudes using personalized mathematics instruction. Educ. Tech. Res. Dev. **50**(1), 21–34 (2002)
7. Anand, P.G., Ross, S.M.: Using computer-assisted instruction to personalize arithmetic for elementary school children. J. Educ. Psychol. **79**(1), 72–78 (1987)
8. Moreno, R., Mayer, R.E.: Engaging students in active learning: the case for personalized multimedia messages. J. Educ. Psychol. **92**(4), 724–733 (2000)
9. Sinatra, A.M., Sims, V.K., Sottilare, R.A.: The Impact of Need for Cognition and Self-Reference on Tutoring a Deductive Reasoning Skill. Technical Report (No. ARL-TR-6961), Army Research Laboratory (2014)
10. Ritter, S., Sinatra, A.M., Fancsali, S.E.: Personalized content in intelligent tutoring systems. In: Design Recommendations for Intelligent Tutoring Systems, pp. 71–78. US Army Research Laboratory, Orlando (2014)
11. Chow, B.: The quest for deeper learning. Education Week (2010). http://www.edweek.org/ew/articles/2010/10/06/06chow_ep.h30.html?qs=Chow
12. Sinatra, A.M.: Using GIFT to support an empirical study on the impact of the self-reference effect on learning. In: AIED 2013 Workshops Proceedings, vol. 7, pp. 80–87 (2013)
13. Sottilare, R.A., Brawner, K.W., Goldberg, B.S., Holden, H.K.: The generalized intelligent framework for tutoring (GIFT) (2012). https://gifttutoring.org/documents/31

Augmented Cognition on the Run: Considerations for the Design and Authoring of Mobile Tutoring Systems

Robert A. Sottilare(⊠)

U.S. Army Research Laboratory, Adelphi, USA
robert.a.sottilare.civ@mail.mil

Abstract. This paper discusses considerations for design and authoring of mobile intelligent tutoring system (ITSs). ITSs are on the rise as tools for desktop tutoring of cognitive tasks (e.g., problem solving and decision making). To become truly ubiquitous, ITSs will be required to leave the desktop and support interactive, adaptive instruction on-the-move via mobile devices. We examined the capabilities of Google Glass as a potential hands-free platform to support mobile tutoring and found many of the functions serviceable as proxies to desktop tutoring functions. The potential of mobile platforms like Google Glass integrated with the Generalized Intelligent Framework for Tutoring (GIFT) provides a practical example on which to discuss limitations and project future capabilities for mobile tutoring.

Keywords: Intelligent tutoring systems · Mobile learning · Distributed learning · Mobile tutoring

1 Introduction

Today, Intelligent Tutoring Systems (ITSs) are generally authored to support desktop training applications with the most common domains being mathematics and physics. In recent years, implementations of ITSs using the Generalized Intelligent Framework for Tutoring (GIFT) [1, 2] have demonstrated adaptive tutoring techniques, strategies, and tactics for desktop training domains, but many training tasks require adaptive instruction beyond the desktop to be compatible with their physical nature [3]. This paper evaluates the interactions and capabilities needed to realize the design and authoring capabilities needed to support mobile tutoring.

Opportunities to expand the capabilities of ITSs may rest beyond the desktop. Commercial products such as Google Glass offer a glimpse of possible trends in adaptive real-time tutoring beyond the desktop. This paper will evaluate how elements of commercial products like Google Glass might be used to support *mobile adaptive tutoring* also known as *tutoring on the run* or *tutoring in the wild*. What we are talking about are tasks that are largely psychomotor tasks in Bloom's taxonomy [4, 5], but may have elements that are cognitive [6], affective [7] and/or social [8]. Examples of psychomotor tasks include most sports in which the learner trains over time to the point of automaticity. The learner must take in information about changing and static

© Springer International Publishing Switzerland 2015
D.D. Schmorrow and C.M. Fidopiastis (Eds.): AC 2015, LNAI 9183, pp. 683–689, 2015.
DOI: 10.1007/978-3-319-20816-9_65

elements in the training or operational environment, quickly make decisions, and then take appropriate action(s). In orienteering, the navigator comes to an area with specific features, analyzes where they might be in the running course, and then determines the best option/direction to reach the next mark in the least amount of time. This part of the task is primarily cognitive and could be trained in a game-based environment. The part of this task which requires physical exertion, stamina, and decision making while under stress cannot always be duplicated in a virtual environment. In American football, the quarterback comes to the line of scrimmage, analyzes the defense, and then determines the best play to take advantage of the situation. The of this task which cannot be duplicated in a game-based or virtual environment is the pressure of the defense, the physical exertion of running multiple plays, and the need to release the ball before the receiver reaches the reception point on the field, and to accurately place the ball where only the receiver can catch it. Finally, presence [9, 10] plays a large part in immersion, engagement learning in real-world physical spaces and are difficult to replicate in virtual environments or computer games.

Discussions will be presented in this paper relative to the capabilities and limitations of the Google Glass technology to support mobile tutoring, as well as recommendations for future capabilities. Google Glass (Fig. 1) will be analyzed specifically with respect to its capability to support a group orienteering task. Google Glass is commercial product that provides interactive exchange of information (e.g., text, alerts, and weather reports) and media (pictures, videos, and livestreaming) via WiFi or cellular phone network.

Fig. 1. Google glass product (left [11]) and capabilities (right [12])

Domain modeling will be introduced as a topic of discussion to project how Google Glass optimally supports the training of tasks in the cognitive, psychomotor, affective, and social/cultural domains. Three dimensions will be evaluated, compared and contrasted with desktop tutoring as it exists today on the desktop. The domain modeling dimensions include: task dynamics, task definition and task complexity as shown below in Fig. 1.

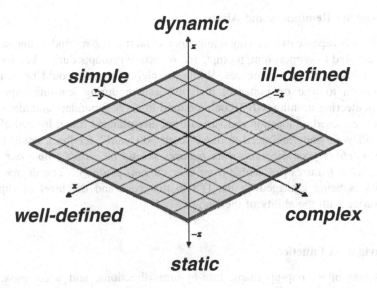

Fig. 2. Representative dimensions of training domains

For our purposes, we have defined the dimensional dichotomics in Fig. 2 as follows:

- Simple tasks – tasks with relatively few steps and generally linear navigation of concepts from beginning to end (e.g., how to apply a tourniquet)
- Complex tasks – task with many steps and substantial branching and parallel processes from beginning to end (e.g., how to evaluate the mental health of an employee)
- Well-defined tasks – tasks with clear measures of success with generally one or few correct paths to success (e.g., how to calculate the area of a circle)
- Ill-defined tasks – tasks without clear measures of success which may have a variety of paths to success (e.g., how to lead a team)

2   Using Google Glass to Support a Psychomotor Task

Google Glass allows users to conduct hands-free interaction across five general functions. While their commercial value is in doubt [11], and their application as a augmented cognition (job aid) or entertainment platform may be more clear [12], their applicability to mobile tutoring tasks and specifically the group orienteering task are just being imagined. Since orienteering is a physical activity, the dynamic aspect of this training task is considered high across the board. The task complexity and definition might be manipulated by the ITS based on the competency of the learner.

2.1 Receiving Reminders and Alerts

Google Glass is capable of receiving reminders and alerts. The reminder function could easily be adapted to support hint, prompt, and reflective prompts during key sequences in adaptive instructional experiences. While the alerts function could be adapted to bring attention to bear on issues of high importance during learning experiences. During orienteering training, GIFT could be used to drive reminders and alerts during key sequences based on location and variance for any planned route. Instead of saying "you are off your route and need to move south 300 yard", feedback could be more reflective – "*check your location; what features should be visible from your current position... what features are visible from your current position*". The degree of task complexity is being managed by the ITS in this case and the level of support is commensurate with the ability of the learner.

2.2 Navigation Functions

Google Glass offers pop-up maps, turn-by-turn directions, and a compass. These functions could be used to support navigation along a course, but might be used to redirect the learner during training when they vary significantly from the planned course. The compass function might be the most useful for the orienteering training task in that it provides information without direction allowing the learner to make their own decisions. In terms of task complexity, very complex orienteering courses could be broken down into small segments to allow novice orienteers the opportunity to realize frequent successes and then scaffolding (reducing support) as their skills grow.

2.3 Augmented Labels of Real Objects

Google Glass also has the capability to provide augmented labels of real objects. This function could be used to aid navigation or other decision-making or problem solving tasks and provide hints or corrective action during training.

2.4 Ability to Share Media

Google Glass can take photos or movies which could be used by the ITS to enhance its situational awareness of the learner. In other words, understanding where the learner is in the context of the orienteering course. In a team orienteering task, this function could be used to share information among team members and allow team members to physically split up in pursuit of an objective. The livestream function allows the user to share a live point of view for analysis of performance by the ITS or to lead other team members to a location based on recognizable features.

2.5   Communication

Probably the most important function in Google Glass is the ability to communicate with the tutor or other team members through texts or shared screens in Google Hangout. Texts can be used to respond to the tutor or other learners in collaborative learning environments. Google Hangout could be used to support in route planning or re-planning with team members. The tutor can capture this communication to determine levels of trust and cooperation within the team. The communication data collected can be used to support after-action reviews and lessons-learned.

3   Discussion and Next Steps

GIFT is readily compatible with the functions in Google Glass to support training in the psychomotor domain and thereby mobile tutoring. The limitations of Google Glass with respect to mobile tutoring are the lack of sensors (e.g., heart rate, blood pressure) to inform critical learner states (e.g., physical exertion) in the learning effect model (Fig. 3). However, this learner data could be made available through other means (e.g., IPhone blood pressure app) and transmitted via Google Glass to GIFT via the cloud.

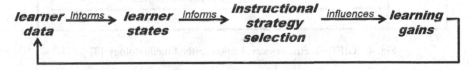

Fig. 3. Learning effect model [1, 3]

Next steps are to evaluate a large cross-section of commercial smart glasses determine which functions are needed to support a wide range of psychomotor tasks. Prototypes would follow along with experimentation to provide empirical evidence of the effect size of these techniques. The testbed methodology used to support this evaluation (Fig. 4) allows for manipulation of learner attributes in the learner model, domain characteristics (e.g., host platform, domain complexity, domain definition, domain dynamics, and training environment conditions), and instructional strategies/tactics/techniques.

Google Glass with GIFT and some sensory augmentation should be able to support complex tasks, but ill-defined tasks may be more challenging as the measures for these tasks as suggested by the name are less defined. Constraint-based or policy-based approaches focused on achievement of goals (go or no-go situations) may provide the best near-term opportunity to tutor in the wild.

The testbed can be used to determine highest reward values for each decision by the adaptive system given the learner state, task type, training or operational conditions under which the task is usually executed, and the definition of the measures or standards for successful completion of the task. Comparative studies are planned to determine the value (cost/benefit) of conducting a wide range of psychomotor tasks in the wild as contrasted with similar training experiences in desktop simulations. While we expect to see differences in performance, learning, and retention, we anticipate the largest effect will be in transfer. Since the training task conditions will be closely aligned with the operational conditions under which the task is normally executed.

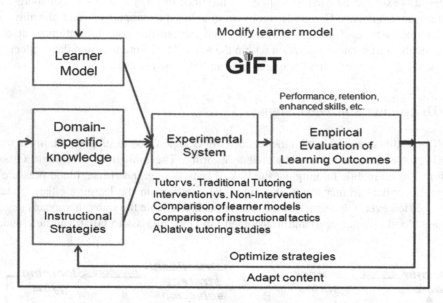

Fig. 4. GIFT effectiveness evaluation testbed methodology [3]

Finally, as we project forward, one objective for augmented cognition on the run is to provide embedded training for dismounted soldiers with dynamic entities and real-time effects [13]. However, limitations not in the adaptive technologies (e.g., intelligent tutoring systems), but limitations in the fields of view (<50°) for a variety of government-off-the-shelf and commercial smart glasses we surveyed [14] may slow adoption of adaptive technologies for embedded training.

Acknowledgments. Research was sponsored by the Army Research Laboratory. The views and conclusions contained in this document are those of the authors and should not be interpreted as representing the official policies, either expressed or implied, of the Army Research Laboratory or the U.S. Government. The U.S. Government is authorized to reproduce and distribute reprints for Government purposes notwithstanding and copyright notation herein.

References

1. Sottilare, R.A., Brawner, K.W., Goldberg, B.S., Holden, H.K.: The Generalized Intelligent Framework for Tutoring (GIFT). U.S. Army Research Laboratory – Human Research & Engineering Directorate (ARL-HRED), Orlando (2012)
2. Sottilare, R., Brawner, K.W., Goldberg, B., Holden, H.: The generalized intelligent framework for tutoring (GIFT). In: Best, C., Galanis, G., Kerry, J., Sottilare, R. (eds.)

Fundamental Issues in Defense Training and Simulation, pp. 223–234. Ashgate Publishing Company, Burlington (2013)

3. Sottilare, R.: Special Report: Adaptive Intelligent Tutoring System (ITS) Research in Support of the Army Learning Model - Research Outline. Army Research Laboratory (ARL-SR-0284), December 2013

4. Anderson, L.W., Krathwohl, D.R. (eds.): A Taxonomy for Learning, Teaching and Assessing: A Revision of Bloom's Taxonomy of Educational Objectives, Complete edition. Longman, New York (2001)

5. Simpson, E.: The Classification of Educational Objectives in the Psychomotor Domain: The Psychomotor Domain, vol. 3. Gryphon House, Washington, D.C. (1972)

6. Bloom, B.S., Krathwohl, D.R.: Taxonomy of Educational Objectives: The Classification of Educational Goals, By a Committee of College and University Examiners. Handbook 1: Cognitive Domain. Longmans, New York (1956)

7. Krathwohl, D.R., Bloom, B.S., Masia, B.B.: Taxonomy of Educational Objectives: Handbook II: Affective Domain. David McKay Co., New York (1964)

8. Soller, A.: Supporting social interaction in an intelligent collaborative learning system. Int. J. Artif. Intell. Educ. 12(1), 40–62 (2001)

9. Lombard, M., Ditton, T.: At the heart of it all: the concept of presence. J. Comput. Mediated Commun. 3(2), (1997)

10. Wirth, W., Hartmann, T., Böcking, S., et al.: A process model of the formation of spatial presence experiences. Media Psychol. 9(3), 493–525 (2007)

11. Mack, E.: Google Glass Is Headed One Of Two Directions Next, Forbes Online. http://www.forbes.com/sites/ericmack/2015/01/15/r-i-p-google-glass-1-0/. Accessed 15 January 2015

12. TechNorms: 10 Amazing Uses For Google Glass To Improve Daily Life in Unique Ways (2015). http://www.technorms.com/33387/10-amazing-uses-for-google-glass

13. Sottilare, R., Marshall, L., Martin, R., Morgan, J.: Injecting realistic human models into the optical display of a future land warrior system for embedded training purposes. J. Def. Model. Simul. 4(2), 97–126 (2007)

14. Sottilare, R., LaViola, J.: Extending intelligent tutoring beyond the desktop to the psychomotor domain: a survey of smart glass technologies. In: Proceedings of the Interservice/Industry Training Simulation and Education Conference, Orlando, Florida, December 2015 (Submitted)

Modeling Shared States for Adaptive Instruction

Robert A. Sottilare[✉]

U.S. Army Research Laboratory, Adelphi, USA
Robert.A.Sottilare.civ@mail.mil

Abstract. This paper discusses methods in which adaptive instructional techniques, strategies and tactics (collectively referred to henceforth as adaptive instruction) might be applied in a multi-learner or team training domain where accurate shared models of cognition and affect are critical to optimizing team performance, and individual learning, retention, and transfer. Application of these models in the Generalized Intelligent Framework for Tutoring (GIFT) is also discussed.

Keywords: Adaptive instruction · Intelligent tutoring systems · Adaptive tutoring · Team modeling · Unit modeling · Shared modeling

1 Introduction

Adaptive instruction is a critical concept in realizing self-regulated instruction where computer-based intelligent tutoring systems (ITSs) jointly manage the pace, flow, and complexity of instruction along with the learner. To begin a discussion of adaptive instruction, we should first discuss what we mean by "adaptive" and how adaptive systems differ from adaptable systems. Adaptable systems may be tailored by the user to support individualized needs or preferences. Adaptable systems offer flexible control of information and system performance resides in the hands of the user [1]. A good example of an adaptable system is a smartphone or tablet where the user can change the interface, layout of applications and decide on specific applications to support the recall of information toward their educational or entertainment goals.

Adaptive systems demonstrate intelligence by altering their behaviors and actions based on their recognition of changing conditions in either the user or the environment. This change is usually managed by software-based agents who use artificial intelligence techniques to guide their decisions and actions [2]. Adaptive instructional systems are "intelligent" in that they are able to observe and interact with both the learner and the training environment (Fig. 1) based on their ability to recognize "learning opportunities" and "teachable moments". Learning opportunities include instances where the adaptive system is aware that the learner is at a point in the instruction where they are able to bridge from existing knowledge to new knowledge. Teachable moments are opportunities for reflection by the learner after a new experience and may be guided by the adaptive system through the use of metacognitive prompts.

© Springer International Publishing Switzerland 2015
D.D. Schmorrow and C.M. Fidopiastis (Eds.): AC 2015, LNAI 9183, pp. 690–696, 2015.
DOI: 10.1007/978-3-319-20816-9_66

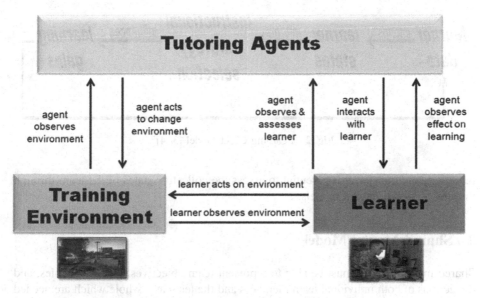

Fig. 1. Adaptive training interaction

The motivation for developing/maintaining shared mental models of cognition is much the same as for maintaining individual models of cognition. For individuals, we refer to the learning effect model (Fig. 2), where selective mining of learner data (e.g., behaviors and physiological sensor inputs) informs learner states (e.g., cognition, affect), which inform strategy and tactics selection by the tutor and ultimately influences learning gains.

Better models of learner cognition are purported to result in more accurate strategy and tactic selection and result in improved learning (e.g., knowledge acquisition, skill acquisition). They most certainly result in more efficient learning as content is tailored to provide instruction on either new material or remediation of old material where the learner is struggling to grasp needed concepts. This results in more efficient learning in terms of instructional contact time and in reduced time to competency when compared to traditional classroom training where everyone is in lockstep.

We define learning gains to include five dimensions: knowledge acquisition, skill acquisition, performance, retention, and transfer. Knowledge and skill acquisition define traditional elements of learning and are elements of learner potential. Performance is a measure of actual ability to apply knowledge and skill to a specific task. Retention is the ability of the learner to recall knowledge so it might be applied. Transfer is the ability to carry learning from training contexts to operational contexts (e.g., from practice to the game as a sports analogy). These concepts may also be applied to teams.

However, "the use of fully automated, computer-based tutoring technologies to provide instruction for teams is as embryonic as the problem space is complex" [5]. In order to determine optimal strategies and tactics for team learning, performance,

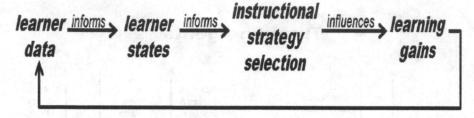

Fig. 2. Learning effect model [3, 4]

retention, and transfer, it is essential to assess the collective states of the team through the use of shared mental models.

2 Shared Mental Models

Shared mental models must be able to represent team objectives, individual roles, and the actions of both individual team members and the team as a whole which are needed to achieve those objectives (Fletcher & Sottilare, 2013). Standards (measures) are needed to determine levels of expectation for learning, performance, retention, and transfer and to assess the effectiveness of the strategies, and tactics implemented by the adaptive system (e.g., intelligent tutoring system – ITS).

These models represent various aspects of the team's perception, decision-making, problem-solving, and interaction. Sottilare, Holden, Brawner & Goldberg [6] suggested the following shared or team models:

- performance (measures of accomplishment during execution of an action, task or function);
- competency (measures of past accomplishments as a guide to probability of success for future performance);
- cognitive states (measures of learning and retention plus engagement and workload as a moderators of learning);
- affective states (assessment of emotion as moderators of cognition/learning);
- trust (measures of confidence in other team members to carry out assigned tasks);
- communication (measures of interaction which may also indicate levels of trust and competency of team members).

As Fig. 3 suggests a learning effect model could be extended for teams and then specifically adapted to focus on shared mental models, but which models are most important to team learning and performance, and which are more than just the sum of the states of individual team members?

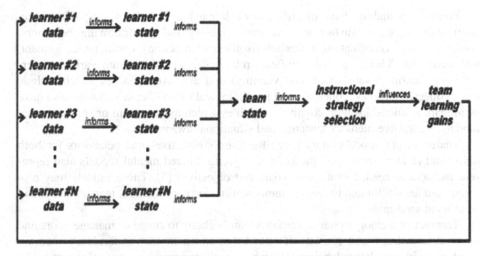

Fig. 3. Notional learning effect model for teams (Fletcher & Sottilare, 2013)

3   Shared Mental Models in GIFT

In this section, we discuss how shared models of cognition and affect might be applied in a tutoring architecture like the Generalized Intelligent Framework for Tutoring (GIFT; [3]) to effectively instruct teams. As mentioned previously, initial analysis of the literature resulted in definitions for performance, competency, cognitive states (e.g., attention, workload, and engagement), affective states (personality, mood, and emotions), trust, and communication.

Additional collaborative research between the US Army Research Laboratory, the University of Central Florida and Iowa State is beginning to uncover an interdependent model of team tutoring strategies based on categories of team behaviors, mutual support, team cognition, and team affect. Each of these categories was analyzed with respect to their influence on team performance, team learning, team satisfaction, and team viability with the goal of implementing viable models as strategies within GIFT.

GIFT is a largely open-source adaptive tutoring architecture whose goals include the reduction of time and skill to author ITSs, automation of instructional management processes during one-to-one and one-to-many tutoring sessions, and the development of tools and methods to evaluate the effectiveness of adaptive tutoring technologies. GIFT development has been fundamentally based on the learning effect model (Fig. 2).

The approach we used is based on a meta-analysis of the team performance and ITS literature and uses structural equation modeling to determine the significance of the relationship of critical team tutoring model variables. The primary search terms used in the meta-analysis were: performance, competency, trust, cognition, affect, communication, intelligent tutoring, human-computer interaction, virtual human, mood, emotion, skill, knowledge, ability, responsibilities, roles, distributed, virtual, after action review, feedback, leadership, cohesion, personality and effectiveness. Each of these primary terms was paired with: team, unit, group, squad, and crew resulting in the selection of over 20,000 articles for inclusion in the meta-analysis.

Preliminary findings have identified key relationships between team performance, team learning, team satisfaction, and team viability and the following behaviors: communication, coordination, reflexivity (self-directed action), conflict management, and leadership. There are also significant relationships between team variables (performance, learning, satisfaction and viability) and affective variables which include trust, collective efficacy, cohesion, and psychological safety. Team variables also have significant relationships with cognitive variables which include team or shared mental models, transactive memory systems, and situational awareness.

Shared mental models characterize the team's objectives and behaviors for both individual team members and the collective group. Shared mental models also represent the actions needed to achieve goals and objectives [5]. These models may represent, but are not limited to team communication and coordination, team efficacy, and situational awareness.

Transactive memory systems support a team's ability to curate or manage (store and retrieve) knowledge and consists of knowledge stored in each individual's memory combined with metadata or labeling information each team members areas of expertise [7].

Team situational awareness involves the perception, comprehension, and projection of activity in the vicinity of the team and an understanding of how these activities might impact team goals and objectives, both immediately and in the near future [8].

4 Discussion and Next Steps

The relationship between team variables, their influence on each other, and their influence on learning, retention, performance, and transfer are not fully understood and merit additional investigation. However, we have identified moderators which influence shared mental models and thereby influence learning. These moderators have been broadly grouped into categories which include:

- team structure, and
- team culture.

Team structure includes variables such as interdependence of team roles, the distribution of team members, the autonomy of team members, the size of the team, the length of the project, and the project's perceived importance.

Team culture influences shared mental models through the values of its members, the collective values of the team, and norms established. The stability of the team and its history of success also influence the confidence and efficacy of the team in tackling new tasks.

Next steps will be to construct team performance and learning models with associated techniques or policies to allow GIFT's intelligent agents to adapt (observe, assess, and act) to address sub-optimal learning states. Identifying shared states or mental models is step one of a multi-step process. Measures or identifying traits of these shared states may be indicated by observation of behaviors demonstrated by individual learners or collective groups of learners. The most difficult question to be answered is what to do once a sub-optimal learning state has been identified. In other

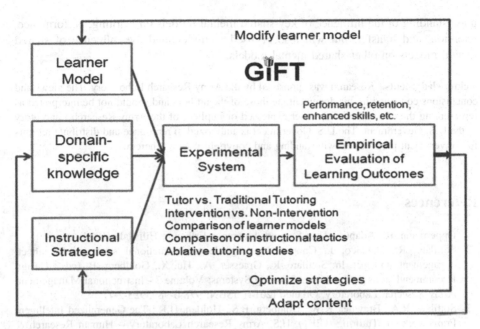

Fig. 4. GIFT effectiveness evaluation testbed methodology

words, what actions are available to the adaptive system and which of these actions provides the highest reward relative to learning and performance outcomes given the state(s) of the team.

The adaptive system must be able to correctly identify the state, analyze trends, formulate a plan for action (e.g., a strategy), and finally execute the plan by implementing a tactic or action per the learning effect model for individuals (Fig. 2) and the learning effect model for teams (Fig. 3). In order to successfully implement a team tutoring structure within GIFT, it must be able to support and uphold policies which are based on sound instructional design principles for both individuals and teams, and which account for individual differences related with learning, performance, retention, and transfer [9]. Just as GIFT's instructional management model for individual training is based on Merrill's Component Display Theory [10], we also anticipate that team tutoring constructs using shared mental models will also support presentation of domain rules and examples of success to the learners, followed by assessment of recall of knowledge related to rules and examples, and finally, immersion in a practice environment to apply knowledge and develop team skills.

Some of these shared states have more obvious action pairs than others. For example, if a task is highly interdependent and the team is relatively new, then communication takes on a higher value. It is simple enough for the ITS to recognize a lack of communication and prompt the team members to keep others informed of their actions. It is more difficult for the ITS to identify specific shared cognitive (e.g., situational awareness) or affective states (e.g., trust). To this end, we are developing a team modeling testbed (Fig. 4) to support experimentation to validate shared mental models developed from the meta-analysis. This testbed will be used to develop an understanding of the influence of key shared mental models on learning, performance, retention, and transfer, but will also be used to understand the influence of shared mental models on other shared mental models.

Acknowledgments. Research was sponsored by the Army Research Laboratory. The views and conclusions contained in this document are those of the authors and should not be interpreted as representing the official policies, either expressed or implied, of the Army Research Laboratory or the U.S. Government. The U.S. Government is authorized to reproduce and distribute reprints for Government purposes notwithstanding and copyright notation herein.

References

1. Oppermann, R.: Adaptive User Support. Lawrence Erlbaum, Hillsdale (1994)
2. Sottilare, R., DeFalco, J., Connor, J.: A guide to instructional strategies for affect, engagement, and grit. In: Sottilare, R., Graesser, A., Hu, X., Goldberg, B. (eds.) Design Recommendations for Intelligent Tutoring Systems: Volume 2 - Instructional Management. Army Research Laboratory, Orlando (2014). ISBN: 978-0-9893923-2-7
3. Sottilare, R.A., Brawner, K.W., Goldberg, B.S., Holden, H.K.: The Generalized Intelligent Framework for Tutoring (GIFT). U.S. Army Research Laboratory – Human Research & Engineering Directorate (ARL-HRED), Orlando (2012)
4. Sottilare, R.: Special Report: Adaptive Intelligent Tutoring System (ITS) Research in Support of the Army Learning Model - Research Outline. Army Research Laboratory (ARL-SR-0284), December 2013
5. Fletcher, J.D., Sottilare, R.: Shared mental models of cognition for intelligent tutoring of teams. In: Sottilare, R., Graesser, A., Hu, X., Holden, H. (eds.) Design Recommendations for Intelligent Tutoring Systems: Volume 1- Learner Modeling. Army Research Laboratory, Orlando (2013). ISBN 978-0-9893923-0-3
6. Sottilare, R., Holden, H., Brawner, K., Goldberg, B.: Challenges and emerging concepts in the development of adaptive, computer-based tutoring systems for team training. In: Proceedings of the Interservice/Industry Training Simulation & Education Conference, Orlando, Florida, December 2011
7. Wegner, D.M.: A computer network model of human transactive memory. Soc. Cogn. **13**(3), 319–339 (1995). doi:10.1521/soco.1995.13.3.319
8. Endsley, M.R.: Toward a theory of situation awareness in dynamic systems. Hum. Factors **37**(1), 32–64 (1995)
9. Sottilare, R., Goldberg, B.: Designing adaptive computer-based tutoring systems to accelerate learning and facilitate retention. J. Cogn. Technol. **17**(1), 19–33 (2012)
10. Merrill, M.D.: The Descriptive Component Display Theory. Educational Technology Publications, Englewood Cliffs (1994)

EEG Coherence Within Tutoring Dyads: A Novel Approach for Pedagogical Efficiency

Bradly Stone$^{(\boxtimes)}$, Kelly Correa, Nandan Thor, and Robin Johnson

Advanced Brain Monitoring, Inc., Carlsbad, CA, USA
{bstone,kcorrea,nthor,rjohnson}@b-alert.com

Abstract. The current study examined EEG coherence across Coach-Learner dyads on a spatial reasoning video game, Tetris®, using an event-locked psychophysiological synching platform. We hypothesized that (1) an intra-individual increase in Theta and a decrease in high Alpha (10-12 Hz) fronto-temporal coherence would occur across increasing difficulty levels, and (2) inter-individual fronto-temporal coherence in high Alpha would increase among lower skilled players. A sample of n = 5 healthy dyads completed the protocol with each learner playing 3 rounds of Tetris®. Across all participants (low-skilled and high-skilled), the intra-individual preliminary results presented herein indicate significant elevation in fronto-parietal coherence. Moreover, the low-skilled players experienced an increase in Theta coherence and high Alpha coherence–the latter not as expected from literature. The high-skilled players had significant reductions in fronto-parietal high Alpha coherence and small increases in Theta. The inter-individual (coach-learner) dyadic coherence results for the low-skilled player showed increased Theta coherence for Coach-Frontal: Learner-Parietal (CF:LP), with no significant change in high Alpha. Meanwhile, an increase in high Alpha coherence was observed in the Coach-Parietal: Learner-Frontal (CP:LF). The high-skilled player experienced decreased Theta coherence for CF:LP, with no significant change in high Alpha, yet a substantial increase in Theta coherence and decrease in high Alpha coherence was observed for CP:LF. These data support the application of coherence analyses for the improvement of pedagogical approaches and provide optimism that further granulated explorations of the data herein could lead to a more thorough understanding of the dynamics of dyadic learning.

Keywords: EEG · Coherence · Dyads · Education · STEM

1 Introduction

Recent pushes to enhance efficiency and efficacy of learning for those involved within Science, Technology, Engineering, and Mathematics (STEM) have encouraged more innovative approaches in teaching, including intelligent tutoring, through the integration of psychophysiology, cognitive processes, and many other factors associated with the learning process. As these approaches are explored, experimental investigations into the underlying constructs of such processes are also being utilized to advance pedagogical research. Researchers have begun to utilize visio-spatial based video games, including Tetris®, as a platform for understanding how to effectively train

© Springer International Publishing Switzerland 2015
D.D. Schmorrow and C.M. Fidopiastis (Eds.): AC 2015, LNAI 9183, pp. 697–706, 2015.
DOI: 10.1007/978-3-319-20816-9_67

individuals' decision-making, problem solving abilities, and increase skill acquisition speed [1, 2],. Tetris® provides an open ended platform that requires optimal attention, perceptual processing, decision making, working memory, and processing speed in order to perform at the highest levels [3].

In recent decades, these processes have been linked with neuronal coherence, a measure of synchrony that taps into both increases in power and phase locking. Neuronal coherence is typically calculated across two brain sites within an individual, using EEG [4, 5], MRI [6–8], and MEG [5]. Coherence analysis utilizing EEG signals enables high resolution of temporal changes, and is associated both with changes in phase coupling and power across regions. The cross-correlation approach of coherence utilizes pairs of signals as a function of frequency in order to provide a means for identifying and isolating frequency bands at which the EEG displays between-channel synchronization [9]. Elevated coherence in parietal Gamma (35-60 Hz) have been shown in both human and animal models to be related to attention processing and prioritization [10, 11], while over the somatosensory cortex, it appears to be related to attentional modality shifting [11, 12]. Higher executive function processes, such as the complex executive processing that occurs during working memory (e.g. encoding and retrieval), have also been associated with neuronal coherence; these are found primarily in the fronto-parietal regions, with elevations in Theta coherence and suppression of high Alpha coherence as the working memory load increases [13, 14]. These findings indicate that attention and working memory are reliant, at least in part, on neuronal coherence within an individual.

Recently, we reported that neurophysiological metrics of attention (B-Alert classifier for engagement), and working memory (workload) correlations across coach-learner dyads related to performance variation [15–17]. We were able to predict a significant amount of the variance in performance by the learner in a coach-learner dyad playing Tetris® using the cross correlations of the B-Alert Classification and Workload models [18, 19]. Taken together, these findings lead to the hypothesis that coherence across individuals may provide even more insight into the tutoring/coaching learning process, particularly in a task requiring attention and working memory.

Others have recently begun to explore cross-individual coherence, and found coherence between a listener and speaker is associated with ability of the listener to recall details from a story [20]. Participant listeners with greater coherence to the speaker had the greatest recall ability. While this study utilized MRI, EEG coherence across individuals has also been explored, and been found in both social interactions [21], and in decision making during card games [22]. Of particular interest is the fronto-parietal coherence found between card players by Astolfi and colleagues, as they found inter-individual coherence in the fronto-parietal regions to occur primarily in the Alpha and higher bandwidths. Given that inter-individual coherence in the fronto-parietal regions are associated with complex executive processing in working memory [13], we proposed to examine these relationships more fully.

Here, we expand upon our original reporting to examine a set of N = 5 dyads with both high-skilled and low-skilled learners to investigate the fronto-parietal coherence both within each learner, and across each learner-coach dyad. We predict that (1) given that intra-individual fronto-temporal coherence is related to working memory, this pattern of increased Theta and decreased high Alpha coherence, across increasing level difficulty, will be present, and (2) that due to the need for the lower skilled player(s) to rely on input from the coach (based on our reported findings [17]), inter-individual fronto-temporal coherence in the Alpha bands will be increased primarily in the lower skilled players.

2 Methods

2.1 Participants

A sample of N = 6 healthy participants (one coach and 5 learners) were enrolled after screening for the following criteria: having taken college level STEM education within 2 years of the study session, self-report of non-use of excessive stimulants, alcohol, prescription or non-prescription drugs, as well as self-report of no prior or existing medical conditions including psychological and neurological disorders that are known to systematically alter EEG signals. Additionally, participants were required to refrain from the following substances prior to their study session: alcoholic beverages 24 h prior, caffeinated beverages 12 h prior, and nicotine 1 h prior. In conjunction with these requirements, participants were also to refrain from using the aforementioned substances for the duration of their study visit (approximately 2 h). The tutor was selected based on both self-report of Tetris® expertise, regular Tetris game play (5 + hr/week), and subsequent confirmation of high levels of Tetris scoring when tested prior to the onset of the study; the tutor was able to clear more than 10 levels consistently (the maximum cleared by the most expert tutee, indicating the tutor had expertise at or above the best tutee).

The final dataset had a mean age of 22.3 yr (range: 21-23 yr); were educationally balanced (33.33 % in college, 50.00 % having received a Bachelor's degree or its equivalent, 16.67 % having received an Associate's degree); computer expertise balanced (33 % reported being Average (proficient at 3-4 applications), 50 % Intermediates (proficient at 5 + applications), and 16.67 % Experts (proficient at 10 + applications)); and ethnicity and gender diverse (66.67 % female, 33.33 % non-white).

The use of human participants was approved by an Institutional Review Board process consisting of external board members and secondary approval through the Department of Navy, prior to participant recruitment. All participants completed the approved consent form before the initiation of the testing. All participants (including the coach) received compensation ($25/hr) for taking part in the study.

2.2 Materials/Equipment

Psychophysiology. Simultaneous and synchronized EEG and ECG were acquired from both the tutor and tutee throughout Tetris® gaming sessions, using the B-Alert® X10 wireless sensor headset connected through the Team Neurodynamics platform shown in Fig. 1 (Advanced Brain Monitoring, Inc, Carlsbad, CA). This system had 9 referential EEG channels located according to the International 10–20 system at Fz, F3, F4, Cz, C3, C4, POz, P3, and P4 and an auxiliary channel for ECG. Linked reference electrodes were located behind each ear on the mastoid bone. ECG electrodes were placed on the right clavicle and the lower left rib. Data were sampled at 256 Hz with a high band pass at 0.1 Hz and a low band bass, fifth order filter, at 100 Hz obtained digitally with Sigma-Delta A/D converters. Data were transmitted wirelessly via Bluetooth to a host computer, where acquisition software then stored the psycho-physiological data. The proprietary acquisition software also included artifact decon-tamination algorithms for eye blink, muscle movement, and environmental/electrical interference such as spikes and saturations.

The architecture for the Team Neurodynamics platform enabled the synchroniza-tion of EEG/ECG for each dyad. Each test subject, referred to as an individual node, was hosted on a portable Windows laptop for unobtrusive, wireless, data acquisition. The set-up, shown in Fig. 1, was used for synchronization of data between the indi-viduals (tutor and tutee) with the task environment (Tetris®). The client-server architecture on the Tetris® platform facilitated data aggregation using a common node, the Aggregator Node. The architecture relies primarily on the passing of simultaneous, real-time markers, otherwise known as beacons, to each individual node in order to provide consistent and reliable timing accuracy for the current task. EEG was acquired at each node using an External Sync Unit (ESU). The ESU not only has a Bluetooth receiver, but also an internal timer that is used to precisely timestamp each EEG packet received from the headset. In addition, the ESU also has serial and parallel ports to accept third party events. Thus, the same timer within the ESU synchronizes both EEG and third party events, providing millisecond level accuracy in alignment. The ESUs of the tutee and the tutor were networked via a serial port network in star topology. The Aggregator node functioned as the hub. Through the star network, a custom hub program generated and transmitted periodic beacons, broadcasted to both individual nodes by the aggregator node at regular intervals, with incremental numbering and the option for manual, time synched annotations.

This structure provides a reliable method for managing synchronization, especially if an individual's node falls out of sync. With ongoing, continuous syncing, all data prior to and after a given node could be salvaged if de-synchronization of individual nodes occur. Beacons were broadcast in ASCII code and each subject node received an individual log that could be altered for offline analysis. Manually annotated, time locked events were also output in ASCII format allowing for individualized com-mentary pertaining to specific session details and/or errors. In addition, the aggregator node uses the beacon intervals to align and decode the EEG with the Tetris® game logging file data from the subject nodes for offline analysis.

Tetris® Game: Objective and Scoring. Programmed in Python by Rensselear Polytechnic Institute (RPI), the Tetris® software used in this preliminary study was designed to replicate the classic 1980 s arcade game [23]. The game is played using seven different geometrically shaped "zoids" composed of four square blocks (see Fig. 2). The objective of Tetris is to manipulate each zoid by moving them left and right and, if necessary, rotating 90 degrees in order to create a horizontal line of 10 blocks without any gaps. As each horizontal line is created, it will disappear, which constitutes as a "cleared line". As the game progresses, the levels increase in speed, ultimately ending when the zoids stack all the way to the top of the playing field. Levels were

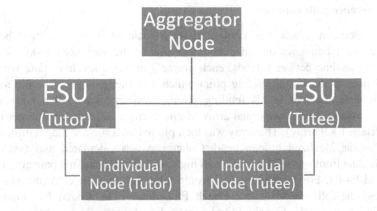

Fig. 1. Team NeuroDynamics architecture

automatically advanced as soon as a player met a certain criteria (lines cleared and/or points obtained). To this end, all players started at Level 0 and continued playing until (1) they reached "Game Over" or (2) they ran out of the pre-set 20 min timeframe. Points are earned based on the number of lines cleared at once and the speed at which a block was placed ("soft drop" versus "hard drop"). For maximum point value, a player should aim to obtain a "tetris" which occurs when four lines are cleared in one simultaneous move.

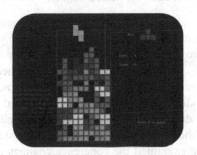

Fig. 2. Tetris (R) game screen shot

2.3 Protocol

EEG and ECG were acquired throughout the testing session, using the B-Alert® X10 wireless sensor headset (Advanced Brain Monitoring, Inc, Carlsbad, CA). Each dyad was positioned in front of one laptop, where the player was coached on the game of Tetris® for 3 games lasting approximately 15 min (or until the player lost nearest to that goal time). The coach gave advice to increase the player's skill. Psychophsyiological data was recorded using ABM's Team NeuroDynamics platform, which synchronized the EEG and ECG with time locked events across each dyad.

2.4   Coherence Calculations

Coherence between dyads was computed on a scale of 0 to 1, with 0 being no coherence and 1 being maximum coherence. Due to the variance in skill level and length of game-time between dyads, each player's first two levels of data were averaged and used as the initial starting point which was then compared to the averaged data from their last two levels (ending point). Coherence was then computed by channel to create a one-dimensional array of one average coherence value per channel (in this case, a 1 × 9 array). The array was then plotted on a surface map template of the channels on an idealized human head. Coherence was calculated and assessed for intra-individual fronto-temporal Theta and high Alpha using channel pairings: Fz-POz, F3-P3, and F4-P4. For inter-individual fronto-temporal coherence, Alpha was examined across the following parings: Coach Fz-Learner POz, Coach F3- Learner P3, Coach F4-Learner P4, Coach POz-Learner Fz, Coach P3-Learner F3, Coach P4-Learner F4.

3   Results

We conducted a preliminary analysis examining the 5 dyads across 3 successive games of Tetris®. These dyads represent a spectrum of skill level in relation to levels completed, total number of lines cleared, and overall score.

3.1   Intra-individual Coherence (Within Subject)

We examined fronto-parietal coherence in the learners, based on initial skill level, which resulted in the 2 least skilled players compared to the 3 most skilled. Skill level was driven by overall score and level obtained in game 1 for each player. Low-skilled players reached level 4–5, while high-skilled players reached levels 9–10. First we examined overall coherence differences in the two groups. Consistent with prior findings [13], both low-skilled and high-skilled players had elevated fronto-parietal coherence. However, this did not exist in the midline channels for the highly skilled players. In comparison to the most skilled players, the least skilled players had weaker coherence. In addition, we examined the coherence changes across the game playing period, and found that as play progressed, the most skilled players had large reductions in fronto-parietal high Alpha, and smaller increases in Theta. In contrast, the least skilled players had the expected increases in Theta coherence, but high Alpha coherence also increased. These findings are demonstrated in Fig. 3.

We also examined overall Theta and High Alpha changes over the course of the game play, but found no significant change (p = .8). Although, there was a trend in both Alpha and Theta for increased power in both bands for the least skilled players, overall (p = .06).

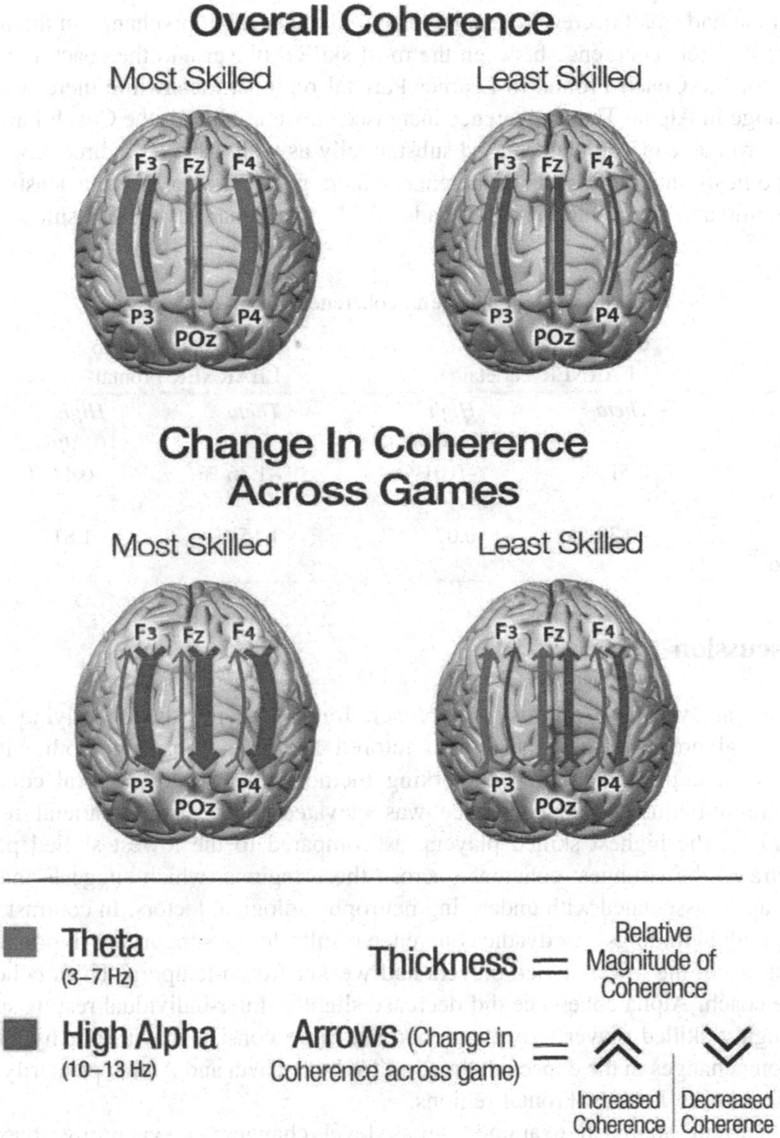

Overall Coherence

Most Skilled   Least Skilled

Change In Coherence
Across Games

Most Skilled   Least Skilled

■ **Theta**
(3–7 Hz)

Thickness = Relative Magnitude of Coherence

■ **High Alpha**
(10–13 Hz)

Arrows (Change in Coherence across game) = ⩚ ⩒

Increased Coherence | Decreased Coherence

Fig. 3. Within individual coherence overall (top) and across game play (bottom) for most skilled player (left) and least skilled player (right).

3.2 Dyadic Coherence (Between Coach-Learner)

In contrast to the individual findings, our dyadic coherence results are less consistent with prior findings [22]. For the least skilled players, we found that Theta coherence from the Coach Frontal to Learner Parietal regions was elevated slightly over the course of game play, but Coach Parietal to Learner Frontal was substantially decreased. High Alpha had small decreases in coherence in the latter, but no change in the former. In contrast, Theta coherence between the most skilled player and the coach decreased slightly for the Coach Frontal to Learner Parietal regions, meanwhile there was minimal change in Alpha. Theta coherence increased substantially for the Coach Parietal to Learner Frontal, and Alpha decreased substantially as well. This is in direct contrast to our hypothesis that the dyadic coherence would grow stronger in the least skilled dyads, compared to the high-skilled dyads. Table 1 summarizes these results.

Table 1. Percent change in coherence during game play

	COACH Frontal to LEARNER Parietal		COACH Parietal to LEARNER Frontal	
	Theta	*High Alpha*	*Theta*	*High Alpha*
Least skilled	0.51 %	−0.01 %	−1.36 %	−0.44 %
Most skilled	−0.30 %	0.07 %	1.15 %	−1.81 %

4 Discussion

Coherence analysis is a promising approach for identifying the underlying neurophysiological processes associated with tutored learning. Consistent both with our hypothesis, and prior literature on working memory and fronto-temporal coherence [13], intra-individual Theta coherence was elevated in the fronto-parietal regions. Interestingly, the highest skilled players, as compared to the lowest skilled players, demonstrated the strongest coherence across these regions, which suggests that skill levels may be associated with underlying neurophysiological factors. In contrast to our intra-individual findings, our dyadic coherence results do not support our hypothesis; as play continued, the lower skilled players had weaker fronto-temporal Theta coherence with the coach. Alpha coherence did decrease slightly. Inter-individual results specific to the highly skilled player's dyadic coherence were consistent with our hypothesis, with strong changes in the expected direction for both Theta and Alpha, primarily in the Coach Parietal to Learner Frontal regions.

The current approach examined gross level changes in synchrony, based on coherence, of initial and highest level attained parts of a coached Tetris gaming session. This approach was successful in identifying the changes and relationships of coherence between and across individuals during the gaming session, and appear to delineate highly skilled from lower skilled players. However, we have the ability to examine whether coherence changes are associated with errors by assessing more granular level changes based on time synchronized markers associated with such errors. Furthermore, future analyses may reveal differences in dyad dynamics based on time lapse and error occurrences. For instance, Lerner et al. (2011) found that synchrony of the listener usually occurred slightly behind that of the speaker [20]. The best listener would even occasionally anticipate the moments of synchrony, as if predicting what was coming next in the story [20]. That level of communication could be a marker of optimized learning, although more work is needed before such interpretations are made. Future analysis will also examine other intra- and inter- individual coherence measures associated with cognitive processes in Tetris®, including attention and attentional shifting.

It should be noted that while elevations in synchrony have been associated with increased performance, attention, and overall improved cognitive processing, synchronization comes at a cost in flexibility and adaptation resources to new information that may have long term influence on the efficacy of learning [24, 25]. As such, retention of learned information and skills that occur during the coached sessions should be examined in future studies.

The work discussed herein supports the need for additional exploration of the role of cross-neuronal synchrony, as measured by coherence in identifying effective training and tutoring approaches. If supported by additional research, these findings can be used to objectively assess new intelligent tutoring approaches, as well as drive the development thereof. Inter-individual and intra-individual neuronal synchrony may also be used to identify (1) those most likely to benefit from tutoring; (2) when a learner has maxed the benefits of the current tutor/tutoring session; and (3) at what time training modalities must be adapted to optimize cognitive processing. This study demonstrates the promise of this approach, yet shows the need for subsequent research to replicate and/or expand upon these findings with larger sample sizes.

Acknowledgments. This work was supported by The Office of Naval Research (contract # N0014-13-P-1068) under Project Officer, Dr. Ray Perez, and in collaboration with Dr. Anna Skinner of Anthrotronix Inc. The views, opinions, and/or findings contained in this article are those of the authors and should not be interpreted as representing the official views or policies, either expressed or implied, of The Office of Naval Research Agency or the Department of Defense.

The authors would like to thank Cole Tran, of Advanced Brain Monitoring, for his help in constructing the figures found herein. Additionally, author Johnson, R. R. is a share holder in Advanced Brain Monitoring, which may benefit financially from the publication of these data.

References

1. Squire, K.: Open-ended video games: a model for developing learning for the interactive age, pp. 167–198 (2008)
2. Gee, J.P.: Why game studies now? Video games: a new art form. Games Cult. 1(1), 58–61 (2006)
3. Gray, W.D., et al.: Tetris as Research Paradigm: An Approach to Studying Complex Cognitive Skills
4. Shaw, J.C.: Correlation and coherence analysis of the EEG: a selective tutorial review. Int. J. Psychophysiol. 1(3), 255–266 (1984)
5. Srinivasan, R., et al.: EEG and MEG coherence: measures of functional connectivity at distinct spatial scales of neocortical dynamics. J. Neurosci. Methods 166(1), 41–52 (2007)

6. Zarahn, E., Aguirre, G.K., D'Esposito, M.: Empirical analyses of BOLD fMRI statistics. Neuroimage **5**(3), 179–197 (1997)
7. He, Y., et al.: Regional coherence changes in the early stages of Alzheimer's disease: a combined structural and resting-state functional MRI study. Neuroimage **35**(2), 488–500 (2007)
8. Hasson, U., et al.: A hierarchy of temporal receptive windows in human cortex. J. Neurosci. **28**(10), 2539–2550 (2008)
9. Ruchkin, D.: EEG coherence. Int. J. Psychophysiol. **57**(2), 83–85 (2005)
10. Fries, P., et al.: Modulation of oscillatory neuronal synchronization by selective visual attention. Science **291**(5508), 1560–1563 (2001)
11. Jensen, O., Kaiser, J., Lachaux, J.-P.: Human gamma-frequency oscillations associated with attention and memory. Trends Neurosci. **30**(7), 317–324 (2007)
12. Bauer, M., et al.: Tactile spatial attention enhances gamma-band activity in somatosensory cortex and reduces low-frequency activity in parieto-occipital areas. J. Neurosci. **26**(2), 490–501 (2006)
13. Sauseng, P., et al.: Fronto-parietal EEG coherence in theta and upper alpha reflect central executive functions of working memory. Int. J. Psychophysiol. **57**(2), 97–103 (2005)
14. Sarnthein, J., et al.: Synchronization between prefrontal and posterior association cortex during human working memory. Proc. Natl. Acad. Sci. **95**(12), 7092–7096 (1998)
15. Johnson, R.R., et al.: Drowsiness/alertness algorithm development and validation using synchronized EEG and cognitive performance to individualize a generalized model. Biol. Psychol. **87**(2), 241–250 (2011)
16. Berka, C., et al.: EEG correlates of task engagement and mental workload in vigilance, learning, and memory tasks. Aviat. Space Environ. Med. **78**(Suppl. 1), B231–B244 (2007)
17. Stone, B., Skinner, A., Stikic, M., Johnson, R.: Assessing neural synchrony in tutoring dyads. In: Schmorrow, D.D., Fidopiastis, C.M. (eds.) AC 2014. LNCS, vol. 8534, pp. 167–178. Springer, Heidelberg (2014)
18. Berka, C., et al.: EEG correlates of task engagement and mental workload in vigilance, learning and memory tasks. Aviat. Space Environ. Med. **78**(5), B231–B244 (2007)
19. Johnson, R.R., et al.: Drowsiness/alertness algorithm development and validation using synchronized EEG and cognitive performance to individualize a generalized model. Biol. Psychol. **87**(2), 241–250 (2011)
20. Lerner, Y., et al.: Topographic mapping of a hierarchy of temporal receptive windows using a narrated story. J. Neurosci. **31**(8), 2906–2915 (2011)
21. Dumas, G., et al.: Inter-brain synchronization during social interaction. PLoS ONE **5**(8), e12166 (2010)
22. Astolfi, L., et al.: Neuroelectrical hyperscanning measures simultaneous brain activity in humans. Brain Topogr. **23**(3), 243–256 (2010)
23. Lindstedt, J.K., Gray, W.D.: Extreme Expertise: Exploring Expert Behavior in Tetris
24. Zohary, E., Shadlen, M.N., Newsome, W.T.: Correlated neuronal discharge rate and its implications for psychophysical performance (1994)
25. Stryker, M.P.: Drums keep pounding a rhythm in the brain. Science **291**(5508), 1506 (2001)

Applications of Augmented Cognition

Contact Activity Visualization for Seniors

Ana Almeida, Micael Carreira, Joaquim Jorge,
and Daniel Gonçalves[✉]

Instituto Superior Técnico/INESC-ID, Rua Alves Redol, 9,
100-029 Lisbon, Portugal
ana.alml37@gmail.com, micaelcarreira@ist.utl.pt,
jorgej@inesc.pt, daniel.goncalves@inesc-id.pt

Abstract. Over the years, people raise their children and watch them as they make their adult lives away from home. Because of that, seniors lose contact and intimacy with their loved ones, as physical presence isn't as possible as desirable. Also, because of physical impairments that may arrive as years pass by, seniors may experience difficulties in communicating and interacting. Thus, a research project called PAELife (Personal Assistant for the Elderly Life) was created with the aim of fighting isolation and exclusion. Our personal contribution to this project is displaying the most active contacts in a visual, powerful way so that they notice which friends are contacting them more and which ones don't contact in a long time. To achieve that, we built a set of prototypes that display contacts' activity from different sources (email, social networks, etc.) and performed two user tests, in order to identify the best alternatives and understand if the senior citizens can correctly perceive the contacts' activity. The tests' feedback allowed us to know what prototypes to choose and the ones to discard. After analyzing the results we implemented a final functional prototype that matched all the requirements collected from the users.

Keywords: Social networks · Contacts · Activity · Senior citizens · Communication

1 Introduction

As time goes by, people tend to become and feel lonely, especially if no family members and/or friends are often around [13, 16]. As children grow up and move out, so does most of the communication with them. This happens especially to senior citizens - who are the people with over 60 years old and, also, the ones who need more medical care and are hospitalized more often [15], who no longer need to support and take care of anyone. Because of this, they adopt a lifestyle that allows them to stay at home and not going out as much as before [6]. As a result, they tend to have less communication and lose intimacy with their loved ones.

In order to best understand how those limitations can impact the daily basis of the seniors, West et al. studied how function and visual impairment are the most problematic [14] and figured out that those limitations can actually promote dependent living. As a result, seniors tend to abandon social living and interaction. Other studies

© Springer International Publishing Switzerland 2015
D.D. Schmorrow and C.M. Fidopiastis (Eds.): AC 2015, LNAI 9183, pp. 709–721, 2015.
DOI: 10.1007/978-3-319-20816-9_68

[2, 12] stated that these kind of limitations are often associated with the decline of quality life and the capability to be with other people.

Nonetheless, technology helps us communicate in many ways, and many people nowadays are already embracing those technologies and making a continuous, effective use of them to narrow the emotional distance between them and their family and friends, that often live apart [10, 11]. As so, technology has proven to be very useful, as it might help in fight isolation and exclusion and can break time-space barriers, which wouldn't be possible without its use. However, senior citizens may have trouble using the technologies described before. When growing up, they hadn't them around, so they aren't used to them. Also, they are commonly resistant to change their lifestyles [6], mainly when it comes to technological aspects, as they appeared late in their lives. We wonder if we can help seniors overcome these time-space barriers, using technology to do so. Even if we could do it, there is a possibility that it wouldn't work, because of the existent gap between seniors and technology; we are going to try to reduce it. Despite that, we believe that these changes would be acceptable to these users, because they might help them become closer to their loved ones.

Taking all this into account, the PAELife project has the goal of preventing and fighting isolation, exclusion and loneliness, promoting new ways of enhancing interaction so that the seniors can experience a more social and fulfilling life. Part of the problems to solve, and the focus of the research described in this paper, is to successfully tackle the remote availability issue, so that users can know how often is a certain person available for online conversation, or has initiated that conversation in a number of different channels. Finding out an effective and efficient way to convey that information led us to study some alternatives, first with low-fidelity prototypes and then, with functional prototypes embodying the lessons from the first study. Our analysis of those studies allowed us to find a suitable solution, as well as a set of design guidelines that could help and guide the creation of similar applications.

2 Related Work

Ozenc and Farnham [9] studied and explored some natural ways of displaying visual representations of groups of people. In the study are represented common lists, pie charts, timelines, geomaps and treemaps. This work compared these ways of organizing and displaying groups of people, giving us an interesting overview of some of the most used representations. The main purpose another study [3] was to display the users' activity so that it would become a way of stimulating users' participation. The authors created IntroText, a new way of displaying the users' activity on a community. This interface is based on multiple actions, as it captures all the interactions that can be performed on a certain online community. Based on those indicators, sentences are formed to let the users know how active a certain contact is. "[Username] is a loyal visitor" and "[Username] eventually shows up" are just a couple of examples of how the activity can be showed.

Another widget is called 'Babble' [4] and it provides cues about the presence and activity in an online conversation. The 'Babble' is a circumference that contains a circle on the center of it and several other colored, smaller circumferences - dots - (each one of the latter representing a contact). The proximity of the dots to that centered circle is a representation of how recently the contact has spoken to the user, which means that the closest a dot is to the center of the 'Babble', the most recently that contact has talked to the user. This way, each user can see what are the most active contacts, and what are the contacts that haven't been talking much.

Morikawa and Aizawa [7] propose a system to facilitate awareness of peoples' contactability and online presence. The framework proposed by this study tries to display the contacts in an innovative way, including a new way to let the users know that a certain contact is actually available for chatting. In the solution proposed by the authors, the contact's avatar is what the user sees. The pictures are displayed in front of a colored background, which indicates the current status of that contact. On top of that, the avatars have their own opacity, whether its owner is in front of the computer or not. If an avatar is opaque, it means that its owner is sitting in front of the computer. As time passes, and if the user leaves its position, the avatar starts to fade out and becomes more trans parent. This approach the problem of the transparency of the avatars, that may not be very noticeable by the senior users, who tend to see fewer details and lose visual perceptiveness, with the ageing process.

There are a few guidelines that developers should take into consideration when designing for seniors. Sizes should be larger than usual, as seniors have difficulty in perceiving small details. Colors are a key point and should be used in as much contrast as possible [8]. Low saturation levels and transparency are to be avoided, but very bright colors might also fatigue the eyes [5], so balance is required. Background patterns should be avoided as well. Also, there is a need to make distinguished and important elements highlighted and visible, but without animations and distracting constituents [5]. These few guidelines are important concepts that are proven to be helpful when designing for seniors and that should be taken into consideration to help seniors take the best advantage of the interface.

3 Low-Fidelity Prototypes

The contacts' activity visualization development was processed in several steps, in order to correctly identify the users' needs and build the visualization prototypes incrementally. The first set of prototypes was made based on some of the implications described in the previous section.

For the general activity, we proposed two different visualizations, which are presented in Fig. 1. Figure 1a shows the activity apart by increasing or decreasing the sizes of the avatars, as the activity is higher or lower, respectively; Fig. 1b, instead, changes the transparency of the pictures, in a way that pictures with lower transparency are the ones that have the highest amount of activity.

Regarding the activity from the sources, we designed seven different ways of displaying this information. The first two, represented by Figs. 2a and b only differ in the shape of the avatars. The first one has a squared representation while the second is rounded, which allows containing more than four sources. The approach on Fig. 2c condenses the bars horizontally in only one place, thus making the visualization cleaner. Figure 2d show vertical bars on the middle, making it is simpler to compare the activity from different sources this way. The three remaining options are very similar between them, as they differ only in the shape of the representation of each source, and are represented on Figs. 3a, b and c.

Regarding notifications, representations with glow, saturation change and numbers were used, as shown in Fig. 4. The representation of the small dots was created because it could be simpler for seniors to count the dots.

Fig. 1. (a) Representation of the activity levels by distinguishing the sizes of the avatars; (b) Representation of the activity levels by distinguishing the transparency of the avatars.

Fig. 2. Squared (a) and rounded (b) representations of the sources' activity; representation of the activity sources only in an horizontal bar (c) and only in vertical bars (d).

Fig. 3. Representation of the activity levels displaying squares (a), circles (b) and semi-circles (c) for each source.

Fig. 4. Representation of the notifications with a glow (a), small dot per notification (b), change in the saturation of the color of the source (c), and with a notification counter (d).

3.1 Results of User Feedback

To find out what was the preferred way of displaying the contacts' activity, we performed user tests with seniors and evaluated the results of those tests. This way, we could collect user feedback and engage seniors in the design process. We interviewed 20 older users for our user study. We sequentially showed participants the several alternatives, and then asked which ones they prefer, which they could understand easier, and some other specific questions such as which was the most active contact.

The results showed that, regarding the general level of activity, 60 % of the users have a preference for the visualization in Fig. 1a. Regarding the visualization of the activity on the different sources, although there was a preference for the representation with inside squares (Fig. 3a), we decided to also implement the alternative with outside rectangles as well (Fig. 2a), since participants reported it was easier to understand the level of activity of contacts. Considering the notification system, the alternative with badges and numbers was the only one that participants could see and understand correctly, and therefore was preferred by 70 % of users (Fig. 4d).

4 Functional Prototypes

The first functional prototypes are the result of the feedback collected from the users study with the low fidelity prototypes. In these functional prototypes we maintained the several types of visualization separated, but incorporated the notifications in the sources' visualization, as there was only one preferred option for that element.

Regarding the different sources of activity, we implemented the two alternatives described before (Figs. 6a and b). We also merged these alternatives with the general activity visualization, as shown in Figs. 7a and b. Each displayed contact is fictitious and its information represents a few activities a person can perform on each source: number of posts on Facebook, tweets, friend requests, emails received, etc. Each of these elements helps composing the length of each bar and, together, they compose the size of the avatar – in the alternatives where that happens (Fig. 5).

Fig. 5. Functional representation of the activity from sources with notifications in bars (a) and in squares (b).

To perceive if the visualization with many contacts was still understandable for users, we created four distinct scenarios: the first one with 20 contacts – a relatively low number of contacts, which is likely the case of most seniors[1] – and just a few contacts that are highly active; a second one with also 20 contacts, but with contacts that have a more uniform level of activity; a third one with 100 contacts, similar in activity as the first one; and a final scenario with 200 contacts, as it is the average number of Facebook friends per user.[1] By creating these different scenarios, we are able to test each alternative with each scenario, making it possible for us to understand if the visualization wasn't reliant to a small number of contacts.

Fig. 6. Functional representation of all the elements in bars (a) and in squares (b)

4.1 Protocol for User Testing

With these intermediate prototypes complete, we also needed to do another session of user testing, in order to understand if these representations made sense and are well perceived by the users, and also, to make a final inquiry on which of the two alternatives for the activity in sources is better, so we are able to choose a final one. We interviewed 15 people, 9 of those were female and 6 were male, from 68 to 90 years old without cognitive disabilities and with none to low knowledge of computers. These are roughly the same characteristics of the participants of the preliminary user tests. Each test was performed individually and the total amount of time spent with each person didn't exceed 15 min. The survey was divided into six categories: general information about the user, the users' perception about the general level of activity, their perception about the activity from each source, their perception about the notification system, perception about the total amount of activity (general and sources) and a few conceptual questions regarding actual tasks that can be performed using our solution.

4.2 Results

In these tests' results, we used a chi-square test to analyze the preferred options when we asked for comparisons and analyzed the general understanding in each alternative. In the perception about the general level of activity, as we only had one option, we asked the users if they understood the concept correctly. More than 65 % of the users were able to understand the concept and make the comparison of the general activity between two contacts correctly. Some of them found it confusing but, after a simple explanation, most of them understood it correctly.

Regarding the perception about the sources of activity, more than 90 % of the users were able to perceive both approaches. However, the comparison of the activity

---

[1] http://www.pewresearch.org/fact-tank/2014/02/03/6-new-facts-about-facebook/.

between two contacts was well perceived in Fig. 6a, as 93 % of the users were able to compare easily and correctly, while only 33 % could identify who was most active on Twitter on Fig. 6b. This happened because humans are better in perceiving changes in length than changes in areas. Also, the results from the preference of the users supported the difficulties they had in analyzing the sources' squares. The users showed a statistically significant preference for the option with the bars (p = 0,004).

Both alternatives from the notification system (the same approach chosen from the previous user testing, but represented inside the bar and inside a small rounded circle) were well accepted and interpreted by the users, as over 85 % of them understood both alternatives. However, the chi-squared test was statistically significant, although with a lower confidence (p = 0,071), which showed us a preference by the representation of the notification's number inside the bar (Fig. 6a).

Finally, we asked the users about their perception about the total activity (general, from each source and with notifications), which is a representation of what the contacts' visualization will probably look like in the final prototype. In this case, the representation with the bars was preferred to the one with the squares (test showed p = 0,004, a preference for Fig. 7a) and the understanding was higher in the alternative with the bars – 80 % - than the one with the squares – only 40 %.

4.3 Conclusions

As we only had one alternative to represent the general level of activity and it was well accepted by the users, we are going to continue to use it. The same goes for the notification system, that was incredibly well perceived; to represent the notifications, we will choose the option that has the number of notification inside the bar, as it was preferred by users and it makes the matching (notification to source) more immediate.

Regarding the activity from each source, it was clear that the users had a preference for the representation with the bars, and it was also clear that this representation made the comparison of the activity of the contacts much easier. Therefore, on the final prototype, we will implement only the representation with squares (Fig. 7a).

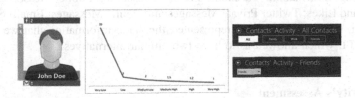

Fig. 7. (a) Contact with sources' activity and notifications inside the bars; (b) Multiplying factor variation regarding the variation of the activity on the sources; (c) Visualization of the groups in an horizontal list and in a dropdown list.

5 Implementation

We implemented the visualization as a Windows Store App, since it was a requirement of the project. We implemented a module to collect users' contacts activity information, but also kept the fictitious for users who did not have social accounts.

5.1 Displaying Contacts

First of all, and when we started to build the first functional prototypes, we had to think about how to design our contacts' avatar, which is represented on Fig. 7a. This element is the base of all the contacts, which all look the same.

5.2 Packing Algorithm

A problem that we had to address was how to pack the contacts' on the canvas. As the size of the avatars isn't always the same (they have different areas correlated with the different level of activity each contact have), we implemented a packing algorithm that packed the squares in the available empty area. We based our implementation in an algorithm that tackles the problem of packing blocks into a fixed rectangle.[2] Our solution was based on setting the maximum height size to the computers' screen resolution. After that, we place an avatar on the first empty space it fits. Then, and instead of horizontally dividing the empty area into two, we do it vertically, so our biggest avatars are placed on the left side on the canvas. Each new avatar is then placed in the leftmost and topmost empty area available where it fits. We do this recursively until we have no more avatars to place on the canvas.

5.3 Information Collection

When we had access to the Social Networks API, in which we could retrieve the actual information that we would be able to use in our work, we found we only had access to the following information: Facebook Private Messages, Public Messages, Unread Messages and Likes; Twitter Private Messages and Public Messages; Emails Sent. This information, stored in a text file, represented the same information that we collected from the API, which allowed us to have two similar alternatives.

5.4 Activity's Assessment

As the contacts may have very low activity levels, it might become tricky to analyze the activity levels on those types of contacts. As so, we decided to calculate the activity level multiplying the original activity by a factor that would change accordingly to the contacts' level of activity. Regarding each source of activity (that is displayed in the

---

[2] http://codeincomplete.com/posts/2011/5/7/bin_packing/.

bars around the contacts' avatar) we used the factor in a way that is represented in Fig. 7b. The X-axis represents the amount of activity that a contact might have in each source. These values were determined empirically, accordingly to the total length of the bars, and are here translated from "Very Low" to "Very High". The multiplying factor was, as well, determined empirically. This solution allows us to prevent the problem described previously, in which we might have contacts that appeared to have no activity at all. A similar approach was used to the calculation of the general activity, which is translated by the total area of the avatar, even though the factors were quite different – also determined empirically.

5.5   Group Visualization

We decided to represent the groups in two different ways, and evaluate these alternatives in a later user test session. A first approach was to display the groups in an horizontal line and the second one with a dropdown, right above the contacts, just as presented on Fig. 7c. The first approach seemed the best to us because it only takes one tap to change the group. However, in this alternative we had to confine the number of groups to be created. The second approach might allow a larger number of groups, but it requires two taps to change to the view of another group. As so, we decided to maintain both alternatives and let the users choose what best fit them.

5.6   Managing Groups and Contacts

Regarding the contacts and groups management, the users can perform several actions: create, rename and delete groups. These actions allowed the users to manage all the groups in the application. So that the users could add contacts to the groups, they could also work on that: move contact to group and remove contact from group. This way, the users could segment their contacts into several groups, easily finding them and analyzing their activity.

6   Evaluation

In this section we explain all the procedures that we followed during the last user test session.

6.1   Protocol

We interviewed 15 people, 6 of whom were male and 9 were female, from 70 to 91 years old without cognitive disabilities. Participants had low or no knowledge of computers or social networks. Each test was performed individually, in a room were the users could sit and interact with the device, and we explained to the users that their participation was anonymous and cost-free. The total time spent with each person didn't exceed 20 min. This survey focused on two main aspects: perception of the users about the contacts' activity using fictitious data and their perception of the contacts' activity regarding their own contacts; thus, with real data. Apart from that, we included some tasks for the users to perform, that tested all the interactions in the application and debriefing questions, for qualitative study.

6.2   Results

The first two questions regarding the perception of activity when comparing two contacts had a task completion of 9/15. It is important to state that the users that couldn't answer those questions were some of the ones who never had any contact with technology. We measured the time that the users took in answering the question. For the first question, the average time to answer was 28 s, and the second one (very similar to first) took only 18 s, in average, as the users already knew what to search for. So, for the first question we estimated a standard deviation of 30.76 s and for the second one, 22.03. Thus, for a level of confidence of 95 %, the confidence interval is [7.904, 48.096] for the first comparison and [3.6, 32.4] for the second. The same applied to the next two questions, in which we asked the users about the contact with higher and lower level of activity. Both the tasks had 6 answers and the average times of response was within a reasonable limit.

The first task that asked the users to create a new group had a completion of 7/15. Typing times were not considered. The average time to perform the task was 62 s, with a standard deviation of 39.48. As so, for a level of confidence of 95 %, the confidence interval for this task is [32.76, 91.24]. The next tasks (all of them had a task completion of 6/15) were performed without major difficulties and were all quite similar. The tasks that required group management were performed with lower average times than the ones that involved contacts management. The tasks about renaming and deleting groups had an average time of 54 and 51 s, respectively. Using the standard deviation of those results (33.1 and 38.2), we calculated the confidence intervals of [27.52, 80.48] and [20.5, 81.5]. The average number of errors for these two tasks was also very low: 1.2 for the renaming of a group and 0.8 for its deleting. Finally, the results for the tasks to move and remove contacts from a group revealed higher average times. These results are also explainable: the users sometimes clicked the wrong contact when they had to choose it, which made them deselect the contact and select the right one. Also, when managing contacts, more taps are required, which undoubtedly increases the completion times.

The final task involved switching the activity visualization time to another period. All the users performed the task with 0 errors and the average completion time was 23.67 s, which translates to a 95 % confidence interval of [13.17, 34.17].

After this, we could analyze the information that we collected from the debriefing questions and from informal conversations with the users. For the two alternatives of visualizing groups, we applied a non-parametric chi-square test. Even though the result of the test wasn't statistically significant ($p = 0.205$), there was a preference for the alternative with the list, even it was by a small margin. Regarding the debriefing questions, which asked about the easiness of performing the tasks, results were satisfying: only around 12 % of the users found any of the tasks difficult or very difficult.

6.3   Conclusions

This final user test sessions allowed us to choose which of the two ways of visualizing the groups we should use. Of course that we opted to eliminate the dropdown, maintaining the very first approach we implemented: the horizontal list, as the results from the user tests showed a preference for the horizontal list.

Also, although the amount of users that were able to complete the tasks were roughly the same amount as the ones that could answer the first questions about the perceiving of activity, the response times were significantly high. The users struggled in opening the bottom bar, and many times they closed the application in the process of pulling the bar up. Also, they felt confused by doing operations whose context isn't familiar to them, as groups creation isn't a very common action. Even though the results weren't very good, we were not extremely concerned: the main focus of the application is to visually show the activity of the contacts, in which many users succeeded in analyzing. The group management was an extra feature that we included in the application due to the addition of the requirements to the project and it can be used separately regarding the contacts' visualization.

However, we could not evaluate with the real data from the users since none of the participants had accounts in which they could login and test the application. This shows us that, probably, only a very small amount of seniors will use the application due to the fact of not having accounts on Gmail, Twitter or Facebook. However, and as many of the users from our session performed surprisingly well in the tasks they were asked to execute, they might have seen the benefits that the application could offer them, and as they didn't struggle much, they wouldn't feel scared to use it.

7   Conclusions and Future Work

The PAELife research was created with the main objective of fighting isolation and loneliness among seniors, promoting new ways of interaction. To achieve that, and focusing on our own contribution, we developed an application that displays the contacts' activity, in order to allow the users to identify their active contacts easily. This way, the users will know with whom they can readily interact with, by the means of the activity analysis. We produced a first set of prototypes that map all the features we needed to include in our system. Those features were tested with users, and the results collected showed us what were the options we clearly needed to discard and what others were good for the seniors to use.

Then, and taking into account the prototypes previously produced, we chose the alternatives that were most understandable and preferred by the users and built the first functional prototypes. This time we made a similar session of user testing, not only to choose a final representation of each element, but also to perceive if the representations chosen before were still accurate and understandable.

In the final work of this project we only had one alternative for each component. Finally, a final session of user testing was required. Apart from questioning the users about the perceptibility of the activity on the three components of the application, we asked the users some qualitative questions, and performed a debriefing questionnaire, in order to perceive and collect feedback in a way that no answer to a task could. The results of the final user test session showed us that the users could interact with the system with relative easiness.

If we could continue with the work, we would have wanted to explore more ways of visualizing the activity, regarding each source and the general activity. This would allow us to determine if there were still better solutions to display the contacts' activity to the users. Also, it would be interesting to develop new ways of display the management groups and contacts. The most difficult action for the users was to pull up the bottom bar that displayed the available actions regarding groups and visualization of activity on other periods of time.

References

1. Coleman, G.W., Gibson, L., Hanson, V.L., Bobrowicz, A., McKay, A.: Engaging the disengaged how do we design technology for digitally excluded older adults? In: Proceedings of the 8th ACM Conference on Designing Interactive Systems, DIS 2010 (2010)
2. Crews, J.E., Campbell, V.A.: Vision impairment and hearing loss among community-dwelling older americans: implications for health and functioning. Am. J. Public Health **94**, 823–829 (2004)
3. Deiml-Seibt, T., Pschetz, L., Müller, B.: A conversational model to display user activity. In: Proceedings of the 23rd British HCI Group Annual Conference on People and Computers: Celebrating People and Technology, BCS-HCI 2009 (2009)
4. Erickson, T., Laff, M.R.: The design of the 'Babble' timeline: a social proxy for visualizing group activity over time. In: CHI '01 Extended Abstracts on Human Factors in Computing Systems, CHI EA 2001 (2001)
5. LCC, Agelight. Interface Design Guidelines for Users of All Ages, pp. 1–17 (2001)
6. Minichiello, V., Browne, J., Kendig, H.: Perceptions and consequences of ageism: views of older people. Ageing Soc. **20**, 253–278 (2000)
7. Morikawa, C., Aizawa, K.: Automated awareness and visualization of online presence. In: Proceedings of the 2012 Joint International Conference on Human-Centered Computer Environments, HCCE 2012 (2012)
8. National Institute on Aging. Making Your Website Senior Friendly Tips from the National Institute on Aging and the National Library of Medicine (2001)
9. Ozenc, F.K., Farnham, S.D.: Life "Modes" in social media. In: Proceedings of the SIGCHI Conference on Human Factors in Computing Systems, CHI 2011 (2011)
10. Satusky, M.J.: Staying connected: Technology Options for Older Adults. Orthopaedic Nursing/National Association of Orthopaedic Nurses (2010)
11. Tollmar, K., Persson, J.: Understanding remote presence. In: Proceedings of the Second Nordic Conference on Human-computer Interaction, NordiCHI 2002 (2002)
12. van de Watering, M.: The impact of computer technology on the elderly. Hum. Comput. Interact. (2005)
13. Victor, C.R., Scambler, S.J., Shah, S., Cook, D.G., Harris, T., Rink, E., De Wilde, S.: Has loneliness amongst older people increased? An investigation into variations between cohorts. Ageing Soc. **22**, 585–597 (2002)
14. West, S.K., Munoz, B., Rubin, G.S., Schein, O., Bandeen-roche, K., Zeger, S., German, P.S., Fried, L.P.: Function and visual impairment in a population-based study of older adults the SEE project. Invest. Ophthalmol. Vis. Sci. **38**, 72–82 (1997)

15. WHO. Healthy ageing profiles: Guidance for producing local health profiles for older people (2008)
16. WRVS, G.N. Loneliness amongst older people and the impact of family connections. WRVS 2012 (2012)

Setting a Privacy and Security Comfort Zone in the Internet of Things

Barbara Endicott-Popovsky[1]([⊠]), Scott David[1], and Martha E. Crosby[2]

[1] University of Washington, Seattle, WA, USA
{endicott,scott.david}@uw.edu
[2] University of Hawaii at Manoa, Honolulu, HI, USA
crosby@hawaii.edu

Abstract. This paper seeks to raise awareness of the potential benefits and detriments resulting from sensor intrusion in the Internet of Things (IoT). The conclusion of this paper is that the IoT has been rendered inevitable as the result of a confluence of historical trends, but that we can make choices regarding its fundamental architecture that can tip the balance of harm and benefit more toward individual or institutional rights and obligations. Once the choices are "baked in" they will be more difficult to alter in future IoT iterations. It is hoped that collective attention to the issues raised in this paper will help to guide these decisions so that the IoT systems we build will result in fewer surprises.

Keywords: Internet of things · Information on top · Insight on time

1 Introduction and Background

1.1 Technology in History

Throughout history, people have created technology to leverage their capacities. Leverage increase and risk reduction are not cost free. Costs include the costs of acquiring or using the technology and the "cost" or loss of liberty when a dependency is developed on the technology. Once we start using hammers, houses are designed to be built with nails, eliminating alternative technologies. Also, various costs of technology are borne by individuals outside the direct supply chain. For example, neighbors of the auto factory experience the noise and pollution of the factory, unregistered alternative energy sources are crowded out, etc. It is typical that reduction of risk in one area frequently requires risk increases somewhere else.

Technology helps mitigate risks. For example, stop lights can mitigate traffic accidents. There are multiple risks borne by individuals and society associated with home heating. Some are immediate risks of comfort and health to the family, while others are broader risks of energy crises on a global level. The thermostat helps to mitigate some existing risks in new ways, but also introduces new risks and benefits associated with the entirely separate world of data commodities, one that is not yet fully developed and therefore more difficult to weigh.

Today's thermostat is a socio-technical feedback loop that is loosely coupled to the information network of the energy markets. Information associated with energy

© Springer International Publishing Switzerland 2015
D.D. Schmorrow and C.M. Fidopiastis (Eds.): AC 2015, LNAI 9183, pp. 722–734, 2015.
DOI: 10.1007/978-3-319-20816-9_69

consumption for home heating is tied to energy information systems subject to security and privacy violations, introducing new risks.

Rules and technical controls are meant to make some element of feedback loops more certain. For instance, when entering a crossroads, drivers perceive other drivers and adjust speed or braking behavior to take their action into account. The red light creates a standard convention to render the behavior of others more predictable, much as the technology of thermostats renders the temperature more predictable by controlling the behavior of a boiler, and therefore more reliable. We need rules and tools to control the new security and privacy risks created by feedback loops connected to information networks.

1.2   IoT Makes the World a Keyboard

The Internet of Things is being realized as the cost of wireless networking, and of data collection, transfer and processing have gone down. As a result, the once unknown details of interactions of people and things can now be collected, transferred and processed for trivial cost and provide insight into consumer behavior. Where that insight has the potential to harm the interests of an individual or entity it is viewed as an "intrusion." In fact, insight and intrusion are two perspectives on the same phenomenon of heightened information.

If you have ever been camping or lived in a home with wood heat, you know that the first person to wake up in the morning stokes the fire to warm up the campsite made cold by inattention during sleep. The colder the campsite, the greater the urgency to get the fire going. The fire and the people form a primitive feedback loop, through which the sensation of cold leads to fire building behaviors, and the achievement of heat signals that those behaviors can stop.

The first electrical thermostat automated the process by providing an artificial heat sensor to replace the human sense of cold and connection to a boiler to replace the wood stove. Such devices were used in settings where consistent temperature had to be maintained, such as incubators for poultry and later human residences. In each case a "feedback loop" was automated to increase efficiency and lower costs.

When the systems operate reliably, they achieve great savings of resources and mitigation of human suffering and inconvenience and increase productivity. That reliability is being threatened by the potential security and privacy breaches that result from being connected online.

1.3   Tech Feedback Loops

Humans have configured a myriad of such feedback loops to increase their comfort, safety and convenience in the physical world. Each of these systems detects a situation through sensors and then performs an assigned task, through "actuators." They are typically one dimensional devices, programmed only to sense a limited range of phenomenon and to actuate a limited response. Each is directed at addressing a specific physical "risk" in the physical world where risk includes inconvenience (heating and elevators) and harm (fire or street crossing).

The Internet of Things is knocking at their door. As processors and radios have gotten smaller and cheaper following Moore's law (2x processor concentration every 18 months) [1], it has become possible to include sensors, processors and transmitters on increasingly prosaic items, to the point where they can be included in food packaging and other single use (disposable/recyclable) items.

This makes it possible to include monitoring equipment in a much greater variety of contexts. As measurements are more relevant, they become more valuable. Relevance is related to risk and leverage opportunities. Data that can best inform my future actions to maximize leverage and reduce risk are most valuable to me, and can also be of most value to those who might wish us harm.

1.4   What We Should Expect of IoT?

Trust is earned. A system must be reliable and serve stakeholder needs to be trusted; however, reliability is not enough since something can be reliably harmful. There is not yet a single performance metric that will answer the question for all stakeholders, "is this system measure relevant to my risk and leverage analysis."

As technology has advanced, it has become cheaper to connect devices. It is at the point where it costs only pennies to add radio technology to a device, depending on the range and bandwidth required, therefore manufacturers are making decisions to include these sensor devices, why not? Moore's law in IoT is driving legal and policy that needs to be revisited periodically to refresh to ensure that we are not introducing overlooked harms.

1.5   Death of Secrecy

Privacy was easy when data wasn't connected. The default was privacy. Secrecy is dead or dying with networked information, but privacy doesn't have to die with it. You don't look into other peoples windows and neither should you look in on other's information. The internet of things will challenge our current notions of secrecy and invite us to employ more positive respect in the provision of privacy (not just an accident), and it will also invite us to act with more intention to understand how our actions affect others and future generations. A call for responsibility and maturity.

As networked information technologies have whittled away at secrecy, we have seen privacy and security diminish. This is not, however, inevitable, but rather a result of our continued reliance on approaches to privacy and security that were developed when there was more secrecy. Our risks have changed, but not our risk mitigation strategies. Faced with rapid change, we look to our old institutions for risk mitigation answers, but the institutions stand mute, completely unable to self-adjust to the new risk circumstances.

Public records of divorces have always been available in county records, but putting them online makes them more accessible. Zillow showed house prices, and contemporary articles talked about privacy intrusions, even though it's public information [2]. One person's intrusion becomes another's insight.

Previously, it was easy to tell if you were "producing" data. With IoT, your participation in the data production process will be less obvious to you. So, how do you know if you are protected from harms? How do you know if someone is intruding on your privacy? Publishing private facts? Defaming reputation? Those are traditional torts. What about new emerging harms? The authors assert that expansion of IoT suggests further demise of secrecy.

The challenge is that data is a dual use technology. It can be used for good or ill. In fact, there are situations in which one party's good is another's bad. When institutions can better tell who you are, that can be both intrusive and empowering depending on how the insight is used by the institution.

1.6 Leverage, Privacy and Security Enhanced or Hindered by IoT?

The question is how can those data flows be rendered reliable? One approach is to render the data non-existent by collection and right-to-be-forgotten type limitations, but these ignore the fundamental value proposition of greater insight that we all enjoy and will seek. They are nostalgic strategies that seek to preserve the type of privacy that was an artifact of accidental secrecy, but which is now dead in the era of networking and ubiquitous simultaneous data collection.

We are information seeking-beings. Every day we seek high quality information on which we can rely. Much of that information involves the current behavior of others. Traffic reports are not useful if we only know about 50 % of the cars, predictions of energy use are not useful if only know about 50 % of houses. Thus we need to have a balance between knowing and not.

It is possible to measure your fuel use directly, but to measure it relative to others, the data about your use has to be compared to that of others. Many communities' energy providers have already had programs through which people are informed about their energy use with others. The latter intrusion is the reason to consider who is handling data about you. Who do you trust, an entity with power with which your interests align, or an entity with medium market power and therefore limited resources to compete reliably.

When a third party is involved, the concept of trust arises. How can you be sure that the insights gathered for you won't be used in ways that harm you?

Giving the system 1000 eyes could be seen as extending neighborhood watch to all of those artificial eyes, thus increasing security. One could see if any part of the system is acting unreliably such as gas leaks, or electricity blackouts, etc. that could be detected quickly. This could help us build more robust systems—thus increasing trust and therefore security. However, these effects are as yet accidental and not designed in. Security and privacy are accidental outcomes in these scenarios.

1.7   The Intimacy of the Grid

As early as 1997, work was being done on computing and emotions. An example is the work of Rosalind Picard at MIT [3]. Reliability and predictability of response enables us to make emotional connections with machines. We want to trust the environmental controls on which we depend. We benefit physically and emotionally if those systems are more reliable and predictable. Thermostats are heat and needed for comfort and survival is a good example. How do we consciously design in the emotional affectiveness of reliability and predictability in this new world of IoT?

1.8   New Forms of Leverage Emerging

What will default structures be for new data and information systems? Systems to date are just baby steps toward a new world of ubiquitous information at all levels. That world is driven by the desire to monetize through advertising, but we don't need to just apply direct monetization rules to all data use. Many uses are not monetized like data that support epidemiology or understanding of social issues.

New possibilities include carbon footprint data for better insight into your energy use which will give better insight into energy use alternatives and better insight into energy use by you relative to others. But that information could also be used to affect your costs—how much you may be allowed to use in the future or what you may pay for fuel. Perhaps you may be compelled to lower your consumption by having an external authority directly lower the thermostat. On the positive side, to lower costs of what you pay, you need to empower the supply chain that feeds you energy. This could enable a local utility to purchase more effectively if they know your pattern of use, creating a benefit to both you and the utility, but it should require your cooperation.

Data about your fuel use is already mixed with data about all use of your fuel supplier. You appear as a part of the gallon purchase by your fuel supplier, and his wholesaler, and how much is produced by APEC. With greater data availability, you will be able to distinguish your use and your impact on the supplier.

2   Risk in the Age of the IOT

2.1   A. New Environment New Risk

Thermostats control local environment against risks from the temperature environment. We have new environments now and new risks. What is the nature of the feedback needed in this information environment? Privacy and security can be viewed as the absence of reliability. Unreliable electricity is a blackout. Unreliable water is a flooded basement. Data is not yet sufficiently boring to be considered reliable. In fact, we don't even have ways to measure reliability of its flows. We need to make data boring – like a thermostat.

2.2 Trust and Individual Outsourcing

This is a time of tremendous distribution of outsourcing causing us to trade new risks for old. Just as businesses once did their own shipping, payroll, tax preparation, data processing, airline reservations. They now outsource those tasks to networks of third party service providers. Individuals also "outsource" those functions to new third party networks on which they depend. We once used travel agents, now we book travel online; we once did our own taxes but now a majority outsource that function to a third party. This opens us up to new risk exposure and proliferation of information about us.

2.3 New Information Risks

With transition to digital, our risks are increasing, so that they include not just physical risk, but also information risk. There was a time when your money could only be stolen in a robbery of your person or your bank by theft of cash or valuables deposited, usually through use of the instrumentality of physical threat of a gun or knife, now data theft is the instrumentality of choice to enable monetary theft with zero physical threat. In this sense, robbery has become different. It is arguably safer for victims with reduced threat of violence, but it is more difficult to detect online and no less economically harmful.

2.4 Exponential Growth of Data

Not only has information become more important, it is also more available as the price of sensors and of networking sensors together have decreased. The rate of capacity of global information collection, transfer and storage has been said to be increasing exponentially [4]. The Internet of Things (IoT) is a concept that is meant to anticipate the emerging setting where the many devices and objects with which we interact can be given a sensory capacity and an actuator capacity to capture and transmit (and sometimes process) data about their environment. Where that environment includes humans, a portion of that data will be "about" that human activity. We need to include in our design conceptualizations that privacy considerations should factor into any application.

2.5 New Responsibilities

Individuals and organizations won't voluntarily assume additional costs unless there are clear benefits. We have an example with the environmental movement and how long it has taken for recycling and limiting energy consumption limitation to become emerging norms that affect behavior beyond mere market or monetary considerations. Individuals now will pay more for green power and organic foods, will spend time and effort to sort their recycling, will turn down their thermostats at night or when out of the house, and purchase fuel efficient cars in a blend of reactions to non-considerations. Similarly, we need to raise awareness of IoT privacy concerns similarly to encourage new behaviors and responsibilities on the part of both individuals and the organizations collecting data.

2.6   IoT Increases Outside Risk by Raising Number of Interactions

Interaction volume is increasing rapidly with IoT. Interactions are indirect since "things" don't exercise discretion, but are programmed, semi-autonomous automatic systems. In the past two decades, technology advances have caused our information environments to become richer, as higher connection speeds and tech have lowered prices, enabling the placement of processing and sensor technologies at increasingly smaller scales. We all benefit from these advances, and all have had to adjust to the implications of being increasingly monitored and observed.

True that data an enormous pile of data is now available to big search engines like Google that can mine for correlation, creating new and increasingly intrusive information, but at least having it in one place better enables audit than if it were in a million places. Like AT&T in 1960's, some natural monopoly is emerging which usually invites regulation. While regulation to preserve privacy may be needed, careful consideration must be given in design because initial reactions to block information flies in the face of creating valuable insights that individuals may wish to have. As stated earlier, a balance must be found between insight and intrusiveness when designing a regulatory regime.

2.7   Interactions Breed Risks and Requires Metrics

We all have more interactions and more perceived risk than ever. Every one of us has this problem, all people and institutions have security challenges, privacy challenges, and unknown risk, cost and liability challenges with IoT. The key is how to create metrics that might provide meaningful ability to measure the level of trust in a system and look to measures of identity integrity.

What is identity integrity? In the physical world, I can recognize my body, my family members, my possessions, my car, my house and other physical objects that are recognized to be within "my control." That is more difficult with intangibles. I own shares of stock of corporation X, I cannot present myself at their office and ask to take home a desk or some office paper—these don't belong to me even though I may "own" a portion of the company. In fact, being a shareholder doesn't even give me a right to be present in their office without permission. Stock rights are specific intangible rights, carefully described under law, regulation and private contract.

Consider the recent headlines describing privacy breaches and harms [5]. Each is a breach of either an input or output channel, in other words an expressive or perceptual channels. When think of it this way we may be able to discover some means of providing tangibility to our personal intangible information. It exists somewhere and is subject to being bounded in some way. This is just the beginning of teasing out the nature of our data presence that will eventually be subject to similar laws, regulation and private contracts that take into account the new nature of the risks and benefits associated with IoT; however, we are a long way from that enlightened view.

3   Solutions

3.1   Privacy is an Operations Problem in IoT Solved with Operational Approaches

How can an individual possibly act to achieve privacy in the context we have just described? How can a company or government protect its interests? By focusing on the actions of privacy and security—seeing them as operations problems–we can design, develop and deploy systems that give greater privacy and security. Consider that all privacy and security violations involve a breach of the input or output channel for data. Reflecting Nissenbaum's contextual appropriateness and distribution norms [6]. While individual and company "calibrations" of these channels may differ, they do so by degree not of kind. If we can deliver channel integrity, we take care of the emergency phenomenon of privacy and security. To do so requires employing reliable systems. Those systems are composed of equipment, software and entities (individuals and organizations) that must be chosen wisely for their ability to take on responsibility to achieve privacy and security expectations. For equipment and software, seek reliability. For entities, seek reliability.

A reliable operator will render service predictable. The big data players have a stake in terms of money and regulation; we can leverage their self-interest to achieve reliability. Do you want a bit player or a significant player to handle your data? The risks are mostly from unauthorized use. Most companies have an interest in preventing unauthorized use in order to deliver reliable services to their B2B and B2D customers. If there is a problem, who can best negotiate with the government, you or the company? Who can best negotiate with another company – you or the company?

3.2   Create a DMZ for Security. Render Externality Innocuous

Sharing information is not a binary issue, not an "either/or." There are myriad levels of sharing in different contexts. As a result, information can be shared in more or less privacy preserving ways. For example, feedback relative information to you on your energy use relative to neighbors, without revealing their identities, and vice versa. This would inform you and others with minimal intrusion. Considering the challenges of coordinating such a broadly distributed system, there are ways to preserve interests and also achieve sharing goals if design intention is there at the beginning.

3.3   Hoarding and Stewardship. Achieve Interdependence

Expect others to abide by their responsibilities set forth in privacy preserving policies, not only is this the best solution for individuals, it is also the only responsible approach when it comes to scarce resources such as energy. No one person gets to be beyond regulation if they are using scarce resources. Hoarding is discouraged and stewardship responsibilities are dominant.

3.4 Achieve the Perspective: My Insight is Your Intrusion

Leverage of information is now available to inform interactions which were never available previously. (The authors couldn't discover others with similar views 100 years ago, but not so today.) This benefit to some individuals is perceived as intrusion to others. As we used to say to our kids when they complained about being in traffic: "We are part of their traffic." Similarly, we are other people's privacy problem, and are part of theirs. It is this co-dependency that is the basis for future governance systems. We should adopt a golden rule of data use: "do unto others as you would have them do unto you." More specifically, this raises the issue of co-management of databases for the purposes of social decisions about relative benefits and harms. To date, the discussion has taken place in developing markets, but the law is frequently out of touch with current reality due to the lag in awareness. Solutions exist, but for earlier problems. Terms of service and other Trust Frameworks are in need of continuous evolution in order to address new and emerging problems that were never conceived of at the time of their drafting.

3.5 Markets and Standards

Internet was built on open standards of technology which allows for remote building in conformity with design, affording interoperability among physical technological components. The Internet was a military technology deployed in civilian context, without consideration of the social implications. Now we get to deal with them.

Legal interoperability is now the challenge. What are open legal standards? What are open legal standard-setting processes? Candidate standards vie for adoption by stakeholders, each making an evaluation of worth and costs. As long as costs are known and accepted, then this process of deliberation is fair. The question of that fairness is broadly described as problem of privacy, but it is more than that. Channel integrity is a precursor to legal interoperability.

Legal systems consist of rules creation, operations and enforcement. There are many different rules in different jurisdictions, and there can be many different cultural and traditional legal approaches in these same jurisdictions. Ultimately standardization for reliability will make inroads into rulemaking processes and enforcement preferences, but the initial impact can be most effective in the middle operations elements, the boring parts of the process of rulemaking and enforcement.

Reliable, consistent service delivery is favored in times of rapid change. Large operations offer some stability as a scaffolding for innovation in rulemaking and enforcement/incentives. The large data providers are the candidates for initiating rulemaking. Once seen as passive presenters of whatever data can be imagined and put online, we now see them beginning to propose and implement rule changes [7].

Increasingly we depend on technologies and people in sociotechnical, social machines to deliver needed services. In the book, "Turning Troubles into Problems: Clientization in Human Services, a collection of essays explores how human service professionals, who must deal with a broad list of challenges including at-risk children, adults and the elderly need to construct the troubles of the groups as standard "problems" that can be dealt with by systems to which they are gatekeepers [8]. The essays consider the challenges of the interface between client "troubles" and administrable "problems" with attention to the multiple dynamic elements that require forms of "mass customization" to achieve scale with empathy and compassion in resource-constrained social services:

> Troubles are present across the life course; they are not the exclusive property of any stage of living. In contemporary society, troubles commonly are muddled and undefined until they are subjected to professional scrutiny. The "gaze" of experts transforms them into certifiable conditions, from specific diseases, disabilities, and dysfunctions, to particular crimes and transgressions [9].

Future IoT systems will need to convert troubles into problems to deal with problem resolution at scale. Insight can be gained from these socio-technical solutions that can be adapted to the problems outlined above.

4   New Paradigm Needed

We call for new architectures of mutual altruism in which participants can act selfishly, but benefit others. You and I rely on these systems to be reliable for our personal and business use. That reliability is dependent on the collective reliability of populations to produce useful and valuable information. You and I need to do our parts as data providers and data handlers.

4.1   Transparency is Mutual

If we want companies to be transparent, should we also be transparent with respect to those same issues. The No More campaign suggests that conversations about interpersonal harms should open up [10]. If 'sunlight is a disinfectant,' why doesn't that apply to people's practices online, including privacy issues with ubiquitous IoT data?

4.2   Be a Good Neighbor: Respect the Right to Be Remembered

'Turning Troubles into Problems' in networked systems, there is the right to not be overlooked. Much is made of the right to be forgotten [11], but at the edges of all bell curves of bureaucracy there are vast populations who suffer from having been long since forgotten. They are the human face of the externalization of costs in scaled systems. Their challenge is to be remembered by systems, not forgotten.

4.3   Responsibility: Empirically-Based Stewardship

Wasteful practices hurt everyone, particularly future generations. Nobody is perfect, but it's better to know behavior standards. What gets measured gets done, and, as an example, until we measure our energy consumption practices, we cannot get climate change mitigation "done." It is not the oil companies that are destroying the earth, it is you and me. We are the consumptive part of the energy production-consumption system. If we exclude ourselves from being counted in the global energy use spectrum, we are part of the problem, not part of the solution.

This doesn't mean that privacy is dead, but neither should social responsibility be dead. Plato declared that an engaged citizen is a public resource. In energy, we are citizens of the world, and we can do something about global problems like climate change from each of our living rooms. The inclusion of our thermostats and other IoT are each small contributions to our collective participation. What provides you with more efficacy– your vote in national elections once every couple of years or your daily "vote" by the consumptive decisions you make? That voice cannot be heard in isolation, it can be included in the conversation when you participate in data gathering.

4.4   Markets and Registries as Risk and Rights Mapping Tools

Markets are the place where Terms of Service are subject to critique and adoption. Positive value propositions are embraced, and those that are not favored are not. When Trust Frameworks of multiple entities change over time to accommodate the needs of broad groups of stakeholders, it is comparable to an open, community development process. Consider that safety equipment in vehicles was in response to market and regulatory pressures. There is a chicken and egg argument about which came first, the market innovation or the consumer need, but ultimately it is a feedback process that moves the market forward.

In order to make this happen, the consumer must be provided with information about choices. For products, it is obvious – purple carrots look different than orange carrots; or this new mobile device is larger, therefore better, etc. As more value is developed in information markets, differences are less obvious without an interface. Registries are the place where we can discern difference. Like securities markets, the differences of value in 100 shares of class A common stock of two companies cannot be found in the Delaware corporate law or even the stock instrument issued by the company, but in information about the company's respective earnings potential and other data about its interactions and performance. Trust Frameworks are at the early stages of standardization. Now there are great differences among these frameworks, but they are standardized by some external laws that sculpt things like DMCA provisions, bankruptcy provisions, etc., and some industry practices, for example similar IP licensing language, etc., mostly developed due to the attorney "herd mentality:" when preparing new documents legal advisors look at examples online for models even though a practice still may not yet be broadly standardized.

Standards emerge in markets. Initiatives like NSTIC and a similar EU initiative are directed at seeking to identify candidate best practices in policy and law to inform future potential standards for deployment in domestic national and global markets [12]. This is a standardization process, but is taking place on the broad scale of global data and identity infrastructures. It is a distributed process that is (frustratingly for countries and companies) not centralized in one place.

Markets are the mechanism and the process for this standardization, and registries and Trust Framework construction tools are important functions to provide for those processes. Registries are where solution discovery, collaboration opportunities and other collaboration and coordination processes take place in loosely coupled system of standard setting. This is the means for addressing the development of practices that will begin to define IoT privacy and security mitigations.

5 Declaration of Interdependence

When our nation was founded, it enshrined its independent coherence through a declaration of independence from the United Kingdom. Our current task is to cohere individuals into responsible communities of interest around issues, such as energy consumption through a declaration of interdependence. Networked information systems are a source of modern problems, and modern solutions. The paradox is resolved when individuals self organize to solve problems, and to help one another. The neighborhood watch has become a model for global citizens to pursue their interests in common with others. Everyone will benefit from greater reliability and less accidental and intentional harm attack which can be the outcome of understanding how interconnected we are and how each of us is responsible for enacting privacy constraints in this new world of IoT. There is no 'other' who can do this for us. It is up to each of us to define ourselves as participants in this new interconnected world and to recognize that we are both demanding consumers and unwitting victims of too much information about us as individuals.

This is not your usual academic paper. It is, instead, a Declaration of Interdependence, which is meant to provide a narrative for the coming Internet of Things. Not everyone is equally enthusiastic about interdependence, but in reality, critics of networks and dependency often ignore the benefits while focusing on the downsides. This narrative seeks to identify paradoxes, which we should knead together until they constitute a balanced approach; that doesn't resolve the paradoxes, but rather accommodates them and taps their risk potential for mutual benefit. While the Internet was designed in the absence of social considerations, the Internet of Things does not have to suffer the same fate. As appetite for more and more information grows, and as more and more personal information is collected, we can get ahead of the consequences by engaging in insightful dialogue about how to define the new rules and tools that we need to exist in this new networked, interdependent world that is being created.

References

1. Cringely, R.X.: Breaking Moore's Law (2014). http://betanews.com/2013/10/15/breaking-moores-law/ (retrieved)
2. Podmolik, M.E.: Know thy neighbor: Zillow adds public data on homes in foreclosure but not yet for sale. Chicago Tribune, 26 October, 2012. http://articles.chicagotribune.com/2012-10-26/business/ct-biz-1026-zillow-20121026_1_zillow-distressed-homes-premarket-inventory (retrieved)
3. Picard, R.: Affective Computing. In: Tatnall, A. (ed.) HC 2013. LNCS, IFIP AICT, vol. 416 (2013)
4. Hilbert, M.: The worlds technological capacity to store, communicate and compute information. Science 332, 60 (2011)
5. Privacy Rights Clearinghouse. Chronology of Data Breaches Security Breaches 2005-Present. http://www.privacyrights.org/data-breach (retrieved)
6. Nissenbaum, H.: Director Information Law Institute. New York University. http://www.nyu.edu/projects/nissenbaum (retrieved)
7. Debt Advice Foundation. Google to impose Strict New Rules on Short-term Lenders, 13 December, 2012. http://www.debtadvicefoundation.org/news/2012/12/13/google-impose-strict-new-rules-short-term-lenders (retrieved)
8. Gubrium, J., Javinem, M. (eds.): Turning Troubles into Problems: Clientization in Human Services. Routledge Press, New York (2014)
9. Ibid. p.3
10. No More: Together we can end domestic violence & sexual assault. Retrieved at: http://nomore.org/
11. Rosen, J.: The Right to Be Forgotten, Stanford Law Review. Online 88, 13 February, 2012. http://www.stanfordlawreview.org/online/privacy-paradox/right-to-be-forgotten (retrieved)
12. National Strategy for Trusted Identities in Cyberspace (NSTIC). http://www.nist.gov/nstic/ (retrieved)

Designing, Developing, and Validating an Adaptive Visual Search Training Platform

Kelly S. Hale[1(⊠)], Katie Del Giudice[1], Jesse Flint[1],
Darren P. Wilson[2], Katherine Muse[3], and Bonnie Kudrick[3]

[1] Design Interactive, Inc., Orlando, FL, USA
{Kelly,Katie,Jesse.Flint}@designinteractive.net
[2] Department of Homeland Security, Houston, USA
Darren.Wilson@HQ.DHS.GOV
[3] Transportation Security Administration, Arlington, USA
{Katherine.Muse,Bonnie.Kudrick}@TSA.DHS.gov

Abstract. Transportation Security Officers (TSOs) are at the forefront of our nation's security, and are tasked with screening every bag boarding a commercial aircraft within the United States. TSOs undergo extensive classroom and simulation-based visual search training to learn how to identify threats within X-ray imagery. Integration of eye tracking technology into simulation-based training could further enhance training by providing in-process measures of traditionally "unobservable" visual search performance. This paper outlines the research and development approach taken to create an innovative training solution for X-ray image threat detection and resolution utilizing advances in eye tracking measurement and training science that provides individualized performance feedback to optimize training effectiveness and efficiency.

1 Introduction

The process of visual search involves finding a target in a field of non-targets or distractors. Visual search is used in a variety of professions, including radiography, surveillance, security, and inspections. It is one of the primary responsibilities of Transportation Security Officers (TSOs) working at airports throughout the United States. Considering that the visual search TSO process alone involves searching for, identifying, and removing potential threat items within passenger carry-on bags, the challenges associated with this task are numerous. First, images presented to TSOs are two-dimensional X-ray interpretations of three-dimensional bags, which differ from photographic visual representations to which most people are accustomed [1]. X-ray images provide information about the inner structure of the object and depict density, whereas photographs created by light reflection provide information about an object's surface. TSOs must thus learn to recognize threats based on an unnatural visual representation, and may utilize different feature components than those that would be used in a real-world visual search task. In addition, the extensive list of prohibited items [2] requires high-cognitive load and attentiveness to evaluate features of a presented image against an extensive internal mental 'library' of features indicative of threat items. Given the low likelihood of encountering a threat during operations compared to the

© Springer International Publishing Switzerland 2015
D.D. Schmorrow and C.M. Fidopiastis (Eds.): AC 2015, LNAI 9183, pp. 735–744, 2015.
DOI: 10.1007/978-3-319-20816-9_70

number of bags screened during a given shift, challenges with sustained attention [3] and vigilance can also impact performance. Furthermore, TSOs operate in a high-stress environment—both physically (e.g., noise, lighting) and psychologically stressful (e.g., passenger throughput, knowing the potentially catastrophic consequences of a missed threat, seeing line lengths increasing).

Because of the complex nature of the task, training TSOs to effectively and efficiently search each carry-on item passing through airport checkpoints requires extensive time and resources. Current training practices include traditional classroom instruction such as lectures, videos, and simulation-based training and mentor-supervised, on-the-job training. Current evaluation methods are often limited to observable behavioral metrics (e.g., detections, false alarms), which are challenging when trying to identify root cause (s) of performance errors (e.g., scan vs. recognition error) and associated influencing factors (e.g., threat type, location, orientation, clutter in bag, etc.). Current evaluation methods need to quantitatively measure details of cognitive states (e.g., inattention) that could negatively affect training outcomes. Due to the challenges with current data collection techniques, diagnosis, and feedback based on *process-level* measures of trainee visual search performance, evaluations and feedback provided by instructors may not address the underlying sources of the trainee's performance level.

Implementing new training methods from visual search research and leveraging emerging technologies can assist in improving the training process and maximize training efficiency and effectiveness. There are multiple reasons this opportunity for improvement exists, including (1) the challenge for an instructor to detect all trainee visual search errors due to the high workload associated with monitoring a complex scenario; (2) the challenge of the instructor to monitor subtle physical behaviors such as scanning patterns or cognitive processes; and (3) the challenge of the instructor to accurately and reliably identify key patterns into which visual search errors fall. As a result, traditional instructor-led training systems may not be capable of identifying the root cause of visual search errors within the baggage screening process.

The training system discussed in this paper was designed to address this gap in performance evaluation by providing instructors with the capability of diagnosing the root cause of performance errors using real-time measures of visual search. The goal of this innovative research and development (R&D) effort was to identify advances in visual search measurement and training science that could be incorporated into a simulation-based training platform to substantially enhance training effectiveness and efficiency of X-ray baggage screening. One advancement was to integrate visual search process measures that 'peer into the mind of the users' to capture perceptual and cognitive processes not otherwise accessible and that are capable of providing quantitative metrics to evaluate trainee cognitive state throughout a training session. Such measures can provide a more comprehensive assessment of progress as a trainee advances through visual search training, and can identify the root cause(s) of training deficiencies/inefficiencies. By understanding specific error patterns in the visual search process, specialized training strategies and training content can be implemented that are tailored to the individual trainee's needs. The resultant training system uses eye tracking measures, which capture where a trainee focused, in conjunction with meta-data available within the image being reviewed, to provide instructors and trainees with individualized feedback such as visual search patterns overlaid on X-ray images and a summary of accuracy across various threat types. This improvement in data collection, diagnosis, and feedback of process-level measures of an individual trainee's real-time visual search performance will address the underlying sources of poor performance in the training process and improve performance.

2 Background

A first primary step in visual search tasks, as well as many other cognitive processing tasks, is attention [4]. Within complex visual scenes, attention is used to select and modulate information based on behavioral relevance to appropriately deal with the problem of too much information. The process of focusing attention involves both parallel and serial mechanisms [5], and this concept forms the basis of many theories of attention. For example, Treisman and Gelade [6] proposed a feature integration theory of attention that follows the idea of guiding attention to a specific location based on a number of underlying processes and factors. Their theory includes a two-step process: an initial, preattentive parallel search where multiple features are registered automatically and a slower, serial search where focal attention is processed to determine what is visible at that location. The Guided Search Theory [7] maintains the two stage process with the distinction that the preattentive stage guides attention to select appropriate objects for the second stage.

Follow-on work and theoretical development has led to a general consensus that attention is primarily driven by one of two processes: stimulus-directed or goal-directed [8–10], where attention is guided either by the stimulus itself or by the goals inherent in the observer completing the visual search. Building on this notion of two distinct control mechanisms of attention, Chun, Golomb, Turk-Browne [11] created a taxonomy of Internal and External attention. External attention refers to a stimulus-driven mode for selection, where—within a visual search task—attention can be directed to spatial locations or time points (assuming some dynamic aspect to the task) alone, or to features or objects that can be selected across space and time. Within this stimulus-driven process, there are two distinct visual search strategies that have been proposed in the literature. The first strategy is Exogenous Search, where specific aspects of the visual scene are captured based on "hard wiring" of humans [10]. In other words, there are certain features that draw attention naturally, such as color, spatial location, and orientation. A second stimulus-based strategy is Endogenous Feature-Based Search, which has been termed habitual [10]. Here, features stand out "automatically" based on specific task knowledge or experience. In the context of baggage screening, there are certain features that are indicative of potential threats (e.g., sharp edge, etc.), and through experience and training, these features naturally 'pop-out' of the visual scene. Internal attention is driven by internal cognitive processes and pulls from representations in working memory and long-term memory based on task rules, decisions, and responses [11]. Here, an Endogenous Goal-Directed Search Strategy is employed where areas within a visual scene are evaluated against specific attentional/perceptual sets to assess relevance to the overarching task goal. In the context of baggage screening, specific areas of the image are compared against known threat 'maps' stored in long-term memory to assess for similarity.

The theoretical framework presented in Fig. 1 builds from Treisman and Gelade's [6] Feature Integration Theory model, and incorporates Chun's [11] taxonomy of Internal and External attention to frame two key search strategies relevant for carry-on baggage screening: exogenous search and endogenous search, with the latter being further subdivided into stimulus driven endogenous search types—feature-based, position-based, and scene-based—and goal-directed endogenous search. Although the literature shows differing support for which strategy comes into play under what circumstances, Neskovic & Cooper [12] promotes that fixations are initially driven by stimulus features, while subsequent fixations are constrained/focused by cognitive expectations during the recognition process. More recent summaries have proposed a 'guiding representation' that guides attention, but is not itself part of the perceptual pathway [13]. Within the guiding representation, a number of attributes have been identified that guide attention without reference to specific pathways (serial or parallel, preattentive). This theoretical model served as the foundation for the training system outlined in this paper, guiding training objectives and system requirements to optimize visual search and detection skills training.

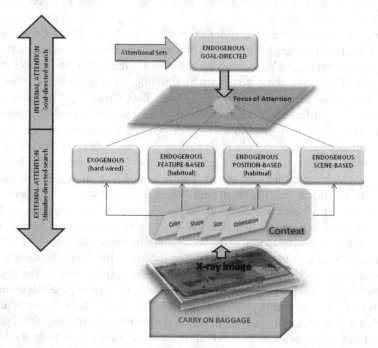

Fig. 1. Conceptual model of visual search strategies for carry-on baggage screening evaluation

3 Development Process

A user-centered training design and development approach [14] was utilized to develop an adaptive visual search training system. This process included: (1) identification of training needs and objectives for the system, (2) system requirements identification, (3) system specifications and architecture development, and (4) graphical user interface and database design. Once the system design was complete, an agile software development process was used to translate the design into functional training software.

3.1 Identification of Training Needs and Objectives

As a first step in the development process, subject matter expert (SME) interviews were completed with representatives from Transportation Security Administration (TSA) to fully understand their current operational and training methods, including the types of visual search challenges included in carry-on baggage screening. The data collected during the SME interviews was used to develop a Concept of Operations for initial system conceptualization and identification of high-level system requirements. Table 1 provides the high-level system requirements developed from SME interview data. This data was also used to identify measures of training effectiveness for both initial training and refresher training that could be used in future system validation.

Table 1. High-level system requirements

A closed-loop, adaptive training system that adapts in real time to user needs based on training strategy, content, and difficulty level
After action review sessions that allow trainees to identify and target areas for improvement
Content control options that allow instructors to maintain up to date images
A flexible image presentation system that reduces image repetition and encourages image novelty
Incremental difficulty levels that allow trainees to advance from novice to expert
Training sessions that allow trainees to increase their exposure to threat images
Training sessions that allow trainees to focus on fine details that distinguish threats from non-threats
System sensors that are portable, lightweight, non-invasive, in an easy-to-use form-factor, and deployable at a reasonable cost

3.2 Developing Detailed Design

Traditional observable training measures do not provide the granularity necessary to diagnose the root cause of visual search performance issues in order to effectively adapt training to address an individual trainee's needs. During this stage of the design process, a combination of observable measures and measures of perceptual and cognitive processes were identified. These measures included both outcomes, such as response accuracy, and processes, such as cognitive activity. An initial analysis of the cognitive activity measurement domain indicated that real-time sensing of task engagement, target awareness, visual attention, and alertness levels could be used to trigger adaptive training interventions.

A literature review was completed that focused on innovative behavioral sensors (e.g., eye tracking), physiological sensors, and brain-based technologies for each process measure. Each sensor category was evaluated to determine the feasibility or ease of near-term (less than three years) deployment within a TSO training environment. Remote eye tracking and electroencephalography (EEG) were considered as sensor inputs for providing real-time, process-level measures of performance. EEG is still considered the preferred method for ambulatory cognitive state sensing due to its relative ease of deployment and high-temporal resolution. However, although commercial EEG systems are available, the technology is not currently suited to the TSA environment due to the high procurement and maintenance costs. Remote eye tracking is a non-invasive method to assess multiple states such as loci of visual attention (gaze position), and level of alertness (blinking behavior). Eye tracking sensors meet the high-level requirements of being portable, lightweight, non-invasive, in an easy-to-use form-factor, and deployable at a reasonable cost, and provide the following measures related to visual perceptual processes [15]:

- Number of overall fixations – inversely correlated with search efficiency
- Gaze percent on each area of interest (AOI) – longer gazes equated with importance or difficulty of information extraction
- Mean Fixation Duration – longer fixations equated with difficulty of extracting information
- Number of fixations on each AOI – reflects importance of that area

The above eye tracking metrics were integrated with trainee responses (threat detection outcomes) to classify each visual image search using an adapted signal detection theory category. Traditional signal detection theory [16] separates visual search responses into four distinct categories in which a searcher can correctly identify a threat (hit), fail to identify a threat (miss), mistakenly identify a safe item as a threat (false alarm), or correctly clear a bag with no threat (correct rejection). These categories are effective at determining the sensitivity of the observer (how good they are at detecting threats). However, these categories are only intended to classify errors at a level needed to determine sensitivity, and are not appropriate for determining the root cause of errors. Including eye tracking metrics in the assessment of performance allows for a more granular breakdown of the miss category to distinguish searches in which the observer fixated on the target and failed to recognize that it was a targeted search item (recognition error), and searches in which the observer did not fixate on the location where the targeted search item was located (scanning error) (Table 2). Recognition and scanning errors can be used to diagnose root cause of errors to develop more focused training.

A diagnostic and adaptation framework was created to monitor eye tracking and behavioral performance in real time, and to determine (1) when, where, and why performance inefficiencies/deficiencies occurred for a given individual; (2) when to continue practice opportunities to increase performance efficiency; and (3) when to advance training to the next stage based on the trainee achievement at a defined task

Table 2. Adapted signal detection theory categories

Threat Present	Behavioral Response	Eye fixation on area of interest	Signal Detection Theory Category
No	No threat	—	Correct Rejection
No	Threat	—	False Alarm
Yes	No threat	No fixation	Miss – scan
Yes	No threat	Fixation	Miss – recognition
Yes	Threat	No fixation	Hit
Yes	Threat	Fixation	Hit

difficulty level. Building on the developer's experience with mitigation strategies [17], training system design [18], and discrimination training theory [19], the current effort conceptualized targeted After Action Review strategies for optimizing and individualizing training to advance training effectiveness and efficiency. At the current stage of development, two types of training have been developed to address the underlying needs of each type of visual search performance error. If a pattern of scan misses are detected, the system provides *exposure training*, which provides the opportunity to view threats and learn what threat items look like when X-rayed. In contrast, if a pattern of recognition misses are detected, the system provides *discrimination training*, which involves pairs of targets with or without salient differences presented in two separate side-by-side bag images. Discrimination training allows trainees to focus on the details of threat items that will enable them to distinguish between threats and non-threats in X-ray images.

These feedback strategies were designed to summarize performance process and outcome measures relative to targeted training goal(s), and the strategies provide suggested next training steps (e.g., proceed to higher difficultly, train specific need [orientation of threat or type of threat that is routinely missed], etc.). These displays may aid instructors in determining readiness for operations, while also allowing individual screeners to train independent of instructors. In addition, adaptive content features were integrated into the training system. Instructors also have the capability to upload updated training images. This provides the user with the capability to dynamically respond to specific operational needs and keep training current and relevant to the threat and security environment.

3.3   Iterative Development Using Agile Process

An agile development process was used to develop the training software. Agile development allows system development to occur in sprints, with development priorities being set at the beginning of the sprint cycle and a working software build being released at the conclusion of each sprint cycle. Two-week sprints were used throughout the development lifecycle, as this allowed adequate time to address the development priorities set at the beginning of the sprint and time for quality assurance testing of each released build. Some of the many benefits of the agile development process as opposed to traditional waterfall or spiral development models include: (1) flexible prioritization of requirements throughout the development lifecycle, (2) a working version of software maintained throughout development that can be used for user testing and feedback, and (3) additional time for quality assurance testing and resolution of identified bugs during sprints instead of at the conclusion of development.

3.4   Empirical Evaluation of Training System Effectiveness

To empirically evaluate training effectiveness, lab-based and field-based studies were completed. Lab-based studies focused on examining how the addition of eye tracking impacted the adaptive training paradigm, and were used to help develop the training platform and content [20, 21]. After initial system development was complete, a training effectiveness evaluation was conducted in the field. Working with the customer, an experimental design was developed that could be executed within operational constraints of space, time, and resources. The effectiveness evaluation was conducted with approximately 128 TSOs across three (3) airports using pre/post-test evaluation of visual search performance compared to control group training sessions. After engaging

Table 3. Critical system development components

Based on theoretical foundations of visual search
Identification of the method by which eye tracking metrics could provide meaningful feedback
Customer input was solicited early and often to:
-   validate high-level requirements
-   inform operational constraints that will limit end-user adoption (in this case, EEG)
-   evaluate feedback screens
Having an internal champion to:
-   identify key stakeholders within the organization
-   provide SMEs
-   coordinate field testing experimentation
Use of agile process to:
-   provide transparency to customer
-   decrease time to integrate new functionality
-   consistently refine and reprioritize based on fluctuating needs
Empirical evaluation of the training effectiveness of the system

in a pretest consisting of 100 X-ray bags to determine baseline performance at the image analysis task, each TSO was then exposed to 4.5 h of training across five consecutive days on the newly developed software or control training software. Results indicated that the training session that used the newly developed software resulted in significantly lower false alarm rates and time to identify threats when compared to the control group.

4 Summary

The R&D process outlined in this paper led to successful development of an innovative simulation-based training system designed to enhance visual search training for carry-on baggage at airport checkpoints. Table 3 highlights the components of the development process that were critical to the successful creation of the system.

5 Conclusion

This paper outlined the R&D process utilized to design and develop an innovative, adaptive training system for visual search. While the focus in this effort was on carry-on baggage screening, the training system framework is applicable to other domains such as radiology, law enforcement, and the military. A user-centered design process was essential to the success of the system, as key stakeholders' and end-users' feedback was captured throughout the effort to adapt and refine system design to meet their needs within operational constraints. Implementing an agile development process allowed for early and often stakeholder review, ensuring design elements discussed were integrated effectively into the end system. The research and development of the resulting system was sponsored by the Department of Homeland Security Science and Technology Directorate's Homeland Security Advanced Research Projects Agency and the TSA Office of Security Capabilities. The system was put through a training effectiveness evaluation in collaboration with the TSA Office of Training and Workforce Engagement, and has been positively received by TSOs.

References

1. Hilscher, M.: Performance Implications of Alternative Color-Codes in Airport X-ray Baggage Screening. University of Central Florida Student Dissertation (2005)
2. TSA.: Prohibited Items List (2011). http://www.tsa.gov/travelers/airtravel/prohibited/permitted-prohibited-items.shtm. Accessed 20 February 2011
3. Green, M.: Inattention blindness and conspicuity (2004). http://www.visualexpert.com/Resources/inattentionalblindness.html. Accessed 8 April 2011
4. Chun, M.M., Golomb, J.D., Turk-Browne, N.B.: A taxonomy of external and internal attention. Annu. Rev. Psychol. 62, 73–101 (2011)
5. Williams, E.: Visual Search: A novel psychophysics for preattentive vision. http://web.mit.edu/rsi/www/pdfs/papers/99/ekwillia.pdf (1999)

6. Treisman, A.M., Gelade, G.: A feature-integration theory of attention. Cogn. Psychol. **12**(1), 97–136 (1980)
7. Wolfe, J.M.: Guided search 2.0 a revised model of visual search. Psychon. Bull. Rev. **1**(2), 202–238 (1994)
8. Theeuwes, J.: Endogenous and exogenous control of visual selection. Perception **23**(4), 429–440 (1994)
9. Theeuwes, J.: Top-down and bottom-up control of visual selection. Acta. Psychol. **135**, 77–99 (2010)
10. Trick, L.M., Enns, J.T., Mills, J., Vavrik, J.: Paying attention behind the wheel: a framework for studying the role of attention in driving. Theor. Issues Ergon. Sci. **5**(5), 385–424 (2004)
11. Chun, M.M., Golomb, J.D., Turk-Browne, N.B.: A taxonomy of external and internal attention. Annu. Rev. Psychol. **62**, 73–101 (2011)
12. Neskovic, P., Cooper, L.N.: Visual search for object features. In: Wang, L., Chen, K., S. Ong, Y. (eds.) ICNC 2005. LNCS, vol. 3610, pp. 877–887. Springer, Heidelberg (2005)
13. Wolfe, J.M., Horowitz, T.S.: What attributes guide the deployment of visual attention and how do they do it? Nat. Rev. Neurosci. **5**(6), 495–501 (2004)
14. Goransson, B., Gulliksen, J., Boivie, I.: The usability design process - integrating user-centered systems design in the software development process. Softw. Process Improv. Pract. **8**, 111–131 (2003)
15. Radach, R., Hyona, J., Deubel, H. (eds.): The Mind's Eye: Cognitive and Applied Aspects of Eye Movement Research. Elsevier, Amsterdam (2003)
16. Macmillan, N.A., Creelman, C.D.: Detection Theory: A User's Guide. Lawrence Erlbaum Associates, Mahwah (2005)
17. Fuchs, S., Hale, K.S., Stanney, K.M., Juhnke, J., Schmorrow, D.D.: Enhancing mitigation in augmented cognition. J. Cogn. Eng. Decis. Making **1**(3), 309–326 (2007)
18. Milham, L.M., Carroll, M.B., Stanney, K.M., Becker, W.: Training requirements analysis. In: Schmorrow, D., Cohn, J., Nicholson, D. (eds.) The Handbook of Virtual Environment Training: Understanding, Predicting and Implementing Effective Training Solutions for Accelerated and Experiential Learning. Ashgate Publishing, Aldershot (2008)
19. Sellers, B., Rivera, J., Fiore, S.M., Schuster, D., Jentsch, F.: Assessing X-ray Security Screening Detection following Training with and without Threat-item Overlap. Proc. Hum. Factors Ergon. Soc. Annu. Meet. **54**(19), 1645–1649 (2010)
20. Hale, K.S., Carpenter, A., Johnston, M., Costello, J., Flint, J.D., Fiore, S.M.: Adaptive Training for Visual Search. In: Proceedings of the Interservice/Industry Training, Simulation & Education Conference (I/ITSEC 2012). Orlando. Paper # 12144 (2012)
21. Winslow, B., Carpenter, A., Flint, J.D., Wang, X., Tomasetti, D., Johnston, M., Hale, K.: Combining EEG and eye tracking: using fixation-locked potentials in visual search. J. Eye Mov. Res. **1**(1), 1–12 (2013)

An Object-Centric Paradigm
for Robot Programming by Demonstration

Di-Wei Huang[1]([✉]), Garrett E. Katz[1], Joshua D. Langsfeld[2], Hyuk Oh[3],
Rodolphe J. Gentili[4], and James A. Reggia[1]

[1] Department of Computer Science, UMIACS, University of Maryland,
College Park, MD 20742, USA
{dwh,reggia}@cs.umd.edu,gkatz12@umd.edu
[2] Department of Mechanical Engineering, University of Maryland,
College Park, MD 20742, USA
jdlangs@umd.edu
[3] Neuroscience and Cognitive Science Program, University of Maryland,
College Park, MD 20742, USA
hyukoh@umd.edu
[4] Department of Kinesiology, Graduate Program in Neuroscience and Cognitive
Science, Maryland Robotics Center, University of Maryland,
College Park, MD 20742, USA
rodolphe@umd.edu

Abstract. In robot programming by demonstration, we hypothesize
that in a class of procedural tasks where the end goal primarily consists of the states of objects that are external to a task performer, one
can significantly reduce complexity of a robot learner by not processing a human demonstrator's motions at all. In this class of tasks, object
behaviors are far more critical than human behaviors. Based on this virtual demonstrator hypothesis, this paper presents a paradigm where a
human demonstrates an object manipulation task in a simulated world
without any of the human demonstrator's body parts being sensed by
a robot learner. Based on the object movements alone, the robot learns
to perform the same task in the physical world. These results provide
strong support for the virtual demonstrator hypothesis.

Keywords: Programming by demonstration · Imitation learning ·
Human-robot interactions

1 Introduction

Programming by demonstration [1,2], or imitation learning, has emerged as a
popular approach for coding behaviors of robots. Essentially, a robot learner
is to observe a human perform a task (i.e., the demonstration), after which
the robot is to autonomously reproduce the human's behavior to complete the
same task (i.e., imitation). This general approach is widely viewed as an intuitive and promising alternative to conventional manual programming of robots.

© Springer International Publishing Switzerland 2015
D.D. Schmorrow and C.M. Fidopiastis (Eds.): AC 2015, LNAI 9183, pp. 745–756, 2015.
DOI: 10.1007/978-3-319-20816-9_71

However, the optimal way in which a demonstrator should interact with an observing robot has not been conclusively determined, and may vary depending on the task and/or the learning robot. Common criteria for evaluating such interactions include minimizing the barriers for humans to demonstrate, minimizing the burdens for a robot's learning algorithms to parse/analyze a demonstration (since imitation learning in itself is already a very difficult problem), and maximizing the types of tasks that are able to be demonstrated.

Existing interaction methods in which a robot learner observes a human demonstration can be classified into two classes. In the first class, the human demonstrator directly drives or manipulates the states of the robot's body, during which the robot stores the state trajectories for learning. The way in which the human drives the robot can be kinesthetic teaching, where a human physically pulls a robot's arms to complete a task [3,4], or teleoperating, where the robot is driven by remotely located controls [5,6]. The robot being driven can also exist in augmented realities [7] or virtual realities [8]. In the second class of interfaces, the human demonstrator performs the target task on his/her own without intervening in creating the states of the robot. The demonstration is captured by a camera and/or spatial markers that detect human motion, the results of which are passed to the robot for learning [9,10]. This method has been used in conjunction with kinesthetic teaching [11]. However, in many cases human motions on their own are vague and do not clearly convey the intention of a demonstration. To remedy this, human motion data are usually furnished with additional information, such as the states of task-related objects [12–14], from which the robot can learn the relations between hand motions and object movements, and speech descriptions about the motions, from which the robot can learn the intentions of the motions from symbolic annotations [15].

Although many demonstration interfaces in the past have emphasized conveying the trajectories of a human's body parts, learning from human motions in this way poses a major burden to the learner as it involves either difficult image processing or requires special equipment for capturing a human's movement. Complex processing is then needed to identify actions from the recorded motions, and to infer the effects the actions have on the task-related objects. Coordinate transformations must also be learned between the demonstrator's and learner's frames of references. Further, since a human's and a robot's bodies are usually very different from each other, it is likely that the robot has to act differently from the human to cause the same effect on an object. In this case, learning from human motions can be ineffective or extremely difficult. To address these issues, we are exploring the following alternative scenario:

Virtual demonstrator hypothesis: In many situations, effective imitation learning of a task can be achieved when the demonstrator is invisible.

In other words, in contrast to past work that deals with humans' physical demonstrations, we hypothesize that for many tasks where the goal is external to a performer's body, most critical information about a target procedure can be learned by ignoring the demonstrator and focusing instead primarily on the behaviors of the objects that are being manipulated, such as assembling a car or fixing a computer. By making the demonstrator a virtual presence, one qualitatively simplifies the motion tracking and understanding needed during learning and eliminates the coordinate transformation problems involved. This approach effectively shifts the problem of programming by demonstration from human motion understanding (i.e., how to do) to object behavior understanding (i.e., what to do). While similar ideas have been considered in a few past studies [12,13], they have either used an over-simplified environment (2D simulated world) or required special equipment. While we do not definitively prove the virtual demonstrator hypothesis in the current paper, we do provide a basic proof-of-concept that this hypothesis is valid in at least some situations and provide strong support for the hypothesis.

In the following, we describe an object-centric paradigm for programming by demonstration based on the virtual demonstrator hypothesis, where a demonstration is composed of object movements only while the human actions that cause these movements are not sensed by a robot learner. The work reported here is mainly about the interaction paradigm, as opposed to describing any specific cognitive robotics approaches to imitation learning. The latter will be the subject of a future paper.

2   Methods

Our object-centric programming by demonstration paradigm can be outlined as the following steps. (1) First, a task space is set up in a software-based simulated environment. (2) A human then demonstrates a task by manipulating objects in this environment via "invisible hands", the process of which is recorded as an object-only demonstration "video" along with information describing the state of the objects. (3) A robot agent processes the object-only video as well as the accompanying information, and forms a plan to reproduce the demonstration. The plan can then be rehearsed and refined in the same environment. (4) Finally, the plan is executed in the real world.

Our initial efforts have focused on a tabletop environment for bimanual object manipulation tasks, one that is being intensely studied such as in [16]. As a result, our software platform contains a 3D simulated world where an invisible demonstrator, a robot, a table, and a variety of task-related objects coexist. An example view of the simulated world as seen by the human demonstrator is given in Fig. 1, which contains a 3D environment and overlaid graphical user interface (GUI) controls (Fig. 1; top-right). The environment can be observed through a freely navigable perspective (Fig. 1; main window) and/or through the robot's perspective (Fig. 1; bottom-right). Real-time rigid body physics simulation is included based on the Bullet physics library[1].

2.1   Task Space Initialization

Task-related objects can be specified by writing XML files in conformance to a predefined XML schema. Our software platform loads such XML files and

---

[1] http://bulletphysics.org.

Fig. 1. An example view of the software simulation. The main screen shows a simulated environment containing a tabletop and a variety of objects (block, boxes, lids, strings, etc.), as they are seen by the human demonstrator. The avatar for a two-armed programmable robot is also embedded in the environment. The bottom-right corner shows the environment as it is seen by the robot. The top-right corner shows a sample GUI window. The user can manipulate the environment, including picking up, moving, rotating, and releasing objects, as well as changing the viewpoint and creating objects.

generates objects in the simulated environment accordingly. The XML schema defines XML elements for generating simple objects including blocks, cylinders, spheres, and containers (Fig. 2a–c), whose size, location, rotation, mass, color, etc., can be specified using XML attributes. Multiple simple objects can also be grouped hierarchically, via XML's hierarchical ordering, to form composite objects, whose center of mass can be specified. For example, the hammer shape in Fig. 2d is composed using three cylinders and a block. Further, more complex objects are included in the XML schema. A string object is simulated by connected solid links (Fig. 2e), which, when cut, will fall to the table (Fig. 2f). A container with a sliding lid can also be created (Fig. 2g). The lidded box can be positioned to become a container with a trap door (Fig. 2h).

2.2   Demonstration

A human demonstrator, while not embodied in the simulated environment, can manipulate objects using keyboard and mouse inputs through a GUI system, and therefore no special hardware is needed. For example, a user can virtually grasp an object by simply clicking on it, and move it by dragging the mouse cursor. A demonstration containing multiple object manipulations can be recorded as a video (a sequence of visual images) and optional text descriptions (object shapes, colors, positions, orientations, etc.), which are then used subsequently for training a robot. Text descriptions enable researchers to opt to work at high-level reasoning about what happens in the scene instead of pure visual learning. A demonstration can be edited as it is created, by undoing unwanted actions. Since

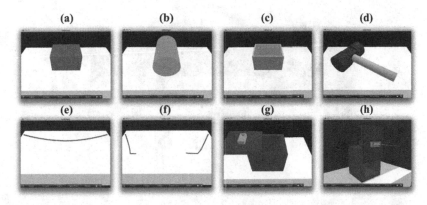

Fig. 2. Sample objects generated via XML files. (a)–(c) show simple objects: a block, a cylinder, and a box container. (d) shows a composite object, a hammer. (e), (f) show a string that when cut dynamically falls onto the table. (g), (h) show a box container with a sliding lid.

the demonstrator is not visible in the simulated world, it is therefore not necessary for the robot to capture and understand human motions or to transform between coordinate systems. Instead, learning can be focused entirely on the consequences of the demonstrator's manipulative movements in the task/object space. That is, from the robot's perspective, the objects in the environment appear to move on their own.

The demonstrator conceptually has two manipulators, or "hands", which can independently manipulate two objects. Each hand can manipulate an object by grasp, move, rotate, and release operations. A manipulation starts by grasping an object, from which point on the object is temporarily unaffected by gravity, i.e., it is held by an invisible hand. A user does so by simply clicking on an object to be moved. The object can then undergo a series of movements and/or rotations. The user can move the object by dragging it. In Fig. 3, the block on the right side is grasped and lifted above the tabletop. To guide the user through moving an object in 3D space using 2D mouse inputs, a rotatable restricting plane and a virtual shadow is added to the demonstrator's perspective (Fig. 3a–b). The object can also be rotated in the three primary axes using GUI controls (Fig. 3c–d). Finally, when the object has been moved/rotated to a desired destination/orientation, it can then be released by clicking the release button. The object resumes being affected by gravity after it is released. The demonstrator can switch between the two hands while manipulating objects. To manipulate two objects in parallel, the demonstrator needs to manually interleave the manipulative actions of the two hands. In the case where the user made an unwanted action, an undo function is provided to restore the previous world state and discard the corresponding segment in the recorded video.

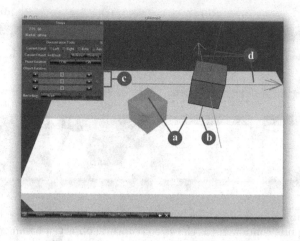

Fig. 3. The demonstration interface. The red block (right) is currently grasped by the demonstrator and raised above the tabletop. (a) A restricting plane perpendicular to the tabletop that guides movement of the grasped object in the 3D world. The plane can be rotated around the vertical axis to select different moving paths. (b) A virtual shadow indicating the location of the object. (c) Sliders that control object rotations around (d) the three primary axes (color coded) (Color figure online).

2.3 Robot Agent

A Matlab application programming interface (API) for controlling a simulated robot is provided. The interface is designed such that a user program serves as the "brain" of the robot that communicates with the body via sensory inputs and motor commands. Specifically, the user program is invoked iteratively at approximately 60 Hz (depending on the computing capacity and complexity of the callback script). In each iteration, the user program is supplied with sensory information in a Matlab variable such as time elapsed since last invocation, current joint angles, current gripper opening, visual images, and end effector positions. The user program can then specify motor commands in another Matlab variable containing joint and gripper velocities. This API resembles a typical perception-action cycle that is adopted by many bio-inspired intelligent agents.

The robot currently built into this system is modeled after Baxter®, a commercial bimanual robot by Rethink Robotics. Each arm of the robot consists of seven joints, two on the shoulder, two on the elbow, and three on the wrist. Physics effects are implemented for the arms to affect objects, making it possible to perform tasks such as pushing an object using a forearm. The robot "sees" the simulated world through a camera mounted on its head, which can pan horizontally. The 3D model and joint configurations of the robot are extracted from data released by the manufacturer[2]. A gripper is attached at the end of each arm, which can act on objects in the environment. The distance between

---

[2] https://github.com/RethinkRobotics/.

the two "fingers" of a gripper can be widened or narrowed, so the gripper can hold or release objects. When a gripper is closing, a simple algorithm is used to determine if an object should be considered grasped by a gripper based on the contact points and normals. If so, the object is attached to the gripper and becomes unaffected by gravity. On the other hand, when the gripper is opening, any grasped objects are considered released and resume being affected by gravity. For debugging purposes, the software provides additional features such as manually controlling robot joints and drawing visual markers in the simulated environment.

2.4 Physical Performance

After a robot controller Matlab program is trained and tested with the simulated robot, it is straightforward to migrate it to control a real Baxter robot through ROS and Robot Raconteur[3]. The latter provides an interface containing methods to read sensor information, such as joint angles and camera images, and to write motor directives, such as new joint velocities or positions, in a similar way to our robot API. Some calibration and parameter tuning is needed to compensate for the differences between the simulated and the physical worlds, such as different camera parameters, lighting conditions, or gripper sizes. Simulated physics can also be different from real physics in complex scenes. It is up to individual robot learning methods to incorporate these factors to build a more generalized controller that reacts to environmental variations.

3 Results: An Example

As a first step in validating the virtual demonstrator hypothesis and to provide an example of our object-centric paradigm, we studied a case of programming by demonstration that involves a simple block stacking task. Initially, there are several blocks in three different sizes lying on the tabletop. The demonstrator manipulates these blocks to build a structure in the simulated environment, and the process is simultaneously recorded as a demonstration. The goal is for a physical robot to start with the same set of blocks placed at different initial positions in the real world, and eventually build the same structure in the same sequence as seen in the demonstration. This example by no means exhausts all possible issues one may encounter in studying robot programming by demonstration, but simply provides a proof of concept: that learning from a virtual demonstrator is viable, at least in certain situations.

First, an XML file was written to generate the initial scene (Fig. 4; left) for the demonstrator to work on. The scene contains ten cubic blocks in red or blue, a $1 \times 1 \times 3$ block in blue, and two $1 \times 1 \times 2$ blocks in red. A human demonstrator then manipulates these blocks to build a structure using only mouse inputs and GUI controls. In this specific example the demonstrator builds what resembles

---

[3] https://robotraconteur.com.

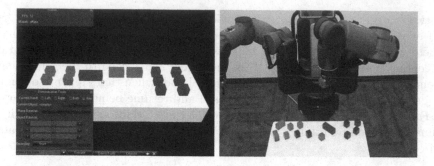

Fig. 4. Left: An initial scene as seen by the demonstrator. Right: A different initial scene for the robot to perform the demonstrated task.

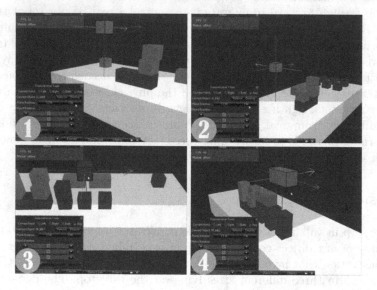

Fig. 5. Screenshots during a demonstration of stacking blocks into the letters "UM" in the virtual environment. The screenshots are temporally ordered in (1)–(4). In (2), the "U" is almost done. In (4), the final piece is going into position.

the letters "UM" (for our institution). A demonstration video is recorded during the demonstration. The demonstrator may elect to undo mistaken actions, in which case the video is updated accordingly. Figure 5 shows four screenshots sampled from a single demonstration. In each screenshot, the human demonstrator acts on the objects in the simulated environment. The demonstrator is invisible to the robot, and thus the blocks appear to be "flying" around from the robot's perspective. Along with the video, symbolic descriptions are generated to indicate which demonstrator's hand is being used and the locations of objects, etc. This symbolic information is optional: a purely vision-based learning system would be able to estimate the locations of objects without referring to symbolic information, but here we intentionally keep our Matlab program simple by using symbolic information to skip some of the complex aspects of image processing.

The physical robot is presented with a new initial scene containing the same blocks from the demonstration (Fig. 4; right). The initial locations of blocks are significantly different from what the human demonstrator started with (Fig. 4; left). In this assessment, the robotic system is learning the intentions/goals of the demonstrator from a single demonstration, and not memorizing the demonstrator's arm trajectories (the demonstrator is invisible as far as the robotic learner is concerned). Thus the robot must immediately generalize to handling a new initial state rather than the initial state used by the demonstrator.

The robot imitation learner[4] is implemented in Matlab and uses the same API to communicate with the physical robot and simulated robot. The Matlab program takes as input the demonstration video (along with symbolic information) and the image capture of the new initial scene (no symbolic information is used). The raw image is "parsed" to determine the locations and orientations of each block, and encode this information in a symbolic form. The Matlab program then generates a plan that best matches what is observed in the demonstration video, including the order in which to stack blocks, the colors and sizes of blocks to be used, the relative positions of blocks in the target structure, and which arm to use. If no arm is specified in the demonstration, the program chooses which arm to use in accordance with the new initial scene. The plan is eventually translated into a

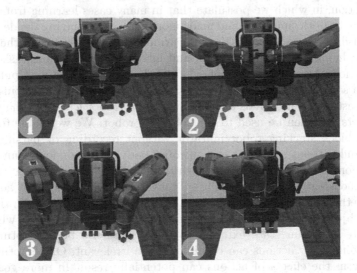

Fig. 6. The robot's successful imitation of stacking blocks into the letters "UM". Pictures are taken in the order of (1)–(4). In (2), arm coordination is being executed as Baxter transfers a block from one hand to the other. In (4), the final "UM" is present (pictures were taken from the opposite side of "UM").

---

[4] We are mainly describing the paradigm here; our robotic learning system will be the subject of a future paper.

Fig. 7. The goal state demonstrated in the virtual environment (left) and the one executed by the robot (right) (Color figure online).

sequence of waypoints for the robot arms to reach, which are then converted to arm joint velocities and passed to the robot for execution. The execution of the plan is shown in Fig. 6 (sampled screenshots). The resulting structure the robot built and the procedure in which the robot built it are qualitatively similar to what the human demonstrated (see Fig. 7), despite that they were started from different initial conditions. The color arrangement of blocks are properly imitated, although the blocks sometimes are not perfectly aligned.

4   Discussion

In summary, we presented an object-centric paradigm for robot programming by demonstration, in which we postulate that in many cases learning from demonstration can be both simplified and made more effective by having the demonstrator be invisible. As such, efforts during learning can be shifted from the difficult problem of human motion perception and interpretation to more task-relevant aspects by focusing only on the behaviors of the objects being manipulated. To this end, a software-based simulated environment was built for creating object-only demonstrations as well as training and testing robot learners. The resulting robot agents can then be used to control a real robot. We were able to quickly develop a block stacking robot imitator without recording or parsing human motions, and without analyzing human-robot body correspondences and coordinate transformations. The "UM" task showed that a software-generated object-centric demonstration can eventually be converted to physical robot actions.

Our method promotes learning based on the effects of actions, i.e., the movements of objects, rather than the actions themselves. In many tasks whose goal is to create a certain state external to the performer's body, capturing and understanding body actions can be difficult and irrelevant. On the other hand, learning from the effects of actions can potentially result in more goal-driven action plans. In fact, since a robot's body configurations are usually very different from those of humans, direct learning from a human's actions is not always possible and may not result in the same effects. In our current result, although the human demonstrator used the same hand throughout the task, the robot decided to transfer blocks from one hand to the other (Fig. 6(2)) due to limitations on which blocks each hand could reach. In this case, imitation strategies that directly mimic human motions may fail. Moreover, highly sophisticated robots may benefit from not mimicking human motions. For example, robots with more arms than humans can potentially complete a task in a way more efficient than a human's approach.

The approach we took heavily relies on software simulations. Compared with physical demonstrations, this simulation-based approach provides a natural way to completely hide the demonstrator's body from the robot observer. The locations and orientations of each object in the simulated world can be obtained easily, instead of having to attach physical markers to each object and/or the demonstrator's body. A simulated environment also reduces human fatigue and risks, as well as managing mental workload and emotional responses. For example, a human can avoid physically demonstrating dangerous tasks in hazardous environments such as a battlefield or underwater. After a robot is trained, it can potentially work with humans as a team while taking over the most dangerous parts of a task, which avoids poor performance caused by human fatigue and critical emotional responses. Furthermore, the simulation abstracts the sizes of objects, so it is now possible to demonstrate what is normally too large or too small to demonstrate in the physical world, such as building a bridge or operating at a nanotechnology level.

The main tradeoff for using our method is that not all tasks can be demonstrated in the software simulation. It is only applicable to a certain class of tasks where object behaviors alone matter. Our method cannot be used in situations where the goal is to mimic human body motions, such as learning a sign language, although it is conceivable that it might be extended to such a challenging task. It does not faithfully capture the trajectory and velocity at which a human would move an object by hand, due to its using a GUI and mouse inputs which inevitably restrict all possible trajectories and velocities to a small subset. It is also not suitable for tasks where the amounts of forces applied to objects are important, although such information is difficult to present even in a physical demonstration environment. Moreover, simulating high-precision physics in real time is generally a hard problem, and thus some simplifications and compromises must be made to reduce computational costs. This requires extra efforts to be put in software implementation and inevitably incurs some unrealistic physical effects in the simulated environment. Currently, our software is limited in simulating only rigid body physics.

Our future work will focus on developing a neurocognitive system that learns from object-centric demonstrations in a complex task scene where it is critical for the robot agent to reason about what happens in a demonstration. We will expand the types of supported task objects including tools.

Acknowledgment. Supported by ONR award N000141310597.

References

1. Argall, B.D., Chernova, S., Veloso, M., Browning, B.: A survey of robot learning from demonstration. Robot. Auton. Syst. **57**(5), 469–483 (2009)

2. Billard, A., Calinon, S., Dillmann, R., Schaal, S.: Robot programming by demonstration. In: Siciliano, B., Khatib, O. (eds.) Springer Handbook of Robotics, pp. 1371–1394. Springer, Heidelberg (2008)
3. Akgun, B., Cakmak, M., Yoo, J.W., Thomaz, A.L.: Trajectories and keyframes for kinesthetic teaching: a human-robot interaction perspective. In: ACM/IEEE International Conference on Human-Robot Interaction, pp. 391–398 (2012)
4. Billard, A.G., Calinon, S., Guenter, F.: Discriminative and adaptive imitation in uni-manual and bi-manual tasks. Robot. Auton. Syst. **54**(5), 370–384 (2006)
5. Chen, J., Haas, E., Barnes, M.: Human performance issues and user interface design for teleoperated robots. IEEE Trans. Syst., Man, Cybern. C **37**(6), 1231–1245 (2007)
6. Sweeney, J., Grupen, R.: A model of shared grasp affordances from demonstration. In: IEEE-RAS International Conference on Humanoid Robots, pp. 27–35 (2007)
7. Chong, J., Ong, S., Nee, A., Youcef-Youmi, K.: Robot programming using augmented reality: an interactive method for planning collision-free paths. Robot. Comput. Integr. Manuf. **25**(3), 689–701 (2009)
8. Martin, R., Sanz, P., Nebot, P., Wirz, R.: A multimodal interface to control a robot arm via the web: a case study on remote programming. IEEE Trans. Ind. Electron. **52**(6), 1506–1520 (2005)
9. Azad, P., Asfour, T., Dillmann, R.: Robust real-time stereo-based markerless human motion capture. In: IEEE-RAS International Conference on Humanoid Robots, pp. 700–707 (2008)
10. Dillmann, R., Asfour, T., Do, M., Jäkel, R., Kasper, A., Azad, P., Ude, A., Schmidt-Rohr, S., Lösch, M.: Advances in robot programming by demonstration. KI - Künstliche Intelligenz **24**(4), 295–303 (2010)
11. Calinon, S., Billard, A.G.: What is the teacher's role in robot programming by demonstration?: toward benchmarks for improved learning. Interact. Stud. **8**(3), 441–464 (2007)
12. Aleotti, J., Caselli, S.: Physics-based virtual reality for task learning and intelligent disassembly planning. Virtual Real. **15**(1), 41–54 (2011)
13. Alissandrakis, A., Nehaniv, C.L., Dautenhahn, K., Saunders, J.: Achieving corresponding effects on multiple robotic platforms: imitating in context using different effect metrics. In: International Symposium on Imitation in Animals and Artifacts (2005)
14. Chella, A., Dindo, H., Infantino, I.: A cognitive framework for imitation learning. Robot. Auton. Syst. **54**(5), 403–408 (2006)
15. Dominey, P.F., Alvarez, M., Gao, B., Jeambrun, M., Cheylus, A., Weitzenfeld, A., Martinez, A., Medrano, A.: Robot command, interrogation and teaching via social interaction. In: IEEE-RAS International Conference on Humanoid Robots, pp. 475–480 (2005)
16. Feniello, A., Dang, H., Birchfield, S.: Program synthesis by examples for object repositioning tasks. In: IEEE/RSJ International Conference on Intelligent Robots and Systems (2014)

Optimization-Based Training in ATM

Amela Karahasanović(✉), Tomas Eric Nordlander,
and Patrick Schittekat

SINTEF ICT, Oslo, Norway
{Amela.Karahasanovic,Tomas.Nordlander,
Patrick.Schittekat}@sintef.no

Abstract. Air Traffic Management is responsible for guiding airplanes as efficiently and safely as possible at and between airports. A team of air traffic controllers is required to make good decisions at all times, even under high stress. The complexity of their tasks requires frequent and high-quality training to ensure constant high performance of the team. In this paper, we present work in progress on a novel training tool based on the *Optimization-based Virtual Instructor*. The tool we propose combines mathematical optimization with visualization, and is expected to improve the training quality while reducing the training cost. We discuss the new Virtual Instructor concept and introduce the necessary state-of-the-art advances needed for both visualization and mathematical optimization to make it work. Two early-stage visualization prototypes are presented. The paper concludes with a possible way forward in the development of the Virtual Instructor.

Keywords: ATM · Training · Optimization

1 Introduction

The increase in air transportation is an important factor for economic growth. However, the current Air Traffic Management (ATM) systems are already approaching their capacity limits and need to be reformed to meet the demands of further growth, sustainability, increased safety, predictability, and efficiency [1]. Coping with these challenges requires not only new automation tools and enhanced procedures, but also a rethinking of Air Traffic Controller (ATCO) training [2].

The real-time simulation (RTS) of work scenarios is considered a cost-effective method of training new and experienced ATCOs to safely manage the efficient flow of aircrafts [3]. One of the great advantages of RTS, compared with other learning aids, is the ability to freeze and replay scenarios directly, enabling instructors to provide timely feedback related to a given traffic situation, as well as on the quality of the decisions made by the trainee [4]. However, there are several disadvantages of RTS: it requires the full attention of an instructor and it disrupts the trainees, making it difficult for them to progress and positively reinforce their learned skills [2]. This can have negative impacts on the achieved learning quality and can consequently affect the operative productivity in Air Traffic Control (ATC) rooms. To overcome this, a self-assessment training tool has been developed that enables ATCOs to review their workflow and

© Springer International Publishing Switzerland 2015
D.D. Schmorrow and C.M. Fidopiastis (Eds.): AC 2015, LNAI 9183, pp. 757–766, 2015.
DOI: 10.1007/978-3-319-20816-9_72

performance at the individual and team level [5]. The results show visual feedback consisting of workflow graphs and radar replays can generate valuable insights that enable self/peer assessments during ATC training. However, the users of the tool expressed a need for the inclusion of a presentation of better (optimal) solutions/decisions that could be used to improve self-learning or group discussions.

In combinatorial complex environments like ATM, it is very unlikely to find optimal solutions/decisions manually. As the many possible decisions and objectives should be considered simultaneously mathematical optimization excels. We believe a training tool based on visualization along with discrete optimization models and algorithms will improve ATCO training. We envisage such a tool will help ATCOs gain an understanding of the effects of their decisions on team performance when using an optimization-based algorithm as a *virtual instructor*.

This paper presents our ongoing development of such a tool. Section 2 describes the related work done in the area of visualization, learning, and optimization. Section 3 presents our optimization-based virtual instructor, and Sect. 4 concludes and proposes future work.

2 Related Work

To develop a training tool capable of presenting an optimal solution, we must draw from the related work in the areas of visualization, learning, and optimization. This section briefly presents the related work and our research questions.

2.1 Visualization and Learning

Whereas traditionally, the term visualization was used to mean 'constructing a visual image in the mind', it now means 'a graphical representation of data or concepts' [9]. Visualization has been used to present the data, support reasoning, and make predictions. With the development of the technology and advancements of our abilities to interact with information, the need to understand the benefits of different presentation forms for human cognition has arisen. Scaife and Rogers proposed a framework to investigate the cognitive value of external graphical presentations, such as maps, diagrams, drawings, and graphs [10]. The main cognitive benefits of using such presentations are externalizing to reduce memory load, computational offloading, annotating, and cognitive tracking. Externalization to reduce memory load includes personal reminders and calendars. Computational offloading includes using a pen and paper for calculations. Annotations and cognitive tracking include modifying representations to reflect changes, such as reordering or crossing tasks off a to-do list [11].

Research has been conducted on understanding the effects of multiple representations. In his Design, Function, Task (DeFT) framework, Ainsworth integrates research in learning, the cognitive science of representation, and constructivist theories of education. He argues that effectiveness of multiple (external) representations can be best understood by considering the characteristics of representations, the role of representations in learning, and the cognitive tasks of learners when interacting with representations [12]. Furthermore, it has been argued that studies evaluating information visualization should focus on the following three aspects, namely users, tasks, and tools (visual representations) [13].

Research has also been done on how visualization techniques can support the teaching and learning of optimization algorithms [14]. To enhance the learning of the Golden Section method, a tool was developed that visualizes the process of bracketing the optimal solution, the iterative reduction of the interval size, and the effectiveness of using the Golden Section ratio. The results indicate the usefulness of such tools.

2.2 Optimization

In optimization, the problem faced by the decision maker is modelled mathematically with the use of constraints, variables, and objectives. When this is done, an algorithm then evaluate a large amount of plausible solutions to the problem to identify the optimal or near-optimal solution. In the context of this paper, a solution describes the decisions that could be implemented.

In more detail, the mathematical model consists of a set of variables, and for each variable, a set of possible values the variable can take. These variables are connected through a set of constraints that restrict which value the variables can take. In general, a feasible solution is the simultaneous assignment of a value to every variable in such a way that no constraints are violated. An objective function is then used to determine the optimal solutions (or good ones) by evaluating the quality of feasible solutions. This objective function consists of a set of decision variables with associated weights of importance (e.g., the importance of route length compared to time used). The feasible solutions are then evaluated through the objective function, and those with the best objective function score are considered the best solution.

Mathematical optimization is used in our daily lives, for example: when asking our GPS navigation system to find the shortest (or fastest) route from point A to point B. Calculating optimal routes manually is a combinatorial, complex, and time-consuming task, while mathematical optimization techniques in our navigation systems often provide the optimal route in mille-seconds.

The ATCO is faced with what mathematicians classify as a hard combinatorial problem where it would be too time-consuming for an ATCO to evaluate all the possible combinations of airplane routes manually. However, while the controller can often find feasible combinations of routes manually (due to the large amount of solutions), it is highly unlikely they would be efficient considering the sheer number of existing combinations—it's a combinatorial problem, where the amount of combinations to investigate increases exponentially with the problem size.

For example, an ATCO assigning existing fixed routes to airplanes from the gate to the runway would have 720 combinations to evaluate when dealing with only six planes and six routes. While some of these combinations (plans) might violate some given constraints (e.g., maximum speed, crossing restricted area, etc.), others do not and are thereby feasible plans. To find the optimal plan, all feasible plans must be evaluated against each other on properties that characterize a good plan (e.g., min. delay, min. distance, preferences, etc.). While six airplanes and six routes is a small

Table 1. Route assignment, a combinatorial problem

Number of airplanes	Number of routes	Number of combinations
6	6	720
12	12	479001600
25	25	15511210043330985984000000
50	50	3.0414093e+64

problem, as the problem grows in size, the combinations grow exponentially (see Table 1). Note that a realistic ATC problem is much more complex.

It is in these types of combinatorial problems where optimization algorithms excel over humans by quickly searching through a large number of combinations and identifying efficient or optimal ones by evaluating each possible solution against others with respect to several (and often conflicting) criteria that characterize a good solution.

The literature on optimized air traffic control for an airport is quite wide, and we refer the reader to recent surveys [6, 7]. Relevant recent progress has been on optimizing different routing phases (surface, departure, and arrival phases) simultaneously and only need on average 15 s (on a laptop) to find the optimal solution. In [8], the authors explain the application and results of the optimization model and algorithms that decide the trajectories of all airplanes in time and space at the Hamburg airport. Afterwards, these optimal trajectories produced by the algorithm were compared with the trajectories made by the controllers during training for three simulation runs. The algorithm and the controllers were given exactly the same input from the simulator to ensure as fair a comparison as possible; the algorithm and controllers considered the same safety rules (runway separations, airplane turning restrictions, etc.) with the objectives of "minimizing total taxi time" and "maximizing punctuality". The results showed optimization-based decision support can provide significant improvements to total taxi time and punctuality, while still maintaining the same level of safety. The improvement potential for the controllers against the algorithm on taxi time was on average 30 %, while punctuality can be improved by 60 %. In addition, without explicitly modelling it, the maximum number of airplanes simultaneously moving on the taxiway can be reduced by 45 %, which would imply a decreased risk of collisions.

The main reason for the performance difference between ATCOs and the algorithm is the capability of the algorithm to make more globally coordinated decisions than the ATCO team. Each individual controller is only responsible for a part of the airport. This compartmentalization of responsibility within the ATCO team is needed to manually cope with the complexity of the task. However, its downside it that it removes the globally view of the problem and most likely also some globally efficient solutions are removed. One really god solutions for one ATC might create havoc ATC down the line. Optimization techniques do not have this disadvantage.

2.3   Research Questions

The research conducted in the areas of visualization and learning forms a solid basis for our understanding of the effects of different presentation forms on learning. However, there is a lack of knowledge on how to present pedagogically alternative solutions in complex domains, such as ATM. According to our knowledge, there is a large research gap when it comes to optimization used for learning.

This leads us to the following research questions:

- **RQ1:** How can we visually present alternative (optimal) decisions and impact of these decisions in order to improve learning?
- **RQ2:** If and how optimal solutions proposed by the mathematical optimization can improve learning? How can we identify the most beneficial and learnable changes to the decisions made by the controller given the optimal solution?

3 Virtual Instructor

To enhance learning in the ATM context, we envisage a tool called the *virtual instructor*, which will enable trainees to replay their decisions, present the impact of these decisions on system performance, and present the alternative solutions in a pedagogical way. This section describes the requirements for such a tool.

An important concept in the ATM context is *situation awareness (SA)*. SA is 'the perception of the elements in the environment within a volume of time and space, the comprehension of their meaning, and the projection of their status in the near future' [8]. Work has been done on the development of design guidelines for SA [9]. In the context of air traffic control, SA usually means the picture, a mental representation of the situation the controllers have on which they base their decisions. A training tool for ATCOs should aim to increase situation awareness.

The above-described frameworks [10–13] identify the main components that should be understood when using visualization in learning. Designing an efficient learning tool for ATCOs should build on:

- A good understanding of users. This includes different levels of expertise in their job, such as general ATCO experience, as well as experience with a particular airport, proficiency with the tools they are using, and cognitive abilities, such as spatial ability and associative memory. Standard tests like *Kit of Factor-Referenced Cognitive tests*[1] can be used.
- A good understanding of the tasks conducted in a learning situation with no instructor.
- A good understanding of potential cognitive benefits of different presentations. The above-described benefits, design objectives, and design heuristics [11, 12] can be used.
- Identifying the learning benefits of different information, presentation forms, and their combinations.

We started by identifying two possible scenarios. In the first scenario, the trainees replay their actions, receive feedback from the system at different decision points based

---

[1] http://trec.nist.gov/data.html.

on the consequences of their decisions, and are presented with an alternative (better) solution. For example, one can present the information on the reduction of taxi time achieved by changing the block-off time and present the movements at the airport in that case. In the other scenario, one can guide trainees to make better decisions by using reminders. For example, one can remind ATCOs of the optimal time for a plane to leave the gate.

The preliminary exploration of the above-described scenarios has been done in two student projects. The first one developed and evaluated a post-simulation training tool that presented an animation of the plane movements based on what the trainees did in the previous training session. The tool presents some critical decision points on a timeline, as well as an explanation of the how these decisions can be improved [14]. During the evaluation, several participants pointed out they would prefer an animated presentation of the optimal solution instead of its textual description (Fig 1).

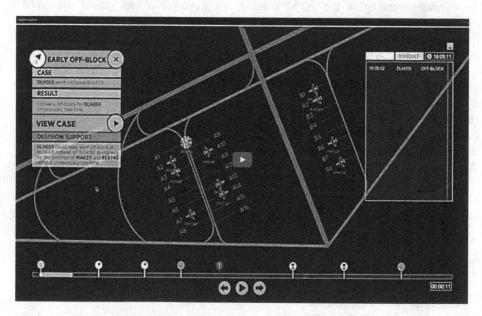

Fig. 1. Flashback tool. from [14]. The green box on the left presents an explanation (early off-block in this case). Different decisions that can be improved are presented on the timeline (Color figure online).

The other project focused on informing the controllers when to leave the gate, as well as which route should they take [15]. Visualizing the state of a plane (more than 5 min to off-block: red; less than 5 min: orange; time for off-block: green) and presenting a timer was proposed. These two scenarios will further be detailed to provide a list of tasks the trainees perform when learning with the help of an optimization tool.

To identify the learning benefits of different information, presentations forms, and their combinations, a set of measures capturing the learning effect in this context must be proposed. Presenting to ATCOs an alternative way of doing their job is not only a question of presentation form, but also a question of the selection of data to be presented. Whereas traditional studies on the usefulness of visualization in learning compare the effects of two different ways of presenting the same information (e.g., comparing an animated and static condition like in [16]), we must also identify the information that will be presented. We assume some solutions generated by an optimization algorithm are more difficult to explain and less intuitive than others.

The virtual instructor would need to suggest the most optimal sequence of changes, starting from the decisions made by the controller. How do we identify this sequence was the subject of research question 2 (Sect. 2.3). Furthermore, for this, we use optimization techniques. A change is defined as a set of decisions that must be modified to move from one solution to another. Two different types of objectives determine whether one change is better than another. The first objective is maximizing performance improvement. In our case, we would like to make changes that improve aspects, such as total taxi time and punctuality. The second objective is more related to the learnability of the changes themselves. Are the proposed changes easily understood by the trainee so that in the future, he or she would take the more performant decision? How this learnability can be measured and formalized is still a subject for future work. However, one can imagine the learnability of the changes depends on multiple factors, such as:

1. The number of decisions that are different from the original decisions;
2. How far into the decision tree the proposed changes propagate;
3. How complex the actions are to perform to implement in practice the change.

We assume a suitable learnability distance measure can be defined based on the above and possibly other factors. The larger the learnability distance between two solutions, the more difficult it would be to learn the changes to move from one solution to another. Hence, the second objective boils down to minimizing this distance from the initial solution when selecting changes to improve the first objective. The two objectives will often be conflicting and a suitable balance between them must be achieved. Furthermore, we want to avoid changing a solution such that it becomes unfeasible, i.e., two airplanes crash. In Fig. 2, the optimization problem to find the optimal sequence of changes is illustrated. In summary, the algorithm must find the best possible solution (in terms of the first objective), which can be reached by applying a sequence of changes from the starting solution. The sequence of changes should result in the lowest possible learnability distance from the starting solution.

This mathematical optimization problem is not easily solved and to the best of our knowledge, not much relevant research exists. Although used in another context (solving vehicle routing problems), distance-based path relinking is an approach [17] that shows potential for several reasons. Path relinking assumes a good solution exists on the path between a so-called "incumbent" solution and the "guiding" solution [18]. The former would be the manual or initial solution, while the optimal solution is the latter. There exists an exponential number of paths or sequences of changes between these solutions. The resulting path is chosen by making local changes to the solution, and a distance measure is used to ensure it moves further away from the incumbent

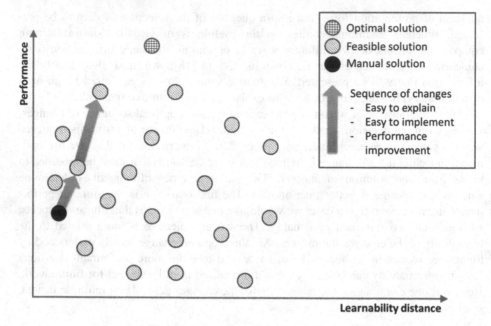

Fig. 2. Finding the optimal sequence of changes

solution. In our case, we would try to stay as close as possible to the incumbent solution. This looks like a promising path to solve such optimization problem but further investigation is needed.

4 Conclusions and Future Work

In this paper, we proposed the development of a novel concept to improve training of decision maker in complex environments. We focused on ATC as a use case and introduced the optimization-based Virtual Instructor. The Virtual Instructor is part of a training tool that can generate challenging scenarios or can replay historic ones. The latter can be used, for example, at team meetings when traffic from the previous day is discussed. The optimization-based Virtual Instructor uses discrete optimization to analyze the decisions made by the trainee and to propose improvements without the need of a physical instructor to be present. The tool is able to run on a standard PC so the training could take place at work, workshops, or at home.

This paper describes relevant concepts from two different research areas, namely HCI and Optimization, to develop such a Virtual Instructor. We argue that it would benefit training to combine and advance the state-of the art in visualization for learning and optimization in a learning environment.

As a first step, we give an initial specification and indicate where the state-of-the-art needs to be advanced. The main challenge is to identify the groups of individual's decisions which can not only significantly improve the team performance, but also be explained and visualized in a way that enhance learning. Therefore, we identified theoretical frameworks and algorithms that form the basis for exploring benefits of optimization in ATCO training. In addition, we prototyped visualizations based on two usage scenarios of the virtual instructor. We presented the improvement potential of using optimization algorithms. Then we identified factors that affect the learnability of the decisions proposed by the algorithm. Finally, we describe a suitable algorithm that would find a sequence of changes to the controller's decisions that are both learnable and result in a solution closer to the optimal one.

We plan to formalize different learnability distance metrics, to develop different algorithms to suggest learnable solutions, and their visualizations. Explorative studies are needed for investigating the effects of: i) the efficiency and the accuracy of the algorithms, ii) the different learnability distances, iii) the different visualization forms, and their combinations on learning. We are going to conduct several studies with ATCO and ATCO trainees to explore this.

Acknowledgements. We are grateful to the students of Department of Informatics, University of Oslo who prototyped the scenarios we described in the paper and to the all participants in our studies.

References

1. EU: Commision of the European Communities: European Transport Policy for 2010, Time to Decide Brussels (2001)
2. Voller, L., Fowler, A.: Human factors longitudinal study to support the improvement of air traffic controller training. In: Kirwan, B., Rodgers, M., Schäfer, D. (eds.) Human Factors Impacts in Air Traffic Management, pp. 153–176. Ashgate Publishing Limited, England (2009)
3. Hitchcock, L.: Air traffic control simulation: Capabilities. In: Smolensky, M.W., Stein, E.S. (eds.) Human Factors in Air Traffic Control, pp. 327–340. Academic Press, USA (1998)
4. Manning, C., Stein, E.: Measuring air traffic controller performance in the 21st century. In: Kirwan, B., Rodgers, M., Schäfer, D. (eds.) Human Factors Impacts in Air Traffic Management. Ashgate Publishing Limited, England, pp. 283–23 (2009)
5. Eide, A.W., Ødegård, S.S., Karahasanović, A.: A Post-simulation Assessment Tool for Training of Air Traffic Controllers. In: Yamamoto, S. (ed.) HCI 2014, Part I. LNCS, vol. 8521, pp. 34–43. Springer, Heidelberg (2014)
6. Atkin, J.A.D.: On-line decision support for the take-off runway scheduling at London Heatrow airport. Ph. D. thesis, University of Nottingham (2008)
7. Bennell, J.A., Mesgarpour, M., Potts, C.N.: Airport runway scheduling. 4OR **9**, 135–138 (2011)
8. Kjenstad, D., Mannino, C., Schittekat, P., Smedsrud, M.: Integrated surface and departure management at airports by optimization. In: 5th International Conference on Modeling, Simulation and Applied Optimization (ICMSAO), pp. 1–5. IEEE Xplore Digital Library (2013)
9. Endsley, M.R.: Designing for Situation Awareness: An Approach to User-Centered Design. Taylor and Francis, New York (2004)

10. Scaife, M., Rogers, Y.: External cognition: how do graphical represenattons work? Int. J. Hum Comput Stud. **45**, 185–213 (1996)
11. Rogers, Y., Sharp, H., Preece, J.: Interaction Design: Beyong Human-Computer Interaction. Wiley, New York (2011)
12. Ainsworth, S.: DeFT: a conceptual framework for considering learning with multiple representations. Learn. Instr. **16**, 183–198 (2006)
13. Chen, C., Yue, Y.: Empirical studies of information visualization: a meta-analysis. Int. J. Hum Comput Stud. **53**, 851–866 (2000)
14. Dahle, T., Bessesen, M.S., Pettersen-Hjelvik, M., Josephsen, A.: Flashback post-simulation tool (in Norwegian). Department of Informatics, UiO, Student report (2014)
15. Fatland, O.G., Furuberg, E., Dijk, L.W.V., Dæhlen, A.K.: Goodgate - Real time air traffic management tool (in Norwegian), Department of Informatics, UiO, Student report (2014)
16. Jones, S., Scaife, M.: Animated diagrams: an investigation into the cognitive effects of using animation to illustrate dynamic processes. In: Anderson, M., Cheng, P., Haarslev, V. (eds.) Diagrams 2000. LNCS (LNAI), vol. 1889, pp. 231–244. Springer, Heidelberg (2000)
17. Sörensen, K., Schittekat, P.: Statistical analysis of distance-based path relinking for the capacitated vehicle routing problem. Comput. Oper. Res. **40**(12), 3197–3205 (2013)
18. Glover, F., Laguna, M.: Fundamentals of scatter search and path relinking. Control Cybern. **29**(3), 653–684 (2000)

Human Factors Within the Transportation Security Administration: Optimizing Performance Through Human Factors Assessments

Bonnie Kudrick[1], Daniel Caggiano[1], and Ann Speed[2(✉)]

[1] Office of Security Capabilities, Mission Analysis Division, Requirements and Systems Engineering Branch, Transportation Security Administration (TSA), Arlington, VA, USA
{bonnie.kudrick, daniel.caggiano}@tsa.dhs.gov
[2] Data Driven and Neural Computing, Sandia National Laboratories, Albuquerque, NM, USA
aespeed@sandia.gov

Abstract. The human factors team in the Mission Analysis Division of TSA's Office of Security Capabilities explores the impact of technology, policies, procedures, and training on human systems performance during transportation security operations. This paper highlights some of the most critical human factors challenges currently facing the aviation security community and provides an overview of innovative on-going human factors projects at TSA that will address some of these challenges by enhancing performance assessment capabilities, improving training opportunities, and optimizing duty rotations and assignments.

Keywords: Aviation · Transportation · Security · Cognition · Workload · Vigilance · Attention · Visual search · Decision making · Personality · Aptitudes · Behavior detection · Image analysis · Training · Human performance · Human factors

1 Introduction

1.1 Session Overview

Often, difficult human factors problems in operational environments are addressed by appealing to the peer-reviewed literature in human factors, cognitive psychology, industrial-organizational psychology, or other related fields. However, it is not always clear that the results from that open literature generalize to the particular operational environments to which they are applied. This session describes just such a series of

© Springer International Publishing Switzerland 2015
D.D. Schmorrow and C.M. Fidopiastis (Eds.): AC 2015, LNAI 9183, pp. 767–776, 2015.
DOI: 10.1007/978-3-319-20816-9_73

situation; specifically the duties and stresses experienced by Transportation Security Officers (TSOs) and Behavior Detection Officers (BDOs) at the airport passenger security checkpoint. Over the last several years, the Human Factors team in the TSA's Office of Security Capabilities has been supporting and funding research on human factors problems specific to TSOs and BDOs. The papers presented in this session describe experimental methods intended to honor the specific constraints experienced by Officers at the checkpoint from stimuli and methods of stimulus presentation to procedures. First, however, is a description of the TSA, the Human Factors Program and its goals, and some of the specific human factors problems encountered in the airport operational environment.

1.2 History and Mission of TSA

The Office of Homeland Security (OHS) was established under the White House in immediate response to the September 11, 2001 terrorist attacks. Two months later, with the passage of the Aviation and Transportation Security Act, the United States Congress created the Transportation Security Administration (TSA) under the Department of Transportation. In order to further align TSA with the nation's security needs, Congress reassigned TSA to the Department of Homeland Security (DHS, formerly OHS) when DHS officially became a Cabinet-level department in March of 2003.

Since its inception, TSA has worked to protect the nation's transportation systems and ensure freedom of movement for people and commerce. While TSA's mission covers all modes of passenger and commercial transportation, including maritime, rail, intercity and commuter bus, and trucking, among others, TSA's presence in aviation security draws disproportionate attention both from the general public and from foreign terrorist groups. The remainder of this paper will focus on TSA's work in the aviation security domain.

1.3 TSA's Approach to Aviation Transportation Security

To counter the diverse and sophisticated threats devised by hostile adversaries, TSA has adopted a layered approach to aviation security. The layered approach has the advantage that it is both *redundant*, providing multiple opportunities to identify the same, specific threat before it reaches an airplane, and *comprehensive*, allowing TSA to detect a wide variety of cues or abnormal behaviors that indicate an adversary's intent to deceive or do harm.

Layers of U.S. Aviation Security

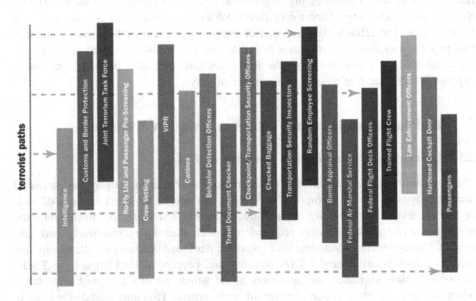

Each layer of security is a system that requires collaboration among a number of elements, including some combination of technology or technologies (such as scanning or imaging devices, automated algorithms, software tools, local and networked databases, and other forms of technology), human beings with different roles and organizational affiliations (security personnel, passengers, analysts, and commercial airline crew members and representatives, among others), and/or trained animals. While a variety of technological innovations have made this layered approach possible, human actors ultimately are the components of each system that are responsible for acquiring, integrating, interpreting, and making decisions based on the information that the other elements of the system provide. Despite this critical role in determining how efficiently and effectively transportation security systems can operate, the human factor is the least well understood and has often been one of the last considerations in the push to develop new ways to address an evolving threat landscape.

1.4   Human Factors Engineering at TSA

TSA's Office of Security Capabilities (OSC) has a team of engineering psychologists and operations analysts with subject-matter expertise in airport security. This team, also called the human factors team, is dedicated to determining how human performance is impacted by the design, implementation, and effectiveness of equipment, human interfaces, software and algorithms, training, policies, and procedures in transportation security systems. The human factors team makes recommendations to TSA stakeholders on how to optimize existing systems for human performance while also influencing human-centered requirements for new procedures and technologies prior to acquisition. To support these efforts, the human factors team works with national laboratories, private companies, universities and other DHS components such as DHS's Science and Technology Directorate (DHS S&T) to conduct assessments that will provide valid and reliable data to assist in improving human performance. Although this paper cannot elaborate on many activities and programs due to security sensitivities, the sections below will provide a non-sensitive overview of OSC's efforts to support TSA's front line officers in a number of ways.

2 The Practice of Human Factors in Aviation Security

2.1 Overview of Human Factors Concerns at TSA

The availability and implementation of technology to screen passengers has increased dramatically since the inception of TSA. Rolling out new or modified versions of tools or procedures can substantially impact how efficiently TSOs are able to integrate the multiple sources of information required to screen passengers effectively and efficiently. Managing the varying levels of cognitive workload that have resulted from new tools is a high priority for the TSA. Sensory and perceptual load impact the TSOs' decision-making, vigilance, and attention, all of which are of the utmost importance when working within an airport checkpoint environment. TSA understands the need to develop techniques to optimize attention allocation; logical reasoning; pattern recognition and classification; visual search and visual memory strategies; and problem solving for TSOs which should include physiological, behavioral, cognitive, and environmental assessments. TSA seeks to maximize human-in-the-loop performance by increasing throughput of screened items or persons; increasing screeners' ability to accurately resolve alarms through improved higher hit rates and lowered false alarm rates; decreasing the time to make a determination; and decreasing the number of secondary searches of carry-on items.

The sections that follow will describe components of one of the most visible and most critical components of TSA's layered security approach, the airport checkpoint, and some of the specific human factors challenges in maximizing the security and efficiency of checkpoint operations.

2.2 Checkpoint Technologies and Personnel

When progressing from the public side to the sterile side of an airport security checkpoint, the first TSO that many passengers encounter is the Travel Document Checker (TDC). The TDC verifies and cross-checks critical information in the traveler's identification document (ID) and boarding pass. At most airports, electronic Boarding Pass Scanning Systems (BPSSs) assist the TDC in verifying the status of boarding passes. In addition, TSA is currently testing and rolling out Credential Authentication Technology (CAT) systems that will assist TDCs in authenticating IDs and eventually will allow the TDC to cross-check the passenger's identity against a list of known travelers for that day at that airport.

Passengers then proceed to a lane where they must place carry-on items onto the conveyor to be scanned through an Advanced Technology (AT) X-ray system. In many cases, a divestiture officer will direct passengers to divest particular items into a bin to be scanned through the X-ray. Passengers then pass through either a walk-through metal detector (WTMD) or an Advanced Imaging Technology (AIT) body scanner designed to detect anomalies that might indicate a failure to divest all property necessary to enter the sterile area. If these systems provide certain types of anomalous readings, checkpoint officers will pat-down the passenger to determine whether the passenger failed to divest an item or whether the system produced a false alarm.

As the passenger is being scanned by either the WTMD or the AIT, a TSO operating the X-ray reviews the image of the passenger's carry-on and divested items. On some X-ray units, automated detection algorithms alert the TSO to areas of concern within the image. X-ray operators can clear or confirm these system alarms, and they also can annotate an image to indicate their own regions of concern within the image. If after final review an X-ray operator clears an image, he or she sends the bag down the exit conveyor where it is picked up by the passenger. The passenger then redresses and proceeds to the gate. If the X-ray operator suspects the image, he or she pulls the suspected item for further inspection by a dynamic officer before the item reaches the passenger-accessible area. The dynamic officer then searches the suspected item with the help of Explosive Trace Detection (ETD) technology. For certain types of passengers and in certain situations, ETDs can also be applied to the hands of passengers as an additional security measure.

2.3 Specific Human Factors Concerns at the Checkpoint

The demands of the checkpoint work environment create a diverse set of human factors challenges. Some duties, such as X-ray image review and checking travel documents, are repetitive tasks in which TSOs must monitor and search cluttered images or documents for subtle, ultra-low frequency threat items. Such tasks can cause eye strain, fatigue, and susceptibility to rapid decrements in performance over time on task and to mind-wandering (i.e. task disengagement). To combat these deleterious effects, officers at the checkpoint rotate through duty positions (TDC, divestiture officer, AIT/WTMD operator, X-ray operator, and dynamic officer) at somewhat regular intervals.

While somewhat short, regular duty cycles can help TSOs to maintain vigilance and focus on the task at hand, they can come at a potential cost. X-ray image analysis is a particularly difficult task, and individuals' ability to perform this task well can vary substantially, even among veteran, well-trained officers. On the other hand, duties such as the TDC and dynamic officer positions require TSOs to interact with passengers on a regular basis. Simplified duty cycles in which all TSOs at the checkpoint rotate through all positions guarantee that, at times, individual officers will not be optimally matched for the particular position they are performing based on their individual profile of knowledge, skills, and attributes.

Training potentially can help reduce the skill gap between the lowest performing and highest performing officers at a given duty position; however, staffing constraints often make it difficult for airports to provide TSOs with one-on-one training opportunities with experts. The most consistently available opportunities for training often are self-paced, computer-based training modules. Traditional computer-based training tools, however, have not always been designed to make a detailed assessment of individual officers' overall skill level and specific areas of weakness. Accurate TSO performance assessment, as it relates specifically to performance on the floor during regular operations, is a prerequisite for determining where TSOs' true training needs are in the first place but has proved to be quite challenging in practice. Establishing and obtaining good performance metrics both during training and during normal operations at the checkpoint is critical to narrowing the skill discrepancies across TSOs.

3   Current TSA Human Factors Studies

As TSA has been funding research in human factors for a number of years, the papers included are only a small subset of the research that has been conducted. However, this sample should provide a reasonable perspective on TSA's attempt to incorporate data from well-designed studies into their decision-making about procedures, technologies, and training methods. (The reader is referred to two papers in another session of this conference, "Domain General and Domain Specific Expert Visual Search" for descriptions of another current TSA project [1, 2].

3.1   Exploring Cognitive Load and Cognitive Fatigue in Behavior Detection Officers

As TSA moves to Risk-Based Security (RBS), one focus of screening activity at the checkpoint is evaluating passenger behavior as well as screening their belongings for threat items. The officers who perform this duty are called Behavior Detection Officers, or BDOs. Initially modeled after the Israeli behavior detection program, and modified for appropriateness within the American culture and Constitution, the BDO program trains its officers to monitor, in real time, behaviors of passengers as they approach and move through the airport security checkpoint. Officers have a list of behaviors they are watching for, and have thresholds of behavior which, when crossed, require additional intervention by either the BDO or a Law Enforcement Officer. The difficulty in the job is that the list of behaviors can be long and watching for these critical behaviors in a crowd of people can be fatiguing, causing decrements in the BDO's performance.

The goal of the project described by Kittinger and Bender [3] is to perform Cognitive Task Analyses (CTAs) on two versions of the BDO Standard Operating Procedure (SOP) to identify areas that cause difficulty for Officers and then to begin to identify areas for which that cognitive load and cognitive/physical fatigue can possibly be reduced. The project will start by augmenting existing Job Analyses and then to design and conduct Cognitive Task Analyses using BDOs from representative airports around the country. Results will provide additional information on ways to make BDOs more effective, and information on how to actually measure cognitive load and fatigue in the field.

3.2   Designing a Method for Quantifying Pat-Down Effectiveness

While TSOs are able to rely on assistance from a variety of technological tools for most current checkpoint security measures, passenger pat-downs are a decidedly 'low-tech' solution for resolving AIT or WTMD anomalies. TSOs performing pat-downs must completely rely on their hands, their eyes, and their judgment to decide whether passengers have fully divested all personal property. To date, the same has been true for training TSOs how to perform proper pat-downs – expert instructors provide qualitative feedback to TSOs during training regarding various aspects of how the TSOs performed the pat-down. These pat-downs often are performed by the TSOs either on the instructors themselves or on other TSOs during training. The instructors have no quantitative or objective measures or tools to refer to when providing feedback to the TSOs; the feedback is based solely on what the instructors see and feel. Furthermore, some passengers may require modified pat-downs based on physical disabilities or chronic pain – current training provides no clear criterion for instructors to determine whether TSOs have modified their pat-down appropriately for any given physical malady.

To address these limitations in current pat-down training methods, the Matteson and colleagues [4] at Johns Hopkins University Applied Physics Laboratory (JHUAPL) are developing the Pat-down Accuracy Training Tool (PATT) for TSA. PATT is a set of anatomically realistic mannequins fitted with pressure sensors that provide objective performance measures to trainees and instructors during pat-down training (see REF TO APL's PAPER). PATT will provide a level of objective feedback that is not currently possible and has the potential to offer new-hire TSOs, as well as TSOs at airports who are approaching annual performance exams, an opportunity to practice pat-downs and receive expert feedback even when instructors or other TSOs might not be available.

3.3   Comparing Visual Search in TSOs and BDOs

Visual search is a key component of the jobs performed by both TSOs and Behavior Detection Officers (BDOs). While there is a growing body of knowledge surrounding the nature of TSO visual search at the X-ray, less is known about how similar that task is to the task of BDOs, who are searching a dynamic field (i.e., passengers moving through the checkpoint) for transient signals (behavioral indicators). Spain and colleagues [5] present a description of method for building on existing research covering similarity between TSO and novice performance in basic visual search tasks to compare BDO performance on these same tasks. The first experiment Spain and colleagues describe involves comparisons between TSOs and BDOs on a task in which subjects search for perfect Ts amidst a field of Ls and approximate Ts (where the vertical bar is offset from the middle). Prior research has illuminated differences between TSOs and novices on this task (accuracy, speed of search termination).

A second experiment focuses on identifying personality characteristics that are predictive of BDO visual search performance (e.g., Big 5 personality, Patriotism) that have been predictive of TSO performance in previous empirical work.

3.4   Adaptive Methods for Training Visual Search Skills

One of the key duties of a TSO is the X-ray image analysis. In order to optimize performance, Hale and colleagues [6] designed, developed and tested and adaptive training system for use both in the laboratory and in the field. This paper outlines the process utilized to design and develop a simulation-based training system to address identified gaps through the integration of process-level measures of individual performance to personalize training, with the goal of enhancing training effectiveness and efficiency. The "ScreenAdapt" prototype's goal is to enhance TSOs ability to detect threats quickly and accurately using behavioral and eye tracking data that records TSO's eye movements during training sessions. Eye tracking data provides insight into performance errors, identifying scan vs. recognition errors, as well as providing visual feedback of scan path and focus areas.

After action review feedback strategies summarize performance process and outcome measures relative to targeted training goal(s), and provide suggested next training steps such as focused training on specific deficits using exposure or discrimination training. Further, individualized image sets are generated based on identified performance deficiencies or inefficiencies, providing endless combinations of image components to avoid image repetition.

3.5   Identifying Cognitive and Psychological Traits Predictive of TSO Performance on Non-X-Ray Duties

TSA employs approximately 55,000 people as Transportation Security Officers (TSOs) to perform a variety of critical security duties as they screen almost 650 million air passengers each year. One of the most studied of these duties is the X-ray operator, for which the TSO has to scan X-ray images of all carry-on bags searching for threat items. However, the X-ray is not the only security duty TSOs perform at the checkpoint. TSO duties include the Travel Document Checker (TDC), the Divest Officer (DO, who prepares passengers and their bags for moving through the relevant imaging technologies), the Walk-through Metal Detector (WTMD), the Advanced Imaging Technology (AIT), and the Dynamic TSO (D-TSO, the person who performs pat-downs, bag checks, etc.). Despite these duties being a lion's share of TSO time at the checkpoint, relatively little research has been done on characteristics that make individual officers successful at these various duties.

Emmanuel and colleagues [7] describe a project with the goal identifying the cognitive and personality characteristics that predict TSO effectiveness at the non-X-ray tasks at the checkpoint. Unlike the X-ray, these other duty stations have an added requirement for success – customer interaction. That is, when they are performing in these roles, TSOs must strike a balance between keeping passengers happy, calm, and compliant without compromising the overall security posture of the checkpoint.

By augmenting two existing job analyses through three TSO subject matter expert workshops, Emmanuel and colleagues identified a list of critical job duties and competencies that were rated as both frequent and critical for the successful performance of these non-X-ray duties. They then identified a group of 32 normed and validated personality and cognitive measures that correspond with these critical TSO characteristics/competencies including Five Factor inventories, measures of the dark side of personality (e.g., narcissism), patriotism, matrix reasoning problems (akin to Raven's Progressive Matrices), and integrity. Their plan is to collect data from ∼ 400 current TSOs and small sample of New Hire TSOs from eight airports on this battery of measures and will be using exploratory and confirmatory factor analysis to test the various hypotheses and to norm the measures for this specific population. The criterion variables to be used include a number of performance measures TSA currently collects on each TSO including annual recertification scores, practical skills evaluations, disciplinary actions, awards, absenteeism, etc.

4 Summary

Over the last several years,TSA has begun an empirically rigorous program for measuring TSO and BDO performance in the field. This effort has provided a respectable and growing body of data that is used by decision-makers to craft policy, training, and to guide the purchase and use of technologies at the checkpoint. Researchers include individuals in academia (Jeremy Wolfe, Steve Mitroff), private companies (Design Interactive, Leigh Fisher, Deloitte, RTI International) and national laboratories (Sandia National Laboratories), enabling TSA to investigate TSO and BDO performance from a variety of perspectives, using a variety of methods, at a variety of information sensitivity levels, yielding a more complete picture of the factors that influence Officer effectiveness, passenger experience, and security posture.

References

1. Stracuzzi, D.J., Speed, A., Silva, A., Haass, M., Trumbo, D.: Exploratory analysis of visual search data. In: Schmorrow, D.D., Fidopiasti, C.M. (eds.) 17th International Conference on Human-Computer Interaction. LNCS, vol. 9183, pp. 537–547. Springer, Heidelberg (2015)
2. Speed, A., Silva, A., Trumbo, D., Stracuzzi, D.J., Warrender, C., Trumbo, M., Divis, K.: Determining the optimal time on X-ray analysis for transportation security officers. In: Schmorrow, D.D., Fidopiastis, C.M. (eds.) 17th International Conference on Human-Computer Interaction. LNCS, vol. 9183, pp. 825–834. Springer, Heidelberg (2015)
3. Kittinger, R., Bender, J.: Methods for determining the role of fatigue and cognitive load on behavior detection officers' (BDOs') performance in the field. In: Schmorrow, D.D., Fidopiastis, C.M. (eds.) 17th International Conference on Human-Computer Interaction. LNCS, vol. 9183, pp. 36–43. Springer, Heidelberg (2015)
4. Matteson, R.: Pat-down accuracy training tool – development and application of a quantitative tool to measure applied pressures during a pat-down. In: 17th International Conference on Human-Computer Interaction. Springer (2015)
5. Spain, R., Hedge, J., Ladd, K.: An examination of visual search success for transportation security officers and behavior detection officers. In: Schmorrow, D.D., Fidopiastis, C.M. (eds.)

17th International Conference on Human-Computer Interaction. LNCS, vol. 9183, pp. 817–824. Springer, Heidelberg (2015)

6. Hale, K., Flint, J., Del Guidice, K., Wilson, D.: Designing, developing, and validating an adaptive visual search training platform. In: Schmorrow, D.D., Fidopiastis, C.M. (eds.) 17th International Conference on Human-Computer Interaction. LNCS, vol. 9183, pp. 735–744. Springer, Heidelberg (2015)

7. Emmanuel, G., Kitinger, R., Speed, A.: A quantitative methodology for identifying attributes which contribute to performance for officers at the transportation security administration. In: Schmorrow, D.D., Fidopiastis, C.M. (eds.) 17th International Conference on Human-Computer Interaction. LNCS, vol. 9183, pp. 373–380. Springer, Heidelberg (2015)

Breathing Life into CPR Training

Dominic Lamboy and Patricia J. Donohue[✉]

Instructional Technologies, San Francisco State University,
San Francisco, CA, USA
pdonohue@sfsu.edu

Abstract. This study reports on our development and prototyping of an accessible, simplified simulation for teaching CPR in classrooms. The prototype involves an inexpensive digitally enhanced dummy that can be constructed from common available materials linked with an iPad or tablet running a customized program. The mobile program targets students at 5th grade and above and faculty for CPR training. iPad sensors register pressure manipulation on the dummy and the program responds with interactive instruction. Several tests with older youth and adults proved the simulation was effective in teaching simple CPR techniques that testers could remember the following week. With an improved dummy, we will conduct empirical tests across different age groups in the coming year.

Keywords: Physical cognition · Game theory · Simulation · Mobile learning

1 Background

The occasional accident happens all too often in K-12 classrooms: an athlete drops to the ground with an unexpected heart attack; the third-grade student chokes on a piece of meat; the swim team member inhales too soon after a dive. There are numerous health emergencies in the K-12 environment on a daily basis. When the accident results in cardiac arrest, staff, students and faculty are rarely prepared to save a life. In the US, the leading cause of natural death is sudden cardiac arrest. Approximately 70 % of Americans do not know how to give Cardio Pulmonary Resuscitation (CPR) or don't remember how. According to the American Heart Association (AHA) 88 % of all cardiac arrests happen at home and less than 8 % of cardiac arrests outside of the hospital survive. By the time emergency medical services (EMS) arrive, it is often too late. The reality is that anyone, from first grade to twelfth, as well as adults, can easily learn enough CPR to restart a heartbeat. One sure method of training for permanent retention is to use simulations [2, 5, 6].

California Congresswoman Lois Capps (CA-24) recently proposed a bill, "Teaching Children to Save Lives" (H.R. 2308) to fund elementary and secondary schools to provide CPR and automated external defibrillator (AED) training. We have developed a prototype dummy that can be used to answer Congresswoman Capps' call. It can be used to teach students and adults a safe and effective method for applying CPR, and as a physical simulation, promises to deliver a skill that can be easily learned and retained for a long duration.

© Springer International Publishing Switzerland 2015
D.D. Schmorrow and C.M. Fidopiastis (Eds.): AC 2015, LNAI 9183, pp. 777–783, 2015.
DOI: 10.1007/978-3-319-20816-9_74

This research proposal hypothesizes that students will learn CPR training with the aid of a simulator dummy and be able to retain what they learn to the end of the semester; with long-term retention possibly as long as one year. Hands-on projects and simulations are effective at reaching underperforming students. With our prototype, we also hypothesize that the intervention will show that underachieving students perform as well or better than their peers in the test classroom. Success with a skill that can help students save lives has the potential to court students into life sciences, engineering or medical career paths.

2 Theoretical Foundations of the Study

The use of an iPad-based learning environment for our study provided access to the benefits of individualized learning, active hands-on learning, and the richness of multimedia and medical simulation technology to foster improved understanding and long-term retention of learning. We therefore joined a hands-on iPad application with a simulation activity for learning CPR in an interactive, kinesthetic environment.

2.1 New Technologies Foster Individualized Learning

James Kaput and Jeremy Roschelle [6] proposed in, *The mathematics of change and variation from a new perspective: New content, new context,* that a Dual Challenge existed with the growth of technology that required teaching "more math to more people" (section *Dual Challenges: Much more mathematics for many more people,* par. (1). They pointed out that, by the turn of the century, teaching mathematics had become increasingly abstract and complex in the face of increasing student diversity and social cost. While pointing out the advantages that new technologies offered, they concluded with the question "Can these new possibilities transform our notion of a core mathematics curriculum for all learners?" Their emphasis on "all learners" alluded early to the inability of mass solutions to meet individual needs. More recent work in artificial intelligence that allows for individualized instruction with solutions such as the Cognitive Tutor [7] or adaptive testing have run into the same constraints of increased cost, learner diversity, and complexity of content. Our challenge was to match individual learners to a learning simulation at reduced cost, thereby meeting Congresswoman Capps' proposal.

We chose to develop a mobile application for the iPad. While the iPad is potentially the most expensive component in the learning system, iPads are increasingly being used in K-12 classrooms. The app would be an additional potential use of an existing technology and one that attracts student interest.

2.2 Constructivism and Authentic, Hands-on Learning

The act of pressing, pushing, tapping and swiping on an iPad provides significant kinesthetic experience and immerses the learner in a hands-on learning experience. S.B. Issenberg [13] identifies ten key features of medical use of simulation that improves learning, including: repetitive practice, immediate feedback, curriculum integration, capture clinical variation, and individualized learning to name those that are relevant. The benefits of constructivist methods that allow learners to explore the meaning of what they learn by studying with others and getting their hands into the lesson have been well documented [4, 10, 12, 14]. In this study, students physically "save a life" through simulation and thereby understand the elements of CPR that allow them to do so. They then teach their peers, their parents, and others, vastly improving their own retention of what they have learned.

2.3 Simulations Aid Learning and Retention

Simulations help bring concepts alive in the hands of every learner. When a student puts hands on the CPR dummy, they understand the life and death situation and they intuitively understand the subtle skills in what they are learning. Research has made great strides in understanding the potential of virtual games and simulations to engage learners and advance their learning as effectively or beyond the traditional lecture [5]. Games, virtual learning environments, and simulations have left laboratories and university classrooms and are being increasingly used in K-12 classrooms to bring the learning benefits to children and young adults and also to give students an introduction to and a taste of career opportunities and environments.

One sure method of training for permanent retention is to use simulations (see [2, 5, 6]). Karl Kapp [6] explains the success of simulations in teaching and uses the example of the T-Haler (a gamified and wifi connected inhaler) that showed "proper use of the inhaler can go from 20 to 60 % by using the T-Haler and playing the computer game to get it right" (p. 4). This study introduces students to the CPR simulation gradually by first involving them in tapping on the CPR mobile application, and then using the simulation in conjunction with a medical dummy.

2.4 Contributions of Multimedia

Richard Mayer's [8] Multimedia Learning Theory states that instructional messages should be developed in light of how the human mind works. Mayer's research shows how words and pictures are qualitatively different yet complement each other and that human understanding occurs when learners are able to integrate visual and verbal representations. Digital interfaces help bridge the gap between the learner and his or her understanding of the content being taught. According to Mayer, building connections between words and pictures, learners are able to create a deeper understanding than from words or pictures alone [8]. The CPR app presents a visual, interactive learning program that joins audio with visual cardiac readings, hands-on manipulation of pressure points, and text-based information all in a smooth simulated experience. Mayer explains that humans have meaningful and transferable learning experiences when they engage in active learning that allows the to pay attention to relevant information and organize it into meaningful mental representations.

We took these challenges and theoretical understandings into consideration in the design and development of the instructional dummy and iPad simulation. We then tested an early prototype simulation using the activities described in the Methods section that follows.

3   Methods

3.1   Creating a Simulation Mobile App

A CPR simulation application (CPR app) was written and developed for delivery on an iPad. The iPad was chosen for its visual screen real estate and sensor capabilities. The CPR app was instructionally designed to match the specifications of current CPR training. One major downfall of any CPR course is that there is not a way to account for how people will react in the real world. Creating a simulation of a real CPR scenario helps overcome that limitation. Also, Pearson [11] reveals that a majority (69 %) of elementary, middle and high school students would like to use mobile devices more in the classroom. The mobile application was developed for two approaches — using the iPad by itself and with a dummy. The basic simulation can be executed using tap gestures. When a dummy is used, the simulation becomes more realistic and has added features; for example, the dummy's eyes may open. The goal of the app is to train students who do not have any prior knowledge of CPR and it is designed to accustom students to the simulation environment by starting with a simple iPad action using tapping gestures, and then moving to the dummy simulation. The learners all have the same goal: the ability to save a life using the techniques learned from the CPR mobile application. The instructional goals are that learners will be able to:

1. Perform one-person adult CPR in an emergency situation;
2. Recognize and know the protocols when dealing with an emergency situation; and
3. Teach others how perform CPR.

The CPR app will maximize the iPad's technology. The application uses aspects of gamification to engage young learners and keep their interest through the hands-on interaction. The app starts with an e-learning module consisting of an interactive presentation with video, audio, and quizzes. The content covers general information about CPR, protocols on what to do in an emergency situation, and directions on how to give compression CPR. Quizzes check for understanding throughout the course. After the initial training, students will perform simulated CPR. Learners use the iPad's touch screen to perform compression CPR in one of the following two ways (see Fig. 1):

1. A simulation finger tap at the appropriate timing; or
2. A full simulation.

The iPad will be connected to a dummy mannequin for the full simulation. The mannequin's heart will stop beating and the students should react and practice by performing a full simulation. The iPad will use its accelerometer technology to determine if the students are compressing the chest at the right depth and pace. If the student is successful, they will have "saved a life." The app is recommended for use in

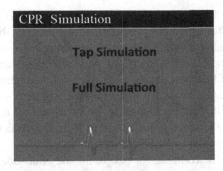

Fig. 1. The CPR app entry to the simulation screen showing a choice between the tap simulation with iPad only, or a full simulation using the medical dummy.

conjunction with teacher input. The students should take advantage of the app to teach others in their family how to give CPR. This is one of the most powerful tools of the app because it allows the student to transfer the knowledge while exposing more people to the life saving skills of compression CPR.

3.2 Teaching by Dummy

The completed simulation prototype will be constructed of a standard medical dummy (i.e., without specialized sensors or artificial responses) and the iPad attached on top (see Fig. 2). The custom iPad program provides the student with the interactive CPR training. The iPad is utilized for its sensitivity and orientation detection. An IEEE Abstract and full paper on haptic technology identifies that a primary application area for haptics has been in surgical simulation and medical training [1]. For our prototype, complex detection is not necessary and would greatly expand the cost. We have shown that the iPad can sense the actions of the learner effectively to render accurate

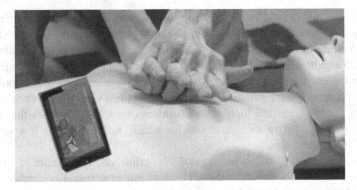

Fig. 2. A standard human dummy will be outfitted with an iPad running the custom CPR training program. The training program was tested and found effective with teenagers and adults showing a one-week retention. When combined with a standard dummy, the iPad capabilities for pressure and time sensing will be utilized to give a more realistic feel for students.

instructional response. The mobile application was built and tested to respond to pressure and counts. The application includes instruction in the CPR methods and provides practice through the simulation until the learner has acquired the skill. The testing environment worked when the iPad was placed on an inflated pillow that mimicked the actions of the chest during CPR. We plan to augment a dummy with the iPad or similar mobile tablet as shown in Fig. 1. We will beta test it in several classes using volunteers. We will retest the volunteers in the same skill in four to six months to determine if there is long term retention. Findings from the alpha iPad tests suggested a high level of skill achievement with small margin of error.

A one-hour training is available for people in the education field and covers the following:

1. Recommended implementation of the app;
2. How to use and update the app;
3. How to evaluate assessments;

4 Implications of the Study

We predicted that giving students and faculty direct hands-on simulated practice in compression CPR would help learners retain the specific procedural skills long term. Informal trials with a medic, a teacher, a nurse, and volunteer students suggested that there was good variety in tasks to maintain attention, the iPad was liked for the content, and the content was appropriate for the training. Changes were also suggested to the application to make it more effective:

1. Make clear the training is for Adult CPR;
2. Switch users out after 2 min;
3. Make the audio directions clearer when to move to the next screen
4. Add a disclaimer that while rate is important in the simulation, depth also is important and is not addressed.

Overall, this proved to be a solid prototype with an app that is effective for introducing students to compression CPR. The designer believes the final product of an e-learning module in an iPad is far more efficient then using an HTML 5 application. The HTML 5 export relies on the Internet as opposed to the app being in the iPad itself. This allowed users to use the app anywhere. This project can provide schools critical instructional content for their iPads and can help local EMS providers reach their goals of educating junior high and high school students on CPR. The fact that the basic mobile app can be used in the classroom for nearly no cost makes it a very viable option for K-12 classrooms.

The statistics on cardiac arrest survival are grim; yet, if a victim is given CPR immediately when EMS arrives, their chance of survival instantly doubles and can possibly triple (American Heart Association, 2013). Yet, the amount of bystanders who know CPR has dropped drastically over the years. In schools, the knowledge rate plummets further. The overall goal of the CPR mobile application is to increase the knowledge base of individuals starting at the Junior High School level in order to help save lives in the community during an emergency. The mobile application has the potential to train people across the world on compression CPR. Although compression only CPR has been taught little in the past, research shows that compression is the most important skill when saving lives. Compression CPR is unique in the sense that it continues to pump blood to the brain (Lurie, et al., 1994). It can prevent a person from going brain dead until EMS arrives. This app will be an invaluable tool for school districts across the US. The mobile application also has the potential to empower students by giving them the skills to save lives.

References

1. Bruner, J.S.: Haptic Technology in Surgical Simulation and Medical Training: A Touch Revolution. IEEE Abstracts and Full Papers, 28 September 2011. http://www.creativeworld9.com/2011/03/abstract-and-full-paper-on-haptic.html
2. Bruner, J.S.:The Rise of Games and High Performance Computing for Modeling and Simulation. National Academies Press (2010). ISBN: 0-309-14778-6, http://www.nap.edu/catalog/12816.html
3. Bruner, J.S.: The act of discovery. Harvard Educ. Rev. 31(1), 21–32 (1961)
4. Jonassen, D., Mayes, T., McAleese, R.: A manifesto for a constructivist approach to uses of technology in higher education. In: Duffy, T.M., Lowyck, J., Jonassen, D.H. (eds.) Designing Environments for Constructive Learning. NATO ASI Series, pp. 231–247. Springer-Verlag, Heidelberg (1993)
5. Kapp, K.M., Blair, L., Mesch, R.: The Gamification of Learning and Instruction Fieldbook: Ideas into Practice. Wiley, San Francisco (2013). ISBN 978-1-118-67443-7
6. Kaput, J., Roschelle, J.: The mathematics of change and variation from a millennial perspective: new content, new context. In: Hoyles, C., Morgan, C., Woodhouse, G. (eds.) Rethinking the Mathematics Curriculum. Falmer Press, London (1998)
7. Koedinger, K.R.: Intelligent cognitive tutors as modeling tool and instructional model. In: A Position Paper for the NCTM Standards 2000 Technology Conference, 5–6 June 1998. Carnegie Mellon University (1998)
8. Mayer, R.: The Cambridge Handbook of Multimedia Learning. Cambridge University Press, USA (2005)
9. Moyer-Packenham, P.S., Salkind, G., Bolyard, J.J.: Virtual manipulatives used by K-8 teachers for mathematics instruction: considering mathematical, cognitive, and pedagogical fidelity. Contemp. Issues Technol. Teacher Educ. 8(3), 202–218 (2008)
10. Papert, S.: Mindstorms: Children, Computers, and Powerful Ideas. Basic Books, New York (1980)
11. Pearson. New Study Reveals U.S. Students Believe Strongly That Mobile Devices Will Improve Education 29 April 2013, Pearson | Always Learning. http://www.pearsoned.com/new-study-reveals-u-s-students-believe-strongly-that-mobile-devices-will-improve-education/#.UqfWBY2wF56. Accessed
12. Piaget, J.: Six Psychological Studies. Random House, New York (1967)
13. Issenberg, S.B., McGaghie, W.: Features and uses of high-fidelity medical simulations that lead to effective learning: a BEME systematic review. Med. Teach. 27, 10–28 (2005)
14. Vygotsky, L.S.: Mind in Society: The Development Of Higher Mental Processes. Harvard University Press, Cambridge (1978)

Enhanced Physical Security Through a Command-Intent Driven Multi-agent Sensor Network

Joshua Love, Wendy Amai, Timothy Blada, Charles Little,
Jason Neely, and Stephen Buerger[(✉)]

Sandia National Laboratories, Intelligent Systems, Robotics and Cybernetics
Group, P.O. Box 5800 MS 1010, Albuquerque, NM 87185, USA
sbuerge@sandia.gov

Abstract. Sandia's Intelligent Systems, Robotics, and Cybernetics group (ISRC) created the Sandia Architecture for Heterogeneous Unmanned System Control (SAHUC) to demonstrate how heterogeneous multi-agent teams could be used for tactical operations including the protection of high-consequence sites. Advances in multi-agent autonomy and unmanned systems have provided revolutionary new capabilities that can be leveraged for physical security applications. SAHUC applies these capabilities to produce a command-intent driven, autonomously adapting, multi-agent mobile sensor network. This network could enhance the security of high-consequence sites; it can be quickly and intuitively re-tasked to rapidly adapt to changing security conditions.

The SAHUC architecture, GUI, autonomy layers, and implementation are explored. Results from experiments and a demonstration are also discussed.

Keywords: Command intent · Physical security · Heterogeneous · Multi-agent distributed · Hierarchical control · SAHUC

1 Introduction

The Intelligent Systems, Robotics, and Cybernetics group (ISRC) performs research and development in several areas of interest to Sandia [1]. One area is protecting high-consequence sites. Sandia provides cutting-edge physical-security solutions by leveraging emerging technologies. Multi-agent systems are one of these emerging technologies. The Sandia Architecture for Heterogeneous Unmanned System Control (SAHUC) was created to demonstrate how heterogeneous multi-agent systems can enhance the security of high-consequence sites. SAHUC enables a single human to easily and intuitively operate a multi-agent mobile sensor network by specifying command intent.

Recent developments in autonomy have produced sophisticated unmanned systems (UMSs). These impressive UMSs have completed complex tasks while minimally interacting with their human operators. Autonomous navigation across difficult terrain and through urban traffic has been demonstrated in [2] and [3]. These advancements are vital features of future UMS operations. However, securing an entire high-consequence

© Springer International Publishing Switzerland 2015
D.D. Schmorrow and C.M. Fidopiastis (Eds.): AC 2015, LNAI 9183, pp. 784–795, 2015.
DOI: 10.1007/978-3-319-20816-9_75

facility requires a team of agents working together seamlessly, not just one highly-capable agent working alone. Advanced navigation is necessary to move individual agents around the facilities, but collaborative autonomy is also necessary to ensure the entire multi-agent team is working together toward common objectives.

If the multi-agent system's desired behavior is well-known prior to execution, scripted collaborative autonomy can sequence combinations of tasks to form complex choreographed multi-agent missions. However, this cannot flexibly respond to intelligent adversaries looking to exploit any rigidly defined and predictable behaviors [4].

Swarm autonomy enables agents to cooperate with each other on a single unifying objective through consensus methods. These methods work well when controlling large groups of simple, homogeneous agents. They are effective at tasks like plume localization, moving in formations, and spreading around perimeters [5, 6]. However, physical security missions are not single objectives; they are coordinated sets of objectives.

Other collaborative autonomy approaches assign tasks to individual agents, who then execute those tasks independently with minimal coordination (typically after solving the multi-agent traveling salesman problem) [7–9]. While promising for many multi-agent applications, these approaches are not tailored to the physical security scenarios where tasks change rapidly to counter time-critical security threats.

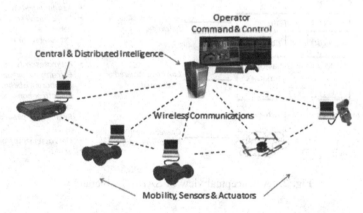

Fig. 1. Human operators intuitively command multi-agent sensor networks with SAHUC

SAHUC adapts the techniques described above to produce a multi-agent system emphasizing responsiveness over optimality, Fig. 1. Other applications may have enough time to calculate an optimal global solution; but the physical security of high-consequence sites does not. Security threats at high-consequence sites must be dealt with immediately.

Sandia's motivation for creating SAHUC has been presented in Sect. 1. SAHUC's architecture is detailed in Sect. 2. Section 3 discusses the current SAHUC proof-of-concept implementation. Section 4 presents the results of two experiments quantifying SAHUC's performance. Section 5 recounts a physical security demonstration, illustrating the potential usefulness of SAHUC. Finally, Sect. 6 concludes.

2 SAHUC Architecture

SAHUC enables a single human to operate a multi-agent mobile network, Fig. 1. This requires several levels of hierarchy, Fig. 2. The Graphical User Interface (GUI) allows the operator to specify command intent by adding, removing, or modifying objectives for the network to accomplish. The human can also specify how the network is expected to perform those objectives by modifying weighting parameters. The high-level autonomy then assigns the objectives to agents. The mid-level autonomy plans paths for the assigned objectives. The mid-level autonomy also estimates metrics characterizing the agent's expected performance. These metric estimates are combined, along with the weighting parameters, to form the costs used in the high-level assignment algorithm. Finally, the lowest level of autonomy tracks the planned path and estimates the agent's state.

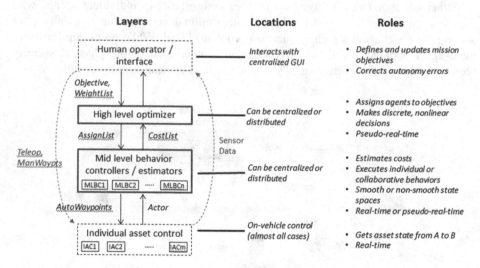

Fig. 2. A conceptual view of SAHUC's hierarchy

2.1 Graphical User Interface

The GUI provides an intuitive 3D view of the current state of the network, Fig. 3. It shows where the agents and adversarial targets currently are positioned and where they have recently been. By right-clicking in the 3D display a user can quickly create a point, multi-segment line, or area of interest. By right-clicking on that point/line/area a new objective can be generated (e.g. look at the point, patrol the border, or search the area). A similarly trivial procedure can be applied to any agent/target icon to create a new objective (e.g. to escort the agent, or follow the target). Through this method, the operator constructs high-level mission behaviors by specifying desired outcomes. If the operator prefers to bypass the autonomy, they can directly command the agents by manually specifying a waypoint or manually teleoperating the vehicle with a joystick. The GUI also displays live sensor streams.

Fig. 3. SAHUC's graphical user interface

2.2 High-Level Autonomy

The highest level of autonomy contains an assignment algorithm. It automatically assigns objectives to agents using metrics computed by the mid-level autonomy. While the assignment algorithm is based upon optimization techniques, approximations are used to speed up the algorithm. Responsiveness and adaptability to changing security threats is more important that being truly "optimal". When a new threat is identified, new objectives are created. The system must respond in seconds; not stop, fully re-plan a truly optimal solution, and then act minutes later.

To ensure assignments occur quickly, metrics are computed in a distributed manner onboard the agents. They are coarse estimations of the true values. The metrics are communicated and combined to form the costs used in the assignment algorithm.

$$C(A_i, O_j) = \beta_1 \cdot M_1(A_i, O_j) + \beta_2 \cdot M_2(A_i, O_j) + \dots \beta_n \cdot M_n(A_i, O_j) \tag{1}$$

The estimated cost of agent A_i performing objective O_j is a weighted combination of the metrics calculated by A_i, Eq. (1). β_k are the weighting parameters defined through the GUI. They enable the human operator to modify how the agents operate (e.g. switch from "fast" to "energy efficient" by modifying the metric weights).

The assignment algorithm minimizes the cost J defined by:

$$J = \sum_i^{N_A} \sum_j^{N_O} z_{ij} \cdot C(A_i, O_j) \tag{2}$$

N_A and N_O are the number of agents and objectives. z_{ij} are a set of binary assignment variables. If agent A_i determined that executing objective O_j was infeasible, a constraint is added to the optimization to prevent this assignment from occurring: $z_{ij} = 0$. Typically, a 1:1 assignment is assumed. That is, each agent is assigned to at most one objective, and one objective has at most one agent assigned to it. In this case, the constraints on Eq. (2) are:

$$\sum_i^{N_A} z_{ij} \le 1 \forall j, \quad \sum_j^{N_O} z_{ij} \le 1 \forall i, \quad \sum_i^{N_A} \sum_j^{N_O} z_{ij} = \min(N_A, N_O) \tag{3}$$

The third constraint prevents agents from being lazy by forcing as many assignments to occur as possible. By allowing the binary decision variable z to be $z \in [0, 1]$, conventional linear programming methods can be applied [10]. These conventional methods can decrease the computation time required for a solution.

In order to prevent the assignment algorithm from suffering "decision chatter" (excessive switching between assignments), a switching cost is assigned to changing from the current assignment, adding hysteresis [11, 12].

If multiple agents are to be assigned to a single objective (e.g. to enable swarm-based objectives), the constraints in (3) must be modified to be:

$$\sum_i^{N_A} z_{ij} \le maxsize(O_j), \sum_j^{N_O} z_{ij} \le 1 \forall i, \sum_i^{N_A} \sum_j^{N_O} z_{ij} = \min\left(N_A, \sum_j^{N_O} maxsize(O_j)\right)$$

Maxsize is the maximum number of agents that can be assigned to each objective.

2.3   Mid-level Autonomy

The mid-level autonomy plans a path to execute the agent's assigned objective. It also considers alternative objectives by: determining if the alternative is feasible, planning a path for the alternative, and estimating metrics for the alternative. These metric estimates are communicated to the high-level optimization layer discussed above.

The mid-level behaviors can determine paths for individuals or teams/swarms. For Physical Security it is necessary to have agents perform behaviors like: move to a point, search an area, patrol a border, protect another asset, follow a target, etc. Heterogeneity in the agent's dynamics or computational capabilities may require different path planning algorithms for the same type of objective. Consider moving to a specific point: the path for a UAV to fly over a building is radically different from the path for a UGV to go around it. The algorithms producing the paths must simply agree on the inputs necessary to define the point to which they are moving.

The mid-level autonomy also produces metric estimates for all objectives. First, feasibility is determined. An objective may be infeasible for an agent because: it may lack a path planning algorithm for that type of objective, it may not have the necessary sensor suite, its limited resources may not allow it to complete the objective.

If the agent could feasibly execute the objective, a path is planned using the mid-level behavior's algorithm. The fidelity of the path is not constrained within SAHUC. Computationally limited agents can use very coarse approximations while computationally rich agents can use highly-accurate predictions. This allows all agents to rapidly approximate the paths for all alternative objectives. The metrics are then calculated for each alternative objective. These metrics include transient and steady-state effects: time to arrival, cycle time, energy to arrival, cycle energy, distance to arrival, cycle distance. For example, the border patrol in Fig. 4 has a distance to arrive at the border (segment a), and then a different distance to perform one complete cycle of that patrol (segments b through g).

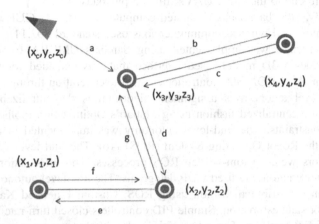

Fig. 4. An example of a border patrol, segments b-through-g would repeat indefinitely

2.4 Low-Level Autonomy

The low-level autonomy follows the planned paths and produces state estimates. The algorithms chosen also depend on the computation available. Heterogeneous agents have heterogeneous capabilities and dynamics. SAHUC does not mandate which algorithms are used in the low-level autonomy.

SAHUC's control algorithms can vary from PIDs to Model-Predictive Controllers to Rapidly-expanding Random Trees. Vehicle-specific controllers are used to fully exploit knowledge of the agent's dynamics (e.g. skid-steered vs unicycle UGVs).

Similarly, the state estimation algorithms vary based on sensor suite and computational capability. Computationally limited agents can use simple Kalman Filters with GPS and IMU measurements. More capable agents can use full SLAM solutions. If the state estimation algorithms include local environment representations, obstacle avoidance can be incorporated within the low-level autonomy.

3   Proof-of-Concept Implementation

SAHUC's proof-of-concept implementation leveraged Commercial-Off-The-Shelf hardware and open-source software. Three highly-modified Jaguar UGVs from Dr. Robot are shown in Fig. 5 [13]. Dr. Robot's GPS receivers were replaced with better-performing NovAtel receivers and pinwheel antennas. The pinwheel antennas and the Jaguar's IMUs where moved outside of the main vehicle bodies to reduce EMF and multi-path interference from the motors and the ground. Asus netbooks with a 1.6 GHz Atom processors running Ubuntu 12.04 were added to each vehicle. Webcams and Hokuyo URG-04LX lidars were also added.

Figure 5 shows three 3DR Arducopter UAVs [14]. The Arducopters have onboard GPS/IMU, 2.4 GHz RC control links, 1.3 GHz video links, and 900 MHz base station links. The UAV base stations operated on 1.6 GHz Asus netbooks. This allowed the UAVs to have identical processing capabilities as the UGVs, but the processing was located offboard due to the small UAVs' limited payloads.

Additionally, GPS backpacks simulated computer vision. The GUI was run on a Windows 7 laptop. All wireless communications used standard 802.11 g hardware.

The user interface was implemented using Sandia's UMBRA framework [15]. UMBRA provides a 3D model-based interface that was extended for the SAHUC implementation. An XBOX 360 controller enabled teleoperation through the GUI.

The high-level autonomy's assignment algorithm is de-centralizable, but was implemented in a centralized fashion using Matlab's Optimization toolbox, primarily due to time constraints. The mid-level autonomy was implemented in a distributed fashion using the Robot Operating System (ROS) [16]. The mid-level behaviors and metric estimators were custom-written ROS processes. The information exchanged with the high-level autonomy used UDP datagrams. The low-level autonomy was also implemented in a distributed fashion using ROS. Custom Extended Kalman Filters were written for state estimation. Simple PID controllers closed turn-rate and velocity loops for waypoint tracking. These two simple algorithms were computationally efficient alternatives to ROS's slam_gmapping and move_base packages. Those packages were also integrated to enable SLAM and advanced path following (including obstacle avoidance). However, they taxed the netbooks to their computational limits and the lidars needed for SLAM did not function well outdoors during daylight hours.

Fig. 5. UGVs and UAVs for SAHUC's proof-of-concept implementation

4 Experiments

Two simple experiments were performed to verify SAHUC's anticipated performance. Each experiment was performed ten times to gather sufficient statistical data.

4.1 Experiment 1

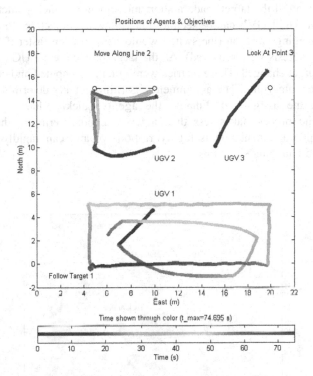

Fig. 6. Experiment 1 had three UGVs performing three objectives: follow a target, move along a line, and look at a point from the north. Time is indicated through color.

The first experiment, shown in Fig. 6, had three UGVs and three objectives: follow a target (that walked in a predefined box pattern), move along a 2-segment line, and look at a point from the North. The assignment algorithm was set to run every 0.1 s and the measured rate was 0.101 s (std dev 0.046). The slight drop and variability can be attributed to running Matlab on a non-real time operating system (Windows 7). The agents were set to compute and broadcast their information every 0.5 s; the measured rate was 0.506 s (std dev 0.077). Experiment 1 verified that SAHUC's proof-of-concept implementation can calculate the metrics and the assignment algorithm's solution as quickly as expected. It also confirmed that the assignment algorithm produced the obviously correct assignments.

4.2 Experiment 2

The second experiment, shown in Fig. 7, had two identical UGVs and two objectives: look at a point from any direction, and follow a target. At the beginning of the experiment, UGV 1 was best suited to follow the target (because it was closest and requires the shortest time, distance, and energy). UGV 2 was similarly best suited to look at the point. Figure 7's initial trajectories demonstrate that this is what the assignment was, until the target made a short movement to quickly alter the obvious best assignment. The UGV's can be seen to quickly switch objectives to automatically adapt to the changing situation (the switch would happen even faster if the switching costs adding hysteresis were removed). As the target moved, each UGV's metrics for following the target changed. These metrics were quickly computed and communicated to the assignment algorithm. The assignment algorithm quickly determined that it was best to switch the assignment. Finally, the agents quickly changed course. The entire end-to-end process takes less than a few seconds, verifying that SAHUC's proof-of-concept implementation is highly responsive and can rapidly and autonomously adapt to changing situations.

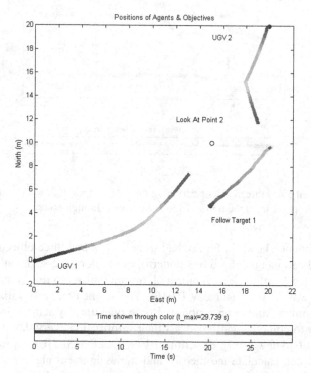

Fig. 7. Experiment 2 had two UGVs and two objectives: look at a point from any direction, follow a target. The target made a short quick move, causing a change in the assignment.

5 Physical Security Demonstration

SAHUC's physical security potential was demonstrated at Sandia's Robotic Vehicle Range (RVR). The RVR includes buildings, towers, paved areas, gravel areas, dirt paths, and a fenced perimeter; making it an ideal physical security test site, Fig. 8.

All three UGVs were used in the demonstration, but only one UAV was flown, in order to satisfy safety concerns. The UAV had a safety pilot to take over RC control in the event of an emergency. The UAV also had a FAA licensed private pilot-in-command to monitor the UAV, communicate with the control tower, and monitor the sky.

The pilot-in-command and safety pilot were not active participants in the system, just necessary to ensure safe testing. The human operator ran the GUI from inside a control room in the RVR, having no line-of-sight to the agents being commanded. The agents operated inside and outside of the fenced security perimeter. Finally, an intruder approached the RVR from the Southeast, sneaked through an open gate on the Southeast end of the RVR, and attempted to gather intelligence about the facility.

Fig. 8. GUI screenshot right after the intruder passed through the open gate

The human operator began by distributing the UGVs throughout the facility. A border patrol objective was created at the open gate because the operator knew this was a weak point in the current security. The tracked UGV began to immediately move back and forth along the open gate, streaming video back to the operator. Then, the operator manually spread the other two UGVs throughout the facility. A visit point objective and an additional border patrol objective were created to place the other UGVs at strategic locations (near the corners of buildings) in the RVR facility.

At this point, the intruder sneaked through the open gate behind the patrolling UGV, but was detected with the camera once the UGV turned around upon reaching the North end of the gate. In practice, machine vision would be used to detect the intruder; however, due to time constraints this was simulated through a GPS backpack. Figure 8 is just after this moment.

Upon the detection of an intruder, the human operator created a track target objective. This was automatically assigned to the UAV, because the UAV was significantly faster at getting to and continuing to track the person. The UAV continued to track the intruder until the intruder disappeared from sight by moving under a tarp, Fig. 9.

Fig. 9. GUI screenshot when the intruder is hiding under the blue tarp

The human operator created a new look-at-point objective to get streaming video of what was under the blue tarp. The closest UGV was assigned and provided video of the intruder. Finally, the human operator informed the intruder that they had been detected and should surrender immediately using speakers on the UGV.

The demonstration illustrated how multiple agents could enhance the physical security of a high-consequence site. The need for heterogeneity was shown when the UAV could better track the intruder in the open, but the UGV could easily see under the blue tarp. The impact of multi-agent autonomy was clear; the single human operator controlled all 4 UMSs simultaneously, and monitored the live sensor feeds, while also explaining the system and answering questions to demonstration attendees.

6   Conclusions

SAHUC enables multi-agent mobile sensor networks for securing high-consequence sites. Multi-agent algorithms have been adapted to emphasize timely responsiveness over optimality, producing a system that can adapt in seconds to constantly evolving security conditions. The capability leverages autonomy where possible and enables operator attention to be focused on the highest-level tasks, such as tactical reasoning.

As processors improve, more computationally expensive algorithms (e.g. SLAM and obstacle avoidance) can be run on the agents. These algorithms should continue to maintain SAHUC's responsiveness. The distributed computation of metrics is a major strength of the architecture. The ability to plan paths and estimate metrics at varying levels of coarseness further ensure responsiveness by allowing customization to the individual agent's computational capability. SAHUC's major drawback is its dependence upon communications, but the bandwidth required for SAHUC's information is significantly lower than that of streaming the live video feeds.

Future work includes larger scale demonstrations, potentially including of all three UAVs, which will yield more complete and realistic demonstrations. The video feeds should be directly overlaid onto the 3D map, making it more intuitive to see what the agents are seeing. Real computer vision algorithms should be run onboard the agents to replace the GPS backpacks. These algorithms may require the increasing the onboard computing. Finally, communications should be intentionally degraded to evaluate how the multi-agent network performs while operating under interference.

Acknowledgments. This research was funded by the Laboratory Directed Research and Development (LDRD) program at Sandia National Laboratories. Sandia National Laboratories is a multi-program laboratory managed and operated by Sandia Corporation, a wholly owned subsidiary of Lockheed Martin Corporation, for the U.S. Department of Energy's National Nuclear Security Administration under contract DE-AC04-94AL85000.

References

1. Intelligent Systems, Robotics, & Cybernetics. http://www.sandia.gov/research/robotics/index.html
2. Urmson, C., et al.: A robust approach to high-speed navigation for unrehearsed desert terrain. J. Field Rob. **23**(8), 467–508 (2006)
3. Montemerlo, M., et al.: Junior: the stanford entry in the urban challenge. J. Field Rob. **25**(9), 569–597 (2008)
4. Kira, Z., et al.: A design process for robot capabilities and missions applied to micro-autonomous platforms. In: Proceedings of SPIE. vol. 7679, pp. 767911 (2010)
5. Vincent, R., et al.: Distributed multirobot exploration, mapping, and task allocation. Ann. Math. Artif. Intell. **52**(2), 229–255 (2009)
6. Scardovi, L., et al.: Stabilization of three-dimensional collective motion. Commun. Inf. Syst. **8**(4), 473–500 (2008)
7. Ryan, A., et al.: Decentralized control of unmanned aerial vehicle sensing missions. In: Proceedings of IEEE American Control Conference, pp. 4672–4677 (2007)
8. Garvey, J., et al.: An autonomous unmanned aerial vehicle system for sensing and tracking. In: Infotech@ Aerospace Conference (2011)
9. Bertucelli, L.F., et al.: Robust planning for coupled cooperative UAV missions. In: Proceedings of IEEE Conference on Decision and Control, pp. 2917–2922 (2004)
10. Linear Programming Relaxation, Wikipedia. http://en.wikipedia.org/wiki/Linear_programming_relaxation
11. Dusonchet, F., Hongler, M.O.: Optimal hysteresis for a class of deterministic deteriorating two-armed bandit problem with switching costs. Automatica **39**(11), 1947–1955 (2003)
12. Kitaev, A., Yu, M., Serfozo, A., Richard, F.: M/M/1 queues with switching costs and hysteretic optimal control. J. Oper. Res. **47**(2), 310–312 (1999)
13. http://jaguar.drrobot.com
14. http://3drobotics.com
15. http://umbra.sandia.gov
16. http://www.ros.org

Technology-Supported Health Measures and Goal-Tracking for Older Adults in Everyday Living

Blaine Reeder[1(✉)], Angela Richard[1], and Martha E. Crosby[2]

[1] University of Colorado Anschutz Medical Campus, Aurora, CO, USA
{blaine.reeder,angela.richard}@ucdenver.edu
[2] University of Hawaii at Manoa, Honolulu, HI, USA
crosby@hawaii.edu

Abstract. In this paper, we review in-home technologies for use by older adults and the potential for technology-supported health measures to support independent living by connecting older adults, informal caregivers, and health care providers. We outline areas for new research that include platforms for technology integration, software for integrated data analytics, design for usability, and patient goal elicitation. Within this research agenda, meaningful health measurements must be defined, stakeholder interactions must be understood, and technologies must be standardized to enable large-scale community-based field studies beyond small-scale feasibility studies.

Keywords: Sensors · Independent living · Older adults · Home care · Heart failure

1 Introduction

1.1 Population Aging

The U.S., along with other countries, is facing a "silver tsunami", wherein the growth of the older adult population (age 65 and older) is expected to increase rapidly over the next four decades. Between 2010 and 2050, the number of older adults in the United States is projected to more than double to approximately 88.5 million [1]. The United Nations reported that globally, the percentage of individuals older than 80 is projected to grow from 14 % in 2013 to 19 % in 2015 [2]. This "graying" of the population will coincide with a projected shortage of gerontological health care workers [3]. The use of existing in-home services to support functional independence at home has been identified as a challenge due to rising numbers of chronically ill and disabled older adults [4]. These factors, coupled with continuously rising health care costs, will require innovative ways of supporting health and independence for older adults. New technology development [5], new models of chronic care delivery for older adults [6], and changes to public policy regarding elder care [7] have been put forth as ways to meet increased demand for aging care services. In this paper, we will discuss how technology-supported health measures can assist older adults, their family members,

© Springer International Publishing Switzerland 2015
D.D. Schmorrow and C.M. Fidopiastis (Eds.): AC 2015, LNAI 9183, pp. 796–806, 2015.
DOI: 10.1007/978-3-319-20816-9_76

and health care providers (HCPs) in decision-making to maintain independence using the United States home health care context as an example.

1.2   Accountable Care Organizations

The passage of the Affordable Care Act in the United States included provisions for the establishment of accountable care organizations (ACOs) [8, 9]. ACOs are entities that consist of groups of integrated HCPs (e.g.: physicians, nurse practitioners, and hospitals) which jointly hold accountability for health care outcomes and costs for a defined patient population across the continuum of care. ACOs are reimbursed through a combination of fee-for-service payments and shared savings that result from greater efficiencies in care provision and reduced costs. Expected advantages of ACOs include the ability to emphasize quality across care settings and individual providers, greater sharing of clinical information, and ability to provide data on costs, care processes and outcomes [8, 9].

1.3   Home Care Context

Home health care in the United States is provided to patients recuperating from an acute illness or surgery, and/or chronic condition(s) that limit the ability to function independently in the home. The primary payer for home health services in the U.S. is Medicare [10]. In 2014, the Medicare Payment Advisory Commission reported that over 12,000 Home Health Agencies (HHAs) in the U.S. provided skilled nursing and therapy services to nearly 3.4 million Medicare beneficiaries [11]. Moreover, the Centers for Medicare & Medicaid Services estimates that home health care expenditures will more than double over the next 10 years [12], representing the highest annual percent change among all types of expenditures from 2015 through 2022. The growth of the home health care industry is fueled by patient preferences, lower costs of care, and technology improvements that expand the types of care that can be provided in home settings [10, 13–15].

The majority of patients admitted to Medicare-certified home health care services are discharged from hospitals or acute rehabilitation facilities, although patients may be referred from primary care physicians, nursing homes, outpatient providers, and patient/family [16, 17]. While the most frequently seen diagnoses for home health care patients are chronic conditions including diabetes, hypertension, heart failure, chronic skin ulcers and osteoarthritis [10], it is common for home care patients to have multiple co-morbid health conditions [18]. Formal home health care services include care provided by nurses; physical, occupational, and speech language therapists; social workers; and home health aides. Patients requiring home health care assistance (e.g., personal care, housekeeping, and other activities but not skilled services), may receive those services through Medicaid waiver programs, private insurance or self-pay. Depending on the condition of the patient and availability of caregiver support, overall goals of home health care services include: promotion of health status improvements; education and support for chronic care self-management; and provision of long-term assistance that can postpone or eliminate the need for the patient to be placed in a skilled nursing facility [14, 15].

2 Independence and Task Advantages

Independence is a complex concept with numerous definitions that include physical, cognitive, emotional, behavioral, and psychosocial factors [19–22]. Our previous work defined independence as the interactions between personal capacity (i.e.,: ability to perform tasks) and environmental resources in relation to a hypothetical threshold for independent living [23]. When results of these interactions fall below this threshold, a person's ability to live independently may be negatively impacted and he or she may become *disabled*. Those individuals who function at a level slightly above the threshold of independence are *vulnerable* to disability and loss of independence. Individuals who have an abundance of personal capacity and support through environmental resources are considered *high functioning*. Figure 1 illustrates this conceptual view of independence, which is congruent with health trajectory models such as the disablement process [24].

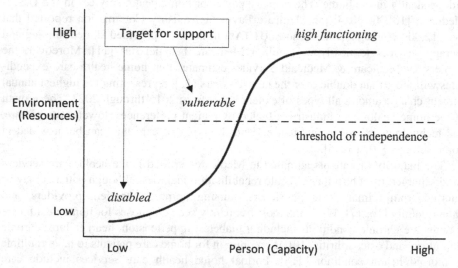

Fig. 1. A conceptual view of independence resulting from the interactions between *person (capacity)* and *environment (resources)* in relation to a hypothetical *threshold of independence* [23].

Within this conceptual view, efforts to help vulnerable or disabled persons should target person-environment interactions with the aim of increasing functional status to a level of independence for disabled persons, or improving personal capacity for vulnerable individuals at-risk for loss of independence. Specifically, technology should support person-environment interactions by creating *task advantages* – the relative ease with which a technology-supported task is performed compared to performance of the task without technology [23] - that enable independence. These task advantages can involve the vulnerable or disabled person only, or can also involve an informal care-giver or health care provider in the form of sharing the burden of task.

3   Patient Activation and Technology

Patient activation is a "patient's knowledge, skills, ability, and willingness to manage his or her own health and care" [25]. Non-contact sensors embedded in the environment [26], body-worn sensors [27], and other personal information devices have great potential for engaging older adults in the management of their own health. By creating task advantages, they are connected to both informal and formal caregiving networks. Telemedicine is the use of technology to bring clinical support delivered by HCPs into the home [28]. Beyond telemedicine, we are concerned with what happens when home care ends. Below, we describe a typical condition (congestive heart failure - CHF) to illustrate potential technology uses to support patients, informal caregivers, and HCPs after home care ends.

3.1   Congestive Heart Failure

Congestive heart failure is one of the most prevalent chronic health conditions among adults 65 and older in the U.S. [29], affecting approximately 5.1 million older adults [30]. Heart failure is one of the leading causes of death [31] resulting in death within five years for approximately 50 % of diagnosed individuals [30]. It is caused by weakness of the cardiac muscle resulting in inadequate oxygenation and fluid overload, leading to shortness of breath and fatigue [32], and is one of the most frequently-seen diagnoses in home health care patients [33], with an average length of stay of 44 days [34]. Home health care interventions focus on the self-management education, close monitoring of physiological parameters, medication adherence, and therapies to increase functional strength and endurance. Discharge from home care typically occurs after certain clinical goals are met, including: patient/family ability to self-monitor symptoms and manage the medical regimen; and stability of physiologic parameters. Patient activation and self-management of health and wellness is crucial to maintaining independence at home after home health care discharge, and to reduce the risk of costly re-hospitalizations. Technology has the potential to support patient activation and self-management.

3.2   Potential for Technology to Support Independence

Technology can create task advantages for independence in everyday living by augmenting personal capacity, increasing affordances in the environment, or a combination of both. In addition, technology can enable independence and goal-tracking through information sourced by older adults and shared with family members and HCPs. Body-worn sensors have the advantage of collecting individual-level data but have the disadvantage of adherence issues [27]. Smart homes are home settings equipped with sensors that allow passive monitoring of residents' health status [35]. These non-contact technologies have the advantage of freeing older adults from engaging with the technology for data collection. Personal computers, tablets, and mobile devices enable collection of self-reported health measures. This data can then be correlated with sensor-based measures and assist with patient goal-tracking.

With regard to congestive heart failure, important physiological factors that can be measured automatically by sensors are heart rate [36–38] and respiratory rate [36, 38, 39]. While many physiological measures may require patients to enter values such as oxygen levels [40], weight [40] and blood pressure [40]. Behavioral factors that can be automatically measured by sensors are activity levels using motion sensors [38]. Devices that require patient-interaction are body-worn sensors such as a smart watch to track activity levels (http://www.getpebble.com) and medication management devices for medication adherence [41, 42]. Reminders can be sent via smart phone [43] or smart watch.

Personal computers, tablets, and mobile devices offer tremendous opportunities for collecting standardized measures of health that can be correlated with physiological and behavioral measures taken with sensors and networked equipment. For example, PROMIS measures (http://www.nihpromis.org/patients/measures) are freely available standardized measures for patient reporting of what they can do or how they feel. PROMIS measures come in short form tools that are especially useful for data collection in the home via electronic means. Useful examples of PROMIS 4-item short form instruments are: Fatigue (4 items), Physical Function (4 items), Sleep Disturbance (4 items), Emotional Distress – Anxiety (4 items), Emotional Distress - Depression (4 items). In addition, shared calendars [44] have potential to enhance coordination and communication for older adults, informal caregivers, and HCPs. In addition, these computing devices, as well as digital pens, can be used to keep health diaries or manage dietary information to promote adherence with dietary recommendations [45]. Table 1 shows potential technology benefits by stakeholder.

4   Future Research

4.1   Platforms for Technology Integration

Patient monitoring systems with advanced features, especially wireless or remote capability, are among the fastest-growing medical devices. These personal medical sensors are broadly available, affordable and allow patients to take measurements at home. As a result, there is a healthy market for these devices because of improvements in their accuracy of measurement. For example, the market for health sensing devices grew from $4.2 billion USD in 2007 to more than $10 billion USD in 2012, a 237 % increase within 5 years (http://www.kaloramainformation.com/Advanced-Remote-Patient-7450566/). Efforts such as those led by the Continua Health Alliance (http://www.continuaalliance.org/) to build health monitoring systems using personal medical

Table 1. Technology types and support opportunities for different stakeholders

Technology	Older Adults	Informal Caregiver	HCPs
Automated physiological measures (heart rate & respiratory sensors)	For interactions about health status with HCPs	Alerts sent if measures drop below predefined threshold	Alerts if measures drop below predefined threshold
Patient-initiated physiological measures (pulse oximeter, blood pressure cuff, scale)	Goal tracking & self-management, and interactions with HCPs	Alerts if measures drop or are not taken	For interactions about self-monitoring and management
Automated behavioral measures (motion sensors)	Goal tracking and self-management	Alerts if activity measures drop	For interactions about self-management
Patient-initiated behavioral measures (phone, smart watch, medication devices)	Goal tracking and self-management	Alerts can be sent if measures drop or are not taken	For interactions about self-management
Electronic self-reports (PROMIS and others)	To correlate perceptions & objective measures	For interactions related to shared decision-making	For interactions about symptom management
Shared calendars	For care coordination	Useful for care coordination	Useful for care coordination
Activity and medication reminders (laptop, tablet, phone, smart watch)	For adherence to goals & correlation with sensor-based measures	Alerts can be sent if measures drop or are not taken	For interactions about self-management and health status

devices are becoming more acceptable. In addition, infrastructure to securely transfer and manage data must be developed. Opportunities exist for applied research and dissemination of new knowledge, based on information gleaned from intelligent sensors. The Internet of Things may be useful toward this end [46, 47]. Improved technology has made these devices available to consumers for home use. Testing these devices in the home setting is required for their validity and reliability in "real world" settings.

Software for Analytics. Applications utilizing intelligent recognition technologies have the potential to solve a broad variety of significant problems faced by elderly people worldwide. Academic and industrial partners from fields such as medicine, nursing, biology, computer science, information science, engineering, mathematics and statistics are collaborating to develop new computational techniques and applications in life science domains. Directly related to platforms for technology integration are software packages to analyze and represent the deluge of data from connected devices [48]. Advances made in visualizations of information; data modeling; data integration; machine learning; data mining; text analysis; pattern recognition and knowledge representation can be utilized or developed. In particular, studies that solicit requirements of different stakeholders are needed.

4.2 Design for Usability

Research that includes participants early in the development process is essential. Studies should investigate behavior, attitude change, motivation, goal setting and adherence with digital interactive interventions. User studies are particularly necessary if the activities involve the use of mobile or wearable technologies with the targeted population. The accurate assessment of cognitive states is vital to identifying and defining cognitive processes and testing models of how cognitive processes operate and interact. Physiological sensors can be used to assess not only the users' health but also their mental status. Health and mental status can each be subdivided into multiple factors. These factors along with the ability to automatically identify the cognitive load of the user from physiological measures will allow a level of interface customization in real-time. Usability studies about data input modalities are important for older adults. For instance, how usable are touch and voice input modalities for data collection in the homes of older adults? Much of the research focus is on the sensors and what we can build rather than the user experience. As more and more information is collected from a greater number of elderly patients, caregivers may get overwhelmed and data analytics will be more expensive. Research activities based on the convergence of technologies such as intelligent sensors; knowledge building; pattern recognition; and secure networking is useful technical research but do the extensive networks of sensors contribute to information overload for the caregiver and the participant?

4.3 Elicitation of Patient Goals

The sensor-based and self-reported measures discussed thus far have been framed primarily from the clinical perspective. The goals of the clinician may not necessarily mesh with the goals of older adult patients, or even family members. New models of patient-directed care are currently being developed to accommodate older adults who want to stay independent in the community [49]. Identification of patient goals of care have practical value for decision-making when considering the trade-offs inherent in many medical treatments, and allows patients more control over their care regimen [50]. Sensor and self-report technologies have the potential to improve patient and family independence and prolong the amount of time that elders can remain in their own home. In addition, these technologies have the potential to reduce costs of care by preventing hospital admissions or readmissions. Further research is needed about the extent to which technology can support patient-identified goals, along with addressing and minimizing perceptions of discomfort or invasiveness that the technology may bring.

5 Conclusion

In this paper we have reviewed technology for use by older adults and the potential for technology to support independent living. In addition, we have described several areas for research to reach this potential. While we have focused on a specific condition as an example (congestive heart failure), technology research should focus on support for independent living, regardless of health condition. Indeed, many older adults contend with multiple morbidities that must be managed to maintain independence in the community. In order to support this population, meaningful health measurements must be defined, interactions between different stakeholders must be understood, and smart home technologies must be standardized [23]. Beyond this, large community-based field studies must be conducted as research-to-date with smart home technologies primarily has been characterized by small feasibility studies [51].

References

1. Vincent, G.K., Velkoff, V.A.: The next four decades: the older population in the United States: 2010 to 2050. US Department of Commerce, Economics and Statistics Administration, US Census Bureau (2010)
2. United Nations Department of Economic and Social Affairs Population Division: World Population Ageing (2013)
3. Cohen, S.A.: A review of demographic and infrastructural factors and potential solutions to the physician and nursing shortage predicted to impact the growing US elderly population. J. Public Health Manag. Pract. 15, 352–362 (2009)
4. Rice, D.P., Fineman, N.: Economic implications of increased longevity in the United States. Annu. Rev. Public Health 25, 457–473 (2004)
5. Koch, S., Hägglund, M.: Health informatics and the delivery of care to older people. Maturitas 63, 195–199 (2009)
6. Boult, C., Green, A.F., Boult, L.B., Pacala, J.T., Snyder, C., Leff, B.: Successful models of comprehensive care for older adults with chronic conditions: evidence for the institute of medicine's "retooling for an aging America" report. J. Am. Geriatr. Soc. 57, 2328–2337 (2009)
7. Houde, S.C., Melillo, K.D.: Public policy - caring for an aging population: review of policy initiatives. J. Gerontological Nurs. 138, 8 (2009)
8. Bodenheimer, T.S., Grumbach, K.: Understanding Health Policy: A Clinical Approach. McGraw-Hill Medical, New York (2012)
9. Burke, T.: Accountable care organizations. Public Health Rep. 126(6), 875–878 (2011)
10. National Association for Home Care and Hospice: Basic statistics about home care (2010)

11. Medicare Payment Advisory Committee (MedPAC 2014): Chapter 9 in Report to Congress: Medicare Payment Policy (2014)
12. Centers for Medicare, and Medicaid Services: National Health Expenditure Projections, pp. 2012–2022 (2012)
13. Bowles, K.H., Naylor, M.D., Foust, J.B.: Patient characteristics at hospital discharge and a comparison of home care referral decisions. J. Am. Geriatr. Soc. **50**, 336–342 (2002)
14. Dieckmann, J.L.: Home health care: an historical perspective and overview. In: Harris, M.D. (ed.) Handbook of Home Health Care Administration, pp. 3–19. Jones and Bartlett Publishers, Sudbury (2010)
15. Murkofsky, R.L., Alston, K.: The past, present, and future of skilled home health agency care. Clin. Geriatr. Med. **25**, 1–17 (2009)
16. Brega, A.G., Jordan, A.K., Schlenker, R.E.: Practice variations in home health care. Home Health Care Serv Q **22**, 41–64 (2003)
17. Park-Lee, E.Y., Decker, F.H.: Comparison of home health and hospice care agencies by organizational characteristics and services provided: United States, 2007. Natl. Health Stat. Rep. **30**, 1–23 (2010)
18. Boling, P.A.: Care transitions and home health care. Clin. Geriatr. Med. **25**(1), 135–148 (2009)
19. Law, M.: The person-environment-occupation model: a transactive approach to occupational performance. Can. J. Occup. Ther. **63**, 9–23 (1996)
20. Lawton, M.P.: An ecological theory of aging applied to elderly housing. Environ. Aging **31**(1), 8–10 (1977)
21. Iwarsson, S., Stahl, A.: Accessibility, usability and universal design–positioning and definition of concepts describing person-environment relationships. Disabil. Rehabil. **25**, 57 (2003)
22. Demiris, G.: Independence and shared decision making: the role of smart home technology in empowering older adults. In: Annual International Conference of the IEEE on Engineering in Medicine and Biology Society EMBC 2009, pp. 6432–6436 (2009)
23. Reeder, B., Demiris, G., Thompson, H.J.: Smart built environments and independent living: a public health perspective. In: Bodine, C., Helal, S., Gu, T., Mokhtari, M. (eds.) ICOST 2014. LNCS, vol. 8456, pp. 219–224. Springer, Heidelberg (2015)
24. Verbrugge, L.M., Jette, A.M.: The disablement process. Soc. Sci. Med. **38**, 1–14 (1994)
25. James, J.: Health Policy Brief: Patient Engagement. Health Affairs (2013)
26. Rantz, M.J., Skubic, M., Popescu, M., Galambos, C., Koopman, R.J., Alexander, G.L., Phillips, L.J., Musterman, K., Back, J., Miller, S.J.: A new paradigm of technology-enabled 'vital signs' for early detection of health change for older adults. Gerontology (2014)
27. Allet, L., Knols, R.H., Shirato, K., de Bruin, E.D.: Wearable systems for monitoring mobility-related activities in chronic disease: a systematic review. Sensors **10**(10), 9026–9052 (2010)
28. Wootton, R.: Twenty years of telemedicine in chronic disease management – an evidence synthesis. J. Telemedicine Telecare **18**, 211–220 (2012)
29. Medicare, C.f., Services, M.: Chronic Conditions among Medicare Beneficiaries. Chartbook, Baltimore (2012)
30. Go, A.S., Mozaffarian, D., Roger, V.L., Benjamin, E.J., Berry, J.D., Borden, W.B., Bravata, D.M., Dai, S., Ford, E.S., Fox, C.S., Franco, S., Fullerton, H.J., Gillespie, C., Hailpern, S.M., Heit, J.A., Howard, V.J., Huffman, M.D., Kissela, B.M., Kittner, S.J., Lackland, D.T., Lichtman, J.H., Lisabeth, L.D., Magid, D., Marcus, G.M., Marelli, A., Matchar, D.B., McGuire, D.K., Mohler, E.R., Moy, C.S., Mussolino, M.E., Nichol, G., Paynter, N.P., Schreiner, P.J., Sorlie, P.D., Stein, J., Turan, T.N., Virani, S.S., Wong, N.D., Woo, D., Turner, M.B.: American heart association statistics, C., stroke statistics, S.: heart disease and stroke statistics–2013 update: a report from the American heart association. Circulation **127**(1), e6–e245 (2013)

31. Kochanek, K.D., Xu, J., Murphy, S.L., Minino, A.M., Kung, H.C.: Deaths: final data for 2009. Natl. Vital Stat. Rep. **60**(3), 1–116 (2011)
32. Institute for Healthcare Improvement: 5 Million Lives Campaign. Improved Care for Patients with Congestive Heart Failure How-to Guide, Getting Started Kit (2008)
33. Care, N.A.f.H., Hospice: Basic statistics about home care. Washington, DC: National Association for Home Care and Hospice, pp. 1–14 (2010)
34. Madigan, E.A.: People with heart failure and home health care resource use and outcomes. J. Clin. Nurs. **17**, 253–259 (2008)
35. Demiris, G., Hensel, B.K.: Technologies for an aging society: a systematic review of "smart home" applications. Yearb. Med. Inform. **47**(Suppl 1), 33–40 (2008)
36. Massagram, W., Lubecke, V.M., Host-Madsen, A., Boric-Lubecke, O.: Assessment of heart rate variability and respiratory sinus arrhythmia via Doppler radar. IEEE Trans. Microw. Theory Tech. **57**, 2542–2549 (2009)
37. Droitcour, A.D., Boric-Lubecke, O., Lubecke, V.M., Lin, J., Kovacs, G.T.: Range correlation and I/Q performance benefits in single-chip silicon Doppler radars for noncontact cardiopulmonary monitoring. IEEE Trans. Microw. Theory Tech. **52**, 838–848 (2004)
38. Skubic, M., Alexander, G., Popescu, M., Rantz, M., Keller, J.: A smart home application to eldercare: current status and lessons learned. Technol. Health Care **17**, 183–201 (2009)
39. Droitcour, A.D., Seto, T.B., Park, B.-K., Yamada, S., Vergara, A., El Hourani, C., Shing, T., Yuen, A., Lubecke, V.M., Boric-Lubecke, O.: Non-contact respiratory rate measurement validation for hospitalized patients, EMBC 2009. In: Annual International Conference of the IEEE on Engineering in Medicine and Biology Society, pp. 4812–4815. IEEE (2009)
40. Demiris, G., Thompson, H.J., Reeder, B., Wilamowska, K., Zaslavsky, O.: Using informatics to capture older adults' wellness. Int. J. Med. Inform. **82**, e232–e241 (2013)
41. Marek, K.D., Stetzer, F., Ryan, P.A., Bub, L.D., Adams, S.J., Schlidt, A., Lancaster, R., O'Brien, A.-M.: Nurse care coordination and technology effects on health status of frail elderly via enhanced self-management of medication: randomized clinical trial to test efficacy. Nurs. Res. **62**, 269–278 (2013)
42. Ligons, F.M., Mello-Thoms, C., Handler, S.M., Romagnoli, K.M., Hochheiser, H.: Assessing the impact of cognitive impairment on the usability of an electronic medication delivery unit in an assisted living population. Int. J. Med. Inform. **83**, 841–848 (2014)
43. Vervloet, M., Linn, A.J., van Weert, J.C.M., de Bakker, D.H., Bouvy, M.L., van Dijk, L.: The effectiveness of interventions using electronic reminders to improve adherence to chronic medication: a systematic review of the literature. J. Am. Med. Inform. Assoc.: JAMIA **19**, 696–704 (2012)
44. Neustaedter, C., Brush, A.J.B., Greenberg, S.: The calendar is crucial: coordination and awareness through the family calendar. ACM Trans. Comput.-Hum. Interact. **16**(1), 1–48 (2009)
45. Lind, L., Karlsson, D.: Telehealth for "the digital illiterate"–elderly heart failure patients experiences. Stud. Health Technol. Inform. **205**, 353–357 (2014)
46. Brush, A., Filippov, E., Huang, D., Jung, J., Mahajan, R., Martinez, F., Mazhar, K., Phanishayee, A., Samuel, A., Scott, J.: Lab of things: a platform for conducting studies with connected devices in multiple homes. In: Proceedings of the 2013 ACM Conference on Pervasive and Ubiquitous Computing Adjunct Publication, pp. 35–38. ACM (2013)
47. Feminella, J., Pisharoty, D., Whitehouse, K.: Piloteur: a lightweight platform for pilot studies of smart homes. In: Proceedings of the 1st ACM Conference on Embedded Systems for Energy-Efficient Buildings, pp. 110–119. ACM, Memphis, Tennessee (2014)
48. Demiris, G., Thompson, H.: Smart homes and ambient assisted living applications: from data to knowledge - empowering or overwhelming older adults? contribution of the IMIA smart homes and ambiant assisted living working group. IMIA Yearb. 2011 Towards Health Inf. **6**(1), 51–57 (2011)

49. Szanton, S.L., Wolff, J.L., Leff, B., Roberts, L., Thorpe, R.J., Tanner, E.K., Boyd, C.M., Xue, Q.L., Guralnik, J., Bishai, D., Gitlin, L.N.: Preliminary data from community aging in place, advancing better living for elders, a patient-directed, team-based intervention to improve physical function and decrease nursing home utilization: the first 100 individuals to complete a centers for medicare and medicaid services innovation project. J. Am. Geriatr. Soc. **63**(2), 371–374 (2015)

50. Reuben, D.B., Tinetti, M.E.: Goal-oriented patient care–an alternative health outcomes paradigm. N. Engl. J. Med. **366**, 777–779 (2012)

51. Reeder, B., Meyer, E., Lazar, A., Chaudhuri, S., Thompson, H.J., Demiris, G.: Framing the evidence for health smart homes and home-based consumer health technologies as a public health intervention for independent aging: a systematic review. Int. J. Med. Inform. **82**, 565–579 (2013)

The Use of Eye Tracking
in Software Development

Bonita Sharif$^{(\boxtimes)}$ and Timothy Shaffer

Youngstown State University, Youngstown, OH 44555, USA
bsharif@ysu.edu, trshaffer@student.ysu.edu

Abstract. Eye trackers have been routinely used in psychology reading experiments and in website usability studies for many years. However, it is only recently that they have been used by more researchers in the software engineering community. In this paper, we categorize two broad areas in which eye tracking technology can benefit software development in a practical way. The first area includes using the eye tracker as an assessment tool for software artifacts, tools, and techniques. The second area deals with using eye tracking data from developers to inform certain software tools and software development tasks such as providing developer recommendations and software traceability tasks. Examples of experiments and studies done in each of these broad areas is presented and discussed along with future work. The results point towards many benefits that eye trackers provide to augment the daily lives of programmers during software development.

Keywords: Eye tracking · Software development · Software traceability · Assessing software artifacts · Program comprehension

1 Introduction

Software development is an integral part of software engineering. Developing software is an intertwined process that involves multiple tasks such as program comprehension, concept/feature location [1], impact analysis, writing code, and testing to match requirements. The above tasks certainly do not encompass all the activities but the core ones that a software developer is faced with on a daily basis. In order to make the task of a software developer a little easier, there has been a lot of work done in trying to understand how a developer interacts with his or her environment. Several researchers have conducted studies, such as the one by Ko et al. [2], to determine the types of questions software developers ask and the knowledge they seek to find while they work on their daily tasks. The end goal is to develop tools to help the developer in the highly complex and intricate skill of software development. The methods used to collect such information are mainly surveys, questionnaires, interviewing, and think-aloud methods.

In this paper, we posit that besides the above methods, a new method of data collection using an eye tracker provides additional benefits to the already existing methods in use. Besides using eye trackers for assessment – which seems to be the most obvious way to use them – they can also be used to inform various software tasks such as providing recommendations based on what the developers should look at next

© Springer International Publishing Switzerland 2015
D.D. Schmorrow and C.M. Fidopiastis (Eds.): AC 2015, LNAI 9183, pp. 807–816, 2015.
DOI: 10.1007/978-3-319-20816-9_77

based on what they have just been looking at. Past data of an eye tracking session can also be used to determine if and when the developer is facing difficulty. There has been one study [3] that tried to determine task difficulty based on psycho-physiological measures (including eye tracking) and the results seem to be quite promising. These directions in using eye tracking data as part of algorithms to inform other software tasks have only recently been explored by a few researchers [3–5]. Seigmund et al. [6] (although not related to eye tracking) recently used functional magnetic resonance imaging to understand how developers read source code. We expect more work to be conducted using biometrics including eye tracking in the future as more software engineering researchers tackle this important human aspect of software engineering.

One viable alternative to eye tracking sessions is developer-session recording models such as Mylyn. Mylyn is an Eclipse plugin that records developer interactions such as mouse clicks, selection and searching within the source code while the developer works on tasks. The main difference between the Mylyn and eye tracking approach is that with Mylyn, one has to click on a source code entity such as an "if statement" or a method call for it to register as something that was selected. With eye tracking, we do not need the developer to click on a method call or a method signature to know that they looked at it. In other words, eye tracking provides much more fine-grained data into what a developer is actually looking at.

We believe eye tracking technology can help software developers in their daily tasks. The goal is to reduce the effort developers have to put in. One instance would be to reduce effort to search by find relevant places in the code to begin their change task solely based on past behavior of eye movements. This approach is very developer centric. The cost of eye tracking equipment has also reduced by many factors of magnitude compared to a few years ago, making this a reality in the near future. The eye trackers we refer to are the remote eye trackers where a person is not required to wear anything, making it more attractive to be adopted by a developer.

In this position paper, we put forth the idea that eye tracking has potential in future software development tasks in software engineering by first outlining the need for eye-aware integrated development environments to make these claims a reality. Next, we provide examples of eye tracking being used in the software engineering realm. We close with the current state of eye trackers, challenges, and a call for more work in this area.

2   Eye-Aware Integrated Development Environments

In order for eye tracking to be adopted in the software engineering community and in the daily life of a developer, we first need to have the working environment of developers support eye gaze recording. Most developers work within an integrated development environment (IDE) such as Eclipse or Visual Studio. For eye tracking to be most useful, the feature of tracking developers' eyes while they work should be available to them from within the IDE itself or else it is less likely to be adopted or used.

2.1 The Problem

The problem with eye tracking so far was that most studies as discussed in the following sections were conducted with small snippets of code that fit on one screen. Every study that was done in software engineering (including some of our own), made use of small code snippets that fit on one screen. These studies mainly used eye tracking for assessing tools and techniques. The nature of the eye tracker is such that it gives you an *(x,y)* pixel coordinate on the screen of where a person is looking at. That *(x,y)* pixel coordinate is not mapped intrinsically to what the stimulus under the coordinate is. In other words, the eye tracker does not know if you scrolled in Eclipse. This is a big problem because when one scrolls, a different element will now appear under the pixel coordinates the person is looking at. So scrolling is not intrinsically captured and the underlying document you are scrolling is not mapped to the pixel coordinate. All the eye tracker will record is the *(x,y)* pixel coordinate. If a source code file is 300 lines long and the user scrolled many times through the file, there is no way for the eye tracker to tell which line in the document (source code) scrolled was under which *(x,y)* pixel coordinate in time without doing some kind of video analysis of the eye tracking session (which we did not want to do as it was not scalable).

This lack of context awareness between the eye tracker and the stimulus needed to be addressed due to the following reasons. First, developers do not just read small snippets of code in a realistic setting. They are more likely to work with an entire system with several hundred classes and long methods, so scrolling support for eye tracking with proper context is extremely important. Second, developers work with many files at a time for even a single change task. This means the eye tracker needs to know when the developer was looking at different source code files or bug reports for instance, as developers might move from reading a text file to writing source code, all of which should be captured by the eye tracking system. None of these features were available with current IDEs.

2.2 The Solution

We recognized this as a problem and decided that we had to find a better way to make eye tracking part of a developers work environment. This is when *iTrace* was born. Since there was no IDE that was eye aware (for scrolling support), we decided to build our own plugin to make eye tracking implicit within the IDE. This breaks the barrier of having small toy code snippets in future studies. It enables us to truly understand what developers are looking at while they develop software in a realistic setting. Currently, we are working on a stable version of *iTrace* and a formal tool demonstration along with an update installation package. Once this is created, it will be available in the open source domain for researchers to use as well as contribute to. We envision that *iTrace* will make an experimenter's job a lot easier since a lot of the groundwork on collecting the data and mapping the data to appropriate code elements is already taken care of by the tool. We believe *iTrace* is a huge step forward in making eye tracking accessible to software engineers as well as experimenters. See Fig. 1 for a snapshot of *iTrace*. It is written in Java and currently supports Java projects.

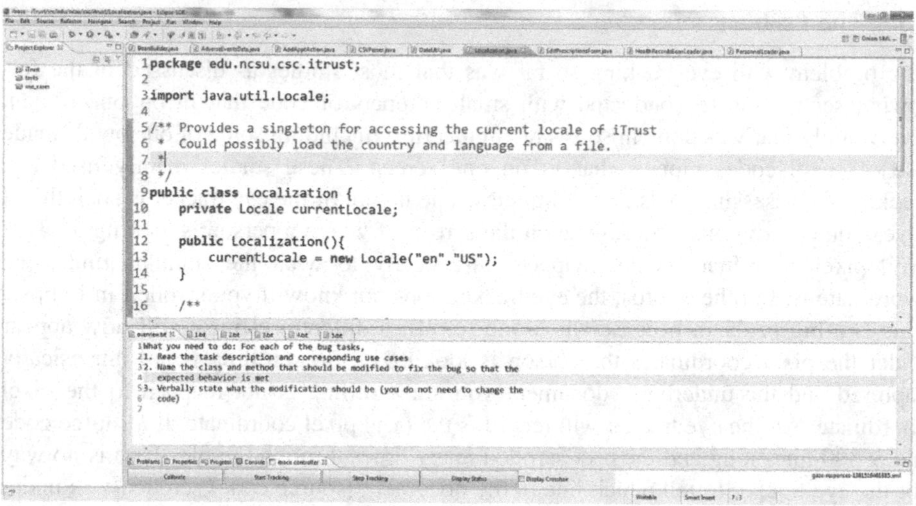

Fig. 1. A snapshot of iTrace

In the figure, we see the Eclipse window with the *iTrace* perspective open. At the very bottom is the *iTrace* dashboard (horizontal set of buttons) to perform a calibration, start tracking, stop tracking, and export sessions. Before an eye tracking session, it is essential that the eye tracker is first calibrated for each individual. During calibration a sequence of nine dots appear on the screen and the user is instructed to look at them. After the calibration is successful, the start tracking button can be activated. From then on, whatever the developer looks at is recorded and mapped to the corresponding source element (if they are looking at source code) until they click Stop tracking. For example, if the developer looked at the Locale object created in the Localization constructor, this gaze would be mapped to that new object created on line 13 in the figure. All context is also maintained i.e., it would also record that the new object was inside the constructor which was inside the class Localization. All of this data is exported in both XML and JSON (user configurable). The amount of data exported per second depends on the frequency of samples taken by the eye tracker. We have successfully used *iTrace* with 30 fps and 60 fps eye trackers for extended periods of time up to 50 or 60 min while collecting data on studies involving real change tasks.

iTrace currently works with the Tobii series eye trackers but supports any other eye tracker as it was designed to be extensible. Recently, we also developed an interface for the EyeTribe Mirametrix S2 eye tracker. In order to use another eye tracker, one needs to write an interface to communicate with the eye tracker and *iTrace*.

In a nutshell, *iTrace* provides a seamless way to collect eye tracking data from inside an IDE while keeping the context even when scrolling. The detailed architecture and design decisions of *iTrace* are out of scope of the current paper and have been left as a future formal tool description and demonstration.

3 Eye Tracking as Assessment

This section describes how eye tracking has been used as an assessment tool in software engineering studies. This is the first broad area in which eye tracking directly benefits daily software engineering activities, tools, and processes by studying if they are useful and how to make them better by directly studying developer eye gaze while they are at work doing the activity, or using the tool or following the process.

Crosby and Stelovksy explored the way subjects viewed algorithms for comprehension and discovered that the eye movements of experts and novices differ in the way they looked at English and Pascal versions of an algorithm [7]. They found that experts spend more time viewing complex statements. They also discovered that while both groups devoted time to viewing comments, novices spent significantly more time doing so.

Bednarik et al. investigated the visual attention of experts versus novices in debugging code [8]. Subjects used a debugger with multiple views to track down one or more defects in each program. No significant correlation was found between patterns of eye movement and performance in using the debugger. In a separate study, Bednarik et al. [9] also gave subjects a choice between viewing code and viewing an alternative representation of programs and asked whether the role of program representation differs over the course of time. They found that many experts choose to look at code ahead of an alternative representation. Subsequently, they studied the eye gaze of pair programmers [10].

Uwano et al. [11] also studied eye gaze patterns of five individuals while they were detecting defects in source code. They also studied eye movements of subjects who looked for inconsistencies in comparing requirements/design documents to source code [12]. The study in [11] was later replicated by Sharif et al. to give similar results [13]. Sharif et al. [14, 15] study the impact of identifier style (i.e., camel case or underscore) on code reading and comprehension using an eye-tracker. They find camel case to be an overall better choice for comprehension. Sharafi et al. [16] replicated the identifier study but tried to determine if gender played a role in identifier style selection for source code reading. They found that males and females follow different comprehension methods. For example: females tend to thoroughly check all answers to make sure they have selected the correct one whereas males do not. This was an interesting finding and nice extension to the studies done in [14, 15].

Yusuf et al. [17] conducted a study to determine if different class diagram layouts with stereotype information help in solving certain tasks. Guehénéuc [18] investigated the comprehension of UML class diagrams. Jeanmart et al. [19] conducted a study on the effect of the Visitor design pattern on comprehension using an eye tracker.

Sharif et al. also conducted several eye tracking studies assessing the role layouts have in the comprehension of design pattern roles [20], assessing a 3D tool [21] and, assessing the comprehension of C ++ and Python programs [22]. A statement advocating the use of eye tracking in assessing software visualizations is given in [23].

Recently, Busjahn et al. [24] used eye tracking in the field of computing education to assess how experts read and understand code. Another study [25] by the same group by authors extends the work and looks in the linearity of natural language text reading and how this linear order is not followed when reading source code. They look at both experts and novices and show that novices also exhibit a less linear order when they read source code compared to natural language text. They also found that experts tend to be much more non-linear than novices.

4   Eye Tracking as Informing Software Tasks

In the previous section, we presented and highlighted a few studies that use eye tracking as a means to assess if the software tool, process, or technique is useful. We have seen examples of studies comparing different layouts in UML diagrams, different identifier styles, and different programming languages to name a few. The bulk of work done in the field of eye tracking in software engineering is in this first area of assessment as it is the most intuitive and reasonable one to perform especially on visual artifacts such as diagrams and well as source code.

The second broad category in software engineering that can benefit from eye tracking is to make eye gazes directly inform the software tools and tasks developers are working on. Decisions can be based not only on the artifacts in question but also on what and how long the developer looks at these artifacts. Note that we are not implying using eye gaze as input to interact with the environment. This is a different concept that is applicable to natural user interfaces (using gestures, voice, and eye gaze to issue commands) and one that is not touched on in this paper.

We describe a few studies in this paper that touch on the aspect of using eye tracking as a means of informing and improving existing software tasks.

Fritz et al. [3] used eye movements along with EEG signals to determine task (reading source code) difficulty in professional programmers adding additional evidence that eye tracking is indeed a viable and useful source of information. They were able to use the pupil dilation as one of the features to predict if a developer found the task to be difficult. Here eye tracking was used in a unique way to help determine if a programmer should possibly take a break if they are finding the task difficult.

Ali et al. [26] used eye tracking in the field of software traceability. They first asked a few developers to read small code snippets and noted where the developers looked at most to understand them. They found that developer look mainly at method names and not class names. They used this information to change the weighting scheme of a software traceability link retrieval algorithm that emphasizes methods more as this is what developers look at more. Here eye tracking was not used to assess an artifact, rather it was used as evidence to modify a weighting scheme in information retrieval methods such as Latent Semantic Indexing (LSI) to get better results.

Rodeghero et al. [5] took an approach similar to [26] and also used eye tracking on small snippets on code to determine what developers are looking at. In their study the task was to summarize about 60 methods from open source Java systems. They then used this information on what developers look at to build better summaries for the methods. Again this approach uses eye gaze to inform a software engineering task namely, method summarization.

In the field of software traceability, Sharif et al. propose to use eye gaze as input to generate traceability links for change tasks [27]. They first proposed this idea of moving towards an eye aware IDE in [28]. In 2014, they conducted a pilot study [4] to determine if it was feasible to generate traceability links from eye gaze alone. The results they found were very promising and eye gaze does indeed seem to work really well to find links between relevant code entities and the task at hand. They developed an algorithm to find relevant entities using a weighting scheme based on time. This helps weed out entities that are looked at initially but later abandoned.

There is still a lot more work to be done in the area of having eye tracking inform more software engineering tasks.

5 Discussion and Future Work

Eye trackers have become more accessible to researchers who are using them to gain additional insights into software development activities. Modern eye trackers implicitly collect developers' eye gaze data on the visual display (stimulus) in an unobtrusive way while they are performing a given task. This eye movement data could provide much valuable insight as to how and why subjects arrive at a certain solution. We believe these measures can add a new additional dimension in supporting software engineering tasks. In March 2012, Tobii received $21 M from Intel to continue R&D investments in making eye-tracking mainstream in personal computers. It is not farfetched to say that we will eventually find an eye tracker inbuilt in every PC in the near future.

The goal is to use an eye tracker that is suitable for the task at hand and the accuracy needed. Not every study is in need of a high-end cye tracker. There are many options to choose from. The main vendors are Tobii, Facelab, SmartEye, and SMI but there have been many more emerging cheaper alternatives on the market in the past couple of years such as the EyeTribe and Mirametrix trackers among others. Tobii also recently put out a less than $100 eye tracker (Tobii EyeX) in 2014 that works with USB 3.0 ports.

Imagine a scenario where a developer would turn eye tracking on with the click of a button within their work environment, just before they start to work on fixing a bug. Then, they go about working in their environment and fix the bug. When they are done with the bug fix, they click another button to stop the eye data being recorded. The amount of data collected for this one change task i.e., fixing a bug is useful for a variety of tasks (summarization, recommendations to name a few). Later, at some point he or she would like to see what and for how long they looked at certain source code elements to learn about their behavior. Another possibility is to detect via eye gaze when the developer is having a difficult time understanding the code and provide some recommendations for him/her to make it easier to proceed. The possibilities are limitless.

The data generated from such sessions is extremely valuable since it is not just the bug fix classes that are important but also the classes that were required to be read and understood in order to find the final set of lines that needed to be changed and committed. With eye tracking data, we are able to see all the places that the developer looked to get to the answer and not just the final answer. Eye tracking is able to give us the fine grained line-level gaze data of a developer while they work. Given that we now have a tool (*iTrace*) that seamlessly integrates with an IDE, the possibilities are endless as to what task can benefit from eye gaze.

One can envision the possibility of recording all gaze activity to help for future bug fixes that are all related to the same feature. Of course we are not there yet. We need an integrated set of tools including a visualization suite for eye tracking data built into the environment to help make sense of all the data that is generated. A 20 min session with a 60 fps eye tracker can easily generate data that is approximately 50 megabytes. An efficient and useful algorithm [4] to weed out stray glances is also necessary.

Since 2006, there has been a surge in eye tracking studies in the software engineering community. The field and technology used is quite intriguing making this an attractive area for young researchers. Even though there are approximately 35 papers using eye tracking in software engineering, we expect this number to drastically increase as more researchers enter the field.

6   Conclusions

The paper presents two broad views on how eye tracking has currently been used in software engineering. The first deals with using an eye tracker as a tool to assess where and for how long a person looks at certain software artifacts. The second area deals with using eye gaze to improve existing software tasks such as software traceability link generation and code summarization. A short description of an eye aware plugin for Eclipse, namely *iTrace* is given that makes larger more realistic studies possible. Eye tracking has potential to greatly enhance a software developer's experience as shown by the studies conducted. The benefit is even more noticeable if researchers use eye gaze to inform software tasks by developing new and innovative algorithms that are developer centric thereby bringing the human aspect back into the more artifact-driven nature of software engineering studies.

References

1. Gethers, M., Dit, B., Revelle, M., Poshyvanyk, D.: Feature location in source code: A taxonomy and survey. J. Softw. Maint. Evolut: Res. Pract. **25**, 53–95 (2013)
2. Ko, A.J., Myers, B.A., Coblenz, M.J., Aung, H.H.: An exploratory study of how developers seek, relate, and collect relevant information during software maintenance tasks. IEEE Trans. Softw. Eng. **32**, 971–987 (2006)
3. Fritz, T., Begel, A., Müller, S., Yigit-Elliott, S., Züger, M.: Using psycho-physiological measures to assess task difficulty in software development. In: International Conference on Software Engineering (ICSE), pp. 402–413. IEEE, Hyderabad (2014)
4. Walters, B., Shaffer, T., Sharif, B., Kagdi, H.: Capturing software traceability links from developers' eye gazes. In: 22nd International Conference on Program Comprehension (ICPC), Hyderabad, India, pp. 201–204 (2014)
5. Rodeghero, P., McMillan, C., McBurney, P.W., Bosch, N., D'Mello, S.: Improving automated source code summarization via an eye-tracking study of programmers. In: 36th

IEEE/ACM International Conference on Software Engineering (ICSE 2014), Hyderabad, India, (2014)

6. Siegmund, J., Kästner, C., Apel, S., Parnin, C., Bethmann, A., Leich, T., Saake, G., Brechmann, A.: Understanding understanding source code with functional magnetic resonance imaging. In: Proceedings of the 36th International Conference on Software Engineering, pp. 378–389. ACM (2014)

7. Crosby, M.E., Stelovsky, J.: How do we read algorithms? a case study. IEEE Comput. **23**, 24–35 (1990)

8. Bednarik, R., Tukiainen, M.: Temporal eye-tracking data: evolution of debugging strategies with multiple representations. In: Symposium on Eye Tracking Research & Applications (ETRA), pp. 99–102. ACM, Savannah (2008)

9. Bednarik, R., Tukiainen, M.: An eye-tracking methodology for characterizing program comprehension processes. In: Symposium on Eye Tracking Research & Applications (ETRA), pp. 125–132. ACM Press, San Diego (2006)

10. Pietinen, S., Bednarik, R., Glotova, T., Tenhunen, V., Tukiainen, M.: A method to study visual attention aspects of collaboration: eye-tracking pair programmers simultaneously. In: 2008 Symposium on Eye Tracking Research & Applications, New York, NY, USA, pp. 39–42 (2008)

11. Uwano, H., Nakamura, M., Monden, A., Matsumoto, K.: Analyzing individual performance of source code review using reviewers' eye movement. In: 2006 Symposium on Eye Tracking Research & Applications (ETRA), pp. 133–140. ACM Press, San Diego (2006)

12. Uwano, H., Monden, A., Matsumoto, K.-i.: DRESREM 2: An analysis system for multi-document software review using reviewers' eye movements. In: 3rd International Conference on Software Engineering Advances (ICSEA), Sliema, Malta, pp. 177–183 (2008)

13. Sharif, B., Falcone, M., Maletic, J.I.: An eye-tracking study on the role of scan time in finding source code defects. In: Symposium on Eye Tracking Research and Applications (ETRA), Santa Barbara, CA, pp. 381–384 (2012)

14. Sharif, B., Maletic, J.I.: An eye tracking study on camelcase and under_score identifier styles. In: 18th IEEE International Conference on Program Comprehension (ICPC 2010), Braga, Portugal, pp. 196–205 (2010)

15. Binkley, D., Davis, M., Lawrie, D., Maletic, J.I., Morrell, C., Sharif, B.: The impact of identifier style on effort and comprehension. Empir. Softw. Eng. J. **18**, 219–276 (2013)

16. Sharafi, Z., Soh, Z., Gueheneuc, Y.-G., Antoniol, G.: Women and men - different but equal: on the impact of identifier style on source code reading. In: International Conference on Program Comprehension (ICPC 2012), pp. 27–36. IEEE, Passau (2012)

17. Yusuf, S., Kagdi, H., Maletic, J.I.: Assessing the comprehension of UML class diagrams via eye tracking. In: IEEE International Conference on Program Comprehension (ICPC 2007), Banff, AB, pp. 113–122 (2007)

18. Guéhéneuc, Y.-G.: TAUPE: towards understanding program comprehension. In: 16th IBM Centers for Advanced Studies on Collaborative Research (CASCON), pp. 1–13. ACM Press, Canada (2006)

19. Jeanmart, S., Guéhéneuc, Y.-G., Sahraoui, H., Habra, N.: Impact of the visitor pattern on program comprehension and maintenance. In: 3rd International Symposium on Empirical Software Engineering and Measurement, Lake Buena Vista, Florida, pp. 69–78 (2009)

20. Sharif, B., Maletic, J.I.: An eye tracking study on the effects of layout in understanding the role of design patterns. In: 26th IEEE International Conference on Software Maintenance (ICSM 2010), Timisoara, Romania, pp. 1–10 (2010)

21. Sharif, B., Jetty, G., Aponte, J., Parra, E.: An empirical study assessing the effect of SeeIT 3D on comprehension. In: 1st IEEE International Working Conference on Software Visualization (VISSOFT 2013), Eindhoven, Netherlands, pp. 1–10 (2013)
22. Turner, R., Sharif, B., Lazar, A.: An eye-tracking study assessing the comprehension of C++ and Python source code. Symposium on Eye Tracking Research & Applications (ETRA 2014), Safety Harbor, Florida, USA, pp. 231–234 (2014)
23. Kagdi, H., Yusuf, S., Maletic, J.I.: On using eye tracking in empirical assessment of software visualizations. In: ACM Workshop on Empirical Assessment of Software Engineering Languages and Technologies, Atlanta, GA, pp. 21–22, (2007)
24. Busjahn, T., Schulte, C., Sharif, B., Simon, Begel, A., Hansen, M., Bednarik, R., Orlov, P., Ihantola, P.: Eye tracking in computing education. In: International Computing Education Research (ICER 2014), Glasgow, Scotland, pp. 3–10 (2014)
25. Busjahn, T., Bednarik, R., Begel, A., Crosby, M., Paterson, J.H., Schulte, C., Sharif, B., Tamm, S.: Eye Movements in Code Reading: Relaxing the Linear Order. In: Proceedings of ICPC, Florence, Italy (2015)
26. Ali, N., Sharafi, Z., Guéhéneuc, Y.-G., Antoniol, G.: An empirical study on requirements traceability using eye-tracking. In: 28th International Conference on Software Maintenance (ICSM), pp. 191–200. IEEE Computer Society Press (2012)
27. Sharif, B., Kagdi, H.: On the use of eye tracking in software traceability. In: 6th ACM International Workshop on Traceability in Emerging Forms of Software Engineering (TEFSE 2011), Honolulu, Hawaii, USA, pp. 67–70 (2011)
28. Walters, B., Falcone, M., Shibble, A., Sharif, B.: Towards an eye-tracking enabled ide for software traceability tasks. In: 7th International Workshop on Traceability in Emerging Forms of Software Engineering (TEFSE), San Francisco, CA, pp. 51–54 (2013)

An Examination of Visual Search Success for Transportation Security Officers and Behavior Detection Officers

Randall D. Spain[✉], Jerry W. Hedge, and Katrina M. Ladd

RTI International, Workforce and Organizational Effectiveness Program
Research, Triangle Park, NC, USA
{rspain, jhedge, kladd}@rti.org

Abstract. This paper discusses ongoing research that seeks to better understand the core visual search skills and requirements of Transportation Security Officers (TSOs) and Behavior Detection Officers (BDOs). The purpose of the first phase of research is to compare TSO and BDO visual search performance on a simple visual search task and to determine whether certain personality and demographic characteristics are related to search performance. The goal of the second phase of research is to identify measures and assessment devices that are more applicable to the visual search requirements of the BDO position. Methods and approaches used to answer key questions related to each phase of research are described, as are potential implications of the research.

Keywords: Visual search · Human performance · Individual differences · Assessments

1 Introduction

Visual search, the act of looking for a target among distractors, is a vital component of the security screening tasks conducted at airports. Both Transportation Security Officers (TSOs) and Behavior Detection Officers (BDOs) are required to visually search their environments for cues that might be indicative of a threat. However, whereas TSOs are responsible for searching x-ray images of luggage on a computer screen, BDOs are required to visually scan crowds and identify behavior cues of mal-intent. In both positions, the success of visual search is ultimately determined by human performance [1]. As such, understanding the nature of visual search itself and the human factors that affect search performance is critical to ensuring that security personnel perform their jobs effectively.

1.1 Visual Search Performance of TSOs and BDOs

As part of its ongoing research with the Transportation Security Administration (TSA), RTI International has been actively involved in evidence-based research to better understand the factors that affect the visual search performance of airport security personnel. The purpose of this research has been to explore aspects of the x-ray search

© Springer International Publishing Switzerland 2015
D.D. Schmorrow and C.M. Fidopiastis (Eds.): AC 2015, LNAI 9183, pp. 817–824, 2015.
DOI: 10.1007/978-3-319-20816-9_78

process itself (e.g., how often targets occur) and to identify predictive markers of search success. Initial phases of research with TSOs examined differences among professional (TSOs) and nonprofessional searchers (college students) on a basic visual search task. Results indicated that professionals were more accurate in their search performance compared to nonprofessional searchers, but nonprofessionals were quicker to locate a target and to terminate their search [2]. Results also showed that the search performance of professionals and nonprofessionals was predicted by different factors. The performance of nonprofessional searchers was best explained by search speed, whereas the performance of professional searchers was best explained by search consistency, or how much time was spent searching images from trial to trial. The researchers concluded that professional searchers were more diligent in their search, which may have resulted from experience or training, leading to better search accuracy [2].

Building on these findings, additional research has examined visual search performance in paradigms wherein more than one target is present within an image. Results of this research have shown that visual search speed and consistency vary among professional and nonprofessional searchers with professionals being more diligent and consistent in their search compared to nonprofessionals. Further results have also shown that professionals are less influenced by target salience (i.e., how difficult a target was to find) than nonprofessionals, which helps them to locate multiple targets, particularly targets that are harder to spot [3].

More recent research conducted with TSOs has also examined how individual differences in traits, abilities, and interests correlate to search performance. Specifically, results indicate that visual search performance of professional searchers can be partially explained by differences in visual working memory capacity; differences in feelings of patriotism; and differences in personality traits such as openness, agreeableness, and conscientiousness [4].

In summary, previous research with TSOs has examined the factors that may moderate search success. The differences in predictors that determine search accuracy among professional and nonprofessional searchers may suggest that professional searchers use unique strategies to examine images or possess unique traits that make them better at visual search. These differences may have implications for the selection and training of professional searchers.

To date, less is known about the visual search skills of BDOs and the factors that contribute to BDO visual search performance. BDOs are former TSOs who have been selected to perform a set of unique job responsibilities, unlike current TSO responsibilities. It is the job of the BDO to accurately and consistently identify and examine suspicious behaviors of travelers. This task requires BDOs to observe passenger behavior and compare what they see to an established environmental baseline of other passengers in the same general location and in the same general timeframe, looking for anomalous behaviors and signs of mal-intent. It seems reasonable to assume that certain core visual search skills and abilities are common to luggage screening and crowd scanning but that other skills and abilities may be unique to the type of work performed by BDOs. It also seems reasonable to assume that BDOs may perform just as well as, or better than, TSOs at visual search, particularly if BDOs have prior experience operating in the role of a TSO. The purpose of this research was to empirically examine these possibilities. Specifically, the aim was to compare the results of TSO and BDO visual search performance on a simple visual search task and on a larger battery of individual difference questionnaires to identify where differences might exist between the two groups and whether certain traits, abilities, and preferences correlate with visual search performance. In line with these goals, the first phase of research was guided by the following research questions:

Research Question 1a: Do BDOs and TSOs perform similarly on a basic visual search task?

Research Question 1b: Do the same traits and abilities that correlate with TSO visual search also correlate with BDO visual search performance?

The following section contains a summary of the approach the research team took toward answering these research questions.

1.2   Research Approach

A critical goal of this effort was to replicate the existing tasks and assessment items used in previous research in a new research effort with TSOs and BDOs. As such, one of the first steps was to review the previous research to identify the tasks and measurements that were to be included in the current effort. Initial studies conducted by RTI [4] and Biggs and colleagues [2] used a simple computer-based visual search task written in MATLAB[1] to examine the visual search skills of professional and non-professional searchers. The task required officers to locate a target T in an array of distractor L shapes (see Fig. 1). Participants completed multiple trials over the course of each testing session and the speed and accuracy of their decisions were reported for each trial.

To support the current research effort, a new version of the visual search software was created to provide a more cost-effective, robust, and flexible solution for collecting visual search data. The visual search task was developed using the Unity3D game development software and was based on the schematics of a visual search task used by Biggs et al. [2] and RTI [4]. The program presents participants with images that contain a random assortment of Ts and Ls. Similar to the Biggs et al. program, Ts, the target item, have a short bar directly in the middle of the T, whereas for Ls, the distractor items, the short bar is slid a variable distance away from center. Some of the distractor Ls approximate the shape of the target T. This manipulation is intentional and serves to increase the difficulty of the task so that participants will not perform perfectly. Each T and L is placed slightly off-center within a randomly selected cell of an invisible 8-by-7 grid. The Ts and Ls are rotated in one of four cardinal directions and are presented against a white background. Each image contains either 8, 16, 24, or 32 objects. All images presented to the participant through this application are generated randomly, with no repeats, at runtime. This method ensures a unique image presentation for each participant.

---

[1] MATLAB is a software program that can be used in conjunction with the Psychophysics toolbox function to design visual cognition experiments.

The program presents participants with 256 images; half of the images contain a target. Participants acknowledge whether a target is present or absent by pressing the corresponding key on the computer keyboard. After making their decision, the program advances to the next visual search image. The accuracy and timing of participants' decisions for each trial is recorded and scored to examine visual search performance.

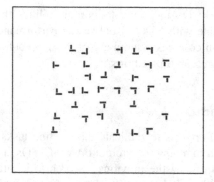

Fig. 1. Example of image from visual search task. Participants are required to find the target T in an array of distractor pseudo Ls.

The second step in our research approach was to build a battery of surveys and questionnaires that would be used to examine the traits, abilities, and preferences of TSOs and BDOs that might correlate with visual search performance. To aid this process we reviewed the measures, questionnaires, and surveys used in the previous studies and the associated data [4]. The purpose of this review was to see if any measures correlated highly with one another and to determine which measures were statistically correlated with visual search performance. By removing duplicative questions and irrelevant or poor predictors of search performance from the battery, the goal was to make the questionnaires more relevant and concise and as a result, reduce respondent burden. The review showed that the measures from the TSO battery did not overlap and most were related to visual search performance; therefore, many of the measures were retained from the previous battery.

The revised battery contains nine measures, including the Big Five Inventory [5], which measures an individual's level of openness, conscientiousness, extraversion, agreeableness, and neuroticism; the maximization scale [6], which measures the degree to which individuals try to maximize decision outcomes; the autism spectrum [7] quotient, which measures the degree to which an adult with normal intelligence has the traits associated with the autistic spectrum (i.e., exceptional attention to detail, poor attention switching, strong focus of attention); and the patriotism scale [8], which includes a series of subscales that measure facets of loyalty and patriotism. Results of the previous visual search research conducted with TSOs shows that each of these measures relates to search performance [4]. The battery also contains items that measure mental abilities and questionnaires that measure basic demographic and work-related information of TSOs and BDOs, including normal daily work activities, past work experiences, academic achievements, and typical hobbies. The research plan is to administer these questionnaires to TSOs and BDOs in addition to the visual search task. Collecting these data will allow the research team to identify personality measures and traits and abilities that might correlate with performance.

1.3   Current Status and Implications

Data collection is currently underway, with plans to collect data from 150 BDOs and 150 TSOs at two airports. Once data have been collected, a critical task will be to compare visual search performance between BDOs and TSOs. Such analysis will allow the research team to make distinct comparisons between these two groups on visual search performance. Another task will be to assess visual search performance in relation to the survey measures and assessments to determine whether search performance is related to certain traits, abilities, and preferences. By examining the individual markers of search performance, the research team will be able to determine whether core traits predict visual search performance for each group.

2   Identifying Assessments for BDO Visual Search

A second goal of this effort was to identify assessments that were more germane to the visual search requirements of the BDO position and to collect data from BDOs using these tests. The visual search task used in previous visual search research with the TSO population, and in the first phase of this experiment, simulates a simple visual search task in which participants search for a target in an array of distractors on a computer screen. Although this task may be representative of the baggage screening performed by TSOs, it is likely to exclude key constructs required for successful BDO visual search. The research questions guiding the second phase of research include the following:

Research Question 2a: Are there tests or assessments available that are more tailored toward the search requirements of the BDO position?

Research Question 2b: How well do BDOs perform on available tests or questionnaires that are more germane to their jobs?

2.1   Approach

To answer these questions, the tasks performed under the second phase of this effort included a review of the cognitive psychology literature as it relates to BDO-relevant visual search; a review of previous job analyses of the BDO position to identify job-relevant dimensions and the knowledge, skills, and abilities that make up the job of the BDO; a review of available tests that have been used and validated to predict job performance of BDOs; gathering and preparing these tests; and finally data collection. Figure 2 contains a general overview of the steps involved in this phase of research. A more detailed account of each step is provided below.

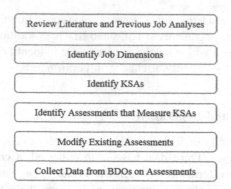

Fig. 2. Overview of steps performed to support the second phase of research

To help identify the visual search requirements of BDOs, the first task undertaken in this second phase of research was to conduct a systematic review of the literature in cognitive psychology as it relates to BDO-relevant visual search. As previously noted, although TSOs rely on visual scanning of computer images, BDOs more routinely engage in crowd-scanning behavior to identify appearance and behavior anomalies of the traveling public. Although both activities require officers to engage in visual search activities, the types of cues that are relevant to the search process and the skills needed to identify those cues may differ. The goal of this task was to critically examine the literature to determine the core visual search skills and abilities pertinent to behavior detection tasks, to identify behavioral cues professionals search for, and to identify extant assessments that have been used to examine behavior detection performance.

In addition to reviewing the relevant scientific literature, it was also important to understand more clearly the job characteristics and job requirements of the BDO position. As such, the second step undertaken during this phase was a thorough review of available position descriptions, job manuals, and previous job analyses for the BDO position, and available training documents, materials, programs. By reviewing these documents the research team sought to develop a better understanding of the processes involved in performing the tasks of the BDO position and the unique requirements and approaches for training BDO visual search. Another goal of this task was to gather further insights about the knowledge, skills, and abilities required for successful BDO job performance. Gaining this understanding helped the research team identify the critical skill and ability requirements of the BDO position and identify gaps in the existing visual search task battery. In addition to reviewing these documents, the research team also reviewed published and unpublished reports that sought to validate different predictors of BDO performance. The information in these reports provided the team with insights about the behavioral and cognitive constructs relevant to the BDO position and with information about assessments that could be used to measures these constructs.

Following the review of the job-related information and pertinent scientific litera-ture, the third step was to interview subject matter experts selected from academia or the field with a background in the type of visual search conducted by BDOs. The purpose of these interviews was to identify critical factors potentially related to BDO performance and the performance of individuals with similar "crowd scanning" job requirements and identify assessments that may align with the knowledge, skills, and abilities pertinent to visual search requirements of BDOs. These three activities— review of the relevant scientific literature, review of pertinent job-related information, and input from the expert panel—aimed to help identify relevant job performance dimensions and shed light on the types of tests or assessments that could be used to support a new research battery tailored to the position of the BDO.

The fourth step toward developing a more tailored set of assessments for BDOs was to select a set of available assessment tools that reflect the state of the science in visual search and behavior detection for modification and preliminary development. Because of the limited duration of this project, new tests could not be developed and validated; therefore, specific emphasis was placed on selecting measures, surveys, and work sample tests that were either ready for use off the shelf or ones that required only minor alterations before being readied for use. Similar to previous research looking at the predictors of TSO visual search performance, the assessments and surveys selected for this phase of experimentation aimed to cover a broad range of instruments including mental and spatial abilities tests, personality assessment inventories, and visual search work sample tests and simulations relevant to BDO job performance.

Once the components of the BDO-relevant test battery were identified and finalized the final step in this phase of research was to test the assessments with a pool of BDOs. After data collection is complete, data will be analyzed to determine how well BDOs perform on the new BDO battery; determine which traits, abilities, and preferences correlate with task performance; and determine whether detection performance can be predicted by BDO experience or other factors.

2.2 Current Status and Implications

At the time of this writing, several initial steps have been taken toward meeting the goals of this phase of research. The research team is currently reviewing the available literature and available job-related information to better understand the job require- ments of the BDO position and identify the core visual search knowledge skills and abilities required for BDO visual search. The BDO tailored measures will be identified next, the assessments will be readied, and data collection will start soon thereafter. Our current plan is to collect data from a sample of BDOs at two airports in the spring and late summer. If possible, we will also run a small sample of TSOs through the new BDO assessment battery. Running TSOs through the battery and comparing their performance to BDOs would allow the research team to empirically determine whether the battery adequately discriminates between BDOs and TSOs. If differences are found between the two types officers, and BDOs perform better than TSOs, it would suggest that the set of items and tasks within the BDO is sensitive to the skill differences between TSOs and BDOs.

3 Summary and Conclusions

This paper discusses ongoing experimentation to examine the visual search perfor- mance of BDOs. The goal of the first phase of research was to establish a baseline of visual search performance for BDOs using a simple visual search task and to make distinctions in performance between BDOs and TSOs. A key approach to this phase was replicating the TSO battery from the previous line of research with BDOs to compare search performance between the two groups of security personnel. Building on this phase, the goal of the second phase was to identify tests and assessments more tailored toward the job requirements of the BDO position. The BDO test battery aims to provide a set of measures that researchers can use to examine and better understand the visual search skills of the BDO position. Foundational to our approach was conducting a review of the existing scientific literature and available job descriptions, job analyses, and training information to determine the core visual search requirements of BDOs. We also sought to collect information from subject matter experts about relevant skills and available assessment approaches. After identifying available assessments relevant to the skills and abilities required for BDO search, our team readied these questionnaires and exercises for use. Data collection using these newly tailored BDO measures is slated to begin in the coming months.

In conclusion, this research will provide foundational information about the visual search skills of BDOs. Understanding the core search requirements of BDOs is essential for making appropriate selection and staffing decisions. As TSA continues to transform its workforce, similar forms of research will need to be conducted to ensure that personnel have the appropriate knowledge, skills, and experience to perform their jobs effectively.

References

1. Wickens, C.D., Hollands, J.G.: Engineering Psychology and Human Performance. Prentice Hall, Upper Saddle River (2000)
2. Biggs, A.T., Cain, M.S., Clark, K., Darling, E.F., Mitroff, S.R.: Assessing visual search performance differences between transportation security administration officers and nonprofessional searchers. Vis. Cogn. **21**, 330–352 (2013)
3. Cain, M.S., Adamo, S.H., Mitroff, S.R.: A taxonomy of multiple-target search errors. Vis. Cogn. **21**(7), 899–921 (2013)
4. RTI International: Basic Research Final Report. Prepared for Resilient Systems Division, Science and Technology Directorate, U.S. Department of Homeland Security, December 2014
5. John, O.P., Naumann, L.P., Soto, C.J.: Paradigm shift to the integrative big five trait taxonomy: history, measurement, and conceptual issues. In: John, O.P., Robins, R.W., Pervin, L.A. (eds.) Handbook of Personality: Theory and Research, pp. 114–158. Guilford, New York (2008)
6. Schwartz, B., Ward, A., Monterosso, J., Lyubomirsky, S., White, K., Lehman, D.R.: Maximizing versus satisficing: happiness is a matter of choice. J. Pers. Soc. Psychol. **83**(5), 1178 (2002)
7. Baron-Cohen, S., Wheelwright, S., Skinner, R., Martin, J., Clubley, E.: The autism-spectrum quotient (AQ): evidence from Asperger syndrome/high-functioning autism, males and females, scientists and mathematicians. J. Autism Dev. Disord. **31**(1), 5–17 (2001)
8. Huddy, L., Khatib, N.: American patriotism, national identity, and political involvement. Am. J. Polit. Sci. **51**(1), 63–77 (2007)

Determining the Optimal Time on X-Ray Analysis for Transportation Security Officers

Ann Speed(✉), Austin Silva, Derek Trumbo, David Stracuzzi,
Christina Warrender, Michael Trumbo, and Kristin Divis

Sandia National Laboratories, Albuquerque, NM 87185, USA
aespeed@sandia.gov

Abstract. The Transportation Security Administration has a large workforce of Transportation Security Officers, most of whom perform interrogation of x-ray images at the passenger checkpoint. To date, TSOs on the x-ray have been limited to a 30-min session at a time, however, it is unclear where this limit originated. The current paper outlines methods for empirically determining if that 30-min duty cycle is optimal and if there are differences between individual TSOs. This work can inform scheduling TSOs at the checkpoint and can also inform whether TSOs should continue to be cross-trained (i.e., performing all 6 checkpoint duties) or whether specialization makes more sense.

Keywords: Visual search · Fatigue · Vigilance · Transportation security agency

1 Introduction

One of the key tasks that Transportation Security Officers (TSOs) must perform is interrogation of passenger bags at the airport security checkpoint using an x-ray system. This is a difficult task for a number of reasons, and requires the TSO to sustain focused attention for a period of time. Currently, TSOs perform x-ray duties for 30 min at a time, with approximately an hour break in between each x-ray session.

The Transportation Security Administration (TSA) is currently examining how they staff security checkpoints and, as such, is curious about how long TSOs can actually spend performing x-ray imagery analysis and whether this differs from TSO to TSO. Such information can impact scheduling and can inform any questions around specializing TSOs for particular duties.

This paper details experimental methods aimed at answering these questions. First is a review of relevant peer-reviewed literature on vigilance, visual search, and inspection. Then, the experimental design and methods for the current study are presented.

1.1 Vigilance

Research on the ability for individuals to sustain attention on a task for an extended period of time started with Mackworth's [1] seminal study of Royal Air Force radar

© Springer International Publishing Switzerland 2015
D.D. Schmorrow and C.M. Fidopiastis (Eds.): AC 2015, LNAI 9183, pp. 825–834, 2015.
DOI: 10.1007/978-3-319-20816-9_79

operators using his "clock" paradigm in which RAF operators monitored the movement of the hands of a clock-type apparatus for low probability jumps as the hands moved around the dial. He found that after about 10–15 min, subjects were increasingly likely to miss such jumps during the first 30 min and that performance bottomed out after that. He also found that short breaks restored performance, that response to an event inhibited response to a subsequent event proximal in time, that an additional monitoring task (e.g., monitoring for a phone call) also further inhibited performance, and that a small dose of amphetamine helped performance.

Similar studies have found similar results – for example Molloy and Parasuraman [2] found that performance degraded during the course of a 30-min vigil of a monitoring task, especially when that task involved attending to multiple complex tasks. However, even a single, complex task, which had the highest performance, still demonstrated some decrement in detection accuracy.

When the number of events to be detected is of sufficient number, the results are often reported in terms of signal detection theory metrics such as d' and a measure of response bias (c or A'). In these cases, a dissociation is often seen between changes in d' and changes in response bias over time, with d' generally declining over time (the *sensitivity decrement*) and positive response bias (i.e., the tendency to say "no target") increasing over time *[the bias increment; 3]*.

Such a sensitivity decrement has been shown repeatedly in numerous paradigms over the course of several decades. See, Howe [4] performed a meta-analysis of 42 vigilance studies and found that the sensitivity decrement is substantially impacted by both the type of discrimination being made (a *successive* one that requires the subject to recall the target from memory or one that simply requires the subject to compare two *simultaneously* occurring stimuli) as well as the rate of the event (higher rates of events lead to greater decrements). They also found that distinguishing between primarily sensory stimuli (e.g., lines of different lengths) and primarily cognitive stimuli (e.g., letters and numbers) also made a difference in the sensitivity decrement. Specifically, type of stimuli (sensory or cognitive) interacted with event rate and type of discrimination (simultaneous or successive). For simultaneous tasks that were also sensory, the sensitivity decrement decreased as event rate increased while the opposite was true for simultaneous cognitive tasks. When the discrimination was successive, that is when subjects had to recall from memory the target stimulus they were maintaining a vigil for, event rate increased the sensitivity decrement for sensory tasks and only slightly decreased it for cognitive tasks.

One key difference between what will be called the "traditional" vigilance literature in the current review and the tasks TSOs face at the checkpoint is the transience of the signal in the traditional vigilance tasks. In the See, Howe [4] meta-analysis all of the studies included in the analysis had a stimulus duration measured in milliseconds – the longest such stimulus was 1.5 s. Thus, as Wolfe, Horowitz [5] point out, a temporary distraction drawing the subject's attention from the display can cause them to miss an event. This is not true in the TSO's case – even in the case of a continuously moving x-ray belt.

1.2   Visual Search

Turning now to another relevant literature, the work on visual search does not often consider performance over time as a critical variable. Wolfe and colleagues [5, 6] reported data for d' and response bias as a function of time and failed to see definitive effects, although Wolfe, Horowitz [5] reported one instance of a bias increment.

There are a few sources of information about domain-specific visual search performance over time in the TSA environment and what literature does exist is sensitive. However it does bear mentioning that those results are mixed with some resulting in a decrement in d' or response bias, some an increment in d' or response bias, and some showing no change in performance over time.

1.3   Inspection

There is a separate literature from the Human Factors world on inspection that also informs the current study. Often, this work has been done with aircraft inspectors looking for fuselage defects (i.e., much of the work Colin Drury and colleagues have done over the years), but some of the work also includes inspection in manufacturing, food inspection, printed circuits, medical, and nuclear weapons domains [7]. In the studies of inspection that don't utilize a dynamic search task, the findings of performance decrements as a function of time in field studies are mixed. Some, such as Hartley, Arnold [8] found significant decrements in airborne inspectors looking for noxious weeds over the course of several hours in the field. Others, such as Spencer and Schurman [9] found no differences in Pd for a four-hour, self-paced eddy current inspection task [also see 3 for a review].

In a review of the literature at the time, Craig [10] offers an interesting observation several of the articles included in his review make – that although inspection tasks in the field can last for quite a long time, inspectors often only perform sustained inspection for short periods – between 5 and 15 min at a time. Presumably this is because inspection tasks in operational environments involve more than just visual inspection. In the TSA domain, this also seems to be the case. In addition to searching x-ray images for threats or prohibited items, the TSO performing x-ray analysis also has to indicate bag checks, can ask for advice from other TSOs, might have to wait for passengers to remove their bags from the exit of the x-ray before moving the belt along, etc.

1.4   Summary

Thus, while there may be an impact of time on task on performance, the TSA x-ray screening task is most likely not cognitively identical to a traditional vigilance task of the Mackworth or radar operator variety. Table 1 outlines some other key differences between these types of tasks.

Ultimately, the question at hand is not whether there is a performance decrement – it would be hard to believe that there would not be after some period of time, which may differ from individual to individual [11]. What is currently at issue is the time-course of this decrement and whether any of the factors that might be under the TSA's

Table 1. Comparison between traditional vigilance tasks (e.g., Mackworth, 1948) and x-ray screening or inspection tasks.

Traditional Visual Search or Inspection tasks	Traditional Vigilance tasks
Complex scenes under the control of the searcher (i.e., the TSO can stop the moving x-ray belt at will to examine a potential target)	Complex dynamic scene not under the control of the searcher
Can have multiple targets/classes of targets simultaneously	Usually has only one event at a time (e.g., appearance of a radar return, clock hand jump, etc.) that is transient target
In TSA it is self-paced in terms of how long the TSO spends making his decision about whether the scene contains a target or not– and the scene doesn't change until the TSO advances the belt	The task is usually task-paced in that targets appear and disappear as a function of the task timing, not as a function of the observer's decision process
Momentary lapse of attention won't result in an error with the Standard SOP (stopping the belt for every bag), but even in SOPs allowing a continuous moving belt, the TSO has the option to reverse the belt and stop it on a bag, thus a momentary lapse of attention can be corrected. Length of signal presence is measured in seconds and is under the control of the TSO	Momentary lapse of attention can result in a miss error that is not correctable, stimulus durations typically measured in milliseconds [e.g., in the 4 meta-analysis, stimulus durations ranged from 2 to 1500 ms]

control could have a mitigating effect on this decrement over a large number of TSOs (e.g., whether continuous belt results in a more dramatic performance decrement over time than does the static belt).

In studies employing a dynamic task in which subjects have to constantly monitor some screen or device for a transient signal, decrements often show up in the first 10–15 min [1, 2, 4]. For tasks with a less dynamic nature, such as inspection or bag screening, decrements sometimes show up that fast [11], sometimes they are slower to appear [7], and sometimes they don't appear at all [5, re-analysis of 12–15]. Thus, while decrements do occur, the timecourse is often different – and timecourse is of preeminent importance for the TSA operational environment for scheduling and personnel specialization reasons. Whether a longer-term decrement that might occur in the x-ray task is a result of the same underlying cognitive or physiological processes as that in the more traditional vigilance tasks is an interesting question – qualitative differences might point to different mitigations, for example – however, this question is not empirically addressed in the current work.

Rather, the goal of this work is to first determine whether there is a reliable decrement in performance during a 2-h task, measured in increments of 5 min [cf. 16 who present data in hour-long increments], whether there are reliable individual differences in the presence and timecourse of this decrement, and whether there are indicators of a change in performance that precede changes in Pd, Pfa, d' or c (such as patterns in eye movements, search patterns, patterns in image manipulation tool use, etc.).

2 Methods

Overall, ∼ 240 TSOs from 6 airports will interrogate x-ray images of mock carryon items using software designed to emulate the look, feel, and a good proportion of the key functionality of one of the x-ray systems currently in use at the TSA checkpoint. Mock items were constructed by the TSA's Transportation Security Integration Facility (TSIF), located at Reagan International Airport in the Washington DC area. They will interrogate these images for 2 h without breaks. After the 2 h bag search task, they then will perform a 45-min battery of general visual cognition tasks (e.g., attention beam, a variant of Raven's progressive matrices, a version of the T and L task, and a pop-out task). The details of this cognitive battery are provided in Matzen [17] and won't be discussed further here. Each aspect of the bag search task is presented in the sections below.

2.1 Experimental Design

This will be a 6x2x2x2x24 mixed experimental design, illustrated in Table 2. The factors include:

- Airport – between subjects, 6 total airports
- SOP – 2 (PreCheck,[1] Standard) – between subjects
- Belt condition – 2 (static, continuous) – between subjects
- Threat Type – 2 (Clear, explosive) – within subjects
- 5-min epoch – 24, (with the possibility of increasing time epoch to 10 min in the event that we have too few observations per subject per 5-min epoch).

The rationale for including static belt on the PreCheck is to simply measure the separate effects of the static belt on TSOs' accuracy/response bias/decision time within the PreCheck context at the actual checkpoint. The rationale for including continuous belt in the Standard checkpoint lane is to explore the effects of this condition on our various dependent measures in anticipation of the inclusion of continuous belt in Standard lanes.

It is estimated that we will collect data from approximately 240 TSOs: approximately 40 TSOs from each of the 6 airports. The only requirements TSOs must meet is that the must have been a TSO for at least a year, they must regularly perform the x-ray task at the checkpoint, and they must be certified to function in both PreCheck and Standard lanes. Otherwise, no attempt will be made to select for gender, age, education, or other such demographic variables although this information will be collected in order to include it in the statistical analysis.

---

[1] PreCheck and Standard refer to the two different screening lanes currently in use at American airports. Passengers who are screened via PreCheck lanes have either registered with the TSA or have been opted in via airline status programs, because of their military service, or because they are a known crew member. In PreCheck lanes, the belt on the x-ray is run continuously unless the TSO sees something he or she wants to inspect futhrer, whereas in the Standard lanes, the TSO is required to stop the belt on every passenger item.

Table 2. Experimental design

Experimental Design		
SOP/Belt (Between Ss)	Threat Type (Within Ss)	5-min Epoch (Within Ss)
PreCheck - static	Clear	1–24
	Threat	1–24
PreCheck - continuous	Clear	1–24
	Threat	1–24
Standard - static	Clear	1–24
	Threat	1–24
Standard - continuous	Clear	1–24
	Threat	1–24

Dependent variables include (all calculated overall in addition to as a function of 5-min epoch):

- Image manipulation tool use (zoom, color changes, etc.)
- Probability of Detection (Pd), Probability of False Alarm (Pfa)
- Decision Time
- Eye Tracking – time to first fixation, number of fixations, types of errors, etc.
- Calculated variables – including d', c, search time consistency [18]
- Image product use (e.g., order of image manipulation tools, which tools selected, eye tracking patterns associated with each bag, etc.).

2.2 Stimuli

Stimulus Creation. All images were created using a Rapiscan AT-2 system. Threat prevalence was set at 10 %. We assumed TSOs would spend 10 s per image on average, thus a 120 min study will require images for at least 720 bags. However, in order to ensure all TSOs spent the entire 120 min interrogating bags we created image sets containing 1,000 unique items.

Stimuli were created by using an existing set of 500 items (including briefcases, rollerboards, car seats, etc.) from the Transportation Security Integration Facility (TSIF). Those items were imaged using the Rapiscan AT-2, then were re-packed adding and subtracting benign prohibited items and threats. Because of the differences in stream of commerce between PreCheck and Standard lanes at the airport, a total of 1,327 item images were created in order to have the stimulus sets closely mirror the expected stream of commerce for the two different types of lanes. The raw X-ray data from the Rapiscan imaging system were then transferred to an emulator that provided a full suite of X-ray data interpretation algorithms.

Each image was then manipulated using 31 manipulation tools on the emulator (32 in the event the emulator imposed target detection boxes around suspect items in the bag), and those image products were then saved as PNG files and transferred to a standard computer system. Each item was also imaged from the top and side, thus each item had either 62 or 64 images associated with it, for a total of 83,624 PNG images generated. Note that this is not the complete set of images available to TSO's at the checkpoint, as the full set would have been prohibitive to collect. However, it does represent the most frequently used subset of image products (determined by a survey conducted of 10 airports from around the country).

In terms of the characteristics of the 1,327 items, there are three general classes of items:

- Threat items - 133 will have IEDs or IED components
- Cleared threat items - Those same 133 items will be re-imaged without the IED/component
- Clear items - The remaining 1061 items will not have threats

Note that each subject will only be able to interrogate 1,000 bags and that the additional bags were generated to reflect differences between what is permitted in bags in the PreCheck and Standard lanes. Thus, for each set of 1,000 bags, 99 contain threat items and those same 99 are cleared threat items. Thus, the threat prevalence rate in a given TSO's stimulus set is 9.9 %.

Across these three classes of bags, 3 % contain benign prohibited items (e.g., water bottles with water in them). 10 % of the items with benign prohibited items contain two benign prohibited items; the rest contain only one benign prohibited item. Overall, an effort was made to match the stimulus set characteristics to what TSA knows about the stream of commerce (in terms of numbers of laptops, iPads, types of bags, etc.).

Target detection boxes were included on images when they were generated by the Rapiscan emulator, and subjects were asked to clear them as a group (rather than individually). In this way, collection and analysis of dependent measures becomes fairly straightforward because for bags with target detection boxes there were two decisions (decision about the target detection boxes, decision about the overall bag) and for those bags without target detection boxes, there was one decision.

The presence and number of target detection boxes was not manipulated as a separate independent variable, but the number of target detection boxes (0 through N) will be entered as a covariate in the statistical model built to analyze the data. Target detection boxes for threat bags and for clear bags were those generated by the Rapiscan AT-2 system used to generate the images. For the cleared threat bags (i.e., threat bags with the threat removed and re-imaged), we re-generated target detection boxes around the same areas of the bags as the Rapiscan system generated for the threat versions of each bag, in order to hold that aspect of those bags constant. In this way, the cleared threat bags were as close to identical to the threat bags, with the exception of the threat presence, as possible, making an ideal stimulus set for the calculation of signal detection measures (d', c).

Stimulus Validation. Because we wound up actually generating 83,624 separate image files, we needed to validate that we had not duplicated any of the images and that we had generated all 31 or 32 image products for each separate X-ray data file. We did this in three ways.

First, we developed a naming convention that created a unique label for each image file that indicated which X-ray data file it belonged to, what view it was (top or side), and which of the 31 or 32 image manipulation tools was applied. This enabled us to validate that we had, at least in filename, all of the image files we expected to have for each X-ray file.

Second, we used hash values to determine whether we had any duplicate images. Each image has a unique hash value, which is essentially a character string that uniquely describes a file's content. Hash values are unique to images in much the same way that fingerprints are unique to individual humans.

Finally, we compared the pixel values of the PNG versions of the original false color image (provided by TSA alongside the corresponding X-ray files) with the pixel values for the normal false color images captured via the emulator by Sandia to determine if we had, in fact, matched all of the original files provided by TSA. After several iterations through the errors we found in these three ways, we reduced the error rate to zero. While this does not guarantee that there are no errors in the stimulus set, it does provide a certain amount of confidence that errors are rare.

2.3 Stimulus Presentation and Data Collection Platform

In the spirit of attempting to measure TSO performance in an environment as similar as possible to a live checkpoint, we developed custom x-ray emulation software that enabled us to collect a wide range of dependent measures. This software emulated the look and feel of the Rapiscan AT-2, and used a keyboard that was mocked up to look and operate like the Rapiscan operator control panel (OCP). While users did not have access to all of the image manipulation tools available on the actual Rapiscan system, a poll conducted of TSOs at several airports yielded the most common image manipulation tools used, and those were included in the functionality of the software.

The emulator software is designed to present each subject with a demographic questionnaire, instructions, practice bag images, and finally the experiment bag images. During both the practice images and experiment images the subject may perform similar operations to the Rapiscan AT-2 system, including: zoom in/out, start/stop image motion, change image variant (CC, BW, etc.), toggle target detection boxes, and reset the view. For each image the subject can indicate whether or not they believe the bag contains a threat. They are also prompted to count the number of threat and prohibited items they believe were in the bag.

The emulator collects detailed information about experiment state and subject behavior during the experiment. The system keeps track of which image is currently being displayed and its current position on the screen at every moment. Each command the subject issues to during the experiment is time-stamped in nanoseconds and associated with the bag and image being displayed at that time. Each of the subject's responses are also collected alongside subject demographics and experiment conditions such as subject ID, SOP and belt mode.

The emulator software is platform independent and can be installed on a machine with any operating system. It can operate with as few as two monitors, though a third monitor can greatly assist the operator with a detailed diagnostics display showing the experiment's state at any point in time. The monitors used were the same monitors currently in use at the TSA checkpoints and operated at a 1280x768 resolution.

Integrated into the x-ray emulation software is a three-camera eye tracking system created by SmartEye. The system operates at 60 Hz. Data collected from the system includes screen intersection (x- and y- coordinates of gaze), fixation locations, and duration. A screen recorder also captures the video that is displayed to each subject so that the eye tracking information can be imposed on top. The software used for screen capture is EyesDX's Video Streamer and Record Manager.

2.4 Procedure

After providing informed consent, TSOs who volunteered to participate are seated at one of two instrumented stations. Before beginning the simulated task, the eye tracking cameras re repositioned and adjusted to ensure the subject is fully within the frame of the camera. The system is then further calibrated using an eight-point gaze calibration where subjects stare at eight strategically placed visual markers places across the two screens.

With the eye trackers and the display screen capture software recording, the subjects then answer an electronic demographic questionnaire. Upon completion, the TSOs re guided through instructions on the display regarding the task and information regarding the keyboard layout. Following the guided instructions, the subjects complete a ten-bag practice session where the experimenter walks them through the first few bags to ensure they understand the task and controls. Before beginning the main 2-h session,, the subjects have one last time to ask questions regarding the task. If no further questions remain, the main task begins.

After the participants complete the 2-h bag search task, are given a 15-min break during which they can leave the instrumentation station. Subjects then return to the stations for a visual cognitive battery with seven tasks. These tasks are detailed in Matzen [17].

3 Results

Statistical Analysis of the Behavioral Data. The data will be analyzed using multilevel growth modeling because of the hierarchical structure of the design and because of the interest in subject behaviors over time. Specifically, for all behavioral independent measures (Pd, Pfa, d', response bias, decision time), except for calculating signal detection measures (d', c), the cleared threat bags will be treated as clear bags in the analysis.

In addition to these more traditional statistical analyses, several machine learning techniques will be applied to the data in order to best exploit the millisecond-level eye tracking and state change logs being collected. These methods are detailed in Stracuzzi, Speed [19].

Acknowledgements. Sandia National Laboratories is a multi-program laboratory managed and operated by Sandia Corporation, a wholly owned subsidiary of Lockheed Martin Corporation, for the U.S. Department of Energy's National Nuclear Security Administration under Contract DE-AC04-94AL85000. This research was funded by an Interagency Agreement between the Transportation Security Administration and the Department of Energy.

References

1. Mackworth, N.H.: The breakdown of vigilance during prolonged visual search. Q. J. Exp. Psychol. **1**, 6–21 (1948)
2. Molloy, R., Parasuraman, R.: Monitoring an automated system for a single failure: Vigilance and task complexity effects. Hum. Factors **38**, 311–322 (1996)
3. Drury, C.G., M. Saran, Schultz, J.: Effect of fatigue / vigilance / environment on inspectors performing floursecent penetrant and/or magnetic particle inspection: Year 1 interim report, F.A. Administration, Editor (2004)
4. See, J.E., et al.: Meta-analysis of the sensitivity decrement in vigilance. Psychol. Bull. **117** (2), 230–249 (1995)
5. Wolfe, J.M., et al.: Low target prevalence is a stubborn source of errors in visual search tasks. J. Exp. Psychol. Gen. **136**(4), 623–638 (2007)
6. Wolfe, J.M., Van Wert, M.J.: Varying target prevalence reveals two dissociable decision criteria in visual search. Curr. Biol. **20**, 121–124 (2010)
7. See, J.E.: Visual Inspection: A Review of the Literature. S.N. Laboratories, Mexico (2012)
8. Hartley, L.R., et al.: Vigilance, visual search and attention in an agricultural task. Appl. Ergonomics **20**(1), 9–16 (1989)
9. Spencer, F., Schurman, D.: Reliability assessment at airline inspection facilities Vol III: Results of an eddy current inspection reliability experiment. F.A. Administration, Editor (1995)
10. Craig, A.: Field studies of human inspection: the application of vigilance research. In: Folkard, S., Monk, T.H. (eds.) Hours of Work: Temporal Factors in Work Scheduling, pp. 133–145. Wiley, New York (1985)
11. Washburn, D.A., et al.: Individual differences in sustained attention and threat detection. Cogn. Technol. **9**(2), 30–33 (2004)
12. Speed, A.: The possible effects of judge-advisor groups on local baggage screener accuracy. Transportation Security Administration (2011)
13. Speed, A., Gaspelin, N., Ruthruff, E.: The effects of social pressure and image resolution on x-ray screener accuracy. Transportation Security Administration (2012)
14. Smith, V.J.: Test and evaluation report for the screener workload fatigue study. Transportation Security Administration (2005)
15. Haass, M.J., et al.: Understanding expert visual search (2014)
16. Ghylin, K.M., et al.: Temporal effects in a security inspection task: breakdown of performance components. In: Proceedings of the Human Factors and Ergonomics Society 51st Annual Meeting (2007)
17. Matzen, L.E.: Effects of professional visual search experience on domain-general and domain-specific visual. In: HCI International. Los Angeles, CA (2015)
18. Biggs, A.T., et al.: Assessing visual search performance differences between transportation security administration officers and non-professional visual searchers. Vis. Cogn. **21**, 330–352 (2013)
19. Stracuzzi, D.S., et al.: Exploratory analysis of visual search data. In: HCI International, Los Angeles, CA (2015)

Author Index

Printed in the United States
By Bookmasters